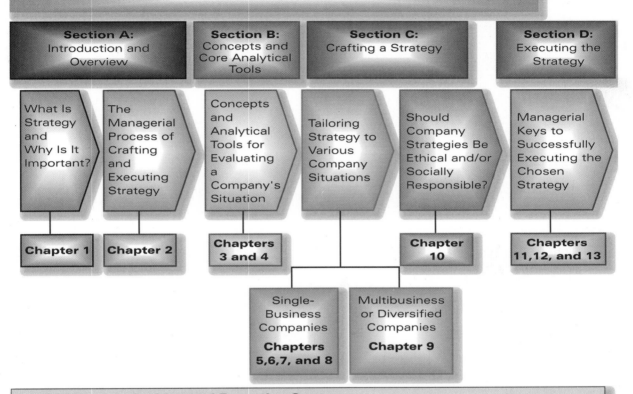

Part I: Concepts and Techniques for Crafting and Executing Strategy

Section A: Introduction and Overview

Section B: Concepts and Core Analytical Tools

Section C: Crafting a Strategy

Section D: Executing the Strategy

What Is Strategy and Why Is It Important?

The Managerial Process of Crafting and Executing Strategy

Concepts and Analytical Tools for Evaluating a Company's Situation

Tailoring Strategy to Various Company Situations

Should Company Strategies Be Ethical and/or Socially Responsible?

Managerial Keys to Successfully Executing the Chosen Strategy

Chapter 1

Chapter 2

Chapters 3 and 4

Chapter 10

Chapters 11,12, and 13

Single-Business Companies

Chapters 5,6,7, and 8

Multibusiness or Diversified Companies

Chapter 9

Part II: Cases in Crafting and Executing Strategy

Section A: Crafting Strategy in Single Business Companies (24 cases)
Section B: Crafting Strategy in Diversified Companies (3 cases)
Section C: Implementing and Executing Strategy (8 cases)
Section D: Strategy, Ethics, and Social Responsibility (2 cases)

Crafting and Executing Strategy

The Quest for Competitive Advantage

Concepts and Cases

Crafting and Executing Strategy

The Quest for Competitive Advantage

Concepts and Cases

Fourteenth Edition

Arthur A. Thompson, Jr.
University of Alabama

A. J. Strickland III
University of Alabama

John E. Gamble
University of South Alabama

Boston   Burr Ridge, IL   Dubuque, IA   Madison, WI   New York   San Francisco   St. Louis
Bangkok   Bogotá   Caracas   Kuala Lumpur   Lisbon   London   Madrid   Mexico City
Milan   Montreal   New Delhi   Santiago   Seoul   Singapore   Sydney   Taipei   Toronto

McGraw-Hill
Irwin

CRAFTING AND EXECUTING STRATEGY, THE QUEST FOR COMPETITIVE ADVANTAGE:
CONCEPTS AND CASES

Published by McGraw-Hill/Irwin, a business unit of The McGraw-Hill Companies, Inc., 1221
Avenue of the Americas, New York, NY, 10020. Copyright © 2005, 2003, 2001, 1999, 1998,
1996, 1995, 1993, 1992, 1990, 1987, 1984, 1981, 1978 by The McGraw-Hill Companies, Inc. All
rights reserved. No part of this publication may be reproduced or distributed in any form or by
any means, or stored in a database or retrieval system, without the prior written consent of The
McGraw-Hill Companies, Inc., including, but not limited to, in any network or other electronic
storage or transmission, or broadcast for distance learning.

Some ancillaries, including electronic and print components, may not be available to customers
outside the United States.

This book is printed on acid-free paper.

1 2 3 4 5 6 7 8 9 0 DOW/DOW 0 9 8 7 6 5 4

ISBN 0-07-288444-4

Editorial director: *John E. Biernat*
Executive editor: *John Weimeister*
Managing developmental editor: *Laura Hurst Spell*
Senior marketing manager: *Lisa Nicks*
Producer, Media technology: *Mark Molsky*
Project manager: *Harvey Yep*
Senior production supervisor: *Rose Hepburn*
Director of design BR: *Keith J. McPherson*
Photo research coordinator: *Kathy Shive*
Supplement producer: *Joyce J. Chappetto*
Senior digital content specialist: *Brian Nacik*
Cover design: *Tamada Brown and Associates*
Interior design: *Kay Fulton*
Typeface: *10.5/12 Times Roman*
Compositor: *Cenveo*
Printer: *R. R. Donnelley*

Library of Congress Cataloging-in-Publication Data
Thompson, Arthur A. 1940–
     Crafting and executing strategy : the quest for competitive advantage : concepts and cases
/ Arthur A. Thompson, Jr., A. J. Strickland III, John E. Gamble.—14th ed.
         p. cm.
     Rev. ed. of: Strategic management. 13th ed. c2003.
     Includes bibliographical references and indexes.
     ISBN 0-07-288444-4 (alk. paper)
     1. Strategic planning. 2. Strategic planning—Case studies. I. Strickland, A. J. (Alonzo
J.) II. Gamble, John (John E.) III. Thompson, Arthur A., 1940– Strategic management. IV.
Title.
HD30.28.T53 2005
658.4′012—dc22
                                                                                           2004049855

http://www.mhhe.com

To our families and especially our wives:
Hasseline, Kitty, and Debra

about the authors

Arthur A. Thompson, Jr., earned his BS and PhD degrees in economics from the University of Tennessee in 1961 and 1965, respectively; spent three years on the economics faculty at Virginia Tech; and served on the faculty of the University of Alabama's College of Commerce and Business Administration for 24 years. In 1974 and again in 1982, Dr. Thompson spent semester-long sabbaticals as a visiting scholar at the Harvard Business School.

His areas of specialization are business strategy, competition and market analysis, and the economics of business enterprises. He has published over 30 articles in some 25 different professional and trade publications and has authored or co-authored five textbooks and four computer-based simulation exercises.

Dr. Thompson is a frequent speaker and consultant on the strategic issues confronting the electric utility industry, particularly as concerns the challenges posed by industry restructuring, re-regulation, competition, and customers' freedom of choice. He spends much of his off-campus time giving presentations to electric utility groups and conducting management development programs for electric utility executives all over the world.

Dr. Thompson and his wife of 43 years have two daughters, two grandchildren, and a Yorkshire terrier.

Dr. A. J. (Lonnie) Strickland, a native of North Georgia, attended the University of Georgia, where he received a bachelor of science degree in math and physics in 1965. Afterward he entered the Georgia Institute of Technology, where he received a master of science in industrial management. He earned a PhD in business administration from Georgia State University in 1969. He currently holds the title of Professor of Strategic Management in the Graduate School of Business at the University of Alabama.

Dr. Strickland's experience in consulting and executive development is in the strategic management area, with a concentration in industry and competitive analysis. He has developed strategic planning systems for such firms as the Southern Company, BellSouth, South Central Bell, American Telephone and Telegraph, Gulf States Paper, Carraway Methodist Medical Center, Delco Remy, Mark IV Industries, Amoco Oil Company, USA Group, General Motors, and Kimberly Clark Corporation (Medical Products). He is a very popular speaker on the subject of implementing strategic change and serves on several corporate boards.

He has served as director of marketing for BellSouth, where he had responsibility for $1 billion in revenues and $300 million in profits.

In the international arena, Dr. Strickland has done extensive work in Europe, the Middle East, Central America, Malaysia, Australia, and Africa. In France he developed a management simulation of corporate decision making that enables management to test various strategic alternatives.

In the area of research, he is the author of 15 books and texts. His management simulations, Tempomatic IV and Micromatic, were pioneering innovations that enjoyed prominent market success for two decades.

Recent awards for Dr. Strickland include the Outstanding Professor Award for the Graduate School of Business and the Outstanding Commitment to Teaching Award for the University of Alabama, in which he takes particular pride. He is a member of various honor leadership societies: Mortar Board, Order of Omega, Beta Gamma Sigma, Omicron Delta Kappa, and Jasons. He is past national president of Pi Kappa Phi social fraternity.

John E. Gamble is currently Chairman of the Department of Management and Associate Professor of Management in the Mitchell College of Business at The University of South Alabama. His teaching specialty at USA is strategic management and he also conducts a course in strategic management in Germany through a collaborative MBA program sponsored by the University of Applied Sciences in Ludwigshafen/Worms, the State of Rhineland Westphalia, and the University of South Alabama.

Dr. Gamble's research interests center on strategic issues in entrepreneurial, health care, and manufacturing settings. His work has been published in such scholarly journals as *Journal of Business Venturing, Journal of Labor Research, Health Care Management Review,* and *Labor Studies Journal.* He is the author or co-author of more than 20 case studies published in various strategic management and strategic marketing texts. He has done consulting on industry and market analysis and strategy formulation and implementation issues with clients in public utilities, technology, non-profit, and entrepreneurial businesses.

Professor Gamble received his Ph.D. in management from the University of Alabama in 1995. Dr. Gamble also has a Bachelor of Science degree and a Master of Arts degree from The University of Alabama.

the|preface

There's a different look and feel to this 14th edition, starting with a more descriptive title—*Crafting and Executing Strategy: The Quest for Competitive Advantage*—that more clearly conveys the central thrust of basic courses in business and competitive strategy. The new face we've put on this edition includes a modified chapter organization, streamlined chapter presentations, more coverage of some topics and less coverage of others, and an all-new and very timely chapter: "Strategy, Ethics, and Social Responsibility." Yet the fundamental character that has driven the text's success over the years remains firmly intact. The treatment of basic concepts and analytical tools is solidly mainstream, very much in step with both theory and practice, and laced with the best examples we could muster. As is traditional in all of our new editions, there is a fresh line-up of the best and most current cases available. And we've prepared a comprehensive package of support materials that truly work in the classroom and that provide maximum flexibility in custom-tailoring a course to particular needs and preferences.

A TEXT WITH ON-TARGET CONTENT

In our view, for a senior/MBA-level strategy text to qualify as having on-target content, it must:

- Explain core concepts and provide examples of their relevance and use by actual companies.
- Present understandable explanations of essential analytical tools, how they are used, and where they fit into the managerial process of crafting and executing strategy.
- Be up-to-date and comprehensive, with solid coverage of the landmark changes in competitive markets and company strategies being driven by globalization and Internet technology.
- Focus squarely on what every student needs to know about crafting, implementing, and executing business strategies in today's market environments.
- Contain fresh, value-adding cases that feature interesting products and companies, illustrate the important kinds of strategic challenges managers face, embrace valuable teaching points, and spark student interest.

We believe the 14th edition measures up on all five of these criteria. Chapter discussions cut straight to the chase about what students really need to know—despite the addition of a new 33-page chapter, the 13 chapters of this edition are 50 pages shorter than the 13 chapters of the previous edition. Our explanations of core concepts and analytical tools are, however, covered in enough depth to make them understandable and usable, the rationale being that a shallow explanation carries little punch and has almost no pedagogical value. We have chosen current examples to which students can easily relate. We have striven to incorporate all relevant state-of-the-art research that is pertinent in a first course in strategy. And we were quite fortunate in assembling a truly fine lineup of interesting, relevant, and challenging cases to drive home valuable lessons in the whys and hows of successfully crafting and executing strategy.

ORGANIZATION, CONTENT, AND FEATURES OF THE TEXT CHAPTERS

The 13 chapters in this edition reflect not only the normal updating and shifts in topical emphasis and coverage but also a modestly different organization of chapters and topics. There's a much improved two-chapter introduction to the concept of strategy and the managerial process of crafting and executing strategy. Chapters 3 and 4 lay out the concepts and tools of analyzing a company's external environment and internal resources and capabilities. There is a four-chapter module on a single-business company's strategy alternatives and a single chapter (condensed from two chapters in prior editions) covering multibusiness diversification. The chapter on Internet strategy that was a prominent feature in the 12th and 13th editions has been dropped; now that Internet technology and use of the Internet have become standard strategy components at most companies worldwide, we think Internet strategy no longer justifies separate chapter-length treatment. However, the material in this deleted chapter that continues to be relevant has been included as a prominent part of Chapters 3, 4, and 6. The all-new Chapter 10, "Strategy, Ethics and Social Responsibility," fills a much-needed gap in coverage and can be assigned at any of several places in the course. We continue with our three-chapter coverage of what managerial actions underlie effective strategy execution.

In all 13 chapters, we have diligently kept the presentations aligned with latest developments in the theory and practice of strategic management. We've gone all-out to incorporate the latest advances in the conceptual underpinning of strategic management and to clearly describe the changes in business strategies, value chain operations, business practices, and competitive conditions being wrought by the continuing march toward globalization and the rapid adoption of Internet technology applications by companies worldwide. The chapter discussions mirror the growing scope and strategic importance of collaborative alliances, the continuing spread of high-velocity change to more industries and company environments, and the recently heightened imperatives of linking strategy and operating practices to what is ethically and socially acceptable. Much is made of the need to match a company's strategy *both* to its external market circumstances and to its internal resources and competitive capabilities. The resource-based view of the firm is prominently integrated into the discussion of crafting both single-business and multibusiness strategies. The three-chapter module on executing strategy embraces a strong resource-based perspective, stressing the importance of intellectual capital, core competencies, and competitive capabilities.

The following rundown summarizes the noteworthy chapter features and topical emphasis in this edition:

- Chapter 1 has been extensively rewritten and revised to focus on the central questions of "What is strategy?" and "Why is it important?" It defines what is meant by the term *strategy* and describes the identifying elements of a company's strategy, why a company's strategy tends to change and evolve over time, why a company's strategy is partly planned and partly reactive, and why management efforts to craft a company's strategy entail a quest for competitive advantage. In addition, there are sections discussing the importance of ethical considerations in crafting strategy, how a company's strategy relates to its "business model," and why good strategy + good strategy execution = good management. The role of this first chapter is to give readers a solid grasp of what the term *strategy* means, pique their interest, and convince them that the ins and outs of crafting and executing a winning strategy are things every business student should know. We intend for this chapter to be a perfect accompaniment for a first day's lecture on what the course is all about and why it matters.

- Chapter 2 delves into the managerial process of actually crafting and executing a strategy—it makes a great assignment for the second day of class. This chapter is structured around the five-step managerial process of crafting and executing strategy: (1) forming a strategic vision of where the company is headed and why, (2) setting objectives and performance targets that measure the company's progress, (3) crafting a strategy to achieve these targets and move the company toward its market destination, (4) implementing and executing the strategy, and (5) monitoring progress and making corrective adjustments as needed. This chapter is also introductory in nature and presents such core concepts as strategic visions and business missions, strategic versus financial objectives, strategic plans, and strategic intent. There's a section underscoring that a company's strategic plan is a collection of strategies devised by different managers at different levels in the organizational hierarchy. We've taken pains to explain why *all managers are on a company's strategy-making, strategy-executing team,* why managers are well advised to make the concepts and techniques of strategic management a basic part of their toolkit, and why the best companies want their personnel to be true "students of the business." The chapter winds up with a section on corporate governance.

- Chapter 3 presents the now-standard tools of industry and competitive analysis and makes a case for why it is important for management to tailor strategy to fit the circumstances of a company's industry and competitive environment. The standout feature of this chapter is a dramatically enhanced and more visual presentation of Michael E. Porter's five-forces model of competition—we think it is the clearest, most compelling five-forces model discussion of any text in the field. Globalization and Internet technology are treated as potent driving forces capable of reshaping industry competition—their roles as change agents have become factors that most companies in most industries must reckon with in forging winning strategies.

- Chapter 4 establishes the equal importance of doing solid company situation analysis as a basis for matching strategy to organizational resources, competencies, and competitive capabilities. The roles of core competencies and organizational resources and capabilities in creating customer value and helping build competitive advantage are *center stage* in the discussions of company resource strengths and weaknesses. SWOT analysis is cast as a simple, easy-to-use way to assess a company's resources and overall situation. There is solid coverage of the now-standard tools of value chain analysis, benchmarking, and competitive strength assessments—all of which, we believe, provide insight into a company's relative cost position and market standing vis-à-vis rivals. There's solid coverage of how company implementation of Internet technology applications is altering company and industry value chains and the performance of particular value chain activities.

- Chapter 5 deals with a company's quest for competitive advantage and is framed around the five generic competitive strategies: low-cost leadership, differentiation, best-cost provider, focused differentiation, and focused low-cost.

- Chapter 6 extends the coverage of the previous chapter and deals with what *other strategic actions* a company can take to complement its choice of a basic competitive strategy. The chapter features sections on what use to make of strategic alliances and collaborative partnerships; what use to make of mergers and acquisitions in strengthening the company's competitiveness; when to integrate backward or forward into more stages of the industry value chain; the merits of outsourcing certain value chain activities from outside specialists; whether and when to employ offensive and defensive moves; and the different ways a company can use the Internet as a distribution channel to position itself in the marketplace.

- Chapter 7 explores a company's strategy options for expanding beyond its domestic boundary and competing in the markets of either a few or a great many countries—options ranging from an export strategy to licensing and franchising to multicountry strategies to global strategies to heavy reliance on strategic alliances and joint ventures. Four strategic issues unique to competing multinationally are given special attention: (1) whether to customize the company's offerings in each different country market to match the tastes and preferences of local buyers or whether to offer a mostly standardized product worldwide; (2) whether to employ essentially the same basic competitive strategy in the markets of all countries where it operates or whether to modify the company's competitive approach country-by-country as may be needed to fit the specific market conditions and competitive circumstances it encounters; (3) locating production facilities, distribution centers, and customer service operations to maximum competitive advantage; and (4) efficient cross-border transfer of a company's resource strengths and capabilities to build competitive advantage. There's also coverage of concepts of profit sanctuaries and cross-market subsidization, the special problems associated with entry into the markets of emerging countries; and strategies that local companies in such emerging countries as India, China, Brazil, and Mexico can use to defend against the invasion of opportunity-seeking, resource-rich global giants.

- Chapter 8 looks at the broad strategy options for companies competing in five different industry environments: (1) emerging industries of the future; (2) turbulent high-velocity markets; (3) mature, slow-growth industries; (4) stagnant and declining industries; and (5) fragmented industries. And it covers the strategy-making challenges that confront companies pursuing rapid growth, companies in industry-leading positions, companies in runner-up positions, and crisis-ridden companies. These nine situations merit special attention in strategy courses because of their widely representative nature and because they reinforce the points made in Chapters 3 and 4 that winning strategies have to be matched both to industry and competitive conditions and to company resources and capabilities.

- In this edition we have combined our two-chapter treatment of diversification into a single streamlined but meaty chapter. The treatment of diversification strategies for multibusiness enterprises in Chapter 9 begins by laying out the various paths for becoming diversified, explains how a company can use diversification to create or compound competitive advantage for its business units, and examines the strategic options an already-diversified company has to improve its overall performance. In the middle part of the chapter, the analytical spotlight is on the techniques and procedures for assessing the strategic attractiveness of a diversified company's business portfolio—the relative attractiveness of the various businesses the company has diversified into, a multi-industry company's competitive strength in each of its lines of business, and the *strategic fits* and *resource fits* among a diversified company's different businesses. The chapter concludes with a brief survey of a company's four main postdiversification strategy alternatives: (1) broadening the diversification base, (2) divesting some businesses and retrenching to a narrower diversification base, (3) restructuring the makeup of the company's business lineup, and (4) multinational diversification.

- Chapter 10 examines the controversial issues of whether and why a company's strategy should pass the test of moral scrutiny. Students usually acknowledge that a company and its personnel have a legal duty to obey the law and play by the rules of fair competition. But today's students seem to be much less clear on (1) whether a company has a *duty* to operate according to the ethical norms of the societies in which it operates and (2) whether a company has a *duty* or *obligation* to contribute to the betterment of society independent of the needs and preferences of the customers it serves. Is it in the best interests of shareholders for a company to operate ethically and/or to operate in a socially responsible manner? The focus of this chapter is squarely on what link, if any, there should be between a company's efforts to craft and execute a winning strategy and its duties to (*a*) conduct its activities in an ethical manner and (*b*) demonstrate socially responsible behavior by being a committed corporate citizen and attending to the needs of nonowner stakeholders—employees, the communities in which it operates, the disadvantaged, and society as a whole. The chapter reflects the very latest in the literature and contains a section on moral, immoral, and amoral managerial behavior, a section addressing "the business of business is business, not ethics" kind of thinking, a section on the concept of social responsibility, and sections that explore the business case for ethical and socially responsible behavior. The chapter has been written as a stand-alone chapter that can be assigned in the early, middle, or late part of the course.

- The three-chapter module on executing strategy (Chapters 11–13) is anchored around a pragmatic, compelling conceptual framework: (1) building the resource strengths and organizational capabilities needed to execute the strategy in competent fashion; (2) allocating ample resources to strategy-critical activities; (3) ensuring that policies and procedures facilitate rather than impede strategy execution; (4) instituting best practices and pushing for continuous improvement in how value chain activities are performed; (5) installing information and operating systems that enable company personnel to better carry out their strategic roles proficiently; (6) tying rewards and incentives directly to the achievement of performance targets and good strategy execution; (7) shaping the work environment and corporate culture to fit the strategy; and (8) exerting the internal leadership needed to drive execution forward. The recurring theme of these three chapters is that executing strategy entails figuring out the specific actions, behaviors, and conditions that are needed for a smooth strategy-supportive operation and then following through to get things done and deliver results—the goal here is to ensure that students understand the strategy-implementing/strategy-executing phase is a make-things-happen and make-them-happen-right kind of managerial exercise.

Our top priority has been to ensure that the 13 chapters of text hit the bull's-eye with respect to content and represent the best thinking of both academics and practitioners. All the chapters contain enough relevant examples to make the presentation convincing, pertinent, and worthwhile to readers preparing for careers in management and business. The boxed Illustration Capsules in each chapter relate stories aimed at both informing students and persuading them that the discipline of strategy merits their rapt attention. We believe our enthusiasm for and dedication to the subject matter will come across to readers.

THE CASE COLLECTION

The 37 cases included in this edition are the very latest and best that we could find. The lineup is flush with examples of strategy in action and valuable lessons for students in the art and science of crafting and executing strategy. And there's a good blend of cases from a length perspective—close to a fourth are under 15 pages yet offer plenty for students to chew on; about a third are medium-length cases; and the remainder are longer, detail-rich cases. At least 23 of the 37 cases involve high-profile companies, products, or people that students will have heard of, know about from personal experience, or can easily identify with. There are four dot-com company cases, plus several others that will provide students with insight into the special demands of competing in industry environments where technological developments are an everyday event, product life cycles are short, and competitive maneuvering among rivals comes fast and furious. At least 27 of the cases involve situations where company resources and competitive capabilities play as large a role in the strategy-making, strategy-implementing scheme of things as industry and competitive conditions do. Scattered throughout the lineup are 16 cases concerning non-U.S. companies, globally competitive industries, and/or cross-cultural situations; these cases, in conjunction with the globalized content of the text chapters, provide ample material for tightly linking the study of crafting and executing strategy to the ongoing globalization of the world economy. You'll also find 5 cases dealing with the strategic problems of family-owned or relatively small entrepreneurial businesses and 22 cases involving public companies about which students can do further research on the Internet. Eleven of the cases (Starbucks, Competition in the Bottled Water Industry, Dell Computer, McDonald's, eBay, Harley-Davidson, Land O' Lakes, Kmart, Continental Airlines, Southwest Airlines, and Beringer Family Winery) have accompanying videotape segments. We believe you will find the collection of 37 cases quite appealing, eminently teachable, and very suitable for drilling students in the use of the concepts and analytical treatments in Chapters 1 through 13. It is a case lineup that should stimulate student interest from beginning to end.

In addition, five other recent cases researched and written by the authors of the text can be downloaded from the Internet using the unique code provided with the purchase of a new text. This extends the number of cases available in the total package to 42.

TWO ACCOMPANYING SIMULATION EXERCISES: *THE BUSINESS STRATEGY GAME* AND *GLO-BUS*

Two strategy-related simulations—*The Business Strategy Game* (the new online 8th edition and the older disk-based 7.2 version) and *GLO-BUS: Developing Winning Competitive Strategies*—are available as companion supplements for use with this and other texts in the field. *The Business Strategy Game* is the world's leading strategy simulation, having been played by well over 350,000 students, and the new online 8th edition is far and away the best and the simplest to administer of any previous version. *GLO-BUS,* a somewhat less complicated online simulation that was introduced in the fall of 2003, has been favorably received (having been played by some 6,000 students in over 100 sections) and is equally suitable for courses in business strategy. Table 1 provides a comparison of the industry and competitive features of *BSG Online* and *GLO-BUS.*

table 1   **A Comparison of *GLO-BUS* versus *The Business Strategy Game***

	GLO-BUS	The Business Strategy Game
Industry setting	Digital camera industry	Athletic footwear industry
Market scope	Worldwide. Production occurs at a single plant in Taiwan and sales are made to retailers in 4 regions: North America, Latin America, Europe-Africa, and Asia Pacific	Worldwide. Both production and sales activities can be pursued in North America, Latin America, Europe-Africa, and Asia Pacific
Number of market segments	A total of 8—4 geographic segments for entry-level cameras and 4 geographic segments for multifeatured cameras	A total of 12—4 geographic segments each for branded footwear sales to retailers, for online footwear sales direct to consumers, and for private-label sales to multistore retailers
Number of decision variables	• Character and performance of the camera line (10 decisions) • Production operations and worker compensation (15 decisions) • Pricing and marketing (15 decisions in 4 geographic regions) • Financing of company operations (4 decisions)	• Production operations and worker compensation (16 decisions each plant, with a maximum of 4 plants) • Shipping (up to 8 decisions each plant) • Pricing and marketing (13 decisions in 4 geographic regions) • Financing of company operations (5 decisions)
Competitive variables used to determine market share (All sales and market share differences are the result of differing competitive efforts among rival companies)	• Price • Performance/quality rating • Number of quarterly sales promotions • Length of promotions in weeks • Promotional discounts • Advertising • Number of camera models • Size of dealer network • Warranty period • Technical support	• Price • Number of models/styles • Styling/quality rating • Advertising • Size of retailer network • Celebrity endorsements • Delivery time • Retailer support • Mail-in rebates • Shipping charges (Internet sales only)
Time frame of decisions	One year, with an option to update as many as 8 of the 44 decisions quarterly	One year
Strategy options (Which options deliver the best performance hinges on the interaction and competitive strength of the strategies employed by rival companies—not on "silver bullet" decision combinations that players are challenged to discover.)	Companies can pursue competitive advantage based on (*a*) low-cost or differentiation, (*b*) competing globally or in select segments, and (*c*) using largely the same strategy across all regions or strategies that are tailored to conditions in each market segment.	Companies have the widest possible strategy-making latitude—striving for competitive advantage based on (*a*) low cost or differentiation, (*b*) competing globally or in select segments, and (*c*) using largely the same strategy across all regions or strategies that are tailored to conditions in each market segment.

(continues)

table 1 **(concluded)**

	GLO-BUS	The Business Strategy Game
Degree of complexity	• *GLO-BUS* Basic (easy to moderate) • *GLO-BUS* Plus (easy to moderate) • *GLO-BUS* Total (medium) Less complex than *BSG* because all production is in a single plant, there are no finished goods inventories (newly assembled cameras are built to order and shipped directly to retailers), and sales forecasting is simpler	More complex than *GLO-BUS* because companies can operate up to four plants, there are 12 market segments (as compared to 8 in *GLO-BUS*), finished goods inventories have to be managed at four distribution centers, and players have to develop a sales forecast based on their competitive strategy and the expected competitive efforts of rivals
Time required to make a complete decision	About 1.5 hours per decision (once players gain familiarity with software and reports). *GLO-BUS* Plus requires about 10 minutes more than *GLO-BUS* Basic per decision and *GLO-BUS* Total can entail up to 30 minutes additional time per decision	2 to 2.5 hours per decision (once players gain familiarity with software and reports)

Both simulations have attractive operating and administrative characteristics that make them a breeze to use in giving students valuable practice in thinking strategically and applying basic strategy concepts and analytical tools:

- Both students and instructors have *anytime, anywhere* access on PCs connected to the Internet and loaded with Internet Explorer and Microsoft Excel (2000, XP, or 2003 versions), a delivery format that is perfect for either on-campus classes or distance learning.

- Time requirements for instructors to administer the simulations are minimal. Instructors must go through Industry Setup and specify a decision schedule and desired scoring weights (which can be altered later). Setting up the simulation for your course is done online and takes about 10–15 minutes. Once setup is completed, no other administrative actions are required beyond that of moving participants to a different team (should the need arise) and monitoring the progress of the simulation (to whatever extent desired). Instructors who wish to do so can track happenings in the simulation by printing copies of the Industry and Company reports (done online), change selected costs and rates to introduce different operating conditions (players are automatically notified of any changes if instructors so choose), and serve as a consultant to troubled companies.

- There's no software for students or administrators to download and no disks to fool with. When participants log on to the Web site, the needed programming and company data is automatically transferred into Excel on the user's PC for the duration of the session and then automatically saved and uploaded back to the server on exit. All work must be done online and the speed for participants using dial-up modems is quite satisfactory.

- The results of each decision are processed automatically on the simulation's server and made available to all participants *within 1 hour following the decision deadline* specified by the instructor/game administrator. There is a state-of-the-art server dedicated to the simulation; the server has ample backup capability and is maintained by a highly reliable Web-hosting service that guarantees 99.9 percent reliability on a 24/7 basis.

- Participants and instructors are notified via e-mail when the results are ready; the e-mail contains highlights of the results.

- Decision schedules are determined by the instructor (done online and automatically communicated to all players). Decisions can be made once a week, twice a week, or even twice daily, depending on how instructors want to conduct the exercise). One popular decision schedule involves 1 or 2 practice decisions, 6–10 regular decisions, and decisions made once a week across the whole term. A second popular schedule is 1 or 2 practice decisions, 6–8 regular decisions, and biweekly decisions, all made during last four or five weeks of the course (when it can be assumed that students have pretty much digested the contents of Chapters 1–8, gotten somewhat comfortable with what is involved in crafting strategy for a single-business company situation, and prepared several assigned cases.

- Instructors have the flexibility to prescribe 0, 1, or 2 practice decisions and from 3 to 10 regular decisions.

- Company teams can be composed of 1 to 5 players each and the number of teams in a single industry can range from 4 to 12. If your class size is too large for a single industry, then it is a simple matter to create two or more industries for a single class section. You'll find that having more than one industry per class presents no significant change in administrative requirements, because everything is processed automatically and all company and individual performances are automatically recorded in your online grade book. Thus it turns out not to be an extra administrative burden to divide a large class into two or more industries.

- Participant's Guides are delivered at the Web site—students can read the guide on their monitors or print out a copy, as they prefer. The Player's Guide for *The Business Strategy Game* is 32 pages, and the Participant's Guide for *GLO-BUS* is 25 pages. There are built-in help screens and on-screen information that provide students with the instructions and information needed to guide them to enter wise decisions. Students make all decisions online and access all the results online.

- Following each decision, participants are provided with a complete set of reports— a six-page Industry Report, a one-page Competitive Intelligence report for each geographic region that includes strategic group maps and bulleted lists of competitive strengths and weaknesses, and a set of Company Reports (income statement, balance sheet, cash flow statement, and assorted production, marketing, and cost statistics).

- There are extensive built-in "Help" screens explaining (*a*) each decision entry, (*b*) the information on each page of the Industry Reports, and (*c*) the numbers presented in the Company Reports. The Help screens allow company co-managers to figure things out for themselves, thereby curbing the need for students to always run to the instructor with questions about how things work.

- Two open-book multiple-choice tests of 20 questions (optional, but strongly recommended) are included as part of each of the two simulations. The quizzes are taken online and automatically graded, with scores reported instantaneously to participants and automatically recorded in instructor's electronic grade book. Quiz 1 has a time limit of 45 minutes and covers contents of the Participant's Guide. Quiz 2 has a time limit of 75 minutes and checks whether players understand what the numbers in the company reports mean and how they are calculated. Students are automatically provided with three sample questions for each test.

- At the end of the simulation exercises, there are peer evaluations that instructors can have students complete. The peer evaluations are optional but strongly recommended; they are completed online and automatically recorded in instructor's electronic grade book. Results can be reviewed by clicking on each co-manager's peer scores in grade book.

All three coauthors of this book are avid longtime simulation users. Our own experiences, together with numerous discussions with colleagues around the world, have convinced us that competition-based simulation games are *the single most effective, most stimulating exercise available* for giving students valuable practice in being active strategic thinkers and in reading the signs of industry change, reacting to the moves of competitors, evaluating strengths and weaknesses in their company's competitive position, and deciding what to do to improve a company's financial performance. We see two big reasons why simulations like *The Business Strategy Game* and *GLO-BUS* are rapidly growing in popularity and merit a place in today's strategy courses:

- Both simulations were carefully designed to connect directly to the chapter material and give students the experience of putting what they read in the chapters into play. Moreover, instructors have opportunity after opportunity to draw upon the industry and company circumstances in the simulation for examples to use in lectures on the text chapters—examples that all students in the class can relate to because of their personal experience in running their companies.

- The market and competitive dynamics of an industry simulation—which makes the simulation a "live case" in which class members are active managerial participants—force class members to wrestle with charting a long-term direction for their company, setting strategic and financial objectives, and crafting strategies that produce good results and perhaps lead to competitive advantage. In both *The Business Strategy Game* and *GLO-BUS,* students are provided with strategic group maps and lists of competitive strengths and weaknesses, as well as an assortment of benchmarks and comparative financial statistics, allowing them to diagnose their company's market standing and decide on a course of action to improve it. And by having to live with the decisions they make, players experience what it means to be accountable for their decisions and achieving satisfactory results. All this serves to drill students in responsible decision making and to improve their business acumen and managerial judgment.

To learn more about these two simulations, please visit www.bsg-online.com or www.glo-bus.com. A "Guided Tour" link on these Web sites provides a quick bird's-eye view and takes about five minutes—enough to determine whether there's sufficient interest on your part to explore further. If you call the senior author of this text, the simulation authors will be glad to provide you with a personal tour of either or both simulations (while you are on your PC) and walk you through the many features.

STUDENT SUPPORT MATERIALS IN THE 14TH EDITION PACKAGE

Key Points Summaries

At the end of each chapter is a synopsis of the core concepts, analytical tools, and other key points discussed in the chapter. These chapter-end synopses, along with the margin notes scattered throughout each chapter, help students focus on basic strategy principles, digest the messages of each chapter, and prepare for tests.

Chapter-End Exercises

Each chapter contains a select number of exercises, most related to research on the Internet, that reinforce key concepts and topics covered in the chapters.

A Value-Added Web Site

The student section of www.mhhe.com/thompson contains a number of helpful aids:

- Self-scoring 20-question chapter tests that students can take to measure their grasp of the material presented in each of the 13 chapters.
- A "Guide to Case Analysis" containing sections on what a case is, why cases are a standard part of courses in strategy, preparing a case for class discussion, doing a written case analysis, doing an oral presentation, and using financial ratio analysis to assess a company's financial condition.
- A table containing formulas and brief explanations of all the various financial ratios that are commonly used in evaluating a company's financial statements and financial strengths.
- A select number of PowerPoint slides for each chapter.

PowerWeb

PowerWeb is now available within the Online Learning Center. Links to PowerWeb articles, news updates, and weekly updates archive are available within each chapter and organized by topic.

Case-TUTOR Software

Accompanying the 37 cases is a downloadable software package containing assignment questions for all 37 cases in the text, plus analytically structured exercises for 13 of the cases that coach students in doing the strategic thinking needed to arrive at solid answers to the assignment questions for that case. Conscientious completion of the case preparation exercises helps students gain quicker command of the concepts and analytical techniques and points them toward doing good strategic analysis—each of the 13 cases for which there is a case preparation exercise is indicated by the Case-TUTOR logo in the case listing section of the Table of Contents (the Case-TUTOR logo also appears on the first page of cases for which there is an exercise). Students can download the Case-TUTOR software at the publisher's Web site.

INSTRUCTOR SUPPORT MATERIALS IN THE 14TH EDITION PACKAGE

Test Bank

There is an 1100-question test bank prepared by the coauthors containing multiple-choice questions and suggested essay questions for each chapter.

Computest

A computerized version of the test bank allows you to generate tests quite conveniently and to add in your own questions.

Instructor's Manual

There's a *comprehensive* two-volume Instructor's Manual that contains a lengthy section on suggestions for organizing and structuring your course, advice on making effective use of a simulation, sample syllabi and daily course outlines, lecture outlines, test questions, and comprehensive teaching notes for each of the 37 cases.

PowerPoint Slides

To facilitate preparation of your lectures and to serve as chapter outlines, you'll have access to approximately 500 colorful, professional-looking slides displaying core concepts, analytical procedures, key points, and all the figures in the text chapters. The slides are the creation of Professor Jana Kuzmicki of Troy State University.

Accompanying Case Videos

Eleven of the cases—Starbucks, Competition in the Bottled Water Industry, Dell Computer, McDonald's, eBay, Harley-Davidson, Land O' Lakes, Kmart, Continental Airlines, Southwest Airlines, and Beringer Family Winery—have accompanying videotape segments that you can show during the course of the case discussions. Suggestions for using each video are contained in the teaching note for that case.

Instructor Resource CD-ROM

The Instructor's Manual, the PowerPoint Slides, various video clips, teaching notes for the 37 cases in the text, and the five supplemental e-cases and their corresponding teaching notes have all been installed on a CD available to adopters. The CD (or the hard copy of the Instructor's Manual) is a useful aid for compiling a syllabus and daily course schedule, preparing customized lectures, and developing tests on the text chapters.

The Business Strategy Game *and* GLO-BUS Online Simulations

Using one of the two companion simulations is a powerful and constructive way of emotionally connecting students to the subject matter of the course. We know of no more effective and interesting way to stimulate the competitive energy of students and prepare them for the rigors of real-world business decision making than to have them match strategic wits with classmates in running a company in head-to-head competition for global market leadership.

Web Site: www.mhhe.com/thompson

The instructor portion of the Web site contains a password-protected section that provides epilogue updates on the 37 cases contained in this text, along with downloadable files of the Instructor's Manual, the PowerPoint slides, and other support-related materials.

With the 14th edition, we've done our level best to satisfy the market's legitimate yearning for a comprehensive teaching/learning package that squarely targets what every business student needs to know about crafting and executing business strategies, that fulfills instructor expectations, that works magic in the classroom, and that wins the applause of students. Our goal has been to raise the bar for what a text package in the discipline of strategy ought to deliver. We have gone the extra mile to equip you with a smorgasbord of teaching/learning opportunities and keep the nature of student assignments varied and interesting. We've pursued every avenue we know to provide you with all the resources and materials you'll need to design and deliver a course that is on the cutting edge and delivers what you are looking for.

ACKNOWLEDGMENTS

We heartily acknowledge the contributions of the case researchers whose casewriting efforts appear herein and the companies whose cooperation made the cases possible. To each one goes a very special thank-you. We cannot overstate the importance of timely, carefully researched cases in contributing to a substantive study of strategic management issues and practices. From a research standpoint, strategy-related cases are invaluable in exposing the generic kinds of strategic issues that companies face, in forming hypotheses about strategic behavior, and in drawing experienced-based generalizations about the practice of strategic management. From an instructional standpoint, strategy cases give students essential practice in diagnosing and evaluating the strategic situations of companies and organizations, in applying the concepts and tools of strategic analysis, in weighing strategic options and crafting strategies, and in tackling the challenges of successful strategy execution. Without a continuing stream of fresh, well-researched, and well-conceived cases, the discipline of strategic management would lose its close ties to the very institutions whose strategic actions and behavior it is aimed at explaining and guiding. There's no question, therefore, that first-class case research makes a valuable scholarly contribution to the theory and practice of managing the strategy-making, strategy-executing process.

In addition, a great number of colleagues and students at various universities, business acquaintances, and people at McGraw-Hill provided inspiration, encouragement, and counsel during the course of this project. Like all text authors in the strategy field, we are intellectually indebted to the many academics whose research and writing have blazed new trails and advanced the discipline of crafting and executing organizational strategies. The following reviewers provided seasoned advice and suggestions that further guided our preparation of this particular edition:

Seyda Deligonul, *St. John Fisher College* and *Michigan State University*
David Flanagan, *Western Michigan University*
Esmeralda Garbi, *Florida Atlantic University*
Mohsin Habib, *University of Massachusetts–Boston*
Kim Hester, *Arkansas State University*
Jeffrey E. McGee, *The University of Texas at Arlington*
Diana J. Wong, *Eastern Michigan University*

We also express our thanks to those reviewers who provided valuable guidance in steering our efforts to improve earlier editions: F. William Brown, Anthony F. Chelte, Gregory G. Dess, Alan B. Eisner, John George, Carle M. Hunt, Theresa Marron-Grodsky, Sarah Marsh, Joshua D. Martin, William L. Moore, Donald Neubaum, George M. Puia, Amit Shah, Lois M. Shelton, Mark Weber, Steve Barndt, J. Michael Geringer, Ming-Fang Li, Richard Stackman, Stephen Tallman, Gerardo R. Ungson, James Boulgarides, Betty Diener, Daniel F. Jennings, David Kuhn, Kathryn Martell, Wilbur Mouton, Bobby Vaught, Tuck Bounds, Lee Burk, Ralph Catalanello, William Crittenden, Vince Luchsinger, Stan Mendenhall, John Moore, Will Mulvaney, Sandra Richard, Ralph Roberts, Thomas Turk, Gordon VonStroh, Fred Zimmerman, S. A. Billion, Charles Byles, Gerald L. Geisler, Rose Knotts, Joseph Rosenstein, James B. Thurman, Ivan Able, W. Harvey Hegarty, Roger Evered, Charles B. Saunders, Rhae M. Swisher, Claude I. Shell, R. Thomas Lenz, Michael C. White, Dennis Callahan, R. Duane Ireland, William E. Burr II, C. W. Millard, Richard Mann, Kurt Christensen, Neil W. Jacobs, Louis W. Fry, D. Robley Wood, George J. Gore, and William R. Soukup.

As always, we value your recommendations and thoughts about the book. Your comments regarding coverage and contents will be taken to heart, and we always are grateful for the time you take to call our attention to printing errors, deficiencies, and other shortcomings. Please e-mail us at athompso@cba.ua.edu, astrickl@cba.ua.edu, or jgamble@usouthal.edu; fax us at (205) 348-6695; or write us at P.O. Box 870225; Department of Management and Marketing; The University of Alabama; Tuscaloosa, Alabama 35487-0225.

Arthur A. Thompson

A. J. Strickland

John E. Gamble

guided tour

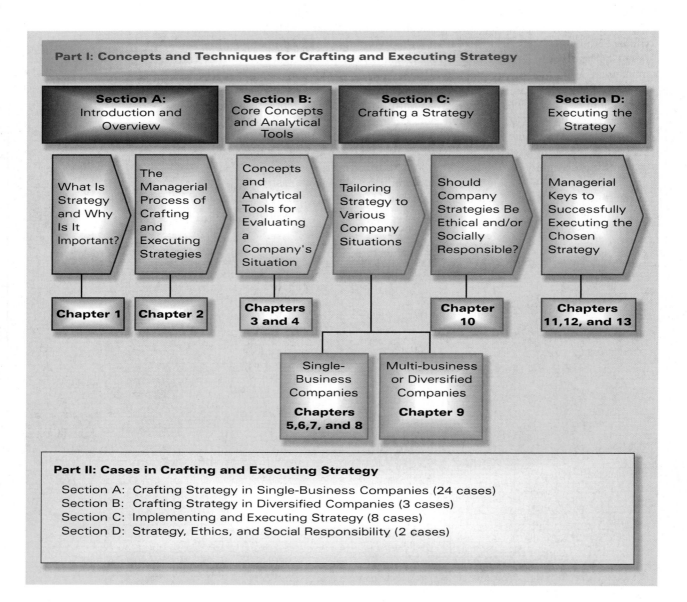

Part I: Concepts and Techniques for Crafting and Executing Strategy

Section A: Introduction and Overview	Section B: Core Concepts and Analytical Tools	Section C: Crafting a Strategy	Section D: Executing the Strategy

What Is Strategy and Why Is It Important?

The Managerial Process of Crafting and Executing Strategies

Concepts and Analytical Tools for Evaluating a Company's Situation

Tailoring Strategy to Various Company Situations

Should Company Strategies Be Ethical and/or Socially Responsible?

Managerial Keys to Successfully Executing the Chosen Strategy

Chapter 1

Chapter 2

Chapters 3 and 4

Chapter 10

Chapters 11, 12, and 13

Single-Business Companies

Chapters 5, 6, 7, and 8

Multi-business or Diversified Companies

Chapter 9

Part II: Cases in Crafting and Executing Strategy

Section A: Crafting Strategy in Single-Business Companies (24 cases)
Section B: Crafting Strategy in Diversified Companies (3 cases)
Section C: Implementing and Executing Strategy (8 cases)
Section D: Strategy, Ethics, and Social Responsibility (2 cases)

chapter one 1

What Is Strategy and Why Is It Important?

(©Images.com/CORBIS)

A strategy is a commitment to undertake one set of actions rather than another.

—**Sharon Oster**
Professor, Yale University

The process of developing superior strategies is part planning, part trial and error, until you hit upon something that works.

—**Costas Markides**
Professor, London Business School

Without a strategy the organization is like a ship without a rudder.

—**Joel Ross and Michael Kami**
Business authors and consultants

Managers at all companies face three central questions in thinking strategically about their company's present circumstances and prospects: Where are we now? Where do we want to go? How will we get there? The question "Where are we now?" concerns the ins and outs of the company's present situation—its market standing, how appealing its products or services are to customers, the competitive pressures it confronts, its strengths and weaknesses, and its current performance. The question "Where do we want to go?" deals with the direction in which management believes the company should be headed in terms of growing the business and strengthening the company's market standing and financial performance in the years ahead. The question "How will we get there?" concerns crafting and executing a strategy to get the company from where it is to where it wants to go.

In this opening chapter, we define the concept of strategy and introduce its many elements and facets. We will explain how a strategy originates, the kinds of actions that determine what a company's strategy is, why strategies are partly proactive and partly reactive, and why company strategies tend to evolve over time. We will look at what sets a winning strategy apart from an ordinary strategy or one that is a sure loser and why the caliber of a company's strategy determines whether it will enjoy a competitive advantage or be burdened by competitive disadvantage. By the end of this chapter, you will have a pretty clear idea of why the tasks of crafting and executing strategy are core management functions and why excellent execution of an excellent strategy is the most reliable recipe for turning a company into a standout performer.

WHAT IS STRATEGY?

A company's **strategy** is management's game plan for growing the business, staking out a market position, attracting and pleasing customers, competing successfully, conducting operations, and achieving targeted objectives. In crafting a strategy, management is in effect saying, "Among all the paths we could have chosen, we have decided to focus on these markets and customer needs, compete in this fashion, allocate our resources and energies in these ways, and use these particular approaches to doing business." A company's strategy thus indicates the choices its managers have made about *how* to attract and please customers, *how* to respond to changing market conditions, *how* to compete successfully, *how* to grow the business, *how* to manage each

> **core concept**
> A company's **strategy** consists of the competitive moves and business approaches that managers employ to attract and please customers, compete successfully, grow the business, conduct operations, and achieve targeted objectives.

3

Each chapter begins with a series of pertinent **quotes** and an introductory preview of its contents.

---

illustration capsule 1.2
Microsoft and Red Hat Linux: Two Contrasting Business Models

The strategies of rival companies are often predicated on strikingly different business models. Consider, for example, the business models for Microsoft and Red Hat Linux in operating system software for PCs.

Microsoft's business model for making money from its operating system products is based on the following revenue-cost-profit economics:

- Employ a cadre of highly skilled programmers to develop proprietary code; keep the source code hidden from users and lock them in to using Microsoft's proprietary software.
- Sell the resulting operating system and software package to personal computer (PC) makers and to PC users at relatively attractive prices (around $75 to PC makers and about $100 at retail to PC users) and achieve large unit sales.
- Most of Microsoft's costs arise on the front end in developing the software and are thus "fixed"; the variable costs of producing and packaging the CDs provided to users are only a couple of dollars per copy—once the break-even volume is reached, Microsoft's revenues from additional sales are almost pure profit.
- Provide technical support to users at no cost.

Red Hat Linux, a company formed to market its own version of the open-source Linux operating system, employs a business model based on sharply different revenue-cost-profit economics:

- Rely on the collaborative efforts of volunteer programmers from all over the world who contribute bits and pieces of code to improve and polish the Linux system. The global community of thousands of programmers who work on Linux in their spare time do what they do because they love it, because they are fervent believers that all software should be free (as in free speech), and, in some cases, because they are anti-Microsoft and want to have a part in undoing what they see as a Microsoft monopoly.
- Collect and test enhancements and new applications submitted by the open-source community of volunteer

programmers. Linux's originator, Linus Torvalds, and a team of 300-plus Red Hat engineers and software developers evaluate which incoming submissions merit inclusion in new releases of Red Hat Linux—the evaluation and integration of new submissions are Red Hat's only up-front product development costs.

- Charge a modest fee to those who prefer to subscribe to the upgraded and tested family of Red Hat Linux products. Subscription fees include a limited number of days of service, support, patches, and updates.
- Release updated versions of Red Hat Linux every 4–6 months to small users and every 12–18 months to corporate users.
- Make the source code open and available to all users, allowing them to create a customized version of Linux.
- Capitalize on the specialized expertise required to use Linux in multiserver, multiprocessor applications by providing fees-based training, consulting, support, engineering, and content management services to Red Hat Linux users. Red Hat offers Linux certification training programs at all skill levels at more than 60 global locations—Red Hat certification in the use of Linux is considered the best in the world.

Microsoft's business model—sell proprietary code software and give service away free—is a proven money maker that generates billions in profits annually. On the other hand, the jury is still out on Red Hat's business model of marketing open-source software developed mainly by volunteers and depending heavily on sales of technical support services, training, and consulting to generate revenues sufficient to cover costs and yield a profit; Red Hat posted losses of $140 million on revenues of $79 million in fiscal year 2002 and losses of $6.6 million on revenues of $91 million in fiscal year 2003. But in the first 9 months of fiscal 2004, Red Hat earned a $9 million profit on revenues of $89 million. And the profits came from a shift in Red Hat's business model that involved putting more emphasis on selling subscriptions to the latest Red Hat Linux updates to corporate users.

Source: Company documents. Reprinted by permission from Microsoft Corporation, http://www.microsoft.com.

In-depth examples— **Illustration Capsules**—appear in boxes throughout each chapter to illustrate important chapter topics, connect the text presentation to real world companies, and convincingly demonstrate "strategy in action."

A Company's Strategy Emerges Incrementally and Then Evolves over Time   A company's strategy should always be viewed as a work in progress. Most of the time a company's strategy emerges in bits and pieces, the result of trial and error, experimentation, deliberate management design, and ongoing management actions to fine-tune this or that piece of the strategy and to adjust certain strategy elements in response to unfolding events. Nonetheless, on occasion, fine-tuning the existing strategy is not enough and major strategy shifts are called for, such as when a strategy is clearly failing and the company faces a financial crisis, when market conditions or buyer preferences change significantly and new opportunities arise, when competitors do something unexpected, or when important technological breakthroughs occur. Some industries are more volatile than others. Industry environments characterized by *high-velocity change* require companies to rapidly adapt their strategies.[3] For example, during the Internet gold rush and subsequent dot-com crash of 1997–2002, technology companies and e-commerce firms found it essential to revise demand forecasts, adjust key elements of their strategies, and update their financial projections at least quarterly and sometimes more frequently.

> **core concept**
> Changing circumstances and ongoing management efforts to improve the strategy cause a company's strategy to emerge and evolve over time—a condition that makes the task of crafting a strategy a work in progress, not a one-time event.

But regardless of whether a company's strategy changes gradually or swiftly, the important point is that a company's present strategy is temporary and on trial, pending new ideas for improvement from management, changing competitive conditions, and any other changes in the company's situation that managers believe warrant strategic adjustments. A company's strategy at any given point is fluid, representing the temporary outcome of an ongoing process that, on the one hand, involves reasoned and intuitive management efforts to design an effective strategy (a well-thought-out plan) and, on the other hand, involves responses to market change and constant experimentation and tinkering (adaptations to new conditions and learning about what has worked well enough to continue and what didn't work and has been abandoned).

> A company's strategy is driven partly by management analysis and choice and partly by the necessity of adapting and learning by doing.

Crafting Strategy Calls for Good Entrepreneurship   The constantly evolving nature of a company's situation puts a premium on management's ability to exhibit astute entrepreneurship. The faster a company's business environment is changing, the more critical it becomes for its managers to be adept in reading the winds of change and making timely strategic adjustments.[4] Managers are always under the gun to pick up on happenings in the external environment and steer company activities in directions that are aligned with unfolding market conditions. This means studying market trends and competitors' actions, listening to customers and anticipating their changing needs and expectations, scrutinizing the business possibilities that spring from new technological developments, building the firm's market position via acquisitions or new product introductions, and pursuing ways to strengthen the firm's competitive capabilities. It means paying attention to early warnings of future change and being willing to experiment with dare-to-be-different ways to establish a market position in that future. It means proactively searching out opportunities to do new things or to do existing things in new or better ways. When obstacles unexpectedly appear in a company's path, it means adapting rapidly and innovatively. *Masterful strategies come partly (maybe mostly) by doing things differently from competitors where it counts— outinnovating them, being more efficient, being more imaginative, adapting faster— rather than running with the herd.* Good strategy making is therefore inseparable from good business entrepreneurship. One cannot exist without the other.

Margin notes define core concepts and call attention to important ideas and principles.

Figures placed throughout the chapters provide conceptual and analytical frameworks.

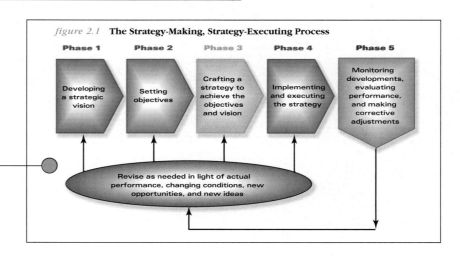

figure 2.1   **The Strategy-Making, Strategy-Executing Process**

Phase 1	Phase 2	Phase 3	Phase 4	Phase 5
Developing a strategic vision	Setting objectives	Crafting a strategy to achieve the objectives and vision	Implementing and executing the strategy	Monitoring developments, evaluating performance, and making corrective adjustments

Revise as needed in light of actual performance, changing conditions, new opportunities, and new ideas

key|points

The tasks of crafting and executing company strategies are the heart and soul of managing a business enterprise and winning in the marketplace. A company's **strategy** is the game plan management is using to stake out a market position, conduct its operations, attract and please customers, compete successfully, and achieve organizational objectives. The central thrust of a company's strategy is undertaking moves to build and strengthen the company's long-term competitive position and financial performance and, ideally, gain a competitive advantage over rivals that then becomes a company's ticket to above-average profitability. A company's strategy typically evolves and reforms over time, emerging from a blend of (1) proactive and purposeful actions on the part of company managers and (2) as-needed reactions to unanticipated developments and fresh market conditions.

Closely related to the concept of strategy is the concept of a company's **business model.** A company's business model is management's storyline for how and why the company's product offerings and competitive approaches will generate a revenue stream and have an associated cost structure that produces attractive earnings and return on investment—in effect, a company's business model sets forth the economic logic for making money in a particular business, given the company's current strategy.

A winning strategy fits the circumstances of a company's external situation and its internal resource strengths and competitive capabilities, builds competitive advantage, and boosts company performance.

Crafting and executing strategy are core management functions. Whether a company wins or loses in the marketplace is directly attributable to the caliber of a company's strategy and the proficiency with which the strategy is executed.

| exercises

1. Go to www.redhat.com and check whether the company's business model is working. Is the company sufficiently profitable to validate its business model and strategy? Is its revenue stream from selling technical support services growing or declining as a percentage of total revenues? Does your review of the company's recent financial performance suggest that its business model and strategy are changing? Read the company's latest statement about its business model.
2. Go to www.levistrauss.com/about/vision and read what the company says about how its corporate values of originality, empathy, integrity, and courage are connected to its vision of clothing the world by marketing the most appealing and widely worn casual clothing in the world. Do you believe what the company says, or are its statements just a bunch of nice pontifications that represent the chief executive officer's personal values (and also good public relations)?

Key Points sections at the end of each chapter provide a handy summary of essential ideas and things to remember.

Several short, mostly Internet-research-related **exercises** at the end of each chapter provide a supplement to assigned cases and a further way to reinforce core concepts.

37 cases detail the strategic circumstances of actual companies and provide practice in applying the concepts and tools of strategic analysis.

Part II: Cases in Crafting and Executing Strategy
Section A: Crafting Strategy in Single-Business Companies (24 cases)
Section B: Crafting Strategy in Diversified Companies (3 cases)
Section C: Implementing and Executing Strategy (8 cases)
Section D: Strategy, Ethics, and Social Responsibility (2 cases)

FOR STUDENTS: An Assortment of Support Materials

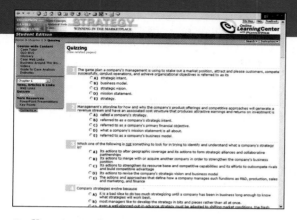

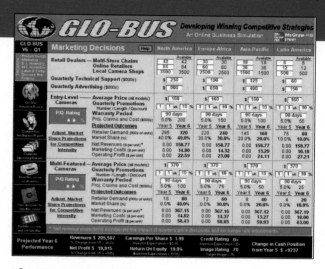

Online Learning Center:
www.mhhe.com/thompson The student portion of the Web site features a "Guide to Case Analysis," with special sections on describing what a case is, explaining why cases are a standard part of courses in strategy, preparing a case for class discussion, doing a written case analysis, performing an oral presentation, and using financial ratio analysis to assess a company's financial condition. In addition, there are 20-question self-scoring chapter tests and a select number of PowerPoint slides for each chapter.

Case-TUTOR Software
Accompanying the 37 cases is a software package containing assignment questions for all 37 cases in the text, plus analytically structured exercises for 13 of the cases that coach students in doing the strategic thinking needed to arrive at solid answers to the assignment questions for that case. Conscientious completion of the exercises help students gain quicker command of the concepts and analytical techniques and points them toward doing good strategic analysis.

The *GLO-BUS* Online Simulation
This course supplement emotionally connects you to the subject matter of the course by having teams of students in your class assigned to manage companies in a head-to-head contest for global market leadership in the digital camera industry. The simulation puts you in a situation where you and co-managers have to make decisions relating to product design, production, work force compensation, pricing, advertising, warranties, sales promotions, and finance. It is your job to craft and execute a strategy for your companpy that is powerful enough to deliver good bottom-line performance despite the efforts of rival companies to take away your company's sales and market share. Each company competes in North America, Latin America, Europe, and Asia.

PowerWeb With each new book, students gain access to PowerWeb news feeds and articles, now organized by topic and chapter within the Online Learning Center.

brief|contents

endnotes

table of|contents

Section B: Core Concepts and Analytical Tools

3. Analyzing a Company's External Environment   44

7. Competing in Foreign Markets   172

8. Tailoring Strategy to Fit Specific Industry and Company Situations   202

9. Diversification: Strategies for Managing a Group of Businesses   234

10. Strategy, Ethics, and Social Responsibility 282

Section D: Executing the Strategy

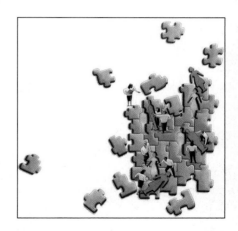

endnotes

part | one

1

Concepts and Techniques for Crafting and Executing Strategy

What Is Strategy and Why Is It Important?

(©Images.com/CORBIS)

A strategy is a commitment to undertake one set of actions rather than another.

—Sharon Oster
Professor, Yale University

The process of developing superior strategies is part planning, part trial and error, until you hit upon something that works.

—Costas Markides
Professor, London Business School

Without a strategy the organization is like a ship without a rudder.

—Joel Ross and Michael Kami
Business authors and consultants

anagers at all companies face three central questions in thinking strategically about their company's present circumstances and prospects: Where are we now? Where do we want to go? How will we get there? The question "Where are we now?" concerns the ins and outs of the company's present situation—its market standing, how appealing its products or services are to customers, the competitive pressures it confronts, its strengths and weaknesses, and its current performance. The question "Where do we want to go?" deals with the direction in which management believes the company should be headed in terms of growing the business and strengthening the company's market standing and financial performance in the years ahead. The question "How will we get there?" concerns crafting and executing a strategy to get the company from where it is to where it wants to go.

In this opening chapter, we define the concept of strategy and introduce its many elements and facets. We will explain how a strategy originates, the kinds of actions that determine what a company's strategy is, why strategies are partly proactive and partly reactive, and why company strategies tend to evolve over time. We will look at what sets a winning strategy apart from an ordinary strategy or one that is a sure loser and why the caliber of a company's strategy determines whether it will enjoy a competitive advantage or be burdened by competitive disadvantage. By the end of this chapter, you will have a pretty clear idea of why the tasks of crafting and executing strategy are core management functions and why excellent execution of an excellent strategy is the most reliable recipe for turning a company into a standout performer.

WHAT IS STRATEGY?

A company's **strategy** is management's game plan for growing the business, staking out a market position, attracting and pleasing customers, competing successfully, conducting operations, and achieving targeted objectives. In crafting a strategy, management is in effect saying, "Among all the paths we could have chosen, we have decided to focus on these markets and customer needs, compete in this fashion, allocate our resources and energies in these ways, and use these particular approaches to doing business." A company's strategy thus indicates the choices its managers have made about *how* to attract and please customers, *how* to respond to changing market conditions, *how* to compete successfully, *how* to grow the business, *how* to manage each

> **core concept**
> A company's *strategy* consists of the competitive moves and business approaches that managers employ to attract and please customers, compete successfully, grow the business, conduct operations, and achieve targeted objectives.

3

functional piece of the business and develop needed capabilities, and *how* to achieve performance targets. It puts the spotlight on the products/services, buyer segments, geographic areas, and business approaches management intends to emphasize.

Normally, markets are diverse enough to give companies a wide degree of strategic freedom in choosing the hows of strategy.[1] Some rivals have wide product lines while others have a narrow product focus, some target the high end of the market while others go after the middle or low end. Some strive for a competitive advantage based on low cost while others aim for a competitive edge based on product superiority or personalized customer service or added convenience. Some competitors position themselves in only one part of the industry's chain of production/distribution activities (preferring to be just in manufacturing or wholesale distribution or retailing), while others are partially or fully integrated, with operations ranging from components production to manufacturing and assembly to wholesale distribution or company-owned retail stores. Some rivals deliberately confine their operations to local or regional markets; others opt to compete nationally, internationally, or globally. Some companies decide to operate in only one industry, while others diversify broadly or narrowly, into related or unrelated industries, via acquisitions, joint ventures, strategic alliances, or internal start-ups.

At companies intent on gaining sales and market share at the expense of competitors, managers lean toward mostly offensive strategies, frequently launching fresh initiatives of one kind or another to make the company's product offering more distinctive and appealing to buyers. Conservative, risk-avoiding companies prefer a sound defense to an aggressive offense; their strategies emphasize gradual gains in the marketplace, fortifying the company's market position, and defending against the latest maneuvering of rivals and other developments that threaten the company's well-being.

There is no shortage of opportunity to fashion a strategy that tightly fits a company's own particular situation and that is discernibly different from the strategies of rivals. Carbon-copy strategies among companies in the same industry are the exception rather than the rule.

For a concrete example of the actions and approaches that comprise strategy, read the description of Southwest Airlines' strategy in Illustration Capsule 1.1.

Identifying a Company's Strategy

A company's strategy is reflected in its actions in the marketplace and the statements of senior managers about the company's current business approaches, future plans, and efforts to strengthen its competitiveness and performance. Figure 1.1 shows what to look for in identifying the substance of a company's overall strategy.

Once it is clear what to look for, the task of identifying a company's strategy is mainly one of researching information about the company's actions in the marketplace and business approaches. In the case of publicly owned enterprises, the strategy is often openly discussed by senior executives in the company's annual report and 10-K report, in press releases and company news (posted on the company's Web site), and in the information provided to investors at the company's Web site. To maintain the confidence of investors and Wall Street, most public companies have to be fairly open about their strategies. Company executives typically lay out key elements of their strategies in presentations to securities analysts (such presentations are usually posted in the investor relations section of the company's Web site). Hence, except for some about-to-be-launched moves and changes that remain under wraps and in the planning stage, there's usually nothing secret or undiscoverable about what a company's present strategy is.

illustration capsule 1.1
The Chief Elements of Southwest Airlines' Strategy

Southwest Airlines pursues a low-cost/low-price/no-frills strategy that features offering passengers a single class of service at the lowest possible fares. Southwest's market focus is flying between pairs of cities ranging anywhere from 150 to 700 miles apart where there is high traffic potential, but recently Southwest has also begun offering longer-range flights, using its low-cost advantage to horn in on the most profitable routes of American, United, Northwest, Delta, and US Airways. The company's strategy in 2003 included the following elements:

- *Grow the business by gradually adding more flights on existing routes and by initiating service to new airports.* The objective was steady growth year after year, not rapid growth for a few years that was impossible to sustain.

- *Make friendly service a company trademark.* Company personnel worked hard at creating a positive, fun flying experience for passengers. Southwest's casually dressed gate personnel and flight attendants, all screened carefully for fun-loving and outgoing personalities, warmly greeted passengers, entertained those in the gate area with trivia questions or contests, directed boarding passengers to open seats and helped with luggage storage, and sometimes sang the announcements on takeoff and landing.

- *Maintain an aircraft fleet of only Boeing 737s.* A fleet with only one type of plane minimized spare parts inventories, made it easier to train maintenance and repair personnel, improved the proficiency and speed with which maintenance routines could be done, and simplified the task of scheduling planes for particular flights.

- *Encourage customers to make reservations and purchase tickets at the company's Web site.* Selling a ticket on its Web site cost Southwest a tenth as much as delivering a ticket through a travel agent and about half of the cost of processing a paper ticket through its own internal reservation system.

- *Avoid flying into congested airports, stressing instead routes between medium-sized cities and small airports close to major metropolitan areas.* This strategy element improved on-time performance and reduced the fuel costs associated with planes sitting in line on crowded taxiways or circling airports waiting for clearance to land, plus it allowed the company to avoid paying the higher landing fees and terminal gate costs at high-traffic airports.

- *Employ a point-to-point route system (as compared to hub-and-spoke systems of rival carriers).* The point-to-point system promoted higher utilization of aircraft and terminal facilities and reduced the number of both aircraft and terminal gates needed to support flight operations.

- *Economize on the amount of time it takes terminal personnel to check passengers in and on-load passengers.* Southwest did not assign each passenger a reserved seat; instead, passengers were given boarding passes imprinted with A, B, or C at check-in and then boarded in groups of 30 according to the letter on their card, sitting in whatever seat was open when they got on the plane. This method sped up the boarding process.

- *Economize on costs.* Southwest served no meals on flights, had no fancy clubs for its frequent flyers to relax in at terminals, and provided no baggage transfer services to other carriers. Whereas other carriers hired cleaning crews, Southwest required flight attendants to clean up trash left by deplaning passengers and get the plane presentable for passengers to board for the next flight. On occasion, pilots pitched in to help with facilitating turnarounds and keeping the ground time between flights to less than 30 minutes. Short turnaround times allowed Southwest planes to fly more flights per day.

Southwest's strategy is a proven winner. Going into 2004, the company had earned a profit every quarter of every year since mid-1974—in an industry chronically riddled with money-losing companies.

Source: Company documents.

Strategy and the Quest for Competitive Advantage

Generally, a company's strategy should be aimed either at providing a product or service that is distinctive from what competitors are offering or at developing competitive

figure 1.1   **Identifying a Company's Strategy—What to Look For**

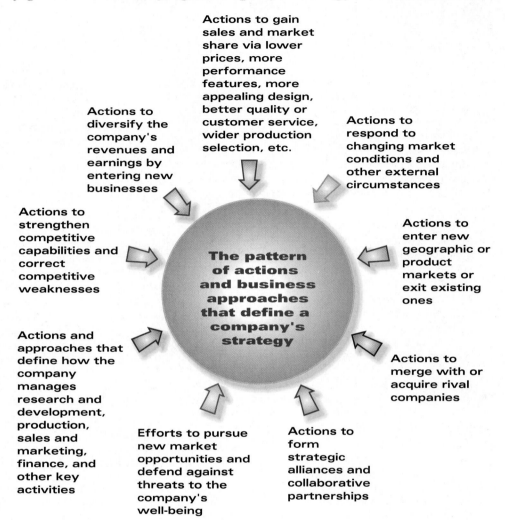

Actions to gain sales and market share via lower prices, more performance features, more appealing design, better quality or customer service, wider production selection, etc.

Actions to diversify the company's revenues and earnings by entering new businesses

Actions to respond to changing market conditions and other external circumstances

Actions to strengthen competitive capabilities and correct competitive weaknesses

Actions to enter new geographic or product markets or exit existing ones

The pattern of actions and business approaches that define a company's strategy

Actions and approaches that define how the company manages research and development, production, sales and marketing, finance, and other key activities

Actions to merge with or acquire rival companies

Efforts to pursue new market opportunities and defend against threats to the company's well-being

Actions to form strategic alliances and collaborative partnerships

capabilities that rivals can't quite match. For instance, while such car rental companies as Hertz, Avis, National, and Dollar slug it out head-to-head trying to woo business and vacation travelers at airports, Enterprise Rent-A-Car has become the world's most profitable car rental company by focusing on people who need a car for ordinary use—for example, while their own is being repaired. Furthermore, instead of hiring low-paid service employees to staff its rental locations, Enterprise recruits recent college graduates and compensates them well for growing the volume of business at Enterprise's locations. Enterprise can also deliver a car to the renter's home and pick it up at the end of the rental. With its distinctive strategy and customer focus, Enterprise operates the biggest car rental fleet in the world and has more locations than any other car rental company.

What separates a powerful strategy from an ordinary or weak one is management's ability to forge a series of moves, both in the marketplace and internally, that makes the company *distinctive,* tilts the playing field in the company's favor by giving buyers reason to prefer its products or services, and produces a *sustainable competitive advantage* over rivals. With a durable competitive advantage, a company has good prospects for winning in the marketplace and realizing above-average profitability. Without competitive advantage, a company risks being beaten by stronger rivals and/or locked into mediocre financial performance.

Four of the most frequently used strategic approaches to setting a company apart from rivals and achieving a sustainable competitive advantage are:

> **core concept**
> A company achieves sustainable competitive advantage when an attractive number of buyers prefer its products or services over the offerings of competitors and when the basis for this preference is durable.

1. *Being the industry's low-cost provider* (thereby gaining a cost-based competitive advantage over rivals). Wal-Mart and Southwest Airlines have earned strong market positions because of the low-cost advantages they have achieved over their rivals and their consequent ability to underprice their competitors.

2. *Outcompeting rivals based on such differentiating features as higher quality, wider product selection, added performance, better service, more attractive styling, technological superiority, or unusually good value for the money.* Successful adopters of differentiation strategies include Johnson & Johnson in baby products (product reliability), Harley-Davidson (bad-boy image and king-of-the-road styling), Chanel and Rolex (top-of-the-line prestige), Mercedes and BMW (engineering design and performance), L. L. Bean (good value), and Amazon.com (wide selection and convenience).

3. *Focusing on a narrow market niche* and winning a competitive edge by doing a better job than rivals of serving the special needs and tastes of niche buyers. Prominent companies that enjoy competitive success in a specialized market niche include eBay in online auctions, Jiffy Lube International in quick oil changes, McAfee in virus protection software, Starbucks in premium coffees and coffee drinks, Whole Foods Market in natural and organic foods, and Krispy Kreme in doughnuts.

4. *Developing expertise and resource strengths that give the company competitive capabilities that rivals can't easily imitate or trump with capabilities of their own.* FedEx has superior capabilities in next-day delivery of small packages, Walt Disney has hard-to-beat capabilities in theme park management and family entertainment, and IBM has wide-ranging capabilities in supporting the information systems and information technology needs of large corporations.

Most companies recognize that winning a durable competitive edge over rivals hinges more on building competitively valuable expertise and capabilities than it does on having a distinctive product. Rivals can nearly always copy the attributes of a popular or innovative product, but for rivals to match experience, know-how, and specialized competitive capabilities that a company has developed and perfected over a long period of time is substantially harder to duplicate and takes much longer—despite years of trying, Kmart, Sears, and other discount retailers and supermarket chains have struck out trying to match Wal-Mart's sophisticated distribution systems and its finely honed merchandising expertise. Company initiatives to build competencies and capabilities that rivals don't have and cannot readily match can relate to greater product innovation capabilities than rivals (3M Corporation), better mastery of a complex technological process (Michelin in making radial tires), expertise in defect-free manufacturing (Toyota and Honda), specialized marketing and merchandising know-how (Coca-Cola), global sales and distribution capability (Black & Decker in power tools), superior e-commerce capabilities (Dell Computer), unique ability to deliver personalized customer service (Ritz Carlton and Four Seasons hotels), or anything else that constitutes a competitively valuable strength in creating, producing, distributing, or marketing the company's product or service.

figure 1.2   **A Company's Actual Strategy Is Partly Proactive and Partly Reactive**

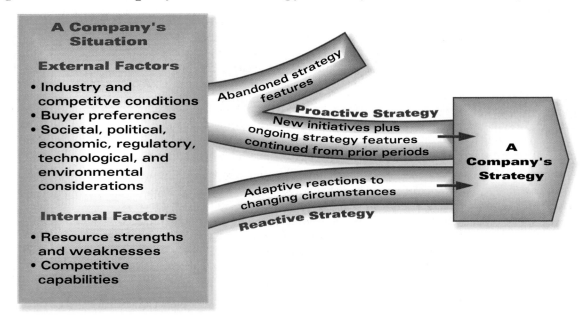

Strategy Is Partly Proactive and Partly Reactive

A company's strategy is typically a blend of (1) proactive actions on the part of managers to improve the company's market position and financial performance and (2) as-needed reactions to unanticipated developments and fresh market conditions—see Figure 1.2.[2] The biggest portion of a company's current strategy flows from previously initiated actions and business approaches that are working well enough to merit continuation and newly launched managerial initiatives to strengthen the company's overall position and performance. This part of management's game plan is deliberate and proactive, standing as the product of management's analysis and strategic thinking about the company's situation and its conclusions about how to position the company in the marketplace and tackle the task of competing for buyer patronage.

But not every strategic move is the result of proactive plotting and deliberate management design. Things happen that cannot be fully anticipated or planned for. When market and competitive conditions take an unexpected turn or some aspect of a company's strategy hits a stone wall, some kind of strategic reaction or adjustment is required. Hence, a portion of a company's strategy is always developed on the fly, coming as a reasoned response to unforeseen developments—fresh strategic maneuvers on the part of rival firms, shifting customer requirements and expectations, new technologies and market opportunities, a changing political or economic climate, or other unpredictable or unanticipated happenings in the surrounding environment. But apart from adapting strategy to changes in the market, there is also a need to adapt strategy as new learning emerges about which pieces of the strategy are working well and which aren't and as management hits upon new ideas for improving the strategy. Crafting a strategy thus involves stitching together a *proactive/intended strategy* and then adapting first one piece and then another as circumstances surrounding the company's situation change or better options emerge—a *reactive/adaptive strategy*.

A Company's Strategy Emerges Incrementally and Then Evolves over Time

A company's strategy should always be viewed as a work in progress. Most of the time a company's strategy emerges in bits and pieces, the result of trial and error, experimentation, deliberate management design, and ongoing management actions to fine-tune this or that piece of the strategy and to adjust certain strategy elements in response to unfolding events. Nonetheless, on occasion, fine-tuning the existing strategy is not enough and major strategy shifts are called for, such as when a strategy is clearly failing and the company faces a financial crisis, when market conditions or buyer preferences change significantly and new opportunities arise, when competitors do something unexpected, or when important technological breakthroughs occur. Some industries are more volatile than others. Industry environments characterized by *high-velocity change* require companies to rapidly adapt their strategies.[3] For example, during the Internet gold rush and subsequent dot-com crash of 1997–2002, technology companies and e-commerce firms found it essential to revise demand forecasts, adjust key elements of their strategies, and update their financial projections at least quarterly and sometimes more frequently.

> **core concept**
> Changing circumstances and ongoing management efforts to improve the strategy cause a company's strategy to emerge and evolve over time—a condition that makes the task of crafting a strategy a work in progress, not a one-time event.

But regardless of whether a company's strategy changes gradually or swiftly, the important point is that a company's present strategy is temporary and on trial, pending new ideas for improvement from management, changing competitive conditions, and any other changes in the company's situation that managers believe warrant strategic adjustments. A company's strategy at any given point is fluid, representing the temporary outcome of an ongoing process that, on the one hand, involves reasoned and intuitive management efforts to design an effective strategy (a well-thought-out plan) and, on the other hand, involves responses to market change and constant experimentation and tinkering (adaptations to new conditions and learning about what has worked well enough to continue and what didn't work and has been abandoned).

> A company's strategy is driven partly by management analysis and choice and partly by the necessity of adapting and learning by doing.

Crafting Strategy Calls for Good Entrepreneurship

The constantly evolving nature of a company's situation puts a premium on management's ability to exhibit astute entrepreneurship. The faster a company's business environment is changing, the more critical it becomes for its managers to be adept in reading the winds of change and making timely strategic adjustments.[4] Managers are always under the gun to pick up on happenings in the external environment and steer company activities in directions that are aligned with unfolding market conditions. This means studying market trends and competitors' actions, listening to customers and anticipating their changing needs and expectations, scrutinizing the business possibilities that spring from new technological developments, building the firm's market position via acquisitions or new product introductions, and pursuing ways to strengthen the firm's competitive capabilities. It means paying attention to early warnings of future change and being willing to experiment with dare-to-be-different ways to establish a market position in that future. It means proactively searching out opportunities to do new things or to do existing things in new or better ways. When obstacles unexpectedly appear in a company's path, it means adapting rapidly and innovatively. *Masterful strategies come partly (maybe mostly) by doing things differently from competitors where it counts— outinnovating them, being more efficient, being more imaginative, adapting faster— rather than running with the herd.* Good strategy making is therefore inseparable from good business entrepreneurship. One cannot exist without the other.

Strategy and Ethics: Passing the Test of Moral Scrutiny

In choosing among strategic alternatives, company managers are well advised to embrace actions that are aboveboard and can pass the test of moral scrutiny. Crafting an ethical strategy means more than keeping a company's strategic actions within the bounds of what is legal. Ethical and moral standards go beyond the prohibitions of law and the language of "thou shalt not" to the issues of "right" versus "wrong" and *duty*—what one *should* do. A strategy is ethical only if: (1) it does not entail actions and behaviors that cross the line from "can do" to "should not do" and "unsavory" and (2) it allows management to fulfill its ethical duties to all stakeholders—owners/shareholders, employees, customers, suppliers, the communities in which it operates, and society at large.

Admittedly, it is not always easy to categorize a given strategic behavior as definitely ethical or definitely unethical; many strategic actions fall in a gray zone in between. Whether they are deemed ethical or unethical hinges on how high one sets the bar. For example, is it ethical for advertisers of alcoholic products to place ads in media having an audience of as much as 50 percent underage viewers? (In 2003, growing concerns about underage drinking prompted some beer and distilled spirits companies to agree to place ads in media with an audience at least 70 percent adult, up from a standard of 50 percent adult.) Is it ethical for an apparel retailer attempting to keep prices attractively low to source clothing from foreign manufacturers who pay substandard wages, employ child labor, or engage in unsavory sweatshop practices? Many people would say no, but some might argue that a company is not unethical simply because it does not police the business practices of its suppliers. Is it ethical for the manufacturers of firearms (in hopes of gaining a supply of resalable weapons) to encourage retired police officers to trade in or return automatic weapons whose manufacture has since been banned by Congress? Several firearms makers have been said to take advantage of a loophole in the law allowing them to traffic in such weapons. Is it ethical for a meatpacker to export meat products that do not meet safe standards in its home country to those countries where the safety and standards are low and inspection is lax? Several consumer groups have protested that certain meatpackers engage in this practice, but the meatpackers defend their actions by saying that none of the exported products constitute a danger to consumers (cross-country meat inspection standards and procedures vary considerably, such that products passing inspection in one country may not pass in another country).

Senior executives with strong character and ethical convictions are generally proactive in linking strategic action and ethics; they forbid the pursuit of ethically questionable business opportunities and insist that all aspects of company strategy reflect high ethical standards.[5] They make it clear that all company personnel are expected to act with integrity, and they put organizational checks and balances into place to monitor behavior, enforce ethical codes of conduct, and provide guidance to employees regarding any gray areas. Their commitment to conducting the company's business in an ethical manner is genuine, not hypocritical lip service.

Recent instances of corporate malfeasance, ethical lapses, and misleading or fraudulent accounting practices at Enron, WorldCom, Tyco, Adelphia, Dynegy, HealthSouth, and other companies leave no room to doubt the damage to a company's reputation and business that can result from ethical misconduct, corporate misdeeds, and even criminal behavior on the part of company personnel. Aside from just the embarrassment and black marks that accompany headline exposure of a company's unethical practices, the hard fact is that many customers and many suppliers are wary of doing business with a company that engages in sleazy practices or that turns a blind eye to illegal or unethical behavior on the part of employees. They are turned off by unethical strategies or behavior and, rather than become victims or get burned themselves, wary customers will quickly take their business elsewhere and wary suppliers will tread carefully. Moreover, employees with character and integrity do not want to work for a company whose strategies are shady or whose executives lack character and integrity. There's little lasting benefit to unethical strategies and behavior, and the downside risks can be substantial. Besides, such actions are plain wrong.

THE RELATIONSHIP BETWEEN A COMPANY'S STRATEGY AND ITS BUSINESS MODEL

Closely related to the concept of strategy is the concept of a company's **business model.** While the word *model* conjures up images of ivory-tower ideas set apart from the real world, such images do not apply here. A company's business model sets forth the economic logic of how an enterprise's strategy can deliver value to customers at a price and cost that yields acceptable profitability.[6] A company's business model thus is management's storyline for how and why the company's product offerings and competitive approaches will generate a revenue stream and have an associated cost structure that produces attractive earnings and return on investment. The nitty-gritty issue surrounding a company's business model is whether the chosen strategy makes good business sense from a money-making perspective. The concept of a company's business model is, consequently, more narrowly focused than the concept of a company's business strategy. A company's strategy *relates broadly to its competitive initiatives and business approaches (irrespective of the financial outcomes it produces), while* a company's business model *deals with whether the revenues and costs flowing from the strategy demonstrate business viability.* Companies that have been in business for a while and are making acceptable profits have a "proven" business model—there is clear evidence that their strategy is capable of profitability and that they have a viable business enterprise. Companies that are in a start-up mode or that are losing money have "questionable" business models; their strategies have yet to produce good bottom-line results, putting their storyline about how they intend to make money and their viability as business enterprises in doubt. Illustration Capsule 1.2 discusses the contrasting business models of Microsoft and Red Hat Linux.

> **core concept**
> A company's **business model** relates to whether the revenue-cost-profit economics of its strategy demonstrate the viability of the business enterprise as a whole.

WHAT MAKES A STRATEGY A WINNER?

Three questions can be used to test the merits of one strategy versus another and distinguish a winning strategy from a losing or mediocre strategy:

1. *How well does the strategy fit the company's situation?* To qualify as a winner, a strategy has to be well matched to industry and competitive conditions, a company's best market opportunities, and other aspects of the enterprise's external environment. At the same time, it has to be tailored to the company's resource strengths and weaknesses, competencies, and competitive capabilities. Unless a strategy exhibits tight fit with both the external and internal aspects of a company's overall situation, it is likely to produce less than the best possible business results.

illustration capsule 1.2
Microsoft and Red Hat Linux: Two Contrasting Business Models

The strategies of rival companies are often predicated on strikingly different business models. Consider, for example, the business models for Microsoft and Red Hat Linux in operating system software for PCs.

Microsoft's business model for making money from its operating system products is based on the following revenue-cost-profit economics:

- Employ a cadre of highly skilled programmers to develop proprietary code; keep the source code hidden from users and lock them in to using Microsoft's proprietary software.

- Sell the resulting operating system and software package to personal computer (PC) makers and to PC users at relatively attractive prices (around $75 to PC makers and about $100 at retail to PC users) and achieve large unit sales.

- Most of Microsoft's costs arise on the front end in developing the software and are thus "fixed"; the variable costs of producing and packaging the CDs provided to users are only a couple of dollars per copy—once the break-even volume is reached, Microsoft's revenues from additional sales are almost pure profit.

- Provide technical support to users at no cost.

Red Hat Linux, a company formed to market its own version of the open-source Linux operating system, employs a business model based on sharply different revenue-cost-profit economics:

- Rely on the collaborative efforts of volunteer programmers from all over the world who contribute bits and pieces of code to improve and polish the Linux system. The global community of thousands of programmers who work on Linux in their spare time do what they do because they love it, because they are fervent believers that all software should be free (as in free speech), and, in some cases, because they are anti-Microsoft and want to have a part in undoing what they see as a Microsoft monopoly.

- Collect and test enhancements and new applications submitted by the open-source community of volunteer programmers. Linux's originator, Linus Torvalds, and a team of 300-plus Red Hat engineers and software developers evaluate which incoming submissions merit inclusion in new releases of Red Hat Linux—the evaluation and integration of new submissions are Red Hat's only up-front product development costs.

- Charge a modest fee to those who prefer to subscribe to the upgraded and tested family of Red Hat Linux products. Subscription fees include a limited number of days of service, support, patches, and updates.

- Release updated versions of Red Hat Linux every 4–6 months to small users and every 12–18 months to corporate users.

- Make the source code open and available to all users, allowing them to create a customized version of Linux.

- Capitalize on the specialized expertise required to use Linux in multiserver, multiprocessor applications by providing fees-based training, consulting, support, engineering, and content management services to Red Hat Linux users. Red Hat offers Linux certification training programs at all skill levels at more than 60 global locations—Red Hat certification in the use of Linux is considered the best in the world.

Microsoft's business model—sell proprietary code software and give service away free—is a proven money maker that generates billions in profits annually. On the other hand, the jury is still out on Red Hat's business model of marketing open-source software developed mainly by volunteers and depending heavily on sales of technical support services, training, and consulting to generate revenues sufficient to cover costs and yield a profit; Red Hat posted losses of $140 million on revenues of $79 million in fiscal year 2002 and losses of $6.6 million on revenues of $91 million in fiscal year 2003. But in the first 9 months of fiscal 2004, Red Hat earned a $9 million profit on revenues of $89 million. And the profits came from a shift in Red Hat's business model that involved putting more emphasis on selling subscriptions to the latest Red Hat Linux updates to corporate users.

Source: Company documents. Reprinted by permission from Microsoft Corporation, http://www.microsoft.com.

2. *Is the strategy helping the company achieve a sustainable competitive advantage?* Winning strategies enable a company to achieve a competitive advantage that is durable. The bigger and more durable the competitive edge that a strategy helps build, the more powerful and appealing it is.

3. *Is the strategy resulting in better company performance?* A good strategy boosts company performance. Two kinds of performance improvements tell the most about the caliber of a company's strategy: (1) gains in profitability and financial strength and (2) gains in the company's competitive strength and market standing.

Once a company commits to a particular strategy and enough time elapses to assess how well it fits the situation and whether it is actually delivering competitive advantage and better performance, then one can determine what grade to assign its strategy. Strategies that come up short on one or more of the above questions are plainly less appealing than strategies passing all three test questions with flying colors.

Managers can also use the same questions to pick and choose among alternative strategic actions. A company evaluating which of several strategic options to employ can size up how well each option measures up against each of the three questions. The strategic option with the highest prospective passing scores on all three questions can be regarded as the best or most attractive strategic alternative.

> **core concept**
> A winning strategy must fit the enterprise's external and internal situation, build sustainable competitive advantage, and improve company performance.

Other criteria for judging the merits of a particular strategy include internal consistency and unity among all the pieces of strategy, the degree of risk the strategy poses as compared to alternative strategies, and the degree to which it is flexible and adaptable to changing circumstances. These criteria are relevant and merit consideration, but they seldom override the importance of the three test questions posed above.

WHY ARE CRAFTING AND EXECUTING STRATEGY IMPORTANT?

Crafting and executing strategy are top-priority managerial tasks for two very big reasons. First, there is a compelling need for managers to *proactively shape,* or *craft,* how the company's business will be conducted. A clear and reasoned strategy is management's prescription for doing business, its road map to competitive advantage, its game plan for pleasing customers and achieving performance targets. Winning in the marketplace requires a well-conceived, opportunistic strategy, usually one characterized by strategic offensives to outinnovate and outmaneuver rivals and secure sustainable competitive advantage, then using this market edge to achieve superior financial performance. A powerful strategy that delivers a home run in the marketplace can propel a firm from a trailing position into a leading one, clearing the way for its products/services to become the industry standard. High-achieving enterprises are nearly always the product of astute, proactive strategy making—companies don't get to the top of the industry rankings or stay there with strategies built around timid actions to try to do better. And only a handful of companies can boast of strategies that hit home runs in the marketplace due to lucky breaks or the good fortune of having stumbled into the right market at the right time with the right product. So there can be little argument that a company's strategy matters—and matters a lot.

Second, a *strategy-focused organization* is more likely to be a strong bottom-line performer. There's no escaping the fact that the quality of managerial strategy making and strategy execution has a positive impact on revenue growth, earnings, and return on investment. A company that lacks clear-cut direction, has vague or undemanding performance targets, has a muddled or flawed strategy, or can't seem to execute its strategy competently is a company whose financial performance is probably suffering, whose business is at long-term risk, and whose management is sorely lacking. In contrast, when crafting and executing a winning strategy drive management's whole approach to operating the company, the odds are much greater that the initiatives and activities of different divisions, departments, managers, and work groups will be unified into a *coordinated, cohesive effort*. Mobilizing the full complement of company resources in a total team effort behind good execution of the chosen strategy and achievement of the targeted performance allows a company to operate at full power. The chief executive officer of one successful company put it well when he said:

> In the main, our competitors are acquainted with the same fundamental concepts and techniques and approaches that we follow, and they are as free to pursue them as we are. More often than not, the difference between their level of success and ours lies in the relative thoroughness and self-discipline with which we and they develop and execute our strategies for the future.

Good Strategy + Good Strategy Execution = Good Management

Crafting and executing strategy are thus core management functions. Among all the things managers do, nothing affects a company's ultimate success or failure more fundamentally than how well its management team charts the company's direction, develops competitively effective strategic moves and business approaches, and pursues what needs to be done internally to produce good day-in, day-out strategy execution and operating excellence. Indeed, *good strategy and good strategy execution are the most trustworthy signs of good management.* Managers don't deserve a gold star for designing a potentially brilliant strategy but failing to put the organizational means in place to carry it out in high-caliber fashion—weak implementation and execution—undermine the strategy's potential and pave the way for shortfalls in customer satisfaction and company performance. Competent execution of a mediocre strategy scarcely merits enthusiastic applause for management's efforts either. The rationale for using the twin standards of good strategy making and good strategy execution to determine whether a company is well managed is therefore compelling: *The better conceived a company's strategy and the more competently it is executed, the more likely it is that the company will be a standout performer in the marketplace.*

core concept
Excellent execution of an excellent strategy is the best test of managerial excellence—and the most reliable recipe for turning companies into standout performers.

Throughout the text chapters to come and the accompanying case collection, the spotlight is trained on the foremost question in running a business enterprise: What must managers do, and do well, to make a company a winner in the marketplace? The answer that emerges, and that becomes the message of this book, is that doing a good job of managing inherently requires good strategic thinking and good management of the strategy-making, strategy-executing process.

The mission of this book is to explore what good strategic thinking entails; to present the core concepts and tools of strategic analysis; to describe the ins and outs of crafting and executing strategy; and, via the cases that have been included, to build your skills both in diagnosing how well the strategy-making, strategy-executing task is being performed in actual companies and in prescribing actions for how the companies in question can improve their approaches to crafting and executing their strategies.

As you tackle the following pages, ponder the following observation by the essayist and poet Ralph Waldo Emerson: "Commerce is a game of skill which many people play, but which few play well." The overriding objective of this book is to help you become a more savvy player and equip you to succeed in business.

key|points

The tasks of crafting and executing company strategies are the heart and soul of managing a business enterprise and winning in the marketplace. A company's **strategy** is the game plan management is using to stake out a market position, conduct its operations, attract and please customers, compete successfully, and achieve organizational objectives. The central thrust of a company's strategy is undertaking moves to build and strengthen the company's long-term competitive position and financial performance and, ideally, gain a competitive advantage over rivals that then becomes a company's ticket to above-average profitability. A company's strategy typically evolves and reforms over time, emerging from a blend of (1) proactive and purposeful actions on the part of company managers and (2) as-needed reactions to unanticipated developments and fresh market conditions.

Closely related to the concept of strategy is the concept of a company's **business model.** A company's business model is management's storyline for how and why the company's product offerings and competitive approaches will generate a revenue stream and have an associated cost structure that produces attractive earnings and return on investment—in effect, a company's business model sets forth the economic logic for making money in a particular business, given the company's current strategy.

A winning strategy fits the circumstances of a company's external situation and its internal resource strengths and competitive capabilities, builds competitive advantage, and boosts company performance.

Crafting and executing strategy are core management functions. Whether a company wins or loses in the marketplace is directly attributable to the caliber of a company's strategy and the proficiency with which the strategy is executed.

| exercises

1. Go to www.redhat.com and check whether the company's business model is working. Is the company sufficiently profitable to validate its business model and strategy? Is its revenue stream from selling technical support services growing or declining as a percentage of total revenues? Does your review of the company's recent financial performance suggest that its business model and strategy are changing? Read the company's latest statement about its business model.

2. Go to www.levistrauss.com/about/vision and read what the company says about how its corporate values of originality, empathy, integrity, and courage are connected to its vision of clothing the world by marketing the most appealing and widely worn casual clothing in the world. Do you believe what the company says, or are its statements just a bunch of nice pontifications that represent the chief executive officer's personal values (and also good public relations)?

The Managerial Process of Crafting and Executing Strategy

(©Dale O'Dell/CORBIS)

Unless we change our direction we are likely to end up where we are headed.

—Ancient Chinese proverb

If we can know where we are and something about how we got there, we might see where we are trending—and if the outcomes which lie naturally in our course are unacceptable, to make timely change.

—Abraham Lincoln

If you don't know where you are going, any road will take you there.

—The Koran

Management's job is not to see the company as it is . . . but as it can become.

—John W. Teets
Former CEO

rafting and executing strategy are the heart and soul of managing a business enterprise. But exactly what is involved in developing a strategy and executing it proficiently? And who besides top management has strategy-making, strategy-executing responsibility? In this chapter we present an overview of the managerial ins and outs of crafting and executing company strategies. Special attention will be given to management's direction-setting responsibilities—charting a strategic course, setting performance targets, and choosing a strategy capable of producing the desired outcomes. We will also examine which kinds of strategic decisions are made at which levels of management and the roles and responsibilities of the company's board of directors in the strategy-making, strategy-executing process.

WHAT DOES THE PROCESS OF CRAFTING AND EXECUTING STRATEGY ENTAIL?

Crafting and executing a company's strategy is a five-phase managerial process:

1. Developing a strategic vision of where the company needs to head and what its future product-customer-market-technology focus should be.
2. Setting objectives and using them as yardsticks for measuring the company's performance and progress.
3. Crafting a strategy to achieve the desired outcomes and move the company along the strategic course that management has charted.
4. Implementing and executing the chosen strategy efficiently and effectively.
5. Monitoring developments and initiating corrective adjustments in the company's long-term direction, objectives, strategy, or execution in light of the company's actual performance, changing conditions, new ideas, and new opportunities.

Figure 2.1 displays this process. Let's examine this five-phase strategy-making, strategy-executing framework in enough detail to set the stage for the forthcoming chapters and to give you a bird's-eye view of what the rest of this book is about.

DEVELOPING A STRATEGIC VISION: PHASE 1 OF THE STRATEGY-MAKING, STRATEGY-EXECUTING PROCESS

Very early in the strategy-making process, a company's senior managers must wrestle with the issue of what directional path the company should take and what changes in the company's product-market-customer-technology focus would improve its current market position and future prospects. Deciding to commit the company to one path

figure 2.1   **The Strategy-Making, Strategy-Executing Process**

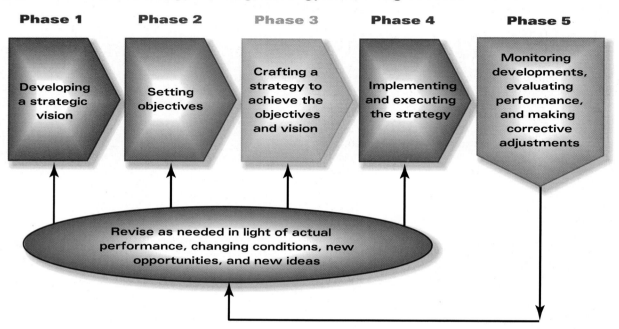

versus another pushes managers to draw some carefully reasoned conclusions about how to try to modify the company's business makeup and the market position it should stake out. A number of direction-shaping factors need to be considered in deciding where to head and why such a direction makes good business sense—see Table 2.1.

Top management's views and conclusions about the company's direction and the product-customer-market-technology focus constitute a **strategic vision** for the company. A strategic vision delineates management's aspirations for the business, providing a panoramic view of "where we are going" and a convincing rationale for why this makes good business sense for the company. A strategic vision thus points an organization in a particular direction, charts a strategic path for it to follow in preparing for the future, and molds organizational identity. A clearly articulated strategic vision communicates management's aspirations to stakeholders and helps steer the energies of company personnel in a common direction. For instance, Henry Ford's vision of a car in every garage had power because it captured the imagination of others, aided internal efforts to mobilize the Ford Motor Company's resources, and served as a reference point for gauging the merits of the company's strategic actions.

core concept
A *strategic vision* is a road map showing the route a company intends to take in developing and strengthening its business. It paints a picture of a company's destination and provides a rationale for going there.

Well-conceived visions are distinctive and specific to a particular organization; they avoid generic, feel-good statements like "We will become a global leader and the first choice of customers in every market we choose to serve"—which could apply to any of hundreds of organizations.[1] And they are not the product of a committee charged with coming up with an innocuous but well-meaning one sentence vision that wins consensus approval from various stakeholders. Nicely worded vision statements with no specifics about the company's product-market-customer-technology focus are suspect. A strategic vision proclaiming management's quest "to be the market leader" or "to be the first choice of customers" or "to be the most innovative" or "to be recog-

table 2.1   **Factors to Consider in Deciding to Commit the Company to One Directional Path versus Another**

External Considerations	Internal Considerations
• Is the outlook for the company promising if it simply maintains its present product/market/customer/technology focus? Does sticking with the company's present strategic course present attractive growth opportunities?	• What are our ambitions for the company? What industry standing does management want the company to have?
• Are changes under way in the market and competitive landscape enhancing or weakening the outlook for the company's present business?	• Will the company's present business generate sufficient growth and profitability in the years ahead to please shareholders?
• What, if any, new customer groups and/or geographic markets should the company get in position to serve?	• What organizational strengths ought the company be trying to leverage in terms of adding new products or services and/or getting into new businesses?
• Which emerging market opportunities should the company pursue and which ones should it avoid?	• Is the company stretching its resources too thin by trying to compete in too many markets or segments? Are some pieces of the company's business unprofitable?
• Should the company plan to abandon any of the markets, market segments, or customer groups we are currently serving?	• Is the company's technological focus too broad or too narrow? Are any changes needed?

nized as the best company in the industry" offer scant guidance about a company's directions and what management intends to do to get there.

For a strategic vision to function as a valuable managerial tool, it must provide understanding of what management wants its business to look like and provide managers with a reference point in making strategic decisions and preparing the company for the future. It must say something definitive about how the company's leaders intend to position the company beyond where it is today. A good vision always needs to be a bit beyond a company's reach, but progress toward the vision is what unifies the efforts of company personnel. Table 2.2 lists some characteristics of an effective vision statement.

A sampling of vision statements currently in use shows a range from strong and clear to bland and ill-conceived. A surprising number of the vision statements found on company Web sites and in annual reports are dull, blurry, and uninspiring—they come across as having been written by a committee to attract consensus from a variety of organizational stakeholders and having been developed only because it is fashionable for companies to have an official vision statement.[2] Few corporate executives want to risk the embarrassment of being without a vision statement. The one- or two-sentence vision statement a company makes available to the public, of course, provides only a glimpse of what company executives are really thinking and where the company is headed and why. Having a vision is not a panacea but rather a useful management tool for giving an organization a sense of direction. Like any tool, it can be used properly or improperly, either strongly conveying a company's strategic course or not. Table 2.3 provides a list of the most common shortcomings in company vision statements.

Illustration Capsule 2.1 contains the strategic vision for Exelon, one of the leading and best-managed electric and gas utility companies in the United States. Illustration Capsule 2.2 provides examples of strategic visions of several prominent companies and nonprofit organizations. See if you can tell which ones are mostly meaningless or nice-sounding and which ones are managerially useful in communicating "where we are headed and the kind of company we are trying to become".

table 2.2   **Characteristics of an Effectively Worded Vision Statement**

Graphic	A well-stated vision paints a picture of the kind of company that management is trying to create and the market position the company is striving to stake out.
Directional	A well-stated vision says something about the company's journey or destination and signals the kinds of business and strategic changes that will be forthcoming.
Focused	A well-stated vision is specific enough to provide managers with guidance in making decisions and allocating resources.
Flexible	A well-stated vision is not a once-and-for-all-time pronouncement— visions about a company's future path may need to change as events unfold and circumstances change.
Feasible	A well-stated vision is within the realm of what the company can reasonably expect to achieve in due time.
Desirable	A well-stated vision appeals to the long-term interests of stakeholders— particularly shareowners, employees, and customers.
Easy to communicate	A well-stated vision is explainable in less than 10 minutes and ideally can be reduced to a simple, memorable slogan (like Henry Ford's famous vision of "a car in every garage").

Source: Reprinted by permission of Harvard Business School Press. From *Leading Change* by John P. Kotter. Boston, MA, p. 72. Copyright © 1996 by the Harvard Business School Publishing Corporation; all rights reserved.

A Strategic Vision Is Different from a Mission Statement   Whereas the chief concern of a strategic vision is with "where we are going and why," a company mission statement usually deals with a company's *present* business scope and purpose— "who we are, what we do, and why we are here." *A company's mission is defined by the buyer needs it seeks to satisfy, the customer groups and market segments it is endeavoring to serve, and the resources and technologies that it is deploying in trying to please its customers.* (Many companies prefer the term business purpose to mission statement, but the two phrases are essentially conceptually identical and are used interchangeably.) A typical example is the mission statement of Trader Joe's (a unique grocery chain):

> The mission of Trader Joe's is to give our customers the best food and beverage values that they can find anywhere and to provide them with the information required for informed buying decisions. We provide these with a dedication to the highest quality of customer satisfaction delivered with a sense of warmth, friendliness, fun, individual pride, and company spirit.

> The distinction between a strategic vision and a mission statement is fairly clear-cut: A strategic vision portrays a company's future business scope ("where we are going") whereas a company's mission typically describes its present business scope and purpose ("who we are, what we do, and why we are here").

The mission statements that one finds in company annual reports or posted on company Web sites typically provide a brief overview of the company's present business purpose and raison d'être and sometimes its geographic coverage or standing as a market leader. They may or may not single out the company's present products/services, the buyer needs it is seeking to satisfy, the customer groups it serves, or its technological and business capabilities. But company mission statements almost never say anything about where the company is headed, the anticipated changes in its business, or its aspirations.

Occasionally, companies couch their mission in terms of making a profit. The notion that a company's mission or business purpose is to make a profit is misguided—profit is more correctly an *objective* and a *result* of what a company does. Making a profit is the obvious intent of every com-

table 2.3   **Common Shortcomings in Company Vision Statements**

1. Incomplete—short on specifics about where the company is headed or what kind of company management is trying to create.
2. Vague—doesn't provide much indication of whether or how management intends to alter the company's current product/market/customer/technology focus.
3. Bland—lacking in motivational power.
4. Not distinctive—could apply to most any company (or at least several others in the same industry).
5. Too reliant on such superlatives as *best, most successful, recognized leader, global or worldwide leader,* or *first choice of customers.*
6. Too generic—fails to identify the business or industry to which it is supposed to apply. The statement could apply to companies in any of several industries.
7. So broad that it really doesn't rule out most any opportunity that management might opt to pursue.

mercial enterprise. It is management's answer to "make a profit doing what and for whom?" that reveals the substance of a company's mission and gives it an identity apart from any other profit-seeking company. Such companies as Charles Schwab, Caterpillar, Toyota, Wal-Mart, and Nokia are each striving to earn a profit for shareholders; but plainly the fundamentals of their business are substantially different when it comes to "who we are and what we do." If a company's mission statement is to have any managerial value or reveal anything useful about its business, it must direct attention to the particular market arena in which it operates—the buyer needs it seeks to satisfy, the customer groups and market segments it is endeavoring to serve, and the types of resources and technologies that it is deploying in trying to please its customers.

Linking the Vision with Company Values

In the course of deciding "who we are and where we are going," many companies also come up with a statement of values to guide the company's pursuit of its vision. By **values,** we means the beliefs, business principles, and practices that are incorporated into the way the company operates and the behavior of company personnel. Values relate to such things as treatment of employees and customers, integrity, ethics, innovativeness, emphasis on quality or service, social responsibility, and community citizenship. Company values statements tend to contain between four and eight values, which, ideally, are tightly connected to and reinforce the company's vision, strategy,

> **core concept**
> A company's **values** are the beliefs, business principles, and practices that guide the conduct of its business, the pursuit of its strategic vision, and the behavior of company personnel.

and operating practices. Home Depot has embraced eight values (entrepreneurial spirit, excellent customer service, giving back to the community, respect for all people, doing the right thing, taking care of people, building strong relationships, and creating shareholder value) in its quest to become the world's largest home improvement retailer by operating warehouse stores filled with a wide assortment of products at the lowest prices with trained associates giving absolutely the best customer service in the industry. Intel's corporate values of discipline, risk taking, quality, customer orientation, a results-oriented atmosphere, and being a great place to work guide the company's business behavior and pursuit of its "core mission" of "being the building block supplier to the Internet economy." At Intel, all employee badges are emblazoned with the company's values and employees are trained in over 40 behaviors exemplifying those values. DuPont, which calls itself "a science company" and makes a wide array of

illustration capsule 2.1
Exelon's Strategic Vision

Exelon, an electric and gas utility company recently created by the merger of Philadelphia Electric Company and Commonwealth Edison, has the following vision statement:

EXELON—ONE COMPANY, ONE VISION

Exelon strives to build exceptional value—by becoming the best and most consistently profitable electricity and gas company in the United States. To succeed, we must . . .

Live up to our commitments	• Keep the lights on. • Perform safely—especially nuclear operations. • Constantly improve our environmental performance. • Act honorably and treat everyone with respect, decency, and integrity. • Continue building a high performance culture that reflects the diversity of our communities. • Report our results, opportunities, and problems honestly and reliably.
Perform at world-class levels	• Relentlessly pursue greater productivity, quality, and innovation. • Understand the relationships among our businesses and optimize the whole. • Promote and implement policies that build effective markets. • Adapt rapidly to changing markets, politics, economics and technology to meet our customers' needs. • Maximize the earnings and cash flow from our assets and businesses and sell those that do not meet our goals.
Invest in our consolidating industry	• Develop strategies based on learning from past successes and failures. • Implement systems and best practices that can be applied to future acquisitions. • Prioritize acquisition opportunities based on synergies from scale, scope, generation and delivery integration, and our ability to profitably satisfy . . . regulatory obligations. • Make acquisitions that will best employ our limited investment resources to produce the most consistent cash flow and earnings accretion. • Return earnings to shareholders when higher returns are not available from acquisition opportunities.

COMMENTARY ON EXELON'S VISION

While the one-sentence vision is definitely overly general and void of direction, what rescues it (and makes the overall vision statement managerially useful) are the specifics that follow. The three things that management says the company must do to succeed and the accompanying bullet points convey a reasonably clear sense of where management intends to take the company and what the company is endeavoring to do in order to deliver exceptional value to stakeholders. But Exelon's vision statement is still somewhat vague on where management is trying to take the company in terms of its future product/market/customer/technology focus.

Source: Company documents.

products, stresses four values—safety, ethics, respect for people, and environmental stewardship; the first three have been in place since the company was founded over 200 years ago by E. I. du Pont. Loblaw, a major grocery chain in Canada, focuses on just two main values in operating its stores—competence and honesty; it expects employees to display both, and top management strives to promote only those employees who are smart and honest.

illustration capsule 2.2
Examples of Strategic Visions—How Well Do They Measure Up?

Using the information in Tables 2.2 and 2.3, critique the adequacy and merit of the following eight vision statements, ranking them from 1 (best) to 8 (in need of substantial improvement).

RED HAT LINUX

To extend our position as the most trusted Linux and open source provider to the enterprise. We intend to grow the market for Linux through a complete range of enterprise Red Hat Linux software, a powerful Internet management platform, and associated support and services.

WELLS FARGO

We want to satisfy all of our customers' financial needs, help them succeed financially, be the premier provider of financial services in every one of our markets, and be known as one of America's great companies.

WYETH

Our vision is to lead the way to a healthier world. By carrying out this vision at every level of our organization, we will be recognized by our employees, customers, and shareholders as the best pharmaceutical company in the world, resulting in value for all. We will achieve this by:

- Leading the world in innovation by linking pharmaceutical, biotech, and vaccines technologies

- Making quality, integrity, and excellence hallmarks of the way we do business

- Attracting, developing, and motivating the best people

- Continually growing and improving our business

GENERAL ELECTRIC

We will become number one or number two in every market we serve, and revolutionize this company to have the speed and agility of a small enterprise.

THE DENTAL PRODUCTS DIVISION OF 3M CORPORATION

Become THE supplier of choice to the global dental professional markets, providing world-class quality and innovative products. [All employees of the division wear badges bearing these words, and whenever a new product or business procedure is being considered, management asks "Is this representative of THE leading dental company?"]

NIKE

To bring innovation and inspiration to every athlete in the world.

HEINZ

Our vision, quite simply, is to be the world's premier food company, offering nutritious, superior tasting foods to people everywhere. Being the premier food company does not mean being the biggest but it does mean being the best in terms of consumer value, customer service, employee talent, and consistent and predictable growth.

INTEL

Our vision: Getting to a billion connected computers worldwide, millions of servers, and trillions of dollars of e-commerce. Intel's core mission is being the building block supplier to the Internet economy and spurring efforts to make the Internet more useful. Being connected is now at the center of people's computing experience. We are helping to expand the capabilities of the PC platform and the Internet . . . We have seen only the early stages of deployment of digital technologies.

Sources: Company documents and Web sites.

Company managers connect values to the strategic vision in one of two ways. In companies with long-standing and deeply entrenched values, managers go to great lengths to explain how the vision is compatible with the company's value set, occasionally reinterpreting the meaning of existing values to indicate their relevance in pursuing the strategic vision. In new companies or companies with weak or incomplete sets of values, top management considers what values, beliefs, and operating principles will help drive the vision forward. Then new values that fit the vision are drafted and circulated among managers and employees for discussion and possible modification.

A final values statement that connects to the vision and that reflects the beliefs and principles the company wants to uphold is then officially adopted. A number of companies combine their vision and values into a single statement or document that is provided to all company personnel and often posted on the company's Web site.

Of course, sometimes there is a wide gap between a company's stated values and its actual conduct. Enron, for example, touted four corporate values—respect, integrity, communication, and excellence—but flagrant disregard for these values by some top officials in their management of the company's financial and accounting practices and energy-trading activities triggered the company's implosion. Once one of the world's Big Five public accounting firms, Arthur Andersen was renowned for its commitment to the highest standards of audit integrity, but its high-profile audit failures and partner approval of shady accounting at Enron, WorldCom, and other companies led to Andersen's demise.

Communicating the Strategic Vision

Developing a well-conceived vision is necessary but not sufficient. Effectively communicating the strategic vision down the line to lower-level managers and employees is as important as the strategic soundness of the journey and destination for which top management has opted. If company personnel don't know what management's vision is and don't buy into the rationale for the direction management wants the company to head, they are unlikely to wholeheartedly commit themselves to making the vision a reality. Furthermore, company personnel need to believe that top management has a sound basis for where it is trying to take the company, and they need to understand why the strategic course that management has charted is both reasonable and beneficial.

Winning the support of organization members for the vision nearly always means putting "where we are going and why" in writing, distributing the statement organizationwide, and having executives personally explain the vision and its rationale to as many people as feasible. Ideally, executives should present their vision for the company in a manner that reaches out and grabs people. An engaging and convincing vision can have enormous motivational value—for the same reason that a stonemason finds building a magnificent cathedral more inspiring than laying stones. When top management articulates a vivid and compelling picture of what the company needs to do and why, organizational members begin to say, "This has a lot of merit. I want to be involved and contribute to making it happen." The more that a vision evokes positive support and excitement, the greater its impact in terms of arousing a committed organizational effort and getting people to move in a common direction.[3]

> **core concept**
> An effectively communicated vision is management's most valuable tool for enlisting the commitment of company personnel to actions that will make the vision a reality.

Most organization members will rise to the challenge of pursuing a path that may significantly enhance the company's competitiveness and market prominence, win big applause from buyers and turn them into loyal customers, or produce important benefits for society as a whole. Presenting the vision as an endeavor that could make the company the world leader or greatly improve the well-being of customers and/or society is far more motivating than stressing the payoff for shareholders—it goes without saying that the company intends to profit shareholders. Unless most managers and employees are also shareholders (because the company incentivizes employees via a stock ownership plan), they are unlikely to be energized by a vision that does little more than enrich shareholders.

> Executive ability to paint a convincing and inspiring picture of a company's journey and destination is an important element of effective strategic leadership.

Expressing the Essence of the Vision in a Slogan   The task of effectively conveying the vision to company personnel is made easier when management's vision of where to head is captured in a catchy slogan. A number of organizations have summed up their visions in a brief phrase:

- Levi Strauss & Company: "We will clothe the world by marketing the most appealing and widely worn casual clothing in the world."
- Microsoft Corporation: "Empower people through great software—any time, any place, and on any device."
- Mayo Clinic: "The best care to every patient every day."
- Scotland Yard: "To make London the safest major city in the world."
- Greenpeace: "To halt environmental abuse and promote environmental solutions."
- Charles Schwab: "To provide customers with the most useful and ethical financial services in the world."

Creating a short slogan to illuminate an organization's direction and purpose and then using it repeatedly as a reminder of the "where we are headed and why" helps keep organization members on the chosen path. But it is important to bear in mind that developing a strategic vision is not a wordsmithing exercise to come up with a snappy slogan. Rather, it is an exercise in thinking carefully about where a company needs to head to be successful. It involves selecting the market arenas in which to participate, putting the company on a clearly defined strategic course, and making a commitment to follow that course.

Breaking Down Resistance to a New Strategic Vision It is particularly important for executives to provide a compelling rationale for a dramatically *new* strategic vision and company direction. When company personnel don't understand or accept the need for redirecting organizational efforts, they are prone to resist change. Hence, reiterating the basis for the new direction, addressing employee concerns head-on, calming fears, lifting spirits, and providing updates and progress reports as events unfold all become part of the task in mobilizing support for the vision and winning commitment to needed actions. Just stating the case for a new direction once is not enough. Executives must repeat the reasons for the new direction often and convincingly at company gatherings and in company publications, and they must reinforce their pronouncements with updates about how the latest information confirms the choice of direction and the validity of the vision. Unless and until more and more people are persuaded of the merits of management's new vision and the vision gains wide acceptance, it will be a struggle to move the organization down the newly chosen path.

Recognizing Strategic Inflection Points Sometimes there's an order-of-magnitude change in a company's environment that dramatically alters its prospects and mandates radical revision of its strategic course. Intel's chairman Andrew Grove calls such occasions *strategic inflection points*—Illustration Capsule 2.3 relates Intel's two encounters with strategic inflection points and the resulting alterations in its strategic vision. As the Intel example forcefully demonstrates, when a company reaches a strategic inflection point, management has some tough decisions to make about the company's course. Often it is a question of what to do to sustain company success, not just how to avoid possible disaster. Responding to unfolding changes in the marketplace in timely fashion lessens a company's chances of becoming trapped in a stagnant or declining business or letting attractive new growth opportunities slip away.

The Payoffs of a Clear Vision Statement In sum, a well-conceived, forcefully communicated strategic vision pays off in several respects: (1) it crystallizes senior executives' own views about the firm's long-term direction; (2) it reduces the risk

illustration capsule 2.3
Intel's Two Strategic Inflection Points

Intel Corporation has encountered two strategic inflection points within the past 20 years. The first came in the mid-1980s, when memory chips were Intel's principal business and Japanese manufacturers, intent on dominating the memory chip business, began cutting their prices 10 percent below the prices charged by Intel and other U.S. memory chip manufacturers. Each time U.S. companies matched the Japanese price cuts, the Japanese manufacturers responded with another 10 percent price cut. Intel's management explored a number of strategic options to cope with the aggressive pricing of its Japanese rivals—building a giant memory chip factory to overcome the cost advantage of Japanese producers, investing in research and development (R&D) to come up with a more advanced memory chip, and retreating to niche markets for memory chips that were not of interest to the Japanese.

At the time, Gordon Moore, Intel's chairman and cofounder, and Andrew Grove, Intel's chief executive officer (CEO), jointly concluded that none of these options offered much promise and that the best long-term solution was to abandon the memory chip business even though it accounted for 70 percent of Intel's revenue. Grove, with the concurrence of both Moore and the board of directors, then proceeded to commit Intel's full energies to the business of developing ever more powerful microprocessors for personal computers. (Intel had invented microprocessors in the early 1970s but had recently been concentrating on memory chips because of strong competition and excess capacity in the market for microprocessors.)

Grove's bold decision to withdraw from memory chips, absorb a $173 million write-off in 1986, and go all out in microprocessors produced a new strategic vision for Intel—becoming the preeminent supplier of microprocessors to the personal computing industry, making the personal computer (PC) the central appliance in the workplace and the home, and being the undisputed leader in driving PC technology forward. Grove's new vision for Intel and the strategic course he charted in 1985 produced spectacular results. Since 1996, over 80 percent of the world's PCs have been made with Intel microprocessors and Intel has become the world's most profitable chip maker.

The company encountered a second inflection point in 1998, opting to refocus on becoming the preeminent building block supplier to the Internet economy (see Illustration Capsule 2.2) and spurring efforts to make the Internet more useful. Starting in early 1998 and responding to the mushrooming importance of the Internet, Intel's senior management launched major new initiatives to direct attention and resources to expanding the capabilities of both the PC platform and the Internet. It was this strategic inflection point that led to Intel's latest strategic vision of playing a major role in getting a billion computers connected to the Internet worldwide, installing millions of servers, and building an Internet infrastructure that would support trillions of dollars of e-commerce and serve as a worldwide communication medium.

Source: Andrew S. Grove, *Only the Paranoid Survive,* (New York: Doubleday-Currency, 1996) and information posted at www.intel.com.

of rudderless decision making; (3) it is a tool for winning the support of organizational members for internal changes that will help make the vision a reality; (4) it provides a beacon for lower-level managers in forming departmental missions, setting departmental objectives, and crafting functional and departmental strategies that are in sync with the company's overall strategy; and (5) it helps an organization prepare for the future. When management is able to demonstrate significant progress in achieving these five benefits, the first step in organizational direction setting has been successfully completed.

SETTING OBJECTIVES: PHASE 2 OF THE STRATEGY-MAKING, STRATEGY-EXECUTING PROCESS

The managerial purpose of setting **objectives** is to convert the strategic vision into specific performance targets—results and outcomes the company's management wants to achieve—and then use these objectives as yardsticks for tracking the company's progress and performance. Well-stated objectives are *quantifiable,* or *measurable,* and contain a *deadline for achievement.* As Bill Hewlett, cofounder of Hewlett-Packard, shrewdly observed, "You cannot manage what you cannot measure . . . And what gets measured gets done."[4] The experiences of countless companies and managers teach that precisely spelling out *how much* of *what kind* of performance *by when* and then pressing forward with actions and incentives calculated to help achieve the targeted outcomes will boost a company's actual performance. It definitely beats setting vague targets like "increase profits," "reduce costs," "become more efficient," or "boost sales," which specify neither how much nor by when, and then living with whatever results company personnel deliver.

> **core concept**
> **Objectives** are an organization's performance targets—the results and outcomes it wants to achieve. They function as yardsticks for tracking an organization's performance and progress.

Ideally, managers ought to use the objective-setting exercise as a tool for truly *stretching an organization to reach its full potential.* Challenging company personnel to go all out and deliver big gains in performance pushes an enterprise to be more inventive, to exhibit some urgency in improving both its financial performance and its business position, and to be more intentional and focused in its actions. *Stretch objectives* help build a firewall against contentment with slow, incremental improvements in organizational performance. As Mitchell Leibovitz, CEO of the auto parts and service retailer Pep Boys, once said, "If you want to have ho-hum results, have ho-hum objectives."

What Kinds of Objectives to Set: The Need for a Balanced Scorecard

Two very distinct types of performance yardsticks are required: those relating to *financial performance* and those relating to *strategic performance*—outcomes that indicate a company is strengthening its marketing standing, competitive vitality, and future business prospects. The following are examples of commonly used financial and strategic objectives:

Financial Objectives	Strategic Objectives
• An *x* percent increase in annual revenues	• Winning an *x* percent market share
• Annual increases in after-tax profits of *x* percent	• Achieving lower overall costs than rivals
• Annual increases in earnings per share of *x* percent	• Overtaking key competitors on product performance or quality or customer service
• Annual dividend increases of *x* percent	• Deriving *x* percent of revenues from the sale of new products introduced within the past five years
• Profit margins of *x* percent	
• An *x* percent return on capital employed (ROCE) or shareholders' equity (ROE)	• Achieving technological leadership
• Increased shareholder value—in the form of an upward-trending stock price and annual dividend increases	• Having better product selection than rivals
• Strong bond and credit ratings	• Strengthening the company's brand-name appeal
• Sufficient internal cash flows to fund new capital investment	• Having stronger national or global sales and distribution capabilities than rivals
• Stable earnings during periods of recession	• Consistently getting new or improved products to market ahead of rivals

illustration capsule 2.4
Examples of Company Objectives

UNILEVER
(Strategic and Financial Objectives)

Grow annual revenues by 5%–6% annually; increase operating profit margins from 11%–16% percent within 5 years; trim the company's 1200 food, household, and personal care products down to 400 core brands; focus sales and marketing efforts on those brands with potential to become respected, market-leading global brands; and streamline the company's supply chain.

THE KROGER COMPANY
(Strategic and Financial Objectives)

Reduce our operating and administrative cost by $500 million by year-end 2003; leverage our $51 billion size to achieve greater economies of scale; reinvest in our core business to increase sales and market share; and grow earnings per share by 10%–12% in 2002–2003 and by 13%–15% annually starting in 2004.

DUPONT
(Financial and Strategic Objectives)

To achieve annual revenue growth of 5%–6% and annual earnings-per-share growth averaging 10%. Grow per-share profits faster than revenues by (a) increasing productivity, (b) selling enough new products each year that average prices and average margins rise, and (c) using surplus cash to buy back shares. Sell the company's low-margin textiles and interiors division (with sales of $6.6 billion and operating profits of only $114 million); this division makes Lycra and other synthetic fibers for carpets and clothes.

HEINZ
(Financial and Strategic Objectives)

Achieve earnings per share in the range of $2.15–$2.25 in 2004; increase operating cash flow by 45% to $750 million; reduce net debt by $1.3 billion in 2003 and further strengthen the company's balance sheet in 2004; continue to introduce new and improved food products; remove the clutter in company product offerings by reducing the number of SKUs (stock keeping units); increase spending on trade promotion and advertising by $200 million to strengthen the recognition and market shares of the company's core brands; and divest non-core underperforming product lines.

SEAGATE TECHNOLOGY
(Strategic Objectives)

Solidify the company's No. 1 position in the overall market for hard-disk drives; get more Seagate drives into popular consumer electronics products (i.e. video recorders); take share away from Western Digital in providing disk drives for Microsoft's Xbox; and capture a 10% share of the market for 2.5-inch hard drives for notebook computers by 2004.

3M CORPORATION
(Financial and Strategic Objectives)

To achieve annual growth in earnings per share of 10% or better, on average; a return on stockholders' equity of 20%–25%; a return on capital employed of 27% or better; and have at least 30% of sales come from products introduced in the past four years.

Sources: Company documents; *Business Week* (July 28, 2003), p. 106; *Business Week* (September 8, 2003), p. 108.

Achieving acceptable financial results is a must. Without adequate profitability and financial strength, a company's pursuit of its strategic vision, as well as its long-term health and ultimate survival, is jeopardized. Further subpar earnings and a weak balance sheet alarm shareholders and creditors and put the jobs of senior executives at risk.

But good financial performance, by itself, is not enough. Of equal or greater importance is a company's strategic performance—outcomes that indicate whether a company's market position and competitiveness are deteriorating, holding steady, or improving. Illustration Capsule 2.4 shows selected objectives of several prominent companies.

Improved Strategic Performance Fosters Better Financial Performance   A company's financial performance measures are really *lagging indicators* that reflect the results of past decisions and organizational activities. But a company's past or current financial performance is not a reliable indicator of its future prospects—poor financial performers often turn things around and do better, while good financial performers can fall on hard times. The best and most reliable *leading indicators* of a company's future financial performance and business prospects are strategic outcomes that indicate whether the company's competitiveness and market position are stronger or weaker. For instance, if a company has set aggressive strategic objectives and is achieving them—such that its competitive strength and market position are on the rise—then there's reason to expect that its future financial performance will be better than its current or past performance. If a company is losing ground to competitors and its market position is slipping—outcomes that reflect weak strategic performance (and, very likely, failure to achieve its strategic objectives)—then its ability to maintain its present profitability is highly suspect. Hence, the degree to which a company's managers set, pursue, and achieve stretch strategic objectives tends to be a reliable leading indicator of its ability to generate higher profits from business operations.

The Balanced Scorecard Approach: A Combination of Strategic and Financial Objectives   The balanced scorecard approach for measuring company performance requires setting both financial and strategic objectives and tracking their achievement. Unless a company is in deep financial difficulty, such that its very survival is threatened, company managers are well advised to put more emphasis on achieving strategic objectives than on achieving financial objectives whenever a trade-off has to be made. *The surest path to sustained future profitability quarter after quarter and year after year is to relentlessly pursue strategic outcomes that strengthen a company's business position and, ideally, give it a growing competitive advantage over rivals.* What ultimately enables a company to deliver better financial results from operations is the achievement of strategic objectives that improve its competitiveness and market strength.

Illustration Capsule 2.5 describes why a growing number of companies are utilizing both financial and strategic objectives to create a "balanced scorecard" approach to measuring company performance.

A Need for Both Short-Term and Long-Term Objectives   As a rule, a company's set of financial and strategic objectives ought to include both short-term and long-term performance targets. Having quarterly or annual objectives focuses attention on delivering immediate performance improvements. Targets to be achieved within three to five years prompt considerations of what to do *now* to put the company in position to perform better down the road. A company that has an objective of doubling its sales within five years can't wait until the third or fourth year to begin growing its sales and customer base. By spelling out annual (or perhaps quarterly) performance targets, management indicates the *speed* at which longer-range targets are to be approached.

Short-range objectives can be identical to long-range objectives if an organization is already performing at the targeted long-term level. For instance, if a company has an ongoing objective of 15 percent profit growth every year and is currently achieving this objective, then the company's long-range and short-range objectives for increasing profits coincide. The most important situation in which short-range objectives differ from long-range objectives occurs when managers are trying to elevate organizational performance and cannot reach the long-range target in just one year. Short-range objectives then serve as stairsteps or milestones.

The Concept of Strategic Intent   A company's objectives sometimes play another role—that of signaling unmistakable **strategic intent** to make quantum gains in

illustration capsule 2.5
Organizations That Use a Balanced Scorecard Approach to Objective Setting

In recent years organizations like Exxon Mobil, CIGNA, United Parcel Service, Sears, Nova Scotia Power, Duke Children's Hospital, and the City of Charlotte, North Carolina—among numerous others—have used the "Balanced Scorecard" approach to objective setting in all or parts of their operations. This approach, developed and fine-tuned by two Harvard professors, stems from the recognition that exclusive reliance on financial performance measures, which really are lag indicators (i.e., they report the consequences of past actions), induced company managers to take actions that make the company's near-term financial performance look good and to neglect the lead indicators (i.e., the drivers of future financial performance). The solution: measure the performance of a company's strategy and make strategic objectives an integral part of a company's set of performance targets. The balanced scorecard approach to objective setting advocates using a company's strategic vision and strategy as the basis for determining what specific strategic and financial outcomes are appropriate measures of the progress a company is making. The intent is to use the balanced scorecard (containing a carefully chosen combination of strategic and financial performance indicators tailored to the company's particular

business) as a tool for managing strategy and measuring its effectiveness.

Four of the initial users of the balanced scorecard approach were money-losing operations that were trailing the industry. Each had new management teams that were implementing strategies that required market repositioning and becoming more customer-driven. All four needed to adopt a new set of cultural values and priorities as well as cost reduction measures. At these four companies, use of a balanced scorecard, consisting of both financial targets (the lag indicators) and strategic targets (the lead indicators of future financial performance), not only served as a vehicle for helping communicate the strategy to organization personnel but also caused the organization to become more strategy-focused.

During the past decade, growing numbers of companies have adopted a balanced scorecard approach, believing that a mix of financial and strategic performance targets is superior to a purely financial set of performance measures and that winning in the marketplace requires paying close attention to whether the company's present strategy is boosting its competitiveness and promoting the development of a sustainable competitive advantage.

core concept
A company exhibits *strategic intent* when it relentlessly pursues an ambitious strategic objective and concentrates its full resources and competitive actions on achieving that objective.

competing against key rivals and establish itself as a clear-cut winner in the marketplace, often against long odds.[5] A company's strategic intent can entail becoming the dominant company in the industry, unseating the existing industry leader, delivering the best customer service of any company in the industry (or the world), or turning a new technology into products capable of changing the way people work and live. Ambitious companies almost invariably begin with strategic intents that are out of proportion to their immediate capabilities and market positions. But they are undeterred by a grandiose objective that may take a sustained effort of 10 years or more to achieve. So intent are they on reaching the target that they set aggressive stretch objectives and pursue them relentlessly, sometimes even obsessively. Capably managed, up-and-coming enterprises with strategic intents exceeding their present reach and resources often prove to be more formidable competitors over time than larger cash-rich rivals with modest market ambitions. Nike's strategic intent during the 1960s was to overtake Adidas, which connected nicely with Nike's core purpose "to experience the emotion of competition, winning, and crushing competitors." Throughout the 1980s, Wal-Mart's strategic intent was to "overtake Sears" as the largest U.S. retailer (a feat accomplished in 1991). For some years, Toyota has been driving to overtake General Motors as the world's largest motor vehicle producer (and it surpassed Ford Motor Company in total vehicles sold in 2003, to rank in second place).

Sometimes a company's strategic intent serves as a rallying cry for managers and employees. When Yamaha overtook Honda in the motorcycle market, Honda responded with "*Yamaha wo tsubusu*" ("We will crush, squash, slaughter Yamaha"). Canon's strategic intent in copying equipment was to "beat Xerox." In the 1960s, Komatsu, Japan's leading earth-moving equipment company, had little market presence outside Japan, depended on its small bulldozers for most of its revenue, and was less than one-third the size of its U.S. rival Caterpillar. But Komatsu's strategic intent was to eventually "encircle Caterpillar" with a broader product line and then compete globally against Caterpillar—its motivating battle cry among managers and employees was "beat Caterpillar." By the late 1980s, Komatsu was the industry's second-ranking company, with a strong sales presence in North America, Europe, and Asia plus a product line that included industrial robots and semiconductors as well as a broad selection of earth-moving equipment.

The Need for Objectives at All Organizational Levels   Objective setting should not stop with top management's establishing of companywide performance targets. Company objectives need to be broken down into performance targets for each separate business, product line, functional department, and individual work unit. Company performance can't reach full potential unless each area of the organization does its part and contributes directly to the desired companywide outcomes and results. This means setting performance targets for each organization unit that support—rather than conflict with or negate—the achievement of companywide strategic and financial objectives.

The ideal situation is a team effort in which each organizational unit strives to produce results in its area of responsibility that contribute to the achievement of the company's performance targets and strategic vision. Such consistency signals that organizational units know their strategic role and are on board in helping the company move down the chosen strategic path and produce the desired results.

The Need for Top-Down Rather Than Bottom-Up Objective Setting
To appreciate why a company's objective-setting process needs to be more top-down than bottom-up, consider the following example: Suppose that the senior executives of a diversified corporation establish a corporate profit objective of $500 million for next year. Suppose further that, after discussion between corporate management and the general managers of the firm's five different businesses, each business is given a stretch profit objective of $100 million by year-end (i.e., if the five business divisions contribute $100 million each in profit, the corporation can reach its $500 million profit objective). A concrete result has thus been agreed on and translated into measurable action commitments at two levels in the managerial hierarchy. Next, suppose that the general manager of business unit A, after some analysis and discussion with functional area managers, concludes that reaching the $100 million profit objective will require selling 1 million units at an average price of $500 and producing them at an average cost of $400 (a $100 profit margin times 1 million units equals $100 million profit). Consequently, the general manager and the manufacturing manager settle on a production objective of 1 million units at a unit cost of $400, and the general manager and the marketing manager agree on a sales objective of 1 million units and a target selling price of $500. In turn, the marketing manager, after consultation with regional sales

personnel, breaks the sales objective of 1 million units into unit sales targets for each sales territory, each item in the product line, and each salesperson. It is logical for organizationwide objectives and strategy to be established first so that they can guide objective setting and strategy making at lower levels.

A top-down process of setting objectives ensures that the financial and strategic performance targets established for business units, divisions, functional departments, and operating units are directly connected to the achievement of companywide objectives. This integration of objectives has two powerful advantages: (1) it helps produce *cohesion* among the objectives and strategies of different parts of the organization, and (2) it helps *unify internal efforts* to move the company along the chosen strategic path. Bottom-up objective setting, with little or no guidance from above, nearly always signals an absence of strategic leadership on the part of senior executives.

CRAFTING A STRATEGY: PHASE 3 OF THE STRATEGY-MAKING, STRATEGY-EXECUTING PROCESS

A company's senior executives obviously have important strategy-making roles. An enterprise's chief executive officer (CEO), as captain of the ship, carries the mantles of chief direction setter, chief objective setter, chief strategy maker, and chief strategy implementer for the total enterprise. Ultimate responsibility for *leading* the strategy-making, strategy-executing process rests with the CEO. In some enterprises the CEO or owner functions as strategic visionary and chief architect of strategy, personally deciding which of several strategic options to pursue, although senior managers and key employees may well assist with gathering and analyzing background data and advising the CEO on which way to go. Such an approach to strategy development is characteristic of small owner-managed companies and sometimes large corporations that have been founded by the present CEO—Michael Dell at Dell Computer, Bill Gates at Microsoft, and Howard Schultz at Starbucks are prominent examples of corporate CEOs who exert a heavy hand in shaping their company's strategy.

In most companies, however, the heads of business divisions and major product lines; the chief financial officer; and vice presidents (VPs) for production, marketing, human resources, and other functional departments have influential strategy-making roles. Normally, a company's chief financial officer is in charge of devising and implementing an appropriate financial strategy; the production VP takes the lead in developing and executing the company's production strategy; the marketing VP orchestrates sales and marketing strategy; a brand manager is in charge of the strategy for a particular brand in the company's product lineup, and so on.

But it is a mistake to view strategy-making as exclusively a top management function, the province of owner-entrepreneurs, CEOs, and other senior executives. The

core concept
Every company manager has a strategy-making, strategy-executing role—it is flawed thinking to look on the tasks of managing strategy as something only high-level managers do.

more wide-ranging a company's operations are, the more that strategy making is a collaborative team effort involving managers (and sometimes key employees) down through the whole organizational hierarchy. Take a company like Toshiba—a $43 billion corporation with 300 subsidiaries, thousands of products, and operations extending across the world. It would be a far-fetched error to assume that a few senior executives in Toshiba headquarters have either the expertise or a sufficiently detailed understanding of all the relevant factors to wisely craft all the strategic initiatives taken in Toshiba's numerous and diverse organizational units. Rather, it takes involvement on the part of Toshiba's whole management team to craft and execute the thousands of strategic initiatives that constitute the whole of Toshiba's strategy.

Major organizational units in a company—business divisions, product groups, functional departments, plants, geographic offices, distribution centers—normally have a leading or supporting role in the company's strategic game plan. Because senior executives in the corporate office seldom know enough about the situation in every geographic area and operating unit to direct every strategic move made in the field, it is common practice for top-level managers to delegate strategy-making authority to middle- and lower-echelon managers who head the organizational subunits where specific strategic results must be achieved. The more that a company's operations cut across different products, industries, and geographical areas, the more that headquarters executives are prone to delegate considerable strategy-making authority to on-the-scene personnel who have firsthand knowledge of customer requirements, can better evaluate market opportunities, and are better able to keep the strategy responsive to changing market and competitive conditions. While managers farther down in the managerial hierarchy obviously have a narrower, more specific strategy-making, strategy-executing role than managers closer to the top, the important understanding here is that in most of today's companies *every company manager typically has a strategy-making, strategy-executing role—ranging from minor to major—for the area he or she heads.* Hence, the notion that an organization's strategists are at the top of the management hierarchy and that midlevel and frontline managers and employees merely carry out their directives is misguided.

With decentralized decision making becoming common at companies of all stripes, it is now typical for key pieces of a company's strategy to originate in a company's middle and lower ranks.[6] For example, in a recent year, Electronic Data Systems conducted a yearlong strategy review involving 2,500 of its 55,000 employees and coordinated by a core of 150 managers and staffers from all over the world.[7] J. M. Smucker Company, well known for its jams and jellies, formed a team of 140 employees (7 percent of its 2,000-person workforce) who spent 25 percent of their time over a six-month period looking for ways to rejuvenate the company's growth. Involving teams of people to dissect complex situations and come up with strategic solutions is becoming increasingly necessary in many businesses. Not only are many strategic issues too far-reaching or too involved for a single manager to handle, but they often cut across functional areas and departments, thus requiring the contributions of many disciplinary experts and the collaboration of managers from different parts of the organization. A valuable strength of collaborative strategy making is that the group of people charged with crafting the strategy can easily include the very people who will also be charged with implementing and executing it. Giving people an influential stake in crafting the strategy they must later help implement and execute not only builds motivation and commitment but also allows them to be held accountable for putting the strategy into place and making it work—the oft-used excuse of "It wasn't my idea to do this" won't fly.

In some companies, top management makes a regular practice of encouraging individuals and teams to develop and champion proposals for new product lines and new business ventures. The idea is to unleash the talents and energies of promising "corporate intrapreneurs," letting them try out untested business ideas and giving them the room to pursue new strategic initiatives. Executives serve as judges of which proposals merit support, give company intrapreneurs the needed organizational and budgetary support, and let them run with the ball. Thus, important pieces of company strategy originate with those intrapreneuring individuals and teams who succeed in championing a proposal through the approval stage and then end up being charged with the lead role in launching new products, overseeing the company's entry into new geographic markets, or heading up new business ventures. W. L. Gore and Associates, a privately owned company famous for its Gore-Tex waterproofing film, is an avid and highly successful practitioner of the corporate intrapreneur approach to strategy making. Gore expects all employees to initiate improvements and to display innovativeness. Each employee's intrapreneuring contributions are prime considerations in determining raises, stock option bonuses, and promotions. W. L. Gore's commitment to intrapreneuring has produced a stream of product innovations and new strategic initiatives that has kept the company vibrant and growing for nearly two decades.

The Strategy-Making Pyramid

It thus follows that *a company's overall strategy is really a collection of strategic initiatives and actions* devised by managers and key employees up and down the whole organizational hierarchy. The larger and more diverse the operations of an enterprise, the more points of strategic initiative it has and the more managers and employees at more levels of management that have a relevant strategy-making role. Figure 2.2 shows who is generally responsible for devising what pieces of a company's overall strategy.

In diversified, multibusiness companies where the strategies of several different businesses have to be managed, the strategy-making task involves four distinct types or levels of strategy, each of which involves different facets of the company's overall strategy:

1. *Corporate strategy* consists of the kinds of initiatives the company uses to establish business positions in different industries, the approaches corporate executives pursue to boost the combined performance of the set of businesses the company has diversified into, and the means of capturing cross-business synergies and turning them into competitive advantage. Senior corporate executives normally have lead responsibility for devising corporate strategy and for choosing among whatever recommended actions bubble up from the organization below. Key business-unit heads may also be influential, especially in strategic decisions affecting the businesses they head. Major strategic decisions are usually reviewed and approved by the company's board of directors. We will look deeper into the strategy-making process at diversified companies when we get to Chapter 9.

2. *Business strategy* concerns the actions and the approaches crafted to produce successful performance in one specific line of business. The key focus here is crafting responses to changing market circumstances and initiating actions to strengthen market position, build competitive advantage, and develop strong competitive capabilities. Orchestrating the development of business-level strategy is the responsibility of the manager in charge of the business. The business head has at least two other strategy-related roles: (1) seeing that lower-level strategies are well conceived, consistent with each other, and adequately matched to the overall business strategy, and (2) getting major business-level strategic moves approved by corporate-level officers (and sometimes the board of directors) and keeping them informed of market developments and emerging strategic issues. In diversified companies, business-unit heads may have the additional obligation of making sure business-level objectives and strategy conform to corporate-level objectives and strategy themes.

figure 2.2 **A Company's Strategy-Making Hierarchy**

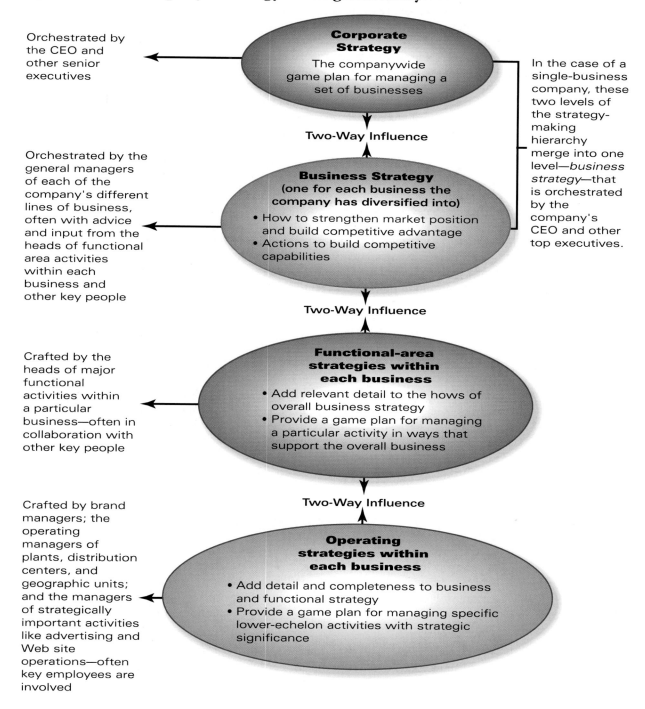

Orchestrated by the CEO and other senior executives

Corporate Strategy
The companywide game plan for managing a set of businesses

In the case of a single-business company, these two levels of the strategy-making hierarchy merge into one level—*business strategy*—that is orchestrated by the company's CEO and other top executives.

Two-Way Influence

Orchestrated by the general managers of each of the company's different lines of business, often with advice and input from the heads of functional area activities within each business and other key people

Business Strategy
(one for each business the company has diversified into)
• How to strengthen market position and build competitive advantage
• Actions to build competitive capabilities

Two-Way Influence

Crafted by the heads of major functional activities within a particular business—often in collaboration with other key people

Functional-area strategies within each business
• Add relevant detail to the hows of overall business strategy
• Provide a game plan for managing a particular activity in ways that support the overall business

Two-Way Influence

Crafted by brand managers; the operating managers of plants, distribution centers, and geographic units; and the managers of strategically important activities like advertising and Web site operations—often key employees are involved

Operating strategies within each business
• Add detail and completeness to business and functional strategy
• Provide a game plan for managing specific lower-echelon activities with strategic significance

3. *Functional-area strategies* concern the actions, approaches, and practices to be employed in managing particular functions or business processes or key activities within a business. A company's marketing strategy, for example, represents the managerial game plan for running the sales and marketing part of the business. A company's new product development strategy represents the managerial game plan for keeping the company's product lineup fresh and in tune with what buyers are looking for. Functional-area strategies add specifics to the hows of business-level strategy. Plus, they aim at establishing or strengthening a business unit's competencies and capabilities in performing strategy-critical activities so as to enhance the business's market position and standing with customers. The primary role of a functional-area strategy is to *support* the company's overall business strategy and competitive approach.

Lead responsibility for functional-area strategies within a business is normally delegated to the heads of the respective functions, with the general manager of the business having final approval and perhaps even exerting a strong influence over the content of particular pieces of functional-area strategies. To some extent, functional managers have to collaborate and coordinate their strategy-making efforts to avoid uncoordinated or conflicting strategies. For the overall business strategy to have maximum impact, a business's marketing strategy, production strategy, finance strategy, customer service strategy, new product development strategy, and human resources strategy should be compatible and mutually reinforcing rather than serving their own narrower purposes. If inconsistent functional-area strategies are sent up the line for final approval, the business head is responsible for spotting the conflicts and getting them resolved.

4. *Operating strategies* concern the relatively narrow strategic initiatives and approaches for managing key operating units (plants, distribution centers, geographic units) and specific operating activities with strategic significance (advertising campaigns, the management of specific brands, supply chain–related activities, and Web site sales and operations). A plant manager needs a strategy for accomplishing the plant's objectives, carrying out the plant's part of the company's overall manufacturing game plan, and dealing with any strategy-related problems that exist at the plant. A company's advertising manager needs a strategy for getting maximum audience exposure and sales impact from the ad budget. Operating strategies, while of limited scope, add further detail and completeness to functional-area strategies and to the overall business strategy. Lead responsibility for operating strategies is usually delegated to frontline managers, subject to review and approval by higher-ranking managers.

Even though operating strategy is at the bottom of the strategy-making hierarchy, its importance should not be downplayed. A major plant that fails in its strategy to achieve production volume, unit cost, and quality targets can undercut the achievement of company sales and profit objectives and wreak havoc with strategic efforts to build a quality image with customers. Frontline managers are thus an important part of an organization's strategy-making team because many operating units have strategy-critical performance targets and need to have strategic action plans in place to achieve them. One cannot reliably judge the strategic importance of a given action simply by the strategy level or location within the managerial hierarchy where it is initiated.

In single-business enterprises, the corporate and business levels of strategy making merge into one level—business strategy—because the strategy for the whole company involves only one distinct line of business. Thus, a single-business enterprise has only three levels of strategy: (1) business strategy for the company as a whole, (2) functional-area strategies for each main area within the business, and (3) operating strategies undertaken by lower-echelon managers to flesh out strategically significant aspects for the company's business and functional area strategies. Proprietorships, partnerships, and owner-managed enterprises may have only one or two strategy-making levels since in small-scale enterprises the whole strategy-making, strategy-executing function can be handled by just a few key people.

Uniting the Strategy-Making Effort

Ideally, the pieces and layers of a company's strategy should fit together like a jigsaw puzzle. To achieve this unity, the strategizing process generally has proceeded from the corporate level to the business level and then from the business level to the functional and operating levels. *Midlevel and frontline managers cannot do good strategy making without understanding the company's long-term direction and higher-level strategies.* The strategic disarray that occurs in an organization when senior managers don't set forth a clearly articulated companywide strategy is akin to what would happen to a football team's offensive performance if the quarterback decided not to call a play for the team but instead let each player pick whatever play he thought would work best at his respective position. In business, as in sports, all the strategy makers in a company are on the same team and the many different pieces of the overall strategy crafted at various organizational levels need to be in sync and united. Anything less than a unified collection of strategies weakens company performance.

> **core concept**
> A company's strategy is at full power only when its many pieces are united.

Achieving unity in strategy making is partly a function of communicating the company's basic strategy themes effectively across the whole organization and establishing clear strategic principles and guidelines for lower-level strategy making. Cohesive strategy making down through the hierarchy becomes easier to achieve when company strategy is distilled into pithy, easy-to-grasp terminology that can be used to drive consistent strategic action throughout the company.[8] The greater the numbers of company personnel who know, understand, and buy in to the company's basic direction and strategy, the smaller the risk that people and organization units will go off in conflicting strategic directions when decision making is pushed down to frontline levels and many people are given a strategy-making role. Good communication of strategic themes and guiding principles thus serves a valuable strategy-unifying purpose.

Merging the Strategic Vision, Objectives, and Strategy into a Strategic Plan

Developing a strategic vision, setting objectives, and crafting a strategy are basic direction-setting tasks. They map out the company's direction, its short-range and long-range performance targets, and the competitive moves and internal action approaches to be used in achieving the targeted business results. Together, they constitute a **strategic plan** for coping with industry and competitive conditions, the expected actions of the industry's key players, and the challenges and issues that stand as obstacles to the company's success.[9]

> **core concept**
> A company's *strategic plan* lays out its future direction, performance targets, and strategy.

In companies committed to regular strategy reviews and the development of explicit strategic plans, the strategic plan may take the form of a written document that is circulated to managers (and perhaps to selected employees). In small privately owned companies, strategic plans exist mostly in the form of oral understandings and commitments among managers and key employees about where to head, what to accomplish, and how to proceed. Short-term performance targets are the part of the strategic plan most often spelled out explicitly and communicated to managers and employees. A number of companies summarize key elements of their strategic plans in the company's annual report to shareholders, in postings on their Web site, in press releases, or in statements provided to the business media. Other companies, perhaps for reasons of competitive sensitivity, make only vague, general statements about their strategic plans that could apply to most any company.

IMPLEMENTING AND EXECUTING THE STRATEGY: PHASE 4 OF THE STRATEGY-MAKING, STRATEGY-EXECUTING PROCESS

Managing strategy implementation and execution is an operations-oriented, make-things-happen activity aimed at shaping the performance of core business activities in a strategy-supportive manner. It is easily the most demanding and time-consuming part of the strategy-management process. To convert strategic plans into actions and results, a manager must be able to direct organizational change, motivate people, build and strengthen company competencies and competitive capabilities, create a strategy-supportive work climate, and meet or beat performance targets.

Management's action agenda for implementing and executing the chosen strategy emerges from assessing what the company, given its particular operating practices and organizational circumstances, will have to do differently or better to execute the strategy proficiently and achieve the targeted performance. Each company manager has to think through the answer to "What has to be done in my area to execute my piece of the strategic plan, and what actions should I take to get the process under way?" How much internal change is needed depends on how much of the strategy is new, how far internal practices and competencies deviate from what the strategy requires, and how well the present work climate/culture supports good strategy execution. Depending on the amount of internal change involved, full implementation and proficient execution of company strategy (or important new pieces thereof) can take several months to several years.

In most situations, managing the strategy-execution process includes the following principal aspects:

- Staffing the organization with the needed skills and expertise, consciously building and strengthening strategy-supportive competencies and competitive capabilities, and organizing the work effort.
- Developing budgets that steer ample resources into those activities critical to strategic success.
- Ensuring that policies and operating procedures facilitate rather than impede effective execution.
- Using the best-known practices to perform core business activities and pushing for continuous improvement. Organizational units have to periodically reassess how things are being done and diligently pursue useful changes and improvements in how the strategy is being executed.
- Installing information and operating systems that enable company personnel to better carry out their strategic roles day in and day out.

- Motivating people to pursue the target objectives energetically and, if need be, modifying their duties and job behavior to better fit the requirements of successful strategy execution.

- Tying rewards and incentives directly to the achievement of performance objectives and good strategy execution.

- Creating a company culture and work climate conducive to successful strategy implementation and execution.

- Exerting the internal leadership needed to drive implementation forward and keep improving strategy execution. When the organization encounters stumbling blocks or weaknesses, management has to see that they are addressed and rectified quickly.

Good strategy execution involves creating strong "fits" between strategy and organizational capabilities, between strategy and the reward structure, between strategy and internal operating systems, and between strategy and the organization's work climate and culture. The stronger these fits—that is, the more that the company's capabilities, reward structure, internal operating systems, and culture facilitate and promote proficient strategy execution—the better the execution and the higher the company's odds of achieving its performance targets. Furthermore, deliberately shaping the performance of core business activities around the strategy helps unite the organization.

INITIATING CORRECTIVE ADJUSTMENTS: PHASE 5 OF THE STRATEGY-MAKING, STRATEGY-EXECUTING PROCESS

The fifth phase of the strategy-management process—evaluating the company's progress, assessing the impact of new external developments, and making corrective adjustments—is the trigger point for deciding whether to continue or change the company's vision, objectives, strategy, and/or strategy-execution methods. So long as the company's direction and strategy seem well matched to industry and competitive conditions and performance targets are being met, company executives may decide to stay the course. Simply fine-tuning the strategic plan and continuing with ongoing efforts to improve strategy execution are sufficient.

But whenever a company encounters disruptive changes in its external environment, questions need to be raised about the appropriateness of its direction and strategy. If a company experiences a downturn in its market position or shortfalls in performance, then company managers are obligated to ferret out whether the causes relate to poor strategy, poor execution, or both and then to take timely corrective action. A company's direction, objectives, and strategy have to be revisited anytime external or internal conditions warrant. It is to be expected that a company will modify its strategic vision, direction, objectives, and strategy over time.

> **core concept**
> A company's vision, objectives, strategy, and approach to strategy execution are never final; managing strategy is an ongoing process, not an every now and then task.

Likewise, it is not unusual for a company to find that one or more aspects of implementing and executing the strategy are not going as well as intended. Proficient strategy execution is always the product of much organizational learning. It is achieved unevenly—coming quickly in some areas and proving nettlesome and problematic in others. Periodically assessing what aspects of strategy execution are working well and what needs improving is normal and desirable. Successful strategy execution entails vigilantly searching for ways *to continuously improve* and then making corrective adjustments whenever and wherever it is useful to do so.

CORPORATE GOVERNANCE: THE ROLE OF THE BOARD OF DIRECTORS IN THE STRATEGY-MAKING, STRATEGY-EXECUTING PROCESS

Although senior managers have *lead responsibility* for crafting and executing a company's strategy, it is the duty of the board of directors to exercise strong oversight and see that the five tasks of strategic management are done in a manner that benefits shareholders (in the case of investor-owned enterprises) or stakeholders (in the case of not-for-profit organizations). In watching over management's strategy-making, strategy-executing actions and making sure that executive actions are not only proper but also aligned with the interests of stakeholders, a company's board of directors have three obligations to fulfill:

1. *Be inquiring critics and overseers.* Board members must ask probing questions and draw on their business acumen to make independent judgments about whether strategy proposals have been adequately analyzed and whether proposed strategic actions appear to have greater promise than alternatives. If executive management is bringing well-supported and reasoned strategy proposals to the board, there's little reason for board members to aggressively challenge and try to pick apart everything put before them. Asking incisive questions is usually sufficient to test whether the case for management's proposals is compelling and to exercise vigilant oversight. However, when the company's strategy is failing or is plagued with faulty execution, and certainly when there is a precipitous collapse in profitability, board members have a duty to be proactive, expressing their concerns about the validity of the strategy and/or operating methods, initiating debate about the company's strategic path, having one-on-one discussions with key executives and other board members, and perhaps directly intervening as a group to alter the company's executive leadership and, ultimately, its strategy and business approaches.

2. *Evaluate the caliber of senior executives' strategy-making and strategy-executing skills.* The board is always responsible for determining whether the current CEO is doing a good job of strategic leadership (as a basis for awarding salary increases and bonuses and deciding on retention or removal). Boards must also exercise due diligence in evaluating the strategic leadership skills of other senior executives in line to succeed the CEO. When the incumbent CEO steps down or leaves for a position elsewhere, the board must elect a successor, either going with an insider or deciding that an outsider is needed to perhaps radically change the company's strategic course.

3. *Institute a compensation plan for top executives that rewards them for actions and results that serve stakeholder interests, and most especially those of shareholders.* A basic principle of corporate governance is that the owners of a corporation delegate operating authority and managerial control to top management in return for compensation. In their role as an agent of shareholders, top executives have a clear and unequivocal *duty* to make decisions and operate the company in accord with shareholder interests (but this does not mean disregarding the interests of other stakeholders, particularly those of employees, with whom they also have an agency relationship). Most boards of directors have a compensation committee, composed entirely of outside directors, to develop a salary and incentive compensation plan that makes it in the self-interest of executives to operate the business in a manner that benefits the owners; the compensation committee's recommendations are presented to the full board for approval. But in addition to creating compensation plans intended to align executive actions with owner interests, it is incumbent on the board of directors to put a halt to self-serving executive perks and privileges that simply enrich the personal welfare of executives. Numerous media reports have recounted instances in which boards of directors have gone along with opportunistic executive efforts to secure excessive, if not downright obscene, compensation of one kind or another (multimillion-dollar interest-free loans, personal use of corporate aircraft, lucrative severance and retirement packages, outsized stock incentive awards, and so on).

The number of prominent companies that have fallen on hard times because of the actions of scurrilous or out-of-control CEOs, the growing propensity of disgruntled stockholders to file lawsuits alleging director negligence, and the escalating costs of liability insurance for directors all underscore the responsibility that a board of directors has for overseeing a company's strategy-making, strategy-executing process and ensuring that management actions are proper and responsible. Moreover, holders of large blocks of shares (mutual funds and pension funds), regulatory authorities, and the financial press consistently urge that board members, especially outside directors, be active and diligent in their oversight of company strategy and maintain a tight rein on executive actions.

Every corporation should have a strong, independent board of directors that has the courage to curb management actions they believe are inappropriate or unduly risky.[10] Boards of directors that lack the backbone to challenge a strong-willed or "imperial" CEO or that rubber-stamp most anything the CEO recommends without probing inquiry and debate (perhaps because the board is stacked with the CEO's cronies) abdicate their duty to represent shareholder interests. The whole fabric of effective corporate governance is undermined when boards of directors shirk their responsibility to maintain ultimate control over the company's strategic direction, the major elements of its strategy, and the business approaches management is using to implement and execute the strategy. Boards of directors thus have a very important oversight role in the strategy-making, strategy-executing process.

key|points

The managerial process of crafting and executing a company's strategy consists of five interrelated and integrated tasks:

1. *Developing a strategic vision of where the company needs to head and what its product-market-customer-technology focus should be.* The vision must provide long-term direction, infuse the organization with a sense of purposeful action, and communicate to stakeholders what management's aspirations for the company are.

2. *Setting objectives.* The role of objectives is to convert the strategic vision into specific performance outcomes for the company to achieve. Objectives need to spell out *how much* of *what kind* of performance *by when,* and they need to require a significant amount of organizational stretch. A balanced scorecard approach to measuring company performance entails setting both *financial objectives* and

strategic objectives. Judging how well a company is doing by its financial performance is not enough—financial outcomes are "lagging indicators" that reflect the impacts of past decisions and organizational activities. But the "lead indicators" of a company's future financial performance are its current achievement of strategic targets that indicate a company is strengthening its marketing standing, competitive vitality, and business prospects.

3. *Crafting a strategy to achieve the desired outcomes and move the company toward where it wants to go.* Crafting strategy is concerned principally with forming responses to changes under way in the external environment, devising competitive moves and market approaches aimed at producing sustainable competitive advantage, building competitively valuable competencies and capabilities, and uniting the strategic actions initiated in various parts of the company. The more wide-ranging a company's operations, the more that strategy making is a team effort. The overall strategy that emerges in such companies is really a collection of strategic actions and business approaches initiated partly by senior company executives, partly by the heads of major business divisions, partly by functional-area managers, and partly by operating managers on the frontlines. The larger and more diverse the operations of an enterprise, the more points of strategic initiative it has and the more managers and employees at more levels of management that have a relevant strategy-making role. A single business enterprise has three levels of strategy—business strategy for the company as a whole, functional-area strategies for each main area within the business, and operating strategies undertaken by lower-echelon managers to flesh out strategically significant aspects for the company's business and functional area strategies. In diversified, multibusiness companies, the strategy-making task involves four distinct types or levels of strategy: corporate strategy for the company as a whole, business strategy (one for each business the company has diversified into), functional-area strategies within each business, and operating strategies. Typically, the strategy-making task is more top-down than bottom-up, with higher-level strategies serving as the guide for developing lower-level strategies.

4. *Implementing and executing the chosen strategy efficiently and effectively.* Managing the implementation and execution of strategy is an operations-oriented, make-things-happen activity aimed at shaping the performance of core business activities in a strategy-supportive manner. Converting a company's strategy into actions and results tests a manager's ability to direct organizational change, motivate people with a reward and incentive compensation system tied to good strategy execution and the achievement of target outcomes, build and strengthen company competencies and competitive capabilities, create a strategy-supportive work climate, and deliver the desired results. The quality of a company's operational excellence in executing the chosen strategy is a major driver of how well the company ultimately performs.

5. *Evaluating performance and initiating corrective adjustments in vision, long-term direction, objectives, strategy, or execution in light of actual experience, changing conditions, new ideas, and new opportunities.* This phase of the strategy management process is the trigger point for deciding whether to continue or change the company's vision, objectives, strategy, and/or strategy execution methods. Sometimes it suffices to simply fine-tune the strategic plan and continue with efforts to improve strategy execution. At other times, major overhauls are required.

Developing a strategic vision and mission, setting objectives, and crafting a strategy are basic direction-setting tasks; together, they constitute a *strategic plan* for coping with industry and competitive conditions, the actions of rivals, and the challenges and issues that stand as obstacles to the company's success.

Boards of directors have a duty to shareholders to play a vigilant supervisory role in a company's strategy-making, strategy-executing process. They are obligated to (1) critically appraise and ultimately approve strategic action plans, (2) evaluate the strategic leadership skills of the CEO and others in line to succeed the incumbent CEO, and (3) institute a compensation plan for top executives that rewards them for actions and results that serve stakeholder interests, and most especially those of shareholders. Boards of directors that are not aggressive and forceful in fulfilling these responsibilities undermine the fabric of effective corporate governance.

exercise

1. Go to the investors section of www.heinz.com and read the letter to the shareholders in the company's fiscal 2003 annual report. Is the vision for Heinz articulated by Chairman and CEO William R. Johnson sufficiently clear and well defined? Why or why not? Are the company's objectives well stated and seemingly appropriate? What about the strategy that Johnson outlines for the company? If you were a shareholder, would you be satisfied with what Johnson has told you about the company's direction, performance targets, and strategy?

chapter three 3

Analyzing a Company's External Environment

(©Royalty-Free/CORBIS)

Analysis is the critical starting point of strategic thinking.

—Kenichi Ohmae
consultant and author

Things are always different—the art is figuring out which differences matter.

—Laszlo Birinyi
investments manager

Competitive battles should be seen not as one-shot skirmishes but as a dynamic multiround game of moves and countermoves.

—Anil K. Gupta
professor

M anagers are not prepared to act wisely in steering a company in a new direction or altering its strategy until they have a deep understanding of the company's situation. This understanding requires thinking strategically about two facets of the company's situation: (1) the industry and competitive environment in which the company operates and the forces acting to reshape this environment, and (2) the company's own market position and competitiveness—its resources and capabilities, its strengths and weaknesses vis-à-vis rivals, and its windows of opportunity.

Managers must be able to perceptively diagnose a company's external and internal environments to succeed in crafting a strategy that is an excellent fit with the company's situation, is capable of building competitive advantage, and promises to boost company performance—the three criteria of a winning strategy. Developing a strategy begins with an appraisal of the company's external and internal situations (to form a strategic vision of where the company needs to head), then moves toward an evaluation of the most promising strategy options, and finally culminates in a choice of a strategy and business model (see Figure 3.1).

This chapter presents the concepts and analytical tools for assessing a single-business company's external environment. Attention centers on the competitive arena in which a company operates, together with the technological, societal, regulatory, or demographic influences in the macroenvironment that are acting to reshape the company's future market arena. In Chapter 4 we explore the methods of evaluating a company's internal circumstances and competitiveness.

THE STRATEGICALLY RELEVANT COMPONENTS OF A COMPANY'S EXTERNAL ENVIRONMENT

All companies operate in a "macroenvironment" shaped by influences emanating from the economy at large, population demographics, societal values and lifestyles, governmental legislation and regulation, technological factors, and, closer to home, the industry and competitive arena in which the company operates (see Figure 3.2). Strictly speaking, a company's macroenvironment includes *all relevant factors and influences* outside the company's boundaries; by *relevant,* we mean important enough to have a bearing on the decisions the company ultimately makes about its direction, objectives, strategy, and business model. For the most part, influences coming from the outer ring

figure 3.1   **From Thinking Strategically about the Company's Situation to Choosing a Strategy**

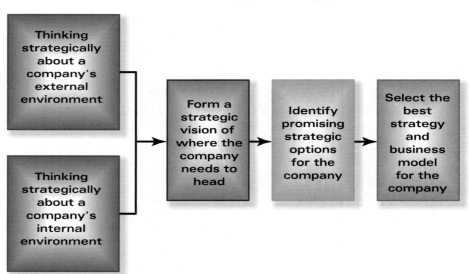

of the macroenvironment have a low impact on a company's business situation and shape only the edges of the company's direction and strategy. (There are notable exceptions, though. Cigarette producers have found their strategic opportunities to be greatly reduced by antismoking ordinances and the growing cultural stigma attached to smoking; the market growth potential for health care and prescription drug companies is quite favorably affected by the demographics of an aging population and longer life expectancies; and companies in most all industries, seeking to capitalize on the benefits of Internet technology applications, are rushing to incorporate e-commerce elements into their strategies.) But while the strategy-shaping impact of outer-ring influences is normally low, there are enough strategically relevant trends and developments in the outer ring of the macroenvironment to justify a watchful eye. As company managers scan the external environment, they must watch for potentially important outer-ring forces, assess their impact and influence, and adapt the company's direction and strategy as needed.

However, the factors and forces in a company's macroenvironment having the biggest strategy-shaping impact almost always pertain to the company's immediate industry and competitive environment. Consequently, it is on these factors that we concentrate our attention in this chapter.

THINKING STRATEGICALLY ABOUT A COMPANY'S INDUSTRY AND COMPETITIVE ENVIRONMENT

Industries differ widely in their economic features, competitive character, and profit outlook. The economic features and competitive character of the trucking industry bear little resemblance to those of discount retailing. The fast-food business has little in common with the business of developing software for Internet applications. The cable TV business is shaped by industry and competitive considerations radically different from

figure 3.2 **The Components of a Company's Macroenvironment**

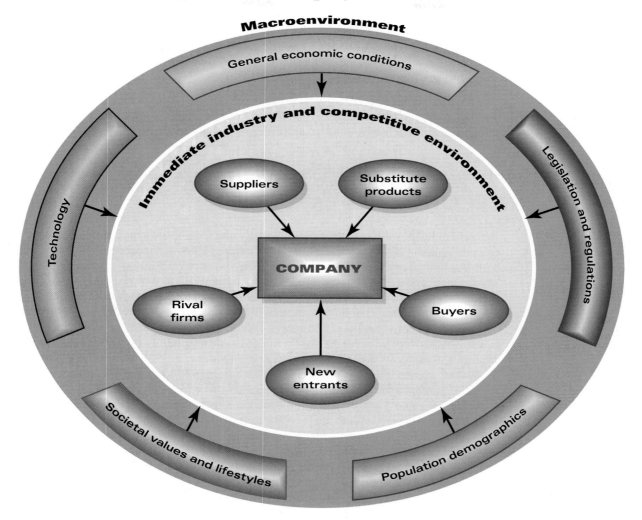

those that dominate the soft-drink business. An industry's economic traits and competitive conditions—and how they are expected to change—determine whether its future profit prospects will be poor, average, or excellent.

To gain a deep understanding of a company's industry and competitive environment, managers do not need to gather all the information they can find and spend lots of time digesting it. Rather, the task is much more focused. Thinking strategically about a company's competitive environment entails using some well-defined concepts and analytical tools to get clear answers to seven questions:

1. What are the dominant economic features of the industry in which the company operates?
2. What kinds of competitive forces are industry members facing, and how strong is each force?
3. What forces are driving changes in the industry, and what impact will these changes have on competitive intensity and industry profitability?

4. What market positions do industry rivals occupy—who is strongly positioned and who is not?

5. What strategic moves are rivals likely to make next?

6. What are the key factors for future competitive success?

7. Does the outlook for the industry present the company with sufficiently attractive prospects for profitability?

The answers to these questions provide managers with a solid diagnosis of the industry and competitive environment. The remainder of this chapter describes the methods of analyzing a company's industry and competitive environment.

QUESTION 1: WHAT ARE THE INDUSTRY'S DOMINANT ECONOMIC FEATURES?

Because industries differ so significantly, analyzing a company's industry and competitive environment begins with identifying the industry's dominant economic features and forming a picture of the industry landscape. An industry's dominant economic features are defined by such factors as overall size and market growth rate, the geographic boundaries of the market (which can extend from local to worldwide), the number and sizes of competitors, what buyers are looking for and the attributes that cause them to choose one seller over another, the pace of technological change and/or product innovations, whether sellers' products are virtually identical or highly differentiated, and the extent to which costs are affected by *scale economies* (i.e., situations in which higher production volumes mean a lower cost for each item produced) and *learning curve* effects (i.e., situations in which efficiency increases as the company gains knowledge and experience). Table 3.1 provides a convenient summary of what economic features to look at and the corresponding questions to consider in profiling an industry's landscape.

Getting a handle on an industry's distinguishing economic features not only sets the stage for the analysis to come but also promotes understanding of the kinds of strategic moves that industry members are likely to employ. For example, in industries characterized by one product advance after another, companies must invest in R&D and develop strong product innovation capabilities—a strategy of continuous product innovation becomes a condition of survival in such industries as video games, computers, and pharmaceuticals. An industry that has recently passed through the rapid-growth stage and is looking at only single-digit percentage increases in buyer demand is likely to be experiencing a competitive shake-out and much stronger strategic emphasis on cost reduction and improved customer service.

In industries like semiconductors, strong learning/experience effects in manufacturing cause unit costs to decline about 20 percent each time *cumulative* production volume doubles. With a 20 percent experience curve effect, if the first 1 million chips cost $100 each, by a production volume of 2 million the unit cost would be $80 (80 percent of $100), by a production volume of 4 million the unit cost would be $64 (80 percent of $80), and so on.[1] The bigger the learning or experience curve effect, the bigger the cost advantage of the company with the largest *cumulative* production volume. Thus, when an industry is characterized by important learning-experience curve effects, industry members are driven to pursue increased sales volumes and capture the resulting cost-saving economies; moreover, low-volume firms come under considerable pressure to grow sales in order to gain the experience needed to become more

table 3.1 **What to Consider in Identifying an Industry's Dominant Economic Features**

Economic Feature	Questions to Answer
Market size and growth rate	• How big is the industry and how fast is it growing? • What does the industry's position in the business life cycle (early development, rapid growth and takeoff, early maturity, maturity, saturation and stagnation, decline) reveal about the industry's growth prospects?
Scope of competitive rivalry	• Is the geographic area over which most companies compete local, regional, national, multinational, or global? • Is having a presence in foreign markets becoming more important to a company's long-term competitive success?
Number of rivals	• Is the industry fragmented into many small companies or dominated by a few large companies? • Is the industry going through a period of consolidation to a smaller number of competitors?
Buyer needs and requirements	• What are buyers looking for—what attributes prompt buyers to choose one brand over another? • Are buyer needs or requirements changing? If so, what is driving such changes?
Production capacity	• Is a surplus of capacity pushing prices and profit margins down? • Is the industry overcrowded with too many competitors?
Pace of technological change	• What role does advancing technology play in this industry? • Are ongoing upgrades of facilities/equipment essential because of rapidly advancing production process technologies? • Do most industry members have or need strong technological capabilities? Why?
Vertical integration	• Are some competitors in this industry partially or fully integrated? • Are there important cost differences among fully versus partially versus nonintegrated firms? • Is there any competitive advantage or disadvantage associated with being fully or partially integrated?
Product innovation	• Is the industry characterized by rapid product innovation and short product life cycles? • How important is R&D and product innovation? • Are there opportunities to overtake key rivals by being first-to-market with next-generation products?
Degree of product differentiation	• Are the products of rivals becoming more differentiated or less differentiated? • Are increasingly look-alike products of rivals causing heightened price competition?
Economies of scale	• Is the industry characterized by economies of scale in purchasing, manufacturing, advertising, shipping, or other activities? • Do companies with large-scale operations have an important cost advantage over small-scale firms?
Learning and experience curve effects	• Are certain industry activities characterized by strong learning and experience effects ("learning by doing") such that unit costs decline as a company's experience in performing the activity builds? • Do any companies have significant cost advantages because of their experience in performing particular activities?

cost-competitive with large-volume rivals. Competitors are also forced to race to build unit volume when larger-scale operations are more economical than smaller-scale operations. The bigger the learning curve effects and/or scale economies in an industry, the more imperative it becomes for competing sellers to pursue strategies to win additional sales and market share—the company with the biggest sales volume gains sustainable competitive advantage as the low-cost producer.

QUESTION 2: WHAT KINDS OF COMPETITIVE FORCES ARE INDUSTRY MEMBERS FACING?

The character, mix, and subtleties of competitive forces are never the same from one industry to another. Far and away the most powerful and widely used tool for systematically diagnosing the principal competitive pressures in a market and assessing the strength and importance of each is the *five-forces model of competition*.[2] This model, depicted in Figure 3.3, holds that the state of competition in an industry is a composite of competitive pressures operating in five areas of the overall market:

1. Competitive pressures associated with the market maneuvering and jockeying for buyer patronage that goes on among *rival sellers* in the industry.
2. Competitive pressures associated with the threat of *new entrants* into the market.
3. Competitive pressures coming from the attempts of companies in other industries to win buyers over to their own *substitute products*.
4. Competitive pressures stemming from *supplier* bargaining power and supplier–seller collaboration.
5. Competitive pressures stemming from *buyer* bargaining power and seller–buyer collaboration.

The way one uses the five-forces model to determine what competition is like in a given industry is to build the picture of competition in three steps:

*   *Step 1*: Identify the specific competitive pressures associated with each of the five forces.
*   *Step 2*: Evaluate how strong the pressures comprising each of the five forces are (fierce, strong, moderate to normal, or weak).
*   *Step 3*: Determine whether the collective strength of the five competitive forces is conducive to earning attractive profits.

The Rivalry among Competing Sellers

core concept
Competitive jockeying among industry rivals is ever changing, as fresh offensive and defensive moves are initiated and rivals emphasize first one mix of competitive weapons and tactics, then another.

The strongest of the five competitive forces is nearly always the market maneuvering and jockeying for buyer patronage that goes on among rival sellers of a product or service. In effect, *a market is a competitive battlefield* where it is customary and expected that rival sellers will employ whatever resources and weapons they have in their business arsenal to improve their market positions and performance. The strategy-making challenge of managers is to craft a competitive strategy that, at the very least, allows their company to hold its own against rivals and that, ideally, strengthens the company's standing with buyers, delivers good profitability, and *produces a competitive edge over rivals*. But when one firm makes a strategic move that produces

figure 3.3 **The Five Forces Model of Competition: A Key Tool for Diagnosing the Competitive Environment**

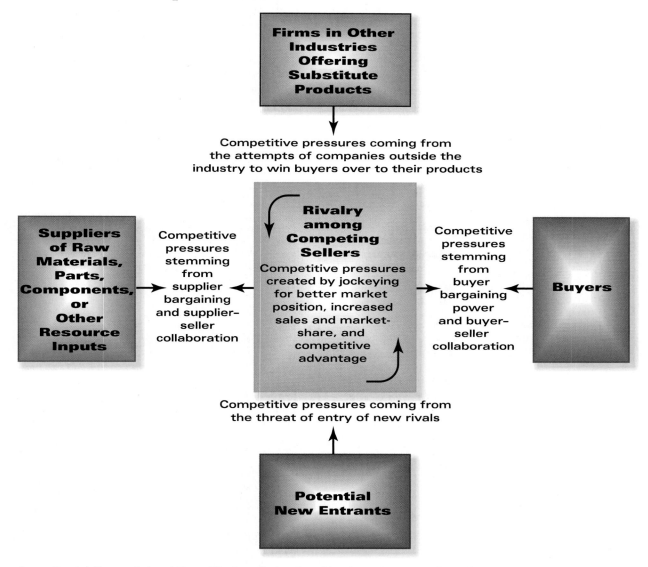

good results, its rivals often respond with offensive or defensive countermoves, shifting their strategic emphasis from one combination of product attributes, marketing tactics, and competitive capabilities to another. This pattern of action and reaction, move and countermove, adjust and readjust, is what makes competitive rivalry a combative, ever-changing contest. The market battle for buyer patronage in an industry takes on a life of its own, with one or another rivals gaining or losing market momentum according to whether their latest strategic adjustments succeed or fail.

figure 3.4   **Weapons for Competing and Factors Affecting the Strength of Rivalry**

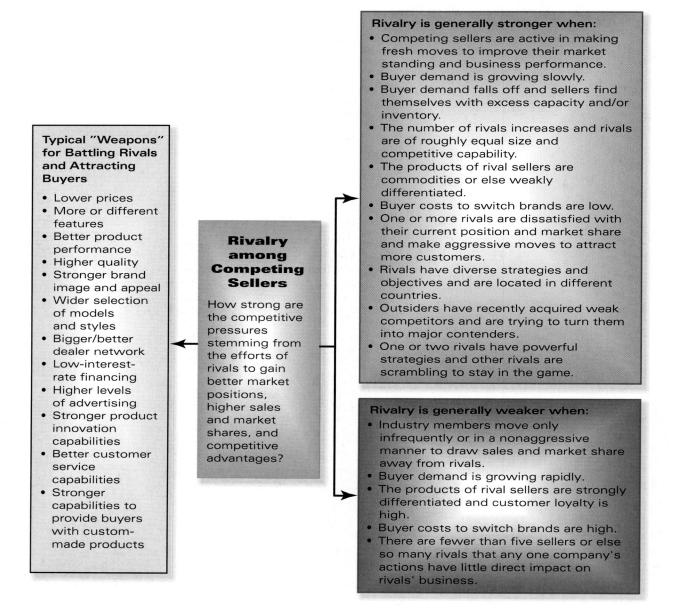

Typical "Weapons" for Battling Rivals and Attracting Buyers

- Lower prices
- More or different features
- Better product performance
- Higher quality
- Stronger brand image and appeal
- Wider selection of models and styles
- Bigger/better dealer network
- Low-interest-rate financing
- Higher levels of advertising
- Stronger product innovation capabilities
- Better customer service capabilities
- Stronger capabilities to provide buyers with custom-made products

Rivalry among Competing Sellers

How strong are the competitive pressures stemming from the efforts of rivals to gain better market positions, higher sales and market shares, and competitive advantages?

Rivalry is generally stronger when:

- Competing sellers are active in making fresh moves to improve their market standing and business performance.
- Buyer demand is growing slowly.
- Buyer demand falls off and sellers find themselves with excess capacity and/or inventory.
- The number of rivals increases and rivals are of roughly equal size and competitive capability.
- The products of rival sellers are commodities or else weakly differentiated.
- Buyer costs to switch brands are low.
- One or more rivals are dissatisfied with their current position and market share and make aggressive moves to attract more customers.
- Rivals have diverse strategies and objectives and are located in different countries.
- Outsiders have recently acquired weak competitors and are trying to turn them into major contenders.
- One or two rivals have powerful strategies and other rivals are scrambling to stay in the game.

Rivalry is generally weaker when:

- Industry members move only infrequently or in a nonaggressive manner to draw sales and market share away from rivals.
- Buyer demand is growing rapidly.
- The products of rival sellers are strongly differentiated and customer loyalty is high.
- Buyer costs to switch brands are high.
- There are fewer than five sellers or else so many rivals that any one company's actions have little direct impact on rivals' business.

Figure 3.4 shows a sampling of competitive weapons that firms can deploy in battling rivals and indicates the factors that influence the intensity of their rivalry. A brief discussion of some of the factors that influence the tempo of rivalry among industry competitors is in order:[3]

- *Rivalry among competing sellers intensifies the more frequently and more aggressively that industry members undertake fresh actions to boost their market standing and performance—perhaps at the expense of rivals.* Rivalry tends to be fairly intense whenever sellers actively engage in vigorous price competition. Lively price competition pressures rival companies to aggressively pursue ways to drive costs out of the business; high-cost companies are hard-pressed to survive. Other indicators of the intensity of rivalry among industry members include:

- Whether industry members are racing to offer better performance features, higher quality, improved customer service, or a wider product selection.
- How frequently rivals resort to such marketing tactics as sales promotions, new advertising campaigns, rebates, or low-interest-rate financing to drum up additional sales.
- How actively industry members are pursuing efforts to build stronger dealer networks or establish positions in foreign markets or otherwise expand their distribution capabilities and market presence.
- The frequency with which rivals introduce new and improved products (and thus are competing on the basis of their product innovation capabilities).
- How hard companies are striving to gain a market edge by developing valuable expertise and capabilities that rivals cannot match.

Normally, industry members are proactive in drawing on their arsenal of competitive weapons and deploying their organizational resources in a manner calculated to strengthen their market positions and performance.

- *Rivalry is usually stronger in slow-growing markets and weaker in fast-growing markets.* Rapidly expanding buyer demand produces enough new business for all industry members to grow. Indeed, in a fast-growing market, a company may find itself stretched just to keep abreast of incoming orders, let alone devote resources to stealing customers away from rivals. But in markets where growth is sluggish or where buyer demand drops off unexpectedly, expansion-minded firms and/or firms with excess capacity often are quick to cut prices and initiate other sales-increasing tactics, thereby igniting a battle for market share that can result in a shake-out of weak, inefficient firms.

- *Rivalry intensifies as the number of competitors increases and as competitors become more equal in size and capability.* The greater the number of competitors, the higher the probability that one or more companies will be busily engaged in a strategic offensive intended to enhance their marketing standing, thereby heating up competition and putting new pressures on rivals to respond with offensive or defensive moves of their own. In addition, when rivals are nearly equal in size and capability, they can usually compete on a fairly even footing, making it harder for one or two firms to emerge as victorious over the others. Consequently, markets tend to be more hotly contested as the number of resourceful and capable rivals increases.

- *Rivalry is usually weaker in industries comprised of so many rivals that the impact of any one company's actions is spread thinly across all industry members; likewise, it is often weak when there are fewer than five competitors.* A progressively larger number of competitors can actually begin to weaken head-to-head rivalry once an industry becomes populated with so many rivals that the impact of successful moves by any one company is spread thinly across many industry members. To the extent that a company's strategic moves ripple out to have little discernible impact on the businesses of its many rivals, then industry members quickly learn that it is not imperative to respond every time one or another rival does something to enhance its market position—an outcome that weakens the intensity of head-to-head battles for market share. Rivalry also tends to be weak if an industry consists of just two or three or four sellers. In a market with few rivals, each competitor soon learns that aggressive moves to grow its sales and market share can have immediate adverse impact on rivals' businesses, almost certainly provoking vigorous retaliation and risking an all-out battle that is likely to lower the profits of all concerned. Thus, although occasional warfare can break out (the current fierce battle between Linux and Microsoft is a prime example), competition among the few normally produces a live-and-let-live approach to competing because rivals see the merits of *restrained* efforts to wrest sales and market share from competitors as opposed to undertaking hard-hitting offensives that escalate into a profit-eroding arms race or price war.

- *Rivalry increases as the products of rival sellers become more standardized.* When the offerings of rivals are identical or only weakly differentiated, buyers have less reason to be brand loyal—a condition that makes it easier for rivals to convince buyers to switch to their offering. And since the brands of different sellers have comparable attributes, buyers can shop the market for the best deal and switch brands at will. In contrast, rivalry typically weakens as the products of rival sellers become more strongly differentiated. Significantly different product attributes from seller to seller breed higher brand loyalty on the part of buyers. The attachment that buyers have to their present brand, coupled with convictions that certain attributes or brands better suit their needs than others, make it tougher for competing companies to steal one another's customers. Unless meaningful numbers of buyers are open to considering new or different product attributes being offered by rivals, strong product differentiation works against fierce rivalry among competing sellers.

- *Rivalry increases as it becomes less costly for buyers to switch brands.* The less expensive it is for buyers to switch their purchases from one seller to another, the easier it is for sellers to steal customers away from rivals. But the higher the costs buyers incur to switch brands, the less prone they are to brand switching. Even if buyers view one or more rival brands as more attractive, they may not believe that switching is worth the costs they will incur. Consequently, unless buyers are dissatisfied with the brand they are presently purchasing, high switching costs can significantly weaken the rivalry among competing sellers.

- *Rivalry is more intense when industry conditions tempt competitors to use price cuts or other competitive weapons to boost unit volume.* When a product is perishable, seasonal, or costly to hold in inventory, or when buyer demand slacks off, competitive pressures build quickly anytime one or more rivals decide to cut prices and dump excess supplies on the market. Likewise, whenever fixed costs account for a large fraction of total cost so that unit costs tend to be lowest at or near full capacity, then industry rivals come under significant pressure to cut prices or otherwise try to boost sales. Unused capacity imposes a significant cost-increasing penalty because there are fewer units over which to spread fixed costs. The pressure of high fixed costs can push rival firms into price concessions, special discounts, rebates, low-interest-rate financing, and other volume-boosting tactics.

- *Rivalry increases when one or more competitors become dissatisfied with their market position and launch moves to bolster their standing at the expense of rivals.* Firms that are losing ground or in financial trouble often react aggressively by acquiring smaller rivals, introducing new products, boosting advertising, discounting prices, and so on. Such actions heighten rivalry and can trigger a hotly contested battle for market share. The market maneuvering among rivals usually heats up when a competitor makes new offensive moves—because it sees an opportunity to better please customers or is under pressure to improve its market share or profitability.

- *Rivalry increases in proportion to the size of the payoff from a successful strategic move.* The greater the benefits of going after a new opportunity, the more likely that one or more rivals will initiate moves to capture it. Competitive pressures nearly always intensify when several rivals start pursuing the same opportunity. For example, competition in music CD e-tailing heated up with the entries of Amazon.com, Barnesandnoble.com, and Buy.com. Furthermore, the size of the strategic payoff can vary with the speed of retaliation. When competitors respond slowly (or not at all), the initiator of a fresh competitive strategy can reap benefits in the intervening period and perhaps gain a first-mover advantage that is not easily surmounted. The greater the benefits of moving first, the more likely some competitor will accept the risk and try it.

- *Rivalry becomes more volatile and unpredictable as the diversity of competitors increases in terms of visions, strategic intents, objectives, strategies, resources, and countries of origin.* A diverse group of sellers often contains one or more mavericks willing to try novel, high-risk, rule-breaking market approaches, thus generating a livelier and less predictable competitive environment. Globally competitive markets often contain rivals with different views about where the industry is headed and a willingness to employ perhaps radically different competitive approaches. Attempts by cross-border rivals to gain stronger footholds in each other's domestic markets usually boost the intensity of rivalry, especially when the aggressors have lower costs or products with more attractive features.

- *Rivalry increases when strong companies outside the industry acquire weak firms in the industry and launch aggressive, well-funded moves to transform their newly acquired competitors into major market contenders.* A concerted effort to turn a weak rival into a market leader nearly always entails launching well-financed strategic initiatives to dramatically improve the competitor's product offering, excite buyer interest, and win a much bigger market share—actions that, if successful, put added pressure on rivals to counter with fresh strategic moves of their own.

- *A powerful, successful competitive strategy employed by one company greatly intensifies the competitive pressures on its rivals to develop effective strategic responses or be relegated to also-ran status.*

Rivalry can be characterized as *cutthroat* or *brutal* when competitors engage in protracted price wars or habitually employ other aggressive tactics that are mutually destructive to profitability. Rivalry can be considered *fierce* to *strong* when the battle for market share is so vigorous that the profit margins of most industry members are squeezed to bare-bones levels. Rivalry can be characterized as *moderate* or *normal* when the maneuvering among industry members, while lively and healthy, still allows most industry members to earn acceptable profits. Rivalry is *weak* when most companies in the industry are relatively well satisfied with their sales growth and market shares, rarely undertake offensives to steal customers away from one another, and have comparatively attractive earnings and returns on investment.

The Potential Entry of New Competitors

Several factors affect the strength of the competitive threat of potential entry in a particular industry (see Figure 3.5). One factor relates to the size of the pool of likely entry candidates and the resources at their command. As a rule, competitive pressures intensify as the pool of entry candidates increases in size. This is especially true when some of the

figure 3.5   **Factors Affecting the Strength of Threat of Entry**

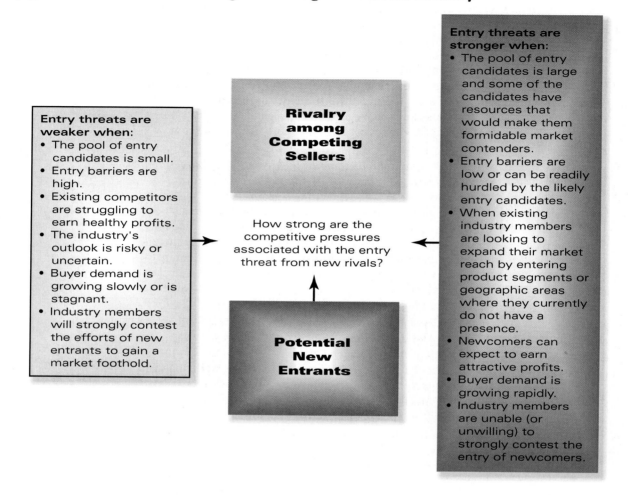

likely entry candidates have ample resources and the potential to become formidable contenders for market leadership. Frequently, the strongest competitive pressures associated with potential entry come not from outsiders but from current industry participants looking for growth opportunities. *Existing industry members are often strong candidates to enter market segments or geographic areas where they currently do not have a market presence.* Companies already well established in certain product categories or geographic areas often possess the resources, competencies, and competitive capabilities to hurdle the barriers of entering a different market segment or new geographic area.

A second factor concerns whether the likely entry candidates face high or low entry barriers. The most common barriers that entry candidates must hurdle include:[4]

- *The presence of sizable economies of scale in production or other areas of operation*—When incumbent companies enjoy cost advantages associated with large-scale operation, outsiders must either enter on a large scale (a costly and perhaps risky move) or accept a cost disadvantage and consequently lower profitability. Trying to overcome the disadvantages of small size by entering on a large scale at the outset can result in long-term overcapacity problems for the new entrant (until sales volume builds up), and it can so threaten the market shares of existing firms that they launch strong defensive maneuvers (price cuts, increased advertising and sales promotion, and similar blocking actions) to maintain their positions and make things hard on a newcomer.

- *Cost and resource disadvantages not related to size*—Existing firms may have low unit costs as a result of experience or learning-curve effects, key patents, partnerships with the best and cheapest suppliers of raw materials and components, proprietary technology know-how not readily available to newcomers, favorable locations, and low fixed costs (because they have older plants that have been mostly depreciated).

- *Brand preferences and customer loyalty*—In some industries, buyers are strongly attached to established brands. Japanese consumers, for example, are fiercely loyal to Japanese brands of motor vehicles, electronics products, cameras, and video games. European consumers have traditionally been loyal to European brands of major household appliances. High brand loyalty means that a potential entrant must commit to spending enough money on advertising and sales promotion to overcome customer loyalties and build its own clientele. Establishing brand recognition and building customer loyalty can be a slow and costly process. In addition, if it is costly or inconvenient for a customer to switch to a new brand, a new entrant must persuade buyers that its brand is worth the switching costs. To overcome switching-cost barriers, new entrants may have to offer buyers a discounted price or an extra margin of quality or service. All this can mean lower expected profit margins for new entrants, which increases the risk to start-up companies dependent on sizable early profits to support their new investments.

- *Capital requirements*—The larger the total dollar investment needed to enter the market successfully, the more limited the pool of potential entrants. The most typical capital requirements for new entrants are those associated with investing in the necessary manufacturing facilities and equipment, being able to finance the introductory advertising and sales promotion campaigns to build brand awareness and establish a clientele, securing the working capital to finance inventories and customer credit, and having sufficient cash reserves to cover start-up losses.

- *Access to distribution channels*—In consumer goods industries, a potential entrant may face the barrier of gaining adequate access to consumers. Wholesale distributors may be reluctant to take on a product that lacks buyer recognition. A network of retail dealers may have to be set up from scratch. Retailers have to be convinced to give a new brand ample display space and an adequate trial period. Entry is tough when existing producers have strong, well-functioning distributor–dealer networks and a newcomer must struggle to squeeze its way into existing distribution channels. To overcome the barrier of gaining adequate access to consumers, potential entrants may have to "buy" their way into wholesale or retail channels by cutting their prices to provide dealers and distributors with higher markups and profit margins or by giving them big advertising and promotional allowances. As a consequence, a potential entrant's own profits may be squeezed unless and until its product gains enough consumer acceptance that distributors and retailers want to carry it.

- *Regulatory policies*—Government agencies can limit or even bar entry by requiring licenses and permits. Regulated industries like cable TV, telecommunications, electric and gas utilities, radio and television broadcasting, liquor retailing, and railroads entail government-controlled entry. In international markets, host governments commonly limit foreign entry and must approve all foreign investment applications. Stringent government-mandated safety regulations and environmental pollution standards are entry barriers because they raise entry costs.

- *Tariffs and international trade restrictions*—National governments commonly use tariffs and trade restrictions (antidumping rules, local content requirements, quotas, etc.) to raise entry barriers for foreign firms and protect domestic producers from outside competition.

Whether an industry's entry barriers ought to be considered high or low and how hard it is for new entrants to compete on a level playing field depend on the resources and competencies possessed by the pool of potential entrants. Entry barriers can be formidable for newly formed enterprises that have to find some way to gain a market foothold and then over time make inroads against well-established companies. But opportunity-seeking companies in other industries, if they have suitable resources, competencies, and brand-name recognition, may be able to hurdle an industry's entry barriers rather easily. In evaluating the potential threat of entry, company managers must look at (1) how formidable the entry barriers are for each type of potential entrant—start-up enterprises, specific candidate companies in other industries, and current industry participants looking to expand their market reach—and (2) how attractive the growth and profit prospects are for new entrants. *Rapidly growing market demand and high potential profits act as magnets, motivating potential entrants to commit the resources needed to hurdle entry barriers.*[5]

> The threat of entry is stronger when entry barriers are low, when there's a sizable pool of entry candidates, when industry growth is rapid and profit potentials are high, and when incumbent firms are unable or unwilling to vigorously contest a newcomer's entry.

However, even if a potential entrant has or can acquire the needed competencies and resources to attempt entry, it still faces the issue of how existing firms will react.[6] Will incumbent firms offer only passive resistance, or will they aggressively defend their market positions using price cuts, increased advertising, product improvements, and whatever else they can think of to give a new entrant (as well as other rivals) a hard time? A potential entrant can have second thoughts when financially strong incumbent firms send clear signals that they will stoutly defend their market positions against newcomers. A potential entrant may also turn away when incumbent firms can leverage distributors and customers to retain their business.

The best test of whether potential entry is a strong or weak competitive force in the marketplace is to ask if the industry's growth and profit prospects are strongly attractive to potential entry candidates. When the answer is no, potential entry is a weak competitive force. When the answer is yes and there are entry candidates with sufficient expertise and resources, then potential entry adds significantly to competitive pressures in the marketplace. The stronger the threat of entry, the more that incumbent firms are driven to seek ways to fortify their positions against newcomers, pursuing strategic moves not only to protect their market shares but also to make entry more costly or difficult.

One additional point: *The threat of entry changes as the industry's prospects grow brighter or dimmer and as entry barriers rise or fall.* For example, in the pharmaceutical industry the expiration of a key patent on a widely prescribed drug virtually guarantees that one or more drug makers will enter with generic offerings of their own. Use of the Internet for shopping is making it much easier for e-tailers to enter into competition against some of the best-known retail chains. In international markets, entry barriers for foreign-based firms fall as tariffs are lowered, as host governments open up their domestic markets to outsiders, as domestic wholesalers and dealers seek out lower-cost foreign-made goods, and as domestic buyers become more willing to purchase foreign brands.

Competitive Pressures from the Sellers of Substitute Products

Companies in one industry come under competitive pressure from the actions of companies in a closely adjoining industry whenever buyers view the products of the two industries as good substitutes. For instance, the producers of sugar experience competitive pressures from the sales and marketing efforts of the makers of artificial sweeteners. Similarly, the producers of eyeglasses and contact lenses are currently facing mounting competitive pressures from growing consumer interest in corrective laser surgery. Newspapers are feeling the competitive force of the general public turning to cable news channels for late-breaking news and using Internet sources to get information about sports results, stock quotes, and job opportunities.

Just how strong the competitive pressures are from the sellers of substitute products depends on three factors: (1) whether substitutes are readily available and attractively priced; (2) whether buyers view the substitutes as being comparable or better in terms of quality, performance, and other relevant attributes; and (3) how much it costs end users to switch to substitutes. Figure 3.6 lists factors affecting the strength of competitive pressures from substitute products and signs that indicate substitutes are a strong competitive force.

The presence of readily available and attractively priced substitutes creates competitive pressure by placing a ceiling on the prices industry members can charge without giving customers an incentive to switch to substitutes and risking sales erosion.[7] At the same time, this price ceiling puts a lid on the profits that industry members can earn unless they find ways to cut costs. When substitutes are cheaper than an industry's product, industry members come under heavy competitive pressure to reduce their prices and find ways to absorb the price cuts with cost reductions.

The availability of substitutes inevitably invites customers to compare performance, features, ease of use, and other attributes as well as price. For example, the makers of films and film-based cameras are experiencing strong competition from the makers of digital cameras because consumers like the convenience and low operating costs of digital cameras. The users of paper cartons constantly weigh the performance trade-offs with plastic containers and metal cans. Competition from well-performing substitute products pushes industry participants to incorporate new performance features and heighten efforts to convince customers their product has attributes that are superior to those of substitutes.

The strength of competition from substitutes is significantly influenced by how difficult or costly it is for the industry's customers to switch to a substitute.[8] Typical switching costs include the time and inconvenience that may be involved, the costs of additional equipment, the time and cost in testing the quality and reliability of the substitute, the psychological costs of severing old supplier relationships and establishing new ones, payments for technical help in making the changeover, and employee retraining costs. When buyers incur high costs in switching to substitutes, the competitive pressures that industry members experience from substitutes are usually lessened unless the sellers of substitutes begin offering price discounts or major performance benefits that entice the industry's customers away. When switching costs are low, it's much easier for sellers of substitutes to convince buyers to change to their products.

As a rule, then, the lower the price of substitutes, the higher their quality and performance, and the lower the user's switching costs, the more intense the competitive pressures posed by substitute products. Good indicators of the competitive strength of substitute products are the rate at which their sales and profits are growing, the market inroads they are making, and their plans for expanding production capacity.

figure 3.6   **Factors Affecting Competition from Substitute Products**

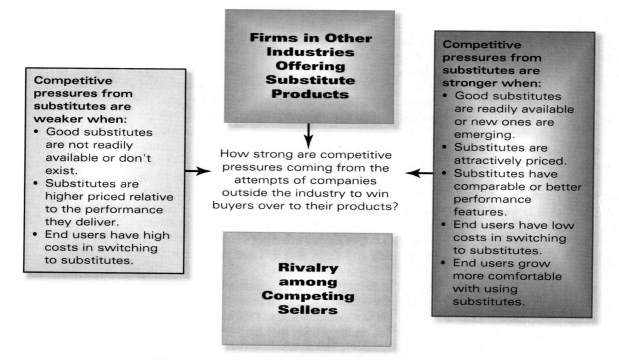

Signs That Competition from Substitutes Is Strong
- Sales of substitutes are growing faster than sales of the industry being analyzed (an indication that the sellers of substitutes are drawing customers away from the industry in question).
- Producers of substitutes are moving to add new capacity.
- Profits of the producers of substitutes are on the rise.

Competitive Pressures Stemming from Supplier Bargaining Power and Supplier–Seller Collaboration

Whether supplier–seller relationships represent a weak or a strong competitive force depends on (1) whether major suppliers can exercise sufficient bargaining power to influence the terms and conditions of supply in their favor, and (2) the nature and extent of supplier–seller collaboration in the industry.

How Supplier Bargaining Power Can Create Competitive Pressures

When the major suppliers to an industry have considerable leverage in determining the terms and conditions of the item they are supplying, they are in a position to exert competitive pressure on one or more rival sellers. For instance, Microsoft and Intel, both of which supply personal computer (PC) makers with products that most PC users consider essential, are known for using their dominant market status not only to charge PC makers premium prices but also to leverage PC makers in other ways. Microsoft pressures PC makers to load only Microsoft products on the PCs they ship and to position the icons for Microsoft software prominently on the screens of new computers that come with factory-loaded software. Intel pushes greater use of Intel microprocessors in PCs by granting PC makers sizable advertising allowances on PC models equipped with "Intel Inside" stickers; it also tends to give PC makers that use the biggest percentages of Intel chips in their PC models top priority in filling orders for newly introduced Intel chips. Being on Intel's list of preferred customers helps a PC maker get an allocation of the first production runs of Intel's latest and greatest chips and thus get new PC models equipped with these chips to market ahead of rivals who are heavier users of chips made by Intel's rivals. The ability of Microsoft and Intel to pressure PC makers for preferential treatment of one kind or another in turn affects competition among rival PC makers.

Several other instances of supplier bargaining power are worth citing. Small-scale retailers must often contend with the power of manufacturers whose products enjoy prestigious and well-respected brand names; when a manufacturer knows that a retailer needs to stock the manufacturer's product because consumers expect to find the product on the shelves of retail stores where they shop, the manufacturer usually has some degree of pricing power and can also push hard for favorable shelf displays. Motor vehicle manufacturers typically exert considerable power over the terms and conditions with which they supply new vehicles to their independent automobile dealerships. The operators of franchised units of such chains as Krispy Kreme Doughnuts, Burger King, Pizza Hut, and Hampton Inns must frequently agree not only to source some of their supplies from the franchisor at prices and terms favorable to that franchisor but also to operate their facilities in a manner largely dictated by the franchisor. Strong supplier bargaining power is a competitive factor in industries where unions have been able to organize the workforces of some industry members but not others; those industry members that must negotiate wages, fringe benefits, and working conditions with powerful unions (which control the supply of labor) often find themselves with higher labor costs than their competitors with nonunion labor forces. The bigger the gap between union and nonunion labor costs in an industry, the more that unionized industry members must scramble to find ways to relieve the competitive pressure associated with their disadvantage on labor costs.

The factors that determine whether any of the suppliers to an industry are in a position to exert substantial bargaining power or leverage are fairly clear-cut:[9]

- *Whether the item being supplied is a commodity that is readily available from many suppliers at the going market price.* Suppliers have little or no bargaining power or leverage whenever industry members have the ability to source their requirements at competitive prices from any of several alternative and eager suppliers, perhaps dividing their purchases among two or more suppliers to promote lively competition for orders. The suppliers of commoditylike items have market power only when supplies become quite tight and industry members are so eager to secure what they need that they agree to terms more favorable to suppliers.

- *Whether a few large suppliers are the primary sources of a particular item.* The leading suppliers may well have pricing leverage unless they are plagued with excess capacity and are scrambling to secure additional orders for their products. Major suppliers with good reputations and strong demand for the items they supply are harder to wring concessions from than struggling suppliers striving to broaden their customer base or more fully utilize their production capacity.

- *Whether it is difficult or costly for industry members to switch their purchases from one supplier to another or to switch to attractive substitute inputs.* High switching costs signal strong bargaining power on the part of suppliers, whereas low switching costs and ready availability of good substitute inputs signal weak bargaining power. Soft-drink bottlers, for example, can counter the bargaining power of aluminum-can suppliers by shifting or threatening to shift to greater use of plastic containers and introducing more attractive plastic container designs.

- *Whether certain needed inputs are in short supply.* Suppliers of items in short supply have some degree of pricing power, whereas a surge in the availability of particular items greatly weakens supplier pricing power and bargaining leverage.

- *Whether certain suppliers provide a differentiated input that enhances the performance or quality of the industry's product.* The more valuable a particular input is in terms of enhancing the performance or quality of the products of industry members or of improving the efficiency of their production processes, the more bargaining leverage its suppliers are likely to possess.

- *Whether certain suppliers provide equipment or services that deliver valuable cost-saving efficiencies to industry members in operating their production processes.* Suppliers who provide cost-saving equipment or other valuable or necessary production-related services are likely to possess bargaining leverage. Industry members that do not source from such suppliers may find themselves at a cost disadvantage and thus under competitive pressure to do so (on terms that are favorable to the suppliers).

- *Whether suppliers provide an item that accounts for a sizable fraction of the costs of the industry's product.* The bigger the cost of a particular part or component, the more opportunity for the pattern of competition in the marketplace to be affected by the actions of suppliers to raise or lower their prices.

- *Whether industry members are major customers of suppliers.* As a rule, suppliers have less bargaining leverage when their sales to members of this one industry constitute a big percentage of their total sales. In such cases, the well-being of suppliers is closely tied to the well-being of their major customers. Suppliers then have a big incentive to protect and enhance their customers' competitiveness via reasonable prices, exceptional quality, and ongoing advances in the technology of the items supplied.

- *Whether it makes good economic sense for industry members to integrate backward and self-manufacture items they have been buying from suppliers.* The make-or-buy issue generally boils down to whether suppliers who specialize in the production of a particular part or component and make them in volume for many different customers have the expertise and scale economies to supply as good or better component at a lower cost than industry members could achieve via self-manufacture. Frequently, it is difficult for industry members to self-manufacture parts and components more economically than they can obtain them from suppliers who specialize in making such items. For instance, most producers of outdoor power equipment (lawn mowers, rotary tillers, leaf blowers, etc.) find it cheaper to source the small engines they need from outside manufacturers who specialize in small-engine manufacture rather than make their own engines because the quantity of engines they need is too small to justify the investment in manufacturing facilities, master the production process, and capture scale economies. Specialists in small-engine manufacture, by supplying many kinds of engines to the whole power equipment industry, can obtain a big enough sales volume to fully realize scale economies, become proficient in all the manufacturing techniques, and keep costs low. As a rule, suppliers are safe from the threat of self-manufacture by their customers *until* the volume of parts a customer needs becomes large enough for the customer to justify backward integration into self-manufacture of the component. Suppliers also gain bargaining power when

figure 3.7   **Factors Affecting the Bargaining Power of Suppliers**

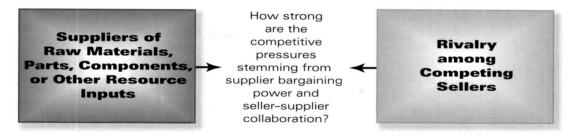

Supplier bargaining power is stronger when:
- Industry members incur high costs in switching their purchases to alternative suppliers.
- Needed inputs are in short supply (which gives suppliers more leverage in setting prices).
- A supplier has a differentiated input that enhances the quality or performance of sellers' products or is a valuable or critical part of sellers' production process.
- There are only a few suppliers of a particular input.
- Some suppliers threaten to integrate forward into the business of industry members and perhaps become a powerful rival.

Supplier bargaining power is weaker when:
- The item being supplied is a commodity that is readily available from many suppliers at the going market price.
- Seller switching costs to alternative suppliers are low.
- Good substitute inputs exist or new ones emerge.
- There is a surge in the availability of supplies (thus greatly weakening supplier pricing power).
- Industry members account for a big fraction of suppliers' total sales and continued high volume purchases are important to the well-being of suppliers.
- Industry members are a threat to integrate backward into the business of suppliers and to self-manufacture their own requirements.
- Seller collaboration or partnering with selected suppliers provides attractive win–win opportunities.

they have the resources and profit incentive to integrate forward into the business of the customers they are supplying and thus become a strong rival.

Figure 3.7 summarizes the conditions that tend to make supplier bargaining power strong or weak.

How Seller–Supplier Partnerships Can Create Competitive Pressures

In more and more industries, sellers are forging strategic partnerships with select suppliers in efforts to (1) reduce inventory and logistics costs (e.g., through just-in-time deliveries); (2) speed the availability of next-generation components; (3) enhance the quality of the parts and components being supplied and reduce defect rates; and (4) squeeze out important cost savings for both themselves and their suppliers. Numerous Internet technology applications are now available that permit real-time data sharing, eliminate paperwork, and produce cost savings all along the supply chain. The many benefits of effective seller–supplier collaboration can translate into competitive advantage for industry members who do the best job of managing supply chain relationships.

Dell Computer has used strategic partnering with key suppliers as a major element in its strategy to be the world's lowest-cost supplier of branded PCs, servers, and workstations. Because Dell has managed its supply chain relationships in ways that contribute to a low-cost, high-quality competitive edge in components supply, it has put enormous pressure on its PC rivals to try to imitate its supply chain management practices. Effective partnerships with suppliers on the part of one or more industry members can thus become a major source of competitive pressure for rival firms.

The more opportunities that exist for win–win efforts between a company and its suppliers, the less their relationship is characterized by who has the upper hand in bargaining with the other. So long as the relationship is producing valuable benefits for both parties, it will last; only if a supply partner is falling behind alternative suppliers is a company likely to switch suppliers and incur the costs and trouble of building close working ties with a different supplier.

Competitive Pressures Stemming from Buyer Bargaining Power and Seller–Buyer Collaboration

Whether seller–buyer relationships represent a weak or strong competitive force depends on (1) whether some or many buyers have sufficient bargaining leverage to obtain price concessions and other favorable terms and conditions of sale, and (2) the extent and competitive importance of seller–buyer strategic partnerships in the industry.

How Buyer Bargaining Power Can Create Competitive Pressures
As with suppliers, the leverage that certain types of buyers have in negotiating favorable terms can range from weak to strong. Individual consumers, for example, rarely have much bargaining power in negotiating price concessions or other favorable terms with sellers; the primary exceptions involve situations in which price haggling is customary, such as the purchase of new and used motor vehicles, homes, and certain big-ticket items like luxury watches, jewelry, and pleasure boats. For most consumer goods and services, individual buyers have no bargaining leverage—their option is to pay the seller's posted price or take their business elsewhere.

In contrast, large retail chains like Wal-Mart, Circuit City, Target, and Home Depot typically have considerable negotiating leverage in purchasing products from manufacturers because of manufacturers' need for broad retail exposure and the most appealing shelf locations. Retailers may stock two or three competing brands of a product but rarely all competing brands, so competition among rival manufacturers for visibility on the shelves of popular multistore retailers gives such retailers significant bargaining strength. Major supermarket chains like Kroger, Safeway, and Royal Ahold, which provide access to millions of grocery shoppers, have sufficient bargaining power to demand promotional allowances and lump-sum payments (called slotting fees) from food products manufacturers in return for stocking certain brands or putting them in the best shelf locations. Motor vehicle manufacturers have strong bargaining power in negotiating to buy original equipment tires from Goodyear, Michelin, Bridgestone/ Firestone, Continental, and Pirelli not only because they buy in large quantities but also because tire makers believe they gain an advantage in supplying replacement tires to vehicle owners if their tire brand is original equipment on the vehicle. "Prestige" buyers have a degree of clout in negotiating with sellers because a seller's reputation is enhanced by having prestige buyers on its customer list.

Even if buyers do not purchase in large quantities or offer a seller important market exposure or prestige, they gain a degree of bargaining leverage in the following circumstances:[10]

- *If buyers' costs of switching to competing brands or substitutes are relatively low*—Buyers who can readily switch brands or source from several sellers have more negotiating leverage than buyers who have high switching costs. When the products of rival sellers are virtually identical, it is relatively easy for buyers to switch from seller to seller at little or no cost and anxious sellers may be willing to make concessions to win or retain a buyer's business.

- *If the number of buyers is small or if a customer is particularly important to a seller*—The smaller the number of buyers, the less easy it is for sellers to find alternative buyers when a customer is lost to a competitor. The prospect of losing a customer not easily replaced often makes a seller more willing to grant concessions of one kind or another.

- *If buyer demand is weak and sellers are scrambling to secure additional sales of their products*—Weak or declining demand creates a "buyers' market" and shifts bargaining power to buyers; conversely, strong or rapidly growing demand creates a "sellers' market" and shifts bargaining power to sellers.

- *If buyers are well informed about sellers' products, prices, and costs*—The more information buyers have, the better bargaining position they are in. The mushrooming availability of product information on the Internet is giving added bargaining power to individuals. Buyers can easily use the Internet to compare prices and features of vacation packages, shop for the best interest rates on mortgages and loans, and find the best prices on big-ticket items such as digital cameras. Bargain-hunting individuals can shop around for the best deal on the Internet and use that information to negotiate a better deal from local retailers; this method is becoming commonplace in buying new and used motor vehicles. Further, the Internet has created opportunities for manufacturers, wholesalers, retailers, and sometimes individuals to join online buying groups to pool their purchasing power and approach vendors for better terms than could be gotten individually. A multinational manufacturer's geographically scattered purchasing groups can use Internet technology to pool their orders with parts and components suppliers and bargain for volume discounts. Purchasing agents at some companies are banding together at third-party Web sites to pool corporate purchases to get better deals or special treatment.

- *If buyers pose a credible threat of integrating backward into the business of sellers*—Companies like Anheuser-Busch, Coors, and Heinz have integrated backward into metal-can manufacturing to gain bargaining power in obtaining the balance of their can requirements from otherwise powerful metal-can manufacturers. Retailers gain bargaining power by stocking and promoting their own private-label brands alongside manufacturers' name brands. Wal-Mart, for example, has elected to compete against Procter & Gamble, its biggest supplier, with its own brand of laundry detergent, called Sam's American Choice, which is priced 25 to 30 percent lower than Procter & Gamble's Tide.

- *If buyers have discretion in whether and when they purchase the product*—If consumers are unhappy with the present deals offered on major appliances, hot tubs, home entertainment centers, or other goods for which time is not a critical purchase factor, they may be in a position to delay purchase until prices and financing terms improve. If business customers are not happy with the prices or security features of bill-payment software systems, they can either delay purchase until next-generation products become available or attempt to develop their own software in-house. If college students believe that the prices of new textbooks are too high, they can purchase used copies.

figure 3.8   **Factors Affecting the Bargaining Power of Buyers**

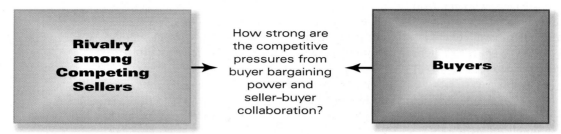

Buyer bargaining power is stronger when:
- Buyer switching costs to competing brands or substitute products are low.
- Buyers are large and can demand concessions when purchasing large quantities.
- Large-volume purchases by buyers are important to sellers.
- Buyer demand is weak or declining.
- There are only a few buyers—so that each one's business is important to sellers.
- Identity of buyer adds prestige to the seller's list of customers.
- Quantity and quality of information available to buyers improves.
- Buyers have the ability to postpone purchases until later if they do not like the present deals being offered by sellers.
- Some buyers are a threat to integrate backward into the business of sellers and become an important competitor.

Buyer bargaining power is weaker when:
- Buyers purchase the item infrequently or in small quantities.
- Buyer switching costs to competing brands are high.
- There is a surge in buyer demand that creates a "sellers' market."
- A seller's brand reputation is important to a buyer.
- A particular seller's product delivers quality or performance that is very important to buyers and that is not matched in other brands.
- Buyer collaboration or partnering with selected sellers provides attractive win–win opportunities.

Figure 3.8 summarizes the circumstances that make for strong or weak bargaining power on the part of buyers.

A final point to keep in mind about buyer bargaining power is that *not all buyers of an industry's product have equal degrees of bargaining power with sellers*, and some may be less sensitive than others to price, quality, or service differences. For example, independent tire retailers have less bargaining power in purchasing tires than do Honda, Ford, and DaimlerChrysler (which buy in much larger quantities), and they are also less sensitive to quality. Motor vehicle manufacturers are very particular about tire quality and tire performance because of the effects on vehicle performance, and they drive a hard bargain with tire manufacturers on both price and quality. Apparel manufacturers confront significant bargaining power when selling to retail chains like JCPenney, Sears, or Target, but they can command much better prices selling to small owner-managed apparel boutiques.

How Seller–Buyer Partnerships Can Create Competitive Pressures

Partnerships between sellers and buyers are an increasingly important element of the competitive picture in *business-to-business relationships* (as opposed to business-to-consumer relationships). Many sellers that provide items to business customers have found it in their mutual interest to collaborate closely on such matters as just-in-time deliveries, order processing, electronic invoice payments, and data sharing. Wal-Mart, for example, provides the manufacturers with whom it does business (like Procter & Gamble) with daily sales at each of its stores so that the manufacturers can maintain sufficient inventories at Wal-Mart's distribution centers to keep the shelves at each Wal-Mart store amply stocked. Dell Computer has partnered with its largest customers to create online systems for over 50,000 corporate customers, providing their employees with information on approved product configurations, global pricing, paperless purchase orders, real-time order tracking, invoicing, purchasing history, and other efficiency tools. Dell also loads a customer's software at the factory and installs asset tags so that customer setup time is minimal; it also helps customers upgrade their PC systems to next-generation hardware and software. Dell's partnerships with its corporate customers have put significant competitive pressure on other PC makers.

Determining Whether the Collective Strength of the Five Competitive Forces Promotes Profitability

Scrutinizing each of the five competitive forces one by one provides a powerful diagnosis of what competition is like in a given market. Once company managers understand the specific competitive pressures comprising each force and determine whether these pressures constitute a strong or weak competitive force, the next step is to evaluate the collective strength of the five forces and determine whether the state of competition promotes profitability. Is the collective impact of the five competitive forces stronger than normal? Are some of the competitive forces sufficiently strong to undermine industry profitability? Can companies in this industry reasonably expect to earn decent profits in light of the prevailing competitive forces?

Does the State of Competition Promote Profitability?

As a rule, the stronger the collective impact of the five competitive forces, the lower the combined profitability of industry participants. The most extreme case of a competitively unattractive industry is when all five forces are producing strong competitive pressures: rivalry among sellers is vigorous, low entry barriers allow new rivals to gain a market foothold, competition from substitutes is intense, and both suppliers and customers are able to exercise considerable bargaining leverage.

> The stronger the forces of competition, the harder it becomes for industry members to earn attractive profits.

Fierce to strong competitive pressures coming from all five directions nearly always drive industry profitability to unacceptably low levels, frequently producing losses for many industry members and forcing some out of business. But an industry can be competitively unattractive without all five competitive forces being strong. Intense competitive pressures from just two or three of the five forces may suffice to destroy the conditions for good profitability and prompt some companies to exit the business. The manufacture of disk drives, for example, is brutally competitive; IBM recently announced the sale of its disk drive business to Hitachi, taking a loss of over $2 billion on its exit from the business. Especially intense competitive conditions seem to be the norm in tire manufacturing and apparel, two industries where profit margins have historically been thin.

In contrast, when the collective impact of the five competitive forces is moderate to weak, an industry is competitively attractive in the sense that industry members can reasonably expect to earn good profits and a nice return on investment. The ideal competitive environment for earning superior profits is one in which both suppliers and customers are in weak bargaining positions, there are no good substitutes, high barriers block further entry, and rivalry among present sellers generates only moderate competitive pressures. Weak competition is the best of all possible worlds for also-ran companies because even they can usually eke out a decent profit—if a company can't make a decent profit when competition is weak, then its business outlook is indeed grim.

In most industries, the collective strength of the five competitive forces is somewhere near the middle of the two extremes of very intense and very weak, typically ranging from slightly stronger than normal to slightly weaker than normal and typically allowing well-managed companies with sound strategies to earn attractive profits.

> A company's strategy is increasingly effective the more it provides some insulation from competitive pressures and shifts the competitive battle in the company's favor.

Does Company Strategy Match Competitive Conditions? Working through the five-forces model step by step not only aids strategy makers in assessing whether the intensity of competition allows good profitability but also promotes sound strategic thinking about how to better match company strategy to the specific competitive character of the marketplace. Effectively matching a company's strategy to the particular competitive pressures and competitive conditions that exist has two aspects:

1. Pursuing actions to shield the firm, as much as possible, from the prevailing competitive pressures.
2. Initiating actions calculated to produce sustainable competitive advantage, thereby shifting competition in the company's favor, putting added competitive pressure on rivals, and perhaps even defining the business model for the industry.

But making headway on these two fronts first requires identifying competitive pressures, gauging the relative strength of each, and gaining a deep enough understanding of the state of competition in the industry to know which strategy buttons to push.

QUESTION 3: WHAT FACTORS ARE DRIVING INDUSTRY CHANGE AND WHAT IMPACTS WILL THEY HAVE?

An industry's present conditions don't necessarily reveal much about the strategically relevant ways in which the industry environment is changing. All industries are characterized by trends and new developments that gradually or speedily produce changes important enough to require a strategic response from participating firms. The popular hypothesis that industries go through a life cycle of takeoff, rapid growth, early maturity, market saturation, and stagnation or decline helps explain industry change—but it is far from complete.[11] An industry's normal progression through the life cycle is by no means the only cause of industry change.

The Concept of Driving Forces

Although it is important to judge what growth stage an industry is in, there's more analytical value in identifying the specific factors causing fundamental industry and

competitive adjustments. Industry and competitive conditions change because certain forces are enticing or pressuring industry participants to alter
their actions.[12] **Driving forces** are those that have the biggest influence on
what kinds of changes will take place in the industry's structure and competitive environment. Some driving forces originate in the company's macroenvironment; some originate from within the company's more immediate
industry and competitive environment. Driving-forces analysis has two steps:
(1) identifying what the driving forces are, and (2) assessing the impact they
will have on the industry.

> **core concept**
> Industry conditions change
> because important forces are
> *driving* industry participants
> (competitors, customers, or
> suppliers) to alter their actions;
> the *driving forces* in an indus-
> try are the *major underlying
> causes* of changing industry
> and competitive conditions—
> some driving forces originate in
> the macroenvironment and
> some originate from within a
> company's immediate industry
> and competitive environment.

Identifying an Industry's Driving Forces

Many events can affect an industry powerfully enough to qualify as driving
forces. Some are unique and specific to a particular industry situation, but
most drivers of change fall into one of the following categories:[13]

- *Growing use of the Internet and emerging new Internet technology applications*—The Internet and the adoption of Internet technology applications represent a driving force of historical and revolutionary proportions. The Internet is
  proving to be an important new distribution channel, allowing manufacturers to access customers directly rather than distribute exclusively through traditional wholesale and retail channels, and also making it easy for companies of all types to
  extend their geographic reach and vie for sales in areas where they formerly did not
  have a presence. Being able to reach consumers via the Internet can increase the
  number of rivals a company faces and escalate rivalry among sellers, sometimes
  pitting pure online sellers against combination brick-and-click sellers against pure
  brick-and-mortar sellers. The Web sites of rival sellers are only a few clicks apart
  and are open for business 24 hours a day every day of the year, giving buyers unprecedented ability to research the product offerings of competitors and shop the
  market for the best value. Companies can use the Internet to reach beyond their borders to find the best suppliers and, further, to collaborate closely with them to
  achieve efficiency gains and cost savings. Moreover, companies across the world
  are using a host of Internet technology applications to revamp internal operations
  and squeeze out cost savings. Internet technology has so many business applications that companies across the world are pursuing its operational benefits and making online systems a normal part of everyday operations. But the impacts vary from
  industry to industry and company to company, and the industry and competitive implications are continuously evolving. The challenges here are to assess precisely
  how the Internet and Internet technology applications are altering a particular industry's landscape and to factor these impacts in to the strategy-making equation.

- *Increasing globalization*—Competition begins to shift from primarily a regional or
  national focus to an international or global focus when industry members begin
  seeking out customers in foreign markets or when production activities begin to migrate to countries where costs are lowest. Globalization of competition really starts
  to take hold when one or more ambitious companies precipitate a race for worldwide
  market leadership by launching initiatives to expand into more and more country
  markets. Globalization can also be precipitated by the blossoming of consumer demand in more and more countries and by the actions of government officials in many
  countries to reduce trade barriers or open up once-closed markets to foreign competitors, as is occurring in many parts of Europe, Latin America, and Asia. Signifi-

cant differences in labor costs among countries give manufacturers a strong incentive to locate plants for labor-intensive products in low-wage countries and use these plants to supply market demand across the world. Wages in China, India, Singapore, Mexico, and Brazil, for example, are about one-fourth those in the United States, Germany, and Japan. The forces of globalization are sometimes such a strong driver that companies find it highly advantageous, if not necessary, to spread their operating reach into more and more country markets. Globalization is very much a driver of industry change in such industries as credit cards, mobile phones, motor vehicles, steel, refined petroleum products, public accounting, and textbook publishing.

- *Changes in the long-term industry growth rate*—Shifts in industry growth up or down are a driving force for industry change, affecting the balance between industry supply and buyer demand, entry and exit, and the character and strength of competition. An upsurge in buyer demand triggers a race among established firms and newcomers to capture the new sales opportunities; ambitious companies with trailing market shares may see the upturn in demand as a golden opportunity to broaden their customer base and move up several notches in the industry standings to secure a place among the market leaders. A slowdown in the rate at which demand is growing nearly always portends mounting rivalry and increased efforts by some firms to maintain their high rates of growth by taking sales and market share away from rivals. If industry sales suddenly turn flat or begin to shrink after years of rising steadily, competition is certain to intensify as industry members scramble for the available business and as mergers and acquisitions result in industry consolidation to a smaller number of competitively stronger participants. Dimming sales prospects usually prompt both competitively weak and growth-oriented companies to sell their business operations to those industry members who elect to stick it out; as demand for the industry's product continues to shrink, the remaining industry members may be forced to close inefficient plants and retrench to a smaller production base—all of which results in a much-changed competitive landscape.

- *Changes in who buys the product and how they use it*—Shifts in buyer demographics and new ways of using the product can alter the state of competition by opening the way to market an industry's product through a different mix of dealers and retail outlets; prompting producers to broaden or narrow their product lines; bringing different sales and promotion approaches into play; and forcing adjustments in customer service offerings (credit, technical assistance, maintenance and repair). The mushrooming popularity of downloading music from the Internet, storing music files on PC hard drives, and burning custom discs has forced recording companies to reexamine their distribution strategies and raised questions about the future of traditional retail music stores; at the same time, it has stimulated sales of disc burners and blank discs. Longer life expectancies and growing percentages of relatively well-to-do retirees are driving changes in such industries as health care, prescription drugs, recreational living, and vacation travel. The growing percentage of households with PCs and Internet access is opening opportunities for banks to expand their electronic bill-payment services and for retailers to move more of their customer services online.

- *Product innovation*—Competition in an industry is always affected by rivals racing to be first to introduce one new product or product enhancement after another. An ongoing stream of product innovations tends to alter the pattern of competition in an industry by attracting more first-time buyers, rejuvenating industry growth, and/or creating wider or narrower product differentiation among rival sellers.

Successful new product introductions strengthen the market positions of the innovating companies, usually at the expense of companies that stick with their old products or are slow to follow with their own versions of the new product. Product innovation has been a key driving force in such industries as digital cameras, golf clubs, video games, toys, and prescription drugs.

- *Technological change and manufacturing process innovation*—Advances in technology can dramatically alter an industry's landscape, making it possible to produce new and better products at lower cost and opening up whole new industry frontiers. Technological developments can also produce competitively significant changes in capital requirements, minimum efficient plant sizes, distribution channels and logistics, and experience or learning-curve effects. In the steel industry, ongoing advances in electric arc minimill technology (which involve recycling scrap steel to make new products) have allowed steelmakers with state-of-the-art minimills to gradually expand into the production of more and more steel products, steadily taking sales and market share from higher-cost integrated producers (which make steel from scratch using iron ore, coke, and traditional blast furnace technology). Nucor, the leader of the minimill technology revolution in the United States, came from nowhere in 1970 to emerge as the nation's biggest and the lowest-cost steel producer as of 2002, having overtaken U.S. Steel and Bethlehem Steel, both integrated producers and the longtime market leaders. In a space of 30 years, advances in minimill technology have changed the face of the steel industry worldwide.

- *Marketing innovation*—When firms are successful in introducing new ways to market their products, they can spark a burst of buyer interest, widen industry demand, increase product differentiation, and lower unit costs—any or all of which can alter the competitive positions of rival firms and force strategy revisions. In today's world, Internet marketing is shaking up competition in such industries as electronics retailing, stock brokerage (where online brokers have taken significant business away from traditional brokers), and office supplies (where Office Depot, Staples, and Office Max are using their Web sites to market office supplies to corporations, small businesses, schools and universities, and government agencies).

- *Entry or exit of major firms*—The entry of one or more foreign companies into a geographic market once dominated by domestic firms nearly always shakes up competitive conditions. Likewise, when an established domestic firm from another industry attempts entry either by acquisition or by launching its own start-up venture, it usually applies its skills and resources in some innovative fashion that pushes competition in new directions. Entry by a major firm thus often produces a new ball game, not only with new key players but also with new rules for competing. Similarly, exit of a major firm changes the competitive structure by reducing the number of market leaders (perhaps increasing the dominance of the leaders who remain) and causing a rush to capture the exiting firm's customers.

- *Diffusion of technical know-how across more companies and more countries*—As knowledge about how to perform a particular activity or execute a particular manufacturing technology spreads, the competitive advantage held by firms originally possessing this know-how erodes. Knowledge diffusion can occur through scientific journals, trade publications, on-site plant tours, word of mouth among suppliers and customers, employee migration, and Internet sources. It can also occur when those possessing technological know-how license others to use it for a royalty fee or team up with a company interested in turning the technology into a new business venture. Quite often, technological know-how can be acquired by simply buying a company that has the wanted skills, patents, or manufacturing capabilities. In recent years, *rapid technology transfer across national boundaries has been a prime factor in causing industries to become more globally competitive.* As companies worldwide gain access to valuable technical know-how, they upgrade their manufacturing capabilities in a long-term effort to compete head-on with established companies. Cross-border technology transfer has made the once domestic industries of automobiles, tires, consumer electronics, telecommunications, computers, and others increasingly global.

- *Changes in cost and efficiency*—Widening or shrinking differences in the costs among key competitors tend to dramatically alter the state of competition. The low cost of e-mail and fax transmission has put mounting competitive pressure on the relatively inefficient and high-cost operations of the U.S. Postal Service—sending a one-page fax is cheaper and far quicker than sending a first-class letter; sending e-mail is faster and cheaper still. In the electric power industry, sharply lower costs to generate electricity at newly constructed combined-cycle generating plants during 1998–2001 forced older coal-fired and gas-fired plants to lower their production costs to remain competitive. Shrinking cost differences in producing multifeatured mobile phones is turning the mobile phone market into a commodity business and causing more buyers to base their purchase decisions on price.

- *Growing buyer preferences for differentiated products instead of a commodity product (or for a more standardized product instead of strongly differentiated products)*—When buyer tastes and preferences start to diverge, sellers can win a loyal following with product offerings that stand apart from those of rival sellers. In recent years, beer drinkers have grown less loyal to a single brand and have begun to drink a variety of domestic and foreign beers; as a consequence, beer manufacturers have introduced a host of new brands and malt beverages with different tastes and flavors. Buyer preferences for motor vehicles are becoming increasingly diverse, with few models generating sales of more than 250,000 units annually. When a shift from standardized to differentiated products occurs, the driver of change is the contest among rivals to cleverly outdifferentiate one another.

  However, buyers sometimes decide that a standardized, budget-priced product suits their requirements as well as or better than a premium-priced product with lots of snappy features and personalized services. Online brokers, for example, have used the lure of cheap commissions to attract many investors willing to place their own buy–sell orders via the Internet; growing acceptance of online trading has put significant competitive pressures on full-service brokers whose business model has always revolved around convincing clients of the value of asking for personalized advice from professional brokers and paying their high commission fees to make trades. Pronounced shifts toward greater product standardization usually spawn lively price competition and force rival sellers to drive down their costs to maintain profitability. The lesson here is that competition is driven partly by whether the market forces in motion are acting to increase or decrease product differentiation.

- *Reductions in uncertainty and business risk*—An emerging industry is typically characterized by much uncertainty over potential market size, how much time and money will be needed to surmount technological problems, and what distribution channels and buyer segments to emphasize. Emerging industries tend to attract only risk-taking entrepreneurial companies. Over time, however, if the business model of industry pioneers proves profitable and market demand for the product appears durable, more conservative firms are usually enticed to enter the market.

Often, these later entrants are large, financially strong firms looking to invest in attractive growth industries.

Lower business risks and less industry uncertainty also affect competition in international markets. In the early stages of a company's entry into foreign markets, conservatism prevails and firms limit their downside exposure by using less risky strategies like exporting, licensing, joint marketing agreements, or joint ventures with local companies to accomplish entry. Then, as experience accumulates and perceived risk levels decline, companies move more boldly and more independently, making acquisitions, constructing their own plants, putting in their own sales and marketing capabilities to build strong competitive positions in each country market, and beginning to link the strategies in each country to create a more globalized strategy.

- *Regulatory influences and government policy changes*—Government regulatory actions can often force significant changes in industry practices and strategic approaches. Deregulation has proved to be a potent pro-competitive force in the airline, banking, natural gas, telecommunications, and electric utility industries. Government efforts to reform Medicare and health insurance have become potent driving forces in the health care industry. In international markets, host governments can drive competitive changes by opening their domestic markets to foreign participation or closing them to protect domestic companies. Note that this driving force is spawned by forces in a company's macroenvironment.

- *Changing societal concerns, attitudes, and lifestyles*—Emerging social issues and changing attitudes and lifestyles can be powerful instigators of industry change. Growing antismoking sentiment has emerged as a major driver of change in the tobacco industry; concerns about terrorism are having a big impact on the travel industry. Consumer concerns about salt, sugar, chemical additives, saturated fat, cholesterol, and nutritional value have forced food producers to revamp food-processing techniques, redirect R&D efforts into the use of healthier ingredients, and compete in developing nutritious, good-tasting products. Safety concerns have transformed the automobile, toy, and outdoor power equipment industries, to mention a few. Increased interest in physical fitness has spawned new industries in exercise equipment, mountain biking, outdoor apparel, sports gyms and recreation centers, vitamin and nutrition supplements, and medically supervised diet programs. Social concerns about air and water pollution have forced industries to incorporate expenditures for controlling pollution into their cost structures. Shifting societal concerns, attitudes, and lifestyles alter the pattern of competition, usually favoring those players that respond quickly and creatively with products targeted to the new trends and conditions. As with the preceding driving force, this driving force springs from factors at work in a company's macroenvironment.

These most common driving forces are summarized in Table 3.2.

That there are so many different *potential driving forces* explains why it is too simplistic to view industry change only in terms of the life-cycle model and why a full understanding of the *causes* underlying the emergence of new competitive conditions is a fundamental part of industry analysis. However, while many forces of change may be at work in a given industry, no more than three or four are likely to be true driving forces powerful enough to qualify as the *major determinants* of why and how the industry is changing. Thus company strategists must resist the temptation to label every change they see as a driving force; the analytical task is to evaluate the forces of industry and competitive change carefully enough to separate major factors from minor ones.

table 3.2   **The Most Common Driving Forces**

1. Growing use of the Internet and emerging new Internet technology applications.
2. Increasing globalization of the industry.
3. Changes in the long-term industry growth rate.
4. Changes in who buys the product and how they use it.
5. Product innovation.
6. Technological change and manufacturing process innovation.
7. Marketing innovation.
8. Entry or exit of major firms.
9. Diffusion of technical know-how across more companies and more countries.
10. Changes in cost and efficiency.
11. Growing buyer preferences for differentiated products instead of standardized commodity products (or for a more standardized product instead of strongly differentiated products).
12. Reductions in uncertainty and business risk.
13. Regulatory influences and government policy changes.
14. Changing societal concerns, attitudes, and lifestyles.

Assessing the Impact of the Driving Forces

The second phase of driving-forces analysis is to determine whether the driving forces are, on the whole, acting to make the industry environment more or less attractive. Answers to three questions are needed here:

1. Are the driving forces causing demand for the industry's product to increase or decrease?
2. Are the driving forces acting to make competition more or less intense?
3. Will the driving forces lead to higher or lower industry profitability?

Getting a handle on the collective impact of the driving forces usually requires looking at the likely effects of each force separately, since the driving forces may not all be pushing change in the same direction. For example, two driving forces may be acting to spur demand for the industry's product while one driving force may be working to curtail demand. Whether the net effect on industry demand is up or down hinges on which driving forces are the more powerful. The analyst's objective here is to get a good grip on what external factors are shaping industry change and what difference these factors will make.

The Link between Driving Forces and Strategy

Sound analysis of an industry's driving forces is a prerequisite to sound strategy making. Without understanding the forces driving industry change and the impacts these forces will have on the character of the industry environment and on the company's business over the next one to three years, managers are ill-prepared to craft a strategy tightly matched to emerging conditions. Similarly, if managers are uncertain about the implications of each driving force, or if their views are incomplete or off base, it's difficult for them to craft a strategy that is responsive to the driving forces and their consequences for the industry. So driving-forces analysis is not something to take lightly; it has practical value and is basic to the task of thinking strategically about where the industry is headed and how to prepare for the changes.

QUESTION 4: WHAT MARKET POSITIONS DO RIVALS OCCUPY—WHO IS STRONGLY POSITIONED AND WHO IS NOT?

Since competing companies commonly sell in different price/quality ranges, emphasize different distribution channels, incorporate product features that appeal to different types of buyers, have different geographic coverage, and so on, it stands to reason that some companies enjoy stronger or more attractive market positions than other companies. Understanding which companies are strongly positioned and which are weakly positioned is an integral part of analyzing an industry's competitive structure. The best technique for revealing the market positions of industry competitors is **strategic group mapping**.[14] This analytical tool is useful for comparing the market positions of each firm separately or for grouping them into like positions when an industry has so many competitors that it is not practical to examine each one in depth.

> **core concept**
> **Strategic group mapping** is a technique for displaying the different market or competitive positions that rival firms occupy in the industry.

Using Strategic Group Maps to Assess the Market Positions of Key Competitors

A **strategic group** consists of those industry members with similar competitive approaches and positions in the market.[15] Companies in the same strategic group can resemble one another in any of several ways: they may have comparable product-line breadth, sell in the same price/quality range, emphasize the same distribution channels, use essentially the same product attributes to appeal to similar types of buyers, depend on identical technological approaches, or offer buyers similar services and technical assistance.[16] An industry contains only one strategic group when all sellers pursue very similar strategies and have comparable market positions. At the other extreme, an industry may contain as many strategic groups as there are competitors when each rival pursues a distinctively different competitive approach and occupies a substantially different market position.

> **core concept**
> A **strategic group** is a cluster of firms in an industry with similar competitive approaches and market positions.

The procedure for constructing a *strategic group map* is straightforward:

- Identify the competitive characteristics that differentiate firms in the industry; typical variables are price/quality range (high, medium, low), geographic coverage (local, regional, national, global), degree of vertical integration (none, partial, full), product-line breadth (wide, narrow), use of distribution channels (one, some, all), and degree of service offered (no-frills, limited, full).
- Plot the firms on a two-variable map using pairs of these differentiating characteristics.
- Assign firms that fall in about the same strategy space to the same strategic group.
- Draw circles around each strategic group, making the circles proportional to the size of the group's share of total industry sales revenues.

This produces a two-dimensional diagram like the one for the retailing industry in Illustration Capsule 3.1.

Several guidelines need to be observed in mapping the positions of strategic groups in the industry's overall strategy space.[17] First, the two variables selected as axes for the map should *not* be highly correlated; if they are, the circles on the map will fall

illustration capsule 3.1
Comparative Market Positions of Selected Retail Chains: A Strategic Group Map Application

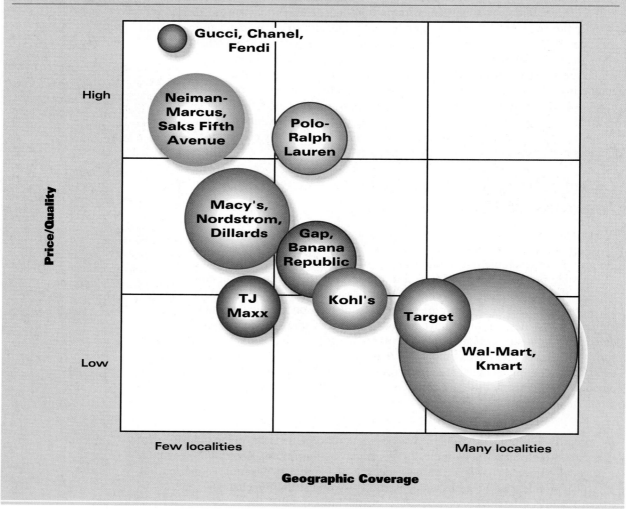

Note: Circles are drawn roughly proportional to the sizes of the chains, based on revenues.

along a diagonal and strategy makers will learn nothing more about the relative positions of competitors than they would by considering just one of the variables. For instance, if companies with broad product lines use multiple distribution channels while companies with narrow lines use a single distribution channel, then looking at broad versus narrow product lines reveals just as much about who is positioned where as looking at single versus multiple distribution channels; that is, one of the variables is redundant. Second, the variables chosen as axes for the map should expose big differences in how rivals position themselves to compete in the marketplace. This, of course, means that analysts must identify the characteristics that differentiate rival firms and use these differences as variables for the axes and as the basis for deciding which firm belongs in which strategic group. Third, the variables used as axes don't have to be either quantitative or continuous; rather, they can be discrete variables or defined in terms of distinct classes and combinations. Fourth, drawing the sizes of the circles on the map proportional to the combined sales of the firms in each strategic group allows the map to reflect the relative sizes of each strategic group. Fifth, if more than two good competitive variables can be used as axes for the map, several maps can be drawn to give different exposures to the competitive positioning relationships present in the industry's structure. Because there is not necessarily one best map for portraying how competing firms are positioned in the market, it is advisable to experiment with different pairs of competitive variables.

What Can Be Learned from Strategic Group Maps

One thing to look for in assessing rivals' market positions is to what extent *industry driving forces and competitive pressures favor some strategic groups and hurt others.*[18] Firms in adversely affected strategic groups may try to shift to a more favorably situated group; how hard such a move proves to be depends on whether entry barriers for the target strategic group are high or low. Attempts by rival firms to enter a new strategic group nearly always increase competitive pressures. If certain firms are known to be trying to change their competitive positions on the map, then attaching arrows to the circles showing the targeted direction helps clarify the picture of competitive maneuvering among rivals.

> Driving forces and competitive pressures do not affect all strategic groups evenly. Profit prospects vary from group to group according to the relative attractiveness of their market positions.

Another consideration is to what extent *the profit potential of different strategic groups varies due to the strengths and weaknesses in each group's market position.* Differences in profitability can occur because of differing degrees of bargaining leverage or collaboration with suppliers and/or customers, differing degrees of exposure to competition from substitute products outside the industry, differing degrees of competitive rivalry within strategic groups, and differing growth rates for the principal buyer segments served by each group.

Generally speaking, *the closer strategic groups are to each other on the map, the stronger the cross-group competitive rivalry tends to be.* Although firms in the same strategic group are the closest rivals, the next closest rivals are in the immediately adjacent groups.[19] Often, firms in strategic groups that are far apart on the map hardly compete at all. For instance, Tiffany & Co. and Wal-Mart both sell gold and silver jewelry, but their clientele and the prices and quality of their products are much too different to justify calling them competitors. For the same reason, Timex is not a meaningful competitive rival of Rolex, and Subaru is not a close competitor of Lincoln or Mercedes-Benz.

QUESTION 5: WHAT STRATEGIC MOVES ARE RIVALS LIKELY TO MAKE NEXT?

Unless a company pays attention to what competitors are doing and knows their strengths and weaknesses, it ends up flying blind into competitive battle. As in sports, scouting the opposition is essential. *Competitive intelligence* about rivals' strategies, their latest actions and announcements, their resource strengths and weaknesses, the efforts being made to improve their situation, and the thinking and leadership styles of

> Good scouting reports on rivals provide a valuable assist in anticipating what moves rivals are likely to make next and outmaneuvering them in the marketplace.

their executives is valuable for predicting or anticipating the strategic moves competitors are likely to make next in the marketplace. Having good information to predict the strategic direction and likely moves of key competitors allows a company to prepare defensive countermoves, to craft its own strategic moves with some confidence about what market maneuvers to expect from rivals, and to exploit any openings that arise from competitors' missteps or strategy flaws.

Identifying Competitors' Strategies and Resource Strengths and Weaknesses

Keeping close tabs on a competitor's strategy entails monitoring what the rival is doing in the marketplace, what its management is saying in company press releases, information posted on the company's Web site (especially press releases and the presentations management has recently made to securities analysts), and such public documents as annual reports and 10-K filings, articles in the business media, and the reports of securities analysts. (Figure 1.1 in Chapter 1 indicates what to look for in identifying a company's strategy.) Company personnel may be able to pick up useful information from a rival's exhibits at trade shows and from conversations with a rival's customers, suppliers, and former employees.[20] Many companies have a competitive intelligence unit that sifts through the available information to construct up-to-date strategic profiles of rivals—their current strategies, their resource strengths and competitive capabilities, their competitive shortcomings, and the latest pronouncements and leadership styles of their executives. Such profiles are typically updated regularly and made available to managers and other key personnel.

Those who gather competitive intelligence on rivals, however, can sometimes cross the fine line between honest inquiry and unethical or even illegal behavior. For example, calling rivals to get information about prices, the dates of new product introductions, or wage and salary levels is legal, but misrepresenting one's company affiliation during such calls is unethical. Pumping rivals' representatives at trade shows is ethical only if one wears a name tag with accurate company affiliation indicated. Avon Products at one point secured information about its biggest rival, Mary Kay Cosmetics (MKC), by having its personnel search through the garbage bins outside MKC's headquarters.[21] When MKC officials learned of the action and sued, Avon claimed it did nothing illegal, since a 1988 Supreme Court case had ruled that trash left on public property (in this case, a sidewalk) was anyone's for the taking. Avon even produced a videotape of its removal of the trash at the MKC site. Avon won the lawsuit—but Avon's action, while legal, scarcely qualifies as ethical.

In sizing up the strategies and the competitive strengths and weaknesses of competitors, it makes sense for company strategists to make three assessments:

1. Which competitor has the best strategy? Which competitors appear to have flawed or weak strategies?
2. Which competitors are poised to gain market share, and which ones seem destined to lose ground?
3. Which competitors are likely to rank among the industry leaders five years from now? Do one or more up-and-coming competitors have powerful strategies and sufficient resource capabilities to overtake the current industry leader?

The industry's *current* major players are generally easy to identify, but some of the leaders may be plagued with weaknesses that are causing them to lose ground; others may lack the resources and capabilities to remain strong contenders given the superior strategies and capabilities of up-and-coming companies. In evaluating which competitors are favorably or unfavorably positioned to gain market ground, company strategists need to focus on why there is potential for some rivals to do better or worse than other rivals. Usually, a competitor's prospects are a function of its vulnerability to driving forces and competitive pressures, whether its strategy has resulted in competitive advantage or disadvantage, and whether its resources and capabilities are well suited for competing on the road ahead.

> Today's market leaders don't automatically become tomorrow's.

Predicting Competitors' Next Moves

Predicting the next strategic moves of competitors is the hardest yet most useful part of competitor analysis. Good clues about what actions a specific company is likely to undertake can often be gleaned from how well it is faring in the marketplace, the problems or weaknesses it needs to address, and how much pressure it is under to improve its financial performance. Content rivals are likely to continue their present strategy with only minor fine-tuning. Ailing rivals can be performing so poorly that fresh strategic moves are virtually certain. Ambitious rivals looking to move up in the industry ranks are strong candidates for launching new strategic offensives to pursue emerging market opportunities and exploit the vulnerabilities of weaker rivals.

Since the moves a competitor is likely to make are generally predicated on the views their executives have about the industry's future and their beliefs about their firm's situation, it makes sense to closely scrutinize the public pronouncements of rival company executives about where the industry is headed and what it will take to be successful, what they are saying about their firm's situation, information from the grapevine about what they are doing, and their past actions and leadership styles. Other considerations in trying to predict what strategic moves rivals are likely to make next include the following:

- Which rivals badly need to increase their unit sales and market share? What strategic options are they most likely to pursue: lowering prices, adding new models and styles, expanding their dealer networks, entering additional geographic markets, boosting advertising to build better brand-name awareness, acquiring a weaker competitor, or placing more emphasis on direct sales via their Web site?
- Which rivals have a strong incentive, along with the resources, to make major strategic changes, perhaps moving to a different position on the strategic group map? Which rivals are probably locked in to pursuing the same basic strategy with only minor adjustments?
- Which rivals are good candidates to be acquired? Which rivals may be looking to make an acquisition and are financially able to do so?
- Which rivals are likely to enter new geographic markets?
- Which rivals are strong candidates to expand their product offerings and enter new product segments where they do not currently have a presence?

To succeed in predicting a competitor's next moves, company strategists need to have a good feel for each rival's situation, how its managers think, and what its best options are. Doing the necessary detective work can be tedious and time-consuming, but scouting competitors well enough to anticipate their next moves allows managers to prepare effective countermoves (perhaps even beat a rival to the punch) and to take rivals' probable actions into account in crafting their own best course of action.

> Managers who fail to study competitors closely risk being caught napping by the new strategic moves of rivals.

QUESTION 6: WHAT ARE THE KEY FACTORS FOR FUTURE COMPETITIVE SUCCESS?

core concept

Key success factors (KSFs) are the product attributes, competencies, competitive capabilities, and market achievements with the greatest impact on future competitive success in the marketplace.

An industry's **key success factors (KSFs)** are those competitive factors that most affect industry members' ability to prosper in the marketplace—the particular strategy elements, product attributes, resources, competencies, competitive capabilities, and market achievements that spell the difference between being a strong competitor and a weak competitor. KSFs by their very nature are so important to future competitive success that *all firms* in the industry must be competent at performing or achieving them or risk becoming an industry also-ran. How well a company's product offering, resources, and capabilities measure up against an industry's KSFs determines just how financially and competitively successful that company will be. Identifying KSFs, in light of the prevailing and anticipated industry and competitive conditions, is therefore always a top priority analytical and strategy-making consideration. Company strategists need to understand the industry landscape well enough to separate the factors most important to competitive success from those that are less important.

In the beer industry, the KSFs are full utilization of brewing capacity (to keep manufacturing costs low), a strong network of wholesale distributors (to get the company's brand stocked and favorably displayed in retail outlets where beer is sold), and clever advertising (to induce beer drinkers to buy the company's brand and thereby pull beer sales through the established wholesale/retail channels). In apparel manufacturing, the KSFs are appealing designs and color combinations (to create buyer interest) and low-cost manufacturing efficiency (to permit attractive retail pricing and ample profit margins). In tin and aluminum cans, because the cost of shipping empty cans is substantial, one of the keys is having can-manufacturing facilities located close to end-use customers. KSFs thus vary from industry to industry, and even from time to time within the same industry, as driving forces and competitive conditions change. Table 3.3 lists the most common types of KSFs.

An industry's KSFs can usually be deduced from what was learned from the previously described analysis of the industry and competitive environment. Which factors are most important to future competitive success flow directly from the industry's dominant characteristics, what competition is like, the impacts of the driving forces, the comparative market positions of industry members, and the likely next moves of key rivals. In addition, the answers to three questions help identify an industry's key success factors:

1. On what basis do buyers of the industry's product choose between the competing brands of sellers? That is, what attributes of competitors' product offerings are crucial?

2. Given the nature of competitive rivalry and the competitive forces prevailing in the marketplace, what resources and competitive capabilities does a company need to have to be competitively successful?

3. What shortcomings are almost certain to put a company at a significant competitive disadvantage?

Only rarely are there more than five or six key factors for future competitive success. And even among these, two or three usually outrank the others in importance. Managers should therefore bear in mind that identifying KSFs requires judgments about which factors are *most important* to future competitive success—temptations to designate each minor factor as a KSF must be resisted. To compile a list of every factor that matters even a little bit defeats the purpose of concentrating management attention on the factors truly critical to long-term competitive success.

table 3.3   **Common Types of Industry Key Success Factors (KSFs)**

Technology-related KSFs	• Expertise in a particular technology or in scientific research (important in pharmaceuticals, Internet applications, mobile communications, and most high-tech industries) • Proven ability to improve production processes (important in industries where advancing technology opens the way for higher manufacturing efficiency and lower production costs)
Manufacturing-related KSFs	• Ability to achieve scale economies and/or capture learning-curve effects (important to achieving low production costs) • Quality control know-how (important in industries where customers insist on product reliability) • High utilization of fixed assets (important in capital-intensive/high-fixed-cost industries) • Access to attractive supplies of skilled labor • High labor productivity (important for items with high labor content) • Low-cost product design and engineering (reduces manufacturing costs) • Ability to manufacture or assemble products that are customized to buyer specifications
Distribution-related KSFs	• A strong network of wholesale distributors/dealers • Strong direct sales capabilities via the Internet and/or having company-owned retail outlets • Ability to secure favorable display space on retailer shelves
Marketing-related KSFs	• Breadth of product line and product selection • A well-known and well-respected brand name • Fast, accurate technical assistance • Courteous, personalized customer service • Accurate filling of buyer orders (few back orders or mistakes) • Customer guarantees and warranties (important in mail-order and online retailing, big-ticket purchases, new product introductions) • Clever advertising
Skills and capability-related KSFs	• A talented workforce (superior talent is important in professional services like accounting and investment banking) • National or global distribution capabilities • Product innovation capabilities (important in industries where rivals are racing to be first to market with new product attributes or performance features) • Design expertise (important in fashion and apparel industries) • Short-delivery-time capability • Supply chain management capabilities • Strong e-commerce capabilities—a user-friendly Web site and/or skills in using Internet technology applications to streamline internal operations
Other types of KSFs	• Overall low costs (not just in manufacturing) so as to be able to meet low-price expectations of customers • Convenient locations (important in many retailing businesses) • Ability to provide fast, convenient after-the-sale repairs and service • A strong balance sheet and access to financial capital (important in newly emerging industries with high degrees of business risk and in capital-intensive industries) • Patent protection

Correctly diagnosing an industry's KSFs raises a company's chances of crafting a sound strategy. The goal of company strategists should be to design a strategy aimed at stacking up well on all of the industry's future KSFs and trying to be *distinctively*

core concept

A sound strategy incorporates the intent to stack up well on all of the industry's KSFs and to excel on one (or two) in particular.

better than rivals on one (or possibly two) of the KSFs. Indeed, companies that stand out or excel on a particular KSF are likely to enjoy a stronger market position—*being distinctively better than rivals on one or two key success factors tends to translate into competitive advantage.* Hence, using the industry's KSFs as *cornerstones* for the company's strategy and trying to gain sustainable competitive advantage by excelling at one particular KSF is a fruitful competitive strategy approach.[22]

QUESTION 7: DOES THE OUTLOOK FOR THE INDUSTRY PRESENT AN ATTRACTIVE OPPORTUNITY?

The final step in evaluating the industry and competitive environment is to use the preceding analysis to decide whether the outlook for the industry presents the company with sufficiently attractive prospects for profitability and growth. The important factors on which to base such a conclusion include:

- The industry's growth potential.
- Whether powerful competitive forces are squeezing industry profitability to subpar levels and whether competition appears destined to grow stronger or weaker.
- Whether industry profitability will be favorably or unfavorably affected by the prevailing driving forces.
- The degrees of risk and uncertainty in the industry's future.
- Whether the industry as a whole confronts severe problems—regulatory or environmental issues, stagnating buyer demand, industry overcapacity, mounting competition, and so on.
- The company's competitive position in the industry vis-à-vis rivals. (Being an entrenched leader or strongly positioned contender in a lackluster industry may present adequate opportunity for good profitability; however, having to fight a steep uphill battle against much stronger rivals may hold little promise of eventual market success or good return on shareholder investment, even though the industry environment is attractive.)
- The company's potential to capitalize on the vulnerabilities of weaker rivals (perhaps converting a relatively unattractive *industry* situation into a potentially rewarding *company* opportunity).
- Whether the company has sufficient competitive strength to defend against or counteract the factors that make the industry unattractive.
- Whether continued participation in this industry adds importantly to the firm's ability to be successful in other industries in which it may have business interests.

As a general proposition, *if an industry's overall profit prospects are above average, the industry environment is basically attractive; if industry profit prospects are below average, conditions are unattractive.* However, it is a mistake to think of a particular industry as being equally attractive or unattractive to all industry participants and all potential entrants. Attractiveness is relative, not absolute, and conclusions one way or the other have to be drawn from the perspective of a particular company. Industries attractive to insiders may be unattractive to outsiders. Companies on the outside may look at an industry's environment and conclude that it is an unattractive business for them to get into, given the prevailing entry barriers, the difficulty of challenging current market leaders with their particular resources and competencies, and the opportunities they have elsewhere. Industry environments unattractive to weak competitors may be attractive to strong competitors. A favorably positioned company may survey a business environment and see a host of opportunities that weak competitors cannot capture.

> **core concept**
> The degree to which an industry is attractive or unattractive is not the same for all industry participants and all potential entrants; the opportunities an industry presents depends partly on a company's ability to capture them.

When a company decides an industry is fundamentally attractive and presents good opportunities, a strong case can be made that it should invest aggressively to capture the opportunities it sees and to improve its long-term competitive position in the business. When a strong competitor concludes an industry is relatively unattractive and lacking in opportunity, it may elect to simply protect its present position, investing cautiously if at all and looking for opportunities in other industries. A competitively weak company in an unattractive industry may see its best option as finding a buyer, perhaps a rival, to acquire its business.

key|points

Thinking strategically about a company's external situation involves probing for answers to the following seven questions:

1. *What are the industry's dominant economic features?* Industries differ significantly on such factors as market size and growth rate, the geographic scope of competitive rivalry, the number and relative sizes of both buyers and sellers, ease of entry and exit, the extent of vertical integration, how fast basic technology is changing, the extent of scale economies and learning-curve effects, the degree of product standardization or differentiation, and overall profitability. While setting the stage for the analysis to come, identifying an industry's economic features also promotes understanding of the kinds of strategic moves that industry members are likely to employ.

2. *What kinds of competitive forces are industry members facing, and how strong is each force?* The strength of competition is a composite of five forces: the rivalry among competing sellers, the presence of attractive substitutes, the potential for new entry, the competitive pressures stemming from supplier bargaining power and supplier–seller collaboration, and the competitive pressures stemming from buyer bargaining power and seller–buyer collaboration. These five forces have to be examined one by one to identify the specific competitive pressures they each comprise and to decide whether these pressures constitute a strong or weak competitive force. The next step in competition analysis is to evaluate the collective strength of the five forces and determine whether the state of competition is conducive to good profitability. Working through the five-forces model step by step not only aids strategy makers in assessing whether the intensity of competition allows good profitability but also promotes sound strategic thinking about how to better match company strategy to the specific competitive character of the marketplace. Effectively matching a company's strategy to the particular competitive pressures and competitive conditions that exist has two aspects: (1) pursuing avenues that shield the firm from as many of the prevailing competitive pressures as possible, and (2) initiating actions calculated to produce sustainable competitive advantage, thereby shifting competition in the company's favor, putting added competitive pressure on rivals, and perhaps even defining the business model for the industry.

3. *What forces are driving changes in the industry, and what impact will these changes have on competitive intensity and industry profitability?* Industry and competitive conditions change because forces are in motion that create incentives or pressures for change. The first phase is to identify the forces that are driving change in the industry; the most common **driving forces** include the Internet and Internet technology applications, globalization of competition in the industry, changes in the long-term industry growth rate, changes in buyer composition, product innovation, entry or exit of major firms, changes in cost and efficiency, changing buyer preferences for standardized versus differentiated products or services, regulatory influences and government policy changes, changing societal and lifestyle factors, and reductions in uncertainty and business risk. The second phase of driving-forces analysis is to determine whether the driving forces, taken together, are acting to make the industry environment more or less attractive. Are the driving forces causing demand for the industry's product to increase or decrease? Are the driving forces acting to make competition more or less intense? Will the driving forces lead to higher or lower industry profitability?

4. *What market positions do industry rivals occupy—who is strongly positioned and who is not?* **Strategic group mapping** is a valuable tool for understanding the similarities, differences, strengths, and weaknesses inherent in the market positions of rival companies. Rivals in the same or nearby **strategic groups** are close competitors, whereas companies in distant strategic groups usually pose little or no immediate threat. The lesson of strategic group mapping is that some positions on the map are more favorable than others. The profit potential of different strategic groups varies due to strengths and weaknesses in each group's market position. Often, industry driving forces and competitive pressures favor some strategic groups and hurt others.

5. *What strategic moves are rivals likely to make next?* This analytical step involves identifying competitors' strategies, deciding which rivals are likely to be strong contenders and which are likely to be weak, evaluating rivals' competitive options, and predicting their next moves. Scouting competitors well enough to anticipate their actions can help a company prepare effective countermoves (perhaps even beating a rival to the punch) and allows managers to take rivals' probable actions into account in designing their own company's best course of action. Managers who fail to study competitors risk being caught unprepared by the strategic moves of rivals.

6. *What are the key factors for competitive success?* An industry's **key success factors (KSFs)** are the particular strategy elements, product attributes, competitive capabilities, and business outcomes that spell the difference between being a strong competitor and a weak competitor—and sometimes between profit and loss. KSFs by their very nature are so important to competitive success that *all firms* in the industry must pay close attention to them or risk becoming an industry also-ran. Correctly diagnosing an industry's KSFs raises a company's chances of crafting a sound strategy. The goal of company strategists should be to design a strategy aimed at stacking up well on all of the industry KSFs and trying to be *distinctively better* than rivals on one (or possibly two) of the KSFs. Indeed, using the industry's KSFs as *cornerstones* for the company's strategy and trying to gain sustainable competitive advantage by excelling at one particular KSF is a fruitful competitive strategy approach.

7. *Does the outlook for the industry present the company with sufficiently attractive prospects for profitability?* The answer to this question is a major driver of company strategy. An assessment that the industry and competitive environment is fun-

damentally attractive typically suggests employing a strategy calculated to build a stronger competitive position in the business, expanding sales efforts, and investing in additional facilities and equipment as needed. If the industry is relatively unattractive, outsiders considering entry may decide against it and look elsewhere for opportunities, weak companies in the industry may merge with or be acquired by a rival, and strong companies may restrict further investments and employ cost-reduction strategies or product innovation strategies to boost long-term competitiveness and protect their profitability. On occasion, an industry that is unattractive overall is still very attractive to a favorably situated company with the skills and resources to take business away from weaker rivals.

A competently conducted industry and competitive analysis generally tells a clear, easily understood story about the company's external environment. But different analysts can still have different judgments about competitive intensity, the impacts of driving forces, how industry conditions will evolve, how good the outlook is for industry profitability, and the degree to which the industry environment offers the company an attractive business opportunity. However, while no method can guarantee a single conclusive diagnosis about the state of industry and competitive conditions and an industry's future outlook, this doesn't justify shortcutting hardnosed strategic analysis and relying instead on opinion and casual observation. Managers become better strategists when they know what questions to pose and what tools to use. This is why this chapter has concentrated on suggesting the right questions to ask, explaining concepts and analytical approaches, and indicating the kinds of things to look for. There's no substitute for staying on the cutting edge of what's happening in the industry—anything less weakens managers' ability to craft strategies that are well matched to the industry and competitive situation.

exercises

1. As the owner of a new fast-food enterprise seeking a loan from a bank to finance the construction and operation of three new store locations, you have been asked to provide the loan officer with a brief analysis of the competitive environment in fast food. Draw a five-forces diagram for the fast-food industry, and briefly discuss the nature and strength of each of the five competitive forces in fast food.

2. Use the strategic group map in Illustration Capsule 3.1 to answer the following: Who are Wal-Mart's two closest competitors? Between which two strategic groups is competition the weakest? Which strategic group faces the weakest competition from the members of other strategic groups?

3. Based on your knowledge of the ice cream industry, which of the following factors might qualify as possible driving forces capable of causing fundamental change in the industry's structure and competitive environment:

    a. Increasing sales of frozen yogurt and frozen sorbets.
    b. The potential for additional makers of ice cream to enter the market.
    c. Growing consumer interest in low-calorie/low-fat dessert alternatives.
    d. A slowdown in the rate of consumer demand for ice cream products.
    e. An increase in the prices of milk and sugar.
    f. A decision by Häagen-Dazs to increase its prices by 10 percent.
    g. A decision by Ben & Jerry's to add five new flavors to its product line.
    h. A trend among ice cream manufacturers to promote their brands on the Internet.

chapter four

Analyzing a Company's Resources and Competitive Position

(©Images.com/CORBIS)

Before executives can chart a new strategy, they must reach common understanding of the company's current position.

—W. Chan Kim and Rene Mauborgne

The real question isn't how well you're doing today against your own history, but how you're doing against your competitors.

—Donald Kress

Organizations succeed in a competitive marketplace over the long run because they can do certain things their customers value better than can their competitors.

—Robert Hayes, Gary Pisano, and David Upton

Only firms who are able to continually build new strategic assets faster and cheaper than their competitors will earn superior returns over the long term.

—C. C. Markides and P. J. Williamson

In Chapter 3 we described how to use the tools of industry and competitive analysis to assess a company's external environment and lay the groundwork for matching a company's strategy to its external situation. In this chapter we discuss the techniques of evaluating a company's internal circumstances—its resource capabilities, relative cost position, and competitive strength versus rivals. The analytical spotlight will be trained on five questions:

1. How well is the company's present strategy working?
2. What are the company's resource strengths and weaknesses, and its external opportunities and threats?
3. Are the company's prices and costs competitive?
4. Is the company competitively stronger or weaker than key rivals?
5. What strategic issues and problems merit front-burner managerial attention?

In probing for answers to these questions, four analytical tools—SWOT analysis, value chain analysis, benchmarking, and competitive strength assessment—will be used. All four are valuable techniques for revealing a company's competitiveness and for helping company managers match their strategy to the company's own particular circumstances.

QUESTION 1: HOW WELL IS THE COMPANY'S PRESENT STRATEGY WORKING?

In evaluating how well a company's present strategy is working, a manager has to start with what the strategy is. Figure 4.1 shows the key components of a single-business company's strategy. The first thing to pin down is the company's competitive approach. Is the company striving to be a low-cost leader *or* stressing ways to differentiate its product offering from rivals? Is it concentrating its efforts on serving a broad spectrum of customers *or* a narrow market niche? Another strategy-defining consideration is the firm's competitive scope within the industry—what its geographic market coverage is and whether it operates in just a single stage of the industry's production/distribution chain or is vertically integrated across several stages. Another good indication of the company's strategy is whether the company has made moves recently to improve its competitive position and performance—for instance, by cutting prices, improving design, stepping up advertising, entering a new geographic market (domestic or foreign), or merging with a competitor. The company's functional strategies in R&D, production, marketing, finance, human resources, information technology, and so on further characterize company strategy.

figure 4.1 **Identifying the Components of a Single-Business Company's Strategy**

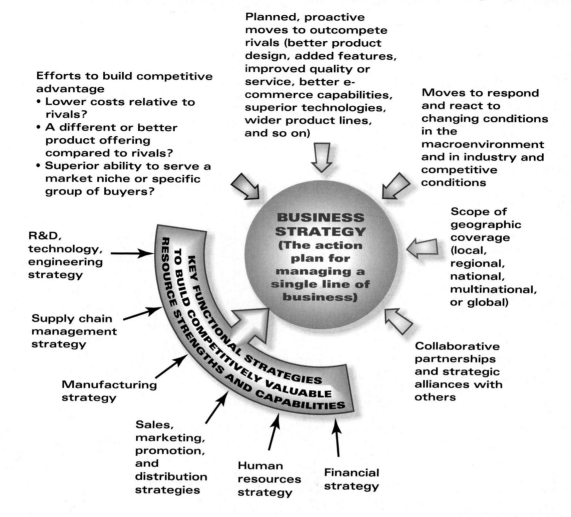

While there's merit in evaluating the strategy from a *qualitative* standpoint (its completeness, internal consistency, rationale, and relevance), the best *quantitative* evidence of how well a company's strategy is working comes from its results. The two best empirical indicators are (1) whether the company is achieving its stated financial and strategic objectives, and (2) whether the company is an above-average industry performer. Persistent shortfalls in meeting company performance targets and weak performance relative to rivals are reliable warning signs that the company suffers from poor strategy making, less-than-competent strategy execution, or both. Other indicators of how well a company's strategy is working include:

- Whether the firm's sales are growing faster, slower, or about the same pace as the market as a whole, thus resulting in a rising, eroding, or stable market share.
- Whether the company is acquiring new customers at an attractive rate as well as retaining existing customers.
- Whether the firm's profit margins are increasing or decreasing and how well its margins compare to rival firms' margins.

- Trends in the firm's net profits and return on investment and how these compare to the same trends for other companies in the industry.
- Whether the company's overall financial strength and credit rating are improving or on the decline.
- Whether the company can demonstrate continuous improvement in such internal performance measures as days of inventory, employee productivity, unit cost, defect rate, scrap rate, misfilled orders, delivery times, warranty costs, and so on.
- How shareholders view the company based on trends in the company's stock price and shareholder value (relative to the stock price trends at other companies in the industry).
- The firm's image and reputation with its customers.
- How well the company stacks up against rivals on technology, product innovation, customer service, product quality, delivery time, price, getting newly developed products to market quickly, and other relevant factors on which buyers base their choice of brands.

The stronger a company's current overall performance, the less likely the need for radical changes in strategy. The weaker a company's financial performance and market standing, the more its current strategy must be questioned. Weak performance is almost always a sign of weak strategy, weak execution, or both.

> The stronger a company's financial performance and market position, the more likely it has a well-conceived, well-executed strategy.

QUESTION 2: WHAT ARE THE COMPANY'S RESOURCE STRENGTHS AND WEAKNESSES AND ITS EXTERNAL OPPORTUNITIES AND THREATS?

Appraising a company's resource strengths and weaknesses and its external opportunities and threats, commonly known as **SWOT analysis,** provides a good overview of whether its overall situation is fundamentally healthy or unhealthy. Just as important, a first-rate SWOT analysis provides the basis for crafting a strategy that capitalizes on the company's resources, aims squarely at capturing the company's best opportunities, and defends against the threats to its well-being.

> **core concept**
> **SWOT analysis** is a simple but powerful tool for sizing up a company's resource capabilities and deficiencies, its market opportunities, and the external threats to its future well-being.

Identifying Company Resource Strengths and Competitive Capabilities

A *strength* is something a company is good at doing or an attribute that enhances its competitiveness. A strength can take any of several forms:

- *A skill or important expertise*—low-cost manufacturing capabilities, strong e-commerce expertise, technological know-how, skills in improving production processes, a proven track record in defect-free manufacture, expertise in providing consistently good customer service, excellent mass merchandising skills, or unique advertising and promotional talents.
- *Valuable physical assets*—state-of-the-art plants and equipment, attractive real estate locations, worldwide distribution facilities, or ownership of valuable natural resource deposits.

- *Valuable human assets*—an experienced and capable workforce, talented employees in key areas, cutting-edge knowledge and intellectual capital, collective learning embedded in the organization and built up over time, or proven managerial know-how.[1]
- *Valuable organizational assets*—proven quality control systems, proprietary technology, key patents, mineral rights, a cadre of highly trained customer service representatives, sizable amounts of cash and marketable securities, a strong balance sheet and credit rating (thus giving the company access to additional financial capital), or a comprehensive list of customers' e-mail addresses.
- *Valuable intangible assets*—a powerful or well-known brand name, a reputation for technological leadership, or strong buyer loyalty and goodwill.
- *Competitive capabilities*—product innovation capabilities, short development times in bringing new products to market, a strong dealer network, cutting-edge supply chain management capabilities, quickness in responding to shifting market conditions and emerging opportunities, or state-of-the-art systems for doing business via the Internet.
- *An achievement or attribute that puts the company in a position of market advantage*—low overall costs relative to competitors, market share leadership, a superior product, a wider product line than rivals, wide geographic coverage, a well-known brand name, superior e-commerce capabilities, or exceptional customer service.
- *Competitively valuable alliances or cooperative ventures*—fruitful partnerships with suppliers that reduce costs and/or enhance product quality and performance; alliances or joint ventures that provide access to valuable technologies, competencies, or geographic markets.

> **core concept**
> A company is better positioned to succeed if it has a competitively valuable complement of resources at its command.

Taken together, a company's strengths determine the complement of competitively valuable *resources* with which it competes—a company's resource strengths represent *competitive assets*. The caliber of a firm's resource strengths and competitive capabilities, along with its ability to mobilize them in the pursuit of competitive advantage, are big determinants of how well a company will perform in the marketplace.[2]

Company Competencies and Competitive Capabilities   Sometimes a company's resource strengths relate to fairly specific skills and expertise (like just-in-time inventory control) and sometimes they flow from pooling the knowledge and expertise of different organizational groups to create a company competence or competitive capability. Competence or capability in continuous product innovation, for example, comes from teaming the efforts of people and groups with expertise in market research, new product R&D, design and engineering, cost-effective manufacturing, and market testing.[3] Company competencies can range from merely a competence in performing an activity to a core competence to a distinctive competence:

> **core concept**
> A *competence* is something an organization is good at doing; it is nearly always the product of learning and experience.

1.   A competence is something an organization is good at doing. It is nearly always the product of experience, representing an accumulation of learning and the buildup of proficiency in performing an internal activity. Usually a company competence originates with deliberate efforts to develop the organizational ability to do something, however imperfectly or inefficiently. Such efforts involve selecting people with the requisite knowledge and skills, upgrading or expanding individual abilities as needed, and then molding the efforts and work products of individuals into a cooperative group effort to create organizational ability. Then, as experience builds, such that the company gains proficiency in performing the activity consistently well and at an acceptable cost, the ability evolves into a true competence and company capability. Examples of competencies include proficiency in merchandising and product display, the capability to create attractive and easy-to-use Web sites, expertise in a specific technology, proven capabilities in selecting good locations for retail outlets, and a proficiency in working with customers on new applications and uses of the product.

2.   A **core competence** is a proficiently performed internal activity that is *central* to a company's strategy and competitiveness. A core competence is a more valuable resource strength than a competence because of the well-performed activity's core role in the company's strategy and the contribution it makes to the company's success in the marketplace. A core competence can relate to any of several aspects of a company's business: expertise in integrating multiple technologies to create families of new products, know-how in creating and operating a cost-efficient supply chain, the capability to speed new or next-generation products to market, good after-sale service capabilities, skills in manufacturing a high-quality product at a low cost, or the capability to fill customer orders accurately and swiftly. A company may have more than one core competence in its resource portfolio, but rare is the company that can legitimately claim more than two or three core competencies. Most often, *a core competence is knowledge-based, residing in people and in a company's intellectual capital and not in its assets on the balance sheet.* Moreover, a core competence is more likely to be grounded in cross-department combinations of knowledge and expertise rather than being the product of a single department or work group.

> **core concept**
> A *core competence* is a competitively important activity that a company performs better than other internal activities.

3.   A **distinctive competence** is a competitively valuable activity that a company *performs better than its rivals.* A distinctive competence thus represents a *competitively superior resource strength.* A company may perform some competitively important activity well enough to claim that activity as a core competence. But what a company does best internally doesn't translate into a distinctive competence unless the company enjoys *competitive superiority in performing that activity.* For instance, most retailers believe they have core competencies in product selection and in-store merchandising, but many retailers run into trouble in the marketplace because they encounter rivals whose core competencies in product selection and in-store merchandising are better than theirs. Consequently, *a core competence becomes a basis for competitive advantage only when it rises to the level of a distinctive competence.* Sharp Corporation's distinctive competence in flat-panel display technology has enabled it to dominate the worldwide market for liquid crystal displays (LCDs). The distinctive competencies of Toyota and Honda in low-cost, high-quality manufacturing and in short design-to-market cycles for new models have proved to be considerable competitive advantages in the global market for motor vehicles. Intel's distinctive competence in rapidly developing new generations of ever-more-powerful semiconductor chips for PCs and network servers has helped give the company a dominating presence in the semiconductor industry. Starbucks' distinctive competence in store ambience and innovative coffee drinks has propelled it to the forefront among coffee retailers.

> **core concept**
> A *distinctive competence* is a competitively valuable activity that a company performs better than its rivals.

The conceptual differences between a competence, a core competence, and a distinctive competence draw attention to the fact that competitive capabilities are not all equal. Some competencies and competitive capabilities merely enable market survival because most rivals have them—indeed, not having a competence or capability that rivals have can result in competitive disadvantage. Core competencies are *competitively* more important than simple competencies because they add power to the company's strategy and have a bigger positive impact on its market position and profitability. On occasion, a company may have a uniquely strong competitive capability that holds the potential for creating competitive advantage if it meets the criterion for a distinctive competence and delivers value to buyers.[4] *The importance of a distinctive competence to strategy-making rests with (1) the competitively valuable capability it gives a company, (2) its potential for being the cornerstone of strategy, and (3) the competitive edge it can produce in the marketplace.* It is always easier to build competitive advantage when a firm has a distinctive competence in performing an activity important to market success, when rival companies do not have offsetting competencies, and when it is costly and time-consuming for rivals to imitate the competence. A distinctive competence is thus potentially the mainspring of a company's success—unless it is trumped by more powerful resources of rivals.

What Is the Competitive Power of a Resource Strength?   It is not enough to simply compile a list of a company's resource strengths and competitive capabilities. What is most telling about a company's strengths, individually and collectively, is how powerful they are in the marketplace. The competitive power of a company strength is measured by how many of the following four tests it can pass:[5]

1. *Is the resource strength hard to copy?* The more difficult and more expensive it is to imitate a company's resource strength, the greater its potential competitive value. Resources tend to be difficult to copy when they are unique (a fantastic real estate location, patent protection); when they must be built over time in ways that are difficult to imitate (a brand name, mastery of a technology); and when they carry big capital requirements (a cost-effective plant to manufacture cutting-edge microprocessors). Wal-Mart's competitors have failed miserably in their attempts over the past two decades to match Wal-Mart's superefficient state-of-the-art distribution and store operations capabilities. Hard-to-copy strengths and capabilities are valuable competitive assets, adding to a company's market prowess and contributing to sustained profitability.

2. *Is the resource strength durable—does it have staying power?* The longer the competitive value of a resource lasts, the greater its value. Some resources lose their clout in the marketplace quickly because of the rapid speeds at which technologies or industry conditions are moving. The value of Eastman Kodak's resources in film and film processing is rapidly being undercut by the growing popularity of digital cameras. The investments that commercial banks have made in branch offices is a rapidly depreciating asset because of growing use of direct deposits, automated teller machines, and telephone and Internet banking options.

3. *Is the resource really competitively superior?* Companies have to guard against pridefully believing that their core competencies are distinctive competencies or that their brand name is more powerful than the brand names of rivals. Who can really say whether Coca-Cola's consumer marketing know-how is better than Pepsi-Cola's or whether the Mercedes-Benz brand name is more powerful than that of BMW or Lexus?

4. *Can the resource strength be trumped by the different resource strengths and competitive capabilities of rivals?* Many commercial airlines (American Airlines, Delta Airlines, Continental Airlines, Singapore Airlines) have attracted large numbers of passengers because of their resources and capabilities in offering safe, convenient, reliable air transportation services and in providing an array of amenities to passengers. However, Southwest Airlines has consistently been a more profitable air carrier because it provides safe, reliable, basic services at radically lower fares. The prestigious brand names of Cadillac and Lincoln have faded in the market for luxury cars because Mercedes, BMW, Audi, Lexus, Acura, and Infiniti have

introduced the most appealing luxury vehicles in recent years. Amazon.com is putting a big dent in the business prospects of brick-and-mortar bookstores; likewise, Wal-Mart (with its lower prices) is putting major competitive pressure on Toys "R" Us, at one time the leading toy retailer in the United States, and on traditional supermarket chains like Kroger, Albertson's, and Safeway, which have struggled to hold their own against Wal-Mart's march into supermarket retailing (where it now is the market leader).

The vast majority of companies are not well endowed with competitively valuable resources, much less with competitively superior resources capable of passing all four tests with high marks. Most firms have a mixed bag of resources—one or two quite valuable, some good, many satisfactory to mediocre. Only a few companies, usually the strongest industry leaders or up-and-coming challengers, possess a distinctive competence or competitively superior resource.

But even if a company doesn't possess a competitively superior resource, it can still marshal potential for winning in the marketplace. Sometimes a company derives significant competitive vitality, maybe even competitive advantage, from a collection of good-to-adequate resources that collectively have competitive power in the marketplace. Toshiba's laptop computers were the global market leader throughout most of the 1990s—an indicator that Toshiba had competitively valuable resource strengths. Yet Toshiba's laptops were not demonstrably faster than rivals' laptops; nor did they have bigger screens, more memory, longer battery power, a better pointing device, or other superior performance features; nor did Toshiba provide clearly superior technical support services to buyers of its laptops. Further, Toshiba laptops were definitely not cheaper, model for model, than the comparable models of its rivals, and they seldom ranked first in the overall performance ratings done by various organizations. Rather, Toshiba's market share leadership stemmed from a *combination* of *good* resource strengths and capabilities—its strategic partnerships with suppliers of laptop components, efficient assembly capability, design expertise, skills in choosing quality components, a wide selection of models, the attractive mix of built-in performance features found in each model when balanced against price, the better-than-average reliability of its models (based on buyer ratings), and good technical support services (based on buyer ratings). The verdict from the marketplace was that PC buyers considered Toshiba laptops to be better, all things considered, than competing brands. (More recently, however, Toshiba has been overtaken by Dell Computer, the present global leader in laptop PCs.)

> A company's success in the marketplace becomes more likely when it has appropriate and ample resources with which to compete, and especially when it has strengths and capabilities with competitive advantage potential.

Identifying Company Resource Weaknesses and Competitive Deficiencies

A *weakness,* or *competitive deficiency,* is something a company lacks or does poorly (in comparison to others) or a condition that puts it at a disadvantage in the marketplace. A company's weaknesses can relate to (1) inferior or unproven skills, expertise, or intellectual capital in competitively important areas of the business; (2) deficiencies in competitively important physical, organizational, or intangible assets; or (3) missing or competitively inferior capabilities in key areas. *Internal weaknesses are thus shortcomings in a company's complement of resources and represent competitive liabilities.* Nearly all companies have competitive liabilities of one kind or another. Whether a company's resource weaknesses make it competitively vulnerable depends on how much they matter in the marketplace and whether they are offset by the company's resource strengths.

> **core concept**
> A company's resource strengths represent *competitive assets;* its resource weaknesses represent *competitive liabilities.*

Table 4.1 lists the kinds of factors to consider in compiling a company's resource strengths and weaknesses. Sizing up a company's complement of resource capabilities and deficiencies is akin to constructing a *strategic balance sheet,* on which resource strengths represent *competitive assets* and resource weaknesses represent *competitive liabilities.* Obviously, the ideal condition is for the company's competitive assets to outweigh its competitive liabilities by an ample margin—a 50–50 balance is definitely not the desired condition!

Identifying a Company's Market Opportunities

Market opportunity is a big factor in shaping a company's strategy. Indeed, managers can't properly tailor strategy to the company's situation without first identifying its opportunities and appraising the growth and profit potential each one holds. Depending on the prevailing circumstances, a company's opportunities can be plentiful or scarce and can range from wildly attractive (an absolute "must" to pursue) to marginally interesting (because the growth and profit potential are questionable) to unsuitable (because there's not a good match with the company's strengths and capabilities). A checklist of potential market opportunities is included in Table 4.1.

In evaluating a company's market opportunities and ranking their attractiveness, managers have to guard against viewing every *industry* opportunity as a *company* opportunity. Not every company is equipped with the resources to successfully pursue each opportunity that exists in its industry. Some companies are more capable of going after particular opportunities than others, and a few companies may be hopelessly outclassed. Occasionally managers may have to deliberately adapt a company's resources to position it to contend for attractive growth opportunities. *But the market opportunities most relevant to a company are those that match up well with the company's financial and organizational resource capabilities, offer the best growth and profitability, and present the most potential for competitive advantage.*

> A company is well advised to pass on a particular market opportunity unless it has or can acquire the resources to capture it.

Identifying Threats to a Company's Future Profitability

Often, certain factors in a company's external environment pose *threats* to its profitability and competitive well-being. Examples of threats include the emergence of cheaper or better technologies, rivals' introduction of new or improved products, lower-cost foreign competitors' entry into a company's market stronghold, new regulations that may be more burdensome to a company than to its competitors, vulnerability to a rise in interest rates, the potential of a hostile takeover, unfavorable demographic shifts, adverse changes in foreign exchange rates, political upheaval in a foreign country where the company has facilities, and so on (Table 4.1). External threats may pose no more than a moderate degree of adversity (all companies confront some threatening elements in the course of doing business), or they may be so imposing as to make a company's situation and outlook quite tenuous. It is management's job to identify the threats to the company's future profitability and to evaluate what strategic actions can be taken to neutralize or lessen their impact.

> Simply making lists of a company's strengths, weaknesses, opportunities, and threats is not enough; the payoff from SWOT analysis comes from the conclusions about a company's situation and the implications for strategy improvement that flow from the four lists.

What Do the SWOT Listings Reveal?

SWOT analysis involves more than making four lists. The two most important parts of SWOT analysis are *drawing conclusions* from the SWOT listings

table 4.1 **What to Look for in Identifying a Company's Strengths, Weaknesses, Opportunities, and Threats**

Potential Resource Strengths and Competitive Capabilities	Potential Resource Weaknesses and Competitive Deficiencies
• A powerful strategy • Core competencies in _____ • A distinctive competence in _____ • A product that is strongly differentiated from those of rivals • Competencies and capabilities that are well matched to industry key success factors • A strong financial condition; ample financial resources to grow the business • Strong brand-name image/company reputation • An attractive customer base • Economy of scale and/or learning and experience curve advantages over rivals • Proprietary technology/superior technological skills/important patents • Superior intellectual capital relative to key rivals • Cost advantages over rivals • Strong advertising and promotion • Product innovation capabilities • Proven capabilities in improving production processes • Good supply chain management capabilities • Good customer service capabilities • Better product quality relative to rivals • Wide geographic coverage and/or strong global distribution capability • Alliances/joint ventures with other firms that provide access to valuable technology, competencies, and/or attractive geographic markets	• No clear strategic direction • Resources that are not well matched to industry key success factors • No well-developed or proven core competencies • A weak balance sheet; too much debt • Higher overall unit costs relative to key competitors • Weak or unproven product innovation capabilities • A product/service with ho-hum attributes or features inferior to those of rivals • Too narrow a product line relative to rivals • Weak brand image or reputation • Weaker dealer network than key rivals and/or lack of adequate global distribution capability • Behind on product quality, R&D, and/or technological know-how • In the wrong strategic group • Losing market share because _____ • Lack of management depth • Inferior intellectual capital relative to leading rivals • Subpar profitability because _____ • Plagued with internal operating problems or obsolete facilities • Behind rivals in e-commerce capabilities • Short on financial resources to grow the business and pursue promising initiatives • Too much underutilized plant capacity
Potential Market Opportunities	**Potential External Threats to a Company's Well-Being**
• Openings to win market share from rivals • Sharply rising buyer demand for the industry's product • Serving additional customer groups or market segments • Expanding into new geographic markets • Expanding the company's product line to meet a broader range of customer needs • Utilizing existing company skills or technological know-how to enter new product lines or new businesses • Online sales • Integrating forward or backward • Falling trade barriers in attractive foreign markets • Acquiring rival firms or companies with attractive technological expertise or capabilities • Entering into alliances or joint ventures that can expand the firm's market coverage or boost its competitive capability • Openings to exploit emerging new technologies	• Increasing intensity of competition among industry rivals—may squeeze profit margins • Slowdowns in market growth • Likely entry of potent new competitors • Loss of sales to substitute products • Growing bargaining power of customers or suppliers • A shift in buyer needs and tastes away from the industry's product • Adverse demographic changes that threaten to curtail demand for the industry's product • Vulnerability to industry driving forces • Restrictive trade policies on the part of foreign governments • Costly new regulatory requirements

figure 4.2   **The Three Steps of SWOT Analysis: Identify, Draw Conclusions, Translate into Strategic Action**

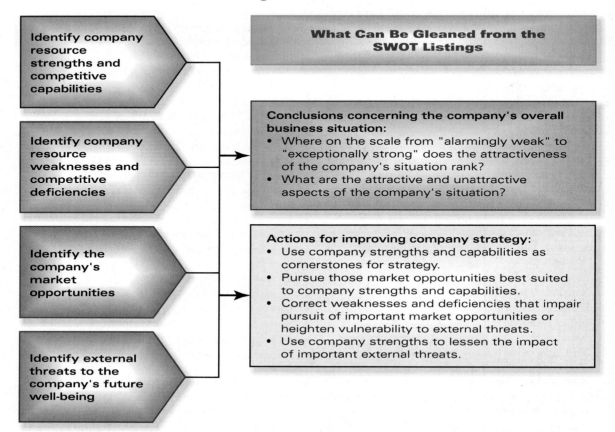

about the company's overall situation, and *acting on those conclusions* to better match the company's strategy to its resource strengths and market opportunities, to correct the important weaknesses, and to defend against external threats. Figure 4.2 shows the three steps of SWOT analysis.

Just what story the SWOT analysis tells about the company's overall situation is often revealed in the answers to the following sets of questions.

- Does the company have an attractive set of resource strengths? Does it have any strong core competencies or a distinctive competence? Are the company's strengths and capabilities well matched to the industry key success factors? Do they add adequate power to the company's strategy, or are more or different strengths needed? Will the company's current strengths and capabilities matter in the future?

- How serious are the company's weaknesses and competitive deficiencies? Are they mostly inconsequential and readily correctable, or could one or more prove fatal if not remedied soon? Are some of the company's weaknesses in areas that relate to the industry's key success factors? Are there any weaknesses that if uncorrected, would keep the company from pursuing an otherwise attractive opportunity? Does the company have important resource gaps that need to be filled for it to move up in the industry rankings and/or boost its profitability?

- Do the company's resource strengths and competitive capabilities (its competitive assets) outweigh its resource weaknesses and competitive deficiencies (its competitive liabilities) by an attractive margin?
- Does the company have attractive market opportunities that are well suited to its resource strengths and competitive capabilities? Does the company lack the resources and capabilities to pursue any of the most attractive opportunities?
- Are the threats alarming, or are they something the company appears able to deal with and defend against?
- All things considered, how strong is the company's overall situation? Where on a scale of 1 to 10 (where 1 is alarmingly weak and 10 is exceptionally strong) should the firm's position and overall situation be ranked? What aspects of the company's situation are particularly attractive? What aspects are of the most concern?

The final piece of SWOT analysis is to translate the diagnosis of the company's situations into actions for improving the company's strategy and business prospects. The following questions point to implications the SWOT listings have for strategic action:

- Which competitive capabilities need to be strengthened immediately (so as to add greater power to the company's strategy and boost sales and profitability)? Do new types of competitive capabilities need to be put in place to help the company better respond to emerging industry and competitive conditions? Which resources and capabilities need to be given greater emphasis, and which merit less emphasis? Should the company emphasize leveraging its existing resource strengths and capabilities, or does it need to create new resource strengths and capabilities?
- What actions should be taken to reduce the company's competitive liabilities? Which weaknesses or competitive deficiencies are in urgent need of correction?
- Which market opportunities should be top priority in future strategic initiatives (because they are good fits with the company's resource strengths and competitive capabilities, present attractive growth and profit prospects, and/or offer the best potential for securing competitive advantage)? Which opportunities should be ignored, at least for the time being (because they offer less growth potential or are not suited to the company's resources and capabilities)?
- What should the company be doing to guard against the threats to its well-being?

A company's resource strengths should generally form the cornerstones of strategy because they represent the company's best chance for market success.[6] As a rule, strategies that place heavy demands on areas where the company is weakest or has unproven ability are suspect and should be avoided. If a company doesn't have the resources and competitive capabilities around which to craft an attractive strategy, managers need to take decisive remedial action either to upgrade existing organizational resources and capabilities and add others as needed or to acquire them through partnerships or strategic alliances with firms possessing the needed expertise. Plainly, managers have to look toward correcting competitive weaknesses that make the company vulnerable, hold down profitability, or disqualify it from pursuing an attractive opportunity.

At the same time, sound strategy making requires sifting through the available market opportunities and aiming strategy at capturing those that are most attractive and suited to the company's circumstances. Rarely does a company have the resource depth to pursue all available market opportunities simultaneously without spreading itself too thin. In deciding how much attention to devote to defending against external threats to the company's market position and future performance, managers must determine how vulnerable the company is, whether there are attractive defensive moves that can be taken to lessen their impact, and whether the costs of undertaking such moves represent the best use of company resources.

QUESTION 3: ARE THE COMPANY'S PRICES AND COSTS COMPETITIVE?

Managers are often stunned when a competitor cuts its price to "unbelievably low" levels or when a new market entrant comes on strong with a very low price. The competitor may not, however, be "dumping" (an economic term for selling large amounts of goods below market price), buying market share, or waging a desperate move to gain sales; it may simply have substantially lower costs. One of the most telling signs of whether a company's business position is strong or precarious is whether its prices and costs are competitive with industry rivals. Price–cost comparisons are especially critical in a commodity-product industry where the value provided to buyers is the same from seller to seller, price competition is typically the ruling market force, and lower-cost companies have the upper hand.

> **The higher a company's costs are above those of close rivals, the more competitively vulnerable it becomes.**

But even in industries where products are differentiated and competition centers on the different attributes of competing brands as much as on price, rival companies have to keep their costs *in line* and make sure that any added costs they incur, and any price premiums they charge, create ample buyer value. While some cost disparity is justified so long as the products or services of closely competing companies are sufficiently differentiated, a high-cost firm's market position becomes increasingly vulnerable the more its costs exceed those of close rivals.

Two analytical tools are particularly useful in determining whether a company's prices and costs are competitive and thus conducive to winning in the marketplace: value chain analysis and benchmarking.

The Concept of a Company Value Chain

> **core concept**
> A company's *value chain* identifies the primary activities that create customer value and the related support activities.

Every company's business consists of a collection of activities undertaken in the course of designing, producing, marketing, delivering, and supporting its product or service. A company's **value chain** consists of the linked set of value-creating activities the company performs internally. As shown in Figure 4.3, the value chain consists of two broad categories of activities: the *primary activities* that are foremost in creating value for customers and the requisite *support activities* that facilitate and enhance the performance of the primary activities.[7] The value chain includes a profit margin because a markup over the cost of performing the firm's value-creating activities is customarily part of the price (or total cost) borne by buyers—a fundamental objective of every enterprise is to create and deliver a value to buyers whose margin over cost yields an attractive profit.

Disaggregating a company's operations into primary and secondary activities exposes the major elements of the company's cost structure. Each activity in the value chain gives rise to costs and ties up assets; assigning the company's operating costs and assets to each individual activity in the chain provides cost estimates and capital requirements. Quite often, there are links between activities such that the manner in which one activity is done can affect the costs of performing other activities. For in-

figure 4.3 **A Representative Company Value Chain**

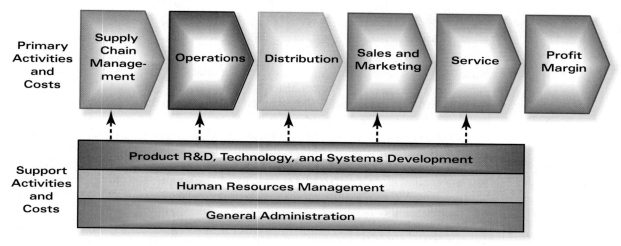

PRIMARY ACTIVITIES

- **Supply Chain Management**—activities, costs, and assets associated with purchasing fuel, energy, raw materials, parts and components, merchandise, and consumable items from vendors; receiving, storing, and disseminating inputs from suppliers; inspection; and inventory management.
- **Operations**—activities, costs, and assets associated with converting inputs into final products.

SUPPORT ACTIVITIES

- **Product R&D, Technology, and Systems Development**—activities, costs, and assets relating to product R&D, process R&D, process design improvement, equipment design, computer software development, telecommunications systems, computer-assisted design and engineering, database capabilities, and development of computerized support systems.
- **Human Resources Management**—activities, costs, and assets associated with the recruitment, hiring, training, development, and compensation of all types of personnel; labor relations activities; and development of knowledge-based skills and core competencies.
- **General Administration**—activities, costs, and assets relating to general management, accounting and finance, legal and regulatory affairs, safety and security, management information systems, forming strategic alliances and collaborating with strategic partners, and other "overhead" functions.

Source: Adapted from Michael E. Porter, *Competitive Advantage* (New York: Free Press, 1985), pp. 37–43.

stance, Japanese producers of videocassette recorders (VCRs) were able to reduce prices from around $1,300 in 1977 to under $300 in 1984 by spotting the impact of an early step in the value chain (product design) on a later step (production) and deciding to change the product design to drastically reduce the number of parts in each VCR.[8]

The combined costs of all the various activities in a company's value chain define the company's internal cost structure. Further, the cost of each activity contributes to whether the company's overall cost position relative to rivals is favorable or unfavorable. The tasks of value chain analysis and benchmarking are to develop the data for comparing a company's costs activity by activity against the costs of key rivals and to learn which internal activities are a source of cost advantage or disadvantage. A company's relative cost position is a function of how the overall costs of the activities it performs in conducting business compare to the overall costs of the activities performed by rivals.

Why the Value Chains of Rival Companies Often Differ

A company's value chain and the manner in which it performs each activity reflect the evolution of its own particular business and internal operations, its strategy, the approaches it is using to execute its strategy, and the underlying economics of the activities themselves.[9] Because these factors differ from company to company, the value chains of rival companies sometimes differ substantially—a condition that complicates the task of assessing rivals' relative cost positions. For instance, competing companies may differ in their degrees of vertical integration. Comparing the value chains of a fully integrated rival and a partially integrated rival requires adjusting for differences in the scope of activities performed. Clearly the costs of internally performed activities for a manufacturer that *makes* all of its own parts and components will be greater than the costs of internally performed activities of a producer that *buys* the needed parts and components from outside suppliers and only performs assembly operations.

Likewise, there is legitimate reason to expect value chain and cost differences between a company that is pursuing a low-cost/low-price strategy and a rival that is positioned on the high end of the market. The costs of certain activities along the low-cost company's value chain should indeed be below those of the high-end firm that understandably has to devote more resources to performing activities that create the added quality and extra features of its products.

Moreover, cost and price differences among rival companies can have their origins in activities performed by suppliers or by distribution channel allies involved in getting the product to end users. Suppliers or wholesale/retail dealers may have excessively high cost structures or profit margins that jeopardize a company's cost-competitiveness even though its costs for internally performed activities are competitive. For example, when determining Michelin's cost-competitiveness vis-à-vis Goodyear and Bridgestone in supplying replacement tires to vehicle owners, we have to look at more than whether Michelin's tire manufacturing costs are above or below Goodyear's and Bridgestone's. Let's say that a buyer has to pay $400 for a set of Michelin tires and only $350 for a comparable set of Goodyear or Bridgestone tires; Michelin's $50 price disadvantage can stem not only from higher manufacturing costs (reflecting, perhaps, the added costs of Michelin's strategic efforts to build a better-quality tire with more performance features) but also from (1) differences in what the three tire makers pay their suppliers for materials and tire-making components, and (2) differences in the operating efficiencies, costs, and markups of Michelin's wholesale–retail dealer outlets versus those of Goodyear and Bridgestone. Thus, determining whether a company's prices and costs are competitive from an end user's standpoint requires looking at the activities and costs of competitively relevant suppliers and forward allies, as well as the costs of internally performed activities.

The Value Chain System for an Entire Industry

As the tire industry example makes clear, a company's value chain is embedded in a larger system of activities that includes the value chains of its suppliers and its distribution channel allies engaged in getting its product or service to end users.[10] *Accurately assessing a company's competitiveness in end-use markets requires that company managers understand the entire value chain system for delivering a product or service to end users, not just the company's own value chain*. At the very least, this means considering the value chains of suppliers and forward channel allies (if any), as shown in Figure 4.4.

Suppliers' value chains are relevant because suppliers perform activities and incur costs in creating and delivering the purchased inputs used in a company's own value

figure 4.4 **A Representative Value Chain for an Entire Industry**

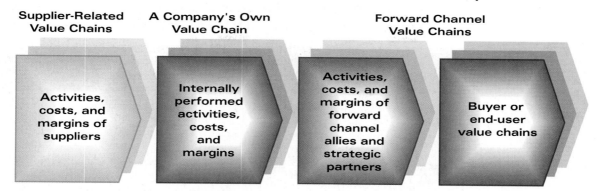

Supplier-Related Value Chains	A Company's Own Value Chain	Forward Channel Value Chains	
Activities, costs, and margins of suppliers	Internally performed activities, costs, and margins	Activities, costs, and margins of forward channel allies and strategic partners	Buyer or end-user value chains

chain. The costs, performance features, and quality of these inputs influence a company's own costs and product differentiation capabilities. Anything a company can do to help its suppliers take costs out of their value chain activities or improve the quality and performance of the items being supplied can enhance its own competitiveness—a powerful reason for working collaboratively with suppliers in managing supply chain activities.

Forward channel and customer value chains are relevant because (1) the costs and margins of a company's distribution allies are part of the price the end user pays, and (2) the activities that distribution allies perform affect the end user's satisfaction. For these reasons, companies normally work closely with their forward channel allies (who are their direct customers) to perform value chain activities in mutually beneficial ways. For instance, some aluminum-can producers have constructed plants next to beer breweries and deliver cans on overhead conveyors directly to the breweries' can-filling lines; this has resulted in significant savings in production scheduling, shipping, and inventory costs for both container producers and breweries.[11] Many automotive parts suppliers have built plants near the auto assembly plants they supply to facilitate just-in-time deliveries, reduce warehousing and shipping costs, and promote close collaboration on parts design and production scheduling. Irrigation equipment companies, suppliers of grape-harvesting and winemaking equipment, and firms making barrels, wine bottles, caps, corks, and labels all have facilities in the California wine country to be close to the nearly 700 winemakers they supply.[12] The lesson here is that a company's value chain activities are often closely linked to the value chains of their suppliers and the forward allies or customers to whom they sell.

> A company's cost-competitiveness depends not only on the costs of internally performed activities (its own value chain) but also on costs in the value chains of its suppliers and forward channel allies.

Although the value chains in Figures 4.3 and 4.4 are representative, actual value chains vary by industry and by company. The primary value chain activities in the pulp and paper industry (timber farming, logging, pulp mills, and papermaking) differ from the primary value chain activities in the home appliance industry (parts and components manufacture, assembly, wholesale distribution, retail sales). The value chain for the soft-drink industry (processing of basic ingredients and syrup manufacture, bottling and can filling, wholesale distribution, advertising, and retail merchandising) differs from that for the computer software industry (programming, disk loading, marketing, distribution). A producer of bathroom and kitchen faucets depends heavily on the activities of wholesale distributors and building supply retailers in winning sales to homebuilders and do-it-yourselfers; a producer of small gasoline engines internalizes its distribution activities by selling directly to the makers of lawn and garden equipment. A wholesaler's most important activities and costs deal with purchased goods, inbound logistics, and

table 4.2   **The Difference between Traditional Cost Accounting and Activity-Based Cost Accounting: A Purchasing Department Example**

Traditional Cost Accounting Categories in Purchasing Department Budget		Cost of Performing Specific Purchasing Department Activities Using Activity-Based Cost Accounting	
Wages and salaries	$340,000	Evaluate supplier capabilities	$100,300
Employee benefits	95,000	Process purchase orders	82,100
Supplies	21,500	Collaborate with suppliers on just-in-time deliveries	140,200
Travel	12,400		
Depreciation	19,000	Share data with suppliers	59,550
Other fixed charges (office space, utilities)	112,000	Check quality of items purchased	94,100
Miscellaneous operating expenses	40,250	Check incoming deliveries against purchase orders	48,450
		Resolve disputes	15,250
Total	$640,150	Conduct internal administration	100,200
		Total	$640,150

Source: Terence P. Par, "A New Tool for Managing Costs," *Fortune,* June 14, 1993, pp. 124–129. © 1993 Time Inc. All rights reserved.

outbound logistics. A hotel's most important activities and costs are in operations—check-in and check-out, maintenance and housekeeping, dining facilities and room service, conventions and meetings, and accounting. Supply chain management and distribution are crucial value chain activities at Amazon.com but comparatively insignificant at Yahoo or a hair salon. Advertising and promotion are dominant activities at Anheuser-Busch but only minor activities at interstate gas pipeline companies. Thus, generic value chains like those in Figures 3.3 and 3.4 are illustrative, not absolute, and have to be drawn to fit the activities of a particular company or industry.

Developing the Data to Measure a Company's Cost Competitiveness

Once the major value chain activities are identified, the next step in evaluating a company's cost competitiveness involves disaggregating, or breaking down, departmental cost accounting data into the costs of performing specific activities.[13] The appropriate degree of disaggregation depends on the economics of the activities and how valuable it is to develop cross-company cost comparisons for narrowly defined activities as opposed to broadly defined activities. A good guideline is to develop separate cost estimates for activities having different economics and for activities representing a significant or growing proportion of cost.[14]

Traditional accounting identifies costs according to broad categories of expenses—wages and salaries, employee benefits, supplies, maintenance, utilities, travel, depreciation, R&D, interest, general administration, and so on. A newer method, *activity-based costing,* entails defining expense categories according to the specific activities being performed and then assigning costs to the activity responsible for creating the cost. An illustrative example is shown in Table 4.2.[15] Perhaps 25 percent of the companies that have explored the feasibility of activity-based costing have adopted this accounting approach. To fully understand the costs of activities all along the industry value chain, cost estimates for activities performed in the competitively relevant portions of suppliers'

illustration capsule 4.1
Value Chain Costs for Companies in the Business of Recording and Distributing Music CDs

The table below presents the representative costs and markups associated with producing and distributing a music CD retailing for $15.

Value Chain Activities and Costs in Producing and Distributing a CD		
1. Record company direct production costs:		$ 2.40
Artists and repertoire	$0.75	
Pressing of CD and packaging	1.65	
2. Royalties		.99
3. Record company marketing expenses		1.50
4. Record company overhead		1.50
5. Total record company costs		6.39
6. Record company's operating profit		1.86
7. Record company's selling price to distributor/wholesaler		8.25
8. Average wholesale distributor markup to cover distribution activities and profit margins		1.50
9. Average wholesale price charged to retailer		9.75
10. Average retail markup over wholesale cost		5.25
11. Average price to consumer at retail		$15.00

Source: "Fight the Power—MP3," a Babson College Case Study, by Adrian Alleyne, under the supervision of Bill Lawler and David Wylie, 1999.

and customers' value chains also have to be developed—an advanced art in competitive intelligence. But despite the tediousness of developing cost estimates activity by activity and the imprecision of some of the estimates, the payoff in exposing the costs of particular activities makes activity-based costing a valuable analytical tool.[16] Illustration Capsule 4.1 shows representative costs for various activities performed by the producers and marketers of music CDs.

The most important application of value chain analysis is to expose how a particular firm's cost position compares with the cost positions of its rivals. What is needed are competitor-versus-competitor cost estimates for supplying a product or service to a well-defined customer group or market segment. The size of a company's cost advantage or disadvantage can vary from item to item in the product line, from customer group to customer group (if different distribution channels are used), and from geographic market to geographic market (if cost factors vary across geographic regions).

Benchmarking the Costs of Key Value Chain Activities

Many companies today are **benchmarking** their costs of performing a given activity against competitors' costs (and/or against the costs of a noncompetitor in another industry that efficiently and effectively performs much the same activity). Benchmarking is a tool that allows a company to determine whether the manner in which it performs particular functions and activities represents industry "best practices" when both cost and effectiveness are taken into account.

Benchmarking entails comparing how different companies perform various value chain activities—how materials are purchased, how suppliers are paid, how inventories are managed, how products are assembled, how fast the company can get new products to market, how the quality control function is performed, how customer orders are filled and shipped, how employees are trained, how payrolls are processed, and how maintenance is performed—and then making cross-company comparisons of the costs of these activities.[17] The objectives of benchmarking are to identify the best practices in performing an activity, to learn how other companies have actually achieved lower costs or better results in performing benchmarked activities, and to take action to improve a company's competitiveness whenever benchmarking reveals that its costs and results of performing an activity do not match those of other companies (either competitors or noncompetitors).

In 1979, Xerox became an early pioneer in the use of benchmarking when Japanese manufacturers began selling midsize copiers in the United States for $9,600 each—less than Xerox's production costs.[18] Although Xerox management suspected its Japanese competitors were dumping, it sent a team of line managers to Japan, including the head of manufacturing, to study competitors' business processes and costs. Fortunately, Xerox's joint venture partner in Japan, Fuji-Xerox, knew the competitors well. The team found that Xerox's costs were excessive due to gross inefficiencies in the company's manufacturing processes and business practices; the study proved instrumental in Xerox's efforts to become cost-competitive and prompted Xerox to embark on a long-term program to benchmark 67 of its key work processes against companies identified as having the best practices in performing these processes. Xerox quickly decided not to restrict its benchmarking efforts to its office equipment rivals but to extend them to any company regarded as "world class" in performing *any activity* relevant to Xerox's business.

In the years since Xerox's pioneering effort to benchmark its costs, benchmarking has become a popular and widely used tool for comparing a company against rivals not only on cost but also on most any relevant activity or competitively important measure. Toyota managers got their idea for just-in-time inventory deliveries by studying how U.S. supermarkets replenished their shelves. Southwest Airlines reduced the turnaround time of its aircraft at each scheduled stop by studying pit crews on the auto racing circuit. Over 80 percent of Fortune 500 companies reportedly engage in some form of benchmarking.

The tough part of benchmarking is not whether to do it but rather how to gain access to information about other companies' practices and costs. Sometimes benchmarking can be accomplished by collecting information from published reports, trade groups, and industry research firms and by talking to knowledgeable industry analysts, customers, and suppliers. On occasion, customers, suppliers, and joint-venture partners often make willing benchmarking allies. Usually, though, benchmarking requires field trips to the facilities of competing or noncompeting companies to observe how things are done, ask questions, compare practices and processes, and perhaps exchange data on productivity, staffing levels, time requirements, and other cost components. The problem is that, because benchmarking involves competitively sensitive cost information,

close rivals can't be expected to be completely open, even if they agree to host facilities tours and answer questions. Making reliable cost comparisons is complicated by the fact that participants often use different cost accounting systems.

illustration capsule 4.2
Benchmarking and Ethical Conduct

Because discussions between benchmarking partners can involve competitively sensitive data, conceivably raising questions about possible restraint of trade or improper business conduct, many benchmarking organizations urge all individuals and organizations involved in benchmarking to abide by a code of conduct grounded in ethical business behavior. One of the most widely used codes of conduct is the one advocated by the International Benchmarking Clearinghouse; it is based on the following principles and guidelines:

- Avoid discussions or actions that could lead to or imply an interest in restraint of trade, market and/or customer allocation schemes, price fixing, dealing arrangements, bid rigging, or bribery. Don't discuss costs with competitors if costs are an element of pricing.

- Refrain from the acquisition of trade secrets from another by any means that could be interpreted as improper including the breach or inducement of a breach of any duty to maintain secrecy. Do not disclose or use any trade secret that may have been obtained through improper means or that was disclosed by another in violation of duty to maintain its secrecy or limit its use.

- Be willing to provide the same type and level of information that you request from your benchmarking partner to your benchmarking partner.

- Communicate fully and early in the relationship to clarify expectations, avoid misunderstanding, and establish mutual interest in the benchmarking exchange.

- Be honest and complete.

- Treat benchmarking interchange as confidential to the individuals and companies involved. Information must not be communicated outside the partnering organizations without the prior consent of the benchmarking partner who shared the information.

- Use information obtained through benchmarking only for purposes stated to the benchmarking partner.

- The use or communication of a benchmarking partner's name with the data obtained or practices observed requires the prior permission of that partner.

- Respect the corporate culture of partner companies and work within mutually agreed procedures.

- Use benchmarking contacts, designated by the partner company, if that is their preferred procedure.

- Obtain mutual agreement with the designated benchmarking contact on any hand-off of communication or responsibility to other parties.

- Make the most of your benchmarking partner's time by being fully prepared for each exchange.

- Help your benchmarking partners prepare by providing them with a questionnaire and agenda prior to benchmarking visits.

- Follow through with each commitment made to your benchmarking partner in a timely manner.

- Understand how your benchmarking partner would like to have the information he or she provides handled and used, and handle and use it in that manner.

Note: Identification of firms, organizations contacted/visited is prohibited without advance approval from the organization.
Source: The International Benchmarking Clearinghouse, September 2003.

However, the explosive interest of companies in benchmarking costs and identifying best practices has prompted consulting organizations (e.g., Accenture, A. T. Kearney, Best Practices Benchmarking & Consulting, Towers Perrin, and Benchmarking Partners); several councils and associations (the International Benchmarking Clearinghouse, the Strategic Planning Institute's Council on Benchmarking); and online benchmarking organizations (Benchnet—the Benchmarking Exchange and the Benchmarking Network) to gather benchmarking data, do benchmarking studies, and distribute information about best practices without identifying the sources. Having an independent group gather the information and report it in a manner that disguises the names of individual companies permits participating companies to avoid disclosing competitively sensitive data to rivals and reduces the risk of ethical problems. Illustration Capsule 4.2 lists some guidelines with regard to benchmarking and ethical conduct.

Strategic Options for Remedying a Cost Disadvantage

Value chain analysis and benchmarking can reveal a great deal about a firm's cost competitiveness. Examining the costs of a company's own value chain activities and comparing them to rivals' indicates who has how much of a cost advantage or disadvantage and which cost components are responsible. Such information is vital in strategic actions to eliminate a cost disadvantage or create a cost advantage. One of the fundamental insights of value chain analysis and benchmarking is that a company's competitiveness on cost depends on how efficiently it manages its value chain activities relative to how well competitors manage theirs.[19] There are three main areas in a company's overall value chain where important differences in the costs of competing firms can occur: a company's own activity segments, suppliers' part of the industry value chain, and the forward channel portion of the industry chain.

When the source of a firm's cost disadvantage is internal, managers can use any of the following eight strategic approaches to restore cost parity:[20]

1. Implement the use of best practices throughout the company, particularly for high-cost activities.

2. Try to eliminate some cost-producing activities altogether by revamping the value chain. Examples include cutting out low-value-added activities or bypassing the value chains and associated costs of distribution allies and marketing directly to end users (the approach used by Dell in PCs and Napster in selling downloads of music files online).

3. Relocate high-cost activities (such as R&D or manufacturing) to geographic areas where they can be performed more cheaply.

4. Search out activities that can be outsourced from vendors or performed by contractors more cheaply than they can be done internally.

5. Invest in productivity-enhancing, cost-saving technological improvements (robotics, flexible manufacturing techniques, state-of-the-art electronic networking).

6. Innovate around the troublesome cost components—computer chip makers regularly design around the patents held by others to avoid paying royalties; automakers have substituted lower-cost plastic and rubber for metal at many exterior body locations.

7. Simplify the product design so that it can be manufactured or assembled quickly and more economically.

8. Try to make up the internal cost disadvantage by achieving savings in other two parts of the value chain system—usually a last resort.

If a firm finds that it has a cost disadvantage stemming from costs in the supplier or forward channel portions of the industry value chain, then the task of reducing its costs to levels more in line with competitors usually has to extend beyond the firm's own in-house operations. Table 4.3 presents the strategy options for attacking high costs associated with supply chain activities or forward channel allies.

Translating Proficient Performance of Value Chain Activities into Competitive Advantage

A company that does a first-rate job of managing its value chain activities relative to competitors stands a good chance of leveraging its competitively valuable competencies and capabilities into sustainable competitive advantage. With rare exceptions,

table 4.3 **Options for Attacking Cost Disadvantages Associated with Supply Chain Activities or Forward Channel Allies**

Options for Attacking the High Costs of Items Purchased from Suppliers	Options for Attacking the High Costs of Forward Channel Allies
• Negotiate more favorable prices with suppliers. • Work with suppliers on the design and specifications for what is being supplied to identify cost savings that will allow them to lower their prices. • Switch to lower-priced substitute inputs. • Collaborate closely with suppliers to identify mutual cost-saving opportunities. For example, just-in-time deliveries from suppliers can lower a company's inventory and internal logistics costs and may also allow its suppliers to economize on their warehousing, shipping, and production scheduling costs—a win–win outcome for both. • Integrate backward into the business of high-cost suppliers to gain control over the costs of purchased items—seldom an attractive option. • Try to make up the difference by cutting costs elsewhere in the chain—usually a last resort.	• Push distributors and other forward channel allies to reduce their markups. • Work closely with forward channel allies to identify win–win opportunities to reduce costs. A chocolate manufacturer learned that by shipping its bulk chocolate in liquid form instead of in 10-pound molded bars, it could not only save its candy-bar manufacturing customers the costs associated with unpacking and melting but also eliminate its own costs of molding and packing bars. • Change to a more economical distribution strategy, including switching to cheaper distribution channels (perhaps direct sales via the Internet) or perhaps integrating forward into company-owned retail outlets. • Try to make up the difference by cutting costs earlier in the cost chain—usually a last resort.

Source: Adapted with permission of The Free Press, a Division of Simon & Schuster Adult Publishing Group, from *Competitive Advantage: Creating and Sustaining Supplier Performance,* by Michael E. Porter. Copyright © 1995, 1998 by Michael E. Porter. All rights reserved.

company attempts to achieve competitive advantage with unique attributes and performance features seldom result in a durable competitive advantage. It is too easy for resourceful competitors to clone, improve on, or find an effective substitute for any unique features of a product or service.[21] A more fruitful approach to achieving and sustaining a competitive edge over rivals is for a company to develop competencies and capabilities that please buyers and that rivals don't have or can't quite match.

The process of translating proficient company performance of value chain activities into competitive advantage is shown in Figure 4.5. The road to competitive advantage begins with management efforts to build more organizational expertise in performing certain competitively important value chain activities, deliberately striving to develop competencies and capabilities that add power to its strategy and competitiveness. If management begins to make one or two of these competencies and capabilities cornerstones of its strategy and continues to invest resources in building greater and greater proficiency in performing them, then over time one (or maybe both) of the targeted competencies/capabilities may rise to the level of a core competence. Later, following additional organizational learning and investments in gaining still greater proficiency, the core competence could evolve into a distinctive competence, giving the company superiority over rivals. Such superiority, if it gives the company significant competitive clout in the marketplace, could produce an attractive competitive edge over rivals and, more important, prove difficult for rivals to match or offset with competencies and capabilities of their own making. As a general rule, it is substantially harder for rivals to achieve best-in-industry proficiency in performing a key value chain activity than it is for them to clone the features and attributes of a hot-selling product or service. This is especially true when a company with a distinctive competence avoids becoming complacent and works diligently to stay ahead of rivals by continuously improving its expertise and capability in the activity where it has a distinctive competence.

> Performing value chain activities in ways that give a company the capabilities to outmatch rivals is a source of competitive advantage.

figure 4.5 **Translating Company Performance of Value Chain Activities into Competitive Advantage**

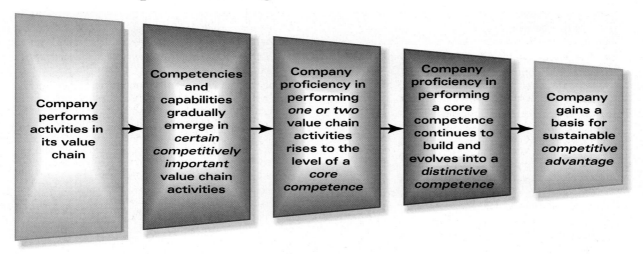

There are numerous examples of companies that have gained a competitive edge by building competencies and capabilities that outmatch those of rivals. Merck and Glaxo, two of the world's most competitively capable pharmaceutical companies, built their business positions around expert performance of a few competitively crucial activities: extensive R&D to achieve first discovery of new drugs, a carefully constructed approach to patenting, skill in gaining rapid and thorough clinical clearance through regulatory bodies, and unusually strong distribution and sales-force capabilities.[22] FedEx has linked and integrated the performance of its aircraft fleet, truck fleet, support systems, and personnel so tightly and smoothly across the company's different value chain activities that it has created the capability to provide customers with guaranteed overnight delivery services. McDonald's can turn out identical-quality fast-food items at some 25,000-plus outlets around the world—an impressive demonstration of its capability to replicate its operating systems at many locations via an omnibus manual of detailed rules and procedures for each activity and intensive training of franchise operators and outlet managers.

QUESTION 4: IS THE COMPANY COMPETITIVELY STRONGER OR WEAKER THAN KEY RIVALS?

Using value chain analysis and benchmarking to determine a company's competitiveness on price and cost is necessary but not sufficient. A more comprehensive assessment needs to be made of the company's overall competitive strength. The answers to two questions are of particular interest: First, how does the company rank relative to competitors on each of the important factors that determine market success? Second, all things considered, does the company have a net competitive advantage or disadvantage vis-à-vis major competitors?

An easy-to-use method for answering the two questions posed above involves developing quantitative strength ratings for the company and its key competitors on each industry key success factor and each competitively decisive resource capability. Much of the information needed for doing a competitive strength assessment comes from previous analyses. Industry and competitive analysis reveals the key success factors and competitive capabilities that separate industry winners from losers. Benchmarking data and scouting key competitors provide a basis for judging the competitive strength of rivals on such factors as cost, key product attributes, customer service, image and reputation, financial strength, technological skills, distribution capability, and other competitively important resources and capabilities. SWOT analysis reveals how the company in question stacks up on these same strength measures.

Step 1 in doing a competitive strength assessment is to make a list of the industry's key success factors and most telling measures of competitive strength or weakness (6 to 10 measures usually suffice). Step 2 is to rate the firm and its rivals on each factor. Numerical rating scales (e.g., from 1 to 10) are best to use, although ratings of stronger (+), weaker (−), and about equal (=) may be appropriate when information is scanty and assigning numerical scores conveys false precision. Step 3 is to sum the strength ratings on each factor to get an overall measure of competitive strength for each company being rated. Step 4 is to use the overall strength ratings to draw conclusions about the size and extent of the company's net competitive advantage or disadvantage and to take specific note of areas of strength and weakness.

Table 4.4 provides two examples of competitive strength assessment, using the hypothetical ABC Company against four rivals. The first example employs an *unweighted rating system*. With unweighted ratings, each key success factor/competitive strength measure is assumed to be equally important (a rather dubious assumption). Whichever company has the highest strength rating on a given measure has an implied competitive edge on that factor; the size of its edge is mirrored in the margin of difference between its rating and the ratings assigned to rivals—a rating of 9 for one company versus ratings of 5, 4, and 3, respectively, for three other companies indicates a bigger advantage than a rating of 9 versus ratings of 8, 7, and 6. Summing a company's ratings on all the measures produces an overall strength rating. The higher a company's overall strength rating, the stronger its overall competitiveness versus rivals. The bigger the difference between a company's overall rating and the scores of *lower-rated* rivals, the greater its implied *net competitive advantage*. Conversely, the bigger the difference between a company's overall rating and the scores of *higher-rated* rivals, the greater its implied *net competitive disadvantage*. Thus, ABC's total score of 61 (see the top half of Table 4.4) signals a much greater net competitive advantage over Rival 4 (with a score of 32) than over Rival 1 (with a score of 58) but indicates a moderate net competitive disadvantage against Rival 2 (with an overall score of 71).

However, a better method is a *weighted rating system* (shown in the bottom half of Table 4.4) because the different measures of competitive strength are unlikely to be equally important. In an industry where the products/services of rivals are virtually identical, for instance, having low unit costs relative to rivals is nearly always the most important determinant of competitive strength. In an industry with strong product differentiation, the most significant measures of competitive strength may be brand awareness, amount of advertising, product attractiveness, and distribution capability. In a weighted rating system each measure of competitive strength is assigned a weight based on its perceived importance in shaping competitive success. A weight could be as high as 0.75 (maybe even higher) in situations where one particular competitive variable is overwhelmingly decisive, or a weight could be as low as 0.20 when two or three strength measures are more important than the rest. Lesser competitive strength indicators can carry weights of 0.05 or 0.10. No matter whether the differences between the importance weights are big or little, *the sum of the weights must equal 1.0.*

> A weighted competitive strength analysis is conceptually stronger than an unweighted analysis because of the inherent weakness in assuming that all the strength measures are equally important.

table 4.4   **Illustrations of Unweighted and Weighted Competitive Strength Assessments**

A. Sample of an Unweighted Competitive Strength Assessment

Rating scale: 1 = Very weak; 10 = Very strong

Key Success Factor/Strength Measure	ABC Co.	Rival 1	Rival 2	Rival 3	Rival 4
Quality/product performance	8	5	10	1	6
Reputation/image	8	7	10	1	6
Manufacturing capability	2	10	4	5	1
Technological skills	10	1	7	3	8
Dealer network/distribution capability	9	4	10	5	1
New product innovation capability	9	4	10	5	1
Financial resources	5	10	7	3	1
Relative cost position	5	10	3	1	4
Customer service capabilities	5	7	10	1	4
Unweighted overall strength rating	61	58	71	25	32

B. Sample of a Weighted Competitive Strength Assessment

Rating scale: 1 = Very weak; 10 = Very strong

Key Success Factor/Strength Measure	Importance Weight	ABC Co. Rating/ Score	Rival 1 Rating/ Score	Rival 2 Rating/ Score	Rival 3 Rating/ Score	Rival 4 Rating/ Score
Quality/product performance	0.10	8/0.80	5/0.50	10/1.00	1/0.10	6/0.60
Reputation/image	0.10	8/0.80	7/0.70	10/1.00	1/0.10	6/0.60
Manufacturing capability	0.10	2/0.20	10/1.00	4/0.40	5/0.50	1/0.10
Technological skills	0.05	10/0.50	1/0.05	7/0.35	3/0.15	8/0.40
Dealer network/distribution capability	0.05	9/0.45	4/0.20	10/0.50	5/0.25	1/0.05
New product innovation capability	0.05	9/0.45	4/0.20	10/0.50	5/0.25	1/0.05
Financial resources	0.10	5/0.50	10/1.00	7/0.70	3/0.30	1/0.10
Relative cost position	0.30	5/1.50	10/3.00	3/0.95	1/0.30	4/1.20
Customer service capabilities	0.15	5/0.75	7/1.05	10/1.50	1/0.15	4/0.60
Sum of importance weights	1.00					
Weighted overall strength rating		5.95	7.70	6.85	2.10	3.70

Weighted strength ratings are calculated by rating each competitor on each strength measure (using the 1 to 10 rating scale) and multiplying the assigned rating by the assigned weight (a rating of 4 times a weight of 0.20 gives a weighted rating, or score, of 0.80). Again, the company with the highest rating on a given measure has an implied competitive edge on that measure, with the size of its edge reflected in the difference between its rating and rivals' ratings. The weight attached to the measure indicates how important the edge is. Summing a company's weighted strength ratings for all the measures yields an overall strength rating. Comparisons of the weighted overall strength scores indicate which competitors are in the strongest and weakest competitive positions and who has how big a net competitive advantage over whom.

Note in Table 4.4 that the unweighted and weighted rating schemes produce different orderings of the companies. In the weighted system, ABC Company drops from second to third in strength, and Rival 1 jumps from third into first because of its high strength ratings on the two most important factors. Weighting the importance of the strength measures can thus make a significant difference in the outcome of the assessment.

Competitive strength assessments provide useful conclusions about a company's competitive situation. The ratings show how a company compares against rivals, factor by factor or capability by capability, thus revealing where it is strongest and weakest, and against whom. Moreover, the overall competitive strength scores indicate how all the different factors add up— whether the company is at a net competitive advantage or disadvantage against each rival. The firm with the largest overall competitive strength rating enjoys the strongest competitive position, with the size of its net competitive advantage reflected by how much its score exceeds the scores of rivals.

> High competitive strength ratings signal a strong competitive position and possession of competitive advantage; low ratings signal a weak position and competitive disadvantage.

Knowing where a company is competitively strong and where it is weak in comparison to specific rivals is valuable in deciding on specific actions to strengthen its ability to compete. As a general rule, a company should try to leverage its competitive strengths (areas where it scores higher than rivals) into sustainable competitive advantage. Furthermore, it makes sense for the company to initiate actions to remedy its important competitive weaknesses (areas where its scores are below those of rivals); at the very least, it should try to narrow the gap against companies with higher strength ratings—when the leader is at 10, improving from a rating of 3 to a rating of 7 can be significant.

In addition, the competitive strength ratings point to which rival companies may be vulnerable to competitive attack and the areas where they are weakest. When a company has important competitive strengths in areas where one or more rivals are weak, it makes sense to consider offensive moves to exploit rivals' competitive weaknesses.

QUESTION 5: WHAT STRATEGIC ISSUES AND PROBLEMS MERIT FRONT-BURNER MANAGERIAL ATTENTION?

The final and most important analytical step is to zero in on exactly what strategic issues that company managers need to address—and resolve—for the company to be more financially and competitively successful in the years ahead. This step involves drawing on the results of both industry and competitive analysis and the evaluations of the company's own competitiveness. The task here is to get a clear fix on exactly what strategic and competitive challenges confront the company, which of the company's competitive shortcomings need to be corrected, what obstacles stand in the way of improving the company's competitive position in the marketplace, and what specific problems merit front-burner attention by company managers. *Pinpointing the precise problems that management needs to worry about sets the agenda for deciding what actions to take next to improve the company's performance and business outlook.*

> Zeroing in on the strategic issues a company faces and compiling a "worry list" of problems and roadblocks creates a strategic agenda of problems that merit prompt managerial attention.

The "worry list" of issues and problems can include such things as *how* to stave off market challenges from new foreign competitors, *how* to combat rivals' price discounting, *how* to reduce the company's high costs to pave the way for price reductions, *how* to sustain the company's present growth rate in light of slowing buyer demand, *whether* to expand the company's product line, *whether* to acquire a rival company to correct the company's competitive deficiencies, *whether* to expand into foreign markets rapidly or cautiously, *whether* to reposition the company and move to a different strategic group, and *what to do* about the aging demographics of the company's customer base.

> A good strategy must contain ways to deal with all the strategic issues and obstacles that stand in the way of the company's financial and competitive success in the years ahead.

If the worry list is relatively minor, suggesting the company's strategy is mostly on track and reasonably well matched to the company's overall situation, managers will seldom need to go much beyond fine-tuning of the present strategy. If, however, the issues and problems confronting the company are serious—indicating the present strategy is not well suited for the road ahead—the task of crafting a better strategy has to go to the top of management's action agenda.

key|points

There are five key questions to consider in analyzing a company's own particular competitive circumstances and its competitive position vis-à-vis key rivals:

1. *How well is the present strategy working?* This involves evaluating the strategy from a qualitative standpoint (completeness, internal consistency, rationale, and suitability to the situation) and also from a quantitative standpoint (the strategic and financial results the strategy is producing). The stronger a company's current overall performance, the less likely the need for radical strategy changes. The weaker a company's performance and/or the faster the changes in its external situation (which can be gleaned from industry and competitive analysis), the more its current strategy must be questioned.

2. *What are the company's resource strengths and weaknesses, and its external opportunities and threats?* A **SWOT analysis** provides an overview of a firm's situation and is an essential component of crafting a strategy tightly matched to the company's situation. The two most important parts of SWOT analysis are (1) drawing conclusions about what story the compilation of strengths, weaknesses, opportunities, and threats tells about the company's overall situation, and (2) acting on those conclusions to better match the company's strategy to its resource strengths and market opportunities, to correct the important weaknesses, and to defend against external threats. A company's resource strengths (which include its **competencies, core competencies,** and **distinctive competencies**) and competitive capabilities are strategically relevant because they are the most logical and appealing building blocks for strategy; resource weaknesses are important because they may represent vulnerabilities that need correction. External opportunities and threats come into play because a good strategy necessarily aims at capturing a company's most attractive opportunities and at defending against threats to its well-being.

3. *Are the company's prices and costs competitive?* One telling sign of whether a company's situation is strong or precarious is whether its prices and costs are competitive with those of industry rivals. **Value chain** analysis and **benchmarking** are essential tools in determining whether the company is performing particular functions and activities cost-effectively, learning whether its costs are in line with competitors, and deciding which internal activities and business processes need to be scrutinized for improvement. Value chain analysis teaches that how competently a

company manages its value chain activities relative to rivals is a key to building valuable competencies and competitive capabilities and then leveraging them into sustainable competitive advantage.

4. *Is the company competitively stronger or weaker than key rivals?* The key appraisals here involve how the company matches up against key rivals on industry key success factors and other chief determinants of competitive success and whether and why the company has a competitive advantage or disadvantage. Quantitative competitive strength assessments, using the method presented in Table 4.4, indicate where a company is competitively strong and weak, and provide insight into the company's ability to defend or enhance its market position. As a rule a company's competitive strategy should be built around its competitive strengths and should aim at shoring up areas where it is competitively vulnerable. Also, the areas where company strengths match up against competitor weaknesses represent the best potential for new offensive initiatives.

5. *What strategic issues and problems merit front-burner managerial attention?* This analytical step zeros in on the strategic issues and problems that stand in the way of the company's success. It involves using the results of both industry and competitive analysis and company situation analysis to identify a "worry list" of issues to be resolved for the company to be financially and competitively successful in the years ahead.

Good company situation analysis, like good industry and competitive analysis, is a valuable precondition for good strategy making. A competently done evaluation of a company's resource capabilities and competitive strengths exposes strong and weak points in the present strategy and how attractive or unattractive the company's competitive position is and why. Managers need such understanding to craft a strategy that is well suited to the company's competitive circumstances.

| exercise

Review the information in Illustration Capsule 4.1 concerning the costs of the different value chain activities associated with recording and distributing music CDs through traditional brick-and-mortar retail outlets. Then answer the following questions:

1. Does the growing popularity of downloading music from the Internet give rise to a new music industry value chain that differs considerably from the traditional value chain? Explain why or why not.

2. What costs are being cut out of the traditional value chain or bypassed as recording studios begin to sell downloadable files of artists' recordings and buyers make their own custom CDs (or play music directly from their PCs)?

3. How much more cost-effective is the value chain for selling downloadable files direct to consumers than the traditional industry value chain?

4. What do you think the growing popularity of downloading music from the Internet is doing to the competitiveness and future business prospects of brick-and-mortar retail music chains?

The Five Generic Competitive Strategies

Which One to Employ?

(©Photowood Inc./CORBIS)

Competitive strategy is about being different. It means deliberately choosing to perform activities differently or to perform different activities than rivals to deliver a unique mix of value.

—**Michael E. Porter**

Strategy . . . is about first analyzing and then experimenting, trying, learning, and experimenting some more.

—**Ian C. McMillan and Rita Gunther McGrath**

The essence of strategy lies in creating tomorrow's competitive advantages faster than competitors mimic the ones you possess today.

—**Gary Hamel and C. K. Prahalad**

T his chapter describes the five *basic competitive strategy options*—which of the five to employ is a company's first and foremost choice in crafting an overall strategy and beginning its quest for competitive advantage. By **competitive strategy** we mean the specifics of management's game plan for competing successfully—how it plans to position the company in the marketplace, its specific efforts to please customers and improve its competitive strength, and the type of competitive advantage it wants to establish. Companies the world over are imaginative in conceiving competitive strategies to win customer favor. At most companies the aim, quite simply, is to do a better job of providing what buyers are looking for and thereby gain the upper hand over rivals.

> **core concept**
> A *competitive strategy* concerns the specifics of management's game plan for competing successfully and achieving a competitive edge over rivals.

A company achieves competitive advantage whenever it has some type of edge over rivals in attracting buyers and coping with competitive forces. There are many routes to competitive advantage, but they all involve giving buyers what they perceive as superior value—a good product at a low price; a superior product that is worth paying more for; or a best-value offering that represents an attractive combination of price, features, quality, service, and other appealing attributes. Delivering superior value—whatever form it takes—nearly always requires performing value chain activities differently than rivals and building competencies and resource capabilities that are not readily matched.

THE FIVE GENERIC COMPETITIVE STRATEGIES

There are countless variations in the competitive strategies that companies employ, mainly because each company's strategic approach entails custom-designed actions to fit its own circumstances and industry environment. The custom-tailored nature of each company's strategy makes the chances remote that any two companies—even companies in the same industry—will employ strategies that are exactly alike in every detail. Managers at different companies always have a slightly different spin on future market conditions and how to best align their company's strategy with these conditions; moreover, they have different notions of how they intend to outmaneuver rivals and what strategic options make the most sense for their particular company. However, when one strips away the details to get at the real substance, the biggest and most important differences among competitive strategies boil down to (1) whether a company's market target is broad or narrow, and (2) whether the company is pursuing a competitive advantage linked to low costs or product differentiation. Five distinct competitive strategy approaches stand out:[1]

1. *A low-cost provider strategy*—appealing to a broad spectrum of customers by being the overall low-cost provider of a product or service.

2. *A broad differentiation strategy*—seeking to differentiate the company's product/service offering from rivals' in ways that will appeal to a broad spectrum of buyers.

3. *A best-cost provider strategy*—giving customers more value for the money by incorporating good-to-excellent product attributes at a lower cost than rivals; the target is to have the lowest (best) costs and prices compared to rivals offering products with comparable attributes.

4. *A focused (or market niche) strategy based on lower cost*—concentrating on a narrow buyer segment and outcompeting rivals by serving niche members at a lower cost than rivals.

5. *A focused (or market niche) strategy based on differentiation*—concentrating on a narrow buyer segment and outcompeting rivals by offering niche members customized attributes that meet their tastes and requirements better than rivals' products.

Each of these five generic competitive approaches stakes out a different market position, as shown in Figure 5.1. Each involves distinctly different approaches to competing and operating the business. The remainder of this chapter explores these five types of competitive strategies and how they differ.

figure 5.1 **The Five Generic Competitive Strategies—Each Stakes Out a Different Position in the Marketplace**

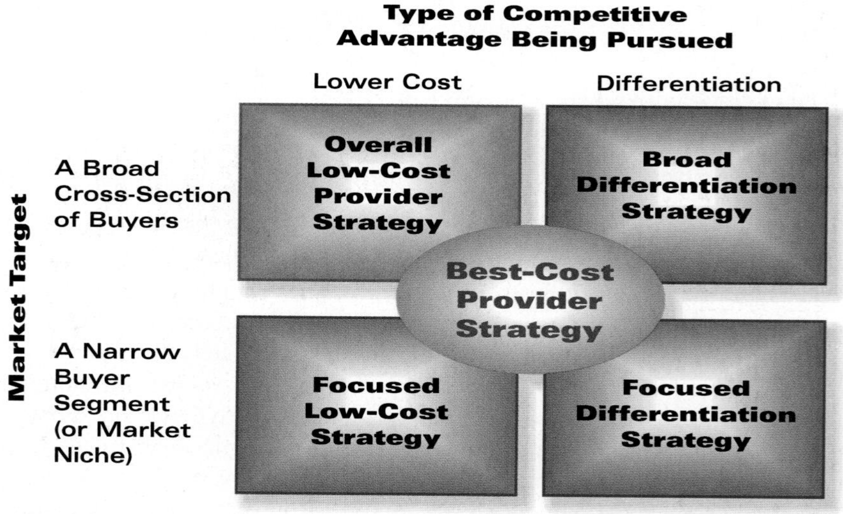

Source: Adapted from Michael E. Porter, *Competitive Strategy: Techniques for Analyzing Industries and Competitors* (New York: Free Press, 1980), pp. 35–40.

LOW-COST PROVIDER STRATEGIES

A company achieves low-cost leadership when it becomes the industry's lowest-cost provider rather than just being one of perhaps several competitors with comparatively low costs. A low-cost provider's strategic target is meaningfully lower costs than rivals—but not necessarily the absolute lowest possible cost. In striving for a cost advantage over rivals, managers must take care to include features and services that buyers consider essential—*a product offering that is too frills-free sabotages the attractiveness of the company's product and can turn buyers off even if it is cheaper than competing products.* For maximum effectiveness, companies employing a low-cost provider strategy need to achieve their cost advantage in ways difficult for rivals to copy or match. If rivals find it relatively easy or inexpensive to imitate the leader's low-cost methods, then the leader's advantage will be too short-lived to yield a valuable edge in the marketplace.

> **core concept**
> A low-cost leader's basis for competitive advantage is lower overall costs than competitors. Successful low-cost leaders are exceptionally good at finding ways to drive costs out of their businesses.

A company has two options for translating a low-cost advantage over rivals into attractive profit performance. Option 1 is to use the lower-cost edge to underprice competitors and attract price-sensitive buyers in great enough numbers to increase total profits. The trick to profitably underpricing rivals is either to keep the size of the price cut smaller than the size of the firm's cost advantage (thus reaping the benefits of both a bigger profit margin per unit sold and the added profits on incremental sales) or to generate enough added volume to increase total profits despite thinner profit margins (larger volume can make up for smaller margins provided the underpricing of rivals brings in enough extra sales). Option 2 is to maintain the present price, be content with the present market share, and use the lower-cost edge to earn a higher profit margin on each unit sold, thereby raising the firm's total profits and overall return on investment. Illustration Capsule 5.1 describes Nucor Corporation's strategy for gaining low-cost leadership in manufacturing a variety of steel products.

The Two Major Avenues for Achieving a Cost Advantage

To achieve a cost advantage, a firm must make sure that its cumulative costs across its overall value chain are lower than competitors' cumulative costs. There are two ways to accomplish this:[2]

1. Outmanage rivals in the efficiency with which value chain activities are performed and in controlling the factors that drive the costs of value chain activities.

2. Revamp the firm's overall value chain to eliminate or bypass some cost-producing activities.

Let's look at each of the two approaches to securing a cost advantage.

Controlling the Cost Drivers   There are nine major cost drivers that come into play in determining a company's costs in each activity segment of the value chain:[3]

1. *Economies or diseconomies of scale*—The costs of a particular value chain activity are often subject to economies or diseconomies of scale. Economies of scale arise whenever activities can be performed more cheaply at larger volumes than smaller volumes and from the ability to spread out certain costs like R&D and advertising over a greater sales volume. Astute management of activities subject to

illustration capsule 5.1
Nucor Corporation's Low-Cost Provider Strategy

Nucor Corporation is the world's leading minimill producer of such steel products as rolled steel, finished steel, steel joists, joist girders, steel decks, and grinding balls. It has close to $6 billion in sales and annual production capacity of 18.6 million tons, making it one of the three largest steel companies in the United States. The company has pursued a strategy that has made it among the lowest-cost producers of steel in the world and has allowed the company to consistently outperform its rivals in terms of sales growth and financial performance.

Nucor's low-cost strategy aims to give it a cost and pricing advantage in the commodity-like steel industry and leaves no part of the company's value chain neglected. The key elements of the strategy include the following:

- Using electric arc furnaces to melt scrap steel and directly reduced iron ore and then conveying the molten metal to a continuous caster and rolling mill to be shaped into steel products, thereby eliminating an assortment of production processes from the value chain used by traditional integrated steel mills. Nucor's minimill value chain makes the use of coal, coke, and iron ore unnecessary; cuts investment in facilities and equipment (eliminating coke ovens, blast furnaces, basic oxygen furnaces, and ingot casters); and requires fewer employees than integrated mills.

- Striving hard for continuous improvement in the efficiency of its plants and frequently investing in state-of-the-art equipment to reduce unit costs. Nucor is known for its technological leadership and its aggressive pursuit of innovation.

- Carefully selecting plant sites to minimize inbound and outbound shipping costs and to take advantage of low rates for electricity (electric arc furnaces are heavy users of electricity). Nucor also avoids geographic areas where labor unions are a strong influence.

- Hiring a nonunion workforce that uses team-based incentive compensation systems (often opposed by unions). Operating and maintenance employees and supervisors are paid weekly bonuses based on the productivity of their work group. The size of the bonus is based on the capabilities of the equipment employed and ranges from 80 percent to 150 percent of an employee's base pay; no bonus is paid if the equipment is not operating. Nucor's compensation program has boosted the company's labor productivity to levels nearly double the industry average while rewarding productive employees with annual compensation packages that exceed what their union counterparts earn by as much as 20 percent. Nucor has been able to attract and retain highly talented, productive, and dedicated employees. In addition, the company's results-oriented culture and self-managed work teams allow the company to employ fewer supervisors than what would be needed with an hourly union workforce.

- Heavily emphasizing consistent product quality and maintaining rigorous quality systems.

- Minimizing general and administrative expenses by maintaining a lean staff at corporate headquarters (fewer than 125 employees) and allowing only four levels of management between the CEO and production workers. Headquarters offices are modestly furnished and located in an inexpensive building. The company minimizes reports, paperwork, and meetings to keep managers focused on value-adding activities. Nucor is noted not only for its streamlined organizational structure but also for its frugality in travel and entertainment expenses—the company's top managers set the example by flying coach class, avoiding pricey hotels, and refraining from taking customers out for expensive dinners.

In 2001–2002, when many U.S. producers of steel products were in dire economic straits because of weak demand for steel and deep price-discounting by foreign rivals, Nucor began acquiring state-of-the-art steelmaking facilities from bankrupt or nearly bankrupt rivals at bargain-basement prices, often at 20 to 25 percent of what it cost to construct the facilities. This gave Nucor much lower depreciation costs than rivals with comparable plants.

Nucor management's outstanding execution of its low-cost strategy and its commitment to drive out non-value-adding costs throughout its value chain has allowed it to grow at a considerably faster rate than its integrated steel mill rivals and maintain high industry-relative profit margins while aggressively competing on price.

Source: Company annual reports, news releases, and Web site.

scale economies or diseconomies can be a major source of cost savings. For example, manufacturing economies can usually be achieved by simplifying the product line, scheduling longer production runs for fewer models, and using common parts and components in different models. In global industries, making separate products for each country market instead of selling a mostly standard product worldwide tends to boost unit costs because of lost time in model changeover, shorter production runs, and inability to reach the most economic scale of production for each country model.

2. *Learning-curve effects*—The cost of performing an activity can decline over time as the experience of company personnel builds. Learning-curve economies can stem from debugging and mastering newly introduced technologies, finding ways to improve plant layout and work flows, and making product design modifications that streamline the assembly process. Speed and knowledge accrue from repeatedly siting and building new plants, retail outlets, or distribution centers. Aggressively managed low-cost providers pay diligent attention to capturing the benefits of learning and experience and to keeping the benefits proprietary to whatever extent possible.

3. *The cost of key resource inputs*—The cost of performing value chain activities depends in part on what a firm has to pay for key resource inputs. Competitors do not all incur the same costs for items purchased from suppliers or for other resources. How well a company manages the costs of acquiring key resource inputs is often a big driver of costs. Input costs are a function of four factors:

   - *Union versus nonunion labor*—Avoiding the use of union labor is often a key to keeping labor input costs low, not just because unions demand high wages but also because union work rules can stifle productivity. Such highly regarded low-cost manufacturers as Nucor and Cooper Tire are noted for their incentive compensation systems that promote very high levels of labor productivity—at both companies, nonunion workers earn more than their unionized counterparts at rival companies, but their high productivity results in lower labor costs per unit produced.

   - *Bargaining power vis-à-vis suppliers*—Many large enterprises (e.g., Wal-Mart, Home Depot, the world's major motor vehicle producers) have used their bargaining clout in purchasing large volumes to wrangle good prices on their purchases from suppliers. Having greater buying power than rivals can be an important source of cost advantage.

   - *Locational variables*—Locations differ in their prevailing wage levels, tax rates, energy costs, inbound and outbound shipping and freight costs, and so on. Opportunities may exist for reducing costs by relocating plants, field offices, warehousing, or headquarters operations.

   - *Supply chain management expertise*—Some companies have more efficient supply chain expertise than others and are able to squeeze out cost savings via partnerships with suppliers that lower the costs of purchased materials and components, e-procurement systems, and inbound logistics.

4. *Links with other activities in the company or industry value chain*—When the cost of one activity is affected by how other activities are performed, costs can be managed downward by making sure that linked activities are performed in cooperative and coordinated fashion. For example, when a company's materials inventory costs

or warranty costs are linked to the activities of suppliers, cost savings can be achieved by working cooperatively with key suppliers on the design of parts and components, quality-assurance procedures, just-in-time delivery, and integrated materials supply. The costs of new product development can often be managed downward by setting up cross-functional task forces (perhaps including representatives of suppliers and key customers) to work on R&D, product design, manufacturing plans, and market launch. Links with forward channels tend to center on location of warehouses, materials handling, outbound shipping, and packaging. Nail manufacturers, for example, learned that delivering nails in prepackaged 1-pound, 5-pound, and 10-pound assortments instead of 100-pound bulk cartons could reduce a hardware dealer's labor costs in filling individual customer orders. The lesson here is that effective coordination of linked activities anywhere in the value chain holds potential for cost reduction.

5. *Sharing opportunities with other organizational or business units within the enterprise*—Different product lines or business units within an enterprise can often share the same order processing and customer billing systems, maintain a common sales force to call on customers, share the same warehouse and distribution facilities, or rely on a common customer service and technical support team. Such combining of like activities and sharing of resources across sister units can create significant cost savings. Furthermore, there are times when the know-how gained in one division or geographic unit can be used to help lower costs in another; sharing know-how across organizational lines has significant cost-saving potential when cross-unit value chain activities are similar and know-how is readily transferred from one unit to another.

6. *The benefits of vertical integration versus outsourcing*—Vertical integration (expanding backward into sources of supply, forward toward end users, or both) allows a firm to bypass suppliers or buyers with considerable bargaining power. Vertical integration, forward or backward, also has potential if there are significant cost savings from having a single firm perform adjacent activities in the industry value chain. But more often it is cheaper to outsource, or hire outside specialists to perform certain functions and activities, since by virtue of their expertise and volume these specialists can perform the activities/functions more cheaply than the company can perform them in-house.

7. *First-mover advantages and disadvantages*—Sometimes the first major brand in the market is able to establish and maintain its brand name at a lower cost than later brand arrivals. Competitors looking to go head-to-head against such first-movers as eBay, Yahoo, and Amazon.com have to spend heavily to come close to achieving the same brand awareness and name recognition. On other occasions, such as when technology is developing fast, late-purchasers can benefit from waiting to install second- or third-generation equipment that is both cheaper and more efficient; first-generation users often incur added costs associated with debugging and learning how to use an immature and unperfected technology. Likewise, companies that follow rather than lead new product development efforts sometimes avoid many of the costs that pioneers incur in performing pathbreaking R&D and opening up new markets.

8. *The percentage of capacity utilization*—Capacity utilization is a big cost driver for those value chain activities associated with substantial fixed costs. Higher rates of capacity utilization allow depreciation and other fixed costs to be spread over a larger unit volume, thereby lowering fixed costs per unit. The more capital-

intensive the business, or the higher the percentage of fixed costs as a percentage of total costs, the more important this cost driver becomes because there's such a stiff unit-cost penalty for underutilizing existing capacity. In such cases, finding ways to operate close to full capacity year-round can be an important source of cost advantage.

9. *Strategic choices and operating decisions*—A company's costs can be driven up or down by a fairly wide assortment of managerial decisions:

   - Adding/cutting the services provided to buyers.
   - Incorporating more/fewer performance and quality features into the product.
   - Increasing/decreasing the number of different channels utilized in distributing the firm's product.
   - Lengthening/shortening delivery times to customers.
   - Putting more/less emphasis than rivals on the use of incentive compensation, wage increases, and fringe benefits to motivate employees and boost worker productivity.
   - Raising/lowering the specifications for purchased materials.

For a company to outmanage rivals in performing value chain activities cost-effectively, its managers must possess a sophisticated understanding of the factors that drive the costs of each activity. And then they must not only use their knowledge about the cost drivers to squeeze out cost savings all along the value chain but also be so much more ingenious and committed than rivals in achieving cost-saving efficiencies that the company ends up with a sustainable cost advantage.

> Outperforming rivals in controlling the factors that drive costs is a very demanding managerial exercise.

Revamping the Value Chain   Dramatic cost advantages can emerge from finding innovative ways to eliminate or bypass cost-producing value chain activities. The primary ways companies can achieve a cost advantage by reconfiguring their value chains include:

- *Making greater use of Internet technology applications*—In recent years the Internet has become a powerful and pervasive tool for reengineering company and industry value chains. For instance, Internet technology has revolutionized supply chain management. Using software packages from any of several vendors, company procurement personnel can—with only a few mouse clicks within one seamless system—check materials inventories against incoming customer orders, check suppliers' stocks, check the latest prices for parts and components at auction and e-sourcing Web sites, and check FedEx delivery schedules. Electronic data interchange software permits the relevant details of incoming customer orders to be instantly shared with the suppliers of needed parts and components. All this lays the foundation for just-in-time deliveries of parts and components, and for the production of parts and components to be matched closely to assembly-plant requirements and production schedules—and such coordination produces savings for both suppliers and manufacturers. Via the Internet, manufacturers can collaborate closely with parts and components suppliers in designing new products and reducing the time it takes to get them into production. Warranty claims and product performance problems involving supplier components can be made available instantly to the relevant suppliers so that corrections can be expedited. Various e-procurement software packages streamline the purchasing process by eliminating much of the manual handling of data and by substituting electronic communication for paper documents such as requests for quotations, purchase orders, order acceptances, and shipping notices.

Manufacturers are using Internet applications to link customer orders to production at their plants and to deliveries of components from suppliers. Real-time sharing of customer orders with suppliers facilitates just-in-time deliveries of parts and slices parts inventory costs. It also allows both manufacturers and their suppliers to gear production to match demand for both components and finished goods. Online systems that monitor actual sales permit more accurate demand forecasting, thereby helping both manufacturers and their suppliers adjust their production schedules as swings in buyer demand are detected. Data sharing, starting with customer orders and going all the way back to components production, coupled with the use of enterprise resource planning (ERP) and manufacturing execution system (MES) software, can make custom manufacturing just as cheap as mass production—and sometimes cheaper. It can also greatly reduce production times and labor costs. J. D. Edwards, a specialist in ERP software, teamed with Camstar Systems, a specialist in MES software, to cut Lexmark's production time for inkjet printers from four hours to 24 minutes.

The instant communications features of the Internet, combined with all the real-time data sharing and information availability, have the further effect of breaking down corporate bureaucracies and reducing overhead costs. The whole "back-office" data management process (order processing, invoicing, customer accounting, and other kinds of transaction costs) can be handled fast, accurately, and with less paperwork and fewer personnel. The time savings and transaction cost reductions associated with doing business online can be quite significant across both company and industry value chains. Illustration Capsule 5.2 describes how one company is using Internet technology to improve both the effectiveness and the efficiency of the activities comprising its potato chip business.

- *Using direct-to-end-user sales and marketing approaches*—Costs in the wholesale/retail portions of the value chain frequently represent 35–50 percent of the price final consumers pay. Software developers are increasingly using the Internet to market and deliver their products directly to buyers; allowing customers to download software directly from the Internet eliminates the costs of producing and packaging CDs and cuts out the host of activities, costs, and markups associated with shipping and distributing software through wholesale and retail channels. By cutting all these costs and activities out of the value chain, software developers have the pricing room to boost their profit margins and still sell their products below levels that retailers would have to charge. The major airlines have stopped paying commissions to travel agents on ticket sales, thereby saving hundreds of millions of dollars in commissions. Airlines now sell most of their tickets directly to passengers via their Web sites, ticket counter agents, and telephone reservation systems.

- *Simplifying product design*—Using computer-assisted design techniques, reducing the number of parts, standardizing parts and components across models and styles, and shifting to an easy-to-manufacture product design can all simplify the value chain.

- *Stripping away the extras*—Offering only basic products or services can help a company cut costs associated with multiple features and options. Stripping extras is a favorite technique of the no-frills airlines like Southwest Airlines.

illustration capsule 5.2
Utz Quality Foods' Use of Internet Technology to Reengineer Value Chain Activities

Utz Quality Foods, the number three maker of salty snacks in the United States, with annual sales of over $200 million, recently implemented an Internet-based sales-tracking system called UtzFocus that monitors sales of the company's chips and pretzel products at each supermarket and convenience store that carries the brand. The 500 drivers/salespeople who deliver Utz snacks directly to retail stores scattered from Massachusetts to North Carolina use handheld computers to upload daily sales data (product by product and store by store) to headquarters. Managers carefully monitor the results to spot missed deliveries, pinpoint stores with lagging sales, and measure the effectiveness of special promotions.

The UtzFocus system also keeps delivery personnel up-to-date on which stores are running specials on Utz products so that drivers can make sure they have ample supplies of the right products on their trucks—and since drivers get a 10 percent commission on sales, they have a stake in making UtzFocus work. The company has also installed machines with monitoring capabilities in all of its plants, and efforts are under way to hook them up to the company's intranet to generate real-time data on the usage of ingredients, measure how close chip-slicing machines are coming to the ideal thickness of 0.057 of an inch, track how many bags of chips the main factory's seven lines are turning out, and keep inventories of ingredients and plastic bags matched to production and sales requirements. This reengineering of the value chain has produced cost-saving efficiencies, improved the effectiveness of Utz's operations, and helped boost sales.

Source: Timothy J. Mullaney, "Using the Net to Stay Crisp: How Utz Tracks Its Snacks from Oven to Grocery Shelf," *Business Week,* April 16, 2001, p. EB34.

- *Shifting to a simpler, less capital-intensive, or more streamlined or flexible technological process*—Computer-assisted design and manufacture, or other flexible manufacturing systems, can accommodate both low-cost efficiency and product customization.

- *Bypassing the use of high-cost raw materials or component parts*—High-cost raw materials and parts can be designed out of the product.

- *Relocating facilities*—Moving plants closer to suppliers, customers, or both can help curtail inbound and outbound logistics costs.

- *Dropping the "something for everyone" approach*—Pruning slow-selling items from the product lineup and being content to meet the needs of most buyers rather than all buyers can eliminate activities and costs associated with numerous product versions.

Examples of Companies That Created New Value Chain Systems and Reduced Costs   One example of accruing significant cost advantages from creating altogether new value chain systems can be found in the beef-packing industry. The traditional cost chain involved raising cattle on scattered farms and ranches, shipping them live to labor-intensive unionized slaughtering plants, and then transporting whole sides of beef to grocery retailers whose butcher departments cut them into smaller pieces and packaged them for sale to grocery shoppers. Iowa Beef Packers revamped the traditional chain with a radically different strategy—large automated plants employing nonunion workers were built near economically transportable supplies of cattle, and the meat was partially butchered at the processing plant into small, high-yield cuts (sometimes sealed in plastic casing ready for purchase) before being boxed and shipped to retailers. Iowa Beef's inbound cattle transportation expenses, traditionally a major cost item, were cut significantly by avoiding the weight losses that occurred when live animals were shipped long distances; major outbound shipping cost savings were achieved by not having to ship whole sides of beef, which had a high waste factor. The company's strategy was so successful that Iowa Beef became the largest U.S. meat-packer, surpassing the former industry leaders, Swift, Wilson, and Armour.[4]

Southwest Airlines has reconfigured the traditional value chain of commercial airlines to lower costs and thereby offers dramatically lower fares to passengers. Its mastery of fast turnarounds at the gates (about 25 minutes versus 45 minutes for rivals) allows its planes to fly more hours per day; by scheduling more flights per day with fewer aircraft, Southwest achieves greater utilization of its investment in aircraft. Southwest chose not to offer in-flight meals, assigned seating, baggage transfer to connecting airlines, or first-class seating and service, thereby eliminating all the cost-producing activities associated with these features. The company's online reservation system and e-ticketing capability encourage customers to bypass travel agents and also reduce staffing requirements at telephone reservation centers. Its use of automated check-in equipment reduces staffing requirements at terminal check-in counters.

Dell Computer has proved a pioneer in redesigning its value chain architecture in assembling and marketing personal computers (PCs). Whereas Dell's major rivals (Compaq, Hewlett-Packard, Sony, and Toshiba) produce their models in volume and sell them through independent resellers and retailers, Dell has elected to market directly to customers, building its PCs as customers order them and shipping them to customers within a few days of receiving the order. Dell's value chain approach has proved cost-effective in coping with the PC industry's blink-of-an-eye product life cycle. The build-to-order strategy enables the company to avoid misjudging buyer demand for its various models and being saddled with quickly obsolete excess components and finished-goods inventories. Also, Dell's sell-direct strategy slices reseller/retailer costs and margins out of the value chain (although some of these savings are offset by the cost of Dell's direct marketing and customer support activities—functions that would otherwise be performed by resellers and retailers). Partnerships with suppliers that facilitate just-in-time deliveries of components and minimize Dell's inventory costs, coupled with Dell's extensive use of e-commerce technologies further reduce Dell's costs. Dell's value chain approach is widely considered to have made it the global low-cost leader in the PC industry.

The Keys to Success in Achieving Low-Cost Leadership

> Success in achieving a low-cost edge over rivals comes from exploring all the avenues for cost reduction and pressing for continuous cost reductions across all aspects of the company's value chain year after year.

To succeed with a low-cost-provider strategy, company managers have to scrutinize each cost-creating activity and determine what drives its cost. Then they have to use this knowledge about the cost drivers to manage the costs of each activity downward, exhaustively pursuing cost savings throughout the value chain. They have to be proactive in restructuring the value chain to eliminate nonessential work steps and low-value activities. Normally, low-cost producers work diligently to create cost-conscious corporate cultures that feature broad employee participation in continuous cost-improvement efforts and limited perks and frills for executives. They strive to operate with exceptionally small corporate staffs to keep administrative costs to a minimum. Many successful low-cost leaders also benchmark costs against best-in-class performers of an activity to keep close tabs on how well they are doing at cost control.

But while low-cost providers are champions of frugality, they are usually aggressive in investing in resources and capabilities that promise to drive costs out of the business. Wal-Mart, one of the foremost practitioners of low-cost leadership, employs state-of-the-art technology throughout its operations—its distribution facilities are an automated showcase, it uses online systems to order goods from suppliers and manage inventories, it equips its stores with cutting-edge sales-tracking and check-out systems, and it operates a private satellite communications system that daily sends point-of-sale data to 4,000 vendors. Wal-Mart's information and communications systems and capabilities are more sophisticated than those of virtually any other retail chain in the world.

Other companies noted for their successful use of low-cost provider strategies include Lincoln Electric in arc welding equipment, Briggs & Stratton in small gasoline engines, Bic in ballpoint pens, Black & Decker in power tools, Stride Rite in footwear, Beaird-Poulan in chain saws, and General Electric and Whirlpool in major home appliances.

When a Low-Cost Provider Strategy Works Best

A competitive strategy predicated on low-cost leadership is particularly powerful when:

1. *Price competition among rival sellers is especially vigorous*—Low-cost providers are in the best position to compete offensively on the basis of price, to use the appeal of lower price to grab sales (and market share) from rivals, to remain profitable in the face of strong price competition, and to survive price wars.

2. *The products of rival sellers are essentially identical and supplies are readily available from any of several eager sellers*—Commodity-like products and/or ample supplies set the stage for lively price competition; in such markets, it is less efficient, higher-cost companies whose profits get squeezed the most.

3. *There are few ways to achieve product differentiation that have value to buyers*—When the differences between brands do not matter much to buyers, buyers are nearly always very sensitive to price differences and shop the market for the best price.

4. *Most buyers use the product in the same ways*—With common user requirements, a standardized product can satisfy the needs of buyers, in which case low selling price, not features or quality, becomes the dominant factor in causing buyers to choose one seller's product over another's.

5. *Buyers incur low costs in switching their purchases from one seller to another*—Low switching costs give buyers the flexibility to shift purchases to lower-priced sellers having equally good products or to attractively priced substitute products. A low-cost leader is well positioned to use low price to induce its customers not to switch to rival brands or substitutes.

6. *Buyers are large and have significant power to bargain down prices*—Low-cost providers have partial profit-margin protection in bargaining with high-volume buyers, since powerful buyers are rarely able to bargain price down past the survival level of the next most cost-efficient seller.

7. *Industry newcomers use introductory low prices to attract buyers and build a customer base*—The low-cost leader can use price cuts of its own to make it harder for a new rival to win customers; the pricing power of the low-cost provider acts as a barrier for new entrants.

> A low-cost provider is in the best position to win the business of price-sensitive buyers, set the floor on market price, and still earn a profit.

As a rule, the more price-sensitive buyers are, the more appealing a low-cost strategy becomes. A low-cost company's ability to set the industry's price floor and still earn a profit erects protective barriers around its market position.

The Pitfalls of a Low-Cost Provider Strategy

Perhaps the biggest pitfall of a low-cost provider strategy is getting carried away with overly aggressive price cutting and ending up with lower, rather than higher, profitability. A low-cost/low-price advantage results in superior profitability only if (1) prices are cut by less than the size of the cost advantage or (2) the added gains in unit sales are large enough to bring in a bigger total profit despite lower margins per unit sold. A company with a 5 percent cost advantage cannot cut prices 20 percent, end up with a volume gain of only 10 percent, and still expect to earn higher profits!

A second big pitfall is not emphasizing avenues of cost advantage that can be kept proprietary or that relegate rivals to playing catch-up. The value of a cost advantage depends on its sustainability. Sustainability, in turn, hinges on whether the company achieves its cost advantage in ways difficult for rivals to copy or match.

> A low-cost provider's product offering must always contain enough attributes to be attractive to prospective buyers—low price, by itself, is not always appealing to buyers.

A third pitfall is becoming too fixated on cost reduction. Low cost cannot be pursued so zealously that a firm's offering ends up being too features-poor to generate buyer appeal. Furthermore, a company driving hard to push its costs down has to guard against misreading or ignoring increased buyer interest in added features or service, declining buyer sensitivity to price, or new developments that start to alter how buyers use the product. A low-cost zealot risks losing market ground if buyers start opting for more upscale or features-rich products.

Even if these mistakes are avoided, a low-cost competitive approach still carries risk. Cost-saving technological breakthroughs or the emergence of still-lower-cost value chain models can nullify a low-cost leader's hard-won position. The current leader may have difficulty in shifting quickly to the new technologies or value chain approaches because heavy investments lock it in (at least temporarily) to its present value chain approach.

DIFFERENTIATION STRATEGIES

> **core concept**
> The essence of a broad differentiation strategy is to be unique in ways that are valuable to a wide range of customers.

Differentiation strategies are attractive whenever buyers' needs and preferences are too diverse to be fully satisfied by a standardized product or by sellers with identical capabilities. A company attempting to succeed through differentiation must study buyers' needs and behavior carefully to learn what buyers consider important, what they think has value, and what they are willing to pay for. Then the company has to incorporate buyer-desired attributes into its product or service offering that will clearly set it apart from rivals. Competitive advantage results once a sufficient number of buyers become strongly attached to the differentiated attributes.

Successful differentiation allows a firm to:

- Command a premium price for its product, and/or
- Increase unit sales (because additional buyers are won over by the differentiating features), and/or

- Gain buyer loyalty to its brand (because some buyers are strongly attracted to the differentiating features and bond with the company and its products).

Differentiation enhances profitability whenever the extra price the product commands outweighs the added costs of achieving the differentiation. Company differentiation strategies fail when buyers don't value the brand's uniqueness and/or when a company's approach to differentiation is easily copied or matched by its rivals.

Types of Differentiation Themes

Companies can pursue differentiation from many angles: a unique taste (Dr Pepper, Listerine); multiple features (Microsoft Windows, Microsoft Office); wide selection and one-stop shopping (Home Depot, Amazon.com); superior service (FedEx); spare parts availability (Caterpillar guarantees 48-hour spare parts delivery to any customer anywhere in the world or else the part is furnished free); engineering design and performance (Mercedes, BMW); prestige and distinctiveness (Rolex); product reliability (Johnson & Johnson in baby products); quality manufacture (Karastan in carpets, Michelin in tires, Honda in automobiles); technological leadership (3M Corporation in bonding and coating products); a full range of services (Charles Schwab in stock brokerage); a complete line of products (Campbell's soups); and top-of-the-line image and reputation (Ralph Lauren and Starbucks).

The most appealing approaches to differentiation are those that are hard or expensive for rivals to duplicate. Indeed, resourceful competitors can, in time, clone almost any product or feature or attribute. If Coca-Cola introduces a vanilla-flavored soft drink, so can Pepsi; if Ford offers a 50,000-mile bumper-to-bumper warranty on its new vehicles, so can Volkswagen and Nissan. This is why *sustainable* differentiation usually has to be linked to core competencies, unique competitive capabilities, and superior management of value chain activities that competitors cannot readily match. As a rule, differentiation yields a longer-lasting and more profitable competitive edge when it is based on product innovation, technical superiority, product quality and reliability, comprehensive customer service, and unique competitive capabilities. Such differentiating attributes tend to be tough for rivals to copy or offset profitably, and buyers widely perceive them as having value.

> Easy-to-copy differentiating features cannot produce sustainable competitive advantage.

Where along the Value Chain to Create the Differentiating Attributes

Differentiation is not something hatched in marketing and advertising departments, nor is it limited to the catchalls of quality and service. Differentiation opportunities can exist in activities all along an industry's value chain; possibilities include the following:

- *Supply chain activities* that ultimately spill over to affect the performance or quality of the company's end product. Starbucks gets high ratings on its coffees partly because it has very strict specifications on the coffee beans it purchases from suppliers.
- *Product R&D activities* that aim at improved product designs and performance features, expanded end uses and applications, more frequent first-on-the-market victories, wider product variety and selection, added user safety, greater recycling capability, or enhanced environmental protection.

- *Production R&D and technology-related activities* that permit custom-order manufacture at an efficient cost; make production methods safer for the environment; or improve product quality, reliability, and appearance. Many manufacturers have developed flexible manufacturing systems that allow different models to be made or different options to be added on the same assembly line. Being able to provide buyers with made-to-order products can be a potent differentiating capability.

- *Manufacturing activities* that reduce product defects, prevent premature product failure, extend product life, allow better warranty coverages, improve economy of use, result in more end-user convenience, or enhance product appearance. The quality edge enjoyed by Japanese automakers stems partly from their distinctive competence in performing assembly-line activities.

- *Outbound logistics and distribution activities* that allow for faster delivery, more accurate order filling, lower shipping costs, and fewer warehouse and on-the-shelf stockouts.

- *Marketing, sales, and customer service activities* that result in superior technical assistance to buyers, faster maintenance and repair services, more and better product information provided to customers, more and better training materials for end users, better credit terms, quicker order processing, or greater customer convenience.

Managers need keen understanding of the sources of differentiation and the activities that drive uniqueness to devise a sound differentiation strategy and evaluate various differentiation approaches.

Achieving a Differentiation-Based Competitive Advantage

While it is easy enough to grasp that a successful differentiation strategy must entail creating buyer value in ways unmatched by rivals, the big question is which of four basic differentiating approaches to take in delivering unique buyer value. One approach is to *incorporate product attributes and user features that lower the buyer's overall costs of using the company's product.* Making a company's product more economical for a buyer to use can be done by reducing the buyer's raw materials waste (providing cut-to-size components), reducing a buyer's inventory requirements (providing just-in-time deliveries), increasing maintenance intervals and product reliability so as to lower a buyer's repair and maintenance costs, using online systems to reduce a buyer's procurement and order processing costs, and providing free technical support.

core concept
A differentiator's basis for competitive advantage is either a product/service offering whose attributes differ significantly from the offerings of rivals or a set of capabilities for delivering customer value that rivals don't have.

A second approach is to *incorporate features that raise product performance.*[5] This can be accomplished with attributes that provide buyers greater reliability, durability, convenience, or ease of use. Other performance-enhancing options include making the company's product or service cleaner, safer, quieter, or more maintenance-free than rival brands. A third approach is to *incorporate features that enhance buyer satisfaction in noneconomic or intangible ways.* Goodyear's Aquatread tire design appeals to safety-conscious motorists wary of slick roads. BMW, Ralph Lauren, and Rolex have differentiation-based competitive advantages linked to buyer desires for status, image, prestige, upscale fashion, superior craftsmanship, and the finer things in life. L. L. Bean makes its mail-order customers feel secure in their purchases by providing an unconditional guarantee with no time limit: "All of our products are guaranteed to give 100 percent satisfaction in every way. Return anything purchased from us at any time if it proves otherwise. We will replace it, refund your purchase price, or credit your credit card, as you wish."

A fourth approach is to differentiate on the basis of capabilities—*to deliver value to customers via competitive capabilities that rivals don't have or can't afford to match.*[6] Japanese automakers can bring new models to market faster than American and European automakers, thereby allowing the Japanese companies to satisfy changing consumer preferences for one vehicle style versus another. CNN has the capability to cover breaking news stories faster and more completely than the major networks. Microsoft has stronger capabilities to design, create, distribute, and advertise an array of software products for PC applications than any of its rivals.

The Importance of Perceived Value

Buyers seldom pay for value they don't perceive, no matter how real the unique extras may be.[7] Thus, the price premium commanded by a differentiation strategy reflects *the value actually delivered* to the buyer and *the value perceived* by the buyer (even if not actually delivered). Actual and perceived value can differ whenever buyers have trouble assessing what their experience with the product will be. Incomplete knowledge on the part of buyers often causes them to judge value based on such signals as price (where price connotes quality), attractive packaging, extensive ad campaigns (i.e., how well known the product is), ad content and image, the quality of brochures and sales presentations, the seller's facilities, the seller's list of customers, the firm's market share, the length of time the firm has been in business, and the professionalism, appearance, and personality of the seller's employees. Such signals of value may be as important as actual value (1) when the nature of differentiation is subjective or hard to quantify, (2) when buyers are making a first-time purchase, (3) when repurchase is infrequent, and (4) when buyers are unsophisticated.

Keeping the Cost of Differentiation in Line

Company efforts to achieve differentiation usually raise costs. The trick to profitable differentiation is either to keep the costs of achieving differentiation below the price premium the differentiating attributes can command in the marketplace (thus increasing the profit margin per unit sold) or to offset thinner profit margins with enough added volume to increase total profits. It usually makes sense to incorporate differentiating features that are not costly but that add to buyer satisfaction. FedEx installed systems that allowed customers to track packages in transit by connecting to the company's Web site and entering the airbill number; some hotels and motels provide free continental breakfasts, exercise facilities, and in-room coffeemaking amenities; publishers are using their Web sites to deliver complementary educational materials to the buyers of their textbooks.

When a Differentiation Strategy Works Best

Differentiation strategies tend to work best in market circumstances where:

- *There are many ways to differentiate the product or service and many buyers perceive these differences as having value*—Unless buyers have strong preferences about certain features, profitable differentiation opportunities are very restricted.
- *Buyer needs and uses are diverse*—The more diverse buyer preferences are, the more room firms have to pursue different approaches to differentiation.

- *Few rival firms are following a similar differentiation approach*—There is less head-to-head rivalry when differentiating rivals go separate ways in pursuing uniqueness and try to appeal to buyers on different combinations of attributes.
- *Technological change is fast-paced and competition revolves around rapidly evolving product features*—Rapid product innovation and frequent introductions of next-version products help maintain buyer interest and provide space for companies to pursue separate differentiating paths.

The Pitfalls of a Differentiation Strategy

There are, of course, no guarantees that differentiation will produce a meaningful competitive advantage. If buyers see little value in the unique attributes or capabilities of a product, then the company's differentiation strategy will get a ho-hum market reception. In addition, attempts at differentiation are doomed to fail if competitors can quickly copy most or all of the appealing product attributes a company comes up with. Rapid imitation means that no rival achieves differentiation, since whenever one firm introduces some aspect of uniqueness that strikes the fancy of buyers, fast-following copycats quickly reestablish similarity. Thus, to build competitive advantage through differentiation a firm must search out sources of uniqueness that are time-consuming or burdensome for rivals to match. Other common pitfalls and mistakes in pursuing differentiation include:[8]

> **core concept**
> Any differentiating feature that works well is a magnet for imitators.

- Trying to differentiate on the basis of something that does not lower a buyer's cost or enhance a buyer's well-being, as perceived by the buyer.
- Overdifferentiating so that the product quality or service level exceeds buyers' needs.
- Trying to charge too high a price premium. (The bigger the price differential, the harder it is to keep buyers from switching to lower-priced competitors.)
- Being timid and not striving to open up meaningful gaps in quality or service or performance features vis-à-vis the products of rivals—tiny differences between rivals' product offerings may not be visible or important to buyers.

A low-cost provider strategy can defeat a differentiation strategy when buyers are satisfied with a basic product and don't think "extra" attributes are worth a higher price.

BEST-COST PROVIDER STRATEGIES

Best-cost provider strategies aim at giving customers *more value for the money.* The objective is to deliver superior value to buyers by satisfying their expectations on key quality/service/features/performance attributes and beating their expectations on price (given what rivals are charging for much the same attributes). A company achieves best-cost status from an ability to incorporate attractive attributes at a lower cost than rivals. To become a best-cost provider, a company must have the resources and capabilities to achieve good-to-excellent quality, incorporate appealing features, match product performance, and provide good-to-excellent customer service—all at a lower cost than rivals.

As Figure 5.1 indicates (see p. 116), best-cost provider strategies stake out a middle ground between pursuing a low-cost advantage and a differentiation advantage and

illustration capsule 5.3
Toyota's Best-Cost Producer Strategy for Its Lexus Line

Toyota Motor Company is widely regarded as a low-cost producer among the world's motor vehicle manufacturers. Despite its emphasis on product quality, Toyota has achieved low-cost leadership because it has developed considerable skills in efficient supply chain management and low-cost assembly capabilities, and because its models are positioned in the low-to-medium end of the price spectrum, where high production volumes are conducive to low unit costs. But when Toyota decided to introduce its new Lexus models to compete in the luxury-car market, it employed a classic best-cost provider strategy. Toyota took the following four steps in crafting and implementing its Lexus strategy:

- *Designing an array of high-performance characteristics and upscale features into the Lexus models* so as to make them comparable in performance and luxury to other high-end models and attractive to Mercedes, BMW, Audi, Jaguar, Cadillac, and Lincoln buyers.

- *Transferring its capabilities in making high-quality Toyota models at low cost to making premium-quality Lexus models at costs below other luxury-car makers.* Toyota's supply chain capabilities and low-cost assembly know-how allowed it to incorporate high-tech performance features and upscale quality into Lexus models at substantially less cost than Mercedes and BMW.

- *Using its relatively lower manufacturing costs to underprice comparable Mercedes and BMW models.* Toyota believed that with its cost advantage it could price attractively equipped Lexus cars low enough to draw price-conscious buyers away from Mercedes and BMW and perhaps induce dissatisfied Lincoln and Cadillac owners to move up to a Lexus.

- *Establishing a new network of Lexus dealers, separate from Toyota dealers, dedicated to providing a level of personalized, attentive customer service unmatched in the industry.*

Lexus models have consistently ranked among the top 10 models in the widely watched J. D. Power & Associates quality survey, and the prices of Lexus models are typically several thousand dollars below those of comparable Mercedes and BMW models—clear signals that Toyota has succeeded in becoming a best-cost producer with its Lexus brand.

between appealing to the broad market as a whole and a narrow market niche. From a competitive positioning standpoint, best-cost strategies are a *hybrid,* balancing a strategic emphasis on low cost against a strategic emphasis on differentiation (superior value). *The target market is value-conscious buyers,* perhaps a very sizable part of the overall market. *The competitive advantage of a best-cost provider is lower costs than rivals* in incorporating good-to-excellent attributes, putting the company in a position to underprice rivals whose products have similar appealing attributes.

A best-cost provider strategy can be quite powerful in markets where buyer diversity makes product differentiation the norm *and* where many buyers are also sensitive to price and value. This is because a best-cost provider can position itself near the middle of the market with either a medium-quality product at a below-average price or a high-quality product at an average price. Often, substantial numbers of buyers prefer midrange products rather than the cheap, basic products of low-cost producers or the expensive products of top-of-the-line differentiators. But unless a company has the resources, know-how, and capabilities to incorporate upscale product or service attributes at a lower cost than rivals, this strategy is ill-advised.

Illustration Capsule 5.3 describes how Toyota has used a best-cost approach with its Lexus models.

The Big Risk of a Best-Cost Provider Strategy

The danger of a best-cost provider strategy is that a company using it will get squeezed between the strategies of firms using low-cost and differentiation strategies. Low-cost leaders may be able to siphon customers away with the appeal of a lower price. High-end differentiators may be able to steal customers away with the appeal of better product attributes. Thus, to be successful, a best-cost provider must offer buyers *significantly* better product attributes in order to justify a price above what low-cost leaders are charging. Likewise, it has to achieve *significantly* lower costs in providing upscale features so that it can outcompete high-end differentiators on the basis of an attractively lower price.

FOCUSED (OR MARKET NICHE) STRATEGIES

What sets focused strategies apart from low-cost leadership or broad differentiation strategies is concentrated attention on a narrow piece of the total market. The target segment, or niche, can be defined by geographic uniqueness, by specialized requirements in using the product, or by special product attributes that appeal only to relatively small numbers of buyers. Examples of firms that concentrate on a well-defined market niche include eBay (in online auctions); Porsche (in sports cars); Cannondale (in top-of-the-line mountain bikes); Jiffy Lube International (a specialist in quick oil changes and simple maintenance for motor vehicles); Google (a specialist in Internet search engine software); Pottery Barn Kids (a retail chain featuring children's furniture and accessories); and Bandag (a specialist in truck tire recapping that promotes its recaps aggressively at over 1,000 truck stops). Microbreweries, local bakeries, bed-and-breakfast inns, and local owner-managed retail boutiques are all good examples of enterprises that have scaled their operations to serve narrow or local customer segments.

A Focused Low-Cost Strategy

A focused strategy based on low cost aims at securing a competitive advantage by serving buyers in the target market niche at a lower cost and lower price than rival competitors. This strategy has considerable attraction when a firm can lower costs significantly by limiting its customer base to a well-defined buyer segment. The avenues to achieving a cost advantage over rivals also serving the target market niche are the same as for low-cost leadership—outmanage rivals in controlling the factors that drive costs and reconfigure the firm's value chain in ways that yield a cost edge over rivals.

Focused low-cost strategies are fairly common. Producers of private-label goods are able to achieve low costs in product development, marketing, distribution, and advertising by concentrating on making generic items imitative of name-brand merchandise and selling directly to retail chains wanting a basic house brand to sell to price-sensitive shoppers. Several small printer-supply manufacturers have begun making low-cost clones of the premium-priced replacement ink and toner cartridges sold by Hewlett-Packard, Lexmark, Canon, and Epson; the clone manufacturers dissect the cartridges of the name-brand companies and then reengineer a similar version that won't violate patents. The components for remanufactured replacement cartridges are acquired from various outside sources, and the clones are then marketed at prices as much as 50 percent below the name-brand cartridges. Cartridge remanufacturers have

illustration capsule 5.4
Motel 6's Focused Low-Cost Strategy

Motel 6 caters to price-conscious travelers who want a clean, no-frills place to spend the night. To be a low-cost provider of overnight lodging, the company (1) selects relatively inexpensive sites on which to construct its units (usually near interstate exits and high-traffic locations but far enough away to avoid paying prime-site prices); (2) builds only basic facilities (no restaurant or bar and only rarely a swimming pool); (3) relies on standard architectural designs that incorporate inexpensive materials and low-cost construction techniques; and (4) provides simple room furnishings and decorations. These approaches lower both investment costs and operating costs. Without restaurants,

bars, and all kinds of guest services, a Motel 6 unit can be operated with just front-desk personnel, room cleanup crews, and skeleton building-and-grounds maintenance.

To promote the Motel 6 concept with travelers who have simple overnight requirements, the chain uses unique, recognizable radio ads done by nationally syndicated radio personality Tom Bodett; the ads describe Motel 6's clean rooms, no-frills facilities, friendly atmosphere, and dependably low rates (usually under $40 a night).

Motel 6's basis for competitive advantage is lower costs than competitors in providing basic, economical overnight accommodations to price-constrained travelers.

been lured to focus on this market because replacement cartridges constitute a multibillion-dollar business with considerable profit potential given their low costs and the premium pricing of the name-brand companies. Illustration Capsule 5.4 describes how Motel 6 has kept its costs low in catering to budget-conscious travelers.

A Focused Differentiation Strategy

A focused strategy based on differentiation aims at securing a competitive advantage by offering niche members a product they perceive as well suited to their own unique tastes and preferences. Successful use of a focused differentiation strategy depends on the existence of a buyer segment that is looking for special product attributes or seller capabilities and on a firm's ability to stand apart from rivals competing in the same target market niche.

Companies like Godiva Chocolates, Chanel, Gucci, Rolex, Rolls-Royce, Häagen-Dazs, and W. L. Gore (the maker of Gore-Tex) employ successful differentiation-based focused strategies targeted at upscale buyers wanting products and services with world-class attributes. Indeed, most markets contain a buyer segment willing to pay a big price premium for the very finest items available, thus opening the strategic window for some competitors to pursue differentiation-based focused strategies aimed at the very top of the market pyramid. Another successful focused differentiator is "fashion food retailer" Trader Joe's, a 150-store East and West Coast chain that is a combination gourmet deli and food warehouse.[9] Customers shop Trader Joe's as much for entertainment as for conventional grocery items—the store stocks out-of-the-ordinary culinary treats like raspberry salsa, salmon burgers, and jasmine fried rice, as well as the standard goods normally found in supermarkets. What sets Trader Joe's apart is not just its unique combination of food novelties and competitively priced grocery items but also its capability to turn an otherwise mundane grocery excursion into a whimsical treasure hunt that is just plain fun. For details about another company's focused differentiation strategy, see Illustration Capsule 5.5.

illustration capsule 5.5

Progressive Insurance's Focused Differentiation Strategy in Auto Insurance

Progressive Insurance has fashioned a strategy in auto insurance focused on people with a record of traffic violations who drive high-performance cars, drivers with accident histories, motorcyclists, teenagers, and other so-called high-risk categories of drivers that most auto insurance companies steer away from. Progressive discovered that some of these high-risk drivers are affluent and pressed for time, making them less sensitive to paying premium rates for their car insurance. Management learned that it could charge such drivers high enough premiums to cover the added risks, plus it differentiated Progressive from other insurers by expediting the process of obtaining insurance and decreasing the annoyance that such drivers faced in obtaining insurance coverage.

In further differentiating and promoting Progressive policies, management created teams of roving claims adjusters who would arrive at accident scenes to assess claims and issue checks for repairs on the spot. Progressive also studied the market segments for insurance carefully enough to discover that some motorcycle owners were not especially risky (middle-aged suburbanites who sometimes commuted to work or used their motorcycles mainly for recreational trips with their friends). Progressive's strategy allowed it to become a leader in the market for luxury-car insurance for customers who appreciated Progressive's streamlined approach to doing business.

Source: Ian C. McMillan, Alexander van Putten, and Rita Gunther McGrath, "Global Gamesmanship," *Harvard Business Review* 81, no. 5 (May 2003), p. 68.

When a Focused Low-Cost or Focused Differentiation Strategy Is Attractive

A focused strategy aimed at securing a competitive edge based either on low cost or differentiation becomes increasingly attractive as more of the following conditions are met:

- The target market niche is big enough to be profitable and offers good growth potential.

- Industry leaders do not see that having a presence in the niche is crucial to their own success—in which case focusers can often escape battling head-to-head against some of the industry's biggest and strongest competitors.

- It is costly or difficult for multisegment competitors to put capabilities in place to meet the specialized needs of the target market niche and at the same time satisfy the expectations of their mainstream customers.

- The industry has many different niches and segments, thereby allowing a focuser to pick a competitively attractive niche suited to its resource strengths and capabilities. Also, with more niches there is more room for focusers to avoid each other in competing for the same customers.

- Few, if any, other rivals are attempting to specialize in the same target segment—a condition that reduces the risk of segment overcrowding.

- The focuser can compete effectively against challengers based on the capabilities and resources it has to serve the targeted niche and the customer goodwill it may have built up.

When an industry has many different niches and segments, the strength of competition varies across and within segments, a condition that makes it important for a focuser to pick a niche that is both competitively attractive and well suited to its resource strengths and capabilities. A focuser's specialized competencies and capabilities in serving the target market niche provide the strongest and most dependable basis for contending successfully with competitive forces. Rivalry in the target niche is weaker when there are comparatively few players in the niche and when multisegment rivals have trouble truly meeting the expectations of the focused firm's target clientele along with the expectations of the other types of customers they cater to. A focuser's unique capabilities in serving the market niche also act as an entry barrier—difficulties in matching a focuser's capabilities can dissuade potential newcomers from entering the niche. They also present a hurdle that makers of substitute products must overcome. Even if some niche buyers have substantial bargaining leverage, their power is blunted somewhat by the downside of shifting their business to rival companies less capable of meeting their expectations.

> Even though a focuser may be small, it still may have substantial competitive strength because of the attractiveness of its product offering and its strong expertise and capabilities in meeting the needs and expectations of niche members.

The Risks of a Focused Low-Cost or Focused Differentiation Strategy

Focusing carries several risks. One is the chance that competitors will find effective ways to match the focused firm's capabilities in serving the target niche—perhaps by coming up with more appealing product offerings or by developing expertise and capabilities that offset the focuser's strengths. A second is the potential for the preferences and needs of niche members to shift over time toward the product attributes desired by the majority of buyers. An erosion of the differences across buyer segments lowers entry barriers into a focuser's market niche and provides an open invitation for rivals in adjacent segments to begin competing for the focuser's customers. A third risk is that the segment may become so attractive it is soon inundated with competitors, intensifying rivalry and splintering segment profits.

THE CONTRASTING FEATURES OF THE FIVE GENERIC COMPETITIVE STRATEGIES: A SUMMARY

Deciding which generic competitive strategy should serve as the framework for hanging the rest of the company's strategy is not a trivial matter. Each of the five generic competitive strategies positions the company differently in its market and competitive environment. Each establishes a central theme for how the company will endeavor to outcompete rivals. Each creates some boundaries or guidelines for maneuvering as market circumstances unfold and as ideas for improving the strategy are debated. Each points to different ways of experimenting and tinkering with the basic strategy—for example, employing a low-cost leadership strategy means experimenting with ways that costs can be cut and value chain activities can be streamlined whereas a broad differentiation strategy means exploring ways to add new differentiating features or to perform value chain activities differently if the result is to add value for customers in ways they are willing to pay for. Each entails differences in terms of product line, production emphasis, marketing emphasis, and means of sustaining the strategy—as shown in Table 5.1. Thus a choice of which generic strategy to employ spills over to affect several aspects of how the business will be operated and the manner in which value chain activities must be managed. Deciding which generic strategy to employ is perhaps the most important strategic commitment a company makes—it tends to drive the rest of the strategic actions a company decides to undertake.

One of the big dangers here is that managers, torn between the pros and cons of the various generic strategies, will opt for *"stuck in the middle" strategies* that represent compromises between lower costs and greater differentiation and between broad and narrow market appeal. Compromise or middle-ground strategies rarely produce sustainable competitive advantage or a distinctive competitive position—well-executed best-cost-producer strategies are the only exception where a compromise between low cost and differentiation succeeds. Usually, companies with compromise strategies end up with a middle-of-the-pack industry ranking—they have average costs, some but not a lot of product differentiation relative to rivals, an average image and reputation, and little prospect of industry leadership. Having a competitive edge over rivals is the single most dependable contributor to above-average company profitability. Hence, only if a company makes a strong and unwavering commitment to one of the five generic competitive strategies does it stand much chance of achieving sustainable competitive advantage that such strategies can deliver if properly executed.

key|points

Early in the process of crafting a strategy company managers have to decide which of the five basic competitive strategies to employ—overall low-cost, broad differentiation, best-cost, focused low-cost, or focused differentiation.

A strategy of trying to be the industry's low-cost provider works well in situations where:

1. The industry's product is essentially the same from seller to seller (brand differences are minor).
2. Many buyers are price-sensitive and shop for the lowest price.
3. There are only a few ways to achieve product differentiation that have much value to buyers.
4. Most buyers use the product in the same ways and thus have common user requirements.
5. Buyers' costs in switching from one seller or brand to another are low or even zero.
6. Buyers are large and have significant power to negotiate pricing terms.

To achieve a low-cost advantage, a company must become more skilled than rivals in controlling the cost drivers and/or it must find innovative ways to eliminate or bypass cost-producing activities. Successful low-cost providers usually achieve their cost advantages by imaginatively and persistently ferreting out cost savings throughout the value chain. They are good at finding ways to drive costs out of their businesses year after year after year. A low-cost company's ability to set the industry's price floor and still earn a profit erects protective barriers around its market position, and it is in by far the strongest position to compete on the basis of a low price.

table 5.1   **Distinguishing Features of the Five Generic Competitive Strategies**

	Low-Cost Provider	Broad Differentiation	Best-Cost Provider	Focused Low-Cost Provider	Focused Differentiation
Strategic target	• A broad cross-section of the market	• A broad cross-section of the market	• Value-conscious buyers	• A narrow market niche where buyer needs and preferences are distinctively different	• A narrow market niche where buyer needs and preferences are distinctively different
Basis of competitive advantage	• Lower overall costs than competitors	• Ability to offer buyers something attractively different from competitors	• Ability to give customers more value for the money	• Lower overall cost than rivals in serving niche members	• Attributes that appeal specifically to niche members
Product line	• A good basic product with few frills (acceptable quality and limited selection)	• Many product variations, wide selection; emphasis on differentiating features	• Items with appealing attributes; assorted upscale features	• Features and attributes tailored to the tastes and requirements of niche members	• Features and attributes tailored to the tastes and requirements of niche members
Production emphasis	• A continuous search for cost reduction without sacrificing acceptable quality and essential features	• Whatever differentiating features buyers are willing to pay for; strive for product superiority	• Upscale features and appealing attributes at lower cost than rivals	• A continuous search for cost reduction while incorporating features and attributes matched to niche member preferences	• Custom-made products that match the tastes and requirements of niche members
Marketing emphasis	• Try to make a virtue out of product features that lead to low cost	• Tout differentiating features • Charge a premium price to cover the extra costs of differentiating features	• Tout delivery of best value • Either deliver comparable features at a lower price than rivals or match rivals on prices and provide better features	• Communicate attractive features of a budget-priced product offering that fits niche buyers' expectations	• Communicate how product offering does the best job of meeting niche buyers' expectations
Keys to sustaining the strategy	• Economical prices/ good value • Low costs, year after year, in every area of the business	• Stress constant innovation to stay ahead of imitative competitors • A few key differentiating features	• Unique expertise in simultaneously managing costs down while incorporating upscale features and attributes	• Stay committed to serving the niche at lowest overall cost; don't blur the firm's image by entering other market segments or adding other products to widen market appeal	• Stay committed to serving the niche better than rivals; don't blur the firm's image by entering other market segments or adding other products to widen market appeal

Differentiation strategies seek to produce a competitive edge by incorporating attributes and features into a company's product/service offering that rivals don't have. Anything a firm can do to create buyer value represents a potential basis for differentiation. Successful differentiation is usually keyed to lowering the buyer's cost of using the item, raising the performance the buyer gets, or boosting a buyer's psychological satisfaction. To be sustainable, differentiation usually has to be linked to unique internal expertise, core competencies, and resources that translate into capabilities rivals can't easily match. Differentiation tied just to unique features seldom is lasting because resourceful competitors are adept at cloning, improving on, or finding substitutes for almost any feature that appeals to buyers.

Best-cost provider strategies combine a strategic emphasis on low cost with a strategic emphasis on more than minimal quality, service, features, or performance. The aim is to create competitive advantage by giving buyers more value for the money; this is done by matching close rivals on key quality/service/features/performance attributes and beating them on the costs of incorporating such attributes into the product or service. To be successful with a best-cost provider strategy, a company must be able to incorporate upscale product or service attributes at a lower cost than rivals. Sustaining a best-cost provider strategy generally means having the capability to simultaneously manage unit costs down and product/service caliber up.

A focus strategy delivers competitive advantage either by achieving lower costs in serving the target market niche or by developing an ability to offer niche buyers something different from rival competitors. A focused strategy based on either low cost or differentiation becomes increasingly attractive as more of the following conditions are met:

1. The target market niche is big enough to be profitable and offers good growth potential.

2. Industry leaders do not see that having a presence in the niche is crucial to their own success—in which case focusers can often escape battling head-to-head against some of the industry's biggest and strongest competitors.

3. It is costly or difficult for multisegment competitors to put capabilities in place to meet the specialized needs of the target market niche and at the same time satisfy the expectations of their mainstream customers.

4. The industry has many different niches and segments, thereby allowing a focuser to pick a competitively attractive niche suited to its resource strengths and capabilities. Also, with more niches there is more room for focusers to avoid each other in competing for the same customers.

5. Few, if any, other rivals are attempting to specialize in the same target segment—a condition that reduces the risk of segment overcrowding.

6. The focuser can compete effectively against challengers based on the capabilities and resources it has to serve the targeted niche and the customer goodwill it may have built up.

Deciding which generic strategy to employ is perhaps the most important strategic commitment a company makes—it tends to drive the rest of the strategic actions a company decides to undertake and it sets the whole tone for the pursuit of a competitive advantage over rivals.

exercises

1. Go to www.google.com and do a search for "low-cost producer." See if you can identify five companies that are pursuing a low-cost strategy in their respective industries.

2. Using the advanced search engine function at www.google.com, enter "best-cost producer" as an exact phrase and see if you can locate three companies that indicate they are employing a best-cost producer strategy.

chapter six

Beyond Competitive Strategy

Other Important Strategy Choices

(© Royalty-Free / CORBIS)

Strategies for taking the hill won't necessarily hold it.

—Amar Bhide

The sure path to oblivion is to stay where you are.

—Bernard Fauber

Successful business strategy is about actively shaping the game you play, not just playing the game you find.

—Adam M. Brandenburger and Barry J. Nalebuff

Don't form an alliance to correct a weakness and don't ally with a partner that is trying to correct a weakness of its own. The only result from a marriage of weaknesses is the creation of even more weaknesses.

—Michel Robert

O nce a company has settled on which of the five generic strategies to employ, attention turns to what other *strategic actions* it can take to complement its choice of a basic competitive strategy. Several decisions have to be made:

- What use to make of strategic alliances and collaborative partnerships.

- Whether to bolster the company's market position via merger or acquisitions.

- Whether to integrate backward or forward into more stages of the industry value chain.

- Whether to outsource certain value chain activities or perform them in-house.

- Whether and when to employ offensive and defensive moves.

- Which of several ways to use the Internet as a distribution channel in positioning the company in the marketplace.

This chapter contains sections discussing the pros and cons of each of the above complementary strategic options. The next-to-last section in the chapter discusses the competitive importance of timing strategic moves—when it is advantageous to be a first-mover and when it is better to be a fast-follower or late-mover. The chapter concludes with a brief look at the need for strategic choices in each functional area of a company's business (R&D, production, sales and marketing, finance, and so on) to support its basic competitive approach and complementary strategic moves.

Figure 6.1 shows the menu of strategic options a company has in crafting a strategy and the order in which the choices should generally be made. The portion of Figure 6.1 below the competitive strategy options illustrates the structure of this chapter and the topics that will be covered.

STRATEGIC ALLIANCES AND COLLABORATIVE PARTNERSHIPS

During the past decade, companies in all types of industries and in all parts of the world have elected to form strategic alliances and partnerships to complement their own strategic initiatives and strengthen their competitiveness in domestic and international markets. This is an about-face from times past, when the vast majority of companies were content to go it alone, confident that they already had or could independently

figure 6.1   **A Company's Menu of Strategy Options**

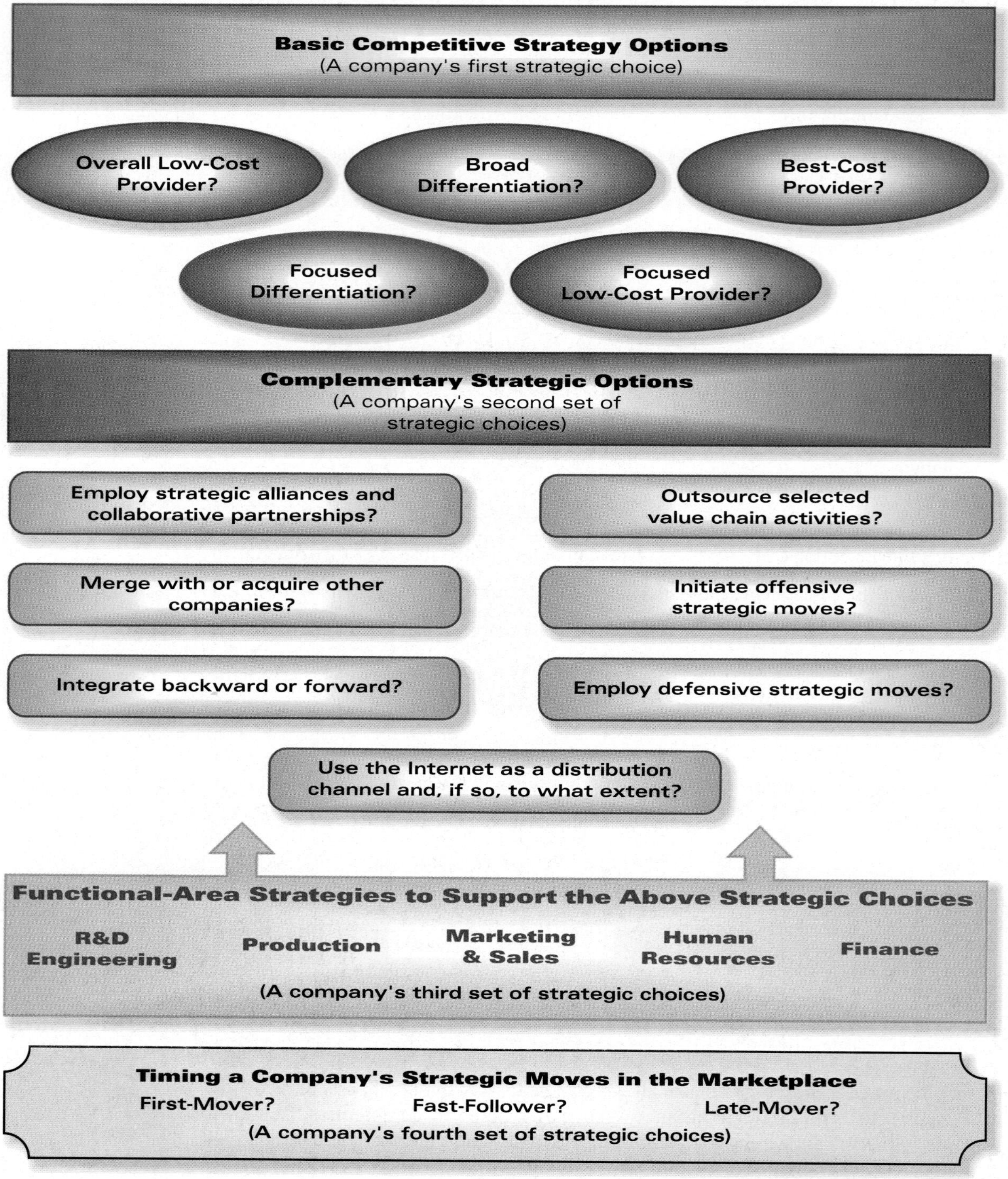

Basic Competitive Strategy Options
(A company's first strategic choice)

Overall Low-Cost Provider?

Broad Differentiation?

Best-Cost Provider?

Focused Differentiation?

Focused Low-Cost Provider?

Complementary Strategic Options
(A company's second set of strategic choices)

Employ strategic alliances and collaborative partnerships?

Outsource selected value chain activities?

Merge with or acquire other companies?

Initiate offensive strategic moves?

Integrate backward or forward?

Employ defensive strategic moves?

Use the Internet as a distribution channel and, if so, to what extent?

Functional-Area Strategies to Support the Above Strategic Choices

| R&D Engineering | Production | Marketing & Sales | Human Resources | Finance |

(A company's third set of strategic choices)

Timing a Company's Strategic Moves in the Marketplace

First-Mover?   Fast-Follower?   Late-Mover?

(A company's fourth set of strategic choices)

develop whatever resources and know-how were needed to be successful in their markets. But globalization of the world economy, revolutionary advances in technology across a broad front, and untapped opportunities in national markets in Asia, Latin America, and Europe that are opening up, deregulating, and/or undergoing privatization have made partnerships of one kind or another integral to competing on a broad geographic scale.

Many companies now find themselves thrust into two very demanding competitive races: (1) *the global race to build a presence in many different national markets* and join the ranks of companies recognized as global market leaders, and (2) *the race to seize opportunities on the frontiers of advancing technology* and build the resource strengths and business capabilities to compete successfully in the industries and product markets of the future.[1] Even the largest and most financially sound companies have concluded that simultaneously running the races for global market leadership and for a stake in the industries of the future requires more diverse and expansive skills, resources, technological expertise, and competitive capabilities than they can assemble and manage alone. Such companies, along with others that are missing the resources and competitive capabilities needed to pursue promising opportunities, have determined that the fastest way to fill the gap is often to form alliances with enterprises having the desired strengths. Consequently, these companies form **strategic alliances** or collaborative partnerships in which two or more companies join forces to achieve mutually beneficial strategic outcomes. Strategic alliances go beyond normal company-to-company dealings but fall short of merger or full joint venture partnership with formal ownership ties. (Some strategic alliances, however, do involve arrangements whereby one or more allies have minority ownership in certain of the other alliance members.)

> **core concept**
> *Strategic alliances* are collaborative partnerships where two or more companies join forces to achieve mutually beneficial strategic outcomes.

The Pervasive Use of Alliances

Strategic alliances and collaborative partnerships have thus emerged as an attractive means of breaching technology and resource gaps. More and more enterprises, especially in fast-changing industries, are making strategic alliances a core part of their overall strategy. Alliances are so central to Corning's strategy that the company describes itself as a "network of organizations." Toyota has forged long-term strategic partnerships with many of its suppliers of automotive parts and components. Microsoft collaborates very closely with independent software developers that create new programs to run on the next-generation versions of Windows. Oracle is said to have over 15,000 alliances. Time Warner, IBM, and Microsoft each have over 200 partnerships with e-business enterprises. Genentech, a leader in biotechnology and human genetics, has a partnering strategy to increase its access to novel biotherapeutics products and technologies and has formed alliances with over 30 companies to strengthen its research and development (R&D) pipeline. Since 1998, Samsung, a South Korean corporation with $34 billion in sales, has entered into 34 major strategic alliances involving such companies as Sony, Yahoo, Hewlett-Packard, Intel, Microsoft, Dell, Mitsubishi, and Rockwell Automation. Studies indicate that large corporations are commonly involved in 30 to 50 alliances and that a number have hundreds of alliances. One recent study estimated that about 35 percent of corporate revenues in 2003 came from activities involving strategic alliances, up from 15 percent in 1995.[2]

> Alliances have become so essential to the competitiveness of companies in many industries that they are a core element of today's business strategies.

In the personal computer (PC) industry, alliances are pervasive because the different components of PCs and the software to run them are supplied by so many different companies—one set of companies provides the microprocessors, another group makes the motherboards, another the monitors, another the disk drives, another the memory chips, and so on. Moreover, their facilities are scattered across the United States, Japan, Taiwan, Singapore, Malaysia, and parts of Europe. Close collaboration is required on product development, logistics, production, and the timing of new product releases. To bring all these diverse enterprises together in a common effort to advance PC technology and PC capabilities, Intel has formed collaborative partnerships with numerous makers of PC components and software developers. Intel's strategic objective has been to foster collaboration on bringing next-generation PC-related products to market in parallel so that PC users can get the maximum benefits from new PCs running on Intel's next-generation microprocessors. Without extensive cooperation among Intel, the makers of other key PC components, PC makers, and software developers in both new technology and new product development, there would be all kinds of delays and incompatibility problems in introducing better-performing PC hardware and software products—obstacles that would dampen the benefits that PC users could get from utilizing Intel's latest generations of chips and lower Intel's chip sales.

> While a few companies have the resources and capabilities to pursue their strategies alone, it is becoming increasingly common for companies to pursue their strategies in collaboration with suppliers, distributors, makers of complementary products, and sometimes even select competitors.

Why and How Strategic Alliances Are Advantageous

The value of a strategic alliance stems not from the agreement or deal itself but rather from the capacity of the partners to defuse organizational frictions, collaborate effectively over time, and work their way through the maze of changes that lie in front of them—technological and competitive surprises, new market developments (which may come at a rapid-fire pace), and changes in their own priorities and competitive circumstances. Collaborative partnerships nearly always entail an *evolving* relationship whose benefits and competitive value ultimately depend on mutual learning, cooperation, and adaptation to changing industry conditions. *The best alliances are highly selective, focusing on particular value chain activities and on obtaining a particular competitive benefit.* Competitive advantage can emerge if the combined resources and capabilities of a company and its allies give it an edge over rivals.

The most common reasons why companies enter into strategic alliances are to collaborate on technology or the development of promising new products, to overcome deficits in their technical and manufacturing expertise, to acquire altogether new competencies, to improve supply chain efficiency, to gain economies of scale in production and/or marketing, and to acquire or improve market access through joint marketing agreements.[3] A company that is racing for global market leadership can enhance its chances for success by using alliances to:

- *Get into critical country markets quickly* and accelerate the process of building a potent global market presence.

- *Gain inside knowledge about unfamiliar markets and cultures* through alliances with local partners. For example, U.S., European, and Japanese companies wanting to build market footholds in the fast-growing Chinese market have pursued partnership arrangements with Chinese companies to help in dealing with government regulations, to supply knowledge of local markets, to provide guidance on adapting their products to better match the buying preferences of Chinese consumers, to set up local manufacturing capabilities, and to assist in distribution, marketing, and promotional activities.

- *Access valuable skills and competencies* that are concentrated in particular geographic locations, such as software design competencies in the United States, fashion design skills in Italy, and efficient manufacturing skills in Japan.

A company that is racing to stake out a strong position in a technology or industry of the future can enhance its market standing by using alliances to:

- *Establish a stronger beachhead* for participating in the target technology or industry.
- *Master new technologies and build new expertise and competencies faster* than would be possible through internal efforts.
- *Open up broader opportunities* in the target industry by melding the firm's own capabilities with the expertise and resources of partners.

Allies can learn much from one another in performing joint research, sharing technological know-how, and collaborating on complementary new technologies and products—sometimes enough to enable them to pursue other new opportunities on their own. Manufacturers typically pursue alliances with parts and components suppliers to gain the efficiencies of better supply chain management and to speed new products to market. By joining forces in components production and/or final assembly, companies may be able to realize cost savings not achievable with their own small volumes—Volvo, Renault, and Peugeot formed an alliance to join forces in making engines for their large car models because none of the three needed enough such engines to operate its own engine plant economically. Manufacturing allies can also learn much about how to improve their quality control and production procedures by studying one another's manufacturing methods. IBM and Dell Computer formed an alliance whereby Dell agreed to purchase $16 billion in parts and components from IBM for use in Dell's PCs, servers, and workstations over a three-year period; Dell determined that IBM's growing expertise and capabilities in PC components justified using IBM as a major supplier even though Dell and IBM competed in supplying laptop computers and servers to corporate customers. Johnson & Johnson and Merck entered into an alliance to market Pepcid AC; Merck developed the stomach distress remedy and Johnson & Johnson functioned as marketer—the alliance made Pepcid products the best-selling remedies for acid indigestion and heartburn. United Airlines, American Airlines, Continental, Delta, and Northwest created an alliance to form Orbitz, an Internet travel site designed to compete with Expedia and Travelocity to provide consumers with low-cost airfares, rental cars, lodging, cruises, and vacation packages.

> The competitive attraction of alliances is in allowing companies to bundle competencies and resources that are more valuable in a joint effort than when kept within a single company.

Strategic cooperation is a much-favored, indeed necessary, approach in industries where new technological developments are occurring at a furious pace along many different paths and where advances in one technology spill over to affect others (often blurring industry boundaries). Whenever industries are experiencing high-velocity technological change in many areas simultaneously, firms find it virtually essential to have cooperative relationships with other enterprises to stay on the leading edge of technology and product performance even in their own area of specialization.

Alliances and Partnerships with Foreign Companies

Cooperative strategies and alliances to penetrate international markets are also common between domestic and foreign firms. Such partnerships are useful in putting together the capabilities to do business over a wider number of country markets. For example, the policy of the Chinese government has long been one of giving privileged market access to only a few select outsiders and requiring the favored outsiders to partner in one way or another with local enterprises. This policy has made alliances with local Chinese companies a strategic necessity for outsiders desirous of gaining a foothold in the vast and fast-growing Chinese market.

Why Many Alliances Are Unstable or Break Apart

The stability of an alliance depends on how well the partners work together, their success in adapting to changing internal and external conditions, and their willingness to renegotiate the bargain if circumstances so warrant. A successful alliance requires real in-the-trenches collaboration, not merely an arm's-length exchange of ideas. Unless partners place a high value on the skills, resources, and contributions each brings to the alliance and the cooperative arrangement results in valuable win–win outcomes, it is doomed. A surprisingly large number of alliances never live up to expectations. A 1999 study by Accenture, a global business consulting organization, revealed that 61 percent of alliances either were outright failures or were "limping along." Many alliances are dissolved after a few years. The high "divorce rate" among strategic allies has several causes—diverging objectives and priorities, an inability to work well together, changing conditions that render the purpose of the alliance obsolete, the emergence of more attractive technological paths, and marketplace rivalry between one or more allies.[4] Experience indicates that alliances stand a reasonable chance of helping a company reduce competitive disadvantage but very rarely have they proved a durable device for achieving a competitive edge.

> Many alliances break apart without reaching their potential because of frictions and conflicts among the allies.

The Strategic Dangers of Relying Heavily on Alliances and Collaborative Partnerships

The Achilles heel of alliances and cooperative strategies is the danger of becoming dependent on other companies for *essential* expertise and capabilities over the long term. To be a market leader (and perhaps even a serious market contender), a company must ultimately develop its own capabilities in areas where internal strategic control is pivotal to protecting its competitiveness and building competitive advantage. Moreover, some alliances hold only limited potential because the partner guards its most valuable skills and expertise; in such instances, acquiring or merging with a company possessing the desired resources is a better solution.

MERGER AND ACQUISITION STRATEGIES

> No company can afford to ignore the strategic and competitive benefits of acquiring or merging with another company to strengthen its market position and open up avenues of new opportunity.

Mergers and acquisitions are much-used strategic options. They are especially suited for situations in which alliances and partnerships do not go far enough in providing a company with access to the needed resources and capabilities. Ownership ties are more permanent than partnership ties, allowing the operations of the merger/acquisition participants to be tightly integrated and creating more in-house control and autonomy. A **merger** is a pooling of equals, with the newly created company often taking on a new name. An **acquisition** is a combination in which one company, the acquirer, purchases and absorbs the operations of another, the acquired. The difference between a merger and an acquisition relates more to the details of ownership, management control, and financial arrangements than to strategy and competitive advantage. The resources, competencies, and competitive capabilities of the newly created enterprise end up much the same whether the combination is the result of acquisition or merger.

Many mergers and acquisitions are driven by strategies to achieve one of five strategic objectives:[5]

> **core concept**
> A **merger** is a pooling of two or more companies as equals, with the newly created company often taking on a new name. An **acquisition** is a combination in which one company purchases and absorbs the operations of another.

1. *To pave the way for the acquiring company to gain more market share and, further, create a more efficient operation out of the combined companies by closing high-cost plants and eliminating surplus capacity industrywide*—The merger that formed DaimlerChrysler was motivated in large part by the fact that the motor vehicle industry had far more production capacity worldwide than was needed; management at both Daimler Benz and Chrysler believed that the efficiency of the two companies could be significantly improved by shutting some plants and laying off workers, realigning which models were produced at which plants, and squeezing out efficiencies by combining supply chain activities, product design, and administration. Quite a number of acquisitions are undertaken with the objective of transforming two or more otherwise high-cost companies into one lean competitor with average or below-average costs.

2. *To expand a company's geographic coverage*—Many industries exist for a long time in a fragmented state, with local companies dominating local markets and no company having a significantly visible regional or national presence. Eventually, though, expansion-minded companies will launch strategies to acquire local companies in adjacent territories. Over time, companies with successful growth via acquisition strategies emerge as regional market leaders and later perhaps as a company with national coverage. Often the acquiring company follows up on its acquisitions with efforts to lower the operating costs and improve the customer service capabilities of the local businesses it acquires.

3. *To extend the company's business into new product categories or international markets*—PepsiCo acquired Quaker Oats chiefly to bring Gatorade into the Pepsi family of beverages, and PepsiCo's Frito-Lay division has made a series of acquisitions of foreign-based snack foods companies to begin to establish a stronger presence in international markets. Companies like Nestlé, Kraft, Unilever, and Procter & Gamble—all racing for global market leadership—have made acquisitions an integral part of their strategies to widen their geographic reach and broaden the number of product categories in which they compete.

4. *To gain quick access to new technologies and avoid the need for a time-consuming R&D effort*—This type of acquisition strategy is a favorite of companies racing to establish attractive positions in emerging markets. Such companies need to fill in technological gaps, extend their technological capabilities along some promising new paths, and position themselves to launch next-wave products and services. Cisco Systems purchased over 75 technology companies to give it more technological reach and product breadth, thereby buttressing its standing as the world's biggest supplier of systems for building the infrastructure of the Internet. Intel has made over 300 acquisitions since 1997 to broaden its technological base, put it in a stronger position to be a major supplier of Internet technology, and make it less dependent on supplying microprocessors for PCs. Between 1996 and 2001, Lucent Technologies acquired 38 companies in the course of its strategic drive to be the technology leader in telecommunications networking. Gaining access to desirable

technologies via acquisition enables a company to build a market position in attractive technologies quickly and serves as a substitute for extensive in-house R&D programs.

5. *To try to invent a new industry and lead the convergence of industries whose boundaries are being blurred by changing technologies and new market opportunities*—In such acquisitions, the company's management is betting that a new industry is on the verge of being born and wants to establish an early position in this industry by bringing together the resources and products of several different companies. Examples include the merger of AOL and media giant Time Warner and Viacom's purchase of Paramount Pictures, CBS, and Blockbuster—both of which reflected bold strategic moves predicated on beliefs that all entertainment content will ultimately converge into a single industry and be distributed over the Internet. (Neither of these mergers and strategic bets, however, have proved successful.)

In addition to the above objectives, there are instances in which acquisitions are motivated by a company's desire to fill resource gaps, thus allowing the new company to do things it could not do before. Illustration Capsule 6.1 describes how Clear Channel Worldwide has used mergers and acquisitions to build a leading global position in outdoor advertising and radio and TV broadcasting.

All too frequently, mergers and acquisitions do not produce the hoped-for outcomes. Combining the operations of two companies, especially large and complex ones, often entails formidable resistance from rank-and-file organization members, hard-to-resolve conflicts in management styles and corporate cultures, and tough problems of integration. Cost savings, expertise sharing, and enhanced competitive capabilities may take substantially longer than expected or, worse, may never materialize at all. Integrating the operations of two fairly large or culturally diverse companies is hard to pull off—only a few companies that use merger and acquisition strategies have proved they can consistently make good decisions about what to leave alone and what to meld into their own operations and systems. In the case of mergers between companies of roughly equal size, the management groups of the two companies frequently battle over which one is going to end up in control.

A number of previously applauded mergers/acquisitions have yet to live up to expectations—the merger of AOL and Time Warner, the merger of Daimler Benz and Chrysler, Hewlett-Packard's acquisition of Compaq Computer, and Ford's acquisition of Jaguar. The AOL Time Warner merger has proved to be mostly a disaster, partly because AOL's rapid growth has evaporated, partly because of a huge clash of corporate cultures, and partly because most of the expected benefits have yet to materialize. Ford paid a handsome price to acquire Jaguar but has yet to make the Jaguar brand a major factor in the luxury-car segment in competition against Mercedes, BMW, and Lexus. Novell acquired WordPerfect for $1.7 billion in stock in 1994, but the combination never generated enough punch to compete against Microsoft Word and Microsoft Office—Novell sold WordPerfect to Corel for $124 million in cash and stock less than two years later. In 2001 electronics retailer Best Buy paid $685 million to acquire Musicland, a struggling 1300-store music retailer that included stores operating under the Musicland, Sam Goody, Suncoast, Media Play, and On Cue names. But Musicland's sales, already declining, dropped even further. In June 2003 Best Buy "sold" Musicland to a Florida investment firm. No cash changed hands and the "buyer" received shares of stock in Best Buy in return for assuming Musicland's liabilities.

illustration capsule 6.1

How Clear Channel Has Used Mergers and Acquisitions to Become a Global Market Leader

In 2003, Clear Channel Worldwide was the fourth largest media company in the world behind Disney, Time Warner, and Viacom/CBS. The company, founded in 1972 by Lowry Mays and Billy Joe McCombs, got its start by acquiring an unprofitable country-music radio station in San Antonio, Texas. Over the next 10 years, Mays learned the radio business and slowly bought other radio stations in a variety of states. Going public in 1984 helped the company raise the equity capital needed to fuel its strategy of expanding by acquiring radio stations in additional geographic markets.

In the late 1980s, following the decision of the Federal Communications Commission to loosen the rules regarding the ability of one company to own both radio and TV stations, Clear Channel broadened its strategy and began acquiring small, struggling TV stations. Soon thereafter, Clear Channel became affiliated with the Fox network, which was starting to build a national presence and challenge ABC, CBS, and NBC. Meanwhile, the company began selling programming services to other stations, and in some markets where it already had stations it took on the function of selling advertising for crosstown stations it did not own.

By 1998, Clear Channel had used acquisitions to build a leading position in radio and television stations. Domestically, it owned, programmed, or sold airtime for 69 AM radio stations, 135 FM stations, and 18 TV stations in 48 local markets in 24 states. The TV stations included affiliates of FOX, UPN, ABC, NBC, and CBS. Clear Channel was also beginning to expand internationally. It purchased an ownership interest in a domestic Spanish-language radio broadcaster; owned two radio stations and a cable audio channel in Denmark; and acquired ownership interests in radio stations in Australia, Mexico, New Zealand, and the Czech Republic.

In 1997, Clear Channel acquired Phoenix-based Eller Media Company, an outdoor advertising company with over 100,000 billboard facings. This was quickly followed by additional acquisitions of outdoor advertising compa-

nies, the most important of which were ABC Outdoor in Milwaukee, Wisconsin; Paxton Communications (with operations in Tampa and Orlando, Florida); Universal Outdoor; and the More Group, with outdoor operations and 90,000 displays in 24 countries.

Then in October 1999, Clear Channel merged with AM-FM, Inc. After divesting some 125 properties needed to gain regulatory approval, Clear Channel Communications (the name adopted by the merged companies) operated in 32 countries and included 830 radio stations, 19 TV stations, and more than 425,000 outdoor displays. Several additional acquisitions were completed during the 2000–2002 period.

Clear Channel's strategy was to buy radio, TV, and outdoor advertising properties with operations in many of the same local markets; share facilities and staffs to cut costs; improve programming; and sell advertising to customers in packages for all three media simultaneously. Packaging ads for two or three media not only helped Clear Channel's advertising clients distribute their messages more effectively but also allowed the company to combine its sales activities and have a common sales force for all three media, achieving significant cost savings and boosting profit margins.

In 2003, Clear Channel Worldwide (the company's latest name) owned radio and television stations, outdoor displays, and entertainment venues in 66 countries around the world. Clear Channel operated 1,184 radio and 34 television stations in the United States and had equity interests in over 240 radio stations internationally. It also operated a national radio network in the United States with about 180 million weekly listeners. In addition, the company operated over 700,000 outdoor advertising displays, including billboards, street furniture, and transit panels around the world. The company's Clear Channel Entertainment division was a leading promoter, producer, and marketer of about 30,000 live entertainment events annually and also owned leading athlete management and marketing companies.

Sources: www.clearchannel.com, September 2003, and *Business Week,* October 19, 1999, p. 56

VERTICAL INTEGRATION STRATEGIES: OPERATING ACROSS MORE STAGES OF THE INDUSTRY VALUE CHAIN

Vertical integration extends a firm's competitive and operating scope within the same basic industry. It involves expanding the firm's range of activities backward into sources of supply and/or forward toward end users. Thus, if a manufacturer invests in facilities to produce certain component parts that it formerly purchased from outside suppliers, it remains in essentially the same industry as before. The only change is that it has operations in two stages of the industry value chain. Similarly, if a paint manufacturer, Sherwin-Williams for example, elects to integrate forward by opening a national chain of retail stores to market its paint products directly to consumers, it remains in the paint business even though its competitive scope extends from manufacturing to retailing.

Vertical integration strategies can aim at *full integration* (participating in all stages of the industry value chain) or *partial integration* (building positions in selected stages of the industry's total value chain). A firm can pursue vertical integration by starting its own operations in other stages in the industry's activity chain or by acquiring a company already performing the activities it wants to bring in-house.

The Strategic Advantages of Vertical Integration

core concept
A vertical integration strategy has appeal *only* if it significantly strengthens a firm's competitive position.

The only good reason for investing company resources in vertical integration is to strengthen the firm's competitive position.[6] Vertical integration has no real payoff profitwise or strategywise unless it produces sufficient cost savings to justify the extra investment, adds materially to a company's technological and competitive strengths, or truly helps differentiate the company's product offering.

Integrating Backward to Achieve Greater Competitiveness   Integrating backward generates cost savings only when the volume needed is big enough to capture the same scale economies suppliers have and when suppliers' production efficiency can be matched or exceeded with no drop-off in quality and new product development capability. Backward integration is most likely to reduce costs when suppliers have sizable profit margins, the item being supplied is a major cost component, and the needed technological skills and product development capability are easily mastered or can be gained by acquiring a supplier with the desired expertise. Integrating backward can sometimes significantly enhance a company's technological capabilities and give it expertise needed to stake out positions in the industries and products of the future. Intel, Cisco, and many other Silicon Valley companies have been active in acquiring companies that will help them speed the advance of Internet technology and pave the way for next-generation families of products and services.

Backward vertical integration can produce a differentiation-based competitive advantage when a company, by performing activities in-house that were previously outsourced, ends up with a better-quality offering, improves the caliber of its customer service, or in other ways enhances the performance of its final product. On occasion, integrating into more stages along the industry value chain can add to a company's differentiation capabilities by allowing it to build or strengthen its core competencies, better master key skills or strategy-critical technologies, or add features that deliver greater customer value. Smithfield Foods, the largest pork processing company in the United States, has integrated backward into hog production because by having direct control over genetics, feed, and other aspects of the hog-raising process, it can introduce branded products—such as Smithfield Lean Generation Pork—that stand out from other pork products on the market.

Other potential advantages of backward integration include decreasing the company's dependence on suppliers of crucial components and lessening the company's vulnerability to powerful suppliers inclined to raise prices at every opportunity. Stockpiling, contracting for fixed prices, multiple sourcing, forming long-term cooperative partnerships, and using substitute inputs are not always attractive ways for dealing with uncertain supply conditions or with economically powerful suppliers. Companies that are low on a key supplier's customer priority list can find themselves waiting on shipments every time supplies get tight. If this occurs often and wreaks havoc in a company's own production and customer relations activities, backward integration can be an advantageous strategic solution.

Integrating Forward to Enhance Competitiveness   The strategic impetus for forward integration is to gain better access to end users and better market visibility. In many industries, independent sales agents, wholesalers, and retailers handle competing brands of the same product; having no allegiance to any one company's brand, they tend to push whatever sells and earns them the biggest profits. Halfhearted commitments by distributors and retailers can frustrate a company's attempt to boost sales and market share, give rise to costly inventory pileups and frequent underutilization of capacity, and disrupt the economies of steady near-capacity production. In such cases, it can be advantageous for a manufacturer to integrate forward into wholesaling or retailing via company-owned distributorships or a chain of retail stores. But often a company's product line is not broad enough to justify stand-alone distributorships or retail outlets. This leaves the option of integrating forward into the activity of selling directly to end users—perhaps via the Internet. Bypassing regular wholesale/retail channels in favor of direct sales and Internet retailing may lower distribution costs, produce a relative cost advantage over certain rivals, and result in lower selling prices to end users.

The Strategic Disadvantages of Vertical Integration

Vertical integration has some substantial drawbacks, however. It boosts a firm's capital investment in the industry, increasing business risk (what if industry growth and profitability go sour?) and perhaps denying financial resources to more worthwhile pursuits. A vertically integrated firm has vested interests in protecting its technology and production facilities. Because of the high costs of abandoning such investments before they are worn out, fully integrated firms tend to adopt new technologies slower than partially integrated or nonintegrated firms. Second, integrating forward or backward locks a firm into relying on its own in-house activities and sources of supply (which later may prove more costly than outsourcing) and potentially results in less flexibility in accommodating buyer demand for greater product variety. In today's world of close working relationships with suppliers and efficient supply chain management systems, very few businesses can make a case for integrating backward into the business of suppliers just for the purposes of ensuring a reliable supply of materials and components or to reduce production costs.

Third, vertical integration poses all kinds of capacity-matching problems. In motor vehicle manufacturing, for example, the most efficient scale of operation for making axles is different from the most economic volume for radiators, and different yet again for both engines and transmissions. Building the capacity to produce just the right number of axles, radiators, engines, and transmissions in-house—and doing so at the lowest unit costs for each—is much easier said than done. If internal capacity for making transmissions is deficient, the difference has to be bought externally. Where internal capacity for radiators proves excessive, customers need to be found for the surplus. And if by-products are generated—as occurs in the processing of many chemical products—they require arrangements for disposal.

Fourth, integration forward or backward often calls for radically different skills and business capabilities. Parts and components manufacturing, assembly operations, wholesale distribution and retailing, and direct sales via the Internet are different businesses with different key success factors. A manufacturer that integrates backward into components production may find that its expertise in advancing the technology of such components is deficient compared to the capabilities of companies that specialize in the manufacture of particular components. Most automakers, for example, have learned that they lack the capabilities to develop next-generation parts and components for their vehicles compared to what can be achieved by partnering with components specialists who have greater depth of knowledge and expertise. Managers of a manufacturing company should consider carefully whether it makes good business sense to invest time and money in developing the expertise and merchandising skills to integrate forward into wholesaling and retailing. Many manufacturers learn the hard way that company-owned wholesale/retail networks present many headaches, fit poorly with what they do best, and don't always add the kind of value to their core business they thought they would. Selling to customers via the Internet poses still another set of problems—it is usually easier to use the Internet to sell to business customers than to consumers.

Integrating backward into parts and components manufacture isn't as simple or profitable as it sounds, either. Producing some or all of the parts and components needed for final assembly can reduce a company's flexibility to make desirable changes in using certain parts and components—it is one thing to design out a component made by a supplier and another to design out a component being made in-house. Companies that alter designs and models frequently in response to shifting buyer preferences often find outsourcing the needed parts and components cheaper and less complicated than in-house manufacturing. Most of the world's automakers, despite their expertise in automotive technology and manufacturing, have concluded that purchasing many of their key parts and components from manufacturing specialists results in higher quality, lower costs, and greater design flexibility than does the vertical integration option.

Weighing the Pros and Cons of Vertical Integration   All in all, a strategy of vertical integration can have both important strengths and weaknesses. Which way the scales tip depends on (1) whether vertical integration can enhance the performance of strategy-critical activities in ways that lower cost, build expertise, or increase differentiation; (2) the impact of vertical integration on investment costs, flexibility and response times, and the administrative costs of coordinating operations across more value chain activities; and (3) whether vertical integration substantially enhances a company's competitiveness. Vertical integration strategies have merit according to which capabilities and value chain activities truly need to be performed in-house and which can be performed better or cheaper by outsiders. Absent solid benefits, integrating forward or backward is not likely to be an attractive competitive strategy option. In a growing number of instances, companies are proving that focusing on a narrower portion of the industry value chain and relying on outsiders to perform the remaining value chain activities is a more flexible and economical strategy.

OUTSOURCING STRATEGIES: NARROWING THE BOUNDARIES OF THE BUSINESS

Over the past decade, outsourcing the performance of some value chain activities traditionally performed in-house has become increasingly popular. Some companies have found vertical integration to be so competitively burdensome that they have deintegrated and withdrawn from some stages of the industry value chain. Moreover, a number of single-business enterprises have begun outsourcing a variety of value chain activities formerly performed in-house to enable them to better concentrate their energies on a narrower, more strategy-critical portion of the overall value chain. Outsourcing strategies thus involve a conscious decision to abandon or forgo attempts to perform certain value chain activities internally and instead to farm them out to outside specialists and business partners. The two driving themes behind outsourcing are that (1) outsiders can often perform certain activities better or cheaper and (2) outsourcing allows a firm to focus its entire energies on its core business—those activities at the center of its expertise (its core competencies) and that are the most critical to its competitive and financial success.

Advantages of Outsourcing

Outsourcing pieces of the value chain to narrow the boundaries of a firm's business makes strategic sense whenever:

- *An activity can be performed more cheaply by outside specialists.* Many PC makers, for example, have shifted from assembling units in-house to using contract assemblers because of the sizable scale economies associated with purchasing PC components in large volumes and assembling PCs. Cisco outsources most all production and assembly of its routers and switching equipment to contract manufacturers that together operate 37 factories, all linked to Cisco facilities via the Internet.

- *An activity can be performed better by outside specialists.* An automaker can obtain higher-caliber navigation systems and audio systems for its cars by sourcing them from companies with specialized know-how and manufacturing expertise than it can from trying to make them in-house.

- *The activity is not crucial to the firm's ability to achieve sustainable competitive advantage and won't hollow out its core competencies, capabilities, or technical know-how.* Outsourcing of maintenance services, data processing, customer billing, employee benefits administration, Web site operations, and other administrative support activities to specialists has become commonplace. American Express, for instance, recently entered into a seven-year, $4 billion deal whereby IBM's Services division will host American Express's Web site, network servers, data storage, and help-desk support; American Express indicated that it would save several hundred million dollars by paying only for the services it needed when it needed them (as opposed to funding its own full-time staff).

- *It reduces the company's risk exposure to changing technology and/or changing buyer preferences.* Outsourcing, for example, puts the burden on outside suppliers of components to keep pace with advancing technology as it affects their component business; should a components supplier fall behind on developing next-generation components or should its component lose out to a different type of component incorporating another type of technology, then the outsourcing company can simply shift suppliers. Likewise, a PC maker that decides to outsource rather than make monitors for its PCs can readily shift its purchases to liquid crystal display (LCD) or flat-panel monitors as more and more buyers of its PCs shift away from ordering conventional cathode ray tube (CRT) monitors. Had a PC maker opted years ago to produce CRT monitors in-house, then it would have less flexibility in accommodating growing buyer preferences for LCD monitors and its investment in facilities to produce CRT monitors would be at risk.

- *It streamlines company operations in ways that cut the time it takes to get newly developed products into the marketplace, lower internal coordination costs, or improve organizational flexibility.* Hewlett-Packard can speed the introduction of next-generation printers by collaborating with outside suppliers of printer components on both new printer design and new model release dates and then holding suppliers accountable for meeting the established specifications and deadlines. Were Hewlett-Packard to make all its printer components in-house, its lead times for getting newly designed models to market would be longer and more cumbersome in terms of bureaucratic hassle, internal resistance, and coordination costs. Major advances in the methods of supply chain management are allowing companies to employ very efficient and effective outsourcing strategies; moreover, outside suppliers tend to be more responsive to requests from their major customers than internal company groups are to requests from another internal group.

- *It allows a company to concentrate on strengthening and leveraging its core competencies.* Ideally, outsourcing allows a company to focus on a distinctive competence in some competitively important activity that results in sustainable competitive advantage over rivals.

core concept

A company should generally *not* perform any value chain activity internally that can be performed more efficiently or effectively by its outside business partners—the chief exception is when an activity is strategically crucial and internal control over that activity is deemed essential.

Often, many of the advantages of performing value chain activities in-house can be captured and many of the disadvantages avoided by forging close, long-term cooperative partnerships with key suppliers and tapping into the important competitive capabilities that able suppliers have painstakingly developed. In years past, many companies maintained arm's-length relationships with suppliers, insisting on items being made to precise specifications and negotiating long and hard over price.[7] Although a company might place orders with the same supplier repeatedly, there was no firm expectation that the orders would continue; price usually determined which supplier was awarded an order, and companies maneuvered for leverage over suppliers to get the lowest possible prices. The threat of switching suppliers was the company's primary weapon. To make this threat credible, sourcing from several suppliers was preferred to dealing with only a single supplier.

Today, most companies are abandoning such approaches in favor of alliances and strategic partnerships with a small number of highly capable suppliers. Cooperative relationships are replacing contractual, purely price-oriented relationships. Relying on outside specialists to perform certain value chain activities offers a number of strategic advantages:[8]

- Obtaining higher quality and/or cheaper components or services than internal sources can provide.

- Improving the company's ability to innovate by allying with "best-in-world" suppliers who have considerable intellectual capital and innovative capabilities of their own.

- Enhancing the firm's strategic flexibility should customer needs and market conditions suddenly shift—seeking out new suppliers with the needed capabilities already in place is frequently quicker, easier, less risky, and cheaper than hurriedly retooling internal operations to disband obsolete capabilities and put new ones in place.

- Increasing the firm's ability to assemble diverse kinds of expertise speedily and efficiently.

- Allowing the firm to concentrate its resources on performing those activities internally that it can perform better than outsiders and/or that it needs to have under its direct control.

Dell Computer's partnerships with the suppliers of PC components have allowed it to operate with fewer than four days of inventory, to realize substantial savings in inventory costs, and to get PCs equipped with next-generation components into the marketplace in less than a week after the newly upgraded components start shipping. Cisco's contract suppliers work so closely with Cisco that they can ship Cisco products to Cisco customers without a Cisco employee ever touching the gear; Cisco management claims its system of alliances saves $500 million to $800 million annually.[9] Hewlett-Packard, IBM, Silicon Graphics (now SGI), and others have sold plants to suppliers and then contracted to purchase the output. Starbucks finds purchasing coffee beans from independent growers to be far more advantageous than trying to integrate backward into the coffee-growing business.

The Pitfalls of Outsourcing

The biggest danger of outsourcing is that a company will farm out too many or the wrong types of activities and thereby hollow out its own capabilities. In such cases, a company loses touch with the very activities and expertise that over the long run determine its success. Cisco guards against loss of control and protects its manufacturing expertise by designing the production methods that its contract manufacturers must use. Cisco keeps the source code for its designs proprietary so it can remain the source of all improvements and innovations. Further, Cisco utilizes online technology to monitor the factory operations of contract manufacturers around the clock, enabling it to know immediately when problems arise and whether to get involved.

USING OFFENSIVE STRATEGIES TO SECURE COMPETITIVE ADVANTAGE

Competitive advantage is nearly always achieved by successful *offensive* strategic moves—initiatives calculated to yield a cost advantage, a differentiation advantage, or a resource advantage. In contrast, *defensive* strategies, discussed later in this chapter, can protect competitive advantage but rarely are the basis for creating the advantage. How long it takes for a successful offensive to create an edge varies with the competitive circumstances.[10] It can be short if the requisite resources and capabilities are already in place awaiting deployment or if buyers respond immediately (as can occur with a dramatic price cut, an imaginative ad campaign, or an especially appealing new product). Securing a competitive edge can take much longer if winning consumer acceptance of an innovative product will take some time or if the firm may need several years to debug a new technology or put new network systems or production capacity in place. Ideally, an offensive move builds competitive advantage quickly; the longer it takes, the more likely it is that rivals will spot the move, see its potential, and begin a counterresponse. The size of the advantage can be large (as in pharmaceuticals, where patents on an important new drug produce a substantial advantage) or small (as in apparel, where popular new designs can be imitated quickly).

However, competent, resourceful competitors can be counted on to counterattack with initiatives to overcome any market disadvantage they face—few companies will allow themselves to be outcompeted without a fight.[11] Thus, to sustain an initially won competitive advantage, a firm must come up with follow-on offensive and defensive moves. Unless the firm initiates one series of offensive and defensive moves after another to protect its market position and retain customer favor, its market advantage will erode.

> **core concept**
> Competent, resourceful rivals will exert strong efforts to overcome any competitive disadvantage they face—they won't be outcompeted without a fight.

Basic Types of Offensive Strategies

Most every company must at times go on the offensive to improve its market position. While offensive attacks may or may not be aimed at particular rivals, they usually are motivated by a desire to win sales and market share at the expense of other companies in the industry. There are six basic types of strategic offensives:[12]

1. Initiatives to match or exceed competitor strengths.
2. Initiatives to capitalize on competitor weaknesses.
3. Simultaneous initiatives on many fronts.
4. End-run offensives.
5. Guerrilla offensives.
6. Preemptive strikes.

Initiatives to Match or Exceed Competitor Strengths   There are two instances in which it makes sense to mount offensives aimed at neutralizing or overcoming the strengths and capabilities of rival companies. The first is when a company has no choice but to try to whittle away at a strong rival's competitive advantage. The second is when it is possible to gain profitable market share at the expense of rivals despite whatever resource strengths and capabilities they have. Attacking a powerful rival's strengths may be necessary when the rival has either a *superior product offering* or *superior organizational resources and capabilities*. Advanced Micro Devices (AMD), wanting to grow its sales of microprocessors for PCs, has on several occasions elected to attack Intel head-on, offering a faster alternative to Intel's Pentium chips at a lower price. Believing that the company's survival depends on eliminating the performance gap between AMD chips and Intel chips, AMD management has been willing to risk that a head-on offensive might prompt Intel to counter with lower prices of its own and accelerated development of faster Pentium chips.

The classic avenue for attacking a strong rival is to offer an equally good product at a lower price.[13] This can produce market share gains if the targeted competitor has sound reasons for not resorting to price cuts of its own and if the challenger convinces buyers that its product is just as good. However, such a strategy increases total profits only if the gains in additional unit sales are enough to offset the impact of lower prices and thinner margins per unit sold. A more potent and sustainable basis for mounting a price-aggressive challenge is to *first achieve a cost advantage* and then hit competitors with a lower price.[14]

Other strategic options for attacking a competitor's strengths include leapfrogging into next-generation technologies to make the rival's products obsolete, adding new features that appeal to the rival's customers, running comparison ads, constructing major new plant capacity in the rival's backyard, expanding the product line to match the rival model for model, and developing customer service capabilities that the targeted rival doesn't have.

As a rule, challenging a rival on competitive grounds where it is strong is an uphill struggle. Success can be long in coming and usually hinges on developing some kind of important edge over the target rival, whether it be lower cost, better service, a product with attractive differentiating features, or unique competitive capabilities (fast design-to-market times, greater technical know-how, or agility in responding to shifting customer requirements). Absent good prospects for added profitability and a more solid competitive position, offensives aimed at attacking a stronger rival head-on are ill-advised. General Motors, for instance, repeatedly attacked rival carmakers with aggressive rebates and 0 percent financing (at a cost of about $3,100 per vehicle sold) in 2001–2002, but it failed to gain more than 1 percent additional market share.[15]

Initiatives to Capitalize on Competitor Weaknesses   Initiatives that exploit competitor weaknesses stand a better chance of succeeding than do those that challenge competitor strengths, especially if the weaknesses represent important vulnerabilities and the rival is caught by surprise with no ready defense.[16] Options for attacking the competitive weaknesses of rivals include:

- Going after the customers of those rivals whose products lag on quality, features, or product performance.

- Making special sales pitches to the customers of those rivals who provide subpar customer service.

- Trying to win customers away from rivals with weak brand recognition (an attractive option if the aggressor has strong marketing skills and a recognized brand name).

- Emphasizing sales to buyers in geographic regions where a rival has a weak market share or is exerting less competitive effort.

- Paying special attention to buyer segments that a rival is neglecting or is weakly equipped to serve.

There are times when a defender facing a direct attack from a strong rival will be motivated to look for opportunities elsewhere rather than counterattack with strong moves of its own.[17]

Simultaneous Initiatives on Many Fronts   On occasion a company may see merit in launching a grand offensive involving multiple initiatives (price cuts, increased advertising, additional performance features, new models and styles, customer service improvements, and such promotions as free samples, coupons, rebates, and in-store displays) launched more or less concurrently across a wide geographic front. Such all-out campaigns can force a rival into many defensive actions to protect different pieces of its customer base simultaneously and thus divide its attention. Multifaceted offensives have their best chance of success when a challenger not only comes up with an especially attractive product or service but also has the brand awareness and distribution clout to get buyers' attention. A high-profile market blitz, buttressed with advertising and special deals, may well entice large numbers of buyers to switch their brand allegiance.

End-Run Offensives   The idea of an end-run offensive is to maneuver *around* competitors, capture unoccupied or less contested market territory, and change the rules of the competitive game in the aggressor's favor.[18] Examples include:

- *Introducing new products that redefine the market and the terms of competition*— Digital cameras have changed the rules of competition for members of the film-based camera and photo-processing industries. Wireless communications firms are employing end-run offensives to wreak havoc with the landline businesses of AT&T and the regional Bells.

- *Launching initiatives to build strong positions in geographic areas where close rivals have little or no market presence*—The race for global market leadership in PCs, servers, and Internet infrastructure products is prompting some contenders to launch early end-run offensives to build positions in less contested markets in Latin America and Asia (China and India have one-third of the world's population).

- *Trying to create new segments by introducing products with different attributes and performance features to better meet the needs of selected buyers*—Witness the success that Lexus, Acura, Infinity, and BMW have had with carlike sport-utility vehicles. This initiative works well when new product versions satisfy certain buyer needs that heretofore have been ignored or neglected.

- *Leapfrogging into next-generation technologies to supplant existing technologies, products and/or services*—The makers of thin, trim flat-panel monitors and LCD TVs are moving aggressively to improve the cost-effectiveness of their technology and production processes to leapfrog the technology of heavier, more bulky CRT monitors and TVs.

Guerrilla Offensives   Guerrilla offensives are particularly well suited to small challengers who have neither the resources nor the market visibility to mount a full-fledged attack on industry leaders.[19] Guerrilla offensives use the hit-and-run principle—an underdog tries to grab sales and market share wherever and whenever it catches rivals napping or spots an opening through which to lure customers away. Guerrilla offensives can involve making scattered, random raids on the leaders' customers with such tactics as occasional lowballing on price (to win a big order or steal a key account); surprising key rivals with sporadic but intense bursts of promotional activity (offering a 20 percent discount for one week to draw customers away from rival brands); or undertaking special campaigns to attract buyers away from rivals plagued with a strike or problems in meeting delivery schedules.[20] Guerrillas can promote the quality of their products when rivals have quality control problems or announce guaranteed delivery times when competitors' deliveries are running behind or significantly boost their commitment to prompt technical support when buyers are frustrated by the caliber of the support offered by industry leaders.

Preemptive Strikes   Preemptive strategies involve moving first to secure an advantageous position that rivals are prevented or discouraged from duplicating. What makes a move preemptive is its one-of-a-kind nature—whoever strikes first stands to acquire competitive assets that rivals can't readily match. There are several ways a firm can bolster its competitive capabilities with preemptive moves: (1) securing exclusive or dominant access to the best distributors in a particular geographic region or country; (2) moving to obtain the most favorable site along a heavily traveled thoroughfare, at a new interchange or intersection, in a new shopping mall, in a natural beauty spot, close to cheap transportation or raw material supplies or market outlets, and so on; and (3) tying up the most reliable, high-quality suppliers via exclusive partnership, long-term contracts, or acquisition.[21] To be successful, a preemptive move doesn't have to totally block rivals from following or copying; it merely needs to give a firm a prime position that is not easily circumvented.

Choosing Which Rivals to Attack

Offensive-minded firms need to analyze which of their rivals to challenge as well as how to mount that challenge. The following are the best targets for offensive attacks:[22]

- *Market leaders that are vulnerable*—Offensive attacks make good sense when a company that leads in terms of size and market share is not a true leader in terms of serving the market well. Signs of leader vulnerability include unhappy buyers, an inferior product line, a weak competitive strategy with regard to low-cost leadership or differentiation, strong emotional commitment to an aging technology the leader has pioneered, outdated plants and equipment, a preoccupation with diversification into other industries, and mediocre or declining profitability. Offensives to erode the positions of market leaders have real promise when the challenger is able to revamp its value chain or innovate to gain a fresh cost-based or differentiation-based competitive advantage.[23] To be judged successful, attacks on leaders don't have to result in making the aggressor the new leader; a challenger may "win" by simply becoming a stronger runner-up. Caution is well advised in challenging strong market leaders—there's a significant risk of squandering valuable resources in a futile effort or precipitating a fierce and profitless industrywide battle for market share.
- *Runner-up firms with weaknesses where the challenger is strong*—Runner-up firms are an especially attractive target when a challenger's resource strengths and competitive capabilities are well suited to exploiting their weaknesses.
- *Struggling enterprises that are on the verge of going under*—Challenging a hard-pressed rival in ways that further sap its financial strength and competitive position can weaken its resolve and hasten its exit from the market.
- *Small local and regional firms with limited capabilities*—Because small firms typically have limited expertise and resources, a challenger with broader capabilities is well positioned to raid their biggest and best customers—particularly those who are growing rapidly, have increasingly sophisticated requirements, and may already be thinking about switching to a supplier with more full-service capability.

Choosing the Basis for Attack

A firm's strategic offensive should, at a minimum, be tied to what it does best—its core competencies, resource strengths, and competitive capabilities. Otherwise the prospects for success are indeed dim. The centerpiece of the offensive can be an important core competence, a unique competitive capability, much-improved performance features, an innovative new product, technological superiority, a cost advantage in manufacturing or distribution, or some kind of differentiation advantage. If the challenger's resources and competitive strengths amount to a competitive advantage over the targeted rivals, so much the better.

USING DEFENSIVE STRATEGIES TO PROTECT THE COMPANY'S POSITION

> It is just as important to discern when to fortify a company's present market position with defensive actions as it is to seize the initiative and launch strategic offensives.

In a competitive market, all firms are subject to offensive challenges from rivals. The purposes of defensive strategies are to lower the risk of being attacked, weaken the impact of any attack that occurs, and influence challengers to aim their efforts at other rivals. While defensive strategies usually don't enhance a firm's competitive advantage, they can definitely help fortify its competitive position, protect its most valuable resources and capabilities from imitation, and defend whatever competitive advantage it might have. Defensive strategies can take either of two forms: blocking challengers and signaling the likelihood of strong retaliation.

Blocking the Avenues Open to Challengers

The most frequently employed approach to defending a company's present position involves actions that restrict a challenger's options for initiating competitive attack. There

> There are many ways to throw obstacles in the path of challengers.

are any number of obstacles that can be put in the path of would-be challengers.[24] A defender can participate in alternative technologies to reduce the threat that rivals will attack with a better technology. A defender can introduce new features, add new models, or broaden its product line to close off gaps and vacant niches to would-be challengers. It can thwart the efforts of rivals to attack with a lower price by maintaining economy-priced options of its own. It can try to discourage buyers from trying competitors' brands via such actions as lengthening warranty coverages, offering free training and support services, developing the capability to deliver spare parts to users faster than rivals can, providing coupons and sample giveaways to buyers most prone to experiment, and making early announcements about impending new products or price changes to induce potential buyers to postpone switching. It can challenge the quality or safety of rivals' products in regulatory proceedings—a favorite tactic of the pharmaceutical firms in trying to delay the introduction of competing prescription drugs. Finally, a defender can grant dealers and distributors volume discounts or better financing terms to discourage them from experimenting with other suppliers, or it can convince them to handle its product line *exclusively* and force competitors to use other distribution outlets.

Signaling Challengers That Retaliation Is Likely

The goal of signaling challengers that strong retaliation is likely in the event of an attack is either to dissuade challengers from attacking at all or to divert them to less threatening options. Either goal can be achieved by letting challengers know the battle will cost more than it is worth. Would-be challengers can be signaled by:[25]

- Publicly announcing management's commitment to maintain the firm's present market share.
- Publicly committing the company to match competitors' terms or prices.
- Maintaining a war chest of cash and marketable securities.
- Making an occasional strong counterresponse to the moves of weak competitors to enhance the firm's image as a tough defender.

STRATEGIES FOR USING THE INTERNET AS A DISTRIBUTION CHANNEL

As the Internet continues to weave its way into the fabric of everyday business and personal life, and as the second wave of Internet entrepreneurship takes root, companies of all types are addressing how best to make the Internet a fundamental part of their business and their competitive strategies. Few if any businesses can escape making some effort to use Internet applications to improve their value chain activities. This much is a given—anything less risks competitive disadvantage. Companies across the world are deep into the process of implementing a variety of Internet technology applications; the chief question companies face at this point is what additional Internet technology applications to incorporate into day-to-day operations. But the larger and much tougher *strategic* issue is how to make the Internet a fundamental part of a company's competitive strategy—in particular, how much emphasis to place on the Internet as a distribution channel for accessing buyers. *Managers must decide how to use the Internet in positioning the company in the marketplace*—whether to use the company's Web site as *simply a means of disseminating product information* (with traditional distribution channel partners making all sales to end users), as a *secondary* or *minor* channel for making sales, as *one of several important distribution channels for generating sales to end users,* as *the primary distribution channel,* or as *the exclusive channel for accessing customers.*[26] Let's look at each of these strategic options in turn.

> Companies today must wrestle with the issue of how to use the Internet in positioning themselves in the marketplace—whether to use their Web site as a way to disseminate product information, as a minor distribution channel, as one of several important distribution channels, as the primary distribution channel, or as the company's only distribution channel.

Using the Internet Just to Disseminate Product Information

Operating a Web site that only disseminates product information—but that relies on click-throughs to the Web sites of distribution channel partners for sales transactions (or that informs site users where nearby retail stores are located)—is an attractive market positioning option for manufacturers and wholesalers that already have retail dealer networks and face nettlesome channel conflict issues if they try to sell online in direct competition with their dealers. A manufacturer or wholesaler that aggressively pursues online sales to end users is signaling both a weak strategic commitment to its dealers and a willingness to cannibalize dealers' sales and growth potential. To the extent that strong partnerships with wholesale and/or retail dealers are critical to accessing end users, selling direct to end users via the company's Web site is a very tricky road to negotiate. A manufacturer's efforts to use its Web site to sell around its dealers is certain to anger its wholesale distributors and retail dealers may respond by putting more effort into marketing the brands of rival manufacturers who don't sell online. In sum, the manufacturer may stand to lose more sales through its dealers than it gains from its own online sales effort. Moreover, dealers may be in better position to employ a brick-and-click strategy than a manufacturer because dealers have a local presence to complement their online sales approach (which consumers may find appealing). Consequently, in industries where the strong support and goodwill of dealer networks is essential, manufacturers may conclude that their Web site should be designed to partner with dealers rather than compete with them—just as the auto manufacturers are doing with their franchised dealers.

Using the Internet as a Minor Distribution Channel

A second strategic option is to use online sales as a relatively minor distribution channel for achieving incremental sales, gaining online sales experience, and doing marketing research. If channel conflict poses a big obstacle to online sales, or if only a small fraction of buyers can be attracted to make online purchases, then companies are well advised to pursue online sales with the strategic intent of gaining experience, learning more about buyer tastes and preferences, testing reaction to new products, creating added market buzz about their products, and boosting overall sales volume a few percentage points. Nike, for example, has begun selling some of its footwear online, giving buyers the option of specifying certain colors and features. Such a strategy is unlikely to provoke much resistance from dealers and could even prove beneficial to dealers if footwear buyers become enamored with custom-made shoes that can be ordered through and/or picked up at Nike retailers. A manufacturer may be able to glean valuable marketing research data from tracking the browsing patterns of Web site visitors and incorporating what generates the most interest into its mainstream product offerings. The behavior and actions of Web surfers are a veritable gold mine of information for companies seeking to respond more precisely to buyer preferences.

Brick-and-Click Strategies: An Appealing Middle Ground

Employing a brick-and-click strategy to sell directly to consumers while at the same time using traditional wholesale and retail channels can be an attractive market positioning option in the right circumstances. With a brick-and-click strategy, sales at a company's Web site can serve as either one of several important distribution channels through which the company accesses end users or as its primary distribution channel. Software developers, for example, have come to rely on the Internet as a highly effective distribution channel to complement sales through brick-and-mortar wholesalers and retailers. Selling online directly to end users has the advantage of cutting out the costs and margins of software wholesalers and retailers (often 35 to 50 percent of the retail price). In addition, allowing customers to download their software purchases immediately eliminates the costs of producing and packaging CDs. However, software developers are still strongly motivated to continue to distribute their products through wholesalers and retailers (to maintain broad access to existing and potential users who, for whatever reason, may be reluctant to buy online).

Despite the channel conflict that exists when a manufacturer sells directly to end users at its Web site in head-to-head competition with its distribution channel allies, there are three major reasons why manufacturers might want to aggressively pursue online sales and establish the Internet as an important distribution channel alongside traditional channels:

1. The manufacturer's profit margin from online sales is bigger than that from sales through wholesale/retail channels.
2. Encouraging buyers to visit the company's Web site helps educate them to the ease and convenience of purchasing online, thus encouraging more and more buyers to migrate to buying online (where company profit margins are greater).
3. Selling directly to end users allows a manufacturer to make greater use of build-to-order manufacturing and assembly as a basis for bypassing traditional distribution channels entirely. Dell Computer, for instance, has used online sales to make

build-to-order options a cost-effective reality. Similarly, several motor vehicle companies have initiated actions to streamline build-to-order manufacturing capabilities and reduce delivery times for custom orders from 30–60 days to as few as 5–10 days; most vehicle manufacturers already have software on their Web sites that permits motor vehicle shoppers to select the models, colors, and optional equipment they would like to have. In industries where build-to-order options can result in substantial cost savings along the industry value chain and permit sizable price reductions to end users, companies have to consider making build-to-order and sell-direct an integral part of their market positioning strategy. Over time, such a strategy could increase the rate at which sales migrate from distribution allies to the company's Web site.

A combination brick-and-click market positioning strategy is highly suitable when on-line sales have a good chance of *evolving* into a manufacturer's primary distribution channel. In such instances, incurring channel conflict in the short term and competing against traditional distribution allies makes good strategic sense.

Many brick-and-mortar companies can enter online retailing at relatively low cost—all they need is a Web store and systems for filling and delivering individual customer orders. Brick-and-click strategies have two big strategic appeals for wholesale and retail enterprises: They are an economic means of expanding a company's geographic reach, and they give both existing and potential customers another choice of how to communicate with the company, shop for product information, make purchases, or resolve customer service problems. Brick-and-mortar distributors and retailers (as well as manufacturers with company-owned retail stores) can shift to brick-and-click strategies by using their current distribution centers and/or retail stores for picking orders from on-hand inventories and making deliveries. Walgreen's, a leading drugstore chain, allows customers to order a prescription online and then pick it up at a local store (using the drive-through window, in some cases). In banking, a brick-and-click strategy allows customers to use local branches and ATMs for depositing checks and getting cash while using online systems to pay bills, check account balances, and transfer funds. Many industrial distributors are finding it efficient for customers to place their orders over the Web rather than phoning them in or waiting for salespeople to call in person. Illustration Capsule 6.2 describes how Office Depot has successfully migrated from a traditional brick-and-mortar distribution strategy to a combination brick-and-click distribution strategy.

Strategies for Online Enterprises

A company that elects to use the Internet as its exclusive channel for accessing buyers is essentially an online business from the perspective of the customer. The company's Web site becomes its online store for making sales and delivering customer services. Except for advertising, the company's Web site functions as the sole point of all buyer–seller contact. Many so-called pure dot-com enterprises have chosen this strategic approach—prominent examples include eBay, Amazon.com, Yahoo, Buy.com, and Priceline.com. For a company to succeed in using the Internet as its exclusive distribution channel, its product or service must be one for which buying online holds strong appeal. Furthermore, judging from the evidence thus far, an online company's strategy must incorporate the following features:

- *The capability to deliver unique value to buyers*—Winning strategies succeed in drawing buyers because of the value being delivered. This means that online

illustration capsule 6.2
Office Depot's Brick-and-Click Strategy

Office Depot was in the first wave of retailers to adopt a combination brick-and-click strategy. In 1996, it began allowing business customers to use the Internet to place orders. Businesses could thus avoid having to make a call, generate a purchase order, and pay an invoice—while still getting same-day or next-day delivery from one of Office Depot's local stores.

Office Depot built its Internet business around its existing network of 1,059 retail stores in 12 countries plus its 22 delivery centers and warehouses, 1,900 delivery trucks, 1,400 account managers, 60 sales offices, and 13 regional call centers that handled large business customers. It already had a solid brand name and enough purchasing power with its suppliers to counter discount-minded online rivals trying to attract buyers of office supplies on the basis of superlow prices. Office Depot's incremental investment to enter the e-commerce arena was minimal since all it needed to add was a Web site where customers could see pictures and descriptions of the 14,000 items it carried, their prices, and in-stock availability. Office Depot's marketing costs to make customers aware of its Web store option ran less than $10 million.

In setting up customized Web pages for 37,000 corporate and educational customers, Office Depot designed sites that allowed the customer's employees varying degrees of freedom to buy supplies. A clerk might be able to order only copying paper, toner cartridges, computer disks, and paper clips up to a preset dollar limit per order, while a vice president might have carte blanche to order any item Office Depot sold. Office Depot's online prices were the same as its store prices; the company's strategy was to promote Web sales on the basis of service, convenience, and lower customer costs for order processing and inventories.

In 2003, over 50 percent of Office Depot's major customers were ordering most of their supplies online because of the convenience and the savings in transactions costs. Bank of America, for example, was ordering 85 percent of its office supplies online from Office Depot.

Customers reported that using the Web site cut their transaction costs by up to 80 percent; plus, Office Depot's same-day or next-day delivery capability allowed them to reduce the amount of office supplies they kept in inventory.

Web site sales cost Office Depot less than $1 per $100 of goods ordered, compared with about $2 for phone and fax orders. And since Web sales eliminate the need to key in transactions, order-entry errors have been virtually eliminated and product returns cut by 50 percent. Billing is handled electronically.

Office Depot's online unit accounted for $2.1 billion in sales in 2002, up sharply from $982 million in 2000, making Office Depot the second-largest online retailer behind Amazon.com. Online sales were about 20 percent of the Office Depot's overall sales. Its online operations have been profitable from the start. Industry experts believe that Office Depot's success is based on the company's philosophy of maintaining a strong link between the Internet and its stores. "Office Depot gets it," noted one industry analyst. "It used the Net to build deeper relationships with customers."

Sources: www.officedepot.com, September 2003, and "Office Depot's e-Diva," *Business Week Online* (www.businessweek.com), August 6, 2001; Laura Lorek, "Office Depot Site Picks Up Speed," *Interactive Week* (www.zdnet.com/intweek), June 25, 2001; "Why Office Depot Loves the Net," *Business Week,* September 27, 1999, pp. EB 66, EB 68; and *Fortune,* November 8, 1999, p. 17.

businesses must usually attract buyers on the basis of something more than just low price—indeed, many dot-coms are already working to tilt the basis for competing away from low price and toward build-to-order systems, convenience, superior product information, attentive online service, and other ways to attract customers to buying online.

- *Deliberate efforts to engineer a value chain that enables differentiation, lower costs, or better value for the money*—For a company to win in the marketplace with an online-only distribution strategy, its value chain approach must hold potential for low-cost leadership, competitively valuable differentiating attributes, or a best-cost provider advantage. If a firm's strategy is to attract customers by selling at cut-rate prices, then it must possess cost advantages in those activities it performs, and it must outsource the remaining activities to low-cost specialists. If an online seller is going to differentiate itself on the basis of a superior buying experience and top-notch customer service, then it needs to concentrate on having an easy-to-navigate Web site, an array of functions and conveniences for customers, "Web reps" who can answer questions online, and logistical capabilities to deliver products quickly and accommodate returned merchandise. If it is going to deliver more value for the money, then it must manage value chain activities so as to deliver upscale products and services at lower costs than rivals. Absent a value chain that puts the company in an attractive position to compete head-to-head against other online and brick-and-mortar rivals, such a distribution strategy is unlikely to produce attractive profitability.

- *An innovative, fresh, and entertaining Web site*—Just as successful brick-and-mortar retailers employ merchandising strategies to keep their stores fresh and interesting to shoppers, Web merchandisers must exert ongoing efforts to add innovative site features and capabilities, enhance the look and feel of their sites, heighten viewer interest with audio and video, and have fresh product offerings and special promotions. Web pages need to be easy to read and interesting, with lots of eye appeal. Web site features that are distinctive, engaging, and entertaining add value to the experience of spending time at the site and are thus strong competitive assets.

- *A clear focus on a limited number of competencies and a relatively specialized number of value chain activities in which proprietary Internet applications and capabilities can be developed*—Low-value-added activities can be delegated to outside specialists. A strong market position is far more likely to emerge from efforts to develop proprietary Internet applications than from using third-party developers' software packages, which are also readily available to imitative rivals. Outsourcing value chain activities for which there is little potential for proprietary advantage allows an enterprise to concentrate on the ones for which it has the most expertise and through which it can gain competitive advantage.

- *Innovative marketing techniques that are efficient in reaching the targeted audience and effective in stimulating purchases (or boosting ancillary revenue sources like advertising)*—Web sites have to be cleverly marketed. Unless Web surfers hear about the site, like what they see on their first visit, and are intrigued enough to return again and again, the site will not generate enough revenue to allow the company to survive. Marketing campaigns that result only in heavy site traffic and lots of page views are seldom sufficient; the best test of effective marketing is the ratio at which page views are converted into revenues (the "look-to-buy" ratio). For example, in 2001 Yahoo's site traffic averaged 1.2 *billion* page views daily but generated only about $2 million in daily revenues; in contrast, the traffic at brokerage firm Charles Schwab's Web site averaged only 40 *million* page views per day but resulted in an average of $5 million daily in online commission revenues.

- *Minimal reliance on ancillary revenues*—Online businesses have to charge fully for the value delivered to customers rather than subsidizing artificially low prices with revenues collected from advertising and other ancillary sources. Companies should view site-advertising revenues and other revenue extras as a way to boost the profitability of an already profitable core businesses, *not* as a means of covering core business losses.

The Issue of Broad versus Narrow Product Offerings   Given that shelf space on the Internet is unlimited, online sellers have to make shrewd decisions about how to position themselves on the spectrum of broad versus narrow product offerings.

A one-stop shopping strategy like that employed by Amazon.com has the appealing economics of helping spread fixed operating costs over a wide number of items and a large customer base. Amazon has diversified its product offerings beyond books to include electronics, computers, housewares, music, DVDs, videos, cameras, toys, baby items and baby registry, software, computer and video games, cell phones and service, tools and hardware, travel services, magazine subscriptions, and outdoor-living items; it has also allowed small specialty-item e-tailers to market their products on the Amazon Web site. The company's tag line "Earth's Biggest Selection" seems accurate: In 2002, Amazon offered some 34 million items at its Web sites in the United States, Britain, France, Germany, Denmark, and Japan. Other e-tailers, such as Expedia and Hotel.com, have adopted classic focus strategies—building a Web site aimed at a sharply defined target audience shopping for a particular product or product category. "Focusers" seek to build customer loyalty based on attractively low prices, better value, wide selection of models and styles within the targeted category, convenient service, nifty options, or some other differentiating attribute. They pay special attention to the details that will please their narrow target audience.

The Order Fulfillment Issue   Another big strategic issue for dot-com retailers is whether to perform order fulfillment activities internally or to outsource them. Building central warehouses, stocking them with adequate inventories, and developing systems to pick, pack, and ship individual orders all require substantial start-up capital but may result in lower overall unit costs than would paying the fees of order fulfillment specialists who make a business of providing warehouse space, stocking inventories, and shipping orders for e-tailers. Outsourcing is likely to be economical unless an e-tailer has high unit volume and the capital to invest in its own order fulfillment capabilities. Buy.com, an online superstore consisting of some 30,000 items, obtains products from name-brand manufacturers and uses outsiders to stock and ship those products; thus, its focus is not on manufacturing or order fulfillment but rather on selling.

CHOOSING APPROPRIATE FUNCTIONAL-AREA STRATEGIES

A company's strategy is not complete until company managers have made strategic choices about how the various functional parts of the business—R&D, production, human resources, sales and marketing, finance, and so on—will be managed in support of its basic competitive strategy approach and the other important competitive moves being taken. Normally, functional-area strategy choices rank third on the menu of choosing among the various strategy options, as shown in Figure 6.1 (see p. 142). But whether commitments to particular functional strategies are made before or after the choices of complementary strategic options shown in Figure 6.1 is beside the point— what's really important is what the functional strategies are and how they mesh to enhance the success of the company's higher-level strategic thrusts.

In many respects, the nature of functional strategies is dictated by the choice of competitive strategy. For example, a manufacturer employing a low-cost provider strategy needs an R&D and product design strategy that emphasizes cheap-to-incorporate features and facilitates economical assembly and a production strategy that stresses capture of scale economies and actions to achieve low-cost manufacture (such as high labor productivity, efficient supply chain management, and automated production processes), and a low-budget marketing strategy. A business pursuing a high-end differentiation strategy needs a production strategy geared to top-notch quality and a marketing strategy aimed at touting differentiating features and using advertising and a trusted brand name to "pull" sales through the chosen distribution channels. A company using a focused differentiation strategy (like Krispy Kreme) needs a marketing strategy that stresses growing the niche (getting more people hooked on Krispy Kreme doughnuts), keeping buyer interest at a high level, and protecting the niche against invasion by outsiders.

Beyond very general prescriptions, it is difficult to say just what the content of the different functional-area strategies should be without first knowing what higher-level strategic choices a company has made, the industry environment in which it operates, the resource strengths that can be leveraged, and so on. Suffice it to say here that company personnel—both managers and employees charged with strategy-making responsibility down through the organizational hierarchy—must be clear about which higher-level strategies top management has chosen and then must tailor the company's functional-area strategies accordingly.

FIRST-MOVER ADVANTAGES AND DISADVANTAGES

When to make a strategic move is often as crucial as *what* move to make. Timing is especially important when *first-mover advantages* or *disadvantages* exist.[27] Being first to initiate a strategic move can have a high payoff in terms of strengthening a company's market position and competitiveness when (1) pioneering helps build a firm's image and reputation with buyers; (2) early commitments to new technologies, new-style components, distribution channels, and so on can produce an absolute cost advantage over rivals; (3) first-time customers remain strongly loyal to pioneering firms in making repeat purchases; and (4) moving first constitutes a preemptive strike, making imitation extra hard or unlikely. The bigger the first-mover advantages, the more attractive making the first move becomes.[28] In the Internet gold-rush era, several companies that were first with a new technology, network solution, or business model enjoyed lasting first-mover advantages in gaining the visibility and reputation needed to emerge as the dominant market leader—America Online, Amazon.com, Yahoo, eBay, and Priceline.com are cases in point. But a first-mover also needs to be a fast learner (so as to sustain any advantage of being a pioneer), and it helps immensely if the first-mover has deep financial pockets, important competencies and competitive capabilities, and high-quality management. Just being a first-mover by itself is seldom enough to yield competitive advantage. The proper target in timing a strategic move is not that of being the first company to do something but rather that of being the first competitor to put together the precise combination of features, customer value, and sound revenue-cost-profit economics that gives it an edge over rivals in the battle for market leadership.[29]

> **core concept**
> Because there are often important advantages to being a first-mover, competitive advantage can spring from *when* a move is made as well as from *what* move is made.

However, being a fast-follower or even a wait-and-see late-mover doesn't always carry a significant or lasting competitive penalty. There are times when a first-mover's skills, know-how, and actions are easily copied or even surpassed, allowing late-movers to catch or overtake the first-mover in a relatively short period. And there are times when there are actually *advantages* to being an adept follower rather than a first-mover. Late-mover advantages (or first-mover disadvantages) arise when (1) pioneering leadership is more costly than imitating followership and only negligible experience or learning-curve benefits accrue to the leader—a condition that allows a follower to end up with lower costs than the first-mover; (2) the products of an innovator are somewhat primitive and do not live up to buyer expectations, thus allowing a clever follower to win disenchanted buyers away from the leader with better-performing next-generation products; and (3) technology is advancing rapidly, giving fast-followers the opening to leapfrog a first-mover's products with more attractive and full-featured second- and third-generation products.

In weighing the pros and cons of being a first-mover versus a fast-follower, it is important to discern when the race to market leadership in a particular industry is a marathon rather than a sprint. In marathons, a slow-mover is not unduly penalized—first-mover advantages can be fleeting, and there's ample time for followers to play catch-up.[30] For instance, it took seven years for videocassette recorders to find their way into 1 million U.S. homes but only a year and a half for 10 million users to sign up for Hotmail. The lesson here is that there is a market-penetration curve for every emerging opportunity; typically, the curve has an inflection point at which all the pieces of the business model fall into place, buyer demand explodes, and the market takes off. The inflection point can come early on a fast-rising curve or farther on up a slow-rising curve. Any company that seeks competitive advantage by being a first-mover should thus first pose some hard questions: Does market takeoff depend on the development of complementary products or services that currently are not available? Is new infrastructure required before buyer demand can surge? Will buyers need to learn new skills or adopt new behaviors? Will buyers encounter high switching costs? Are there influential competitors in a position to derail the efforts of a first-mover? When the answers to any of these questions are yes, then a company must be careful not to pour too many resources into getting ahead of the market opportunity—the race is likely going to be more of a 10-year marathon than a 2-year sprint. But being first out of the starting block is competitively important if it produces clear and substantial benefits to buyers and competitors will be compelled to follow.

While being an adept fast-follower has the advantages of being less risky and skirting the costs of pioneering, rarely does a company have much to gain from being a slow-follower and concentrating on avoiding the "mistakes" of first-movers. Habitual late-movers, while often able to survive, are usually fighting to retain their customers and scrambling to keep pace with more progressive and innovative rivals. For a habitual late-mover to catch up, it must count on first-movers to be slow learners—plus it has to hope that buyers will be slow to gravitate to the products of first-movers, again giving it time to catch up. And it has to have competencies and capabilities that are sufficiently strong to allow it to close the gap fairly quickly once it makes its move. Counting on all first-movers to stumble or otherwise be easily overtaken is usually a bad bet that puts a late-mover's competitive position at risk.

Illustration Capsule 6.3 describes the challenges that late-moving telephone companies have in winning the battle to supply high-speed Internet access and overcoming the first-mover advantages of cable companies.

key|points

Once a company has selected which of the five basic competitive strategies to employ in its quest for competitive advantage, it must then decide whether to supplement its choice of a basic competitive strategy approach with strategic actions relating to forming alliances and collaborative partnerships, pursuing mergers and acquisitions, integrating forward or backward, outsourcing certain value chain activities, making offensive and defensive moves, and what use to make of the Internet in selling directly to end users, as shown in Figure 6.1.

illustration capsule 6.3

The Battle in Consumer Broadband: First-Movers versus Late-Movers

In 1988 an engineer at the Bell companies' research labs figured out how to rush signals along ordinary copper wire at high speed using digital technology, thus creating the digital subscriber line (DSL). But the regional Bells, which dominated the local telephone market, showed little interest over the next 10 years, believing it was more lucrative to rent T-1 lines to businesses that needed fast data transmission capability and rent second phone lines to households wanting an Internet connection that didn't disrupt their regular telephone service. Furthermore, telephone executives were skeptical about DSL technology—there were a host of technical snarls to overcome, and early users encountered annoying glitches. Many executives doubted that it made good sense to invest billions of dollars in the infrastructure needed to roll out DSL to residential and small business customers, given the success they were having with T-1 and second-line rentals. As a consequence, the Bells didn't seriously begin to market DSL until the late 1990s, two years after the cable TV companies began their push to market cable broadband.

Cable companies were more than happy to be the first-movers in marketing broadband service via their copper cable wires, chiefly because their business was threatened by satellite TV technology and they saw broadband as an innovative service they could provide that the satellite companies could not. (Delivering broadband service via satellite has yet to become a factor in the marketplace, winning only a 1 percent share in 2003.) Cable companies were able to deploy broadband on their copper wire economically because during the 1980s and early 1990s most cable operators had spent about $60 billion to upgrade their systems with fiber-optic technology in order to handle two-way traffic rather than just one-way TV signals and thereby make good on their promises to local governments to develop "interactive" cable systems if they were awarded franchises. Although the early interactive services were duds, technicians discovered in the mid-1990s that the two-way systems enabled high-speed Internet hookups.

With Internet excitement surging in the late 1990s, cable executives saw high-speed Internet service as a no-brainer and began rolling it out to customers in 1998, securing about 362,000 customers by year-end versus only about 41,000 for DSL. Part of the early success of cable broadband was due to a cost advantage in modems—cable

executives, seeing the potential of cable broadband several years earlier, had asked CableLabs to standardize the technology for cable modems, a move that lowered costs and made cable modems marketable in consumer electronics stores. DSL modems were substantially more complicated, and it took longer to drive the costs down from several hundred dollars each to under $100—today, both cable and phone companies pay about $50 for modems, but cable modems got there much sooner.

As cable broadband began to attract more and more attention, the regional Bells continued to move slowly on DSL. The technical problems lingered, and early users were disgruntled by a host of annoying and sometimes horrendous installation difficulties and service glitches. Not only did providing users with convenient and reliable service prove to be a formidable challenge, but some regulatory issues stood in the way as well. And it continues to be hard to justify multibillion-dollar investments to install the necessary equipment and support systems to offer, market, manage, and maintain DSL service on the vast scale of a regional Bell company. SBC Communications figured it would cost at least $6 billion to roll out DSL to its customers. Verizon estimated that it would take 3.5 to 4 million customers to make DSL economics work, a number it would probably not reach until the end of 2005.

In 2003, high-speed consumer access to the Internet was a surging business with a bright outlook and cable broadband was the preferred choice—70 percent of the market was opting for cable modems supplied by cable TV companies instead of DSL service offered by the local phone companies. While only about 13 million of the 115 million U.S. households had cable Internet access and only 7.3 million had DSL in June 2003, the number of Internet users upgrading to high-speed service was growing by several hundred thousand monthly. Moreover, over half of the households subscribing to cable broadband and DSL were disconnecting their second phone lines, once used to connect to the Internet. While an additional 25 to 30 million households and small businesses were expected to upgrade to broadband in the next several years, it was questionable whether DSL broadband would be able to catch cable broadband in the marketplace. Phone company executives were hopeful that DSL could close the gap, despite its late start.

Source: Shawn Young and Peter Grant, "How Phone Firms Lost to Cable in Consumer Broadband Market," *The Wall Street Journal,* March 13, 2003, pp. A1, A6.

Many companies are using strategic alliances and collaborative partnerships to help them in the race to build a global market presence and in the technology race. Even large and financially strong companies have concluded that simultaneously running both races requires more diverse and expansive skills and competitive capabilities than they can assemble and manage alone. Strategic alliances are an attractive, flexible, and often cost-effective means by which companies can gain access to missing technology, expertise, and business capabilities. The competitive attraction of alliances is to bundle competencies and resources that are more valuable in a joint effort than when kept separate. Competitive advantage emerges when a company acquires valuable resources and capabilities through alliances that it could not readily obtain on its own and that give it an edge over rivals.

Mergers and acquisitions are another attractive strategic option for strengthening a firm's competitiveness. Companies racing for global market leadership frequently make acquisitions to build a market presence in countries where they currently do not compete. Similarly, companies racing to establish attractive positions in the industries of the future merge or make acquisitions to close gaps in resources or technology, build important technological capabilities, and move into position to launch next-wave products and services. When the operations of two companies are combined via merger or acquisition, the new company's competitiveness can be enhanced in any of several ways—lower costs; stronger technological skills; more or better competitive capabilities; a more attractive lineup of products and services; wider geographic coverage; and/or greater financial resources with which to invest in R&D, add capacity, or expand into new areas.

Vertically integrating forward or backward makes strategic sense only if it strengthens a company's position via either cost reduction or creation of a differentiation-based advantage. Otherwise, the drawbacks of vertical integration (increased investment, greater business risk, increased vulnerability to technological changes, and less flexibility in making product changes) outweigh the advantages (better coordination of production flows and technological know-how from stage to stage, more specialized use of technology, greater internal control over operations, greater scale economies, and matching production with sales and marketing). Collaborative partnerships with suppliers and/or distribution allies often permit a company to achieve the advantages of vertical integration without encountering the drawbacks.

Outsourcing pieces of the value chain formerly performed in-house can enhance a company's competitiveness whenever (1) an activity can be performed better or more cheaply by outside specialists; (2) the activity is not crucial to the firm's ability to achieve sustainable competitive advantage and won't hollow out its core competencies, capabilities, or technical know-how; (3) outsourcing reduces the company's risk exposure to changing technology and/or changing buyer preferences; (4) outsourcing streamlines company operations in ways that improve organizational flexibility, cut cycle time, speed decision making, and reduce coordination costs; and/or (5) outsourcing allows a company to concentrate on its core business and do what it does best. In many situations outsourcing is a superior strategic alternative to vertical integration.

A variety of offensive strategic moves can be used to secure a competitive advantage. Strategic offensives can be aimed either at competitors' strengths or at their weaknesses; they can involve end runs or grand offensives on many fronts; they can be designed as guerrilla actions or as preemptive strikes; and the target of the offensive can be a market leader, a runner-up firm, or the smallest and/or weakest firms in the industry.

Defensive strategies to protect a company's position usually take the form of making moves that put obstacles in the path of would-be challengers and fortify the company's present position while undertaking actions to dissuade rivals from even trying to attack (by signaling that the resulting battle will be more costly to the challenger than it is worth).

One of the most pertinent strategic issues that companies face is how to use the Internet in positioning the company in the marketplace—as *only a means of disseminating product information* (with traditional distribution channel partners making all sales to end users), as a *secondary channel,* as *one of several important distribution channels,* as the company's *primary distribution channel,* or as the company's *exclusive channel for accessing customers.*

The timing of strategic moves also has relevance in the quest for competitive advantage. Because of the competitive importance that is sometimes associated with when a strategic move is made, company managers are obligated to carefully consider the advantages or disadvantages that attach to being a first-mover versus a fast-follower versus a wait-and-see late-mover. At the end of the day, though, the proper objective of a first-mover is that of being the first competitor to put together the precise combination of features, customer value, and sound revenue/cost/profit economics that puts it ahead of the pack in capturing an attractive market opportunity. Sometimes the company that first unlocks a profitable market opportunity is the first-mover and sometimes it is not—but the company that comes up with the key is surely the smart mover.

| exercises

1. Go to www.google.com and do a search on "strategic alliances." Identify at least two companies in different industries that are making a significant use of strategic alliances as a core part of their strategies. In addition, identify who their alliances are with and describe the purpose of the alliances.

2. Go to www.google.com and do a search on "acquisition strategy." Identify at least two companies in different industries that are using acquisitions to strengthen their market positions. Identify some of the companies that have been acquired, and describe the purpose behind the acquisitions.

chapter seven

Competing in Foreign Markets

(© Julie Nicholls/CORBIS)

You have no choice but to operate in a world shaped by globalization and the information revolution. There are two options: Adapt or die.

—Andrew S. Grove
Chairman, Intel Corporation

You do not choose to become global. The market chooses for you; it forces your hand.

—Alain Gomez
CEO, Thomson, S.A.

Industries actually vary a great deal in the pressures they put on a company to sell internationally.

—Niraj Dawar and Tony Frost
Professors, Richard Ivey School of Business

A ny company that aspires to industry leadership in the 21st century must think in terms of global, not domestic, market leadership. The world economy is globalizing at an accelerating pace as countries previously closed to foreign companies open up their markets, as the Internet shrinks the importance of geographic distance, and as ambitious growth-minded companies race to build stronger competitive positions in the markets of more and more countries. Companies in industries that are already globally competitive or in the process of becoming so are under the gun to come up with a strategy for competing successfully in foreign markets.

This chapter focuses on strategy options for expanding beyond domestic boundaries and competing in the markets of either a few or a great many countries. The spotlight will be on four strategic issues unique to competing multinationally:

1. Whether to customize the company's offerings in each different country market to match the tastes and preferences of local buyers or to offer a mostly standardized product worldwide.

2. Whether to employ essentially the same basic competitive strategy in all countries or modify the strategy country by country.

3. Where to locate the company's production facilities, distribution centers, and customer service operations so as to realize the greatest location advantages.

4. How to efficiently transfer the company's resource strengths and capabilities from one country to another in an effort to secure competitive advantage.

In the process of exploring these issues, we will introduce a number of core concepts—multicountry competition, global competition, profit sanctuaries, and cross-market subsidization. The chapter includes sections on cross-country differences in cultural, demographic, and market conditions; strategy options for entering and competing in foreign markets; the growing role of alliances with foreign partners; the importance of locating operations in the most advantageous countries; and the special circumstances of competing in such emerging markets as China, India, and Brazil.

WHY COMPANIES EXPAND INTO FOREIGN MARKETS

A company may opt to expand outside its domestic market for any of four major reasons:

1. *To gain access to new customers*—Expanding into foreign markets offers potential for increased revenues, profits, and long-term growth and becomes an especially attractive option when a company's home markets are mature. Firms like Cisco Systems, Dell, Sony, Nokia, Avon, and Toyota, which are racing for global leadership in their respective industries, are moving rapidly and aggressively to extend their market reach into all corners of the world.

2. *To achieve lower costs and enhance the firm's competitiveness*—Many companies are driven to sell in more than one country because domestic sales volume is not large enough to fully capture manufacturing economies of scale or learning-curve effects and thereby substantially improve the firm's cost-competitiveness. The relatively small size of country markets in Europe explains why companies like Michelin, BMW, and Nestlé long ago began selling their products all across Europe and then moved into markets in North America and Latin America.

3. *To capitalize on its core competencies*—A company may be able to leverage its competencies and capabilities into a position of competitive advantage in foreign markets as well as just domestic markets. Nokia's competencies and capabilities in mobile phones have propelled it to global market leadership in the wireless telecommunications business.

4. *To spread its business risk across a wider market base*—A company spreads business risk by operating in a number of different foreign countries rather than depending entirely on operations in its domestic market. Thus, if the economies of certain Asian countries turn down for a period of time, a company with operations across much of the world may be sustained by buoyant sales in Latin America or Europe.

In a few cases, companies in industries based on natural resources (e.g., oil and gas, minerals, rubber, and lumber) often find it necessary to operate in the international arena because attractive raw material supplies are located in foreign countries.

The Difference between Competing Internationally and Competing Globally

Typically, a company will *start* to compete internationally by entering just one or maybe a select few foreign markets. Competing on a truly global scale comes later, after the company has established operations on several continents and is racing against rivals for global market leadership. Thus, there is a meaningful distinction between the competitive scope of a company that operates in a few foreign countries (with perhaps modest ambitions to enter several more country markets) and a company that markets its products in 50 to 100 countries and is expanding its operations into additional country markets annually. The former is most accurately termed an *international competitor* while the latter qualifies as a *global competitor*. In the discussion that follows, we'll continue to make a distinction between strategies for competing internationally and strategies for competing globally.

CROSS-COUNTRY DIFFERENCES IN CULTURAL, DEMOGRAPHIC, AND MARKET CONDITIONS

Regardless of a company's motivation for expanding outside its domestic markets, the strategies it uses to compete in foreign markets must be *situation-driven*. Cultural, demographic, and market conditions vary significantly among the countries of the world. Cultures and lifestyles are the most obvious areas in which countries differ; market demographics are close behind. Consumers in Spain do not have the same tastes, preferences, and buying habits as consumers in Norway; buyers differ yet again in Greece, Chile, New Zealand, and Taiwan. Less than 10 percent of the populations of Brazil, India, and China have annual purchasing power equivalent to $20,000. Middle-class consumers represent a much smaller portion of the population in these and other emerging countries than in North America, Japan, and much of Western Europe.[1] Sometimes, product designs suitable in one country are inappropriate in another—for example, in the United States electrical devices run on 110-volt electrical systems, but in some European countries the standard is a 240-volt electric system, necessitating the use of different electrical designs and components. In France consumers prefer top-loading washing machines, while in most other European countries consumers prefer front-loading machines. Northern Europeans want large refrigerators because they tend to shop once a week in supermarkets; southern Europeans can get by on small refrigerators because they shop daily. In parts of Asia refrigerators are a status symbol and may be placed in the living room, leading to preferences for stylish designs and colors—in India bright blue and red are popular colors. In other Asian countries household space is constrained and many refrigerators are only four feet high so that the top can be used for storage. In Hong Kong the preference is for compact European-style appliances, but in Taiwan large American-style appliances are more popular.

Similarly, market growth varies from country to country. In emerging markets like India, China, Brazil, and Malaysia, market growth potential is far higher than in the more mature economies of Britain, Denmark, Canada, and Japan. In automobiles, for example, the potential for market growth is explosive in China, where sales amount to only 1 million vehicles annually in a country with 1.3 billion people. In India there are efficient, well-developed national channels for distributing trucks, scooters, farm equipment, groceries, personal care items, and other packaged products to the country's 3 million retailers, whereas in China distribution is primarily local and there is no national network for distributing most products. The marketplace is intensely competitive in some countries and only moderately contested in others. Industry driving forces may be one thing in Italy, quite another in Canada, and different yet again in Israel or Argentina or South Korea.

One of the biggest concerns of companies competing in foreign markets is whether to customize their offerings in each different country market to match the tastes and preferences of local buyers or whether to offer a mostly standardized product worldwide. While the products of a company that is responsive to local tastes will appeal to local buyers, customizing a company's products country by country *may* have the effect of raising production and distribution costs due to the greater variety of designs and components, shorter production runs, and the complications of added inventory handling and distribution logistics. Greater standardization of a global company's product offering, on the other hand, can lead to scale economies and learning-curve effects, thus contributing to the achievement of a low-cost advantage. The tension between the market pressures to customize and the competitive pressures to lower costs is one of the big strategic issues that participants in foreign markets have to resolve.

Aside from the basic cultural and market differences among countries, a company also has to pay special attention to location advantages that stem from country-to-country variations in manufacturing and distribution costs, the risks of shifting exchange rates, and the economic and political demands of host governments.

The Potential for Locational Advantages

Differences in wage rates, worker productivity, inflation rates, energy costs, tax rates, government regulations, and the like create sizable variations in manufacturing costs from country to country. Plants in some countries have major manufacturing cost advantages because of lower input costs (especially labor), relaxed government regulations, the proximity of suppliers, or unique natural resources. In such cases, the low-cost countries become principal production sites, with most of the output being exported to markets in other parts of the world. Companies that build production facilities in low-cost countries (or that source their products from contract manufacturers in these countries) have a competitive advantage over rivals with plants in countries where costs are higher. The competitive role of low manufacturing costs is most evident in low-wage countries like China, India, Pakistan, Cambodia, Vietnam, Mexico, Brazil, Guatemala, the Philippines, and several countries in Africa that have become production havens for manufactured goods with high labor content (especially textiles and apparel). China is fast becoming the manufacturing capital of the world—virtually all of the world's major manufacturing companies now have facilities in China, and China attracted more foreign direct investment in 2002 and 2003 than any other country in the world. Likewise, concerns about short delivery times and low shipping costs make some countries better locations than others for establishing distribution centers.

The quality of a country's business environment also offers locational advantages—the governments of some countries are anxious to attract foreign investments and go all-out to create a business climate that outsiders will view as favorable. A good example is Ireland, which has one of the world's most pro-business environments. Ireland offers companies very low corporate tax rates, has a government that is responsive to the needs of industry, and aggressively recruits high-tech manufacturing facilities and multinational companies. Such policies were a significant force in making Ireland the most dynamic, fastest-growing nation in Europe during the 1990s. The single biggest foreign investment in Ireland's history is Intel's largest non-U.S. chip manufacturing plant, a $2.5 billion facility employing over 4,000 people. Another locational advantage is the clustering of suppliers of components and capital equipment; infrastructure suppliers (universities, vocational training providers, research enterprises); trade associations; and makers of complementary products in a geographic area—such clustering can be an important source of cost savings in addition to facilitating close collaboration with key suppliers.

The Risks of Adverse Exchange Rate Shifts

The volatility of exchange rates greatly complicates the issue of geographic cost advantages. Currency exchange rates often move up or down 20 to 40 percent annually. Changes of this magnitude can either totally wipe out a country's low-cost advantage or transform a former high-cost location into a competitive-cost location. For instance, in the mid-1980s, when the dollar was strong relative to the Japanese yen (meaning that $1 would purchase, say, 125 yen as opposed to only 100 yen), Japanese heavy-equipment maker Komatsu was able to undercut U.S.-based Caterpillar's prices by as much as 25 percent, causing Caterpillar to lose sales and market share. But starting in 1985, when exchange rates began to shift and the dollar grew steadily weaker against the yen (meaning that $1 was worth fewer and fewer yen), Komatsu had to raise its prices six times over two years as its yen-based costs in terms of dollars soared. With its competitiveness against Komatsu restored, Caterpillar regained sales and market share. The lesson of fluctuating exchange rates is that companies that export goods to foreign countries always gain in competitiveness when the currency of the country in which the goods are manufactured is weak. Exporters are disadvantaged when the currency of the country where goods are being manufactured grows stronger. Sizable long-term shifts in exchange rates thus shuffle the global cards of which rivals have the upper hand in the marketplace and which countries represent the low-cost manufacturing location.

As a further illustration of the risks associated with fluctuating exchange rates, consider the case of a U.S. company that has located manufacturing facilities in Brazil (where the currency is *reals*—pronounced ray-alls) and that exports most of the Brazilian-made goods to markets in the European Union (where the currency is *euros*). To keep the numbers simple, assume that the exchange rate is 4 Brazilian reals for 1 euro and that the product being made in Brazil has a manufacturing cost of 4 Brazilian reals (or 1 euro). Now suppose that for some reason the exchange rate shifts from 4 reals per euro to 5 reals per euro (meaning that the real has declined in value and that the euro is stronger). Making the product in Brazil is now more cost-competitive because a Brazilian good costing 4 reals to produce has fallen to only 0.8 euros at the new exchange rate. If, in contrast, the value of the Brazilian real grows stronger in relation to the euro—resulting in an exchange rate of 3 reals to 1 euro—the same good costing 4 reals to produce now has a cost of 1.33 euros. Clearly, the attraction of manufacturing a good in Brazil and selling it in Europe is far greater when the euro is strong (an exchange rate of 1 euro for 5 Brazilian reals) than when the euro is weak and exchanges for only 3 Brazilian reals.

> Companies with manufacturing facilities in Brazil are more cost-competitive in exporting goods to world markets when the Brazilian real is weak; their competitiveness erodes when the Brazilian real grows stronger relative to the currencies of the countries where the Brazilian-made goods are being sold.

Insofar as U.S.-based manufacturers are concerned, declines in the value of the U.S. dollar against foreign currencies reduce or eliminate whatever cost advantage foreign manufacturers might have over U.S. manufacturers and can even prompt foreign companies to establish production plants in the United States. Likewise, a weak euro enhances the cost-competitiveness of companies manufacturing goods in Europe for export to foreign markets; a strong euro versus other currencies weakens the cost-competitiveness of European plants that manufacture goods for export.

In 2002, when the Brazilian real declined in value by about 25 percent against the dollar, the euro, and several other currencies, the ability of companies with manufacturing plants in Brazil to compete in world markets was greatly enhanced—of course, in the future years this windfall gain in cost advantage might well be eroded by sustained rises in the value of the Brazilian real against these same currencies. Herein lies the risk: Currency exchange rates are rather unpredictable, swinging first one way and then another way, so the competitiveness of any company's facilities in any country is partly dependent on whether exchange rate changes over time have a favorable or

> **core concept**
> Shifting exchange rates pose significant risks to a company's competitiveness in foreign markets. Exporters win when the currency of the country where goods are being manufactured grows weaker, and they lose when the currency grows stronger. Domestic companies under pressure from lower-cost imports are benefited when their government's currency grows weaker in relation to the countries where the imported goods are being made.

unfavorable cost impact. Companies making goods in one country for export to foreign countries always gain in competitiveness as the currency of that country grows weaker. Exporters are disadvantaged when the currency of the country where goods are being manufactured grows stronger. On the other hand, domestic companies that are under pressure from lower-cost imported goods gain in competitiveness when their currency grows weaker in relation to the currencies of the countries where the imported goods are made.

Host Government Policies

National governments enact all kinds of measures affecting business conditions and the operation of foreign companies in their markets. Host governments may set local content requirements on goods made inside their borders by foreign-based companies, put restrictions on exports to ensure adequate local supplies, regulate the prices of imported and locally produced goods, and impose tariffs or quotas on the imports of certain goods—until 2002, when it joined the World Trade Organization, China imposed a 100 percent tariff on motor vehicle imports. Governments may or may not have burdensome tax structures, stringent environmental regulations, or strictly-enforced worker safety standards. Sometimes outsiders face a web of regulations regarding technical standards, product certification, prior approval of capital spending projects, withdrawal of funds from the country, and required minority (sometimes majority) ownership of foreign company operations by local citizens. A few governments may be hostile to or suspicious of foreign companies operating within their borders. Some governments provide subsidies and low-interest loans to domestic companies to help them compete against foreign-based companies. Other governments, anxious to obtain new plants and jobs, offer foreign companies a helping hand in the form of subsidies, privileged market access, and technical assistance. All of these possibilities explain why the managers of companies opting to compete in foreign markets have to take a close look at a country's politics and policies toward business in general, and foreign companies in particular, in deciding which country markets to participate in and which ones to avoid.

THE CONCEPTS OF MULTICOUNTRY COMPETITION AND GLOBAL COMPETITION

core concept

Multicountry competition exists when competition in one national market is not closely connected to competition in another national market—there is no global or world market, just a collection of self-contained country markets.

There are important differences in the patterns of international competition from industry to industry.[2] At one extreme is **multicountry competition,** in which there's so much cross-country variation in market conditions and in the companies contending for leadership that the market contest among rivals in one country is not closely connected to the market contests in other countries. The standout features of multicountry competition are that (1) buyers in different countries are attracted to different product attributes, (2) sellers vary from country to country, and (3) industry conditions and competitive forces in each national market differ in important respects. Take the banking industry in Italy, Brazil, and Japan as an example—the requirements and expectations of banking customers vary among the three countries, the lead banking competitors in Italy differ from those in Brazil or in Japan, and the competitive battle going on among the leading banks in Italy is unrelated to the rivalry taking place in Brazil or Japan. Thus, *with multicountry competition, rival firms battle for national championships and winning in one country does not necessarily signal the* *ability to fare well in other countries.* In multicountry competition, the power of a company's strategy and resource capabilities in one country may not enhance its competitiveness to the same degree in other countries where it operates. Moreover, any competitive advantage a company secures in one country is largely confined to that country; the spillover effects to other countries are minimal to nonexistent. Industries characterized by multicountry competition include radio and TV broadcasting, consumer banking, life insurance, apparel, metals fabrication, many types of food products (coffee, cereals, breads, canned goods, frozen foods), and retailing.

At the other extreme is **global competition,** in which prices and competitive conditions across country markets are strongly linked and the term *global* or *world market* has true meaning. In a globally competitive industry, much the same group of rival companies competes in many different countries, but especially so in countries where sales volumes are large and where having a competitive presence is strategically important to building a strong global position in the industry. Thus, a company's competitive position in one country both affects and is affected by its position in other countries. In global competition, a firm's overall competitive advantage grows out of its entire worldwide operations; the competitive advantage it creates at its home base is supplemented by advantages growing out of its operations in other countries (having plants in low-wage countries, being able to transfer expertise from country to country, having the capability to serve customers who also have multinational operations, and brand-name recognition in many parts of the world). *Rival firms in globally competitive industries vie for worldwide leadership.* Global competition exists in motor vehicles, television sets, tires, mobile phones, personal computers, copiers, watches, digital cameras, bicycles, and commercial aircraft.

> **core concept**
> *Global competition* exists when competitive conditions across national markets are linked strongly enough to form a true international market and when leading competitors compete head to head in many different countries.

An industry can have segments that are globally competitive and segments in which competition is country by country.[3] In the hotel/motel industry, for example, the low- and medium-priced segments are characterized by multicountry competition—competitors mainly serve travelers within the same country. In the business and luxury segments, however, competition is more globalized. Companies like Nikki, Marriott, Sheraton, and Hilton have hotels at many international locations, use worldwide reservation systems, and establish common quality and service standards to gain marketing advantages in serving businesspeople and other travelers who make frequent international trips. In lubricants, the marine engine segment is globally competitive—ships move from port to port and require the same oil everywhere they stop. Brand reputations in marine lubricants have a global scope, and successful marine engine lubricant producers (Exxon Mobil, BP Amoco, and Shell) operate globally. In automotive motor oil, however, multicountry competition dominates—countries have different weather conditions and driving patterns, production of motor oil is subject to limited scale economies, shipping costs are high, and retail distribution channels differ markedly from country to country. Thus, domestic firms—like Quaker State and Pennzoil in the United States and Castrol in Great Britain—can be leaders in their home markets without competing globally.

It is also important to recognize that an industry can be in transition from multicountry competition to global competition. In a number of today's industries—beer and major home appliances are prime examples—leading domestic competitors have begun expanding into more and more foreign markets, often acquiring local companies or brands and integrating them into their operations. As some industry members start to build global brands and a global presence, other industry members find themselves pressured to follow the same strategic path—especially if establishing multinational operations results in important scale economies and a powerhouse brand name. As the industry consolidates to fewer players, such that many of the same companies find themselves in head-to-head competition in more and more country markets, global competition begins to replace multicountry competition.

At the same time, consumer tastes in a number of important product categories are converging across the world. Less diversity of tastes and preferences opens the way for companies to create global brands and sell essentially the same products in most all countries of the world. Even in industries where consumer tastes remain fairly diverse, companies are learning to use "custom mass production" to economically create different versions of a product and thereby satisfy the tastes of people in different countries.

In addition to taking the obvious cultural and political differences between countries into account, a company has to shape its strategic approach to competing in foreign markets according to whether its industry is characterized by multicountry competition, global competition, or a transition from one to the other.

STRATEGY OPTIONS FOR ENTERING AND COMPETING IN FOREIGN MARKETS

There are a host of generic strategic options for a company that decides to expand outside its domestic market and compete internationally or globally:

1. *Maintain a national (one-country) production base and export goods to foreign markets,* using either company-owned or foreign-controlled forward distribution channels.

2. *License foreign firms to use the company's technology or to produce and distribute the company's products.*

3. *Employ a franchising strategy.*

4. *Follow a multicountry strategy,* varying the company's strategic approach (perhaps a little, perhaps a lot) from country to country in accordance with local conditions and differing buyer tastes and preferences.

5. *Follow a global strategy,* using essentially the same competitive strategy approach in all country markets where the company has a presence.

6. *Use strategic alliances or joint ventures with foreign companies as the primary vehicle for entering foreign markets* and perhaps also using them as an ongoing strategic arrangement aimed at maintaining or strengthening its competitiveness.

The following sections discuss the first five options in more detail; the sixth option is discussed in a separate section later in the chapter.

Export Strategies

Using domestic plants as a production base for exporting goods to foreign markets is an excellent *initial strategy* for pursuing international sales. It is a conservative way to test the international waters. The amount of capital needed to begin exporting is often quite minimal; existing production capacity may well be sufficient to make goods for export. With an export strategy, a manufacturer can limit its involvement in foreign markets by contracting with foreign wholesalers experienced in importing to handle the entire distribution and marketing function in their countries or regions of the world. If it is more advantageous to maintain control over these functions, however, a manufacturer can establish its own distribution and sales organizations in some or all of the target foreign markets. Either way, a home-based production and export strategy helps the firm minimize its direct investments in foreign countries. Such strategies are commonly favored by Chinese, Korean, and Italian companies—products are designed and manufactured at home and then distributed through local channels in the importing countries; the primary functions performed abroad relate chiefly to establishing a network of distributors and perhaps conducting sales promotion and brand awareness activities.

Whether an export strategy can be pursued successfully over the long run hinges on the relative cost-competitiveness of the home-country production base. In some industries, firms gain additional scale economies and learning-curve benefits from centralizing production in one or several giant plants whose output capability exceeds demand in any one country market; obviously, a company must export to capture such economies. However, an export strategy is vulnerable when (1) manufacturing costs in the home country are substantially higher than in foreign countries where rivals have plants, (2) the costs of shipping the product to distant foreign markets are relatively high, or (3) adverse shifts occur in currency exchange rates. Unless an exporter can both keep its production and shipping costs competitive with rivals and successfully hedge against unfavorable changes in currency exchange rates, its success will be limited.

Licensing Strategies

Licensing makes sense when a firm with valuable technical know-how or a unique patented product has neither the internal organizational capability nor the resources to enter foreign markets. Licensing also has the advantage of avoiding the risks of committing resources to country markets that are unfamiliar, politically volatile, economically unstable, or otherwise risky. By licensing the technology or the production rights to foreign-based firms, the firm does not have to bear the costs and risks of entering foreign markets on its own, yet it is able to generate income from royalties. The big disadvantage of licensing is the risk of providing valuable technological know-how to foreign companies and thereby losing some degree of control over its use; monitoring licensees and safeguarding the company's proprietary know-how can prove quite difficult in some circumstances. But if the royalty potential is considerable and the companies to whom the licenses are being granted are both trustworthy and reputable, then licensing can be a very attractive option. Many software and pharmaceutical companies use licensing strategies.

Franchising Strategies

While licensing works well for manufacturers and owners of proprietary technology, franchising is often better suited to the global expansion efforts of service and retailing enterprises. McDonald's, Yum! Brands (the parent of Pizza Hut, KFC, and Taco Bell), the UPS Store, Jani-King International (the world's largest commercial cleaning franchisor), Roto-Rooter, 7-Eleven, and Hilton Hotels have all used franchising to build a presence in foreign markets. Franchising has much the same advantages as licensing. The franchisee bears most of the costs and risks of establishing foreign locations; a franchisor has to expend only the resources to recruit, train, support, and monitor franchisees. The big problem a franchisor faces is maintaining quality control; foreign franchisees do not always exhibit strong commitment to consistency and standardization, especially when the local culture does not stress the same kinds of quality concerns. Another problem that can arise is whether to allow foreign franchisees to make modifications in the franchisor's product offering so as to better satisfy the tastes and expectations of local buyers. Should McDonald's allow its franchised units in Japan to modify Big Macs slightly to suit Japanese tastes? Should the franchised KFC units in China be permitted to substitute spices that appeal to Chinese consumers? Or should the same menu offerings be rigorously and unvaryingly required of all franchisees worldwide?

A Multicountry Strategy or a Global Strategy?

The need for a *multicountry strategy* derives from the sometimes vast differences in cultural, economic, political, and competitive conditions in different countries. The more diverse national market conditions are, the stronger the case for a multicountry strategy, in which the company tailors its strategic approach to fit each host country's market situation. Usually, but not always, companies employing a multicountry strategy use the same basic competitive theme (low-cost, differentiation, or best-cost) in each country, making whatever country-specific variations are needed to best satisfy customers and to position themselves against local rivals. They may aim at broad market targets in some countries and focus more narrowly on a particular niche in others. The bigger the country-to-country variations, the more a company's overall international strategy becomes a collection of its individual country strategies. But variations still allow room to connect the strategies in different countries by making an effort to transfer ideas, technologies, competencies, and capabilities that work successfully in one country market to other fairly similar country markets. Toward this end, it is useful to view operations in each country as experiments that result in learning and in capabilities that may merit transfer to other country markets.[4]

> A multicountry strategy is appropriate for industries where multicountry competition dominates and local responsiveness is essential. A global strategy works best in markets that are globally competitive or beginning to globalize.

While multicountry strategies are best suited for industries where multicountry competition dominates and a fairly high degree of local responsiveness is competitively imperative, *global strategies* are best suited for globally competitive industries. A global strategy is one in which the company's approach is *predominantly the same* in all countries. Although relatively *minor* country-to-country differences in a company's global strategy may be incorporated to accommodate specific situations in a few host countries, the company's fundamental competitive approach (low-cost, differentiation, best-cost, or focused) remains very much intact worldwide. Moreover, a global strategy involves (1) integrating and coordinating the company's strategic moves worldwide, and (2) selling in many if not all nations where there is significant buyer demand. Figure 7.1 provides a point-by-point comparison of multicountry versus global strategies. *The issue of whether to employ essentially the same basic competitive strategy in the markets of all countries or whether to vary the company's competitive approach to fit specific market conditions and buyer preferences in each host country is perhaps the foremost strategic issue firms face when they compete in foreign markets.*

The strength of a multicountry strategy is that it matches the company's competitive approach to host-country circumstances and accommodates the differing tastes and expectations of buyers in each country. A multicountry strategy is essential when there are significant country-to-country differences in customers' needs and buying habits (see Illustration Capsule 7.1); when buyers in a country insist on special-order or highly customized products; when host governments enact regulations requiring that

figure 7.1 **How a Multicountry Strategy Differs from a Global Strategy**

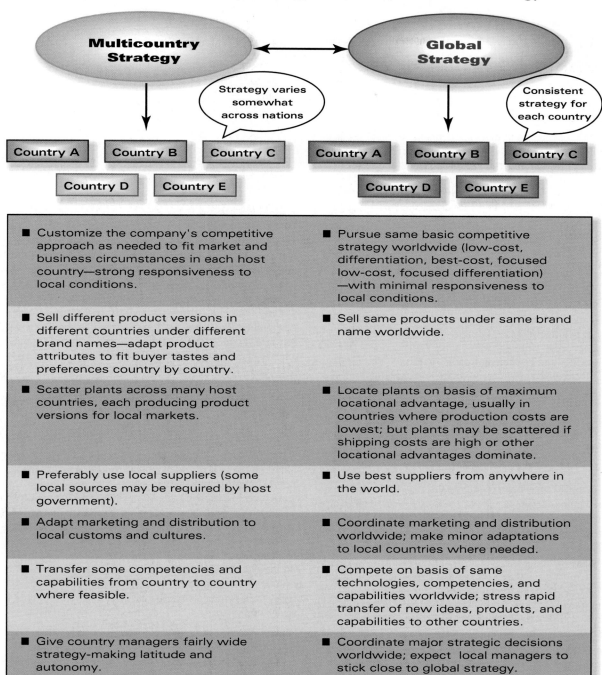

illustration capsule 7.1
Coca-Cola, Microsoft, McDonald's, and Nestlé: Users of Multicountry Strategies

COCA-COLA'S MULTICOUNTRY STRATEGY IN BEVERAGES

Coca-Cola strives to meet the demands of local tastes and cultures, offering 300 brands in some 200 countries. Its network of bottlers and distributors is distinctly local, and the company's products and brands are formulated to cater to local tastes. The ways in which Coca-Cola's local operating units bring products to market, the packaging that is used, and the advertising messages that are employed are all intended to match the local culture and fit in with local business practices. Many of the ingredients and supplies for Coca-Cola's products are sourced locally.

MICROSOFT'S MULTICOUNTRY STRATEGY IN PC SOFTWARE

In order to best serve the needs of users in foreign countries, Microsoft localizes many of its software products to reflect local languages. In France, for example, all user messages and documentation are in French and all monetary references are in euros. In the United Kingdom, monetary references are in British pounds and user messages and documentation reflect certain British conventions. Various Microsoft products have been localized into more than 30 languages.

MCDONALD'S MULTICOUNTRY STRATEGY IN FAST FOOD

McDonald's has been highly successful in markets outside the United States, partly because it has been adept in altering its menu offerings to cater to local tastes. In Taiwan and Singapore, McDonald's outlets offer a bone-in fried chicken dish called Chicken McCrispy. In Great Britain, there's McChicken Tikka Naan to appeal to British cravings for Indian food. In India, McDonald's features the Maharajah Mac sandwich (an Indian version of the Big Mac); in Japan, there's the Chicken Tatsuta sandwich and a Teriyaki Burger sandwich; in Australia, there's a McOz Burger. However, the infrastructure and operating systems that are employed in the outlets are largely the same, enabling McDonald's to achieve low-cost leadership status once it builds volume up at its outlets (sometimes a 5-year process) and once it has enough outlets operating in a country to achieve full economies of scale (sometimes a 5- to 10-year process in the largest foreign markets).

NESTLÉ'S MULTICOUNTRY STRATEGY IN INSTANT COFFEE

Swiss-based Nestlé, the largest food company in the world, is also the largest marketer of coffee, with about a 22 percent share of the world coffee market. Chief executive Peter Brabeck-Letmathe advocates understanding the distinctions between the cultures in which Nestlé markets its products. "[If] you are open to new languages, you are also open to new cultures," he explains. Thus, instant coffee names like Nescafé, Taster's Choice, Ricore, and Ricoffy line grocery shelves in various countries. If customers prefer roast or ground coffee, they can purchase Nespresso, Bonka, Zoegas, or Loumidis, depending on where they live.

Nestlé produces 200 types of instant coffee, from lighter blends for the U.S. market to dark espressos for Latin America; it has 27 factories in 24 countries making instant coffee varieties. To keep its instant coffees matched to consumer tastes in different countries (and areas within some countries), Nestlé operates four coffee research labs that experiment with new blends in aroma, flavor, and color. The strategy is to match the blends marketed in each country to the tastes and preferences of coffee drinkers in that country, introducing new blends to develop new segments when opportunities appear and altering blends as needed to respond to changing tastes and buyer habits. In Britain, Nescafé was promoted extensively to build a wider base of instant-coffee drinkers. In Japan, where Nescafé was considered a luxury item, the company made its Japanese blends available in fancy containers suitable for gift-giving.

Sources: www.cocacola.com, accessed September 19, 2003; www.nestle.com, accessed August 15, 2001; "Nestlé S.A.," Hoover's Online (www.hoovers.com), accessed August 15, 2001; Tom Mudd, "Nestlé Plays to Global Audience," *Industry Week* (www.industryweek.com), August 13, 2001; company annual reports; Shawn Tully, "Nestlé Shows How to Gobble Markets," *Fortune,* January 16, 1989, pp. 74–78; and "Nestlé: A Giant in a Hurry," *Business Week,* March 22, 1993, pp. 50–54.

products sold locally meet strict manufacturing specifications or performance standards; and when the trade restrictions of host governments are so diverse and complicated that they preclude a uniform, coordinated worldwide market approach. Sony markets a different Walkman in Norway than in Sweden to better meet the somewhat different needs of the users in each market. Castrol, a specialist in oil lubricants has over 3,000 different formulas of lubricants, many of which have been tailored for different climates, vehicle types and uses, and equipment applications that characterize different country markets.

However, a multicountry strategy has two big drawbacks: It hinders transfer of a company's competencies and resources across country boundaries (since different competencies and capabilities may be used in different host countries), and it does not promote building a single, unified competitive advantage—especially one based on low cost. Companies employing a multicountry strategy face big hurdles in achieving low-cost leadership unless they find ways to customize their products and still be in position to capture scale economies and learning-curve effects—the capability to implement mass customization at relatively low cost (as Dell and Toyota have demonstrated) greatly facilitates effective use of a multicountry approach.

As a rule, most multinational competitors endeavor to employ as global a strategy as customer needs permit. Philips Electronics, the Netherlands-based electronics and consumer products company, operated successfully with a multicountry strategy for many years but has recently begun moving more toward a unified strategy within the European Union and within North America.[5] A global strategy can concentrate on building the resource strengths to secure a sustainable low-cost or differentiation-based competitive advantage over both domestic rivals and global rivals racing for world market leadership. Whenever country-to-country differences are small enough to be accommodated within the framework of a global strategy, a global strategy is preferable to a multicountry strategy because of the value of creating both a uniform brand offering and strong competencies and capabilities not readily matched by rivals.

THE QUEST FOR COMPETITIVE ADVANTAGE IN FOREIGN MARKETS

There are three ways in which a firm can gain competitive advantage (or offset domestic disadvantages) by expanding outside its domestic market.[6] First, it can use location to lower costs or achieve greater product differentiation. Second, it can transfer competitively valuable competencies and capabilities from its domestic markets to foreign markets. Third, it can use cross-border coordination in ways that a domestic-only competitor cannot.

Using Location to Build Competitive Advantage

To use location to build competitive advantage, a company must consider two issues: (1) whether to concentrate each activity it performs in a few select countries or to disperse performance of the activity to many nations, and (2) in which countries to locate particular activities.

Companies tend to concentrate their activities in a *limited number of locations* in the following circumstances:

- *When the costs of manufacturing or other activities are significantly lower in some geographic locations than in others*—For example, much

> Companies can pursue competitive advantage in world markets by locating activities in the most advantageous nations; a domestic-only competitor has no such opportunities.

of the world's athletic footwear is manufactured in Asia (China and Korea) because of low labor costs; much of the production of motherboards for PCs is located in Taiwan because of both low costs and the high-caliber technical skills of the Taiwanese labor force.

- *When there are significant scale economies*—The presence of significant economies of scale in components production or final assembly means that a company can gain major cost savings from operating a few superefficient plants as opposed to a host of small plants scattered across the world. Important marketing and distribution economies associated with multinational operations can also yield low-cost leadership. In situations where some competitors are intent on global dominance, being the worldwide low-cost provider is a powerful competitive advantage. Achieving low-cost provider status often requires a company to have the largest worldwide *manufacturing share,* with production centralized in one or a few world-scale plants in low-cost locations. Some companies even use such plants to manufacture units sold under the brand names of rivals. Manufacturing share (as distinct from brand share or market share) is significant because it provides more certain access to production-related scale economies. Japanese makers of VCRs, microwave ovens, TVs, and DVD players have used their large manufacturing share to establish a low-cost advantage.[7]

- *When there is a steep learning curve associated with performing an activity in a single location*—In some industries learning-curve effects in parts manufacture or assembly are so great that a company establishes one or two large plants from which it serves the world market. The key to riding down the learning curve is to concentrate production in a few locations to increase the accumulated volume at a plant (and thus the experience of the plant's workforce) as rapidly as possible.

- *When certain locations have superior resources, allow better coordination of related activities, or offer other valuable advantages*—A research unit or a sophisticated production facility may be situated in a particular nation because of its pool of technically trained personnel. Samsung became a leader in memory chip technology by establishing a major R&D facility in Silicon Valley and transferring the know-how it gained back to headquarters and its plants in South Korea. Where just-in-time inventory practices yield big cost savings and/or where an assembly firm has long-term partnering arrangements with its key suppliers, parts manufacturing plants may be clustered around final assembly plants. An assembly plant may be located in a country in return for the host government's allowing freer import of components from large-scale, centralized parts plants located elsewhere. A customer service center or sales office may be opened in a particular country to help cultivate strong relationships with pivotal customers located nearby.

However, *there are instances when dispersing activities is more advantageous than concentrating them.* Buyer-related activities—such as distribution to dealers, sales and advertising, and after-sale service—usually must take place close to buyers. This means physically locating the capability to perform such activities in every country market where a global firm has major customers (unless buyers in several adjoining countries can be served quickly from a nearby central location). For example, firms that make mining and oil-drilling equipment maintain operations in many international locations to support customers' needs for speedy equipment repair and technical assistance. The four biggest public accounting firms have numerous international offices to service the foreign operations of their multinational corporate clients. A global competitor that effectively disperses its buyer-related activities can gain a service-based competitive edge in world markets over rivals whose buyer-related activities are more concentrated—this is one reason the Big Four public accounting firms (PricewaterhouseCoopers, KPMG, Deloitte & Touche, and Ernst & Young) have been so successful relative to second-tier firms. Dispersing activities to many locations is also competitively advantageous when high transportation costs, diseconomies of large size, and trade barriers make it too expensive to operate from a central location. Many companies distribute their products from multiple locations to shorten delivery times to customers. In addition, it is strategically advantageous to disperse activities to hedge against the risks of fluctuating exchange rates; supply interruptions (due to strikes, mechanical failures, and transportation delays); and adverse political developments. Such risks are greater when activities are concentrated in a single location.

The classic reason for locating an activity in a particular country is low cost.[8] Even though multinational and global firms have strong reason to disperse buyer-related activities to many international locations, such activities as materials procurement, parts manufacture, finished goods assembly, technology research, and new product development can frequently be decoupled from buyer locations and performed wherever advantage lies. Components can be made in Mexico; technology research done in Frankfurt; new products developed and tested in Phoenix; and assembly plants located in Spain, Brazil, Taiwan, or South Carolina. Capital can be raised in whatever country it is available on the best terms.

Using Cross-Border Transfers of Competencies and Capabilities to Build Competitive Advantage

Expanding beyond domestic borders is a way for companies to leverage their core competencies and resource strengths, using them as a basis for competing successfully in additional country markets and growing sales and profits in the process. Transferring competencies, capabilities, and resource strengths from country to country contributes to the development of broader or deeper competencies and capabilities— ideally helping a company achieve *dominating depth* in some competitively valuable area. Dominating depth in a competitively valuable capability, resource, or value chain activity is a strong basis for sustainable competitive advantage over other multinational or global competitors and especially so over domestic-only competitors. A one-country customer base is too small to support the resource buildup needed to achieve such depth; this is particularly true when the market is just emerging and sophisticated resources have not been required.

Whirlpool, the leading global manufacturer of home appliances, with plants in 14 countries and sales in 170 countries, has used the Internet to create a global information technology platform that allows the company to transfer key product innovations and production processes across regions and brands quickly and effectively. Wal-Mart is slowly but forcefully expanding its operations with a strategy that involves transferring its considerable domestic expertise in distribution and discount retailing to other countries. Its status as the largest, most resource-deep, and most sophisticated user of distribution-retailing know-how has served it well in building its foreign sales and profitability. But Wal-Mart is not racing madly to position itself in many foreign markets; rather, it is establishing a strong presence in select country markets and learning how to be successful in these before tackling entry into other major markets.

However, cross-border resource transfers are not a guaranteed recipe for success. Philips Electronics sells more color TVs and DVD recorders in Europe than any other company does; its biggest technological breakthrough was the compact disc, which it invented in 1982. Philips has worldwide sales of about 32 billion euros, but as of 2002 Philips had lost money for 15 consecutive years in its U.S. consumer electronics business. In the United States, the company's color TVs and DVD recorders (sold under the Magnavox and Philips brands) are slow sellers. Philips is notoriously slow in introducing new products into the U.S. market and has been struggling to develop an able sales force that can make inroads with U.S. electronics retailers and change its image as a clunky brand.

Using Cross-Border Coordination to Build Competitive Advantage

Coordinating company activities across different countries contributes to sustainable competitive advantage in several different ways. Multinational and global competitors can choose where and how to challenge rivals. They may decide to retaliate against an aggressive rival in the country market where the rival has its biggest sales volume or its best profit margins in order to reduce the rival's financial resources for competing in other country markets. They may also decide to wage a price-cutting offensive against weak rivals in their home markets, capturing greater market share and subsidizing any short-term losses with profits earned in other country markets.

If a firm learns how to assemble its product more efficiently at, say, its Brazilian plant, the accumulated expertise can be easily transferred via the Internet to assembly plants in other world locations. Knowledge gained in marketing a company's product in Great Britain can readily be exchanged with company personnel in New Zealand or Australia. A global or multinational manufacturer can shift production from a plant in one country to a plant in another to take advantage of exchange rate fluctuations, to enhance its leverage with host-country governments, and to respond to changing wage rates, components shortages, energy costs, or changes in tariffs and quotas. Production schedules can be coordinated worldwide; shipments can be diverted from one distribution center to another if sales rise unexpectedly in one place and fall in another.

Using Internet technology applications, companies can collect ideas for new and improved products from customers and sales and marketing personnel all over the world, permitting informed decisions about what can be standardized and what should be customized. Likewise, Internet technology can be used to involve the company's best design and engineering personnel (wherever they are located) in collectively coming up with next-generation products—it is becoming increasingly easy for company personnel in one location to use the Internet to collaborate closely with personnel in other locations in performing strategically relevant activities. Efficiencies can also be achieved by shifting workloads from where they are unusually heavy to locations where personnel are underutilized.

A company can enhance its brand reputation by consistently incorporating the same differentiating attributes in its products worldwide. The reputation for quality that Honda established worldwide first in motorcycles and then in automobiles gave it competitive advantage in positioning Honda lawn mowers at the upper end of the U.S. outdoor power equipment market—the Honda name gave the company instant credibility with U.S. buyers. Whirlpool's efforts to link its product R&D and manufacturing operations in North America, Latin America, Europe, and Asia allowed it to accelerate the discovery of innovative appliance features, coordinate the introduction of these features in the appliance products marketed in different countries, and create a cost-efficient worldwide supply chain. Whirlpool's conscious efforts to integrate and coordinate its various operations around the world have helped it become a low-cost producer and also speed product innovations to market, both of which have helped give Whirlpool advantages over rivals in designing and rapidly introducing innovative and attractively priced appliances worldwide.

PROFIT SANCTUARIES, CROSS-MARKET SUBSIDIZATION, AND GLOBAL STRATEGIC OFFENSIVES

Profit sanctuaries are country markets in which a company derives substantial profits because of its strong or protected market position. Japan, for example, is a profit sanctuary for most Japanese companies because trade barriers erected by the Japanese government effectively block foreign companies from competing for a large share of Japanese sales. Protected from the threat of foreign competition in their home market, Japanese companies can safely charge somewhat higher prices to their Japanese customers and thus earn attractively large profits on sales made in Japan. In most cases, a company's biggest and most strategically crucial profit sanctuary is its home market, but international and global companies may also enjoy profit sanctuary status in other nations where they have a strong competitive position, big sales volume, and attractive profit margins. Companies that compete globally are likely to have more profit sanctuaries than companies that compete in just a few country markets; a domestic-only competitor, of course, can have only one profit sanctuary (see Figure 7.2).

> **core concept**
> Companies with large, protected *profit sanctuaries*—country markets in which a company derives substantial profits because of its strong or protected market position—have competitive advantage over companies that don't have a protected sanctuary. Companies with multiple profit sanctuaries have a competitive advantage over companies with a single sanctuary.

Using Cross-Market Subsidization to Wage a Strategic Offensive

Profit sanctuaries are valuable competitive assets, providing the financial strength to support strategic offensives in selected country markets and aid a company's race for global market leadership. The added financial capability afforded by multiple profit sanctuaries gives a global or multicountry competitor the financial strength to wage a market offensive against a domestic competitor whose only profit sanctuary is its home market. Consider the case of a purely domestic company in competition with a company that has multiple profit sanctuaries and that is racing for global market leadership. The global company has the flexibility of lowballing its prices in the domestic company's home market and grabbing market share at the domestic company's expense, subsidizing razor-thin margins or even losses with the healthy profits earned in its profit sanctuaries—a practice called **cross-market subsidization.** The global company can adjust the depth of its price cutting to move in and capture market share quickly, or it can shave prices slightly to make gradual market inroads (perhaps over a

> **core concept**
> *Cross-market subsidization*—supporting competitive offensives in one market with resources and profits diverted from operations in other markets—is a powerful competitive weapon.

figure 7.2   **Profit Sanctuary Potential of Domestic-Only, Multicountry, and Global Competitors**

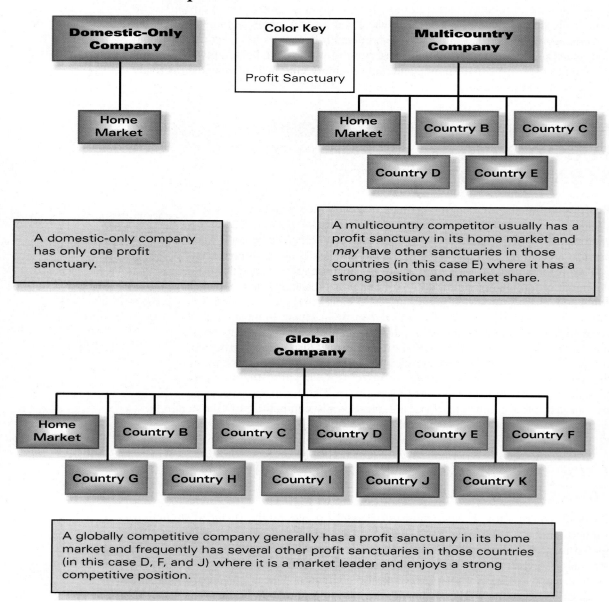

A domestic-only company has only one profit sanctuary.

A multicountry competitor usually has a profit sanctuary in its home market and *may* have other sanctuaries in those countries (in this case E) where it has a strong position and market share.

A globally competitive company generally has a profit sanctuary in its home market and frequently has several other profit sanctuaries in those countries (in this case D, F, and J) where it is a market leader and enjoys a strong competitive position.

decade or more) so as not to threaten domestic firms precipitously or trigger protectionist government actions. If the domestic company retaliates with matching price cuts, it exposes its entire revenue and profit base to erosion; its profits can be squeezed substantially and its competitive strength sapped, even if it is the domestic market leader.

Global Strategic Offensives

One of the most frequently used offensives is dumping goods at unreasonably low prices in the markets of foreign rivals. Such a strategy, if used repeatedly in the same country, can put domestic firms in dire financial straits or drive them out of business. Many governments have antidumping laws aimed at protecting domestic firms from unfair pricing by foreign rivals. In 2002, for example, the U.S. government imposed tariffs of up to 30 percent on selected steel products that Asian and European steel manufacturers were said to be selling at ultralow prices in the U.S. market.

But more usually the offensive strategies of companies that compete in multiple country markets with multiple products (several brands of cigarettes or different brands of food products) are more sophisticated. In deciding how to attack a multinational rival, a company needs to be alert to a competitor's incentive to react strongly and forcefully (often indicated by the size of the rival's market share or the growth potential of the market) and the rival's ability to defend its position (who has more clout in this arena—the attacker or the defender?).[9] The company also has to decide just how important it is to defeat the rival—how much is there to be gained?

If the offensive appears attractive, there are at least three options. One is a *direct onslaught,* in which the objective is to capture a major slice of market share and force the rival to retreat. Such onslaughts nearly always involve (1) price cutting (often without regard to immediate profits), (2) heavy expenditures on marketing, advertising, and promotion, and (3) attempts to gain the upper hand in one or more distribution channels. Direct onslaughts require a massive commitment of resources and make sense only if the market arena is highly attractive to the attacker.

A second type of offensive is the *contest,* which is more subtle and more focused than an onslaught. A contest offensive zeros in on a particular market segment that is unsuited to the capabilities and strengths of the defender and in which the attacker has a new next-generation or breakthrough product. Warner Brothers recently slashed the prices of its DVDs to such low levels that rivals were loath to follow suit; the move put enormous pressure on movie rental companies like Blockbuster. Warner Brothers' motive was to get people accustomed to buying DVDs instead of renting them. Such offensives often become a contest of whose strategy and business model will prevail.

A third offensive is the *feint,* a move designed to divert the defender's attention away from the attacker's main target. A good example of a feint offensive is Philip Morris's move in 1993 to reduce the U.S. price of its best-selling Marlboro cigarettes by 20 percent. Its rival R. J. Reynolds, which at the time was strapped for resources, was forced to institute matching price cuts on its Camel and Winston brands and scramble to defend its already eroding market share. But while Reynolds was busily engaged protecting its turf in the U.S. market, Philip Morris launched a major offensive into Russia and Eastern Europe (where cigarette sales were on the rise) and spent $800 million to get its brands established there. Philip Morris won the battle for market share in Eastern Europe hands down over Reynolds.

STRATEGIC ALLIANCES AND JOINT VENTURES WITH FOREIGN PARTNERS

Strategic alliances, joint ventures, and other cooperative agreements with foreign companies are a favorite and potentially fruitful means for entering a foreign market or strengthening a firm's competitiveness in world markets. Historically, export-minded firms in industrialized nations sought alliances with firms in less-developed countries to import and market their products locally—such arrangements were often necessary to win approval for entry from the host country's government. More recently, companies from different parts of the world have formed strategic alliances and partnership arrangements to strengthen their mutual ability to serve whole continents and move toward more global market participation. Both Japanese and American companies are actively forming alliances with European companies to strengthen their ability to compete in the 25-nation European Union and to capitalize on the opening up of Eastern European markets. Many U.S. and European companies are allying with Asian companies in their efforts to enter markets in China, India, and other Asian countries.

Of late, the number of alliances, joint ventures, and other collaborative efforts has exploded. Cooperative arrangements between domestic and foreign companies have strategic appeal for reasons besides gaining wider access to attractive country markets.[10] One is to capture economies of scale in production and/or marketing—cost reduction can be the difference that allows a company to be cost-competitive. By joining forces in producing components, assembling models, and marketing their products, companies can realize cost savings not achievable with their own small volumes. A second reason is to fill gaps in technical expertise and/or knowledge of local markets (buying habits and product preferences of consumers, local customs, and so on). Allies learn much from one another in performing joint research, sharing technological know-how, studying one another's manufacturing methods, and understanding how to tailor sales and marketing approaches to fit local cultures and traditions. A third reason is to share distribution facilities and dealer networks, thus mutually strengthening their access to buyers. Fourth, allied companies can direct their competitive energies more toward mutual rivals and less toward one another; teaming up may help them close the gap on leading companies. Fifth, companies opt to form alliances with local companies (even where not legally required) because of the partner's local market knowledge and working relationships with key officials in the host-country government.[11] And, finally, alliances can be a particularly useful way to gain agreement on important technical standards—they have been used to arrive at standards for DVD players, assorted PC devices, Internet-related technologies, high-definition televisions, and mobile phones.

> Strategic alliances can help companies in globally competitive industries strengthen their competitive positions while still preserving their independence.

The Risks of Strategic Alliances with Foreign Partners

Alliances and joint ventures have their pitfalls, however. Achieving effective collaboration between independent companies, each with different motives and perhaps conflicting objectives, is not easy.[12] It requires many meetings of many people working in good faith over a period of time to iron out what is to be shared, what is to remain proprietary, and how the cooperative arrangements will work. Cross-border allies typically have to overcome language and cultural barriers; the communication, trust-building, and coordination costs are high in terms of management time. Often, once the bloom is off the rose, partners discover they have conflicting objectives and strategies and/or deep differences of opinion about how to proceed. Tensions build up, working relationships cool, and the hoped-for benefits never materialize.[13]

Another major problem is getting alliance partners to make decisions fast enough to respond to rapidly advancing technological developments. Large telecommunications companies striving to achieve "global connectivity" have made extensive use of alliances and joint ventures with foreign counterparts, but they are encountering serious difficulty in reaching agreements on which of several technological approaches to employ and how to adapt to the swift pace at which all of the alternatives are advancing. AT&T and British Telecom, which formed a $10 billion joint venture to build an Internet-based global network linking 100 major cities, took eight months to find a CEO to head the project and even longer to come up with a name; the joint venture was abandoned in 2002.

Allies often find it difficult to collaborate effectively in competitively sensitive areas, thus raising questions about mutual trust and forthright exchanges of information and expertise. There can also be clashes of egos and company cultures. The key people on whom success or failure depends may have little personal chemistry, be unable to work closely together or form a partnership, or be unable to come to consensus. For example, an alliance between Northwest Airlines and KLM Royal Dutch Airlines linking their hubs in Detroit and Amsterdam resulted in a bitter feud among both companies' top officials (who, according to some reports, refused to speak to each other) and precipitated a battle for control of Northwest engineered by KLM. The dispute was rooted in a clash of business philosophies (the American way versus the European way), basic cultural differences, and an executive power struggle.[14]

> Strategic alliances are more effective in helping establish a beachhead of new opportunity in world markets than in achieving and sustaining global leadership.

Another danger of collaborative partnerships is that of becoming overly dependent on another company for essential expertise and capabilities over the long term. To be a serious market contender, a company must ultimately develop internal capabilities in all areas important to strengthening its competitive position and building a sustainable competitive advantage. When learning from allies holds only limited potential (because those allies guard their most valuable skills and expertise), acquiring or merging with a company possessing the desired know-how and resources is a better solution. If a company is aiming for global market leadership, then cross-border merger or acquisition may be a better alternative than cross-border alliances or joint ventures. Illustration Capsule 7.2 relates the experiences of various companies with cross-border strategic alliances.

Making the Most of Strategic Alliances with Foreign Partners

Whether or not a company realizes the potential of alliances and collaborative partnerships with foreign enterprises seems to be a function of six factors:[15]

1. *Picking a good partner*—A good partner not only has the desired expertise and capabilities but also shares the company's vision about the purpose of the alliance. Experience indicates that it is generally wise to avoid a partnership in which there is strong potential of direct competition because of overlapping product lines or other conflicting interests—agreements to jointly market each other's products hold much potential for conflict unless the products are complements rather than substitutes and unless there is good chemistry among key personnel.

2. *Being sensitive to cultural differences*—Unless the outsider exhibits respect for the local culture and local business practices, productive working relationships are unlikely to emerge.

3. *Recognizing that the alliance must benefit both sides*—Information must be shared as well as gained, and the relationship must remain forthright and trustful. Many

illustration capsule 7.2
Cross-Border Strategic Alliances

As the chairman of British Aerospace recently observed, a strategic alliance with a foreign company is "one of the quickest and cheapest ways to develop a global strategy." High-profile global alliances include the following:

- Two auto firms, Renault of France and Nissan of Japan, formed a global partnership in 1999 and then strengthened and the alliance in 2002 for the purpose of gaining sales for new Nissan vehicles introduced in the European market.

- Verizon Wireless and Vodaphone AirTouch PLC (a leader in wireless communications in Europe) entered into cooperative agreements in 2003 to jointly develop and co-brand a data card (based on technology in Vodaphone's Mobile Connect card) to provide international travelers with both Internet and corporate network access throughout Verizon's U.S. network and Vodaphone's 28-country network; the Verizon-Vodaphone alliance also involved cooperative development efforts in card hardware, roaming, and interconnectivity of services and billing.

- Toyota and First Automotive Works, China's biggest automaker, entered into an alliance in 2002 to make luxury sedans, sport-utility vehicles, and minivehicles for the Chinese market. The intent was to make as many as 400,000 vehicles annually by 2010, an amount equal to the number that Volkswagen, the company with the largest share of the Chinese market, was making as of 2002. The alliance envisioned a joint investment of about $1.2 billion. At the time of the announced alliance, Toyota was lagging behind Honda, General Motors, and Volkswagen in setting up production facilities in China. Capturing a bigger share of the Chinese market was seen as crucial to Toyota's success in

achieving its strategic objective of having a 15 percent share of the world's automotive market by 2010.

- Airbus Industrie was formed by an alliance of aerospace companies from Britain, Spain, Germany, and France that included British Aerospace, Daimler-Benz Aerospace, and Aerospatiale. The objective of the alliance was to create a European aircraft company capable of competing with U.S.-based Boeing Corporation. The alliance has proved highly successful, infusing Airbus with the know-how and resources to compete head-to-head with Boeing for world leadership in large commercial aircraft.

- General Electric (GE) and SNECMA, a French maker of jet engines, have had a long-standing 50–50 partnership in two ventures, one called CFM International, which makes jet engines to power aircraft made by Boeing and Airbus Industrie, and a second called CFAN, which functions as the exclusive supply source for wide-chord blades for commercial jet engines made by GE. The GE/SNECMA has enjoyed great success since the 1970s. SNECMA was an attractive alliance partner from GE's perspective because it gave GE a France-based connection to help market the alliance's products to Airbus Industrie; likewise, SNECMA found the alliance attractive because it could serve as an entrée for marketing the alliance's products to Boeing. CFM International has sold over 15,000 jet engines since the early 1980s, winning market shares for large commercial aircraft of about 35 percent through the 1980s and market shares approaching 50 percent since 1995. As of mid-2003, CFM56 jet engines powered some 5,000 aircraft deployed by 340 customers.

Sources: Company Web sites and press releases; and Yves L. Doz and Gary Hamel, *Alliance Advantage: The Art of Creating Value through Partnering* (Boston, MA: Harvard Business School Press, 1998).

alliances fail because one or both partners grow unhappy with what they are learning. Also, if either partner plays games with information or tries to take advantage of the other, the resulting friction can quickly erode the value of further collaboration.

4. *Ensuring that both parties live up to their commitments*—Both parties have to deliver on their commitments for the alliance to produce the intended benefits. The division of work has to be perceived as fairly apportioned, and the caliber of the benefits received on both sides has to be perceived as adequate.

5. *Structuring the decision-making process so that actions can be taken swiftly when needed*—In many instances, the fast pace of technological and competitive changes dictates an equally fast decision-making process. If the parties get bogged down in discussion or in gaining internal approval from higher-ups, the alliance can turn into an anchor of delay and inaction.

6. *Managing the learning process and then adjusting the alliance agreement over time to fit new circumstances*—In today's fast-moving markets, few alliances can succeed by holding only to initial plans. One of the keys to long-lasting success is learning to adapt to change; the terms and objectives of the alliance must be adjusted as needed.

Most alliances with foreign companies that aim at technology-sharing or providing market access turn out to be temporary, fulfilling their purpose after a few years because the benefits of mutual learning have occurred and because the businesses of both partners have developed to the point where they are ready to go their own ways. In such cases, it is important for the company to learn thoroughly and rapidly about a partner's technology, business practices, and organizational capabilities and then transfer valuable ideas and practices into its own operations promptly. Although long-term alliances sometimes prove mutually beneficial, most partners don't hesitate to terminate the alliance and go it alone when the payoffs run out.

Alliances are more likely to be long-lasting when (1) they involve collaboration with suppliers or distribution allies and each party's contribution involves activities in different portions of the industry value chain, or (2) both parties conclude that continued collaboration is in their mutual interest, perhaps because new opportunities for learning are emerging or perhaps because further collaboration will allow each partner to extend its market reach beyond what it could accomplish on its own.

COMPETING IN EMERGING FOREIGN MARKETS

Companies racing for global leadership have to consider competing in *emerging markets* like China, India, Brazil, Indonesia, and Mexico—countries where the business risks are considerable but where the opportunities for growth are huge, especially as their economies develop and living standards climb toward levels in the industrialized world.[16] With the world now comprising more than 6 billion people—fully one-third of whom are in India and China, and hundreds of millions more in other less-developed countries of Asia and Latin America—a company that aspires to world market leadership (or to sustained rapid growth) cannot ignore the market opportunities or the base of technical and managerial talent such countries offer. This is especially true given that the once-high protectionist barriers in most of these countries are in the process of crumbling. Coca-Cola, for example, has predicted that its $2 billion investment in China, India, and Indonesia—which together hold 40 percent of the world's population—can produce sales in those countries that double every three years for the foreseeable future (compared to a modest 4 percent growth rate that Coca-Cola averaged in the United States during the 1990s and to only 1–2 percent U.S. growth in 2000–2002).[17]

Tailoring products for these big emerging markets often involves more than making minor product changes and becoming more familiar with local cultures.[18] Ford's attempt to sell a Ford Escort in India at a price of $21,000—a luxury-car price, given that India's best-selling Maruti-Suzuki model sold at the time for $10,000 or less, and that fewer than 10 percent of Indian households have annual purchasing power greater than

$20,000—met with a less-than-enthusiastic market response. McDonald's has had to offer vegetable burgers in parts of Asia and to rethink its prices, which are often high by local standards and affordable only by the well-to-do. Kellogg has struggled to introduce its cereals successfully because consumers in many less-developed countries do not eat cereal for breakfast—changing habits is difficult and expensive. In several emerging countries, Coca-Cola has found that advertising its world image does not strike a chord with the local populace. Single-serving packages of detergents, shampoos, pickles, cough syrup, and cooking oils are very popular in India because they allow buyers to conserve cash by purchasing only what they need immediately.

Strategy Implications

Consumers in emerging markets are highly focused on price, in many cases giving local low-cost competitors the edge. Companies wishing to succeed in these markets

> Profitability in emerging markets rarely comes quickly or easily—new entrants have to be very sensitive to local conditions, be willing to invest in developing the market for their products over the long term, and be patient in earning a profit.

have to attract buyers with bargain prices as well as better products—an approach that can entail a radical departure from the strategy used in other parts of the world. If building a market for the company's products is likely to be a long-term process and involve reeducation of consumers, a company must not only be patient with regard to sizable revenues and profits but also prepared in the interim to invest sizable sums to alter buying habits and tastes. Also, specially designed or packaged products may be needed to accommodate local market circumstances. For example, when Unilever entered the market for laundry detergents in India, it realized that 80 percent of the population could not afford the brands it was selling to affluent consumers there (as well as in wealthier countries). To compete against a very low-priced detergent made by a local company, Unilever came up with a low-cost formula that was not harsh to the skin, constructed new low-cost production facilities, packaged the detergent (named Wheel) in single-use amounts so that it could be sold very cheaply, distributed the product to local merchants by hand carts, and crafted an economical marketing campaign that included painted signs on buildings and demonstrations near stores—the new brand captured $100 million in sales in a relatively short time. Unilever later replicated the strategy in South America with a brand named Ala.

Because managing a new venture in an emerging market requires a blend of global knowledge and local sensitivity to the culture and business practices, the management team must usually consist of a mix of expatriate and local managers. Expatriate managers are needed to transfer technology, business practices, and the corporate culture and to serve as conduits for the flow of information between the corporate office and local operations; local managers bring needed understanding of the area's nuances and deep commitment to its market.

Strategies for Local Companies in Emerging Markets

If large, opportunity-seeking, resource-rich companies are looking to enter emerging markets, what strategy options can local companies use to survive? As it turns out, the prospects for local companies facing global giants are by no means grim. Their optimal strategic approach hinges on (1) whether their competitive assets are suitable only for the home market or can be transferred abroad, and (2) whether industry pressures to move toward global competition are strong or weak. The four generic options are shown in Figure 7.3.

figure 7.3 **Strategy Options for Local Companies in Competing against Global Companies**

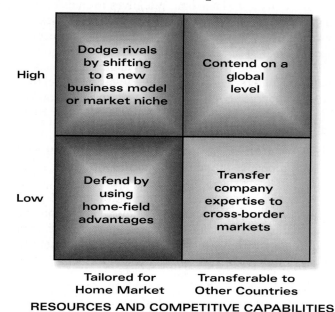

INDUSTRY
PRESSURES
TO GLOBALIZE

High — Dodge rivals by shifting to a new business model or market niche | Contend on a global level

Low — Defend by using home-field advantages | Transfer company expertise to cross-border markets

Tailored for Home Market | Transferable to Other Countries

RESOURCES AND COMPETITIVE CAPABILITIES

Using Home-Field Advantages When the pressures for global competition are low and a local firm has competitive strengths well suited to the local market, a good strategy option is to concentrate on the advantages enjoyed in the home market, cater to customers who prefer a local touch, and accept the loss of customers attracted to global brands.[19] A local company may be able to astutely exploit its local orientation—its familiarity with local preferences, its expertise in traditional products, its long-standing customer relationships. A local company, in many cases, enjoys a significant cost advantage over global rivals (perhaps because of simpler product design or lower operating and overhead costs), allowing it to compete on the basis of price. Its global competitors often aim their products at upper- and middle-income urban buyers, who tend to be more fashion-conscious, more willing to experiment with new products, and more attracted to global brands. Bajaj Auto, India's largest producer of scooters, has defended its turf against Honda (which entered the Indian market with a local joint venture partner to sell scooters, motorcycles, and other vehicles on the basis of its superior technology, quality, and brand appeal) by focusing on buyers who wanted low-cost, durable scooters and easy access to maintenance in the countryside. Bajaj designed a rugged, cheap-to-build scooter for India's rough roads, increased its investments in R&D to improve reliability and quality, and created an extensive network of distributors and roadside-mechanic stalls, a strategic approach that served it well—while Honda captured about an 11 percent market share, Bajaj maintained a share above 70 percent, close to its 77 percent share prior to Honda's entry. In the fall of 1998, Honda announced it was pulling out of its scooter manufacturing joint venture with its Indian partner.

Transferring the Company's Expertise to Cross-Border Markets
When a company has resource strengths and capabilities suitable for competing in other country markets, launching initiatives to transfer its expertise to cross-border markets becomes a viable strategic option.[20] Televisa, Mexico's largest media company, used its expertise in Spanish culture and linguistics to become the world's most prolific producer of Spanish-language soap operas. Jollibee Foods, a family-owned company with 56 percent of the fast-food business in the Philippines, combated McDonald's entry first by upgrading service and delivery standards and then by using its expertise in seasoning hamburgers with garlic and soy sauce and making noodle and rice meals with fish to open outlets catering to Asian residents in Hong Kong, the Middle East, and California.

Shifting to a New Business Model or Market Niche   When industry pressures to globalize are high, any of the following three options makes the most sense: (1) shift the business to a piece of the industry value chain where the firm's expertise and resources provide competitive advantage, (2) enter into a joint venture with a globally competitive partner, or (3) sell out to (be acquired by) a global entrant into the home market who concludes the company would be a good entry vehicle.[21] When Microsoft entered China, local software developers shifted from cloning Windows products to developing Windows application software customized to the Chinese market. When the Russian PC market opened to IBM, Compaq, and Hewlett-Packard, local Russian PC maker Vist focused on assembling very low-cost models, marketing them through exclusive distribution agreements with selected local retailers, and opening company-owned full-service centers in dozens of Russian cities. Vist focused on providing low-cost PCs, giving lengthy warranties, and catering to buyers who felt the need for local service and support. Vist's strategy allowed it to remain the market leader, with a 20 percent share.

Contending on a Global Level   If a local company in an emerging market has transferable resources and capabilities, it can sometimes launch successful initiatives to meet the pressures for globalization head-on and start to compete on a global level itself.[22] When General Motors (GM) decided to outsource the production of radiator caps for all of its North American vehicles, Sundaram Fasteners of India pursued the opportunity; it purchased one of GM's radiator cap production lines, moved it to India, and became GM's sole supplier of radiator caps in North America—at 5 million units a year. As a participant in GM's supplier network, Sundaram learned about emerging technical standards, built its capabilities, and became one of the first Indian companies to achieve QS 9000 certification, a quality standard that GM now requires for all suppliers. Sundaram's acquired expertise in quality standards enabled it then to pursue opportunities to supply automotive parts in Japan and Europe.

key|points

Most issues in competitive strategy that apply to domestic companies apply also to companies that compete internationally. But there are four strategic issues unique to competing across national boundaries:

1.   Whether to customize the company's offerings in each different country market to match the tastes and preferences of local buyers or offer a mostly standardized product worldwide.

2. Whether to employ essentially the same basic competitive strategy in all countries or modify the strategy country by country to fit the specific market conditions and competitive circumstances it encounters.

3. Where to locate the company's production facilities, distribution centers, and customer service operations so as to realize the greatest locational advantages.

4. Whether and how to efficiently transfer the company's resource strengths and capabilities from one country to another in an effort to secure competitive advantage.

Companies opt to expand outside their domestic market for any of four major reasons: to gain access to new customers for their products or services, to achieve lower costs and become more competitive on price, to leverage their core competencies, and to spread their business risk across a wider market base. A company is an *international* or *multinational competitor* when it competes in several foreign markets; it is a *global competitor* when it has or is pursuing a market presence in virtually all of the world's major countries.

The strategies a company uses to compete in foreign markets have to be *situation-driven*—cultural, demographic, and market conditions vary significantly from country to country. One of the biggest concerns of competing in foreign markets is whether to customize the company's offerings to cater to the tastes and preferences of local buyers in all or most different country markets or whether to offer a mostly standardized product worldwide. While being responsive to local tastes makes a company's products more appealing to local buyers, customizing a company's products country by country may have the effect of raising production and distribution costs due to the greater variety of designs and components, shorter production runs, and the complications of added inventory handling and distribution logistics. In contrast, greater standardization of the company's product offering, enhances the capture of scale economies and learning-experience curve effects, contributing to the achievement of a low-cost advantage. The tension between the market pressures to customize and the competitive pressures to lower costs is one of the big strategic issues that participants in foreign markets have to resolve.

Multicountry competition exists when competition in one national market is independent of competition in another national market—there is no "international market," just a collection of self-contained country markets. **Global competition** exists when competitive conditions across national markets are linked strongly enough to form a true world market and when leading competitors compete head-to-head in many different countries. A multicountry strategy is appropriate for industries where multicountry competition dominates, but a global strategy works best in markets that are globally competitive or beginning to globalize. Other strategy options for competing in world markets include maintaining a national (one-country) production base and exporting goods to foreign markets, licensing foreign firms to use the company's technology or produce and distribute the company's products, employing a franchising strategy, and using strategic alliances or other collaborative partnerships to enter a foreign market or strengthen a firm's competitiveness in world markets.

The number of global strategic alliances, joint ventures, and other collaborative arrangements has exploded in recent years. Cooperative arrangements with foreign partners have strategic appeal from several angles: gaining wider access to attractive country markets, allowing capture of economies of scale in production and/or marketing, filling gaps in technical expertise and/or knowledge of local markets, saving on costs by sharing distribution facilities and dealer networks, helping gain agreement on important technical standards, and helping combat the impact of alliances that rivals have formed. Cross-border strategic alliances are fast reshaping competition in world markets, pitting one group of allied global companies against other groups of allied global companies.

There are three ways in which a firm can gain competitive advantage (or offset domestic disadvantages) in global markets. One way involves locating various value chain activities among nations in a manner that lowers costs or achieves greater product differentiation. A second way involves efficient and effective transfer of competitively valuable competencies and capabilities from its domestic markets to foreign markets. A third way draws on a multinational or global competitor's ability to deepen or broaden its resource strengths and capabilities and to coordinate its dispersed activities in ways that a domestic-only competitor cannot.

Profit sanctuaries are country markets in which a company derives substantial profits because of its strong or protected market position. They are valuable competitive assets, providing the financial strength to support competitive offensives in one market with resources and profits diverted from operations in other markets, and aid a company's race for global market leadership. Companies with large, protected profit sanctuaries have competitive advantage over companies that don't have a protected sanctuary. Companies with multiple profit sanctuaries have a competitive advantage over companies with a single sanctuary. The **cross-market subsidization** capabilities provided by multiple profit sanctuaries gives a global or international competitor a powerful offensive weapon.

Companies racing for global leadership have to consider competing in *emerging markets* like China, India, Brazil, Indonesia, and Mexico—countries where the business risks are considerable but the opportunities for growth are huge. To succeed in these markets, it is usually necessary to attract buyers with bargain prices as well as better products—an approach that can entail a radical departure from the strategy used in other parts of the world. Moreover, building a market for the company's products in these markets is likely to be a long-term process, involving the investment of sizable sums to alter buying habits and tastes and reeducate consumers. Profitability is unlikely to come quickly or easily.

The outlook for local companies in emerging markets wishing to survive against the entry of global giants is by no means grim. The optimal strategic approach hinges on whether a firm's competitive assets are suitable only for the home market or can be transferred abroad and on whether industry pressures to move toward global competition are strong or weak. Local companies can compete against global newcomers by (1) defending on the basis of home-field advantages, (2) transferring their expertise to cross-border markets, (3) dodging large rivals by shifting to a new business model or market niche, or (4) launching initiatives to compete on a global level themselves.

exercises

1. Log on to www.caterpillar.com and search for information about Caterpillar's strategy in foreign markets. Is the company pursuing a global strategy or a multi-country strategy? Support your answer.

2. Assume you are in charge of developing the strategy for a multinational company selling products in some 50 different countries around the world. One of the issues you face is whether to employ a multicountry strategy or a global strategy.

a. If your company's product is personal computers, do you think it would make better strategic sense to employ a multicountry strategy or a global strategy? Why?

b. If your company's product is dry soup mixes and canned soups, would a multicountry strategy seem to be more advisable than a global strategy? Why?

c. If your company's product is washing machines, would it seem to make more sense to pursue a multicountry strategy or a global strategy? Why?

d. If your company's product is basic work tools (hammers, screwdrivers, pliers, wrenches, saws), would a multicountry strategy or a global strategy seem to have more appeal? Why?

chapter eight

Tailoring Strategy to Fit Specific Industry and Company Situations

(©Images.com/CORBIS)

The best strategy for a given firm is ultimately a unique construction reflecting its particular circumstances.

—**Michael E. Porter**

Competing in the marketplace is like war. You have injuries and casualties, and the best strategy wins.

—**John Collins**

It is much better to make your own products obsolete than allow a competitor to do it.

—**Michael A. Cusamano and Richard W. Selby**

In a turbulent age, the only dependable advantage is reinventing your business model before circumstances force you to.

—**Gary Hamel and Liisa Välikangas**

P rior chapters have emphasized the analysis and options that go into matching a company's choice of strategy to (1) industry and competitive conditions and (2) its own resource strengths and weaknesses, competitive capabilities, opportunities and threats, and market position. But there's more to be revealed about the hows of matching the choices of strategy to a company's circumstances. This chapter looks at the strategy-making task in nine other commonly encountered situations:

1. Companies competing in emerging industries.
2. Companies competing in turbulent, high-velocity markets.
3. Companies competing in mature, slow-growth industries.
4. Companies competing in stagnant or declining industries.
5. Companies competing in fragmented industries.
6. Companies pursuing rapid growth.
7. Companies in industry leadership positions.
8. Companies in runner-up positions.
9. Companies in competitively weak positions or plagued by crisis conditions.

We selected these situations to shed still more light on the factors that managers need to consider in tailoring a company's strategy. When you finish this chapter, you will have a stronger grasp of the factors that managers have to weigh in choosing a strategy and what the pros and cons are for some of the heretofore unexplored strategic options that are open to a company.

STRATEGIES FOR COMPETING IN EMERGING INDUSTRIES

An *emerging industry* is one in the formative stage. Examples include wireless Internet communications, high-definition TV and liquid crystal display (LCD) TV screens, assisted living for the elderly, online education, organic food products, e-book publishing, and electronic banking. Many companies striving to establish a strong foothold in an emerging industry are in a start-up mode; they are busily perfecting technology, adding people, acquiring or constructing facilities, gearing up operations, and trying to broaden distribution and gain buyer acceptance. The business models and strategies of companies in an emerging industry are unproved—what appears to be a promising business concept and strategy may never generate attractive bottom-line profitability. Often, there are important product design problems and technological problems that remain to be worked out.

Challenges When Competing in Emerging Industries

Competing in emerging industries presents managers with some unique strategy-making challenges:[1]

- Because the market is new and unproved, there may be much speculation about how it will function, how fast it will grow, and how big it will get. The little historical information available is virtually useless in making sales and profit projections. There's lots of guesswork about how rapidly buyers will be attracted and how much they will be willing to pay. For example, there is still uncertainty about how quickly the demand for high-definition TV sets will grow following the 2003 law requiring all U.S. TV stations to broadcast digital programs.

- In many cases, much of the technological know-how underlying the products of emerging industries is proprietary and closely guarded, having been developed in-house by pioneering firms; patents and unique technical expertise are key factors in securing competitive advantage. In other cases, the technology is multifaceted, entailing parallel or collaborative efforts on the part of several enterprises and perhaps competing technological approaches.

- Often, there is no consensus regarding which of several competing technologies will win out or which product attributes will prove decisive in winning buyer favor—as is the case in high-speed Internet access where cable modems, digital subscriber line (DSL), and wireless technologies are competing vigorously. Until market forces sort these things out, wide differences in product quality and performance are typical. Rivalry therefore centers on each firm's efforts to get the market to ratify its own strategic approach to technology, product design, marketing, and distribution.

- Entry barriers tend to be relatively low, even for entrepreneurial start-up companies. Large, well-known, opportunity-seeking companies with ample resources and competitive capabilities are likely to enter if the industry has promise for explosive growth or if its emergence threatens their present business. For instance, many traditional local telephone companies, seeing the potent threat of wireless communications technology, have opted to enter the mobile communications business in one way or another.

- Strong learning and experience curve effects may be present, allowing significant price reductions as volume builds and costs fall.

- Since in an emerging industry all buyers are first-time users, the marketing task is to induce initial purchase and to overcome customer concerns about product features, performance reliability, and conflicting claims of rival firms.

- Many potential buyers expect first-generation products to be rapidly improved, so they delay purchase until technology and product design mature and second- or third-generation products appear on the market.

- Sometimes, firms have trouble securing ample supplies of raw materials and components (until suppliers gear up to meet the industry's needs).
- Undercapitalized companies, finding themselves short of funds to support needed R&D and get through several lean years until the product catches on, end up merging with competitors or being acquired by financially strong outsiders looking to invest in a growth market.

The two critical strategic issues confronting firms in an emerging industry are (1) how to finance initial operations until sales and revenues take off, and (2) what market segments and competitive advantages to go after in trying to secure a front-runner position.[2] Competitive strategies keyed either to low cost or differentiation are usually viable. Focusing makes good sense when resources and capabilities are limited and the industry has too many technological frontiers or too many buyer segments to pursue at once. The lack of established "rules of the game" gives industry participants considerable freedom to experiment with a variety of different strategic approaches. Nonetheless, a firm with solid resource capabilities, an appealing business model, and a good strategy has a golden opportunity to shape the rules and establish itself as the recognized industry front-runner.

Strategic Avenues for Competing in an Emerging Industry

Dealing with all the risks and opportunities of an emerging industry is one of the most challenging business strategy problems. To be successful in an emerging industry, companies usually have to pursue one or more of the following strategic avenues:[3]

1. Try to win the early race for industry leadership with risk-taking entrepreneurship and a bold creative strategy. Broad or focused differentiation strategies keyed to technological or product superiority typically offer the best chance for early competitive advantage.

2. Push to perfect the technology, improve product quality, and develop additional attractive performance features.

3. As technological uncertainty clears and a dominant technology emerges, adopt it quickly. (However, while there's merit in trying to be the industry standard-bearer on technology and to pioneer the dominant product design, firms have to beware of betting too heavily on their own preferred technological approach or product design—especially when there are many competing technologies, R&D is costly, and technological developments can quickly move in surprising new directions.)

> Strategic success in an emerging industry calls for bold entrepreneurship, a willingness to pioneer and take risks, an intuitive feel for what buyers will like, quick response to new developments, and opportunistic strategy making.

4. Form strategic alliances with key suppliers to gain access to specialized skills, technological capabilities, and critical materials or components.

5. Acquire or form alliances with companies that have related or complementary technological expertise as a means of helping outcompete rivals on the basis of technological superiority.

6. Try to capture any first-mover advantages associated with early commitments to promising technologies.

7. Pursue new customer groups, new user applications, and entry into new geographical areas (perhaps using strategic partnerships or joint ventures if financial resources are constrained).

8. Make it easy and cheap for first-time buyers to try the industry's first-generation product. Then, as the product becomes familiar to a wide portion of the market, begin to shift the advertising emphasis from creating product awareness to increasing frequency of use and building brand loyalty.

9. Use price cuts to attract the next layer of price-sensitive buyers into the market.

The short-term value of winning the early race for growth and market share leadership has to be balanced against the longer-range need to build a durable competitive edge and a defendable market position.[4] Well-financed outsiders are certain to move in with aggressive strategies as industry sales start to take off and the perceived risk of investing in the industry lessens. A rush of new entrants, attracted by the growth and profit potential, may crowd the market and force industry consolidation to a smaller number of players. Resource-rich latecomers, aspiring to industry leadership, may be able to become major players by acquiring and merging the operations of weaker competitors and then launching strategic offensives to build market share and gain quick brand-name recognition. Strategies must be aimed at competing for the long haul; often, this means sacrificing some degree of short-term profitability in order to invest in the resources, capabilities, and market recognition needed to sustain early successes.

> The early leaders in an emerging industry cannot rest on their laurels; they must drive hard to strengthen their resource capabilities and build a position strong enough to ward off newcomers and compete successfully for the long haul.

Young companies in fast-growing markets face three strategic hurdles: (1) managing their own rapid expansion, (2) defending against competitors trying to horn in on their success, and (3) building a competitive position extending beyond their initial product or market. Up-and-coming companies can help their cause by selecting knowledgeable members for their boards of directors, by hiring entrepreneurial managers with experience in guiding young businesses through the start-up and takeoff stages, by concentrating on out-innovating the competition, and perhaps by merging with or acquiring another firm to gain added expertise and a stronger resource base.

STRATEGIES FOR COMPETING IN TURBULENT, HIGH-VELOCITY MARKETS

More and more companies are finding themselves in industry situations characterized by rapid technological change, short product life cycles because of entry of important new rivals into the marketplace, frequent launches of new competitive moves by rivals, and fast-evolving customer requirements and expectations—all occurring at once. Since news of this or that important competitive development arrives daily, it is an imposing task just to monitor and assess developing events. High-velocity change is plainly the prevailing condition in personal computer hardware and software, video games, networking, wireless telecommunications, medical equipment, biotechnology, prescription drugs, and virtually all Internet industries.

Strategic Postures for Coping with Rapid Change

The central strategy-making challenge in a turbulent market environment is managing change.[5] As illustrated in Figure 8.1, a company can assume any of three strategic postures in dealing with high-velocity change:[6]

- *It can react to change.* The company can respond to a rival's new product with a better product. It can counter an unexpected shift in buyer tastes and buyer demand

figure 8.1   **Meeting the Challenge of High-Velocity Change**

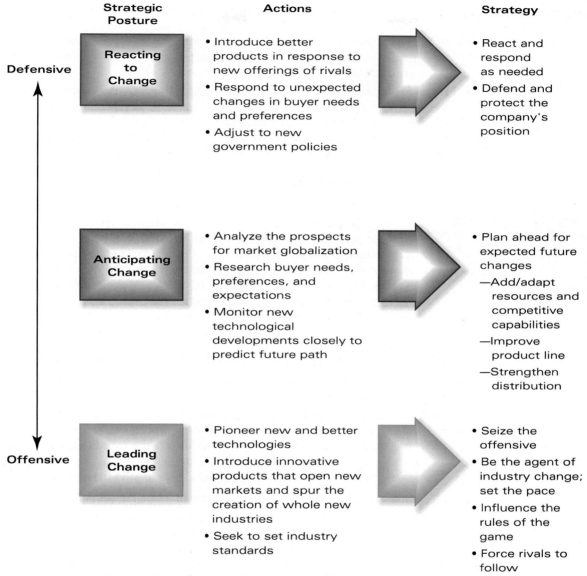

by redesigning or repackaging its product, or shifting its advertising emphasis to different product attributes. Reacting is a defensive strategy and is therefore unlikely to create fresh opportunity, but it is nonetheless a necessary component in a company's arsenal of options.

- *It can anticipate change, make plans for dealing with the expected changes, and follow its plans as changes occur (fine-tuning them as may be needed).* Anticipation entails looking ahead to analyze what is likely to occur and then preparing and positioning for that future. It entails studying buyer behavior, buyer needs, and buyer expectations to get insight into how the market will evolve, then lining up the necessary production and distribution capabilities ahead of time. Like reacting to change, anticipating change is still fundamentally defensive in that forces outside the enterprise are in the driver's seat. Anticipation, however, can open up new opportunities and thus is a better way to manage change than just pure reaction.

> *Reacting to change and anticipating change are basically defensive postures; leading change is an offensive posture.*

- *It can lead change.* Leading change entails initiating the market and competitive forces that others must respond to—*it is an offensive strategy aimed at putting a company in the driver's seat.* Leading change means being first to market with an important new product or service. It means being the technological leader, rushing next-generation products to market ahead of rivals, and having products whose features and attributes shape customer preferences and expectations. It means proactively seeking to shape the rules of the game.

> *Industry leaders are proactive agents of change, not reactive followers and analyzers. Moreover, they improvise, experiment, develop options, and adapt rapidly.*

As a practical matter, a company's approach to managing change should, ideally, incorporate all three postures (though not in the same proportion). The best-performing companies in high-velocity markets consistently seek to lead change with proactive strategies that often entail the flexibility to pursue any of several strategic options, depending on how the market actually evolves. Even so, an environment of relentless change makes it incumbent on any company to anticipate and prepare for the future and to react quickly to unpredictable or uncontrollable new developments.

Strategic Moves for Fast-Changing Markets

Competitive success in fast-changing markets tends to hinge on a company's ability to improvise, experiment, adapt, reinvent, and regenerate as market and competitive conditions shift rapidly and sometimes unpredictably.[7] It has to constantly reshape its strategy and its basis for competitive advantage. While the process of altering offensive and defensive moves every few months or weeks to keep the overall strategy closely matched to changing conditions is inefficient, the alternative—a fast-obsolescing strategy—is worse. The following five strategic moves seem to offer the best payoffs:

1. *Invest aggressively in R&D to stay on the leading edge of technological know-how.* Translating technological advances into innovative new products (and remaining close on the heels of whatever advances and features are pioneered by rivals) is a necessity in industries where technology is the primary driver of change. But it is often desirable to focus the R&D effort on a few critical areas, not only to avoid stretching the company's resources too thin but also to deepen the firm's expertise, master the technology, fully capture learning-curve effects, and become the dominant leader in a particular technology or product category.[8] When a fast-evolving market environment entails many technological areas and product categories, competitors have little choice but to employ some type of focus strategy and concentrate on being the leader in a particular product/technology category.

2. *Develop quick-response capability.* Because no company can predict all of the changes that will occur, it is crucial to have the organizational capability to be able to react quickly, improvising if necessary. This means shifting resources internally, adapting existing competencies and capabilities, creating new competencies and capabilities, and not falling far behind rivals. Companies that are habitual late-movers are destined to be industry also-rans.

3. *Rely on strategic partnerships with outside suppliers and with companies making tie-in products.* In many high-velocity industries, technology is branching off to create so many new technological paths and product categories that no company has the resources and competencies to pursue them all. Specialization (to promote the necessary technical depth) and focus (to preserve organizational agility and leverage the firm's expertise) are desirable strategies. Companies build their competitive position not just by strengthening their own internal resource base but also by partnering with those suppliers making state-of-the-art parts and components and by collaborating closely with both the developers of related technologies and the makers of tie-in products. For example, personal computer companies like Gateway, Dell, Compaq, and Acer rely heavily on the developers and manufacturers of chips, monitors, hard drives, DVD players, and software for innovative advances in PCs. None of the PC makers have done much in the way of integrating backward into parts and components because they have learned that the most effective way to provide PC users with a state-of-the-art product is to outsource the latest, most advanced components from technologically sophisticated suppliers who make it their business to stay on the cutting edge of their specialization and who can achieve economies of scale by mass-producing components for many PC assemblers. An outsourcing strategy also allows a company the flexibility to replace suppliers that fall behind on technology or product features or that cease to be competitive on price. The managerial challenge here is to strike a good balance between building a rich internal resource base that, on the one hand, keeps the firm from being at the mercy of its suppliers and allies and, on the other hand, maintains organizational agility by relying on the resources and expertise of capable (and perhaps "best-in-world") outsiders.

4. *Initiate fresh actions every few months, not just when a competitive response is needed.* In some sense, change is partly triggered by the passage of time rather than solely by the occurrence of events. A company can be proactive by making *time-paced moves*—introducing a new or improved product every four months, rather than when the market tapers off or a rival introduces a next-generation model.[9] Similarly, a company can expand into a new geographic market every six months rather than waiting for a new market opportunity to present itself; it can also refresh existing brands every two years rather than waiting until their popularity wanes. The keys to successfully using time pacing as a strategic weapon are choosing intervals that make sense internally and externally, establishing an internal organizational rhythm for change, and choreographing the transitions. 3M Corporation has long pursued an objective of having 25 percent of its revenues come from products less than four years old, a force that established the rhythm of change and created a relentless push for new products. Recently, the firm's CEO upped the tempo of change at 3M by increasing the percentage from 25 percent to 30 percent.

5. *Keep the company's products and services fresh and exciting enough to stand out in the midst of all the change that is taking place.* One of the risks of rapid change is that products and even companies can get lost in the shuffle. The marketing challenge here is to keep the firm's products and services in the limelight and, further, to keep them innovative and well matched to the changes that are occurring in the marketplace.

Cutting-edge know-how and first-to-market capabilities are very valuable competitive assets in fast-evolving markets. Moreover, action-packed competition demands that a company have quick reaction times and flexible, adaptable resources—organizational

In fast-paced markets, in-depth expertise, speed, agility, innovativeness, opportunism, and resource flexibility are critical organizational capabilities.

agility is a huge competitive asset. Even so, companies will make mistakes and some things a company does are going to work better than others. When a company's strategy doesn't seem to be working well, it has to quickly regroup—probing, experimenting, improvising, and trying again and again until it finds something that strikes the right chord with buyers and that puts it in sync with market and competitive realities.

STRATEGIES FOR COMPETING IN MATURING INDUSTRIES

A maturing industry is one that is moving from rapid growth to significantly slower growth. An industry is said to be mature when nearly all potential buyers are already users of the industry's products. In a mature market, demand consists mainly of replacement sales to existing users, with growth hinging on the industry's abilities to attract the few remaining new buyers and to convince existing buyers to up their usage. Consumer goods industries that are mature typically have a growth rate under 5 percent—roughly equal to the growth of the customer base or economy as a whole.

Industry Changes Resulting from Market Maturity

An industry's transition to maturity does not begin on an easily predicted schedule. Industry maturity can be forestalled by the emergence of new technological advances, product innovations, or other driving forces that keep rejuvenating market demand. Nonetheless, when growth rates do slacken, the onset of market maturity usually produces fundamental changes in the industry's competitive environment:[10]

1. *Slowing growth in buyer demand generates more head-to-head competition for market share.* Firms that want to continue on a rapid-growth track start looking for ways to take customers away from competitors. Outbreaks of price cutting, increased advertising, and other aggressive tactics to gain market share are common.

2. *Buyers become more sophisticated, often driving a harder bargain on repeat purchases.* Since buyers have experience with the product and are familiar with competing brands, they are better able to evaluate different brands and can use their knowledge to negotiate a better deal with sellers.

3. *Competition often produces a greater emphasis on cost and service.* As sellers all begin to offer the product attributes buyers prefer, buyer choices increasingly depend on which seller offers the best combination of price and service.

4. *Firms have a "topping-out" problem in adding new facilities.* Reduced rates of industry growth mean slowdowns in capacity expansion for manufacturers and slowdowns in new store growth for retail chains. With slower industry growth, adding too much capacity too soon can create oversupply conditions that adversely affect company profits well into the future.

5. *Product innovation and new end-use applications are harder to come by.* Producers find it increasingly difficult to create new product features, find further uses for the product, and sustain buyer excitement.

6. *International competition increases.* Growth-minded domestic firms start to seek out sales opportunities in foreign markets. Some companies, looking for ways to cut costs, relocate plants to countries with lower wage rates. Greater product

standardization and diffusion of technological know-how reduce entry barriers and make it possible for enterprising foreign companies to become serious market contenders in more countries. Industry leadership passes to companies that succeed in building strong competitive positions in most of the world's major geographic markets and in winning the biggest global market shares.

7. *Industry profitability falls temporarily or permanently.* Slower growth, increased competition, more sophisticated buyers, and occasional periods of overcapacity put pressure on industry profit margins. Weaker, less-efficient firms are usually the hardest hit.

8. *Stiffening competition induces a number of mergers and acquisitions among former competitors, drives the weakest firms out of the industry, and produces industry consolidation in general.* Inefficient firms and firms with weak competitive strategies can achieve respectable results in a fast-growing industry with booming sales. But the intensifying competition that accompanies industry maturity exposes competitive weakness and throws second- and third-tier competitors into a survival-of-the-fittest contest.

Strategic Moves in Maturing Industries

As the new competitive character of industry maturity begins to hit full force, any of several strategic moves can strengthen a firm's competitive position: pruning the product line, improving value chain efficiency, trimming costs, increasing sales to present customers, acquiring rival firms, expanding internationally, and strengthening capabilities.[11]

Pruning Marginal Products and Models   A wide selection of models, features, and product options sometimes has competitive value during the growth stage, when buyers' needs are still evolving. But such variety can become too costly as price competition stiffens and profit margins are squeezed. Maintaining many product versions works against achieving design, parts inventory, and production economies at the manufacturing levels and can increase inventory stocking costs for distributors and retailers. In addition, the prices of slow-selling versions may not cover their true costs. Pruning marginal products from the line opens the door for cost savings and permits more concentration on items whose margins are highest and/or where a firm has a competitive advantage.

More Emphasis on Value Chain Innovation   Efforts to reinvent the industry value chain can have a fourfold payoff: lower costs, better product or service quality, greater capability to turn out multiple or customized product versions, and shorter design-to-market cycles. Manufacturers can mechanize high-cost activities, redesign production lines to improve labor efficiency, build flexibility into the assembly process so that customized product versions can be easily produced, and increase use of advanced technology (robotics, computerized controls, and automatic guided vehicles). Suppliers of parts and components, manufacturers, and distributors can collaborate on the use of Internet technology and e-commerce techniques to streamline various value chain activities and implement cost-saving innovations.

Trimming Costs   Stiffening price competition gives firms extra incentive to drive down unit costs. Company cost-reduction initiatives can cover a broad front. Some of the most frequently pursued options are pushing suppliers for better prices, implementing tighter supply chain management practices, cutting low-value activities out of the value chain, developing more economical product designs, reengineering internal processes using e-commerce technology, and shifting to more economical distribution arrangements.

Increasing Sales to Present Customers   In a mature market, growing by taking customers away from rivals may not be as appealing as expanding sales to existing customers. Strategies to increase purchases by existing customers can involve adding more sales promotions, providing complementary items and ancillary services, and finding more ways for customers to use the product. Convenience stores, for example, have boosted average sales per customer by adding video rentals, automated teller machines, gasoline pumps, and deli counters.

Acquiring Rival Firms at Bargain Prices   Sometimes a firm can acquire the facilities and assets of struggling rivals quite cheaply. Bargain-priced acquisitions can help create a low-cost position if they also present opportunities for greater operating efficiency. In addition, an acquired firm's customer base can provide expanded market coverage and opportunities for greater scale economies. The most desirable acquisitions are those that will significantly enhance the acquiring firm's competitive strength.

Expanding Internationally   As its domestic market matures, a firm may seek to enter foreign markets where attractive growth potential still exists and competitive pressures are not so strong. Many multinational companies are expanding into such emerging markets as China, India, Brazil, Argentina, and the Philippines, where the long-term growth prospects are quite attractive. Strategies to expand internationally also make sense when a domestic firm's skills, reputation, and product are readily transferable to foreign markets. For example, even though the U.S. market for soft drinks is mature, Coca-Cola has remained a growth company by upping its efforts to penetrate emerging markets where soft-drink sales are expanding rapidly.

Building New or More Flexible Capabilities   The stiffening pressures of competition in a maturing or already mature market can often be combated by strengthening the company's resource base and competitive capabilities. This can mean adding new competencies or capabilities, deepening existing competencies to make them harder to imitate, or striving to make core competencies more adaptable to changing customer requirements and expectations. Microsoft has responded to competitors' challenges by expanding its already large cadre of talented programmers. Chevron has developed a best-practices discovery team and a best-practices resource map to enhance the speed and effectiveness with which it is able to transfer efficiency improvements from one oil refinery to another.

Strategic Pitfalls in Maturing Industries

One of the greatest strategic mistakes a firm can make in a maturing industry is pursuing a compromise strategy that leaves it stuck in the middle.

Perhaps the biggest strategic mistake a company can make as an industry matures is steering a middle course between low cost, differentiation, and focusing—blending efforts to achieve low cost with efforts to incorporate differentiating features and efforts to focus on a limited target market. Such strategic compromises typically leave the firm stuck in the middle with a fuzzy strategy, too little commitment to winning a competitive advantage, an average image with buyers, and little chance of springing into the ranks of the industry leaders.

Other strategic pitfalls include being slow to mount a defense against stiffening competitive pressures, concentrating more on protecting short-term profitability than on building or maintaining long-term competitive position, waiting too long to respond to price cutting by rivals, overexpanding in the face of slowing growth, overspending on advertising and sales promotion efforts in a losing effort to combat the growth slow-down, and failing to pursue cost reduction soon enough or aggressively enough.

STRATEGIES FOR FIRMS IN STAGNANT OR DECLINING INDUSTRIES

Many firms operate in industries where demand is growing more slowly than the economy-wide average or is even declining. Although harvesting the business to obtain the greatest cash flow, selling out, or preparing for closedown are obvious end-game strategies for uncommitted competitors with dim long-term prospects, strong competitors may be able to achieve good performance even in a stagnant market environment.[12] Stagnant demand by itself is not enough to make an industry unattractive. Selling out may or may not be practical, and closing operations is always a last resort.

Businesses competing in stagnant or declining industries must resign themselves to performance targets consistent with available market opportunities. Cash flow and return-on-investment criteria are more appropriate than growth-oriented performance measures, but sales and market-share growth are by no means ruled out. Strong competitors may be able to take sales from weaker rivals, and the acquisition or exit of weaker firms creates opportunities for the remaining companies to capture greater market share.

In general, companies that succeed in stagnant industries employ one or more of three strategic themes:[13]

1. *Pursue a focused strategy aimed at the fastest-growing market segments within the industry.* Stagnant or declining markets, like other markets, are composed of numerous segments or niches. Frequently, one or more of these segments is growing rapidly, despite stagnation in the industry as a whole. An astute competitor who zeroes in on fast-growing segments and does a first-rate job of meeting the needs of buyers comprising these segments can often escape stagnating sales and profits and even gain decided competitive advantage. For instance, both Ben & Jerry's and Häagen-Dazs have achieved success by focusing on the growing luxury or superpremium segment of the otherwise stagnant market for ice cream; revenue growth and profit margins are substantially higher for high-end ice creams sold in supermarkets and in scoop shops than is the case in other segments of the ice cream market.

2. *Stress differentiation based on quality improvement and product innovation.* Either enhanced quality or innovation can rejuvenate demand by creating important new growth segments or inducing buyers to trade up. Successful product innovation opens up an avenue for competing that bypasses meeting or beating rivals' prices. Differentiation based on successful innovation has the additional advantage of being difficult and expensive for rival firms to imitate. Sony has built a solid business selling high-quality multifeatured TVs, an industry where market demand has been relatively flat in the world's industrialized nations for some years. New Covent Garden Soup has met with success by introducing packaged fresh soups for sale in major supermarkets, where the typical soup offerings are canned or dry mixes.

> Achieving competitive advantage in stagnant or declining industries usually requires pursuing one of three competitive approaches: focusing on growing market segments within the industry, differentiating on the basis of better quality and frequent product innovation, or becoming a lower-cost producer.

3. *Strive to drive costs down and become the industry's low-cost leader.* Companies in stagnant industries can improve profit margins and return on investment by pursuing innovative cost reduction year after year. Potential cost-saving actions include (*a*) cutting marginally beneficial activities out of the value chain; (*b*) outsourcing functions and activities that can be performed more cheaply by outsiders; (*c*) redesigning internal business processes to exploit cost-reducing e-commerce technologies; (*d*) consolidating underutilized production facilities; (*e*) adding more distribution channels to ensure the unit volume needed for low-cost production; (*f*) closing low-volume, high-cost retail outlets; and (*g*) pruning marginal products from the firm's offerings. Japan-based Asahi Glass (a low-cost producer of flat glass), PotashCorp and IMC Global (two low-cost leaders in potash production), Alcan Aluminum, Nucor Steel, and Safety Components International (a low-cost producer of air bags for motor vehicles) have all been successful in driving costs down in competitively tough and largely stagnant industry environments.

These three strategic themes are not mutually exclusive.[14] Introducing innovative versions of a product can *create* a fast-growing market segment. Similarly, relentless pursuit of greater operating efficiencies permits price reductions that create price-conscious growth segments. Note that all three themes are spinoffs of the generic competitive strategies, adjusted to fit the circumstances of a tough industry environment. The most attractive declining industries are those in which sales are eroding only slowly, there is large built-in demand, and some profitable niches remain.

The most common strategic mistakes companies make in stagnating or declining markets are (1) getting trapped in a profitless war of attrition, (2) diverting too much cash out of the business too quickly (thus further eroding performance), and (3) being overly optimistic about the industry's future and spending too much on improvements in anticipation that things will get better.

Illustration Capsule 8.1 describes the creative approach taken by Yamaha to combat the declining demand in the piano market.

STRATEGIES FOR COMPETING IN FRAGMENTED INDUSTRIES

A number of industries are populated by hundreds, even thousands, of small and medium-sized companies, many privately held and none with a substantial share of total industry sales.[15] The standout competitive feature of a fragmented industry is the absence of market leaders with king-sized market shares or widespread buyer recognition. Examples of fragmented industries include book publishing, landscaping and plant nurseries, real estate development, convenience stores, banking, health and medical care, mail order catalog sales, computer software development, custom printing, kitchen cabinets, trucking, auto repair, restaurants and fast food, public accounting, apparel manufacture and apparel retailing, paperboard boxes, hotels and motels, and furniture.

Reasons for Supply-Side Fragmentation

Any of several reasons can account for why the supply side of an industry is fragmented:

- Market demand is so extensive and so diverse that very large numbers of firms can easily coexist trying to accommodate the range and variety of buyer preferences

illustration capsule 8.1
Yamaha's Strategy in the Stagnant Piano Industry

For some years now, worldwide demand for pianos has been declining—in the mid-1980s the decline was 10 percent annually. Modern-day parents have not put the same stress on music lessons for their children as prior generations of parents did. In an effort to see if it could revitalize its piano business, Yamaha conducted a market research survey to learn what use was being made of pianos in households that owned one. The survey revealed that the overwhelming majority of the 40 million pianos in American, European, and Japanese households were seldom used. In most cases, the reasons the piano had been purchased no longer applied. Children had either stopped taking piano lessons or were grown and had left the household; adult household members played their pianos sparingly, if at all—only a small percentage were accomplished piano players. Most pianos were serving as a piece of fine furniture and were in good condition despite not being tuned regularly. The survey also confirmed that the income levels of piano owners were well above average.

Beginning in the late 1980s, Yamaha's piano strategists saw the idle pianos in these upscale households as a potential market opportunity. The strategy that emerged entailed marketing an attachment that would convert the piano into an old-fashioned automatic player piano capable of playing a wide number of selections recorded on disks. Concurrently, Yamaha introduced Disklavier, an upright acoustic player piano model that could record and play back performances up to 90 minutes long, making it simple to monitor student progress.

Over the past 15 years, Yamaha has introduced a host of Disklavier pianos—grand pianos, minigrand, upright, and console designs in a variety of styles and finishes. It has partnered with recording artists and music studios to make thousands of digital disks available for Yamaha piano owners, allowing them to enjoy concert-caliber performances in their home. And it has created a global music education program for both teachers and students—in 2003 Yamaha had about 750,000 students enrolled in its music education programs at some 7,500 locations across the world. Together, these efforts have helped rejuvenate and sustain Yamaha's piano business.

Source: www.yamaha.com.

and requirements and to cover all the needed geographic locations. This is true in the hotel and restaurant industry in New York City, London, or Tokyo, and the market for apparel. Likewise, there is ample room in the marketplace for numerous auto repair outlets, gasoline and convenience store retailers, and real estate firms.

- Low entry barriers allow small firms to enter quickly and cheaply.
- An absence of scale economies permits small companies to compete on an equal cost footing with larger firms.
- Buyers require relatively small quantities of customized products (as in business forms, interior design, kitchen cabinets, and advertising). Because demand for any particular product version is small, sales volumes are not adequate to support producing, distributing, or marketing on a scale that yields advantages to a large firm.
- The market for the industry's product or service is becoming more global, putting companies in more and more countries in the same competitive market arena (as in apparel manufacture).
- The technologies embodied in the industry's value chain are exploding into so many new areas and along so many different paths that specialization is essential just to keep abreast in any one area of expertise.
- The industry is young and crowded with aspiring contenders, with no firm having yet developed the resource base, competitive capabilities, and market recognition to command a significant market share (as in business-to-consumer retailing via the Internet).

Some fragmented industries consolidate over time as growth slows and the market matures. The stiffer competition that accompanies slower growth produces a shake-out of weak, inefficient firms and a greater concentration of larger, more visible sellers. Others remain atomistic because it is inherent in the nature of their businesses. And still others remain stuck in a fragmented state because existing firms lack the resources or ingenuity to employ a strategy powerful enough to drive industry consolidation.

Competitive rivalry in fragmented industries can vary from moderately strong to fierce. Low barriers tend to make entry of new competitors an ongoing threat. Competition from substitutes may or may not be a major factor. The relatively small size of companies in fragmented industries puts them in a relatively weak position to bargain with powerful suppliers and buyers, although sometimes they can become members of a cooperative formed for the purpose of using their combined leverage to negotiate better sales and purchase terms. In such an environment, the best a firm can expect is to cultivate a loyal customer base and grow a bit faster than the industry average. Competitive strategies based on either low cost or product differentiation are viable unless the industry's product is highly standardized or a commodity (like sand, concrete blocks, or paperboard boxes). Focusing on a well-defined market niche or buyer segment usually offers more competitive advantage potential than striving for broad market appeal.

> In fragmented industries competitors usually have wide enough strategic latitude (1) to either compete broadly or focus and (2) to pursue a low-cost, differentiation-based, or best-cost competitive advantage.

Strategy Options for a Fragmented Industry

Suitable competitive strategy options in a fragmented industry include:

- *Constructing and operating "formula" facilities*—This strategic approach is frequently employed in restaurant and retailing businesses operating at multiple locations. It involves constructing standardized outlets in favorable locations at minimum cost and then operating them cost-effectively. Yum! Brands (the parent of Pizza Hut, Taco Bell, KFC, Long John Silver's, and A&W restaurants), Home Depot, Staples, and 7-Eleven pursue this strategy.

- *Becoming a low-cost operator*—When price competition is intense and profit margins are under constant pressure, companies can stress no-frills operations featuring low overhead, high-productivity/low-cost labor, lean capital budgets, and dedicated pursuit of total operating efficiency. Successful low-cost producers in a fragmented industry can play the price-discounting game and still earn profits above the industry average. Many e-tailers compete on the basis of bargain prices; so do local tire retailers and supermarkets and off-brand gasoline stations.

- *Specializing by product type*—When a fragmented industry's products include a range of styles or services, a strategy to focus on one product or service category can be effective. Some firms in the furniture industry specialize in only one furniture type such as brass beds, rattan and wicker, lawn and garden, or early American. In auto repair, companies specialize in transmission repair, body work, or speedy oil changes.

- *Specializing by customer type*—A firm can stake out a market niche in a fragmented industry by catering to those customers who are interested in low prices, unique product attributes, customized features, carefree service, or other extras. A number of restaurants cater to take-out customers; others specialize in fine dining, and still others cater to the sports bar crowd.

- *Focusing on a limited geographic area*—Even though a firm in a fragmented industry can't win a big share of total industrywide sales, it can still try to dominate a local or regional geographic area. Concentrating company efforts on a limited territory can produce greater operating efficiency, speed delivery and customer services, promote strong brand awareness, and permit saturation advertising, while avoiding the diseconomies of stretching operations out over a much wider area. Supermarkets, banks, convenience stores, and sporting goods retailers successfully operate multiple locations within a limited geographic area.

In fragmented industries, firms generally have the strategic freedom to pursue broad or narrow market targets and low-cost or differentiation-based competitive advantages. Many different strategic approaches can exist side by side.

STRATEGIES FOR SUSTAINING RAPID COMPANY GROWTH

Companies that are focused on growing their revenues and earnings at a rapid or above-average pace year after year generally have to craft a portfolio of strategic initiatives covering three horizons:[16]

- *Horizon 1: "Short-jump" strategic initiatives to fortify and extend the company's position in existing businesses*—Short-jump initiatives typically include adding new items to the company's present product line, expanding into new geographic areas where the company does not yet have a market presence, and launching offensives to take market share away from rivals. The objective is to capitalize fully on whatever growth potential exists in the company's present business arenas.

- *Horizon 2: "Medium-jump" strategic initiatives to leverage existing resources and capabilities by entering new businesses with promising growth potential*—Growth companies have to be alert for opportunities to jump into new businesses where there is promise of rapid growth and where their experience, intellectual capital, and technological know-how will prove valuable in gaining rapid market penetration. While Horizon 2 initiatives may take a back seat to Horizon 1 initiatives as long as there is plenty of untapped growth in the company's present businesses, they move to the front as the onset of market maturity dims the company's growth prospects in its present business(es).

- *Horizon 3: "Long-jump" strategic initiatives to plant the seeds for ventures in businesses that do not yet exist*—Long-jump initiatives can entail pumping funds into long-range R&D projects, setting up an internal venture capital fund to invest in promising start-up companies attempting to create the industries of the future, or acquiring a number of small start-up companies experimenting with technologies and product ideas that complement the company's present businesses. Intel, for example, set up a multibillion-dollar venture fund to invest in over 100 different projects and start-up companies, the intent being to plant seeds for Intel's future, broadening its base as a global leader in supplying building blocks for PCs and the worldwide Internet economy. Royal Dutch/Shell, with over $140 billion in revenues and over 100,000 employees, spent over $20 million on rule-breaking, game-changing ideas put forth by free-thinking employees; the objective was to inject a new spirit of entrepreneurship into the company and sow the seeds of faster growth.[17]

figure 8.2   **The Three Strategy Horizons for Sustaining Rapid Growth**

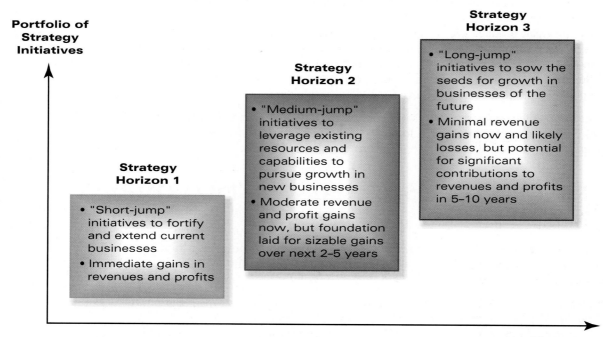

Source: Adapted from Eric D. Beinhocker, "Robust Adaptive Strategies," *Sloan Management Review* 40, No. 3 (Spring 1999), p. 101.

The three strategy horizons are illustrated in Figure 8.2. Managing such a portfolio of strategic initiatives to sustain rapid growth is not easy, however. The tendency of most companies is to focus on Horizon 1 strategies and devote only sporadic and uneven attention to Horizon 2 and 3 strategies. But a recent McKinsey & Company study of 30 of the world's leading growth companies revealed a relatively balanced portfolio of strategic initiatives covering all three horizons. The lesson of successful growth companies is that keeping a company's record of rapid growth intact over the long term entails crafting a diverse population of strategies, ranging from short-jump incremental strategies to grow present businesses to long-jump initiatives with a 5- to 10-year growth payoff horizon.[18] Having a mixture of short-jump, medium-jump, and long-jump initiatives not only increases the odds of hitting a few home runs but also provides some protection against unexpected adversity in present or newly entered businesses.

The Risks of Pursuing Multiple Strategy Horizons

There are, of course, risks to pursuing a diverse strategy portfolio aimed at sustained growth. A company cannot, of course, place bets on every opportunity that appears on its radar screen, lest it stretch its resources too thin. And medium-jump and long-jump initiatives can cause a company to stray far from its core competencies and end up trying to compete in businesses for which it is ill-suited. Moreover, it can be difficult to achieve competitive advantage in medium- and long-jump product families and businesses that prove not to mesh well with a company's present businesses and resource strengths. The payoffs of long-jump initiatives often prove elusive; not all of the seeds a company sows will bear fruit, and only a few may evolve into truly significant contributors to the company's revenue and profit growth. The losses from those long-jump ventures that do not take root may significantly erode the gains from those that do, resulting in disappointingly modest gains in overall profits.

STRATEGIES FOR INDUSTRY LEADERS

The competitive positions of industry leaders normally range from "stronger than average" to "powerful." Leaders typically are well known, and strongly entrenched leaders have proven strategies (keyed either to low-cost leadership or to differentiation). Some of the best-known industry leaders are Anheuser-Busch (beer), Starbucks (coffee drinks), Microsoft (computer software), Callaway (golf clubs), McDonald's (fast food), Gillette (razor blades), Campbell's Soup (canned soups), Gerber (baby food), Hewlett-Packard (printers), Nokia (cell phones), AT&T (long-distance telephone service), Eastman Kodak (camera film), Wal-Mart (discount retailing), Amazon.com (online shopping), eBay (online auctions), and Levi Strauss (jeans).

The main strategic concern for a leader revolves around how to defend and strengthen its leadership position, perhaps becoming the *dominant* leader as opposed to just *a* leader. However, the pursuit of industry leadership and large market share is primarily important because of the competitive advantage and profitability that accrue to being the industry's biggest company. Three contrasting strategic postures are open to industry leaders:[19]

1. Stay-on-the-offensive strategy—The central goal of a stay-on-the-offensive strategy is to be a first-mover and a proactive market leader.[20] It rests on the principle that staying a step ahead and forcing rivals into a catch-up mode is the surest path to industry prominence and potential market dominance—as the saying goes, the best defense is a good offense. Being the industry standard setter entails relentless pursuit of continuous improvement and innovation—being out front with technological improvements, new or better products, more attractive performance features, quality enhancements, improved customer service, ways to cut operating costs, and ways to make it easier and less costly for potential customers to switch their purchases from runner-up firms to its own products. A low-cost leader must set the pace for cost reduction, and a differentiator must constantly initiate new ways to keep its product set apart from the brands of imitative rivals in order to be the standard against which rivals' products are judged. The array of options for a potent stay-on-the-offensive strategy can also include initiatives to expand overall industry demand—spurring the creation of new families of products, making the product more suitable for consumers in emerging-country markets, discovering new uses for the product, attracting new users of the product, and promoting more frequent use.

> The two best tests of success of a stay-on-the-offensive strategy are (1) the extent to which it keeps rivals in a reactive mode, scrambling to keep up, and (2) whether the leader is growing faster than the industry as a whole and wresting market share from rivals.

Furthermore, unless a leader's market share is already so dominant that it presents a threat of antitrust action (a market share under 60 percent is usually safe), a potent stay-on-the-offensive strategy entails actions aimed at growing faster than the industry as a whole and wresting market share from rivals. A leader whose growth does not equal or outpace the industry average is losing ground to competitors.

2. *Fortify-and-defend strategy*—The essence of "fortify and defend" is to make it harder for challengers to gain ground and for new firms to enter. The goals of a strong defense are to hold on to the present market share, strengthen current market position, and protect whatever competitive advantage the firm has. Specific defensive actions can include:

- Attempting to raise the competitive ante for challengers and new entrants via increased spending for advertising, higher levels of customer service, and bigger R&D outlays.
- Introducing more product versions or brands to match the product attributes that challenger brands have or to fill vacant niches that competitors could slip into.
- Adding personalized services and other extras that boost customer loyalty and make it harder or more costly for customers to switch to rival products.
- Keeping prices reasonable and quality attractive.
- Building new capacity ahead of market demand to discourage smaller competitors from adding capacity of their own.
- Investing enough to remain cost-competitive and technologically progressive.
- Patenting the feasible alternative technologies.
- Signing exclusive contracts with the best suppliers and dealer distributors.

> Industry leaders can strengthen their long-term competitive positions with strategies keyed to aggressive offense, aggressive defense, or muscling smaller rivals and customers into behaviors that bolster its own market standing.

A fortify-and-defend strategy best suits firms that have already achieved industry dominance and don't wish to risk antitrust action. It is also well suited to situations where a firm wishes to milk its present position for profits and cash flow because the industry's prospects for growth are low or because further gains in market share do not appear profitable enough to go after. But a fortify-and-defend strategy always entails trying to grow as fast as the market as a whole (to stave off market-share slippage) and requires reinvesting enough capital in the business to protect the leader's ability to compete.

3. *Muscle-flexing strategy*—Here a dominant leader plays competitive hardball (presumably in an ethical and competitively legal manner) when smaller rivals rock the boat with price cuts or mount new market offensives that directly threaten its position. Specific responses can include quickly matching and perhaps exceeding challengers' price cuts, using large promotional campaigns to counter challengers' moves to gain market share, and offering better deals to their major customers. Dominant leaders may also court distributors assiduously to dissuade them from carrying rivals' products, provide salespersons with documented information about the weaknesses of competing products, or try to fill any vacant positions in their own firms by making attractive offers to the better executives of rivals that get out of line.

The leader may also use various arm-twisting tactics to pressure present customers not to use the products of rivals. This can range from simply forcefully communicating its displeasure should customers opt to use the products of rivals to pushing them to agree to exclusive arrangements in return for better prices to charging them a higher price if they use any competitors' products. As a final resort, a leader may grant certain customers special discounts or preferred treatment if they do not use any products of rivals.

The obvious risks of a muscle-flexing strategy are running afoul of the antitrust laws (as Microsoft did—see Illustration Capsule 8.2), alienating customers with bullying tactics, and arousing adverse public opinion. A company that tries to throw its weight around to protect and enhance its market dominance has got to be judicious, lest it cross the line from allowable tactics to unethical or illegal competitive practices.

illustration capsule 8.2
How Microsoft Uses Its Muscle to Maintain Its Market Leadership

U.S. district judge Thomas Penfield Jackson concluded in 1999 in *U.S.* v. *Microsoft* that Microsoft repeatedly had used heavy-handed tactics to routinely pressure customers, crush competitors, and throttle competition. Judge Jackson painted Microsoft as a domineering company that rewarded its friends and punished its enemies, pointing to the following examples:

- Gateway and IBM, both of which resisted Microsoft's efforts to dissuade them from using or promoting competitors' products on their PCs, were forced to pay higher prices for installing Microsoft's Windows operating system on their PCs than several other PC makers had to pay.

- Microsoft tried to persuade Netscape to halt its development of platform-level technologies for Windows 95, arguing that Netscape's Navigator browser should be designed to run on Windows 95 only rather than be designed in a way that could serve as an alternative operating system platform and substitute for use of Windows. Microsoft wanted Netscape to agree to a special alliance with Microsoft that would allow Microsoft to incorporate Navigator's functionality into Windows. When Netscape refused, Microsoft withheld information about its Windows 95 code until after it released the new operating system and its own new version of Internet Explorer. Microsoft also refused to give Netscape a license to one of its scripting tools, thereby preventing Netscape from doing business with certain Internet service providers for a time. Simultaneously, Microsoft pressured PC makers to install Internet Explorer as the preferred alternative to Netscape Navigator. When Compaq removed the Internet Explorer icon from the opening screen of its

computers and preinstalled the Navigator icon, Microsoft threatened to revoke Compaq's license to install Windows 95.

- Microsoft tried to convince Intel not to ship its newly developed Native Signal Processing (NSP) software (intended to help spark demand for Intel's most advanced microprocessors) because Microsoft felt that NSP represented an incursion into Microsoft's operating system platform territory. It also asked Intel to reduce the number of people working on software at Intel. Microsoft assured Intel that if it would stop promoting NSP, Microsoft would accelerate its own work to incorporate the functions of NSP into Windows. At the same time, Microsoft pressured PC makers not to install Intel's NSP software on their PCs.

- When Compaq Computer entered into an agreement with America Online (AOL) to promote AOL above all other online services and began to ship its computers with the Microsoft Network (MSN) icon removed and the AOL icon installed, Microsoft wrote Compaq a letter stating its intention to terminate Compaq's license for Windows 95 if it did not restore the MSN icon to its original position on the opening screen.

Despite the 1999 decision, Microsoft has continued to flex its muscles. In 2001, the company reduced its support for the language Java in its release of the new Windows XP operating system—Java is favored by Microsoft's longtime rival Sun Microsystems. Microsoft also pressured PC makers to display three of its own icons—for MSN online, Windows Media player, and Internet Explorer—on the Windows XP desktop. And it has consistently used harassing tactics against RealNetworks, a maker of media software that competes directly with Microsoft's Windows Media Player.

Sources: Don Clark, "Microsoft Raises Requirements on Icon Use by Computer Makers," *The Wall Street Journal* (www.wsj.com), August 9, 2001; D. Ian Hopper, "Microsoft Appeals to Supreme Court," Associated Press, August 8, 2001; John R. Wilke and Don Clark, "Senate Judiciary Committee Plans Microsoft Hearings," *The Wall Street Journal* (http://public.wsj.com), July 24, 2001; John R. Wilke and Don Clark, "Microsoft Pulls Back Support for Java," *The Wall Street Journal* (www.wsj.com), July 19, 2001; and transcript of Judge Jackson's findings of fact in *U.S.* v. *Microsoft,* November 5, 1999.

STRATEGIES FOR RUNNER-UP FIRMS

Runner-up or "second-tier" firms have smaller market shares than "first-tier" industry leaders. Some runner-up firms are up-and-coming *market challengers,* employing offensive strategies to gain market share and build a stronger market position. Other runner-up competitors are *focusers*, seeking to improve their lot by concentrating their attention on serving a limited portion of the market. There are, of course, always a number of firms in any industry that are destined to be *perennial runners-up*, lacking the resources and competitive strengths to do more than continue in trailing positions and/or content to follow the trendsetting moves of the market leaders.

Obstacles for Firms with Small Market Shares

In industries where big size is definitely a key success factor, firms with small market shares have some obstacles to overcome: (1) less access to economies of scale in manufacturing, distribution, or marketing and sales promotion; (2) difficulty in gaining customer recognition; (3) weaker ability to use mass media advertising; and (4) difficulty in funding capital requirements.[21] When significant scale economies give large-volume competitors a *dominating* cost advantage, small-share firms have only two viable strategic options: initiate offensive moves to gain sales and market share (so as to build the volume of business needed to approach the scale economies enjoyed by larger rivals) or withdraw from the business (gradually or quickly).

The competitive strategies most underdogs use to build market share and achieve critical scale economies are based on (1) using lower prices to win customers from weak higher-cost rivals; (2) merging with or acquiring rival firms to achieve the size needed to capture greater scale economies; (3) investing in new cost-saving facilities and equipment, perhaps relocating operations to countries where costs are significantly lower; and (4) pursuing technological innovations or radical value chain revamping to achieve dramatic cost savings.

But *it is erroneous to view runner-up firms as inherently less profitable or unable to hold their own against the biggest firms.* Many small and medium-sized firms earn healthy profits and enjoy good reputations with customers.

Strategic Approaches for Runner-Up Companies

Assuming that scale economies or learning-curve effects are relatively small and result in no important cost advantage for big-share firms, runner-up companies have considerable strategic flexibility and can consider any of the following seven approaches.

Offensive Strategies to Build Market Share   A challenger firm needs a strategy aimed at building a competitive advantage of its own. Rarely can a runner-up improve its competitive position by imitating the strategies of leading firms. A cardinal rule in offensive strategy is to avoid attacking a leader head-on with an imitative strategy, regardless of the resources and staying power an underdog may have.[22] Moreover, if a challenger has a 5 percent market share and needs a 20 percent share to earn attractive returns, it needs a more creative approach to competing than just "Try harder."

> Rarely can a runner-up firm successfully challenge an industry leader with a copycat strategy.

Ambitious runner-up companies have to make some waves in the marketplace if they want to make big market share gains. The best "mover-and-shaker" offensives usually involve one of the following approaches:

- Pioneering a leapfrog technological breakthrough.
- Getting new or better products into the market consistently ahead of rivals and building a reputation for product leadership.

- Being more agile and innovative in adapting to evolving market conditions and customer expectations than slower-to-change market leaders.

- Forging attractive strategic alliances with key distributors, dealers, or marketers of complementary products.

- Finding innovative ways to dramatically drive down costs and then using the attraction of lower prices to win customers from higher-cost, higher-priced rivals. A challenger firm can pursue aggressive cost reduction by eliminating marginal activities from its value chain, streamlining supply chain relationships, improving internal operating efficiency, using various e-commerce techniques, and merging with or acquiring rival firms to achieve the size needed to capture greater scale economies.

- Crafting an attractive differentiation strategy based on premium quality, technological superiority, outstanding customer service, rapid product innovation, or convenient online shopping options.

Without a potent offensive strategy to capture added market share, runner-up companies have to patiently nibble away at the lead of market leaders and build sales at a moderate pace over time.

Growth-via-Acquisition Strategy   One of the most frequently used strategies employed by ambitious runner-up companies is merging with or acquiring rivals to form an enterprise that has greater competitive strength and a larger share of the overall market. For an enterprise to succeed with this strategic approach, senior management must have the skills to assimilate the operations of the acquired companies, eliminating duplication and overlap, generating efficiencies and cost savings, and structuring the combined resources in ways that create substantially stronger competitive capabilities. Many banks owe their growth during the past decade to acquisition of smaller regional and local banks. Likewise, a number of book publishers have grown by acquiring small publishers. Cisco Systems has used acquisitions to become a leader in Internet networking products.

Vacant-Niche Strategy   This version of a focused strategy involves concentrating on specific customer groups or end-use applications that market leaders have bypassed or neglected. An ideal vacant niche is of sufficient size and scope to be profitable, has some growth potential, is well suited to a firm's own capabilities, and for one reason or another is hard for leading firms to serve. Two examples where vacant-niche strategies have worked successfully are (1) regional commuter airlines serving cities with too few passengers to fill the large jets flown by major airlines and (2) health-food producers (like Health Valley, Hain, and Tree of Life) that cater to local health-food stores—a market segment traditionally given little attention by Kraft, General Mills, Nestlé, Unilever, Campbell Soup, and other leading food products firms.

Specialist Strategy   A specialist firm trains its competitive effort on one technology, product or product family, end use, or market segment (often one in which buyers have special needs). The aim is to train the company's resource strengths and capabilities on building competitive advantage through leadership in a specific area. Smaller companies that successfully use this focused strategy include Formby's (a specialist in stains and finishes for wood furniture, especially refinishing); Blue Diamond (a California-based grower and marketer of almonds); Canada Dry (known for its ginger ale, tonic water, and carbonated soda water); and American Tobacco (a leader in chewing tobacco and snuff). Many companies in high-tech industries concentrate their energies on being the clear leader in a particular technological niche; their competitive advantage is superior technological depth, technical expertise that is highly valued by customers, and the capability to consistently beat out rivals in pioneering technological advances.

Superior Product Strategy   The approach here is to use a differentiation-based focused strategy keyed to superior product quality or unique attributes. Sales and marketing efforts are aimed directly at quality-conscious and performance-oriented buyers. Fine craftsmanship, prestige quality, frequent product innovations, and/or close contact with customers to solicit their input in developing a better product usually undergird the superior product approach. Some examples include Samuel Adams in beer, Tiffany in diamonds and jewelry, Chicago Cutlery in premium-quality kitchen knives, Baccarat in fine crystal, Cannondale in mountain bikes, Bally in shoes, and Patagonia in apparel for outdoor recreation enthusiasts.

Distinctive-Image Strategy   Some runner-up companies build their strategies around ways to make themselves stand out from competitors. A variety of distinctive-image strategies can be used: creating a reputation for charging the lowest prices, providing prestige quality at a good price, going all-out to give superior customer service, designing unique product attributes, being a leader in new product introduction, or devising unusually creative advertising. Examples include Dr Pepper's strategy in calling attention to its distinctive taste, Apple Computer's making it easier and more interesting for people to use its Macintosh PCs, and Mary Kay Cosmetics' distinctive use of the color pink.

Content Follower Strategy   Content followers deliberately refrain from initiating trendsetting strategic moves and from aggressive attempts to steal customers away from the leaders. Followers prefer approaches that will not provoke competitive retaliation, often opting for focus and differentiation strategies that keep them out of the leaders' paths. They react and respond rather than initiate and challenge. They prefer defense to offense. And they rarely get out of line with the leaders on price. They are content to simply maintain their market position, albeit sometimes struggling to do so. Followers have no urgent strategic questions to confront beyond "What strategic changes are the leaders initiating and what do we need to do to follow along and maintain our present position?" The marketers of private-label products tend to be followers, imitating many of the features of name-brand products and content to sell to price-conscious buyers at prices modestly below those of well-known brands.

STRATEGIES FOR WEAK AND CRISIS-RIDDEN BUSINESSES

A firm in an also-ran or declining competitive position has four basic strategic options. If it can come up with the financial resources, it can launch an *offensive turnaround strategy* keyed either to low-cost or "new" differentiation themes, pouring enough money and talent into the effort to move up a notch or two in the industry rankings and become a respectable market contender within five years or so. It can employ a *fortify-and-defend strategy,* using variations of its present strategy and fighting hard to keep sales, market share, profitability, and competitive position at current levels. It can opt for a *fast-exit strategy* and get out of the business, either by selling out to another firm or by closing down operations if a buyer cannot be found. Or it can employ an *end-game or slow-exit strategy,* keeping reinvestment to a bare-bones minimum and taking actions to maximize short-term cash flows in preparation for an orderly market exit.

> The strategic options for a competitively weak company include waging a modest offensive to improve its position, defending its present position, being acquired by another company, or employing an end-game strategy.

Turnaround Strategies for Businesses in Crisis

Turnaround strategies are needed when a business worth rescuing goes into crisis; the objective is to arrest and reverse the sources of competitive and financial weakness as quickly as possible. Management's first task in formulating a suitable turnaround strategy is to diagnose what lies at the root of poor performance. Is it an unexpected downturn in sales brought on by a weak economy? An ill-chosen competitive strategy? Poor execution of an otherwise workable strategy? High operating costs? Important resource deficiencies? An overload of debt? The next task is to decide whether the business can be saved or whether the situation is hopeless. Understanding what is wrong with the business and how serious its strategic problems are is essential because different diagnoses lead to different turnaround strategies.

Some of the most common causes of business trouble are taking on too much debt, overestimating the potential for sales growth, ignoring the profit-depressing effects of an overly aggressive effort to "buy" market share with deep price cuts, being burdened with heavy fixed costs because of an inability to use plant capacity, betting on R&D efforts but failing to come up with effective innovations, betting on technological long shots, being too optimistic about the ability to penetrate new markets, making frequent changes in strategy (because the previous strategy didn't work out), and being overpowered by more successful rivals. Curing these kinds of problems and achieving a successful business turnaround can involve any of the following actions:

- Selling off assets to raise cash to save the remaining part of the business.
- Revising the existing strategy.
- Launching efforts to boost revenues.
- Pursuing cost reduction.
- Using a combination of these efforts.

Selling Off Assets   Asset-reduction strategies are essential when cash flow is a critical consideration and when the most practical ways to generate cash are (1) through sale of some of the firm's assets (plant and equipment, land, patents, inventories, or profitable subsidiaries) and (2) through retrenchment (pruning of marginal products from the product line, closing or selling older plants, reducing the workforce, withdrawing from outlying markets, cutting back customer service). Sometimes crisis-ridden companies sell off assets not so much to unload losing operations as to raise funds to save and strengthen the remaining business activities. In such cases, the choice is usually to dispose of noncore business assets to support strategy renewal in the firm's core businesses.

Strategy Revision   When weak performance is caused by bad strategy, the task of strategy overhaul can proceed along any of several paths: (1) shifting to a new competitive approach to rebuild the firm's market position; (2) overhauling internal operations and functional-area strategies to better support the same overall business strategy; (3) merging with another firm in the industry and forging a new strategy keyed to the newly merged firm's strengths; and (4) retrenching into a reduced core of products and customers more closely matched to the firm's strengths. The most appealing path depends on prevailing industry conditions, the firm's particular strengths and weaknesses, its competitive capabilities vis-à-vis rival firms, and the severity of the crisis. A situation analysis of the industry, the major competitors, and the firm's own competitive position is a prerequisite for action. As a rule, successful strategy revision must be tied to the ailing firm's strengths and near-term competitive capabilities and directed at its best market opportunities.

Boosting Revenues   Revenue-increasing turnaround efforts aim at generating increased sales volume. There are a number of revenue-building options: price cuts, increased promotion, a bigger sales force, added customer services, and quickly achieved product improvements. Attempts to increase revenues and sales volumes are necessary (1) when there is little or no room in the operating budget to cut expenses and still break even, and (2) when the key to restoring profitability is increased use of existing capacity. If buyers are not especially price-sensitive because of differentiating features, the quickest way to boost short-term revenues may be to raise prices rather than opt for volume-building price cuts.

Cutting Costs   Cost-reducing turnaround strategies work best when an ailing firm's value chain and cost structure are flexible enough to permit radical surgery, when operating inefficiencies are identifiable and readily correctable, when the firm's costs are obviously bloated, and when the firm is relatively close to its break-even point. Accompanying a general belt-tightening can be an increased emphasis on paring administrative overheads, elimination of nonessential and low-value-added activities in the firm's value chain, modernization of existing plant and equipment to gain greater productivity, delay of nonessential capital expenditures, and debt restructuring to reduce interest costs and stretch out repayments.

Combination Efforts   Combination turnaround strategies are usually essential in grim situations that require fast action on a broad front. Likewise, combination actions frequently come into play when new managers are brought in and given a free hand to make whatever changes they see fit. The tougher the problems, the more likely it is that the solutions will involve multiple strategic initiatives—see the story of turnaround efforts at Lucent Technologies in Illustration Capsule 8.3.

Turnaround efforts tend to be high-risk undertakings, and they often fail. A landmark study of 64 companies found no successful turnarounds among the most troubled companies in eight basic industries.[23] Many of the troubled businesses waited too long to begin a turnaround. Others found themselves short of both the cash and entrepreneurial talent needed to compete in a slow-growth industry characterized by a fierce battle for market share. Better-positioned rivals simply proved too strong to defeat in a long, head-to-head contest. Even when successful, turnaround may involve numerous attempts and management changes before long-term competitive viability and profitability are finally restored. A recent study found that troubled companies that did nothing and elected to wait out hard times had only a 10 percent chance of recovery.[24] This same study also found that, of the companies studied, the chances of recovery

illustration capsule 8.3
Lucent Technologies' Turnaround Strategy: Slow to Produce Results

In the fall of 2001, the situation was becoming desperate at Lucent Technologies, an AT&T spinoff that had been heralded as a superstar of the telecommunications equipment industry. The combination of lost sales to competitors and a steep downturn in capital spending for telecommunications equipment had thrown the company into a nosedive, driving its stock price from over $80 a share down to under $10. Revenues had dropped from $38 billion in the fiscal year ending September 1999 to just $21 billion in fiscal year ending September 2001; profits had declined even more precipitously, falling from a positive $3.5 billion to a stunning $14.2 billion loss. Some observers predicted the company could not survive, and most everyone agreed that Lucent's recovery would be slow at best because of a capacity glut in fiber-optic telecommunications systems.

To bolster its sagging outlook, top executives engineered a turnaround strategy that featured:

- Eliminating 15,000 to 20,000 jobs worldwide immediately and eventually cutting the workforce by more than half, from 150,000 to 60,000.

- Consolidating production at a fewer plants and closing the unneeded plants.

- Selling the company's fiber-optic business (for about $4 billion).

- Raising additional cash by selling $1.8 billion in convertible preferred stock.

- Reaching an agreement with its group of banks to realign the terms of $4 billion in loans.

- Dropping certain product lines.

- Spinning off its microelectronics business, Agere Systems, as a separate company.

- Pursuing a number of cost-cutting initiatives aimed at making Lucent a leaner, more efficient maker of telecommunications equipment.

Top executives were confident in predicting that these moves would return Lucent to profitability in 2002, even without a recovery in telecommunications spending. But Lucent's turnaround proved considerably more problematic than expected. In fiscal 2002 (ending September 2002), revenues fell further, to $12.3 billion, and losses amounted to $12 billion. Lucent's struggles to get its business back on track included restoring lost confidence in top management by brining in a new president and CEO, Pat Russo. Russo continued with the restructuring efforts previously announced but also spurred company efforts to grow the company's revenues and reduce the company's break-even sales volumes via additional streamlining of operations.

In the fall of 2003, the company was continuing to lose money and was also experiencing further revenue declines. In the third quarter of fiscal 2003, Lucent reported revenues of $1.96 billion and a loss of $254 million. The company's stock was trading in the $2.00–$2.50 range. Russo forecast that the company would not return to profitability until sometime in 2004. The bright spot in Lucent's outlook was its strong position in third-generation (3G) wireless technology. Lucent management expected that the company would get a major boost from sales of 3G technology products as wireless communications companies began to more aggressively upgrade their networks.

Sources: www.lucent.com, accessed September 22, 2003; Yuki Noguchi, "Lucent Closes Herndon's Chromatis," *Washington Post* (www.washingtonpost.com), August 29, 2001; Simon Romero, "Lucent Maps Out Route to Profit by the End of Next Year," *New York Times* (www.nytimes.com), August 24, 2001; Peter J. Howe, "Lucent Fires 290 More at Massachusetts Sites," *Boston Globe* (www.boston.com), August 24, 2001; and Sara Silver, "Lucent Cuts 2,200 Jobs," Associated Press, August 23, 2001.

were boosted 190 percent if the turnaround strategy involved buying assets that strengthened the company's business in its core markets; companies that both bought assets or companies in their core markets and sold off noncore assets increased their chances of recovery by 250 percent.

Liquidation—the Strategy of Last Resort

Sometimes a business in crisis is too far gone to be salvaged. The problem, of course, is determining when a turnaround is achievable and when it isn't. It is easy for owners or managers to let their emotions and pride overcome sound judgment when a business gets in such deep trouble that a successful turnaround is remote. Closing down a crisis-ridden business and liquidating its assets, however, is sometimes the best and wisest strategy. Of all the strategic alternatives, liquidation is the most unpleasant and painful because of the hardships of job eliminations and the effects of business closings on local communities. Nonetheless, in hopeless situations, an early liquidation effort usually serves owner-stockholder interests better than an inevitable bankruptcy. Prolonging the pursuit of a lost cause merely exhausts an organization's resources further and leaves less to salvage, not to mention the added stress and potential career impairment for all the people involved.

End-Game Strategies

An *end-game, slow-exit,* or *harvesting strategy* steers a middle course between preserving the status quo and exiting as soon as possible. This type of strategy involves a gradual phasing down of the business and even sacrificing market position in return for bigger near-term cash flows or current profitability. The overriding financial objective of a slow-exit or harvest strategy is to reap the greatest possible harvest of cash to deploy to other business endeavors. The operating budget is chopped to a rock-bottom level; reinvestment in the business is held to a bare minimum. Capital expenditures for new equipment are put on hold or given low financial priority (unless replacement needs are unusually urgent); instead, efforts are made to stretch the life of existing equipment and make do with present facilities as long as possible. Promotional expenses may be cut gradually, quality reduced in not-so-visible ways, nonessential customer services curtailed, and the like. Although such actions may result in shrinking sales and market share, if cash expenses can be cut even faster, then after-tax profits and cash flows are bigger (at least temporarily). The business gradually declines, but not before sizable amounts of cash have been harvested.

An end-game, slow-exit, or harvest strategy is a reasonable strategic option for a weak business in the following circumstances:[25]

1. *When the industry's long-term prospects are unattractive*—as seems to be the case for the cigarette industry, for the manufacture and sale of VCRs and videocassettes (which are now being replaced by DVD players and both CDs and DVDs), and for the 3.5-inch floppy disk business.

2. *When rejuvenating the business would be too costly or at best marginally profitable*—as could be the case at Iomega, which is struggling to maintain sales of its Zip drives in the face of rapidly expanding hard disk drives on PCs, or at Polaroid, which has experienced stagnant sales for its instant cameras and film.

3. *When the firm's market share is becoming increasingly costly to maintain or defend*—as could be the case with the makers of film for traditional cameras.

4. *When reduced levels of competitive effort will not trigger an immediate or rapid falloff in sales*—the makers of printers will not likely experience much of a decline in sales of either dot-matrix printers or ribbons if they spend all of their ad budgets on promoting their lines of laser printers.

5. *When the enterprise can redeploy the freed resources in higher-opportunity areas*—the makers of CD players and CDs are better off devoting their resources to the production and sale of DVD players/recorders and DVDs.

6. *When the business is not a crucial or core component of a diversified company's overall lineup of businesses*—gradually letting a sideline business decay is strategically preferable to deliberately letting a mainline or core business decline.

7. *When the business does not contribute other desired features to a company's overall business portfolio*—such features include sales stability, prestige, and a well-rounded product line.

The more of these seven conditions that are present, the more ideal the business is for harvesting and a slow-exit or end-game strategy.

End-game strategies make the most sense for diversified companies that have sideline or noncore business units in weak competitive positions or in unattractive industries. Such companies can withdraw the cash flows from unattractive, noncore business units and reallocate them to business units with greater profit potential or spend them on the acquisition of new businesses.

10 COMMANDMENTS FOR CRAFTING SUCCESSFUL BUSINESS STRATEGIES

Company experiences over the years prove again and again that disastrous strategies can be avoided by adhering to good strategy-making principles. We've distilled the lessons learned from the strategic mistakes companies most often make into 10 commandments that serve as useful guides for developing sound strategies:

1. *Place top priority on crafting and executing strategic moves that enhance the company's competitive position for the long term.* The glory of meeting one quarter's or one year's financial performance targets quickly fades, but an ever-stronger competitive position pays off year after year. Shareholders are never well served by managers who let short-term financial performance considerations rule out strategic initiatives that will meaningfully bolster the company's longer-term competitive position and competitive strength. The best way to ensure a company's long-term profitability is with a strategy that strengthens the company's long-term competitiveness and market position.

2. *Be prompt in adapting to changing market conditions, unmet customer needs, buyer wishes for something better, emerging technological alternatives, and new initiatives of competitors.* Responding late or with too little often puts a company in the precarious position of having to play catch-up. While pursuit of a consistent strategy has its virtues, adapting strategy to changing circumstances is normal and necessary. Moreover, long-term strategic commitments to achieve top quality or lowest cost should be interpreted relative to competitors' products as well as customers' needs and expectations; the company should avoid singlemindedly striving to make the absolute highest-quality or lowest-cost product no matter what.

3. *Invest in creating a sustainable competitive advantage.* Having a competitive edge over rivals is the single most dependable contributor to above-average profitability.

As a general rule, a company must play aggressive offense to build competitive advantage and aggressive defense to protect it.

4. *Avoid strategies capable of succeeding only in the most optimistic circumstances.* Expect competitors to employ countermeasures and expect times of unfavorable market conditions. A good strategy works reasonably well and produces tolerable results even in the worst of times.

5. *Don't underestimate the reactions and the commitment of rival firms.* Rivals are most dangerous when they are pushed into a corner and their well-being is threatened.

6. *Consider that attacking competitive weakness is usually more profitable and less risky than attacking competitive strength.* Attacking capable, resourceful rivals is likely to fail unless the attacker has deep financial pockets and a solid basis for competitive advantage over stronger rivals.

7. *Be judicious in cutting prices without an established cost advantage.* Only a low-cost producer can win at price cutting over the long term.

8. *Strive to open up very meaningful gaps in quality or service or performance features when pursuing a differentiation strategy.* Tiny differences between rivals' product offerings may not be visible or important to buyers.

9. *Avoid stuck-in-the-middle strategies that represent compromises between lower costs and greater differentiation and between broad and narrow market appeal.* Compromise strategies rarely produce sustainable competitive advantage or a distinctive competitive position—a well-executed best-cost producer strategy is the only exception where a compromise between low cost and differentiation succeeds. Usually, companies with compromise strategies end up with average costs, average differentiation, an average image and reputation, a middle-of-the-pack industry ranking, and little prospect of industry leadership.

10. *Be aware that aggressive moves to wrest market share away from rivals often provoke retaliation in the form of a price war—to the detriment of everyone's profits.* Aggressive moves to capture a bigger market share invite cutthroat competition, particularly when the market is plagued with high inventories and excess production capacity.

MATCHING STRATEGY TO ANY INDUSTRY AND COMPANY SITUATION

It is not enough to understand a company's basic competitive strategy options—overall low-cost leadership, broad differentiation, best-cost, focused low-cost, and focused differentiation—and that there are a variety of offensive, defensive, first-mover, and late-mover initiatives and actions to choose from. The lessons of this chapter are (1) that some strategic options are better suited to certain specific industry and competitive environments than others and (2) that some strategic options are better suited to certain specific company situations than others. This chapter portrays the multifaceted task of matching strategy to a firm's external and internal circumstances in nine types of situations.

Rather than try to summarize the main points we made about choosing strategies for these nine sets of circumstances (the relevant principles are not readily capsuled in three or four sentences each), we think it more useful to conclude this chapter by outlining a broader framework for matching strategy to *any* industry and company situation. Aligning a company's strategy with its overall situation starts with a quick diagnosis of the industry environment and the firm's competitive standing in the industry:

1. What basic type of industry environment (emerging, rapid-growth, high-velocity, mature, global, commodity-product) does the company operate in? What strategic options and strategic postures are usually best suited to this generic type of environment?

2. What position does the firm have in the industry (leader, runner-up, or also-ran; strong, weak, or crisis-ridden)? How does the firm's market standing influence its strategic options given the industry and competitive environment—in particular, which courses of action have to be ruled out?

Next, strategists need to factor in the primary external and internal situational considerations (as discussed in Chapters 3 and 4) and decide how all the factors add up. Nearly always, weighing the various considerations makes it clear that some strategic options can be ruled out. Listing the pros and cons of the remaining options can help managers choose the best overall strategy.

The final step is to custom-tailor the chosen generic competitive strategy approach (low-cost, broad differentiation, best-cost, focused low-cost, focused differentiation) to fit *both* the industry environment and the firm's standing vis-à-vis competitors. Here, it is important to be sure that (1) the customized aspects of the proposed strategy are well matched to the firm's competencies and competitive capabilities, and (2) the strategy addresses all issues and problems the firm confronts.

In weeding out less-attractive strategic alternatives and weighing the pros and cons of the most attractive ones, the answers to the following questions often help point to the best course of action:

*   What kind of competitive edge can the company *realistically* achieve? Can the company execute the strategic moves necessary to secure this edge?

*   Does the company have the organizational capabilities and financial resources to succeed in these moves and approaches? If not, can they be acquired?

*   Once built, how can the competitive advantage be protected? Is the company in a position to lead industry change and set the rules by which rivals must compete? What defensive strategies need to be employed? Will rivals counterattack? What will it take to blunt their efforts?

*   Are any rivals particularly vulnerable? Should the firm mount an offensive to capitalize on these vulnerabilities? What offensive moves need to be employed?

*   What additional strategic moves are needed to deal with driving forces in the industry, specific threats and weaknesses, and any other issues/problems unique to the firm?

table 8.1   **Sample Format for a Strategic Action Plan**

1. Strategic Vision and Mission
2. Strategic Objectives
  • Short-term
  • Long-term
3. Financial Objectives
  • Short-term
  • Long-term
4. Overall Business Strategy
	5. Supporting Functional Strategies
	  • Production
	  • Marketing/sales
	  • Finance
	  • Personnel/human resources
	  • Other
	6. Recommended Actions to Improve
	    Company Performance
	  • Immediate
	  • Longer-range

In crafting the overall strategy, there are several pitfalls to avoid:

• Designing an overly ambitious strategic plan—one that overtaxes the company's resources and capabilities.

• Selecting a strategy that represents a radical departure from or abandonment of the cornerstones of the company's prior success—a radical strategy change need not be rejected automatically, but it should be pursued only after careful risk assessment.

• Choosing a strategy that goes against the grain of the organization's culture or conflicts with the values and philosophies of the most senior executives.

• Being unwilling to *commit wholeheartedly* to one of the five competitive strategies—picking and choosing features of the different strategies usually produces so many compromises between low cost, best cost, differentiation, and focusing that the company fails to achieve any kind of advantage and ends up stuck in the middle.

Table 8.1 provides a generic format for outlining a strategic action plan for a single-business enterprise. It contains all of the pieces of a comprehensive strategic action plan that we discussed at various places in these first eight chapters.

| exercises

1. Listed below are eight industries. Classify each one as (a) emerging, (b) turbulent or high-velocity, (c) mature/slow-growth, (d) stagnant/declining, or (e) fragmented. Do research on the Internet, if needed, to locate information on industry conditions and reach a conclusion on what classification to assign each of the following:

   (1) DVD player industry

   (2) Dry cleaning industry

   (3) Poultry industry

   (4) Camera film and film-developing industry

   (5) Wine, beer, and liquor retailing

   (6) Personal computer industry

   (7) Cell phone industry

   (8) Recorded music industry (DVDs, CDs, tapes)

2. Toyota overtook Ford Motor Company in 2003 to become the second largest maker of motor vehicles, behind General Motors. Toyota is widely regarded as having aspirations to overtake General Motors as the global leader in motor vehicles within the next 10 years. Do research on the Internet or in the library to determine what strategy General Motors is pursuing to maintain its status as the industry leader. Then research Toyota's strategy to overtake General Motors.

chapter nine

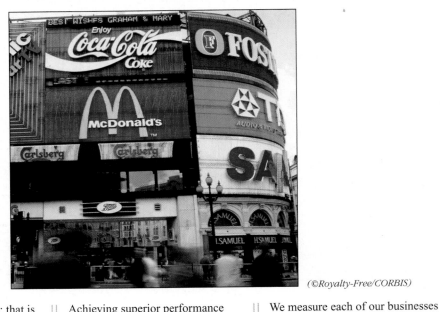

Diversification

Strategies for Managing a Group of Businesses

(©Royalty-Free/CORBIS)

To acquire or not to acquire: that is the question.

—Robert J. Terry

Fit between a parent and its businesses is a two-edged sword: a good fit can create value; a bad one can destroy it.

—Andrew Campbell, Michael Goold, and Marcus Alexander

Achieving superior performance through diversification is largely based on relatedness.

—Philippe Very

Make winners out of every business in your company. Don't carry losers.

—Jack Welch
Former CEO, General Electric

We measure each of our businesses against strict criteria: growth, margin, and return-on-capital hurdle rate, and does it have the ability to become number one or two in its industry? We are quite pragmatic. If a business does not contribute to our overall vision, it has to go.

—Richard Wambold
CEO, Pactiv

In this chapter we move up one level in the strategy-making hierarchy, from strategy making in a single-business enterprise to strategy making in a diversified enterprise. Because a diversified company is a collection of individual businesses, the strategy-making task is a more complicated exercise. In a one-business company, managers have to contend with assessing only one industry environment and the question of how to compete successfully in it—the result is what we labeled in Chapter 2 as *business strategy* (or *business-level strategy*). But in a diversified company, the strategy-making challenge involves assessing multiple industry environments and coming up with a *set* of business strategies, one for each industry arena in which the diversified company operates. And top executives at a diversified company must still go one step further and devise a companywide or *corporate strategy.*

In most diversified companies, corporate-level executives delegate considerable strategy-making authority to the heads of each business, usually giving them the latitude to craft a business strategy suited to their particular industry and competitive circumstances and holding them accountable for producing good results. But the task of crafting a diversified company's overall or corporate strategy falls squarely on the shoulders of top-level executives.

Devising a corporate strategy has four distinct facets:

1. *Picking new industries to enter and deciding on the means of entry*—The first concerns in diversifying are what new industries to get into and whether to enter by starting a new business from the ground up, acquiring a company already in the target industry, or forming a joint venture or strategic alliance with another company. A company can diversify narrowly into a few industries or broadly into many industries. These choices shape what positions the company will initially stake out for itself.

2. *Initiating actions to boost the combined performance of the businesses the firm has entered*—As positions are created in the chosen industries, corporate strategists typically zero in on ways to strengthen the long-term competitive positions and profits of the businesses the firm has invested in. Corporate parents can help their business subsidiaries by providing financial resources, by supplying missing

skills or technological know-how or managerial expertise to better perform key value chain activities, and by providing new avenues for cost reduction. They can also acquire another company in the same industry and merge the two operations into a stronger business, or acquire new businesses that strongly complement existing businesses. Typically, a company will pursue rapid-growth strategies in its most promising businesses, initiate turnaround efforts in weak-performing businesses with potential, and divest businesses that are no longer attractive or that don't fit into management's long-range plans.

3. *Pursuing opportunities to leverage cross-business value chain relationships and strategic fits into competitive advantage*—A company that diversifies into businesses with related value chain activities (pertaining to technology, supply chain logistics, production, overlapping distribution channels, or common customers) gains competitive advantage potential not open to a company that diversifies into businesses whose value chains are totally unrelated. Related diversification presents opportunities to transfer skills, share expertise, share facilities, or share a common brand name, thereby reducing overall costs, strengthening the competitiveness of some of the company's products, and enhancing the capabilities of particular business units.

4. *Establishing investment priorities and steering corporate resources into the most attractive business units*—A diversified company's different businesses are usually not equally attractive from the standpoint of investing additional funds. It is incumbent on corporate management to (*a*) decide on the priorities for investing capital in the company's different businesses, (*b*) channel resources into areas where earnings potentials are higher, and (*c*) divest business units that are chronically poor performers or are in an increasingly unattractive industry. Divesting poor performers and businesses in unattractive industries frees up unproductive investments either for redeployment to promising business units or for financing attractive new acquisitions.

The demanding and time-consuming nature of these four tasks explains why corporate executives generally refrain from becoming immersed in the details of crafting and implementing business-level strategies, preferring instead to delegate lead responsibility for business strategy to the heads of each business unit.

In the first portion of this chapter, we describe the various paths through which a company can become diversified and explain how a company can use diversification to create or compound competitive advantage for its business units. In the second part of the chapter, we examine the techniques and procedures for assessing the strategic attractiveness of a diversified company's business portfolio and survey the strategic options open to already-diversified companies.

WHEN TO DIVERSIFY

So long as a company has its hands full trying to capitalize on profitable growth opportunities in its present industry, there is no urgency to pursue diversification. Companies that concentrate on a single business can achieve enviable success over many decades—good examples include McDonald's, Southwest Airlines, Domino's Pizza, Apple Computer, Wal-Mart, FedEx, Hershey, Timex, Anheuser-Busch, Xerox, and Ford Motor

Company. In the nonprofit sector, continued emphasis on a single activity has proved successful for the Red Cross, the Salvation Army, the Christian Children's Fund, the Girl Scouts, Phi Beta Kappa, and the American Civil Liberties Union. Concentrating on a single line of business (totally or with a small dose of diversification) has important advantages. A single-business company has less ambiguity about who it is, what it does, and where it is headed. It can devote the full force of its resources to improving its competitiveness, expanding into geographic markets it doesn't serve, and responding to changing market conditions and evolving customer preferences. The more successful a single-business enterprise is, the more able it is to parlay its accumulated know-how, competitive capabilities, and reputation into a sustainable position as a leading firm in its industry.

The big risk of a single-business company, of course, is having all of the firm's eggs in one industry basket. If the market is eroded by the appearance of new technologies, new products, or fast-shifting buyer preferences, then a company's prospects can quickly dim. Consider, for example, what digital cameras are doing to the market for film and film processing, what CD and DVD technology has done to the market for cassette tapes and floppy disks, and what mobile phones are doing to the local and long-distance landline businesses. Where there are substantial risks that a single-business company's market will dry up or when opportunities to grow revenues and earnings in the company's mainstay business begin to peter out, managers usually have to make diversifying into other businesses a top consideration.

Factors That Signal It Is Time to Diversify

Diversification merits strong consideration whenever a single-business company is faced with diminishing market opportunities and stagnating sales in its principal business.[1] But there are four other instances in which a company becomes a prime candidate for diversifying:

1. When it can expand into industries whose technologies and products complement its present business.
2. When it can leverage existing competencies and capabilities by expanding into businesses where these same resource strengths are valuable competitive assets.
3. When diversifying into closely related businesses opens new avenues for reducing costs.
4. When it has a powerful and well-known brand name that can be transferred to the products of other businesses.

As part of the decision to diversify, the company must ask itself, "What kind and how much diversification?" The strategic possibilities are wide open. A company can diversify into closely related businesses or into totally unrelated businesses. It can diversify its present revenue and earning base to a small extent (such that new businesses account for less than 15 percent of companywide revenues and profits) or to a major extent (such that new businesses produce 30 or more percent of revenues and profits). It can move into one or two large new businesses or a greater number of small ones. It can achieve diversification by acquiring an existing company, creating an internal start-up, or entering a joint venture. There's no tried-and-true method for determining when it is time for a company to diversify. Judgments about the timing of a company's diversification effort are best made case by case, according to the company's own unique situation.

Building Shareholder Value: The Ultimate Justification for Diversifying

Diversification must do more for a company than simply spread its business risk across various industries. Shareholders can easily diversify risk on their own by purchasing stock in companies in different industries or investing in mutual funds, so they don't need a company to diversify merely to spread their risk across different industries. In principle, diversification makes good strategic and business sense only if it results in added shareholder value—value that shareholders cannot capture through their ownership of different companies in different industries.

For there to be reasonable expectations that a diversification move can produce added value for shareholders, the move must pass three tests:[2]

1. *The industry attractiveness test*—The industry chosen for diversification must be attractive enough to yield consistently good returns on investment. Industry attractiveness depends chiefly on favorable competitive conditions and a market environment conducive to earning profits that are as good or better than the company is earning in its present business(es). It is hard to imagine declaring an industry to be attractive if profit expectations are *lower* than in the company's present businesses.

2. *The cost-of-entry test*—The cost to enter the target industry must not be so high as to erode the potential for profitability. A catch-22 can prevail here, however. The more attractive an industry's prospects are for growth and good long-term profitability, the more expensive it can be to get into. Entry barriers for start-up companies are likely to be high in attractive industries; were barriers low, a rush of new entrants would soon erode the potential for high profitability. And buying an existing, well-positioned company in an appealing industry often entails a high acquisition cost. Paying too much to acquire a company in an attractive industry reduces a company's rate of return on the acquisition price and erodes the potential for enhanced shareholder value.

3. *The better-off test*—Diversifying into a new business must offer potential for the company's existing businesses and the new business to perform better together under a single corporate umbrella than they would perform operating as independent, stand-alone businesses. For example, let's say that company A diversifies by purchasing company B in another industry. If A and B's consolidated profits in the years to come prove no greater than what each could have earned on its own, then A's diversification won't provide its shareholders with added value. Company A's shareholders could have achieved the same $1 + 1 = 2$ result by merely purchasing stock in company B. Diversification does not create shareholder value unless it produces a $1 + 1 = 3$ effect where sister businesses perform better together as part of the same firm than they could have performed as independent companies. The best chance of a $1 + 1 = 3$ outcome occurs when a company diversifies into businesses that have competitively important value chain matchups with its existing businesses—matchups that offer opportunities to reduce costs, to transfer skills or technology from one business to another, to create valuable new competencies and capabilities, or to leverage existing resources (such as brand-name reputation).

Diversification moves that satisfy all three tests have the greatest potential to grow shareholder value over the long term. Diversification moves that can pass only one or two tests are suspect.

STRATEGIES FOR ENTERING NEW BUSINESSES

Entry into new businesses can take any of three forms: acquisition, internal start-up, or joint ventures/strategic partnerships.

Acquisition of an Existing Business

Acquisition is the most popular means of diversifying into another industry. Not only is it quicker than trying to launch a brand-new operation, but it also offers an effective way to hurdle such entry barriers as acquiring technological know-how, establishing supplier relationships, becoming big enough to match rivals' efficiency and unit costs, having to spend large sums on introductory advertising and promotions, and securing adequate distribution. Whether friendly or hostile, acquisitions allow the acquirer to move directly to the task of building a strong market position in the target industry, rather than getting bogged down in going the internal start-up route and trying to develop the knowledge, resources, scale of operation, and market reputation necessary to become an effective competitor within a few years.

However, finding the right kind of company to acquire sometimes presents a challenge.[3] The big dilemma an acquisition-minded firm faces is whether to pay a premium price for a successful company or to buy a struggling company at a bargain price. If the buying firm has little knowledge of the industry but ample capital, it is often better off purchasing a capable, strongly positioned firm—unless the price of such an acquisition is prohibitive and flunks the cost-of-entry test. However, when the acquirer sees promising ways to transform a weak firm into a strong one and has the resources, the know-how, and the patience to do it, a struggling company can be the better long-term investment.

The cost-of-entry test requires that the expected profit stream of an acquired business provide an attractive return on the total acquisition cost and on any new capital investment needed to sustain or expand its operations. A high acquisition price can make meeting that test improbable or difficult. For instance, suppose that the price to purchase a company is $3 million and that the company is earning after-tax profits of $200,000 on an equity investment of $1 million (a 20 percent annual return). Simple arithmetic requires that the profits be tripled if the purchaser is to earn the same 20 percent return. Building the acquired firm's annual earnings from $200,000 to $600,000 could take several years—and require additional investment, on which the purchaser would also have to earn a 20 percent return. Since the owners of a successful and growing company usually demand a price that reflects their business's profit prospects, it's easy for such an acquisition to fail the cost-of-entry test. A would-be diversifier can't count on being able to acquire a desirable company in an appealing industry at a price that still permits attractive returns on investment.

Internal Start-Up

Achieving diversification through internal start-up involves building a new business subsidiary from scratch. This entry option takes longer than the acquisition option and poses some hurdles. A newly formed business unit not only has to overcome entry barriers but also has to invest in new production capacity, develop sources of supply, hire and train employees, build channels of distribution, grow a customer base, and so on. Generally, forming a start-up subsidiary to enter a new business has appeal only when (1) the parent

> The biggest drawbacks to entering an industry by forming an internal start-up are the costs of overcoming entry barriers and the extra time it takes to build a strong and profitable competitive position.

company already has most or all of the skills and resources it needs to piece together a new business and compete effectively; (2) there is ample time to launch the business; (3) the costs are lower than those of acquiring another firm; (4) the targeted industry is populated with many relatively small firms such that the new start-up does not have to compete head-to-head against larger, more powerful rivals; (5) adding new production capacity will not adversely impact the supply–demand balance in the industry; and (6) incumbent firms are likely to be slow or ineffective in responding to a new entrant's efforts to crack the market.[4]

Joint Ventures and Strategic Partnerships

Joint ventures typically entail forming a new corporate entity owned by the partners, whereas strategic partnerships usually can be terminated whenever one of the partners so chooses. Most joint ventures involve two partners and, historically, were formed to pursue opportunities that were somewhat peripheral to the strategic interests of the partners; very few companies have used joint ventures to enter new industries central to their diversification strategy. In recent years, strategic partnerships/alliances have replaced joint ventures as the favored mechanism for joining forces to pursue strategically important diversification opportunities because they can readily accommodate multiple partners and are more adaptable to rapidly changing technological and market conditions than a formal joint venture.

A strategic partnership or joint venture can be useful in at least three types of situations.[5] First, a strategic partnership/joint venture is a good way to pursue an opportunity that is too complex, uneconomical, or risky for a single organization to pursue alone. Second, strategic partnerships/joint ventures make sense when the opportunities in a new industry require a broader range of competencies and know-how than any one organization can marshal. Many of the opportunities in satellite-based telecommunications, biotechnology, and network-based systems that blend hardware, software, and services, for example, call for the coordinated development of complementary innovations and integrating a host of financial, technical, political, and regulatory factors. In such cases, pooling the resources and competencies of two or more independent organizations is essential to generate the capabilities needed for success.

Third, joint ventures are sometimes the only way to gain entry into a desirable foreign market, especially when the foreign government requires companies wishing to enter the market to secure a local partner; for example, the Chinese government closed entry in the automotive industry to all but a few select automakers, and in the elevator industry it originally permitted only Otis, Schindler, and Mitsubishi to establish joint ventures with local partners. Although permission was later granted to other companies, the three early entrants were able to retain a market advantage.[6] Alliances with local partners have become a favorite mechanism for global companies not only to establish footholds in desirable foreign country markets but also to surmount tariff barriers and import quotas. Local partners offer outside companies the benefits of local knowledge about market conditions, local customs and cultural factors, and customer buying habits; they can also be a source of managerial and marketing personnel and provide access to distribution outlets. The foreign partner's role is usually to provide specialized skills, technological know-how, and other resources needed to crack the local market and serve it efficiently.

However, strategic alliances/joint ventures have their difficulties, often posing complicated questions about how to divide efforts among the partners and about who has effective control.[7] Conflicts between foreign and domestic partners can arise over whether to use local sourcing of components, how much production to export, whether operating procedures should conform to the local partner's or the foreign company's standards, and to what extent the local partner is entitled to make use of the foreign partner's technology and intellectual property. As the foreign partner acquires experience, its need for the local partner typically diminishes, posing the strategic issue of whether the partnership should be dissolved. This happens frequently in alliances between global manufacturers and local distributors.[8]

Joint ventures are generally the least durable of the entry options, usually lasting only until the partners decide to go their own ways. Japanese automakers have abandoned their European distribution partners and set up their own dealer networks; BMW did the same in Japan. However, the temporary character of joint ventures is not always bad. Several ambitious local partners have used their alliances with global companies to master technologies and build key competitive skills, then capitalized on the acquired know-how to launch their own entry into the international arena. Taiwan's Acer Computer Group used its alliance with Texas Instruments as a stepping-stone for entering the world market for desktop and laptop computers.

CHOOSING THE DIVERSIFICATION PATH: RELATED VERSUS UNRELATED BUSINESSES

Once the decision is made to pursue diversification, the firm must choose whether to diversify into **related businesses, unrelated businesses,** or some mix of both (see Figure 9.1). *Businesses are said to be related when their value chains possess competitively valuable cross-business value chain matchups or strategic fits.* The appeal of related diversification is exploiting these matchups to realize a $1 + 1 = 3$ performance outcome and thus build shareholder value. *Businesses are said to be unrelated when the activities comprising their respective value chains are so dissimilar that no competitively valuable cross-business relationships are present.*

> **core concept**
> *Related businesses* possess competitively valuable cross-business value chain matchups; *unrelated businesses* have dissimilar value chains, containing no competitively useful cross-business relationships.

Most companies favor related diversification strategies because of the performance-enhancing potential of cross-business synergies. However, some companies have, for one reason or another, opted to try to build shareholder value with unrelated diversification strategies. And a few have diversified into both related and unrelated businesses. The next two sections explore the ins and outs of related and unrelated diversification.

THE CASE FOR DIVERSIFYING INTO RELATED BUSINESSES

A related diversification strategy involves building the company around businesses whose value chains possess competitively valuable strategic fits, as shown in Figure 9.2. **Strategic fit** exists whenever one or more activities comprising the value chains of different businesses are sufficiently similar as to present opportunities for:[9]

> **core concept**
> *Strategic fit* exists when the value chains of different businesses present opportunities for cross-business resource transfer, lower costs through combining the performance of related value chain activities, cross-business use of a potent brand name, and cross-business collaboration to build new or stronger competitive capabilities.

- Transferring competitively valuable expertise, technological know-how, or other capabilities from one business to another.
- Combining the related activities of separate businesses into a single operation to achieve lower costs.

figure 9.1   **Strategy Alternatives for a Company Looking to Diversify**

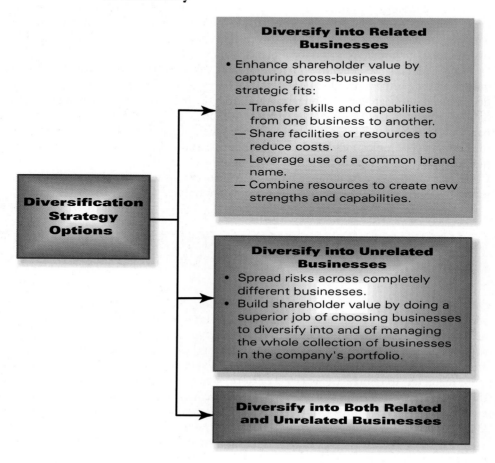

Diversification Strategy Options

Diversify into Related Businesses

- Enhance shareholder value by capturing cross-business strategic fits:
  — Transfer skills and capabilities from one business to another.
  — Share facilities or resources to reduce costs.
  — Leverage use of a common brand name.
  — Combine resources to create new strengths and capabilities.

Diversify into Unrelated Businesses

- Spread risks across completely different businesses.
- Build shareholder value by doing a superior job of choosing businesses to diversify into and of managing the whole collection of businesses in the company's portfolio.

Diversify into Both Related and Unrelated Businesses

- Exploiting common use of a well-known brand name.
- Cross-business collaboration to create competitively valuable resource strengths and capabilities.

Related diversification thus has strategic appeal from several angles. It allows a firm to reap the competitive advantage benefits of skills transfer, lower costs, common brand names, and/or stronger competitive capabilities and still spread investor risks over a broad business base. Furthermore, the relatedness among the different businesses provides sharper focus for managing diversification and a useful degree of strategic unity across the company's various business activities.

Cross-Business Strategic Fits along the Value Chain

Cross-business strategic fits can exist anywhere along the value chain—in R&D and technology activities, in supply chain activities and relationships with suppliers, in manufacturing, in sales and marketing, in distribution activities, or in administrative support activities.[10]

figure 9.2 **Related Businesses Possess Related Value Chain Activities and Competitively Valuable Strategic Fits**

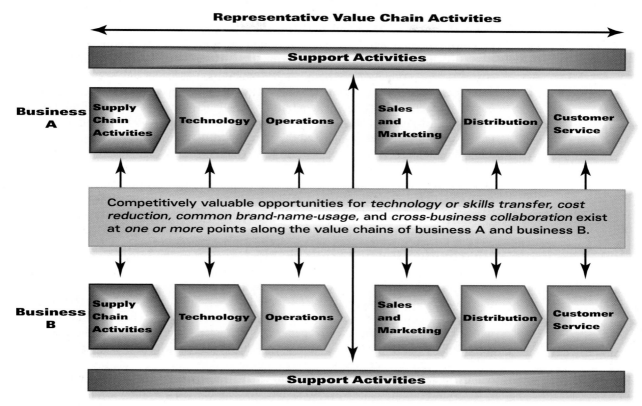

Strategic Fits in R&D and Technology Activities Diversifying into businesses where there is potential for sharing common technology, exploiting the full range of business opportunities associated with a particular technology and its derivatives, or transferring technological know-how from one business to another has considerable appeal. Businesses with technology-sharing benefits can perform better together than apart because of potential cost savings in R&D and potentially shorter times in getting new products to market; also, technological advances in one business can lead to increased sales for both. Technological innovations have been the driver behind the efforts of cable TV companies to diversify into high-speed Internet access (via the use of cable modems) and, further, to explore providing local and long-distance telephone service to residential and commercial customers in a single wire.

Strategic Fits in Supply Chain Activities Businesses that have supply chain strategic fits can perform better together because of the potential for skills transfer in procuring materials, greater bargaining power in negotiating with common suppliers, the benefits of added collaboration with common supply chain partners, and/or added leverage with shippers in securing volume discounts on incoming parts and components. Dell Computer's strategic partnerships with leading suppliers of microprocessors, motherboards, disk drives, memory chips, monitors, modems, flat-panel displays, long-life batteries, and other desktop and laptop components have been an important component of the company's strategy to diversify into servers, data storage devices, and LCD TVs—products that include many components common to PCs and that can be sourced from the same strategic partners that provide Dell with PC components.

Manufacturing-Related Strategic Fits   Cross-business strategic fits in manufacturing-related activities can represent an important source of competitive advantage in situations where a diversifier's expertise in quality manufacture and cost-efficient production methods can be transferred to another business. When Emerson Electric diversified into the chain-saw business, it transferred its expertise in low-cost manufacture to its newly acquired Beaird-Poulan business division; the transfer drove Beaird-Poulan's new strategy—to be the low-cost provider of chain-saw products—and fundamentally changed the way Beaird-Poulan chain saws were designed and manufactured. Another benefit of value chain matchups comes from the ability to perform manufacturing or assembly activities jointly in the same facility rather than independently, thus making it feasible to consolidate production into a smaller number of plants and significantly reduce overall production costs. When snowmobile maker Bombardier diversified into motorcycles, it was able to set up motorcycle assembly lines in the same manufacturing facility where it was assembling snowmobiles.

Distribution-Related Strategic Fits   Businesses with closely related distribution activities can perform better together than apart because of potential cost savings in sharing the same distribution facilities or using many of the same wholesale distributors and retail dealers to access customers. When Sunbeam acquired Mr. Coffee, it was able to consolidate its own distribution centers for small household appliances with those of Mr. Coffee, thereby generating considerable cost savings. Likewise, since Sunbeam products were sold to many of the same retailers as Mr. Coffee products (Wal-Mart, Kmart, department stores, home centers, hardware chains, supermarket chains, and drugstore chains), Sunbeam was able to convince many of the retailers carrying Sunbeam appliances to also take on the Mr. Coffee line and vice versa.

Strategic Fits in Sales and Marketing Activities   Various cost-saving opportunities spring from diversifying into businesses with closely related sales and marketing activities. Sales costs can often be reduced by using a single sales force for the products of both businesses rather than having separate sales forces for each business. When the products are distributed through many of the same wholesale and retail dealers or are sold directly to the same customers, it is usually feasible to give one salesperson the responsibility for handling the sales of both products. The products of related businesses can be promoted at the same Web site and included in the same media ads and sales brochures.

After-sale service and repair organizations for the products of closely related businesses can often be consolidated into a single operation. There may be opportunities to reduce costs by coordinating delivery and shipping, consolidating order processing and billing, and using common promotional tie-ins (cents-off couponing, free samples and trial offers, seasonal specials, and the like). When global power-tool maker Black & Decker acquired General Electric's domestic small-appliance business, it was able to use its own global sales force and distribution facilities to sell and distribute toasters, irons, mixers, and coffeemakers because the types of customers that carried its power tools (discounters like Wal-Mart and Kmart, home centers, and hardware stores) also stocked small appliances. The economies Black & Decker achieved for both product lines were substantial.

A second category of benefits arises when different businesses use similar sales and marketing approaches; in such cases, there may be competitively valuable opportunities to transfer selling, merchandising, advertising, and product differentiation skills from one business to another. Procter & Gamble's product lineup includes Folgers coffee, Tide laundry detergent, Crest toothpaste, Ivory soap, Charmin toilet tissue, and Head & Shoulders shampoo. All of these have different competitors and different supply chain and production requirements, but they all move through the same wholesale distribution systems, are sold in common retail settings to the same shoppers, are advertised and promoted in much the same ways, and require the same marketing and merchandising skills.

A third set of benefits arises from related sales and marketing activities when a company's brand name and reputation in one business is transferable to other businesses. Honda's name in motorcycles and automobiles gave it instant credibility and recognition in entering the lawn-mower business, allowing it to achieve a significant market share without spending large sums on advertising to establish a brand identity for its lawn mowers. Canon's reputation in photographic equipment was a competitive asset that facilitated the company's diversification into copying equipment. Panasonic's name in consumer electronics (radios, TVs) was readily transferred to microwave ovens, making it easier and cheaper for Panasonic to diversify into the microwave oven market.

Strategic Fits in Managerial and Administrative Support Activities

Often, different businesses require comparable types of skills, competencies, and managerial know-how, thereby allowing know-how in one line of business to be transferred to another. At General Electric (GE), managers who were involved in the company's expansion into Russia were able to expedite entry because of information they gained from GE managers involved in expansions into other emerging markets. The lessons GE managers learned in China were passed along to GE managers in Russia, allowing them to anticipate that the Russian government would demand that GE build production capacity in the country rather than enter the market through exporting or licensing. In addition, GE's managers in Russia were better able to develop realistic performance expectations and make tough up-front decisions since experience in China and elsewhere warned them (1) that there would likely be increased short-term costs during the early years of start-up and (2) that if GE committed to the Russian market for the long term and aided the country's economic development it could eventually expect to be given the freedom to pursue profitable penetration of the Russian market.[11]

Likewise, different businesses sometimes use the same sorts of administrative support facilities. For instance, an electric utility that diversifies into natural gas, appliance sales and repair services, and power line broadband can use the same customer data network, the same customer call centers and local offices, the same billing and customer accounting systems, and the same customer service infrastructure to support all of its products and services.

Illustration Capsule 9.1 lists the businesses of five companies that have pursued a strategy of related diversification.

Strategic Fit, Economies of Scope, and Competitive Advantage

What makes related diversification an attractive strategy is the opportunity to convert the strategic fit between the value chains of different businesses into a competitive

illustration capsule 9.1
Five Companies That Have Diversified into Related Businesses

GILLETTE

- Blades and razors
- Toiletries (Right Guard, Foamy, Dry Idea, Soft & Dry, White Rain)
- Oral-B toothbrushes
- Braun shavers, coffeemakers, alarm clocks, mixers, hair dryers, and electric toothbrushes
- Duracell batteries

DARDEN RESTAURANTS

- Olive Garden restaurant chain (Italian-themed)
- Red Lobster restaurant chain (seafood-themed)
- Bahama Breeze restaurant chain (Caribbean-themed)
- Smokey Bones BBQ Sports Bar restaurants

L'ORÉAL

- Maybelline, Lancôme, Helena Rubenstein, Kiehl's, Garner, and Shu Uemura cosmetics
- L'Oréal and Soft Sheen/Carson hair care products
- Redken, Matrix, L'Oréal Professional, and Kerastase Paris professional hair care and skin care products
- Ralph Lauren and Giorgio Armani fragrances
- Biotherm skin care products
- La Roche–Posay and Vichy Laboratories dermo-cosmetics

JOHNSON & JOHNSON

- Baby products (powder, shampoo, oil, lotion)
- Band-Aids and other first-aid products
- Women's health and personal care products (Stayfree, Carefree, Sure & Natural)
- Neutrogena and Aveeno skin care products
- Nonprescription drugs (Tylenol, Motrin, Pepcid AC, Mylanta, Monistat)
- Prescription drugs
- Prosthetic and other medical devices
- Surgical and hospital products
- Accuvue contact lenses

PEPSICO

- Soft drinks (Pepsi, Diet Pepsi, Pepsi One, Mountain Dew, Mug, Slice)
- Fruit juices (Tropicana and Dole)
- Sports drinks (Gatorade)
- Other beverages (Aquafina bottled water, SoBe, Lipton ready-to-drink tea, Frappucino—in partnership with Starbucks, international sales of 7UP)
- Snack foods (Fritos, Lay's, Ruffles, Doritos, Tostitos, Santitas, Smart Food, Rold Gold pretzels, Chee-tos, Grandma's cookies, Sun Chips, Cracker Jack, Frito-Lay dips and salsas)
- Cereals, rice, and breakfast products (Quaker oatmeal, Cap'n Crunch, Life, Rice-A-Roni, Quaker rice cakes, Aunt Jemima mixes and syrups, Quaker grits)

Source: Company annual reports.

advantage. The greater the relatedness among the businesses of a diversified company, the greater the opportunities for combining related value chain activities, leveraging use of a respected brand name and/or collaborating to create new resource strengths and capabilities. The more competitively important the strategic fit relationships across related businesses, the bigger the window for converting strategic fits into competitive advantage over rivals lacking comparable strategic fits in their own operations.

Economies of Scope: A Path to Competitive Advantage   One of the most important competitive advantages that a related diversification strategy can produce is lower costs than competitors. Related businesses often present opportunities to consolidate certain value chain activities or use common resources, and thereby eliminate costs. Such cost savings are termed **economies of scope**—a concept distinct from *economies of scale*. Economies of *scale* are cost savings that accrue directly from a larger-sized operation; for example, unit costs may be lower in a large plant than in a small plant, lower in a large distribution center than in a small one, lower for large-volume purchases of components than for small-volume purchases. Economies of *scope,* however, stem directly from cost-saving strategic fits along the value chains of related businesses; such economies are open only to multibusiness enterprises and are very much a phenomenon of related diversification. Most usually, economies of scope are the result of two or more businesses sharing technology, performing R&D together, using common manufacturing or distribution facilities, sharing a common sales force or distributor/dealer network, using the same established brand name, and/or sharing the same administrative infrastructure. *The greater the economies associated with cost-saving strategic fits, the greater the potential for a related diversification strategy to yield a competitive advantage based on lower costs.*

> **core concept**
> ***Economies of scope*** are cost reductions that flow from operating in multiple businesses; such economies stem directly from strategic-fit efficiencies along the value chains of related businesses.

From Competitive Advantage to Added Profitability and Gains in Shareholder Value Armed with the competitive advantages that come from economies of scope and the capture of other strategic-fit benefits, a company with a portfolio of related businesses is poised to achieve a $1 + 1 = 3$ financial performance and the hoped-for gains in shareholder value. The business logic is compelling: A company that succeeds in capturing strategic fits along the value chains of its related businesses has a clear path to achieving competitive advantage over undiversified competitors and competitors whose own diversification efforts don't offer equivalent strategic-fit benefits. With such competitive advantage, a company then has a dependable basis for earning better-than-average profits—in particular, profits and a return on investment that exceed what the company's businesses could earn as stand-alone enterprises. In turn, above-average profitability is what fuels $1 + 1 = 3$ gains in shareholder value—the necessary outcome for satisfying the better-off test and proving the business merit of a company's diversification effort.

> **core concept**
> A company that leverages the strategic fit of its related businesses into competitive advantage has a clear avenue to producing gains in shareholder value.

Consequently, a strategy of diversifying into related businesses where competitively valuable strategic fit benefits can be captured has strong potential for putting sister businesses in position to perform better financially as part of the same company than they could have performed as independent enterprises. This makes a strategy of related diversification a very appealing vehicle for building shareholder value in ways that shareholders cannot undertake by simply owning a portfolio of stocks of companies in different industries. The capture of strategic-fit benefits is possible only via a strategy of related diversification.[12]

A Word of Caution Diversifying into related businesses is no guarantee of gains in shareholder value. Many companies have stumbled with related diversification because they overpaid for the acquired companies, failing the cost-of-entry test. And two problems commonly arise in passing the better-off test: One occurs when the likely cost savings of combining related value chain activities and capturing economies of scope are overestimated; in such cases, the realized cost savings and gains in profitability prove too small to justify the acquisition price. The second occurs when transferring resources from one business to another is fraught with unforeseen obstacles that delay or diminish the strategic-fit benefits actually captured. Experience indicates that it is easy to be overly optimistic about the value of the cross-business synergies—realizing them is harder than first meets the eye.

THE CASE FOR DIVERSIFYING INTO UNRELATED BUSINESSES

A strategy of diversifying into unrelated businesses discounts the value and importance of the strategic-fit benefits associated with related diversification and instead focuses on building and managing a portfolio of business subsidiaries capable of delivering good financial performance in their respective industries. Companies that pursue a strategy of unrelated diversification generally exhibit a willingness to diversify into *any industry* where there's potential for a company to realize consistently good financial results. Decisions to diversify into one industry versus another are the product of an opportunistic search for good companies to acquire—*the basic premise of unrelated diversification is that any company that can be acquired on good financial terms and that has satisfactory earnings potential represents a good acquisition.* While companies pursuing unrelated diversification may well look for companies that can satisfy the industry attractiveness and cost-of-entry tests, they either disregard the better-off test or relegate it to secondary status. *A strategy of unrelated diversification involves no deliberate effort to seek out businesses having strategic fit with the firm's other businesses* (see Figure 9.3). Rather, the company spends much time and effort screening new acquisition candidates and deciding whether to keep or divest existing businesses, using such criteria as:

- Whether the business can meet corporate targets for profitability and return on investment.
- Whether the business will require substantial infusions of capital to replace out-of-date plants and equipment, fund expansion, and provide working capital.

figure 9.3 Unrelated Businesses Have Unrelated Value Chains and No Strategic Fits

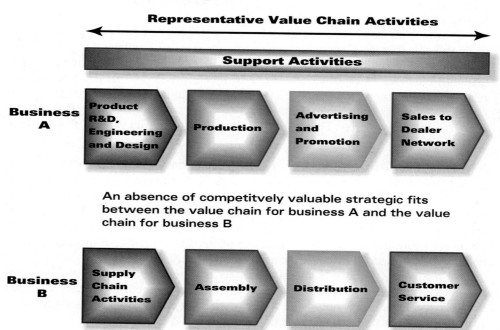

Representative Value Chain Activities

Support Activities

Business A

Product R&D, Engineering and Design | Production | Advertising and Promotion | Sales to Dealer Network

An absence of competitvely valuable strategic fits between the value chain for business A and the value chain for business B

Business B

Supply Chain Activities | Assembly | Distribution | Customer Service

- Whether the business is in an industry with significant growth potential.
- Whether the business is big enough to contribute *significantly* to the parent firm's bottom line.
- Whether there is a potential for union difficulties or adverse government regulations concerning product safety or the environment.
- Whether there is industry vulnerability to recession, inflation, high interest rates, or shifts in government policy.

Some acquisition candidates offer quick opportunities for financial gain because of their "special situation." Three types of businesses may hold such attraction:

- *Companies whose assets are undervalued*—Opportunities may exist to acquire undervalued companies and resell their assets for more than the acquisition costs.
- *Companies that are financially distressed*—Businesses in financial distress can often be purchased at a bargain price, their operations turned around with the aid of the parent company's financial resources and managerial know-how, and then either held as long-term investments in the acquirer's business portfolio (because of their strong earnings or cash flow potential) or sold at a profit, whichever is more attractive.
- *Companies that have bright growth prospects but are short on investment capital*—Cash-poor but opportunity-rich companies are usually coveted acquisition candidates for a financially strong opportunity-seeking firm.

Companies that pursue unrelated diversification nearly always enter new businesses by acquiring an established company rather than by forming a start-up subsidiary within their own corporate structures. The premise of acquisition-minded corporations is that growth by acquisition can deliver enhanced shareholder value through upward-trending corporate revenues and earnings and a stock price that *on average* rises enough year after year to amply reward and please shareholders.

A key issue in unrelated diversification is how wide a net to cast in building a portfolio of unrelated businesses. In other words, should a company pursuing unrelated diversification seek to have few or many unrelated businesses? How much business diversity can corporate executives successfully manage? A reasonable way to resolve the issue of how much diversification comes from answering two questions: "What is the least diversification it will take to achieve acceptable growth and profitability?" and "What is the most diversification that can be managed, given the complexity it adds?"[13] The optimal amount of diversification usually lies between these two extremes.

Illustration Capsule 9.2 lists the businesses of five companies that have pursued unrelated diversification. Such companies are frequently labeled *conglomerates* because their business interests range broadly across diverse industries.

The Merits of an Unrelated Diversification Strategy

A strategy of unrelated diversification has appeal from several angles:

1. Business risk is scattered over a set of truly *diverse* industries. In comparison to related diversification, unrelated diversification more closely approximates *pure* diversification of financial and business risk because the company's investments are spread over businesses whose technologies and value chain activities bear no close relationship and whose markets are largely disconnected.[14]

illustration capsule 9.2
Five Companies That Have Diversified into Unrelated Businesses

UNITED TECHNOLOGIES, INC.

- Pratt & Whitney aircraft engines
- Carrier heating and air-conditioning equipment
- Otis elevators
- Sikorsky helicopters
- Hamilton Substrand aerospace subsystems and components

THE WALT DISNEY COMPANY

- Theme parks
- Disney Cruise Line
- Resort properties
- Movie, video, and theatrical productions (for both children and adults)
- Television broadcasting (ABC, Disney Channel, Toon Disney, Classic Sports Network, ESPN and ESPN2, E!, Lifetime, and A&E networks)
- Radio broadcasting (Disney Radio)
- Musical recordings and sales of animation art
- Anaheim Mighty Ducks NHL franchise
- Anaheim Angels major league baseball franchise (25 percent ownership)
- Books and magazine publishing
- Interactive software and Internet sites
- The Disney Store retail shops

COOPER INDUSTRIES

- Crescent wrenches, pliers, and screwdrivers
- Nicholson files and saws
- Diamond horseshoes and farrier tools
- Lufkin measuring and layout products

- Gardner-Denver electric power tools
- Electrical construction materials
- Lighting fixtures, fuses, and circuit protection devices
- Electric utility products (transformers, relays, capacitor controls, switches)
- Emergency lighting, fire detection, and security systems

TEXTRON, INC.

- Bell helicopters
- Cessna Aircraft
- E-Z-Go golf carts
- Textron Automotive (instrument panels, plastic fuel tanks, plastic interior and exterior trim)
- Textron Fastening Systems (the global leader)
- Fluid and power systems
- Textron Financial Services
- Jacobsen turf care equipment
- Ransomes turf care and utility vehicles
- Tools and testing equipment for the wire and cable industry

AMERICAN STANDARD

- Trane and American Standard furnaces, heat pumps, and air conditioners
- Plumbing products (American Standard, Ideal Standard, Standard, Porcher lavatories, toilets, bath tubs, faucets, whirlpool baths, and shower basins)
- Automotive products (commercial and utility vehicle braking and control systems)
- Medical systems (DiaSorin disease assessment and management products)

Source: Company annual reports.

2. The company's financial resources can be employed to maximum advantage by investing in *whatever industries* offer the best profit prospects. Specifically, cash flows from company businesses with lower growth and profit prospects can be diverted to acquiring and expanding businesses with higher growth and profit potentials.

3. To the extent that corporate managers are exceptionally astute at spotting bargain-priced companies with big upside profit potential, shareholder wealth can be enhanced by buying distressed businesses at a low price, turning their operations around fairly quickly with infusions of cash and managerial know-how supplied by the parent company, and then riding the crest of the profit increases generated by the newly acquired businesses.

4. Company profitability may prove somewhat more stable over the course of economic upswings and downswings—in a broadly diversified company, there's a chance that market downtrends in some of the company's businesses will be partially offset by cyclical upswings in its other businesses, thus producing somewhat less earnings volatility. (In actual practice, however, there's no convincing evidence that the consolidated profits of firms with unrelated diversification strategies are more stable or less subject to reversal in periods of recession and economic stress than the profits of firms with related diversification strategies.)

Unrelated diversification can be appealing in several other circumstances. It certainly merits consideration when a firm needs to diversify away from an endangered or unattractive industry and has no distinctive competencies or capabilities it can transfer to an adjacent industry. There's also a rationale for unrelated diversification to the extent that owners have a strong preference for spreading business risks widely and not restricting themselves to investing in a family of closely related businesses.

Building Shareholder Value via Unrelated Diversification   Building shareholder value via unrelated diversification is predicated on executive skill in managing a group of unrelated businesses. For a strategy of unrelated diversification to generate gains in shareholder value, corporate-level managers must produce company-wide financial results above and beyond what business-level managers could produce if the businesses operated as stand-alone entities. Corporate executives add value to a diversified enterprise by shrewdly deciding which businesses to get into and which ones to get out of, cleverly allocating the corporate parent's financial resources to businesses with the best profit potential, and consistently providing high-caliber decision-making guidance to the general managers of the company's business subsidiaries. In more specific terms, this means corporate-level executives must:

- Do a superior job of diversifying into new businesses that can produce consistently good earnings and returns on investment (thereby satisfying the attractiveness test).
- Do an excellent job of negotiating favorable acquisition prices (thereby satisfying the cost-of-entry test).
- Discern when it is the "right" time to sell a particular business (when a business subsidiary is on the verge of confronting adverse industry and competitive conditions and probable declines in long-term profitability), and determine the "right" selling price—ideally one higher than the company's net investment in the business.
- Shift corporate financial resources out of businesses where profit opportunities are dim and into businesses with the potential for above-average earnings growth and returns on investment.
- Do such a good job overseeing the firm's business subsidiaries and contributing to how they are managed—by providing expert problem-solving skills, creative strategy suggestions, decision-making guidance to business-level managers, and needed infusions of investment capital—that the subsidiaries perform at a higher level than they would otherwise be able to do (a possible way to satisfy the better-off test).

To the extent that corporate executives are able to craft and execute a strategy of unrelated diversification that produces enough of the above outcomes to produce a stream of dividends and capital gains for stockholders greater than a $1 + 1 = 2$ outcome, a case can be made that shareholder value has truly been enhanced.

The Drawbacks of Unrelated Diversification

Unrelated diversification strategies have two important negatives that undercut the positives: very demanding managerial requirements and limited competitive advantage potential.

Demanding Managerial Requirements   Successfully managing a set of fundamentally different businesses operating in fundamentally different industry and competitive environments is a very challenging and exceptionally difficult proposition for corporate-level managers. Key executives at the corporate level, while perhaps having personally worked in one or two of the company's businesses, cannot possibly have in-depth familiarity with each of the company's businesses—the prevailing competitive market conditions, driving forces, industry key success factors, each business's competitive strengths and weaknesses, and so on. The greater the number of businesses a company is in and the more diverse those businesses are, the harder it is for corporate managers to (1) stay abreast of what's happening in each industry and each subsidiary and thus judge whether a particular business has bright prospects or is headed for trouble, (2) know enough about the issues and problems facing each subsidiary to pick business-unit heads having the requisite combination of managerial skills and know-how, (3) be able to tell the difference between those strategic proposals of business-unit managers that are prudent and those that are risky or unlikely to succeed, and (4) know what to do if a business unit stumbles and its results suddenly head downhill.[15]

> **core concept**
> The two biggest drawbacks to unrelated diversification are the difficulties of competently managing many different businesses and being without the added source of competitive advantage that cross-business strategic fit provides.

In a company like Walt Disney (see Illustration Capsule 6.2) or Tyco International (which acquired over 1,000 companies during the 1990–2001 period), corporate executives are constantly scrambling to stay on top of fresh industry developments and the strategic progress and plans of each subsidiary, often depending on briefings by business-level managers for many of the details. As a rule, the more unrelated businesses that a company has diversified into, the more corporate executives are reduced to "managing by the numbers"—that is, keeping a close track on the financial and operating results of each subsidiary and assuming that everything is under control in a business as long as the latest key financial and operating measures look good. Managing by the numbers can work if the heads of the various business units are quite capable, but there's still ample room for strategic issues to be glossed over and for impending downturns in some of the company's key businesses to go unnoticed. Just one or two unforeseen declines or big strategic mistakes (misjudging the importance of certain competitive forces or the impact of driving forces or key success factors, encountering unexpected problems in a newly acquired business, or being too optimistic about turning around a struggling subsidiary) can cause a precipitous drop in corporate earnings and crash the parent company's stock price. As the former chairman of a Fortune 500 company advised, "Never acquire a business you don't know how to run." Because every business tends to encounter rough sledding, a good way to gauge the merits of acquiring a company in an unrelated industry is to ask, "If the business got into trouble, is corporate management likely to know how to bail it out?" When the answer is no (or even maybe), growth via acquisition into unrelated businesses is a chancy strategy.[16]

Hence, overseeing a set of widely diverse businesses may turn out to be much harder than it sounds. In practice, comparatively few companies have proved that they have top management capabilities that are up to the task. Far more companies have failed at unrelated diversification than have succeeded. It is simply very difficult for corporate executives to build shareholder value based on their expertise in (1) picking which industries to diversify into and which companies in these industries to acquire, (2) shifting resources from low-performing business into high-performing businesses, and (3) giving high-caliber decision-making guidance to the general managers of their business subsidiaries. Instead of achieving $1 + 1 = 3$ gains in shareholder value, the odds are that the result of unrelated diversification will be $1 + 1 = 2$ or less.

Limited Competitive Advantage Potential   The second big negative is that *unrelated diversification offers no potential for competitive advantage beyond that of what each individual business can generate on its own.* Unlike a related diversification strategy, there are no cross-business strategic fits to draw on for reducing costs, beneficially transferring skills and technology, leveraging use of a powerful brand name, or collaborating to build mutually beneficial competitive capabilities. Yes, a cash-rich corporate parent pursuing unrelated diversification can provide cash-short subsidiaries with much-needed capital, and maybe even added managerial know-how to help resolve problems in particular business units but otherwise it has little to offer in the way of enhancing the competitive strength of its individual business units. *Without the competitive advantage potential of strategic fits, consolidated performance of an unrelated group of businesses stands to be little or no better than the sum of what the individual business units could achieve if they were independent.*

> Relying solely on the expertise of corporate executives to wisely manage a set of unrelated businesses is *a much weaker foundation for enhancing shareholder value* than is a strategy of related diversification where corporate performance can be boosted by competitively valuable cross-business strategic fits.

COMBINATION RELATED–UNRELATED DIVERSIFICATION STRATEGIES

There's nothing to preclude a company from diversifying into both related and unrelated businesses. Indeed, in actual practice the business makeup of diversified companies varies considerably. Some diversified companies are really *dominant-business enterprises*—one major "core" business accounts for 50 to 80 percent of total revenues and a collection of small related or unrelated businesses accounts for the remainder. Some diversified companies are *narrowly diversified* around a few (two to five) related or unrelated businesses. Others are *broadly diversified* around a wide-ranging collection of related businesses, unrelated businesses, or a mixture of both. And a number of multibusiness enterprises have diversified into unrelated areas but have a collection of related businesses within each area—thus giving them a business portfolio consisting of *several unrelated groups of related businesses.* There's ample room for companies to customize their diversification strategies to incorporate elements of both related and unrelated diversification, as may suit their own risk preferences and strategic vision.

Figure 9.4 indicates what to look for in identifying the main elements of a company's diversification strategy. Having a clear fix on the company's current corporate strategy sets the stage for evaluating how good the strategy is and proposing strategic moves to boost the company's performance.

figure 9.4   **Identifying a Diversified Company's Strategy**

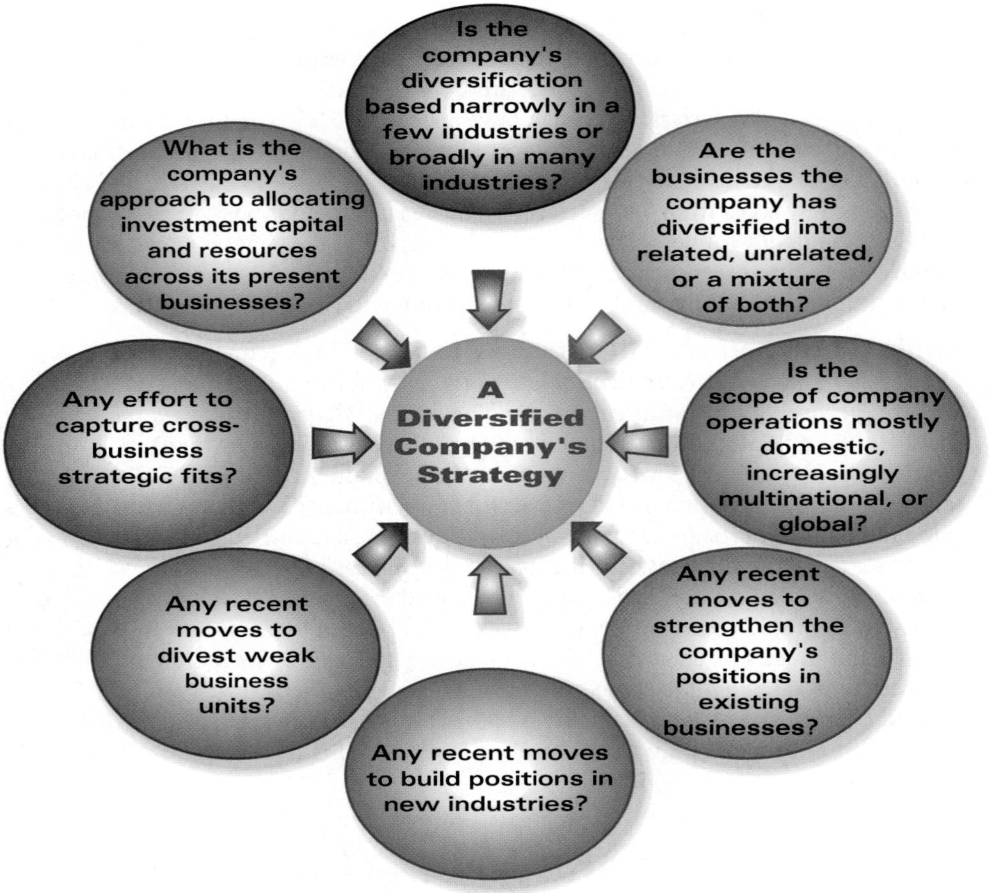

EVALUATING THE STRATEGY OF A DIVERSIFIED COMPANY

Strategic analysis of diversified companies builds on the concepts and methods used for single-business companies. But there are some additional aspects to consider and a couple of new analytical tools to master. The procedure for evaluating a diversified company's strategy and deciding how to improve the company's performance involves six steps:

1. Evaluating industry attractiveness.
2. Evaluating business-unit competitive strength.
3. Checking the competitive advantage potential of cross-business strategic fits.
4. Checking for resource fit.
5. Ranking the business units on the basis of performance and priority for resource allocation.
6. Crafting new strategic moves to improve overall corporate performance.

The core concepts and analytical techniques underlying each of these steps merit further discussion.

Step 1: Evaluating Industry Attractiveness

A principal consideration in evaluating a diversified company's business makeup and the caliber of its strategy is the attractiveness of the industries in which it has business operations. Answers to several questions are required:

1. *Does each industry the company has diversified into represent a good business for the company to be in?* Ideally, each industry in which the firm operates will pass the attractiveness test.

2. *Which of the company's industries are most attractive and which are least attractive?* Comparing the attractiveness of the industries and ranking them from most to least attractive is a prerequisite to deciding how to allocate corporate resources across the various businesses.

3. *How appealing is the whole group of industries in which the company has invested?* The answer to this question points to whether the group of industries holds promise for attractive growth and profitability or whether the company may be in too many slow-growing, intensely competitive, highly cyclical businesses. A company whose revenues and profits come chiefly from businesses in relatively unattractive industries probably needs to look at building positions in additional industries that qualify as highly attractive.

The more attractive the industries (both individually and as a group) a diversified company is in, the better its prospects for good long-term performance.

Calculating Industry Attractiveness Scores for Each Industry into Which the Company Has Diversified

A simple and reliable analytical tool involves calculating quantitative industry attractiveness scores, which can then be used to gauge each industry's attractiveness, rank the industries from most to least attractive, and make judgments about the attractiveness of all the industries as a group. A sample calculation is shown in Table 9.1. The following measures of industry attractiveness are likely to come into play for most companies:

*   *Market size and projected growth rate*—Big industries are more attractive than small industries, and fast-growing industries tend to be more attractive than slow-growing industries, other things being equal.

*   *The intensity of competition*—Industries where competitive pressures are relatively weak are more attractive than industries where competitive pressures are strong.

*   *Emerging opportunities and threats*—Industries with promising opportunities and minimal threats on the near horizon are more attractive than industries with modest opportunities and imposing threats.

*   *The presence of cross-industry strategic fits*—The more the industry's value chain and resource requirements match up well with the value chain activities of other industries in which the company has operations, the more attractive the industry is to a firm pursuing related diversification. However, cross-industry strategic fits may be of no consequence to a company committed to a strategy of unrelated diversification.

*   *Resource requirements*—Industries having resource requirements within the company's reach are more attractive than industries where capital and other resource requirements could strain corporate financial resources and organizational capabilities.

table 9.1   **Calculating Weighted Industry Attractiveness Scores**

Industry Attractiveness Measure	Importance Weight	Industry A Rating/ Score	Industry B Rating/ Score	Industry C Rating/ Score	Industry D Rating/ Score
Market size and projected growth rate	0.10	8/0.80	5/0.50	7/0.70	3/0.30
Intensity of competition	0.25	8/2.00	7/1.75	3/0.75	2/0.50
Emerging opportunities and threats	0.10	2/0.20	9/0.90	4/0.40	5/0.50
Cross-industry strategic fits	0.20	8/1.60	4/0.80	8/1.60	2/0.40
Resource requirements	0.10	9/0.90	7/0.70	10/1.00	5/0.50
Seasonal and cyclical influences	0.05	9/0.45	8/0.40	10/0.50	5/0.25
Societal, political, regulatory, and environmental factors	0.05	10/1.00	7/0.70	7/0.70	3/0.30
Industry profitability	0.10	5/0.50	10/1.00	3/0.30	3/0.30
Industry uncertainty and business risk	0.05	5/0.25	7/0.35	10/0.50	1/0.05
Sum of the assigned weights	1.00				
Overall industry attractiveness scores		**7.70**	**7.10**	**5.45**	**3.10**

Rating scale: 1 = Very unattractive to company; 10 = Very attractive to company

- *Seasonal and cyclical influences*—Industries where buyer demand is relatively steady year-round and not unduly vulnerable to economic ups and downs tend to be more attractive than industries where there are wide swings in buyer demand within or across years. However, seasonality may be a plus for a company that is in several seasonal industries, if the seasonal highs in one industry correspond to the lows in another industry, thus helping even out monthly sales levels. Likewise, cyclical market demand in one industry can be attractive if its up-cycle runs counter to the market down-cycles in another industry where the company operates, thus helping reduce revenue and earnings volatility.

- *Social, political, regulatory, and environmental factors*—Industries with significant problems in such areas as consumer health, safety, or environmental pollution or that are subject to intense regulation are less attractive than industries where such problems are not burning issues.

- *Industry profitability*—Industries with healthy profit margins and high rates of return on investment are generally more attractive than industries where profits have historically been low or unstable.

- *Industry uncertainty and business risk*—Industries with less uncertainty on the horizon and lower overall business risk are more attractive than industries whose prospects for one reason or another are quite uncertain, especially when the industry has formidable resource requirements.

After settling on a set of attractiveness measures that suit a diversified company's circumstances, each attractiveness measure is assigned a weight reflecting its relative importance in determining an industry's attractiveness—it is weak methodology to assume that the various attractiveness measures are equally important. The intensity of competition in an industry should nearly always carry a high weight (say, 0.20 to 0.30). Strategic-fit considerations should be assigned a high weight in the case of companies with related diversification strategies; but, for companies with an unrelated diversification strategy, strategic fits with other industries may be given a low weight or even dropped from the list of attractiveness measures altogether. Seasonal and cyclical influences generally are assigned a low weight (or maybe even eliminated from the analysis) unless a company has diversified into industries strongly characterized by seasonal demand and/or heavy vulnerability to cyclical upswings and downswings. The importance weights must add up to 1.0.

Next, each industry is rated on each of the chosen industry attractiveness measures, using a rating scale of 1 to 10 (where a *high* rating signifies *high* attractiveness and a *low* rating signifies *low* attractiveness). Keep in mind here that the more intensely competitive an industry is, the *lower* the attractiveness rating for that industry. Likewise, the higher the capital and resource requirements associated with being in a particular industry, the lower the attractiveness rating. And an industry subject to stringent pollution control regulations or that causes societal problems (like cigarettes or alcoholic beverages) should be given a low attractiveness rating. Weighted attractiveness scores are then calculated by multiplying the industry's rating on each measure by the corresponding weight. For example, a rating of 8 times a weight of 0.25 gives a weighted attractiveness score of 2.00. The sum of the weighted scores for all the attractiveness measures provides an overall industry attractiveness score.

There are two hurdles to using this method of evaluating industry attractiveness. One is deciding on appropriate weights for the industry attractiveness measures. Not only may different analysts have different views about which weights are appropriate for the different attractiveness measures but also different weightings may be appropriate for different companies—based on their strategies, performance targets, and financial circumstances. For instance, placing a low weight on industry resource requirements may be justifiable for a cash-rich company, whereas a high weight may be more appropriate for a financially strapped company. The second hurdle is getting reliable data for use in assigning accurate and objective ratings. Without good information, the ratings necessarily become subjective, and their validity hinges on whether management has probed industry conditions sufficiently to make reliable judgments. Generally, a company can come up with the statistical data needed to compare its industries on such factors as market size, growth rate, seasonal and cyclical influences, and industry profitability. Cross-industry fits and resource requirements are also fairly easy to judge. But the attractiveness measure where judgment weighs most heavily is that of intensity of competition. It is not always easy to conclude whether competition in one industry is stronger or weaker than in another industry because of the different types of competitive influences that prevail and the differences in their relative importance. In the event that the available information is too skimpy to confidently assign a rating value to an industry on a particular attractiveness measure, then it is usually best to use a score of 5, which avoids biasing the overall attractiveness score either up or down.

Nonetheless, industry attractiveness scores are a reasonably reliable method for ranking a diversified company's industries from most to least attractive—quantitative ratings like those shown for the four industries in Table 9.1 tell a valuable story about just how and why some of the industries a company has diversified into are more attractive than others.

Interpreting the Industry Attractiveness Scores   Industries with a score much below 5.0 probably do not pass the attractiveness test. If a company's industry attractiveness scores are all above 5.0, it is probably fair to conclude that the group of industries the company operates in is attractive as a whole. But the group of industries takes on a decidedly lower degree of attractiveness as the number of industries with scores below 5.0 increases, especially if industries with low scores account for a sizable fraction of the company's revenues.

For a diversified company to be a strong performer, a substantial portion of its revenues and profits must come from business units with relatively high attractiveness scores. It is particularly important that a diversified company's principal businesses be in industries with a good outlook for growth and above-average profitability. Having a big fraction of the company's revenues and profits come from industries with slow growth, low profitability, or intense competition tends to drag overall company performance down. Business units in the least attractive industries are potential candidates for divestiture, unless they are positioned strongly enough to overcome the unattractive aspects of their industry environments or they are a strategically important component of the company's business makeup.

Step 2: Evaluating Business-Unit Competitive Strength

The second step in evaluating a diversified company is to appraise how strongly positioned each of its business units are in their respective industry. Doing an appraisal of each business unit's strength and competitive position in its industry not only reveals its chances for industry success but also provides a basis for ranking the units from competitively strongest to competitively weakest and sizing up the competitive strength of all the business units as a group.

Calculating Competitive Strength Scores for Each Business Unit
Quantitative measures of each business unit's competitive strength can be calculated using a procedure similar to that for measuring industry attractiveness (see Table 9.2). There are a host of measures that can be used in assessing the competitive strength of a diversified company's business subsidiaries:

- *Relative market share*—A business unit's relative market share is defined as the ratio of its market share to the market share held by the largest rival firm in the industry, with market share measured in unit volume, not dollars. For instance, if business A has a market-leading share of 40 percent and its largest rival has 30 percent, A's relative market share is 1.33. (Note that only business units that are market share leaders in their respective industries can have relative market shares greater then 1.0.) If business B has a 15 percent market share and B's largest rival has 30 percent, B's relative market share is 0.5. The further below 1.0 a business unit's relative market share is, the weaker its competitive strength and market position vis-à-vis rivals. *Using relative market share is analytically superior to using straight-percentage market share to measure competitive strength.* A 10 percent market share, for example, does not signal much competitive strength if the leader's share is 50 percent (a 0.20 relative market share), but a 10 percent share is actually quite strong if the leader's share is 12 percent (a 0.83 relative market share).

- *Costs relative to competitors' costs*—Business units that have low costs relative to key competitors' costs tend to be more strongly positioned in their industries than business units struggling to maintain cost parity with major rivals. Assuming that the prices charged by industry rivals are about the same, business units with higher relative market shares should have lower unit costs than competitors of economies from larger-scale operations and the benefits of learning-curve effects. In contrast, a business unit with higher costs than its key rivals is likely to be competitively

table 9.2 **Calculating Weighted Competitive Strength Scores for a Diversified Company's Business Units**

Competitive Strength Measure	Importance Weight	Business A in Industry A Rating/Score	Business B in Industry B Rating/Score	Business C in Industry C Rating/Score	Business D in Industry D Rating/Score
Relative market share	0.15	10/1.50	1/0.15	6/0.90	2/0.30
Costs relative to competitors' costs	0.20	7/1.40	2/0.40	5/1.00	3/0.60
Ability to match or beat rivals on key product attributes	0.05	9/0.45	4/0.20	8/0.40	4/0.20
Ability to benefit from strategic fits with sister businesses	0.20	8/1.60	4/0.80	8/0.80	2/0.60
Bargaining leverage with suppliers/buyers; caliber of alliances	0.05	9/0.90	3/0.30	6/0.30	2/0.10
Brand image and reputation	0.10	9/0.90	2/0.20	7/0.70	5/0.50
Competitively valuable capabilities	0.15	7/1.05	2/0.20	5/0.75	3/0.45
Profitability relative to competitors	0.10	5/0.50	1/0.10	4/0.40	4/0.40
Sum of the assigned weights	1.00				
Overall industry attractiveness scores		**8.30**	**2.35**	**5.25**	**3.15**

Rating scale: 1 = Very weak; 10 = Very strong

vulnerable unless its product is strongly differentiated from those of rivals and its customers are willing to pay premium prices for the differentiating features. Another indicator of low cost can be a business unit's supply chain management capabilities.

- *Ability to match or beat rivals on key product attributes*—A company's competitiveness depends in part on being able to satisfy buyer expectations with regard to features, product performance, reliability, service, and other important attributes.
- *Ability to benefit from strategic fits with sister businesses*—Strategic fits with other businesses within the company enhance a business unit's competitive strength and may provide a competitive edge.
- *Ability to exercise bargaining leverage with key suppliers or customers*—Having bargaining leverage signals competitive strength and can be a source of competitive advantage.
- *Caliber of strategic alliances and collaborative partnerships with suppliers and/or buyers*—Well-functioning alliances and partnerships may signal a potential competitive advantage and thus add to a business's competitive strength. Alliances with key suppliers are often the basis for competitive strength in supply chain management.
- *Brand image and reputation*—A strong brand name is a valuable competitive asset in most industries.
- *Competitively valuable capabilities*—Business units recognized for their technological leadership, product innovation, or marketing prowess are usually strong competitors in their industry. Skills in supply chain management can generate valuable cost or product differentiation advantages. So can unique production capabilities. Sometimes a company's business units gain competitive strength because of their knowledge of customers and markets and/or their proven managerial

capabilities. *An important thing to look for here is how well a business unit's competitive assets match industry key success factors.* The more a business unit's resource strengths and competitive capabilities match the industry's key success factors, the stronger its competitive position tends to be.

- *Profitability relative to competitors*—Business units that consistently earn above-average returns on investment and have bigger profit margins than their rivals usually have stronger competitive positions.

After settling on a set of competitive strength measures that are well matched to the circumstances of the various business units, weights indicating each measure's importance need to be assigned. A case can be made for using different weights for different business units whenever the importance of the strength measures differs significantly from business to business, but otherwise it is simpler just to go with a single set of weights and avoid the added complication of multiple weights. As before, the importance weights must add up to 1.0. Each business unit is then rated on each of the chosen strength measures, using a rating scale of 1 to 10 (where a *high* rating signifies competitive *strength* and a *low* rating signifies competitive *weakness*). In the event that the available information is too skimpy to confidently assign a rating value to a business unit on a particular strength measure, then it is usually best to use a score of 5, which avoids biasing the overall score either up or down. Weighted strength ratings are calculated by multiplying the business unit's rating on each strength measure by the assigned weight. For example, a strength score of 6 times a weight of 0.15 gives a weighted strength rating of 0.90. The sum of weighted ratings across all the strength measures provides a quantitative measure of a business unit's overall market strength and competitive standing.

Interpreting the Competitive Strength Scores   Business units with competitive strength ratings above 6.7 (on a scale of 1 to 10) are strong market contenders in their industries. Businesses with ratings in the 3.3 to 6.7 range have moderate competitive strength. Businesses with ratings below 3.3 are in competitively weak market positions. If a diversified company's business units all have competitive strength scores above 5.0, it is fair to conclude that its business units are all fairly strong market contenders in their respective industries. But as the number of business units with scores below 5.0 increases, there's reason to question whether the company can perform well with so many businesses in relatively weak competitive positions. This concern takes on even more importance when business units with low scores account for a sizable fraction of the company's revenues.

Using a Nine-Cell Matrix to Simultaneously Portray Industry Attractiveness and Competitive Strength   The industry attractiveness and business strength scores can be used to portray the strategic positions of each business in a diversified company. Industry attractiveness is plotted on the vertical axis, and competitive strength on the horizontal axis. A nine-cell grid emerges from dividing the vertical axis into three regions (high, medium, and low attractiveness) and the horizontal axis into three regions (strong, average, and weak competitive strength). As shown in Figure 9.5, high attractiveness is associated with scores of 6.7 or greater on a rating scale of 1 to 10, medium attractiveness to scores of 3.3 to 6.7, and low attractiveness to scores below 3.3. Likewise, high competitive strength is defined as a score greater than 6.7, average strength as scores of 3.3 to 6.7, and low strength as scores below 3.3. Each business unit is plotted on the nine-cell matrix according to its overall attractiveness score and strength score, and then shown as a bubble. The size of each bubble is scaled

figure 9.5   **A Nine-Cell Industry Attractiveness–Competitive Strength Matrix**

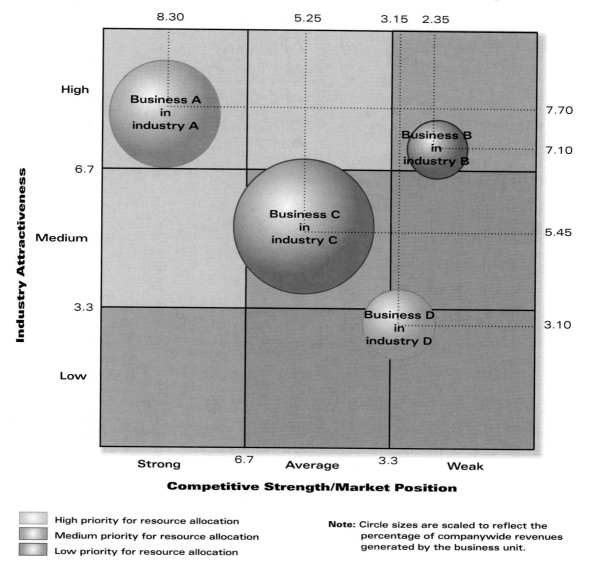

High priority for resource allocation
Medium priority for resource allocation
Low priority for resource allocation

Note: Circle sizes are scaled to reflect the percentage of companywide revenues generated by the business unit.

to what percentage of revenues the business generates relative to total corporate revenues. The bubbles in Figure 9.5 were located on the grid using the attractiveness scores from Table 9.1 and the strength scores for the four business units in Table 9.2.

The locations of the business units on the attractiveness–strength matrix provide valuable guidance in deploying corporate resources to the various business units. In general, *a diversified company's prospects for good overall performance are enhanced by concentrating corporate resources and strategic attention on those business units having the greatest competitive strength*

core concept
In a diversified company, businesses having the greatest competitive strength and positioned in attractive industries should generally have top priority in allocating corporate resources.

and positioned in highly attractive industries—specifically, businesses in the three cells in the upper left portion of the attractiveness–strength matrix, where industry attractiveness and competitive strength/market position are both favorable. The general strategic prescription for businesses falling in these three cells (for instance, business A in Figure 9.5) is "grow and build," with businesses in the high–strong cell standing first in line for resource allocations by the corporate parent.

Next in priority come businesses positioned in the three diagonal cells stretching from the lower left to the upper right (businesses B and C in Figure 9.5). Such businesses usually merit medium or intermediate priority in the parent's resource allocation ranking. However, some businesses in the medium-priority diagonal cells may have brighter or dimmer prospects than others. For example, a small business in the upper right cell of the matrix (like business B), despite being in a highly attractive industry, may occupy too weak a competitive position in its industry to justify the investment and resources needed to turn it into a strong market contender and shift its position leftward in the matrix over time. If, however, a business in the upper right cell has attractive opportunities for rapid growth and a good potential for winning a much stronger market position over time, it may merit a high claim on the corporate parent's resource allocation ranking and be given the capital it needs to pursue a grow-and-build strategy—the strategic objective here would be to move the business leftward in the attractiveness–strength matrix over time.

Businesses in the three cells in the lower right corner of the matrix (like business D in Figure 9.5) typically are weak performers and have the lowest claim on corporate resources. Most such businesses are good candidates for being divested (sold to other companies) or else managed in a manner calculated to squeeze out the maximum cash flows from operations—the cash flows from low-performing/low-potential businesses can then be diverted to financing expansion of business units with greater market opportunities. In exceptional cases where a business located in the three lower right cells is nonetheless fairly profitable (which it might be if it is in the low–average cell) or has the potential for good earnings and return on investment, the business merits retention and the allocation of sufficient resources to achieve better performance.

The nine-cell attractiveness–strength matrix provides clear, strong logic for why a diversified company needs to consider both industry attractiveness and business strength in allocating resources and investment capital to its different businesses. A good case can be made for concentrating resources in those businesses that enjoy higher degrees of attractiveness and competitive strength, being very selective in making investments in businesses with intermediate positions on the grid, and withdrawing resources from businesses that are lower in attractiveness and strength unless they offer exceptional profit or cash flow potential.

Step 3: Checking the Competitive Advantage Potential of Cross-Business Strategic Fits

A company's related diversification strategy derives its power in large part from competitively valuable strategic fits among its businesses. Checking the competitive advantage potential of cross-business strategic fits involves searching for and evaluating how much benefit a diversified company can gain from four types of value chain matchups:

1. *Opportunities to combine the performance of certain activities,* thereby reducing costs. Potential value chain matchups where economies of scope can be realized include purchasing (where combining materials purchases could lead to greater bargaining leverage with suppliers); manufacturing (where it may be possible to share manufacturing facilities); or distribution (where it may be possible to share warehousing, sales forces, distributors, dealers, online sales channels, and after-sale service activities).

2. *Opportunities to transfer skills, technology, or intellectual capital from one business to another,* thereby leveraging use of existing resources. Good candidates for transfer include speed in bringing new products to market, proven R&D skills in generating new products or improving existing technologies, organizational agility in responding to shifting market conditions and emerging opportunities, and state-of-the-art systems for doing business via the Internet.

3. *Opportunities to share use of a well-respected brand name,* thereby gaining credibility with brand-conscious buyers and perhaps commanding prominent display space with retailers.

4. *Opportunities for businesses to collaborate in creating valuable new competitive capabilities* (enhanced quality control capabilities, quicker first-to-market capabilities, greater product innovation capabilities).

Figure 9.6 illustrates the process of searching for competitively valuable cross-business strategic fits and value chain matchups. *But more than just strategic fit identification is needed. The real test is what competitive value can be generated from these fits.* To what extent can cost savings be realized? How much competitive value will come from cross-business transfer of skills, technology, or intellectual capital? Will transferring a potent brand name to the products of other businesses grow sales significantly? Will cross-business collaboration to create or strengthen competitive capabilities lead to significant gains in the marketplace or in financial performance? Without significant strategic fits and dedicated company efforts to capture the benefits, one has to be skeptical about the potential for a diversified company's businesses to perform better together than apart.

> **core concept**
> The greater the value of cross-business strategic fits in enhancing a company's performance in the marketplace or on the bottom line, the more competitively powerful is its strategy of related diversification.

Step 4: Checking for Resource Fit

The businesses in a diversified company's lineup need to exhibit good *resource fit* as well as good strategic fit. Resource fit exists when (1) businesses add to a company's resource strengths, either financially or strategically, and (2) a company has the resources to adequately support its businesses as a group without spreading itself too thin. One important dimension of resource fit concerns whether a diversified company has the financial strength to satisfy the cash flow and investments of its different businesses.

Financial Resource Fits: Cash Cows versus Cash Hogs   Different businesses have different cash flow and investment characteristics. For example, business units in rapidly growing industries are often **cash hogs**—the cash flows they are able to generate from internal operations aren't big enough to fund their expansion. To keep pace with rising buyer demand, rapid-growth businesses frequently need sizable annual capital investments—for new facilities and equipment, for new product development or technology improvements, and for additional working capital to support inventory expansion and a larger base of operations. A business in a fast-growing industry becomes an even bigger cash hog when it has a relatively low market share and is pursuing a strategy to become an industry leader. Because a cash hog's financial

> **core concept**
> A *cash hog* is a business whose internal cash flows are inadequate to fully fund its needs for working capital and new capital investment.

figure 9.6   **Identifying the Competitive Advantage Potential of Cross-Business Strategic Fits**

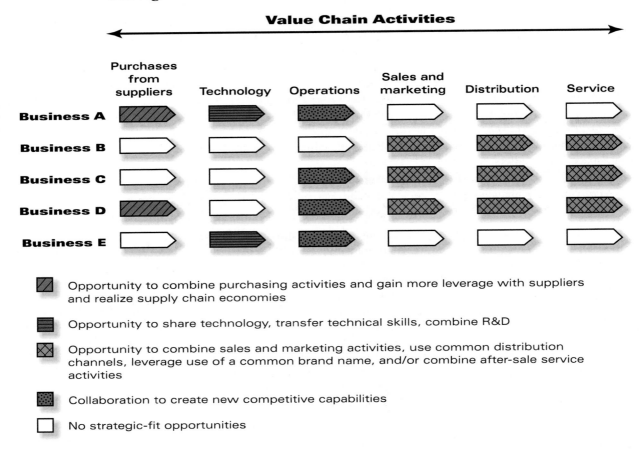

resources must be provided by the corporate parent, corporate managers have to decide whether its investment requirements are strategically and financially worthwhile.

In contrast, business units with leading market positions in mature industries may, however, be **cash cows**—businesses that generate substantial cash surpluses over what is needed for capital reinvestment and competitive maneuvers to sustain their present market position. Market leaders in slow-growth industries often generate sizable positive cash flows *over and above what is needed for reinvestment in operations* because their industry-leading positions tend to give them the sales volumes and reputation to earn attractive profits and because the slow-growth nature of their industry often entails relatively modest annual investment requirements. Though not always attractive from a growth standpoint, cash cows are valuable businesses from a financial resource perspective. The surplus cash flows they generate can be used to pay corporate dividends, finance acquisitions, and provide funds for investing in the company's promising cash hogs. It makes good financial and strategic sense for diversified companies to keep cash cows in healthy condition, fortifying and defending their market position so as to preserve their cash-generating capability over the long term and thereby have an ongoing source of financial resources to deploy elsewhere.

core concept
A *cash cow* is a business that generates cash flows over and above its internal requirements, thus providing a corporate parent with funds for investing in cash hog businesses, financing new acquisitions, or paying dividends.

Viewing a diversified group of businesses as a collection of cash flows and cash requirements (present and future) is a major step forward in understanding what the financial ramifications of diversification are and why having businesses with good financial resource fit is so important. For instance, a diversified company's businesses exhibit good financial resource fit when the excess cash generated by its cash cow businesses is sufficient to fund the investment requirements of promising cash hog businesses. Ideally, investing in cash hogs over time results in growing the hogs into self-supporting "stars." *Star businesses* have strong or market-leading competitive positions in attractive, high-growth markets and high levels of profitability and are often the cash cows of the future—when the markets of star businesses begin to mature and their growth slows, their competitive strength should produce self-generated cash flows more than sufficient to cover their investment needs. The "success sequence" is thus cash hog to young star (but perhaps still a cash hog) to self-supporting star to cash cow.

If, however, a cash hog has questionable promise (either because of low industry attractiveness or a weak competitive position), then it becomes a logical candidate for divestiture. Pursuing an aggressive invest-and-expand strategy for cash hog with an uncertain future seldom makes sense. Such businesses are a financial drain and fail the resource fit test because they strain the corporate parent's ability to adequately fund its other businesses. Divesting a less attractive cash hog business is usually the best alternative unless (1) it has valuable strategic fits with other business units or (2) the capital infusions needed from the corporate parent are modest relative to the funds available and there's a decent chance of growing the business into a solid bottom-line contributor yielding a good return on invested capital.

Aside from cash flow considerations, a business has good financial fit when it contributes to the achievement of corporate performance objectives (growth in earnings per share, above-average return on investment, recognition as an industry leader, etc.) and when it materially enhances shareholder value via helping drive increases in the company's stock price. A business exhibits poor financial fit if it soaks up a disproportionate share of the company's financial resources, makes subpar or inconsistent bottom-line contributions, is unduly risky and failure would jeopardize the entire enterprise, or remains too small to make a material earnings contribution even though it performs well.

A diversified company's strategy also fails the resource fit test when its financial resources are stretched across so many businesses that its credit rating is impaired. Severe financial strain sometimes occurs when a company borrows so heavily to finance new acquisitions that it has to trim way back on capital expenditures for existing businesses and use the big majority of its financial resources to meet interest obligations and to pay down debt. Some diversified companies have found themselves so financially overextended that they have had to sell off certain businesses to raise the money to meet existing debt obligations and fund essential capital expenditures for the remaining businesses.

Competitive and Managerial Resource Fits   A diversified company's strategy must aim at producing a good fit between its resource capability and the competitive and managerial requirements of its businesses.[17] Diversification is more likely to enhance shareholder value when the company has or can develop strong competitive and managerial capabilities. Sometimes the resource strengths crucial to succeeding in one particular business are a poor match with the key success factors in other businesses. For instance, BTR, a multibusiness company in Great Britain, discovered that the company's resources and managerial skills were quite well suited for parenting industrial manufacturing businesses but not for parenting its distribution businesses (National

> A close match between industry key success factors and company resources and capabilities is a solid sign of good resource fit.

Tyre Services and Texas-based Summers Group); as a consequence, BTR decided to divest its distribution businesses and focus exclusively on diversifying around small industrial manufacturing.[18] One company with businesses in restaurants and retailing decided that its resource capabilities in site selection, controlling operating costs, management selection and training, and supply chain logistics would enable it to succeed in the hotel business and in property management; but what management missed was that these businesses had some significantly different key success factors—namely, skills in controlling property development costs, maintaining low overheads, product branding (hotels), and ability to recruit a sufficient volume of business to maintain high levels of facility utilization.[19] A mismatch between the company's resource strengths and the key success factors in a particular business can be serious enough to warrant divesting an existing business or not acquiring a new business. In contrast, when a company's resources and capabilities are a good match with the key success factors of industries it is not presently in, it makes sense to take a hard look at acquiring companies in these industries and expanding the company's business lineup.

A second instance in which a diversified company can fail the resource fit test is by not having sufficient *resource depth* to support all of its businesses. A diversified company has to guard against stretching its resource base too thin and trying to do too many things. The broader the diversification, the greater the concern about whether the company has sufficient managerial depth to cope with the diverse range of operating problems its wide business lineup presents (plus those it may be contemplating getting into). The more a company's diversification strategy is tied to leveraging its resources and capabilities in new businesses, the more it has to develop a big enough and deep enough resource pool to supply these businesses with sufficient capability to create competitive advantage.[20] Otherwise its strengths end up being stretched too thin across too many businesses and the opportunity for competitive advantage is lost.

A Note of Caution   Hitting a home run in one business doesn't mean a company can easily enter a new business with similar resource requirements and hit a second home run.[21] Noted British retailer Marks & Spencer—despite possessing a range of impressive resource capabilities (ability to choose excellent store locations, a supply chain that allows both low costs and high merchandise quality, loyal employees, an excellent reputation with consumers, and strong management expertise) that have made it one of Britain's premier retailers for 100 years—has failed repeatedly in its efforts to diversify into department store retailing in the United States. Even though Philip Morris (now named Altria) had built powerful consumer marketing capabilities in its cigarette and beer businesses, it floundered in soft drinks and ended up divesting its acquisition of 7UP after several frustrating years of competing against strongly entrenched, resource-capable rivals like Coca-Cola and PepsiCo.

Step 5: Ranking the Business Units on the Basis of Performance and Priority for Resource Allocation

Once a diversified company's strategy has been evaluated from the perspective of industry attractiveness, competitive strength, strategic fit, and resource fit, the next step is to rank the performance prospects of the businesses from best to worst and determine which businesses merit top priority for new investments by the corporate parent.

The most important considerations in judging business-unit performance are sales growth, profit growth, contribution to company earnings, and return on capital. Sometimes, cash flow is a big consideration. Information on each business's past performance can be gleaned from a company's financial records. While past performance is not necessarily a good predictor of future performance, it does signal whether a business is in a strong position or a weak one.

The industry attractiveness/business strength evaluations also provide a basis for judging a business's prospects. Normally, strong business units in attractive industries have significantly better prospects than weak businesses in unattractive industries. And, normally, the revenue and earnings outlook for businesses in fast-growing industries is better than for businesses in slow-growing industries—one important exception is when a business has the competitive strength to draw sales and market share away from its rivals and thus achieve much faster growth than the industry as whole. As a rule, the prior analyses, taken together, signal which business units are likely to be strong performers on the road ahead and which are likely to be laggards. And it is a short step from ranking the prospects of business units to drawing conclusions about whether the company as a whole is capable of strong, mediocre, or weak performance in upcoming years.

The rankings of future performance generally determine what priority the corporate parent should give to each business in terms of resource allocation. The task here is to decide which business units should have top priority for corporate resource support and new capital investment and which should carry the lowest priority. *Business subsidiaries with the brightest profit and growth prospects and solid strategic and resource fits generally should head the list for corporate resource support.* However, corporate executives need to give special attention to whether and how corporate resources and capabilities can be used to enhance the competitiveness of particular business units. Opportunities for resource transfer, activity combining, or infusions of new financial capital become especially important when improvement in some key success area could make a big difference to a particular business unit's performance.

For a company's diversification strategy to generate ever-higher levels of performance, corporate managers have to do an effective job of steering resources out of low-opportunity areas into high-opportunity areas. Divesting marginal businesses is one of the best ways of freeing unproductive assets for redeployment. Surplus funds from cash cows also add to the corporate treasury. Figure 9.7 shows the chief strategic and financial options for allocating a diversified company's financial resources. Ideally, a company will have enough funds to do what is needed, both strategically and financially. If not, strategic uses of corporate resources should usually take precedence unless there is a compelling reason to strengthen the firm's balance sheet or divert financial resources to pacify shareholders.

Step 6: Crafting New Strategic Moves to Improve Overall Corporate Performance

The diagnosis and conclusions flowing from the five preceding analytical steps set the agenda for crafting strategic moves to improve a diversified company's overall performance. The strategic options boil down to five broad categories of actions:

1. Sticking closely with the existing business lineup and pursuing the opportunities it presents.
2. Broadening the company's diversification base by making new acquisitions in new industries.

figure 9.7   **The Chief Strategic and Financial Options for Allocating a Diversified Company's Financial Resources**

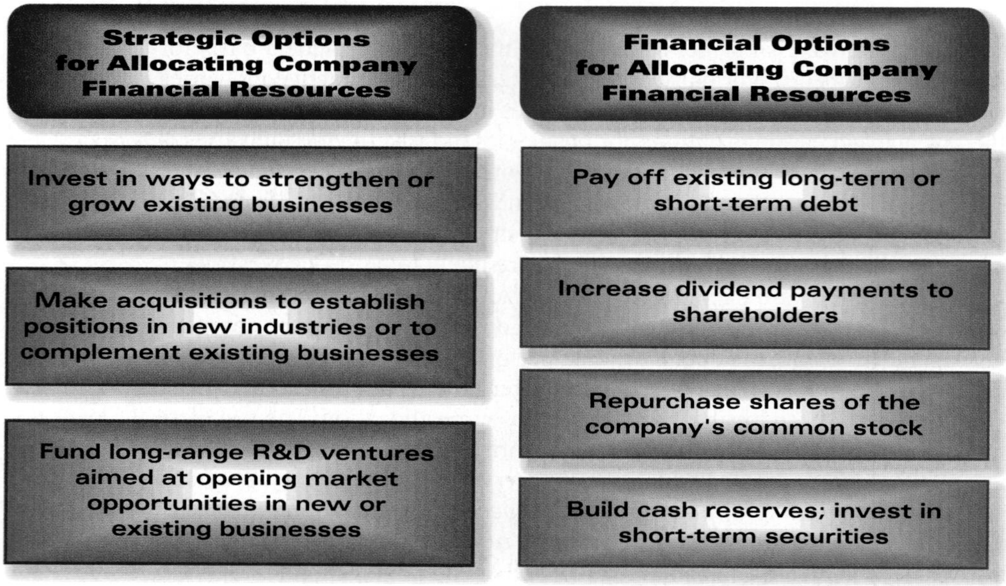

Strategic Options for Allocating Company Financial Resources	Financial Options for Allocating Company Financial Resources
Invest in ways to strengthen or grow existing businesses	Pay off existing long-term or short-term debt
Make acquisitions to establish positions in new industries or to complement existing businesses	Increase dividend payments to shareholders
Fund long-range R&D ventures aimed at opening market opportunities in new or existing businesses	Repurchase shares of the company's common stock
	Build cash reserves; invest in short-term securities

3. Divesting certain businesses and retrenching to a narrower diversification base.
4. Restructuring the company's business lineup and putting a whole new face on the company's business makeup.
5. Pursuing multinational diversification and striving to globalize the operations of several of the company's business units.

The option of sticking with the current business lineup makes sense when the company's present businesses offer attractive growth opportunities and can be counted on to generate dependable earnings and cash flows. As long as the company's set of existing businesses puts it in good position for the future and these businesses have good strategic and/or resource fits, then rocking the boat with major changes in the company's business mix is usually unnecessary. Corporate executives can concentrate their attention on getting the best performance from each of its businesses, steering corporate resources into those areas of greatest potential and profitability. Exactly how to wring better performance from the present business lineup will be dictated by each business's circumstances and the preceding analysis of the corporate parent's diversification strategy.

However, in the event that corporate executives are not entirely satisfied with the opportunities they see in the company's present set of businesses and conclude that changes in the company's direction and business makeup are in order, they can opt for any of the four other strategic alternatives listed above. These options are discussed in the following section.

figure 9.8   **A Company's Four Main Strategic Alternatives After It Diversifies**

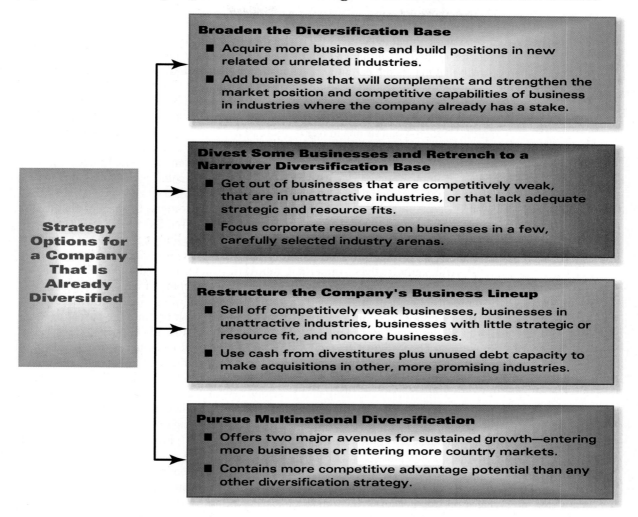

Strategy Options for a Company That Is Already Diversified

Broaden the Diversification Base
- Acquire more businesses and build positions in new related or unrelated industries.
- Add businesses that will complement and strengthen the market position and competitive capabilities of business in industries where the company already has a stake.

Divest Some Businesses and Retrench to a Narrower Diversification Base
- Get out of businesses that are competitively weak, that are in unattractive industries, or that lack adequate strategic and resource fits.
- Focus corporate resources on businesses in a few, carefully selected industry arenas.

Restructure the Company's Business Lineup
- Sell off competitively weak businesses, businesses in unattractive industries, businesses with little strategic or resource fit, and noncore businesses.
- Use cash from divestitures plus unused debt capacity to make acquisitions in other, more promising industries.

Pursue Multinational Diversification
- Offers two major avenues for sustained growth—entering more businesses or entering more country markets.
- Contains more competitive advantage potential than any other diversification strategy.

AFTER A COMPANY DIVERSIFIES: THE FOUR MAIN STRATEGY ALTERNATIVES

Diversifying is by no means the final stage in the evolution of a company's strategy. Once a company has diversified into a collection of related or unrelated businesses and concludes that some overhaul is needed in the company's present lineup and diversification strategy, it can pursue any of the four main strategic paths listed in the preceding section. These four paths are detailed in Figure 9.8 and discussed in the following sections.

Strategies to Broaden a Diversified Company's Business Base

Diversified companies sometimes find it desirable to build positions in new industries, whether related or unrelated. There are several motivating factors. One is sluggish growth that makes the potential revenue and profit boost of a newly acquired business look attractive. A second is vulnerability to seasonal or recessionary influences or to threats from emerging new technologies. A third is the potential for transferring resources and capabilities to other related or complementary businesses. A fourth is rapidly changing conditions in one or more of a company's core businesses brought on by technological, legislative, or new product innovations that alter buyer requirements and preferences. For instance, the passage of legislation in the United States allowing banks, insurance companies, and stock brokerages to enter each other's businesses spurred a raft of acquisitions and mergers to create full-service financial enterprises capable of meeting the multiple financial needs of customers. Citigroup, already the largest U.S. bank with a global banking franchise, acquired Salomon Smith Barney to position itself in the investment banking and brokerage business and acquired insurance giant Travelers Group to enable it to offer customers insurance products.

A fifth, and often very important, motivating factor for adding new businesses is to complement and strengthen the market position and competitive capabilities of one or more of its present businesses. Viacom's acquisition of CBS strengthened and extended Viacom's reach into various media businesses—it became the parent of Paramount Pictures, an assortment of cable TV networks (UPN, MTV, Nickelodeon, VH1, Showtime, The Movie Channel, Comedy Central), Blockbuster video stores, two movie theater chains, and 19 local TV stations. Unilever, a leading maker of food and personal care products, expanded its business lineup by acquiring SlimFast, Ben & Jerry's Homemade Ice Cream, and Bestfoods (whose brands included Knorr's soups, Hellman's mayonnaise, Skippy peanut butter, and Mazola cooking oils). Unilever saw these businesses as giving it more clout in competing against such other diversified food and household products companies as Nestlé, Kraft, Procter & Gamble, Danone, Campbell Soup, and General Mills.

Usually, expansion into new businesses is undertaken by acquiring companies already in the target industry. Some companies depend on new acquisitions to drive a major portion of their growth in revenues and earnings, and thus are always on the acquisition trail. Cisco Systems built itself into a worldwide leader in networking systems for the Internet by making 75 technology-based acquisitions during 1993–2002 to extend its market reach from routing and switching into voice and video over Internet protocol, optical networking, wireless, storage networking, security, broadband, and content networking. Tyco International, recently beset with charges of looting on the part of several top executives, transformed itself from an obscure company in the early 1990s into a $36 billion global manufacturing enterprise with operations in over 100 countries as of 2003 by making over 1,000 acquisitions. The company's far-flung diversification includes businesses in electronics, electrical components, fire and security systems, health care products, valves, undersea telecommunications systems, plastics, and adhesives. Tyco made over 700 acquisitions of small companies in the 1999–2001 period alone. Illustration Capsule 9.3 describes how Johnson & Johnson has used acquisitions to diversify far beyond its well-known Band-Aid and baby care businesses and become a major player in pharmaceuticals, medical devices, and medical diagnostics.

illustration capsule 9.3
Managing Diversification at Johnson & Johnson—The Benefits of Cross-Business Strategic Fits

Johnson & Johnson (J&J), once a consumer products company known for its Band-Aid line and its baby care products, has evolved into a $36 billion diversified enterprise consisting of some 204 different businesses organized into three divisions: drugs, medical devices and diagnostics, and consumer products. Over the past decade J&J has acquired 52 businesses at a cost of about $30 billion; about 10 to 15 percent of J&J's annual growth in revenues has come from acquisitions. Much of the company's recent growth has been in the pharmaceutical division, which in 2002 accounted for about 50 percent of J&J's revenues and 61 percent of its operating profits.

Competitors view J&J as a fierce rival with both scientific expertise and marketing savvy. Each of J&J's business units operates pretty much as an independent enterprise, setting its own strategies and operating with its own finance and human resource departments—such decentralization has resulted in relatively high overhead costs, but corporate management has felt such costs were worth the benefits gained in entrepreneurial attitudes at the business-unit level and the added competitiveness that such attitudes have fostered.

However, corporate management is beginning to champion greater cross-business cooperation and collaboration, believing that many of the advances in 21st century medicine will come from applying advances in one discipline to another. J&J had 9,300 scientists working in 40 research labs in 2003, and the frequency of cross-disciplinary collaboration was increasing. One of J&J's new drug-coated stents grew out of a discussion between a drug researcher and a researcher in the company's stent business. (When stents are inserted to prop open arteries following angioplasty, the drug coating helps prevent infection.) A gene technology database compiled by the company's gene research lab was shared with personnel from the diagnostics division, who developed a test that the drug R&D people could use to predict which patients would most benefit from an experimental cancer therapy. J&J experts in various diseases have been meeting quarterly for the past five years to share information, and top management is setting up cross-disciplinary groups to focus on new treatments for particular diseases. J&J's new liquid Band-Aid product (a liquid coating applied to hard-to-cover places like fingers and knuckles) is based on a material used in a wound-closing product sold by the company's hospital products company.

J&J's corporate management believes that close collaboration among people in its diagnostics, medical devices, and pharmaceuticals businesses—where numerous cross-business strategic fits exist—will give J&J an edge on competitors, most of whom cannot match the company's breadth and depth of expertise.

Source: Amy Barrett, "Staying on Top," *Business Week,* May 5, 2003, pp. 60–68.

Divestiture Strategies Aimed at Retrenching to a Narrower Diversification Base

A number of diversified firms have had difficulty managing a diverse group of businesses and have elected to get out of some of them. Retrenching to a narrower diversification base is usually undertaken when top management concludes that its diversification strategy has ranged too far afield and that the company can improve long-term performance by concentrating on building stronger positions in a smaller number of core businesses and industries. Hewlett-Packard spun off its testing and measurement businesses into a stand-alone company called Agilent Technologies so that it could better concentrate on its PC, workstation, server, printer and peripherals, and electronics businesses. PepsiCo divested its cash-hog group of restaurant businesses, consisting of KFC, Pizza Hut, Taco Bell, and California Pizza Kitchens, to provide more

> Focusing corporate resources on a few core and mostly related businesses avoids the mistake of diversifying so broadly that resources and management attention are stretched too thin.

resources for strengthening its soft-drink business (which was losing market share to Coca-Cola) and growing its more profitable Frito-Lay snack foods business. Kmart divested OfficeMax, Sports Authority, and Borders Bookstores in order to refocus management attention and all of the company's resources on restoring luster to its distressed discount retailing business. (However, Kmart is still being totally outclassed in discount retailing by Wal-Mart and Target.)

But there are other important reasons for divesting one or more of a company's present businesses. Sometimes divesting a business has to be considered because market conditions in a once-attractive industry have badly deteriorated. A business can become a prime candidate for divestiture because it lacks adequate strategic or resource fit, because it is a cash hog with questionable long-term potential, or because it is weakly positioned in its industry with little prospect the corporate parent can realize a decent return on its investment in the business. Sometimes a company acquires businesses that, down the road, just do not work out as expected even though management has tried all it can think of to make them profitable—mistakes cannot be completely avoided because it is hard to foresee how getting into a new line of business will actually work out. Subpar performance by some business units is bound to occur, thereby raising questions of whether to divest them or keep them and attempt a turnaround. Other business units, despite adequate financial performance, may not mesh as well with the rest of the firm as was originally thought.

On occasion, a diversification move that seems sensible from a strategic-fit standpoint turns out to be a poor *cultural fit*.[22] Several pharmaceutical companies had just this experience. When they diversified into cosmetics and perfume, they discovered their personnel had little respect for the "frivolous" nature of such products compared to the far nobler task of developing miracle drugs to cure the ill. The absence of shared values and cultural compatibility between the medical research and chemical-compounding expertise of the pharmaceutical companies and the fashion/marketing orientation of the cosmetics business was the undoing of what otherwise was diversification into businesses with technology-sharing potential, product-development fit, and some overlap in distribution channels.

Recent research indicates that pruning businesses and narrowing a firm's diversification base improves corporate performance.[23] Corporate parents often end up selling off businesses too late and at too low a price, sacrificing shareholder value.[24] A useful guide to determine whether or when to divest a business subsidiary is to ask, "If we were not in this business today, would we want to get into it now?"[25] When the answer is no or probably not, divestiture should be considered. Another signal that a business should become a divestiture candidate is whether it is worth more to another company than to the present parent; in such cases, shareholders would be well served if the company sells the business and collects a premium price from the buyer for whom the business is a valuable fit.[26]

The Two Options for Divesting a Business: Selling It or Spinning It Off as an Independent Company   Selling a business outright to another company is far and away the most frequently used option for divesting a business. But sometimes a business selected for divestiture has ample resource strengths to compete successfully on its own. In such cases, a corporate parent may elect to spin the unwanted business off as a financially and managerially independent company, either by selling shares to the investing public via an initial public offering or by distributing shares in the new company to existing shareholders of the corporate parent. When a corporate parent decides to spin off one of its businesses as a separate company, there's the issue of whether or not to retain partial ownership. Retaining partial ownership makes sense when the business to be divested has a hot product or technological capabilities that give it good profit prospects. When 3Com elected to divest its PalmPilot business, which investors then saw as having very promising profit potential, it elected to retain a substantial ownership interest so as to provide 3Com shareholders a way of participating in whatever future market success that PalmPilot (now Palm, Inc.) might have on its own.

Selling a business outright requires finding a buyer. This can prove hard or easy, depending on the business. As a rule, a company selling a troubled business should not ask, "How can we pawn this business off on someone, and what is the most we can get for it?"[27] Instead, it is wiser to ask, "For what sort of company would this business be a good fit, and under what conditions would it be viewed as a good deal?" Enterprises for which the business is a good fit are likely to pay the highest price. Of course, if a buyer willing to pay an acceptable price cannot be found, then a company must decide whether to keep the business until a buyer appears; spin it off as a separate company; or, in the case of a crisis-ridden business that is losing substantial sums, simply close it down and liquidate the remaining assets. Liquidation is obviously a last resort.

Strategies to Restructure a Company's Business Lineup

Restructuring strategies involve divesting some businesses and acquiring others so as to put a whole new face on the company's business lineup. Performing radical surgery on the group of businesses a company is in becomes an appealing strategy alternative when a diversified company's financial performance is being squeezed or eroded by:

> **core concept**
> *Restructuring* involves divesting some businesses and acquiring others so as to put a whole new face on the company's business lineup.

- Too many businesses in slow-growth, declining, low-margin, or otherwise unattractive industries (a condition indicated by the number and size of businesses with industry attractiveness ratings below 5 and located on the bottom half of the attractiveness–strength matrix—see Figure 9.5).
- Too many competitively weak businesses (a condition indicated by the number and size of businesses with competitive strength ratings below 5 and located on the right half of the attractiveness–strength matrix).
- Ongoing declines in the market shares of one or more major business units that are falling prey to more market-savvy competitors.
- An excessive debt burden with interest costs that eat deeply into profitability.
- Ill-chosen acquisitions that haven't lived up to expectations.

Restructuring can also be mandated by the emergence of new technologies that threaten the survival of one or more of a diversified company's important businesses or by the appointment of a new CEO who decides to redirect the company. On occasion, restructuring can be prompted by special circumstances—as when a firm has a unique opportunity to make an acquisition so big and important that it has to sell several existing business units to finance the new acquisition or when a company needs to sell off some businesses in order to raise the cash for entering a potentially big industry with wave-of-the-future technologies or products.

Candidates for divestiture in a corporate restructuring effort typically include not only weak or up-and-down performers or those in unattractive industries but also business units that lack strategic fit with the businesses to be retained, businesses that are cash hogs or that lack other types of resource fit, and businesses incompatible with the company's revised diversification strategy (even though they may be profitable or in an attractive industry). As businesses are divested, corporate restructuring generally involves aligning the remaining business units into groups with the best strategic fits and then redeploying the cash flows from the divested business to either pay down debt or make new acquisitions to strengthen the parent company's business position in the industries it has chosen to emphasize.[28]

Over the past decade, corporate restructuring has become a popular strategy at many diversified companies, especially those that had diversified broadly into many different industries and lines of business. For instance, one struggling diversified company over a two-year period divested four business units, closed down the operations of four others, and added 25 new lines of business to its portfolio (16 through acquisition and 9 through internal start-up). During Jack Welch's first four years as CEO of General Electric (GE), the company divested 117 business units, accounting for about 20 percent of GE's assets; these divestitures, coupled with several important acquisitions, provided GE with 14 major business divisions and led to Welch's challenge to the managers of GE's divisions to become number one or number two in their industry. Ten years after Welch became CEO, GE was a different company, having divested operations worth $9 billion, made new acquisitions totaling $24 billion, and cut its workforce by 100,000 people. Then, during the 1990–2001 period, GE continued to reshuffle its business lineup, acquiring over 600 new companies, including 108 in 1998 and 64 during a 90-day period in 1999. Most of the new acquisitions were in Europe, Asia, and Latin America and were aimed at transforming GE into a truly global enterprise. PerkinElmer used a series of divestitures and new acquisitions to transform itself from a supplier of low-margin services sold to government agencies into an innovative high-tech company with operations in over 125 countries and businesses in four industry groups—life sciences (drug research and clinical screening), optoelectronics, instruments, and fluid control and containment (for customers in aerospace, power generation, and semiconductors).

Several broadly diversified companies have pursued restructuring by splitting into two or more independent companies. In 1996, AT&T divided itself into three companies—one (which retained the AT&T name) for long-distance and other telecommunications services, one (called Lucent Technologies) for manufacturing telecommunications equipment, and one (called NCR) for computer systems that essentially represented the divestiture of AT&T's earlier acquisition of National Cash Register. A few years after the split-up, AT&T acquired TCI Communications and MediaOne, both leading cable TV providers, in an attempt to restructure itself into a new-age telecommunications company offering bundled local and long-distance service, cable TV, and high-speed Internet access. In 2000, after its bundled services concept flopped and its debt had become excessive, AT&T began splitting itself once again, this time into four businesses—cable TV (later acquired by Comcast), wireless communications (acquired by Cingular in 2004), landlines communications for businesses, and landlines communications for consumers. Before beginning a restructuring effort in 1995, British-based Hanson PLC owned companies with more than $20 billion in revenues in industries as diverse as beer, exercise equipment, tools, construction cranes, tobacco, cement, chemicals, coal mining, electricity, hot tubs and whirlpools, cookware, rock and gravel, bricks, and asphalt. By early 1997, Hanson had restructured itself into a $3.8 billion enterprise focused more narrowly on gravel, crushed rock, cement, asphalt, bricks, and construction cranes; the remaining businesses were divided into four groups and divested.

In a study of the performance of the 200 largest U.S. corporations from 1990 to 2000, McKinsey & Company found that those companies that actively managed their business portfolios through acquisitions and divestitures created substantially more shareholder value than those that kept a fixed lineup of businesses.[29]

Multinational Diversification Strategies

The distinguishing characteristics of a multinational diversification strategy are a *diversity of businesses* and a *diversity of national markets.*[30] Such diversity makes multinational diversification a particularly challenging and complex strategy to conceive and execute. Managers have to develop business strategies for each industry (with as many multinational variations as conditions in each country market dictate). Then they have to pursue and manage opportunities for cross-business and cross-country collaboration and strategic coordination in ways calculated to result in competitive advantage and enhanced profitability.

Moreover, the geographic operating scope of individual businesses within a diversified multinational company can range from one country only to several countries to many countries to global. Thus, each business unit within such a company often competes in a somewhat different combination of geographic markets than the other businesses do—adding another element of strategic complexity, and perhaps an element of opportunity.

Illustration Capsule 9.4 shows the scope of four prominent diversified multinational companies.

The Appeal of Multinational Diversification: More Opportunities for Sustained Growth and Maximum Competitive Advantage Potential

Despite their complexity, multinational diversification strategies have great appeal. They contain two major avenues for growing revenues and profits: (1) to grow by entering additional businesses, and (2) to grow by extending the operations of existing businesses into additional country markets. Moreover, a strategy of multinational diversification also contains six attractive paths to competitive advantage, *all of which can be pursued simultaneously:*

1. *Full capture of economies of scale and experience and learning-curve effects.* In some businesses, the volume of sales needed to realize full economies of scale and/or benefit fully from experience and learning-curve effects is rather sizable, often exceeding the volume that can be achieved operating within the boundaries of a single country market, especially a small one. *The ability to drive down unit costs by expanding sales to additional country markets is one reason why a diversified multinational may seek to acquire a business and then rapidly expand its operations into more and more foreign markets.*

2. *Opportunities to capitalize on cross-business economies of scope.* Diversifying into related businesses offering economies of scope can drive the development of a low-cost advantage over less diversified rivals. For example, a diversified multinational company (DMNC) that uses mostly the same distributors and retail dealers worldwide can diversify into new businesses using these same worldwide distribution channels at relatively little incremental expense. The cost savings of piggybacking distribution activities can be substantial. Moreover, with more business selling more products in more countries, a DMNC acquires more bargaining leverage in its purchases from suppliers and more bargaining leverage with retailers in securing attractive display space for its products. Consider, for example, the competitive power that Sony derived from these very sorts of economies of scope when it decided to diversify into the video game business with its PlayStation

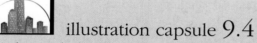

illustration capsule 9.4
The Global Scope of Four Prominent Diversified Multinational Corporations

Company	Global Scope	Businesses into Which the Company Has Diversified
Sony	Operations in more than 100 countries and sales offices in more than 200 countries	• Televisions, VCRs, DVD players, radios, CD players and home stereos, digital cameras and video equipment, PCs and Trinitron computer monitors • PlayStation game consoles and video game software • Columbia, Epic, and Sony Classical prerecorded music • Columbia TriStar motion pictures, syndicated television programs • Other businesses (insurance, financing, entertainment complexes, Internet-related businesses)
Nestlé	Operations in 70 countries and sales offices in more than 200 countries	• Beverages (Nescafé and Taster's Choice coffees, Nestea, Perrier, Arrowhead, and Calistoga mineral and bottled waters) • Milk products (Carnation, Gloria, Neslac, Coffee Mate, Nestlé ice cream and yogurt) • Pet foods (Friskies, Alpo, Fancy Feast, Mighty Dog) • Contadina, Libby's, and Stouffer's food products and prepared dishes • Chocolate and confectionery products (Nestlé Crunch, Smarties, Baby Ruth, Butterfinger, KitKat) • Pharmaceuticals (Alcon ophthalmic products, Galderma dermatological products)
Siemens	Operations in 160 countries and sales offices in more than 190 countries	• Electrical power generation, transmission, and distribution equipment and products • Manufacturing automation systems, industrial motors, industrial computers, industrial machinery, industrial tools, plant construction and maintenance • Information and communications (solutions and services needed for corporate communication networks, telephones, PCs, mainframes, computer network products, consulting services) • Mass transit and light rail systems, rail cars, locomotives • Medical equipment, health care management services • Semiconductors, memory components, microcontrollers, capacitors, resistors • Lighting (bulbs, lamps, theater and television lighting systems) • Home electronics, large home appliances, vacuum cleaners • Financial services (commercial lending, pension administration, venture capital) • Procurement and logistics services, business consulting services

illustration capsule 9.4
(concluded)

Company	Global Scope	Businesses into Which the Company Has Diversified
Samsung	Operations in more than 60 countries and sales in more than 200 countries	• Notebook computers, hard disk drives, DC/DVD-ROM drives, monitors, printers, and fax machines • Televisions (big screen TVs, plasma screen TVs, and LCD screen TVs), DVD and MP3 players • Cell phones and various other telecommunications products • Compressors • Home appliances (refrigerators, air conditioners, microwaves, washing machines, and vacuum cleaners) • Semiconductor products (DRAM chips, flash memory chips, graphics memory chips, and others) • Optical fibers, fiber-optic cables, and fiber-optic connectors

Source: Company annual reports and Web sites.

product line. Sony had in-place capability to go after video game sales in all country markets where it presently did business in other product categories (TVs, computers, DVD players, VCRs, radios, CD players, and digital and video cameras). And it had the marketing clout and brand-name credibility to persuade retailers to give Sony's PlayStation products prime shelf space and visibility. These strategic-fit benefits helped Sony quickly overtake longtime industry leaders Nintendo and Sega and fortify its position against Microsoft's entry with its new Xbox offerings.

3. *Opportunities to transfer competitively valuable resources both from one business to another and from one country to another.* A company pursuing related diversification can gain a competitive edge over less diversified rivals by transferring competitively valuable resources from one business to another; a multinational company can gain competitive advantage over rivals with narrower geographic coverage by transferring competitively valuable resources from one country to another. But a strategy of multinational diversification enables simultaneous pursuit of both sources of competitive advantage.

4. *Ability to leverage use of a well-known and competitively powerful brand name.* Diversified multinational companies whose businesses have brand names that are well known and respected across the world possess a valuable strategic asset with competitive advantage potential. For example, Sony's well-established global brand-name recognition gives it an important marketing and advertising advantage over rivals with lesser-known brands. When Sony goes into a new marketplace with the stamp of the Sony brand on new businesses or product families, it can command prominent display space with retailers. It can expect to win sales and market share simply on the confidence that

> Transferring a powerful brand name from one product or business to another can usually be done very economically.

buyers place in products carrying the Sony name. While Sony may spend money to make consumers aware of the availability of its new products, it does not have to spend nearly as much on achieving brand recognition and market acceptance as would a lesser-known competitor. Further, if Sony moves into a new country market for the first time and does well selling Sony PlayStations and video games, it is easier to sell consumers in that country Sony TVs, digital cameras, PCs, and so on—plus, the related advertising costs are likely to be less than they would be without having already established the Sony brand strongly in the minds of buyers.

5. *Ability to capitalize on opportunities for cross-business and cross-country collaboration and strategic coordination.*[31] A multinational diversification strategy allows competitively valuable cross-business and cross-country coordination of certain value chain activities. For instance, by channeling corporate resources directly into a combined R&D/technology effort for all related businesses, as opposed to letting each business unit fund and direct its own R&D effort however it sees fit, a DMNC can merge its expertise and efforts *worldwide* to advance core technologies, expedite cross-business and cross-country product improvements, speed the development of new products that complement existing products, and pursue promising technological avenues to create altogether new businesses—all significant contributors to competitive advantage and better corporate performance.[32] Honda has been very successful in building R&D expertise in gasoline engines and transferring the resulting technological advances to its businesses in automobiles, motorcycles, outboard engines, snow blowers, lawn mowers, garden tillers, and portable power generators. Further, a DMNC can reduce costs through cross-business and cross-country coordination of purchasing and procurement from suppliers, from collaborative introduction and shared use of e-commerce technologies and online sales efforts, and from coordinated product introductions and promotional campaigns.

6. *Opportunities to use cross-business or cross-country subsidization to outcompete rivals.* A financially successful DMNC has potentially valuable organizational resources and multiple profit sanctuaries in both certain country markets and certain businesses that it can draw on to wage a market offensive. In comparison, a one-business domestic company has only one profit sanctuary—its home market. A diversified one-country competitor may have profit sanctuaries in several businesses, but all are in the same country market. A one-business multinational company may have profit sanctuaries in several country markets, but all are in the same business. All three are vulnerable to an offensive in their more limited profit sanctuaries by an aggressive DMNC willing to lowball its prices and/or spend extravagantly on advertising to win market share at their expense. A DMNC's ability to keep hammering away at competitors with low prices year after year may reflect either a cost advantage growing out of its related diversification strategy or a willingness to accept low profits or even losses in the market being attacked because it has ample earnings from its other profit sanctuaries. For example, Sony's global-scale diversification strategy gives it unique competitive strengths in outcompeting Nintendo and Microsoft. If need be, Sony can maintain low prices on its PlayStations or fund high-profile promotions for its latest video game products, using earnings from its other business lines to fund its offensive to wrest market share away from Nintendo and Microsoft in video games. At the same time, Sony can draw on its considerable resources in R&D, its ability to transfer electronics technology from one electronics product family to another, and its expertise in product innovation to introduce better and better video game players, perhaps multifunctional

players that do more than just play video games. Such competitive actions not only enhance Sony's own brand image but also make it very tough for Nintendo and Microsoft to match Sony's prices, advertising, and product development efforts and still earn acceptable profits.

The Combined Effects of These Advantages Is Potent A strategy of diversifying into *related* industries and then competing *globally* in each of these industries thus has great potential for being a winner in the marketplace because of the long-term growth opportunities it offers and the multiple corporate-level competitive advantage opportunities it contains. Indeed, *a strategy of multinational diversification contains more competitive advantage potential than any other diversification strategy.* The strategic key to maximum competitive advantage is for a DMNC to concentrate its diversification efforts in those industries where there are resource-sharing and resource-transfer opportunities and where there are important economies of scope and brand-name benefits. These strategic-fit benefits will make the more powerful a competitor and improve its profit and growth performance.

> **core concept**
> A strategy of multinational diversification has more built-in potential for competitive advantage than any other diversification strategy.

However, it is important to recognize that cross-subsidization can only be used sparingly. It is one thing to *occasionally* divert a portion of the profits and cash flows from existing businesses to help fund entry into a new business or country market or wage a competitive offensive against select rivals. It is quite another thing to *regularly* use cross-subsidization tactics and thereby weaken overall company performance. A DMNC is under the same pressures as any other company to demonstrate consistently acceptable profitability across its whole operation.[33] At some juncture, every business and every country market needs to make a profit contribution or become a candidate for abandonment. As a general rule, *cross-subsidization tactics are justified only when there is a good prospect that the short-term impairment to corporate profitability will be offset by stronger competitiveness and better overall profitability over the long term.*

> **core concept**
> Although cross-subsidization is a potent competitive weapon, it can only be used infrequently because of its adverse impact on overall corporate profitability.

key|points

Most companies have their business roots in a single industry. Even though they may have since diversified into other industries, a substantial part of their revenues and profits still usually comes from the original or core business. Diversification becomes an attractive strategy when a company runs out of profitable growth opportunities in its original business. The purpose of diversification is to build shareholder value. Diversification builds shareholder value when a diversified group of businesses can perform better under the auspices of a single corporate parent than they would as independent, stand-alone businesses—the goal is to achieve not just a $1 + 1 = 2$ result but rather to realize important $1 + 1 = 3$ performance benefits. Whether getting into a new business has potential to enhance shareholder value hinges on whether a company's entry into that business can pass the attractiveness test, the cost-of-entry test, and the better-off test.

Entry into new businesses can take any of three forms: acquisition, internal start-up, or joint venture/strategic partnership. Each has its pros and cons, but acquisition is the most frequently used; internal start-up takes the longest; and joint venture/strategic partnership, though used second most frequently, is the least durable.

There are two fundamental approaches to diversification—into related businesses and into unrelated businesses. The rationale for *related* diversification is strategic:

Diversify into businesses with strategic fits along their respective value chains, capitalize on strategic-fit relationships to gain competitive advantage, and then use competitive advantage to achieve the desired $1 + 1 = 3$ impact on shareholder value. Businesses have strategic fit when their value chains offer potential (1) for realizing economies of scope or cost-saving efficiencies associated with sharing technology, facilities, functional activities, distribution outlets, or brand names; (2) for competitively valuable cross-business transfers of technology, skills, know-how, or other resource capabilities; (3) for leveraging use of a well-known and trusted brand name, and (4) for competitively valuable cross-business collaboration to build new or stronger resource strengths and competitive capabilities.

The basic premise of *unrelated* diversification is that any business that has good profit prospects and can be acquired on good financial terms is a good business to diversify into. Unrelated diversification strategies surrender the competitive advantage potential of strategic fit in return for such advantages as (1) spreading business risk over a variety of industries and (2) providing opportunities for financial gain (if candidate acquisitions have undervalued assets, are bargain-priced and have good upside potential given the right management, or need the backing of a financially strong parent to capitalize on attractive opportunities). In theory, unrelated diversification also offers greater earnings stability over the business cycle (a third advantage), but this advantage is very hard to realize in practice. The greater the number of businesses a conglomerate is in and the more diverse these businesses are, the harder it is for corporate executives to select capable managers to run each business, know when the major strategic proposals of business units are sound, or decide on a wise course of recovery when a business unit stumbles. Unless corporate managers are exceptionally shrewd and talented, unrelated diversification is a dubious and unreliable approach to building shareholder value when compared to related diversification.

Analyzing a company's diversification strategy is a six-step process:

- *Step 1:* Evaluate the long-term attractiveness of the industries into which the firm has diversified.
- *Step 2:* Evaluate the relative competitive strength of each of the company's business units.
- *Step 3:* Check for cross-business strategic fits.
- *Step 4:* Check whether the firm's resource strengths fit the resource requirements of its present business lineup.
- *Step 5:* Rank the performance prospects of the businesses from best to worst and determine what the corporate parent's priority should be in allocating resources to its various businesses.
- *Step 6:* Craft new strategic moves to improve overall corporate performance.

Once a company has diversified, corporate management's task is to manage the collection of businesses for maximum long-term performance. There are four different strategic paths for improving a diversified company's performance: (1) broadening the firm's business base by diversifying into additional businesses, (2) retrenching to a narrower diversification base by divesting some of its present businesses, (3) corporate restructuring, and (4) multinational diversification.

Broadening the diversification base is attractive when growth is sluggish and the company needs the revenue and profit boost of a newly acquired business, when it has resources and capabilities that are eminently transferable to related or complementary businesses, or when the opportunity to acquire an attractive company unexpectedly lands on its doorstep. Furthermore, there are occasions when a diversified company makes new acquisitions to complement and strengthen the market position and competitive capabilities of one or more of its present businesses.

Retrenching to a narrower diversification base is usually undertaken when corporate management concludes that the firm's diversification efforts have ranged too far afield and that the best avenue for improving long-term performance is to concentrate on building strong positions in a smaller number of businesses. Retrenchment is usually accomplished by divesting businesses that are no longer deemed suitable for the company to be in.

Corporate restructuring strategies involve divesting some businesses and acquiring new businesses so as to put a whole new face on the company's business lineup. Performing radical surgery on the group of businesses a company is in becomes an appealing strategy alternative when a diversified company's financial performance is being squeezed or eroded by (1) too many businesses in slow-growth or declining or low-margin or otherwise unattractive industries, (2) too many competitively weak businesses, (3) ongoing declines in the market shares of one or more major business units that are falling prey to more market-savvy competitors, (4) an excessive debt burden with interest costs that eat deeply into profitability, or (5) ill-chosen acquisitions that haven't lived up to expectations.

Multinational diversification strategies feature a diversity of businesses and a diversity of national markets. Despite the complexity of having to devise and manage so many strategies (at least one for each industry, with as many variations for country markets as may be needed), multinational diversification strategies have considerable appeal. They offer two avenues for long-term growth in revenues and profitability—one is to grow by entering additional businesses and the other is to grow by extending the operations of existing businesses into additional country markets. Moreover, multinational diversification offers six ways to build competitive advantage: (1) full capture of economies of scale and learning-curve effects, (2) opportunities to capitalize on cross-business economies of scope, (3) opportunity to transfer competitively valuable resources from one business to another and from one country to another, (4) ability to leverage use of a well-known and competitively powerful brand name, (5) ability to capitalize on opportunities for cross-business and cross-country collaboration and strategic coordination, and (6) opportunities to use cross-business or cross-country subsidization to wrest sales and market share from rivals. A strategy of multinational diversification contains more competitive advantage potential than any other diversification strategy.

| exercises

1. What do you see as the strategic fits that exist among the value chains of the diversified companies listed in Illustration Capsule 9.1?

2. Consider the business lineup of the Walt Disney Company shown in Illustration Capsule 9.2. What problems do you think the top executives at Disney would encounter in trying to stay on top of all the businesses the company is in? How might they decide the merits of adding new businesses or divesting poorly performing businesses? What types of advice might they give to the general managers of each of Disney's business units?

chapter ten

Strategy, Ethics, and Social Responsibility

(©Raymond Gehman/ CORBIS)

When morality comes up against profit, it is seldom profit that loses.

—Shirley Chisholm
Former Congresswoman

But I'd shut my eyes in the sentry box so I didn't see nothing wrong.

—Rudyard Kipling
Author

The marketplace, for all its splendors, may produce value but not values.

—E. J. Dionne
Washington Post *columnist*

There is one and only one social responsibility of business—to use its resources and engage in activities designed to increase its profits so long as it stays within the rules of the game, which is to say engages in free and open competition, without deception or fraud.

—Milton Friedman
Nobel Prize–winning economist

Corporations are economic entities, to be sure, but they are also social institutions that must justify their existence by their overall contribution to society.

—Henry Mintzberg, Robert Simons, and Kunal Basu
Professors

learly, a company has a responsibility to make a profit and grow the business—in capitalistic or market economies, management's fiduciary duty to create value for shareholders is not a matter for serious debate. Clearly, a company and its personnel also have a duty to obey the law and play by the rules of fair competition. But does a company have a duty to operate according to the ethical norms of the societies in which it operates—should it be held to some standard of ethical conduct? And does it have a duty or obligation to contribute to the betterment of society independent of the needs and preferences of the customers it serves? Should a company display a social conscience and devote a portion of its resources to bettering society?

The focus of this chapter is to examine what link, if any, there should be between a company's efforts to craft and execute a winning strategy and its duties to (1) conduct its activities in an ethical manner and (2) demonstrate socially responsible behavior by being a committed corporate citizen and attending to the needs of nonowner stakeholders—employees, the communities in which it operates, the disadvantaged, and society as a whole.

STRATEGY AND ETHICS

Ethics involves concepts of right and wrong, fair and unfair, moral and immoral. Most people and most societies consider lying, cheating, stealing, and harming others to be unethical, immoral, and socially unacceptable. Honesty, integrity, keeping one's word, respecting the rights of others, and practicing the Golden Rule are generally considered ethical and virtuous—they are traits that a good person is supposed to believe in and to display. Beliefs about what is ethical serve as a *moral compass* in guiding the actions and behaviors of individuals and organizations. The issue here is how do notions of right and wrong, fair and unfair, moral and immoral, ethical and unethical translate into judging management decisions and the strategies and actions of companies in the marketplace.

What Do We Mean by Business Ethics?

Business ethics is the application of general ethical principles and standards to business behavior.[1] Business ethics does not really involve a special set of ethical standards applicable only to business situations. Ethical principles in business are not materially different from ethical principles in general. Why? Because business must draw its ideas of "the right thing to do" and "the wrong thing to do" from the same sources as anyone else. A business should not

> **core concept**
> By **business ethics**, we mean the application of general ethical principles and standards to business behavior.

Business actions are judged by the general ethical standards of society, not by a special set of more permissive standards.

make its own rules about what is right and wrong. If dishonesty is considered to be unethical and immoral, then dishonest behavior in business—whether it relates to customers, suppliers, employees or shareholders—qualifies as equally unethical and immoral. If being ethical entails not harming others, then recalling a defective or unsafe product is ethically necessary and failing to undertake such a recall or correct the problem in future shipments of the product is likewise unethical. If society deems bribery to be unethical, then it follows that it is unethical for company personnel to make payoffs to government officials to facilitate business transactions or bestow gifts and other favors on prospective customers to win or retain their business.

The Three Categories of Management Morality

Three categories of managers stand out with regard to ethical and moral principles in business affairs:[2]

- *The moral manager*—Moral managers are dedicated to high standards of ethical behavior, both in their own actions and in their expectations of how the company's business is to be conducted. They see themselves as stewards of ethical behavior and believe it is important to exercise ethical leadership. Moral managers may well be ambitious and have a powerful urge to succeed, but they pursue success in business within the confines of both the letter and the spirit of the law—they typically regard the law as an ethical minimum and have a habit of operating well above what the law requires.

- *The immoral manager*—Immoral managers are actively opposed to ethical behavior in business and willfully ignore ethical principles in their decision making. They view legal standards as barriers that must be skirted or overcome. Prone to pursuing their own self-interest, immoral managers are living examples of capitalistic greed, caring only about their own or their organization's gains and successes. Their philosophy is that good businesspeople cannot spend time watching out for the interests of others when what really matters is the bottom line and making one's numbers. In the minds of immoral managers, nice guys come in second and the competitive nature of business requires that you either trample on others or get trampled yourself. Immoral managers are thus the bad guys and relish wearing the black hats.

- *The amoral manager*—Amoral managers appear in two forms: the intentionally amoral manager and the unintentionally amoral manager. *Intentionally amoral managers* consciously believe business and ethics are not to be mixed because different rules apply in business versus other realms of life. They think it is fine not to factor ethical considerations into their decisions and actions since business activity lies outside the sphere of moral judgment. Intentionally amoral managers view ethics as inappropriate and too Sunday-schoolish for the tough competitive world of business. Their concept of right and wrong tends to be lawyer-driven—how much can we get by with and still be in compliance? *Unintentionally amoral managers* do not pay much attention to the concept of business ethics either, but for different reasons. They are simply casual about, careless about, or inattentive to the fact that certain kinds of business decisions or company activities are unsavory or may have deleterious effects on others—in short, they are blind to the ethical dimension of decisions and business actions. Some may be so ethically unconscious that they have just never stopped to consider whether ethics applies to business decisions or company actions. Some unintentionally amoral managers may see themselves as well-intentioned and even personally ethical. *Amoral managers of both types view it necessary to comply with the law, but they see little reason to do more because government provides the legal framework that says what society will put up with— businesses ought to be able to do whatever the law allows them to do.*

By some accounts, the population of managers is said to be distributed among all three types in a bell-shaped curve, with immoral managers and moral managers occupying the two tails of the curve, and the amoral managers (especially the intentionally amoral managers) occupying the broad middle ground.[3] Furthermore, within the population of managers, there is experiential evidence to support that while the average manager may be amoral most of the time, he or she may slip into a moral or immoral mode on occasion, based on a variety of impinging factors and circumstances.

A landscape that is apparently so cluttered with amoral and immoral managers does not bode well for the *frequency* with which company managers ground their strategies on exemplary ethical principles or for the *vigor* with which they try to ingrain ethical behavior into company personnel. And, as many business school professors have noted, there are considerable numbers of amoral business students in our classrooms. So efforts to root out business corruption and implant high ethical principles into the managerial process of crafting and executing strategy is unlikely to produce an ethically strong global business climate anytime in the near future, barring major effort to address and correct the ethical amorality and immorality of company managers.

What Are the Drivers of Unethical Strategies and Business Behavior?

The apparent pervasiveness of immoral and amoral businesspeople is one obvious reason why ethical principles are an ineffective moral compass in business dealings and why companies may resort to unethical strategic behavior. But apart from "the business of business is business, not ethics" kind of thinking, three other main drivers of unethical business behavior also stand out:

- Overzealous or obsessive pursuit of personal gain, wealth, and other selfish interests.
- Heavy pressures on company managers to meet or beat earnings targets.
- A company culture that puts the profitability and good business performance ahead of ethical behavior.

Overzealous Pursuit of Personal Gain, Wealth, and Selfish Interests

People who are obsessed with wealth accumulation, greed, power, status, and other selfish interests often push ethical principles aside in their quest for self-gain. Driven by their ambitions, they exhibit few qualms in doing whatever is necessary to achieve their goals. Their first and only priority is to look out for their own best interests and if climbing the ladder of success means having few scruples and ignoring the welfare of others, so be it. A general disregard for business ethics can prompt all kinds of unethical strategic maneuvers and behaviors at companies. Top executives, directors, and majority shareholders at cable-TV company Adelphia Communications ripped off the company for amounts totaling well over $1 billion, diverting hundreds of millions of dollars to fund their Buffalo Sabres hockey team, build a private golf course, and buy timber rights—among other things—and driving the company into bankruptcy. Their actions, which represent one of the biggest instances of corporate looting and self-dealing in American business, took place despite the company's public pontifications about the principles it would observe in trying to care for customers, employees, stockholders, and the local communities where it operated. Providian Financial Corporation, despite an otherwise glowing record of social responsibility and service to many of its stakeholders, paid $150 million in December 2001 to settle class-action lawsuits alleging that its strategy included attempts to systematically cheat credit card holders. Andrew Fastow, Enron's chief financial officer (CFO), set himself up as the manager of one of Enron's off-the-books partnerships and as the part-owner of another, allegedly earning extra compensation of $30 million for his owner-manager roles in the two partnerships; Enron's board of directors agreed to suspend the company's conflict-of-interest rules designed to protect the company from this very kind of executive self-dealing.

According to a civil complaint filed by the Securities and Exchange Commission, the chief executive officer (CEO) of Tyco International, a well-known $35.6 billion manufacturing and services company, conspired with the company's CFO to steal more than $170 million, including a company-paid $2 million birthday party for the CEO's wife held on Sardinia, an island off the coast of Italy; a $7 million Park Avenue apartment for his wife; and secret low-interest and interest-free loans to fund private businesses and investments and purchase lavish artwork, yachts, estate jewelry, and vacation homes in New Hampshire, Connecticut, Nantucket, and Park City, Utah. The CEO allegedly lived rent-free in a $31 million Fifth Avenue apartment that Tyco purchased in his name, directed millions of dollars of charitable contributions in his own name using Tyco funds, diverted company funds to finance his personal businesses and investments, and sold millions of dollars of Tyco stock back to Tyco itself through Tyco subsidiaries located in offshore bank-secrecy jurisdictions. Tyco's CEO and CFO were further charged with conspiring to reap more than $430 million from sales of stock, using questionable accounting to hide their actions, and engaging in deceptive accounting practices to distort the company's financial condition from 1995 to 2002. At the trial on the charges filed by the SEC, the prosecutor told the jury in his opening statement, "This case is about lying, cheating and stealing. These people didn't win the jackpot—they stole it." Defense lawyers countered that "every single transaction . . . was set down in detail in Tyco's books and records" and that the authorized and disclosed multimillion-dollar compensation packages were merited by the company's financial performance and stock price gains.

Heavy Pressures on Company Managers to Meet or Beat Earnings Targets   When companies find themselves scrambling to achieve ambitious earnings growth and meet the quarterly and annual performance expectations of Wall Street analysts and investors, managers often feel enormous pressure *to do whatever it takes* to sustain the company's reputation for delivering good financial performance. Executives at high-performing companies know that investors will see the slightest sign of a slowdown in earnings growth as a red flag and drive down the company's stock price. The company's credit rating could be downgraded if it has used lots of debt to finance its growth. The pressure to watch the scoreboard and "never miss a quarter"—so as not to upset the expectations of Wall Street analysts and fickle stock market investors—prompts managers to cut costs wherever savings show up immediately, squeeze extra sales out of early deliveries, and engage in other short-term maneuvers to make the numbers. As the pressure builds to keep performance numbers looking good, company personnel start stretching the rules further and further, until the limits of ethical conduct are overlooked.[4] Once ethical boundaries are crossed in efforts to "meet or beat the numbers," the threshold for making more extreme ethical compromises becomes lower.

Several top executives at WorldCom, a company built with scores of acquisitions in exchange for WorldCom stock, allegedly concocted a fraudulent $11 billion accounting scheme to hide costs and inflate revenues and profit over several years; the scheme was said to have helped the company keep its stock price propped up high enough to make additional acquisitions, support its nearly $30 billion debt load, and allow executives to cash in on their lucrative stock options. At Qwest Communications, a company created by the merger of a go-go telecom start-up and U.S. West (one of the regional Bell companies), management was charged with scheming to improperly book $2.4 billion in revenues from a variety of sources and deals, thereby inflating the company's profits and deceiving shareholders about how well the company's strategy to create a telecommunications company of the future was actually working. Scrambling to find ways to hit its earnings targets in 1999–2000, Enron entered into a partnership with Blockbuster to provide movies to homes directly over phone lines; months after the partnership was formed, Enron used "creative accounting" to book $110.9 million in profits based on the projected performance of its Blockbuster partnership (the profits were never realized because the venture was called off after a 1,000-home pilot test).

At Bristol-Myers Squibb, the world's fifth largest drug maker, management apparently engaged in a series of numbers-game maneuvers to meet earnings targets, including such actions as:

- Offering special end-of-quarter discounts to induce distributors and local pharmacies to stock up on certain prescription drugs—a practice known as "channel stuffing."
- Issuing last-minute price increase alerts to spur purchases and beef up operating profits.
- Setting up excessive reserves for restructuring charges and then reversing some of the charges as needed to bolster operating profits.
- Making repeated asset sales small enough that the gains could be reported as additions to operating profit rather than being flagged as one-time gains. (Some accountants have long used a rule of thumb that says a transaction that alters quarterly profits by less than 5 percent is "immaterial" and need not be disclosed in the company's financial reports.)

Such numbers games were said to be a common "earnings management" practice at Bristol-Myers and, according to one former executive, "sent a huge message across the organization that you make your numbers at all costs."[5]

Company executives often feel pressured to hit financial performance targets because their compensation depends heavily on the company's performance. During the late 1990s, it became fashionable for boards of directors to grant lavish bonuses, stock option awards, and other compensation benefits to executives for meeting specified performance targets. So outlandishly large were these rewards that executives had strong personal incentives to bend the rules and engage in behaviors the allowed the targets to be met. Much of the accounting hocus-pocus at the root of recent corporate scandals has entailed situations in which executives benefited enormously from misleading accounting or other shady activities that allowed them to hit the numbers and receive incentive awards ranging from $10 million to $100 million. At Bristol-Myers Squibb, for example, the pay-for-performance link spawned strong rules-bending incentives. About 94 percent of one top executive's $18.5 million in total compensation in 2001 came from stock-option grants, a bonus, and long-term incentive payments linked to corporate performance; about 92 percent of a second executive's $12.9 million of compensation was incentive-based.[6]

The fundamental problem with a "make the numbers and move on" syndrome is that a company doesn't really serve its customers or its shareholders by putting top priority on the bottom line. Shareholder interests are best served by doing a really good job of serving customers (observing the rule that customers are "king") and by improving the company's competitiveness in the marketplace. Cutting ethical corners or stooping to downright illegal actions in the name of profits first is convoluted and misguided—when the spotlight is shined on such scurrilous behavior, the resulting fallout actually depreciates shareholder value rather than enhancing it.

Company Cultures That Put the Bottom Line Ahead of Ethical Behavior   When a company's culture spawns an ethically corrupt or amoral work climate, people have a company-approved license to ignore "what's right" and engage in most any behavior or employ most any strategy they think they can get away with. In such an environment, ethically immoral or amoral people are certain to play down the relevance of ethical strategic actions and business conduct. Moreover, the pressures to conform to the norms of the corporate culture can prompt otherwise honorable people to make ethical mistakes and succumb to the many opportunities around them to engage in unethical practices.

A perfect example of a company culture gone awry on ethics is Enron.[7] Enron's leaders encouraged company personnel to focus on the current bottom line and to be innovative and aggressive in figuring out what could be done to grow current revenues and earnings. Employees were expected to pursue opportunities to the utmost in the electric utility industry that at the time was undergoing looser regulation. Enron executives viewed the company as a laboratory for innovation; the company hired the best and brightest people and pushed them to be creative, look at problems and opportunities in new ways, and exhibit a sense of urgency in making things happen. Employees were encouraged to make a difference and do their part in creating an entrepreneurial environment where creativity flourished, people could achieve their full potential, and everyone had a stake in the outcome. Enron employees got the message—pushing the limits and meeting one's numbers were viewed as survival skills. Enron's annual "rank and yank" formal evaluation process where the 15 to 20 percent lowest-ranking employees were let go or encouraged to seek other employment made it abundantly clear that bottom-line results and being the "mover-and-shaker" in the marketplace were what counted. The name of the game at Enron became devising clever ways to boost revenues and earnings, even if it sometimes meant operating outside established policies and without the knowledge of superiors. In fact, outside-the-lines behavior was celebrated if it generated profitable new business. Enron's energy contracts and its trading and hedging activities grew increasingly more complex and diverse as employees pursued first this avenue and then another to help keep Enron's financial performance looking good.

As a consequence of Enron's well-publicized successes in creating new products and businesses and leveraging the company's trading and hedging expertise into new market arenas, Enron came to be regarded as an exceptionally innovative company. It was ranked by its corporate peers as the most innovative U.S. company for three consecutive years in *Fortune* magazine's annual surveys of the most admired companies. A high-performance/high-rewards climate came to pervade the Enron culture, as the best workers (determined by who produced the best bottom-line results) received impressively large incentives and bonuses (amounting to as much as $1 million for traders and even more for senior executives). On Car Day at Enron, an array of luxury sports cars arrived for presentation to the most successful employees. Understandably, employees wanted to be seen as part of Enron's star team and partake in the benefits that being one of Enron's best and smartest employees entailed. The high monetary rewards, the ambitious and hard-driving people that the company hired and promoted, and the competitive, results-oriented culture combined to give Enron a reputation not only for trampling competitors at every opportunity but also for internal ruthlessness.

The company's super-aggressiveness and win-at-all-costs mind-set nurtured a culture that gradually and then more rapidly fostered the erosion of ethical standards, eventually making a mockery of the company's stated values of integrity and respect. When it became evident in the fall of 2001 that Enron was a house of cards propped up by deceitful accounting and a myriad of unsavory practices, the company imploded in a matter of weeks—the biggest bankruptcy of all time cost investors $64 billion in losses (between August 2000, when the stock price was at its five-year high, and November 2001), and Enron employees lost their retirement assets, which were almost totally invested in Enron stock.

Business Ethics in the Global Community

Notions of right and wrong, fair and unfair, moral and immoral, ethical and unethical are present in all societies, organizations, and individuals. Some concepts of what is right and what is wrong are *universal* and *transcend most all cultures.* For instance, being truthful (or not lying) strikes a chord of what's right in the peoples of all nations. Demonstrating integrity of character, not cheating, and treating people with dignity and respect are concepts that resonate with people of most religions and cultures. Most people believe that companies should not pillage or degrade the environment in the course of conducting their operations. Most people would concur that it is unethical to expose workers to toxic chemicals and hazardous materials. But the school of *ethical relativism* holds that there are important instances in which what is deemed fair or unfair, what constitutes proper regard for human rights, and what is considered ethical or unethical in business situations varies from one society or country to another. Hence, so this school of thought contends, there are occasions when cultural norms and the circumstances of the situation determine whether certain actions or behaviors are right or wrong.

> **core concept**
> The school of *ethical universalism* holds that human nature is the same everywhere and thus that ethical rules are cross-cultural; the school of *ethical relativism* holds that different societal cultures and customs give rise to divergent values and ethical principles of right and wrong.

Cross-Culture Variability in Ethical Standards   Religious beliefs, historic traditions, social customs, and prevailing political and economic doctrines (whether a country leans more toward a capitalistic market economy or one heavily dominated by socialistic or communistic principles) all affect what is deemed ethical or unethical in a particular society or country. Moreover, there are differences in the degree to which some ethical behaviors are considered more important than others. In Japan, China, and other Asian societies, for instance, there's a strong ethic of loyalty to work groups and corporations; such fidelity stems from Confucianism and centuries-long traditions that hold that one's primary obligation is not to oneself but rather to family, clan, government, and employer.[8] In Japan, such beliefs translate into high cultural expectations that company personnel will exhibit strong loyalty to superiors and to their employer. Japanese employees, believing in the importance of loyalty to their employer, are therefore unlikely to blow the whistle when they see their company engage in wrongdoing. Moreover, some Japanese corporations will fire an employee for breach of loyalty if the employee simply interviews for a job with another firm. In Italy, people are relatively carefree; they live for the moment and are generally willing to take chances about what the future will bring. As a consequence, an Italian manager may be disinclined to keep a promise or fulfill contractual obligations; further, there are often low levels of trust between parties in business deals and honest communications are frequently lacking.[9] In China, there's greater societal toleration of child labor, dangerous working conditions, and passing off fake or inferior products than in some other parts of the world. In addition, since China's history is more tied to the functioning of a planned or socialist economy, there is no strong concept of what constitutes moral or ethical behavior in free market transactions—some Chinese ethicists even contend that traditional concepts of morality are irrelevant insofar as behavior in a market economy is concerned because the manner in which competitive markets operate is inherently amoral.[10] One study revealed that managers in Hong Kong rank taking credit for another's work and accomplishments at the top of a list of unethical behaviors and, in contrast to managers in Western cultures, considered it more unethical than bribery or illicitly obtaining information about competitors.[11] In Mexico, nepotism (favoritism based on family or social ties) is more acceptable than in the United States or many other countries.

In the former Soviet Union, decades of authoritarian government rule and socialistic traditions created a system where Communist Party officials issued a blizzard of rules and orders about how industries were to operate in the planned economy. Bribes and favors were frequently used to get governmental officials to act favorably. Because Soviet managers found it onerous and sometimes impossible to comply with all the various dictates, many of which were conflicting or inefficient, they routinely broke rules, manipulated production data, fabricated accounts, and traded favors in the course of conducting operations. Since the collapse of communist rule and the breakup of the Soviet Union in the late 1980s, many Russian people, long accustomed to the communist idea that people are supposed to work for the collective good of society, have exhibited considerable mistrust of how business is conducted in Russia. Such views are particularly understandable given that the actions of some Russian businesspeople have proved wildly corrupt based on ethical standards in the U.S. and Western Europe, with unethical practices being more the norm than the exception.

Thus, apart from certain universal basics—honesty, trustworthiness, fairness, avoiding unnecessary harm, and respecting the environment—there are variations in what societies generally agree to be right and wrong in the conduct of business activities, and certainly there are cross-country variations in the *degree* to which certain behaviors are considered unethical.[12] As a consequence of these cross-country variations and conflicting interpretations of what exactly constitutes fairness, trustworthiness, integrity, and so on, some people argue that there are few absolutes when it comes to business ethics and thus few ethical absolutes for consistently judging a company's conduct in various countries and markets. See Illustration Capsule 10.1 for examples of business situations in which cultures and local customs have clashed on ethical standards.

The view that what constitutes ethical or unethical conduct can vary according to time, circumstance, local cultural norms, and religious convictions leads to the conclusion that there is no objective way to *prove* that some countries or cultures are correct and others are wrong about proper business ethics. *To some extent,* therefore, there is merit in the school of ethical relativism's view that what is deemed right or wrong, fair or unfair, moral or immoral, ethical or unethical in business situations has to be viewed in the context of each country's local customs, religious traditions, and societal norms. On the one hand, a company has to be very cautious about exporting its home-country values and ethics to foreign countries where it operates—"photocopying" ethics is disrespectful of other countries and neglects the important role of moral free space. On the other hand, there are occasions when the rule of "When in Rome, do as the Romans do" is ethically and morally wrong regardless of local customs, traditions, and norms.

Consider, for instance, the following example: In 1992, the owners of the SS *United States,* an aging luxury ocean liner constructed with asbestos in the 1940s, had the liner towed to Turkey, where a contractor had agreed to remove the asbestos for $2 million (versus a far higher cost in the United States, where asbestos removal safety

illustration capsule 10.1
When Cultures Clash on Ethical Standards: Some Examples

The following three examples illustrate the perplexing gray zone that global managers must navigate when two sets of ethical standards meet across cultures:

- You are a manager of a chain of fast-food restaurants in Russia, in partnership with a Russian company. One day you discover that a senior officer of your Russian joint venture partner has been "borrowing" equipment from the joint venture company and utilizing it in another of his business ventures. When you confront him, the Russian partner defends his actions, arguing that as an owner of both companies he is entitled to share use of the equipment.

- In preparing a bid for a multimillion-dollar contract in a foreign country, you are introduced to a "consultant" who offers to help you in submitting the bid and negotiating with the customer company. You learn in conversing with the consultant that she is well connected in local government and business circles and knows key personnel in the customer company extremely well. The consultant quotes you a six-figure fee. Later,

your local coworkers tell you that the use of such consultants is normal in this country—and that a large fraction of the fee will go directly to people working for the customer company. They further inform you that bidders who reject the help of such consultants have lost contracts to competitors who employed them.

- You are the sales manager at a U.S. sleepwear manufacturing company. Company personnel discover that the chemicals used to flameproof your line of children's pajamas might cause cancer if absorbed through the skin. After these pajamas are banned from sale in the United States, you discover that the children's pajamas in inventory and the remaining flameproof material can be sold to sleepwear distributors in Asia, where there are no restrictions against the material's use. The senior executives of the company learn of this opportunity and expect you to sell the inventories of banned pajamas and flameproof materials to the foreign distributors.

Sources: Thomas Donaldson and Thomas W. Dunfee, "When Ethics Travel: The Promise and Peril of Global Business Ethics," *California Management Review* 41, no. 4 (Summer 1999), p. 45; and James E. Post, Anne T. Lawrence, and James Weber, *Business and Society: Corporate Strategy, Public Policy, Ethics,* 10th ed. (Burr Ridge, IL: McGraw-Hill/Irwin, 2002), p. 115.

standards were much more stringent).[13] When Turkish officials blocked the asbestos removal because of the dangers to workers of contracting cancer, the owners had the liner towed to the Black Sea port of Sevastopol, in the Crimean Republic, where the asbestos removal standards were quite lax and where a contractor had agreed to remove more than 500,000 square feet of carcinogenic asbestos for less than $2 million.

Few people would argue that exposing workers to carcinogenic asbestos is ethically correct, irrespective of what a country's law allows or the value the country places on worker safety. Likewise, many would argue that standards for judging honesty, integrity, trustworthiness, and fairness travel quite well across countries and are *universal.* According to this view, basic moral standards really do not vary *significantly* according to time, circumstance, local cultural beliefs, and religious convictions, thus making it feasible for a multinational company to have a code of ethics that can be applied more or less evenly across countries.[14]

The Payment of Bribes and Kickbacks   One of the thorniest ethical problems that multinational companies face is the degree of cross-country variability in paying bribes as part of business transactions. In many countries in Eastern Europe, Africa, Latin America, and Asia, it is customary to pay bribes to government officials in order to win a government contract or to facilitate a business transaction. In some developing nations, it is difficult for any company, foreign or domestic, to move goods through customs without paying off low-level officials.[15] Likewise, in many countries it is normal

table 10.1   **Perceived Degree of Governmental Corruption in Selected Countries, as Measured by a Composite Corruption Perceptions Index (CPI), 2002** (A CPI Score of 10 is "highly clean" and a score of 0 is "highly corrupt.")

Country	2002 CPI Score*	90% Confidence Range	Number of Surveys Used	Country	2002 CPI Score*	90% Confidence Range	Number of Surveys Used
Finland	9.7	9.5–9.9	8	Uruguay	5.1	4.6–5.6	5
Denmark	9.5	9.3–9.7	8	Malaysia	4.9	4.6–5.2	11
New Zealand	9.5	9.3–9.6	8	South Africa	4.8	4.5–5.0	11
Sweden	9.3	9.2–9.4	10	South Korea	4.5	3.9–5.1	12
Canada	9.0	8.9–9.2	10	Brazil	4.0	3.8–4.2	10
Netherlands	9.0	8.8–9.1	9	Peru	4.0	3.7–4.4	7
Great Britain	8.7	8.4–8.9	11	Czech Republic	3.7	3.3–4.2	10
Australia	8.6	8.0–9.0	11	Mexico	3.6	3.3–3.9	10
Norway	8.5	8.0–8.9	8	China	3.5	3.1–4.1	11
Switzerland	8.5	7.9–8.9	9	Argentina	2.7	2.5–3.1	10
Hong Kong	8.2	7.8–8.6	11	India	2.7	2.5–2.9	12
United States	7.7	7.2–8.0	12	Russia	2.7	2.3–3.3	12
Chile	7.5	7.0–7.9	10	Pakistan	2.6	1.7–3.3	3
Germany	7.3	6.7–7.7	10	Philippines	2.6	2.4–2.9	11
Israel	7.3	6.7–7.7	9	Vietnam	2.4	2.0–2.9	7
Japan	7.1	6.6–7.4	12	Indonesia	1.9	1.7–2.2	12
Spain	7.1	6.5–7.6	10	Kenya	1.9	1.7–2.2	5
France	6.3	5.9–6.8	10	Paraguay	1.7	1.5–1.8	3
Italy	5.2	4.6–5.7	11	Bangladesh	1.2	0.7–1.6	5

Note: The CPI score ranges between 10 (highly clean) and 0 (highly corrupt); the data were collected between 2000 and 2002 and represent a composite of multiple sources, as indicated in the number of surveys used. The CPI represents the perceptions of well-informed people regarding the frequency of corrupt payments, the value of bribes paid, and the resulting obstacles to businesses.

Source: Transparency International, *2003 Global Corruption Report,* www.globalcorruptionreport.org, accessed October 1, 2003, pp. 265–66.

to make payments to prospective customers in order to win or retain their business. According to a 1999 *Wall Street Journal* report, 30 to 60 percent of all business transactions in Eastern Europe involved paying bribes, and the costs of bribe payments averaged 2 to 8 percent of revenues.[16] The 2003 *Global Corruption Report,* sponsored by Berlin-based Transparency International, found that corruption among public officials and in business transactions is widespread across the world. Table 10.1 shows some of the countries where corruption is believed to be lowest and highest. Table 10.2 presents data showing the perceived likelihood that companies in the 21 largest exporting countries are paying bribes to win business in the markets of 15 emerging markets. Table 10.3 indicates that bribery was perceived to occur most often in public works contracts and construction and in the arms and defense industry. On a scale of 1 to 10, where 10 indicates negligible bribery, even the "cleanest" industry sectors—agriculture, light manufacturing, and fisheries—only had "passable" scores of 5.9, indicating that bribes are quite likely a common occurrence in these sectors as well.

Companies that forbid the payment of bribes and kickbacks in their codes of ethical conduct and that are serious about enforcing this prohibition face a formidable challenge in those countries where bribery and kickback payments have been

table 10.2 **The Degree to Which Companies in Major Exporting Countries Are Perceived to Be Paying Bribes in Doing Business Abroad**

Rank/ Country	Bribe Payers Index (10 = low; 0 = high)	Rank/ Country	Bribe Payers Index (10 = low; 0 = high)
1. Australia	8.5	12. France	5.5
2. Sweden	8.4	13. United States	5.3
3. Switzerland	8.4	14. Japan	5.3
4. Austria	8.2	15. Malaysia	4.3
5. Canada	8.1	16. Hong Kong	4.3
6. Netherlands	7.8	17. Italy	4.1
7. Belgium	7.8	18. South Korea	3.9
8. Britain	6.9	19. Taiwan	3.8
9. Singapore	6.3	20. China (excluding Hong Kong)	3.5
10. Germany	6.3	21. Russia	3.2
11. Spain	5.8		

Note: The Bribe Payers Index is based on a questionnaire developed by Transparency International and a survey of some 835 private sector leaders in 15 emerging countries accounting for 60 percent of all imports into non–Organization for Economic Cooperation and Development countries—actual polling was conducted by Gallup International.
Source: Transparency International, *2003 Global Corruption Report,* www.globalcorruptionreport.org, accessed October 1, 2003, p. 267.

entrenched as a local custom for decades and are not considered unethical by many people. The same goes for multinational companies that do business in countries where bribery is illegal and also in countries where bribery and kickbacks are tolerated or customary. Some people say that bribes and kickbacks are no different from tipping for service at restaurants—whether you tip for service at dinner, make payments to government officials to get goods through customs, or give kickbacks to customers to retain their business, you pay for a service rendered.

U.S. companies are prohibited by the Foreign Corrupt Practices Act (FCPA) from paying bribes to government officials, political parties, political candidates, or others in all countries where they do business; the FCPA requires U.S. companies with foreign operations to adopt accounting practices that ensure full disclosure of a company's transactions so that illegal payments can be detected. The 35 member countries of the Organization for Economic Cooperation and Development (OECD) in 1997 adopted a convention to combat bribery in international business transactions; the Anti-Bribery Convention obligated the countries to criminalize the bribery of foreign public officials, including payments made to political parties and party officials. However, so far there has been little or no enforcement of the OECD convention and the payment of bribes in global business transactions remains a common practice in many countries.

Cross-country variability in business conduct and ethical standards makes it a formidable challenge for multinational companies to educate and motivate their employees worldwide to respect the customs and traditions of other nations and, at the same time, adhere to the company's own particular code of ethical behavior. At the level most managers confront it, bribery has no satisfactory solution.[17] Refusing to pay bribes or kickbacks is very often tantamount to losing business. Frequently, the sales and profits are lost to more unscrupulous companies, with the result that both ethical companies and ethical individuals are penalized. Sometimes subtle cross-country differences in what is deemed ethically right or wrong make it tough to draw a line in the sand between right and wrong decisions, actions, and business practices.

table 10.3   **Bribery in Different Industries**

Business Sector	Bribery Score (10 = low bribery; 0 = high bribery)
Agriculture	5.9
Light manufacturing	5.9
Fisheries	5.9
Information technology	5.1
Forestry	5.1
Civilian aerospace	4.9
Banking and finance	4.7
Heavy manufacturing	4.5
Pharmaceuticals/medical care	4.3
Transportation/storage	4.3
Mining	4.0
Power generation/transmission	3.7
Telecommunications	3.7
Real estate/property	3.5
Oil and gas	2.7
Arms and defense	1.9
Public works/construction	1.3

Note: The bribery scores for each industry are based on a questionnaire developed by Transparency International and a survey of some 835 private sector leaders in 15 emerging countries accounting for 60 percent of all imports into non–Organization for Economic Cooperation and Development countries—actual polling was conducted by Gallup International.

Source: Transparency International, *2003 Global Corruption Report*, www.globalcorruption-report.org, accessed October 1, 2003, p. 268.

Determining What Is Ethical When Local Standards Vary   But while it is indisputable that cultural differences abound in global business activities and that these cultural differences sometimes give rise to differences in ethical principles and standards, might it be the case that in many instances of cross-country differences one side is "more right" than the other? If so, then the task of the multinational manager is to discover what the right ethical standards are and act accordingly. A good example is the payment of bribes and kickbacks. Yes, bribes and kickbacks seem to be common in some countries, but does this justify paying them? Just because bribery flourishes in a country does not mean that it is an authentic or legitimate ethical norm. Virtually all of the world's major religions (Buddhism, Christianity, Confucianism, Hinduism, Islam, Judaism, Sikhism, and Taoism) and moral schools of thought condemn bribery and corruption.[18] Bribery is commonplace in India but interviews with Indian CEOs whose companies constantly engaged in payoffs indicated disgust for the practice and they expressed no illusions about its impropriety.[19] Therefore, a multinational company might reasonably conclude that the right ethical standard is one of refusing to engage in bribery and kickbacks no matter what the local custom is.

> Managers in multinational enterprises have to figure out how to navigate the gray zone that arises when operating in two cultures with two sets of ethics.

A company that elects to conform to local ethical standards necessarily assumes that what prevails as local morality is an adequate guide to ethical behavior. This can be ethically dangerous—it leads to the conclusion that if a country's culture is accepting of bribery or environmental degradation or exposing workers to dangerous conditions (toxic chemicals or bodily harm), then so much the worse for honest people and protection of the environment and safe working conditions. Granting an *automatic* preference to local country ethical norms can thus present vexing problems to company managers when the ethical standards followed in a foreign country are lower than those in its home country or in the company's code of ethics —sometimes there can be no compromise on what is ethical and what is not. Yet the notion of a self-righteous multinational company as the standard-bearer of moral truth is also scary—common sense suggests there ought to be room for *legitimate* local norms and opportunity for host country cultures to exert some influence in setting their own moral and ethical standards.

Approaches to Managing a Company's Ethical Conduct

The stance a company takes in dealing with or managing ethical conduct at any given point can take any of four basic forms:[20]

- The unconcerned or nonissue approach.
- The damage control approach.
- The compliance approach.
- The ethical culture approach.

The differences in these four approaches are discussed briefly below and summarized in Table 10.4.

The Unconcerned or Nonissue Approach   The unconcerned approach is prevalent at companies whose executives are immoral and unintentionally amoral. Companies using this approach ascribe to the view that business ethics is an oxymoron in a dog-eat-dog, survival-of-the-fittest world and that under-the-table dealing can be good business. They believe the business of business is business, not ethics and that if the law permits so-called "unethical behavior" and if others are doing it too, why stand on ethical principles (when in Rome do as the Romans do). Companies in this mode are usually out to make the greatest possible profit at most any cost and the strategies they employ, while legal, may well embrace elements that are ethically shady or unsavory—for them, ethics is a nonissue.

The Damage Control Approach   Damage control is favored at companies whose managers are intentionally amoral but who fear scandal and are desirous of containing any adverse fallout from claims that the company's strategy has unethical components or that company personnel engage in unethical practices. Companies using this approach, not wanting to risk tarnishing the reputations of key personnel or the company, usually make some concession to window-dressing ethics, going so far as to adopt a code of ethics—so that their executives can point to it as evidence of their ethical commitment should any ethical lapses on the company's part be exposed. Managers at these companies may opt to incorporate unethical elements into the company's strategy as long as those elements can be explained away or kept under wraps. Although unethical practices are not endorsed, executives look the other way when shady behavior occurs—management's stance is one of "See no evil, hear no evil, speak no evil" (except when there's great risk of fallout from inaction). Thus they may condone questionable actions that help the company reach earnings targets or bolster its market standing—such as pressuring customers to stock up on the company's product (channel stuffing), making under-the-table payments to win new business, stonewalling the recall of products claimed to be unsafe, bad-mouthing the products of rivals, or trying to keep prices low by sourcing goods from disreputable suppliers in low-wage countries that run sweatshop operations or use child labor.

table 10.4   **Four Approaches to Managing Business Ethics**

	Unconcerned Approach	Damage Control Approach	Compliance Approach	Ethical Culture Approach
Underlying beliefs	• The business of business is business, not ethics. • Ethics has no place in the conduct of business. • Companies should not be morally accountable for their actions.	• Need to make a token gesture in the direction of ethical standards (a code of ethics).	• Company must be committed to ethical standards and monitoring ethics performance. • Unethical behavior must be prevented and punished if discovered. • A reputation for high ethical standards is important.	• Ethics is basic to the culture. • Behaving ethically must be a deeply held corporate value and become a way of life. • Everyone is expected to walk the talk.
Means of dealing with ethics issues	• There's no need to make decisions concerning business ethics—if it's legal, it is okay. • No intervention regarding the ethical component of decisions is needed.	• Act to protect the company against the dangers of unethical strategies and behavior. • Ignore unethical behavior or allow it to go unpunished unless the situation is extreme and requires action.	• Establish a clear, comprehensive code of ethics. • Prevent unethical behavior. • Provide ethics training for all personnel. • The company has an ethics compliance office, a chief ethics officer, and formal ethics compliance procedures.	• Ethical behavior is ingrained and reinforced as part of the culture. • Rely on coworker peer pressure— "That's not how we do things here." • Everyone is an ethics watchdog— whistle-blowing is required. • Ethics heroes are celebrated; ethics stories are told.
Challenges in trying to make the approach work	• Financial consequences can become unaffordable. • Some stakeholders are alienated.	• Credibility problems with stakeholders can arise. • The company is susceptible to ethical scandal. • The company has a subpar ethical reputation— executives don't walk the talk.	• Organization members come to rely on the existing rules for moral guidance—fosters a mentality of what is not forbidden is allowed. • Rules and guidelines proliferate. • The locus of moral control resides in the code and in the ethics compliance system rather than in an individual's own moral responsibility for ethical behavior.	• New employees must receive an ethics induction. • Formal ethics management systems receive less emphasis. • Relying on peer pressures and cultural norms to enforce ethical standards can result in eliminating some or many of the compliance trappings and, over time, induce moral laxness.

Source: Adapted from Gedeon J. Rossouw and Leon J. van Vuuren, "Modes of Managing Morality: A Descriptive Model of Strategies for Managing Ethics," *Journal of Business Ethics* 46, no. 4 (September 2003), pp. 392–93. Reprinted with kind permission of Kluwer Academic Publishers.

The main objective of the damage control approach is to protect against adverse publicity brought on by angry or vocal stakeholders, outside investigation, threats of litigation, or punitive government action—hence the need to make token gestures toward rejecting unethical behavior and instituting modest corporate governance safeguards. But at companies in a damage-control mode, employees do not operate within a strong ethical context. There's a gap between talking ethics and walking ethics. The company's code of ethics, if any, exists merely as nice words on paper. Employees quickly get the message that rule-bending is tolerated, if not condoned, and that unethical behavior will go unpunished (or may even be rewarded) unless it results in egregious harm or scandal that cannot be ignored.

The Compliance Approach   Anywhere from light to forceful compliance is favored at companies whose managers (1) lean toward being somewhat amoral but are highly concerned about having ethically upstanding reputations or (2) are moral and see strong compliance methods as the best way to impose and enforce ethical rules and high ethical standards. Companies that adopt a compliance mode usually do some or all of the following to display their commitment to ethical conduct: make the code of ethics a visible and regular part of communications with employees, implement ethics training programs, appoint a chief ethics officer or ethics ombudsperson, have ethics committees to give guidance on ethics matters, institute formal procedures for investigating alleged ethics violations, conduct ethics audits to measure and document compliance, give ethics awards to employees for outstanding efforts to create an ethical climate and improve ethical performance, and/or try to deter violations by setting up ethics hotlines for anonymous callers to use in reporting possible violations.

Emphasis here is usually on securing broad compliance and measuring the degree to which ethical standards are upheld and observed. However, violators are disciplined and sometimes subjected to public reprimand and punishment (including dismissal). The driving force behind the company's commitment to eradicate unethical behavior normally stems from a desire to avoid the cost and damage associated with unethical conduct or else a quest to gain favor from stakeholders (especially ethically conscious customers, employees, and investors) for having a highly regarded reputation for ethical behavior. One of the weaknesses of the compliance approach is that moral control resides in the company's code of ethics and in the ethics compliance system rather than in an individual's own moral responsibility for ethical behavior.

The Ethical Culture Approach   At some companies, top executives believe that high ethical principles must be deeply ingrained in the corporate culture and function as guides for "how we do things around here." A company using the ethical culture approach seeks to gain employee buy-in to the company's ethical standards, business principles, and corporate values. The ethical principles embraced in the company's code of ethics and/or in its statement of corporate values are seen as integral to the company's identity and ways of operating—they are at the core of the company's soul and are promoted as part of "business as usual." The integrity of the ethical culture approach depends heavily on the ethical integrity of the executives who create and nurture the culture—it is incumbent on them to determine how high the bar is to be set and to exemplify ethical standards in their own decisions and behavior. Further, it is essential that the strategy be ethical in all respects and that ethical behavior be ingrained in the means that company personnel employ to execute the strategy.

Many of the trappings used in the compliance approach are also manifest in the ethical culture mode, but one other is added—strong peer pressure from coworkers to observe ethical norms. Thus, responsibility for ethics compliance is widely dispersed throughout all levels of management and the rank-and-file. Stories of former and current moral heroes are kept in circulation, and the deeds of company personnel who display ethical values and are dedicated to walking the talk are celebrated at internal company events. The message that ethics matters—and matters a lot—resounds loudly and clearly throughout the organization and in its strategy and decisions. However, one of the challenges to overcome in the ethical culture approach is relying too heavily on peer pressures and cultural norms to enforce ethics compliance rather than on an individual's own moral responsibility for ethical behavior—absent unrelenting peer pressure or strong internal compliance systems, there is a danger that over time company personnel may become lax about its ethical standards.

Why a Company Can Change Its Ethics Management Approach   Regardless of the approach they have used to managing ethical conduct, a company's executives may sense they have exhausted a particular mode's potential for managing ethics and that they need to become more forceful in their approach to ethics management. Such changes typically occur when the company's ethical failures have made the headlines and created an embarrassing situation for company officials or when the business climate changes. For example, the recent raft of corporate scandals, coupled with aggressive enforcement of anticorruption legislation such as the Sarbanes-Oxley Act of 2002 (which addresses corporate governance and accounting practices), has prompted numerous executives and boards of directors to clean up their acts in accounting and financial reporting, review their ethical standards, and tighten up ethics compliance procedures. Intentionally amoral managers using the unconcerned or nonissue approach to ethics management may see less risk in shifting to the damage control approach (or, for appearance's sake, maybe a "light" compliance mode). Senior managers who have employed the damage control mode may be motivated by bad experiences to mend their ways and shift to a compliance mode. In the wake of so many corporate scandals, companies in the compliance mode may move closer to the ethical culture approach.

Why Should Company Strategies Be Ethical?

There are two reasons why a company's strategy should be ethical: (1) because a strategy that is unethical in whole or in part is morally wrong and reflects badly on the character of the company personnel involved and (2) because an ethical strategy is good business and in the self-interest of shareholders.

Managers do not dispassionately assess what strategic course to steer. Ethical strategy making generally begins with managers who themselves have strong character (i.e., who are honest, have integrity, are ethical, and truly care about how they conduct the company's business). Managers with high ethical principles and standards are usually advocates of a corporate code of ethics and strong ethics compliance, and they are typically genuinely committed to certain corporate values and business principles. They walk the talk in displaying the company's stated values and living up to its business principles and ethical standards. They understand there's a big difference between adopting values statements and codes of ethics that serve merely as window dressing and those that truly paint the white lines for a company's actual strategy and business conduct. As a consequence, ethically strong managers consciously opt for strategic actions that can pass moral scrutiny—they display no tolerance for strategies with ethically controversial components.

But there are solid business reasons to adopt ethical strategies even if most company managers are not of strong moral character and personally committed to high ethical standards. Pursuing unethical strategies puts a company's reputation at high risk and can do lasting damage. The experiences at Enron, WorldCom, Tyco, HealthSouth, Rite Aid, Qwest Communications, Arthur Andersen, and several other companies illustrate that when top executives devise shady strategies or wink at unethical behavior, the impact on the company can be severe and sometimes devastating. Coca-Cola was sorely embarrassed when it came to light that company personnel had rigged a marketing test of Frozen Coke at several Burger King restaurants to make it appear that consumer response was better than it really was—an outside firm was hired to spend up to $10,000 to goose demand for Frozen Coke and other frozen drinks at Burger King restaurants taking part in the test promotion. Given the results of the test, Burger King invested $65 million to make Frozen Coke and other frozen carbonated beverages a standard menu item starting in 1999. The marketing fraud came to light in February 2003 when a Coca-Cola finance manager sent a letter to Coca-Cola's CEO with detailed claims that metal shavings were getting into its Frozen Coke drinks and that there were assorted other problems with the company's marketing programs and accounting. A month later the employee was laid off, along with 1,000 other Coke employees, as part of a restructuring effort. In July 2003, four months after the marketing test fraud came to light and following several years of disappointing sales, Burger King began phasing out Frozen Coke. Coca-Cola later paid $540,000 to settle a lawsuit filed by the laid-off finance manager and offered Burger King $21 million as part of an apology.

Rehabilitating a company's shattered reputation is time-consuming and costly. Customers shun companies known for their shady behavior. Companies with reputations for unethical conduct have considerable difficulty in recruiting and retaining talented employees. Most hardworking, ethically upstanding people are repulsed by a work environment where unethical behavior is condoned; they don't want to get entrapped in a compromising situation, nor do they want their personal reputations tarnished by the actions of an unsavory employer. A 1997 survey revealed that 42 percent of the respondents took into account a company's ethics when deciding whether to accept a job.[21] Creditors are usually unnerved by the unethical actions of a borrower because of the potential business fallout and subsequent risk of default on any loans. To some significant degree, therefore, companies recognize that ethical strategies and ethical conduct are good business. Most companies have strategies that pass the test of being ethical, and most companies are aware that both their reputations and their long-term well-being are tied to conducting their business in a manner that wins the approval of suppliers, employees, investors, and society at large.

> Conducting business in an ethical fashion is in a company's enlightened self-interest.

Illustration Capsule 10.2 describes elements of the strategies that three of the world's most prominent investment banking firms employed to attract new clients and reward the executives of existing clients—judge for yourself whether what they did was ethical or shady.

Linking a Company's Strategy to Its Ethical Principles and Core Values

Many companies have officially adopted a code of ethical conduct and a statement of company values. But there's a big difference between having a code of ethics and a values statement that serve merely as a public window dressing and having ethical standards and corporate values that truly paint the white lines for a company's actual strategy and business conduct. If ethical standards and statements of core values are to

illustration capsule 10.2
Strategies to Gain New Business at Wall Street Investment Banking Firms: Ethical or Unethical?

At Salomon Smith Barney (a subsidiary of Citigroup), Credit Suisse First Boston (CSFB), and Goldman Sachs (three of the world's most prominent investment banking companies), part of the strategy for securing the investment banking business of large corporate clients (to handle the sale of new stock issues or new bond issues or advise on mergers and acquisitions) involved (1) hyping the stocks of companies that were actual or prospective customers of their investment banking services, and (2) allocating hard-to-get shares of hot new initial public offerings (IPOs) to select executives and directors of existing and potential client companies, who then made millions of dollars in profits when the stocks went up once public trading began. Former WorldCom CEO Bernie Ebbers reportedly made more than $11 million in trading profits over a four-year period on shares of IPOs received from Salomon Smith Barney; Salomon served as WorldCom's investment banker on a variety of deals during this period. Jack Grubman, Salomon's top-paid research analyst at the time, enthusiastically touted WorldCom stock and was regarded as the company's biggest cheerleader on Wall Street.

To help draw in business from new or existing corporate clients, CSFB established brokerage accounts for corporate executives who steered their company's investment banking business to CSFB. Apparently, CSFB's strategy for acquiring more business involved promising the CEO and/or CFO of companies about to go public for the first time or needing to issue new long-term bonds that if CSFB was chosen to handle their company's new initial public offering of common stock or a new bond issue, then CSFB would ensure they would be allocated shares at the initial offering price of all subsequent IPOs in which CSFB was a participant. During 1999–2000, it was common for the stock of a hot new IPO to rise 100 to 500 percent above the

initial offering price in the first few days or weeks of public trading; the shares allocated to these executives were then sold for a tidy profit over the initial offering price. According to investigative sources, CSFB increased the number of companies whose executives were allowed to participate in its IPO offerings from 26 companies in January 1999 to 160 companies in early 2000; executives received anywhere from 200 to 1,000 shares each of every IPO in which CSFB was a participant in 2000. CSFB's accounts for these executives reportedly generated profits of about $80 million for the participants. Apparently, it was CSFB's practice to curtail access to IPOs for some executives if their companies didn't come through with additional securities business for CSFB or if CSFB concluded that other securities offerings by these companies would be unlikely.

Goldman Sachs also used an IPO-allocation scheme to attract investment banking business, giving shares to executives at 21 companies—among the participants were the CEOs of eBay, Yahoo, and Ford Motor Company. EBay's CEO was a participant in over 100 IPOs managed by Goldman during the 1996–2000 period and was on Goldman's board of directors part of this time; eBay paid Goldman Sachs $8 million in fees for services during the 1996–2001 period.

QUESTIONS TO CONSIDER:

1. If you were a top executive at Salomon Smith Barney, CSFB, or Goldman Sachs, would you be proud to defend your company's actions?

2. Would you want to step forward and take credit for having been a part of the group who designed or approved of the strategy for gaining new business at any of these three firms?

Sources: Charles Gasparino, "Salomon Probe Includes Senior Executives," *The Wall Street Journal,* September 3, 2002, p. C1; Randall Smith and Susan Pulliam, "How a Star Banker Pressed for IPOs," *The Wall Street Journal,* September 4, 2002, pp. C1, C14; Randall Smith and Susan Pulliam, "How a Technology-Banking Star Doled Out Shares of Hot IPOs," *The Wall Street Journal,* September 23; 2002, pp. A1, A10; and Randall Smith, "Goldman Sachs Faces Scrutiny for IPO-Allocation Practices," *The Wall Street Journal,* October 3, 2002, pp. A1, A6.

have more than a cosmetic role, boards of directors and top executives must work diligently to see that they are scrupulously observed in crafting the company's strategy and conducting every facet of the company's business. In other words, living up to the ethical principles and displaying the core values in actions and decisions must become a way of life at the company.

Indeed, the litmus test of whether a company's code of ethics and statement of core values are cosmetic is the extent to which they are embraced in crafting strategy and in operating the business on a day-to-day basis. It is up to senior executives to walk the talk and make a point of considering two sets of questions whenever a new strategic initiative is under review:

- Is what we are proposing to do fully compliant with our code of ethical conduct? Is there anything here that could be considered ethically objectionable?
- Is it apparent that this proposed action is in harmony with our core values? Are any conflicts or concerns evident?

Unless questions of this nature are posed—either in open discussion or by force of habit in the minds of strategy makers—then there's room for strategic initiatives to become disconnected from the company's code of ethics and stated core values. If a company's executives are ethically principled and believe strongly in living up to the company's stated core values, there's a good chance they will pose these types of questions and reject strategic initiatives that don't measure up. There's also a good chance that strategic actions will be scrutinized for their compatibility with ethical standards and core values when the latter are so deeply ingrained in a company's culture and in the everyday conduct of company personnel that they are automatically taken into account in all that the company does. However, in companies with window-dressing ethics and core values or in companies headed by immoral or amoral managers, any strategy-ethics-values linkage stems mainly from a desire to avoid the risk of embarrassment, scandal, and possible disciplinary action should strategy-makers get called on the carpet and held accountable for approving an unethical strategic initiative.

> **core concept**
> More attention is paid to linking strategy with ethical principles and core values in companies headed by moral executives and in companies where ethical principles and core values are a way of life.

STRATEGY AND SOCIAL RESPONSIBILITY

The idea that businesses have an obligation to foster social betterment, a much-debated topic in the past 40 years, took root in the 19th century when progressive companies in the aftermath of the industrial revolution began to provide workers with housing and other amenities. The notion that corporate executives should balance the interests of all stakeholders—shareholders, employees, customers, suppliers, the communities in which they operated, and society at large—began to blossom in the 1960s. A group of chief executives of America's 200 largest corporations, calling themselves the Business Roundtable, promoted the concept of corporate social responsibility. In 1981, the Roundtable's "Statement on Corporate Responsibility" said:[22]

> **core concept**
> The notion of *social responsibility* as it applies to businesses concerns a company's *duty* to operate by means that avoid harm to stakeholders and the environment and, further, to consider the overall betterment of society in its decisions and actions.

> Balancing the shareholder's expectations of maximum return against other priorities is one of the fundamental problems confronting corporate management. The shareholder must receive a good return but the legitimate concerns of other constituencies (customers, employees, communities, suppliers and society at large) also must have the appropriate attention . . . [Leading managers] believe that by giving enlightened consideration to balancing the legitimate claims of all its constituents, a corporation will best serve the interest of its shareholders.

Today, corporate social responsibility is a concept that resonates in Western Europe, the United States, Canada, and such developing nations as Brazil and India.

figure 10.1   **Categories of Socially Responsible Business Behavior**

Source: Adapted from material in Ronald Paul Hill, Debra Stephens, and Iain Smith, "Corporate Social Responsibility: An Examination of Individual Firm Behavior," *Business and Society Review* 108, no. 3 (September 2003), p. 348.

What Do We Mean by Social Responsibility?

The essence of socially responsible business behavior is that a company should strive to balance the benefits of strategic actions to benefit shareholders against any possible adverse impacts on other stakeholders (employees, suppliers, customers, local communities, and society at large) and, further, to proactively mitigate any harmful effects on the environment that its actions and business may have. Social responsibility includes corporate philanthropy and actions to earn the trust and respect of stakeholders for the firm's efforts to improve the general well-being of customers, employees, local communities, society at large, and the environment. As depicted in Figure 10.1, a company's menu for crafting its social responsibility strategy includes:

- *Efforts to employ an ethical strategy and observe ethical principles in operating the business*—A genuine commitment to observing ethical principles is necessary here simply because unethical strategies and conduct are incompatible with the concept of socially responsible business behavior.

- *Making charitable contributions, donating money and the time of company personnel to community service endeavors, supporting various worthy organizational causes, and reaching out to make a difference in the lives of the disadvantaged*—Some companies fulfill their corporate citizenship and community outreach obligations by spreading their efforts over a multitude of charitable and community activities; for instance, Microsoft and Johnson & Johnson support a broad variety of community art, social welfare, and environmental programs. Others prefer to focus their energies more narrowly. McDonald's, for example, concentrates on sponsoring the Ronald McDonald House program (which provides a home away from home for the families of seriously ill children receiving treatment at nearby hospitals), preventing child abuse and neglect, and participating in local community service activities; in 2003, there were 212 Ronald McDonald Houses in 20 countries and more than 5,000 bedrooms available nightly. British Telecom gives 1 percent of its profits directly to communities, largely for education—teacher training, in-school workshops, and digital technology. Leading prescription drug maker GlaxoSmithKline and other pharmaceutical companies either donate or heavily discount medicines for distribution in the least-developed nations. Numerous health-related businesses take a leading role in community activities that promote effective health care. Many companies work closely with community officials to minimize the impact of hiring large numbers of new employees (which could put a strain on local schools and utility services) and to provide outplacement services for laid-off workers. Companies frequently reinforce their philanthropic efforts by encouraging employees to support charitable causes and participate in community affairs, often through programs to match employee contributions.

> Business leaders who want their companies to be regarded as exemplary corporate citizens must not only see that their companies operate ethically but also display a social conscience in decisions that affect employees, the environment, the communities in which they operate, and society at large.

- *Actions to protect or enhance the environment and, in particular, to minimize or eliminate any adverse impact on the environment stemming from the company's own business activities*—Social responsibility as it applies to environmental protection means doing more than what is legally required. From a social responsibility perspective, companies have an obligation to be *stewards of the environment*. This means using the best available science and technology to achieve higher-than-required environmental standards. Even more ideally, it means putting time and money into improving the environment in ways that extend past a company's own industry boundaries—such as participating in recycling projects, adopting energy conservation practices, and supporting efforts to clean up local water supplies. Retailers such as Home Depot in the United States and B&Q in the United Kingdom have pressured their suppliers to adopt stronger environmental protection practices.[23]

- *Actions to create a work environment that enhances the quality of life for employees and makes the company a great place to work*—Numerous companies go beyond providing the ordinary kinds of compensation and exert extra efforts to enhance the quality of life for their employees, both at work and at home. This can include varied and engaging job assignments, career development programs and mentoring, rapid career advancement, appealing compensation incentives, ongoing training to ensure future employability, added decision-making authority, on-site day care, flexible work schedules for single parents, workplace exercise facilities, special leaves to care for sick family members, work-at-home opportunities, gender pay equity, showcase plants and offices, special safety programs, and the like.

- *Actions to build a workforce that is diverse with respect to gender, race, national origin, and perhaps other aspects that different people bring to the workplace*—Most large companies in the United States have established workforce diversity programs, and some go the extra mile to ensure that their workplaces are attractive to ethnic minorities and inclusive of all groups and perspectives. The pursuit of workforce diversity can be good business—Johnson & Johnson, Pfizer, and Coca-Cola believe that a reputation for workforce diversity makes recruiting employees easier (talented employees from diverse backgrounds often seek out such companies). And at Coca-Cola, where strategic success depends on getting people all over the world to become loyal consumers of the company's beverages, efforts to build a public persona of inclusiveness for people of all races, religions, nationalities, interests, and talents has considerable strategic value. Multinational companies are particularly inclined to make workforce diversity a visible strategic component; they recognize that respecting individual differences and promoting inclusiveness resonate well with people all around the world. At a few companies the diversity initiative extends to suppliers—sourcing items from small businesses owned by women or ethnic minorities.

Linking Strategy and Social Responsibility

While striving to be socially responsible entails choosing from the menu outlined in the preceding section, there can be no generic approach to linking a company's strategy and business conduct to social responsibility. It is logical for management to match the company's social responsibility strategy to its core values, business mission, and overall strategy. There's plenty of room for every company to make its own statement about what charitable contributions to make, what kinds of community service projects to emphasize, what environmental actions to support, how to make the company a good place to work, where and how workforce diversity fits into the picture, and what else it will do to support worthy causes and projects that benefit society. Thus, *the combination of socially responsible endeavors a company elects to pursue defines its social responsibility strategy.* However, unless a company's social responsibility initiatives become part of the way it operates its business every day, the initiatives are unlikely to catch fire and be fully effective. As an executive at Royal Dutch/Shell put it, corporate social responsibility "is not a cosmetic; it must be rooted in our values. It must make a difference to the way we do business."[24] Thus some companies are integrating social responsibility objectives into their missions and overall performance targets—they see social performance and environmental metrics as an essential component of judging the company's overall future performance.

> **core concept**
> A company's social responsibility strategy is defined by the specific combination of socially beneficial activities it opts to support with its contributions of time, money, and other resources.

At Starbucks, the commitment to social responsibility is linked to the company's strategy and operating practices via the tagline "Giving back to our communities is the way we do business"; top management makes the theme come alive via the company's extensive community building activities, efforts to protect the welfare of coffee growers and their families (in particular, making sure they receive a fair price), a variety of recycling and environmental conservation practices, and the financial support it provides to charities and the disadvantaged through the Starbucks Foundation. At Green Mountain Coffee Roasters, social responsibility includes fair dealing with suppliers and trying to do something about the poverty of small coffee growers; in its dealings with suppliers at small farmer cooperatives in Peru, Mexico, and Sumatra, Green Mountain pays "fair trade" prices for coffee beans (in 2002, the fair trade prices were a minimum of $1.26 per pound for conventional coffee and $1.41 for organically grown versus market prices of 24 to 50 cents per pound). Green Mountain also purchases about 25 percent of its coffee direct from farmers so as to cut out intermediaries and see that farmers realize a higher price for their efforts—coffee is the world's second most heavily traded commodity after oil, requiring the labor of some 20 million people, most of whom live at the poverty level.[25] At Whole Foods Market, a $3 billion supermarket chain specializing in organic and natural foods, the social responsibility emphasis is on supporting organic farming and sustainable agriculture, recycling, sustainable seafood practices, giving employees paid time off to participate in worthy community service endeavors, and donating 5 percent of after-tax profits in cash or products to charitable causes. At General Mills the social responsibility focus is on service to the community and bettering the employment opportunities for minorities and women. Stonyfield Farm, a producer of yogurt and ice cream products, employs a social responsibility strategy focused on wellness, good nutrition, and "earth-friendly" actions (10 percent of profits are donated to help protect and restore the earth, and yogurt lids are used as mini-billboards to help educate people about environmental issues); in addition, it is stressing the development of an environmentally friendly supply chain, sourcing from farmers that grow organic products and refrain from using artificial hormones in milk production. Chick-Fil-A, an Atlanta-based fast-food chain with 1,000 outlets, has a charitable foundation, supports 12 foster homes and a summer camp (for some 1,500 campers from 22 states and several foreign countries), funds two scholarship programs (including one for employees that has awarded more than $17 million in scholarships), and a closed-on-Sunday policy to ensure that every Chick-Fil-A employee and restaurant operator has an opportunity to worship, spend time with family and friends, or just plain rest from the workweek.[26] Toys "R" Us supports initiatives addressing the issues of child labor and fair labor practices around the world. Community Pride Food Stores is assisting in revitalizing the inner city of Richmond, Virginia, where the company is based.

> Each company's strategic efforts to operate in a socially responsible manner should be custom-tailored, matched to its core values and business mission, thereby representing its own statement about "how we do business and how we intend to fulfill our duties to all stakeholders and society at large."

It is common for companies engaged in natural resource extraction, electric power production, forestry and paper products, motor vehicles, and chemicals production to place more emphasis on addressing environmental concerns than, say, software and electronics firms or apparel manufacturers. Companies whose business success is heavily dependent on high employee morale or attracting and retaining the best and brightest employees are somewhat more prone to stress the well-being of their employees and foster a positive, high-energy workplace environment that elicits the dedication and enthusiastic commitment of employees, thus putting real meaning behind the claim "Our people are our greatest asset." Ernst & Young, one of the four largest global accounting firms, stresses its "People First" workforce diversity strategy that is all about respecting differences, fostering individuality, and promoting inclusiveness so that its 105,000 employees in 140 countries can feel valued, engaged, and empowered in developing creative ways to serve the firm's clients.

Thus, while the strategies and actions of all socially responsible companies have a sameness in the sense of drawing on the five categories of socially responsible behavior shown in Figure 10.1, each company's version of being socially responsible is unique.

The Moral Case for Corporate Social Responsibility

The moral case for why businesses should actively promote the betterment of society and act in a manner that benefits all of the company's stakeholders—not just the interests of shareholders—boils down to "It's the right thing to do." Ordinary decency, civic-mindedness, and concern for the well-being of society should be expected of any business. In today's social and political climate most business leaders can be expected to acknowledge that socially responsible actions are important and that businesses have a duty to be good corporate citizens. But there is a complementary school of thought that business operates on the basis of an implied *social contract* with the members of society. According to this contract, society grants a business the right to conduct its business affairs and agrees not to unreasonably restrain its pursuit of a fair profit for the goods or services it sells; in return for this "license to operate," a business is obligated to act as a responsible citizen and do its fair share to promote the general welfare. Such a view clearly puts a moral burden on a company to take corporate citizenship into consideration and to act in the overall best interests of society as well as shareholders.

> Every action a company takes can be interpreted as a statement of what the company stands for.

The Business Case for Socially Responsible Behavior

Whatever the merits of the moral case for socially responsible business behavior, it has long been recognized that it is in the enlightened self-interest of companies to be good citizens and devote some of their energies and resources to the betterment of such stakeholders as employees, the communities in which it operates, and society in general. In short, there are several reasons why the exercise of social responsibility is good business:

- *It generates internal benefits* (particularly as concerns employee recruiting, workforce retention, and training costs)—Companies with deservedly good reputations for contributing time and money to the betterment of society are better able to attract and retain employees compared to companies with tarnished reputations. Some employees just feel better about working for a company committed to improving society.[27] This can contribute to lower turnover and better worker productivity. Other direct and indirect economic benefits include lower costs for staff recruitment and training. For example, Starbucks is said to enjoy much lower rates of employee turnover because of its full benefits package for both full-time and part-time employees, management efforts to make Starbucks a great place to work, and the company's socially responsible practices. When a U.S. manufacturer of recycled paper, taking eco-efficiency to heart, discovered how to increase its fiber recovery rate, it saved the equivalent of 20,000 tons of waste paper—a factor that helped the company become the industry's lowest-cost producer.[28] Various benchmarking and measurement mechanisms have shown that workforce diversity initiatives promote the success of companies that stay behind them. Making a company a great place to work pays dividends in the form of higher worker productivity, more creativity and energy on the part of workers, and greater employee commitment to the company's business mission/vision and success in the marketplace.

- *It reduces the risk of reputation-damaging incidents and can lead to increased buyer patronage*—Firms may well be penalized by employees, consumers, and shareholders for actions that are not considered socially responsible. When a major oil company suffered damage to its reputation on environmental and social grounds, the CEO repeatedly said that the most negative impact the company suffered—and the one that made him fear for the future of the company—was that bright young graduates were no longer attracted to work for the company.[29] Consumer, environmental, and human rights activist groups are quick to criticize businesses whose behavior they consider to be out of line, and they are adept at getting their message into the media and onto the Internet. Pressure groups can generate widespread adverse publicity, promote boycotts, and influence like-minded or sympathetic buyers to avoid an offender's products. Research has shown that product boycott announcements are associated with a decline in a company's stock price.[30] Outspoken criticism of Royal Dutch/Shell by environmental and human rights groups and associated boycotts were said to be major factors in the company's decision to tune in to its social responsibilities. For many years, Nike received stinging criticism for not policing sweatshop conditions in the Asian factories of its contractors, causing Nike CEO Phil Knight to observe that "Nike has become synonymous with slave wages, forced overtime, and arbitrary abuse."[31] In 1997, Nike began an extensive effort to monitor conditions in the 800 overseas factories from which it outsourced its shoes; Knight said, "Good shoes come from good factories and good factories have good labor relations." Nonetheless, Nike has continually been plagued by complaints from human rights activists that its monitoring procedures are flawed and that it is not doing enough to correct the plight of factory workers. In contrast, to the extent that a company's socially responsible behavior wins applause from consumers and fortifies its reputation, the company may win additional patronage; Ben & Jerry's, Whole Foods Market, Stonyfield Farm, and the Body Shop have definitely expanded their customer bases because of their visible and well-publicized activities as socially conscious companies. More and more companies are recognizing the strategic value of social responsibility strategies that reach out to people of all cultures and demographics—in the United States, women are said to having buying power of $3.7 trillion, retired and disabled people close to $4.1 trillion, Hispanics nearly $600 billion, African Americans some $500 billion, and Asian Americans about $255 billion.[32] So reaching out in ways that appeal to such groups can pay off at the cash register. Some observers and executives are convinced that a strong, visible social responsibility strategy gives a company an edge in differentiating itself from rivals and in appealing to those consumers who prefer to do business with companies that are solid corporate citizens. Yet there is only limited evidence that consumers go out of their way to patronize socially responsible companies if it means paying a higher price or purchasing an inferior product.[33]

> The higher the public profile of a company or brand, the greater the scrutiny of its activities and the higher the potential for it to become a target for pressure group action.

- *It is in the best interest of shareholders*—Well-conceived social responsibility strategies work to the advantage of shareholders in several ways. Socially responsible business behavior helps avoid or preempt legal and regulatory actions that could prove costly and otherwise burdensome. Increasing numbers of mutual funds and pension benefit managers are restricting their stock purchases to companies that meet social responsibility criteria. According to one survey, one out of every eight dollars under professional management in the United States involved socially responsible investing.[34] Moreover, the growth in socially responsible investing and identifying socially responsible companies has led to a substantial increase in the number of companies that publish formal reports on their social and environmental activities.[35] The stock prices of companies that rate high on social and environmental performance criteria have been found to perform 35 to 45 percent better than the average of the 2,500 companies comprising the Dow Jones Global Index.[36] A two-year study of leading companies found that improving environmental compliance and developing environmentally friendly products can enhance earnings per share, profitability, and the likelihood of winning contracts.[37] Nearly 100 studies have examined the relationship between corporate citizenship and corporate financial performance over the past 30 years; the majority point to a positive relationship. Of the 80 studies that examined whether a company's social performance is a good predictor of its financial performance, 42 concluded yes, 4 concluded no, and the remainder reported mixed or inconclusive findings.[38] To the extent that socially responsible behavior is good business, then, a social responsibility strategy that

> There's little hard evidence indicating shareholders are disadvantaged in any meaningful or substantive way by a company's actions to be socially responsible.

packs some punch and is more than rhetorical flourish turns out to be in the best interest of shareholders.

In sum, companies that take social responsibility seriously can improve their business reputations and operational efficiency while also reducing their risk exposure and encouraging loyalty and innovation. Overall, companies that take special pains to protect the environment (beyond what is required by law), are active in community affairs, and are generous supporters of charitable causes and projects that benefit society are more likely to be seen as good investments and as good companies to work for or do business with. Shareholders are likely to view the business case for social responsibility as a strong one, even though they certainly have a right to be concerned whether the time and money their company spends to carry out its social responsibility strategy outweighs the benefits and reduces the bottom line by an unjustified amount.

Companies are, of course, sometimes rewarded for bad behavior—a company that is able to shift environmental and other social costs associated with its activities onto society as a whole can reap large short-term profits. The major cigarette producers for many years were able to earn greatly inflated profits by shifting the health-related costs of smoking onto others and escaping any responsibility for the harm their products caused to consumers and the general public. But the profitability of shifting costs onto society is a risky practice because it attracts scrutiny from pressure groups, raises the threat of regulation and/or legislation to correct the inequity, and prompts socially conscious buyers to take their business elsewhere.

The Controversy over Do-Good Executives

While there is substantial agreement that businesses have stakeholder and societal obligations and that these must be incorporated into a company's overall strategy and into the conduct of its business operations, there is much less agreement about the extent to which "do-good" executives should pursue their personal vision of a better world using company funds. One view holds that any money executives authorize for so-called social responsibility initiatives is effectively theft from a company's shareholders who can, after all, decide for themselves what and how much to give to charity and other causes they deem worthy. A related school of thought says that companies should be wary of taking on an assortment of societal obligations because doing so diverts valuable resources and weakens a company's competitiveness. Many academics and businesspeople believe that businesses best satisfy their social responsibilities through conventional business activities, primarily producing needed goods and services at prices that people can afford. They further argue that spending shareholders' or customers' money for social causes not only muddies decision making by diluting the focus on the company's business mission but also thrusts business executives into the role of social engineers—a role more appropriately performed by charitable and nonprofit organizations and duly-elected government officials. Do we really want corporate executives deciding how to best balance the different interests of stakeholders and functioning as social engineers? Are they competent to make such judgments?

Take the case of Coca-Cola and Pepsi bottlers. Local bottlers of both brands have signed contracts with public school districts that provide millions of dollars of support for local schools in exchange for vending machine distribution rights in the schools.[39] While such contracts would seem to be a win–win proposition, protests from parents concerned about children's sugar-laden diets and commercialism in the schools make such contracts questionable. Opponents of these contracts claim that it is the role of government to provide adequate school funding and that the learning environment in local schools should be free of commercialism and the self-serving efforts of businesses to hide behind providing support for education.

In September 1997, the Business Roundtable changed its stance from one of support for social responsibility and balanced consideration of stakeholder interests to one of skepticism with regard to such actions:

> The notion that the board must somehow balance the interests of stockholders against the interests of other stakeholders fundamentally misconstrues the role of directors. It is, moreover, an unworkable notion because it would leave the board with no criteria for resolving conflicts between the interest of stockholders and of other stakeholders or among different groups of stakeholders.[40]

The new Business Roundtable view implied that the paramount duty of management and of boards of directors is to the corporation's stockholders. Customers may be "king," and employees may be the corporation's "greatest asset" (at least in the rhetoric), but the interests of shareholders rule.[41]

But there are real problems with disconnecting business behavior from the well-being of nonowner stakeholders and the well-being of society at large.[42] Isolating business from the rest of society when the two are inextricably intertwined and interdependent is unrealistic. Most business decisions spill over to impact nonowner stakeholders and society. Furthermore, the notion that businesses must be managed *solely* to serve the interests of shareholders is something of a stretch. Clearly, a business's first priority must be to deliver value to customers. Unless a company does a creditable job of satisfying buyer needs and expectations of reliable and attractively priced goods and services, it cannot survive. While shareholders provide capital and are certainly entitled to a return on their investment, fewer and fewer shareholders are truly committed to the companies whose stock they own. Shareholders can dispose of their holdings in a moment's whim or at the first sign of a downturn in the stock price. Mutual funds buy and sell shares daily, adding and dropping companies whenever they see fit. Day traders buy and sell within hours. Such buying and selling of shares is nothing more than a financial transaction and results in no capital being provided to the company to fund operations except when it entails the purchase of newly issued shares of stock. So why should shareholders—a group distant from the company's operations and adding little to its operations except when new shares of stock are purchased—lay such a large claim on how a company should be managed? Are most shareholders really interested in or knowledgeable about the companies they own? Or do they just own a stock for whatever financial returns it is expected to provide?

While there is legitimate concern about the use of company resources for do-good purposes and the motives and competencies of business executives in functioning as social engineers, it is tough to argue that businesses have *no obligations* to nonowner stakeholders or to society at large. If one looks at the category of activities that fall under the umbrella of socially responsible behavior (Figure 10.1), there's really very little for shareholders or others concerned about the do-good attempts of executives to object to in principle. Certainly, it is legitimate for companies to minimize or eliminate any adverse impacts of their operations on the environment. It is hard to argue against efforts to make the company a great place to work or to promote workforce diversity. And with regard to charitable contributions, community service projects, and the like, it would be hard to find a company where spending on such activities is so out of control that shareholders might rightfully complain or that the company's competitiveness is being eroded. What is likely to prove most objectionable in the social responsibility arena are the specific activities a company elects to engage in and/or the manner in which a company carries out its attempts to behave in a socially responsible manner.

How Much Attention to Social Responsibility Is Enough?

What is an appropriate balance between the imperative to create value for shareholders and the obligation to proactively contribute to the larger social good? What fraction of a company's resources ought to be aimed at addressing social concerns and bettering the well-being of society and the environment? A few companies have a policy of setting aside a specified percentage of their profits (typically 5 percent or maybe 10 percent) to fund their social responsibility strategy; they view such percentages as a fair amount to return to the community as a kind of thank-you or a tithe to the betterment of society. Other companies shy away from a specified percentage of profits or revenues because it entails upping the commitment in good times and cutting back on social responsibility initiatives in hard times (even cutting out social responsibility initiatives entirely if profits temporarily turn into losses). If social responsibility is an ongoing commitment rooted in the corporate culture and enlists broad participation on the part of company personnel, then a sizable portion of the funding for the company's social responsibility strategy has to be viewed as simply a regular and ongoing cost of doing business.

But judging how far a particular company should go in pursuing particular social causes is a tough issue. Consider, for example, Nike's commitment to monitoring the workplace conditions of its contract suppliers.[43] The scale of this monitoring task is significant: Nike has over 800 contract suppliers employing over 600,000 people in 50 countries. How frequently should sites be monitored? How should it respond to the use of underage labor? If only children above a set age are to be employed by suppliers, should suppliers still be required to provide schooling opportunities? At last count, Nike had some 80 people engaged in site monitoring. Should Nike's monitoring budget be $2 million, $5 million, $10 million, or whatever it takes?

Consider another example: If pharmaceutical manufacturers donate or discount their drugs for distribution to low-income people in less developed nations, what safeguards should they put in place to see that the drugs reach the intended recipients and are not diverted by corrupt local officials for reexport to markets in other countries? Should drug manufacturers also assist in drug distribution and administration in these less-developed countries? How much should a drug company invest in R&D to develop medicines for tropical diseases commonly occurring in less-developed countries when it is unlikely to recover its costs in the foreseeable future?

And how much should a company allocate to charitable contributions? Is it falling short of its responsibilities if its donations are less than 1 percent of profits? Is a company going too far if it allocates 5 percent or even 10 percent of its profits to worthy causes of one kind or another? The point here is that there is no simple or widely accepted standard for judging when a company has or has not gone far enough in fulfilling its citizenship responsibilities.

Linking Social Performance Targets to Executive Compensation

Perhaps the most surefire way to enlist a genuine commitment to corporate social responsibility initiatives is to link the achievement of social performance targets to executive compensation. If a company's board of directors is serious about corporate citizenship, then it will incorporate measures of the company's social and environmental performance into its evaluation of top executives, especially the CEO. And if the

CEO uses compensation incentives to further enlist the support of down-the-line company personnel in effectively crafting and executing a social responsibility strategy, the company will over time build a culture rooted in social responsible and ethical behavior. At Verizon Communications, 10 percent of the annual bonus of the company's top 2,500 managers is tied directly to the achievement of social responsibility targets; for the rest of the staff, there are corporate recognition awards in the form of cash for employees who have made big contributions towards social causes—Verizon paid out $1.24 million in such awards to its 227,000 employees in 2002.

According to one survey, 80 percent of surveyed CEOs believe that environmental and social performance metrics are a valid part of measuring a company's overall performance. To further heighten executive focus on the role and importance of socially responsible behavior, companies such as Safeway, Ford Motor, Sony, Vodaphone, DaimlerChrysler, and Prudential have begun issuing a special "corporate social responsibility report," much like an annual report, detailing their social responsibility initiatives and the results achieved.

key|points

Ethics involves concepts of right and wrong, fair and unfair, moral and immoral. Beliefs about what is ethical serve as a *moral compass* in guiding the actions and behaviors of individuals and organizations. Ethical principles in business are not materially different from ethical principles in general. Business actions are judged by the general ethical standards of society, not by a special set of standards that is either more permissive or less permissive.

Three categories of managers stand out as concerns their prevailing beliefs in and commitments to ethical and moral principles in business affairs: the moral manager; the immoral manager, and the amoral manager. By some accounts, the population of managers is said to be distributed among all three types in a bell-shaped curve, with immoral managers and moral managers occupying the two tails of the curve, and the amoral managers, especially the intentionally amoral managers, occupying the broad middle ground.

The apparently large numbers of immoral and amoral businesspeople are one obvious reason why some companies resort to unethical strategic behavior. Three other main drivers of unethical business behavior also stand out:

- Overzealous or obsessive pursuit of personal gain, wealth, and other selfish interests.
- Heavy pressures on company managers to meet or beat earnings targets.
- A company culture that puts the profitability and good business performance ahead of ethical behavior.

Ethical universalism holds that human nature is the same everywhere and thus that ethical rules are cross-cultural. *Ethical relativism* holds that different societal cultures and customs give rise to divergent values and ethical principles of right and wrong. *To some extent,* there is merit in the view that business ethics have to be viewed in the context of each country's local customs, religious traditions, and societal norms. A company has to be very cautious about exporting its home-country values and ethics to foreign countries where it operates—"photocopying" ethics is disrespectful of other countries' values and traditions. However, there are occasions when the rule of "When in Rome, do as the Romans do" is ethically and morally wrong irrespective of local customs, traditions and norms—one such case is the payment of bribes and kickbacks. Managers in multinational enterprises have to figure out how to navigate the gray zone that arises when operating in two cultures with two sets of ethics.

The stance a company takes in dealing with or managing ethical conduct at any given time can take any of four basic forms:

- The unconcerned or nonissue approach.
- The damage control approach.
- The compliance approach.
- The ethical culture approach.

The challenges that arise in each of the four approaches provide an explanation of why a company's executives may sense they have exhausted a particular mode's potential for managing ethics and that they need to move to a stronger, more forceful approach to ethics management.

There are two reasons why a company's strategy should be ethical: (1) because a strategy that is unethical in whole or in part is morally wrong and reflects badly on the character of the company personnel involved, and (2) because an ethical strategy is good business and in the self-interest of shareholders.

Corporate social responsibility is defined as a company's *duty* to operate its business by means that avoid harm to other stakeholders and the environment and, further, to consider the overall betterment of society in its decisions and actions. The essence of *socially responsible business behavior* is that a company should strive to *balance* the benefits of strategic actions to benefit shareholders against any possible adverse impacts on other stakeholders (employees, suppliers, customers, local communities, and society at large) and, further, to proactively mitigate any harmful effects on the environment that its actions and business may have. The menu of actions and behavior for demonstrating social responsibility includes:

- Employing an ethical strategy and observing ethical principles in operating the business.
- Making charitable contributions, donating money and the time of company personnel to community service endeavors, supporting various worthy organizational causes, and making a difference in the lives of the disadvantaged; corporate commitments are further reinforced by encouraging employees to support charitable and community activities.
- Protecting or enhancing the environment and, in particular, striving to minimize or eliminate any adverse impact on the environment stemming from the company's own business activities.
- Creating a work environment that makes the company a great place to work.
- Employing a workforce that is diverse with respect to gender, race, national origin, and perhaps other aspects that different people bring to the workplace.

While striving to be socially responsible entails selecting from the above menu, there can be no generic approach to linking a company's strategy and business conduct to social responsibility. Each company's social responsibility strategy should logically be matched to its core values and business mission and thus be somewhat different from the approaches to social responsibility taken by even other companies in the same industry.

The moral case for social responsibility boils down to a simple concept: It's the right thing to do. The business case for social responsibility holds that it is in the enlightened self-interest of companies to be good citizens and devote some of their energies and resources to the betterment of such stakeholders as employees, the communities in which it operates, and society in general. There are three reasons why the exercise of social responsibility is good business:

- It generates internal benefits (particularly as concerns employee recruiting, workforce retention, and training costs).

- It reduces the risk of reputation-damaging incidents and can lead to increased buyer patronage. The higher the public profile of a company or brand, the greater the scrutiny of its activities and the higher the potential for it to become a target for pressure group action.

- It is in the best interest of shareholders.

Companies that take social responsibility seriously can improve their business reputations and operational efficiency while also reducing their risk exposure and encouraging loyalty and innovation. Overall, they are more likely to be seen as a good investment and as a good company to work for or do business with.

However, there is a school of thought that says companies should be very cautious in their endeavors to better the overall well-being of society because it diverts valuable resources and weakens a company's competitiveness. According to this view, businesses best satisfy their social responsibilities through conventional business activities—producing needed goods and services at prices consistent with the lowest feasible costs. They further argue that spending shareholders' or customers' money for social causes not only muddies decision making by diluting the focus on the company's business mission but also thrusts business executives into the role of social engineers—a role more appropriately performed by charitable and nonprofit organizations and duly-elected government officials. Yet, it is tough to argue that businesses have *no obligations* to nonowner stakeholders or to society at large. If one looks at the category of activities that fall under the umbrella of socially responsible behavior (refer to Figure 10.1), there's really very little to object to in principle. The main problems come in judging the specifics of how well a company goes about the particular social betterment and corporate citizenship activities that it opts to pursue. Are the actions self-serving? Do the actions go far enough? Were the actions done in an appropriate fashion?

In sum, the case for ethical and socially responsible behavior are about attracting and retaining talented staff, about managing risk, and about assuring a company's reputation with customers, suppliers, local communities, and society.

exercises

1. Consider the following portrayal of strategies employed by the major recording studios:[44]

> Some recording artists and the Recording Artists' Coalition claim that the world's five major music recording studios—Universal, Sony, Time Warner, EMI/Virgin, and Bertlesmann—deliberately employ strategies calculated to take advantage of musicians who record for them. One practice to which they strenuously object is that the major-label record companies frequently require artists to sign contracts committing them to do six to eight albums, an obligation that some artists say can entail an indefinite term of indentured servitude. Further, it is claimed that audits routinely detect unpaid royalties to musicians under contract; according to one music industry attorney, record companies misreport and underpay artist royalties by 10 to 40 percent and are "intentionally fraudulent." One music writer was recently quoted as saying the process was "an entrenched system whose prowess and conniving makes Enron look like amateur hour." Royalty calculations are based on complex formulas that are paid only after artists pay for recording costs and other expenses and after any advances are covered by royalty earnings.

A *Baffler* magazine article outlined a hypothetical but typical record deal in which a promising young band is given a $250,000 royalty advance on a new album. The album subsequently sells 250,000 copies, earning $710,000 for the record company; but the band, after repaying the record company for $264,000 in expenses ranging from recording fees and video budgets to catering, wardrobe, and bus tour costs for promotional events related to the album, ends up $14,000 in the hole, owes the record company money, and is thus paid no royalties on any of the $710,000 in revenues the recording company receives from the sale of the band's music. It is also standard practice in the music industry for recording studios to sidestep payola laws by hiring independent promoters to lobby and compensate radio stations for playing certain records. Record companies are often entitled to damages for undelivered albums if an artist leaves a recording studio for another label after seven years. Record companies also retain the copyrights in perpetuity on all music recorded under contract, a practice that artists claim is unfair. The Dixie Chicks, after a year-long feud with Sony over contract terms, ended up refusing to do another album; Sony sued for breach of contract, prompting a countersuit by the Dixie Chicks charging "systematic thievery" to cheat them out of royalties. The suits were settled out of court. One artist said, "The record companies are like cartels."

Recording studios defend their strategic practices by pointing out that fewer than 5 percent of the signed artists ever deliver a hit and that they lose money on albums that sell poorly. According to one study, only 1 of 244 contracts signed during 1994–1996 was negotiated without the artists being represented by legal counsel, and virtually all contracts renegotiated after a hit album added terms more favorable to the artist.

a. If you were a recording artist, would you be happy with some of the strategic practices of the recording studios? Would you feel comfortable signing a recording contract with studios engaging in any of the practices? Which, if any, of their practices do you believe are unethical?

b. Would you want to be an employee of any of the companies described above? Would you be proud of the company you worked for if you were an employee?

2. Consider the following portrayal of the turnaround strategy employed by Fleming Companies, which at the time was the largest U.S. distributor of consumer packaged goods to retailers of all sizes and formats:[45]

Dozens of manufacturers that used Fleming as a channel for distributing their products to supermarkets and grocery retailers claimed that Fleming habitually deducted arbitrary sums (amounting to perhaps $100 million annually) from the billings they submitted. The practice was said to be a part of Fleming's turnaround strategy to boost its own margins and restore profitability after five money-losing years (1996–2000). According to a food industry consultant who once worked for Fleming, the company's practice was to "deduct and deduct until a vendor cuts them off, then they pay. Then they start deducting again."

Former high-level Fleming employees claimed that the company played games with slotting fees, sometimes taking slotting fee deductions from manufacturer billings for products it never stocked in its warehouse or put on retailers' shelves. Fleming's standing as the largest wholesale grocery products distributor, with some 50,000 retail customers (including Kmart), gave it powerful gatekeeper status because many grocery products manufacturers use a third-party distributor to access small independent grocery chains and because many small grocers get most of their merchandise through a grocery distributor (unlike Wal-Mart, Safeway, and many other large chains that buy directly from the manufacturers). Thus manufacturers that sold through Fleming were hesitant to cut off deliveries to Fleming or protest its deductions too vociferously because they didn't have effective alternatives to getting their products to Fleming's 50,000 customers.

Relationships with some of Fleming's retail customers, most notably Kmart (its biggest customer) and several small independent supermarkets, were also said to be strained because of recurring service and billing issues.

a. Is Fleming engaging in anything unethical here? If you were a Fleming executive, on what grounds would you defend the company's actions?

b. Is the company unfairly using its muscle of serving some 50,000 retail accounts to take advantage of its suppliers?

c. If you were a manufacturer that sold through Fleming, would you be looking for other distributors to handle your products?

d. If you were a Fleming shareholder, would you be pleased with the manner in which the company is being managed and the reputation that such practices are giving the company? Is what is going on here sufficient grounds for selling the shares you own?

(*Special note:* Shortly after Fleming's practices came to light in a front-page *Wall Street Journal* article on September 5, 2002, things at Fleming began to go downhill quickly. The company's profits on sales of $15.5 billion in 2002 were marginal, despite having acquired Target, Albertson's, and 100 other supermarkets as new customers. In February 2003, Kmart terminated its supply relationship with Fleming. In April 2003, Fleming filed for Chapter 11 bankruptcy protection and began a program to dispose of most all of its business assets to pay off creditors. By mid-2003, the company had sold all of its retail grocery operations and all of its wholesale grocery distribution business. Only two small divisions remained, and they were up for sale. The company was history.)

3. Log on to www.business-ethics.com. Review the companies listed as the 100 Best Corporate Citizens and criteria for earning a spot on this list. Do the criteria seem reasonable? Is there ample reason to believe that the 100 companies on this list pursue strategies that are ethical? Or do the criteria used to determine the 100 Best Corporate Citizens point more to companies that have some standout socially responsible practices?

4. Recently, it came to light that three of the world's four biggest public accounting firms may have overbilled clients for travel-related expenses. Pricewaterhouse-Coopers, KPMG, and Ernst & Young were sued for systematically charging their clients full price for airline tickets, hotel rooms and car-rental expenses, even though they received volume discounts and rebates of up to 40 percent under their contracts with various travel companies. Large accounting firms, law firms and medical practices have in recent years used their size and purchasing volumes to negotiate sizable discounts and rebates on up-front travel costs; some of these contracts apparently required that the discounts not be disclosed to other parties, which seemingly included clients.

However, it has long been the custom for accounting and law firms to bill their clients for actual out-of-pocket expenses. The three accounting firms, so the lawsuit alleges, billed clients for the so-called full prices of the airline tickets, hotel rooms and car-rental expenses rather than for the out-of-pocket discounted amounts. They pocketed the differences to the tune of several million dollars annually in additional profits. Several clients, upon learning of the full-price billing practices, claimed fraud and sued.

Do you consider the accounting firms' billing practice to be unethical? Why or why not?

chapter eleven

Building Resource Strengths and Organizational Capabilities

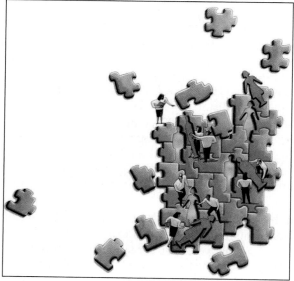

(©Images.com/CORBIS)

The best game plan in the world never blocked or tackled anybody.

—Vince Lombardi

Strategies most often fail because they aren't executed well.

—Larry Bossidy and Ram Charan
CEO Honeywell International; author and consultant

Organizing is what you do before you do something, so that when you do it, it is not all mixed up.

—A. A. Milne

O nce managers have decided on a strategy, the emphasis turns to converting it into actions and good results. Putting the strategy into place and getting the organization to execute it well call for different sets of managerial skills. Whereas crafting strategy is largely a market-driven activity, executing strategy is primarily an operations-driven activity revolving around the management of people and business processes. Whereas successful strategy making depends on business vision, solid industry and competitive analysis, and shrewd market positioning, successful strategy execution depends on doing a good job of working with and through others, building and strengthening competitive capabilities, motivating and rewarding people in a strategy-supportive manner, and instilling a discipline of getting things done. Executing strategy is an action-oriented, make-things-happen task that tests a manager's ability to direct organizational change, achieve continuous improvement in operations and business processes, create and nurture a strategy-supportive culture, and consistently meet or beat performance targets.

Experienced managers are emphatic in declaring that it is a whole lot easier to develop a sound strategic plan than it is to execute the plan and achieve the desired outcomes. According to one executive, "It's been rather easy for us to decide where we wanted to go. The hard part is to get the organization to act on the new priorities."[1] What makes executing strategy a tougher, more time-consuming management challenge than crafting strategy is the wide array of managerial activities that have to be attended to, the many ways managers can proceed, the demanding people-management skills required, the perseverance necessary to get a variety of initiatives launched and moving, the number of bedeviling issues that must be worked out, the resistance to change that must be overcome, and the difficulties of integrating the efforts of many different work groups into a smoothly functioning whole.

Just because senior managers announce a new strategy doesn't mean that organizational members will agree with it or enthusiastically move forward in implementing it. Senior executives cannot simply tell their immediate subordinates to undertake new strategic initiatives and expect the needed actions and changes to occur rapidly and deliver the intended results. Skeptical managers and employees may see the strategy as contrary to the organization's best interests, unlikely to succeed, or threatening to their

> Companies don't implement and execute strategies; people do.

departments or careers. Moreover, individual employees may have different ideas about what internal changes are needed to execute the strategy. Long-standing attitudes, vested interests, inertia, and ingrained organizational practices don't melt away when managers decide on a new strategy and begin efforts to implement it—especially when only comparatively few people have been involved in crafting the strategy and when the rationale for strategic change has to be sold to enough organizational members to root out the status quo. It takes adept managerial leadership to convincingly communicate the new strategy and the reasons for it, overcome pockets of doubt and disagreement, build consensus on all the hows of implementation and execution, secure the commitment and energetic cooperation of organizational units, and get all the pieces into place and working well. Depending on how much consensus building, motivating, and organizational change is involved, the process of implementing strategy changes can take several months to several years.

Like crafting strategy, executing strategy is a job for the whole management team, not just a few senior managers. While an organization's chief executive officer and the heads of major units (business divisions, functional departments, and key operating units) are ultimately responsible for seeing that strategy is executed successfully, the process typically affects every part of the firm, from the biggest operating unit to the smallest frontline work group. Top-level managers have to rely on the active support and cooperation of middle and lower managers to push strategy changes into functional areas and operating units and to see that the organization actually operates in accordance with the strategy on a daily basis. Middle and lower-level managers not only are responsible for initiating and supervising the execution process in their areas of authority but also are instrumental in getting subordinates to continuously improve on how strategy-critical value chain activities are being performed and in producing the operating results that allow company performance targets to be met—their role on the company's strategy execution team is by no means minimal. *Strategy execution thus requires every manager to think through the answer to "What does my area have to do to implement its part of the strategic plan, and what should I do to get these things accomplished effectively and efficiently?"*

> **core concept**
> All managers have strategy-executing responsibility in their areas of authority, and all employees are participants in the strategy execution process.

A FRAMEWORK FOR EXECUTING STRATEGY

Implementing and executing strategy entails figuring out all the hows—the specific techniques, actions, and behaviors that are needed for a smooth strategy-supportive operation—and then following through to get things done and deliver results. The idea is to make things happen and make them happen right. The first step in implementing strategic changes is for management to communicate the case for organizational change so clearly and persuasively to organizational members that a determined commitment takes hold throughout the ranks to find ways to put the strategy into place, make it work, and meet performance targets. The ideal condition is for managers to arouse enough enthusiasm for the strategy to turn the implementation process into a companywide crusade. *Management's handling of the strategy implementation process can be considered successful if and when the company achieves the targeted strategic and financial performance and shows good progress in making its strategic vision a reality.*

The specific hows of executing a strategy—the exact items that need to be placed on management's action agenda—always have to be customized to fit the particulars of a company's situation. Making minor changes in an existing strategy differs from implementing radical strategy changes. The hot buttons for successfully executing a low-cost provider strategy are different from those in executing a high-end differentiation strategy. Implementing and executing a new strategy for a struggling company in the midst of a financial crisis is different from improving strategy execution in a company where the execution is already pretty good. Moreover, some managers are more adept than others at using this or that approach to achieving the desired kinds of organizational changes. Hence, there's no definitive 10-step checklist or managerial recipe for successful strategy execution. Strategy execution varies according to individual company situations and circumstances, the strategy implementer's best judgment, and the implementer's ability to use particular organizational change techniques effectively.

THE PRINCIPAL MANAGERIAL COMPONENTS OF THE STRATEGY EXECUTION PROCESS

While a company's strategy-executing approaches always have to be tailored to the company's situation, certain managerial bases have to be covered no matter what the circumstances. Eight managerial tasks crop up repeatedly in company efforts to execute strategy (see Figure 11.1):

1. Building an organization with the competencies, capabilities, and resource strengths to execute strategy successfully.
2. Marshaling resources behind the drive for good strategy execution and operating excellence.
3. Instituting policies and procedures that facilitate strategy execution.
4. Adopting best practices and striving for continuous improvement in how value chain activities are performed.
5. Installing information and operating systems that enable company personnel to carry out their strategic roles proficiently.
6. Tying rewards and incentives directly to the achievement of strategic and financial targets and to good strategy execution.
7. Shaping the work environment and corporate culture to fit the strategy.
8. Exerting the internal leadership needed to drive implementation forward and keep improving on how the strategy is being executed.

How well managers perform these eight tasks has a decisive impact on whether the outcome is a spectacular success, a colossal failure, or something in between.

In devising an action agenda for implementing and executing strategy, the place for managers to start is with *a probing assessment of what the organization must do differently and better to carry out the strategy successfully.* They should then consider *precisely how to make the necessary internal changes as rapidly as possible.* Successful strategy implementers have a knack for diagnosing what their organizations need to do to execute the chosen strategy well and figuring out how to get things done—they are masters in promoting results-oriented behaviors on the part of company personnel and following through on making the right things happen.[2]

> When strategies fail, it is often because of poor execution—things that were supposed to get done slip through the cracks.

The bigger the organization, the more that successful strategy execution depends on the cooperation and implementing skills of operating managers who can push

figure 11.1   **The Eight Components of the Strategy Execution Process**

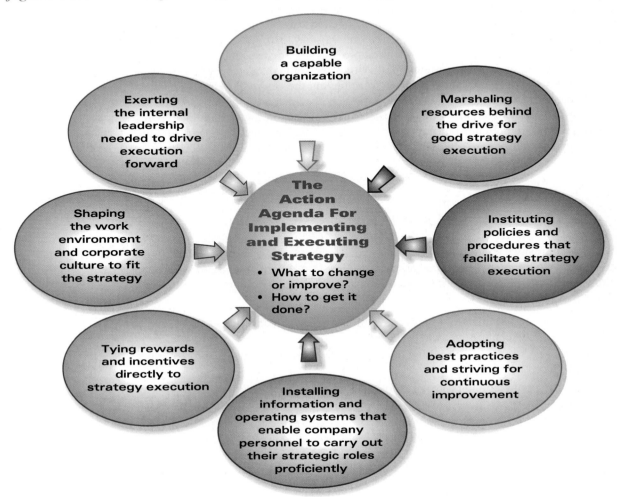

needed changes at the lowest organizational levels and deliver results. In a company with geographically scattered operating units, the action agenda of senior executives mostly involves communicating the case for change to others, building consensus for how to proceed, installing strong allies in positions where they can push implementation along in key organizational units, urging and empowering subordinates to keep the process moving, establishing measures of progress and deadlines, recognizing and rewarding those who achieve implementation milestones, directing resources to the right places, and personally leading the strategic change process. In small organizations, by contrast, top managers can deal directly with frontline managers and employees, personally orchestrating the action steps and implementation sequence, observing firsthand how implementation is progressing, and deciding how hard and how fast to push the process along. Regardless of the organization's size and the scope of the changes, the most important leadership trait is a strong, confident sense of what to do and how to do it. Such confidence comes from understanding the circumstances of the organization and the requirements for effective strategy execution. It then remains for those

figure 11.2   **The Three Components of Building a Capable Organization**

Staffing the Organization

- Putting together a strong management team
- Recruiting and retaining talented employees

Building Core Competencies and Competitive Capabilities

- Developing a set of competencies and capabilities suited to the current strategy
- Updating and revising this set as external conditions and strategy change
- Training and retraining employees as needed to maintain skills-based competencies

Matching the Organization Structure to Strategy

- Designing an organization structure that facilitates good strategy execution
- Deciding how much decision-making authority to push down to lower-level managers and front line employees

A Company with the Organizational Capability Needed for Proficient Strategy Execution

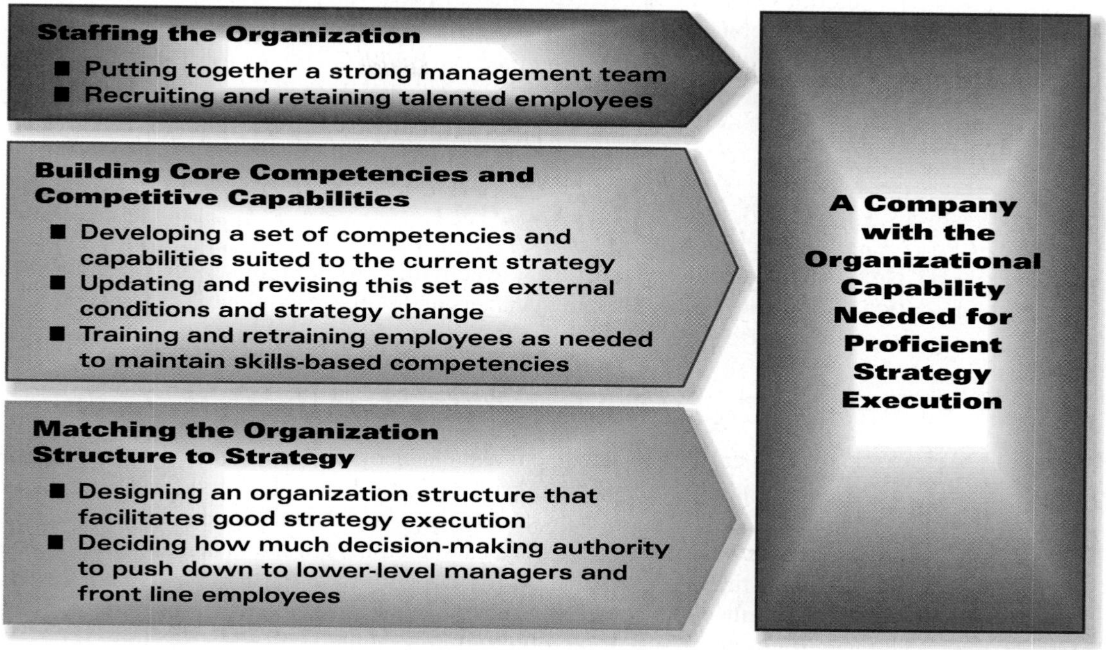

managers and company personnel in strategy-critical areas to step up to the plate and produce the desired results.

Managing the Strategy Execution Process: What's Covered in Chapters 11, 12, and 13   In the remainder of this chapter and the next two chapters, we will discuss what is involved in managing the process of implementing and executing strategy. The discussion of executing strategy in Chapters 11, 12, and 13 is framed around the eight managerial tasks shown in Figure 11.1 and the most common issues associated with each. This chapter explores the task of building strategy-supportive competencies, capabilities, and resource strengths. Chapter 12 looks at allocating sufficient money and people to the performance of strategy-critical activities, establishing strategy-facilitating policies and procedures, instituting best practices, installing operating systems, and tying rewards to the achievement of good results. Chapter 13 deals with creating a strategy-supportive corporate culture and exercising appropriate strategic leadership.

BUILDING A CAPABLE ORGANIZATION

Proficient strategy execution depends heavily on competent personnel, better-than-adequate competitive capabilities, and effective internal organization. Building a capable organization is thus always a top priority in strategy execution. As shown in Figure 11.2, three types of organization-building actions are paramount:

1. *Staffing the organization*—putting together a strong management team and recruiting and retaining employees with the needed experience, technical skills, and intellectual capital.

2. *Building core competencies and competitive capabilities*—developing a set of abilities that will enable good strategy execution and updating them as strategy and external conditions change.

3. *Structuring the organization and work effort*—organizing value chain activities and business processes and deciding how much decision-making authority to push down to lower-level managers and frontline employees.

STAFFING THE ORGANIZATION

No company can hope to perform the activities required for successful strategy execution without attracting capable managers and without employees that give it a suitable knowledge base and portfolio of *intellectual capital.*

Putting Together a Strong Management Team

Assembling a capable management team is a cornerstone of the organization-building task.[3] Different strategies and company circumstances often call for different mixes of backgrounds, experiences, know-how, values, beliefs, management styles, and personalities. The personal chemistry among the members of the management team needs to be right, and the talent base needs to be appropriate for the chosen strategy. But the most important condition is to fill key managerial slots with people who can be counted on to get things done; otherwise the implementation-execution process can't proceed at full speed. Sometimes the existing management team is suitable; at other times it may need to be strengthened or expanded by promoting qualified people from within or by bringing in outsiders whose experience, skills, and leadership styles better suit the situation. In turnaround and rapid-growth situations, and in instances when a company doesn't have insiders with the requisite experience or know-how, filling key management slots from the outside is a fairly standard organization-building approach. Illustration Capsule 11.1 describes General Electric's widely acclaimed approach to developing a high-caliber management team.

> **core concept**
> Putting together a talented management team with the right mix of skills and experiences is one of the first strategy-implementing steps.

Recruiting and Retaining Capable Employees

Assembling a capable management team is not enough. Staffing the organization with the right kinds of people must go much deeper than managerial jobs in order to build an organization capable of effective strategy execution. Companies like Electronic Data Systems (EDS), McKinsey & Company, Cisco Systems, Southwest Airlines, Procter & Gamble, PepsiCo, Nike, Microsoft, and Intel make a concerted effort to recruit the best and brightest people they can find and then retain them with excellent compensation packages, opportunities for rapid advancement and professional growth, and challenging and interesting assignments. Having a cadre of people with strong skill sets and budding management potential is essential to their business. EDS requires college graduates to have at least a 3.5 grade point average (on a 4.0 scale) just to qualify for an interview, believing that having a high-caliber pool of employees is crucial to operating the information technology systems of its customers. Microsoft makes a point of hiring the very brightest and most talented programmers it can find and motivating them with both good monetary incentives and the challenge of working on cutting-edge software design projects. McKinsey & Company, one of the world's premier management consulting companies, recruits only cream-of-the-crop master's degree candidates at the nation's

illustration capsule 11.1
How General Electric Develops a Talented and Deep Management Team

General Electric (GE) is widely considered to be one of the best-managed companies in the world, partly because of its concerted effort to develop outstanding managers. For starters, GE strives to hire talented people with high potential for executive leadership; it then goes to great lengths to expand the leadership, business, and decision-making capabilities of all its managers. Four key elements underpin GE's efforts to build a talent-rich stable of managers:

1. GE makes a practice of transferring managers across divisional, business, or functional lines for sustained periods of time. Such transfers allow managers to develop relationships with colleagues in other parts of the company, help break down insular thinking in business "silos," and promote the sharing of cross-business ideas and best practices. There is an enormous emphasis at GE on transferring ideas and best practices from business to business and making GE a "boundaryless" company.

2. In selecting executives for key positions, GE is strongly disposed to candidates who exhibit what are called the four E's—enormous personal *energy,* the ability to motivate and *energize* others, *edge* (a GE code word for instinctive competitiveness and the ability to make tough decisions in a timely fashion, saying yes or no instead of maybe), and *execution* (the ability to carry things through to fruition).

3. All managers are expected to be proficient at what GE calls *workout*—a process in which managers and employees come together to confront issues as soon as they come up, pinpoint the root cause of the issues, and bring about quick resolutions so the business can move forward. Workout is GE's way of training its managers to diagnose what to do and how to do it.

4. Each year GE sends about 10,000 newly hired and longtime managers to its Leadership Development Center (generally regarded as one of the best corporate training centers in the world) for a three-week course on the company's Six Sigma quality initiative. More than 5,000 "master black belt" and "black belt" Six Sigma experts have graduated from the program to drive forward thousands of quality initiatives throughout GE. Six Sigma training is an ironclad requirement for promotion to any professional and managerial position and any stock option award. GE's Leadership Development Center also offers advanced courses for senior managers that may focus on a single management topic for a month. All classes involve managers from different GE businesses and different parts of the world. Some of the most valuable learning comes in between formal class sessions when GE managers from different businesses trade ideas about how to improve processes and better serve the customer. This knowledge sharing not only spreads best practices throughout the organization but also improves each GE manager's knowledge.

Each of GE's 85,000 managers and professionals is graded in an annual process that divides them into five tiers: the top 10 percent, the next 15 percent, the middle 50 percent, the next 15 percent, and the bottom 10 percent. Everyone in the top tier gets stock awards, nobody in the fourth tier gets shares of stock, and most of those in the fifth tier become candidates for being weeded out. Business heads are pressured to wean out "C" players. GE's CEO personally reviews the performance of the top 3,000 managers. Senior executive compensation is heavily weighted toward Six Sigma commitment and producing successful business results.

According to Jack Welch, GE's CEO from 1980 to 2001, "The reality is, we simply cannot afford to field anything but teams of 'A' players."

Sources: 1998 annual report; www.ge.com; John A. Byrne, "How Jack Welch Runs GE," *Business Week,* June 8, 1998, p. 90; Miriam Leuchter, "Management Farm Teams," *Journal of Business Strategy,* May 1998, pp. 29–32; and "The House That Jack Built, *The Economist,* September 18, 1999.

top 10 business schools; such talent is essential to McKinsey's strategy of performing high-level consulting for the world's top corporations. The leading global accounting firms screen candidates not only on the basis of their accounting expertise but also on whether they possess the people skills needed to relate well with clients and colleagues. Southwest Airlines goes to considerable lengths to hire people who can have fun on the job; it uses special interviewing and screening methods to gauge whether applicants for customer-contact jobs have outgoing personality traits that match its strategy of creating a high-spirited, fun-loving, in-flight atmosphere for passengers; it is so selective that only about 3 percent of the people who apply are offered jobs.

In high-tech companies, the challenge is to staff work groups with gifted, imaginative, and energetic people who can bring life to new ideas quickly and inject into the organization what one Dell Computer executive called "hum."[4] The saying "People are our most important asset" may seem hollow, but it fits high-technology companies dead-on. Besides checking closely for functional and technical skills, Dell Computer tests applicants for their tolerance of ambiguity and change, their capacity to work in teams, and their ability to learn on the fly. Companies like Amazon.com and Cisco Systems have broken new ground in recruiting, hiring, cultivating, developing, and retaining talented employees—most all of whom are in their 20s and 30s. Cisco goes after the top 10 percent, raiding other companies and endeavoring to retain key people at the companies it acquires so as to maintain a cadre of star engineers, programmers, managers, salespeople, and support personnel in executing its strategy to remain the world's leading provider of Internet infrastructure products and technology.

> **core concept**
> In many industries adding to a company's talent base and building intellectual capital is more important to strategy execution than additional investments in plants, equipment, and other hard assets.

Where intellectual capital is crucial in building a strategy-capable organization, companies have instituted a number of practices in staffing their organizations and developing a strong knowledge base:

1. Spending considerable effort in screening and evaluating job applicants, selecting only those with suitable skill sets, energy, initiative, judgment, and aptitudes for learning and adaptability to the company's work environment and culture.

2. Putting employees through training programs that continue throughout their careers.

3. Providing promising employees with challenging, interesting, and skill-stretching assignments.

4. Rotating people through jobs that not only have great content but also span functional and geographic boundaries. Providing people with opportunities to gain experience in a variety of international settings is increasingly considered an essential part of career development in multinational or global companies.

5. Encouraging employees to be creative and innovative, to challenge existing ways of doing things and offer better ways, and to submit ideas for new products or businesses. Progressive companies work hard at creating an environment in which ideas and suggestions bubble up from below rather than proceed from the top down. Employees are made to feel that their opinions count.

6. Fostering a stimulating and engaging work environment such that employees will consider the company a great place to work.

7. Exerting efforts to retain high-potential, high-performing employees with salary increases, performance bonuses, stock awards and equity ownership, and other long-term incentives.

8. Coaching average performers to improve their skills and capabilities, while weeding out underperformers and benchwarmers.

BUILDING CORE COMPETENCIES AND COMPETITIVE CAPABILITIES

A top organization-building priority in the strategy implementing/executing process is the need to build and strengthen competitively valuable core competencies and organizational capabilities. Whereas managers identify the desired competencies and capabilities in the course of crafting strategy, good strategy execution requires putting the desired competencies and capabilities in place, upgrading them as needed, and then modifying them as market conditions evolve. Sometimes a company already has the needed competencies and capabilities, in which case managers can concentrate on nurturing them to promote better strategy execution. More often, however, company managers have to add new competencies and capabilities to implement strategic initiatives and promote proficient strategy execution.

A number of prominent companies have succeeded in establishing core competencies and capabilities that have been instrumental in making them winners in the marketplace. Honda's core competence is its depth of expertise in gasoline engine technology and small engine design. Intel's is in the design of complex chips for personal computers and servers. Procter & Gamble's core competencies reside in its superb marketing/distribution skills and its R&D capabilities in five core technologies—fats, oils, skin chemistry, surfactants, and emulsifiers. Sony's core competencies are its expertise in electronic technology and its ability to translate that expertise into innovative products (cutting-edge video game hardware, miniaturized radios and video cameras, TVs and DVDs with unique features, attractively designed PCs). Dell Computer can deliver state-of-the-art products to its customers within days of next-generation components becoming available—and at attractively low costs (it has leveraged its collection of competencies and capabilities into being the global low-cost leader in PCs).

The Three-Stage Process of Developing and Strengthening Competencies and Capabilities

Building core competencies and competitive capabilities is a time-consuming, managerially challenging exercise. While some organization-building assist can be gotten from discovering how best-in-industry or best-in-world companies perform a particular activity, trying to replicate and then improve on those competencies and capabilities of others is, however, much easier said than done—for the same reasons that one cannot become a good golfer just by watching Tiger Woods. Putting a new capability in place is more complicated than just forming a new team or department and charging it with becoming highly competent in performing the desired activity, using whatever it can learn from other companies having similar competencies or capabilities. Rather, it takes a series of deliberate and well-orchestrated organizational steps to achieve mounting proficiency in performing an activity. The capability-building process has three stages:

> *Stage 1*—First, the organization must develop the *ability* to do something, however imperfectly or inefficiently. This entails selecting people with the requisite skills and experience, upgrading or expanding individual abilities as needed, and then molding the efforts and work products of individuals into a collaborative effort to create organizational ability.
>
> *Stage 2*—As experience grows and company personnel learn how to perform the activity *consistently well and at an acceptable cost,* the ability evolves into a tried-and-true *competence or capability.*
>
> *Stage 3*—Should the organization continue to polish and refine its know-how and otherwise sharpen its performance such that it becomes *better than rivals* at performing the activity, the core competence rises to the rank of a *distinctive competence* (or the capability becomes a competitively superior capability), thus providing a path to competitive advantage.

Many companies manage to get through stages 1 and 2 in performing a strategy-critical activity, but comparatively few achieve sufficient proficiency in performing strategy-critical activities to qualify for the third stage.

Managing the Process   Four traits concerning core competencies and competitive capabilities are important in successfully managing the organization-building process:[5]

1. *Core competencies and competitive capabilities are bundles of skills and know-how that most often grow out of the combined efforts of cross-functional work groups and departments performing complementary activities at different locations in the firm's value chain.* Rarely does a core competence or capability consist of narrow skills attached to the work efforts of a single department. For instance, a core competence in speeding new products to market involves the collaborative efforts of personnel in R&D, engineering and design, purchasing, production, marketing, and distribution. Similarly, the capability to provide superior customer service is a team effort among people in customer call centers (where orders are taken and inquiries are answered), shipping and delivery, billing and accounts receivable, and after-sale support. Complex activities (like designing and manufacturing a sport-utility vehicle or creating the capability for secure credit card transactions over the Internet) usually involve a number of component skills, technological disciplines, competencies, and capabilities—some performed in-house and some provided by suppliers/allies. An important part of the organization-building function is to think about which activities of which groups need to be linked and made mutually reinforcing and then to forge the necessary collaboration both internally and with outside resource providers.

2. *Normally, a core competence or capability emerges incrementally out of company efforts either to bolster skills that contributed to earlier successes or to respond to customer problems, new technological and market opportunities, and the competitive maneuverings of rivals.* Migrating from the one-time ability to do something up the ladder to a core competence or competitively valuable capability is usually an organization-building process that takes months and often years to accomplish—it is definitely not an overnight event.

3. *The key to leveraging a core competence into a distinctive competence (or a capability into a competitively superior capability) is concentrating more effort and more talent than rivals on deepening and strengthening the competence or capability, so as to achieve the dominance needed for competitive advantage.* This does not necessarily mean spending more money on such activities than competitors, but it does mean consciously focusing more talent on them and striving for best-in-industry, if not best-in-world, status. To achieve dominance on lean financial resources, companies like Cray in large computers and Honda in gasoline engines have leveraged the expertise of their talent pool by frequently re-forming high-intensity teams and reusing key people on special projects. The experiences of these and other companies indicate that the usual keys to successfully building core competencies and valuable capabilities are superior employee selection, thorough training and retraining, powerful cultural influences, effective cross-functional collaboration, empowerment, motivating incentives, short deadlines, and good databases—not big operating budgets.

4. *Evolving changes in customers' needs and competitive conditions often require tweaking and adjusting a company's portfolio of competencies and intellectual capital to keep its capabilities freshly honed and on the cutting edge.* This is particularly important in high-tech industries and fast-paced markets where important developments occur weekly. As a consequence, wise company managers work at anticipating changes in customer-market requirements and staying ahead of the

curve in proactively building a package of competencies and capabilities that can win out over rivals.

Managerial actions to develop core competencies and competitive capabilities generally take one of two forms: either strengthening the company's base of skills, knowledge, and intellect, or coordinating and networking the efforts of the various work groups and departments. Actions of the first sort can be undertaken at all managerial levels, but actions of the second sort are best orchestrated by senior managers who not only appreciate the strategy-executing significance of strong competencies/capabilities but also have the clout to enforce the necessary networking and cooperation among individuals, groups, departments, and external allies.

One organization-building question is whether to develop the desired competencies and capabilities internally or to outsource them by partnering with key suppliers or forming strategic alliances. The answer depends on what can be safely delegated to outside suppliers or allies versus what internal capabilities are key to the company's long-term success. Either way, though, calls for action. Outsourcing means launching initiatives to identify the most attractive providers and to establish collaborative relationships. Developing the capabilities in-house means marshaling personnel with relevant skills and experience, networking the individual skills and related cross-functional activities to form organizational capability, and building the desired levels of proficiency through repetition (practice makes perfect).[6]

Sometimes the tediousness of internal organization building can be shortcut by buying a company that has the requisite capability and integrating its competencies into the firm's value chain. Indeed, a pressing need to acquire certain capabilities quickly is one reason to acquire another company—an acquisition aimed at building greater capability can be every bit as competitively valuable as an acquisition aimed at adding new products or services to the company's business lineup. Capabilities-motivated acquisitions are essential (1) when a market opportunity can slip by faster than a needed capability can be created internally, and (2) when industry conditions, technology, or competitors are moving at such a rapid clip that time is of the essence. But usually there's no good substitute for ongoing internal efforts to build and strengthen the company's competencies and capabilities in performing strategy-critical value chain activities.

Updating and Reshaping Competencies and Capabilities as External Conditions and Company Strategy Change   Even after core competencies and competitive capabilities are in place and functioning, company managers can't relax. Competencies and capabilities that grow stale can impair competitiveness unless they are refreshed, modified, or even replaced in response to ongoing market changes and shifts in company strategy. Indeed, the buildup of knowledge and experience over time, coupled with the imperatives of keeping capabilities in step with ongoing strategy and market changes, makes it appropriate to view a company as *a bundle of evolving competencies and capabilities.* Management's organization-building challenge is one of deciding when and how to recalibrate existing competencies and capabilities, and when and how to develop new ones. Although the task is formidable, ideally it produces a dynamic organization.

From Competencies and Capabilities to Competitive Advantage

While strong core competencies and competitive capabilities are a major assist in executing strategy, they are an equally important avenue for securing a competitive edge over rivals in situations where it is relatively easy for rivals to copy smart strategies. Any time rivals can readily duplicate successful strategy features, making it difficult or impossible to beat rivals in the marketplace with a superior strategy, the chief way to achieve lasting competitive advantage is to beat them by performing certain value chain activities in superior fashion. Building core competencies, resource strengths, and organizational capabilities that rivals can't match is thus one of the best and most reliable ways to beat them. Moreover, cutting-edge core competencies and organizational capabilities are not easily duplicated by rival firms; thus, any competitive edge they produce is likely to be sustainable, paving the way for above-average organizational performance.

The Strategic Role of Employee Training

Training and retraining are important when a company shifts to a strategy requiring different skills, competitive capabilities, managerial approaches, and operating methods. Training is also strategically important in organizational efforts to build skills-based competencies. And it is a key activity in businesses where technical know-how is changing so rapidly that a company loses its ability to compete unless its skilled people have cutting-edge knowledge and expertise. Successful strategy implementers see to it that the training function is both adequately funded and effective. If the chosen strategy calls for new skills, deeper technological capability, or building and using new capabilities, training should be placed near the top of the action agenda.

The strategic importance of training has not gone unnoticed. Over 600 companies have established internal "universities" to lead the training effort, facilitate continuous organizational learning, and help upgrade company competencies and capabilities. Many companies conduct orientation sessions for new employees, fund an assortment of competence-building training programs, and reimburse employees for tuition and other expenses associated with obtaining additional college education, attending professional development courses, and earning professional certification of one kind or another. A number of companies offer online, just-in-time training courses to employees around the clock. Increasingly, employees at all levels are expected to take an active role in their own professional development, assuming responsibility for keeping their skills and expertise up-to-date and in sync with the company's needs.

MATCHING ORGANIZATION STRUCTURE TO STRATEGY

There are few hard-and-fast rules for organizing the work effort to support strategy. Every firm's organization chart is partly a product of its particular situation, reflecting prior organizational patterns, varying internal circumstances, executive judgments about reporting relationships, and the politics of who gets which assignments. Moreover, every strategy is grounded in its own set of key success factors and value chain activities. But some considerations are common to all companies. These are summarized in Figure 11.3 and discussed in turn in the following sections.

Deciding Which Value Chain Activities to Perform Internally and Which to Outsource

In any business, some activities in the value chain are always more critical to strategic success and competitive advantage than others. Among the primary value chain activ-

figure 11.3   **Structuring the Work Effort to Promote Successful Strategy Execution**

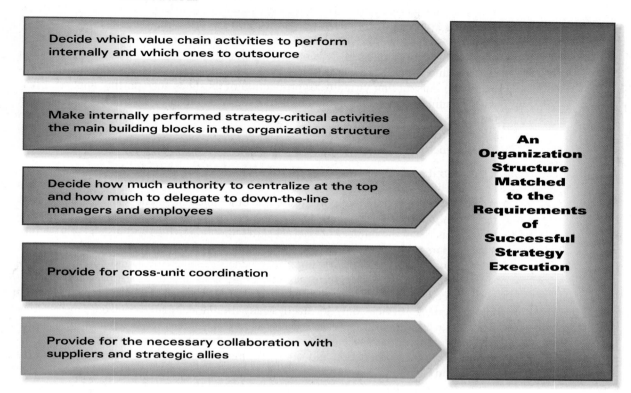

Decide which value chain activities to perform internally and which ones to outsource

Make internally performed strategy-critical activities the main building blocks in the organization structure

Decide how much authority to centralize at the top and how much to delegate to down-the-line managers and employees

Provide for cross-unit coordination

Provide for the necessary collaboration with suppliers and strategic allies

An Organization Structure Matched to the Requirements of Successful Strategy Execution

ities are certain crucial business processes that have to be performed either exceedingly well or in closely coordinated fashion for the organization to deliver on the capabilities needed for strategic success. For instance, hotel/motel enterprises have to be good at fast check-in/check-out, room maintenance, food service, and creating a pleasant ambience. For a manufacturer of chocolate bars, buying quality cocoa beans at low prices is vital and reducing production costs by a fraction of a cent per bar can mean a seven-figure improvement in the bottom line. In discount stock brokerage, the strategy-critical activities are fast access to information, accurate order execution, efficient record keeping, and good customer service. In specialty chemicals, the critical activities are R&D, product innovation, getting new products onto the market quickly, effective marketing, and expertise in assisting customers. In consumer electronics, where advancing technology drives new product innovation, rapidly getting cutting-edge, next-generation products to market is a critical organizational capability.

As a general rule, strategy-critical activities need to be performed internally so that management can directly control their performance. Less important activities—like routine administrative housekeeping (doing the payroll, administering employee benefit programs, providing corporate security, managing stockholder relations, maintaining fleet vehicles) and some support functions (information technology and data processing, training, public relations, market research, legal and legislative affairs)—may be strong candidates for outsourcing. Two questions help pinpoint an organization's strategy-critical activities: "What functions or business processes have to be performed extra well or in timely fashion to achieve sustainable competitive advantage?" and "In what value chain activities would poor execution seriously impair strategic success?"[7]

However, a number of companies have found ways to successfully rely on outside components suppliers, product designers, distribution channels, advertising agencies, and financial services firms to perform strategically significant value chain activities.[8] For years Polaroid Corporation bought its film from Eastman Kodak, its electronics from Texas Instruments, and its cameras from Timex and others, while it concentrated on producing its unique self-developing film packets and designing its next-generation cameras and films. Nike concentrates on design, marketing, and distribution to retailers, while outsourcing virtually all production of its shoes and sporting apparel. Likewise, a number of personal computer manufacturers outsource assembly, concentrating their energies instead on product design, sales and marketing, and distribution. So while performing strategy-critical activities in-house normally makes good sense, there can be times when outsourcing some of them works to good advantage.

The Merits of Outsourcing Noncritical Value Chain Activities   Managers too often spend inordinate amounts of time, mental energy, and financial resources wrestling with functional support groups and other internal bureaucracies, which diverts their attention from the company's strategy-critical activities. One way to reduce such distractions is to cut the number of internal staff-support activities and instead rely on outside vendors with specialized expertise to supply such noncritical support services as Web site operations, data processing, fringe benefits management, and training. An outsider, by concentrating specialists and technology in its area of expertise, can frequently perform certain services as well or better, and often more cheaply, than a company that performs these services only for itself. Many mining companies outsource geological work, assaying, and drilling. E. & J. Gallo Winery outsources 95 percent of its grape production, letting farmers take on the weather and other grape-growing risks while it concentrates on wine production and sales.[9] Eastman Kodak, Ford, Exxon Mobil, Merrill Lynch, and Chevron have outsourced their data processing activities to computer service firms, believing that outside specialists can perform the needed services at lower costs and equal or better quality. A relatively large number of companies outsource the operation of their Web sites to Web design and hosting enterprises.

But besides less internal hassle and lower costs there are other strong reasons to consider outsourcing. Approached from a strategic point of view, outsourcing noncrucial support activities can decrease internal bureaucracies, flatten the organization structure, speed decision making, heighten the company's strategic focus, improve its innovative capacity (through interaction with best-in-world suppliers), and increase competitive responsiveness.[10] Outsourcing has considerable merit when it allows a company to concentrate its own energies and resources on those value chain activities for which it can create unique value and thus become best in the industry (or, better still, best in the world). It also has merit when the company needs strategic control to build core competencies, achieve competitive advantage, and manage key customer/supplier/distributor relationships.

> **core concept**
> Outsourcing has many strategy-executing advantages—lower costs, less internal bureaucracy, speedier decision-making, and heightened strategic focus.

The Merits of Partnering with Others to Gain Added Competitive Capabilities   There is another equally important reason to look outside for resources to compete effectively aside from just the cost savings and agility that outsourcing can permit. *Partnerships can add to a company's arsenal of capabilities and contribute to better strategy execution.* By building, continually improving, and then leveraging partnerships, a company enhances its overall organizational capabilities and builds resource strengths—strengths that deliver value to customers and consequently pave the way for competitive success.

Automobile manufacturers, for example, work closely with their suppliers to advance the design and functioning of engine cooling systems, transmission systems, electrical systems, and so on—all of which helps shorten the cycle time for new models, improve the quality and performance of those models, and lower overall production costs. Prior to merging with Germany's Daimler-Benz, Chrysler transformed itself from a high-cost producer into a low-cost producer by abandoning internal production of many parts and components and instead outsourcing them from more efficient parts/components suppliers; greater reliance on outsourcing enabled Chrysler to shorten its design-to-market cycle for new models and drive down its production costs. Soft-drink and beer manufacturers all cultivate their relationships with their bottlers and distributors to strengthen access to local markets and build the loyalty, support, and commitment for corporate marketing programs, without which their own sales and growth are weakened. Similarly, fast-food enterprises like McDonald's and Taco Bell find it essential to work hand-in-hand with franchisees on outlet cleanliness, consistency of product quality, in-store ambience, courtesy and friendliness of store personnel, and other aspects of store operations. Unless franchisees continuously deliver sufficient customer satisfaction to attract repeat business, a fast-food chain's sales and competitive standing will suffer quickly. Companies like Ford, Boeing, Aerospatiale, AT&T, BMW, and Dell Computer have learned that their central R&D groups cannot begin to match the innovative capabilities of a well-managed network of supply chain partners having the ability to advance the technology, lead the development of next-generation parts and components, and supply them at a relatively low price.[11]

> **core concept**
> Strategic partnerships, alliances, and close collaboration with suppliers, distributors, makers of complementary products, and even competitors all make good strategic sense whenever the result is to enhance organizational resources and capabilities.

The Dangers of Excessive Outsourcing   Critics contend that *a company that goes overboard on outsourcing can hollow out its knowledge base and capabilities, putting itself at the mercy of outside suppliers and leaving it short of the resource strengths to be master of its own destiny.*[12] The point is well taken. Outsourcing strategy-critical activities must be done judiciously and with safeguards against losing control over the performance of key value chain activities and becoming overly dependent on outsiders. Thus, many companies refuse to source key components from a single supplier, opting to use two or three suppliers as a way to avoid becoming overly dependent on any one supplier and giving any one supplier too much bargaining power. Moreover, they regularly evaluate their suppliers, looking not only at the supplier's overall performance but also at whether they should switch to another supplier or even bring the activity back in-house. To avoid loss of control, companies typically work closely with key suppliers, endeavoring to make sure that suppliers' activities are closely integrated with their own requirements and expectations. Most companies appear alert to the primary danger of excessive outsourcing: being caught without the internal strengths and capabilities needed to protect their well-being in the marketplace.

Making Strategy-Critical Activities the Main Building Blocks of the Organization Structure

The rationale for making strategy-critical activities the main building blocks in structuring a business is compelling: If activities crucial to strategic success are to have the resources, decision-making influence, and organizational impact they need, they have to be centerpieces in the organizational scheme. Plainly, implementing a new or changed strategy is likely to entail new or different key activities, competencies, or capabilities and therefore to require new or different organizational arrangements. If workable organizational adjustments are not forthcoming, the resulting mismatch between strategy and structure can open the door to execution and performance problems.[13] Hence, attempting to carry out a new strategy with an old organizational structure is usually unwise.

Although the stress here is on designing the organization structure around the needs of effective strategy execution, it is worth noting that structure can and does influence the choice of strategy. A good strategy must be doable. When an organization's present structure is so far out of line with the requirements of a particular strategy that the organization would have to be turned upside down to implement it, the strategy may not be doable and should not be given further consideration. In such cases, structure shapes the choice of strategy. The thing to remember, however, is that *once a strategy is chosen, structure must be modified to fit the strategy if, in fact, an approximate fit does not already exist.* Any influences of structure on strategy should, logically, come before the point of strategy selection rather than after it.

The Primary Building Blocks of the Organization Structure

The primary organizational building blocks within a business are usually *traditional functional departments* (R&D, engineering and design, production and operations, sales and marketing, information technology, finance and accounting, and human resources) and *process-complete departments* (supply chain management, filling customer orders, customer service, quality control, direct sales via the company's Web site).[14] In enterprises with operations in various countries around the world (or with geographically scattered organizational units within a country), the basic building blocks may also include *geographic organizational units,* each of which has profit/loss responsibility for its assigned geographic area. In vertically integrated firms, the major building blocks are *divisional units performing one or more of the major processing steps along the value chain* (raw materials production, components manufacture, assembly, wholesale distribution, retail store operations); each division in the value chain may operate as a profit center for performance measurement purposes.

The typical building blocks of a diversified company are its *individual businesses,* with each business unit usually operating as an independent profit center and with corporate headquarters performing assorted support functions for all of its business units.

Why Functional Organization Structures Often Impede Strategy Execution

A big weakness of traditional functionally organized structures is that pieces of strategically relevant activities and capabilities often end up scattered across many departments, with the result that no one group or manager is accountable. Consider, for example, how a functional structure results in fragmented performance of the following strategy-critical activities:

- *Filling customer orders accurately and promptly*—a process that cuts across sales (which wins the order); finance (which may have to check credit terms or approve special financing); production (which must produce the goods and replenish warehouse inventories as needed); warehousing (which has to verify whether the items are in stock, pick the order from the warehouse, and package it for shipping); and shipping (which has to choose a carrier to deliver the goods and release the goods to the carrier).[15]

- *Speeding new products to market*—a cross-functional process involving personnel in R&D, design and engineering, purchasing, manufacturing, and sales and marketing.

- *Improving product quality*—a process that often involves the collaboration of personnel in R&D, engineering and design, components purchasing from suppliers, in-house components production, manufacturing, and assembly.
- *Supply chain management*—a collaborative process that cuts across such functional areas as purchasing, engineering and design, components purchasing, inventory management, manufacturing and assembly, and warehousing and shipping.
- *Building the capability to conduct business via the Internet*—a process that involves personnel in information technology, supply chain management, production, sales and marketing, warehousing and shipping, customer service, finance, and accounting.
- *Obtaining feedback from customers and making product modifications to meet their needs*—a process that involves personnel in customer service and after-sale support, R&D, engineering and design, components purchasing, manufacturing and assembly, and marketing research.

Handoffs from one department to another lengthen completion time and frequently drive up administrative costs, since coordinating the fragmented pieces can soak up hours of effort on the parts of many people.[16] This is not a fatal flaw of functional organization—organizing around specific functions has worked to good advantage in support activities like finance and accounting, human resource management, and engineering, and in such primary activities as R&D, manufacturing, and marketing. But fragmentation is an important weakness of functional organization, accounting for why we indicated that a company's competencies and capabilities are usually cross-functional and don't reside in the activities of a single functional department.

Increasingly during the past decade, companies have found that rather than continuing to scatter related pieces of a strategy-critical business process across several functional departments and scrambling to integrate their efforts, it is better to reengineer the work effort and create *process departments*. This is done by pulling the people who performed the pieces in functional departments into a group that works together to perform the whole process. Pulling the pieces of strategy-critical processes out of the functional silos and creating process departments or cross-functional work groups charged with performing all the steps needed to produce a strategy-critical result has been termed **business process reengineering.**

> **core concept**
> *Business process reengineering* involves pulling the pieces of a strategy-critical process out of various functional departments and integrating them into a streamlined, cohesive series of work steps performed within a single work unit.

In the electronics industry, where product life cycles run only three to six months due to the speed of advancing technology, companies have formed process departments charged with cutting the time it takes to bring new technologies and products to commercial fruition. Northwest Water, a British utility, used business process reengineering to eliminate 45 work depots that served as home bases to crews who installed and repaired water and sewage lines and equipment. Now crews work directly from their vehicles, receiving assignments and reporting work completion from computer terminals in their trucks. Crew members are no longer employees but contractors to Northwest Water. These reengineering efforts not only eliminated the need for the work depots but also allowed Northwest Water to eliminate a big percentage of the bureaucratic personnel and supervisory organization that managed the crews.[17] At acute care hospitals such as Lee Memorial in Fort Myers, Florida, and St. Vincent's in Melbourne, Australia, medical care has been reengineered so that it is delivered by interdisciplinary teams of health care professionals organized around the needs of the patients and their families rather than around functional departments within the hospital. Both hospitals created treatment-specific wards within the hospital to handle most of a patient's needs, from admission to discharge. Patients are no longer wheeled from department to department for procedures and tests; instead, teams have the equipment and resources within each focused care unit to provide total care for the patient. While the hospitals had some concern about functional inefficiency in the use of some facilities, process organization has resulted in substantially lower operating costs, faster patient recovery, and greater satisfaction on the part of patients and caregivers.

Reengineering strategy-critical business processes to reduce fragmentation across traditional departmental lines and cut bureaucratic overhead has proved to be a legitimate organization design tool, not a passing fad. Process organization is every bit as valid an organizing principle as functional specialization. Strategy execution is improved when the pieces of strategy-critical activities and core business processes performed by different departments are properly integrated and coordinated.

Companies that have reengineered some of their business processes have ended up compressing formerly separate steps and tasks into jobs performed by a single person and integrating jobs into team activities. Reorganization then follows as a natural consequence of task synthesis and job redesign. When done properly, reengineering can produce dramatic gains in productivity and organizational capability. In the order-processing section of General Electric's circuit breaker division, elapsed time from order receipt to delivery was cut from three weeks to three days by consolidating six production units into one, reducing a variety of former inventory and handling steps, automating the design system to replace a human custom-design process, and cutting the organizational layers between managers and workers from three to one. Productivity rose 20 percent in one year, and unit manufacturing costs dropped 30 percent.[18]

Determining the Degree of Authority and Independence to Give Each Unit and Each Employee

In executing strategy and conducting daily operations, companies must decide how much authority to delegate to the managers of each organization unit—especially the heads of business subsidiaries; functional and process departments; and plants, sales offices, distribution centers; and other operating units—and how much decision-making latitude to give individual employees in performing their jobs. The two extremes are to *centralize decision making* at the top (the CEO and a few close lieutenants) or to *decentralize decision making* by giving managers and employees considerable decision-making latitude in their areas of responsibility. As shown in Table 11.1, the two approaches are based on sharply different underlying principles and beliefs, with each having its pros and cons.

Centralized Decision-Making   *In a highly centralized organization structure, top executives retain authority for most strategic and operating decisions and keep a tight rein on business-unit heads, department heads, and the managers of key operating units; comparatively little discretionary authority is granted to frontline supervisors and rank-and-file employees.* The command-and-control paradigm of centralized structures is based on the underlying assumption that frontline personnel have neither the time nor the inclination to direct and properly control the work they are performing, and that they lack the knowledge and judgment to make wise decisions about how best to do it—hence the need for managerially prescribed policies and procedures, close supervision, and tight control. The thesis underlying authoritarian structures is that strict enforcement of detailed procedures backed by rigorous managerial oversight is the most reliable way to keep the daily execution of strategy on track.

There are disadvantages to having a small number of top-level managers micromanage the business by personally making decisions or by requiring they approve the recommendations of lower-level subordinates before actions can be taken.

table 11.1   **Advantages and Disadvantages of Centralized versus Decentralized Decision-Making**

Centralized Organizational Structures	Decentralized Organizational Structures
Basic Tenets • Decisions on most matters of importance should be pushed to managers up the line who have the experience, expertise, and judgment to decide what is the wisest or best course of action. • Frontline supervisors and rank-and-file employees can't be relied on to make the right decisions because they seldom know what is best for the organization and because they do not have the time or the inclination to properly manage the tasks they are performing. **Chief Advantage** • Tight control from the top allows for accountability. **Primary Disadvantages** • Lengthens response times because management bureaucracy must decide on a course of action. • Does not encourage responsibility among lower-level managers and rank-and-file employees. • Discourages lower-level managers and rank-and-file employees from exercising any initiative—they are expected to wait to be told what to do.	**Basic Tenets** • Decision-making authority should be put in the hands of the people closest to and most familiar with the situation and these people should be trained to exercise good judgment. • A company that draws on the combined intellectual capital of all its employees can outperform a command-and-control company. **Chief Advantages** • Encourages lower-level managers and rank-and-file employees to exercise initiative and act responsibly. • Promotes greater motivation and involvement in the business on the part of more company personnel. • Spurs new ideas and creative thinking. • Allows fast response times. • Reduces layers of management. **Primary Disadvantages** • Puts the organization at risk if many bad decisions are made at lower levels. • Impedes cross-unit coordination and capture of strategic fits.

The big advantage of an authoritarian structure is tight control by the manager in charge—it is easy to know who is accountable when things do not go well. But there are some serious disadvantages. Hierarchical command-and-control structures make an organization sluggish in responding to changing conditions because of the time it takes for the review/approval process to run up all the layers of the management bureaucracy. Furthermore, to work well, centralized decision making requires top-level managers to gather and process whatever information is relevant to the decision. When the relevant knowledge resides at lower organizational levels (or is technical, detailed, or hard to express in words), it is difficult and time-consuming to get all of the facts and nuances in front of a high-level executive located far from the scene of the action—full under-standing of the situation cannot be readily copied from one mind to another. Hence, centralized decision making is often impractical—the larger the company and the more scattered its operations, the more that decision-making authority has to be delegated to managers closer to the scene of the action.

Decentralized Decision-Making   *In a highly decentralized organization, decision-making authority is pushed down to the lowest organizational level capable of making timely, informed, competent decisions.* The objective is to put adequate decision-making authority in the hands of the people closest to and most familiar with the situation and train them to weigh all the factors and exercise good judgment. The case for empowering down-the-line managers and employees to make decisions related to daily operations and executing the strategy is based on the belief that a company that

> The ultimate goal of decentralized decision making is not to push decisions down to lower levels but to put decision-making authority in the hands of those persons or teams closest to and most knowledgeable about the situation.

draws on the combined intellectual capital of all its employees can outperform a command-and-control company. Decentralized decision making means, for example, that in a diversified company the various business-unit heads have broad authority to execute the agreed-on business strategy with comparatively little interference from corporate headquarters; moreover, the business-unit heads delegate considerable decision-making latitude to functional and process department heads and the heads of the various operating units (plants, distribution centers, sales offices) in implementing and executing their pieces of the strategy. In turn, work teams may be empowered to manage and improve their assigned value chain activity, and employees with customer contact may be empowered to do what it takes to please customers. At Starbucks, for example, employees are encouraged to exercise initiative in promoting customer satisfaction—there's the story of a store employee who, when the computerized cash register system went offline, enthusiastically offered free coffee to waiting customers.[19] With decentralized decision making, top management maintains control by limiting empowered managers' and employees' discretionary authority and holding people accountable for the decisions they make.

Decentralized organization structures have much to recommend them. Delegating greater authority to subordinate managers and employees creates a more horizontal organization structure with fewer management layers. Whereas in a centralized vertical structure managers and workers have to go up the ladder of authority for an answer, in a decentralized horizontal structure they develop their own answers and action plans—making decisions in their areas of responsibility and being accountable for results is an integral part of their job. Pushing decision-making authority down to middle and lower-level managers and then further on to work teams and individual employees shortens organizational response times and spurs new ideas, creative thinking, innovation, and greater involvement on the part of subordinate managers and employees. In worker-empowered structures, jobs can be defined more broadly, several tasks can be integrated into a single job, and people can direct their own work. Fewer managers are needed because deciding how to do things becomes part of each person's or team's job. Further, today's electronic communication systems make it easy and relatively inexpensive for people at all organizational levels to have direct access to data, other employees, managers, suppliers, and customers. They can access information quickly (via the Internet or company intranet), readily check with superiors or others as needed, and take responsible action. Typically, there are genuine gains in morale and productivity when people are provided with the tools and information they need to operate in a self-directed way.

Insofar as all five tasks of strategic management are concerned, a decentralized approach to decision making means that the managers of each organizational unit should not only lead the crafting of their unit's strategy but also lead the decision making on how to execute it. Decentralization thus requires selecting strong managers to head each organizational unit and holding them accountable for crafting and executing appropriate strategies for their units. Managers who consistently produce unsatisfactory results have to be weeded out.

The past decade has seen a growing shift from authoritarian, multilayered hierarchical structures to flatter, more decentralized structures that stress employee empowerment. There's strong and growing consensus that authoritarian, hierarchical organization structures are not well suited to implementing and executing strategies in an era when extensive information and instant communication are the norm and when a big fraction of the organization's most valuable assets consists of intellectual capital and resides in the knowledge and capabilities of its employees. Many companies have therefore begun empowering lower-level managers and employees throughout their organizations, giving them greater discretionary authority to make strategic adjustments in their areas of responsibility and to decide what needs to be done to put new strategic initiatives into place and execute them proficiently.

Maintaining Control in a Decentralized Organization Structure
Pushing decision-making authority deep down into the organization structure presents its own challenge: *how to exercise adequate control over the actions of empowered employees so that the business is not put at risk at the same time that the benefits of empowerment are realized.*[20] Maintaining adequate organizational control over empowered employees is generally accomplished by placing limits on the authority that empowered personnel can exercise, holding people accountable for their decisions, instituting compensation incentives that reward people for doing their jobs in a manner to contributes to good company performance, and creating a corporate culture where there's strong peer pressure on individuals to act responsibly.

Capturing Strategic Fits in a Decentralized Structure Diversified companies striving to capture cross-business strategic fits have to beware of giving business heads full rein to operate independently when cross-business collaboration is essential in order to gain strategic fit benefits. Cross-business strategic fits typically have to be captured either by enforcing close cross-business collaboration or by centralizing performance of functions having strategic fits at the corporate level.[21] For example, if businesses with overlapping process and product technologies have their own independent R&D departments—each pursuing their own priorities, projects, and strategic agendas—it's hard for the corporate parent to prevent duplication of effort, capture either economies of scale or economies of scope, or broaden the company's R&D efforts to embrace new technological paths, product families, end-use applications, and customer groups. Where cross-business R&D fits exist, the best solution is usually to centralize the R&D function and have a coordinated corporate R&D effort that serves both the interests of individual business and the company as a whole. Likewise, centralizing the related activities of separate businesses makes sense when there are opportunities to share a common sales force, use common distribution channels, rely on a common field service organization to handle customer requests for technical assistance or provide maintenance and repair services, use common e-commerce systems and approaches, and so on.

The point here is that efforts to decentralize decision making and give organizational units leeway in conducting operations have to be tempered with the need to maintain adequate control and cross-unit coordination—decentralization doesn't mean delegating authority in ways that allow organization units and individuals to do their own thing. The strategic importance of cross-unit collaboration creates numerous instances when decision-making authority needs to be retained at high levels in the organization and ample cross-unit coordination strictly enforced.

Providing for Internal Cross-Unit Coordination

The classic way to coordinate the activities of organizational units is to position them in the hierarchy so that the most closely related ones report to a single person (a functional department head, a process manager, a geographic area head, a senior executive). Managers higher up in the ranks generally have the clout to coordinate, integrate, and arrange for the cooperation of units under their supervision. In such structures, the chief executive officer, chief operating officer, and business-level managers end up as central points of coordination because of their positions of authority over the whole unit. When a firm is pursuing a related diversification strategy, coordinating the related activities of independent business units often requires the centralizing authority of a single corporate-level officer. Also, diversified companies commonly centralize such staff support functions as public relations, finance and accounting, employee benefits, and information technology at the corporate level both to contain the costs of support activities and to facilitate uniform and coordinated performance of such functions within each business unit.

But, as explained earlier, the functional organization structures employed in most businesses often result in fragmentation. Close cross-unit collaboration is usually needed to build core competencies and competitive capabilities in such strategically important activities as speeding new products to market and providing superior customer service. To combat fragmentation and achieve the desired degree of cross-unit cooperation and collaboration, most companies supplement their functional organization structures. Sometimes this takes the form of creating process departments to bring together the pieces of strategically important activities previously performed in separate functional units. And sometimes the coordinating mechanisms involve the use of cross-functional task forces, dual reporting relationships, informal organizational networking, voluntary cooperation, incentive compensation tied to group performance measures, and strong executive-level insistence on teamwork and cross-department cooperation (including removal of recalcitrant managers who stonewall collaborative efforts). At one European-based company, a top executive promptly replaced the managers of several plants who were not fully committed to collaborating closely on eliminating duplication in product development and production efforts among plants in several different countries. Earlier, the executive, noting that negotiations among the managers had stalled on which labs and plants to close, had met with all the managers, asked them to cooperate to find a solution, discussed with them which options were unacceptable, and given them a deadline to find a solution. When the asked-for teamwork wasn't forthcoming, several managers were replaced.

See Illustration Capsule 11.2 for how 3M Corporation puts the necessary organizational arrangements into place to create worldwide coordination on technology matters.

Providing for Collaboration with Outside Suppliers and Strategic Allies

Someone or some group must be authorized to collaborate as needed with each major outside constituency involved in strategy execution. Forming alliances and cooperative relationships presents immediate opportunities and opens the door to future possibilities, but nothing valuable is realized until the relationship grows, develops, and blossoms. Unless top management sees that constructive organizational bridge-building with strategic partners occurs and that productive working relationships emerge, the value of alliances is lost and the company's power to execute its strategy is weakened. If close working relationships with suppliers are crucial, then supply chain management must be given formal status on the company's organization chart and a significant position in the pecking order. If distributor/dealer/franchisee relationships are important, someone must be assigned the task of nurturing the relationships with forward channel allies. If working in parallel with providers of complementary products and services contributes to enhanced organizational capability, then cooperative organizational arrangements have to be put in place and managed to good effect.

Building organizational bridges with external allies can be accomplished by appointing "relationship managers" with responsibility for making particular strategic

illustration capsule 11.2
Cross-Unit Coordination on Technology at 3M Corporation

At 3M, technology experts in more than 100 laboratories around the world have come to work openly and cooperatively without resorting to turf-protection tactics or not-invented-here mindsets. 3M management has been successful in creating a collegial working environment in which the scientists call on one another for assistance and advice and in rapid technology transfer.

Management formed a Technical Council, composed of the heads of the major labs; the council meets monthly and has a three-day annual retreat to discuss ways to improve cross-unit transfer of technology and other issues of common interest. In addition, management created a broader-based Technical Forum, composed of scientists and technical experts chosen as representatives, to facilitate grassroots communication among employees in all the labs. One of the forum's responsibilities is to organize employees with similar technical interests from all the labs into chapters; chapter members attend regular seminars with experts from outside the company. There's also an annual three-day technology fair at which 3M scientists showcase their latest findings for colleagues and expand their network of acquaintances.

As a result of these collaborative efforts, 3M has developed a portfolio of more than 100 technologies and created the capability to routinely use these technologies in product applications in three different divisions that each serve multiple markets.

partnerships or alliances generate the intended benefits. Relationship managers have many roles and functions: getting the right people together, promoting good rapport, seeing that plans for specific activities are developed and carried out, helping adjust internal organizational procedures and communication systems, ironing out operating dissimilarities, and nurturing interpersonal cooperation. Multiple cross-organization ties have to be established and kept open to ensure proper communication and coordination.[22] There has to be enough information sharing to make the relationship work and periodic frank discussions of conflicts, trouble spots, and changing situations.[23]

Perspectives on Structuring the Work Effort

All organization designs have their strategy-related strengths and weaknesses. To do a good job of matching structure to strategy, strategy implementers first have to pick a basic design and modify it as needed to fit the company's particular business lineup. They must then (1) supplement the design with appropriate coordinating mechanisms (cross-functional task forces, special project teams, self-contained work teams, and so on), and (2) institute whatever networking and communication arrangements it takes to support effective execution of the firm's strategy. Some companies may avoid setting up "ideal" organizational arrangements because they do not want to disturb certain existing reporting relationships or because they need to accommodate other situational idiosyncrasies, yet they must still work toward the goal of building a competitively capable organization.

> There is no perfect or ideal way of structuring the work effort.

The ways and means of developing stronger core competencies and organizational capabilities (or creating altogether new ones) have to fit a company's own circumstances. Not only do different companies and executives tackle the capabilities-building challenge in different ways, but the task of

> Organizational capabilities emerge from a process of consciously knitting together the efforts of different work groups, departments, and external allies, not from how the boxes on the organization chart are arranged.

building different capabilities requires different organizing techniques. Thus, generalizing about how to build capabilities has to be done cautiously. What can be said unequivocally is that building a capable organization entails a process of consciously knitting together the efforts of individuals and groups. Competencies and capabilities emerge from establishing and nurturing cooperative working relationships among people and groups to perform activities in a more customer-satisfying fashion, not from rearranging boxes on an organization chart. Furthermore, organization building is a task in which senior management must be deeply involved. Indeed, effectively managing both internal organization processes and external collaboration to create and develop competitively valuable competencies and capabilities is a top challenge for senior executives in today's companies.

ORGANIZATIONAL STRUCTURES OF THE FUTURE

Many of today's companies are winding up the task of remodeling their traditional hierarchical structures once built around functional specialization and centralized authority.

> Revolutionary changes in how companies are organizing the work effort have been occurring since the early 1990s.

Much of the corporate downsizing movement in the late 1980s and early 1990s was aimed at recasting authoritarian, pyramidal organizational structures into flatter, decentralized structures. The change was driven by growing realization that command-and-control hierarchies were proving a liability in businesses where customer preferences were shifting from standardized products to custom orders and special features, product life cycles were growing shorter, custom mass-production methods were replacing standardized mass-production techniques, customers wanted to be treated as individuals, technological change was ongoing, and market conditions were fluid. Layered management hierarchies with lots of checks and controls that required people to look upward in the organizational structure for answers and approval were failing to deliver responsive customer service and timely adaptations to changing conditions. Likewise, functional silos, task-oriented work, and fragmentation of strategy-critical activities further contributed to an erosion of competitiveness in fluid or volatile business environments.

The organizational adjustments and downsizing of companies in 2001–2002 brought further refinements and changes to streamline organizational activities and shake out inefficiencies. The goals have been to make the organization leaner, flatter, and more responsive to change. Many companies are drawing on five tools of organizational design: (1) empowered managers and workers, (2) reengineered work processes, (3) self-directed work teams, (4) rapid incorporation of Internet technology applications, and (5) networking with outsiders to improve existing organization capabilities and create new ones. Considerable management attention is being devoted to building a company capable of outcompeting rivals on the basis of superior resource strengths and competitive capabilities—capabilities that are increasingly based on intellectual capital. The organizations of the future will have several new characteristics:

- Fewer barriers between different vertical ranks, between functions and disciplines, between units in different geographic locations, and between the company and its suppliers, distributors/dealers, strategic allies, and customers.
- A capacity for change and rapid learning.
- Collaborative efforts among people in different functional specialties and geographic locations—essential to create organization competencies and capabilities.

- Extensive use of Internet technology and e-commerce business practices—real-time data and information systems, greater reliance on online systems for transacting business with suppliers and customers, and Internet-based communication and collaboration with suppliers, customers, and strategic partners.

key|points

The job of strategy implementation and execution is to convert strategic plans into actions and good results. The test of successful strategy execution is whether actual organization performance matches or exceeds the targets spelled out in the strategic plan. Shortfalls in performance signal weak strategy, weak execution, or both.

In deciding how to implement a new or revised strategy, managers have to determine what internal conditions are needed to execute the strategic plan successfully. Then they must create these conditions as rapidly as practical. The process of implementing and executing strategy involves:

1. Building an organization with the competencies, capabilities, and resource strengths to execute strategy successfully.
2. Marshaling resources to support the strategy execution effort.
3. Instituting policies and procedures that facilitate strategy execution.
4. Adopting best practices and striving for continuous improvement.
5. Installing information and operating systems that enable company personnel to carry out their strategic roles proficiently.
6. Tying rewards and incentives directly to the achievement of strategic and financial targets and to good strategy execution.
7. Shaping the work environment and corporate culture to fit the strategy.
8. Exerting the internal leadership needed to drive implementation forward and to keep improving on how the strategy is being executed.

The place for managers to start in implementing and executing a new or different strategy is with *a probing assessment of what the organization must do differently and better to carry out the strategy successfully.* They should then consider *precisely how to make the necessary internal changes* as rapidly as possible. Successful strategy implementers have a knack for diagnosing what their organizations need to do to execute the chosen strategy well and figuring out how to get things done—they are masters in promoting results-oriented behaviors on the part of company personnel and following through on making the right things happen.

Like crafting strategy, executing strategy is a job for a company's whole management team, not just a few senior managers. Top-level managers have to rely on the active support and cooperation of middle and lower managers to push strategy changes into functional areas and operating units and to see that the organization actually operates in accordance with the strategy on a daily basis. Middle and lower-level managers are not only responsible for initiating and supervising the execution process in their areas of authority but also instrumental in getting subordinates to continuously improve on critical value chain activities. Thus, all managers need *an action agenda.*

Building a capable organization is always a top priority in strategy execution, and three types of organization-building actions are paramount:

1. *Staffing the organization.*
2. *Building core competencies and competitive capabilities.*
3. *Structuring the organization and work effort.*

Selecting able people for key positions tends to be one of the earliest strategy implementation steps. No company can hope to perform the activities required for successful strategy execution without attracting capable managers and without employees that give it a suitable knowledge base and portfolio of intellectual capital.

Building core competencies and competitive capabilities involves three stages: (1) developing the *ability* to do something, however imperfectly or inefficiently, by selecting people with the requisite skills and experience, upgrading or expanding individual abilities as needed, and then molding the efforts and work products of individuals into a collaborative group effort; (2) coordinating group efforts to learn how to perform the activity *consistently well and at an acceptable cost,* thereby transforming the ability into a tried-and-true *competence* or *capability;* and (3) continuing to polish and refine the organization's know-how and otherwise sharpen performance such that it becomes *better than rivals* at performing the activity, thus raising the core competence (or capability) to the rank of a *distinctive competence* (or competitively superior capability) and opening an avenue to competitive advantage. Many companies manage to get through stages 1 and 2, but comparatively few qualify for the third stage.

Managerial actions to develop core competencies and competitive capabilities generally take one of two forms: either strengthening the company's base of skills, knowledge, and intellect, or coordinating and networking the efforts of the various work groups and departments. Actions of the first sort can be undertaken at all managerial levels, but actions of the second sort are best orchestrated by senior managers who not only appreciate the strategy-executing significance of strong competencies/capabilities but also have the clout to enforce the necessary networking and cooperation among individuals, groups, departments, and external allies.

Strong core competencies and competitive capabilities are an important avenue for securing a competitive edge over rivals in situations where it is relatively easy for rivals to copy smart strategies. Anytime rivals can readily duplicate successful strategy features, making it difficult or impossible to beat rivals in the marketplace with a superior strategy, the chief way to achieve lasting competitive advantage is to beat rivals by performing certain value chain activities in superior fashion. Building core competencies, resource strengths, and organizational capabilities that rivals can't match is one of the best and most reliable ways to beat them.

Structuring the organization and organizing the work effort in a strategy-supportive fashion has five aspects:

1. Deciding which value chain activities to perform internally and which ones to outsource.
2. Making internally performed strategy-critical activities the main building blocks in the organization structure.
3. Deciding how much authority to centralize at the top and how much to delegate to down-the-line managers and employees.
4. Providing for internal cross-unit coordination and collaboration to build and strengthen internal competencies/capabilities.
5. Providing for the necessary collaboration and coordination with suppliers and strategic allies.

The primary organizational building blocks within a business are usually *traditional functional departments* and *process-complete departments.* In enterprises with operations in various countries around the world (or with geographically scattered organizational units within a country), the basic building blocks may also include *geographic organizational units,* each of which has profit/loss responsibility for its assigned geographic area. In vertically integrated firms, the major building blocks are *divisional units performing one or more of the major processing steps along the value chain* (raw materials production, components manufacture, assembly, wholesale distribution, retail store operations); each division in the value chain may operate as a profit center for performance measurement purposes. The typical building blocks of a diversified company are its *individual businesses,* with each business unit usually operating as an independent profit center and with corporate headquarters performing assorted support functions for all the businesses.

Whatever basic structure is chosen, it usually has to be supplemented with interdisciplinary task forces, incentive compensation schemes tied to measures of joint performance, empowerment of cross-functional and/or self-directed work teams to perform and unify fragmented processes and strategy-critical activities, special project teams, relationship managers, and special top management efforts to knit the work of different individuals and groups into valuable competitive capabilities.

In more and more companies, efforts to match structure to strategy involve fewer layers of management authority; managers and workers are empowered to act on their own judgment; work processes are being reengineered to reduce cross-department fragmentation; collaborative partnerships exist with outsiders (suppliers, distributors/dealers, companies with complementary products/services, and even select competitors); and there's increased outsourcing of selected value chain activities, leaner staffing of internal support functions, and rapidly growing use of Internet technology applications to streamline operations and expedite cross-unit communication.

| exercise

As the new owner of a local ice cream store located in a strip mall adjacent to a university campus, you are contemplating how to organize your business—whether to make your ice cream in-house or outsource its production to a nearby ice cream manufacturer whose brand is in most of the local supermarkets, and how much authority to delegate to the two assistant store managers and to employees working the counter and the cash register. You plan to sell 20 flavors of ice cream.

1. What are the pros and cons of contracting with the local company to custom-produce your product line?

2. Since you do not plan to be in the store during all of the hours it is open, what specific decision-making authority would you delegate to the two assistant store managers?

3. To what extent, if any, should store employees—many of whom will be university students working part-time—be empowered to make decisions relating to store operations (opening and closing, keeping the premises clean and attractive, keeping the work area behind the counter stocked with adequate supplies of cups, cones, napkins, and so on)?

4. Should you create a policies and procedures manual for the assistant managers and employees, or should you just give oral instructions and have them learn their duties and responsibilities on the job?

5. How can you maintain control during the times you are not in the store?

chapter twelve

Managing Internal Operations
Actions That Promote Better Strategy Execution

(© Images.com/CORBIS)

Winning companies know how to do their work better.

—**Michael Hammer and James Champy**

If you talk about change but don't change the reward and recognition system, nothing changes.

—**Paul Allaire**
Former CEO, Xerox Corporation

If you want people motivated to do a good job, give them a good job to do.

—**Frederick Herzberg**

You ought to pay big bonuses for premier performance . . . Be a top payer, not in the middle or low end of the pack.

—**Lawrence Bossidy**
CEO, Honeywell International

In Chapter 11 we emphasized the importance of building organization capabilities and structuring the work effort so as to perform strategy-critical activities in a coordinated and highly competent manner. In this chapter we discuss five additional managerial actions that facilitate the success of a company's strategy execution efforts:

1. Marshaling ample resources behind the drive for good strategy execution and operating excellence.

2. Instituting policies and procedures that facilitate strategy execution.

3. Adopting best practices and striving for continuous improvement in how value chain activities are performed.

4. Installing information and operating systems that enable company personnel to carry out their strategic roles proficiently.

5. Tying rewards and incentives directly to the achievement of strategic and financial targets and to good strategy execution.

MARSHALING RESOURCES BEHIND THE DRIVE FOR GOOD STRATEGY EXECUTION

Early in the process of implementing and executing a new or different strategy, managers need to determine what resources will be needed and then consider whether the current budgets of organizational units are suitable. Plainly, organizational units must have the budgets and resources for executing their parts of the strategic plan effectively and efficiently. Developing a strategy-driven budget requires top management to determine what funding is needed to execute new strategic initiatives and to strengthen or modify the company's competencies and capabilities. This includes careful screening of requests for more people and more or better facilities and equipment, approving those that hold promise for making a cost-justified contribution to strategy execution, and turning down those that don't. Should internal cash flows prove insufficient to fund the planned strategic initiatives, then management must raise additional funds through borrowing or selling additional shares of stock to willing investors.

A company's ability to marshal the resources needed to support new strategic initiatives and steer them to the appropriate organizational units has a major impact on the strategy execution process. Too little funding (stemming either from constrained financial resources or from sluggish management action to adequately increase the budgets of strategy-critical organizational units) slows progress and impedes the efforts of organizational units to execute their pieces of the strategic plan proficiently. Too much funding wastes

core concept
The funding requirements of a new strategy must drive how capital allocations are made and the size of each unit's operating budgets. Underfunding organizational units and activities pivotal to strategic success impedes execution and the drive for operating excellence.

organizational resources and reduces financial performance. Both outcomes argue for managers to be deeply involved in reviewing budget proposals and directing the proper kinds and amounts of resources to strategy-critical organization units.

A change in strategy nearly always calls for budget reallocations. Units important in the prior strategy but having a lesser role in the new strategy may need downsizing. Units that now have a bigger and more critical strategic role may need more people, new equipment, additional facilities, and above-average increases in their operating budgets. Strategy implementers need to be active and forceful in shifting resources, downsizing some areas and upsizing others, not only to amply fund activities with a critical role in the new strategy but also to avoid inefficiency and achieve profit projections. They have to exercise their power to put enough resources behind new strategic initiatives to make things happen, and they have to make the tough decisions to kill projects and activities that are no longer justified.

Visible actions to reallocate operating funds and move people into new organizational units signal a determined commitment to strategic change and frequently are needed to catalyze the implementation process and give it credibility. Microsoft has made a practice of regularly shifting hundreds of programmers to new high-priority programming initiatives within a matter of weeks or even days. At Harris Corporation, where the strategy was to diffuse research ideas into areas that were commercially viable, top management regularly shifted groups of engineers out of government projects and into new commercial venture divisions. Fast-moving developments in many markets are prompting companies to abandon traditional annual or semiannual budgeting and resource allocation cycles in favor of cycles that match the strategy changes a company makes in response to newly developing events.

Just fine-tuning the execution of a company's existing strategy, however, seldom requires big movements of people and money from one area to another. The desired improvements can usually be accomplished through above-average budget increases to organizational units where new initiatives are contemplated and below-average increases (or even small cuts) for the remaining organizational units. The chief exception occurs where a prime ingredient of strategy is to create altogether new capabilities or to generate fresh products and business opportunities within the existing budget. Then, as proposals and business plans worth pursuing bubble up from below, managers have to decide where the needed capital expenditures, operating budgets, and personnel will come from. Companies like 3M, General Electric, and Boeing shift resources and people from area to area as needed to support the launch of new products and new business ventures. They empower "product champions" and small bands of would-be entrepreneurs by giving them financial and technical support and by setting up organizational units and programs to help new ventures blossom more quickly.

INSTITUTING POLICIES AND PROCEDURES THAT FACILITATE STRATEGY EXECUTION

core concept
Well-conceived policies and procedures aid strategy execution; out-of-sync ones are barriers.

Changes in strategy generally call for some changes in work practices and operations. Asking people to alter established procedures always upsets the internal order of things. It is normal for pockets of resistance to develop and for people to exhibit some degree of stress and anxiety about how the changes will affect them, especially when the changes may eliminate jobs. Questions are also likely to arise over what activities need to be rigidly prescribed and where there ought to be leeway for independent action.

figure 12.1   **How Prescribed Policies and Procedures Facilitate Strategy Execution**

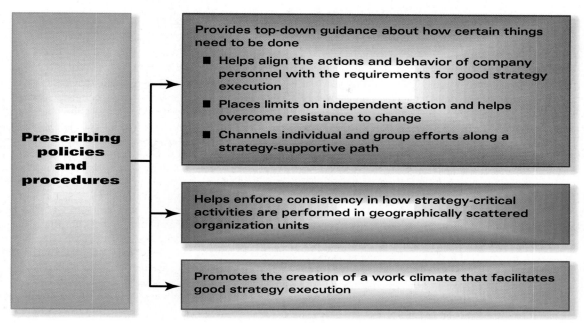

As shown in Figure 12.1, prescribing new policies and operating procedures designed to facilitate strategy execution has merit from several angles:

1. *It provides top-down guidance regarding how certain things now need to be done.* New policies and operating practices can help align actions with strategy throughout the organization, placing limits on independent behavior and channeling individual and group efforts along a path in tune with the new strategy. They also help counteract tendencies for some people to resist change—most people refrain from violating company policy or going against recommended practices and procedures without first gaining clearance or having strong justification.

2. *It helps enforce needed consistency in how particular strategy-critical activities are performed in geographically scattered operating units.* Eliminating significant differences in the operating practices of different plants, sales regions, customer service centers, or the individual outlets in a chain operation is frequently desirable to avoid sending mixed messages to internal personnel and to customers who do business with the company at multiple locations.

3. *It promotes the creation of a work climate that facilitates good strategy execution.* Because dismantling old policies and procedures and instituting new ones invariably alter the internal work climate, strategy implementers can use the policy-changing process as a powerful lever for changing the corporate culture in ways that produce a stronger fit with the new strategy.

Company managers therefore need to be inventive in devising policies and practices that can provide vital support to effective strategy implementation and execution.

In an attempt to steer "crew members" into stronger quality and service behavior patterns, McDonald's policy manual spells out procedures in detail; for example,

illustration capsule 12.1

Graniterock's "Short Pay" Policy: An Innovative Way to Promote Strategy Execution

In 1987, the owners of Graniterock, a 100-plus-year-old supplier of crushed gravel, sand, concrete, and asphalt in Watsonville, California, set two big, hairy, audacious goals (BHAGs) for the company: total customer satisfaction and a reputation for service that met or exceeded that of Nordstrom, the upscale department store famous for pleasing its customers. To drive the internal efforts to achieve these two objectives, top management instituted "short pay," a policy designed to signal both employees and customers that Graniterock was deadly serious about its two strategic commitments. At the bottom of every Graniterock invoice was the following statement:

> If you are not satisfied for any reason, don't pay us for it. Simply scratch out the line item, write a brief note about the problem, and return a copy of this invoice along with your check for the balance.

Customers did not have to call and complain and were not expected to return the product. They were given complete discretionary power to decide whether and how much to pay based on their satisfaction level.

The policy has worked exceptionally well, providing unmistakable feedback and spurring company managers to correct any problems quickly in order to avoid repeated short payments. Graniterock has enjoyed market share increases, while charging a 6 percent price premium for its commodity products in competition against larger rivals. Its profit margins and overall financial performance have improved. Graniterock won the prestigious Malcolm Baldrige National Quality Award in 1992, about five years after instituting the policy. *Fortune* rated Graniterock as one of the 100 best companies to work for in America in 2001 (ranked 17th) and 2002 (ranked 16th). Company employees receive an average of 43 hours of training annually. Entry-level employees, called job owners, start at $16 an hour and progress to such positions as "accomplished job owner" and "improvement champion" (base pay of $26 an hour). The company has a no-layoff policy, provides employees with 12 massages a year, and sends positive customer comments about employees home for families to read.

Source: Based on information in Robert Levering and Milton Moskowitz, "The 100 Best Companies to Work For," *Fortune*, February 4, 2002, p. 73, and Jim Collins, "Turning Goals into Results: The Power of Catalytic Mechanisms," *Harvard Business Review* 77, no. 4 (July–August 1999), pp. 72–73.

"Cooks must turn, never flip, hamburgers … If they haven't been purchased, Big Macs must be discarded in 10 minutes after being cooked and French fries in 7 minutes … Cashiers must make eye contact with and smile at every customer." Hewlett-Packard requires R&D people to make regular visits to customers to learn about their problems, talk about new product applications, and in general keep the company's R&D programs customer-oriented. Mrs. Fields Cookies has a policy of establishing hourly sales quotas for each store outlet; furthermore, it is company policy that cookies not sold within two hours after being baked have to be removed from the case and given to charitable organizations. Illustration Capsule 12.1 describes how Graniterock's "short pay" policy spurs employee focus on providing total customer satisfaction and building the company's reputation for superior customer service.

Thus, there is a definite role for new and revised policies and procedures in the strategy implementation process. Wisely constructed policies and procedures help channel actions, behavior, decisions, and practices in directions that promote good strategy execution. When policies and practices aren't strategy-supportive, they become a barrier to the kinds of attitudinal and behavioral changes strategy implementers are trying to promote. Sometimes people hide behind or vigorously defend long-standing policies and operating procedures in an effort to stall implementation or force it along a different route. Anytime a company alters its strategy, managers should review existing policies and operating procedures, proactively revise or discard those that are out of sync, and formulate new ones to facilitate execution of new strategic initiatives.

None of this implies that companies need thick policy manuals to direct the strategy execution process and prescribe exactly how daily operations are to be conducted. Too much policy can erect as many obstacles as wrong policy or be as confusing as no policy. There is wisdom in a middle approach: *Prescribe enough policies to give organization members clear direction in implementing strategy and to place desirable boundaries on their actions; then empower them to act within these boundaries however they think makes sense.* Allowing company personnel to act anywhere between the "white lines" is especially appropriate when individual creativity and initiative are more essential to good strategy execution than standardization and strict conformity. Instituting strategy-facilitating policies can therefore mean more policies, fewer policies, or different policies. It can mean policies that require things to be done a certain way or policies that give employees leeway to do activities the way they think best.

ADOPTING BEST PRACTICES AND STRIVING FOR CONTINUOUS IMPROVEMENT

Company managers can significantly advance the cause of competent strategy execution by pushing organization units and company personnel to identify and adopt the best practices for performing value chain activities and, further, insisting on continuous improvement in how internal operations are conducted. One of the most widely used and effective tools for gauging how well a company is executing pieces of its strategy entails benchmarking the company's performance of particular activities and business processes against "best-in-industry" and "best-in-world" performers.[1] It can also be useful to look at "best-in-company" performers of an activity if a company has a number of different organizational units performing much the same function at different locations. Identifying, analyzing, and understanding how top companies or individuals perform particular value chain activities and business processes provides useful yardsticks for judging the effectiveness and efficiency of internal operations and setting performance standards for organization units to meet or beat.

> **core concept**
> Managerial efforts to identify and adopt best practices are a powerful tool for promoting operating excellence and better strategy execution.

How the Process of Identifying and Incorporating Best Practices Works

A **best practice** is a technique for performing an activity or business process that at least one company has demonstrated works particularly well. To qualify as a legitimate best practice, the technique must have a proven record in significantly lowering costs, improving quality or performance, shortening time requirements, enhancing safety, or delivering some other highly positive operating outcome. Best practices thus identify a path to operating excellence. For a best practice to be valuable and transferable, it must demonstrate success over time, deliver quantifiable and highly positive results, and be repeatable.

> **core concept**
> A **best practice** is any practice that at least one company has proved works particularly well.

Benchmarking is the backbone of the process of identifying, studying, and implementing outstanding practices. A company's benchmarking effort looks outward to find best practices and then proceeds to develop the data for measuring how well a company's own performance of an activity stacks up against the best-practice standard.

figure 12.2   **From Benchmarking and Best-Practice Implementation to Operating Excellence**

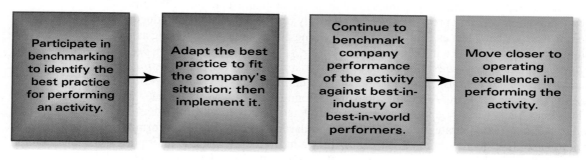

Informally, benchmarking involves being humble enough to admit that others have come up with world-class ways to perform particular activities yet wise enough to try to learn how to match, and even surpass, them. But, as shown in Figure 12.2, the payoff of benchmarking comes from applying the top-notch approaches pioneered by other companies in the company's own operation and thereby spurring dramatic improvements in the proficiency with which value chain tasks are performed. The goal of benchmarking is to promote the achievement of operating excellence in a variety of strategy-critical and support activities.

However, benchmarking is more complicated than simply identifying which companies are the best performers of an activity and then trying to exactly copy other companies' approaches—especially if these companies are in other industries. Normally, the outstanding practices of other organizations have to be adapted to fit the specific circumstances of a company's own business and operating requirements. Since most companies believe "our work is different" or "we are unique," the telling part of any best-practice initiative is how well the company puts its own version of the best practice into place and makes it work.

Indeed, a best practice remains little more than an interesting success story unless company personnel buy into the task of translating what can be learned from other companies into real action and results. The agents of change must be frontline employees who are convinced of the need to abandon the old ways of doing things and switch to a best-practice mind-set. The more that organizational units use best practices in performing their work, the closer a company moves toward performing its value chain activities as effectively and efficiently as possible. This is what operational excellence is all about.

Legions of companies across the world now engage in benchmarking to improve their strategy execution efforts and, ideally, gain a strategic, operational, and financial advantage over rivals. A survey of over 4,000 managers in 15 countries indicated that over 85 percent were using benchmarking to measure the efficiency and effectiveness of their internal activities.[2] Since 1990, the number of companies instituting best-practice programs as an integral part of their efforts to improve strategy execution has grown significantly. Scores of trade associations and special interest organizations have undertaken efforts to collect best-practice data relevant to a particular industry or business function and make their databases available online to members. Benchmarking and best-practice implementation have clearly emerged as legitimate and valuable managerial tools for promoting operational excellence.

TQM and Six Sigma Quality Programs: Tools for Promoting Operational Excellence

Best-practice implementation has stimulated greater management awareness of the importance of business process reengineering, total quality management (TQM) programs, Six Sigma quality control techniques, and other continuous improvement methods. Indeed, quality improvement processes of one kind or another have become globally pervasive management tools for implementing strategies keyed to defect-free manufacture, superior product quality, superior customer service, and total customer satisfaction. The following paragraphs describe two specific types of programs and then discuss the difference between process reengineering and continuous improvement.

Total Quality Management Programs   *Total quality management (TQM) is a philosophy of managing a set of business practices that emphasizes continuous improvement in all phases of operations, 100 percent accuracy in performing tasks, involvement and empowerment of employees at all levels, team-based work design, benchmarking, and total customer satisfaction.*[3] While TQM concentrates on the production of quality goods and fully satisfying customer expectations, it achieves its biggest successes when it is also extended to employee efforts in *all departments*—human resources, billing, R&D, engineering, accounting and records, and information systems—that may lack pressing, customer-driven incentives to improve. It involves reforming the corporate culture and shifting to a total quality/continuous improvement business philosophy that permeates every facet of the organization.[4] TQM aims at instilling enthusiasm and commitment to doing things right from the top to the bottom of the organization. It entails a restless search for continuing improvement, the little steps forward each day that the Japanese call *kaizen.* TQM is thus a race without a finish. The managerial objective is to kindle a burning desire in people to use their ingenuity and initiative to progressively improve their performance of value chain activities. TQM doctrine preaches that there's no such thing as "good enough" and that everyone has a responsibility to participate in continuous improvement. TQM takes a fairly long time to show significant results—very little benefit emerges within the first six months. The long-term payoff of TQM, if it comes, depends heavily on management's success in implanting a culture within which TQM philosophies and practices can thrive.

> **core concept**
> TQM entails creating a total quality culture bent on continuously improving the performance of every task and value chain activity.

Six Sigma Quality Control   *Six Sigma quality control consists of a disciplined, statistics-based system aimed at producing not more than 3.4 defects per million iterations for any business process—from manufacturing to customer transactions.* The Six Sigma process of define, measure, analyze, improve, and control (DMAIC) is an improvement system for existing processes falling below specification and needing incremental improvement. The Six Sigma process of define, measure, analyze, design, and verify (DMADV) is an improvement system used to develop new processes or products at Six Sigma quality levels. Both Six Sigma processes are executed by personnel who have earned Six Sigma "green belts" and Six Sigma "black belts," and are overseen by personnel who have completed Six Sigma "master black belt" training. According to the Six Sigma Academy, personnel with black belts can save companies approximately $230,000 per project and can complete four to six projects a year.[5]

   The statistical thinking underlying Six Sigma is based on the following three principles: All work is a process, all processes have variability, and all processes create data that explains variability.[6] To illustrate how these three principles drive the metrics of DMAIC, consider the case of a janitorial company that wants to improve the caliber of work done by its cleaning crews and thereby boost customer satisfaction. The janitorial company's Six Sigma team can pursue quality enhancement and continuous improvement via the DMAIC process as follows:

- *Define.* Because Six Sigma is aimed at reducing defects, the first step is to define what constitutes defect. Six Sigma team members might decide that leaving streaks on windows is a defect because it is a source of customer dissatisfaction.
- *Measure.* The next step is to collect data to find out why, how, and how often this defect occurs. This might include a process flow map of the specific ways that cleaning crews go about the task of cleaning a commercial customer's windows. Other metrics may include recording what tools and cleaning products the crews use to clean windows.
- *Analyze.* After the data are gathered and the statistics analyzed, the company's Six Sigma team discovers that the tools and window cleaning techniques of certain employees are better than those of other employees because their tools and procedures leave no streaked windows—a "best practice" for avoiding window streaking is thus identified and documented.
- *Improve.* The Six Sigma team implements the documented best practice as a standard way of cleaning windows.
- *Control.* The company teaches new and existing employees the best practice technique for window cleaning. Over time, there's significant improvement in customer satisfaction and increased business.

Six Sigma's DMAIC process is a particularly good vehicle for improving performance when there are *wide variations* in how well an activity is performed.[7] For instance, airlines striving to improve the on-time performance of their flights have more to gain from actions to curtail the number of flights that are late by more then 30 minutes than from actions to reduce the number of flights that are late by less than 5 minutes. Likewise, FedEx might have a 16-hour average delivery time for its overnight package service operation, but if the actual delivery time varies around the 16-hour average from a low of 12 hours to a high of 26 hours such that 10 percent of its packages are delivered over 6 hours late, then it has a huge *reliability* problem.

A problem tailor-made for Six Sigma occurs in the insurance industry, where it is common for top agents to outsell poor agents by a factor of 10 to 1 or more. If insurance executives offer a trip to Hawaii in a monthly contest to motivate low-performing agents, the typical result is to motivate top agents to be even more productive and make the performance gap even wider. A DMAIC Six Sigma project to reduce the variation in the performance of agents and correct the problem of so many low-performing agents would begin by measuring the performance of all agents, perhaps discovering that the top 20 percent sell 7 times more policies than the bottom 40 percent. Six Sigma analysis would then consider such steps as mapping how top agents spend their day, investigating the factors that distinguish top performers from low performers, learning what techniques training specialists have employed in converting low-performing agents into high performers, and examining how the hiring process could be improved to avoid hiring underperformers in the first place.

The next step would be to *test* proposed solutions—better training methods or psychological profiling to identify and weed out candidates likely to be poor performers—to identify and measure which alternative solutions really work, which don't, and why. Only those actions that prove statistically beneficial are then introduced on a wide scale. The DMAIC method thus entails empirical analysis to diagnose the problem

illustration capsule 12.2
Whirlpool's Use of Six Sigma to Promote Operating Excellence

Top management at Whirlpool Corporation, the leading global manufacturer and marketer of home appliances in 2003, with production operations in 14 countries and sales in some 170 countries, has a vision of Whirlpool appliances in "Every Home, Everywhere." One of management's chief objectives in pursuing this vision is to build unmatched customer loyalty to the Whirlpool brand. Whirlpool's strategy to win the hearts and minds of appliance buyers the world over has been to produce and market appliances with top-notch quality and innovative features that users will find appealing. In addition, Whirlpool's strategy has been to offer a wide selection of models (recognizing that buyer tastes and needs differ) and to strive for low-cost production efficiency, thereby enabling Whirlpool to price its products very competitively. Executing this strategy at Whirlpool's operations in North America (where it is the market leader), Latin America (where it is also the market leader), Europe (where it ranks third), and Asia (where it is number one in India and has a foothold with huge growth opportunities elsewhere) has involved a strong focus on continuous improvement and a drive for operating excellence. To marshal the efforts of its 68,000 employees in executing the strategy successfully, management developed a comprehensive Operational Excellence program with Six Sigma as one of the centerpieces.

The Operational Excellence initiative, which began in the 1990s, incorporated Six Sigma techniques to improve the quality of Whirlpool products, while at the same time lowering costs and trimming the time it took to get product innovations into the marketplace. The Six Sigma program helped Whirlpool save $175 million in manufacturing costs in its first three years.

To sustain the productivity gains and cost savings, Whirlpool embedded Six Sigma practices within each of its manufacturing facilities worldwide and instilled a culture based on Six Sigma and lean manufacturing skills and capabilities. Beginning in 2002, each of Whirlpool's operating units began taking the Six Sigma initiative to a higher level by first placing the needs of the customer at the center of every function—R&D, technology, manufacturing, marketing, and administrative support—and then striving to consistently improve quality levels while eliminating all unnecessary costs. The company has systematically gone through every aspect of its business with the view that company personnel should perform every activity at every level in a manner that focuses on delivering value to the customer and that leads to continuous improvement. Whirlpool management believes that the companywide Six Sigma program and emphasis on continuous improvement has been a major contributor in sustaining the company's global leadership in appliances.

Source: www.whirlpool.com, accessed September 25, 2003.

(*design, measure, analyze*), test alternative solutions (*improve*) and then *control* the variability in how well the activity is performed by implementing actions shown to truly fix the problem.

General Electric (GE), one of the most successful companies implementing Six Sigma training and pursuing Six Sigma perfection, estimated benefits on the order of $10 billion during the first five years of implementation. GE first began Six Sigma in 1995 after Motorola and Allied Signal blazed the Six Sigma trail. Since the mid-1990s, thousands of companies and nonprofit organizations around the world have begun utilizing Six Sigma programs to promote operating excellence. Illustration Capsule 12.2 describes Whirlpool's use of Six Sigma in its appliance business.

Six Sigma is, however, not just a quality-enhancing tool for manufacturers. At one company, product sales personnel typically wined and dined customers to close their deals. But the costs of such entertaining were viewed as excessively high in many instances. A Six Sigma project that examined sales data found that although face time with customers was important, wining, dining, and other types of entertainment were not.[8] The data showed that regular face time helped close sales, but that time could be spent over a cup of

core concept
Using Six Sigma to improve the performance of strategy-critical activities enhances strategy execution.

coffee instead of golfing at a resort or taking clients to expensive restaurants. In addition, analysis showed that too much face time with customers was counterproductive. A regularly scheduled customer picnic was found to be detrimental to closing sales because it was held at a busy time of year, when customers preferred not to be away from their offices. Changing the manner in which prospective customers were wooed resulted in a 10 percent increase in sales. A financial services firm utilized Six Sigma techniques to determine whether it was paying an inordinate amount of money to provide customer service.[9] The company knew that it could save money by encouraging customers to use its Web site to get information about their accounts, but customers continued to contact the company's call center for information they could have gotten online. A Six Sigma team examined call center and Web site data and discovered that if the Web site was reconfigured to mirror the questions being asked at the call center, the company could cut costs and increase the quality of customer service. The result was the movement of customers to the Web, rather than the phone, to get account information. A Milwaukee hospital used Six Sigma to map the process as prescriptions originated with a doctor's writeup, were filled by the hospital pharmacy, and then administered by nurses. DMAIC analysis revealed that most mistakes came from misreading the doctor's handwriting.[10] The hospital implemented a program requiring doctors to type the prescription into a computer, which slashed the number of errors dramatically.

The point here is that Six Sigma can be a valuable and potent management tool for achieving operating excellence in both manufacturing and nonmanufacturing situations. A company that systematically applies Six Sigma methods to its value chain, activity by activity, can make major strides in improving the proficiency with which its strategy is executed.

The Difference between Process Reengineering and Continuous Improvement Programs   Business process reengineering and continuous improvement efforts like TQM and Six Sigma both aim at improved efficiency and reduced costs, better product quality, and greater customer satisfaction. The essential difference between business process reengineering and continuous improvement programs is that reengineering aims at *quantum gains* on the order of 30 to 50 percent or more whereas total quality programs stress *incremental progress*, striving for inch-by-inch gains again and again in a never-ending stream. The two approaches to improved performance of value chain activities and operating excellence are not mutually exclusive; it makes sense to use them in tandem. Reengineering can be used first to produce a good basic design that yields quick, dramatic improvements in performing a business process. Total quality programs can then be used as a follow-on to reengineering and/or best-practice implementation, delivering gradual improvements. Such a two-pronged approach to implementing operational excellence is like a marathon race in which you run the first four miles as fast as you can, then gradually pick up speed the remainder of the way.

> Business process reengineering aims at one-time quantum improvement; TQM and Six Sigma aim at incremental progress.

Capturing the Benefits of Best-Practice and Continuous Improvement Programs

Research indicates that some companies benefit from reengineering and continuous improvement programs and some do not.[11] Usually, the biggest beneficiaries are companies that view such programs not as ends in themselves but as tools for implementing and executing company strategy more effectively. The skimpiest payoffs from best practices, TQM, Six Sigma, and reengineering occur when company managers seize them as something worth trying—novel ideas that could improve things. In most such instances, they result in strategy-blind efforts to simply manage better. There's an important lesson here. Best practices, TQM, Six Sigma quality, and reengineering all need to be seen and used as part of a bigger-picture effort to execute strategy proficiently. Only strategy can point to which value chain activities matter and what performance targets make the most sense. Absent a strategic framework, managers lack the context in which to fix things that really matter to business-unit performance and competitive success.

To get the most from programs for facilitating better strategy execution, managers must have a clear idea of what specific outcomes really matter. Examples of such performance indicators include a Six Sigma defect rate (fewer than 3.4 errors per million iterations), high on-time delivery percentages, low overall costs relative to rivals, high percentages of pleased customers and few customer complaints, shorter cycle times, and a higher percentage of revenues coming from recently introduced products. Benchmarking best-in-industry and best-in-world performance of most or all value chain activities provides a realistic basis for setting internal performance milestones and longer-range targets.

Then comes the managerial task of building a total quality culture and instilling the necessary commitment to achieving the targets and performance measures that the strategy requires. Managers can take the following action steps to realize full value from TQM or Six Sigma initiatives:[12]

1. Visible, unequivocal, and unyielding commitment to total quality and continuous improvement, including a quality vision and specific, measurable objectives for boosting quality and making continuous improvement.

2. Nudging people toward quality-supportive behaviors by:
   a. Screening job applicants rigorously and hiring only those with attitudes and aptitudes right for quality-based performance.
   b. Providing quality training for most employees.
   c. Using teams and team-building exercises to reinforce and nurture individual effort (the creation of a quality culture is facilitated when teams become more cross-functional, multitask oriented, and increasingly self-managed).
   d. Recognizing and rewarding individual and team efforts regularly and systematically.
   e. Stressing prevention (doing it right the first time), not inspection (instituting ways to correct mistakes).

3. Empowering employees so that authority for delivering great service or improving products is in the hands of the doers rather than the overseers.

4. Using online systems to provide all relevant parties with the latest best practices and actual experiences with them, thereby speeding the diffusion and adoption of best practices throughout the organization and also allowing them to exchange data and opinions about how to upgrade the prevailing best practices.

5. Preaching that performance can, and must, be improved because competitors are not resting on their laurels and customers are always looking for something better.

If the targeted performance measures are appropriate to the strategy and if all organizational members (top executives, middle managers, professional staff, and line employees) buy into the process of continuous improvement, then the work climate becomes decidedly more conducive to proficient strategy execution.

When used effectively, TQM, Six Sigma and other similar continuous improvement techniques can greatly enhance a company's product design, cycle time, production costs, product quality, service, customer satisfaction, and other operating capabilities—

and it can even deliver competitive advantage.[13] Not only do ongoing incremental improvements add up over time and strengthen organizational capabilities, but continuous improvement programs have hard-to-imitate aspects. While it is relatively easy for rivals to undertake benchmarking, process improvement, and quality training, it is much more difficult and time-consuming for them to instill a total quality culture (as occurs when TQM or Six Sigma techniques are religiously employed) and generate lasting management commitment to operational excellence throughout their organizations.

INSTALLING INFORMATION AND OPERATING SYSTEMS

Company strategies can't be executed well without a number of internal systems for business operations. Southwest, American, Northwest, Delta, and other major airlines cannot hope to provide passenger-pleasing service without a user-friendly online reservation system, an accurate and speedy baggage handling system, and a strict aircraft maintenance program that minimizes equipment failures requiring at-the-gate service and delaying plane departures. FedEx has internal communication systems that allow it to coordinate its nearly 60,000 vehicles in handling an average of 5.2 million packages a day. Its leading-edge flight operations systems allow a single controller to direct as many as 200 of FedEx's 650-plus aircraft simultaneously, overriding their flight plans should weather or other special emergencies arise. In addition, FedEx has created a series of e-business tools for customers that allow them to ship and track packages online (either at FedEx's Web site or on their own company intranets or Web sites), create address books, review shipping history, generate custom reports, simplify customer billing, reduce internal warehousing and inventory management costs, purchase goods and services from suppliers, and respond quickly to changing customer demands. All of FedEx's systems support the company's strategy of providing businesses and individuals with a broad array of package delivery services (from premium next-day to economical five-day deliveries) and boosting its competitiveness against United Parcel Service, Airborne Express, and the U.S. Postal Service.

Otis Elevator has a 24-hour centralized communications center called OtisLine to coordinate its maintenance efforts in North America.[14] Trained operators take all trouble calls, input critical information on a computer screen, and dispatch people directly via a beeper system to the local trouble spot. Also, much of the information needed for repairs is provided directly from faulty elevators through internally installed microcomputer monitors, helping keep the outage time on Otis elevators and escalators to less than two and a half hours. From the trouble-call inputs, problem patterns across North America are identified and the information communicated to design and manufacturing personnel, allowing them to quickly alter design specifications or manufacturing procedures when needed to correct recurring problems.

Wal-Mart is generally considered to have the most sophisticated retailing systems of any company in the world. For example, Wal-Mart's computers transmit daily sales data to Wrangler, a supplier of blue jeans; Wrangler then uses a model that interprets the data, and software applications that act on these interpretations, in order to ship specific quantities of specific sizes and colors to specific stores from specific warehouses—the system lowers logistics and inventory costs and leads to fewer stockouts.[15] Domino's Pizza has computerized systems at each outlet to facilitate ordering, inventory, payroll, cash flow, and work control functions, thereby freeing managers to spend more time on supervision, customer service, and business development activities.[16] Most telephone companies, electric utilities, and TV broadcasting systems have online monitoring systems to spot transmission problems within seconds and increase the reliability of their services. At eBay, there are systems for real-time monitoring of new listings, bidding activity, Web site traffic, and page views.

Amazon.com ships customer orders from fully computerized, 1,300-by-600-foot warehouses containing about 3 million books, CDs, toys, and houseware items.[17] The warehouses are so technologically sophisticated that they require about as many lines of code to run as Amazon's Web site does. Using complex picking algorithms, computers initiate the order-picking process by sending signals to workers' wireless receivers, telling them which items to pick off the shelves in which order. Computers also generate data on misboxed items, chute backup times, line speed, worker productivity, and shipping weights on orders. Systems are upgraded regularly, and productivity improvements are aggressively pursued. In 2003 Amazon's six warehouses were able to handle three times the volume handled in 1999 at costs averaging 10 percent of revenues (versus 20 percent in 1999); in addition, they turned their inventory over 20 times annually in an industry whose average was 15 turns. Amazon's warehouse efficiency and cost per order filled was so low that one of the fastest-growing and most profitable parts of Amazon's business was using its warehouses to run the e-commerce operations of Toys "R" Us and Target.

Well-conceived state-of-the-art operating systems not only enable better strategy execution but also strengthen organizational capabilities—perhaps enough to provide a competitive edge over rivals. For example, a company with a differentiation strategy based on superior quality has added capability if it has systems for training personnel in quality techniques, tracking product quality at each production step, and ensuring that all goods shipped meet quality standards. A company striving to be a low-cost provider is competitively stronger if it has a benchmarking system that identifies opportunities to implement best practices and drive costs out of the business. Fast-growing companies get an important assist from having capabilities in place to recruit and train new employees in large numbers and from investing in infrastructure that gives them the capability to handle rapid growth as it occurs.

It is nearly always better to put infrastructure and support systems in place before they are actually needed than to have to scramble to catch up to customer demand. In businesses such as public accounting and management consulting, where large numbers of professional staff need cutting-edge technical know-how, companies need well-functioning systems for training and retraining employees regularly and keeping them supplied with up-to-date information. Companies that rely on empowered customer service employees to act promptly and creatively in pleasing customers need state-of-the-art information systems that put essential data in front of employees with a few keystrokes. Many companies have cataloged best-practice information on their intranets to promote faster transfer and implementation organizationwide.[18]

> **core concept**
> State-of-the-art support systems can be a basis for competitive advantage if they give a firm capabilities that rivals can't match.

Instituting Adequate Information Systems, Performance Tracking, and Controls

Accurate and timely information about daily operations is essential if managers are to gauge how well the strategy execution process is proceeding. Information systems need to cover five broad areas: (1) customer data, (2) operations data, (3) employee data, (4) supplier/partner/collaborative ally data, and (5) financial performance data. All key strategic performance indicators have to be tracked and reported as often as practical. Monthly profit-and-loss statements and monthly statistical summaries, long the norm, are fast being replaced by daily statistical updates and even up-to-the-minute performance monitoring that online technology makes possible. Many retail companies have automated online systems that generate daily sales reports for each store and maintain up-to-the-minute inventory and sales records on each item. Manufacturing plants typically generate daily production reports and track labor productivity on every shift. Many retailers and manufacturers have online data systems connecting them with their suppliers that monitor the status of inventories, track shipments and deliveries, and measure defect rates.

Real-time information systems permit company managers to stay on top of implementation initiatives and daily operations, and to intervene if things seem to be drifting off course. Tracking key performance indicators, gathering information from operating personnel, quickly identifying and diagnosing problems, and taking corrective actions are all integral pieces of the process of managing strategy implementation and execution and exercising adequate organization control. Telephone companies have elaborate information systems to measure signal quality, connection times, interrupts, wrong connections, billing errors, and other measures of reliability that affect customer service and satisfaction. To track and manage the quality of passenger service, airlines have information systems to monitor gate delays, on-time departures and arrivals, baggage handling times, lost baggage complaints, stockouts on meals and drinks, overbookings, and maintenance delays and failures. Virtually all companies now provide customer-contact personnel with computer access to customer databases so that they can respond effectively to customer inquiries and deliver personalized customer service.

Statistical information gives managers a feel for the numbers, briefings and meetings provide a feel for the latest developments and emerging issues, and personal contacts add a feel for the people dimension. All are good barometers. Managers have to identify problem areas and deviations from plan before they can take actions to get the organization back on course, by either improving the approaches to strategy execution or fine-tuning the strategy. Jeff Bezos, Amazon's CEO, is an ardent proponent of managing by the numbers—as he puts it "math-based decisions always trump opinion and judgment . . . The trouble with most corporations is that they make judgment-based decisions when data-based decisions could be made."[19]

> **core concept**
> Good information systems and operating data are essential components of good strategy execution and operating excellence.

Exercising Adequate Controls over Empowered Employees

Another important aspect of effectively managing and controlling the strategy execution process is monitoring the performance of empowered workers to see that they are acting within the specified limits.[20] Leaving empowered employees to their own devices in meeting performance standards without appropriate checks and balances can expose an organization to excessive risk.[21] Instances abound of employees' decisions or behavior having gone awry, sometimes costing a company huge sums or producing lawsuits aside from just generating embarrassing publicity.

Managers can't devote big chunks of their time to making sure that the decisions and behavior of empowered employees stay between the white lines—this would defeat the major purpose of empowerment and, in effect, lead to the reinstatement of a managerial bureaucracy engaged in constant over-the-shoulder supervision. Yet management has a clear responsibility to exercise sufficient control over empowered employees to protect the company against out-of-bounds behavior and unwelcome surprises. Scrutinizing daily and weekly operating statistics is one of the important ways in which managers can monitor the results that flow from the actions of empowered subordinates—if the operating results flowing from the actions of empowered employees look good, then it is reasonable to assume that empowerment is working.

One of the main purposes of tracking daily operating performance is to relieve managers of the burden of constant supervision and give them time for other issues. But managerial control is only part of the answer. Another valuable lever of control in companies that rely on empowered employees, especially in those that use self-managed work groups or other such teams, is peer-based control.[22] The big majority of team members feel responsible for the success of the whole team and tend to be relatively intolerant of any team member's behavior that weakens team performance or puts team accomplishments at risk. Because peer evaluation is such a powerful control device, companies organized into teams can remove some layers of the management hierarchy. This is especially true when a company has the information systems capability to closely monitor team performance.

TYING REWARDS AND INCENTIVES TO STRATEGY EXECUTION

It is important for both organization units and individuals to be enthusiastically committed to executing strategy and achieving performance targets. Company managers typically use an assortment of motivational techniques and rewards to enlist organizationwide commitment to executing the strategic plan. A manager has to do more than just talk to everyone about how important new strategic practices and performance targets are to the organization's well-being. No matter how inspiring, talk seldom commands people's best efforts for long. *To get employees' sustained, energetic commitment, management has to be resourceful in designing and using motivational incentives—both monetary and nonmonetary.* The more a manager understands what motivates subordinates and the more he or she relies on motivational incentives as a tool for achieving the targeted strategic and financial results, the greater will be employees' commitment to good day-in, day-out execution of the company's strategic plan.

> **core concept**
> A properly designed reward structure is management's most powerful tool for mobilizing organizational commitment to successful strategy execution.

Strategy-Facilitating Motivational Practices

Financial incentives generally head the list of motivating tools for trying to gain wholehearted employee commitment to good strategy execution and operating excellence. Monetary rewards generally include some combination of base pay increases, performance bonuses, profit sharing plans, stock awards, company contributions to employee 401(k) or retirement plans, and piecework incentives (in the case of production workers). But successful companies and managers normally make extensive use of such nonmonetary carrot-and-stick incentives as frequent words of praise (or constructive criticism), special recognition at company gatherings or in the company newsletter, more (or less) job security, stimulating assignments, opportunities to transfer to attractive locations, increased (or decreased) autonomy, and rapid promotion (or the risk of being sidelined in a routine or dead-end job). In addition, companies use a host of other motivational approaches to spur stronger employee commitment to the strategy execution process; the following are some of the most important:[23]

> **core concept**
> One of management's biggest strategy-executing challenges is to employ motivational techniques that build wholehearted commitment to operating excellence and winning attitudes among employees.

- *Providing attractive perks and fringe benefits*—The various options here include full coverage of health insurance premiums; full tuition reimbursement for work on college degrees; paid vacation time of three or four weeks; on-site child care at major facilities; on-site gym facilities and massage therapists; getaway opportunities at company-owned recreational facilities (beach houses, ranches, resort condos); personal concierge services; subsidized cafeterias and free lunches; casual dress every day; personal travel services; paid sabbaticals; maternity leaves; paid leaves to care for ill family members; telecommuting; compressed workweeks (four 10-hour days instead of five 8-hour days); reduced summer hours; college scholarships for children; on-the-spot bonuses for exceptional performance; and relocation services.

- *Relying on promotion from within whenever possible*—This practice helps bind workers to their employer and employers to their workers; plus, it is an incentive for good performance. Promotion from within also helps ensure that people in positions of responsibility actually know something about the business, technology, and operations they are managing.

- *Making sure that the ideas and suggestions of employees are valued and respected*—Research indicates that the moves of many companies to push decision making down the line and empower employees increases employee motivation and satisfaction, as well as boosting their productivity. The use of self-managed teams has much the same effect.

- *Creating a work atmosphere in which there is genuine sincerity, caring, and mutual respect among workers and between management and employees*—A "family" work environment where people are on a first-name basis and there is strong camaraderie promotes teamwork and cross-unit collaboration.

- *Stating the strategic vision in inspirational terms that make employees feel they are a part of doing something very worthwhile in a larger social sense*—There's strong motivating power associated with giving people a chance to be part of something exciting and personally satisfying. Jobs with noble purpose tend to turn employees on. At Pfizer, Merck, and most other pharmaceutical companies, it is the notion of helping sick people get well and restoring patients to full life. At Whole Foods Market (a natural foods grocery chain), it is helping customers discover good eating habits and thus improving human health and nutrition.

- *Sharing information with employees about financial performance, strategy, operational measures, market conditions, and competitors' actions*—Broad disclosure and prompt communication send the message that managers trust their workers. Keeping employees in the dark denies them information useful to performing their job, prevents them from being "students of the business," and usually turns them off.

- *Having knockout facilities*—An impressive corporate facility for employees to work in usually has decidedly positive effects on morale and productivity.

- *Being flexible in how the company approaches people management (motivation, compensation, recognition, recruitment) in multinational, multicultural environments*—Managers and employees in countries whose customs, habits, values, and business practices vary from those at the home office often become frustrated with insistence on consistent people-management practices worldwide. But the one area where consistency is essential is conveying the message that the organization values people of all races and cultural backgrounds and that discrimination of any sort will not be tolerated.

For specific examples of the motivational tactics employed by several prominent companies, see Illustration Capsule 12.3.

illustration capsule 12.3
Companies with Effective Motivation and Reward Techniques

Companies have come up with a variety of motivational and reward practices to help create a work environment that facilitates better strategy execution. Here's a glimpse of what some companies believe are best practices:

- At Google, the leader in Internet search engine technology and provider of 75 percent of all Web searches as of 2003, there's a sprawling four-building complex known as the Googleplex. The roughly 1,000 employees are provided with free food, unlimited ice cream, pool and Ping-Pong tables, and complimentary massages. Moreover, they are given the ability to spend 20 percent of their work time on any outside activity. Management built the Googleplex to be "a dream environment."

- At Amazon.com one of the most prized awards is Just Do It—winners are employees who do something they think will help Amazon *without* first getting their boss's permission. The action has to be well thought through but doesn't have to succeed.

- Lincoln Electric, a company deservedly famous for its piecework pay scheme and incentive bonus plan, rewards individual productivity by paying workers for each nondefective piece produced. Workers have to correct quality problems on their own time—defects in products used by customers can be traced back to the worker who caused them. Lincoln's piecework plan motivates workers to pay attention to both quality and volume produced. In addition, the company sets aside a substantial portion of its profits above a specified base for worker bonuses. To determine bonus size, Lincoln Electric rates each worker on four equally important performance measures: dependability, quality, output, and ideas and cooperation. The higher a worker's merit rating, the higher the incentive bonus earned; the highest rated workers in good profit years receive bonuses of as much as 110 percent of their piecework compensation.

- Several Japanese automobile producers, believing that providing employment security is a valuable contributor to worker productivity and company loyalty, elect not to lay off factory workers when business slacks off for a period but instead put them out in the field to sell

vehicles. Southwest Airlines, FedEx, Lands' End, and Harley-Davidson (all companies that have been listed among the 100 best companies to work for in America) have also instituted no-layoff policies and use employment security as both a positive motivator and a means of reinforcing good strategy execution.

- Procter & Gamble, Merck, Charles Schwab, General Mills, Amgen, Tellabs, and Eli Lilly provide stock awards to all employees. Having employee-owners who share in a company's success (or failure) via stock ownership is widely viewed as a way to bolster employee commitment to good strategy execution and operational excellence.

- Nordstrom typically pays its retail salespeople an hourly wage higher than the prevailing rates paid by other department store chains plus a commission on each sale. Spurred by a culture that encourages salespeople to go all-out to satisfy customers, to exercise their own best judgment, and to seek out and promote new fashion ideas, Nordstrom salespeople often earn twice the average incomes of sales employees at competing stores. Nordstrom's rules for employees are simple: "Rule #1: Use your good judgment in all situations. There will be no additional rules." Nordstrom is widely regarded for its superior in-house customer service experience.

- Kimberly-Clark spends about $6 million annually on events to celebrate employee successes, and FedEx gives out awards to employees whose job performance is above and beyond expectations (in 2001 the company spent over $13 million on such awards).

- Monsanto, FedEx, AT&T, Whole Foods Markets, Advanced Micro Devices, and W. L. Gore & Associates (the maker of Gore-Tex) have tapped into the motivational power of self-managed teams, recognizing that team members put considerable peer pressure on coworkers to pull their weight and help achieve team goals and expectations. At W. L. Gore (a regular member on annual listings of the 100 best companies to work for), each team member's compensation is based on other team members' rankings of his or her contribution to the enterprise.

Sources: Jeffrey Pfeffer and John F. Veiga, "Putting People First for Organizational Success," *Academy of Management Executive* 13, no. 2 (May 1999), pp. 40–42; *Fortune's* lists of the 100 best companies to work for in America—see the January 12, 1998, January 10, 2000, and February 4, 2002, issues; Jeffrey Pfeffer, "Producing Sustainable Competitive Advantage through the Effective Management of People," *Academy of Management Executive* 9, no. 1 (February 1995), pp. 59–60; and Steven Kerr, "Risky Business: The New Pay Game," *Fortune,* July 22, 1996, p. 95.

Striking the Right Balance between Rewards and Punishment

While most approaches to motivation, compensation, and people management accentuate the positive, companies also embellish positive rewards with the risk of punishment. At General Electric, McKinsey & Company, several global public accounting firms, and other companies that look for and expect top-notch individual performance, there's an "up-or-out" policy—managers and professionals whose performance is not good enough to warrant promotion are first denied bonuses and stock awards and eventually weeded out. A number of companies deliberately give employees heavy workloads and tight deadlines—personnel are pushed hard to achieve "stretch" objectives and expected to put in long hours (nights and weekends if need be). At most companies, senior executives and key personnel in underperforming units are pressured to boost performance to acceptable levels and keep it there or risk being replaced.

As a general rule, it is unwise to take off the pressure for good individual and group performance or play down the stress, anxiety, and adverse consequences of shortfalls in performance. There is no evidence that a no-pressure/no-adverse-consequences work environment leads to superior strategy execution or operating excellence. As the CEO of a major bank put it, "There's a deliberate policy here to create a level of anxiety. Winners usually play like they're one touchdown behind."[24] *High-performing organizations nearly always have a cadre of ambitious people who relish the opportunity to climb the ladder of success, love a challenge, thrive in a performance-oriented environment, and find some competition and pressure useful to satisfy their own drives for personal recognition, accomplishment, and self-satisfaction.*

However, if an organization's motivational approaches and reward structure induce too much stress, internal competitiveness, job insecurity, and unpleasant consequences, the impact on workforce morale and strategy execution can be counterproductive. Evidence shows that managerial initiatives to improve strategy execution should incorporate more positive than negative motivational elements because when cooperation is positively enlisted and rewarded, rather than strong-armed by orders and threats (implicit or explicit), people tend to respond with more enthusiasm, dedication, creativity, and initiative. Something of a middle ground is generally optimal—not only handing out decidedly positive rewards for meeting or beating performance targets but also imposing sufficiently negative consequences (if only withholding rewards) when actual performance falls short of the target. But the negative consequences of underachievement should never be so severe or demoralizing as to impede a renewed and determined effort to overcome existing obstacles and hit the targets in upcoming periods.

Linking the Reward System to Strategically Relevant Performance Outcomes

core concept
A properly designed reward system aligns the well-being of organization members with their contributions to competent strategy execution and the achievement of performance targets.

The most dependable way to keep people focused on strategy execution and the achievement of performance targets is to *generously* reward and recognize individuals and groups who meet or beat performance targets and deny rewards and recognition to those who don't. *The use of incentives and rewards is the single most powerful tool management has to win strong employee commitment to diligent, competent strategy execution and operating excellence.* Decisions on salary increases, incentive compensation, promotions, key assignments, and the ways and means of awarding praise and recognition are potent attention-getting, commitment-generating devices. Such decisions seldom escape

illustration capsule 12.4
Nucor and Bank One: Two Companies That Tie Incentives Directly to Strategy Execution

The strategy at Nucor Corporation, one of the two biggest steel producers in the United States, is to be *the* low-cost producer of steel products. Because labor costs are a significant fraction of total cost in the steel business, successful implementation of Nucor's low-cost leadership strategy entails achieving lower labor costs per ton of steel than competitors' costs. Nucor management uses an incentive system to promote high worker productivity and drive labor costs per ton below rivals'. Each plant's workforce is organized into production teams (each assigned to perform particular functions), and weekly production targets are established for each team. Base pay scales are set at levels comparable to wages for similar manufacturing jobs in the local areas where Nucor has plants, but workers can earn a 1 percent bonus for each 1 percent that their output exceeds target levels. If a production team exceeds its weekly production target by 10 percent, team members receive a 10 percent bonus in their next paycheck; if a team exceeds its quota by 20 percent, team members earn a 20 percent bonus. Bonuses, paid every two weeks, are based on the prior two weeks' actual production levels measured against the targets.

Nucor's piece-rate incentive plan has resulted in labor productivity levels 10 to 20 percent above the average of the unionized workforces of large, integrated steel producers like U.S. Steel and Bethlehem Steel, given Nucor a cost advantage over most rivals, and made Nucor workers among the best-paid in the U.S. steel industry.

At Bank One (one of the 10 largest U.S. banks and also one of the most profitable, according to return on assets), operating in a manner that produces consistently high levels of customer satisfaction makes a big competitive difference in how well the company fares against rivals; customer satisfaction ranks high on Bank One's list of strategic priorities. To enhance employee commitment to the task of pleasing customers, Bank One ties the pay scales in each branch office to that branch's customer satisfaction rating—the higher the branch's ratings, the higher that branch's pay scales. By shifting from a theme of equal pay for equal work to one of equal pay for equal performance, Bank One has focused the attention of branch employees on the task of pleasing, even delighting, their customers.

---

the closest employee scrutiny, saying more about what is expected and who is considered to be doing a good job than about any other factor. Hence, when achievement of the targeted strategic and financial outcomes become *the dominating basis* for designing incentives, evaluating individual and group efforts, and handing out rewards, company personnel quickly grasp that it is in their own self-interest to do their best in executing the strategy competently and achieving key performance targets.[25] Indeed, it is usually through the company's system of incentives and rewards that workforce members emotionally ratify their commitment to the company's strategy execution effort.

Strategy-driven performance targets need to be established for every organization unit, every manager, every team or work group, and perhaps every employee—targets that measure whether strategy execution is progressing satisfactorily. If the company's strategy is to be a low-cost provider, the incentive system must reward actions and achievements that result in lower costs. If the company has a differentiation strategy predicated on superior quality and service, the incentive system must reward such outcomes as Six Sigma defect rates, infrequent need for product repair, low numbers of customer complaints, and speedy order processing and delivery. If a company's growth is predicated on a strategy of new product innovation, incentives should be tied to factors such as the percentages of revenues and profits coming from newly introduced products.

Illustration Capsule 12.4 provides two vivid examples of how companies have designed incentives linked directly to outcomes reflecting good strategy execution.

The Importance of Basing Incentives on Achieving Results, Not on Performing Assigned Functions

To create a strategy-supportive system of rewards and incentives, a company must emphasize rewarding people for accomplishing results, not for just dutifully performing assigned functions. Focusing jobholders' attention and energy on what to *achieve* as opposed to what to *do* makes the work environment

> It is folly to reward one outcome in hopes of getting another outcome.

results-oriented. It is flawed management to tie incentives and rewards to satisfactory performance of duties and activities in hopes that the by-products will be the desired business outcomes and company achievements.[26] In any job, performing assigned tasks is not equivalent to achieving intended outcomes. Diligently attending to assigned duties does not, by itself, guarantee results. As any student knows, the fact that an instructor teaches and students go to class doesn't necessarily mean that the students are learning. The enterprise of education would no doubt take on a different character if teachers were rewarded for the result of student learning rather than for the activity of teaching.

Incentive compensation for top executives is typically tied to company profitability (earnings growth, return on equity investment, return on total assets, economic value added); the company's stock price performance; and perhaps such measures as market share, product quality, or customer satisfaction. However, incentives for department

> **core concept**
> The role of the reward system is to align the well-being of organization members with realizing the company's vision, so that organization members benefit by helping the company execute its strategy competently and fully satisfy customers.

heads, teams, and individual workers may be tied to performance outcomes more closely related to their strategic area of responsibility. In manufacturing, incentive compensation may be tied to unit manufacturing costs, on-time production and shipping, defect rates, the number and extent of work stoppages due to labor disagreements and equipment breakdowns, and so on. In sales and marketing, there may be incentives for achieving dollar sales or unit volume targets, market share, sales penetration of each target customer group, the fate of newly introduced products, the frequency of customer complaints, the number of new accounts acquired, and customer satisfaction. Which performance measures to base incentive compensation on depends on the situation—the priority placed on various financial and strategic objectives, the requirements for strategic and competitive success, and what specific results are needed in different facets of the business to keep strategy execution on track.

Guidelines for Designing Incentive Compensation Systems

The concepts and company experiences discussed above yield the following prescriptive guidelines for creating an incentive compensation system to help drive successful strategy execution:

1. *The performance payoff must be a major, not minor, piece of the total compensation package.* Payoffs must be at least 10 to 12 percent of base salary to have much impact. Incentives that amount to 20 percent or more of total compensation are big attention-getters, likely to really drive individual or team effort; incentives amounting to less than 5 percent of total compensation have comparatively weak motivational impact. Moreover, the payoff for high-performing individuals and teams must be meaningfully greater than the payoff for average performers, and the payoff for average performers meaningfully bigger than for below-average performers.

2. *The incentive plan should extend to all managers and all workers, not just top management.* It is a gross miscalculation to expect that lower-level managers and employees will work their hardest to hit performance targets just so a few senior executives can get lucrative rewards.

3. *The reward system must be administered with scrupulous care and fairness.* If performance standards are set unrealistically high or if individual/group performance

evaluations are not accurate and well documented, dissatisfaction with the system will overcome any positive benefits.

4. *The incentives should be based only on achieving performance targets spelled out in the strategic plan.* Incentives should not be linked to outcomes that get thrown in because they are thought to be nice. Performance evaluation based on factors not tightly related to good strategy execution signal that either the strategic plan is incomplete (because important performance targets were left out) or management's real agenda is something other than the stated strategic and financial objectives.

5. *The performance targets each individual is expected to achieve should involve outcomes that the individual can personally affect.* The role of incentives is to enhance individual commitment and channel behavior in beneficial directions. This role is not well served when the performance measures by which an individual is judged are outside his or her arena of influence.

6. *Keep the time between the performance review and payment of the reward short.* A lengthy interval between review and payment breeds discontent and works against reinforcing cause and effect. Companies like Nucor and Continental Airlines have discovered that weekly or monthly payments for good performance work much better than annual payments. Nucor pays weekly bonuses based on prior-week production levels; Continental awards employees a monthly bonus for each month that on-time flight performance meets or beats a specified percentage companywide.

7. *Make liberal use of nonmonetary rewards; don't rely solely on monetary rewards.* When used properly, money is a great motivator, but there are also potent advantages to be gained from praise, special recognition, handing out plum assignments, and so on.

8. *Absolutely avoid skirting the system to find ways to reward effort rather than results.* Whenever actual performance falls short of targeted performance, there's merit in determining whether the causes are attributable to subpar individual/group performance or to circumstances beyond the control of those responsible. An argument can be made that exceptions should be made in giving rewards to people who've tried hard, gone the extra mile, yet still come up short because of circumstances beyond their control. The problem with making exceptions for unknowable, uncontrollable, or unforeseeable circumstances is that once good excuses start to creep into justifying rewards for subpar results, the door is open for all kinds of reasons why actual performance failed to match targeted performance. A "no excuses" standard is more evenhanded and certainly easier to administer.

Once the incentives are designed, they have to be communicated and explained. Everybody needs to understand how their incentive compensation is calculated and how individual/group performance targets contribute to organizational performance targets. The pressure to achieve the targeted strategic and financial performance and continuously improve on strategy execution should be unrelenting, with few (if any) loopholes for rewarding shortfalls in performance. People at all levels have to be held accountable for carrying out their assigned parts of the strategic plan, and they have to understand their rewards are based on the caliber of results that are achieved. But with the pressure to perform should come meaningful rewards. Without an ample payoff, the system breaks down, and managers are left with the less workable options of barking orders, trying to enforce compliance, and depending on the good will of employees.

> **core concept**
> The unwavering standard for judging whether individuals, teams, and organizational units have done a good job must be whether they achieve performance targets consistent with effective strategy execution.

Performance-Based Incentives and Rewards in Multinational Enterprises   In some foreign countries, incentive pay runs counter to local customs and cultural norms. Professor Steven Kerr cites the time he lectured an executive education class on the need for more performance-based pay and a Japanese manager protested, "You shouldn't bribe your children to do their homework, you shouldn't bribe your wife to prepare dinner, and you shouldn't bribe your employees to work for the company."[27] Singling out individuals and commending them for unusually good effort can also be a problem; Japanese culture considers public praise of an individual an affront to the harmony of the group. In some countries, employees have a preference for nonmonetary rewards—more leisure time, important titles, access to vacation villages, and nontaxable perks. Thus, multinational companies have to build some degree of flexibility into the design of incentives and rewards in order to accommodate cross-cultural traditions and preferences.

key|points

Managers implementing and executing a new or different strategy must identify the resource requirements of each new strategic initiative and then consider whether the current pattern of resource allocation and the budgets of the various subunits are suitable. Every organization unit needs to have the people, equipment, facilities, and other resources to carry out its part of the strategic plan (but no more than what it really needs). Implementing a new strategy often entails shifting resources from one area to another—downsizing units that are overstaffed and overfunded, upsizing those more critical to strategic success, and killing projects and activities that are no longer justified.

Anytime a company alters its strategy, managers should review existing policies and operating procedures, proactively revise or discard those that are out of sync, and formulate new ones to facilitate execution of new strategic initiatives. Prescribing new or freshly revised policies and operating procedures aids the task of strategy execution (1) by providing top-down guidance to operating managers, supervisory personnel, and employees regarding how certain things need to be done and what the boundaries are on independent actions and decisions; (2) by enforcing consistency in how particular strategy-critical activities are performed in geographically scattered operating units; and (3) by promoting the creation of a work climate and corporate culture that promotes good strategy execution. Thick policy manuals are usually unnecessary. Indeed, when individual creativity and initiative are more essential to good execution than standardization and conformity, it is better to give people the freedom to do things however they see fit and hold them accountable for good results rather than try to control their behavior with policies and guidelines for every situation.

Competent strategy execution entails visible, unyielding managerial commitment to best practices and continuous improvement. Benchmarking, the discovery and adoption of best practices, business process reengineering, and continuous improvement initiatives like total quality management (TQM) or Six Sigma programs all aim at improved efficiency, lower costs, better product quality, and greater customer satisfaction. *These initiatives are important tools for learning how to execute a strategy more proficiently.* Benchmarking, part of the process of discovering best practices, provides a realistic basis for setting performance targets. Instituting "best-in-industry" or "best-in-world" operating practices in most or all value chain activities provides a means for taking strategy execution to a higher plateau of competence and nurturing a high-performance work environment. Business process reengineering is a way to make quantum progress toward becoming a world-class organization, while TQM and Six Sigma programs instill a commitment to continuous improvement and operating excellence. An organization bent on continuous improvement is a valuable competitive asset—one that, over time, can yield important competitive capabilities (in reducing costs, speeding new products to market, or improving product quality, service, or customer satisfaction) and be a source of competitive advantage.

Company strategies can't be implemented or executed well without a number of support systems to carry on business operations. Well-conceived state-of-the-art support systems can not only facilitate better strategy execution but also strengthen organizational capabilities enough to provide a competitive edge over rivals. In the age of the Internet, real-time information and control systems, growing use of e-commerce technologies and business practices, company intranets, and wireless communications capabilities, companies can't hope to outexecute their competitors without cutting-edge information systems and technologically sophisticated operating capabilities that enable fast, efficient, and effective organization action.

Strategy-supportive motivational practices and reward systems are powerful management tools for gaining employee commitment. The key to creating a reward system that promotes good strategy execution is to make strategically relevant measures of performance *the dominating basis* for designing incentives, evaluating individual and group efforts, and handing out rewards. Positive motivational practices generally work better than negative ones, but there is a place for both. There's also a place for both monetary and nonmonetary incentives.

For an incentive compensation system to work well (1) the monetary payoff should be a major percentage of the compensation package, (2) the use of incentives should extend to all managers and workers, (3) the system should be administered with care and fairness, (4) the incentives should be linked to performance targets spelled out in the strategic plan, (5) each individual's performance targets should involve outcomes the person can personally affect, (6) rewards should promptly follow the determination of good performance, (7) monetary rewards should be supplemented with liberal use of nonmonetary rewards, and (8) skirting the system to reward nonperformers or subpar results should be scrupulously avoided.

| exercises

1. Go to www.google.com and, using the advanced search feature, enter "best practices." Browse through the search results to identify at least five organizations that have gathered a set of best practices and are making information about them available to members. Explore at least one of the sites to get an idea of the kind of best-practice information that is available.

2. Go to www.google.com and do a search on "Six Sigma" quality programs. Browse through the search results and (*a*) identify several companies that offer Six Sigma training and (*b*) find lists of companies that have implemented Six Sigma programs in their pursuit of operational excellence. In particular, you should go to www.isixsigma.com and explore the Six Sigma Q&A menu option.

3. Go to www.google.com and do a search on "total quality management." Browse through the search results and (*a*) identify companies that offer TQM training, (*b*) identify some books on TQM programs, and (*c*) find lists of companies that have implemented TQM programs in their pursuit of operational excellence.

4. Consult the latest issue of *Fortune* containing the annual "100 Best Companies to Work For" (usually a late-January or early-February issue) and identify at least 5, and preferably 10, compensation incentives that these companies use to enhance employee motivation and reward them for good strategic and financial performance.

chapter thirteen

Corporate Culture and Leadership

Keys to Good Strategy Execution

(©Chase Swift/CORBIS)

The biggest levers you've got to change a company are strategy, structure, and culture. If I could pick two, I'd pick strategy and culture.

—Wayne Leonard
CEO, Entergy

An organization's capacity to execute its strategy depends on its "hard" infrastructure—its organizational structure and systems—and on its "soft" infrastructure—its culture and norms.

—Amar Bhide

Weak leadership can wreck the soundest strategy; forceful execution of even a poor plan can often bring victory.

—Sun Zi

Leadership is accomplishing something through other people that wouldn't have happened if you weren't there . . . Leadership is being able to mobilize ideas and values that energize other people . . . Leaders develop a story line that engages other people.

—Noel Tichy

Seeing people in person is a big part of how you drive any change process. You have to show people a positive view of the future and say "we can do it."

—Jeffrey Immelt
CEO, General Electric

In the previous two chapters we examined six of the managerial tasks that are important to good strategy execution and operating excellence—building a capable organization, marshaling the needed resources and steering them to strategy-critical operating units, instituting policies and procedures that facilitate strategy execution, adopting best practices and striving for continuous improvement in how value chain activities are performed, installing information and operating systems that enable company personnel to carry out their strategic roles proficiently, and tying rewards and incentives directly to the achievement of strategic and financial targets. In this chapter we explore the two remaining managerial tasks that shape the outcome of efforts to execute a company's strategy: creating a strategy-supportive corporate culture and exerting the internal leadership needed to drive good strategy execution and the pursuit of operating excellence.

BUILDING A CORPORATE CULTURE THAT PROMOTES GOOD STRATEGY EXECUTION

Every company has its own unique culture. The character of a company's culture or work climate is a product of the core values and business principles that executives espouse, the standards of what is ethically acceptable and what is not, the behaviors that define "how we do things around here," the stories that get told over and over to illustrate and reinforce values and traditions, the company's approach to people management, and its internal politics. The meshing together of stated beliefs, business principles, style of operating, ingrained behaviors and attitudes, and work climate define a company's **corporate culture.**

core concept
Corporate culture refers to the character of a company's internal work climate and personality—as shaped by its core values, beliefs, business principles, traditions, ingrained behaviors, and style of operating.

Corporate cultures vary widely. For instance, the bedrock of Wal-Mart's culture is dedication to customer satisfaction, zealous pursuit of low costs and frugal operating practices, a strong work ethic, ritualistic Saturday-morning headquarters meetings to exchange ideas and review problems, and company executives' commitment to visiting stores, listening to customers, and soliciting suggestions from employees. At Nordstrom, the corporate culture is centered on delivering exceptional service to customers; the company's motto is "Respond to unreasonable customer requests"—each out-of-the-ordinary request is seen as an opportunity for a "heroic" act by an employee that can further the company's reputation for a customer-pleasing shopping environment. Nordstrom makes a point of promoting employees noted for their heroic acts and dedication to outstanding service; the company motivates its salespeople with a commission-based compensation system that enables Nordstrom's best salespeople to earn more than double what other department stores pay. General Electric's culture is founded on a hard-driving,

369

illustration capsule 13.1
The Culture at Alberto-Culver

The Alberto-Culver Company, with 2003 revenues of about $2.9 billion and over 13,000 employees worldwide, is the producer and marketer of Alberto VO5 hair care products; St. Ives skin care, hair care, and facial care products; and such brands as Molly McButter, Mrs. Dash, Consort, Just for Me, TRESemmé, and Static Guard. Alberto-Culver brands are sold in 120 countries. The company's Sally Beauty Company has 2,700 stores in five countries and is the world's largest distributor of professional salon products.

At the careers section of its Web site, the company described its culture in the following words:

> Building careers is as important to us at Alberto-Culver as building brands. We believe in a values-based workplace. We believe in the importance of families and a life/family balance. We believe in in-your-face-honesty without the taint of corporate politics. There's no talk behind your back. If there are issues you'll know, face-to-face. We believe the best ideas make their way—quickly—up an organization, not down. We believe that we should take advantage of every ounce of your talent, not just assign you to a box. We believe in celebrating our victories. We believe in open communication. We believe you can improve what you measure, so we survey and spot check all the time. For that same reason, everyone has specific goals so that their expectations are in line with their managers and the company. We believe that victory is a team accomplishment. We believe in personal development. We believe if you talk with us, you will catch our enthusiasm and want to be part of us.

Source: Alberto-Culver Web site, December 2, 2002, and March 28, 2004.

results-oriented atmosphere (where all of the company's business divisions are held to a standard of being number one or two in their industries as well as achieving good business results); extensive cross-business sharing of ideas, best practices, and learning; the reliance on "workout sessions" to identify, debate, and resolve burning issues; a commitment to Six Sigma quality; and globalization of the company. At Microsoft, there are stories of the long hours programmers put in, the emotional peaks and valleys in encountering and overcoming coding problems, the exhilaration of completing a complex program on schedule, the satisfaction of working on cutting-edge projects, the rewards of being part of a team responsible for a popular new software program, and the tradition of competing aggressively. Enron's collapse in 2001 was partly the product of a flawed corporate culture—one based on the positives of product innovation, aggressive risk-taking, and a driving ambition to lead global change in the energy business but also on the negatives of arrogance, ego, greed, deliberately obscure accounting practices, and an "ends-justify-the-means" mentality in pursuing stretch revenue and profitability targets. In the end, Enron came unglued because a few top executives chose unethical and illegal paths to pursue corporate revenue and profitability targets—in a company that publicly preached integrity and other notable corporate values but was lax in making sure that key executives walked the talk.

Illustration Capsule 13.1 presents Alberto-Culver's description of its corporate culture.

What to Look for in Identifying a Company's Corporate Culture

The taproot of corporate culture is the organization's beliefs and philosophy about how its affairs ought to be conducted—the reasons why it does things the way it does. A company's culture is manifested in the values and business principles that management preaches and practices, in official policies and procedures, in its revered traditions and oft-repeated stories, in the attitudes and behaviors of employees, in the peer pressures that exist to display core values, in the company's politics, in its approaches to people management and problem solving, in its relationships with external stakeholders (particularly vendors and the communities in which it operates), and in the "chemistry" and the "personality" that permeate its work environment. Some of these sociological forces are readily apparent, and others operate quite subtly.

The values, beliefs, and practices that undergird a company's culture can come from anywhere in the organization hierarchy, sometimes representing the philosophy of an influential executive and sometimes resulting from exemplary actions on the part of a specific employee, work group, department, or division.[1] Key elements of the culture often originate with a founder or other strong leader who articulated them as a set of business principles, company policies, or ways of dealing with employees, customers, vendors, shareholders, and the communities in which it operated. Over time, these cultural underpinnings take root, become embedded in how the company conducts its business, come to be accepted and shared by company managers and employees, and then persist as new employees are encouraged to adopt and follow the professed values and practices.

The Role of Stories Frequently, a significant part of a company's culture is captured in the stories that get told over and over again to illustrate to newcomers the importance of certain values and the depth of commitment that various company personnel have displayed. One of the folktales at FedEx, world renowned for the reliability of its next-day package delivery guarantee, is about a deliveryman who had been given the wrong key to a FedEx drop box. Rather than leave the packages in the drop box until the next day when the right key was available, the deliveryman unbolted the drop box from its base, loaded it into the truck, and took it back to the station. There, the box was pried open and the contents removed and sped on their way for on-time arrival. Nordstrom keeps a scrapbook commemorating the heroic acts of its employees and uses it as a regular reminder of the above-and-beyond-the-call-of-duty behaviors that employees are encouraged to display. At Frito-Lay, there are dozens of stories about truck drivers who went to extraordinary lengths in overcoming adverse weather conditions to keep store shelves stocked with Frito-Lay products. Such stories serve the valuable purpose of illustrating the kinds of behavior the company encourages and reveres. Moreover, each retelling of a legendary story puts a bit more peer pressure on company personnel to go an extra step when the opportunity presents itself, to do their part to display core values, and to uphold company traditions.

Perpetuating the Culture Once established, company cultures are perpetuated in six important ways: (1) by screening and selecting new employees that will mesh well with the culture, (2) by systematic indoctrination of new members in the culture's fundamentals, (3) by the efforts of senior group members to reiterate core values in daily conversations and pronouncements, (4) by the telling and retelling of company legends, (5) by regular ceremonies honoring members who display desired cultural behaviors, and (6) by visibly rewarding those who display cultural norms and penalizing those who don't.[2] The more that new employees are being brought into the organization the more important it becomes to screen job applicants every bit as much for how well their values, beliefs, and personalities match up with the culture as for their technical skills and experience. For example, a company that stresses operating with integrity and fairness has to hire people who themselves have integrity and place a high value on fair play. A company whose culture revolves around creativity, product innovation, and leading change has to screen new hires for their ability to think outside the box, generate new ideas, and thrive in a climate of rapid change and ambiguity. Southwest Airlines, whose two core values "LUV" and fun permeate the work environment and whose objective is to ensure that passengers have a positive and enjoyable flying experience, goes to considerable lengths to hire flight attendants and gate personnel who are witty, cheery, and outgoing and who display "whistle while you work" attitudes. Fast-growing companies risk creating a culture by chance rather than by design if they rush to hire employees mainly for their talents and credentials and neglect to screen out candidates whose values, philosophies, and personalities aren't a good fit with the organizational character, vision, and strategy being articulated by the company's senior executives.

As a rule, companies are attentive to the task of hiring people who will fit in and who will embrace the prevailing culture. Usually, job seekers lean toward accepting jobs at companies where they feel comfortable with the atmosphere and the people they will be working with. Employees who don't hit it off at a company tend to leave quickly, while employees who thrive and are pleased with the work environment stay on, eventually moving up the ranks to positions of greater responsibility. The longer people stay at an organization, the more they come to embrace and mirror the corporate culture—their values and beliefs tend to be molded by mentors, fellow workers, company training programs, and the reward structure. Normally, employees who have worked at a company for a long time play a major role in indoctrinating new employees into the culture.

Forces That Cause a Company's Culture to Evolve   However, even stable cultures aren't static—just like strategy and organization structure, they evolve. New challenges in the marketplace, revolutionary technologies, and shifting internal conditions—especially eroding business prospects, an internal crisis, or top executive turnover—tend to breed new ways of doing things and, in turn, cultural evolution. An incoming CEO who decides to shake up the existing business and take it in new directions often triggers a cultural shift, perhaps one of major proportions. Likewise, diversification into new businesses, expansion into foreign countries, rapid growth, an influx of new employees, and merger with or acquisition of another company can all precipitate cultural changes.

Company Subcultures: The Problems Posed by New Acquisitions and Multinational Operations   Although it is common to speak about corporate culture in the singular, companies typically have multiple cultures or numerous subcultures within the prevailing culture.[3] Values, beliefs, and practices within a company sometimes vary significantly by department, geographic location, division, or business unit. A company's subcultures can clash, or at least not mesh well, if they embrace conflicting business philosophies or operating approaches, or if key executives employ different approaches to people management, or if important differences between a company's culture and those of recently acquired companies have not yet been ironed out. *Global and multinational companies tend to be at least partly multicultural* because cross-country organization units have different operating histories and work climates, as well as members who have grown up under different social customs and traditions and who have different sets of values and beliefs. The human resources manager of a global pharmaceutical company who took on an assignment in the Far East discovered, to his surprise, that one of his biggest challenges was to persuade his company's managers in China, Korea, Malaysia, and Taiwan to accept promotions—their cultural values were such that they did not believe in competing with their peers for career rewards or personal gain, nor did they relish breaking ties to their local communities to assume cross-national responsibilities.[4] Many companies that have merged with or acquired foreign companies have to deal with language- and custom-based cultural differences.

Nonetheless, the existence of subcultures does not preclude important areas of commonality and compatibility. For example, General Electric's cultural components of boundarylessness, workout, and Six Sigma quality can be implanted and practiced successfully in different countries. AES, a global power company with operations in over 20 countries, has found that the four core values of integrity, fairness, fun, and social responsibility underlying its culture are readily embraced by people in most countries. Moreover, AES tries to define and practice its cultural values the same way in all of its locations while still being sensitive to differences that exist among various people groups across the world; top managers at AES express the views that people across the world are more similar than different and that the company's culture is as meaningful in Argentina or Kazakhstan as in the United States.

In today's globalizing world, multinational companies are learning how to make strategy-critical cultural traits travel across country boundaries and create a workably uniform culture worldwide. Likewise, company managements are quite alert to the importance of cultural compatibility in making acquisitions and the need to address how to merge and integrate the cultures of newly acquired companies—cultural due diligence is often as important as financial due diligence in deciding whether to go forward on an acquisition or merger. On a number of occasions, companies have decided to pass on acquiring particular companies because of culture conflicts that they believed would be hard to resolve.

Culture: Ally or Obstacle to Strategy Execution?

A company's present culture and work climate may or may not be compatible with what is needed for effective implementation and execution of the chosen strategy. *When a company's present work climate promotes attitudes and behaviors that are well suited to first-rate strategy execution, its culture functions as a valuable ally in the strategy execution process.* When the culture is in conflict with some aspect of the company's direction, performance targets, or strategy, the culture becomes a stumbling block.[5]

How Culture Can Promote Better Strategy Execution A culture grounded in strategy-supportive values, practices, and behavioral norms adds significantly to the power and effectiveness of a company's strategy execution effort. For example, a culture where frugality and thrift are values widely shared by organizational members nurtures employee actions to identify cost-saving opportunities—the very behavior needed for successful execution of a low-cost leadership strategy. A culture built around such business principles as pleasing customers, fair treatment, operating excellence, and employee empowerment promotes employee behaviors and an esprit de corps that facilitate execution of strategies keyed to high product quality and superior customer service. A culture in which taking initiative, challenging the status quo, exhibiting creativity, embracing change, and being a team player pervade the work climate promotes creative collaboration and a drive to lead market change—outcomes that are conducive to successful execution of product innovation and technological leadership strategies.[6]

A tight culture–strategy alignment furthers a company's strategy execution effort in two ways:[7]

1. *A culture that encourages actions supportive of good strategy execution not only provides company personnel with clear guidance regarding what behaviors and results constitute good job performance but also produces significant peer pressure from coworkers to conform to culturally acceptable norms.* The tighter the

strategy–culture fit, the more that the culture pushes people to display behaviors and observe operating practices that are conducive to good strategy execution. A strategy-supportive culture thus funnels organizational energy toward getting the right things done and delivering positive organizational results. In a company whose strategy and culture are misaligned, some of the very behaviors needed to execute strategy successfully run contrary to the behaviors and values imbedded in the prevailing culture. Such a clash nearly always produces resistance from employees who have strong allegiance to the present culture. Culture-bred resistance to the actions and behaviors needed for good execution, if strong and widespread, poses a formidable hurdle that has to be cleared for strategy execution to get very far.

2. *A culture imbedded with values and behaviors that facilitate strategy execution promotes strong employee identification with and commitment to the company's vision, performance targets, and strategy.* When a company's culture is grounded in many of the needed strategy-executing behaviors, employees feel genuinely better about their jobs, the company they work for, and the merits of what the company is trying to accomplish. As a consequence, company personnel are more inclined to exhibit some passion and exert their best efforts in making the strategy work, trying to achieve the targeted performance, and moving the company closer to realizing its strategic vision.

core concept
Because culturally approved behavior thrives and culturally disapproved behavior gets squashed, company managers are well-advised to spend time creating a culture that supports and encourages the behaviors conducive to good strategy execution.

These aspects of culture–strategy alignment say something important about the task of managing the strategy executing process: *Closely aligning corporate culture with the requirements for proficient strategy execution merits the full attention of senior executives.* The managerial objective is to create and nurture a work culture that mobilizes organizational energy squarely behind efforts to execute strategy. A good job of culture building on management's part promotes can-do attitudes and acceptance of change, instills strong peer pressures for behaviors conducive to good strategy execution, and enlists more enthusiasm and dedicated effort among company personnel for achieving company objectives.

The Perils of Strategy–Culture Conflict Conflicts between behaviors approved by the culture and behaviors needed for good strategy execution send mixed signals to organization members, forcing an undesirable choice. Should organization members be loyal to the culture and company traditions (as well as to their own personal values and beliefs, which are likely to be compatible with the culture) and thus resist or be indifferent to actions and behaviors that will promote better strategy execution? Or should they support the strategy execution effort and engage in actions and behaviors that run counter to the culture?

When a company's culture is out of sync with what is needed for strategic success, the culture has to be changed as rapidly as can be managed—this, of course, presumes that it is one or more aspects of the culture that are out of whack rather than the strategy. While correcting a strategy–culture conflict can occasionally mean revamping strategy to produce cultural fit, more usually it means revamping the mismatched cultural features to produce strategy fit. The more entrenched the mismatched aspects of the culture, the greater the difficulty of implementing new or different strategies until better strategy–culture alignment emerges. A sizable and prolonged strategy–culture conflict weakens and may even defeat managerial efforts to make the strategy work.

Strong versus Weak Cultures

Corporate cultures vary widely in the degree to which they are embedded in company practices and behavioral norms. Strongly embedded cultures go directly to a company's heart and soul; those with shallow roots provide little in the way of a definable corporate character.

Strong-Culture Companies   A company's culture can be strong and cohesive in the sense that the company conducts its business according to a clear and explicit set of principles and values, has managers who devote considerable time to communicating these principles and values to organization members and explaining how they relate to its business environment, and has values shared by senior executives and rank-and-file employees alike.[8] Strong-culture companies have a well-defined corporate character, typically underpinned by a creed or values statement. Executives regularly stress the importance of using company values and business principles as the basis for decisions and actions taken throughout the organization. In strong-culture companies, values and behavioral norms are so deeply rooted that they don't change much when a new CEO takes over—although they can erode over time if the CEO ceases to nurture them. And they

> In a strong-culture company, values and behavioral norms are like crabgrass: deeply rooted and hard to weed out.

may not change much as strategy evolves and the organization acts to make strategy adjustments, either because the new strategies are compatible with the present culture or because the dominant traits of the culture are somewhat strategy-neutral and compatible with evolving versions of the company's strategy.

Three factors contribute to the development of strong cultures: (1) a founder or other strong leader who establishes values, principles, and practices that are consistent and sensible in light of customer needs, competitive conditions, and strategic requirements; (2) a sincere, long-standing company commitment to operating the business according to these established traditions, thereby creating an internal environment that supports decision making and strategies based on cultural norms; and (3) a genuine concern for the well-being of the organization's three biggest constituencies—customers, employees, and shareholders. Continuity of leadership, small group size, stable group membership, geographic concentration, and considerable organizational success all contribute to the emergence and sustainability of a strong culture.[9]

During the time a strong culture is being implanted, there's nearly always a good strategy–culture fit (which partially accounts for the organization's success). Mismatches between strategy and culture in a strong-culture company tend to occur when a company's business environment undergoes significant change, prompting a drastic strategy revision that clashes with the entrenched culture. A strategy–culture clash can also occur in a strong-culture company whose business has gradually eroded; when a new leader is brought in to revitalize the company's operations, he or she may push the company in a strategic direction that requires substantially different cultural and behavioral norms. In such cases, a major culture-changing effort has to be launched.

One of the best examples of an industry in which strategy changes have clashed with deeply implanted cultures is the electric utility industry. Most electric utility companies, long used to operating as slow-moving regulated monopolies with captive customers, are now confronting the emergence of a vigorously competitive market in wholesale power generation and growing freedom on the part of industrial, commercial, and residential customers to choose their own energy supplier (in much the same way as customers choose their long-distance telephone carriers—an industry that once was a heavily regulated market). These new market circumstances are prompting electric companies to shift away from cultures predicated on risk avoidance, centralized control of decision making, and the politics of regulatory relationships toward cultures aimed at entrepreneurial risk taking, product innovation, competitive thinking, greater attention to customer service, cost reduction, and competitive pricing.

Weak-Culture Companies   In direct contrast to strong-culture companies, weak-culture companies are fragmented in the sense that no one set of values is consistently preached or widely shared, few behavioral norms are evident in operating practices, and few traditions are widely revered or proudly nurtured by company personnel. Because top executives don't repeatedly espouse any particular business philosophy or exhibit long-standing commitment to particular values or extol particular operating practices and behavioral norms, organization members at weak-culture companies typically lack any deeply felt sense of corporate identity. While employees may have some bonds of identification with and loyalty toward their department, their colleagues, their union, or their boss, a weak company culture breeds no strong employee allegiance to what the company stands for or to operating the business in well-defined ways. Such lack of a definable corporate character results in many employees viewing their company as just a place to work and their job as just a way to make a living—there's neither passion about the company nor emotional commitment to what it is trying to accomplish. Very often, cultural weakness stems from moderately entrenched subcultures that block the emergence of a well-defined companywide work climate.

As a consequence, *weak cultures provide little or no strategy-implementing assistance* because there are no traditions, beliefs, values, common bonds, or behavioral norms that management can use as levers to mobilize commitment to executing the chosen strategy. While a weak culture does not usually pose a strong barrier to strategy execution, it also provides no support. Without a work climate that channels organizational energy in the direction of good strategy execution, managers are left with the options of either using compensation incentives and other motivational devices to mobilize employee commitment or trying to establish cultural roots that will in time start to nurture the strategy execution process.

Unhealthy Cultures

The distinctive characteristic of an unhealthy corporate culture is the presence of counterproductive cultural traits that adversely impact the work climate and company performance.[10] The following three traits are particularly unhealthy:

1.   A highly politicized internal environment in which many issues get resolved and decisions made on the basis of which individuals or groups have the most political clout to carry the day.
2.   Hostility to change and a general wariness of people who champion new ways of doing things.
3.   A "not-invented-here" mind-set that makes company personnel averse to looking outside the company for best practices, new managerial approaches, and innovative ideas.

What makes a politicized internal environment so unhealthy is that political infighting consumes a great deal of organizational energy, often with the result that political maneuvering takes precedence over what's best for the company. In companies where internal politics pervades the work climate, empire-building managers jealously guard their decision-making prerogatives. They have their own agendas and operate the work units under their supervision as autonomous "fiefdoms," and the positions they take on issues is usually aimed at protecting or expanding their turf. Collaboration with other organizational units is viewed with suspicion (What are "they" up to? How can "we" protect "our" flanks?), and cross-unit cooperation occurs grudgingly. When an important proposal comes up, advocates try to ram it through and opponents try to alter or defeat it. The support or opposition of politically influential executives and/or coalitions among departments with vested interests in a particular outcome typically weigh heavily in deciding what actions the company takes. All this maneuvering takes away from efforts to execute strategy with real proficiency and frustrates those who are less political and more inclined to do what is in the company's best interests.

In less-adaptive cultures where skepticism about the importance of new developments and resistance to change are the norm, managers prefer waiting until the fog of uncertainty clears before steering a new course. They believe in moving cautiously and conservatively, preferring to follow others rather than take decisive action to be in the forefront of change. Change-resistant cultures place a premium on not making mistakes, prompting managers to lean toward safe, don't-rock-the-boat options that will have only a ripple effect on the status quo, protect or advance their own careers, and guard the interests of their immediate work groups.

Change-resistant cultures encourage a number of undesirable or unhealthy behaviors—risk avoidance, timidity regarding emerging opportunities, and laxity in product innovation and continuous improvement. In change-resistant cultures, word quickly gets around that proposals to do things differently face an uphill battle and that people who champion them may be seen as either nuisances or troublemakers. Executives who don't value managers or employees with initiative and new ideas put a damper on product innovation, experimentation, and efforts to improve. At the same time, change-resistant companies have little appetite for being first-movers or fast-followers, believing that being in the forefront of change is too risky and that acting too quickly increases vulnerability to costly mistakes. They are more inclined to adopt a wait-and-see posture, carefully analyze several alternative responses, learn from the missteps of early movers, and then move forward cautiously and conservatively with initiatives that are deemed safe. Hostility to change is most often found in companies with multilayered management bureaucracies that have enjoyed considerable market success in years past and that are wedded to the "We have done it this way for years" syndrome.

When such companies encounter business environments with accelerating change, going slow on altering traditional ways of doing things can be become a liability rather than an asset. General Motors, IBM, Sears, and Eastman Kodak are classic examples of companies whose change-resistant bureaucracies were slow to respond to fundamental changes in their markets; clinging to the cultures and traditions that made them successful, they were reluctant to alter operating practices and modify their business approaches. As strategies of gradual change won out over bold innovation and being an early mover, all four lost market share to rivals that quickly moved to institute changes more in tune with evolving market conditions and buyer preferences. These companies are now struggling to recoup lost ground with cultures and behaviors more suited to market success—the kinds of fit that caused them to succeed in the first place.

The third unhealthy cultural trait—the not-invented-here mind-set—tends to develop when a company reigns as an industry leader or enjoys great market success for so long that its personnel start to believe they have all the answers or can develop them on their own. Such confidence in the correctness of how it does things and in the company's skills and capabilities breeds arrogance—there's a strong tendency for company personnel to discount the merits or significance of what outsiders are doing and what can be learned by studying best-in-class performers. Benchmarking and best-practices programs are seen as offering little payoff. Any market share gains on the part of up-and-coming rivals are regarded as temporary setbacks, soon to be reversed by the company's own forthcoming initiatives. Insular thinking, internally driven solutions, and a must-be-invented-here mindset come to permeate the corporate culture. An inwardly focused corporate culture gives rise to managerial inbreeding and a failure to recruit people who can offer fresh thinking and outside perspectives. The big risk of insular cultural thinking is that the company can underestimate the competencies and accomplishments of rival companies and overestimate its own progress—with a resulting loss of competitive advantage over time.

Unhealthy cultures typically impair company performance. Avon, BankAmerica, Citicorp, Coors, Ford, General Motors, Kmart, Kroger, Sears, and Xerox are examples of companies whose unhealthy cultures during the late 1970s and early 1980s contributed to ho-hum performance on the bottom line and in the marketplace.[11] General Motors, Kmart, and Sears are still struggling to uproot problematic cultural traits and replace them with behaviors having a more suitable strategy–culture fit.

Adaptive Cultures

> **core concept**
>
> In adaptive cultures, there's a spirit of doing what's necessary to ensure long-term organizational success provided the new behaviors and operating practices that management is calling for are seen as legitimate and consistent with the core values and business principles underpinning the culture.

The hallmark of adaptive corporate cultures is willingness on the part of organizational members to accept change and take on the challenge of introducing and executing new strategies.[12] Company personnel share a feeling of confidence that the organization can deal with whatever threats and opportunities come down the pike; they are receptive to risk taking, experimentation, innovation, and changing strategies and practices. In direct contrast to change-resistant cultures, adaptive cultures are very supportive of managers and employees at all ranks who propose or help initiate useful change. Internal entrepreneurship is encouraged and rewarded. Senior executives seek out, support, and promote individuals who exercise initiative, spot opportunities for improvement, and display the skills to implement them. Managers habitually fund product development initiatives, evaluate new ideas openly, and take prudent risks to create new business positions. As a consequence, the company exhibits a proactive approach to identifying issues, evaluating the implications and options, and implementing workable solutions. Strategies and traditional operating practices are modified as needed to adjust to or take advantage of changes in the business environment.

But why is change so willingly embraced in an adaptive culture? Why are organization members not fearful of how change will affect them? Why does an adaptive culture not become unglued with ongoing changes in strategy, operating practices, and behavioral norms? The answers lie in two distinctive and dominant traits of an adaptive culture: (1) Any changes in operating practices and behaviors must *not* compromise core values and long-standing business principles, and (2) the changes that are instituted must satisfy the legitimate interests of stakeholders—customers, employees, shareowners, suppliers, and the communities where the company operates.[13] In other words, what sustains an adaptive culture is that organization members perceive the changes that management is trying to institute as legitimate and in keeping with the core values and business principles that form the heart and soul of the culture.

Thus, for an adaptive culture to remain intact over time, top management must orchestrate the responses in a manner that demonstrates genuine care for the well-being of all key constituencies and tries to satisfy all their legitimate interests simultaneously.

Unless fairness to all constituencies is a decision-making principle and a commitment to doing the right thing is evident to organization members, the changes are not likely to be readily accepted and implemented.[14] Making changes that will please customers and/or protect, if not enhance, the company's long-term well-being is generally seen as legitimate and is often seen as the best way of looking out for the interests of employees, stockholders, suppliers, and communities where the company operates. At companies with adaptive cultures, management concern for the well-being of employees is nearly always a big factor in gaining employee support for change—company personnel are usually receptive to change as long as employees understand that changes in their job assignments are part of the process of adapting to new conditions and that their employment security will not be threatened unless the company's business unexpectedly reverses direction. In cases where workforce downsizing becomes necessary, management concern for employees dictates that separation be handled humanely, making employee departure as painless as possible. Management efforts to make adaptation fair and equitable for customers, employees, stockholders, suppliers, and communities where the company operates, keeping adverse impacts to a minimum insofar as possible, breeds acceptance of and support for change among all organization stakeholders.

Technology, software, and dot-com companies offer good illustrations of organizations with adaptive cultures. Such companies thrive on change—driving it, leading it, and capitalizing on it (but sometimes also succumbing to change when they make the wrong move or are swamped by better technologies or the superior business models of rivals). Companies like Microsoft, Intel, Nokia, Amazon.com, and Dell Computer cultivate the capability to act and react rapidly. They are avid practitioners of entrepreneurship and innovation, with a demonstrated willingness to take bold risks to create altogether new products, new businesses, and new industries. To create and nurture a culture that can adapt rapidly to changing business conditions, they make a point of staffing their organizations with people who are proactive, who rise to the challenge of change, and who have an aptitude for adapting.

In fast-changing business environments, a corporate culture that is receptive to altering organizational practices and behaviors is a virtual necessity. However, adaptive cultures work to the advantage of all companies, not just those in rapid-change environments. Every company operates in a market and business climate that is changing to one degree or another and that, in turn, requires internal operating responses and new behaviors on the part of organization members. As a company's strategy evolves, an adaptive culture is a definite ally in the strategy-implementing, strategy-executing process as compared to cultures that have to be coaxed and cajoled to change. This constitutes a good argument for why managers should strive to build a strong, adaptive corporate culture.

> A good case can be made that a strongly planted, adaptive culture is the best of all corporate cultures.

Creating a Strong Fit between Strategy and Culture

It is the *strategy maker's* responsibility to select a strategy compatible with the sacred or unchangeable parts of the organization's prevailing corporate culture. It is the *strategy implementer's* task, once strategy is chosen, to change whatever facets of the corporate culture hinder effective execution.

Changing a Problem Culture   Changing a company's culture to align it with strategy is among the toughest management tasks because of the heavy anchor of deeply held values and habits—people cling emotionally to the old and familiar. It takes concerted management action over a period of

> Once a culture is established, it is difficult to change.

figure 13.1   **Changing a Problem Culture**

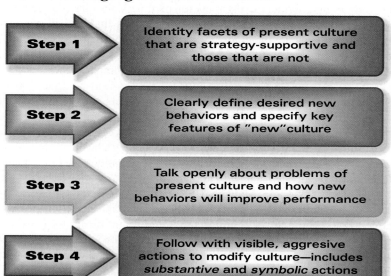

time to replace an unhealthy culture with a healthy culture or to root out certain unwanted behaviors and instill ones that are more strategy-supportive. *The single most
visible factor that distinguishes successful culture-change efforts from failed attempts
is competent leadership at the top.* Great power is needed to force major cultural
change—to overcome the springback resistance of entrenched cultures—and great
power normally resides only at the top.

As shown in Figure 13.1, the first step in fixing a problem culture is to identify
those facets of the present culture that are dysfunctional and explain why they pose obstacles to executing new strategic initiatives and achieving company performance targets. Second, managers have to clearly define the desired new behaviors and specify the
key features of the culture they want to create. Third, managers have to talk openly and
forthrightly to all concerned about problematic aspects of the culture and why and how
new behaviors will improve company performance—the case for cultural change has to
be persuasive and the benefits of a reformed culture made convincing to all concerned.
Finally, and most important, the talk has to be followed swiftly by visible, aggressive actions to promote the desired new behaviors—actions that everyone will understand are
intended to produce behaviors and practices conducive to good strategy execution.

The menu of actions management can take to change a problem culture includes
the following:[15]

1. Making a compelling case for why the company's new direction and a different cultural atmosphere are in the organization's best interests and why individuals and
groups should commit themselves to making it happen despite the obstacles. Skeptics have to be convinced that all is not well with the status quo. This can be done by:

- Challenging the status quo with very basic questions: Are we giving customers
what they really need and want? Why aren't we taking more business away
from rivals? Why do our rivals have lower costs than we do? How can we drive
costs out of the business and be more competitive on price? Why can't

design-to-market cycle time be halved? Why aren't we moving faster to make better use of the Internet and e-commerce technologies and practices? How can we grow company revenues at 15 percent instead of 10 percent? What can we do to speed up our decision making and shorten response times?

- Creating events where everyone in management is forced to listen to angry customers, dissatisfied strategic allies, alienated employees, or disenchanted stockholders.

2. Repeating at every opportunity the messages of why cultural change is good for company stakeholders (particularly customers, employees, and shareholders). Effective culture-change leaders are good at telling stories to convey new values and connect the case for change to organization members.

3. Visibly praising and generously rewarding people who display newly advocated cultural norms and who participate in implementing the desired kinds of operating practices.

4. Altering incentive compensation to reward the desired cultural behavior and deny rewards to those who resist change.

5. Recruiting and hiring new managers and employees who have the desired cultural values and can serve as role models for the desired cultural behavior.

6. Replacing key executives who are strongly associated with the old culture.

7. Revising policies and procedures in ways that will help drive cultural change.

Only with bold leadership and concerted action on many fronts can a company succeed in tackling so large and difficult a task as major cultural change. When only strategic fine-tuning is being implemented, it takes less time and effort to bring values and culture into alignment with strategy, but there is still a lead role for the manager to play in communicating the need for new cultural behaviors and personally launching actions to prod the culture into better alignment with strategy.

Symbolic Culture-Changing Actions Managerial actions to tighten the strategy–culture fit need to be both symbolic and substantive. Symbolic actions are valuable for the signals they send about the kinds of behavior and performance strategy implementers wish to encourage. The most important symbolic actions are those that top executives take to *lead by example.* For instance, if the organization's strategy involves a drive to become the industry's low-cost producer, senior managers must display frugality in their own actions and decisions: inexpensive decorations in the executive suite, conservative expense accounts and entertainment allowances, a lean staff in the corporate office, scrutiny of budget requests, few executive perks, and so on. If the culture change imperative is to be more responsive to customers' needs and to pleasing customers, the CEO can instill greater customer awareness by requiring all officers and executives to spend a significant portion of each week talking with customers about their needs.

Another category of symbolic actions includes the ceremonial events organizations hold to designate and honor people whose actions and performance exemplify what is called for in the new culture. Many universities give outstanding teacher awards each year to symbolize their commitment to good teaching and their esteem for instructors who display exceptional classroom talents. Numerous businesses have employee-of-the-month awards. The military has a long-standing custom of awarding ribbons and medals for exemplary actions. Mary Kay Cosmetics awards an array of prizes—from ribbons to pink automobiles—to its beauty consultants for reaching various sales plateaus.

The best companies and the best executives expertly use symbols, role models, ceremonial occasions, and group gatherings to tighten the strategy–culture fit. Low-cost leaders like Wal-Mart and Nucor are renowned for their spartan facilities, executive frugality, intolerance of waste, and zealous control of costs. Nucor executives make a point of flying coach class and using taxis at airports rather than limousines. Executives sensitive to their role in promoting strategy–culture fits make a habit of appearing at ceremonial functions to praise individuals and groups that get with the program. They honor individuals who exhibit cultural norms and reward those who achieve strategic milestones. They participate in employee training programs to stress strategic priorities, values, ethical principles, and cultural norms. Every group gathering is seen as an opportunity to repeat and ingrain values, praise good deeds, reinforce cultural norms, and promote changes that assist strategy execution. Sensitive executives make sure that current decisions and policy changes will be construed by organizational members as consistent with cultural values and supportive of the company's new strategic direction.[16]

Substantive Culture-Changing Actions   While symbolically leading the push for new behaviors and communicating the reasons for new approaches is crucial, strategy implementers have to convince all those concerned that the culture-changing effort is more than cosmetic. Talk and symbolism have to be complemented by substantive actions and real movement. The actions taken have to be credible, highly visible, and unmistakably indicative of the seriousness of management's commitment to new strategic initiatives and the associated cultural changes. There are several ways to make substantive changes. One is to engineer some quick successes that highlight the benefits of the proposed changes, thus making enthusiasm for them contagious. However, instant results are usually not as important as having the will and patience to create a solid, competent team psychologically committed to pursuing the strategy in a superior fashion. The strongest signs that management is truly committed to creating a new culture include replacing old-culture traditionalist managers with new-breed managers, changing dysfunctional policies and operating practices, instituting new compensation incentives visibly tied to the achievement of freshly set performance targets, and making major budgetary reallocations that shift substantial resources from old-strategy projects and programs to new-strategy projects and programs.

Implanting the needed culture-building values and behavior depends on a sincere, sustained commitment by the chief executive coupled with extraordinary persistence in reinforcing the culture at every opportunity through both word and deed. Neither charisma nor personal magnetism is essential. However, personally talking to many departmental groups about the reasons for change *is* essential; organizational changes are seldom accomplished successfully from an office. Moreover, creating and sustaining a strategy-supportive culture is a job for the whole management team. Major cultural change requires many initiatives from many people. Senior officers, department heads, and middle managers have to reiterate valued behaviors and translate the organization's core values and business principles into everyday practice. In addition, strategy implementers must enlist the support of frontline supervisors and employee opinion leaders, convincing them of the merits of practicing and enforcing cultural norms at the lowest levels in the organization. Until a big majority of employees join the new culture and share an emotional commitment to its basic values and behavioral norms, there's considerably more work to be done in both instilling the culture and tightening the strategy–culture fit.

Changing culture to support strategy is not a short-term exercise. It takes time for a new culture to emerge and prevail. Overnight transformations simply don't occur. The bigger the organization and the greater the cultural shift needed to produce a strategy–culture fit, the longer it takes. In large companies, fixing a problem culture and instilling a new set of attitudes and behaviors can take two to five years. In fact, it is usually tougher to reform an entrenched problematic culture than it is to instill a strategy-supportive culture from scratch in a brand-new organization. Sometimes executives succeed in changing the values and behaviors of small groups of managers and even whole departments or divisions, only to find the changes eroded over time by the actions of the rest of the organization—what is communicated, praised, supported, and penalized by an entrenched majority undermines the new emergent culture and halts its progress. Executives, despite a series of well-intended actions to reform a problem culture, are likely to fail at weeding out embedded cultural traits when widespread employee skepticism about the company's new directions and culture-change effort spawns covert resistance to the cultural behaviors and operating practices advocated by top management. This is why management must take every opportunity to convince employees of the need for culture change and communicate to them how new attitudes, behaviors, and operating practices will benefit the interests of organizational stakeholders.

A company that has done a good job of fixing its problem culture is Alberto-Culver—see Illustration Capsule 13.2.

Grounding the Culture in Core Values and Ethics

A corporate culture grounded in socially approved values and ethical business principles is a vital ingredient in a company's long-term strategic success.[17] Unless a company's executives genuinely care about how the company's business affairs are conducted, the company's reputation and ultimately its performance are put at risk. The recent wave of corporate scandals vividly demonstrates the damage that occurs when the public spotlight is trained on a company's shady business practices and the unethical behavior of certain company personnel. Codes of ethics are not prevalent in large corporations around the world.[18] In the United States, over 90 percent of large companies have a code of ethics, and in Canada the number runs close to 85 percent; over 50 percent of British and German companies have a code, while in France the number is close to 30 percent. Substantial numbers of large companies also have corporate values statements.

While there's no doubt that some companies and some company personnel knowingly engage in unsavory business practices and have little regard for ethical standards, one must be cautious about concluding that a company's core values and ethical standards are just a bunch of high-sounding platitudes that serve only cosmetic purposes. Executives at many companies genuinely care about the values and ethical standards that company personnel exhibit in conducting the company's business; they are aware that their own reputations, as well as the company's reputation, hangs on whether outsiders see the company's actions as ethical or honest or socially acceptable. At such companies, values statements and codes of ethics matter, and they are ingrained to one degree or another in the company's culture—see Table 13.1 for the kinds of topics that are commonly found in values statements and codes of ethics.

Indeed, at companies where executives are truly committed to practicing the values and ethical standards that have been espoused, *the stated core values and ethical*

illustration capsule 13.2
The Culture-Change Effort at Alberto-Culver's North American Division

In 1993, Carol Bernick—vice chairperson of Alberto-Culver, president of its North American division, and daughter of the company's founders—concluded that her division's existing culture had four problems: Employees dutifully waited for marching orders from their bosses, workers put pleasing their bosses ahead of pleasing customers, some company policies were not family-friendly, and there was too much bureaucracy and paperwork. What was needed, in Bernick's opinion, was a culture in which company employees welcomed innovation, took risks, and had a sense of ownership and an urgency to get things done.

To change the culture, Alberto-Culver's management undertook a series of actions:

- In 1993, a new position called growth development leader (GDL) was created to help orchestrate the task of fixing the culture deep in the ranks (there were 70 GDLs in Alberto-Culver's North American division). GDLs came from all ranks of the company's managerial ladder and were handpicked for such qualities as empathy, communication skills, positive attitude, and ability to let their hair down and have fun. GDLs performed their regular jobs in addition to taking on the GDL roles; it was considered an honor to be chosen. Each GDL mentored about 12 people from both a career and a family standpoint. GDLs met with senior executives weekly, bringing forward people's questions and issues and then, afterward, sharing with their groups the topics and solutions that were discussed. GDLs brought a group member as a guest to each meeting. One meeting each year is devoted to identifying "macros and irritations"—attendees are divided into four subgroups and given 15 minutes to identify the company's four biggest challenges (the macros) and the four most annoying aspects of life at the company (the irritations); the whole group votes on which four deserve the company's attention. Those selected are then addressed, and assignments made for follow-up and results.

- Changing the culture was made an issue across the company, starting in 1995 with a two-hour State of the Company presentation to employees covering where the company was and where it wanted to be. The State of the Company address was made an annual event.

- Management created ways to measure the gains in changing the culture. One involved an annual all-employee survey to assess progress against cultural goals and to get 360-degree feedback—the 2000 survey had 180 questions, including 33 relating to the performance of each respondent's GDL. A bonfire celebration was held in the company parking lot to announce that paperwork would be cut 30 percent.

- A list of 10 cultural imperatives was formalized in 1998—honesty, ownership, trust, customer orientation, commitment, fun, innovation, risk taking, speed and urgency, and teamwork. These imperatives came to be known internally as HOT CC FIRST.

- Extensive celebrations and awards programs were instituted. Most celebrations are scheduled, but some are spontaneous (an impromptu thank-you party for a good fiscal year). Business Builder Awards (initiated in 1997) are given to individuals and teams that make a significant impact on the company's growth and profitability. The best-scoring GDLs on the annual employee surveys are awarded shares of company stock. The company notes all work anniversaries and personal milestones with "Alberto-appropriate" gifts; appreciative company employees sometimes give thank-you gifts to their GDLs. According to Carol Bernick, "If you want something to grow, pour champagne on it. We've made a huge effort—maybe even an over-the-top effort—to celebrate our successes and, indeed, just about everything we'd like to see happen again."

The culture change effort at Alberto-Culver North America was viewed as a major contributor to improved performance. From 1993, when the effort first began, to 2001, the division's sales increased from just under $350 million to over $600 million and pretax profits rose from $20 million to almost $50 million.

table 13.1   **The Content of Company Values Statements and Codes of Ethics**

Topics Commonly Appearing in Values Statements	Topics Commonly Appearing in Codes of Ethics
• Commitment to such outcomes as customer satisfaction and customer service, quality, product innovation, and/or technological leadership • Commitment to achievement, excellence, and results • Importance of demonstrating such qualities as honesty, integrity, trust, fairness, quality of life, pride of workmanship, and ethics • Importance of creativity, taking initiative, and accepting responsibility • Importance of teamwork and a cooperative attitude • Importance of Golden Rule behavior and respect for coworkers • Making the company a great place to work • Importance of having fun and creating a fun work environment • Duty to stakeholders—customers, employees, suppliers, shareholders, communities where the company operates, and society at large • Commitment to exercising social responsibility and being a good community citizen • Commitment to protecting the environment • Commitment to workforce diversity	• Mandates that company personnel will display honesty and integrity in their actions • An expectation that all company personnel will comply fully with all laws and regulations, specifically: 　—Antitrust laws prohibiting anticompetitive practices, conspiracies to fix prices, or attempts to monopolize 　—The Foreign Corrupt Practices Act 　—Securities laws and prohibitions against insider trading 　—Environmental and workplace safety regulations 　—Discrimination and sexual harassment regulations • Prohibitions against giving or accepting bribes, kickbacks, or gifts • Avoiding conflicts of interest • Fairness in selling and marketing practices • Supplier relationships and procurement practices • Acquiring and using competitively sensitive information about rivals and others • Political contributions, activities, and lobbying • Avoiding use of company assets, resources, and property for personal or other inappropriate purposes • Responsibility to protect proprietary information and not divulge trade secrets

principles are the cornerstones of the corporate culture. As depicted in Figure 13.2, a company that works hard at putting its stated core values and ethical principles into practice fosters a work climate where company personnel share common convictions about how the company's business is to be conducted and where they are expected to act in accord with stated values and ethical standards. By promoting behaviors that mirror the values and ethics standards, a company's stated values and ethical standards nurture the corporate culture in three highly positive ways: (1) they communicate the company's good intentions and validate the integrity and aboveboard character of its business principles and operating methods, (2) they steer company personnel toward doing the right thing, and (3) they establish a "corporate conscience" and provide yardsticks for gauging the appropriateness of particular actions, decisions, and policies (see Figure 13.3).[19]

> A company's values statement and code of ethics communicate expectations of how employees should conduct themselves in the workplace.

Companies ingrain their values and ethical standards in a number of different ways.[20] Tradition-steeped companies with a rich folklore rely heavily on word-of-mouth indoctrination and the power of tradition to instill values and enforce ethical conduct. But many companies today convey their values and codes of ethics to stakeholders and interested parties in their annual reports, on their Web sites, and in internal

figure 13.2   **The Two Culture-Building Roles of a Company's Core Values and Ethical Standards**

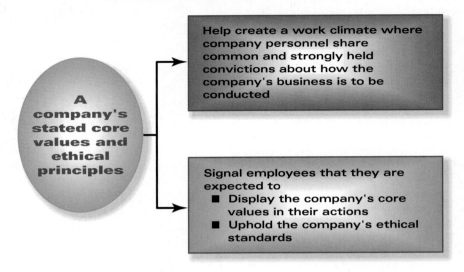

communications to all employees. The standards are hammered in at orientation courses for new employees and in training courses for managers and employees. The trend of making stakeholders aware of a company's commitment to core values and ethical business conduct is attributable to three factors: (1) greater management understanding of the role these statements play in culture building, (2) a renewed focus on ethical standards stemming from the corporate scandals that came to light in 2001–2002, and (3) the growing numbers of consumers who prefer to patronize ethical companies with ethical products.

However, there is a considerable difference between saying the right things (having a well-articulated corporate values statement or code of ethics) and truly managing a company in an ethical and socially responsible way. Companies that are truly committed to the stated core values and to high ethical standards make ethical behavior *a fundamental component of their corporate culture.* They put a stake in the ground, making it unequivocally clear that company personnel are expected to live up to the company's values and ethical standards—how well individuals display core values and adhere to ethical standards is often part of their job performance evaluations. Peer pressures to conform to cultural norms are quite strong, acting as an important deterrent to outside-the-lines behavior. Moreover, values statements and codes of ethical conduct are used as benchmarks for judging the appropriateness of company policies and operating practices.

At Darden Restaurants—a $4.5 billion casual dining company with over 1,200 company-owned Red Lobster, Olive Garden, Bahama Breeze, and Smokey Bones BBQ Sports Bar restaurants—the core values are operating with integrity, treating people fairly, and welcoming and celebrating workforce diversity; the company's practice of these values has been instrumental in creating a culture characterized by trust, exciting jobs and career opportunities for employees, and a passion to be the best in casual dining.[21]

Once values and ethical standards have been formally adopted, they must be institutionalized in the company's policies and practices and ingrained in the conduct of company personnel.[22] Imbedding the values and code of ethics entails several actions:

figure 13.3 **How a Company's Core Values and Ethical Principles Positively Impact the Corporate Culture**

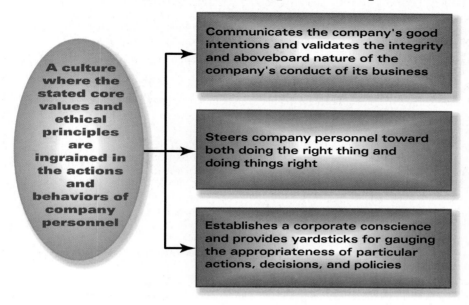

- Incorporation of the statement of values and the code of ethics into employee training and educational programs.
- Explicit attention to values and ethics in recruiting and hiring to screen out applicants who do not exhibit compatible character traits.
- Frequent reiteration of company values and ethical principles at company events and internal communications to employees.
- Active management involvement, from the CEO down to frontline supervisors, in stressing the importance of values and ethical conduct and in overseeing the compliance process.
- Ceremonies and awards for individuals and groups who display the values.
- Instituting ethics enforcement procedures.

In the case of codes of ethics, special attention must be given to sections of the company that are particularly vulnerable—procurement, sales, and political lobbying. Employees who deal with external parties are in ethically sensitive positions and often are drawn into compromising situations. Company personnel assigned to subsidiaries in foreign countries can find themselves trapped in ethical dilemmas if bribery and corruption of public officials are common practices or if suppliers or customers are accustomed to kickbacks of one kind or another. Mandatory ethics training for such personnel is usually desirable.

As a test of your ethics, take the quiz on page 388.

Structuring the Ethics Compliance and Enforcement Process   If a company's executives truly aspire for company personnel to behave ethically, then procedures for enforcing ethical standards and handling potential violations have to be

A Test of Your Business Ethics

As a gauge of your own ethical and moral standards, take the following quiz and see how you stack up against other members of your class. For the test to be valid, you need to answer the questions candidly and not on the basis of what you think the right answer is. When you finish the test, you should compare your answers to how your future employer would likely want you to answer each of these questions. Which are likely to be considered vital?

1. Is it unethical to make up data to justify the introduction of a new product if, when you start to object, your boss tells you, "Just do it"?
    ____Yes ____No ____Unsure (it depends) ____Need more information

2. Do you think that it is acceptable to give your boss a $100 gift to celebrate a birthday or holiday?
    ____Yes ____No ____Unsure (it depends) ____Need more information

3. Would it be wrong to accept a $100 gift from your boss (who is of the opposite sex) to celebrate your birthday?
    ____Yes ____No ____Unsure (it depends) ____Need more information

4. Is it unethical to accept an invitation from a supplier to spend a holiday weekend skiing at the supplier company's resort home in Colorado? (Would your answer be different if you were presently considering a proposal from that supplier to purchase $1 million worth of components?)
    ____Yes ____No ____Unsure (it depends) ____Need more information

5. Is it unethical to give a customer company's purchasing manager free tickets to the Super Bowl if he or she is looking for tickets and is likely to make a large purchase from your company?
    ____Yes ____No ____Unsure (it depends) ____Need more information

6. Is it unethical to use sick days provided in your company benefits plan as personal days so that you can go attend a family event or leave early for a weekend vacation?
    ____Yes ____No ____Unsure (it depends) ____Need more information

7. Would it be wrong to keep quiet if you, as a junior financial analyst, had just calculated that the projected return on a possible project was 18 percent and your boss (a) informed you that no project could be approved without the prospect of a 25 percent return and (b) told you to go back and redo the numbers and "get them right"?
    ____Yes ____No ____Unsure (it depends) ____Need more information

8. Would it be unethical to allow your supervisor to believe that you were chiefly responsible for the success of a new company initiative if it actually resulted from a team effort or major contributions by a coworker?
    ____Yes ____No ____Unsure (it depends) ____Need more information

9. Is it unethical to fail to come forward to support an employee wrongfully accused of misconduct if that person is a source of aggravation for you at work?
    ____Yes ____No ____Unsure (it depends) ____Need more information

10. Is it wrong to use your employer's staff to prepare invitations for a party that you will give when clients or customers are among those invited?
    ____Yes ____No ____Unsure (it depends) ____Need more information

11. Is it wrong to browse the Internet while at work if all your work is done and there is otherwise nothing you ought to be doing? (Would your answer be the same if you were downloading music files using file-sharing software from Kazaa? What if the Web sites you visited were pornographic?)
    ____Yes ____No ____Unsure (it depends) ____Need more information

12. Is it unethical to keep quiet if you are aware that a coworker is being sexually harassed by his or her boss?
    ____Yes ____No ____Unsure (it depends) ____Need more information

13. Is there an ethical problem with using your employer's copier to make a small number of copies for personal use (for example, your tax returns, your child's school project, or personal correspondence)?
    ____Yes ____No ____Unsure (it depends) ____Need more information

14. Is it unethical to install company-owned software on your home computer without the permission of your supervisor and the software vendor?
    ____Yes ____No ____Unsure (it depends) ____Need more information

15. Is it unethical to okay the shipment of products to a customer that do not meet the customer's specifications without first checking with the customer?
    ____Yes ____No ____Unsure (it depends) ____Need more information

Answers: We think a strong case can be made that the answers to questions 1, 3, 4, 5, 6, 7, 8, 9, 10, 11, 12, 13, 14, and 15 are yes and that the answer to question 2 is no. Most employers would consider the answers to questions 10 and 13 to be yes unless company policy allows personal use of company resources under certain specified conditions.

developed. Even in an ethically strong company, there can be bad apples—and some of the bad apples may even rise to the executive ranks. So it is rarely enough to rely on an ethically strong culture to produce ethics compliance.

The compliance effort must permeate the company, extending to every organizational unit. The attitudes, character, and work history of prospective employees must be scrutinized. Company personnel have to be educated about what is ethical and what is not; this means establishing ethics training programs and discussing what to do in gray areas. Everyone must be encouraged to raise issues with ethical dimensions, and such discussions should be treated as a legitimate topic. Line managers at all levels must give serious and continuous attention to the task of explaining how the values and ethical code apply in their areas. In addition, they must insist that company values and ethical standards become a way of life. In general, instilling values and insisting on ethical conduct must be looked on as a continuous culture-building, culture-nurturing exercise. Whether the effort succeeds or fails depends largely on how well corporate values and ethical standards are visibly integrated into company policies, managerial practices, and actions at all levels.

A company's formal ethics compliance and enforcement mechanisms can entail such actions as forming an ethics committee to give guidance on ethics matters, appointing an ethics officer to head the compliance effort, establishing an ethics hotline or Web site that employees can use to either anonymously report a possible violation or get confidential advice on a troubling ethics-related situation, and having an annual ethics audit to measure the extent of ethical behavior and identify problem areas. Increasing numbers of companies, wary of the damage to their reputations from public exposure of unethical behavior by company personnel, have begun openly encouraging employees to blow the whistle on possible ethical violations via toll-free hotlines, e-mail, and special Web sites. If a company is really serious about enforcing ethical behavior, it probably needs to do four things:

1. Have mandatory ethics training programs for employees.
2. Conduct an annual audit of each manager's efforts to uphold ethical standards and require formal reports on the actions taken by managers to remedy deficient conduct.
3. Require all employees to sign a statement annually certifying that they have complied with the company's code of ethics.
4. Openly encourage company personnel to report possible infractions via anonymous calls to a hotline or posting to a special company Web site.

While these actions may seem extreme or objectionable, they leave little room to doubt the seriousness of a company's commitment to ethics compliance. And most company personnel will think twice about knowingly engaging in unethical conduct when they know their actions will be audited and/or when they have to sign statements certifying compliance with the company's code of ethics. Ideally, the company's commitment to its stated values and ethical principles will instill not only a corporate conscience but also a conscience on the part of company personnel that prompts them to report possible ethical violations. While ethically conscious companies have provisions for disciplining violators, *the main purpose of the various means of enforcement is to encourage compliance rather than administer punishment.* Thus, the reason for openly encouraging people to report possible ethical violations is not so much to get someone in trouble as to *prevent further damage* and heighten awareness of operating within ethical bounds.

As was discussed in Chapter 10, transnational companies face a host of challenges in enforcing a common set of ethical standards when what is considered ethical varies either substantially or subtly from country to country. While there are a number of mostly universal and cross-cultural ethical standards—as concerns honesty, trustworthiness, fairness, avoiding unnecessary harm to individuals, and respecting the environment, there are shades and variations in what societies generally agree to be "right" and "wrong" based on the prevailing circumstances, local customs, and predominant religious convictions. And certainly there are cross-country variations in the *degree* or *severity* to which certain behaviors are considered unethical.[23] Thus transnational companies have to make a fundamental decision whether to try to enforce common ethical standards and interpretation of what is ethically right and wrong across their operations in all countries or whether to permit selected "rules bending" on a case-by-case basis.

Establishing a Strategy–Culture Fit in Multinational and Global Companies

In multinational and global companies, where some cross-border diversity in the corporate culture is normal, efforts to establish a tight strategy–culture fit is complicated by the diversity of societal customs and lifestyles from country to country. Company personnel in different countries sometimes fervently insist on being treated as distinctive individuals or groups, making a one-size-fits-all culture potentially inappropriate. Leading cross-border culture-change initiatives requires sensitivity to prevailing cultural differences; managers must discern when diversity has to be accommodated and when cross-border differences can be and should be narrowed.[24] Cross-country cultural diversity in a multinational enterprise is more tolerable if the company is pursuing a multicountry strategy and if the company's culture in each country is well aligned with its strategy in that country. But significant cross-country differences in a company's culture are likely to impede execution of a global strategy and have to be addressed.

As discussed earlier in this chapter, the trick to establishing a workable strategy–culture fit in multinational and global companies is to ground the culture in strategy-supportive values and operating practices that travel well across country borders and strike a chord with managers and workers in many different areas of the world, despite the diversity of local customs and traditions. A multinational enterprise with a misfit between its strategy and culture in certain countries where it operates can attack the problem by reinterpreting, de-emphasizing, or even abandoning those values and cultural traits which it finds inappropriate for some countries where it operates. Problematic values and operating principles can be replaced with values and operating approaches that travel well across country borders but that are still strategy supportive. Many times a company's values statement only has to be reworded so as to express existing values in ways that have more universal appeal. Sometimes certain offending operating practices can be modified to good advantage in all locations where the company operates.

Aside from trying to ground the culture in a set of core values and operating principles that have universal appeal, management can seek to minimize the existence of subcultures and cross-country cultural diversity by:

- Instituting training programs to communicate the meaning of core values and explain the case for common operating principles and practices.
- Drawing on the full range of motivational and compensation incentives to induce personnel to adopt and practice the desired behaviors.
- Allowing some leeway for certain core values and principles to be interpreted and applied somewhat differently, if necessary, to accommodate local customs and traditions.

Generally, a high degree of cross-country homogeneity in a company's culture is desirable and has to be pursued. Having too much variation in the corporate culture from country to country not only makes it difficult to use the culture in helping drive the strategy execution process but also works against the establishment of a one-company mind-set and a consistent corporate identity.

LEADING THE STRATEGY EXECUTION PROCESS

The litany of managing the strategy process is simple enough: Craft a sound strategic plan, implement it, execute it to the fullest, adjust it as needed, and win! But the leadership challenges are significant and diverse. Exerting take-charge leadership, being a "spark plug," ramrodding things through, and achieving results thrusts a manager into a variety of leadership roles in managing the strategy execution process: resource acquirer and allocator, capabilities builder, motivator, policymaker, policy enforcer, head cheerleader, crisis solver, decision maker, and taskmaster, to mention a few. There are times when leading the strategy execution process entails being authoritarian and hardnosed, times when it is best to be a perceptive listener and a compromising decision maker, times when matters are best delegated to people closest to the scene of the action, and times when being a coach is the proper role. Many occasions call for the manager in charge to assume a highly visible role and put in long hours guiding the process, while others entail only a brief ceremonial performance with the details delegated to subordinates.

For the most part, leading the strategy execution process has to be top-down and driven by mandates to get things done and show good results. Just how to go about the specifics of leading organization efforts to put a strategy in place and deliver the intended results has to start with understanding the requirements for good strategy execution, followed by a diagnosis of the organization's capabilities and preparedness to execute the necessary strategic initiatives, and then decisions as to which of several ways to proceed to get things done and achieve the targeted results.[25] In general, leading the drive for good strategy execution and operating excellence calls for several actions on the part of the manager-in-charge:

1. Staying on top of what is happening, closely monitoring progress, ferreting out issues, and learning what obstacles lie in the path of good execution.
2. Putting constructive pressure on the organization to achieve good results.
3. Keeping the organization focused on operating excellence.
4. Leading the development of stronger core competencies and competitive capabilities.
5. Displaying ethical integrity and leading social responsibility initiatives.
6. Pushing corrective actions to improve strategy execution and achieve the targeted results.

Staying on Top of How Well Things Are Going

To stay on top of how well the strategy execution process is going, a manager needs to develop a broad network of contacts and sources of information, both formal and informal. The regular channels include talking with key subordinates, attending presentations and meetings, reading reviews of the latest operating results, talking to customers, watching the competitive reactions of rival firms, exchanging e-mail and holding telephone conversations with people in outlying locations, making onsite visits, and listening to rank-and-file employees. However, some information is more trustworthy than the rest, and the views and perspectives offered by different people can vary widely. Presentations and briefings by subordinates may not represent the whole truth. Bad news or problems may be minimized or in some cases not reported at all as subordinates delay conveying failures and problems in hopes that they can turn things around in time. Hence, managers have to make sure that they have accurate information and a feel for the existing situation. They have to confirm whether things are on track, identify problems, learn what obstacles lie in the path of good strategy execution and develop a basis for determining what, if anything, they can personally do to move the process along.

> **core concept**
> *Management by walking around (MBWA)* is one of the techniques that effective leaders use to stay informed about how well the strategy execution process is progressing.

One of the best ways for executives in charge of strategy execution to stay on top of things is by making regular visits to the field and talking with many different people at many different levels—a technique often labeled **managing by walking around (MBWA).** Wal-Mart executives have had a long-standing practice of spending two to three days every week visiting Wal-Mart's stores and talking with store managers and employees. Sam Walton, Wal-Mart's founder, insisted, "The key is to get out into the store and listen to what the associates have to say." Jack Welch, the highly effective CEO of General Electric (GE) from 1980 to 2001, not only spent several days each month personally visiting GE operations and talking with major customers but also arranged his schedule so that he could spend time exchanging information and ideas with GE managers from all over the world who were attending classes at the company's leadership development center near GE's headquarters. Some companies have weekly get-togethers in each division (often on Friday afternoons), attended by both executives and employees, to create a regular opportunity for tidbits of information to flow freely between down-the-line employees and executives. Many manufacturing executives make a point of strolling the factory floor to talk with workers and meeting regularly with union officials. Some managers operate out of open cubicles in big spaces populated with open cubicles for other personnel so that they can interact easily and frequently with coworkers. Jeff Bezos, Amazon.com's CEO, is noted for his practice of MBWA, firing off a battery of questions when he tours facilities and insisting that Amazon managers spend time in the trenches with their people to avoid abstract thinking and getting disconnected from the reality of what's happening.[26]

Most managers rightly attach great importance to spending time with people at various company facilities and gathering information and opinions firsthand from diverse sources about how well various aspects of the strategy execution process are going. Such contacts give managers a feel for what progress is being made, what problems are being encountered, and whether additional resources or different approaches may be needed. Just as important, MBWA provides opportunities for managers to talk informally to many different people at different organizational levels, give encouragement, lift spirits, shift attention from the old to the new priorities, and create some excitement—all of which generate positive energy and help mobilize organizational efforts behind strategy execution.

Putting Constructive Pressure on the Organization to Achieve Good Results

Managers have to be out front in mobilizing organizational energy behind the drive for good strategy execution and operating excellence. Part of the leadership requirement here entails nurturing a results-oriented work climate. A culture where there's constructive pressure to achieve good results is a valuable contributor to good strategy execution and operating excellence. Results-oriented cultures are permeated with a spirit of achievement and have a good track record in meeting or beating performance targets. If management wants to drive the strategy execution effort by instilling a results-oriented work climate, then senior executives have to take the lead in promoting certain enabling cultural drivers: a strong sense of involvement on the part of company personnel, emphasis on individual initiative and creativity, respect for the contribution of individuals and groups, and pride in doing things right.

Organizational leaders who succeed in creating a results-oriented work climate typically are intensely people-oriented, and they are skilled users of people-management practices that win the emotional commitment of company personnel and inspire them to do their best.[27] They understand that treating employees well generally leads to increased teamwork, higher morale, greater loyalty, and increased employee commitment to making a contribution. All of these foster an esprit de corps that energizes organizational members to contribute to the drive for operating excellence and proficient strategy execution.

Successfully leading the effort to instill a spirit of high achievement into the culture generally entails such leadership actions and managerial practices as:

- Treating employees with dignity and respect. This often includes a strong company commitment to training each employee thoroughly, providing attractive career opportunities, emphasizing promotion from within, and providing a high degree of job security. Some companies symbolize the value of individual employees and the importance of their contributions by referring to them as cast members (Disney), crew members (McDonald's), coworkers (Kinko's and CDW Computer Centers), job owners (Graniterock), partners (Starbucks), or associates (Wal-Mart, Lenscrafters, W. L. Gore, Edward Jones, Publix Supermarkets, and Marriott International). At a number of companies, managers at every level are held responsible for developing the people who report to them.

- Making champions out of the people who turn in winning performances—but doing so in ways that promote teamwork and cross-unit collaboration as opposed to spurring an unhealthy footrace among employees to best one another.

- Encouraging employees to use initiative and creativity in performing their work.

- Setting stretch objectives and clearly communicating an expectation that company personnel are to give their best in achieving performance targets.

- Granting employees enough autonomy to stand out, excel, and contribute.

- Using the full range of motivational techniques and compensation incentives to inspire company personnel, nurture a results-oriented work climate, and enforce high-performance standards.

- Celebrating individual, group, and company successes. Top management should miss no opportunity to express respect for individual employees and their appreciation of extraordinary individual and group effort.[28] Companies like Mary Kay Cosmetics, Tupperware, and McDonald's actively seek out reasons and opportunities to give pins, buttons, badges, and medals for good showings by average performers—the idea being to express appreciation and give a motivational boost to people who stand out in doing ordinary jobs. General Electric and 3M Corporation make a point of ceremoniously honoring individuals who believe so strongly in their ideas that they take it on themselves to hurdle the bureaucracy, maneuver their projects through the system, and turn them into improved services, new products, or even new businesses.

While leadership efforts to instill a results-oriented culture usually accentuate the positive, there are negative reinforcers too. Managers whose units consistently perform poorly have to be replaced. Low-performing workers and people who reject the results-oriented cultural emphasis have to be weeded out or at least moved to out-of-the-way positions. Average performers have to be candidly counseled that they have limited career potential unless they show more progress in the form of more effort, better skills, and ability to deliver better results.

Keeping the Internal Organization Focused on Operating Excellence

Another leadership dimension of the drive for good strategy execution is keeping the organization bubbling with fresh supplies of ideas and suggestions for improvement. Managers cannot mandate innovative improvements by simply exhorting people to "be creative," nor can they make continuous progress toward operating excellence with directives to "try harder." Rather, they have to foster a culture where innovative ideas and experimentation with new ways of doing things can blossom and thrive. There are several actions that organizational leaders can take to promote new ideas for improving the performance of value chain activities:

- *Encouraging individuals and groups to brainstorm, let their imaginations fly in all directions, and come up with proposals for improving how things are done*—Operating excellence requires that everybody be expected to contribute ideas, exercise initiative, and pursue continuous improvement. The leadership trick is to keep a sense of urgency alive in the business so that people see change and innovation as necessities. One year after taking charge at Siemens-Nixdorf Information Systems, Gerhard Schulmeyer produced the first profit in the merged company, which had been losing hundreds of millions of dollars annually since 1991; he credited the turnaround to the creation of 5,000 "change agents," almost 15 percent of the workforce, who volunteered for active roles in the company's change agenda while continuing to perform their regular jobs.

- *Taking special pains to foster, nourish, and support people who are eager for a chance to try turning their ideas into better ways of operating*—People with maverick ideas or out-of-the-ordinary proposals have to be tolerated and given room to operate. Above all, would-be champions who advocate radical or different ideas must not be looked on as disruptive or troublesome. The best champions and change agents are persistent, competitive, tenacious, committed, and fanatic about seeing their idea through to success.

- *Ensuring that the rewards for successful champions are large and visible and that people who champion an unsuccessful idea are not punished or sidelined but rather encouraged to try again*—Encouraging lots of "tries" is important since many ideas won't pan out.

- *Using all kinds of ad hoc organizational forms to support ideas and experimentation*—Venture teams, task forces, "performance shootouts" among different groups working on competing approaches, and informal "bootleg" projects composed of volunteers are just a few of the possibilities.

- *Using the tools of benchmarking, best practices, business process reengineering, TQM, and Six Sigma quality to focus attention on continuous improvement—* These are proven approaches to getting better operating results and facilitating better strategy execution.

Leading the Development of Better Competencies and Capabilities

A third avenue to better strategy execution and operating excellence is proactively strengthening organizational competencies and competitive capabilities. This often requires top management intervention. Senior management usually has to *lead* the strengthening effort because core competencies and competitive capabilities typically reside in the combined efforts of different work groups, departments, and strategic allies. The tasks of managing human skills, knowledge bases, and intellect and then integrating them to forge competitively advantageous competencies and capabilities is an exercise best orchestrated by senior managers who appreciate their strategy-implementing significance and who have the clout to enforce the necessary networking and cooperation among individuals, groups, departments, and external allies. Stronger competencies and capabilities can not only lead to better performance of value chain activities and pave the way for better bottom-line results. Also, in today's globalizing economy, strategy leaders are well positioned to spot opportunities to leverage existing competencies and competitive capabilities across geographical borders.

Aside from leading efforts to strengthen *existing* competencies and capabilities, effective strategy leaders try to anticipate changes in customer-market requirements and proactively build *new* competencies and capabilities that offer a competitive edge over rivals. Senior managers are in the best position to see the need and potential of new capabilities and then to play a lead role in the capability-building, resource-strengthening process. Proactively building new competencies and capabilities ahead of rivals to gain a competitive edge is strategic leadership of the best kind, but strengthening the company's resource base in reaction to newly developed capabilities of pioneering rivals occurs more frequently.

Displaying Ethical Integrity and Leading Social Responsibility Initiatives

For an organization to avoid the pitfalls of scandal and disgrace and consistently display the intent to conduct its business in a principled manner, the CEO and those around the CEO must be openly and unswervingly committed to ethical conduct and socially redeeming business principles and core values. Leading the effort to operate the company's business in an ethically principled fashion has three pieces. First and foremost, the CEO and other senior executives must set an excellent example in their own ethical behavior, demonstrating character and personal integrity in their actions and decisions. The behavior of senior executives is always watched carefully, sending a clear message to company personnel regarding what the "real" standards of personal conduct are. Moreover, the company's strategy and operating decisions have to be seen as ethical—actions speak louder than words here. Second, top management must declare unequivocal support of the company's ethical code and take an uncompromising stand on expecting all company personnel to conduct themselves in an ethical fashion

illustration capsule 13.3

Lockheed Martin's Corrective Actions after Violating U.S. Antibribery Laws

Lockheed Martin Corporation is among the world's leading producers of aeronautics and space systems, with 2002 sales of $26 billion. The company designed and built the P-38 fighter, B-29 bomber, U-2 and SR-71 reconnaissance aircraft, C-130 cargo planes, F-104 Starfighter, F-16 Fighting Falcon, F-22 Raptor, and Titan and Trident missiles. It has been a major contractor on the Mercury, Gemini, Apollo, Skylab, and shuttle space programs.

Lockheed Martin's status as a U.S. government contractor was jeopardized in 1995 when company officials admitted that the company had conspired to violate U.S. antibribery laws. The infraction occurred in 1990 when Lockheed Martin paid an Egyptian lawmaker $1 million to help the company secure a contract to supply Egypt with C-130 cargo planes. The U.S. government fined Lockheed Martin $24.8 million and placed it on three-year probation during which further ethics violations could bar the company from bidding on government contracts.

After the conviction, Lockheed Martin's CEO and other senior executives put a comprehensive ethics compliance program in place to guard against subsequent violations. Completion of an online ethics training course was made mandatory for all employees; the course covered Lockheed Martin's code of ethics and business conduct. The online software system records when employees complete online sessions on such topics as sexual harassment, security, software-license compliance, labor charging, insider trading, and gratuities. It also gives the company the capability to conduct up-to-the-minute ethics audits to determine how many hours of training have been completed by each of Lockheed Martin's 170,000 employees.

Lockheed Martin's ethics software programs provide company managers with a variety of statistics related to ethics violations that do occur at the company—like the number of detected violations of misuse of company resources, conflicts of interest, and security breaches. In addition, the system gives an accounting of the number of Lockheed Martin employees discharged, suspended, and reprimanded for ethics violations. Lockheed Martin managers and the U.S. government use the database to assess the state of business ethics at the company.

Lockheed Martin's renewed commitment to honesty, integrity, respect, trust, responsibility, and citizenship—along with its method for monitoring ethics compliance—paved the way for the company to receive the 1998 American Business Ethics Award. Upon receiving the award, the company's chairman and CEO, Vance Coffman, said, "At Lockheed Martin, we have stressed that the first and most important unifying principle guiding us is ethical conduct, every day and everywhere we do business. Receiving the American Business Ethics Award is a strong signal that we are achieving our goal of putting our Corporation on a firm ethical foundation for the challenges of the 21st century."

Source: The Wall Street Journal, Eastern Edition [Staff Produced Copy Only] by Staff. Copyright 1999 by Dow Jones & Company, Inc. Reproduced with permission of Dow Jones & Company, Inc. in the format textbook via the Copyright Clearance Center.

at all times. This means iterating and reiterating to employees that it is their duty to observe the company's ethical codes. Third, top management must be prepared to act as the final arbiter on hard calls; this means removing people from key positions or terminating them when they are guilty of a violation. It also means reprimanding those who have been lax in monitoring and enforcing ethical compliance. Failure to act swiftly and decisively in punishing ethical misconduct is interpreted as a lack of real commitment.

See Illustration Capsule 13.3 for a discussion of the actions Lockheed Martin's top executives took when the company faced a bribery scandal.

Demonstrating Genuine Commitment to a Strategy of Social Responsibility   As was discussed in Chapter 10, business leaders who want their companies to be regarded as exemplary corporate citizens must not only see that their companies operate ethically but also take a lead role in crafting a social responsibility strategy that positively improves the well-being of employees, the environment, the communities in which they operate, and society at large. The CEO and other senior executives must insist that the company go past the rhetoric and cosmetics of corporate citizenship and employ a genuine strategy of social responsibility. *What separates companies that make a sincere effort to carry their weight in being good corporate citizens from companies that are content to do only what is legally required of them are company leaders who believe strongly that just making a profit is not good enough. Such leaders are committed to a higher standard of performance that includes social and environmental metrics as well as financial and strategic metrics.*

> Companies with socially conscious strategy leaders and a core value of corporate social responsibility move beyond the rhetorical flourishes of corporate citizenship and enlist the full support of company personnel behind social responsibility initiatives.

One of the leadership responsibilities of the CEO and other senior managers, therefore, is to *step out front,* wave the flag of socially responsible behavior for all to see, marshal the support of company personnel, and integrate social responsibility initiatives into an everyday part of how the company conducts its business affairs. Strategy leaders have to insist on the use of social and environmental metrics in evaluating performance and, ideally, the company's board of directors will elect to tie the company's social and environmental performance to executive compensation—a surefire way to make sure that social responsibility efforts are more than window dressing. To help ensure that it has commitment from senior managers, Verizon Communications ties 10 percent of the annual bonus of the company's top 2,500 managers directly to the achievement of social responsibility targets. One survey found over 60 percent of senior managers believed that a portion of executive compensation should be linked to a company's performance on social and environmental measures. The strength of the commitment from the top—typically a company's CEO and board of directors—ultimately determines whether a company will pursue a genuine, full-fledged strategy of social responsibility that embraces some customized combination of actions to protect the environment (beyond what is required by law), actively participate in community affairs, be a generous supporter of charitable causes and projects that benefit society, and have a positive impact on workforce diversity and the overall well-being of employees.

Leading the Process of Making Corrective Adjustments

The leadership challenge of making corrective adjustments is twofold: deciding when adjustments are needed and deciding what adjustments to make. Both decisions are a normal and necessary part of managing the strategy execution process, since no scheme for implementing and executing strategy can foresee all the events and problems that will arise. There comes a time at every company when managers have to fine-tune or overhaul the approaches to strategy execution and push for better results. Clearly, when a company's strategy execution effort is not delivering good results and making measurable progress toward operating excellence, it is the leader's responsibility to step forward and push corrective actions.

The *process* of making corrective adjustments varies according to the situation. In a crisis, it is typical for leaders to have key subordinates gather information, identify and evaluate options (crunching whatever numbers may be appropriate), and perhaps prepare a preliminary set of recommended actions for consideration. The organizational leader then usually meets with key subordinates and personally presides over extended discussions of the proposed responses, trying to build a quick consensus among members of the executive inner circle. If no consensus emerges and action is required immediately, the burden falls on the manager in charge to choose the response and urge its support.

When the situation allows managers to proceed more deliberately in deciding when to make changes and what changes to make, most managers seem to prefer a process of incrementally solidifying commitment to a particular course of action.[29] The process that managers go through in deciding on corrective adjustments is essentially the same for both proactive and reactive changes: They sense needs, gather information, broaden and deepen their understanding of the situation, develop options and explore their pros and cons, put forth action proposals, generate partial (comfort-level) solutions, strive for a consensus, and finally formally adopt an agreed-on course of action.[30] The time frame for deciding what corrective changes to initiate can take a few hours, a few days, a few weeks, or even a few months if the situation is particularly complicated.

Success in initiating corrective actions usually hinges on thorough analysis of the situation, the exercise of good business judgment in deciding what actions to take, and good implementation of the corrective actions that are initiated. Successful managers are skilled in getting an organization back on track rather quickly; they (and their staffs) are good at discerning what actions to take and in ramrodding them through to a successful conclusion. Managers that struggle to show measurable progress in generating good results and improving the performance of strategy-critical value chain activities are candidates for being replaced.

The challenges of leading a successful strategy execution effort are, without question, substantial.[31] But the job is definitely doable. Because each instance of executing strategy occurs under different organizational circumstances, the managerial agenda for executing strategy always needs to be situation-specific—there's no neat generic procedure to follow. And, as we said at the beginning of Chapter 11, executing strategy is an action-oriented, make-the-right-things-happen task that challenges a manager's ability to lead and direct organizational change, create or reinvent business processes, manage and motivate people, and achieve performance targets. If you now better understand what the challenges are, what approaches are available, which issues need to be considered, and why the action agenda for implementing and executing strategy sweeps across so many aspects of administrative and managerial work, then we will look on our discussion in Chapters 11–13 as a success.

A Final Word on Managing the Process of Crafting and Executing Strategy   In practice, it is hard to separate the leadership requirements of executing strategy from the other pieces of the strategy process. As we emphasized in Chapter 2, the job of crafting, implementing, and executing strategy is a five-task process with much looping and recycling to fine-tune and adjust strategic visions, objectives, strategies, capabilities, implementation approaches, and cultures to fit one another and to fit changing circumstances. The process is continuous, and the conceptually separate acts of crafting and executing strategy blur together in real-world situations. The best tests of good strategic leadership are whether the company has a good strategy and whether the strategy execution effort is delivering the hoped-for results. If these two conditions exist, the chances are excellent that the company has good strategic leadership.

key|points

A company's culture is manifested in the values and business principles that management preaches and practices, in the tone and philosophy of official policies and procedures, in its revered traditions and oft-repeated stories, in the attitudes and behaviors of employees, in the peer pressures that exist to display core values, in the organization's politics, in its approaches to people management and problem solving, in its relationships with external stakeholders (particularly vendors and the communities in which it operates), and in the atmosphere that permeates its work environment. Culture thus concerns the personality a company has and the style in which it does things.

Very often, the elements of company culture originate with a founder or other early influential leaders who articulate the values, beliefs, and principles to which the company should adhere. These elements then get incorporated into company policies, a creed or values statement, strategies, and operating practices. Over time, these values and practices become shared by company employees and managers. Cultures are perpetuated as new leaders act to reinforce them, as new employees are encouraged to adopt and follow them, as stories of people and events illustrating core values and practices are told and retold, and as organization members are honored and rewarded for displaying cultural norms.

Company cultures vary widely in strength and in makeup. Some cultures are strongly embedded, while others are weak or fragmented. Some cultures are unhealthy, often dominated by self-serving politics, resistance to change, and inward focus. Unhealthy cultural traits are often precursors to declining company performance. In adaptive cultures, the work climate is receptive to new ideas, experimentation, innovation, new strategies, and new operating practices provided the new behaviors and operating practices that management is calling for are seen as legitimate and consistent with the core values and business principles underpinning the culture. An adaptive culture is a terrific managerial ally, especially in fast-changing business environments, because company personnel are receptive to risk taking, experimentation, innovation, and changing strategies and practices—there's a feeling of confidence that the organization can deal with whatever threats and opportunities come down the pike. In direct contrast to change-resistant cultures, adaptive cultures are very supportive of managers and employees at all ranks who propose or help initiate useful change; indeed, there's a proactive approach to identifying issues, evaluating the implications and options, and implementing workable solutions.

A culture grounded in values, practices, and behavioral norms that match what is needed for good strategy execution helps energize people throughout the company to do their jobs in a strategy-supportive manner, adding significantly to the power of a company's strategy execution effort and the chances of achieving the targeted results. But when the culture is in conflict with some aspect of the company's direction, performance targets, or strategy, the culture becomes a stumbling block. Thus, an important part of managing the strategy execution process is establishing and nurturing a good fit between culture and strategy.

Changing a company's culture, especially a strong one with traits that don't fit a new strategy's requirements, is one of the toughest management challenges. Changing a culture requires competent leadership at the top. It requires symbolic actions and substantive actions that unmistakably indicate serious commitment on the part of top management. The more that culture-driven actions and behaviors fit what's needed for good strategy execution, the less managers have to depend on policies, rules, procedures, and supervision to enforce what people should and should not do.

Healthy corporate cultures are grounded in ethical business principles, socially approved values, and socially responsible decision making. One has to be cautious in jumping to the conclusion that a company's stated values and ethical principles are mere window dressing. While some companies display low ethical standards, many companies are truly committed to the stated core values and to high ethical standards, and they make ethical behavior *a fundamental component of their corporate culture.* If management practices what it preaches, a company's core values and ethical standards nurture the corporate culture in three highly positive ways: (1) they communicate the company's good intentions and validate the integrity and aboveboard character of its business principles and operating methods, (2) they steer company personnel toward both doing the right thing and doing things right, and (3) they establish a corporate conscience that gauges the appropriateness of particular actions, decisions, and policies. Companies that really care about how they conduct their business put a stake in the ground, making it unequivocally clear that company personnel are expected to live up to the company's values and ethical standards—how well individuals display core values and adhere to ethical standards is often part of their job performance evaluations. Peer pressures to conform to cultural norms are quite strong, acting as an important deterrent to outside-the-lines behavior.

To be effective, corporate ethics and values programs have to become a way of life through training, strict compliance and enforcement procedures, and reiterated management endorsements. Moreover, top managers must practice what they preach, serving as role models for ethical behavior, values-driven decision making, and a social conscience.

Successful managers have to do several things in leading the drive for good strategy execution and operating excellence. First, they stay on top of things. They keep a finger on the organization's pulse by spending considerable time outside their offices, listening and talking to organization members, coaching, cheerleading, and picking up important information. Second, they are active and visible in putting constructive pressure on the organization to achieve good results. Generally, this is best accomplished by promoting an esprit de corps that mobilizes and energizes organizational members to execute strategy in a competent fashion and deliver the targeted results. Third, they keep the organization focused on operating excellence by championing innovative ideas for improvement and promoting the use of best practices and benchmarking to measure the progress being made in performing value chain activities in first-rate fashion. Fourth, they exert their clout in developing competencies and competitive capabilities that enable better execution. Fifth, they serve as a role model in displaying high ethical standards, and they insist that company personnel conduct the company's business ethically and in a socially responsible manner. They demonstrate unequivocal and visible commitment to the ethics enforcement process. Sixth and finally, when a company's strategy execution effort is not delivering good results and the organization is not making measurable progress toward operating excellence, it is the leader's responsibility to step forward and push corrective actions.

| exercises

1. Go to www.hermanmiller.com and read what the company has to say about its corporate culture in the careers sections of the Web site. Do you think this statement is just nice window dressing, or, based on what else you can learn about the Herman Miller Company from browsing this Web site, is there reason to believe that management has truly built a culture that makes the stated values and principles come alive? Explain.

2. Go to the careers section at www.qualcomm.com and see what Qualcomm, one of the most prominent companies in mobile communications technology, has to say about "life at Qualcomm." Is what's on this Web site just recruiting propaganda, or does it convey the type of work climate that management is actually trying to create? If you were a senior executive at Qualcomm, would you see merit in building and nurturing a culture like what is described in the section on "life at Qualcomm"? Would such a culture represent a tight fit with Qualcomm's high-tech business and strategy? (You can get an overview of the Qualcomm's strategy by exploring the section for investors and some of the recent press releases.) Is your answer consistent with what is presented in the "Awards and Honors" menu selection in the "About Qualcomm" portion of the Web site?

3. Go to www.jnj.com, the Web site of Johnson & Johnson and read the "J&J Credo," which sets forth the company's responsibilities to customers, employees, the community, and shareholders. Then read the "Our Company" section. Why do you think the credo has resulted in numerous awards and accolades that recognize the company as a good corporate citizen?

part two 2

Cases in Crafting and Executing Strategy

Starbucks in 2004: Driving for Global Dominance

Arthur A. Thompson
The University of Alabama

Thomas F. Hawk
Frostburg State University

Amit J. Shah
Frostburg State University

In early 2004 Howard Schultz, Starbucks' founder and chairman of the board, could look with satisfaction on the company's phenomenal growth and market success. Since 1987, Starbucks had transformed itself from a modest nine-store operation in the Pacific Northwest into a powerhouse multinational enterprise with 7,225 store locations, including some 1,600 stores in 30 foreign countries (see Exhibit 1). During Starbucks' early years, when coffee was a 50-cent morning habit at local diners and fast-food establishments, skeptics had ridiculed the notion of $3 coffee as a yuppie fad. But the popularity of Starbucks' Italian-style coffees, espresso beverages, teas, pastries, and confections had made Starbucks one of the great retailing stories of recent history and the world's biggest specialty coffee chain. In 2003, Starbucks made the Fortune 500, prompting Schultz to remark, "It would be arrogant to sit here and say that 10 years ago we thought we would be on the Fortune 500. But we dreamed from day one and we dreamed big."[1]

Having not only positioned Starbucks as the dominant retailer, roaster, and brand of specialty coffees and coffee drinks in North America but also spawned the creation of the specialty coffee industry, the company's strategic intent was to establish Starbucks as the most recognized and respected brand in

the world. Management expected to have 15,000 Starbucks stores by year-end 2005 and 25,000 locations by 2013. In 2003, new stores were being opened at the rate of three a day. Starbucks reported revenues in 2003 of $4.1 billion, up 128 percent from $1.8 billion in fiscal 2000 ending September 30; after-tax profits in 2003 were $268.3 million, an increase of 184 percent from net earnings of $94.6 million in 2000.

COMPANY BACKGROUND

Starbucks got its start in 1971 when three academics, English teacher Jerry Baldwin, history teacher Zev Siegel, and writer Gordon Bowker—all coffee aficionados—opened Starbucks Coffee, Tea, and Spice in Seattle's touristy Pikes Place Market. The three partners shared a love for fine coffees and exotic teas and believed they could build a clientele in Seattle that would appreciate the best coffees and teas, much like the customer group that had already emerged in the San Francisco Bay area. Baldwin, Siegel, and Bowker each invested $1,350 and borrowed another $5,000 from a bank to open the Pikes Place store. The inspiration and mentor for the Starbucks venture in Seattle was a Dutch immigrant named Alfred Peet, who had opened Peet's Coffee and Tea, in Berkeley, California, in 1966. Peet's store specialized in importing fine coffees and teas and dark-roasting its own beans the European way to bring out the full

[1]As quoted in Cora Daniels, "Mr. Coffee," *Fortune,* April 14, 2003, p. 139.

exhibit 1 **Number of Starbucks Store Locations, 1987–2003**

Year	Number of Store Locations	Year	Number of Store Locations
1987	17	1996	1,015
1988	33	1997	1,412
1989	55	1998	1,886
1990	84	1999	2,135
1991	116	2000	3,501
1992	165	2001	4,709
1993	272	2002	5,886
1994	425	2003	7,225
1995	676		

Licensed Locations of Starbucks Stores Outside the Continental United States, 2003

Asia-Pacific		Europe–Middle East–Africa		Americas	
Japan	486	Saudi Arabia	29	Canada	53
China	116	United Arab Emirates	27	Hawaii	38
Taiwan	113	Germany	25	Mexico	17
South Korea	75	Kuwait	20	Puerto Rico	3
Philippines	54	Spain	15	Chile	3
Malaysia	37	Switzerland	15	Peru	1
New Zealand	35	Greece	12		
Singapore	35	Lebanon	9		
Indonesia	17	Austria	8		
		Qatar	5		
		Bahrain	4		
		Turkey	4		
		Oman	3		
Total	968		176		113

Source: Company records and reports.

flavors. Customers were encouraged to learn how to grind the beans and make their own freshly brewed coffee at home. Baldwin, Siegel, and Bowker were well acquainted with Peet's expertise, having visited his store on numerous occasions and listened to him expound on quality coffees and the importance of proper bean-roasting techniques.

The Pikes Place store featured modest, hand-built classic nautical fixtures. One wall was devoted to whole-bean coffees, while another had shelves of coffee products. The store did not offer fresh-brewed coffee sold by the cup, but tasting samples were sometimes available. Initially, Siegel was the only paid employee. He wore a grocer's apron, scooped out beans for customers, extolled the virtues of fine, dark-roasted coffees, and functioned as the partnership's retail expert. The other two partners kept their day jobs but came by at lunch or after work to help out. During the start-up period, Baldwin kept the books and developed a growing knowledge of coffee; Bowker served as the "magic, mystery, and romance man."[2] The store was an immediate success, with sales exceeding expectations, partly because of interest stirred by a favorable article in the *Seattle Times*. For most of the first year, Starbucks ordered

[2]Howard Schultz and Dori Jones Yang, *Pour Your Heart Into It* (New York: Hyperion, 1997), p. 33.

its coffee beans from Peet's, but then the partners purchased a used roaster from Holland, set up roasting operations in a nearby ramshackle building, and came up with their own blends and flavors.

By the early 1980s, the company had four Starbucks stores in the Seattle area and had been profitable every year since opening its doors. But then Zev Siegel experienced burnout and left the company to pursue other interests. Jerry Baldwin took over day-to-day management of the company and functioned as chief executive officer; Gordon Bowker remained involved as an owner but devoted most of his time to his advertising and design firm, a weekly newspaper he had founded, and a microbrewery that he was launching known as the Redhook Ale Brewery.

Howard Schultz Enters the Picture

In 1981, Howard Schultz, vice president and general manager of U.S. operations for a Swedish maker of stylish kitchen equipment and coffeemakers, decided to pay Starbucks a visit—he was curious about why Starbucks was selling so many of his company's products. The morning after his arrival in Seattle, he was escorted to the Pikes Place store by Linda Grossman, the retail merchandising manager for Starbucks. A solo violinist was playing Mozart at the door, his violin case open for donations. Schultz was immediately taken by the powerful and pleasing aroma of the coffees, the wall displaying coffee beans, and the rows of coffeemakers on the shelves. As he talked with the clerk behind the counter, the clerk scooped out some Sumatran coffee beans, ground them, put the grounds in a cone filter, poured hot water over the cone, and shortly handed Schultz a porcelain mug filled with freshly brewed coffee. After taking only three sips of the brew, Schultz was hooked. He began asking the clerk and Grossman questions about the company, about coffees from different parts of the world, and about the different ways of roasting coffee.

A bit later, he was introduced to Jerry Baldwin and Gordon Bowker, whose offices overlooked the company's coffee-roasting operation. Schultz was struck by their knowledge about coffee, their commitment to providing customers with quality coffees, and their passion for educating customers about the merits of dark-roasted coffees. Baldwin told Schultz, "We don't manage the business to maximize anything other than the quality of the coffee."[3] The company purchased only the finest arabica coffees and put them through a meticulous dark-roasting process to bring out their full flavors. Baldwin explained that the cheap robusta coffees used in supermarket blends burned when subjected to dark roasting. He also noted that the makers of supermarket blends preferred lighter roasts because it allowed higher yields (the longer a coffee was roasted, the more weight it lost).

Schultz was also struck by the business philosophy of the two partners. It was clear that Starbucks stood not just for good coffee but also for the dark-roasted flavor profiles that the founders were passionate about. Top quality, fresh-roasted, whole-bean coffee was the company's differentiating feature and a bedrock value. It was also clear to Schultz that Starbucks was strongly committed to educating its customers to appreciate the qualities of fine coffees. The company depended mainly on word of mouth to get more people into its stores, then built customer loyalty cup by cup as buyers gained a sense of discovery and excitement about the taste of fine coffee.

On his trip back to New York the next day, Howard Schultz could not stop thinking about Starbucks and what it would be like to be a part of the Starbucks enterprise. Schultz recalled, "There was something magic about it, a passion and authenticity I had never experienced in business."[4] The appeal of living in the Seattle area was another strong plus. By the time he landed at Kennedy Airport, he knew in his heart he wanted to go to work for Starbucks. At the first opportunity, Schultz asked Baldwin whether there was any way he could fit into Starbucks. Although the two had established an easy, comfortable personal rapport, it still took a year, numerous meetings at which Schultz presented his ideas, and a lot of convincing to get Baldwin, Bowker, and their silent partner from San Francisco to agree to hire him. Schultz pursued a job at Starbucks far more vigorously than Starbucks pursued hiring Schultz. There was some nervousness about bringing in an outsider, especially a high-powered New Yorker who had not grown up with the values of the company.

[3]Ibid., p. 34.
[4]Ibid., p. 36.

Nonetheless, Schultz continued to press his ideas about the tremendous potential of expanding the Starbucks enterprise outside Seattle and exposing people all over America to Starbucks coffee. Schultz argued that there had to be more than just the few thousand coffee lovers in Seattle who would enjoy the company's products.

At a meeting with the three owners in San Francisco in Spring 1982, Schultz once again presented his ideas and vision for opening Starbucks stores across the United States and Canada. He thought the meeting went well and flew back to New York thinking a job offer was in the bag. However, the next day Jerry Baldwin called Schultz and indicated that the owners had decided against hiring him because geographic expansion was too risky and they did not share Schultz's vision for Starbucks. Schultz was despondent, seeing his dreams of being a part of Starbucks' future go up in smoke. Still, he believed so deeply in Starbucks' potential that he decided to make a last ditch appeal; he called Baldwin back the next day and made an impassioned, reasoned case for why the decision was a mistake. Baldwin agreed to reconsider. The next morning Baldwin called Schultz and told him the job of heading marketing and overseeing the retail stores was his. In September 1982, Schultz took over his new responsibilities at Starbucks.

Starbucks and Howard Schultz: The 1982–1985 Period

In his first few months at Starbucks, Howard Schultz spent most of his waking hours in the four Seattle stores—working behind the counters, tasting different kinds of coffee, talking with customers, getting to know store personnel, and learning the retail aspects of the coffee business. By December, Jerry Baldwin concluded that Schultz was ready for the final part of his training, that of actually roasting the coffee. Schultz spent a week getting an education about the colors of different coffee beans, listening for the telltale second pop of the beans during the roasting process, learning to taste the subtle differences among Jerry Baldwin and Gordon Bowker's various roasts, and familiarizing himself with the roasting techniques for different beans.

Schultz made a point of acclimating himself to the informal dress code at Starbucks, gaining credi-

bility and building trust with colleagues, and making the transition from the high-energy, coat-and-tie style of New York to the more casual, low-key ambience of the Pacific Northwest (see Exhibit 2 for a rundown on Howard Schultz's background). Schultz made real headway in gaining the acceptance and respect of company personnel while working at the Pike Place store one day during the busy Christmas season that first year. The store was packed and Schultz was behind the counter ringing up sales of coffee when someone shouted that a shopper had just headed out the door with some stuff—two expensive coffeemakers it turned out, one in each hand. Without thinking, Schultz leaped over the counter and chased the thief up the cobblestone street outside the store, yelling, "Drop that stuff! Drop it!" The thief was startled enough to drop both pieces he had carried off and ran away. Howard picked up the merchandise and returned to the store, holding the coffeemakers up like trophies. Everyone applauded. When Schultz returned to his office later that afternoon, his staff had strung up a banner that read: "Make my day."[5]

Schultz was overflowing with ideas for the company. Early on, he noticed that first-time customers sometimes felt uneasy in the stores because of their lack of knowledge about fine coffees and because store employees sometimes came across as a little arrogant or superior to coffee novices. Schultz worked with store employees on customer-friendly sales skills and developed brochures that made it easy for customers to learn about fine coffees. However, Schultz's biggest inspiration and vision for Starbucks' future came during the spring of 1983 when the company sent him to Milan, Italy, to attend an international housewares show. While walking from his hotel to the convention center, Schultz spotted an espresso bar and went inside to look around. The cashier beside the door nodded and smiled. The barista behind the counter greeted Howard cheerfully and moved gracefully to pull a shot of espresso for one customer and handcraft a foamy cappuccino for another, all the while conversing merrily with those standing at the counter. Schultz thought the barista's performance was "great theater." Just down the way on a side street, he went in an even more crowded espresso bar where the barista, whom he surmised to

---

[5] As told in ibid., p. 48.

exhibit 2   **Biographical Sketch of Howard Schultz**

- Schultz's parents both came from working-class families residing in Brooklyn, New York, for two generations. Neither completed high school.
- Schultz grew up in a government-subsidized housing project in Brooklyn, was the oldest of three children, played sports with the neighborhood kids, developed a passion for baseball, and became a die-hard Yankees fan.
- Schultz's father was a blue-collar factory worker and taxicab driver who held many low-wage, no benefits jobs; his mother remained home to take care of the children during their preschool years, then worked as an office receptionist. The family was hard pressed to make ends meet.
- Schultz had a number of jobs as a teenager—paper route, counter job at luncheonette, an after-school job in the garment district in Manhattan, a summer job steaming yarn at a knit factory. He always gave part of his earnings to his mother to help with family expenses.
- He saw success in sports as his way to escape life in the projects; he played quarterback on the high school football team.
- He was offered a scholarship to play football at Northern Michigan University (the only offer he got) and took it. When his parents drove him to the campus to begin the fall term, it was his first trip outside New York. It turned out that he didn't have enough talent to play football, but he got loans and worked at several jobs to keep himself in school. He majored in communications, took a few business courses on the side, and graduated in 1975 with a B average—the first person in his family to graduate from college.
- He went to work for a ski lodge in Michigan after graduation, then left to go back to New York, landing a sales job at Xerox Corporation. He left Xerox to work for Swedish coffee-equipment maker Hammarplast, U.S.A., becoming vice president and general manager in charge of U.S. operations and managing 20 independent sales representatives.
- He married Sheri Kersch in July 1982; the couple had two children.
- His father contracted lung cancer in 1982 at age 60 and died in 1988, leaving his mother with no pension, no life insurance, and no savings.
- Schultz became a principal owner of Seattle SuperSonics NBA team in 2001; also a principal owner of Seattle Storm of WNBA.
- He owned about 16 million shares of Starbucks in early 2003 and had an estimated net worth of $700 million.

Source: Howard Schultz and Dori Jones Yang, *Pour Your Heart Into It* (New York: Hyperion, 1997).

be the owner, was greeting customers by name; people were laughing and talking in an atmosphere that plainly was comfortable and familiar. In the next few blocks, he saw two more espresso bars. That afternoon when the trade show concluded for the day, Schultz walked the streets of Milan to explore more espresso bars. Some were stylish and upscale; others attracted a blue-collar clientele. Most had few chairs, and it was common for Italian opera to be playing in the background. What struck Schultz was how popular and vibrant the Italian coffee bars were. Energy levels were typically high, and they seemed to function as an integral community gathering place. Each one had its own unique character, but they all had a barista who performed with flair and maintained a camaraderie with the customers.

Schultz remained in Milan for a week, exploring coffee bars and learning as much as he could about the Italian passion for coffee drinks. Schultz was particularly struck by the fact that there were 1,500 coffee bars in Milan, a city about the size of Philadelphia, and a total of 200,000 in all of Italy. In one bar, he heard a customer order a caffe latte and decided to try one himself—the barista made a shot of espresso, steamed a frothy pitcher of milk, poured the two together in a cup, and put a dollop of foam on the top. Schultz liked it immediately, concluding that lattes should be a feature item on any coffee bar menu even though none of the coffee experts he had talked to had ever mentioned them.

Schultz's 1983 trip to Milan produced a revelation: the Starbucks stores in Seattle completely missed the point. There was much more to the coffee business than just selling beans and getting people to appreciate grinding their own beans and brewing fine coffee in their homes. What Starbucks needed to do was serve fresh brewed coffee, espresso, and cappuccino in its stores (in addition to beans and coffee equipment) and try to create an American version of the Italian coffee bar culture. Going to Starbucks should be an experience, a special treat, a place to meet friends and visit. Re-creating the authentic Italian coffee bar culture in the United States could be Starbucks' differentiating factor.

Schultz Becomes Frustrated

On his return from Italy, Howard Schultz shared his revelation and ideas for modifying the format of Starbucks' stores with Jerry Baldwin and Gordon Bowker. But instead of winning their approval for trying out some of his ideas, Schultz encountered strong resistance. Baldwin and Bowker argued that Starbucks was a retailer, not a restaurant or coffee bar. They feared that serving drinks would put them in the beverage business and diminish the integrity of Starbucks' mission as a purveyor of fine coffees. They pointed out that Starbucks had been profitable every year and there was no reason to rock the boat in a small, private company like Starbucks. But a more pressing reason not to pursue Schultz's coffee bar concept emerged shortly—Baldwin and Bowker were excited by an opportunity to purchase Peet's Coffee and Tea. The acquisition was finalized in early 1984; to fund it, Starbucks had to take on considerable debt, leaving little in the way of financial flexibility to support Schultz's ideas for entering the beverage part of the coffee business or expanding the number of Starbucks stores.

For most of 1984, Starbucks managers were dividing their time between operations in Seattle and the Peet's enterprise in San Francisco. Schultz found himself in San Francisco every other week supervising the marketing and operations of the five Peet's stores. Starbucks employees began to feel neglected and, in one quarter, did not receive their usual bonus due to tight financial conditions. Employee discontent escalated to the point where a union election was called. The union won by three votes. Jerry Baldwin was shocked at the results, concluding that employees no longer trusted him. In the months that followed, he began to spend more of his energy on Peet's operation in San Francisco.

It took Howard Schultz nearly a year to convince Jerry Baldwin to let him test an espresso bar. Baldwin relented when Starbucks opened its sixth store in April 1984. It was the first of the company's stores designed to sell beverages, and it was the first one located in downtown Seattle. Schultz asked for a 1,500-square-foot space to set up a full-scale Italian-style espresso bar, but Baldwin agreed to allocating only 300 square feet in a corner of the new store. The store opened with no fanfare as a deliberate experiment. By closing time on the first day, some 400 customers had been served, well above the 250-customer average of Starbucks' best-performing stores. Within two months the store was serving 800 customers a day. The two baristas could not keep up with orders during the early-morning hours, resulting in lines outside the door onto the sidewalk. Most of the business was at the espresso counter, while sales at the regular retail counter were only adequate.

Schultz was elated at the test results, expecting that Baldwin's doubts about entering the beverage side of the business would be dispelled and that he would gain approval to pursue the opportunity to take Starbucks to a new level. Every day he went into Baldwin's office to show him the sales figures and customer counts at the new downtown store. But Baldwin was not comfortable with the success of the new store, believing that it felt wrong and that espresso drinks were a distraction from the core business of marketing fine arabica coffees at retail. Baldwin rebelled at the thought that people would see Starbucks as a place to get a quick cup of coffee to go. He adamantly told Schultz, "We're coffee roasters. I don't want to be in the restaurant business . . . besides, we're too deeply in debt to consider pursuing this idea."[6] While he didn't deny that the experiment was succeeding, he didn't want to go forward with introducing beverages in other Starbucks stores. Schultz's efforts to persuade Baldwin to change his mind continued to meet strong resistance, although to avoid a total impasse Baldwin finally did agree to let Schultz put espresso machines in the back of possibly one or two other Starbucks stores.

Over the next several months, Schultz made up his mind to leave Starbucks and start his own company. His plan was to open espresso bars in high-traffic downtown locations, serve espresso drinks and coffee by the cup, and try to emulate the friendly, energetic atmosphere he had encountered in Italian espresso bars. Jerry Baldwin and Gordon Bowker, knowing how frustrated Schultz had become, supported his efforts to go out on his own and agreed to let him stay in his current job and office until definitive plans were in place. Schultz left Starbucks in late 1985.

[6]Ibid., pp. 61–62.

Schultz's Il Giornale Venture

With the aid of a lawyer friend who helped companies raise venture capital and go public, Howard Schultz began seeking out investors for the kind of company he had in mind. Ironically, Jerry Baldwin committed to investing $150,000 of Starbucks' money in Schultz's coffee bar enterprise, thus becoming Schultz's first investor. Baldwin accepted Schultz's invitation to be a director of the new company and Gordon Bowker agreed to be a part-time consultant for six months. Bowker, pumped up about the new venture, urged Howard to take pains to make sure that everything about the new stores—the name, the presentation, the care taken in preparing the coffee—be calculated to lead customers to expect something better than competitors offered. Bowker proposed that the new company be named Il Giornale Coffee Company (pronounced *il jor NAHL ee*), a suggestion that Schultz accepted. In December 1985, Bowker and Schultz made a trip to Italy, where they visited some 500 espresso bars in Milan and Verona, observing local habits, taking notes about decor and menus, snapping photographs, and videotaping baristas in action.

About $400,000 in seed capital was raised by the end of January 1986, enough to rent an office, hire a couple of key employees, develop a store design, and open the first store. But it took until the end of 1986 to raise the remaining $1.25 million needed to launch at least eight espresso bars and prove that Schultz's strategy and business model were viable. Schultz made presentations to 242 potential investors, 217 of whom said no. Many who heard Schultz's hour-long presentation saw coffee as a commodity business and thought that Schultz's espresso bar concept lacked any basis for sustainable competitive advantage (no patent on dark roast, no advantage in purchasing coffee beans, no ways to prevent the entry of imitative competitors). Some noted that coffee couldn't be turned into a growth business—consumption of coffee had been declining since the mid-1960s. Others were skeptical that people would pay $1.50 or more for a cup of coffee, and the company's unpronounceable name turned some off. Being rejected by so many of the potential investors he approached was disheartening for Schultz (some who listened to his presentation didn't even bother to call him back; others refused to take his calls). Nonetheless, Schultz maintained an upbeat at-titude and displayed passion and enthusiasm in making his pitch. He ended up raising $1.65 million from about 30 investors, most of which came from nine people, five of whom became directors.

The first Il Giornale store opened in April 1986. It had 700 square feet and was located near the entrance of Seattle's tallest building. The decor was Italian, and the menu had some Italian words. Italian opera music played in the background. The baristas wore white shirts and bow ties. All service was stand-up—there were no chairs. National and international papers were hung on rods on the wall. By closing time on the first day, 300 customers had been served, mostly in the morning hours. But while the core idea worked well, it soon became apparent that several aspects of the format were not appropriate for Seattle. Some customers objected to the incessant opera music, others wanted a place to sit down, and many did not understand the Italian words on the menu. These "mistakes" were quickly fixed, but an effort was made not to compromise the style and elegance of the store. Within six months, the store was serving more than 1,000 customers a day. Regular customers had learned how to pronounce the company's name. Because most customers were in a hurry, it became apparent that speedy service was essential.

Six months after the first Il Giornale opened, a second store was opened in another downtown building. A third store was opened in Vancouver, British Columbia, in April 1987. Vancouver was chosen to test the transferability of the company's business concept outside Seattle. Schultz's goal was to open 50 stores in five years, and he needed to dispel his investors' doubts about geographic expansion early on to achieve his growth objective. By mid-1987 sales at the three stores were running at a rate equal to $1.5 million annually.

Il Giornale Acquires Starbucks

In March 1987 Jerry Baldwin and Gordon Bowker decided to sell the whole Starbucks operation in Seattle—the stores, the roasting plant, and the Starbucks name. Bowker wanted to cash out his coffee business investment to concentrate on his other enterprises; Baldwin, who was tired of commuting between Seattle and San Francisco and wrestling with the troubles created by the two parts of the company, elected to concentrate on the Peet's operation. As he recalls, "My wife and I had a 30-second conversation and decided to keep Peet's. It was the original and it was better."[7]

Schultz knew immediately that he had to buy Starbucks; his board of directors agreed. Schultz and his newly hired finance and accounting manager drew up a set of financial projections for the combined operations and a financing package that included a stock offering to Il Giornale's original investors and a line of credit with local banks. While a rival plan to acquire Starbucks was put together by another Il Giornale investor, Schultz's proposal prevailed. Within weeks, Schultz had raised the $3.8 million needed to buy Starbucks, and the acquisition was completed in August 1987. The new name of the combined companies was Starbucks Corporation. Howard Schultz, at the age of 34, became Starbucks' president and CEO.

STARBUCKS AS A PRIVATE COMPANY: 1987–1992

The Monday morning following the completed acquisition, Howard Schultz returned to the Starbucks offices at the roasting plant, greeted all the familiar faces, and accepted their congratulations. Then he called the staff together for a meeting on the roasting plant floor:

> All my life I have wanted to be part of a company and a group of people who share a common vision . . . I'm here today because I love this company. I love what it represents . . . I know you're concerned . . . I promise you I will not let you down. I promise you I will not leave anyone behind . . . In five years, I want you to look back at this day and say "I was there when it started. I helped build this company into something great."[8]

Schultz told the group that his vision was for Starbucks to become a national company with values and guiding principles that employees could be proud of. He indicated that he wanted to include people in the decision-making process and that he would be open and honest with them.

Schultz believed it was essential, not just an intriguing option, to build a company that valued and respected its people, that inspired them, and that shared the fruits of success with those who contributed to the company's long-term value. His aspiration was for Starbucks to become the most respected brand name in coffee and for the company to be admired for its corporate responsibility. In the next few days and weeks, Schultz came to see that the unity and morale at Starbucks had deteriorated badly in the 20 months he had been at Il Giornale. Some employees were cynical and felt unappreciated. There was a feeling that prior management had abandoned them and a wariness about what the new regime would bring. Schultz decided to make building a new relationship of mutual respect between employees and management a priority.

The new Starbucks had a total of nine stores. The business plan Schultz had presented investors called for the new company to open 125 stores in the next five years—15 the first year, 20 the second, 25 the third, 30 the fourth, and 35 the fifth. Revenues were projected to reach $60 million in 1992. But the company lacked experienced management. Schultz had never led a growth effort of such magnitude and was just learning what the job of CEO was all about, having been the president of a small company for barely two years. Dave Olsen, a Seattle coffee bar owner whom Schultz had recruited to direct store operations at Il Giornale, was still learning the ropes in managing a multistore operation. Ron Lawrence, the company's controller, had worked as a controller for several organizations. Other Starbucks employees had only the experience of managing or being a part of a six-store organization. When Starbucks' key roaster and coffee buyer resigned, Schultz put Dave Olsen in charge of buying and roasting coffee. Lawrence Maltz, who had 20 years' experience in business, including 8 years as president of a profitable public beverage company, was hired as executive vice president and charged with heading operations, finance, and human resources.

In the next several months, a number of changes were instituted. To symbolize the merging of the two companies and the two cultures, a new logo was created that melded the designs of the Starbucks logo and the Il Giornale logo. The Starbucks stores were equipped with espresso machines and remodeled to look more Italian than Old World nautical. Il Giornale green replaced the traditional Starbucks brown.

[7]As quoted in Jennifer Reese, "Starbucks: Inside the Coffee Cult," *Fortune,* December 9, 1996, p. 193.
[8]Schultz and Yang, *Pour Your Heart Into It,* pp. 101–2.

The result was a new type of store—a cross between a retail coffee bean store and an espresso bar/café—that eventually became Starbucks' signature.

By December 1987, the mood of the employees at Starbucks had turned upbeat. They were buying into the changes that Schultz was making, and trust began to build between management and employees. New stores were on the verge of opening in Vancouver and Chicago. One Starbucks store employee, Daryl Moore, who had started working at Starbucks in 1981 and who had voted against unionization in 1985, began to question the need for a union with his fellow employees. Over the next few weeks, Moore began a move to decertify the union. He carried a decertification letter around to Starbucks stores and secured the signatures of employees who no longer wished to be represented by the union. He got a majority of store employees to sign the letter and presented it to the National Labor Relations Board. The union representing store employees was decertified. Later, in 1992, the union representing Starbucks' roasting plant and warehouse employees was also decertified.

Market Expansion Outside the Pacific Northwest

Starbucks' entry into Chicago proved far more troublesome than management anticipated. The first Chicago store opened in October 1987, and three more stores were opened over the next six months. Customer counts at the stores were substantially below expectations. Chicagoans did not take to dark-roasted coffee as fast as Schultz had hoped. The first downtown store opened onto the street rather than into the lobby of the building where it was located; in the winter months, customers were hesitant to go out in the wind and cold to acquire a cup of coffee. It was expensive to supply fresh coffee to the Chicago stores out of the Seattle warehouse (the company solved the problem of freshness and quality assurance by putting freshly roasted beans in special FlavorLock bags that used vacuum packaging techniques with a one-way valve to allow carbon dioxide to escape without allowing air and moisture in). Rents were higher in Chicago than in Seattle, and so were wage rates. The result was a squeeze on store profit margins. Gradually, customer counts improved, but Starbucks lost money on its Chicago stores until, in 1990,

prices were raised to reflect higher rents and labor costs, more experienced store managers were hired, and a critical mass of customers caught on to the taste of Starbucks products.

Portland, Oregon, was the next market the company entered, and Portland coffee drinkers took to Starbucks products quickly. By 1991, the Chicago stores had become profitable and the company was ready for its next big market entry. Management decided on California because of its host of neighborhood centers and the receptiveness of Californians to high-quality, innovative food. Los Angeles was chosen as the first California market to enter. L.A. was selected principally because of its status as a trendsetter and its cultural ties to the rest of the country. L.A. consumers embraced Starbucks quickly, and the *Los Angeles Times* named Starbucks as the best coffee in America even before the first store opened. The entry into San Francisco proved more troublesome because San Francisco had an ordinance against converting stores to restaurant-related uses in certain prime urban neighborhoods; Starbucks could sell beverages and pastries to customers at stand-up counters but could not offer seating in stores that had formerly been used for general retailing. However, the city council was soon convinced by café owners and real estate brokers to change the code. Still, Starbucks faced strong competition from Peet's and local espresso bars in the San Francisco market.

Starbucks' store expansion targets proved easier to meet than Schultz had originally anticipated, and he upped the numbers to keep challenging the organization. Starbucks opened 15 new stores in fiscal 1988, 20 in 1989, 30 in 1990, 32 in 1991, and 53 in 1992—producing a total of 161 stores, significantly above the 1987 objective of 125 stores.

From the outset, the strategy was to open only company-owned stores; franchising was avoided so as to keep the company in full control of the quality of its products and the character and location of its stores. But company-ownership of all stores required Starbucks to raise new venture capital to cover the cost of new store expansion. In 1988 the company raised $3.9 million, in 1990 venture capitalists provided an additional $13.5 million, and in 1991 another round of venture capital financing generated $15 million. Starbucks was able to raise the needed funds despite posting losses of $330,000 in 1987, $764,000 in 1988, and $1.2 million in 1989. While the losses were troubling to Starbucks' board of directors and investors, Schultz's business plan had forecast losses during the early years of expansion. At a particularly tense board meeting where directors sharply questioned Schultz about the lack of profitability, Schultz said:

> Look, we're going to keep losing money until we can do three things. We have to attract a management team well beyond our expansion needs. We have to build a world-class roasting facility. And we need a computer information system sophisticated enough to keep track of sales in hundreds and hundreds of stores.[9]

Schultz argued for patience as the company invested in the infrastructure to support continued growth well into the 1990s. He contended that hiring experienced executives ahead of the growth curve, building facilities far beyond current needs, and installing support systems laid a strong foundation for rapid, profitable growth on down the road. His arguments carried the day with the board and with investors, especially since revenues were growing by approximately 80 percent annually and customer traffic at the stores was meeting or exceeding expectations.

Starbucks became profitable in 1990, and profits increased every year thereafter except for fiscal year 2000. Exhibit 3 provides a financial summary for 1998–2003.

HOWARD SCHULTZ'S STRATEGY TO MAKE STARBUCKS A GREAT PLACE TO WORK

Howard Schultz deeply believed that Starbucks' success was heavily dependent on customers having a very positive experience in its stores. This meant having store employees who were knowledgeable about the company's products, who paid attention to detail in preparing the company's espresso drinks, who eagerly communicated the company's passion for coffee, and who possessed the skills and personality to deliver consistent, pleasing customer service. Many of the baristas were in their 20s and worked part-time, going to college on the side or pursuing

other career activities. The challenge to Starbucks, in Schultz's view, was how to attract, motivate, and reward store employees in a manner that would make Starbucks a company that people would want to work for and that would generate enthusiastic commitment and higher levels of customer service. Moreover, Schultz wanted to send all Starbucks employees a message that would cement the trust that had been building between management and the company's workforce.

One of the requests that employees had made to the prior owners of Starbucks was to extend health care benefits to part-time workers. Their request had been turned down, but Schultz believed that expanding heath care coverage to include part-timers was the right thing to do. His father had recently passed away with cancer and he knew from his own past experience of having grown up in a family that struggled to make ends meet how difficult it was to cope with rising medical costs. In 1988 Schultz went to the board of directors with his plan to expand the company's heath care coverage to include part-timers who worked at least 20 hours a week. He saw the proposal not as a generous gesture but as a core strategy to win employee loyalty and commitment to the company's mission. Board members resisted because the company was unprofitable and the added costs of the extended coverage would only worsen the company's bottom line. But Schultz argued passionately that it was the right thing to do and wouldn't be as expensive as it seemed. He observed that if the new benefit reduced turnover, which he believed was likely, then it would reduce the costs of hiring and training—which equaled about $3,000 per new hire; he further pointed out that it cost $1,500 a year to provide an employee with full benefits. Part-timers, he argued, were vital to Starbucks, constituting two-thirds of the company's workforce. Many were baristas who knew the favorite drinks of regular customers; if the barista left, that connection with the customer was broken. Moreover, many part-time employees were called on to open the stores early, sometimes at 5:30 or 6:00 AM; others had to work until closing, usually 9:00 PM or later. Providing these employees with health care benefits, he argued, would signal that the company honored their value and contribution.

The board approved Schultz's plan, and starting in late 1988 part-timers working 20 or more hours were offered the same health coverage as full-time

[9]Ibid., p. 142.

exhibit 3 **Financial and Operating Summary for Starbucks Corporation, 1998–2003 (dollars in 000s)**

	Fiscal Years Ending[a]					
	September 30, 2003	September 29, 2002	September 30, 2001	October 1, 2000	October 3, 1999	September 27, 1998
Results of operations data						
Net revenues						
Retail	$3,449,624	$2,792,904	$2,229,594	$1,823,607	$1,423,389	$1,102,574
Specialty	625,898	496,004	419,386	354,007	263,439	206,128
Total net revenues	$4,075,522	$3,288,908	$2,648,980	$2,177,614	$1,686,828	$1,308,702
Cost of sales and related company costs	1,685,928	1,350,011	1,112,785	961,885	741,010	578,483
Store operating expenses	1,379,574	1,109,782	867,957	704,898	543,572	418,476
Other operating expenses	141,346	106,084	72,406	78,445	51,374	43,479
Depreciation and amortization expenses	237,807	205,557	163,501	130,232	97,797	72,543
General and administrative expenses	244,550	234,581	179,852	110,202	89,681	77,575
Income from equity investors	38,396	33,445	27,740	20,300	—	
Merger expenses[b]	—	—	—	—	—	8,930
Operating income	$ 424,713	$ 316,338	$ 280,219	$ 212,252	$ 156,711	$ 109,216
Internet-related investment losses				58,792		
Gain on sale of investment		13,361	2,940			
Net earnings	$ 268,346	$ 212,686	$ 180,335	$ 94,564	$ 101,693	$ 68,372
Net earnings per common share—diluted	$ 0.67	$ 0.54	$ 0.46	$ 0.24	$ 0.27	$ 0.19
Cash dividends per share	$ 0	$ 0	$ 0	$ 0	$ 0	$ 0
Balance sheet data						
Current assets	$ 924,029	$ 772,643	$ 593,925	$ 459,819	$ 386,500	$ 337,280
Current liabilities	608,703	462,595	445,264	313,251	251,597	179,475
Working capital	$ 315,326	$ 310,048	$ 148,661	$ 146,568	$ 135,303	$ 157,805
Total assets	$2,729,746	$2,214,392	$1,846,519	$1,491,546	$1,252,514	$ 992,755
Long-term debt (including current portion)	$ 4,354	$ 5,076	$ 6,483	$ 7,168	$ 7,691	$ 1,803
Shareholders' equity	$2,082,427	$1,723,189	$1,375,927	$1,148,399	$ 961,013	$ 794,297

exhibit 3 **(concluded)**

	Fiscal Years Ending[a]					
	September 30, 2003	September 29, 2002	September 30, 2001	October 1, 2000	October 3, 1999	September 27, 1998
Store operations data						
Percentage change in comparable store sales[c]						
United States	9%	7%	5%	9%	6%	5%
International	7%	1%	3%	12%	8%	n.a.
Consolidated	8%	6%	5%	9%	6%	5%
Systemwide retail store sales[d]	n.a.	$3,796,000	$2,950,000	$2,250,000	$1,633,000	$1,190,000
Systemwide stores opened during the year						
United States						
Company-operated stores	506	503	498	388	394	352
Licensed stores	315	264	268	342	42	39
International						
Company-operated stores	96	111	149	96	53	35
Licensed stores	284	299	293	177	1,239	48
Total	1,201	1,177	1,208	1,003	612	474
Systemwide stores open at year end[e]						
United States						
Company-operated stores	3,779	3,209	2,706	2,208	1,820	1,622
Licensed stores	1,422	1,033	769	501	159	133
International						
Company-operated stores	767	671	560	411	315	66
Licensed stores	1,257	973	674	381	204	65
Total	7,225	5,886	4,709	3,501	2,498	1,886

[a]The company's fiscal year ends on the Sunday closest to September 30. All fiscal years presented include 52 weeks, except fiscal 1999, which includes 53 weeks.

[b]Merger expenses relate to the business combination with Seattle Coffee Holdings Limited.

[c]Includes only company-operated stores open 13 months or longer.

[d]Systemwide retail sales include sales at company-operated and licensed stores and are believed by management to measure global penetration of Starbucks retail stores.

[e]Systemwide store openings are reported net of closures.

Source: 10-K reports for 2003, 2002, 2000, and 1999 and company press releases (for 2003 data).

employees. Starbucks paid 75 percent of an employee's health care premium; the employee paid 25 percent. Over the years, Starbucks extended its health coverage to include preventive care, crisis counseling, dental care, eye care, mental health, and chemical dependency. Coverage was also offered for unmarried partners in a committed relationship. Since most Starbucks' employees were young and comparatively healthy, the company had been able to provide broader coverage while keeping monthly payments relatively low. The value of Starbucks' health care program struck home when one of the company's store managers and a former barista walked into Schultz's office and told him he had AIDS:

> I had known he was gay but had no idea he was sick. His disease had entered a new phase, he explained, and he wouldn't be able to work any longer. We sat together and cried, for I could not find meaningful words to console him. I couldn't compose myself. I hugged him.[10]
>
> At that point, Starbucks had no provision for employees with AIDS. We had a policy decision. Because of Jim, we decided to offer health-care coverage to all employees who have terminal illnesses, paying medical costs in full from the time they are not able to work until they are covered by government programs, usually twenty-nine months.
>
> After his visit to me, I spoke with Jim often and visited him at the hospice. Within a year he was gone. I received a letter from his family afterward, telling me how much they appreciated our benefit plan.

In 1994 Howard Schultz was invited to The White House for a one-on-one meeting with President Bill Clinton to brief him on Starbucks' health care program.

The Creation of an Employee Stock Option Plan

By 1991 the company's profitability had improved to the point where Schultz could pursue a stock option plan for all employees, a program he believed would have a positive, long-term effect on the success of Starbucks.[11] Schultz wanted to turn all Starbucks employees into partners, give them a chance to share in the success of the company, and make clear the

connection between their contributions and the company's market value. Even though Starbucks was still a private company, the plan that emerged called for granting stock options to all full-time and part-time employees in proportion to their base pay. In May 1991, the plan, dubbed Bean Stock, was presented to the board. Though board members were concerned that increasing the number of shares might unduly dilute the value of the shares of investors who had put up hard cash, the plan received unanimous approval. The first grant was made in October 1991, just after the end of the company's fiscal year in September; each partner was granted stock options worth 12 percent of base pay. Each October since then, Starbucks has granted employees options equal to 14 percent of base pay, awarded at the stock price at the start of the fiscal year (October 1). When the Bean Stock program was presented to employees, Starbucks dropped the term *employee* and began referring to all of its people as *partners* because everyone, including part-timers working at least 20 hours per week, was eligible for stock options after six months. At the end of fiscal year 2003, Starbucks employee stock option plan included 39 million shares in outstanding options; new options for about 10 million shares were being granted annually.[12]

Starbucks became a public company in 1992; its initial public offering (IPO) of common stock in June proved to be one of the most successful IPOs of 1992 and provided the company access to the capital needed to accelerate expansion of its store network. Exhibit 4 shows the performance of the company's stock price since the 1992 IPO.

Starbucks' Stock Purchase Plan for Employees

In 1995, Starbucks implemented an employee stock purchase plan. Eligible employees could contribute up to 10 percent of their base earnings to quarterly purchases of the company's common stock at 85 percent of the going stock price. As of fiscal 2003, about 5.7 million shares had been issued since inception of the plan, and new shares were being purchased at a rate close to 1 million shares annually by some 11,184 active employee participants (out of almost 35,000 employees who were eligible to partici-

---

[10]Ibid., p. 129.

[11]As related in ibid., pp. 131–36.

[12]Starbucks annual report, 2002, p. 32.

exhibit 4 **The Performance of Starbucks' Stock, 1992–2003**

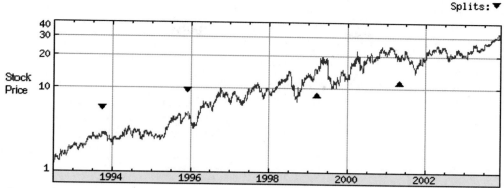

Source: www.finance.yahoo.com.

pate).[13] An employee stock option plan for eligible United Kingdom employees was established in 2002.[14]

The Workplace Environment

Starbucks' management believed that the company's pay scales and fringe benefit package allowed it to attract motivated people with above-average skills and good work habits. Store employees were paid around $9–$12 an hour, several dollars above the hourly minimum wage. Whereas most national retailers and fast-food chains had turnover rates for store employees ranging from 150 to 400 percent a year, the turnover rates for Starbucks' baristas ran about 65 percent. Starbucks' turnover for store managers was about 25 percent, compared to about 50 percent for other chain retailers. Starbucks' executives believed that efforts to make the company an attractive, caring place to work were responsible for its relatively low turnover rates. One Starbucks store manager commented, "Morale is very high in my store among the staff. I've worked for a lot of companies, but I've never seen this level of respect. It's a company that's very true to its workers, and it shows. Our customers always comment that we're happy and having fun. In fact, a lot of people ask if they can work here."[15]

[13]Ibid.

[14]Ibid.

[15]Ben van Houten, "Employee Perks: Starbucks Coffee's Employee Benefit Plan," *Restaurant Business,* May 15, 1997, p. 85.

Starbucks' management used annual "Partner View" surveys to solicit feedback from its workforce of over 74,000 people, learn their concerns, and measure job satisfaction. In the latest sample survey of 1,400 employees, 79 percent rated Starbucks' workplace environment favorably relative to other companies they were familiar with, 72 percent reported being satisfied with their present job, 16 percent were neutral, and 12 percent were dissatisfied. But the 2002 survey revealed that many employees viewed the benefits package as only "average," prompting the company to increase its match of 401(k) contributions for those who had been with the company more than three years and to have these contributions vest immediately.

Exhibit 5 contains a summary of Starbucks' fringe benefit program. Starbucks was named by *Fortune* magazine as one of the "100 Best Companies to Work For" in 1998, 1999, 2000, and 2002. Still, in 2003, Starbucks' management was concerned by field reports of stores that were suffering from slumping employee morale and store manager burnout.

STARBUCKS' CORPORATE VALUES AND BUSINESS PRINCIPLES

During the early building years, Howard Schultz and other Starbucks' senior executives worked to instill some key values and guiding principles into the

exhibit 5   **Elements of Starbucks' Fringe Benefit Program**

- Medical insurance
- Dental and vision care
- Mental health and chemical dependency coverage
- Short- and long-term disability
- Life insurance
- Benefits extended to committed domestic partners of Starbucks employees
- Sick time
- Paid vacations (first-year workers got one vacation week and two personal days)

- 401(k) retirement savings plan—the company matched from 25% to 150%, based on length of service, of each employee's contributions up to the first 4% of compensation
- Stock purchase plan—eligible employees could buy shares at a discounted price through regular payroll deductions
- Free pound of coffee each week
- 30% product discounts
- Stock option plan (Bean Stock)

Source: Compiled by the case researchers from company documents and other sources.

Starbucks culture. The cornerstone value in the effort "to build a company with soul" was that the company would never stop pursuing the perfect cup of coffee by buying the best beans and roasting them to perfection. Schultz remained steadfastly opposed to franchising, so that the company could control the quality of its products and build a culture common to all stores. He was adamant about not selling artificially flavored coffee beans—"We will not pollute our high-quality beans with chemicals"; if a customer wanted hazelnut-flavored coffee, Starbucks would provide it by adding hazelnut syrup to the drink rather than by adding hazelnut flavoring to the beans during roasting. Running flavored beans through the grinders would leave behind chemical residues that would alter the flavor of beans ground afterward; plus, the chemical smell given off by artificially flavored beans was absorbed by other beans in the store. Furthermore, Schultz didn't want the company to pursue supermarket sales because it would mean pouring Starbucks' beans into clear plastic bins where they could get stale, thus compromising the company's legacy of fresh, dark-roasted, full-flavored coffee.

Starbucks' management was also emphatic about the importance of employees paying attention to what pleased customers. Employees were trained to go out of their way, and to take heroic measures if necessary, to make sure customers were fully satisfied. The theme was "Just say yes" to customer requests. Further, employees were encouraged to speak their minds without fear of retribution from upper management—senior executives wanted employees to be vocal about what Starbucks was doing right,

what it was doing wrong, and what changes were needed. Management wanted employees to be involved in and contribute to the process of making Starbucks a better company.

A values and principles "crisis" arose at Starbucks in 1989 when customers started requesting skim (i.e., nonfat) milk in making cappuccinos and lattes. Howard Schultz, who read all customer comments cards, and Dave Olsen, head of coffee quality, conducted taste tests of lattes and cappuccinos made with nonfat milk and concluded they were not as good as those made with whole milk. Howard Behar, recently hired as head of retail store operations, indicated that management's opinions didn't matter; what mattered was giving customers what they wanted. Schultz took the position that "We will never offer nonfat milk. It's not who we are." Behar, however, stuck to his guns, maintaining that use of nonfat milk should at least be tested—otherwise it appeared as if all the statements management had made about the importance of really and truly pleasing customers were a sham. A fierce internal debate ensued. One dogmatic defender of the quality and taste of Starbucks' coffee products buttonholed Behar outside his office and told him that using nonfat milk amounted to "bastardizing" the company's products. Numerous store managers maintained that offering two kinds of milk was operationally impractical. Schultz found himself in a quandary, torn between the company's commitment to quality and its goal of pleasing customers. One day after visiting one of the stores in a residential neighborhood and watching a customer leave to go to a competitor's store because Starbucks did not make lattes with nonfat milk, Schultz authorized Behar to begin testing.[16] Within six months all 30 stores were offering drinks made with nonfat milk. Currently, about half the lattes and cappuccinos Starbucks sells are made with nonfat milk.

Schultz's approach to offering employees good compensation and a comprehensive benefits package was driven by his belief that sharing the company's success with the people who made it happen helped everyone think and act like an owner, build positive long-term relationships with customers, and do things in an efficient way. He had vivid recollection of his father's employment experience—bouncing from one low-paying job to another, working for employers who offered few or no benefits and who conducted their business with no respect for the contributions of the workforce—and he had no intention of Starbucks being that type of company. He vowed that he would never let Starbucks employees suffer a similar fate, saying:

> My father worked hard all his life and he had little to show for it. He was a beaten man. This is not the American dream. The worker on our plant floor is contributing great value to the company; if he or she has low self-worth, that will have an effect on the company.[17]

The company's employee benefits program was predicated on the belief that better benefits attract good people and keep them longer. Schultz's rationale was that if you treat your employees well, that is how they will treat customers.

STARBUCKS' MISSION STATEMENT

In early 1990, the senior executive team at Starbucks went to an off-site retreat to debate the company's values and beliefs and draft a mission statement. Schultz wanted the mission statement to convey a strong sense of organizational purpose and to articulate the company's fundamental beliefs and guiding principles. The draft was submitted to all employees for review, and several changes were made on the basis of employee comments. The resulting mission

[16]As related in Schultz and Yang, *Pour Your Heart Into It*, p. 168.
[17]As quoted in Ingrid Abramovitch, "Miracles of Marketing," *Success* 40, no. 3, p. 26.

exhibit 6   **Starbucks' Mission Statement**

Establish Starbucks as the premier purveyor of the finest coffee in the world while maintaining our uncompromising principles while we grow.

The following six guiding principles will help us measure the appropriateness of our decisions:

- Provide a great work environment and treat each other with respect and dignity.
- Embrace diversity as an essential component in the way we do business.
- Apply the highest standards of excellence to the purchasing, roasting, and fresh delivery of our coffee.
- Develop enthusiastically satisfied customers all of the time.
- Contribute positively to our communities and our environment.
- Recognize that profitability is essential to our future success.

Source: www.starbucks.com, November 2003.

statement, which remained unchanged in 2003, is shown in Exhibit 6.

Following adoption of the mission statement, Starbucks' management implemented a "Mission Review" to solicit and gather employee opinions about whether the company was living up to its stated mission. Employees were urged to report their concerns to the company's Mission Review team if they thought particular management decisions were not supportive of the company's mission statement. Comment cards were given to each newly hired employee and were kept available in common areas with other employee forms. Employees had the option of signing the comment cards or not. Hundreds of cards were submitted to the Mission Review team each year. The company promised that a relevant manager would respond to all signed cards within two weeks. Howard Schultz reviewed all the comments, signed and unsigned.

STARBUCKS' STORE EXPANSION STRATEGY

In 1992 and 1993 Starbucks developed a three-year geographic expansion strategy that targeted areas that not only had favorable demographic profiles but also could be serviced and supported by the company's operations infrastructure. For each targeted region, Starbucks selected a large city to serve as a "hub"; teams of professionals were located in hub cities to support the goal of opening 20 or more stores in the hub in the first two years. Once stores blanketed the hub, then additional stores were opened in smaller, surrounding "spoke" areas in the region. To oversee the expansion process, Starbucks created zone vice presidents to direct the development of each region and to implant the Starbucks culture in the newly opened stores. All of the new zone vice presidents Starbucks recruited came with extensive operating and marketing experience in chain store retailing.

Starbucks' strategy in major metropolitan cities was to blanket the area with stores, even if some stores cannibalized another store's business.[18] While a new store might draw 30 percent of the business of an existing store two or so blocks away, management believed that its "Starbucks everywhere" approach cut down on delivery and management costs, shortened customer lines at individual stores, and increased foot traffic for all the stores in an area.

Starbucks' store launches grew steadily more successful. In 2002, new stores generated an average of $1.2 million in first-year revenues, compared to $700,000 in 1995 and only $427,000 in 1990. The steady increases in new-store revenues were due partly to growing popularity of premium coffee drinks and partly to Starbucks' growing reputation. In more and more instances, Starbucks' reputation reached new markets even before stores opened. Moreover, existing stores continued to post sales gains in the range of 2–10 percent annually. In 2003, Starbucks posted same-store sales increases averaging 8 percent (Exhibit 3), the 12th consecutive year the company had achieved sales growth of 5 percent or greater at existing stores. Starbucks' revenues had climbed an average of 20 percent annually since 1992. In a representative week in 2003, about 20 million people bought a cup of coffee at Starbucks; a typical customer stopped at a Starbucks about 18 times a month—no U.S. retailer had a higher frequency of customer visits.[19]

One of Starbucks' core competencies was identifying good retailing sites for its new stores. The

[18]Daniels, "Mr. Coffee," p. 140.
[19]Ibid.

company was regarded as having the best real estate team in the coffee bar industry and a sophisticated system for identifying not only the most attractive individual city blocks but also the exact store location that was best; it also worked hard at building good relationships with local real estate representatives in areas where it was opening multiple store locations. The company's site location track record was so good that as of 1997 it had closed only 2 of the 1,500 sites it had opened; its track record in finding successful store locations was still intact as of 2003 (although specific figures were not available).

Exhibit 7 shows a timeline of Starbucks' entry into new market areas, along with other accomplishments, milestones, key events, and awards.

International Expansion

In markets outside the continental United States (including Hawaii), Starbucks had a two-pronged store expansion: either open company-owned and company-operated stores or else license a reputable and capable local company with retailing know-how in the target host country to develop and operate new Starbucks stores. In most countries, Starbucks used a local partner/licensee to help it recruit talented individuals, set up supplier relationships, locate suitable store sites, and cater to local market conditions. Starbucks looked for partners/licensees that had strong retail/restaurant experience, had values and a corporate culture compatible with Starbucks, were committed to good customer service, possessed talented management and strong financial resources, and had demonstrated brand-building skills.

Starbucks had created a new subsidiary, Starbucks Coffee International, to orchestrate overseas expansion and begin to build the Starbucks brand name globally via licensees. (See Exhibit 1 for the number of licensed international stores and Exhibit 7 for the years in which Starbucks entered most of these foreign markets.) Starbucks' management expected to have a total of 10,000 stores in 60 countries by the end of 2005. The company's first store in France opened in early 2004 in Paris. China was expected to be Starbucks' biggest market outside the United States in the years to come. Thus far, Starbucks products were proving to be a much bigger hit with consumers in Asia than in Europe. Even so, Starbucks was said to be losing money in both Japan and Britain; moreover, the Starbucks Coffee International division was only marginally profitable, with 2003 pretax earnings of only $5.5 million on sales of $603 million.

Going into 2004, Schultz believed the company's long-range goal of 25,000 store locations by 2013 was achievable. He noted that Starbucks had only a 7 percent share of the coffee-drinking market in the United States and a 1 percent share internationally. According to Schultz, "That still leaves lots of room for growth. Internationally, we are still in our infancy."[20] Although coffee consumption worldwide was stagnant, coffee was still the second most consumed beverage in the world, trailing only water.[21] Starbucks maintained that it would not franchise, although its foreign stores were frequently opened in partnership with local companies.

Employee Training

To accommodate its strategy of rapid store expansion, Starbucks put in systems to recruit, hire, and train baristas and store managers. Starbucks' vice president for human resources used some simple guidelines in screening candidates for new positions: "We want passionate people who love coffee . . . We're looking for a diverse workforce, which reflects our community. We want people who enjoy what they're doing and for whom work is an extension of themselves."[22]

All partners/baristas hired for a retail job in a Starbucks store received at least 24 hours training in their first two to four weeks. The training topics included coffee history, drink preparation, coffee knowledge (four hours), customer service (four hours), and retail skills; there was also a four-hour workshop titled "Brewing the Perfect Cup." Baristas spent considerable time learning about beverage preparation—grinding the beans, steaming milk, learning to pull perfect (18- to 23-second) shots of espresso, memorizing the recipes of all the different drinks, practicing making the different drinks, and learning how to customize drinks to customer specifications. There were sessions on cash register operations, how to clean the milk wand on the espresso machine, explaining the Italian drink names to customers, selling home espresso machines, making eye contact with customers, and taking personal respon-

sibility for the cleanliness of the store. Everyone was drilled in the Star Skills, three guidelines for on-the-job interpersonal relations: (1) maintain and enhance self-esteem, (2) listen and acknowledge, and (3) ask for help. And there were rules to be memorized: milk must be steamed to at least 150 degrees Fahrenheit but never more than 170 degrees; every espresso shot not pulled within 23 seconds must be tossed; never let coffee sit in the pot more than 20 minutes; always compensate dissatisfied customers with a Starbucks coupon for a free drink.

Management trainees attended classes for 8 to 12 weeks. Their training went much deeper, covering not only coffee knowledge and information imparted to baristas but also the details of store operations, practices and procedures as set forth in the company's operating manual, information systems, and the basics of managing people. Starbucks' trainers were all store managers and district managers with on-site experience. One of their major objectives was to ingrain the company's values, principles, and culture and to pass on their knowledge about coffee and their passion about Starbucks.

When Starbucks opened stores in a new market, it launched a major recruiting effort. Eight to 10 weeks before opening, the company placed ads to hire baristas and begin their training. It sent a Star team of experienced managers and baristas from existing stores to the area to lead the store opening effort and to conduct one-on-one training following the company's formal classes and basic orientation sessions at the Starbucks Coffee School in San Francisco.

Real Estate, Store Design, Store Planning, and Construction

Starting in 1991, Starbucks created its own in-house team of architects and designers to ensure that each store would convey the right image and character. Stores had to be custom-designed because, unlike McDonald's or Wal-Mart, the company bought no real estate and built no freestanding structures; rather, each space was leased in an existing structure, meaning that each store differed in size and shape. Most stores ranged in size from 1,000 to 1,500 square feet and were located in office buildings, downtown and suburban retail centers, airport terminals, university campus areas, and busy neighborhood shopping areas convenient for pedestrian foot

---

[20]Starbucks annual report, 2002, Letter to Shareholders.
[21]Ibid.
[22]Kate Rounds, "Starbucks Coffee," *Incentive* 167, no. 7, p. 22.

exhibit 7   **Timeline of Starbucks' Accomplishments, Milestones, Key Events, and Selected Awards, 1987–2003**

Year	Accomplishments/Milestones/Key Events/Awards
1987	• Il Giornale acquires the assets of Starbucks Coffee, Tea, and Spices and changes the company's name to Starbucks Corporation.
	• First stores outside of Seattle are opened in Chicago and Vancouver, British Columbia.
1988	• Starbucks introduces a mail order catalog, with service to all 50 states.
1990	• Starbucks expands Seattle headquarters and builds a new coffee bean roasting plant in Seattle.
1990	• Starbucks' first licensed airport location is opened at Sea-Tac International Airport in partnership with HMS Host.
	• Horizon Air begins serving Starbucks coffee on its flights.
1991	• Starbucks becomes first privately owned U.S. company to offer a stock option program that includes part-time employees.
1992	• Starbucks completes an IPO and becomes a public company trading on the Nasdaq National Market under the symbol SBUX.
1993	• Starbucks enters into an alliance with Barnes & Noble to have Starbucks coffee stores inside B&N's bookstores.
	• Starbucks opens a second roasting plant in Kent, Washington.
1994	• Starbucks wins contract for its coffees to be served at all Sheraton Hotels.
	• Starbucks expands to Minneapolis, Boston, New York, Atlanta, and Dallas.
1995	• Starbucks begins selling compact discs of music played in Starbucks stores.
	• United Airlines begins serving Starbucks on its flights.
	• A new $11 million state-of-the-art roasting facility is opened in York, Pennsylvania.
	• A joint venture is formed to open Starbucks stores in Japan.
	• Starbucks expands to Philadelphia, Pittsburgh, Las Vegas, Cincinnati, Baltimore, San Antonio, and Austin.
1996	• First Starbucks locations are opened in Japan, Hawaii, and Singapore.
	• Starbucks wins an account for Westin Hotels.
	• Starbucks' coffee-flavored ice creams are introduced in partnership with Dreyer's Grand Ice Cream.
	• Starbucks-PepsiCo venture begins selling a bottled version of Starbucks Frappuccino.
	• First Starbucks locations are opened in Rhode Island; Idaho; North Carolina; Arizona; Utah; and Ontario, Canada.
	• Starbucks receives 1996 Corporate Conscience Award for International Human Rights from Council on Economic Priorities.
1997	• First Starbucks locations are opened in Florida, Michigan, Wisconsin, and the Philippines.
	• Canadian Airlines begins serving Starbucks coffee on its flights.
	• Starbucks Foundation is established to help support local literacy programs in communities where Starbucks has coffeehouses.
	• Starbucks named one of the "Best Companies to Work for in America for People with Disabilities" by *We* magazine.
1998	• Starbucks enters into an alliance with Kraft Foods to handle the distribution of packaged Starbucks coffee in supermarkets.
	• First Starbucks locations are opened in New Orleans, St. Louis, Kansas City, Portland (Maine), Taiwan, Thailand, New Zealand, and Malaysia.
	• Starbucks enters Great Britain by acquiring 60 Seattle Coffee locations.
	• Starbucks acquires Pasqua, a San Francisco–based coffee retailer.
	• Company Web site, www.starbucks.com, is launched.

exhibit 7 **(concluded)**

Year	Accomplishments/Milestones/Key Events/Awards
1999	• First Starbucks locations are opened in Memphis, Nashville, Saskatchewan, China, Kuwait, South Korea, and Lebanon.
	• Tazo, a Portland, Oregon, tea company is acquired, and sales of Tazo teas at Starbucks locations begins.
	• Starbucks forms an agreement with Albertson's to open more than 100 Starbucks locations in Albertson's supermarkets beginning in 2000.
2000	• Howard Schultz transitions from chairman and CEO to chairman and chief global strategist; Orrin Smith is promoted to president and CEO.
	• Starbucks enters into agreement with Host Marriott International to open locations in select properties.
	• First Starbucks locations are opened in Dubai, Hong Kong, Shanghai, Qatar, Bahrain, Saudi Arabia, and Australia.
	• Starbucks begins marketing Fair Trade Certified coffees.
	• Starbucks acquires Hear Music, a San Francisco music company.
	• *Interbrand Magazine* names Starbucks as one of the "75 Great Global Brands of the 21st Century."
2001	• Starbucks adopts coffee sourcing guidelines developed in partnership with Conservation International and commits to purchase at least 1 million pounds of Fair Trade Certified coffee.
	• Starbucks offers $1 million in support to coffee farmers.
	• Starbucks begins to offer high-speed wireless Internet access in stores.
	• Starbucks begins offering a reloadable Starbucks Card for customers to use in making purchases at Starbucks stores.
	• Starbucks opens 300th location in Japan and first stores in Switzerland, Austria, and Israel.
	• Howard Schultz is named one of the "Top 25 Best Managers" by *Business Week*.
2002	• Starbucks begins selling Fair Trade Certified coffees in select foreign locations.
	• Starbucks opens first stores in Oman, Indonesia, Germany, Spain, Puerto Rico, Mexico, Greece, and southern China.
	• *Fortune* magazine names Starbucks as one of the "100 Best Companies to Work For" (as it also did in 1998, 1999, and 2000).
	• *Business Ethics Magazine* names Starbucks as one of "100 Best Corporate Citizens" (as it also did in 2000 and 2001).
2003	• The company introduces the Starbucks Duetto Visa card, which combines Visa card functionality with the reloadable Starbucks Card functionality.
	• Starbucks acquires Seattle Coffee Company, consisting of 129 company-operated and franchised Seattle's Best Coffee locations, 21 company-operated Torrefazione Italia locations in the United States and Canada, and distribution of Seattle Coffee in some 12,000 supermarket and retail food locations.
	• Starbucks opens its 1,000th store in the Asia Pacific region and its first stores in Turkey, Chile, and Peru; it also announces plans to open stores in France in 2004.
	• Starbucks decides to end venture in Israel (a total of six stores) due to challenging operating conditions.
	• *Brandweek* ranks Starbucks eighth on its "Super Brand List."
	• Starbucks named as one of the "Ten Most Admired Companies in America" in *Fortune* survey.

Source: www.starbucks.com, accessed November 4, 2003.

traffic and/or drivers. Only a select few were in suburban malls.

Over the years, Starbucks had experimented with a broad range of store formats. Special seating areas were added to help make Starbucks a desirable gathering place where customers could meet and chat or simply enjoy a peaceful interlude in their day. Flagship stores in high-traffic, high-visibility locations had fireplaces, leather chairs, newspapers, couches, and lots of ambience. The company also experimented with drive-through windows in locations where speed and convenience were important to customers and with kiosks in supermarkets, building lobbies, and other public places.

A "stores of the future" project team was formed in 1995 to raise Starbucks' store design to a still higher level and come up with the next generation of Starbucks stores. The vision of what a Starbucks store should be like included such concepts as an authentic coffee experience that conveyed the artistry of espresso making, a place to think and imagine, a spot where people could gather and talk over a great cup of coffee, a comforting refuge that provided a sense of community, a third place for people to congregate beyond work or the home, a place that welcomes people and rewards them for coming, and a layout that could accommodate both fast service and quiet moments. The team researched the art and literature of coffee throughout the ages, studied coffee-growing and coffee-making techniques, and looked at how Starbucks' stores had already evolved in terms of design, logos, colors, and mood. The team came up with four store designs—one for each of the four stages of coffee making: growing, roasting, brewing, and aroma—each with its own color combinations, lighting scheme, and component materials. Within each of the four basic store templates, Starbucks could vary the materials and details to adapt to different store sizes and settings (downtown buildings, college campuses, neighborhood shopping areas). In late 1996, Starbucks began opening new stores based on one of the four formats and color schemes. But as the number of stores increased rapidly between 2000 and 2003, greater store diversity and layout quickly became necessary. Exhibit 8 shows the diverse nature of Starbucks stores in 2003.

To better control average store opening costs, the company centralized buying, developed standard contracts and fixed fees for certain items, and consolidated work under those contractors who displayed good cost-control practices. The retail operations group outlined exactly the minimum amount of equipment each core store needed so that standard items could be ordered in volume from vendors at 20 to 30 percent discounts, then delivered just in time to the store site either from company warehouses or the vendor. Modular designs for display cases were developed. And the whole store layout was developed on a computer, with software that allowed the costs to be estimated as the design evolved. All this cut store opening costs significantly and reduced store development time from 24 to 18 weeks.

In August 2002, Starbucks teamed up with T-Mobile USA, the largest U.S. carrier-owned Wi-Fi service, to experiment with providing Internet access and enhanced digital entertainment to patrons at over 1,200 Starbucks locations. Customers using a Wi-Fi notebook computer while at Starbucks locations equipped with wireless broadband Internet service could surf the Web or take advantage of special Starbucks-sponsored multimedia promotions (e.g., classic blues performances by Howlin' Wolf and Muddy Waters, an array of great blues tunes, and videos of noteworthy musicians sharing how blues music and artists influenced them). The objective was to heighten the "third place" Starbucks experience, entice customers into perhaps buying a second latte or espresso while catching up on e-mail, listening to digital music, putting the finishing touches on a presentation, or accessing their corporate intranet. Since the August 2002 introduction of Wi-Fi at Starbucks, wireless Internet service had been added at 1,200 more stores and the number of accesses was in the millions; internal research showed that the average connection lasted approximately 45 minutes and more than 90 percent of T-Mobile HotSpot accesses were during the off-peak store hours, after 9:00 AM. In October 2003, Starbucks announced that it was expanding Wi-Fi capability to additional locations and would have 2,700 stores equipped with wireless Internet access by year-end.

During the early start-up years, Starbucks avoided debt and financed new stores entirely with equity capital. But as the company's profitability improved and its balance sheet strengthened, Schultz's opposition to debt as a legitimate financing vehicle softened. In 1996 the company completed its second debt offering, netting $161 million from the sale of convertible debentures for use in its capital construction program. This debt was successfully converted

exhibit 8 **Scenes from Starbucks Stores**

into common stock in 1997. Over the next seven years, strong internal cash flows allowed Starbucks to finance virtually all of its store expansion with internal funds; the company had less than $6 million in long-term debt on its balance sheet despite having invested some $1.3 billion in facilities and equipment.

Store Ambience

Starbucks' management viewed each store as a billboard for the company and as a contributor to building the company's brand and image. Each detail was scrutinized to enhance the mood and ambience of the store, to make sure everything signaled "best of class" and reflected the personality of the community and the neighborhood. The thesis was "Everything matters." The company went to great lengths to make sure that the store fixtures, the merchandise displays, the colors, the artwork, the banners, the music, and the aromas all blended to create a consistent, inviting, stimulating environment that evoked the romance of coffee, that signaled the company's passion for coffee, and that rewarded customers with ceremony, stories, and surprise. Starbucks was recognized for its sensitivity to neighborhood conservation with Scenic America's award for excellent design and "sensitive reuse of spaces within cities."

To try to keep the coffee aromas in the stores pure, Starbucks banned smoking and asked employees to refrain from wearing perfumes or colognes. Prepared foods were kept covered so that customers would smell coffee only. Colorful banners and posters kept the look of Starbucks stores fresh and in season. Company designers came up with artwork for commuter mugs and T-shirts in different cities that were in keeping with each city's personality (peach-shaped coffee mugs for Atlanta, pictures of Paul Revere for Boston and the Statue of Liberty for New York). To make sure that Starbucks stores measured up to standards, the company used "mystery shoppers" who posed as customers and rated each location on a number of criteria.

THE PRODUCT LINE AT STARBUCKS

Starbucks stores offered a choice of regular or decaffeinated coffee beverages, a special "coffee of the day," an assortment of made-to-order Italian-style hot and cold espresso drinks, and hot and iced teas. In addition, customers could choose from a wide selection of fresh-roasted whole-bean coffees (which could be ground or not on the premises for take-home in distinctive packages), fresh pastries, juices, coffee-making equipment, coffee mugs and other accessories, and music CDs. From time to time, stores ran special promotions touting Starbucks' special Christmas Blend coffee, shade-grown coffee from Mexico, organically grown coffees, and various rare and exotic coffees from across the world. In 2003, Starbucks began offering customers a choice of using its exclusive Silk soymilk, specifically designed to accentuate its handcrafted beverages using espresso roast coffee and Tazo Chai teas; the organic, kosher soymilk appealed to some customers as a substitute for milk or skim milk in various coffee and tea beverages.

The company's retail sales mix in 2002 was 77 percent beverages, 13 percent food items, 6 percent whole-bean coffees, and 4 percent coffee-making equipment and accessories.[23] The product mix in each store varied according to the size and location of each outlet. Larger stores carried a greater variety of whole coffee beans, gourmet food items, teas, coffee mugs, coffee grinders, coffee-making equipment, filters, storage containers, and other accessories. Smaller stores and kiosks typically sold a full line of coffee beverages, a limited selection of whole-bean coffees, and a few hardware items.

The idea for selling music CDs (which, in some cases, were special compilations that had been put together for Starbucks to use as store background music) originated with a Starbucks store manager who had worked in the music industry and selected the new "tape of the month" Starbucks played as background in its stores. The manager had gotten compliments from customers wanting to buy the music they heard and suggested to senior executives that there was a market for the company's music tapes. Research through two years of comment cards turned up hundreds asking Starbucks to sell the music it played in its stores. The Starbucks CDs, initially created from the Capitol Records library, proved a significant seller and addition to the product line; some of the CDs were specific collections designed to tie in with new blends of coffee that the company was promoting. In 2000, Starbucks acquired Hear Music, a San Francisco–based company, to give it added capability in enhancing its music CD offerings.

---

[23]Starbucks fiscal 2002 annual report, p. 15.

In 2003, in an average week, about 22 million customers patronized Starbucks stores in North America, up from about 5 million in 1998. Stores did about half of their business by 11:00 AM. Loyal customers patronized a Starbucks store 15 to 20 times a month, spending perhaps $50–$75 monthly. Some Starbucks fanatics came in daily. Baristas became familiar with regular customers, learning their names and their favorite drinks. Christine Nagy, a field director for Oracle Corporation in Palo Alto, California, told a *Wall Street Journal* reporter, "For me, it's a daily necessity or I start getting withdrawals."[24] Her standard order was a custom drink: a decaf grande nonfat no-whip no-foam extra-cocoa mocha; when the barista saw her come through the door, Nagy told the reporter, "They just say 'We need a Christine here.'" Since its inception in 2001, 20 million Starbucks customers had purchased the reloadable Starbucks Card that allowed them to pay for their purchases with a quick swipe at the cash register and also to earn and redeem rewards.

In the fall of 2003 Starbucks, in partnership with Bank One, introduced the Duetto Visa card, which added Visa card functionality to the reloadable Starbucks Cards. By charging purchases to the Visa account of their Duetto card anywhere Visa credit cards were accepted, cardholders earned 1 percent back in Duetto Dollars, which were automatically loaded on their Starbucks Card account after each billing cycle. Duetto Dollars could be used to purchase beverages, food, and store merchandise at any Starbucks location. The Duetto card was the latest in an ongoing effort by Starbucks' management to introduce new products and experiences for customers that belonged exclusively to Starbucks; senior executives drummed the importance of always being open to reinventing the Starbucks experience.

So far, Starbucks had spent very little money on advertising, preferring instead to build the brand cup by cup with customers and depend on word of mouth and the appeal of its storefronts.

Joint Ventures

In 1994, after months of meetings and experimentation, PepsiCo and Starbucks entered into a joint venture to create new coffee-related products for mass distribution through Pepsi channels, including cold coffee drinks in a bottle or can. Howard Schultz saw this as a major paradigm shift with the potential to cause Starbucks' business to evolve in heretofore unimaginable directions; he thought it was time to look for ways to move Starbucks out into more mainstream markets. Cold coffee products had historically met with poor market reception, except in Japan, where there was an $8 billion market for ready-to-drink coffee-based beverages. Nonetheless, Schultz was hoping the partners would hit on a new product to exploit a good-tasting coffee extract that had been developed by Starbucks' recently appointed director of research and development. The joint venture's first new product, Mazagran, a lightly flavored carbonated coffee drink, was a failure; a market test in southern California showed that some people liked it and some hated it. While people were willing to try it the first time, partly because the Starbucks name was on the label, repeat sales proved disappointing.

Despite the clash of cultures and the different motivations of PepsiCo and Starbucks, the partnership held together because of the good working relationship that evolved between Howard Schultz and Pepsi's senior executives. Then Schultz, at a meeting to discuss the future of Mazagran, suggested, "Why not develop a bottled version of Frappuccino?"[25] Starbucks had come up with the new cold coffee drink in the summer of 1995, and it had proved to be a big hot-weather seller; Pepsi executives were enthusiastic. After months of experimentation, the joint venture product research team came up with a shelf-stable version of Frappuccino that tasted quite good. It was tested in West Coast supermarkets in the summer of 1996; sales ran 10 times over projections, with 70 percent being repeat sales. Sales of Frappuccino reached $125 million in 1997 and achieved national supermarket penetration of 80 percent. Starbucks' management believed that the market for Frappuccino would ultimately exceed $1 billion.

In October 1995 Starbucks partnered with Dreyer's Grand Ice Cream to supply coffee extract for a new line of coffee ice cream made and distributed by Dreyer's under the Starbucks brand. The new line, featuring such flavors as Dark Roast Expresso Swirl, JavaChip, Vanilla MochaChip, Biscotti Bliss, and Caffe Almond Fudge, hit supermarket shelves in April 1996, and by July 1996 Starbucks coffee-flavored ice cream was the best-selling super-premium brand in the coffee segment. In 1997, two

---

[24]David Bank, "Starbucks Faces Growing Competition: Its Own Stores," *The Wall Street Journal,* January 21, 1997, p. B1.

[25]As related in Schultz and Yang, *Pour Your Heart Into It,* p. 224.

new low-fat flavors were added to complement the original six flavors, along with two flavors of ice cream bars; all were well received in the marketplace.

In 2003, Starbucks' partnerships with PepsiCo and Dreyer's generated revenues of about $6 million.

Licensed Stores and Specialty Sales

Starbucks had a licensing agreement with Kraft Foods to market and distribute Starbucks' whole-bean and ground coffees in grocery and mass-merchandise channels across the United States. Kraft managed all distribution, marketing, advertising, and promotions and paid a royalty to Starbucks based on a percentage of net sales. Two-thirds of all coffee was sold in supermarkets. Starbucks coffee sold in supermarkets featured distinctive, elegant packaging; prominent positions in grocery aisles; and the same premium quality as that of coffee sold in its stores. Product freshness was guaranteed by Starbucks' FlavorLock packaging, and the price per pound paralleled the prices in Starbucks' retail stores. Flavor selections in supermarkets, however, were more limited than those at Starbucks stores. Starbucks executives recognized that supermarket distribution entailed several risks, especially in exposing Starbucks to first-time customers. Starbucks had built its reputation around the unique retail experience in its stores, where all beverages were properly prepared—it had no control over how customers would perceive Starbucks when they encountered it in grocery aisles. A second risk concerned coffee preparation at home. Rigorous quality control and skilled baristas ensured that store-purchased beverages would measure up, but consumers using poor equipment or inappropriate brewing methods could easily conclude that Starbucks packaged coffees did not live up to their reputation.

Going into 2004, Starbucks coffees were available in some 19,500 supermarkets and warehouse clubs (such as Sam's and Costco) and generated 2003 revenues close to $160 million.

Starbucks had also entered into a limited number of licensing agreements for store locations in areas where it did not have ability to locate its own outlets. The company had an agreement with Marriott Host International that allowed Host to operate Starbucks retail stores in airport locations, and it had an agreement with Aramark Food and Services to put Starbucks stores on university campuses and other locations operated by Aramark. Starbucks received a license fee and a royalty on sales at these locations and supplied the coffee for resale in the licensed locations. All licensed stores had to follow Starbucks' detailed operating procedures and all managers and employees who worked in these stores received the same training given to Starbucks managers and store employees. As of 2003, there were 1,422 licensed or franchised stores in the United States and 1,257 licensed stores internationally. Royalty and license fee revenues from domestic stores generated close to $150 million in revenues in fiscal 2003, with international licensed retail stores accounting for about $250 million in revenues.

Starbucks had a specialty sales group that provided its coffee products to restaurants, airlines, hotels, universities, hospitals, business offices, country clubs, and select retailers. One of the early users of Starbucks coffee was Horizon Airlines, a regional carrier based in Seattle. In 1995, Starbucks entered into negotiations with United Airlines to serve Starbucks coffee on all United flights. There was much internal debate at Starbucks about whether such a move made sense for Starbucks and the possible damage to the integrity of the Starbucks brand if the quality of the coffee served did not measure up. After seven months of negotiation and discussion over coffee-making procedures, United Airlines and Starbucks came up with a mutually agreeable way to handle quality control on 500-plus planes having varying equipment, and Starbucks became the coffee supplier to the 20 million passengers flying United each year. Since then, Starbucks had entered into an agreement to have Starbucks coffee served on Canadian Air flights.

In recent years, the specialty sales group had won the coffee accounts at Sheraton and Westin hotels, resulting in packets of Starbucks coffee being in each room with coffee-making equipment. Starbucks had entered into an agreement with Wells Fargo to provide coffee service at some of the bank's locations in California. A 1997 agreement with U.S. Office Products gave Starbucks an entrée to provide its coffee to workers in 1.5 million business offices. In addition, Starbucks supplied an exclusive coffee blend to Nordstrom's for sale only in Nordstrom stores, operated coffee bars in Barnes & Noble bookstores, and, most recently, had begun coffee bar operations for Chapters, a Toronto book retailer that had sites throughout Canada. In fiscal 2003, Starbucks had approximately 12,800 food-service accounts that generated revenues of about $175 million. Starbucks was in the process of partnering with SYSCO to service the majority of its food-service accounts.

Mail Order Sales

The original Starbucks had begun a small mail order operation in the 1970s to serve travelers who had visited a Seattle store or former store customers who had moved away from Seattle. Sales were solicited by mailing out a simple brochure. In 1988, Starbucks developed its first catalog and began expanding its mail order base to targeted demographic groups. In 1990 a toll-free number was set up. Sales grew steadily as the company's name and reputation began to build. The company's market research indicated that its average mail order customer was a connoisseur, well educated, relatively affluent, well traveled, interested in the arts and cultural events, and usually a loyal buyer of the company's products. As time went on, the cities and neighborhoods where the company's mail order customers were located became beacons the company used to decide where to open new stores.

Starbucks published a mail order catalog that was distributed six times a year and that offered coffee, a selection of candies and pastries, and select coffee-making equipment and accessories. A special gift-giving catalog was mailed to business accounts during the 1997 Christmas holiday season; this practice carried over into 2002. The company also had an electronic store on America Online. In 1997, sales of this division were about $21.2 million, roughly 2 percent of total revenues; almost 50,000 mail order customers were signed up to receive monthly deliveries of Starbucks coffee as of late 1997. The number of mail order consumers steadily increased thereafter, as did sales revenues from online marketing. Starbucks' management believed that its direct response marketing effort helped pave the way for retail expansion into new markets and reinforced brand recognition in existing markets.

However, in 2001–2002 catalog sales fell off as the number of retail stores expanded and as Starbucks coffee began to be sold in supermarkets. The company discontinued its catalog operations in early 2003, along with sales via the company's Web site (online customers could buy selected Starbucks coffees at Amazon.com and several other Web sites).

COFFEE PURCHASING STRATEGY

Starbucks personnel traveled regularly to coffee-producing countries—Colombia, Sumatra, Yemen, Antigua, Indonesia, Guatemala, New Guinea, Costa Rica, Sulawesi, Papua, Kenya, Ethiopia, Java, Mexico—building relationships with growers and exporters, checking on agricultural conditions and crop yields, and searching out varieties and sources that would meet Starbucks' exacting standards of quality and flavor. The coffee-purchasing group, working with personnel in roasting operations, tested new varieties and blends of beans from different sources.

Coffee was grown in 70 tropical countries and was the second most traded commodity in the world after petroleum. The global value of the 2000–2001 coffee bean crop was about $5.6 billion. By World Bank estimates, some 25 million small farmers made their living growing coffee. Commodity-grade coffee, which consisted of robusta and commercial-quality arabica beans, was traded in a highly competitive market as an undifferentiated product. Coffee prices were subject to considerable volatility due to weather, economic and political conditions in the growing countries, new agreements establishing export quotas, and periodic efforts to bolster prices by restricting coffee supplies. Starbucks used fixed-price purchase commitments to limit its exposure to fluctuating coffee prices in upcoming periods and, on occasion, purchased coffee futures contracts to provide price protection. In years past, there had been times when unexpected jumps in coffee prices had put a squeeze on Starbucks' margins, forcing an increase in the prices of the beverages and beans sold at retail.

Starbucks sourced approximately 50 percent of its beans from Latin America, 35 percent from the Pacific Rim, and 15 percent from East Africa. Sourcing from multiple geographic areas not only allowed Starbucks to offer a greater range of coffee varieties to customers but also spread the company's risks regarding weather, price volatility, and changing economic and political conditions in coffee-growing countries.

During 2002, a global oversupply of more than 2 billion pounds drove the prices of commodity coffees to historic lows of $0.40–$0.50 per pound. The specialty coffee market, which represented about 10 percent of worldwide production, consisted primarily of high-quality arabica beans. Prices for specialty coffees were determined by the quality and flavor of the beans and were almost always higher than prevailing prices for commodity-grade coffee beans. Starbucks purchased only high-quality arabica coffee beans, paying an average of $1.20 per pound in 2002. Its purchases represented about 1 percent of the world's coffee-bean crop.

Believing that the continued growth and success of its business depended on gaining access to adequate supplies of high-quality coffees on a year-in, year-out basis, Starbucks had been a leader in promoting environmental and social stewardship in coffee-origin countries. Starbucks' coffee-sourcing strategy was to contribute to the sustainability of coffee growers and help conserve the environment. In sourcing green coffee beans, Starbucks was increasingly dealing directly with farmers and cooperatives, and its policy was to pay prices high enough to ensure that small coffee growers, most of whom lived on the edge of poverty, were able to cover their production costs and provide for their families. About 40 percent of Starbucks' purchases were made under three- to five-year contracts, which management believed enabled the company to purchase its future coffee-bean requirements at predictable prices over multiple crop years. Coffee purchases negotiated through long-term contracts increased from 3 percent in 2001 to 36 percent in 2002. Farmers who met important quality, environmental, social, and economic criteria—which Starbucks had developed with the support of Conservation International's Center for Environmental Leadership in Business— were rewarded with financial incentives and preferred supplier status.

Fair Trade Certified Coffee

A growing number of small coffee growers were members of democratically run cooperatives that were registered with Fairtrade Labelling Organizations International; these growers could sell their beans directly to importers, roasters, and retailers at favorable guaranteed "fair-trade" prices. Buyers of Fair Trade Certified coffee beans had to pay a minimum of $1.26 per pound for nonorganic green arabica coffee and $1.41 for organic green arabica coffee. According to TransFair USA, an independent nonprofit organization that licensed Starbucks to sell Fair Trade coffee imported into the United States, the guaranteed prices for Fair Trade coffees boosted earnings for small coffee growers enough to allow them to afford basic health care, education, and home improvements. In 2003, Starbucks marketed Fair Trade Certified coffee at most of its retail stores and through some 350 university and hotel locations that were licensed to sell Starbucks coffees.

Environmental Best Practices

Since 1998, Starbucks had partnered with Conservation International to promote coffee cultivation methods that protected biodiversity and maintained a healthy environment. A growing percentage of the coffees that Starbucks purchased were grown without the use of pesticides, herbicides, or chemical fertilizers; organic cultivation methods resulted in clean ground water and helped protect against degrading of local ecosystems, many of which were fragile or in areas where biodiversity was under severe threat. Another environmental conservation practice involved growing organic coffee under a natural canopy of shade trees interspersed with fruit trees and other crops; this not only allowed farmers to get higher crop yields from small acreages but also helped protect against soil erosion on mountainsides.

COFFEE-ROASTING OPERATIONS

Starbucks considered the roasting of its coffee beans to be something of an art form, entailing trial-and-error testing of different combinations of time and temperature to get the most out of each type of bean and blend. Recipes were put together by the coffee department once all the components had been tested. Computerized roasters guaranteed consistency. Each batch was roasted in a powerful gas oven for 12 to 15 minutes. Highly trained and experienced roasting personnel monitored the process, using both smell and hearing to help check when the beans were perfectly done—coffee beans make a popping sound when ready. Starbucks' standards were so exacting that roasters tested the color of the beans in a blood-cell analyzer and discarded the entire batch if the reading wasn't on target. After roasting and cooling, the coffee was immediately vacuum-sealed in one-way valve bags that let out gases naturally produced by fresh-roasted beans without letting oxygen in—one-way valve technology extended the shelf life of packaged Starbucks coffee to 26 weeks. As a matter of policy, however, Starbucks removed coffees on its shelves after three months and, in the case of coffee used to prepare beverages in stores, the shelf life was limited to seven days after the bag was opened.

In 2003, Starbucks had roasting plants in Seattle and Kent, Washington; York, Pennsylvania; Minden, Nevada; and the Netherlands. In addition to roasting capability, the Kent, Minden, York, and Netherlands plants also had additional space for warehousing and shipping coffees. The roasting plants and distribution facilities in Kent and Seattle supplied stores west of the Mississippi and in the Asia Pacific region. The newly constructed Minden plant/distribution center was used to supply stores in the Mountain West and Midwest. The roasting and distribution facility in York, which could be expanded to 1 million square feet, supplied stores mainly east of the Mississippi. The 70,000-square-foot facility in the Netherlands supplied stores in Europe and the Middle East.

STARBUCKS' CORPORATE SOCIAL RESPONSIBILITY STRATEGY

Howard Schultz's effort to "build a company with soul" included broad-based initiatives to contribute positively to the communities in which Starbucks had stores and to the environment. The guiding theme of Starbucks' social responsibility strategy was "Giving back to our communities is the way we do business." The Starbucks Foundation was set up in 1997 to orchestrate the company's philanthropic activities. Since 1991 Starbucks had been a major contributor to CARE, a worldwide relief and development organization that sponsored health, education, and humanitarian aid programs in almost all of the third world countries where Starbucks purchased its coffee supplies. Stores featured CARE in promotions and had organized concerts to benefit CARE. A second major philanthropic effort involved pro-

viding financial support to community literacy organizations. In 1995 Starbucks began a program to improve the conditions of workers in coffee-growing countries, establishing a code of conduct for its growers and providing financial assistance for agricultural improvement projects. In 1997, Starbucks formed an alliance with Appropriate Technology International to help poor, small-scale coffee growers in Guatemala increase their income by improving the quality of their crops and their market access; the company's first-year grant of $75,000 went to fund a new processing facility and set up a loan program for a producer cooperative.

Starbucks had an Environmental Committee that looked for ways not only to reduce, reuse, and recycle waste but also to contribute to local community environmental efforts. A Green Store Task Force looked at how Starbucks stores could conserve on water and energy usage and generate less solid waste. Customers who brought their own mugs to stores were given a 10-cent discount on beverage purchases (in 2002, customers used commuter mugs in making purchases about 12.7 million times). Coffee grounds, which made up a big portion of the waste stream in stores, were packaged and given to customers, parks, schools, and plant nurseries as a soil amendment. Company personnel purchased paper products with high levels of recycled content and unbleached fiber to help Starbucks minimize its environmental footprint. Stores participated in Earth Day activities each year with in-store promotions and volunteer efforts to educate employees and customers about the impacts their actions had on the environment. Suppliers were encouraged to provide the most energy-efficient products within their category and eliminate excessive packaging; Starbucks had recently instituted a Code of Conduct for suppliers of noncoffee products that addressed standards for social responsibility, including labor and human rights. No genetically modified ingredients were used in any food or beverage products that Starbucks served, with the exception of milk (U.S. labeling requirements do not require milk producers to disclose the use of hormones aimed at increasing the milk production of dairy herds).

Starbucks stores participated regularly in local charitable projects of one kind or another, donating drinks, books, and proceeds from store-opening benefits. Employees were encouraged to recommend and apply for grants from the Starbucks Foundation to benefit local community literacy organizations.

exhibit 9   **Starbucks' Environmental Mission Statement**

Starbucks is committed to a role of environmental leadership in all facets of our business.
We fulfill this mission by a commitment to:
- Understanding of environmental issues and sharing information with our partners.
- Developing innovative and flexible solutions to bring about change.
- Striving to buy, sell, and use environmentally friendly products.
- Recognizing that fiscal responsibility is essential to our environmental future.
- Instilling environmental responsibility as a corporate value.
- Measuring and monitoring our progress for each project.

On the Fourth of July weekend in 1997, three Starbucks employees were murdered in the company's store in the Georgetown area of Washington, D.C.; Starbucks offered a $100,000 reward for information leading to the arrest of the murderer(s). The company announced that it would reopen the store in early 1998 and donate all future net proceeds of the store to a Starbucks Memorial Fund that would make annual grants to local groups working to reduce violence and aid the victims of violent crimes.

Starbucks felt so deeply about its responsibilities that it even developed an environmental mission statement to expand on its corporate mission statement (see Exhibit 9). In 2002 Starbucks also began issuing an annual "Corporate Social Responsibility Report" (the reports for recent years can be viewed in the Investors section at www.starbucks.com). Going into 2004, Starbucks had received 20 awards from a diverse group of organizations for its philanthropic, community service, and environmental activities.

STARBUCKS' EXCURSION INTO DOT-COM BUSINESSES

In the late 1990s, Howard Schultz became enamored with the potential of the Internet and pushed Starbucks into a series of dot-com investments:

- Cooking.com—a Santa Monica–based e-tailer of kitchenwares, which was still operating in late 2003, although it had not yet earned a profit.
- Living.com, Inc.—an online retailer of furniture and home products in which Starbucks invested $20.3 million. Living.com filed for bankruptcy in mid-2000, even though it had recently been rated as the best online retailer of furniture by e-commerce analyst Gomez.com. Living.com had allied with Amazon.com (which was also an investor) to market its products under the "Home" tab on Amazon's Web site.
- Kozmo.com, Inc.—an Internet start-up that offered fast and free delivery of products such as video games, movies, snacks, and magazines. Starbucks and Kozmo entered into a joint marketing pact in early 2000 that called for Kozmo.com to pay Starbucks $150 million over the next five years for prominent placement in Starbucks shops. Under the terms of the deal, Kozmo would locate "drop boxes" for the return of videos and other items in Starbucks stores throughout the cities where Kozmo operated. Kozmo also agreed to deliver packaged Starbucks coffees, teas, and other products, and look into opportunities to deliver hot beverages. The agreement was a crucial part of Kozmo's planned expansion to 21 U.S. cities by the end of 2000; Kozmo currently offered one-hour delivery of videos, books, magazines, meals, snacks and beverages in the New York, San Francisco, Boston, Seattle, and Washington, D.C., markets. Kozmo, which began operations in March 1998 to deliver videos in the Greenwich Village section of Manhattan, had secured $28 million in venture capital funding in 1999 and reportedly received $60 million from Amazon.com and an additional $30 million from Japanese Internet investor Softbank in January 2000. After burning through some $280 million in capital and getting little interest from consumers, Kozmo closed down operations in April 2001.
- Talk City, Inc.—a 1996 start-up founded by former Apple employees to create chat rooms and online communities on its own Web site as well as for other sites. Starbucks had invested in a $20 million pre-IPO offering of Talk City stock in 1999. Talk City generated most of its revenue from advertising and sponsorships on its sites. Howard Schultz planned to promote Talk City's

Web chats at Starbucks stores offering Internet access to patrons. Talk City shut down its Web site and filed for Chapter 7 bankruptcy in August 2002, after changing its name to LiveWorld in 2001 and then selling its assets to MyESP.com in late 2001. LiveWorld's customers included the Internal Revenue Service, Cisco Systems, Eastman Kodak, Coca-Cola, and Costco; its revenues reached a peak of about $14.8 million, but the company was never profitable, with annual losses running as high as $42 million.

In the fourth quarter of 2000, Starbucks wrote off the full amount of its equity investment in Living.com and the majority of its equity investments in Cooking.com, Kozmo.com, and Talk City—a total of $58.8 million.

THE SPECIALTY COFFEE INDUSTRY

While the market for traditional commercial-grade coffees had stagnated since the 1970s, the specialty coffee segment had expanded as interested, educated, upscale consumers became increasingly inclined to upgrade to premium coffees with more robust flavors. Whereas retail sales of specialty coffees amounted to only $45 million in 1969, by 1994 retail sales of specialty coffees had increased to $2 billion, much of which stemmed from sales in coffee bars or the shops of coffee-bean retailers (like Peet's). The increase was attributed to wider consumer awareness of and appreciation for fine coffee, the emergence of coffee bars featuring a blossoming number of premium coffee beverages, and the adoption of a healthier lifestyle that prompted some consumers to replace alcohol with coffee. Coffee's image changed from one of just a breakfast or after-dinner beverage to a drink that could be enjoyed anytime in the company of others. Many coffee drinkers took to the idea of coffee bars where they could enjoy a high-caliber coffee beverage and sit back and relax with friends or business associates.

Some industry experts expected the gourmet coffee market in the United States to be saturated by 2005. But the international market was much more wide open as of early 2004. The United States, Germany, and Japan were the three biggest coffee-consuming countries.

Competitors

In 2003, there were an estimated 14,000 specialty coffee outlets in the United States, with some observers predicting there would as many as 18,000 locations selling specialty coffee drinks by 2015. Starbucks' success was prompting a number of ambitious rivals to scale up their expansion plans. No other specialty coffee rival had even as many as 250 stores, but there were at least 20 small local and regional chains that aspired to compete against Starbucks in their local market arenas, most notably Tully's Coffee (98 stores in 4 states), Gloria Jean's (280 mall locations in 35 states and several foreign countries), New World Coffee (30 locations), Brew HaHa (15 locations in Delaware and Pennsylvania), Bad Ass Coffee (about 30 locations in 10 states and Canada), Caribou Coffee (241 locations in 9 states), Second Cup Coffee (the largest chain based in Canada), and Qwiky's (India). While it had been anticipated in the late 1990s that local and regional chains would merge to better position themselves as an alternative to Starbucks, such consolidation had not occurred as of 2003. But numerous retail entrepreneurs had picked up on the growing popularity of specialty coffees and opened coffee bars in high-pedestrian-traffic locations to serve espresso, cappuccino, lattes, and other coffee drinks.

In late 2003, McDonald's announced it would begin opening a new type of store called McCafe featuring premium coffee and made-to-order specialty drinks in a café-style setting, with Internet access also available. Krispy Kreme Doughnuts had recently upgraded the number and quality of the coffee drinks it offered at its locations.

Starbucks also faced competition from nationwide coffee manufacturers such as Kraft General Foods (the parent of Maxwell House), Procter & Gamble (the marketer of Folger's and Millstone brands), and Nestlé, all of which distributed their coffees through supermarkets. There were also dozens of specialty coffee companies that sold whole-bean coffees in supermarkets—brands like Green Mountain, Allegro, Peaberry, Brothers, and Millstone. Because many consumers were accustomed to purchasing their coffee supplies at supermarkets, it was easy for them to substitute whatever specialty coffee brand or brands were featured in their local supermarkets for Starbucks. But despite the upsurge of interest in specialty coffees, the National Coffee Association reported that regular coffee still accounted for 87 percent of all coffee consumed in the United States in 2002; some industry experts believed that this statistic signaled that the gourmet coffee segment was still emerging.

Growing numbers of restaurants were upgrading the quality of the coffee they served. And both General Foods and Procter & Gamble had introduced premium blends of their Maxwell House and Folger's coffees on supermarket shelves, pricing them several dollars below Starbucks' offerings.

Future Challenges

In fiscal 2004, Starbucks planned to open approximately 1,300 new stores worldwide and to have comparable store sales growth of 3 to 7 percent. Top management believed that it could grow revenues by about 20 percent annually and net earnings by 20–25 percent annually for the next three to five years. To sustain the company's growth and make Starbucks one of the world's preeminent global brands, Howard Schultz believed that the company had to challenge the status quo, be innovative, take risks, and adapt its vision of who it was, what it did, and where it was headed. He was pushing Starbucks executives to consider a number of fundamental strategic questions. What could Starbucks do to make its stores an even more elegant "third place" that welcomed, rewarded, and surprised customers? What new products and new experiences could Starbucks provide that would uniquely belong to or be associated with Starbucks? How could Starbucks reach people who were not coffee drinkers? What new or different strategic paths should Starbucks pursue to achieve its objective of becoming the most recognized and respected brand in the world?

case 2

Netflix

Braxton Maddox
The University of Alabama

A large customer base and promising business model seemed like a formula for success, but for Reed Hastings, founder and CEO of on-line movie rental pioneer Netflix, the challenges had just begun. As he awaited a morning meeting, Hastings speculated how his company was to sustain itself and be added to the short list of dot-com wonder businesses that made it through the pioneer stages. With such large competitors holding the resources to mount strong, enduring attacks against Netflix, along with the ever-changing movie and entertainment industry, Hastings was faced with the challenge of how to sustain Netflix's growth and determine the best ways to respond to the competition.

So far, Netflix had remained a few steps ahead of its closest competitor, but that certainly didn't calm Hastings's mind. After successfully founding his first company, Pure Software, in 1991, Hastings led several acquisitions that allowed the company to become one of the 50 largest software companies in the world by 1997. Hastings then founded Netflix in 1997, launched the online subscription service in 1999, and led Netflix to a subscriber base of over 1 million in just three and a half years. (Online service AOL took six years to acquire the same number of subscribers.) During the third quarter of 2003, despite a rapidly changing industry, Netflix reported a stronger-than-expected boost in subscribers of 74 percent. Netflix had become not only one of the very few dot-com success stories but also a highly profitable one, growing substantially in the face of increasingly strong competition.

The strong success of Netflix had not gone unnoticed. Since its founding in 1997, Netflix had battled the ever-evolving channels of DVD entertainment and accumulated a steady stream of competitors, including retail giant Wal-Mart and movie rental leader Blockbuster Video. So far, Netflix had remained ahead of the game with, among other things, innovative technology and software to help manage its intricate rental system. Netflix had pioneered the online DVD rental industry when DVDs were rare and had developed a strong lead of customers, revenue, and brand recognition. "No one is going to out-hare Netflix," Hastings said. "Our danger is in a tortoise attack. Wal-Mart has the ability to mount such a steady, relentless attack."

In June 2003, Netflix won a patent that covered much of its business model and could be used to help stifle competition in the future or at least demand licensing fees for the service. Mike Schuh of Foundation Capital, one of Netflix's earliest financial backers, noted that the barriers to entry in the online DVD rental market were very low, but the barriers to profitability were extremely high. Besides new entrants, Netflix also faced a more powerful challenge: the likelihood that DVDs would soon no longer be the medium of choice for home entertainment and that customers would instead download movies to their PCs or TVs.

DVDs

The digital video disc (DVD) player was one of the most successful consumer electronic products of all time (see Exhibit 1). The DVD market was also one of the fastest-growing markets, experiencing unprecedented growth since its debut in 1997 (see Exhibit 2); the growth was largely attributed to dramatically falling component prices. DVD playback had worked its way into a number of electronic

Prepared under the supervision of Professor A. J. Strickland, The University of Alabama. Copyright © 2004 by Braxton Maddox and A. J. Strickland.

exhibit 1 **Revenues, Growth, and Market Share for DVD and VHS Rentals**

	1997	1998	1999	2000	2001	2002 E	2003 E	2004 E	2005 E	2006 E
Revenues ($ millions)										
DVD rental	$ 2	$ 22	$ 110	$ 747	$ 2,348	$ 4,218	$ 6,044	$ 7,429	$ 8,548	$ 9,574
VHS rental	8,973	9,634	10,003	9,537	8,471	7,210	5,951	5,043	4,292	3,433
Total rental	$8,975	$9,657	$10,113	$10,284	$10,819	$11,428	$11,995	$12,472	$12,840	$13,007
Growth										
DVD rental	NA	1,259%	396%	577%	214%	80%	43%	23%	15%	12%
VHS rental	NA	7%	4%	–5%	–11%	–15%	–17%	–15%	–15%	–20%
Total rental	NA	8%	5%	2%	5%	6%	5%	4%	3%	1%
% of total rental market										
DVD rental	0%	0%	1%	7%	22%	37%	50%	60%	67%	74%
VHS rental	100%	100%	99%	93%	78%	63%	50%	40%	33%	26%

exhibit 2 **DVD Growth and Penetration**

	1997	1998	1999	2000	2001	2002 E	2003 E	2004 E	2005 E	2006 E
DVD households (millions)	0.3	1.2	4.6	12.6	24.8	36	45.7	53.6	61.2	69
Growth	—	300%	284%	96%	96%	45%	27%	17%	14%	13%
TV households (millions)	100.2	102.1	103.2	104.8	106	107.2	108.4	109.7	110.9	112.2
Growth	—	2%	1%	2%	1%	1%	1%	1%	1%	1%
DVD penetration	0%	1%	4%	12%	23%	34%	42%	49%	55%	62%

devices, and DVD recording was expected to be an essential driver of the DVD market. DVD recorders were forecast to surpass sales of play-only DVD players by 2007, with an expected compound annual growth rate of 126 percent. DVD sales for 2003 were expected to reach $11.4 billion, up 34 percent from 2002 and double those of 2001.

DVD movies were available through a wide variety of channels to the consumer:

- Physical retail store and stand-alone outlet sales such as Wal-Mart and Best Buy.
- Physical retail store rental outlets such as Movie Gallery and Blockbuster Video.
- Web sites of both brick-and-mortar stores and Internet-only retailers such as Amazon.com.
- Online rental services such as Netflix and Wal-Mart's online service.
- PC downloads from Web sites such as Movielink or file-sharing programs such as Kazaa.

NETFLIX

Netflix was based in Los Gatos, California. As the world's largest online DVD rental service, it had a library of more than 15,000 movies to choose from. The idea was simple: customers signed up for a subscription to Netflix and created a "wish list" of all the movies they wanted to see; the list could be changed at any time. Provided the movies were available in Netflix's inventory, the DVDs were shipped to the customer free of charge. The unique aspect about Netflix was that it provided all the benefits of a typical movie rental store but without the hassle of having to return the rentals at a specific time. For a set fee each month, customers could rent as many DVDs as they wanted and keep them as long as they wanted—there were no due dates or late fees. The catch was that customers were limited to having only a certain number of DVDs in their possession at a time; the number allowed varied according to the customer's subscription level.

Netflix's 2003 pricing levels were as follows:

$13.95—four DVDs a month, two titles out at a time.

$19.95—unlimited DVDs, three out at a time.

$29.95—unlimited DVDs, five out at a time.

$39.95—unlimited DVDs, eight out at a time.

Netflix prided itself on fast, free service. It could reach more than half of its subscribers with next-day delivery and provided prepaid return envelopes for mailing back the DVDs. (See Exhibits 3 and 4 for Netflix income statements.)

In a survey by Netflix, customers said they rented twice as many movies per month as they did prior to joining Netflix. New Netflix customers also said they were immediately more satisfied with their home-entertainment experience than they were prior to joining Netflix. And 9 out of 10 customers said they were so satisfied with the service that they were willing to pitch it to family and friends.

Netflix's service was full of innovative technology designed to make browsing and selecting movies as easy as possible. One such innovative service was CineMatch, an Oracle database that organized Netflix's library of movies into clusters of similar movies and analyzed how customers rated them after they rented them. Those customers who rated similar movies in similar clusters were then matched as like-minded viewers. When a customer was online, Cine-Match looked at the clusters he or she had rented from in the past, determined which movies the customer had yet to rent in that cluster, and recommended only those movies that had been highly rated by matched viewers. "Over 50 percent of our traffic comes via the recommendation system," said Hastings. "It requires a lot of work in real time." Cine-Match ran on two Sun 420 systems and could generate thousands of predictions each second. The dataset of user ratings was stored on a third system. "The key is the quality of the data we use," said Neil Hunt, Netflix's vice president of e-commerce. "The more data we collect about user preferences, the better the recommendations."

Also to help keep customers happy, Netflix developed a sophisticated distribution system to speed up mailing times. It also built a system of 15 distribution centers across the country with the goal of having enough distribution centers to allow most Netflix customers to receive their DVDs within one day. The decentralized distribution system allowed Netflix an advantage over Wal-Mart and Blockbuster, each of which sent their DVDs out of only one warehouse. Sophistication came with the software Netflix used to keep track of its inventory. Netflix's system allowed the distribution centers to communicate to determine the fastest way of getting the DVDs to the customers. For example, suppose a customer placed

exhibit 3   **Netflix's Income Statements, 1999–2002 (in millions)**

	2002	2001	2000	1999
Net sales	$152.81	$ 75.91	$ 35.89	$ 5.01
Cost of goods sold	78.14	49.91	24.86	4.37
Gross profit	$ 74.67	$ 26.01	$ 11.03	$ 0.63
R&D expenditures	14.63	17.73	16.82	7.41
Selling, general, and administrative expenses	61.89	39.14	42.96	18.51
Income before depreciation and amortization	$ (1.84)	$(30.87)	$(48.75)	$(25.29)
Depreciation and amortization	n/a	n/a	n/a	n/a
Nonoperating income	(8.13)	(5.90)	(7.16)	(3.82)
Interest expenses	11.97	1.85	1.45	0.74
Income before tax	$ (21.95)	$(38.62)	$(57.36)	$(29.85)
Provision for income taxes	n/a	n/a	n/a	n/a
Minority interest	n/a	n/a	n/a	n/a
Investment gains (losses)	n/a	n/a	n/a	n/a
Other income	n/a	n/a	n/a	n/a
Net income before extra items	$ (21.95)	$(38.62)	$(57.36)	$(29.85)
Extra items	n/a	n/a	n/a	n/a
Discontinued operations	n/a	n/a	n/a	n/a
Net income	$ (21.95)	$(38.62)	$(57.36)	$(29.85)

an order for a specific DVD. The system first looked for that DVD at the closest distribution center to the customer. If that distribution center didn't have the DVD in stock, the system then moved the next closest center and checked there. This continued until the DVD was found and shipped. If the DVD was unavailable anywhere in the system, it was wait-listed. The system then moved to the customer's next choice and the process started all over. And no matter where the DVD was sent from, the system knew to print the return label to the distribution center closest to the customer to reduce return mail times.

BLOCKBUSTER VIDEO

Blockbuster Video was the world leader in the videocassette, DVD, and video game rental industry, holding a 65 percent market share of the $8.5 billion market. (See Exhibit 5 for the company's income statements, 1999–2002.) It had revenues of more than $5.5 billion in 2002—80 percent of which came from the United States. Founded in Dallas, Texas, in 1985, Blockbuster had grown to more than 8,500 company-operated franchised stores worldwide— with more than 2,600 stores outside the United States. Analysts predicted the movie/video game rental market to grow to more than $30 billion by 2006, and Blockbuster planned to be "the complete source" for movies and games, rental and retail.

In an increasing focus on retail, Blockbuster had developed innovative programs and expanded its in-store movie, DVD, and video game selection, including everything from the newest releases to a wide collection of older titles in a number of genres. One such innovative program was developed in September of 2000, when Blockbuster began to market the pay-per-view service DIRECTV in 3,800 of its stores. After the initial success of the alliance, Blockbuster co-branded with DIRECTV in July 2001 and thus established its presence in the pay-per-view movie industry. The Blockbuster pay-per-view service offered 44 movie selections a day to subscribers.

exhibit 4 **Netflix's Quarterly Income Statements, Quarter 4, 2002–Quarter 3, 2003 (in millions)**

	Quarter 3 2003	Quarter 2 2003	Quarter 1 2003	Quarter 4 2002
Net sales	$72.20	$63.19	$55.67	$40.73
Cost of goods sold	38.65	35.24	30.01	21.50
Gross profit	$33.55	$27.95	$25.66	$19.24
R&D expenditures	4.74	4.12	10.57	3.97
SGA expenses	23.18	19.27	15.46	16.08
Income before depreciation and amortization	$ 5.63	$ 4.55	$ (0.36)	$ (0.81)
Depreciation and amortization	n/a	n/a	n/a	n/a
Nonoperating income	(2.24)	(1.14)	(3.97)	(0.89)
Interest expenses	0.09	0.10	0.19	n/a
Income before tax	3.30	3.31	(4.52)	(1.70)
Provision for income taxes	n/a	n/a	n/a	n/a
Minority interest	n/a	n/a	n/a	n/a
Investment gains (losses)	n/a	n/a	n/a	n/a
Other income	n/a	n/a	n/a	n/a
Net income before extra items	3.30	3.31	(4.52)	(1.70)
Extra items				
Discontinued operations	n/a	n/a	n/a	n/a
Net income	3.30	3.31	(4.52)	(1.70)

Blockbuster also began investigating the online DVD rental market. In 2002 it acquired Film Caddy, one of Netflix's smaller competitors. Blockbuster felt that online rental was a niche market but was nonetheless focused on a program it planned to roll out the following year that would integrate online and in-store rentals.

WAL-MART

Even as Blockbuster gained ground with online rentals, Netflix had an even larger new entrant to contend with. As Netflix's Reed Hastings said, "Wal-Mart has enough money to send a man to the moon; we alternate between stark raving fear and bracing optimism." Wal-Mart Stores, Inc., was the world's largest retailer, with $244.5 billion in sales in the fiscal year ending January 31, 2003. The company was an employer to more than 1.3 million associates worldwide through more than 3,200 facilities in the United States and more than 1,100 abroad.

Wal-Mart developed a rental DVD offer nearly identical to that of Netflix—DVDs, priced at $15.54 for unlimited service—in October 2002 and implemented it in June 2003 through Walmart.com. Its envelopes and movie selections were also nearly identical to Netflix's. Tom Adams, founder of Adams Market Research, said that although Walmart.com was gaining subscribers, it would have, at most, about a fifth of the number of Netflix subscribers at the end of 2003. Wal-Mart operated only 7 distribution centers, versus Netflix's 15, but planned to open more centers at other Wal-Mart facilities. Wal-Mart was also still working out the bugs with its online software, whereas Netflix had already spent several years debugging its software. Wal-Mart was definitely not known for its movie rental expertise.

MOVIE GALLERY

Movie Gallery was formed in 1985 by Joe Malugen and Harrison Parrish in Dothan, Alabama. It began

exhibit 5 **Blockbuster Video Income Statements, 1999–2002 (in millions)**

	2002	2001	2000	1999
Net sales	$ 5,565.90	$5,156.70	$4,960.10	$4,463.50
Cost of goods sold	2,358.70	2,420.70	2,036.00	1,762.50
Gross profit	$ 3,207.20	$2,736.00	$2,924.10	$2,701.00
R&D expenditures	n/a	n/a	n/a	n/a
Selling, general, and administrative expenses	2,636.30	2,531.90	2,389.30	2,187.00
Income before depreciation and amortization	$ 570.90	$ 204.10	$ 534.80	$ 514.00
Depreciation and amortization	233.80	423.70	459.10	392.30
Nonoperating income	7.00	0.90	9.00	3.00
Interest expenses	49.50	78.20	116.50	119.30
Income before tax	$ 294.60	$ (296.90)	$ (31.80)	$ 5.40
Provision for income taxes	103.00	(56.10)	45.40	71.80
Minority interest	n/a	n/a	n/a	n/a
Investment gains (losses)	n/a	n/a	n/a	n/a
Other income	(2.20)	0.50	1.30	(2.80)
Net income before extra items	$ 189.40	$ (240.30)	$ (75.90)	$ (69.20)
Extra items	n/a	n/a	n/a	n/a
Discontinued operations	(1,817.00)	n/a	n/a	n/a
Net income	$(1,627.60)	$ (240.30)	$ (75.90)	$ (69.20)

operating in southern Alabama and the Florida panhandle through its wholly owned subsidiary M.G.A., Inc. By 1992 the company had annual revenues of $6 million and a total of 37 stores. Movie Gallery grew through the acquisition of various mom-and-pop video stores and in 1994 had reached a total of 73 stores and annual revenues of $12 million.

In August of 1994, to further its growth, Movie Gallery completed an initial public offering (IPO) of its stock. The revenue received from this IPO was used to purchase video chains, mainly in the Southeast. The company then raised more public funds to continue the acquisition of stores to add to the Movie Gallery name. As a result of this intense expansion, Movie Gallery had grown to over 850 stores by way of more than 100 separate acquisitions and employed more than 6,000 associates in more than 24 states. This aggressive approach took off with no looking back.

From 1996 through 1998 Movie Gallery focused its attention away from expansion and toward fine-

tuning internal aspects of the company. Because Movie Gallery was essentially a conglomerate of different mom-and-pop and chain stores, the company focused on implementing the Movie Gallery culture and philosophy. The goals were to assimilate all the different movie stores and to differentiate Movie Gallery from the rest of the major movie rental stores. In 1999 the company once again undertook intense expansion, announcing the plans to construct 100 new stores. It then acquired Blowout Entertainment in May, which added 88 more stores to the company's arsenal. By the end of the year, Movie Gallery had taken in $276 million and had more than 950 stores in 31 states. To bring itself into the changing face of movie rental, Movie Gallery launched Moviegallery.com through a separate, wholly owned subsidiary. In 2000, Movie Gallery opened 100 new stores and relocated 25 stores.

Movie Gallery kicked off 2001 by winning the honor of Retailer of the Year (Large Chain) from the

exhibit 6   **Movie Gallery Income Statement and Balance Sheet Data, 2000–2003 (in thousands)**

Income Statement Data	Period Ending		
	January 5, 2003	January 6, 2002	December 31, 2000
Total revenue	$528,988	$369,131	$318,936
Cost of revenue	194,670	126,447	113,171
Gross profit	$334,318	$242,684	$205,765
Operating income	$ 35,881	$ 27,170	$ 19,690
Net income	$ 20,934	$ 14,356	$ 9,486

Balance Sheet Data	January 5, 2003	January 6, 2002	December 31, 2000
Total assets	$363,574	$270,132	$217,536
Total liabilities	104,523	107,950	88,327
Total stockholder equity	$259,051	$162,182	$129,209

Video Software Dealers Association. It followed by completing its largest single-chain acquisition to date, buying Video Update, an international video rental company. The acquisition of 100 retail stores in five Canadian provinces expanded Movie Gallery's store base by 30 percent and gave the company an international presence. By the end of 2001, Movie Gallery's annual revenues had surpassed $369 million.

In 2002 Movie Gallery planned to continue its aggressive expansion through 125 new store openings and multiple acquisitions. Movie Gallery was the third largest video specialty retailer in the United States, with 1,678 stores and more than 8,500 associates in 42 states and five Canadian provinces.

Movie Gallery had not implemented any online DVD rental service, but with its large and diverse geographic spread, entry into the online rental industry was not expected to be far away. (See Exhibit 6 for Movie Gallery's income statements, 2000–2003.)

WALT DISNEY'S MOVIES ON DEMAND

A popular criticism of the Netflix model was that, even though they could have a number of movies always at their disposal, customers had to wait at least a day to receive newly ordered DVDs. A strong upcoming threat against Netflix was the new technology of movies on demand. There were a number of ways companies could market this new idea, and one of these was being pioneered by entertainment titan Walt Disney. The service, called MovieBeam, could transmit a digital-quality movie to a receiver manufactured by Samsung. The movie was then stored on the receiver's hard drive, a process that allowed the customer the opportunity to watch the movie on his or her own schedule. MovieBeam's prices included a $6.99 monthly equipment service fee and a viewing fee of $3.99 each for new releases and $2.49 each for older titles. The viewing fee entitled the customer unlimited viewing of the title for 24 hours. MovieBeam had access to films released by DreamWorks, MGM, Miramax, New Line Cinema, Sony Pictures, Universal Studios, Warner Bros. Entertainment, Twentieth Century Fox, and Walt Disney Pictures.

MOVIELINK'S DOWNLOADABLE MOVIES

Another way consumers could watch movies on demand was by downloading the movies directly to their personal computers (PCs). One company that provided this service was MovieLink, formed in August 2001 as a joint venture between Metro-Goldwyn-Mayer Studios, Paramount Pictures, Sony Pictures, Warner Bros., and Universal Studios. Headquartered in Santa Monica, California, MovieLink had become the leading online movie download delivery service.

The download service offered customers with broadband Internet connections a wide selection of movies. After browsing the selection of movies, customers registered and rented movies using a valid credit card. There were no late fees or return times, and MovieLink did not require a subscription or membership. Instead, each movie was independently priced by the content provider and charged per rental. MovieLink also offered a downloadable program, MovieLink Manager, to help customers manage downloads, which could then be viewed with Windows Media Player or the RealOne Player. Customers could also easily connect their PCs to their TVs with an S-Cable, RCA composite connection, wireless connection, or cable connection to view the movies on a bigger screen, thus eliminating the problem of having to sit in front of a computer to watch a movie at home.

DVD RECORDERS

In addition to having the ability to copy and burn CDs and DVDs on a personal computer, consumers also now had the option to copy DVDs with new home theater DVD recorders. About the size of a VHS or DVD player, these drives allowed the user to quickly burn a digital copy of the DVD on a blank disc. Users could record live TV programs as well. Information from the original DVD or other audiovisual input was stored on an internal hard drive, ranging anywhere from 80 to 120 gigabytes, and could then be burned to the blank DVD.

PIRACY IN THE MOVIE INDUSTRY

In the late 1990s music sales were booming. This was of course before the advent of the infamous Napster and numerous other file-sharing Web sites that together cost the worldwide music industry an estimated $2.6 billion in sales in 2002. The technology used to pirate music files over the Internet was also allowing people to easily pirate movies. Web sites such as Kazaa, Morpheus, and iMesh were being used more and more to download movies that sometimes weren't even released in theaters yet. With the pirates just scratching the surface of the $65-billion-a-year film and TV business, entertainment companies were striving for ways to protect themselves from becoming the victims of the next wave of piracy attacks. Some 600,000 films were being downloaded illegally every day, costing film companies hundreds of millions in lost video sales.

Fortunately, movie and TV companies still had a little time to work. Downloading movies was still quite a large endeavor, requiring a couple of hours per movie. And only about 27 percent of the country's 66 million Internet users had the necessary broadband connections to accomplish downloading a movie in that amount of time. But the growing trend of ripping and burning movies to DVDs was quickly becoming an underground industry that by late 2003 cost the film studios an estimated $3 billion in lost DVDs sales.

It wasn't that film and entertainment companies wanted to keep movie downloads from happening—as Brian Roberts of Comcast noted, "We would certainly like to be able to make our content available in a digital world . . . but we need to feel secure that we're going to get paid for it." This was vitally important to film companies, for which DVD and home video sales were the major sources of revenues, even over theater revenues. The early success of online music stores such as Apple Computer Inc.'s iTunes provided much optimism among entertainment companies. These stores offered a large library of music files that customers could download at 99 cents per song. More than 5 million songs were sold by iTunes in the first two months of its operation—evidence that consumers were willing to accept limits on copyrights of music, and possibly movies, if the price was right.

THE FUTURE OF NETFLIX

Netflix had remained optimistic about the future, taking note of key market trends that indicated a strong, sustaining demand for its products. One such trend was that consumers were becoming more comfortable with the Internet. With the widespread adoption of more broadband technologies, consumers were able to do more on the Internet than ever before. And as the Internet continued to evolve, reaching the consumers in new innovative ways provided strong advantages. As hardware improved and the costs came down, the growth of DVD use as the preferred medium choice for at-home entertainment was accelerating quickly.

As ownership of DVDs had become more mainstream, so had Netflix's subscriber base. Women made up over half of Netflix's subscribers, and the average household income of new subscribers had fallen by approximately half over two years—indicating that online DVD rental was reaching a wider socioeconomic range. Topping it off was the ongoing love of Americans for the movies: 2002 was the highest-grossing box office year ever. And with Netflix providing an easy affordable way to explore the movies, consumers were beginning to make their choice for online DVD rental known. Netflix and Reed Hastings had their goals set: "Our vision is to change the way people access and view the movies they love. To accomplish that, on a large scale, we have to set a long-term goal to acquire 5 million subscribers in the U.S., or 5 percent of the U.S. TV households over the next four to seven years." Hastings was now challenged with how to sustain what Netflix had accomplished so far and how to reach the company's goal of 5 million subscribers, knowing very well that Wal-Mart and Blockbuster were not far behind.

Azalea Seafood Gumbo Shoppe in 2004

John E. Gamble

University of South Alabama

John Addison had just returned from lunch when his partner, Mike Rathle, remarked that Wal-Mart's weekly order for seafood gumbo had reached an all-time high of 200 cases. Addison was elated to hear the good news since, even though Wal-Mart had been Azalea Seafood Gumbo Shoppe's most important customer for several years, orders from the world's largest retailer had all but ceased during November 2003 because of a change in Azalea's shipping method and an accompanying change in Wal-Mart's internal purchasing procedure. Sales had increased considerably during December as Azalea tried to make sure seafood managers knew how to order the company's products using the new system, and by the first week of January 2004, the record order suggested that all of the kinks were finally worked out.

Azalea Seafood Gumbo Shoppe was among the nation's largest producers of ready-to-eat gumbo, with annual revenues in 2003 of more than $1 million. In 2004 the company's products could be found in approximately 1,000 supermarkets and were served in about 300 restaurants in the southeastern United States, but the recent problem with receiving orders from Wal-Mart and the company's slowing growth rate forced the two owners to think about their envisioned future for the company. After hearing of the Wal-Mart order, John Addison commented to Mike Rathle:

> What we've accomplished since we bought Azalea in 1991 is remarkable. We have successfully transitioned from a small retail seafood shop to one of the largest producers of gumbo in the U.S. We've gained

distribution to supermarkets, Wal-Mart Supercenters, Sam's Clubs and probably half the seafood restaurants within 100 miles of here. However, I think that we have several issues to consider. How large do we want to get? We are comfortable now at $1 million a year in sales, but do we want to grow to $1.5 million? Do we want sales of $5 million? $10 million? If we want greater sales, how will we achieve our growth? Should more of our sales come from supermarkets or food service? Do we need a new plant? Should we develop new products? Should we expand our catering business? Should we reestablish retail sales of fresh shrimp and crawfish?

Rathle agreed that Addison's questions were important and believed the two partners should try to settle on a strategic direction before the end of February since a great deal of their free time would be consumed by their catering business beginning at Mardi Gras and running through the end of the summer.

COMPANY HISTORY AND BACKGROUND

Azalea Seafood Gumbo Shoppe was established in Mobile, Alabama, in 1971 by Pat Lodds. Mobile was an attractive market for seafood sales because the city's location on the northern coast of the Gulf of Mexico made fresh seafood readily available and because seafood dishes were staples in most Mobilians' diets. Azalea Seafood Gumbo Shoppe, like other seafood shops in Mobile, offered customers fresh snapper, grouper, flounder, and shrimp caught in Mobile Bay and the Gulf of Mexico, but Azalea differed from its rivals by also selling prepared seafood gumbo that could be taken home for dinner.

The shop was located near the busy McGregor Avenue and Airport Boulevard intersection in a concrete-block building that had been a fried chicken restaurant in the mid-1960s. Azalea's sales of seafood were brisk from almost the day the store opened and its gumbo that was made using Lodds's 100-year-old family recipe became popular within months as word of the prepared gumbo spread. Many Mobilians possessed their own treasured gumbo recipes, but since gumbo was very difficult and time-consuming to prepare, it was much more convenient to drop by Azalea Seafood Gumbo Shoppe to pick up high-quality gumbo for that evening's dinner. The most trying aspect of preparing gumbo was making its roux base—a mixture of flour and oil that was cooked at a very high temperature. The skill took some time for most cooks to master because the flour and oil mixture had to be cooked until it reached a deep brown color without scorching.

Pat Lodds owned and operated Azalea Seafood Gumbo Shoppe until 1981, when it was sold to Jim Hartman. Hartman continued to sell fresh fish and freshly prepared gumbo to walk-in customers but also began to freeze large gallon containers for sale to local seafood restaurants that might not be able to cook a good gumbo. Hartman also began to prepare and sell shrimp creole to walk-in customers and area restaurants because the product required ingredients similar to those found in gumbo and used a similar preparation process. However, gumbo was by far the more popular seller of the two prepared food products. By 1991 Azalea's seafood gumbo was distributed by three food-service suppliers to about 30 restaurants along the Gulf Coast, and its sales remained relatively stable at about $10,000 to $15,000 a month. Even though the store was doing well, Jim Hartman began to grow tired of the daily routine and mentioned to a few business contacts and friends that he would entertain offers on the business. Three of Hartman's previous employees heard that the business was for sale and began to think about the possibility of purchasing Azalea Seafood Gumbo Shoppe.

Mike Rathle, John Addison, and Bill Sibley had been friends since attending McGill-Toolen High School together and working at the seafood shop after school during their senior year. Upon high school graduation, Rathle and Addison attended the University of South Alabama, where Rathle obtained a marketing degree and Addison graduated with a degree in international business. Sibley began a career with International Paper, where he was employed at the company's Mobile mill as a Safety Coordinator when he heard that Jim Hartman was interested in selling his seafood business. The news immediately intrigued Sibley, and he contacted his two longtime friends to discuss a partnership to purchase the business. Rathle and Addison were both busy operating a small construction company at the time, but they were interested in hearing more about the opportunity. After hearing the details, Rathle believed that he could leverage the knowledge he had gained while employed with Brach's Candy as an area sales manager to expand Azalea's gumbo into supermarkets. Addison agreed that Azalea could be an attractive investment opportunity if the company's gumbo sales could be expanded into supermarkets and additional restaurants, so he joined his two friends in the new venture.

The three friends approached Jim Hartman with an offer, and by August 1991 they owned and operated the seafood and gumbo shop where they had worked after school during the 12th grade. Once the three became owners of the business, Bill Sibley oversaw the company's gumbo production, while Mike Rathle immediately began to call on area supermarkets and restaurants to gain access to new customers for the company's prepared gumbo. John Addison was still involved with a number of construction projects but joined Sibley in Azalea's marketing efforts within a few months.

Shortly before the company's first anniversary of new ownership, the three partners were notified that their building lease would not be renewed because a shopping center would be built on the property where Azalea Seafood Gumbo Shoppe had operated since 1971. Relocating would be a problem since it would be difficult to move the kitchen equipment and freezers without disrupting the company's production. The three partners spent the days following the eviction notice dreading the prospects of moving. But before they had an opportunity to look at other properties, a competing gumbo producer who was retiring approached them and offered Azalea his kitchen equipment and freezers for $5,000. In addition, Azalea could assume the former competitor's building lease. Mike Rathle stated that the timing of the offer was a "godsend because we were able to pick up our ingredients and move to a turnkey operation without losing a beat."

The new 2,200-square-foot production facility was much larger than Azalea's previous building and was located on a one-acre parcel of land that also included a frame house built in the 1930s. The house was located only about 100 feet from the concrete-block plant and could be used as an office. The only drawback to the new building was that its location on a quiet street outside the city limits was too far from high-traffic areas to support retail sales of fresh seafood and prepared gumbo. The partners had considered giving up retail sales and focusing on commercial accounts before they knew of their pending lease termination and saw the move as the deciding factor. With a clear vision of Azalea's future business and the new production facility's production capacity of eight tons a day, Rathle and Addison began to aggressively pursue new supermarket and food-service accounts. They were able to land account after account over the next 10 years, and in 2004 Azalea Seafood Gumbo Shoppe produced more than 45 tons of gumbo and other seafood products each month. Bill Sibley sold his interest in the business to John Addison and Mike Rathle in early 2001 to pursue other business opportunities.

OVERVIEW OF THE VALUE-ADDED SEAFOOD INDUSTRY

Value-added seafood products included any type of packaged food item including seafood as an ingredient. Value-added seafood producers purchased fresh, frozen, or cooked seafood to use in creating their products for sale to restaurants, supermarkets, or other types of food retailers. Food companies that sold seafood products either used their own marketing staffs to sell and distribute products to retailers and restaurants or contracted with food brokers to provide the marketing and logistical support needed to distribute their products. Packaged seafood products were also distributed by jobbers, independent sellers who purchased packaged food products directly from manufacturers and sold them to restaurants and grocers after a 15–20 percent markup.

Suppliers

Value-added seafood producers could readily obtain ingredients from seafood processors, fruit and vegetable producers, canned and dry-goods producers, or large food wholesalers that specialized in such ingredients. Large processed-food companies had considerable latitude in their choice of suppliers of ingredients since most ingredients were commodity-like and readily available from multiple sources. In some instances, large food companies were able to further improve their abilities to negotiate with suppliers by their own production of some key ingredients. Many times, smaller value-added producers did not have adequate volume to negotiate directly with the producer of ingredients but were able to select from a variety of wholesalers to obtain the best mix of quality and price for purchased ingredients.

Production

Packaged food production in the United States was regulated and monitored by the U.S. Food and Drug Administration (FDA), the U.S. Department of Agriculture (USDA), and state departments of public health. The latter usually monitored only the cleanliness of food producers' cooking areas and other facilities with monthly inspections, whereas the FDA required food producers to develop and implement a Hazard Analysis Critical Control Point (HACCP) system for their operations and comply with the provisions of the Food and Nutritional Labeling Act. The Nutritional Labeling and Education Act of 1990 required all packaged foods to bear nutrition labels providing a list of ingredients and nutritional facts about the product. The act also established standardized definitions for such terms used on food packaging as *low fat* and *light*. The USDA enforced the Federal Meat Inspection Act, which established sanitation standards for producers of meat and poultry products.

All seafood processors were required to develop an HACCP plan using guidelines provided by the FDA to ensure that packaged foods were free from such health hazards as pathogens and toxins. HACCP plans had to provide general information about the company's product and processes, describe the food, describe method of distribution and storage, identify intended use and consumer, and develop a flow diagram of the company's value chain. Food companies were also required to identify potential species-related and process-related health hazards and identify critical hazard control points. Once a food producer had set critical limits for health hazards, a monitoring procedure was developed and followed. Food companies were required to establish record-keeping and verification procedures that could be evaluated by the FDA during inspections.

Distribution

Processed food items were distributed either by the producer itself or by food wholesalers or brokers who represented a large number of companies producing many types of products. Sometimes a food broker or wholesaler might represent companies producing products in nearly every category found in supermarkets. Food brokers had become larger and their product offerings broader as a wave of acquisitions and mergers during the 1990s had reduced the number of food brokers in the United States from about 2,500 in 1990 to about 200 in 2001. Consolidation among food brokers was driven primarily by consolidation among food producers and food retailers. However, there remained a large number of small food brokers in the industry that focused on representing food companies in the sale of their products to restaurants.

Consolidation of Packaged Food Companies Throughout the 1990s and into the early 2000s, large global food companies like Unilever, Nestlé, and Kraft Foods had acquired smaller companies to fill gaps in their product lines and expand their global presence. Food brokers were forced to alter their business practices as the food industry consolidated, since larger food companies had greater service demands than small independent food producers. Smaller companies were typically pleased with a broker that could deliver products to supermarkets within a limited geographic region and assure that items were in stock and located in appropriate locations within stores. Large food companies that chose to outsource distribution considered contracts with brokers competitive resources that could be used to provide broader geographic coverage for their brands and that could contribute to efficient inventory management and replenishment systems. Global food manufacturers had also begun to demand

in-store marketing services from brokers in return for distributing their multiple brands. Brokers could be required to report stockouts, make price checks, and deliver up-to-the-minute inventory data to manufacturers' distribution centers. Brokers might also be asked to set up in-store displays, discuss new products with store managers, and conduct in-store product sampling. Small food manufacturers had much less ability to demand such services from food brokers. In fact, some small food producers might find it difficult to secure the services of a national food broker and would likely receive only minimal attention to their brand if a large broker did agree to distribute their product.

Consolidation of Supermarkets and Other Grocers Consolidation among grocery retailers also supported the trend toward fewer, larger food brokerages. In 2002, 42.8 percent of the $412 billion supermarket industry was accounted for by Wal-Mart, Kroger, Safeway, Albertson's, and Ahold USA. In 1995 the top five supermarket companies had accounted for only 26.5 percent of industry sales. Between 1997 and 2002 there were more than 75 mergers and acquisitions in the supermarket industry. Much of the industry's merger activity had occurred as a result of traditional supermarket companies' attempts to better compete with Wal-Mart. Wal-Mart did not enter the grocery industry until 1988, with the opening of its first Supercenter, but was crowned the U.S. supermarket leader in 2002 with annual grocery sales of $48.7 billion. Competition in the industry was expected to intensify further with Wal-Mart's planned addition of 1,500 supercenters between 2003 and 2008. In 2003, Wal-Mart operated 1,430 supercenters, 533 Sam's Clubs, and 60 Wal-Mart Neighborhood Markets. The industry's other leading grocery companies believed that mergers between the larger companies and acquisitions of smaller chains would provide greater purchasing power to meet Wal-Mart's discount pricing. Exhibit 1 presents estimated sales and number of stores with annual sales exceeding $2 million for the top 20 U.S. grocers.

Between 1997 and 2001, the grocery industry had experienced more than $15 billion in grocery bankruptcies and analysts believed that bankruptcies totaling another $15 billion would occur in the retail grocery industry between 2002 and 2005. One such

exhibit 1   **Estimated Sales and Number of Supermarket Locations for the Top 20 U.S. Grocers, Year-End 2002**

Rank	Company	Estimated Sales (in millions)	Number of Supermarket Locations (Store sales of $2 million or greater)
1	Wal-Mart*	$48,742	1,336
2	The Kroger Company*	44,782	2,482
3	Safeway	29,355	1,581
4	Albertson's	28,461	1,589
5	Ahold USA	25,010	1,270
6	Delhaize-America	14,733	1,445
7	Publix	14,528	749
8	Winn-Dixie	12,646	1,058
9	SUPERVALU	8,198	582
10	A&P	7,823	488
11	H-E-B Grocery Company	7,744	284
12	Meijer*	6,053	156
13	Military Commissaries	5,541	185
14	Shaw's	4,125	185
15	Pathmark	4,117	145
16	Hy-Vee	4,030	189
17	Aldi	3,739	775
18	Giant Eagle	2,950	122
19	Raley's	2,675	134
20	Wegman's	2,491	64

*Supercenter statistics reduced to include only traditional supermarket items.
Source: Progressive Grocer Annual Report, May 1, 2003.

bankruptcy involved Delchamps, Inc., a former Mobile, Alabama–based grocery chain that was acquired by Jackson, Mississippi's Jitney Jungle in 1997 in an attempt by both companies' management to gain greater purchasing power. In 1999 the Jitney Jungle–Delchamps chain included 198 stores with annual sales of approximately $2 billion, but it was forced to file for bankruptcy protection that same year and was dissolved in late 2000. The new company had been able to achieve some cost savings in purchasing, but any cost savings from lower prices on packaged goods was more than offset by the interest expense and debt service that accompanied the buyout. Jitney Jungle's stores and fixtures were purchased by Winn-Dixie, a chain with more than 1,000 stores in 14 states and by Bruno's, a 187-store chain operating in Alabama, Florida, Georgia, and Mississippi. Bruno's had emerged from its own Chapter 11 bankruptcy protection just months before it purchased 17 of Jitney Jungle's stores.

Like the large global food companies, large national grocers expected food brokers to provide national coverage and take a large role in inventory management and replenishment efforts. The grocery industry's razor-thin margins required that supermarkets have access to cutting-edge information systems to reduce spoilage of perishable items and keep popular items on the shelf while keeping store inventory levels at a minimum. SUPERVALU, the largest distributor of food products to U.S. grocers, offered comprehensive procurement, distribution, and replenishment services to more than 4,000 grocery stores and supermarkets in the United States. The company's logistics services featured activity-based costing, cross-docked warehouses, on-time delivery, 24/7 service, and Web-based ordering and invoicing. In addition to inventory management benefits, both large and small grocery chains profited from SUPERVALU's $19 billion purchasing power. Like many other large food brokers, SUPERVALU had made a number of acquisitions in recent years to boost its ability to provide better service and broader geographic coverage to food companies and grocers. In 2002 SUPERVALU was also the nation's ninth largest supermarket chain, with 582 stores and retail sales of $8.2 billion.

Distribution in the Food Service Industry

Even though the $180 billion U.S. food-service industry was highly fragmented, with more than 3,500 broadline food-service distributors and 15,000 specialty product suppliers that provided various food items to restaurants and other locations where prepared food was served, many industry participants believed that the industry would soon consolidate. Large food-service companies like SYSCO and U.S. Foodservice had begun to acquire food-service distributors of all types and in all geographic locations in the United States. SYSCO, the largest food-service company in the United States, with 2003 sales of $26.1 billion, provided more than 275,000 products to 420,000 different customers in all 50 states and portions of Canada. SYSCO had completed more than 19 acquisitions between 2000 and 2003 to expand its line of fresh and frozen meats, seafood, poultry, fruits and vegetables, canned and dry foods, equipment and supplies, beverages, bakery items, dairy products, disposables, medical and surgical products, and chemical and sanitation items sold to restaurants, hotels, schools, hospitals, and other locations where food was prepared.

U.S. Foodservice was the second largest food-service company in the United States, with 2002 sales of $18.5 billion. U.S. Foodservice had made a number of acquisitions immediately after its 2000 acquisition by Dutch supermarket giant Ahold but had been forced to curtail such investments in 2003 because of Ahold's struggling supermarket business. Ahold had total worldwide sales of more than 62 billion euros in 2002, with supermarkets in Europe, Latin America, and Asia in addition to its food-service business. The company's U.S. subsidiary, Ahold USA, was the fifth largest supermarket chain in the United States, with approximately 1,300 supermarkets and 2002 sales of $25 billion. Ahold's restructuring plan called for the reengineering of its supermarket operations, the divestiture of its stores in Spain, and the closing of poorly performing stores worldwide. U.S. Foodservice did not anticipate any additional acquisitions during Ahold's restructuring.

The growing size and strength of food-service distributors had little effect on jobbers since jobbers had traditionally been forced to call on small accounts or distribute only items needed by restaurants on an infrequent basis. A jobber was usually a one-person operation with company assets limited to a single refrigerated truck. Jobbers lacked any formal relationship with food producers and usually operated on a cash-and-carry basis. Jobbers typically purchased only a few cases of items at any given time for their daily calls to small restaurants that might need a case or two of some food item. Few jobbers had annual sales of over $400,000, but they were important distributors for small restaurants that lacked the sales volume to establish an account with a large food-service company.

Food brokers also played a role in the food-service industry. Many small- and medium-sized food companies would contract with food brokers to promote their products to restaurants that were served by food-service distributors that purchased their products. For example, once a food-service distributor agreed to purchase a food company's product, food brokers could be hired to create pull for that product by marketing the product directly to the food distributor's restaurant customers. In return, food brokers typically received a 5 percent commission on a food company's sales increases to food distributors.

Growth in Sales of Meals Eaten Away from Home

Consolidation of the U.S. food-service industry was also likely because of opportunity presented by the rapid growth in the number of meals eaten away from home. In 2003, nearly 70 billion meals were eaten in more than 850,000 restaurants, schools, work cafeterias, hospitals, nursing homes, and other places where meals were served. Restaurants' share of the food dollar had grown from 33 percent in 1980 to 46 percent in 2003. Americans were projected to spend 53 percent of their food dollars in restaurants by 2010. In addition, the restaurant industry's sales were projected to grow from $421 billion in 2003 to $577 billion in 2010. Companies like SYSCO and Ahold were willing to make further investments in the food-service industry to capture a greater share of the rapidly growing industry. Also, food service offered Ahold business diversification beyond sales of food items in supermarkets while keeping the company from straying too far from its core competencies in the grocery business.

AZALEA SEAFOOD GUMBO SHOPPE IN 2004

In 2004, Azalea Seafood Gumbo Shoppe's seafood gumbo, crawfish étouffée, shrimp creole, and shrimp-and-crabmeat bisque were distributed to more than 1,000 supermarkets, 20 Sam's Clubs, and approximately 300 restaurants in the southeastern United States. The company's sales had grown at a compounded rate of 33 percent between 1992 and 1999. The company's 2000 sales fell by 15 percent after Jitney Jungle filed for Chapter 11 bankruptcy protection and later ceased operations. As an unsecured supplier, Azalea had no ability to recover the outstanding account of more than $100,000. The company's 2000 sales were also adversely affected by a kitchen worker's decision to stamp gumbo containers with a date stamp after a stamp showing a lot number broke. The company had to eventually recall more than $100,000 worth of gumbo when consumers and retailers believed that the date was an expiration date that had passed. Revenues were decreased further when Publix supermarkets stopped placing orders with Azalea because of the recall. Azalea's revenues had grown at a more modest 6.5 percent annual rate between 2001 and 2003 although its profits had grown at a more rapid pace as company management had refined the implementation of its strategy. Azalea Seafood Gumbo Shoppe's income statements for 1996 through 2003 are presented in Exhibit 2. The company's balance sheets for 1996 through 2003 are presented in Exhibit 3.

Azalea's Product Line

Azalea Seafood Gumbo Shoppe produced fully cooked seafood gumbo, crawfish étouffée, shrimp creole, and shrimp-and-crabmeat bisque, all of which were sold in quart, half-gallon, and gallon containers. The company's seafood products were sold frozen and were ready to serve after thawing and heating. Azalea's quart and half-gallon containers were sold in supermarkets and wholesale clubs and its gallon containers were sold to restaurants and other food-service customers. The company's gumbo was its best-selling item, accounting for approximately 90 percent of its annual sales. Azalea's seafood gumbo, like other gumbos, was a stewlike soup containing a roux base, okra, crabmeat, shrimp,

and spices that traced its roots to the Acadians who migrated from Canada to the New Orleans area in the late 1700s. The Acadians borrowed heavily from the Native Americans and the French and Spanish settlers who lived near the Mississippi Delta in perfecting many of today's Cajun recipes. Azalea Seafood Gumbo Shoppe's authentic Louisiana-style seafood gumbo had been featured in the "Taste of America" sponsored by the National Press Club in Washington, D.C., and had been served in the White House during the Reagan presidency.

Azalea added a white cream sauce–based shrimp-and-crabmeat bisque in 1997 and introduced a crawfish étouffée in 1998. Étouffée was another Cajun-style dish that was usually served over rice but could also be served alone or in a bread bowl or pie shell. Azalea's crawfish étouffée received the San Francisco Seafood Show's Silver Award for Best New Product in 1998. Nutritional label information for all four products is presented in Exhibit 4.

Azalea's Production Process

Azalea operated on a just-in-time production schedule with relatively short production runs that were initiated as needed to fill orders from distributors and retailers. Mike Rathle and John Addison shared responsibility for planning and organizing the company's overall production process, but the company's kitchen manager was responsible for running the day-to-day kitchen operations and coordinating the efforts of Azalea's three full-time and two part-time kitchen workers. Rathle's responsibility for planning and organizing the kitchen operations included scheduling the batch-cooking activities and purchasing ingredients used in Azalea's products. The company purchased fresh vegetables, fresh cooked crabmeat, cooked frozen shrimp, and packaging directly from manufacturers; it purchased other ingredients and supplies from one primary and two secondary food distributors. Even though Azalea's production plant was located on the Gulf of Mexico, where seafood was readily available, Addison and Rathle had found that shrimp landed, cooked, and flash-frozen in California could be purchased at better prices. Most of the company's supply of crabmeat and crawfish was landed and processed by Gulf Coast fisheries.

Azalea attempted to eliminate as much preparation as possible and concentrate only on the production of its gumbo, bisque, étouffée, and creole items. The company purchased diced vegetables and cooked shrimp, crabmeat, and crawfish to eliminate labor-intensive cooking preparation activities. In addition, the purchase of processed vegetables and seafood reduced food waste and allowed for shorter cleanup periods.

Gumbo was cooked to order each day in the company's 150-gallon insulated steam kettle. Shrimp-and-crabmeat bisque, shrimp creole, and crawfish étouffée were not cooked every day since orders for those products were less frequent than those for the company's gumbo. The gumbo and other products were cooked for approximately one and a half hours in the steam kettle before being transferred to quart, half-gallon, or gallon plastic tubs that would be stocked in supermarket freezers. Exhibit 5 presents an image of Azalea's products displayed in supermarket cooler, along with pictures of the company's production facility and office, a serving of seafood gumbo, and scenes from a catering event.

Sales and Marketing

John Addison and Mike Rathle were both responsible for the company's sales and marketing efforts. When either partner identified a potential new customer, typically he would give price quotes over the phone and ship samples of the product to the company to evaluate. If the grocer or food-service distributor was interested in the new product, meetings would be set up to finalize the details. Their approach to developing new accounts had been successful with grocery accounts established with Wal-Mart, Bruno's, Winn-Dixie, Publix, Greer's, and Randall's (see Exhibit 6 for a list of Azalea's supermarket accounts). Azalea had also developed a relationship with Associated Grocers, a food distributor that specialized in delivering food and beverage products to small mom-and-pop grocers. The company used the same approach to develop food-service accounts and had been able to gain access to more than 300 restaurants through distribution agreements with U.S. Foodservice and Wood Fruitticher.

Establishing an account with a regional office of a national grocer usually took time, hard work, and some good fortune. Rathle explained how personal contacts, persistence, and salesmanship played a role in Azalea's gaining access to distribution in about 300 Wal-Mart Supercenters and 20 Sam's Clubs in the southeastern United States:

> We got into Wal-Mart because a local Supercenter manager liked our product and asked that we sell to him on a direct delivery basis. Our product was selling well in that one store and I found out that a person I knew while working for Brach's was a grocery manager for Wal-Mart. I called him up and said, "You guys need to get me in the warehouse. Look at the volume I'm selling down here in this one store." Two weeks later we were in the warehouse selling to 300 Wal-Marts and 20 Sam's stores.
>
> We were also lucky in the way that Wood Fruitticher became a distributor for our gumbo. John just called them up one day and told them what volume we could supply and they said, "Ship it." Other accounts are very difficult to land. We've been in Winn-Dixie regionally for a long time, but we've made no progress working with their corporate people to get our gumbo distributed on a national basis.

Addison and Rathle's marketing efforts to grocers also included trying to keep a favorable product placement in its distribution network of 1,000 supermarkets. This was a challenging task since it was impossible for the two partners to call on all 1,000 store managers or seafood managers. Many times, store managers might decide to move items around in the store and Azalea's gumbo might be moved to an unfavorable freezer location without Addison or Rathle's knowledge. The company had hired a number of food brokers to ensure favorable placement but found that most brokers weren't willing to devote much attention to a company with a single product line. Azalea had found one food broker on the Mississippi Gulf Coast who was willing to represent the company and had maintained a good relationship with the broker since 2000. Azalea had also hired a full-time sales person in 2003 to develop new accounts and check product placement in Mobile-area supermarkets. The company's in-store placement in Wal-Mart and Sam's was not a concern since Wal-Mart maintained a Plan-O-Gram that standardized product placement in all stores. Rathle explained how the product's placement in the store had such a large bearing on its sales:

> One of our biggest problems in supermarkets is having our product moved down to the end of a freezer aisle by the bait shrimp or getting stuck at the top right corner of stand-up freezer. The best placement is center face—right at eye level. We usually have

exhibit 2 **Azalea Seafood Gumbo Shoppe, Income Statements, 1996–2003**[1]

	2003	2002	2001	2000	1999	1998	1997	1996
Revenues								
Wholesale sales	$1,019,024	$977,012	$901,343	$1,036,570	$1,222,452	$1,327,346	$944,522	$880,914
Catering	14,838	13,953	10,459	18,937	16,146	10,613	20,575	5,980
Allowances/damages	(8,410)	(8,685)	(8,967)	(11,936)	(5,800)	(4,453)	(1,855)	(1,669)
Sales discounts	(7,579)	(7,369)	(6,239)	(2,004)	(3,627)	(13,683)	(8,291)	(9,742)
Total revenues	1,017,872	$974,911	$896,596	$1,041,567	$1,229,171	$1,319,823	$954,951	$875,484
Cost of goods sold								
Cost of ingredients	336,822	$323,149	$344,793	$440,673	$501,554	$555,873	$449,086	$401,812
Cost of containers	103,082	97,754	95,676	82,813	94,368	97,520	67,120	57,519
Freight and shipping	31,696	31,696	17,605	24,249	26,384	35,925	8,039	10,494
Payroll—officers[2]	11,912	11,912	58,680	84,186	123,260	138,363	108,480	107,873
Payroll—other	92,931	90,702	72,827	97,248	107,016	123,446	50,206	46,101
Commission/brokerage	1,602	1,664	1,805	480	463	4,708	0	2,206
Cost of goods sold	578,045	$556,878	$591,386	$729,650	$853,046	$955,833	$682,931	$626,005
Gross profit	$ 439,827	$418,032	$305,210	$311,917	$376,125	$363,990	$272,020	$249,479
Expenses								
Advertising	$ 0	$ 0	$ 4,786	$ 3,973	$ 16,633	$ 14,626	$ 9,217	$ 2,421
Bad debt expense[3]	1,357	29,303	770	0	5,634	0	0	0
Bank charges	1,523	1,523	954	1,316	5,682	4,367	9,437	1,260
Contract labor	2,436	2,436	2,571	2,071	687	976	1,103	254
Contributions	607	882	331	607	1,646	816	1,081	1,294
Covenant not to compete expense[4]	4,525	4,525	3,770	0	0	0	0	0
Depreciation expense	47,207	45,261	38,470	31,202	39,738	41,000	20,388	19,496
Dues and subscriptions	563	539	335	909	83	286	183	264
Equipment rental	3,702	3,702	2,902	1,265	296	1,658	943	326
Entertainment and meals	760	729	384	1,909	2,414	1,592	342	2,442
Insurance	47,002	45,064	41,647	43,442	28,275	31,741	21,681	21,522
Interest expense	13,372	12,079	13,339	12,133	11,188	12,623	5,298	6,268
Janitorial and pest control	2,833	3,029	3,319	3,177	4,473	4,394	7,102	2,026
Miscellaneous	315	315	829	179	190	0	817	0

exhibit 2 (concluded)

Revenues	2003	2002	2001	2000	1999	1998	1997	1996
Postage	182	144	268	169	356	961	410	334
Office expense	1,456	1,456	1,967	2,510	3,141	4,635	2,884	3,662
Payroll tax expense	9,688	9,288	10,992	16,249	19,911	21,988	12,627	12,341
Penalties	2,153	3,791	1,302	1,134	5,800	847	529	0
Product demo costs	10,867	10,779	3,320	10,368	45,344	105,683	30,520	46,951
Product sampling	69	0	43	250	670	1,785	2,512	0
Professional fees	7,675	7,296	9,543	6,085	5,813	6,457	6,177	7,554
Rent	13,071	13,071	14,560	14,560	14,560	15,718	11,030	14,339
Repairs and maintenance	8,654	8,297	11,029	26,258	19,553	7,799	3,462	11,368
Service charges	2,043	1,298	3,202	3,863	3,662	2,108	1,660	4
Security	844	789	1,064	283	1,692	1,180	728	1,037
Supplies	2,599	2,434	3,085	3,219	9,775	6,360	1,667	1,554
Taxes and licenses	3,930	3,422	4,715	1,222	2,782	1,488	2,103	2,899
Telephone	8,128	7,640	8,119	13,015	16,405	16,899	11,595	12,613
Travel	580	515	636	2,927	4,343	5,333	3,317	864
Truck lease	13,618	13,618	12,414	16,891	15,820	18,894	13,721	13,984
Truck expenses	10,587	10,151	10,501	15,375	10,526	5,543	5,553	8,067
Uniforms and laundry	0	0	0	1,999	3,913	3,664	2,113	1,796
Utilities	23,860	23,011	21,099	21,816	21,527	19,767	17,526	19,445
Total expenses	246,202	$266,387	$232,268	$ 260,376	$ 322,530	$ 361,186	$207,726	$216,384
Net income	$ 193,625	$151,646	$ 72,942	$ 51,541	$ 53,595	$ 2,804	$ 64,294	$ 33,094

[1]Azalea Seafood Gumbo Shoppe's financial statements have been disguised. However, the relationships remain intact.
[2]Azalea Seafood Gumbo Shoppe officers agreed to reduce salaries and take larger distributions in 2002.
[3]Write-off of bad debt associated with bankruptcy of Jitney-Jungle.
[4]Covenant not to compete related to exit of a third business partner.

exhibit 3 **Azalea Seafood Gumbo Shoppe, Balance Sheets, 1999–2003[1]**

	2003	2002	2001	2000	1999	1998	1997	1996
Assets								
Current assets								
Cash	$ (20,146)	$ (18,962)	$ (35,088)	$ (12,249)	$ (22,689)	$ 6,467	$ (23,542)	$ (18,345)
Accounts receivable	72,048	64,794	83,655	98,347	130,043	93,444	99,777	62,143
Other current assets								
Inventory—finished goods	10,991	10,809	10,424	6,337	11,189	11,145	9,134	6,580
Inventory—raw materials	16,570	15,845	17,172	21,503	34,686	33,990	34,223	29,913
Prepaid insurance	10,181	10,250	7,676	10,554	7,771	5,940	6,325	5,316
Total other current assets	37,742	36,904	35,272	38,393	53,646	51,074	49,681	41,810
Total current assets	$ 89,644	$ 82,736	$ 83,839	$124,491	$160,999	$150,985	$125,916	$ 85,608
Fixed assets								
Equipment and machinery	$332,295	$326,858	$289,203	$293,064	$206,477	$198,423	$150,484	$106,616
Office equipment and furniture	9,966	9,966	9,966	9,966	9,966	9,966	7,406	7,406
Leasehold improvements	12,147	12,147	12,147	12,147	12,147	12,147	1,663	1,663
Vehicles	121,944	121,944	31,055	31,055	31,055	17,819	16,134	16,134
Accumulated depreciation	(333,366)	(281,297)	(236,036)	(196,989)	(165,788)	(126,050)	(80,902)	(60,514)
Total fixed assets	$142,986	$189,618	$106,335	$149,243	$ 93,858	$112,305	$ 94,785	$ 71,305
Other assets								
Stockholders' loans	$ 27,310	$ 26,771	$ 27,561	$ 27,624	$ 22,850	$ 28,932	$ 29,055	$ 33,083
Covenant not to compete[2]	67,863	67,863	67,863	0	0	0	0	0
Total other assets	(9,445)	(8,295)	(3,770)	27,624	22,850	28,932	29,055	33,083
Total assets	$223,185	$264,059	$186,404	$301,357	$277,707	$292,222	$249,757	$189,996

	2003	2002	2001	2000	1999	1998	1997	1996
Liabilities and equity								
Liabilities								
Current liabilities								
Accounts payable	$ 100,627	$ 98,895	$117,432	$126,635	$126,100	$119,345	$ 99,874	$ 51,831
Other current liabilities								
Notes payable	$ 13,857	$ 13,141	$ 17,578	$ 13,805	$ 5,261	$ 5,185	$ 46,305	$6,297
Payroll taxes payable	14,967	14,810	12,486	4,411	5,528	8,642	6,728	4,625
Current portion of long-term debt	43,644	42,836	35,182	46,136	64,606	44,692	29,253	19,561
Total other current liabilities	$ 72,467	$ 70,793	$ 65,252	$ 64,352	$ 75,396	$ 58,520	$ 82,286	$ 30,483
Long-term liabilities								
Notes payable	$ 183,034	$200,243	$114,265	$131,222	$ 93,132	$112,834	$ 47,848	$ 60,379
Less current portion	43,644	(42,836)	(35,182)	(46,136)	(64,606)	(44,692)	(29,253)	(19,561)
Total long-term liabilities	$ 226,678	$157,407	$ 79,083	$ 85,085	$ 28,526	$ 68,141	$ 18,595	$ 40,819
Equity								
Common stock	$ 300	$ 300	$ 300	$ 300	$ 300	$ 300	$ 300	$ 300
Paid-in capital	19,698	19,698	19,698	19,698	19,692	19,692	19,692	19,692
Retained earnings	(196,578)	(83,027)	(95,355)	5,286	27,693	26,225	29,009	46,872
Total equity	$(176,580)	$ (63,029)	$ (75,357)	$ 25,284	$ 47,685	$ 46,217	$ 49,001	$ 66,864
Total liabilities and equity	$ 223,192	$264,059	$186,404	$301,357	$277,707	$292,222	$249,757	$189,996

[1]Azalea Seafood Gumbo Shoppe's financial statements have been disguised. However, the relationships remain intact.
[2]Covenant not to compete related to exit of third business partner.

exhibit 4   **Nutritional Facts for Azalea Seafood Gumbo Shoppe's Seafood Dishes**

Seafood Gumbo
  Nutrition Facts
  Serving Size 1 cup (228g)
  Amount Per Serving
  Calories 60   Calories from Fat 15

		% Daily Value*
Total Fat	2g	3%
Saturated Fat	0g	0%
Cholesterol	30mg	11%
Sodium	410mg	17%
Total Carbohydrate	6g	2%
Dietary Fiber	0g	0%
Sugars	5g	
Protein	5g	
Vitamin A	4%	Vitamin C 8%
Calcium	2%	Iron 4%

*Percent Daily Values are based on a 2,000-calorie diet.

Shrimp-and-Crabmeat Bisque
  Nutrition Facts
  Serving Size 2/3 cup (140g)
  Servings Per Container approx. 14
  Amount Per Serving
  Calories 120   Calories from Fat 50

		% Daily Value*
Total Fat	26g	9%
Saturated Fat	1.5g	9%
Cholesterol	50mg	16%
Sodium	580mg	24%
Total Carbohydrate	9g	3%
Dietary Fiber	0g	0%
Sugars less than	1g	
Protein	7g	
Vitamin A	2%	Vitamin C 4%
Calcium	2%	Iron 4%

*Percent Daily Values are based on a 2,000-calorie diet.

Shrimp Creole
  Nutrition Facts
  Serving Size 2/3 cup (139g)
  Amount Per Serving
  Calories 40   Calories from Fat 10

		% Daily Value*
Total Fat	1g	2%
Saturated Fat	0g	0%
Cholesterol	20mg	6%
Sodium	300mg	13%
Total Carbohydrate	5g	2%
Dietary Fiber	0g	0%
Sugars	3g	
Protein	3g	
Vitamin A	6%	Vitamin C 10%
Calcium	2%	Iron 4%

*Percent Daily Values are based on a 2,000-calorie diet.

Crawfish Étouffée
  Nutrition Facts
  Serving Size 2/3 cup (140g)
  Amount Per Serving
  Calories 100   Calories from Fat 40

		% Daily Value*
Total Fat	4.5g	7%
Saturated Fat	1g	4%
Cholesterol	40mg	13%
Sodium	710mg	30%
Total Carbohydrate	9g	3%
Dietary Fiber less than	1g	2%
Sugars	7g	
Protein	7g	
Vitamin A	4%	Vitamin C 8%
Calcium	2%	Iron 6%

*Percent Daily Values are based on a 2,000-calorie diet.

good placement in Wal-Mart or Sam's because we've proven our product sells and we've worked with them to get a good Plan-O-Gram placement. The Plan-O-Gram goes out to every Supercenter and Sam's so that every store has the exact same store schematic. As long as we've got a good spot on the Plan-O-Gram the biggest part of the battle is won.

It's also very hard for us to get a good broker to distribute our products. We just aren't large enough to get the interest of a SUPERVALU. So we've been forced to work with corporate buyers to work on our placement. We have found a broker that is small enough to be interested in us, but yet he has a very good relationship with Winn-Dixie. He's done a great

exhibit 5 **Azalea Seafood Gumbo Shoppe Images: In-Store Product Placement, Catering Scene, and a Gumbo Serving**

job getting us a good Plan-O-Gram placement with Winn-Dixies in Mississippi, but we really need more brokers with relationships like his.

In some ways, Azalea's competition in supermarkets was limited since there were few companies that specialized in gumbo. However, when discussing competition, Addison explained how in other ways everything in the store competed with his gumbo:

Our competitor is every other product in the store or on the menu. A customer can purchase gumbo or they can buy fish. They can buy gumbo or they can buy steak or chicken. But as far as other gumbo producers, there are only about four or five out there. Usually they appear whenever we land a new supermarket account. When we were only in Bruno's we had no real competition. Then we got into Delchamps and here came everyone out of the woodwork trying to

exhibit 6 **Estimated Sales and Number of Locations for Azalea Seafood Gumbo Shoppe's Supermarket Customers, 2002**

Company	Estimated 2002 Sales (in millions)	Number of Stores (store sales of $2 million or greater)
Wal-Mart*	$48,742	1,336
Winn-Dixie	12,646	1,058
Randall's†	—	138
Bruno's‡	1,862	187
Greer's	90	38

*Supercenter statistics reduced to include only traditional supermarket items.

†Revenues are not reported for Randall's by its parent, Safeway.

‡Bruno's is owned by Ahold, USA.

Sources: Progressive Grocer Annual Report, May 1, 2003; company Web sites.

take away the account. The same thing happened when we showed up in Wal-Mart. However, we've never really permanently lost business to a competitor. Sometimes a newcomer or existing competitor will pay a big slotting fee to get on the shelf, but if their product doesn't taste as good as ours or is overpriced, they'll be gone in three or four months. There are a couple of other companies that sell gumbo to food service distributors, but we haven't really experienced any strong price competition in that segment.

Azalea's food-service accounts with food distributors were highly attractive because they required virtually no continued sales and promotion support after the account was established. Once the food distributor began to carry a prepared food item, it promoted the products it carried and placed regular orders with its manufacturers. About 10 percent of Azalea's production volume was dedicated to its food-service accounts. Most of the company's gumbo and other products were sold to large food-service accounts like U.S. Foodservice, but about 20 percent of Azalea's food-service sales were made to jobbers. Addison and Rathle believed that the company's just-in-time production process helped keep its costs low and improved cash flow, but since the company had very little inventory on hand it frequently did not have any cases available to sell to jobbers who stopped by.

Addison and Rathle had also gained some food-service accounts by calling directly on the corporate offices of various restaurant chains. The partners had been able to gain accounts with a few small regional chains but had been unable to land accounts with larger chains even though many chain buyers liked the gumbo samples and were comfortable with Azalea's pricing. Rathle discussed how the company's austere facilities had been a problem for some corporate buyers:

> I made a presentation to Applebee's a couple of years ago to try to get them to serve our gumbo. The meeting was going very well, with the buyer saying how great our gumbo was, but then she started talking about how the manufacturers of their food items had these state-of-the-art facilities. It seemed that she went on forever about the automation that she sees in the plants and manufacturers' use of statistical quality control techniques. I knew that the meeting was a waste of time when she asked when she could come down and inspect our plant.
>
> We later had a similar opportunity with Cracker Barrel. We had sent a sample and they called to say that they liked the product and were coming down to work out the details of a contract. We knew from our meeting with Applebee's that we needed to impress these people with our facility. Well, we did the best we could do. We painted everything, did a lot of yard maintenance, and generally cleaned everything up. They never showed up. Actually, I think that they did show up, but didn't come in. On the day of the meeting, I was sitting in the office when I saw a rental Suburban full of suits pull into our driveway, sit for a while, and then turn around and pull off. Now I don't know if those were the guys from Cracker Barrel, but I never did receive a phone call about why they never showed for the meeting. But I can't really blame them. They probably pulled in here and said, "This is it? These guys can't do anything for us."

Distribution

Azalea Seafood Gumbo Shoppe's seafood gumbo, shrimp creole, and other products were picked up at the plant by food-service distributors and jobbers, but the company was responsible for shipping its products to supermarkets. In most cases, Azalea would ship its products to regional warehouses operated by the supermarket chains and the chain would handle shipments from the warehouses to the stores. Azalea's relationship with Wal-Mart required it not only to pay the freight on shipments to the regional warehouse in Monroe, Georgia, but also to pay freight expenses to ship the products from the warehouse to individual Wal-Mart Supercenters, Neighborhood Markets, and Sam's Clubs.

In mid-2003, Addison and Rathle asked Wal-Mart purchasing agents if there was a less costly method to make their products available in Wal-Mart stores since Azalea Seafood's freight charges had grown dramatically since 1997. Beginning in the fall of 2003, Wal-Mart allowed Azalea to participate in an assembly item program, whereby Azalea shipped products to Tampa Bay Fisheries, a regional seafood wholesaler. Tampa Bay Fisheries then included Azalea's products along with other seafood items it carried in its shipments to individual Wal-Mart stores. Addison and Rathle were excited about the new distribution agreement since it would reduce their shipping costs to Wal-Mart by more than half. The new distribution system did have a short-term cost because seafood managers were not informed of a new ordering process that accompanied the change in distribution. Prior to Azalea's participation in the item assembly program, seafood managers could use handheld scanners to reorder Azalea's seafood gumbo, crawfish étouffée, and other products. However, orders for products shipped by Tampa Bay Fisheries were ordered from an item order form that was sent to Tampa Bay Fisheries every Monday and Thursday morning. The confusion was gradually resolved as seafood managers began to call Azalea in December 2003 to determine why orders placed with their handheld scanners were unfilled.

OPPORTUNITIES FOR FURTHER GROWTH

As the two partners walked from the office to the plant to tell the kitchen workers to schedule the Wal-Mart order for the next morning, Mike Rathle addressed some of the questions John Addison had just raised:

> You know I really think that we're going to have to move to a new facility before we can land many more accounts—especially in food service. It just seems that large customers are worried about our sanitation, which has never been a problem, and our ability to meet their production needs. They see this 2,200-square-foot building and think we can't do as much volume as we can. We'll need about $120,000 in new equipment and our rent will probably go up by about $1,000 to $1,500 per month if we move. But you know, if the people in Bentonville called next week and wanted our product in 100 Sam's locations, I'm not sure we could do it with our current facility.
>
> Also, if we had a larger building specifically designed for food processing, we could become USDA certified. USDA certification would allow us to add new products like chicken gumbo that would sell at a lower price point than seafood gumbo. We could also add new products like red beans and sausage or cajun stuffed chicken breasts. We could also do custom entrées for our food-service customers. None of that will happen in our current building since we don't have 12-foot ceilings, two bathrooms, an office for the USDA inspector to park, or isolation freezers for raw food.

After scheduling the next day's production with the kitchen manager, Rathle returned to his discussion of a new production facility on their walk back to the frame house used as Azalea's office:

> Well, let's say we agree to make the investment in a new plant. We could continue to focus on wholesale gumbo sales to supermarkets and food-service customers or we could find a site with good frontage and get back into retail sales. We could sell crawfish and shrimp during summer months when our gumbo sales fall off some. The margins on retail sales are so-so, and we would probably have to work weekends, but the retail sales would probably help our cash flow situation. However, it could become a real headache.

Addison mentioned to Rathle that Azalea's current production capacity would allow the company to increase annual sales to about $1.5 million without any further investment. He believed that both partners could live very well if the company could grow sales by another 50 percent without the addition of debt or increased rental expenses. Also, their current level of production allowed the two owners adequate time to cater parties and special events, which had nearly 50 percent margins and improved Azalea's cash flows since payments were made in advance. However, Addison went on to comment that the highest return on their investment of time and money hinged on their ability to grow revenues and earnings by an additional 5 to 10 times to become an acquisition candidate for a large food company or food distributor.

Non Stop Yacht, S.L.

Charlene Nicholls-Nixon

The University of Western Ontario

INTRODUCTION

On February 17, 2003, Paul Metcalf, founder of Non Stop Yacht S.L. (NSY), wondered how best to pursue growth for his startup. NSY provided a central, one-stop Internet e-commerce Web site to service the mega-yacht[1] industry. Metcalf's business concept was to provide captains and crew with information and the ability to shop online for any parts or services related to the functioning of their vessel: from finding a light bulb, to selecting a new satellite system, to arranging a photographer in the Cayman Islands.

Based in Barcelona, Spain, NSY grew rapidly, achieving sales of US$200,000[2] in its first year of operation. But second-year sales were below Metcalf's expectations and the two-year-old NSY had yet to post break-even results. With cash becoming an issue and investors reluctant to provide further capital, Metcalf felt it was time to revisit whether he had chosen the most appropriate business model to capture value from the NSY concept. He was keenly aware that he had to make a decision quickly. There would be no margin for error.

THE RECREATIONAL MEGA-YACHT INDUSTRY

A mega-yacht was loosely defined as any yacht greater than 45 metres in length. Owning mega-yachts was a hobby of the immensely wealthy. Despite the global recession, the yachting world was still growing rapidly because "yacht owners were typically high net-worth individuals and corporations with cash to burn."[3] In 2003, there were approximately 5,000 mega-yachts in the world, ranging in cost from an average of $10 million to $50 million and higher. The industry included another 5,000 superyachts[4] in its boat count.

Examples of mega-yachts included the following, rated by Power and Motoryacht as the top two mega-yachts in 2002:[5]

- The Savarona: 124 metres in length, featuring a Turkish bath with 300-ton marble fountains and basins that are more than 200 years old, 39 bathrooms, 17 bedrooms and an exquisite gold and marble balustrade.[6]

- The Alexander: 121 metres in length, launched in 1976 and owned by Greek real estate billion-

Ivey

Richard Ivey School of Business
The University of Western Ontario

Ken Mark and Jordan Mitchell prepared this case under the supervision of Professor Charlene Nicholls-Nixon solely to provide material for class discussion. The authors do not intend to illustrate either effective or ineffective handling of a managerial situation. The authors may have disguised certain names and other identifying information to protect confidentiality.

[1]Defined as yachts over 45 metres in length.

[2]All dollar amounts in U.S. dollars unless otherwise stated.

[3]Christopher Dinsmore, "Yard Gets Off to Quick Start," *The Virginian-Pilot,* February 6, 2002.

[4]Superyachts were defined as being between 25 to 45 metres in length and costing in the million-dollar range.

[5]Michael Field, "Booming Super-Yacht Industry Getting Even More Extravagant," *Agence France-Presse,* June 28, 2002.

[6]A ramp.

aire John Latsis. The mega-yacht was in the headlines in 2000 when Prince Charles of Britain and his lover, Camilla Parker Bowles, were photographed cruising in it.

Economic activity in the mega-yacht industry was estimated at $1,035 million worldwide, of which new builds accounted for $383 million. The maintenance, refit, and repair business sectors accounted for the other $652 million. (At any time, there were about 1,600 mega-yachts docked for service). In September 2002, consultants estimated that demand in the worldwide market would continue to increase by 6 percent per year and even more in the near-term outlook.[7]

Ports of Call

There were a few key ports of call for mega-yachts: South Florida, Majorca, the French Riviera, and St. Maarten. The impact of mega-yachts was not to be underestimated: South Florida alone claimed that mega-yachts were a significant portion of the $9 billion per annum recreational marine industry.[8] Frank Herhold, executive director of the Marine Industries Association of South Florida, a trade group with about 800 members, stated:

> Mega-yachts are a very fragile, mobile community. About 900 mega-yachts visit South Florida each year, and 800 of them stay. They spend about $500,000 per visit.[9]

Various economic impacts included purchases of goods and services, as well as maintenance, repairs, refittings and docking fees (between $7 to $10 per foot per day) billed by local marinas and boatyards. In South Florida, the recreational marine industry directly employed an estimated 39,000 people and generated indirect employment for another 109,000.[10]

To attract visitors and support the community, South Florida also held the Fort Lauderdale Boat Show, displaying $1.6 billion of boats, mega-yachts, and accessories to thousands of visitors. The show's average $500 million annual impact was welcomed by the city.[11]

Customers

Americans purchased 45 percent of all superyachts and mega-yachts, up from 10 percent a decade ago to 12 percent in 2002.[12] Customers bought mega-yachts and superyachts in the same way they bought other large-ticket items. Within their network of contacts and friends, they located yacht brokerages that could equip them with the most impressive yacht they could afford.

Mega-yacht owners typically spent 6 to 10 weeks a year onboard their yacht, frequently entertaining guests with the key but subtle aim of putting their immense wealth on display during this short period of time. Typically, no expense was spared to provide the highest levels of comfort and luxury for guests—fresh, premium food was cooked by chefs, crews were fully staffed, and the mega-yacht had to be in pristine condition at all times. A typical mega-yacht would have six crew members, including a captain, mate, chief engineer, cook, stewardess, and deck hand. In extreme cases, the mega-yacht had 90 to 100 full-time crew.

When not in use by the owner, mega-yachts were often made available for charter. During this three-to-four-month time period, the yacht owner turned over the care of the vessel to the chartering party and the yacht management service. The level of luxury depended on the amount the party was willing to spend.

For the rest of the year, the mega-yacht was moored in port, in dry storage or in dock for repairs. The generally accepted industry rule was that operating expenses accounted for 10 percent of the yacht's value per year. Of this amount, a quarter was due to spare parts, consumables, and upgrades. The other three-quarters covered fuel, food, communication costs, docking fees, crew payroll, and repair and refit yard fees. Every four to five years, a mega-yacht required a major refit costing up to 20 percent of the yacht's value.

---

[7]"United Kingdom Report Says Superyacht Boom is 'Only The Beginning,'" *Advanced Materials and Composite News,* September 7, 2002. (Note: The report uses the words "superyacht" and "mega-yacht" interchangeably.)

[8]Joseph Mann, "Sturgeon Bay, Wis.-Based Marine Firm Focuses on Mega-yachts," *Fort Lauderdale Sun-Sentinel,* June 4, 2002.

[9]Joseph Mann, "Fort Lauderdale, Fla.-Area Summit Seeks to Buoy Recreational Marine Industry," *Fort Lauderdale Sun-Sentinel,* October 18, 2002.

[10]Ibid.

[11]Linda Rawls, "Buoyant Nautical Market Welcomes Lauderdale Show," *The Palm Beach Post,* November 1, 2002.

[12]Angus MacSwan, "Rich Sail Through Troubled Times on Superyachts," *Reuters News,* November 3, 2002.

Yacht Builders

At any time, there were about two dozen specialty yacht builders in the world constructing mega-yachts. Mega-yachts took between one and three years to build. In 2002, 56 percent of new mega-yachts were built in Europe, 35 percent in the United States, and the remainder were built in Asia and South Africa. In 2002, industry observers calculated that yacht builders were completing 482 mega-yachts for 2003, a 4.7 percent drop from the previous year.[13] Although yacht builders focused on construction, related services could add substantially to their bottom line. Rybovich Spencer, a West Palm Beach, Florida–based full-service shipyard and shipbuilder, said its service and dockage business, consisting of repairs and refits for over 80 mega-yachts, brought in an additional $5 million in sales during a six-month period between 2001 and 2002.[14] Yacht builders invested between $2 million to $15 million to upgrade current facilities to serve mega-yachts.[15]

The growth in the industry had led to a proliferation in the number of yacht builders, and in 2002, signs of consolidation appeared. Palmer Johnson Inc., a shipbuilder and refitter based in Sturgeon Bay, Wisconsin, announced its intentions to focus on the mega-yacht industry with its acquisition of two Fort Lauderdale marine companies specializing in supplying parts, equipment and fuel to the yachting sector.[16]

Yacht Management Companies

There were dozens of yacht management companies providing such services as parts procurement, crew hiring and management, co-ordination of yacht maintenance, and organizing charters. As an example of a service provided, organizing charters helped mega-yacht owners recoup some of the investment in their vessel: rental rates ranged from $50,000 per week to $584,000 per week for the 325-foot Christina O, a yacht for up to 36 people that once belonged to the late Aristotle Onassis. These costs did not include tips, food, alcohol, and fuel (which could add another 20 percent to 40 percent to costs).[17] The fees for dockage in the Mediterranean could range from $1,000 to $2,000 per night. The yacht management company's commission, included in the total amount, would be between 10 percent to 20 percent.

Consolidation in this industry was also starting to take place, as transnational players began moving into the lucrative U.S. market. In 2002, the Rodriguez Group, a French yachting services company, purchased Fort Lauderdale–based Bob Saxon Associates Inc., a yacht management and charter company with 27 employees.[18]

THE PARTS PROCUREMENT PROCESS

Given the nature of conspicuous consumption in the mega-yacht industry, most mega-yachts were filled with specially made and expensive parts (see Exhibit 1). There were three main categories of boat parts:

1. *Spare parts*—typically more urgent than anything else, this category referred to parts that had unexpectedly broken down. Examples included: a replacement pump for the head (toilet), a new hydraulic seal for the steering system, a non-standard valve in the sewage system or a new electronics board for the unit that closes the curtains in the owner's stateroom.

2. *Consumables and stock spares*—this category included parts that were less urgent but necessary to have in the case of a breakdown or replacement. Examples included: oil and fuel filters, light bulbs, pump seals, electronic switches, crockery (pots and pans) for the galley (kitchen), charts, and tools.

3. *Upgrades and refits*—this category included a range of products from fire and safety to the entertainment or communication systems.

[13]Dale K. DuPont, "Fort Lauderdale, Fla.-Based Magazine Says Mega-yacht Orders Are Down," *Miami Herald,* October 23, 2002.

[14]Joseph Mann, "West Palm Beach, Fla.-based Boatyard, Boatbuilder, Logs Strong Sales Period," *Fort Lauderdale Sun-Sentinel,* May 31, 2002.

[15]Joseph Mann, "Fort Lauderdale, Fla.-Shipyard Gets Upgrades," *Fort Lauderdale Sun-Sentinel,* November 2, 2002.

[16]Joseph Mann, "Sturgeon Bay, Wis.-Based Marine Firm Focuses on Mega-yachts," *Fort Lauderdale Sun-Sentinel,* June 4, 2002.

[17]Dirk Wittenborn, "Chartered Waters," *Independent on Sunday,* June 2, 2002.

[18]Joseph Mann, "Fort Lauderdale, Fla.-based Yacht Services Company Sold," *Fort Lauderdale Sun-Sentinel,* July 4, 2002.

exhibit 1 **Parts Requirements for Mega-Yachts**

The scope of supply included any parts for the following systems aboard a mega-yacht or superyacht:

- Main Engines
- Propulsion Units
- Generators
- Air Conditioning
- Refrigeration
- Water Makers
- Shorepower Conversion Units
- Sewage Systems
- Stabilization Systems
- Bow Thrusters
- Fuel Purification
- Oil Purification
- Fresh Water System
- Hot Water System
- Communication Systems
- Navigation Electronics

- Compressed Air Systems
- Entertainment Systems
- Fire Fighting Equipment
- Safety Equipment
- Hydraulics
- Sails and Rigging
- Kitchen Equipment
- Cranes
- Tenders
- Jet-skis
- Diving Equipment
- Anchor Handling Equipment
- Alarm Systems
- Charts
- Helicopters
- Other Sea Craft

Because the range of products required by mega-yachts was so great, suppliers were located around the world. The majority of the suppliers were located in the United Kingdom, Germany, Holland, France, United States, Australia, Scandinavia, and Japan. As the industry continued to mature, more standardization and consolidation of suppliers were expected to occur.

There were four main suppliers to mega-yachts:

- Commercial/Industrial—engines, laundry, kitchen, and electrical system suppliers
- Consumer Products—entertainment systems, fixtures in bathrooms, furniture, etc.
- Small Yacht Products—rope handling equipment, navigation equipment, electronic system suppliers
- Dedicated Suppliers—small number of manufacturers that catered to the mega-yacht market

The thousands of parts and equipment manufacturers sold their wares through exclusive distributors.

Analysts indicated that Germany had a 26 percent share of the market, followed by the United Kingdom and the Netherlands each with an 18 percent share, the United States with 14 percent, Norway with 9 percent, France with 6 percent, and Finland 3 percent.[19]

Owners rarely ever dealt with the purchasing of boat parts or servicing, leaving these duties to the crew (40 percent of the time) and yacht repair and refit specialists (60 percent of the time). The crew dealt with ongoing or emergency repairs while yacht repair and refit specialists handled regularly scheduled maintenance. The crew had several ways to deal with parts procurement: They could leave the task to the yacht management company; they could rely on a purchasing agent; or they could approach parts distributors (see Exhibit 2).

Yacht management companies and purchasing agents would locate the products from their database or collection of catalogues. They would then order the part, look after the paperwork and have the part shipped to their warehouse or directly to the yacht. Typically, they would add a percentage fee, ranging between 5 percent to 10 percent of the cost of the part. For important customers, the purchasing agent would have the clout to negotiate a cheaper price than the yacht owner would receive by dealing directly with the manufacturer. Parts could also be obtained through local yacht agents. Like purchasing agents, local yacht agents (who typically also managed many other sideline businesses), generally had local knowledge of their port, any local suppliers, and local import laws. The yacht agent would add a small percentage to the cost of the product or service.

Alternatively, crews could pursue parts procurement independently. This approach usually involved a lengthy investigation period where they would have to track down products and product information through contacts, magazines, catalogues, and the Internet. In some cases, crews were able to contact the distributor or manufacturer directly and arrange to have the product shipped to the yacht. Although contacting parts suppliers was not simple (there were thousands of suppliers), extra commissions for intermediaries would not have to be paid.

[19]"United Kingdom Report Says Superyacht Boom is 'Only The Beginning'," *Advanced Materials and Composite News,* September 7, 2002. (Note: The report uses the words "superyacht" and "mega-yacht" interchangeably.)

exhibit 2 **Traditional Parts Procurement Process**

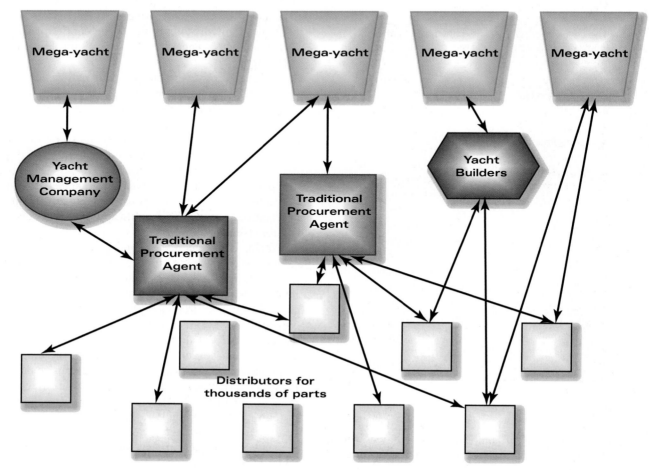

Distributors for
thousands of parts

Crews could also locate and purchase boat parts by directly contacting yacht builders and/or repair and refit yards. Yacht builders would typically specialize in parts they used to equip the vessels they were building. Repair and refit yards did not always have a wide contact base of suppliers and would add 10 percent to 15 percent onto the cost of the product or service. Their businesses were based on charging for the labor component of the refit or repair. In most major ports, there would be one or two major refit yards. For example, the predominant refit yards in Spain included MB 92 in Barcelona and Izar in Cartagena.

THE NSY VALUE PROPOSITION

Because mega-yachts were transient sea craft that sailed frequently from port to port, supplies and equipment were often needed on a last-minute basis. Locating the right spare or replacement part was often a frustrating endeavor for mega-yacht crews; there were literally thousands of manufacturers worldwide, each making nonstandard boat parts. Attempting to describe the boat part while connected to procurement agents on satellite telephone was not the ideal solution. Often, agents themselves had to resort to haphazard guessing to correctly identify the item requested. To compound the problem, most parts suppliers did not have their catalogues online; the catalogues were often in paper form and updated annually.

Metcalf believed that his company's e-commerce Web site had an advantage over traditional methods of procurement. While connected to the Internet, mega-yacht crews could browse the catalogues of a variety of suppliers on the NSY site. Instantaneous access to current product information would virtually eliminate many of the problems crews commonly associated with parts procurement, including how to find and contact the manufacturer and local distributor, describing the part, ensuring appropriate measurements (metric versus imperial), managing time zone differences, dealing with communication problems, locating sending and receiving agents, managing customs clearance, and arranging payment.

Metcalf explained why he chose to operate NSY as an e-commerce site:

> I thought the Internet was the best method of delivery to a customer base that was located all over the world and constantly moving. The fit was perfect! I felt the problem of parts procurement could be better addressed using the Internet. The biggest problem in getting boat parts was getting the right information about the product. So, I figured if I could have an Internet site and an up-to-date catalogue on CD that gave the information *and* delivered the product, it would be better than the current method of finding the parts yourself or by using an agent who is serving dozens of other customers. My plan was to have a huge catalogue of everybody's catalogue. A person from the boat would order a part and say, "Okay, I'm in this place," and the product would be drop-shipped from the supplier in that area. (See Exhibit 3.)

Metcalf believed that NSY's competitive advantage would be its database and network of suppliers, the ability to ship anywhere in the world from Barcelona, the flexibility of its cost structure, and the transparency of billing. Taken together, the benefits provided a compelling value proposition to the crew of superyachts and mega-yachts, which included:

1. Up-to-date catalogue on CD, allowing the crew to browse and shop off-line then upload the order by fax, e-mail, or through the Internet (the hard-copy catalogue of National Marine had some parts not available for the past six years);

2. Automatic accounting for the captain or yacht management company;

3. Password-protected expenditure levels for captain, mate or engineer;

4. Automatic receipt copies, invoice copies and VAT[20] receipts;

5. Links into maintenance scheduling software if used on the yacht;

6. Easy reordering of parts or groups of parts;

7. Intelligent add-on sales with instant access to view the available options;

8. Product pictures and part diagrams; and

9. No time zone issues.

With the NonStopYacht.com Web site, Metcalf aimed to become the Web-based purchasing agent of choice to crew members and yacht management companies. NSY's continually updated Web site could be instantly accessed by customers, with orders placed online or by telephone.

NSY'S BUSINESS MODEL

Initially, Metcalf had envisioned building NSY as a virtual corporation. The Web site would be NSY's only interface with the customer. Supplies would be procured from a growing network of vendors that agreed to post their merchandise with NSY and then have NSY arrange the shipping directly to the customer.

NSY's revenues were generated from dealer margins that were earned when merchandise was sold through the Web site. Suppliers were not required to pay listing fees. The business model worked as follows: NSY would utilize the supplier's country-specific distributor to ship product to customers. In the process, it would earn dealer margins on the wholesale prices of these products. NSY aimed to charge end-customers prices similar to those offered by local dealers. In the rare case that the supplier did not have a distributor, NSY would arrange for the part to be shipped directly to the customer. In these situations, NSY would earn both distributor margins and dealer margins.

Metcalf and his team worked feverishly for months, making over 900 supplier contacts around

---

[20]Value Added Tax (European).

exhibit 3   **Non Stop Yacht Facilitates Parts Procurement**

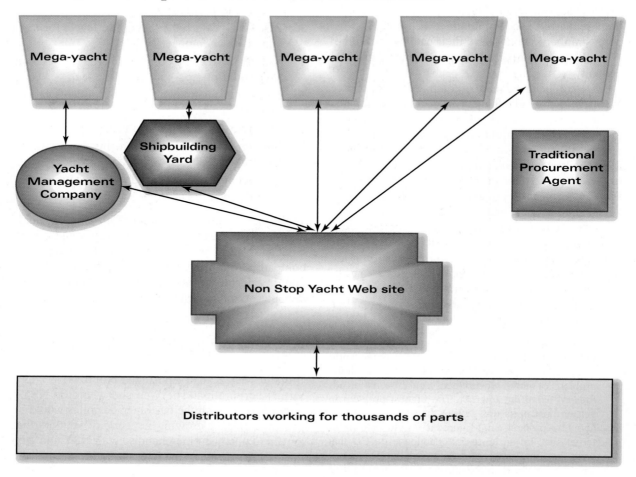

the world with a combined product offering that included over 20,000 branded items. The process of getting all of the suppliers and their products had been an arduous task. Metcalf recalled:

> We basically rang up all the suppliers, told them about the idea and many of them said "great." The biggest challenge was convincing them of our main objective, which was *not* selling *against* their distributors. Once we convinced them that the customer would order from us, then we would go through their designated distributor in that country.

At the same time as agreements were being signed with a critical mass of suppliers, the Web site was developed. Then, attention turned to building traffic on the site:

> When we finished the basic structure of the Web site, we sent out passwords to various mega-yachts and got their feedback on what they liked and didn't like about the site. The site was ugly because I designed it initially. We had three people working on the back end, and before its final release, I hired someone who improved the look and consistency of the appearance.
>
> We opened the Web site to resounding silence in June 2001. We had visitors but not many purchasers. We got the phone calls: "My boss was on your site and he would like to order this." The Web site did not work the way I wanted it to as an e-commerce site. However, it did provide parts information to crews.

Since initial sales had been much slower than Metcalf had anticipated, he decided to move from a hidden office to a publicly accessible area. As soon as he had created a face for NSY to deal directly with customers, sales started to pick up. The business model quickly evolved from an Internet-based venture to a hybrid "bricks and mortar" enterprise:

> What we were finding was that customers were looking on the Web site to find the information; then we'd get a call saying, "Yes, we saw this boat part on your Web site and would like to order it." The decision to move from a strictly e-commerce company to dealing directly with the customer was quite simple, really. We were located upstairs in a non-public area and were trying to operate it as a strictly e-commerce business. But we kept on getting calls. We decided to move downstairs, and put in a free Internet access terminal for the crew to use. That helped out immensely. Once we saw that the e-commerce solution alone wouldn't work, we developed a face to the crews of the mega-yachts. Crews are able to come in, use our Internet, ask us about products and do the order either over the phone, by fax or in person. The site is updated, but it's in hibernation, since most of our sales are generated through the office.

Metcalf and the investors decided to open up the second NSY office in Palma, Mallorca, Spain, in October 2002. Metcalf believed Palma to be a vital hub of activity for superyachts and mega-yachts and was confident that the new office was a natural extension of the Barcelona location.

The accessibility to information within the mega-yacht industry made it possible for Metcalf to obtain the names and lengths of the yachts, the major equipment being installed, the yard where the yacht was built and the present captain's name. The only information that was not available was details relating to the owner. NSY advertised in three publications that were frequently referenced and read by captains and crews: *Professional Yachtman's Association News, The Yacht Report,* and *Showboats.* Another important advertising method was the attendance of Metcalf and his team at the major boat shows in Europe and the United States.

THE NSY TEAM

In February 2003, the NSY management team was composed of Metcalf as chief executive officer (CEO) and president, Stephanie McKay as commercial manager and Sam Jones as marketing and sales specialist. Contract employees such as Robert Franks

performed computing or administrative tasks. Each individual brought a unique and complementary set of skills and experience to NSY.

Metcalf had spent six years in computer sales in his native United Kingdom before pursuing a career in the sailing world in 1993. He worked first as a sailing instructor in Greece, and then went to work on a variety of small- and medium-sized yachts, ranging in size from 12 metres to 52 metres. During this time, Metcalf's travels took him throughout the Caribbean, North America, and the Mediterranean. The experience gave Metcalf a wide base of yachting knowledge including electrical, plumbing, engine rooms, and general maintenance. It also gave him valuable contacts with owners, captains, and engineers within the industry. Metcalf was 30 years old when he began writing the NSY business plan in October 1999. He received his initial seed capital from Riva y Garcia on June 16, 2000 (see Exhibit 4).

In 2003, McKay had worked at NSY for two years. She was responsible for the establishment of many of the relationships with suppliers due to her savvy negotiation skills and ability to speak three languages. Her prior experience had been based in emergency assistance with a leading insurance company, working in both the United Kingdom and France. Being with NSY from the beginning, McKay wrote an entire manual of procedures and established strong ties with yacht refit yards in the Mediterranean.

Jones had worked for NSY for nine months. During this time, he had managed to increase the walk-in traffic and the direct-to-yacht business through his personable selling approach to the 30 to 40 mega-yachts sailing into Barcelona each year. In October 2002, he was placed in charge of the new Palma office. The team used the services of Robert Franks, an experienced U.K. computer programmer based in Barcelona, for any issues with the Web site and for the integration and set-up of any new technologies relevant to NSY.

COMPETITOR REACTION

Metcalf believed that NSY's key competitors would be the major traditional procurement agents, yacht builders or parts-related Web sites, but none of these parties took visible action following the launch of NonStopYacht.com in June 2001.

exhibit 4   **Financing of Non Stop Yacht**

By February 2003, there had been three rounds of investment in Non Stop Yacht:

Round	Investor	Date	Amount (US$)
1	Riva y Garcia + Barcelona EMPREN	06/16/2000	$180,000
2	Riva y Garcia + Barcelona EMPREN	12/16/2000	180,000
3*	Riva y Garcia + Barcelona EMPREN	04/01/2001	51,085
	Total		$411,085

*The third joint small round of financing was in the form of a loan with the plan that the investment would be returned in cash or equity, with valuation based on performance against target.

Riva y Garcia

Riva y Garcia was an investment banking boutique with offices in Barcelona and Madrid. Its primary focus was on corporate finance for Catalonian and Spanish companies as well as the operation of three institutional investment funds, one of which was WebCapital, the fund that invested in Non Stop Yacht.

Sebastian Waldburg, director private equity from Riva y Garcia, commented on why he gave Metcalf the funding:

> He [Metcalf] had worked in the sector and had detected a serious need. He wanted to use the Internet as a tool to fill a gap. We thought it was a good approach and an interesting sector. It's a small sector worth a lot of money. You don't have to talk to a million customers.

> VC firms invest in the person. Paul has the experience and knowledge in the industry. He has a strong capacity in being flexible in terms of where the business will take him.

On his expectations of Non Stop Yacht's financial commitment, Walburg said:

> The financial model we had built showed us a 34 percent return. This year I want to see them break even. That would be sales of 70,000 Euros a month. And I don't mean an average of 70,000 a month. Every month, at least 70, which would cover their fixed costs. By next year, I want to see a 50 percent to 80 percent growth rate in sales.

Barcelona EMPREN

Barcelona Empren was an organization focused on providing start-up and seed capital to companies in telecommunications, biotech, engineering and software companies. Its shareholders included pre-eminent leaders in Spain from the following sectors: public institutions (27.5 percent), telecom (22.5 percent), banks (35 percent), industrial sector (10 percent), and public utilities (5 percent).

Emilio Gómez I. Janer, analyst with Barcelona Empren, commented on giving funding to NSY:

> He's an innovator in the yachting industry, he has an excellent niche in the marketplace and Paul and his team are experts in the sector. He knows what the problem in the industry is and he has the knowledge and experience to make it successful.

On his expectations of financial results, Gómez commented:

> Originally, we had planned a 30 percent IRR.* I wanted to see $500,000 in sales in 2002 and $1 million in 2003.

*Internal Rate of Return.

Very little information was publicly available about the companies that acted as purchasing agents in the mega-yacht industry. Many of these firms were private companies or one-person operations with closely guarded lists of clientele. Worldwide, Metcalf believed there were three major traditional procurement agents:

- *National Marine*, Florida, United States—This competitor was the largest purchasing agent in

the world with annual sales of approximately $10 million, employing 35 people. Its focus was almost entirely U.S.-based and it was not well known in Europe. National Marine published a 1,000-page catalogue annually and sold parts to mega-yachts and superyachts throughout the world.

- *Alex Spares*, United Kingdom—The operation began in 1972 and comprised one principal and one assistant. Annual sales were estimated at approximately $1 million. Spares's competitive advantage was his experience of over 30 years in the industry and his extensive personal network contacts, including many mega-yacht captains and crews.

- *Versillias Supplies,* Viareggio, Italy—The operation relied mostly on dealings with Mediterranean mega-yachts and suppliers. Their sales were approximately $1 million.

In addition to these "majors," there were approximately another 200 small local yacht agents located around the world that did not specialize in locating and sourcing local parts and services for yachts in their locale. Rather, they acted as the "person on the ground" to arrange everything from getting fresh flowers to renting a limousine for the boat's owner. According to Metcalf, none of these small enterprises had the clout or worldwide name recognition that National Marine, Alex Spares, or Versillias had.

By February 2003, there was some industry speculation about the possibility of strategic alliances between NSY and its major competitors, specifically National Marine, Alex Spares, and Palmer Johnson.

Emerging Competitors: Vertically Integrated Yacht Builders?

Two major yacht builders had started to incorporate a completely vertical operation including building, selling, chartering, servicing, refitting and ordering parts for the mega-yachts. Frequently, these parts were required for the building projects in which the yard was involved.

Palmer Johnson Inc.

Started in 1918, this was one of the world's preeminent builders, yacht repair and support services of sailboats, superyachts, and mega-yachts with over $300 million in sales. Palmer Johnson usually built 40 yachts per year. Their subsidiaries included companies that built production, semi-custom, and custom luxury yachts; operated brokerage yacht sales across the United States, United Kingdom, France, and Singapore; refitted, repaired, and painted mega-yachts; and operated a global logistical support unit serving mega-yachts worldwide. Being one of the biggest yacht builders, refit yards, and brokerages in the world, Metcalf be-

lieved Palmer Johnson had a good reputation and significant clout with suppliers. In 2002, Palmer Johnson was expected to seek growth through expanding the service side of their enterprise.

Lurssen

Located in Bremen, Germany, Lurssen had a long history in ship building dating back to 1875, with many of the world's firsts in yachting, including the invention of the first motor boat in 1886. Lurssen was another of the world's major yacht builders with sales of approximately $150 million. A highly diversified company, they were involved in the production, servicing, and logistical support of mega-yachts as well as Naval vessels. They typically built 30 mega-yachts per year. Their competitive advantage was similar to Palmer Johnson's in their worldwide reputation, history and clout with suppliers.

The Failed Alliance Between Palmer Johnson and Lurssen

Palmer Johnson and Lurssen had tried to form a strategic alliance together in the mid-1990s, but it had failed due to differences in business objectives. Both companies were yacht builders, which meant they were competing for the same superyachts and mega-yacht contracts. As well, their repair and refit yards were not complementary and both companies found it challenging to agree upon an efficient way to procure and sell boat parts. Last, management from both companies was unable to reconcile the U.S.–German management styles.

METCALF'S OPTIONS

In 2003, Metcalf was experiencing substantial pressure to raise NSY's performance to meet investor expectations. Moreover, he was also personally motivated to see a payoff for the exhausting schedule he had been keeping since launching the venture two and half years earlier. So far, the results had been disappointing. Metcalf's original plan for growth called for sales of $10 million and profits of $1.97 million by the end of the 2003 fiscal year (see Exhibit 5). In the first full year of operation, NSY generated sales of $200,000, which was consistent with Metcalf's business plan. However, in 2002, the sales were $300,000, or 11 percent of the original business plan. NSY was just cash flow positive.

Metcalf was now wondering whether he should revisit the NSY business model. He believed there

exhibit 5 **Original Financial Projections for Non Stop Yacht**

	Year 1	Year 2	Year 3	Year 4	Year 5
Sales	$214,720	$2,654,484	$10,698,465	$13,908,004	$18,080,406
Sales growth %		1,136%	303%	30%	30%
Profit	$(414,188)	$317,189	$1,973,416	$2,648,157	$3,537,727
Profit growth %		−176.6%	522.2%	34.2%	33.6%
# of yachts	1,600	1,712	1,832	1,960	2,097
Total mega-yacht market size (millions)	$160.0	$171.2	$183.2	$196.0	$209.7
Growth %	7%	7%	7%	7%	7%
NSY market share	0.13%	1.55%	5.84%	7.10%	8.62%

were three alternative business models that had the potential to improve the company's performance. Metcalf's quandary was deciding how to choose from among these options.

Option #1: Signing an Agreement with Palmer Johnson or National Marine

Metcalf felt there were trade-offs associated with entering into a strategic alliance with Palmer Johnson or National Marine:

> The problem is, if we sign an agreement with National or Palmer Johnson to become their European arm, we become a third party. We have to stop dealing direct with the crew of the mega-yachts.
>
> Signing the agreement with National or Palmer would give us high volume and low margin. We would charge them a fixed cost of 5,000 to 6,000 Euros a month and add an additional 5 percent margin. The advantage of the mixture of dealing with agents and direct to the mega-yachts is higher margin . . . an average of about 25 percent versus the current 15 percent. The problem is slow growth.

The decision was not based purely on sales or gross margin dollars as Metcalf was confident that, by signing the agreement, his sales would reach $3 million immediately, with potential for 50 percent growth in the second year, 30 percent in the third, tapering down to 10 percent growth per year in subsequent years.

To accommodate the increased volume, Metcalf would have to contract two extra administrative people at $20,000 a year plus 25 percent in employee

tax. In the second year, he would likely add another person. Metcalf could gain savings of approximately $10,000 per year on his rent by moving into an office without public access. New computers and additional office furniture, which were treated as expenses, would require an additional outlay of $2,000 per terminal, including telephone and Internet hookup. With this option, NSY would likely experience a 5 percent increase in expenses each year. The main investment would be the increased accounts receivables, estimated to represent approximately 20 days. NSY typically paid its bills in 15 days and did not carry any inventory.

Option #2: Growth Through Repair and Refit Yards and Dealing Direct to Yachts—a "Hybrid" Option

Metcalf felt there was a great opportunity to service the yacht refit yards, local yacht agents and yacht management services, while trying to deal directly with the mega-yachts at the same time. But there were two potential problems with this approach. First, if NSY contracted with a refit yard, the company might have to cease dealing directly with the yachts in order to avoid conflict of interest. Second, NSY could lose its name recognition with the end consumer if it relied upon yacht refit yards, agents, or management services to generate sales. Metcalf expected a margin of 5 percent to 15 percent when dealing with a third party and a margin of 25 percent when dealing directly with the yachts, making a blended margin of approximately 20 percent.

With this growth option, Metcalf believed he could generate sales of more than $2 million in three years, with a growth rate of 15 percent for each subsequent year. NSY could accommodate this type of growth with its current team in Barcelona, although Metcalf expected that each additional bricks-and-mortar office would require another two employees at $20,000 per person. It was probable that, in addition to the Palma office, two more offices would be required in Antibes, France, and Monaco.

The start-up for each new office was estimated to be $10,000, plus $2,000 per employee for the computer and office equipment. The yearly amount of telephone, consumables, and miscellaneous expense was estimated at $20,000 per office. Metcalf expected that NSY would require an average increase in travel expense of $5,000 per office. The rent and related expenses for a small office per year in major ports in the Mediterranean was estimated to be about $2,000 per month. Since NSY expensed its computers and office equipment, the only working capital requirement would be an increase in accounts receivable.

Option #3: Organic Growth Through Opening Multiple Locations

Metcalf felt that the recently opened Palma office would generate more walk-in traffic and would continue to present a company "face" to the crew of the mega-yachts. Metcalf further believed that yacht crews would be more apt to deal with NSY if they constantly saw a shop in each major destination. Thus, an alternative business model was to expand by continuing to open locations in key ports around the world. Sebastian Waldburg, from Riva y Garcia, commented on the viability of expanding with a bricks-and-mortar approach:

> Yes, NSY is a relatively low-budget operation. If they replicate the small offices, say in Antibes or Monaco, and before they open up their office, if they can arrange to be the back-office for yacht refit yards and yacht management services, they could cover their fixed costs of running it. They could likely charge the yacht management services or the refit yard a fixed monthly fee with variable charges for purchases.
>
> It's important to have the local touch and the local being-in-touch. With a little office, they can give constant and consistent quality and service.

Emilio Gómez I. Janer from Barcelona Empren commented:

> I'm the biggest proponent of this approach. Yes, I believe it's necessary to have brick-and-mortar presence in each port. You need to have close proximity to where the sales happen.

Without actively pursuing the yacht refit yards and yacht management services, Metcalf felt that he could achieve sales of $500,000 with the Barcelona and Palma office. With two additional offices (each costing $15,000 to set up and $75,000 to run per annum), he felt that he could reach $1.5 million in annual sales five years from now.

Competition in the Bottled Water Industry

John E. Gamble
University of South Alabama

Bottled water was among the world's most attractive beverage categories, with global sales in 2001 exceeding 32 billion gallons and annual growth averaging nearly 9 percent between 1996 and 2001. Bottled water had long been a widely consumed product in Western Europe and Mexico, where annual per capita consumption averaged about 30 gallons in 2001, but until the mid-1990s bottled water had been somewhat of a novelty or prestige product in the United States. In 1990 approximately 2.2 billion gallons of bottled water were consumed in the United States and per capita consumption approximated 9 gallons. U.S. per capita consumption had grown to nearly 20 gallons a year by 2001 and was expected to grow to 26 gallons a year by 2005. The rising popularity of bottled water in the United States during the 1990s allowed the United States to become the world's largest market for bottled water by 1996 (see Exhibit 1).

The growing popularity of bottled water in the United States was attributable to concerns over the safety of municipal drinking water, an increased

---

exhibit 1 **Leading Country Markets for Bottled Water, 1996 and 2001 (In Millions of Gallons)**

2001 Rank	Country	1996	2001	CAGR* (1996–2001)
1	United States	3,495.1	5,425.3	9.2%
2	Mexico	2,674.2	3,496.5	5.5
3	Italy	1,923.9	2,502.6	5.4
4	Germany	2,097.6	2,336.5	2.2
5	France	1,498.9	2,064.6	6.6
6	China	565.0	2,007.8	28.9
7	Indonesia	512.1	1,352.1	21.4
8	Thailand	854.5	1,198.3	7.0
9	Brazil	475.7	1,139.6	19.1
10	Spain	884.0	1,091.4	4.3
All others		4,205.4	7,488.4	12.2
Worldwide total		21,182.4	32,104.1	8.7%

*Compound average growth rate.

Source: Beverage Marketing Corporation, as reported by *Bottled Water Reporter*, April–May 2002.

focus on fitness and health, and the hectic on-the-go lifestyles of American consumers. The convenience, purity, and portability of bottled water made it the natural solution to consumers' dissatisfaction with tap water. The U.S. bottled water market, like most markets outside the United States, was characterized by fierce competitive rivalry as the world's bottled water sellers jockeyed for market share and volume gains. Both the global and U.S. bottled water markets had become dominated by a few international food and beverage producers like Coca-Cola, PepsiCo, Nestlé, and Groupe Danone, but they also included many small regional sellers that were required to develop either low-cost production and distribution capabilities or differentiation strategies keyed to some unique product attributes. At the close of 2002, industry rivals were entering new distribution channels, developing innovative product variations, entering into strategic agreements to penetrate new international markets, and acquiring smaller sellers that might hold strong positions in certain U.S. regional markets or emerging markets. Industry analysts and observers believed the recent moves undertaken by the world's largest sellers of bottled water would alter the competitive dynamics of the bottled water industry and mandate that certain players modify their current strategic approaches to competition in the industry.

INDUSTRY CONDITIONS IN 2002

Even though it was the world's largest market for bottled water, the United States remained among the faster-growing markets for bottled water since per capita consumption of bottled water fell substantially below consumption rates in Western Europe, the Middle East, and Mexico. Bottled water consumption in the United States also lagged per capita consumption of soft drinks by a wide margin. However, many U.S. consumers were making a transition from soft drinks to bottled water as the soft-drink market had grown by less than 1 percent annually between 1996 and 2001 and the market for bottled water had continued to grow at annual rates near 10 percent during the same time period. By 2002, 70 percent of U.S. households purchased bottled water at least once a year and the average water-buying household purchased 22 twelve-ounce bottles a year. Exhibits 2 through 5 illustrate the growing popularity of bottled water among U.S. consumers during the 1990s and through 2001.

Almost one-half of bottled water consumed in the United States in 1990 was bulk water delivered to homes and offices in returnable five-gallon containers and dispensed through coolers. Only 186 million gallons of water were sold in one-liter or smaller single-serving polyethylene terephthalate (PET) bottles. In 2002, bottled water sold in one-liter or smaller PET containers accounted for 36.2 percent of industry volume and 50.8 percent of dollar sales and had grown by 29.1 percent annually between 1995 and 2001. The sales of bulk water sold in 5-gallon containers or 1- or 2.5-gallon high-density polyethylene (HDPE) containers accounted for 60.9 percent of gallonage but only 43.3 percent of dollar sales. Convenience was the primary appeal of smaller, single-serving PET containers since consumers could purchase chilled water they could drink immediately. Water purchased for immediate consumption grew from 8.3 percent of industry sales volume in 1990 to 16.7 percent of sales volume in 2000. Portability also partly explained the appeal of water bottled in PET containers since the small plastic bottles were easier to carry than glasses or cups of tap water. In 2001, consumers began to prefer PET containers not only for immediate consumption but also for home use as the take-home PET market for the first time exceeded the volume sales of chilled PET water sold for immediate consumption. Water packaged in PET containers sold through take-home channels accounted for 28 percent of industry sales volume in 2001 and was expected to account for more than one-half of industry growth between 2002 and 2007.

The convenience and portability of bottled water were two of a variety of reasons U.S. consumers were increasingly attracted to bottled water. An increased emphasis on healthy lifestyles and improved consumer awareness of the need for proper hydration led many consumers to shift traditional beverage preferences toward bottled water. Bottled water consumers frequently claimed drinking more water improved the appearance of their skin and gave them more energy. Bottled water analysts also believed many health-conscious consumers drank bottled water because it was a symbol to others that they were interested in health.

exhibit 2 **Per Capita Consumption of Bottled Water by Country Market, 1996 and 2001**

2001 Rank	Country	Per Capita Consumption (in gallons)		Compound Average Growth Rate
		1996	2001	
1	Italy	33.5	43.4	5.3%
2	France	25.7	34.7	6.2
3	Mexico	28.1	34.3	4.1
4	Belgium-Luxembourg	28.8	32.6	2.5
5	United Arab Emirates	25.7	31.3	4.0
6	Germany	25.6	28.1	1.9
7	Spain	22.3	27.3	4.1
8	Switzerland	21.1	23.8	2.4
9	Lebanon	12.7	22.5	12.1
10	Saudi Arabia	15.1	22.5	8.3
11	Austria	18.5	20.5	2.1
12	Cyprus	14.2	20.2	7.3
13	Czech Republic	12.9	19.6	8.7
14	United States	13.1	19.5	8.3
15	Thailand	14.5	19.4	6.0
Global average		3.3	4.9	8.2%

Source: Beverage Marketing Corporation, as reported by *Bottled Water Reporter,* April–May 2002.

exhibit 3 **U.S. Per Capita Beverage Consumption, 1996 and 2001**

Beverage	Gallons per Person 1996	Gallons per Person 2001	Compound Average Growth Rate
Soft drinks	53.4	55.3	0.7%
Coffee	22.3	21.9	−0.4
Bottled water*	13.0	19.9	8.9
Milk	24.2	19.9	−3.8
Fruit beverages	15.0	15.5	0.7
Tea	9.7	9.3	−0.8
Wine	1.9	2.0	1.0
Beer and spirits	29.3	23.5	−4.3
Tap water/all other	23.2	24.5	1.1
Total	192.0	191.8	

*Note: The per capita consumption of bottled water as presented by *Beverage Aisle* varies slightly from the calculations prepared by Beverage Marketing Corporation presented in Exhibits 2 and 5.
Source: Beverage Aisle, August 15, 2002.

A certain amount of industry growth was attributable to increased concerns over the quality of tap water provided by municipal water sources. Consumers in parts of the world with inadequate water treatment facilities relied on bottled water to provide daily hydration needs, but tap water in the United States was very pure by global standards. Municipal water systems were regulated by the U.S. Environ-

exhibit 4   **Volume Sales and Dollar Value of the U.S. Bottled Water Market, 1991–2001**

Year	Volume Sales (in millions of gallons)	Annual Change	Industry Revenues (in millions of dollars)	Annual Change
1991	2,355.9	2.1%	$2,512.9	−0.6%
1992	2,486.6	5.5	2,658.7	5.8
1993	2,689.4	8.2	2,876.7	8.2
1994	2,966.4	10.3	3,164.3	10.0
1995	3,226.9	8.8	3,521.9	11.3
1996	3,495.1	8.3	3,835.4	8.9
1997	3,794.3	8.6	4,222.7	10.1
1998	4,130.7	8.9	4,666.1	10.5
1999	4,583.4	11.0	5,314.7	13.9
2000	4,904.4	7.0	5,809.0	9.3
2001	5,425.3	10.6	6,477.0	11.5

Source: Beverage Marketing Corporation, as reported by *Bottled Water Reporter,* April–May 2002.

exhibit 5   **U.S. Per Capita Consumption of Bottled Water, 1991–2001**

Year	Per Capita Consumption (in gallons)	Annual Change
1991	9.3	—
1992	9.8	5.4%
1993	10.5	7.1
1994	11.5	9.5
1995	12.2	6.1
1996	13.1	7.4
1997	14.1	7.6
1998	15.3	8.5
1999	16.8	9.8
2000	17.8	6.0
2001	19.5	9.6

Source: Beverage Marketing Corporation, as reported by *Bottled Water Reporter,* April–May 2002.

mental Protection Agency (EPA) and were required to comply with the provisions of the Safe Drinking Water Act Amendments of 2001. Consumer concerns over the quality of drinking water in the United States emerged in 1993 when 400,000 residents of Milwaukee, Wisconsin, became ill with flulike symptoms and almost 100 immune impaired residents died from waterborne bacterial infections. Throughout the 1990s and into the early 2000s, the media sporadically reported cases of municipal water contamination, such as in 2000 when residents of Washington, D.C., became ill after the city's water filtration process caused elevated levels of suspended materials in the water. Consumer attention to the purity of municipal water was also heightened in 2000 when the EPA proposed revising the standard for arsenic content in tap water as specified by the Safe Drinking Water Act Amendments of 1996 from

50 parts per billion (ppb) to 10 ppb. Prior to the congressional discussion of acceptable arsenic levels in drinking water, most Americans were unaware that any arsenic was present in tap water.

Even though some consumers were concerned about the purity of municipal water, most consumers' complaints with tap water centered on its chemical taste, which resulted from treatment processes that included the use of chlorine and other chemicals such as fluoride. In a tap water tasting in Atlanta hosted by *Southpoint* magazine, judges rated municipal water on taste and found some cities' waters very palatable. Water obtained from the municipal source in Memphis was said to have "a refreshing texture" and tap water from New Orleans was commended for "its neutrality." However, other municipal systems did not fare as well with the judges—some of whom suggested Houston's water tasted "like a chemistry lab," while others said Atlanta's municipal water was akin to "a gulp of swimming pool water."[1] However, there were positive attributes to the chemicals added to tap water, as chlorine was necessary to kill any bacteria in the water and fluoride had contributed greatly to improved dental health in the United States. In addition, tap water had been shown to be no less healthy than bottled water in a number of independent studies, including a study publicized in Europe that was commissioned by the World Wide Fund for Nature and conducted by researchers at the University of Geneva.

Bottled water producers in the United States were required to meet the standards of both the EPA and the U.S. Food and Drug Administration (FDA). Like all food and beverage products sold in the United States, bottled water was subject to such food safety and labeling requirements as nutritional labeling provisions and general Good Manufacturing Practices (GMPs). Bottled water GMPs were mandated under the 1962 Kefauver-Harris drug amendments to the Federal Food, Drug and Cosmetic Act of 1938 and established specifications for plant construction and design, sanitation, equipment design and construction, production and process controls, and record keeping. The FDA required bottled water producers to test for the presence of bacteria at least weekly and to test for inorganic contaminants, trace metals, minerals, pesticides, herbicides, and organic compounds annually. Bottled water was also regulated by state agencies that conducted inspections of bottling facilities and certification of testing facilities to ensure that bottled water was bottled under federal GMPs and was safe to drink.

Bottled water producers were also required to comply with the FDA's Standard of Identity, which required bottlers to include source water information on their products' labels. Water labeled as "spring water" must have been captured from a borehole or natural orifice of a spring that naturally flows to the surface. "Artesian water" could be extracted from a confined aquifer (a water-bearing underground layer of rock or sand) where the water level stood above the top of the aquifer. "Sparkling water" was required to have natural carbonation as it emerged from the source, although carbonation could be added to return the carbon dioxide level to what was evident as the water emerged from the source. Even though sparkling water was very popular throughout most of Europe and the Middle East, it accounted for only 9 percent of U.S. bottled water sales in 2001.

The FDA's definition of "mineral water" stated that such water must have at least 250 parts per million of total dissolved solids and its standards required water labeled as "purified" to have undergone distillation, deionization, or reverse osmosis to remove chemicals such as chlorine and fluoride. "Drinking water" required no additional processing beyond what was required for tap water but could not include flavoring or other additives that account for more than 1 percent of the product's total weight. Both "drinking water" and "purified water" had to clearly state that the water originated "from a community water system" or "from a municipal source."

Bottled water producers could also voluntarily become members of the International Bottled Water Association (IBWA) and agree to comply with its Model Code, which went beyond the standards of the EPA, FDA, or state agencies. The Model Code allowed fewer parts per million of certain organic and inorganic chemicals and microbiological contaminants than FDA, EPA, or state regulations and imposed a chlorine limitation on bottled water. Neither the FDA nor the EPA limited chlorine content. IBWA members were monitored for compliance through annual, unannounced inspections administered by an independent third-party organization.

---

[1] As quoted in "The Taste of Water," Bottled Water Web (www.bottledwaterweb.com/watertaste.htm).

Distribution and Sale of Bottled Water

Consumers could purchase bottled water in nearly any location in the United States where food was also sold. Supermarkets, supercenters, and wholesale clubs all stocked large inventories of bottled water, and most convenience stores dedicated at least one stand-up cooler to bottled water. Bottled water could also be purchased in most delis and many restaurants; from vending machines; and at sporting events and other special events like concerts, outdoor festivals, and carnivals. Bottled water could also be delivered directly to consumers' homes or offices.

The distribution of bottled water varied depending on the producer and the distribution channel. Typically, bottled water was distributed to large grocers and wholesale clubs directly by the bottled water producer, while most producers used third parties like beer and wine distributors or food distributors to make sales and deliveries to convenience-store buyers. Similarly, food-service distributors usually handled landing accounts with restaurants and delis and making necessary deliveries to keep the account properly stocked. Most distributors made deliveries of bottled water to convenience stores and restaurants along with their regular scheduled deliveries of other foods and beverages. Therefore, these third-party food and beverage distributors almost never made deliveries to one-time or infrequent events like art festivals or sporting events, since they were better equipped to represent a variety of food and beverage companies that wanted their products available for sale in locations where consumers made frequent food and beverage purchases. Similarly, vending machine servicing did not match the resources and competitive capabilities of most food and beverage distributors.

Because of the difficulty for food-service distributors to restock vending machines and provide bottled water to special events, Coca-Cola and PepsiCo were able to dominate such channels since they could make deliveries of bottled water along with their deliveries of other beverages. Coca-Cola and PepsiCo's vast beverage distribution systems made it easy for the two companies to make Dasani and Aquafina available anywhere Coke or Pepsi could be purchased. In addition, the two cola giants almost always negotiated contracts with sports stadiums, universities, and school systems that made one of them the exclusive supplier of all types of nonalcoholic beverages sold in the venue for some period of time. Under such circumstances, it was nearly impossible for other brands of bottled water to gain access to the account.

Coca-Cola and PepsiCo's soft-drink businesses also aided the two companies in making Aquafina and Dasani available in supermarkets, supercenters, wholesale clubs, and convenience stores. Soft-drink sales were important to all types of food stores since soft drinks made up a sizable percentage of sales and since food retailers frequently relied on soft-drink promotions to generate store traffic. Coca-Cola and PepsiCo were able to encourage their customers to purchase items across their product line to ensure prompt and complete shipment of key soft-drink products. As a diversified food products company, PepsiCo had exploited the popularity of its soft drinks, Gatorade sports drinks, Frito-Lay snack foods, and Tropicana orange juice in persuading grocery accounts to purchase not only Aquafina but also other new brands such as FruitWorks, SoBe, Lipton's iced tea, and Starbucks Frappuccino.

Since most supermarkets, supercenters, and food stores usually carried only three to five branded bottled waters plus a private-label brand, bottled water producers other than Coke and Pepsi were required to compete aggressively on price to gain access to shelf space. Market surveys indicated that wholesale prices for branded bottled water ranged between $3.50 and $7.00 per case—depending on the appeal of the product and the competitive strength of the seller. Some supermarkets and other grocery chains required bottled water suppliers to pay slotting fees in addition to offering low prices to gain shelf space. Grocers expected to pay less for private-label products and typically required private-label suppliers to prepare bids offering both purified and spring water in packaging of various sizes. Contracts were awarded to the low bidder and typically re-bid on an annual or biannual basis.

Convenience-store buyers also aggressively pressed bottled water producers and food distributors for low prices and slotting fees. Most convenience stores carried only two to four brands of bottled water beyond what was distributed by Coca-Cola and Pepsi and required bottlers to pay annual slotting fees of $300 to $400 per store in return for providing 5 to 10 bottle facings on a cooler shelf. Even though bottled water producers were responsible for paying slotting fees to gain shelf space, food-service distributors handled sales transactions with convenience stores and made all deliveries. Food and beverage distributors usually paid the bottlers of lesser-known brands $3.75 to $4.25 per case, while popular national brands commanded wholesale prices in the $5.00–$6.00 range. Typically, a distributor would represent only one or two bottled water producers and required producers to make deliveries to their warehouses. Some bottlers offered to provide retailers with rebates of approximately 25 cents per case to help secure distributors for their brand. Food distributors also asked bottled water suppliers to sponsor annual trade shows at which participating vendors (including bottled water producers) would offer discounts of approximately 25 cents per case to convenience-store customers willing to commit to large quarterly purchases. Food and beverage distributors usually allowed bottled water producers to negotiate slotting fees and rebates directly with convenience-store buyers.

There was not as much competition among bottled water producers to gain shelf space in delis and restaurants since volume was relatively low—making per unit distribution costs exceedingly high unless other beverages were delivered along with bottled water. PepsiCo and Coca-Cola were among the better-suited bottled water producers to economically distribute water to restaurants since they likely provided fountain drinks to such establishments.

Bulk water sold in returnable five-gallon containers was delivered to home and office users directly by bottled water producers. These producers usually specialized in home and office delivery, but might also sell a PET product through convenience and supermarket channels. Retail pricing to bulk water purchasers ranged between $5 and $7 per five-gallon container. Consumers of bulk water were also required to rent a cooler at $10 to $15 per month. Most bulk water sellers used a delivery route system with scheduled visits for deliveries of water and empty container pickup.

Suppliers to the Industry

The suppliers to the bottled water industry included municipal water systems; spring operators; bottling equipment manufacturers; deionization, reverse osmosis, and filtration equipment manufacturers; cooler manufacturers; sellers of racking systems; manufacturers of PET and HDPE bottles and plastic

caps; label printers; and secondary packaging suppliers. Most packaging supplies needed for the production of bottled water were readily available for a large number of suppliers. Large bottlers able to commit to annual purchases of more than 5 million PET bottles could purchase bottles for as little as 5 cents per bottle, while regional bottlers purchasing smaller quantities of bottles or only making one-time purchases of bottles could expect to pay as much as 15 cents per bottle. Most PET and HDPE bottle producers preferred to reward customers choosing to develop ongoing relationships with their lowest prices. Suppliers of secondary packaging (e.g., cardboard boxes, shrink-wrap, and six-pack rings) and suppliers of printed film or paper labels were numerous and aggressively competed for the business of large bottled water producers.

Equipment used for water purification and filling bottles was manufactured and marketed by about 50 different companies in the United States. About 10 manufacturers offered a complete line of filling equipment, filtration equipment, distillation equipment, deionization equipment, bottle washers, labeling equipment, packaging equipment, and reverse osmosis equipment, with others specializing in a few equipment categories. A basic bottle-filling line could be purchased for about $125,000, while a large state-of-the-art bottling facility could require a capital investment of more than $100 million. Bottlers choosing to sell spring water could expect to invest about $300,000 for source certification, road grading, and installation of pumping equipment, fencing, holding tanks, and disinfecting equipment. Bottlers that did not own springs were also required to enter into lease agreements with spring owners that typically ranged from $20,000 to $30,000 a year. Companies selling purified water merely purchased tap water from municipal water systems at industrial rates prior to purifying and bottling the water for sale to consumers. Sellers of purified water were able not only to pay less for water they bottled, but also to avoid spring water's inbound shipping costs of 5 to 15 cents per gallon since water arrived at the bottling facility by pipe rather than by truck.

Key Competitive Capabilities in the Bottled Water Industry

Bottled water did not enjoy the brand loyalty of soft drinks, beer, or many other food and beverage products, but it was experiencing some increased brand loyalty, with 10–25 percent of consumers looking for a specific brand and an additional two-thirds considering only a few brands acceptable. Because of the growing importance of brand recognition, successful sellers of bottled water were required to possess well-developed brand-building skills. Most of the industry's major sellers were global food companies—having built respected brands in soft drinks, dairy products, chocolates, and breakfast cereals prior to entering the bottled water industry. PepsiCo, Coca-Cola, and Nestlé were the most successful sellers at building consumer loyalty in the United States, according to a 2002 brand loyalty study conducted by NFO WorldGroup. The survey found that Aquafina consumers were rather loyal to PepsiCo's brand, as it accounted for 77 percent of regular Aquafina consumers' total bottled water purchases. Nestlé Waters' brands also commanded a 77 percent brand loyalty rating, while the Dasani brand accounted for 62 percent of bottled water consumed by frequent Dasani purchasers. Brands offered by other bottled water sellers achieved far lower levels of brand loyalty.

Bottled water sellers also needed to have efficient distribution systems to supermarket, wholesale club, and convenience store channels to be successful in the industry. It was imperative for bottled water distributors (whether direct store delivery by bottlers or delivery by third parties) to maximize the number of deliveries per driver since distribution included high fixed costs for warehouses, trucks, handheld inventory tracking devices, and labor. It was also critical for distributors and bottlers to provide on-time deliveries and offer responsive customer service to large customers in the highly price-competitive market. Price competition also mandated high utilization of large-scale plants to achieve low production costs. Volume and market share were also key factors in keeping marketing expenses at an acceptable per-unit level.

Recent Trends in the Bottled Water Industry

As the U.S. per capita consumption of bottled water grew to nearly 20 gallons in 2001, industry analysts believed the annual growth rate of bottled water sales in the U.S. would begin to slow. There was some concern among analysts that a slowing industry growth rate might set off stronger price competition in the in-

dustry. As of mid-2002, there had been some modest declines in pricing at both the retail and wholesale levels. Some of the price decline was attributable to Coca-Cola and PepsiCo's use of multipacks in take-home PET channels, which had slightly decreased average revenue per gallon. A July 2002 pricing survey found the average retail price of bottled water sold in supermarkets had declined by 3.4 percent since July 2001, with the price of some brands down by as much as 9 percent from the previous year.

The world's largest sellers of bottled water appeared to be positioning for industry maturity by purchasing smaller regional brands, with Groupe Danone acquiring Naya for $34 million and McKesson for $1.1 billion in 2000, Suntory acquiring Great Pines Water for $19 million in 1999, and Nestlé acquiring Aberfoyle Springs in 2000 and Black Mountain and Aqua Cool in 2001. Most of the leading sellers of bottled water were making similar acquisitions worldwide. Nestlé had acquired bottled water producers in Poland, Hungary, Russia, Greece, France, and Saudi Arabia between 2000 and 2002. Groupe Danone had made a number of acquisitions in attractive global markets and had also entered into strategic alliances and joint ventures to increase penetration of selected emerging and developed markets.

Industry consolidation created a more globally competitive environment in which the top sellers met each other in almost all of the world's markets. Danone and Nestlé had long competed against each other in most country markets, but PepsiCo and Coca-Cola were quickly becoming global sellers as they pushed Aquafina and Dasani into new international markets. In 2001, the top five sellers of bottled water accounted for 75 percent of industry sales; some industry observers believed the industry could consolidate further to three sellers accounting for 75 percent of industry sales by 2005. Exhibits 6 and 7 indicate the degree of industry consolidation in the U.S. bottled water market in 2001.

The introduction of enhanced waters was the most important product innovation since bottled water gained widespread acceptance in the United States, as most sellers in 2002 were moving quickly to introduce variations of their products that included vitamins, carbohydrates, electrolytes, and other supplements. The innovation seemed to be a hit with consumers—the market for enhanced bottled waters expanded from $20 million in 2000 to $85 million in 2001 and was expected to surpass $100

exhibit 6   **Leading U.S. Bottled Water Producers, 2001**

Rank	Company	Wholesale Sales (in millions)	Market Share	2001 Growth
1	Nestlé Waters	$2,103.3	32.5%	23.5%
2	Groupe Danone	879.9	13.6	3.3
3	PepsiCo	645.0	10.0	44.9
4	Coca-Cola	560.0	8.6	105.1
5	Suntory Water Group	507.1	7.8	−0.8
6	Crystal Geyser	235.0	3.6	27.0
7	Culligan International	155.5	2.4	41.4
8	Vermont Pure	67.1	1.0	12.6
9	Glacier Water	60.3	0.9	2.0

Source: Beverage Marketing Corporation, as reported by *Beverage Aisle,* April 15, 2002.

exhibit 7   **Top 10 U.S. Bottled Water Brands, 2001**

Rank	Brand	Parent Company	Wholesale Sales (in millions)	Market Share	2001 Growth
1	Aquafina	PepsiCo	$645.0	10.0%	44.9%
2	Dasani	Coca-Cola	560.0	8.6	105.1
3	Poland Springs	Nestlé Waters	542.0	8.4	20.2
4	Arrowhead	Nestlé Waters	399.6	6.2	18.3
5	Sparkletts	Groupe Danone	361.8	5.6	4.1
6	Deer Park	Nestlé Waters	247.5	3.8	18.6
7	Crystal Geyser	Crystal Geyser	235.0	3.6	27.0
8	Evian	Groupe Danone	211.2	3.3	−4.0
9	Zephyrhills	Nestlé Waters	184.0	2.8	10.8
10	Ozarka	Nestlé Waters	183.9	2.8	11.7

Source: Beverage Marketing Corporation, as reported by *Beverage Aisle,* April 15, 2002.

million in 2002. One of the earliest enhanced waters was Energy Brands' Glaceau Vitamin Water, which was launched in 2000. In 2002, Glaceau came in 20 flavor and supplement varieties that promised mental stimulation, physical rejuvenation, and overall improved health. Glaceau was also the best-selling brand of enhanced water in late 2002, with annual sales growth of 270 percent. Glaceau retailed for about $1.49 per bottle. Baxter International was a $4.7 billion global health care company that offered three scientifically developed and tested vitamin- and nutrient-enriched waters to promote heart health, women's health, and men's health. Brands touting health benefits with wider distribution than Baxter's Pulse or Glaceau Vitamin Water included Clearly Canadian's Reebok Fitness Water, Gatorade's Propel, and PepsiCo's Aquafina Essentials.

Bottled water producers were optimistic about the prospects of selling vitamin-enhanced waters since marketing research had shown consumers (especially female baby boomers) were interested in increasing their intake of vitamins, since enhanced waters were more easily differentiated than purified or spring water, and since enhanced waters carried retail prices as much as 40 percent higher than purified water. Enhanced waters also offered higher margins than typical bottled waters. Even though enhanced waters offered potential benefits, there were some features of enhanced waters that might cause consumers to limit their consumption of such products,

exhibit 8   **Comparison of Product Characteristics of Prominent Enhanced Bottled Water Brands**

Brand	Producer	Additives	Claims to Help . . .
Aquafina Essentials	PepsiCo	Vitamins B6, B12, pantothenic acid, niacin	An active life
Dasani NutriWater	Coca-Cola	Vitamins C, B3, B6, B12	Metabolism, fighting free radicals
Glaceau Vitamin Water	Energy Brands	Guarana, ginseng	Energy level
Propel Fitness Water	PepsiCo	Vitamins B, C, and E	Energy level, fighting free radicals
Pulse Men's Health	Baxter International	Lycophene	Prostate health
Reebok Fitness Water	Clearly Canadian	Chromium	Insulin activity, cholesterol level

Source: "Enhanced Waters Pour onto Shelves," *USA Today,* August 23, 2002, p. M1.

including the need for sweeteners to disguise the taste of added vitamins and supplements and calorie contents that ranged from 20 calories per 16-ounce serving for Propel and Reebok to 100 calories per 16-ounce serving for Glaceau. In addition, some medical researchers had suggested that consumers would need to drink approximately 10 bottles of enhanced water each day to meet minimum dietary requirements for the vitamins promoted on the waters' labels. Exhibit 8 presents a comparison of leading enhanced bottled water brands offered in late 2002.

PROFILES OF THE LEADING BOTTLED WATER PRODUCERS

Nestlé Waters

Nestlé was Switzerland's largest industrial company and the world's largest food company, with 2001 sales of 84.7 billion Swiss francs (approximately $59 billion). The company was broadly diversified into 19 food and beverage categories that were sold in almost every country in the world under such recognizable brand names as Nescafé, Taster's Choice, Perrier, Vittel, Carnation, PowerBar, Friskies, Alpo, Nestea, Libby's, Stouffer's, and of course Nestlé. The company produced bottled water as early as 1843, but its 1992 acquisition of Perrier created the foundation of what has made Nestlé Waters the world's largest seller of bottled water, with 72 brands in 160 countries. In 2001, Nestlé recorded bottled water

sales of 7.5 billion Swiss francs (approximately $5 billion) and held a 16 percent share of the global bottled water market. Nestlé's title as global leader in the bottled water industry was a result of its number one positions in the United States, Canada, Europe, and most Latin American countries. Nestlé was also aggressive in its attempts to build market-leading positions in the Middle East, Asia, and Africa through the introduction of global Nestlé products and acquisitions of established local brands in most geographic regions of the world. Nestlé acquired 11 bottled water producers in 2001 and was expected to purchase several other brands in 2002.

The company's bottled water portfolio in 2002 included 2 global brands (Nestlé Pure Life and Nestlé Aquarel), 4 international premium brands (Perrier, Vittel, Contrex, and San Pellegrino), and 66 local brands. Nestlé Pure Life was a purified water product developed in 1998 for emerging markets and in 2002 was marketed in 12 countries in Asia, Latin America, and the Middle East where safe drinking water was a primary concern. Nestlé Aquarel was developed in 2000 for the European market and was differentiated from other spring waters by its low mineral content, which was more suitable to children's taste preferences. Nestlé's other waters marketed in Europe were either spring water with a higher mineral content or sparkling waters such as Perrier and San Pellegrino. Almost all brands marketed outside of Europe were either spring water or mineral water with no carbonation.

Its brands in the United States included Arrowhead, Ice Mountain, Calistoga, Deer Park, Great Bear, Zephyrhills, Oasis, Ozarka, Poland Springs,

Black Mountain, and Aqua Cool. Nestlé Waters did not market an enhanced-water product. The following table lists the 2001 wholesale sales for Nestlé's leading U.S. brands:

Nestlé's Leading U.S. Bottled Water Brands

Brand	2001 Wholesale Sales (in millions)
Poland Springs	$542.0
Arrowhead	399.6
Deer Park	247.5
Zephyrhills	184.0
Ozarka	183.9
Ice Mountain	106.2
Aberfoyle	102.0
Perrier	85.9

Source: Beverage Marketing Corporation, as reported by Beverage Aisle, April 15, 2002.

Nestlé's brand portfolio in the United States reflected the regional nature of the U.S. market, with most of its brands not competing against each other in specific regional markets. Dasani, Aquafina, Evian, and Perrier were among the few national brands, since most brands began as small regional sellers. For the 52 weeks ending May 12, 2002, Nestlé led most regional markets, as is demonstrated in Exhibit 9. Nestlé's market leading positions in U.S. regional markets and its competitive capabilities developed in Europe allowed it to earn the status of low-cost leader in the United States. Exhibit 10 illustrates Nestlé Waters' cost and wholesale pricing advantages relative to Coca-Cola and PepsiCo in U.S. markets. The company's $100 million bottling plant, which was under construction in Tennessee in 2002, was expected to aid Nestlé in maintaining its low-cost leadership. Nestlé Waters' management stated in mid-2002 that it expected to double the division's revenues by 2010.

Groupe Danone

Groupe Danone was established in 1966 through the merger of two of France's leading glass makers, who foresaw the oncoming acceptability of plastic as a substitute to glass containers. The management of the newly merged company believed that rather than shift its focus to the manufacture of plastic containers, the company should focus on entering markets for products typically sold in glass containers. Groupe Danone's diversification outside of glass containers began in 1969 when the company acquired Evian—France's leading brand of bottled water. Throughout the 1970s and 1980s, Groupe Danone acquired additional food and beverage companies that produced beer, pasta, baby food, cereals, sauces, confectionery, dairy products, and baked goods. In 1997, the company slimmed its portfolio of businesses to dairy products, bottled water, and a baked goods division producing cereal, cookies, and snacks. In 2002, Groupe Danone was a leading global food company, with annual sales of 44.5 billion euros, and was the world's largest producer of dairy products; the number-two producer of cereal, cookies, and baked snacks; and the largest seller of bottled water by volume. (Nestlé was the world's largest bottled water producer based on dollar sales.)

The company's Aqua, Evian, and Volvic brands were three of the world's four best-selling brands of bottled water. Danone also marketed country-specific brands such as Villa del Sur in Argentina, Wahaha in China, and Dannon in the United States. In the United States, Groupe Danone also marketed the regional brands listed in the following table:

Danone's Leading U.S. Bottled Water Brands

Brand	2001 Wholesale Sales (in millions)
Sparkletts	$361.8
Evian	211.2
Dannon	112.4
Pure American	91.5
Alhambra	87.7
Volvic	7.8

Source: Beverage Marketing Corporation, as reported by Beverage Aisle, April 15, 2002.

Groupe Danone's strongest brands sold in the United States during 2002 were Sparkletts, which was the fifth best-selling brand in California, and Dannon, which was the fourth best-selling brand in the Plains States and the fifth best-selling brand in the West, Southeast, Northeast, Mid-South, and Great Lakes (see Exhibit 9). Evian was Danone's

exhibit 9 **Top 5 Brands of Bottled Water, by U.S. Regional Market (52 Weeks Ending May 12, 2002)**

West	South Central	Mid-South	Great Lakes
1. Arrowhead	1. Ozarka	1. Aquafina	1. Aquafina
2. Aquafina	2. Dasani	2. Dasani	2. Ice Mountain
3. Private-label brand	3. Aquafina	3. Private-label brand	3. Private-label brand
4. Dasani	4. Private-label brand	4. Deer Park	4. Dasani
5. Dannon	5. Deja Blue	5. Dannon	5. Dannon

California	Southeast	Northeast	Plains
1. Arrowhead	1. Zephyrhills	1. Poland Spring	1. Aquafina
2. Crystal Geyser	2. Private-label brand	2. Private-label brand	2. Private-label brand
3. Aquafina	3. Dasani	3. Aquafina	3. Dasani
4. Private-label brand	4. Aquafina	4. Dasani	4. Dannon
5. Sparkletts	5. Dannon	5. Dannon	5. Chippewa

Source: IRI InfoScan, as reported by *National Petroleum News,* July 2002.

exhibit 10 **Value Chain Comparison for the Bottled Water Operations of Nestlé, PepsiCo, and Coca-Cola**

	Nestlé Waters	PepsiCo	Coca-Cola
Retailer price per case	$8.44	$8.52	$8.65
Retailer margin	35.0%	17.5%	17.6%
Wholesale price per case	$5.49	$7.03	$7.13
Wholesale sales	$5.49	$7.03	$7.13
Support revenue	0.00	0.41	0.52
Total bottler revenue	$5.49	$7.44	$7.65
Expenses			
Water	$0.01	$1.67	$1.70
PET bottles	1.03	1.16	1.16
Secondary packaging	0.61	0.68	0.68
Closures	0.21	0.23	0.23
Labor/manufacturing	0.70	0.70	0.77
Depreciation	0.07	0.08	0.08
Total cost of goods sold	2.63	4.52	4.62
Gross profit	$2.86	$2.92	$3.03
Selling, general, and administrative costs	2.29	2.25	2.53
EBITA*	$0.57	$0.67	$0.50
EBITA margin	10.4%	9.0%	6.5%

*Earnings before interest, taxes, and amortization.

Source: Goldman Sachs Global Equity Research, as reported by *Beverage World,* April 2002.

second best-selling bottled water brand in the United States but was not among the top five brands in any regional market.

Danone recorded worldwide bottled water sales of 3.8 billion euros in 2001 and produced an operating profit of 321 million euros from its bottled water sales that same year. The company's bottled water sales had grown at an average rate of over 8 percent between 1997 and 2001, but had declined by 8 percent between 2000 and 2001. Danone's capital investments in its bottled water business exceeded 1.4 billion euros between 1997 and 2001, and it, like Nestlé, had made a number of acquisitions of regional bottled water producers during the late 1990s and early 2000s. During 2002, Danone acquired a controlling interest in Poland's leading brand of bottled water for an undisclosed amount and purchased Canada's Sparkling Spring brand of waters for an estimated $300–$400 million. The company also entered into a joint venture with Kirin Beverage Company to strengthen its distribution network in Japan and embarked on a partnership with the Rachid Group, an Egyptian firm, to accelerate its development of market opportunities in North Africa and the Near and Middle East. Also, in mid-2002, Danone and Nestlé were bidding against each other for control of Bisleri, India's leading brand of bottled water, with about a 50 percent share of the market.

Groupe Danone's sales and market share began to decline in the United States beginning in 2000 when Coca-Cola bottlers began distributing Dasani rather than distributing only Evian and other non-Coke brands. Prior to the introduction of Dasani, about 60 percent of Evian's U.S. distribution was handled by Coca-Cola bottlers. Groupe Danone relied on Pepsi bottlers and independent bottlers for distribution to markets not handled by Coca-Cola. With Coca-Cola bottler's attention directed toward the sale of Dasani, Evian lost shelf space in many convenience stores, supermarkets, delis, restaurants, and wholesale clubs.

Groupe Danone and Coca-Cola entered into two new strategic partnerships in mid-2002 that made Coca-Cola the exclusive distributor of Evian, Dannon, and Sparkletts in the United States and Canada. The two companies entered into a distribution agreement in April 2002 whereby Coca-Cola agreed to distribute Evian along with Dasani to convenience stores, supermarkets, and other retail locations serviced by Coca-Cola's bottling operations. The two companies also began a joint venture in June 2002

that made Coke responsible for the production, marketing, and distribution of Dannon and Sparkletts in the United States. Coca-Cola provided Danone an up-front cash payment in return for 51 percent ownership of the joint venture. Danone contributed its five plants and other bottled water assets located in the United States to the joint venture. Coca-Cola also held the license for the use of the Dannon and Sparkletts brands in the United States. Danone's less popular PET brands and its home and office delivery businesses were not included in the agreement.

The Coca-Cola Company

The Coca-Cola Company was the world's leading manufacturer, marketer, and distributor of nonalcoholic beverage concentrates, with 300 brands worldwide. The company produced soft drinks, juice and juice drinks, sports drinks, water, and coffee, but it was best known for Coca-Cola, which had been called the world's most valuable brand. In 2001, the company sold more than 17.8 billion cases of beverages worldwide to record revenues of approximately $20 billion. Coca-Cola's net income for 2001 was nearly $4 billion. Sixty-two percent of Coke's revenues were generated outside of North America, with six international markets (Germany, Brazil, United Kingdom, Japan, and Mexico) each contributing more than $1 billion per year to Coca-Cola's consolidated revenues. The company also sold more than $1 billion worth of beverages in the United States each year.

Along with the universal appeal of the Coca-Cola brand, Coca-Cola's vast global distribution system that included independent bottlers, bottlers partially owned by Coca-Cola, and company-owned bottlers made Coke an almost unstoppable international powerhouse. Coca-Cola held market-leading positions in most countries in the cola segment of the soft-drink industry, and the strength of the Coca-Cola brand aided the company in gaining market share in most other soft-drink segments such as the lemon-lime and diet segments. The company had also been able to leverage Coke's appeal with consumers to gain access to retail distribution channels for new beverages included in its portfolio such as Minute Maid orange juice products, Powerade isotonic beverages, and Dasani purified water.

The Coca-Cola Company did not market and distribute its own brand of bottled water until mid-1999, when it introduced Dasani. The company created a purified water that included a combination of magnesium sulfate, potassium chloride, and salt to re-create what Coke researchers believed were the best attributes of leading spring waters from around the world. The Dasani formula was a closely guarded secret and was sold to bottlers, just as the company sold its Coke concentrate to bottlers. The Dasani name was developed by linguists who suggested the dual *a*'s gave a soothing sound to the name, the *s* conveyed crispness and freshness, and the *i* ending gave a foreign ring to the name. Dasani was supported with an estimated $15 million advertising budget during its first year on the market and was distributed through all retail channels where Coke was available. Coca-Cola's marketing expertise and vast U.S. distribution system allowed Dasani to become the second largest and fastest-growing brand of water sold in the United States by 2001. Dasani did not have significant sales outside the United States, but Coca-Cola did produce and market bottled water in foreign countries under local brand names, such as its Bonaqua brand in the Iberian market.

In late 2002, Coca-Cola was testing four varieties of enhanced bottled waters in New York, Cincinnati, and Charleston. The Dasani Nutriwater line included a lemon-tangerine flavor that promoted "bone strength" with added calcium, magnesium, and B vitamins; pear-cucumber for "balancing" that included B and C vitamins; mandarin orange for "immunity" with vitamin C and zinc; and a multivitamin wild berry variety that included B, C, and E vitamins. Each of the varieties of Nutriwater had about 20 calories per 16-ounce serving. Coke's new product retailed for $1.19–$1.39 per 16-ounce container in test markets. Nutriwater's national rollout was expected for early 2003.

Coca-Cola's 2002 joint venture with Groupe Danone allowed Coca-Cola to jump to the rank of second largest bottled water producer in the United States. The joint venture and Evian distribution agreement provided Coke with bottled water products at all price points with Dasani positioned as an upper-mid-priced product, Evian as a premium-priced bottled water, and Sparkletts and Dannon as value-priced waters. Coke management believed the addition of Sparkletts and Dannon would allow the company to protect Dasani's near-premium pricing while gaining spring water brands that could be marketed nationally to challenge Nestlé's regional brands in the spring water segment. The editor of *Beverage Digest* noted the Coca-Cola–Groupe Danone joint venture would take Coke into several new bottled water markets, including private-label and spring water, and said the deal "has the potential of significantly altering the landscape of the bottled water business in the U.S."[2]

PepsiCo, Inc.

In 2002, PepsiCo was the world's fifth largest food and beverage company, with sales of about $27 billion. The company's brands were sold in more than 200 countries and included such well-known names as Lay's, Tostitos, Mountain Dew, Pepsi, Doritos, Lipton iced tea, Gatorade, Quaker, and Cracker Jack. PepsiCo also produced and marketed Aquafina, which in 2002 was the best-selling brand of bottled water in the United States.

PepsiCo had made attempts to enter the bottled water market as early as 1987 when it purchased a spring water company, but its attempts were unsuccessful until its 1997 introduction of Aquafina. After experimenting with spring water and sparkling water for several years, Pepsi management believed it would be easier to produce a national brand of bottled water that could utilize its water purification facilities used in its soft-drink bottling plants. Pepsi management also believed the company could distinguish its brand of purified bottled water from competing brands by stripping all chlorine and other particles out of tap water that might impart an unpleasant taste or smell. PepsiCo began testing a filtration process for Aquafina in 1994 when it installed $3 million worth of reverse osmosis filtration equipment in its Wichita, Kansas, bottling plant to further purify municipal water used to make soft drinks. The system pushed water through a fiberglass membrane at very high pressure to remove chemicals and minerals before further purifying the water using carbon filters. The water produced by Pepsi's process was so free of chemicals that the company was required to add ozone gas to the water to prevent bacteria growth.

Pepsi sold the purification process to its bottlers who were responsible for the production and distribution of Aquafina. PepsiCo marketed the product

[2]"Coca-Cola Water Deal Creates a Stir," *Atlanta Journal-Constitution,* June 18, 2002, p. 1D.

nationally, spending about $15 million in 2000, $20 million in 2001, and $40 million in 2002 on advertising alone. PepsiCo also developed innovative supermarket displays for Aquafina, employed celebrities to endorse the product, and negotiated contracts to make Aquafina the official beverage of sports organizations such as the Professional Golfers Association of America and major league soccer.

PepsiCo was also moving into international bottled water markets, including Spain and Mexico. In late 2002, PepsiCo's bottling operations acquired Mexico's largest Pepsi bottler, Pepsi-Gemex SA de CV, for $1.26 billion. Gemex not only bottled and distributed Pepsi soft drinks in Mexico but was also Mexico's number one producer of purified water. The company's Electropura was sold only in one-gallon and larger HDPE containers, but it was expected that Pepsi management would introduce bottled water in small PET containers after it took over Gemex operations. PepsiCo also entered the bottled water market in Spain during 2002. Pepsi management supported its Spanish Aquafina launch with a $10 million advertising budget.

PepsiCo launched its Aquafina Essentials enhanced-water line in the United States during the summer of 2002. The line retailed for a suggested price of $1.49 per 20-ounce bottle and included four varieties. Multi-V was a watermelon-flavored beverage containing 25 percent of the daily requirement for vitamins B6, B12, C, E, pantothenic acid, and niacin. Daily-C was a citrus blend fortified with 100 percent of the daily requirement for Vitamin C. B-Power had a wild berry flavoring and provided 25 percent of the daily requirement of vitamins B6, B12, pantothenic acid, and niacin. Aquafina Essentials Calcium+ filled out the line and had a tangy tangerine-pineapple flavoring and provided 25 percent of the daily requirement for calcium and folic acid. The Essentials line was PepsiCo's second attempt at fortified waters. It had attempted to add calcium to Aquafina without any flavoring in 2000, but the company's director of beverage research and development said the beverage's taste was like "chewing on chalk."[3]

---

[3]"Pepsi, Coke Take Opposite Tacks in Bottled Water Marketing Battle," *The Wall Street Journal,* April 18, 2002, p. A1.

Suntory Water Group

Suntory Limited was a diversified Japanese consumer products company with 2001 sales of 833 billion yen (approximately $7.2 billion). The company was Japan's largest producer and distributor of alcoholic and nonalcoholic beverages and was among Japan's largest food distributors. The company also competed in the pharmaceutical and publishing industries, and operated restaurants, bars, and sports clubs in Japan. The company's businesses in the United States included independent Pepsi-Cola bottling operations, a resort management group, Suntory Pharmaceuticals, and Suntory Water Group. Suntory Water Group was the fifth largest producer and distributor of bottled water in the United States, with annual sales of $507 million in 2001. Suntory Water Group's bottled spring water was available nationwide under such regional brands as Crystal Springs, Sierra Springs, Hinckley Springs, Kentwood Springs, Belmont Springs, and Georgia Mountain. The annual sales of its best-selling brands at year-end 2001 are presented in the following table:

Suntory's Leading U.S. Brands

Brand	2001 Wholesale Sales (in millions)
Crystal Springs	$175.4
Sierra Springs	128.7
Hinckley Springs	95.8
Kentwood Springs	63.9

Source: Beverage Marketing Corporation, as reported by *Beverage Aisle,* April 15, 2002.

Suntory had made 30 acquisitions between 1999 and 2001 to increase its overall market share in the United States and to expand its home and office delivery business. In 2002, Suntory Water Group led the direct delivery bulk water segment of the U.S. bottled water industry. The company's home and office delivery business maintained delivery fleets in most parts of the United States and was supported by the company's water.com Web site, which allowed consumers to purchase bulk water and water bottled in PET containers for direct delivery. During 2002, Suntory introduced a calcium-enhanced bottled water and developed the first PET water package capable of being dispensed through 12-ounce can vending machines. The 11.5-ounce PET container won the Institute of Packaging Professionals' 2002 Innovation Award and would be used by all of its regional brands by early 2003.

Other Sellers

In addition to the industry's leading sellers of bottled water, there were hundreds of regional and specialty brands of bottled water in the United States. Most of these companies were privately held bottlers with distribution limited to small geographic regions that competed aggressively on price to make it onto convenience-store and supermarket shelves as third-tier brands. Many of these bottlers also sought out private-label contracts with discounters and large supermarket chains to better ensure full capacity utilization and to achieve sufficient volume to purchase bottles and other packaging at lower prices.

Another group of small bottlers, such as Penta and Trinity, used differentiating features to avoid the fierce price competition at the low end of the market and sold in the superpremium segment, where bottled water retailed from $1.50 to $2.25 per 16-ounce PET container. Penta was among the most successful superpremium brands and had differentiated itself from other brands by using a proprietary purification system that it claimed removed 100 percent of impurities from tap water. In late 2002, Penta was distributed in more than 2,700 health food stores in 48 U.S. states. The product was also available in England and Australia. The company had built brand recognition through product placements in more than 25 television series, including widely watched programs like *Friends, Scrubs,* and *The Practice.* Penta had also entered into agreements during 2002 that would place its product in four upcoming feature films. Trinity's differentiation was based on its water source, which was a 2.2-mile-deep artesian well located in the mountains of Idaho. Trinity claimed its water was incomparable in natural purity since the depth of the natural well maintained water at 138° Fahrenheit and since the water rose to the surface through crystal-lined granite faults in the mountain. Trinity was the best-selling bottled water in U.S. natural foods stores in late 2002.

Dollar General and the Extreme Value Retailing Industry

Sue A. Cullers
Tarleton State University

S. Stephen Vitucci
Tarleton State University–Central Texas

The Dollar General Corporation originated the dollar-store concept: providing discounted items in a small neighborhood store setting to consumers in the low- to middle-income brackets and on fixed incomes. Founders J. L. and Cal Turner opened their first Dollar General store—with no item priced above $1—on an experimental basis in 1955. The Turners' dollar-store concept—providing very inexpensive and deeply discounted items in a small neighborhood store setting to consumers of modest means and income—was so successful that in 10 years the company had grown to 255 stores with annual sales of $25.8 million. Over the next four decades, Dollar General capitalized on low-income consumers' broad interest in its bargain-priced merchandise, growing to over 6,300 stores in 27 states, with 2002 sales of $6.1 billion and more than 54,000 employees. Management believed that its merchandise lineup delivered convenience and value on the basics, thereby helping its clientele save time and money; however, in 2003, Dollar General's merchandise line was no longer comprised of just items priced below $1; most of what it stocked was, however, still priced below $5. Dollar General's mission and values are shown in Exhibit 1. Exhibit 2 shows representative exterior and interior pictures of Dollar General stores.

THE DOLLAR STORE NICHE

One of the most clear-cut segments of the general merchandise retailing business during the 1990–2003 period was extreme-value retailing as represented by so-called dollar discount stores. The three leading extreme-value retailing chains were Dollar General, Family Dollar, and Dollar Tree. During 2002, the three chains combined opened more than 1,300 new stores and by year-end were operating a total of 12,992 stores across the United States:

	Number of Stores, Year-End 2002
Dollar General	6,113
Family Dollar	4,616
Dollar Tree	2,263

These three retailers had combined 2002 sales of $12.6 billion and profits of $630 million. Nationally, sales at dollar stores grew at a rate of 22 percent a year from 1997 through 2001. Dollar stores had broad-based appeal: in 59 percent of American households, someone was a regular dollar-store shopper, up 12 percent from 1998.[1]

The typical dollar store ranged from 3,000 to 10,000 square feet and carried such goods as stationery, gifts, toys, food, household and cleaning

[1]Bob Ingram and Tom Weir, "The Buck Stops There," *Supermarket Business Magazine,* June 15, 2001.

exhibit 1   **Dollar General's Mission and Values, 2003**

Through more than six decades of change, Dollar General's philosophy has remained the same. Our mission is brought to life in the positive attitudes shared by our employees, in the return visit of a satisfied customer, and in the careful thought put into each decision that makes a difference in the lives of Dollar General customers, employees and shareholders.

Dollar General's Mission: Serving Others

- For Customers—A Better Life
- For Shareholders—A Superior Return
- For Employees—Respect and Opportunity

Dollar General's Strategy

A customer-driven distributor of consumable basics

Dollar General's Niche

Profitable small stores delivering convenience and value

Dollar General's Values

- Building our Company with persons who are committed to integrity.
- Promoting leadership that results in team creativity, prompt, effective decision making, and tough expense management.
- Emphasizing strengths and learning from our mistakes.
- Seeking true success that involves mutual gain.

Source: Dollar General Web site, November 2003.

products, health and beauty aids, basic clothing, and school and stationery supplies—all at very low prices and the vast majority under $10. The dollar stores' market was customers who wanted to pay the least amount for products ranging from cereal to socks to motor oil to notebook paper.

The dollar-store category differentiated itself through low prices in convenient small stores. Prices were competitive because of the stores' low-cost operating structure: they minimized labor and advertising costs, offered a limited assortment of merchandise, used a simple merchandise presentation, and located in second-tier shopping strips with low rents. Having few stock keeping units (SKUs) reduced purchasing costs and helped lower the cost of goods sold. Most dollar stores served trade areas no larger than three to five miles in radius, allowing such chains to profitably operate several small stores in an area that might support just one of its rivals' superstores.

Initially, most dollar stores were located in small towns and suburban areas in the southern and southeastern United States. Dollar stores thereby took retail market share not being served by larger retailers such as Wal-Mart, by building stores in communities too small to support a full-sized discount store or supercenter. As the dollar-store chains grew, they built stores in communities that had Wal-Mart or Kmart stores, sometimes across the street from a supercenter. In these communities, dollar stores thrived by offering convenience and competitive prices. By 2003, dollar stores had expanded into other geo-

graphic areas of the United States, becoming a truly national phenomenon. Dollar General's stores were in 27 states in the Midwest, Southeast, and South, while Dollar Tree and Family Dollar had stores in 40 and 42 states, respectively.

Dollar stores had their greatest appeal among large families; low-income, fixed-income, and blue-collar households; and women ages 55 to 64. Leigh Stelmach, Dollar General's executive vice president for operations and merchandising, described the company's customers: "Our customers are salt-of-the-earth people who are savvy about spending money because they have to be. They have to balance their checkbooks every day, at least mentally."[2] Dollar General's CEO, Cal Turner Jr., said, "Our customer doesn't buy until she absolutely has to—she's that stretched. Our agenda has to be to do everything we possibly can to be responsive to her needs."[3]

In 2000, nearly one-third of Americans lived on household incomes of less than $25,000. Such customers had been essential to the discount concept when it emerged in the 1960s, but were then abandoned through the 1980s as discounters moved upscale. Not all dollar-store shoppers had low incomes, however: 13 percent of dollar-store sales were to

[2] As quoted in Laura Heller, "A Singular Sense of Mission," *Discount Store News,* December 8, 1997.

[3] As quoted in Debbie Howell, "The Leader in the Realm of Deep Discount," *Discount Store News,* May 8, 2000.

exhibit 2   **Exterior and Interior Scenes of Dollar General Stores**

female college graduates, and 20 percent were to customers with household income of $50,000 or more.

Competition for extreme-value retailers included other dollar stores, discounters Wal-Mart and Kmart, Goodwill and thrift stores, convenience stores, and supermarkets. Wal-Mart had little reason to worry about the extreme-value segment—Dollar General's revenues for a year equaled Wal-Mart's revenues for a week. Wal-Mart's sales *increase* of $16 billion in 2001 was larger than the annual sales for the entire dollar-store industry. However, in an apparent response to the growth of dollar stores, Wal-Mart introduced departments in some of its stores that sold merchandise similar to that offered by dollar stores at even-dollar price points.

The rapid growth of dollar stores posed a threat for the supermarket industry. In the late 1990s dollar stores began carrying food and other products traditionally sold by grocery stores. A 2000 study on channel blurring found that 57 percent of heavy grocery channel shoppers also shopped in dollar stores. The study also showed a steady decline in the annual number of household visits to grocery stores: 87 in 2000, down from 91 in 1998. Dollar stores were cheaper on the basics and faster for quick trips than supermarkets. Dollar stores also posed a threat for convenience stores, which charged higher prices for similar goods and saw their household penetration drop 7 percentage points, to 45 percent, from 1998 to 2001.[4]

In 2003, the dollar-store industry had significant growth potential because the United States was not saturated with dollar stores. The industry was expected to average 17 percent growth for the foreseeable future. There were still thousands of small towns and neighborhoods that could support a dollar store but did not have one. Extreme-value retailers were not particularly threatened by online retailing because many of their customers did not shop online. Changes in the economy did not tend to hurt dollar stores. In hard times, value prices drew in shoppers who had higher income levels; in a booming economy, lower-income shoppers increased their purchases at dollar stores. Key to the growing success of dollar stores were low capital investment, high return on investment, strong cash flows, careful monitoring of costs, and an abundance of potential new locations.

THE TURNERS AND DOLLAR GENERAL

In 1939, J. L. Turner and his son, Cal Turner, bought a building in Scottsville, Kentucky, and established a wholesaling business. They decided to expand into retailing in 1955 when they spotted opportunities to buy a variety of low-priced merchandise they thought they could resell at attractively low prices. They hit on the idea of a store where everything would be priced at $1 or less—and the concept quickly proved viable. Because their early Dollar General stores carried mostly closeout and discontinued merchandise that the Turners could obtain at bargain prices, customers were likely to find almost anything in the stores.

In the late 1960s, with expansion proceeding at a rapid pace, a third-generation Turner, Cal Turner Jr., joined the Dollar General team as a director. Cal Turner Jr. became president of Dollar General in 1977 and CEO and chairman of the board in 1988, taking over leadership from his father. He described his father and grandfather, the company founders:

> My dad never separated the company from family. The Turners were struggling farmers who were very close to the customer base and never lost that close proximity. That has been a very strong underpinning of the values and the culture of the company.[5]

Cal Turner Jr., who once considered becoming a Methodist minister, said that he followed a ministerial form of management, emphasizing personal values and serving others. Turner believed that by lowering prices, Dollar General allowed its customers to lead better lives and that "those who follow a ministerial approach to management can outsell and outprofit those who don't."[6]

J. L. Turner's father was killed when J.L. was in third grade. J.L. quit school to farm and support his mother and younger siblings, and he never was able to return to school. Because J.L. was functionally illiterate, he relied on his young son Cal to help with business deals. Later, Dollar General established a literacy campaign that was inspired by J.L. and by the desire to make a difference in the lives of Dollar General customers. Since 1987, Dollar General had made each of its stores a place where people could go to find out where to learn to read, take General Education Development (GED) classes or the GED test, or sign up to be a tutor. By 2001, Dollar General's literacy program had helped more than 50,000 people. Dollar General also offered grants of up to $20,000 to nonprofit organizations, including schools and school districts. The funds could be used for programs targeting youth education, literacy, self-esteem, or mentoring.

In 1993, Dollar General became the first retailer in a Nashville housing project. The company worked

---

[4]Ingram and Weir, "The Buck Stops There."

[5]As quoted in Debbie Howell, "Dollar General's Cal Turner Sr. Dead at 85," *DSN Retailing Today,* December 11, 2000.

[6]As quoted in Richard Halverson, "Dollar General Keeps Simplicity Top of Mind," *Discount Store News,* July 3, 1995.

with state and local agencies to develop an educational program designed to reduce the neighborhood's chronic unemployment. Several government agencies were involved in establishing the store, and a federal grant was used to build it. The city provided land and grant money, while a civic agency provided job training and free child care. Several graduates from the job-training program went on to work in Dollar General stores and other businesses.[7]

In 1996, Dollar General opened its second Nashville store serving a public housing development. The facility also contained an employment agency, an entrepreneurial training center, the YWCA/Dollar General Learning Center, a community police station, social services offices, and room for three small businesses.[8] Later in 1996, the company opened its third learning center store, this one in an inner-city neighborhood in Charleston, South Carolina.[9] By 2000, Dollar General had opened seven learning center stores that provided training, educational services, and access to needed merchandise for inner-city residents.

THE GROWTH OF DOLLAR GENERAL

Two acquisitions in 1983 and 1985 added 483 stores to the Dollar General chain and boosted revenues almost 50 percent. Integrating so many new stores into the chain forced the company to examine its operating practices. The new stores had to be stocked with merchandise quickly, so Dollar General chose to carry conventional goods purchased from suppliers rather than closeout goods. From that experience, Cal Turner Jr., concluded that customers wanted Dollar General to have a predictable assortment of merchandise in stock every day.[10] All Dollar General stores then began offering a selection of apparel, school supplies, and household products. Over time, they carried less and less clearance merchandise. Company managers observed that customers always

bought the least expensive choice of any it gave them, and they realized that their customers were having a hard time making ends meet. The company's strategy of selling basic consumable goods at a low price thus evolved from its response to the acquisitions in 1983 and 1985.

The strategy shifts following the two big acquisitions led the company to pursue rapid expansion of its store locations. The rate of growth accelerated, with more stores opened each year from 1991 through 1994 (see Exhibit 3). By the start of 1995, Dollar General had 2,059 stores and annual sales of $1.76 billion. The company's growth and size began to force a transition away from being a relatively small, family-controlled organization. Cal Turner Jr. began to install more professional management and put in the infrastructure and systems to operate Dollar General as a large and fast-growing retail organization.

Still, in 1995, Dollar General's motto could have been "Keep things simple." Company managers believed that the key to achieving high levels of productivity was to make operations simple to run. "Simple" included reducing the number of SKUs. Dollar General customers did not need a wide selection of merchandise—just the lowest prices on the basics. The corporate growth strategy was to keep overhead low and provide greater value to customers, leading to increased sales and greater profits. The company's simple approach to operations had produced same-store sales growth of 13.5 percent and operating profit growth of 51.6 percent in 1994.

In the mid-1990s, the company began to expand store sizes from 5,000 square feet to 6,800 square feet of selling space. The expansion provided more space for hard lines (stationery, school supplies, hardware, and various household items). In earlier store layouts, soft lines (clothing, shoes, and home products such as sheets and towels) had two-thirds of the floor space and 40 percent of sales. However, from 1991 to 1995, hard lines had increased from 60 percent of sales to 70 percent. Hard lines offered faster inventory turns but slightly lower gross margin than soft lines. In 1995, turns per year for hard goods were 4.5; for soft goods, 1.5. Management saw fast inventory turns as critical to Dollar General's profitability. In 1996, Dollar General developed a new consumables-oriented merchandise strategy, emphasizing select food items (candy, snack foods, and

[7]Cyndee Miller, "Rediscovering the Inner City," *Marketing News*, January 17, 1994.

[8]Teresa Andreoli, "Dollar General Expands Community Projects Program," *Discount Store News*, March 18, 1996.

[9]"Dollar General Opens Third Inner City Store," *Discount Store News,* October 7, 1996.

[10]Dollar General Corporation, 10-K report, 2003.

exhibit 3   **Growth in the Number of Dollar General Stores, 1991–2002**

Year	Beginning of Year	Stores Opened	Stores Closed	End of Year
1991	1,461	118	57	1,522
1992	1,522	146	68	1,617
1993	1,617	251	68	1,800
1994	1,800	302	43	2,059
1995	2,059	397	40	2,416
1996	2,416	360	42	2,734
1997	2,734	468	33	3,169
1998	3,169	551	33	3,687
1999	3,687	646	39	4,294
2000	4,294	758	52	5,000
2001	5,000	602	62	5,540
2002	5,540	622	49	6,113

Source: Dollar General 10-K reports, 1996–2003.

other nonperishable packaged foods), pet food, and paper products. Previously, Dollar General had not sold food products.[11]

Dollar General's merchandising approach placed constant downward pressure on operating expenses. Bob Carpenter, executive vice president for Dollar General, described the company's cost strategy:

> If we can control our expenses, we can lower our prices, which increases sales, which in turn lowers the average cost of goods—the classic productivity loop. We have to constantly watch expenses because if they get out of line, and we have to increase prices, sales dip and the same loop comes into play but in the opposite direction.[12]

The strong pressure to keep its margins healthy forced Dollar General to watch its costs very closely and operate very lean. To help hold down distribution expenses, DG concentrated on building stores close to its distribution centers; new distribution centers were built to support expansion into adjoining geographic areas. From 1995 to 1997, the average distance between stores and the nearest distribution center was reduced from 600 miles to just over 300 miles. In the late 1990s, Dollar General's growth strategy was to open an average of one new store each day and to add a new distribution center each year.

[11]Teresa Andreoli, "Dollar General: Bring on the Basics," *Discount Store News,* June 17, 1996.

[12]As quoted in Jay L. Johnson, "Money Machines," *Discount Merchandiser,* September 1998.

Dollar General's marketing and advertising strategy was simple. Consistent with its everyday-low-pricing strategy, it offered no discount promotions or sales; its even-dollar pricing did not change from week to week. In the early 1990s, Dollar General sent out 13 direct-mail advertising circulars per year. Over the next several years, it cut back on advertising costs by eliminating direct mail circulars, with last circular mailed in December 1998.[13] The company did continue direct mailings to support the opening of new stores. Advertising as a percentage of sales dropped from 4 percent to about 0.5 percent, helping to explain the increase in net income as percentage of sales from 0.8 percent in 1986 to 5.7 percent in 1998.

Managing Rapid Growth, 1998–2002

By the start of 1998, Dollar General had 3,169 stores and four distribution centers. The company's stock price had responded to the growth in stores, revenues, and income, making Dollar General the best-performing retailing stock of the 1990s. The company had split its stock 5-for-4 at least once each year since 1993.

In 1998, Dollar General sought to maintain momentum by increasing the capacity and improving the operation of its distribution system. New distribution center capacity was needed to catch up with past

[13]Ibid.

exhibit 4   **Dollar General Stores, by State, as of February 28, 2003**

State	Number of Stores	State	Number of Stores
Alabama	305	Missouri	273
Arkansas	196	Nebraska	75
Delaware	23	New Jersey	20
Florida	354	New York	124
Georgia	352	North Carolina	327
Illinois	260	Ohio	332
Indiana	249	Oklahoma	226
Iowa	136	Pennsylvania	341
Kansas	144	South Carolina	219
Kentucky	251	Tennessee	324
Louisiana	211	Texas	770
Maryland	63	Virginia	230
Michigan	91	West Virginia	115
Mississippi	181	Total	6,192

Source: Dollar General 10-K report, 2003.

growth in sales and number of stores. Supporting its stores had become more difficult in 1997, when the company began carrying 700 fast-turning consumable products in all of its stores. The program was so popular with customers that Dollar General's in-stock position dropped to 80 percent; during 1998 it improved to 89 percent, but the company's goal was 95 percent. Turner commented that Dollar General's growth had created great demands on the company. He announced that during the next 18 months, Dollar General would double its distribution capacity.

Management's priority for 1999 was expanding distribution and technology systems to support the expected addition of 550 new stores in its then 24-state market. The company implemented electronic data interchange (EDI) purchase ordering with 600 core vendors and began installation of a new distribution center merchandise replenishment system. In March 1999 the company began selling bread and milk in its learning center stores to comply with federal guidelines for accepting food stamps; they were the first stores in the chain to sell perishable food items.[14]

In 1999, Dollar General's growth and profitability put the company in the Fortune 500 rankings for the first time; it ranked seventh in 10-year earnings per share growth.[15] Fourth-quarter 1999 profits rose

by 16.2 percent, the 37th consecutive quarter in which earnings increased by more than 15 percent.[16] However, in 2000, Dollar General posted lower earnings for the fourth quarter and the year as a whole. Sales were sharply higher after the company opened 758 new stores during the year, but gross margin dropped by 2.7 percent and operating costs rose by 1.5 percent. Cal Turner Jr., commented:

> Year-over-year declines in earnings are rare for Dollar General. 2000 was an unusual year of poorer implementation of our growth as we undertook more change than could be fully digested in one year.[17]

He predicted that Dollar General would learn valuable lessons from the earnings downturn and position itself for future growth.

Dollar General continued its investment in infrastructure: a new distribution center in Alachua, Florida, opened in August 2000, and its Zanesville, Ohio, distribution center opened in April 2001. This gave the company seven distribution centers across the Southeast and Midwest, four of which were opened between 1998 and 2001. These distribution centers supported some 6,192 stores in 27 states as of February 2003 (see Exhibit 4). Each distribution center served approximately 800 stores, with an

[14]Howell, "The Leader in the Realm of Deep Discount."

[15]Debbie Howell, "Dollar General Hits Milestone," *DSN Retailing Today,* February 19, 2001.

[16]Don Hogsett, "Dollar Gen. 4Q Net Jumps 19%," *Home Textiles Today,* February 28, 2000.

[17]As quoted in "Dollar General Posts 4Q Earnings Decline," *Home Textiles Today,* March 5, 2001.

exhibit 5   **Dollar General Distribution Centers, February 28, 2003**

Location	Year Opened	Number of Stores Served
Scottsville, Kentucky	1959	867
Ardmore, Oklahoma	1994	975
South Boston, Virginia	1997	971
Indianola, Mississippi	1998	696
Fulton, Missouri	1999	912
Alachua, Florida	2000	770
Zanesville, Ohio	2001	1,001

Source: Dollar General 10-K report, 2003.

average distance per delivery of 220 miles (see Exhibit 5). The distribution center in Ohio was built to support growth in Michigan, New York, and New Jersey, states where Dollar General did not yet have stores. The 5,000th Dollar General store, opened early in 2001 in Waterford, Michigan, increased the company's territory to 25 states. Later that year, the company opened its first stores in New York and New Jersey. Bob Carpenter, Dollar General's president, said: "No one else opens as many stores as we do. It's a real task. There's not a model for it." Only Radio Shack (with 7,100 stores) had more retail merchandise stores than Dollar General.[18]

The Accounting Restatement

On April 30, 2001, Dollar General announced that it had discovered accounting irregularities that would force it to restate the financial statements for fiscal years 1998 and 1999 and the interim financial information for 2000. The initial estimate was that the restatements would reduce earnings by $0.07 per share over the period 1998–2000, when reported earnings had totaled $1.81 per share. Turner sought to reassure investors, saying that he did not expect the restatements to affect future profits or the growth of the company. However, the stock market had already been shocked by other companies' restatements, and Dollar General's stock fell by 37 percent upon the news. Uncertainty about Dollar General's accounting records and financial reporting caused investors and

others to question much that the company had accomplished over the preceding decade.

The audit committee of Dollar General's board of directors hired law firm Dechert Price & Rhoads of Philadelphia and accounting firm Arthur Andersen to look into the discrepancies. During the period affected by the restatement, Dollar General's accounting firm had been Deloitte & Touche; the company fired Deloitte & Touche in September 2001, hiring Ernst & Young to serve as its auditor.[19] The U.S. Securities and Exchange Commission (SEC) began its own investigation of Dollar General's accounting problems.

After Dollar General announced the discovery of the accounting irregularities, shareholders filed more than 20 class action lawsuits against the company and current and former officers and directors. The plaintiffs alleged that Dollar General and its officers and directors had made misrepresentations about its financial results in filings with the SEC and other public statements. They sought damages with interest and such other relief as the court would allow. After several months, Dollar General reached a settlement agreement with the plaintiffs for total damages of $162 million.[20]

There were also six shareholder derivative lawsuits against current and former directors and officers of Dollar General and Deloitte & Touche. These suits alleged that directors and officers had breached their fiduciary duties to Dollar General and that Deloitte & Touche had aided and abetted those breaches and was negligent in its service as Dollar General's independent accountant. Dollar General Corporation was a nominal defendant in these actions. A settlement agreement was reached in these lawsuits also. After being fired by Dollar General, Deloitte & Touche sent a letter to the SEC outlining its disagreement with Dollar General. Deloitte & Touche claimed that Dollar General's managers had said there had been significant efforts on the part of Dollar General personnel to withhold information from Deloitte & Touche and to mislead the auditor during the performance of past audits. As part of the restatement, Dollar General changed several leases from operating leases to capital leases. Deloitte & Touche stood by its original findings that the leases should have been treated as operating leases, saying that it had not received enough information from

---

[18]As quoted in Howell, "Dollar General Hits Milestone."

[19]Dollar General Corporation, 8-K/A report, October 9, 2001.
[20]Dollar General Corporation, 8-K report, September 16, 2002.

exhibit 6 **Summary of Changes in Dollar General's Restatement of Its Earnings**

	Before the Changes		After the Restatement	
Year	Net Income (in millions)	Earnings Per Share	Net Income (in millions)	Earnings Per Share
2000	$206.0	$0.62	$ 70.6*	$0.21
1999	219.4	0.65	186.7	0.55
1998	182.0	0.54	150.9	0.45

*Includes effect of $162 million expense associated with shareholder lawsuits.
Source: Dollar General 10-K report, 2002.

Dollar General to conclude that the previous treatment of the leases was incorrect. Deloitte & Touche also said that it had found information that could affect its ability to rely on some members of Dollar General's management.

Dollar General's investigation of its accounting records and restatement of the financial reports delayed the issuance of the 2000 annual report until January 2002. At that time, Dollar General lowered its combined earnings for fiscal years 1998–2000 by $0.60 per share, to $1.21. The correction of accounting errors reduced after-tax earnings for the period by about $100 million, causing about half the decrease in earnings per share. The remainder of the decrease in earnings was due to the cost of settling the shareholder lawsuits. Exhibit 6 provides a summary of the effects on 1998–2000 earnings.

Dollar General's investigation into the financial irregularities found a pattern of numerous accounting errors, which fell into four general categories:

1. Items affecting cost of goods sold that were recorded incorrectly, or for which more accurate estimates became available.
2. Selling, general, and administrative (SG&A) expenses that were incurred but not accrued or were recorded incorrectly.
3. Errors in interest expense caused by misclassifying leases.
4. Errors in the company income tax provision.

Examples of items in category 1 included provision for inventory shrinkage, expenses associated with the company's import program, markdown on excess inventory, and vendor allowances for new store openings. Correction of the errors in category 2 reduced diluted earnings per share by $0.11 over the three-year period (see Exhibit 7). Prior to the restatement,

the company had recorded certain expenses (property taxes, rent, supplies, advertising costs, and utilities) when it paid them, rather than when the activity was actually undertaken. Certain so-called synthetic leases were restated from the operating lease classification to the capital lease category; as a result, depreciation expense had to be recorded on the leased assets. (Synthetic leases are a form of off-balance-sheet financing used for real property. For financial reporting purposes, the lessee treats the lease as an operating lease. Therefore, it does not report the asset or the related debt on its balance sheet. However, for tax purposes the lessee is treated as owning the asset, and it is allowed to deduct depreciation and interest expense on its tax return.) Restatement of the leases increased long-term liabilities by $511 million at the end of 2001. Finally, some expenses had been charged against unrelated liability accounts rather than being categorized as SG&A expenses.

Increases in interest expense reduced diluted earnings per share by $0.11 over the three-year period; these increases were necessary in order to correctly record additional interest expense resulting from the lease-related restatements. Corrections of errors in calculating income tax expense reduced diluted earnings by $0.02 over the three-year period.

The large number of errors raised the question of whether the accounting misstatements were deliberate. Dollar General's April 2001 press release announcing the restatements said that

the company and the audit committee are reviewing allegations of fraudulent behavior in connection with certain of the accounting irregularities and are reviewing the company's internal accounting controls and financial reporting processes.[21]

---

[21]As quoted in Dollar General Corporation, 8-K report, filed with SEC April 30, 2001.

exhibit 7   **Adjustments to Dollar General's Earnings per Share Resulting from the Restatement, 1999–2001**

	Three-Year Cumulative	February 2, 2001	January 28, 2000	January 29, 1999
Cost of goods sold	$(0.05)	$(0.01)	$(0.01)	$(0.03)
Selling, general, and administrative expense	(0.11)	(0.02)	(0.05)	(0.04)
Interest expense	(0.11)	(0.06)	(0.04)	(0.01)
Tax provision	(0.02)	(0.01)	(0.00)	(0.01)
Total	$(0.30)	$(0.11)	$(0.10)	$(0.09)

Note: Totals may not foot due to rounding; includes accounting changes but excludes litigation settlement expense.
Source: Dollar General 10-K report, 2002.

However, when the investigation had been completed, Dollar General declined to state whether fraud was involved, saying the SEC was still conducting an ongoing inquiry.

Following discovery of the misstatements, Dollar General adopted a new reporting structure, with the chief financial officer (CFO), James Hagan, reporting directly to the president and chief operating officer, who in turn reported to the board audit committee. Hagan was hired in February 2001 to replace Brian Burr, who had been CFO since March 1999. Burr lacked experience in retailing finance. He in turn had replaced Phil Richards, who became CFO in 1996. There was some speculation that the rapid turnover of Dollar General's finance executives and its slower adoption of information technology (compared to competitors) may have left it vulnerable to accounting problems.[22]

Turner told company investors that new measures had been adopted to prevent future mistakes, including hiring several new executives and a new financial reporting structure with tighter controls. Dollar General also implemented enhancements to its corporate governance and internal control procedures. It agreed to elect directors every year, with two-thirds of them independent, and to have the independent directors meet at least once a year without the CEO or inside directors in attendance.[23]

[22]Debbie Howell, "Accounting Errors Cast Shadow on Dollar General's Success," *DSN Retailing Today,* May 21, 2001; and Debbie Howell, "Dollar General Re-releases Finances," *DSN Retailing Today,* February 11, 2002.

[23]Bernard Bush, "Dollar General's Debt Rating Lowered a Notch," *The Tennessean,* p. E4, April 11, 2002.

Cal Turner Jr., received a salary of $795,864 for 2001, an $800,000 bonus, and stock options in the amount of 111,785 shares. He was granted the bonus because Dollar General exceeded its earnings goal for the year. Dollar General's earnings rose 32.9 percent in 2001, excluding restatement expenses and costs of settling shareholder lawsuits. However, company stock finished the year down 21 percent because of reaction to the accounting problems. A spokesperson for the company said that Turner's compensation was comparable to the average for similar-sized companies and that the amount of his compensation was recommended by an outside consultant.[24]

In July and August of 2002, Turner made voluntary payments to Dollar General of $6.8 million in cash. Approximately $6 million represented the value of stock options he had exercised and $0.8 million was the value of bonuses paid to Turner in 1999 and 2000. Vesting of the options and payment of the bonuses occurred on the basis of the financial statements originally issued but would not have occurred on the basis of the financial results as restated.[25]

After the Restatement

Dollar General continued with its growth strategy, even while the accounting investigation was underway. From 1998 through 2002, Dollar General's sales revenues doubled (see Exhibits 7 and 8). Dollar General's low-income customers appeared unaffected by and unaware of the financial probe;

[24]Getahn Ward, "Accounting Woes Don't Affect Turner Bonus," *The Tennessean,* May 4, 2002.

[25]www.dollargeneral.com/aboutus/history.aspx. 2003.

exhibit 8 **Dollar General Income Statements, 2001–2003 (in thousands except per-share amounts)**

	For the Year Ended		
	January 31, 2003	February 1, 2002	February 2, 2001
Net sales	$6,100,404	$5,322,895	$4,550,571
Cost of goods sold	4,376,138	3,813,483	3,299,668
Gross profit	1,724,266	1,509,412	1,250,903
Litigation settlement	(29,541)		162,000
Operating profit	457,265	373,611	154,004
Interest expense	42,639	45,789	45,357
Income before taxes	414,626	327,822	108,647
Provision for income taxes	149,680	120,309	38,005
Net income	$ 264,946	$ 207,513	$ 70,642
Diluted earnings per share	$0.79	$0.62	$0.21

Source: Dollar General 10-K report, 2003.

company managers commented that its investing public was different from its customer public.[26]

The sales of perishable food begun in Dollar General's learning center stores in 1997 proved so successful that Dollar General installed coolers (refrigerated merchandise display cases) on a trial basis in 400 stores. The coolers were stocked with perishable food items, including milk, eggs, hot dogs, lunch meat, and frozen foods. Average transaction size was significantly higher in stores with coolers, and Dollar General decided to introduce the coolers in 1,000 additional stores during 2002. The company expected that sale of perishable foods, along with other consumable hard lines, would bring customers to the stores more frequently. For 2002, highly consumable merchandise accounted for 60.2 percent of Dollar General's sales. Seasonal products, home products, and basic clothing accounted for 16.3, 13.3, and 10.2 percent, respectively.[27]

Dollar General continued to capitalize on the income demographic of people earning $25,000 or less a year, the fastest-growing income segment of American society. The aging population added to Dollar General's customer base due to increasing numbers of retirees with fixed incomes. In 2002, *DSN Retailing Today* conducted a market basket study to compare prices at various stores. Researchers bought the lowest-cost item in a category, regardless of brand. The study found that Wal-Mart had lower prices than all the supermarket chains. Dollar General, however, actually beat Wal-Mart by 4 percent: Dollar General's market basket came in at $50.49, compared to $52.62 for Wal-Mart and $61.06 for Super-Target.[28]

The most critical element of the company's strategy for success was keeping its costs to a minimum through product selection, distribution strategy, advertising, and use of technology. Dollar General's annual sales per square foot of selling space were lower than for Wal-Mart, Kmart, or Target, but its expenses per square foot were lower, too. By locating at least half of its stores in small towns, Dollar General took advantage of lower lease rates in those areas. The company estimated that there were 18,000 communities nationwide with populations under 25,000 that would support a Dollar General store. Within the 27 states that Dollar General served as of 2002, there were still many communities and neighborhoods where a Dollar General store would operate profitably. When the company eliminated most of its direct mail advertising, same-store sales seemed to decline initially. However, the change proved beneficial in the long run. Lower costs al-

[26]Dollar General Corporation, 10-K report, January 14, 2002.

[27]www.dollargeneral.com/aboutus/history.aspx. 2003.

[28]Laura Heller, "Wal-Mart, Dollar General Lead Pricing in Atlanta," *DSN Retailing Today,* August 12, 2002.

exhibit 9 **Dollar General's Balance Sheets, 2002–2003 (in thousands)**

	January 31, 2003	February 1, 2002
Assets		
Current assets		
Cash and cash equivalents	$ 121,318	$ 261,525
Merchandise inventories	1,123,031	1,131,023
Deferred income taxes	33,860	105,091
Other current assets	45,699	58,048
Total current assets	$1,323,908	$1,556,047
Net property and equipment	993,822	988,915
Other assets, net	15,423	7,423
Total assets	$2,333,153	$2,552,385
Liabilities and equity		
Current liabilities		
Current portion of long-term obligations	$ 16,209	$ 395,675
Accounts payable	341,303	322,463
Accrued expenses and other	239,898	242,780
Litigation settlement payable		162,000
Income taxes payable	67,091	10,633
Total current liabilities	644,501	1,133,551
Long-term obligations	330,337	339,470
Deferred income taxes	50,247	37,646
Common stock, par value $0.50 per share	166,670	166,359
Additional paid-in capital	313,269	301,848
Retained earnings	812,220	579,265
Accumulated other comprehensive loss	(1,349)	(3,228)
Less treasury stock	(2,742)	(2,395)
Less unearned compensation		(131)
Total shareholders' equity	1,288,068	1,041,718
Total liabilities and shareholders' equity	$2,333,153	$2,552,385

Source: Dollar General 10-K report, 2003.

lowed the company to lower its selling prices, which led to increased sales.

Dollar General's distribution centers were a powerful platform for the company's growth. The entire distribution system was automated with replenishment and allocation systems that kept merchandise in stock and distributed to store locations. The company planned to open its next distribution center late in 2004 or in 2005 to support continued growth.

Early in 2002, systems to support perpetual inventories were installed in approximately 4,800 stores. Dollar General had the systems in all stores by the end of 2002 and began implementation in 2003. The perpetual inventory system allowed the company to track store-level inventory at the SKU level and was expected to result in better inventory management. Investments in technology also included a new merchandise planning system to assist with purchasing and store allocation decisions and satellite technology for improved communication between stores and the corporate office.[29]

[29]Debbie Howell, "Dollar General Expands Perishables Assortment," *DSN Retailing Today,* May 6, 2002, p. 2.

In April 2002, Moody's lowered the debt rating for Dollar General by a notch because of concerns about the SEC investigation of the company and the ability of Dollar General to keep up with its rapid growth. CFO Jim Hagan said the company was disappointed by Moody's move:

> We believe this downgrade by Moody's does not reflect the underlying strength of the Dollar General business model. While we have candidly acknowledged that our infrastructure was strained by our growth during the last 10 years, we believe that the necessary initiatives are under way to strengthen our infrastructure to support the continued growth of the company.[30]

The Turner dynasty at Dollar General ended in November 2002 when Cal Turner Jr. resigned as CEO.[31] The company's spokesperson said that Turner's resignation was not related to the company's accounting problems; Turner simply wished to retire. Referring to the accounting restatements, Turner had said, "Clearly, this ship faltered while I was at the helm. This was the biggest surprise and most jolting disappointment in my 36 years with the company."[32]

Under Turner's leadership, the Dollar General chain had grown from 761 stores in 1977 to more than 5,500 stores, with sales in excess of $6 billion. In April 2003, David Perdue was named CEO for Dollar General. Perdue had extensive experience in manufacturing but not in retailing; he had served as chair and CEO of Pillowtex Corporation and former brand president for Reebok. Turner retired from the company's board of directors in June 2003, and Perdue became chairman of the board, with the responsibility to determine the vision and direction of the company.

DOLLAR GENERAL'S COMPETITORS

Family Dollar

Family Dollar was Dollar General's most direct competitor, targeting the same customers with similar

---

exhibit 10   **The Growth of the Family Dollar Chain, 1998–2002**

Year	Number of Family Dollar Stores
1998	3,017
1999	3,324
2000	3,689
2001	4,141
2002	4,616

Source: Family Dollar 10-K report, 2002.

merchandise and similar strategies. Both chains grew rapidly (see Exhibits 9, 10, and 11). Many small towns and urban neighborhoods had both a Family Dollar store and a Dollar General store, both operating successfully and profitably.

The original predecessor of Family Dollar was formed in 1959 to operate one retail store in Charlotte, North Carolina. As of November 2002, Family Dollar had 4,636 stores in 41 states and the District of Columbia. Family Dollar had expanded geographically more rapidly than Dollar General, and it had stores throughout the United States except in the Northwest.

The typical Family Dollar store had 7,500 to 9,500 square feet of total area. The stores were in both rural and urban areas, generally freestanding or located in shopping centers. Family Dollar had more urban stores than Dollar General had. Historically, about 25 percent of Family Dollar stores were in areas with a population above 75,000. In 2002, 40 percent of new stores were located in urban markets, with an emphasis on large urban markets.

Like Dollar General, Family Dollar employed an everyday-low-price merchandising strategy, with most items priced below $10, and offered a variety of hard-line and soft-line merchandise. In 2002, hard lines accounted for approximately 76 percent of Family Dollar's sales. Like Dollar General, in the late 1990s Family Dollar adjusted its merchandise selection, adding more hard-line consumables and reducing space allocated to hanging apparel and shoes.

In 2001 and 2002, shareholders of U.S. corporations lost billions of dollars in stock value due to accounting errors and earnings restatements. As a result, investors became more attentive to earnings quality. In 2002, nearly 450 large companies were

---

[30]As quoted in Bernard Bush, "Dollar General Settlement Gets Judge's Approval," *The Tennessean*, April 6, 2002.

[31]Dollar General Corporation, 8-K report, filed with SEC September 16, 2002.

[32]As quoted in Howell, "Dollar General Expands Perishables Assortment."

exhibit 11 **Family Dollar Income Statements, 2000–2002 (in thousands except per-share amounts)**

	August 31, 2002	September 1, 2001	August 26, 2000
Net sales	$4,162,652	$3,665,362	$3,132,639
Cost of sales	2,766,733	2,439,261	2,076,916
Selling, general, and administrative expense	1,054,298	927,679	784,812
Total costs and expenses	3,821,031	3,366,940	2,861,728
Income before taxes	341,621	298,422	270,911
Income taxes	124,692	108,917	98,894
Net income	$ 216,929	$ 189,505	$ 172,017
Net income per common share—diluted	$1.25	1.10	1.00

Source: Family Dollar 10-K report, 2002.

exhibit 12 **Family Dollar's Consolidated Balance Sheets, 2001–2002 (in thousands)**

	August 31, 2002	September 1, 2001
Current assets		
Cash and cash equivalents	$ 220,265	$ 21,753
Merchandise inventory	766,631	721,560
Deferred income taxes	49,941	43,985
Income tax refund receivable	6,469	4,936
Prepayments and other current assets	12,553	15,031
Total current assets	1,055,859	807,265
Net property and equipment	685,617	580,879
Other assets	13,143	11,601
Total assets	$1,754,619	$1,399,745
Liabilities and shareholders' equity		
Current liabilities		
Accounts payable	$ 381,164	$ 264,965
Accrued liabilities	149,616	125,329
Total current liabilities	530,780	390,294
Deferred income taxes	68,891	50,436
Shareholders' equity		
Common stock, $0.10 par	18,583	18,454
Capital in excess of par	63,294	40,318
Retained earnings	1,118,015	945,192
Subtotal	1,199,892	1,003,964
Less treasury stock at cost	(44,944)	(44,949)
Total stockholders' equity	1,154,948	959,015
Total liabilities and stockholders' equity	$1,754,619	$1,399,745

Source: Family Dollar 10-K report, 2002.

ranked for the quality of their earnings. Family Dollar Stores topped the earnings quality rankings with a score of 100.[33]

Dollar Tree

Dollar Tree, the smallest of the three large dollar-store chains, employed a strategy substantially different from that of Dollar General and Family Dollar. Dollar Tree described itself as the leading operator of discount variety stores offering merchandise at the fixed price of $1. At Dollar Tree, everything cost exactly $1. Dollar Tree managers believed that the variety and quality of products sold for $1 set it apart from its competitors. Despite its pricing strategy, Dollar Tree aimed for a more upscale customer, with a household income of at least $30,000. Dollar Tree sold items that people want but don't really need, such as hairclips, feather dusters, and bath gel.[34]

Dollar Tree's business strategy was to exceed the customer's expectations of variety and quality of products that could be purchased for $1, offering items that sold for more than $1 elsewhere. Direct relationships with manufacturers allowed the company to select from a broad range of products and to customize packaging and product sizes to meet customers' needs. Dollar Tree's merchandise mix was a balanced selection of products within traditional variety store categories: basic everyday items and seasonal and closeout merchandise (see Exhibit 13). The stores carried certain basic consumable merchandise to bring customers in on a regular basis. Consumable merchandise included candy, food, health and beauty items, and paper and plastics. Variety merchandise included toys, housewares, party goods, gifts, and stationery. Closeout merchandise represented less than 15 percent of purchases.

[33]"Earnings-Quality Leaders," *Dow Theory Forecasts,* November 18, 2002.

[34]Ellen Glanton, "Dollars and Sense," *Forbes,* January 8, 2001.

exhibit 13 **Dollar Tree's Merchandise Mix, 2000–2001**

Merchandise Type	2001	2000
Variety categories	50.7%	51.4%
Consumable	38.2	36.6
Seasonal	11.1	12.0

Source: Dollar Tree 10-K report, 2002.

Dollar Tree stores were successful in large cities and small towns. Stores were designed with bright lighting and colors, uniform decorative signs, and carpeting. The company believed that the store's image attracted new and repeat customers. At the end of 1997, Dollar Tree had 1,059 stores in 28 states and 3.9 million square feet of selling space. By December 31, 2002, Dollar Tree had 2,263 stores in 40 states and 13 million square feet of selling space (Exhibit 14). Store growth came from opening new stores and selective mergers and acquisitions. The company operated stores under the names Dollar Tree, Dollar Express, Dollar Bills, Only One Dollar, and Only $One.

Most retailers can increase the selling price of merchandise to increase same-store sales or to cover increasing costs. As a fixed-price retailer, Dollar Tree could not raise selling prices to increase sales; therefore, sales growth had to come from opening new stores and expanding existing stores. Dollar Tree had to control its merchandise costs, inventory levels, and operating expenses. The efficiency of its distribution system was critical to growth and profitability. Dollar Tree had six distribution centers capable of supporting about $3 billion in annual sales. It intended to add distribution capacity to support opening of new stores, with the aim of staying about one year ahead of distribution needs.

Dollar Tree has not paid dividends on common stock and did not anticipate paying dividends in the foreseeable future, retaining all of its income for development and expansion of the business and repayment of indebtedness.

exhibit 14 **Selected Financial Data for Dollar Tree, 2000–2002**

	2002	2001	2000
Net sales	$2,329 million	$1,990 million	$1,690 million
Gross profit	$ 848 million	$ 716 million	$ 624 million
Selling, general, and administrative expense	$ 594 million	$ 512 million	$ 421 million
Net income	$ 155 million	$ 123 million	$ 122 million
Number of stores at end of period	2,263	1,975	1,729
Selling square feet annual growth	29.0%	29.6%	27.9%
Net sales annual growth	17.0%	17.7%	24.9%
Comparable store sales increase	1.0%	0.1%	5.7%
Net sales per selling square foot	$199	$217	$238
Net sales per store	$ 1.08 million	$ 1.04 million	$ 1.01 million
Return on assets	15.3%	14.9%	17.9%
Return on equity	20.5%	21.0%	29.1%
Store inventory turns	4.5	4.6	4.7
Cash	$ 336 million	$ 237 million	$ 182 million
Working capital	$ 510 million	$ 361 million	$ 303 million
Total assets	$1,116 million	$ 902 million	$ 747 million
Total debt	$ 54 million	$ 62 million	$ 71 million
Shareholders' equity	$ 855 million	$ 652 million	$ 519 million

Source: Dollar Tree 10-K report, 2002.

Growth, Strategy, and Slotting at No Pudge! Foods, Inc.

Chris Robertson
Northeastern University

Call us skeptics, but we didn't believe homemade fat-free brownies could match the addictive flavor of the gooey, traditional kind. That was before we tried moist and fudgy No Pudge! Brownie Mix. —Fitness Magazine

Lindsay Frucci was at a crossroads. Her seven-year-old fat-free brownie mix company, No Pudge! Foods, Inc. (No Pudge!), was just starting to take off, and she was considering a number of options for the future. She was seriously thinking about expanding into fat-free muffin mix. This would break tradition from her narrow, but strong, line of four fat-free brownie mix flavors. She also had an opportunity to develop a ready-made fat-free brownie for fast-food franchises such as Subway. Yet there was still plenty of unfinished business in the

Northeastern
UNIVERSITY

Ivey

Richard Ivey School of Business
The University of Western Ontario

Professor Chris Robertson prepared this case solely to provide material for class discussion. The author does not intend to illustrate either effective or ineffective handling of a managerial situation. The author may have disguised certain names and other identifying information to protect confidentiality.

Ivey Management Services prohibits any form of reproduction, storage or transmittal without its written permission. This material is not covered under authorization from CanCopy or any reproduction rights organization. To order copies or request permission to reproduce materials, contact Ivey Publishing, Ivey Management Services, c/o Richard Ivey School of Business, The University of Western Ontario, London, Ontario, Canada, N6A 3K7; phone (519) 661-3208; fax (519) 661-3882; e-mail cases@ivey.uwo.ca.

brownie world. The U.S. Midwest and Southeast looked extremely promising. Perhaps going international was another viable, yet complicated, option.

THE BIRTH OF THE FAT-FREE BROWNIE MIX

In January of 1995, a New Hampshire brownie-aholic with minimal business experience decided to start a company that would revolutionize the brownie world. Although Lindsay Frucci had tasted various fat-free style brownies in the past, she was enormously displeased with the bland, at best, taste. After a month or so of whipping up experimental batches of different fat-free brownie mixes, she finally came up with a mix that was fudgy, chewy and delicious: everything that a brownie lover looks for in a brownie, but with *no fat*. With the recipe intact, and validated by friends, relatives and the local community, Frucci sailed forward into uncharted waters. Her mission: to take these tasty treats to the general public. Specifically, she wanted to target, "upscale, educated consumers, primarily females between the ages of 20 and 60." Her instinct was to initially go after health-conscious people who wanted to minimize the fat intake in their diets.

Fortunately, while seeking help from a local SCORE[1] (Service Corps of Retired Executives) office, she connected with some key people who would guide her through the arduous process of establishing

[1]SCORE is a division of the U.S. Small Business Administration.

exhibit 1   **Quotes from the Media about No Pudge! Fat-Free Fudge Brownie Mix**

"...all you add to this No Pudge! mix is vanilla yogurt. The best part of the quick and easy process is a fudgy, chewy brownie that has only 90 calories."   —*Muscle & Fitness* magazine

"Very satisfying."   —*Good Morning America*

"Love the taste of brownies but hate the fat? We recommend No Pudge! Fudge brownie mix."   —*Self* magazine

"The Brownie of Your Dreams"   —*Weight Watchers* magazine

". . . simply combine the mix with fat-free yogurt, and the end result is thick, moist and truly delicious brownies."   —*Chocolatier* magazine

"My expectations were low, I must admit....I was surprised at seeing an end product closely resembling the full-fat versions. . . . In my book, they were a winner."   —*Kankakee Daily Journal*

"No Pudge! Brownies, the best fat-free treat we've ever tasted."   —*Teen* magazine

"But the ease of preparation is second to the wonderful smell as the brownies bake, and their rich, moist, hard-to-believe-they're-not-sinful taste and texture"   —*Boston Sunday Globe*

"You have to try this product. . . . I'm telling you, these are good."   —*Hartford Courant*

"While fat-free brownies may seem like the ultimate oxymoron, skeptics beware: No Pudge! makes a thick, tender, fudgy brownie that can stand up proudly and be judged with its peers."   —*Boston Globe* Food Section

"...thick, rich, chewy brownies. With just 100 calories each and no fat, preservatives or artificial ingredients, this dessert definitely qualifies as spa cuisine."   —*Spa* magazine

a viable business and getting her product onto supermarket shelves. Jay Albert, a retired chief executive officer (CEO) of Blanchard and Blanchard (a condiment producer) in Vermont, and Bob Fox, the former associate chief counsel of General Foods, walked Frucci through the multitude of decisions that had to be made to get the firm up and running. Stuart Pompian, a retired venture capitalist, jumped in to carry No Pudge! to the next level. All of the time and effort of these retired executives was complimentary, and none received compensation from No Pudge!

Finally, in August of 1995, the first bags of the No Pudge! Original Fudge Brownie Mix hit the shelves of a few local New Hampshire stores. Less than seven years later, No Pudge! Foods, Inc. offered four different mixes in 48 states (all but Alaska and Hawaii) and Canada (see Exhibit 1 for media quotes about No Pudge!).

GROWING PAINS

In 1995, revenues at No Pudge! totaled a mere $6,000.[2] After experimenting with a number of alter-

native brownie mix flavors, and testing them out on a local mothers' ski group, Frucci decided to introduce the cappuccino- and raspberry-flavored mixes in March of 1996. Gradually, 1996 sales climbed to $42,000, though a profit had yet to be seen. In 1997, Frucci decided that she must be more aggressive if this venture were to survive. She pursued distribution at a fervent pace. Her efforts paid off, and Trader Joe's Company, a successful national supermarket chain with close to $2 billion in sales, agreed to put No Pudge! products on the shelf. As a result, 1997 sales jumped to $250,000. The mint-flavored mix was also introduced in 1997.

In 1998 and 1999, growth was steady, due to the addition of two distributors, with sales of $325,000 and $450,000 respectively. No Pudge! products were gradually finding their way onto more supermarket shelves. By the end of 1999, No Pudge! was offered by three distributors and was on numerous store shelves in eight states. Despite the positive trend, No Pudge! was still financially teetering between the red and the black. Production costs were extremely high, and margins were slim. Frucci was quickly finding out that the only way to turn a solid profit was to increase revenues substantially.

In January of 2000, Frucci decided to attend the National Food Distributors Association annual

---

[2]All financial figures are approximate and based on interviews with L. Frucci.

meeting and present her product to numerous national distributors. Her efforts paid off. In the next year, an additional 23 distributors agreed to sign on and offer No Pudge! products. Revenues in 2000 blossomed about 70 percent to $750,000, and then rose to $1.5 million in 2001. A slim profit was finally realized in 2001. By April of 2002, sales were well ahead of the prior year, and if the trend continued, Frucci expected between $2.3 million and $2.5 million for the year.

OPERATIONS AND STRATEGY

Staffing was a concern for No Pudge!, as the growth projections came in. Initially, the firm was a one-woman show, with Frucci working out of her home in Hopkinton, New Hampshire. Manufacturing was outsourced from the beginning by using a "co-packer," Concord Foods (Concord) of Brockton, Massachusetts. Concord managed the entire manufacturing process and shipped orders directly to distributors nationwide. Supermarkets and specialty stores then placed their orders with their local distributor. This left Frucci primarily with sales, strategy, marketing and financial duties. A bookkeeper was hired in 1996, and by 2002, the headquarters staff, including Frucci, totaled a mere four employees: three full-time and one part-time. With continued growth, staffing changes would clearly be necessary.

Ninety-two percent of sales were realized through the strong distributor network. The remaining 8 percent were essentially online orders placed through the NoPudge.com Web site. Frucci also chose to outsource the bulk of the work related to online orders. An answering service in New Hampshire took down the orders and passed the requests on to No Pudge! No Pudge! staffers then processed credit card authorizations and forwarded all orders to a fulfillment house in Connecticut that managed all distribution and delivery.

The original mix accounted for roughly 65 percent of sales, with the remaining 45 percent spread somewhat equally across the cappuccino-, raspberry-, and mint-flavored mixes. Direct competition in the fat-free brownie mix category for No Pudge! was virtually nonexistent. While major producers such as Betty Crocker and Duncan Hines offered reduced-fat mixes (with five grams of fat), the only other totally fat-free mix was Krusteaz. The uniqueness for No Pudge! was in the just-add-yogurt concept. The distinctively styled No Pudge! box (see Exhibits 2 and 3) also differentiated the product from other mass-produced, generic-style mixes. From a price-point perspective No Pudge! products were usually offered at retail stores in the $2.99 to $3.79 range, which was about $1.00 over the standard price for the reduced-fat mixes.[3]

Frucci believed that online consumers could be extremely helpful in her "guerilla marketing" campaign. Along with every order, she also sent a 50 cent coupon and a "SIRF." A SIRF was a "special item request form" that No Pudge! advocates could deliver to their local grocer if the product was not on the shelf (see Exhibit 4). If enough SIRFs ended up on a store manager's desk, there was a good chance that an order would be placed for the requested item. Frucci went a step further than other SIRF users by listing all of her distributors on the back of the card. This made it much easier for the grocer to identify where to place the order. SIRFs were enormously helpful in No Pudge!'s rapid geographic expansion.

While Frucci's primary target market was the health-conscious consumer, she also targeted overweight individuals, specifically weight-loss groups. According to some experts, more than 40 million U.S. adults were more than 20 percent above their desired weight.[4] While there were strict laws about sending promotions and samples to groups such as Weight Watchers, Frucci found out that if members or instructors initiated a request, then it could be fulfilled. The use of SIRFs helped stimulate interest and requests from weight-loss groups.

THE SLOTTING BLUES

One barrier to entry that Frucci continued to wrestle with was the industry norm of charging slotting fees in exchange for shelf space. This was a clever, profitable method for retailers to put new products on the shelf at no cost. It took the financial risk out of

[3]Typically, distributors added on a 27 percent markup, and retail stores added a markup between 25 and 40 percent.
[4]Obesity: The World's Oldest Metabolic Disorder, by Michael Blumenkrantz, M.D. http://www.quantumhcp.com/obesity.htm

exhibit 2 **Print Advertising**

Source: Company files.

new product offerings for retailers. Slotting occurred in two forms: direct cash disbursements and free fill.

Generally, cash slotting fees ranged from $2,500 to $25,000 per new item. With all of the large supermarket chains, a slotting fee was a given (see Exhibit 5 for a list of the top 20 U.S. supermarkets). This made obtaining shelf space extremely difficult and costly for small firms like No Pudge! Nevertheless, No Pudge! managed to gain entry into 16 of the top 20 chains. Big-time manufacturers such as Kellogg and Kraft spent close to 14 percent of their revenues on various shelf-space costs. A 2001 accounting

exhibit 3   **Product Descriptions**

NO PUDGE! Fat Free Fudge Brownie Mixes are the only brownie mixes that make rich, fudgy REAL brownies with NO FAT. Our mixes are made from the finest natural ingredients using no artificial flavors, colors or preservatives, are low in sodium and contain no cholesterol. They are unique in that the only ingredient that the consumer adds to the mix to make the brownies is fat free vanilla or french vanilla yogurt. This provides a significant benefit to the consumer because they are adding a healthy, natural ingredient that they can feel good about. This is a significant benefit for the retailer as well because for every bag of mix that a consumer buys, they buy a container of yogurt as well. But the very best thing about NO PUDGE! Fat Free Fudge Brownies is the remarkable taste and texture. Weight Watchers Magazine told their readers that our mixes make 'The Brownie of Your Dreams' and TEEN Magazine called them the 'Best fat free treat we've ever tasted'.

BROWNIES WITHOUT GUILT!!
Don't you love it?!

Original Fudge Brownie Mix makes traditional thick, fudgy brownies. Great for folks who don't want anything but a rich, all-chocolate taste.
Raspberry Fudge Brownie Mix captures that delectable combination of sweet, juicy raspberries and dark, fudgy chocolate. A treat that, quite simply, is not to be missed!
Cappuccino Fudge Brownie Mix combines our trademark rich, fudgy chocolate with real Brazilian Dark Roast coffee and a hint of all natural sweet vanilla. A coffee and chocolate lover's dream!
Mint Fudge Brownie Mix combines the dark, fudgy decadent chocolate of our Original Fudge Brownie with the mouth tingling *zing* of mint. If you like chocolate and mint you are going to LOVE these brownies!!

PRODUCT DESCRIPTION	UPC		
Original Fudge Brownie Mix	7 08758 00101 9	**Unit Size:** 13.7 oz	
Raspberry Fudge Brownie Mix	7 08758 00102 6	**Unit Dimensions:** 3.5"l x 2.5"w x 7.5"h	
Cappuccino Fudge Brownie Mix	7 08758 00103 3	**Case Dimensions:** 7.25" x 7.75"w x 7.7"h	
Mint Fudge Brownie Mix	7 08758 00104 0	**Case Pack:** 6	**Case Weight:** 6 lb
		Case Cube: .25	

NO PUDGE! FOODS, Inc.
159 Clarke Lane · Hopkinton, NH 03229-2027 · 1-800-730-7547 · Fax 1-800-730-4726
E-mail: lindsay@nopudge.com · www.nopudge.com

Source: Company files.

adjustment by Kellogg for shelf-space costs totaled $1.3 billion.[5]

Free fill was a request for a free shipment of the first order per store in order to earn the right to shelf space. Major chains such as Stop and Shop had 300 stores, which made free fill, *at each store,* incredibly costly. In 2002, the U.S. government and Federal Trade Commission had begun an investigation into whether paying for shelf space was anticompetitive.[6]

When first confronted with the slotting issue, Frucci knew that there was no way her firm could survive if she agreed to play by industry rules. Eventually, she came up with a barrage of arguments that she presented to retailers: first, her product was unique; second, No Pudge! was a small firm and if it

[5]Julie Forster, "The Hidden Cost of Shelf Space," *Business Week,* April 15, 2002, p. 103

[6]Ibid.

exhibit 4   **Special Item Request Form (SIRF)**

No Pudge! Foods, Inc.
Fat Free Fudge Brownie Mixes

SPECIAL ITEM REQUEST FORM

To the Store Manager:
As a regular customer of your store I would like to ask you to stock No Pudge! Fat Free Brownie Mixes. Please see the back of this paper for a list of distributors that stock No Pudge!. Thank You!!

Your Name: _____

City: _____ Zip: _____

Phone: _____

Date: _____

Store Name/Location _____

Associated Buyers	Kehe
Blooming Prairie	Lomar
Davidson	Millbrook
DPI-Colorado	Nikol Foods
European Imports	Northeast Coop
GAF - Great Lakes	Peter's Imports
GAF - Mid Atlantic	Peyton
GAF - North Central	Tree of Life MW
GAF - Southeast	Tree of Life/GAF N. Calif.
GAF - Southern California	Tree of Life NE
GAF - South Florida	Tree of Life SE
Gourmet Specialties/UWG	Tree of Life SW
Haddon House	Tumbleweed
Hannaford/Progressive	UNFI

Source: Company files.

paid slotting fees, there would be no money left for coupons or demos; third, No Pudge! was a Certified Woman Owned Company (by the Women's Business Enterprise National Council). In addition to these arguments she still had flocks of No Pudge! fanatics delivering their SIRFs to store managers.

Her hardball tactics paid off, and she avoided paying slotting fees. The only free fill she agreed to deliver was for new store openings. Nevertheless, retailers found other ways to dip into No Pudge!'s profits through charge-backs for advertising, reclamations (the return of damaged goods) and broker-paid commissions on net invoices. She felt lucky to survive in such a hostile environment for small businesses. As her firm continued to grow, the pressure to pay slotting fees also began to increase dramatically.

exhibit 5   **The Top 20 U.S. Supermarket Chains, 2001**

		Sales ($mil)	Stores	Stocks No Pudge!	Headquarters
1	The Kroger Co.	$50,098	3,600	Yes	Cincinnati, OH
2	Albertson's, Inc.	36,762	2,400	Yes	Boise, ID
3	Safeway Inc.	34,301	1,770	No	San Francisco, CA
4	Ahold USA, Inc.	27,023	1,475	Yes	Chantilly, VA
5	IGA, INC.	21,000	4,000	Yes	Chicago, IL
6	Publix Super Markets, Inc.	15,370	700	Yes	Lakeland, Fl
7	Delhaize America, Inc.	14,913	1,200	No	Salisbury, NC
8	Fred Meyer, Inc.	14,878	1,300	Yes	Portland, OR
9	Winn-Dixie Stores, Inc.	12,903	1,150	Yes	Jacksonville, FL
10	The Great Atlantic & Pacific Tea Company, Inc.	10,973	750	Yes	Montvale, NJ
11	Meijer, Inc.	10,000	150	Yes	Grand Rapids, MI
12	H. E. Butt Grocery Company	8,965	295	Yes	San Antonio, TX
13	The Stop & Shop Companies, Inc.	7,748	300	Yes	Quincy, MA
14	Ralph's Grocery Company	5,487	450	Yes	Compton, CA
15	The Vons Companies, Inc.	5,407	330	Yes	Arcadia, CA
16	Giant Food Inc.	4,780	180	No	Landover, MD
17	Giant Eagle Inc.	4,435	145	Yes	Pittsburgh, PA
18	Shaw's Supermarkets, Inc.	4,100	185	Yes	West Bridgewater, MA
19	Pathmark Stores, Inc.	3,963	140	No	Carteret, NJ
20	Hy-Vee, Inc.	3,900	210	Yes	West Des Moines, IL

Source: www.hoovers.com.

LOOKING AHEAD

As Frucci considered the many options for No Pudge!'s future, she kept thinking about her target of $15 million in revenues. If she were able to grow the firm to that level, then she would seriously consider selling the firm to one of the major food purveyors such as Kraft. The big question was how could No Pudge! grow that much more without further product extension and new product development? The opportunity to make ready-mix fat-free brownies for a franchise like Subway could produce a huge jolt in revenues. She had already developed fat-free muffin mixes in four flavors (corn, bran, lemon poppy, and banana) that could make it to the market by late 2002.

Geographically, No Pudge! sales were still lagging in various regions of the United States, and more work was needed in those areas to bolster sales (see Exhibit 6). Although she had only just begun to explore expansion to Canada, she recognized that this would be a venerable entrance into international trade. Going international would require additional staffing as well, but might enhance No Pudge!'s perception as a potential acquisition target. All of these options looked viable, and Frucci realized that she needed to maintain a consistent standard, no matter how difficult, with regards to securing shelf space, if her firm were to survive.

exhibit 6   **Regional Breakout of 2001 Sales**

Region	% of Sales
Northeast	46.82
Southeast	10.65
Midwest	15.76
Southwest	3.91
West	21.13
Canada	1.73

case 8

Dell Computer in 2003: Driving for Industry Leadership

Arthur A. Thompson
The University of Alabama

John E. Gamble
University of South Alabama

In 1984, at the age of 19, Michael Dell founded Dell Computer with a simple vision and business concept—that personal computers (PCs) could be built to order and sold directly to customers. Michael Dell believed his approach to the PC business had two advantages: (1) Bypassing distributors and retail dealers eliminated the markups of resellers, and (2) building to order greatly reduced the costs and risks associated with carrying large stocks of parts, components, and finished goods. While at times between 1986 and 1993 the company struggled to refine its strategy, build an adequate infrastructure, and establish market credibility against better-known rivals, Dell Computer's strategy started to click into full gear in the late 1990s. Going into 2003, Dell's sell-direct and build-to-order business model and strategy had provided the company with the most efficient procurement, manufacturing, and distribution capabilities in the global PC industry and given Dell a substantial cost and profit margin advantage over rival PC vendors. Dell's operating costs ran about 10 percent of revenues in 2002, compared to 21 percent of revenues at Hewlett-Packard (HP), 25 percent at Gateway, and 46 percent at Cisco Systems (considered the world's most efficient producer of networking equipment). Dell's low-cost provider status was powering its drive for market leadership in a growing number of product categories.

Dell Computer was solidly entrenched as the market leader in PC sales in the United States, with nearly a 28 percent market share in 2002, comfortably ahead of Hewlett-Packard (16.8 percent) and Gateway (5.7 percent). Dell had moved ahead of IBM into second place during 1998 and then overtaken Compaq Computer as the U.S. sales leader in the third quarter of 1999. Its market share leadership in the United States had widened every year since 2000. Worldwide, Dell Computer was in a neck-and-neck race for global market leadership with HP, which acquired Compaq Computer in May 2002. Dell was the world leader in unit sales in the first and third quarters of 2002, and HP was the sales leader in the second and fourth quarters. Dell had overtaken Compaq as the global market leader in 2001. But when HP, the third-ranking PC seller in the world, acquired Compaq, the second-ranking PC vendor, Dell found itself in a tight battle with HP for the top spot globally. Exhibit 1 shows the shifting domestic and global sales and market share rankings in PCs during the 1996–2002 period.

Since the late 1990s, Dell had also been driving for industry leadership in servers. In 2002 Dell was the number one domestic seller of entry-level servers and high-performance workstations (used for applications with demanding graphics). It was number two in the world in server shipments and within striking distance of global market leadership. In the mid-to-late 1990s, a big fraction of the servers sold were proprietary machines running on customized Unix

exhibit 1 **Leading PC Vendors Worldwide and in the United States, Based on Factory Shipments, 1996–2002**

A. U.S. Market Shares of the Leading PC Vendors, 1998–2002

2002 Rank	Vendor	2002		2001		2000	
		Shipments (in 000s)	Market Share	Shipments (in 000s)	Market Share	Shipments (in 000s)	Market Share
1	Dell	13,324	27.9%	10,817	23.5%	9,645	19.7%
	Compaq*	—	—	5,341	11.6	7,761	15.9
2	Hewlett-Packard*	8,052	16.8	4,374	9.5	5,630	11.5
3	Gateway	2,725	5.7	3,219	7.0	4,237	8.7
4	IBM	2,531	5.3	2,461	5.3	2,668	5.5
5	Apple	1,693	3.5	1,665	3.6	n.a.	n.a.
	Others	19,514	40.8	23,509	51.0	18,959	38.8
	All vendors	47,839	100.0%	46,051	100.0%	48,900	100.0%

B. Worldwide Market Shares of the Leading PC Vendors, 1996–2002[†]

2002 Rank	Vendor	2002		2001		2000	
		Shipments (in 000s)	Market Share	Shipments (in 000s)	Market Share	Shipments (in 000s)	Market Share
1	Dell	20,672	15.2%	17,231	12.9%	14,801	10.6%
	Compaq*	—	—	14,673	11.0	17,399	12.5
2	Hewlett-Packard*	18,432	13.6	9,309	7.0	10,327	7.4
3	IBM	7,996	5.9	8,292	6.2	9,308	6.7
4	Fujitsu Siemens	5,822	4.3	6,022	4.5	6,582	4.7
5	NEC	4,533	3.3	4,702	3.5	n.a.	n.a.
	Others	78,567	57.8	73,237	54.9	80,640	58.0
	All vendors	136,022	100.0%	133,466	100.0%	139,057	100.0%

*Compaq was acquired by Hewlett-Packard in May 2002. The 2002 data for Hewlett-Packard include both Compaq-branded and Hewlett-Packard-branded PCs for the last three quarters of 2002, plus only Hewlett-Packard-branded PCs for Q1 2002. Compaq's worldwide PC shipments during Q1 2002 were 3,367,000; its U.S. PC shipments during Q1 2002 were 1,280,000 units.

†Includes branded shipments only and excludes original equipment manufacturer (OEM) sales for all manufacturers; shipments of Compaq PCs for last three quarters of 2002 are included in 2002 figures for Hewlett-Packard.

Source: International Data Corporation.

operating systems and carrying price tags ranging from $30,000 to $1 million or more. But a seismic shift in server technology, coupled with growing cost-consciousness on the part of server users, produced a radically new server market during 1999–2002. In 2003 about 8 out of 10 servers sold were expected to carry price tags below $10,000 and to run on either Windows or the free Linux operating system rather than more costly Unix systems. The overall share of Unix-based servers shipped in 2003 was expected to be about 10 percent, down from

about 18 percent in 1997. Dell's domestic and global market share in low-priced and midrange servers was climbing rapidly. Dell had over a 30 percent share of the 2002 world market for servers, up from 2 percent in 1995.

In addition, Dell was making market inroads in other product categories. Its sales of data storage devices were growing rapidly, aided by a strategic alliance with EMC, a leader in the data storage. In 2001–2002, Dell began selling low-cost, data-routing switches—a product category where Cisco Systems

1999		1998	
Shipments (in 000s)	Market Share	Shipments (in 000s)	Market Share
7,492	16.6%	4,799	13.2%
7,222	16.0	6,052	16.7
3,955	8.8	2,832	7.8
4,001	8.9	3,039	8.4
3,274	7.2	2,983	8.2
n.a.	n.a.	n.a.	n.a.
19,248	42.6	16,549	45.6
45,192	100.0%	36,254	100.0%

1999		1998		1997		1996	
Shipments (in 000s)	Market Share	Shipments (in 000s)	Market Share	Shipments (in 000s)	Market Share	Shipments (in 000s)	Market Share
11,883	10.5%	7,770	8.5%	4,684	5.8%	2,996	4.3%
15,732	14.0	13,266	14.5	10,064	12.6	7,211	10.4
7,577	6.7	5,743	6.3	4,468	5.6	2,984	4.3
9,287	8.2	7,946	8.7	7,239	9.1	6,176	8.9
n.a.	n.a.	n.a.	n.a.	n.a.	n.a.	n.a.	n.a.
5,989	5.3	5,976	6.5	4,150	5.2	4,230	6.1
62,258	55.2	50,741	55.5	49,333	61.7	45,727	66.0
112,726	100.0%	91,442	100.0%	79,938	100.0%	69,324	100.0%

was the dominant global leader. In late 2002 Dell introduced a new line of handheld PCs—the Axim X5—to compete against the higher-priced products of Palm, HP, and others; the Axim offered a solid but not trendsetting design, was packed with features, and was priced roughly 50 percent below the best-selling models of rivals. Starting in 2003, Dell planned to begin marketing Dell-branded printers and printer cartridges, product categories that provided global leader HP with the lion's share of its profits. In January 2003, Dell announced that it would begin

selling retail-store systems, including electronic cash registers, specialized software, services, and peripherals required to link retail-store checkout lanes to corporate information systems. Since the late 1990s, Dell had been marketing CD and DVD drives, printers, scanners, modems, monitors, digital cameras, memory cards, Zip drives, and speakers made by a variety of manufacturers.

So far, Dell's foray into new products had proved to be profitable; according to Michael Dell, "We believe that all our businesses should make money. If a business doesn't make money, if you can't figure out how to make money in that business, you shouldn't be in that business."[1] In 2002, more than half of Dell's profits came from products other than desktop computers, and the percentage from nondesktop computing was growing.

Moreover, Dell was the world's leading Internet retailer. Dell began Internet sales at its Web site (www.dell.com) in 1995, almost overnight achieving sales of $1 million a day. By early 2003, over 50 percent of Dell's sales were Web-enabled—and the percentage was increasing. Dell's Web site sales exceeded $50 million a day in 2002, up from $35 million daily in early 2000 and $5 million daily in early 1998. The company averaged over 3 million visits weekly at its 80 country-specific sites in 2002. Dell products were sold in more than 170 countries, but sales in 60 countries accounted for 97 percent of total revenues.

In its fiscal year ending January 31, 2003, Dell Computer posted revenues of $35.4 billion, up from $3.4 billion in the year ending January 29, 1995—an eight-year compound average growth rate of 34.0 percent. Over the same period, profits were up from $140 million to $2.1 billion—a 40.5 percent compound average growth rate. A $100 investment in Dell's stock at its initial public offering in June 1988 would have been worth about $28,500 in February 2003. Dell Computer was one of the top 10 best-performing stocks on the New York Stock Exchange and the Nasdaq during the 1990s. Based on 2001 data, Dell ranked number 53 on the Fortune 500, number 131 on the Fortune Global 500, and number 23 on the Fortune Global "most admired" list.

COMPANY BACKGROUND

At age 12, Michael Dell was running a mail order stamp-trading business, complete with a national catalog, and grossing $2,000 a month. At 16 he was selling subscriptions to the *Houston Post,* and at 17 he bought his first BMW with money he had earned. He enrolled at the University of Texas in 1983 as a premed student (his parents wanted him to become a doctor), but he soon became immersed in computers and started selling PC components out of his college

[1]Quoted in "Dell Puts Happy Customers First," *Nikkei Weekly,* December 16, 2002.

dormitory room. He bought random-access memory (RAM) chips and disk drives for IBM PCs at cost from IBM dealers, who at the time often had excess supplies on hand because they were required to order large monthly quotas from IBM. Dell resold the components through newspaper ads (and later through ads in national computer magazines) at 10–15 percent below the regular retail price.

By April 1984 sales were running about $80,000 per month. Michael decided to drop out of college and form a company, PCs Ltd., to sell both PC components and PCs under the brand name PCs Limited. He obtained his PCs by buying retailers' surplus stocks at cost, then powering them up with graphics cards, hard disks, and memory before reselling them. His strategy was to sell directly to end users; by eliminating the retail markup, Dell's new company was able to sell IBM clones (machines that copied the functioning of IBM PCs using the same or similar components) about 40 percent below the price of IBM's best-selling PCs. The discounting strategy was successful, attracting price-conscious buyers and generating rapid revenue growth. By 1985, the company was assembling its own PC designs with a few people working on six-foot tables. The company had 40 employees, and Michael Dell worked 18-hour days, often sleeping on a cot in his office. By the end of fiscal 1986, sales had reached $33 million.

During the next several years, however, PCs Limited was hampered by growing pains—specifically, a lack of money, people, and resources. Michael Dell sought to refine the company's business model; add needed production capacity; and build a bigger, deeper management staff and corporate infrastructure while at the same time keeping costs low. The company was renamed Dell Computer in 1987, and the first international offices were opened that same year. In 1988 Dell added a sales force to serve large customers, began selling to government agencies, and became a public company—raising $34.2 million in its first offering of common stock. Sales to large customers quickly became the dominant part of Dell's business. By 1990 Dell Computer had sales of $388 million, a market share of 2–3 percent, and an R&D staff of over 150 people. Michael Dell's vision was for Dell Computer to become one of the top three PC companies.

Thinking its direct sales business would not grow fast enough, in 1990–93, the company began distributing its computer products through Soft Warehouse

Superstores (now CompUSA), Staples (a leading office products chain), Wal-Mart, Sam's Club, and Price Club (now Price/Costco). Dell also sold PCs through Best Buy stores in 16 states and through Xerox in 19 Latin American countries. But when the company learned how thin its margins were in selling through such distribution channels, it realized it had made a mistake and withdrew from selling to retailers and other intermediaries in 1994 to refocus on direct sales. At the time, sales through retailers accounted for only about 2 percent of Dell's revenues.

Further problems emerged in 1993. In that year Dell reportedly had $38 million in second-quarter losses from engaging in a risky foreign-currency hedging strategy, quality difficulties arose with certain PC lines made by the company's contract manufacturers, profit margins declined, and buyers were turned off by the company's laptop PC models. To get laptop sales back on track, the company took a charge of $40 million to write off its laptop line and suspended sales of laptops until it could get redesigned models into the marketplace. The problems resulted in losses of $36 million for the company's fiscal year ending January 30, 1994.

Because of higher costs and unacceptably low profit margins in selling to individuals and households, Dell Computer did not pursue the consumer market aggressively until sales to individuals at the company's Internet site took off in 1996 and 1997. It became clear that PC-savvy individuals, who were buying their second and third computers, wanted powerful computers with multiple features; did not need much technical support; and liked the convenience of buying direct from Dell, ordering exactly what they wanted, and having it delivered to their door within a matter of days. In early 1997, Dell created an internal sales and marketing group dedicated to serving the individual consumer segment and introduced a product line designed especially for individual users.

By late 1997, Dell had become a low-cost leader among PC vendors by wringing greater and greater efficiency out of its direct sales and build-to-order business model. The company was a pioneer and an acknowledged world leader in incorporating e-commerce technology and use of the Internet into its everyday business practices. The goal was to achieve what Michael Dell called "virtual integration"—a stitching together of Dell's business with its supply partners and customers in real time such that

all three appeared to be part of the same organizational team.[2] The company's mission was "to be the most successful computer company in the world at delivering the best customer experience in the markets we serve."[3]

In early 2002, Dell Computer had 34,600 employees in 34 countries, up from 16,000 at year-end 1997; approximately 42 percent of Dell's employees were located in countries outside the United States, and this percentage was growing. During fiscal years 2001 and 2002, Dell had eliminated some 5,700 employee positions worldwide to better align its cost structure with slowdowns in industrywide PC sales, business cutbacks on information technology (IT) expenditures, and stiffer competitive pressures. The company's headquarters and main office complex was in Round Rock, Texas (an Austin suburb).

Exhibits 2 through 4 provide Dell Computer's recent financial statements and geographic operating performance.

Michael Dell

Michael Dell was widely considered one of the mythic heroes within the PC industry, having been labeled "the quintessential American entrepreneur" and "the most innovative guy for marketing computers in this decade." In 1992, at the age of 27, Michael Dell became the youngest CEO ever to head a Fortune 500 company; he was a billionaire at the age of 31. Once pudgy and bespectacled, in 2003, 38-year-old Michael Dell was physically fit, considered good-looking, wore contact lenses, ate only health foods, and lived in a three-story 33,000-square-foot home on a 60-acre estate in Austin, Texas, with his wife and four children. In early 2003 Michael Dell owned about 11.8 percent of Dell Computer's common stock, worth about $8.5 billion.

In the company's early days Michael Dell hung around mostly with the company's engineers. He was so shy that some employees thought he was stuck up because he never talked to them. But people who worked with him closely described him as a likable

---

[2]This was the term Michael Dell used in an interview published in the *Harvard Business Review*. See Joan Magretta, "The Power of Virtual Integration: An Interview with Dell Computer's Michael Dell," *Harvard Business Review*, March–April 1998, p. 75.

[3]Information posted on www.dell.com, February 1, 2000.

exhibit 2   **Dell Computer's Consolidated Statements of Income, Fiscal Years 1997–2003 (in millions, except per share data)**

	Fiscal Year Ended	
	January 31, 2003	February 1, 2002
Net revenue	$35,404	$31,168
Cost of revenue	29,055	25,661
Gross margin	6,349	5,507
Operating expenses:		
Selling, general and administrative	3,050	2,784
Research, development and engineering	455	452
Special charges	—	482
Total operating expenses	3,505	3,718
Operating income	2,844	1,789
Investment and other income (loss), net	183	(58)
Income before income taxes, extraordinary loss, and cumulative effect of change in accounting principle	3,027	1,731
Provision for income taxes	905	485
Income before extraordinary loss and cumulative effect of change in accounting principle	2,122	1,246
Extraordinary loss, net of taxes	—	—
Income before cumulative effect of change in accounting principle	2,122	1,246
Cumulative effect of change in accounting principle, net	—	—
Net income	$ 2,122	$ 1,246
Basic earnings per common share (in whole dollars):		
Income before extraordinary loss and cumulative effect of change in accounting principle	$0.82	$0.48
Extraordinary loss, net of taxes	—	—
Income before cumulative effect of change in accounting principle	$0.82	$0.48
Cumulative effect of change in accounting principle, net	—	—
Earnings per common share	$0.82	$0.48
Diluted earnings per common share (in whole dollars)	$0.80	$0.46
Weighted average shares outstanding:		
Basic	2,584	2,602
Diluted	2,644	2,726

Source: Dell Computer Corporation annual reports and press release on February 13, 2003.

young man who was slow to warm up to strangers.[4] He was a terrible public speaker and wasn't good at running meetings. But Lee Walker, a 51-year-old venture capitalist brought in by Michael Dell to provide much-needed managerial and financial experience during the company's organization-building years, became Michael Dell's mentor, built up his confidence, and was instrumental in turning him into a polished executive.[5] Walker served as the company's president and chief operating officer during the 1986–1990 period; he had a fatherly image, knew everyone by name, and played a key role in implementing Michael Dell's marketing ideas. Under Walker's tutelage, Michael Dell became intimately

[4]"Michael Dell: On Managing Growth," *MIS Week,* September 5, 1988, p. 1.

[5]"The Education of Michael Dell," *Business Week,* March 22, 1993, p. 86.

		Fiscal Year Ended		
February 2, 2001	**January 28, 2000**	**January 29, 1999**	**February 1, 1998**	**February 2, 1997**
$31,888	$25,265	$18,243	$12,327	$7,759
25,455	20,047	14,137	9,605	6,093
6,443	5,218	4,106	2,722	1,666
3,193	2,387	1,788	1,202	826
482	374	272	204	126
105	194	—	—	—
3,780	2,955	2,060	1,406	952
2,663	2,263	2,046	1,316	714
531	188	38	52	33
3,194	2,451	2,084	1,368	747
958	785	624	424	216
2,236	1,666	1,460	944	531
—	—	—	—	(13)
2,236	1666	1,460	944	518
(59)	—	—	—	—
$ 2,177	$ 1,666	$ 1,460	$ 944	$ 518
$0.87	$0.66	$0.58	$0.36	$0.19
—	—	—	—	(0.01)
$0.87	$0.66	$0.58	$0.36	$0.18
(0.03)	—	—	—	—
$0.84	$0.66	$0.58	$0.36	$0.18
$0.79	$0.61	$0.53	$0.32	$0.17
2,582	2,536	2,531	2,631	2,838
2,746	2,728	2,772	2,952	3,126

familiar with all parts of the business, overcame his shyness, learned to control his ego, and turned into a charismatic leader with an instinct for motivating people and winning their loyalty and respect. When Walker had to leave the company in 1990 because of health reasons, Dell turned to Morton Meyerson, former CEO and president of Electronic Data Systems, for advice and guidance on how to transform Dell Computer from a fast-growing medium-sized company into a billion-dollar enterprise.

Though sometimes given to displays of impatience, Michael Dell usually spoke in a quiet, reflective manner and came across as a person with maturity and seasoned judgment far beyond his age. His prowess was based more on an astute combination of technical knowledge and marketing know-how than on being a technological wizard. By the late 1990s, he was a much-sought-after speaker at industry and company conferences—he received 100 requests to speak in 1997; 800 in 1998; and over

exhibit 3 **Dell Computer's Consolidated Statements of Financial Position, Fiscal Years 1999–2003 (in millions of dollars)**

	February 1, 2003	February 1, 2002	February 2, 2001	January 28, 2000	January 29, 1999
Assets					
Current assets:					
Cash and cash equivalents	$ 4,232	$ 3,641	$ 4,910	$ 3,809	$1,726
Short-term investments	406	273	525	323	923
Accounts receivable, net	2,586	2,269	2,424	2,608	2,094
Inventories	306	278	400	391	273
Other	1,394	1,416	1,467	550	791
Total current assets	8,924	7,877	9,726	7,681	5,807
Property, plant and equipment, net	913	826	996	765	523
Other investments and noncurrent assets	5,633	4,832	2,948	3,025	547
Total assets	$15,470	$13,535	$13,670	$11,471	$6,877
Liabilities and stockholders' equity					
Current liabilities:					
Accounts payable	$ 5,989	$ 5,075	$ 4,286	$ 3,538	$2,397
Accrued and other	2,944	2,444	2,492	1,654	1,298
Total current liabilities	8,933	7,519	6,778	5,192	3,695
Long-term debt	506	520	509	508	512
Other	1,158	802	761	463	349
Total liabilities	10,597	8,841	8,048	6,163	4,556
Stockholders' equity:					
Preferred stock and capital in excess of $.01 par value; shares issued and outstanding: none	—	—	—	—	—
Common stock and capital in excess of $.01 par value; shares authorized: 7,000; shares issued and outstanding: 2,654, 2,601, 2,543 and 2,575, respectively	6,361	5,605	4,795	3,583	1,781
Treasury stock, at cost, 52 shares and no shares, respectively	—	(2,249)	—	—	—
Retained earnings	1,364	1,364	839	1,260	606
Other	(26)	(26)	(12)	465	(66)
Total stockholders' equity	4,873	4,694	5,622	5,308	2,321
Total liabilities and stockholders' equity	$15,470	$13,535	$13,670	$11,471	$6,877

Source: Dell Computer Corporation annual reports and press release, February 13, 2003.

exhibit 4   **Geographic Area Information, Dell Computer, Fiscal 2000–2003 (in millions of dollars)**

	Fiscal Year Ended			
	January 31, 2003	February 1, 2002	February 2, 2001	January 28, 2000
Net revenues				
Americas				
Business	$19,394	$17,275	$18,969	$15,160
U.S. consumer	5,653	4,485	3,902	2,719
Total Americas	25,047	21,760	22,871	17,879
Europe	6,912	6,429	6,399	5,590
Asia-Pacific-Japan	3,445	2,979	2,618	1,796
Total net revenues	$35,404	$31,168	$31,888	$25,265
Operating income				
Americas				
Business	$ 1,945	$ 1,482	$ 1,999	$ 1,800
U.S. consumer	308	260	253	204
Total Americas	2,253	1,742	2,252	2,004
Europe	388	377	347	359
Asia-Pacific-Japan	203	152	169	94
Special charges	—	(482)	(105)	(194)
Total operating income	$ 2,844	$ 1,789	$ 2,663	$ 2,263

Source: Dell Computer Corporation annual reports.

1,200 in 1999. His views and opinions about the future of PCs, the Internet, and e-commerce practices carried considerable weight both in the PC industry and among executives worldwide. His speeches were usually full of usable information about the nuts and bolts of Dell Computer's business model, the compelling advantages of incorporating e-commerce technology and practices into a company's operations, and developments in the IT industry.

Michael Dell was considered a very accessible CEO and a role model for young executives because he had done what many of them were trying to do. He delegated authority to subordinates, believing that the best results came from turning "loose talented people who can be relied upon to do what they're supposed to do." Business associates viewed Michael Dell as an aggressive personality, an extremely competitive risk taker who had always played close to the edge. He spent about 30 percent of his time traveling to company operations and meeting with customers. In a typical year, he would make two or three trips to Europe and two trips to Asia.

DELL COMPUTER'S STRATEGY

The core of Dell Computer's strategy in 2002–2003 was to use its strong capabilities in supply chain management, low-cost manufacturing, and direct sales capabilities to expand into product categories where it could provide added value to its customers in the form of lower prices. Its standard pattern of attack was to identify an IT product with good margins; figure out how to build it (or else have it built by others) cheaply enough to be able to significantly underprice competitive products; market the new product to Dell's steadily growing customer base; and then watch the market share points, incremental revenues, and incremental profits pile up.

Dell management believed it had the industry's most efficient business model. The company's strategy was built around a number of core elements: a cost-efficient approach to build-to-order manufacturing, partnerships with suppliers aimed at squeezing cost savings out of the supply chain, direct sales to customers, award-winning customer service and technical support, pioneering use of the Internet and e-commerce technology, and product-line expansion aimed at capturing a bigger share of the dollars its customers spent for IT products and services.

Cost-Efficient Build-to-Order Manufacturing

Dell built its computers, workstations, and servers to order; none were produced for inventory. Dell customers could order custom-equipped servers and workstations based on the needs of their applications. Desktop and laptop customers ordered whatever configuration of microprocessor speed, random-access memory, hard disk capacity, CD or DVD drives, fax/modem/wireless capabilities, graphics cards, monitor size, speakers, and other accessories they preferred. The orders were directed to the nearest factory. In 2003 Dell had assembly plants in Austin, Texas; Nashville, Tennessee; Limerick, Ireland; Xiamen, China; Penang, Malaysia; and El Dorado do Sul, Brazil. At all locations, the company had the capability to assemble PCs, workstations, and servers; Dell assembled its data storage products at its Austin, Limerick, and Penang plants. In 2002, typical orders were built and delivered in three to five days.

Until 1997, Dell operated its assembly lines in traditional fashion with workers performing a single operation. An order form accompanied each metal chassis across the production floor; drives, chips, and ancillary items were installed to match customer specifications. As a partly assembled PC arrived at a new workstation, the operator, standing beside a tall steel rack with drawers full of components, was instructed what to do by little red and green lights flashing beside the drawers. When the operator was finished, the drawers containing the used components were automatically replenished from the other side, and the PC chassis glided down the line to the next workstation. However, Dell had reorganized its plants in 1997, shifting to "cell manufacturing" techniques whereby a team of workers operating at a group workstation (or cell) assembled an entire PC according to customer specifications. The shift to cell manufacturing reduced Dell's assembly times by 75 percent and doubled productivity per square foot of assembly space. Assembled computers were first

tested and then loaded with the desired software, shipped, and typically delivered five to six business days after the order was placed.

At Dell's newest plant in Austin, the cell manufacturing approach had been abandoned in favor of an even more efficient assembly-line approach. Workers at the new plant in 2002 could turn out about 700 desktop PCs per hour on three assembly lines that took half the floor space of the now-closed cell manufacturing plant in Austin, where production had run about 120 units per hour. Although the new Austin plant was designed for production of 400 units per hour, management believed that it would be able to improve operations enough to boost hourly production from the current 700 units to 1,000 units per hour. The gains in productivity had been achieved partly by redesigning the PCs to permit easier and faster assembly, partly by innovations in the assembly process, and partly by reducing the number of times a computer was touched by workers during assembly and shipping by 50 percent. At both Dell's Austin plant and its plant in Ireland, workers could assemble a PC in two to three minutes. Moreover, just-in-time inventory practices that left pallets of parts sitting around everywhere had been tweaked to just-in-the-nick-of-time delivery by suppliers of the exact parts needed every couple of hours; double-decker conveyor belts moved parts and components to designated assembly points. Newly assembled PCs were routed on conveyors to shipping, where they were boxed and shipped to customers the same day.

Dell was regarded as a world-class manufacturing innovator and a pioneer in how to mass-produce a customized product—its methods were routinely studied in business schools worldwide. Most of Dell's PC rivals—notably, IBM and HP/Compaq—had given up on trying to produce their own PCs as cheaply as Dell and shifted to outsourcing their PCs from contract manufacturers. Dell management believed that its in-house manufacturing delivered about a 6 percent cost advantage versus outsourcing.

Dell's build-to-order strategy meant that the company had no in-house stock of finished goods inventories and that, unlike competitors using the traditional value chain model, it did not have to wait for resellers to clear out their own inventories before it could push new models into the marketplace—resellers typically operated with 30 to 60 days inventory of prebuilt models (see Exhibit 5). Equally important was the fact

exhibit 5 **Comparative Value Chain Models of PC Vendors**

Traditional Build-to-Stock Value Chain Used by Hewlett-Packard, IBM, Sony, and Most Others

| Manufacture and delivery of PC parts and components by suppliers | Assembly of PCs as needed to fill orders from distributors and retailers | Sales and marketing activities of PC vendors to build a brand image and establish a network of resellers | Sales and marketing activities of resellers | Purchases by PC users | Service and support activities provided to PC users by resellers (and some PC vendors) |

Build-to-Order, Sell-Direct Value Chain Developed by Dell Computer

| Manufacture and delivery of PC parts and components by supply partners | Custom assembly of PCs as orders are received from PC buyers | Sales and marketing activities of PC vendor to build brand image and secure orders from PC buyers | Purchases by PC users | Service and support activities provided to PC users by Dell or contract providers |

Close collaboration and real-time data-sharing to drive down costs of supply chain activities, minimize inventories, keep assembly costs low, and respond quickly to changes in the makeup of customer orders

that customers who bought from Dell got the satisfaction of having their computers customized to their particular liking and pocketbook.

Quality Control

All assembly plants had the capability to run testing and quality control processes on components, parts, and subassemblies obtained from suppliers, as well as on the finished products Dell assembled. Suppliers were urged to participate in a quality certification program that committed them to achieving defined quality specifications. Quality control activities were undertaken at various stages in the assembly process.

In addition, Dell's quality control program included testing of completed units after assembly, ongoing production reliability audits, failure tracking for early identification of problems associated with new models shipped to customers, and information obtained from customers through its service and technical support programs. All of the company's plants had been certified as meeting ISO 9002 quality standards.

Partnerships with Suppliers

Michael Dell believed that it made much better sense for Dell Computer to partner with reputable suppliers of PC parts and components than to integrate backward and get into parts and components manufacturing on its own. He explained why:

> If you've got a race with 20 players all vying to make the fastest graphics chip in the world, do you want to be the twenty-first horse, or do you want to evaluate the field of 20 and pick the best one?[6]

Dell evaluated the various makers of each component; picked the best one or two as suppliers; and then stuck with them as long as they maintained their leadership in technology, performance, quality, and cost. Management believed that long-term partnerships with reputable suppliers had at least five advantages. First, using name-brand processors, disk drives, modems, speakers, and multimedia components enhanced the quality and performance of Dell's PCs. Because of varying performance among different brands of components, the brand of the components was quite important to customers concerned about performance and reliability. Second, because Dell partnered with suppliers for the long term and because it committed to purchase a specified percentage of its requirements from each supplier, Dell was assured of getting the volume of components it needed on a timely basis even when overall market demand for a particular component temporarily exceeded the overall market supply. Third, Dell's long-run commitment to its suppliers made it feasible for suppliers to locate their plants or distribution centers within a few miles of Dell assembly plants, putting them in position to make deliveries daily or every few hours, as needed. Dell supplied data on inventories and replenishment needs to its suppliers at least once a day—hourly in the case of components being delivered several times daily from nearby sources.

Fourth, long-term supply partnerships facilitated having some of the supplier's engineers assigned to Dell's product design teams and being treated as part of Dell. When new products were launched, suppliers' engineers were stationed in Dell's plants; if early buyers called with a problem related to design, further assembly and shipments were halted while the supplier's engineers and Dell personnel corrected the flaw on the spot.[7] Fifth, long-term partnerships enlisted greater cooperation on the part of suppliers to seek new ways to drive costs out of the supply chain.

Dell openly shared its daily production schedules, sales forecasts, and new model introduction plans with vendors. Dell also did a three-year plan with each of its key suppliers and worked with suppliers to minimize the number of different stock-keeping units of parts and components in its products and to identify ways to drive costs down.

Commitment to Just-in-Time Inventory Practices

Dell's just-in-time inventory emphasis yielded major cost advantages and shortened the time it took for Dell to get new generations of its computer models into the marketplace. New advances were coming so fast in certain computer parts and components (particularly microprocessors, disk drives, and wireless devices) that any given item in inventory was obsolete in a matter of months, sometimes quicker. Moreover, rapid-fire reductions in the prices of components were not unusual—for example, Intel regularly cut the prices on its older chips when it introduced newer chips, and it introduced new chip generations about every three months. Michael Dell explained the dramatic economics of minimal component inventories as follows:

> If I've got 11 days of inventory and my competitor has 80 and Intel comes out with a new chip, that means I'm going to get to market 69 days sooner.
>
> In the computer industry, inventory can be a pretty massive risk because if the cost of materials is going down 50 percent a year and you have two or three months of inventory versus eleven days, you've got a big cost disadvantage. And you're vulnerable to product transitions, when you can get stuck with obsolete inventory.[8]

For a growing number of parts and components, Dell's close partnership with suppliers was allowing it to operate with no more than two hours of inventory.

Dell's supplier of monitors was Sony. Because the monitors Sony supplied with the Dell name already imprinted were of dependably high quality (a defect rate of fewer than 1,000 per million), Dell didn't even open up the monitor boxes to test them at its Reno, Nevada, monitor distribution center.[9] Utilizing sophisticated data exchange systems, Dell

---

[6]Quoted in Magretta, "The Power of Virtual Integration," p. 74.
[7]Magretta, "The Power of Virtual Integration," p. 75.
[8]Ibid., p. 76.
[9]Ibid.

arranged for its shippers (Airborne Express and United Parcel Service) to pick up computers at U.S. assembly plants, then pick up the accompanying monitors at its Reno distribution center and deliver both to the customer simultaneously. The savings in time and cost were significant.

Dell had been working hard for the past several years to refine and improve its relationships with suppliers and its procedures for operating with smaller inventories. In fiscal year 1995, Dell averaged an inventory turn cycle of 32 days. By the end of fiscal 1997 (January 1997), the average was down to 13 days. The following year, it was 7 days, which compared very favorably with Gateway's 14-day average, Compaq's 23-day average, and the estimated industrywide average of over 50 days. In fiscal year 1999 and 2000, Dell operated with an average of six days' supply in inventory; the average dropped to five days' supply in fiscal year 2001 and to four days' supply in 2002 and 2003.

Dell's Direct Sales Strategy and Marketing Efforts

With thousands of phone, fax, and Internet orders daily and ongoing field sales force contact with customers, the company kept its finger on the market pulse, quickly detecting shifts in sales trends, design problems, and quality glitches. If the company got more than a few of the same complaints, the information was relayed immediately to design engineers who checked out the problem. When design flaws or components defects were found, the factory was notified and the problem corrected within a few days. Management believed Dell's ability to respond quickly gave it a significant advantage over PC makers that operated on the basis of large production runs of variously configured and equipped PCs and sold them through retail channels. Dell saw its direct sales approach as a totally customer-driven system, with the flexibility to transition quickly to new generations of components and PC models.

Dell's Customer-Based Sales and Marketing Focus Unlike technology companies that organized their sales and marketing efforts around product lines, Dell was organized around customer groups. Dell had placed managers in charge of developing sales and service programs appropriate to the needs and expectations of each customer group. Up

until the early 1990s, Dell operated with sales and service programs aimed at just two market segments—high-volume corporate and governmental buyers and low-volume business and individual buyers. But as sales took off in 1995–97, these segments were subdivided into finer, more homogeneous categories that by 2000 included global enterprise accounts, large and midsize companies (over 400 employees), small companies (under 400 employees), health care businesses (over 400 employees), federal government agencies, state and local government agencies, educational institutions, and individual consumers. Many of these customer segments were further subdivided—for instance, within the federal category, Dell had formed separate sales forces and marketing programs for the army, navy, and air force; in education, there were separate sales and marketing programs for K–12 schools; higher education institutions; and personal-use purchases by faculty, staff, and students. Dell's largest global enterprise accounts were assigned their own dedicated sales force—for example, Dell had a sales force of 150 people dedicated to meeting the needs of General Electric's facilities and personnel scattered across the world.

Dell's sales to individuals and small businesses were made by telephone, fax, and the Internet. It had call centers in the United States, Europe, and Asia with toll-free lines; customers could talk with a sales representative about specific models, get information faxed or mailed to them, place an order, and pay by credit card. The Asian and European call centers were equipped with technology that routed calls from a particular country to a particular call center. Thus, for example, a customer calling from Lisbon, Portugal, was automatically directed to a Portuguese-speaking sales rep at the call center in Montpelier, France.

Dell in Japan While NEC, Toshiba, Fujitsu, and Hitachi had the leading shares of the $20 billion PC market in Japan for 2002, Dell was fifth, with a 7.7 percent dollar share, and IBM ranked sixth. Other competitors included Sony, Sharp, and Matshusita. Counting units sold, however, Dell was number one in business desktop computers and was number two in entry-level and midrange servers, with a 19.1 percent share in mid-2002. Dell's 2002 sales in Japan were up about 20 percent, in a market where overall sales were flat. Dell's technical and customer support was ranked the best in Japan in 2002 by *Nikkei PC,* an industry trade magazine. Dell had 200 full-time personnel at its call center in Japan and was tracking Japanese buying habits and preferences with its proprietary software. The head of Dell's consumer PC sales group in Japan had installed 34 kiosks in leading electronics stores around Japan, allowing shoppers to test Dell computers, ask questions of staff, and place orders—about half the sales were to people who did not know about Dell prior to visiting the kiosk.

Dell believed that it was more profitable than any other PC-server vendor selling in the Japanese market. Dell's profit margins in Japan were higher than those in the U.S. market, and sales were rising briskly. Dell overtook NEC in servers to become the second-ranking seller of servers in the fourth quarter of 2002. Japan ranked 20th worldwide in personal computers per capita, with a rate of 31.5 computers per 100 people; the United States ranked 1st, with 58.5 computers per 100 people.[10]

Dell in China   Dell Computer entered China in 1998 and achieved faster growth there than in any other foreign market it had entered. The market for PCs in China was the third largest in the world, behind the United States and Japan, and was on the verge of being the second largest. Unit volume was expanding 20–30 percent annually and with a population of 1.4 billion people (of which some 400 million lived in metropolitan areas where computer use was growing rapidly), the Chinese market for PCs was expected to become the largest in the world by 2010. The market leader in China was Legend, a local company; other major local PC producers were Founder and Great Wall. IBM, Hewlett-Packard, Dell, Toshiba, Acer, and NEC Japan were among the top 10 market share leaders in China. All of the major contenders except Dell relied on resellers to handle sales and service; Dell sold directly to customers in China just as it did elsewhere.

Dell's primary target market in China consisted of large corporate accounts. Management believed that many Chinese companies would find the savings from direct sales appealing, that they would like the idea of having Dell build PCs and servers to their requirements and specifications, and that—once they became a Dell customer—they would like the convenience of Internet purchases and the company's growing array of products and services. Dell recognized that its direct sales approach put it at a short-term disadvantage in appealing to small business customers and individual consumers. According to an executive from rival Legend, "It takes two years of a person's savings to buy a PC in China. And when two years of savings is at stake, the whole family wants to come out to a store to touch and try the machine."[11] But Dell believed that over time, as Chinese consumers became more familiar with PCs and more comfortable with making online purchases, it would be able to attract growing numbers of small business customers and consumers through Internet and telephone sales. In 2002, about 40 percent of Dell's sales in China were over the Internet.

Dell's sales in Asia were expected to surpass those in Europe by year-end 2003 and to become Dell's biggest region outside the United States by 2005.

Dell in Latin America   In 2002 PC sales in Latin America exceeded 5 million units. Latin America had a population of 450 million people. Dell management believed that in the next few years PC use in Latin America would reach 1 for every 30 people (one-tenth the penetration in the United States), pushing annual sales up to 15 million units. The company's plant in Brazil, the largest market in Latin America, was opened to produce, sell, and provide service and technical support for customers in Brazil, Argentina, Chile, Uruguay, and Paraguay.

Using Dell Direct Store Kiosks to Access Individual Consumers   In 2002 Dell began installing Dell Direct Store kiosks in a variety of retail settings. The kiosks did not carry inventory, but customers could talk face-to-face with a knowledgeable Dell sales representative, inspect Dell's products, and order them on the Internet while at the kiosk. The idea for using kiosks had begun in Japan, where Dell sales reps were encountering resistance to Dell's direct sales approach from individual buyers—Japanese consumers were noted for wanting to touch and feel a product before committing to purchase it. When kiosks were installed in Japanese retail settings, they proved quite popular and helped generate a big boost in Dell's share of PC sales to consumers in Japan. The success of kiosks in Japan had inspired Dell to try them in the United States. About 60 kiosks were in place at U.S. locations during the 2002 holi-

---

[10]According to figures cited in Ken Belson, "How Dell Is Defying an Industry's Gravity in Japan," *New York Times,* December 8, 2002, Section 3, p. 4.

[11]Quoted in Neel Chowdhury, "Dell Cracks China," *Fortune,* June 21, 1999, p. 121.

day sales season. In January 2003, Dell announced that it would begin placing Dell Direct Store kiosks in selected Wal-Mart and Sears stores.

Customer Service and Technical Support

Service became a feature of Dell's strategy in 1986 when the company began providing a year's free on-site service with most of its PCs after users complained about having to ship their PCs back to Austin for repairs. Dell contracted with local service providers to handle customer requests for repairs; on-site service was provided on a next-day basis. Dell also provided its customers with technical support via a toll-free phone number and e-mail. Dell received close to 40,000 e-mail messages monthly requesting service and support. Bundled service policies were a major selling point for winning corporate accounts. If customers preferred to work with their own service provider, Dell supplied the provider of choice with training and spare parts needed to service customers' equipment. Recently, Dell had instituted a First Call Resolution initiative to strengthen its capabilities to resolve customer inquiries or difficulties on the first call; first call resolution percentages were made an important measure in evaluating the company's technical support performance.

Value-Added Services   Dell kept close track of the purchases of its large global customers, country by country and department by department—and customers themselves found this purchase information valuable. Dell's sales and support personnel used their knowledge about a particular customer's needs to help that customer plan PC purchases, to configure the customer's PC networks, and to provide value-added services. For example, for its large customers Dell loaded software and placed ID tags on newly ordered PCs at the factory, thereby eliminating the need for the customer's IT personnel to unpack the PC, deliver it to an employee's desk, hook it up, place asset tags on the PC, and load the needed software from an assortment of CD-ROMs and diskettes—a process that could take several hours and cost $200–$300.[12] While Dell charged an extra $15 or $20 for the software-loading and asset-tagging services, the savings to customers were still

considerable—one large customer reported savings of $500,000 annually from this service.[13]

Premier Pages   Dell had developed customized, password-protected Web sites called Premier Pages for over 40,000 corporate, governmental, and institutional customers worldwide. These Premier Pages gave customers' personnel online access to information about all Dell products and configurations the company had purchased or that were currently authorized for purchase. Employees could use Premier Pages to (1) obtain customer-specific pricing for whatever machines and options the employee wanted to consider, (2) place an order online that would be electronically routed to higher-level managers for approval and then on to Dell for assembly and delivery, and (3) seek advanced help desk support. Customers could also search and sort all invoices and obtain purchase histories. These features eliminated paper invoices, cut ordering time, and reduced the internal labor customers needed to staff corporate purchasing and accounting functions. Customer use of Premier Pages had boosted the productivity of Dell salespeople assigned to these accounts by 50 percent. Dell was providing Premier Page service to thousands of additional customers annually and adding more features to further improve functionality.

www.dell.com   At the company's Web site, which underwent a global redesign in late 1999 and had 50 country-specific sites in local languages and currencies, prospective buyers could review Dell's entire product line in detail, configure and price customized PCs, place orders, and track orders from manufacturing through shipping. The closing rate on sales at Dell's Web site was 20 percent higher than that on sales inquiries received via telephone. The company was adding Web-based customer service and support tools to make a customer's online experience pleasant and satisfying.

In February 2003, over 50 percent of Dell's technical support activities were being conducted via the Internet. Dell was aggressively pursuing initiatives to enhance its online technical support tools and reduce the number and cost of telephone support calls (which totaled about 8 million in 2000). Management believed that enhancing www.dell.com to shrink transaction and order fulfillment times, increase accuracy, and provide more personalized content

---

[12]Magretta, "The Power of Virtual Integration," p. 79.

[13]"Michael Dell Rocks," *Fortune,* May 11, 1998, p. 61.

resulted in a higher degree of "e-loyalty" than traditional attributes like price and product selection.

On-Site Services Corporate customers paid Dell fees to provide technical support, on-site service, and help with migrating to new IT technologies. Services were one of the fastest growing part of Dell, accounting for almost $4 billion in sales in 2002. Dell's service business was split about 50–50 between what Michael Dell called close-to-the-box services and management and professional services—but the latter were growing faster, at close to 25 percent annually. Dell estimated that close-to-the-box support services for Dell products represented about a $50 billion market, whereas the market for management and professional services (IT life-cycle services, deployment of new technology, and solutions for greater IT productivity) was about $90 billion. IT consulting services were becoming more standardized, driven primarily by growing hardware and software standardization, reduction in on-site service requirements (partly because of online diagnostic and support tools, growing ease of repair and maintenance, increased customer knowledge, and increased remote management capabilities), and declines in the skills and know-how that were required to perform service tasks on standardized equipment and install new, more standardized systems.

In a fall 2002 speech, Michael Dell explained the company's move into services:

> We developed a couple of years ago an organization we originally called Dell Technology Consulting, and what they do is the kind of technical consulting, the SAN [storage area network] installation and design, the Microsoft Exchange implementation, the Oracle 9i rack, the cluster installation and design. Last year we did about 2000 engagements with Dell Technology Consulting.
>
> We acquired a company called Plural, which is totally focused on the Microsoft application environment, and have combined those resources together to create what we now call Dell Professional Services . . . Our focus here is, first and foremost, to support our thrust into enterprise products. And we know that as customers require those products, you can't have a 70 percent increase in SAN shipments year over year, you can't have a billion dollar external storage business unless you can design and install those products.[14]

Dell's strategy in services, like its strategy in hardware products, was to bring down the cost of IT consulting services for its large enterprise customers. The providers of on-site service, technical support, and other types of IT consulting typically charged premium prices and realized hefty profits for their efforts. During 2001–2002, according to Michael Dell, customers who bought the services being provided by Dell saved 40 to 50 percent over what they would have paid other providers of IT services. Going into 2003, Dell had some 8,000 employees in its services group and top management foresaw services as playing an expanding role in the company's growth. Kevin Rollins, Dell's president, indicated the company's business model "isn't just about making cheap boxes, it's also about freeing customers from overpriced relationships" with such vendors as IBM, Sun Microsystems, and Hewlett-Packard.[15]

While a number of Dell's corporate accounts were large enough to justify dedicated on-site teams of Dell support personnel, Dell generally contracted with third-party providers to make the necessary on-site service calls. Customers notified Dell when they had problems; such notices triggered two electronic dispatches—one to ship replacement parts from Dell's factory to the customer sites and one to notify the contract service provider to prepare to make the needed repairs as soon as the parts arrived.[16] Bad parts were returned so that Dell could determine what went wrong and how to prevent such problems from happening again. Problems relating to faulty components or flawed components design were promptly passed along to the relevant supplier for correction.

Customer Forums In addition to using its sales and support mechanisms to stay close to customers, Dell periodically held regional forums for its best customers. The company formed Platinum and Gold Councils composed of its largest customers in the United States, Europe, Japan, and the Asia-Pacific region; regional meetings were held every six to nine months.[17] Some regions had two meetings—one for chief information officers and one for technical personnel. At the meetings, which frequently

[14]Speech to Gartner Fall Symposium, Orlando, FL, October 9, 2002.

[15]Quoted in Kathryn Jones, "The Dell Way," *Business 2.0,* February 2003.

[16]Kevin Rollins, "Using Information to Speed Execution," *Harvard Business Review,* March–April, 1998, p. 81.

[17]Magretta, "The Power of Virtual Integration," p. 80.

included a presentation by Michael Dell, Dell's senior technologists shared their views on the direction of the latest technological developments, what the flow of technology really meant for customers, and Dell's plans for introducing new and upgraded products over the next two years. There were also break-out sessions on topics of current interest. Dell found that the information gleaned from customers at these meetings assisted the company in forecasting demand for its products.

Pioneering Leadership in Use of the Internet and E-Commerce Technology

Dell Computer was a leader in using the Internet and e-commerce technologies to squeeze greater efficiency out of its supply chain activities, to streamline the order-to-delivery process, to encourage greater customer use of its Web site, and to gather and utilize all types of information. In a 1999 speech to 1,200 customers, Michael Dell said:

> The world will be changed forever by the Internet . . . The Internet will be your business. If your business isn't enabled by providing customers and suppliers with more information, you're probably already in trouble. The Internet provides a dramatic reduction in the cost of transactions and the cost of interaction among people and businesses, and it creates dramatic new opportunities and destroys old competitive advantages. The Internet is like a weapon sitting on a table ready to be picked up by either you or your competitors.[18]

Dell Computer's use of its Web site and various Internet technology applications had proved instrumental in helping the company become the industry's low-cost provider and drive costs out of its business. Internet technology applications were a cornerstone of Dell's collaborative efforts with suppliers. The company provided order-status information quickly and conveniently over the Internet, thereby eliminating tens of thousands of order-status inquiries coming in by phone. It used its Web site as a powerful sales and technical support tool. Few companies could match Dell's competencies and capabilities in the use of Internet technology to im-

[18]Keynote speech given on August 25, 1999, in Austin, Texas, at Dell's DirectConnect Conference.

prove operating efficiency and gain new sales in a cost-efficient manner.

Expansion into New Products

Dell's recent expansion into data storage hardware, switches, handheld PCs, printers, and printer cartridges represented an effort to diversify the company's product base and to use its competitive capabilities in PCs and servers to pursue revenue growth opportunities. Dell had expanded its product line to include storage devices designed to handle a variety of customers' needs for high-speed data storage and retrieval; management saw storage devices as a growth opportunity because the computing systems of corporate and institutional customers were making increasing use of high-speed data storage and retrieval devices. Dell's PowerVault line of storage products had data protection and recovery features that made it easy for customers to add and manage storage and simplify consolidation. Because it relied on standardized technology and components (which were considerably cheaper than customized ones) as building blocks for its storage products, Dell had been able to drive down storage prices for its customers by about 50 percent during 2001–2002.

Dell began selling its own data-routing switches in 2001. As sales of these switches accelerated and as Dell mulled whether to expand into other networking products and Internet gear, Cisco elected to discontinue supplying its switches to Dell for resale as of October 2002. Dell's family of PowerConnect switches—simple commodity-like products generally referred to as layer 2 switches in the industry—carried a price of $20 per port, versus $70–$100 for comparable Cisco switches and $38 for comparable 3Com switches. Most of Dell's sales of switches were to customers who were in the process of buying Dell servers. Michael Dell used Dell's entry into data networking switches to explain the logic behind the company's strategy to expand into products and services that complemented its sales of PCs, workstations, and servers:

> In the United States, Dell has about a 46 percent share of the market for small computer systems sold to large corporations, which does not mean that we sell to 46 percent of corporations; it means we sell to about 90 percent of corporations and one out of two of the products they buy is Dell. So we have pretty profound access and coverage within large corporations.

Every computer that we sell to businesses is attached to a network. So you buy a PC, you buy a server, you attach them with switches, layer 2 and layer 3, into a WAN [wide-area network], into some fiber optic backbone or something that connects out to the broader Internet or intranet or whatever the network may be.

So it's a fairly logical adjacency to say, okay, you're buying PCs from Dell, how about switches from Dell. And it turns out that that's a fairly easy thing for us to sell.[19]

Some observers saw Dell's 2003 entry into the printer market as another deliberate attack on Hewlett-Packard—going after HP's biggest and most profitable business segment at a time when HP management was busy tackling the challenges of merging its operations with those of Compaq and trying to make its acquisition a success. Dell's Axim line of handheld PCs was priced at about 50 percent less than HP's popular iPaq line of handhelds, and Dell's storage and networking products also carried lower prices than comparable HP products. Dell management, however, indicated the company's entry into the printer market was driven by a desire to add value for its customers. Michael Dell explained, "We think we can drive down the entire cost of owning and using printing products. If you look at any other market Dell has gone into, we have been able to significantly save money for customers. We know we can do that in printers; we have looked at the supply chain all the way through its various cycles and we know there are inefficiencies there. I think the price of the total offering when we include the printer and the supplies . . . can come down quite considerably."[20]

When Dell announced it had contracted with Lexmark to make printers and printer and toner cartridges for sale under the Dell label beginning in 2003, HP immediately discontinued supplying HP printers to Dell for resale at Dell's Web site. Dell had been selling Lexmark printers for two years and since 2000 had resold about 4 million printers made by such vendors as HP, Lexmark, and other vendors to its customers. Lexmark designed and made critical parts for its printers but used offshore contract manufacturers for assembly. Gross profit margins on printers (sales minus cost of goods sold) were said to

be in single digits in late 2002, but the gross margins on printer supplies were in the 50–60 percent range—brand-name ink cartridges for printers typically ran $25 to $35.

Dell's Entry into the White-Box PC Segment

In 2002 Dell announced it would begin making so-called white-box (i.e., unbranded) PCs for resale under the private labels of retailers. PC dealers that supplied white-box PCs to small businesses and price-conscious individuals under the dealer's own brand name accounted for about one-third of total PC sales and about 50 percent of sales to small businesses. According to one industry analyst, "Increasingly, Dell's biggest competitor these days isn't big brand-name companies like IBM or HP, it's white-box vendors." Dell's thinking in entering the white-box PC segment was that it was cheaper to reach many small businesses through the white-box dealers that already served them than by using its own sales force and support groups to sell and service businesses with fewer than 100 employees. Dell believed its low-cost supply chain and assembly capabilities would allow it to build generic machines cheaper than white-box resellers could buy components and assemble a customized machine. Management expected that Dell would achieve $380 million in sales of white-box PCs in 2003 and would generate profit margins equal to those on Dell-branded PCs. Some industry analysts were skeptical of Dell's move into white-box PCs because they expected white-box dealers to be reluctant to buy their PCs from a company that had a history of taking their clients. Others believed this was a test effort by Dell to develop the capabilities to take on white-box dealers in Asia and especially in China, where the sellers of generic PCs were particularly strong.

Going into 2003, Dell Computer had a war chest of over $9 billion in cash and liquid investments that it could deploy in its pursuit of attractive revenue growth opportunities. Management had expressed a desire to grow the company revenues to around $60 or $65 billion annually by 2006. The company wanted such products as servers, storage devices, switches and routers, printers, and other peripherals to account for 50 percent of revenues within four or five years. According to Michael Dell, whereas Dell's

[19]Remarks by Michael Dell, MIT Sloan School of Management, September 26, 2002; posted at www.dell.com.
[20]Quoted in the *Financial Times* Global News Wire, October 10, 2002.

unit shipments, revenues, and profits were all up at double-digit rates in the second quarter of 2002, "on average, the rest of the industry was down 4 percent in shipments, down 10 percent in revenue and lost money."[21]

Other Elements of Dell's Business Strategy

Dell's strategy had two other elements that assisted the company's drive for industry leadership: R&D and advertising.

Research and Development   Dell's R&D focus was to track and test new developments in components and software, ascertain which ones would prove most useful and cost-effective for customers, and then design them into Dell products. Management's philosophy was it was Dell's job on behalf of its customers to sort out all the new technology coming into the marketplace and help steer customers to options and solutions most relevant to their needs. The company talked to its customers frequently about "relevant technology," listening carefully to customers' needs and problems and endeavoring to identify the most cost-effective solutions.

Dell was a strong advocate of incorporating standardized components in its products so as not to tie either it or its customers to one company's proprietary technology and components, which almost always carried a price premium and increased costs for its customers. Dell actively promoted the use of industrywide standards and regularly pressed its suppliers of a particular part or component to agree on common standards. Michael Dell and other company officials saw standardized technology as beginning to take over the largest part of the $875 billion spent annually on IT—standardization was very much evident in the areas of servers, storage, networking, and high-performance computing. One example of the impact of standardized technology was at the University of Buffalo, where Dell had installed a 5.6 teraflop cluster of about 2,000 Dell servers containing 4,000 microprocessors that was being used to decode the human genome. The cluster of servers, which were the same as those Dell sold to its business customers, had been installed in about 60 days at a cost of a few million dollars and represented the third most powerful super-

computer in the world. High-performance clusters of PCs and servers were replacing mainframe computers and custom-designed supercomputers because of their much lower cost. Amerada Hess, attracted by Dell's use of standardized and upgradable parts and components, installed a cluster of several hundred Dell workstations and allocated about $300,000 a year to upgrade and maintain it; the cluster had replaced an IBM supercomputer that cost $1.5 million a year to lease and operate. Studies conducted by Dell indicated that, over time, products incorporating standardized technology delivered about twice the performance per dollar of cost as products based on proprietary technology.

Dell's R&D group included over 3,000 engineers, and its annual R&D budget was $450 to $500 million. The company's R&D unit also studied and implemented ways to control quality and to streamline the assembly process. About 15 percent of Dell's 800 U.S. patents were ranked "elite."

Advertising   Michael Dell was a strong believer in the power of advertising and frequently espoused its importance in the company's strategy. His competitive zeal resulted in the company's being the first to use comparative ads, throwing barbs at Compaq's higher prices. Although Compaq won a lawsuit against Dell for making false comparisons, Michael Dell was unapologetic, arguing that the ads were very effective: "We were able to increase customer awareness about value."[22] Dell insisted that the company's ads be communicative and forceful, not soft and fuzzy.

The company regularly had prominent ads describing its products and prices in such leading computer publications as *PC Magazine* and *PC World,* as well as in *USA Today, The Wall Street Journal,* and other business publications. In the spring of 1998, the company debuted a major multiyear, worldwide TV campaign to strengthen its brand image using the theme "Be Direct." Most recently, Dell had been successful in gaining sales to consumers with a popular ad campaign featuring Steven, the "Dude, You're Gettin' a Dell" guy, enthusiastically pitching Dell products. A second popular campaign featured a group of young Dell interns working their way through Dell's operations and talking with workers about their jobs.

[21]Quoted in *Investor's Business Daily,* September 6, 2002.

[22]"The Education of Michael Dell," p. 85.

DELL'S PERFORMANCE IN 2002 AND EARLY 2003

In 2001–2002 Dell added about 16,000 new business customers in North and South America alone—in the United States, Dell had gained about 1,500 new business customers each quarter since mid-2001. In its largest accounts, the portion of revenue coming from new customers had increased 50 percent above 2001 levels, and revenues from existing corporate accounts were up by about 20 percent. The company believed that close to $6 billion of its fiscal 2003 revenues could be attributed to market share gains in the past eight quarters. Management believed that its strategy to acquire new customers, keep its customers satisfied, and sell them a growing array of IT products and services was working well.

According to data compiled by Dell management, in the second quarter of 2002, Dell generated operating income of $75,000 per employee, versus $15,000 for Hewlett-Packard, $10,000 for IBM, and −$1,000 for Sun Microsystems. Whereas Dell's revenues were running close to or above record levels on a quarterly basis in mid-2002, the revenues of its chief competitors were averaging about 62 percent of their all-time peak-quarter revenues—and most were not expected to exceed their previous quarterly peak for at least two years. From the third quarter of 1997 through the first quarter of 2002, Dell's unit worldwide market share had risen 158 percent; during the same period, HP's worldwide unit market share had dropped by 23 percent and IBM's unit share was down 19 percent. From 1998 through the second quarter of 2002, Dell had increased its U.S. share of entry-level and midrange servers from about 12 percent to an industry-leading 29.9 percent, edging out Hewlett-Packard, whose share had dropped from 43 percent in 1998 to 29.8 percent in mid-2002; third-ranked IBM's share had remained relatively constant at around 11 percent. Dell's market share in fiscal 2003 was higher than in fiscal 2002 in all regions of the world.

Dell's strategy was also generating good cash flows. Statistics compiled by Dell indicated that its free cash flow (defined as cash flow from operations minus capital expenditures) had averaged just over 12 percent of revenues during 1997–2002; this compared very favorably with free cash flows at Sun Microsystems (about 9 percent), IBM (about 6 percent),

and Hewlett-Packard (nearly 3 percent). Going into 2003, Dell had $9.9 billion in cash and investments, a company record.

During the November 2002–January 2003 period (the fourth quarter of Dell's 2003 fiscal year), the company posted its best-ever quarterly product shipments, revenues, and operating profits. Management indicated that Dell's global market share in PCs in the last quarter of fiscal 2003 was almost 3 points higher than in its fiscal 2002 fourth quarter, and its U.S. share was 5 points higher—in servers, Dell's market share was over 3 points higher. Unit shipments were up 25 percent, and shipments in China, France, Germany, and Japan increased a combined 39 percent, with server sales in those countries up 47 percent. Despite steadily eroding average selling prices of $1,640 in fiscal 2003; $1,700 in 2002; $2,050 in 2001; $2,250 in 2000; and $2,600 in 1998, Dell's revenues were climbing as the company gained volume and market share in virtually all product categories and geographic areas where it competed.

MARKET CONDITIONS IN THE INFORMATION TECHNOLOGY INDUSTRY IN EARLY 2003

Analysts expected the $875 billion worldwide IT industry to grow roughly 5 percent in 2003, following a 2.3 percent decline in 2002 and close to a 1 percent decline in 2001—corporate spending for IT products accounted for about 45 percent of all capital expenditures of U.S. businesses. From 1980 to 2000, IT spending had grown at an average annual rate of 12 percent and then flattened. The recent slowdown in IT spending reflected a combination of factors: sluggish economic growth worldwide that was prompting businesses to delay upgrades and hold on to aging equipment longer; overinvestment in IT in the 1995–99 period; declining unit prices for many IT products (especially PCs and servers); and a growing preference for lower-priced, standard-component hardware that was good enough to perform a variety of functions using off-the-shelf Windows or Linux operating systems (as opposed to relying on proprietary hardware and customized Unix software). The selling points that appealed most to customers were

exhibit 6 **Actual and Projected Worldwide Shipments of PCs, 1980–2004**

Year	Volume of PC Shipments (millions)
1980	1
1985	11
1990	24
1995	58
1996	69
1997	80
1998	91
1999	112
2000	140
2001	134
2002	136
2003	147*
2004	164*

*Forecast.

Source: International Data Corporation.

standardization, flexibility, modularity, simplicity, economy of use, and value.

Exhibit 6 shows actual and projected PC sales for 1980–2004 as compiled by industry researcher International Data Corporation. According to Gartner Research, the billionth PC was shipped sometime in July 2002; of the billion, an estimated 550 million were still in use. Nearly 82 percent of the 1 billion PCs that had been shipped were desktops, and 75 percent were sold to businesses. With a world population of 6 billion, most industry participants believed there was ample opportunity for further growth in the PC market. Computer usage in Europe was half of that in the United States, even though the combined economies of the European countries were a bit larger than the U.S. economy. Growth potential for PCs was seen as particularly strong in China, India, several other Asian countries, and portions of Latin America. Many industry experts foresaw a time when the installed base of PCs would exceed 1 billion units, and some believed the total would eventually reach 1.5 billion—a ratio of one PC to every four people in the world.

Forecasters also predicted that there would be a strong built-in PC replacement demand as microprocessor speeds continued to escalate. A micro-

processor operating at 450 megahertz could process 600 million instructions per second (MIPS); Intel had forecast that it would be able to produce microprocessors capable of 100,000 MIPS by 2011. Such speeds were expected to spawn massive increases in computing functionality and altogether new uses and applications not only for PCs but also for computing devices of all types. At the same time, forecasters expected full global buildout of the Internet, which would entail the installation of millions of servers.

Currently, there was growing interest in notebook computers; many businesses were turning to notebooks equipped with wireless data communications capability to improve worker productivity and keep workers connected to important information. The emergence of Wireless Fidelity (Wi-Fi) networking technology was fueling the trend—Wi-Fi systems were being used in businesses, on college campuses, in airports, and other locations to link users to the Internet and to private networks. Another next-generation PC, the tablet PC, used a penlike stylus for writing notes on text documents and e-books. The media center PC combined a full-function PC with such consumer electronic devices as a DVD player, music jukebox, and personal video recorder. Two other devices—flat-panel LCD monitors and DVD recorder drives—were also stimulating sales of new PCs.

The Server Market

In the server market, a sea change from proprietary servers running Unix operating systems to much lower-cost Intel/Windows/Linux server technologies was generating a slowdown in dollar revenues from server sales despite rapidly increasing unit volume. Dell was the market leader in the number of low-end and midrange servers shipped but because of its low prices trailed far behind Hewlett-Packard, IBM, and Sun Microsystems in total revenues from server sales. The rapid inroads that Dell was making into the server market had greatly intensified competition in servers in the past three years. In late 2002, HP, IBM, and Sun were in a dead heat for market share leadership based on dollar volume.[23] In the third quarter of 2002, IBM overtook HP as the overall revenue leader in servers, with 30.0 percent of the market versus

[23]Based on data compiled and reported by International Data Corporation.

HP's 27.2 percent. However, HP edged out Sun for the lead in Unix-based servers, with a revenue share of 32.9 percent versus Sun's 30.4 percent.

The Unix share of the server operating system market (based on unit shipments) was said to have decreased by 50 percent over the past five years compared to Windows and Linux, which had almost tripled in use—Dell estimated that Unix-based servers accounted for about 17 percent of unit volume and 55 percent of dollar volume in mid-2002. A number of industry observers believed that Linux was the "new Unix" and that the days of using expensive, proprietary Unix systems were numbered.

COMPETING VALUE CHAIN MODELS IN THE GLOBAL PC INDUSTRY

When the personal computer industry first began to take shape in the early 1980s, the founding companies manufactured many of the components themselves—disk drives, memory chips, graphics chips, microprocessors, motherboards, and software. Subscribing to a philosophy that mandated in-house development of key components, they built expertise in a variety of PC-related technologies and created organizational units to produce components as well as handle final assembly. While certain noncritical items were typically outsourced, if a computer maker was not at least partially vertically integrated and an assembler of some components, then it was not taken seriously as a manufacturer.

But as the industry grew, technology advanced quickly in so many directions on so many parts and components that the early personal computer manufacturers could not keep pace as experts on all fronts. There were too many technological innovations in components to pursue and too many manufacturing intricacies to master for a vertically integrated manufacturer to keep its products on the cutting edge. As a consequence, companies emerged that specialized in making particular components. Specialists could marshal enough R&D capability and resources to either lead the technological developments in their area of specialization or else quickly match the advances made by their competitors. Moreover, specialist firms could mass-produce the component and supply it to several computer manufacturers far

cheaper than any one manufacturer could fund the needed component R&D and then make only whatever smaller volume of components it needed for assembling its own brand of PCs.

Thus, in the early 1990s, computer makers began to abandon vertical integration in favor of a strategy of outsourcing most components from specialists and concentrating on efficient assembly and marketing their brand of computers. Recall Exhibit 5, which shows the value chain model that such manufacturers as Compaq Computer, IBM, Hewlett-Packard, Sony, Toshiba, and Fujitsu-Siemens used in the 1990s. It featured arm's-length transactions between specialist suppliers, manufacturer/assemblers, distributors and retailers, and end users. However, Dell, Gateway, and Micron Electronics employed a shorter value chain model, selling directly to customers and eliminating the time and costs associated with distributing through independent resellers. Building to order avoided (1) having to keep many differently equipped models on retailers' shelves to fill buyer requests for one or another configuration of options and components, and (2) having to clear out slow-selling models at a discount before introducing new generations of PCs. Direct sales eliminated retailer costs and markups (retail dealer margins were typically in the range of 4 to 10 percent).

Because of Dell's success in using its business model and strategy to become the low-cost leader, most other PC makers in 2003 were endeavoring to emulate various aspects of Dell's strategy, but with little notable success. Nearly all vendors were trying to cut days of inventory out of their supply chains and reduce their costs of goods sold and operating expenses to levels that would make them more competitive with Dell. In an effort to cut their assembly costs, several of the leading PC makers (including IBM and Hewlett Packard) had begun outsourcing assembly to contract manufacturers and refocused their internal efforts on product design and marketing. Virtually all vendors were trying to minimize the amount of finished goods in dealer/distributor inventories and shorten the time it took to replenish dealer stocks. Collaboration with contract manufacturers was increasing to develop the capabilities to use a build-to-order model and be able to deliver orders to customers in 7 to 14 days, but this was complicated by the use of offshore contract manufacturers.

While most PC vendors would have liked to adopt Dell's sell-direct strategy for at least some of

exhibit 7 **Dell's Principal Competitors and Dell's Market Share, by Product Category, 2002**

Product Category	Dell's Principal Competitors	Estimated Worldwide Market Size in 2003 (in billions)	Dell's Worldwide Share, 2002
PCs and workstations	Hewlett-Packard (maker of both Compaq and HP brands), IBM, Gateway, Apple, Acer, Sony, Fujitsu-Siemens (in Europe and Japan), Legend (in China)	$162	~16%
Servers	Hewlett-Packard, IBM, Sun Microsystems, Fujitsu	$50	~9
Data storage devices	Hewlett-Packard, IBM, EMC, Hitachi	$31	~6
Networking switches and related equipment	Cisco Systems, Enterasys, Nortel, 3Com	$58	<1
Handheld PCs	Palm, Sony, Hewlett-Packard, Toshiba, Casio	$4	<1
Printers and printer cartridges	Hewlett-Packard, Lexmark, Canon, Epson	$35–$45	0
Cash register systems	IBM, NCR, Wincor Nixdorf, Hewlett-Packard, Sun Microsystems	$4 (in North America)	0
Services	Accenture, IBM, Hewlett-Packard, many others	$350	~2

Source: Compiled by the case authors from a variety of sources, including International Data Corporation and www.dell.com.

their sales, they were reluctant to push direct sales hard for fear of alienating the dealers on whom they depended for the bulk of their sales. Dealers saw sell-direct efforts on the part of a manufacturer whose brand they represented as a move to cannibalize their business and to compete against them. So far, other than Dell and Gateway, the remaining PC vendors had elected, for the most part, to market their products through independent dealers who were responsible for handling sales and service to customers. However, Dell's success in gaining large enterprise customers with its direct sales force had forced growing numbers of PC vendors to supplement the efforts of their independent dealers with direct sales and service efforts of their own. Going into 2003, several of Dell's rivals were selling 15 to 25 percent of their products direct.

PROFILES OF SELECTED COMPETITORS IN THE PC INDUSTRY

This section presents brief profiles of four of Dell's principal competitors. Exhibit 7 summarizes Dell's principal competitors in the various product categories where it competed and the sizes of these product markets.

Hewlett-Packard

In one of the most contentious and controversial acquisitions in U.S. history, Hewlett-Packard shareholders voted by a narrow margin in early 2002 to approve the company's acquisition of Compaq Computer, the world's second largest full-service global computing company (behind IBM) and a company with 2001 revenues of $33.6 billion and a net loss of $785 million. Compaq had passed IBM to become the world leader in PCs in 1995 and remained in first place until it was overtaken by Dell in late 1999. Compaq acquired Tandem Computer in 1997 and Digital Equipment Corporation in 1998 to give it capabilities, products, and service offerings that allowed it to compete in every sector of the computer industry.[24] When Compaq purchased it, Digital was a troubled company with high operating costs, an inability to maintain technological leadership in high-end computing, and a nine-year string of having

[24]"Can Compaq Catch Up?" *Business Week,* May 3, 1999, p. 163.

either lost money or barely broken even.[25] The acquisitions gave Compaq a product line that included PCs, servers, workstations, mainframes, peripherals, and such services as business and e-commerce solutions, hardware and software support, systems integration, and technology consulting. In 2000, Compaq spent $370 million to acquire certain assets of Inacom Corporation that management believed would help Compaq reduce inventories, speed cycle time, and enhance its capabilities to do business with customers via the Internet.

Carly Fiorina, who became HP's CEO in 1999, explained why the acquisition of Compaq was strategically sound:

> With Compaq, we become No. 1 in Windows, No. 1 in Linux and No. 1 in UNIX . . . with our combined market position in servers, we will be able to engage the software community in building the applications that will drive demand for [Intel's] Itanium systems.
>
> Compaq is the leading provider of storage systems in the world on a revenue basis. With Compaq, we become the No. 1 player in storage, and the leader in the fastest growing segment of the storage market—storage area networks.
>
> With Compaq, we double our service and support capacity in the area of mission-critical infrastructure design, outsourcing and support. And while support is frequently considered the boring part of the services business, it produces mid-teens operating margins quarter after quarter. It's like the supplies business—more is better.
>
> Compaq is No. 1 today in high-performance computing as a result of their Tandem acquisition. Between Himalaya, their fault-tolerant computing systems, and our own super-fast Superdome, we will have an incredibly powerful position at the high end of the server market. And we gain access to new customers and markets where fault-tolerant computing is required: national security, the military and the world's largest stock exchanges, for example.
>
> Let's talk about PCs . . . Compaq has been able to improve their turns in that business from 23 turns of inventory per year to 62—100 percent improvement year over year—and they are coming close to doing as well as Dell does. They've reduced operating expenses by $130 million, improved gross margins by three points, reduced channel inventory by more than $800 million. They ship about 70 percent of their commercial volume through their direct channel,

comparable to Dell. We will combine our successful retail PC business model with their commercial business model and achieve much more together than we could alone.

> With Compaq, we will double the size of our sales force to 15,000 strong. We will build our R&D budget to more than $4 billion a year, and add important capabilities to HP Labs. We will become the No. 1 player in a whole host of countries around the world—HP operates in more than 160 countries, with well over 60 percent of our revenues coming from outside the U.S. The new HP will be the No. 1 player in the consumer and small- and medium-business segments. And in the enterprise space, this company will be able to compete for every single customer's business.
>
> We have estimated cost synergies of $2.5 billion by 2004 . . . By 2003, the PC and personal devices business will earn 3 percent operating margin, which more than returns its cost of capital and generates substantial cash. Our enterprise business will earn 9 percent, and our services business will earn 14 percent. All in all, the company will generate $1.5 billion of cash flow net of capital expenditures every quarter.
>
> It is a rare opportunity when a technology company can advance its market position substantially and reduce its cost structure substantially at the same time. And this is possible because Compaq and HP are in the same businesses, pursuing the same strategies, in the same markets, with complementary capabilities.

However, HP's acquisition of Compaq was met with considerable skepticism from both industry analysts and investors. Opponents pointed out that no large mergers of technology companies had proved successful and delivered the promised benefits. The PC businesses of both companies were unprofitable, and skeptics doubted that combining the two would produce a profitable business capable of competing effectively with Dell. In 2001–2002, Compaq was struggling to make a success of several prior acquisitions and was losing market share in many market categories—its revenues in 2001 were almost $9 billion below revenues in 2000. Many also saw the merger as likely to divert management attention and resources away from HP's core imaging and printing business, which generated the bulk of HP's profits.

HP completed its acquisition of Compaq on May 3, 2002, producing a company with combined annual revenues close to $82 billion and transforming HP into a company with four major business groups: imaging and printing; personal computing systems (desktop and notebook PCs, workstations, handheld PCs, and DVD drives); enterprise systems

---

[25]More information on Digital's competitive position can be found in "Compaq-Digital: Let the Slimming Begin," *Business Week,* June 22, 1998.

exhibit 8   **Performance of Hewlett-Packard's Four Major Business Groups, Fiscal Years 2000–2002 (in billions of dollars)**

	Printing and Imaging	Personal Computing Systems*	Enterprise Systems†	HP Services
2002 (fiscal year ending October 31)				
Net revenue	$20,324	$14,733	$11,400	$9,095
Operating income (loss)	3,249	(401)	(968)	1,022
Inventories	3,136	843	1,188	629
2001 (fiscal year ending October 31)				
Net revenue	$19,426	$10,117	$ 8,395	$6,124
Operating income (loss)	1,849	(412)	(291)	647
Inventories	3,433	602	843	342
2000 (fiscal year ending October 31)				
Net revenue	$20,346	$12,008	$ 9,628	$5,730
Operating income (loss)	2,523	335	660	578
Inventories	3,475	685	1,080	337

*Includes desktop and notebook PCs, workstations, handheld PCs, and DVD drives.
†Primarily composed of servers and storage devices.
Note: The figures for 2002 include data for Compaq Computer only for the period May 3 through October 31, 2002, the end of HP's fiscal year.
Source: HP's 2002 10K report.

(composed primarily of servers and storage devices); and IT services—see Exhibit 8 for the performance of these four segments. As of December 2002, HP management had moved aggressively to cut the size of the combined workforces by 17,900 employees (versus a previously announced cut of 15,000) and expected to achieve cost savings of $3 billion in 2003, a year ahead of initial plans. Going into 2003, HP management believed the integration was solidly on track, beating or meeting all its integration milestones to date. Outsiders, however, had heard anecdotal reports of infighting among the various camps in the new company.[26]

HP reported total revenues of $56.6 billion and losses of $903 million for fiscal 2002, versus revenues of $45.2 billion and net profits of $408 million for fiscal 2001. HP had sales of $48.9 billion and net profits of $3.9 billion in 2000. The combined revenues of HP and Compaq in 2002, however, were running close to 10 percent below comparable 2001 levels, indicating that HP and Compaq products were losing ground in the marketplace.

In the fourth quarter of 2002, HP had an estimated 16.1 percent worldwide share of PC sales, versus 15.7 percent for Dell, 5.8 percent for third-place IBM, 4.3 percent for Fujitsu Siemens, and 3.3 percent for NEC. In the United States, HP had a 20.8 percent share, versus 29.2 percent for Dell. Analysts believed that HP retook the top spot in the 2002 fourth quarter because HP's strong presence in retail stores gave it an advantage over Dell in selling to holiday shoppers and because it had aggressive promotions and price cuts. An HP marketing official said, "HP is attacking Dell on price and beating them with new and innovative products. We're growing faster than the market and gaining share across all regions and categories. [Dell] can no longer claim price as a competitive advantage. The momentum is clearly with HP."[27]

While it was true that HP's performance in the fourth quarter of 2002 was better than in the third quarter and might reflect growing momentum on HP's part, its fourth-quarter 2002 revenues for its Personal Computing Systems group were still about

[26]"HP Blames Economy, Not Merger, for Its Soft Sales," *Houston Chronicle,* August 28, 2002, Business section, p. 1.

[27]Quoted in *Investor's Business Daily,* January 17, 2003, p. A1.

8 percent below what HP and Compaq had achieved in the fourth quarter of 2001. Statistics released by both International Data Corporation and Gartner Research showed HP losing market share in the fourth quarter of 2002 compared to what HP and Compaq enjoyed in the fourth quarter of 2001, with Dell's fourth-quarter 2002 share about 20 percent higher than its fourth-quarter 2001 share. What was most encouraging about HP's fourth-quarter performance was management's report that the company had been able to narrow its losses in Personal Computing Systems by year-end 2002 to a −1.7 percent operating margin, reduce total channel inventories to 4.3 weeks, and improve distribution efficiency.

Going into 2003, Hewlett-Packard was

- Number one globally in imaging and printing.
- Number one globally in personal computers (based on fourth-quarter 2002 statistics reported by Gartner Research).
- Number one globally in Unix, Windows, and Linux servers.
- Number one globally in enterprise storage (with revenues about 35 percent greater than the number two vendor as of mid-2002).
- Number one globally in management software.
- Number three globally in IT services.

HP management saw IBM, not Dell, as its biggest competitor.

In an effort to gain market momentum and prove that the Compaq acquisition was going to prove successful, HP had recently introduced a number of new products, including a tablet PC, a media center PC, new iPAQ Pocket PC designs, new monitors, a first-ever mobile workstation, and two Intel Itanium 2–based workstations that would support Unix, Windows, and Linux.

In January 2003, Carly Fiorina provided her take on developments in the world IT market and HP's future strategy and prospects:

The value proposition for IT has to change . . . This industry has been focused on a cyclical economic environment. And we all know that the cyclical economic environment means that there have been substantial declines in growth rates; that smaller start-up players have been struggling to survive; and that in fact, consolidation in the IT industry is happening.

. . . The market trends that we are seeing today are not being driven by cyclical economics, although

clearly that's going on. I believe what we're really seeing in the IT industry today is being driven as much by changes in customer requirements . . . customer requirements are no longer simply about the fastest, hottest box. Customer requirements are no longer simply about the latest killer app. They are no longer about what's the next big thing, or the next coolest piece of technology. Customers are focused on something much more fundamental and much more practical, and that is: How do I get a better return on my technology investment? How do I get real value? How do I make sure that I can live with, not only the initial costs, but the ongoing costs of owning and operating technology?

And just as important, you want to know: do I as a customer, have freedom? Can I choose the pieces I want? Can I make sure that I stay in control of my environment and in control of my investment? How do I stay in control of what is core to my business, because in fact the last thing I want to do as a customer is to hand the keys of the kingdom over to someone else? How do I make sure I have freedom of choice?

So, in the midst of all this change, and in the face of those fundamental, practical, and profound requirements, what is it that HP is focused on?

Our strategy—our investment—our commitment, are focused around four fundamental principles; first, that we will be the company that provides the best return on information technology (RoIT). And by the best return on information technology, we deliver on that commitment through our products, our people, our services, and importantly, our partners. And by return on information technology, what we mean is lowest total cost of ownership, improved productivity, better manageability, better interoperability, reduced complexity, improved reliability, and security.

And we think we come to the table with a portfolio that differentiates us from our competitors and uniquely positions us to meet those goals. Today, we [are] the number one company in supercomputing; number one in network management capability through our OpenView platform and professional services; number one in servers—in Windows and Linux and UNIX; number one in storage; number one in imaging and printing at a time when imaging and printing are critical to [customers'] infrastructure as [they] digitize [their] processes; number one in laptops and PCs; and a leader in IT services.

Our portfolio today runs from desktop to print shop; from palmtop to nonstop computing systems; from printers that sell for $49.99—and by the way, those $49.99 printers have 100 patents associated with them and drop 18 million drops of ink a second, proving that hi-tech and low cost can go together—

everything from $49.99 printers to multimillion dollar commercial publishing systems.

That portfolio has helped us become the number one consumer IT company in the world; the number one small- and medium-business technology company in the world; and the number one or two enterprise IT technology company in the world—depending on how you count . . . We believe it is factually accurate to say that we are the leading technology company in the world.

For a company that does 60 percent of its business outside the United States . . . we believe it is an advantage for our partners and for our customers that we have capabilities in 160 countries, that we do business in 43 currencies and 15 languages around the world . . . More than one billion people around the world use HP technology every day.

For our consumer customers, as our second principle, we're focused on providing what we would call simple, rewarding experiences—technology and solutions that are simple to own, simple to buy, simple to operate, and provide rewarding experiences that make consumers' lives more productive, more communicative, more fun, and more valuable.

Our third principle is to deliver world-class cost structures and world-class capabilities. We believe we are the company that provides the best technology at the lowest cost with the best total customer experience.

. . . In the last six months of 2002, we introduced more than one hundred new products and added 1,400 patents, bringing our patent portfolio to over 17,000 worldwide. This happens to be the fastest rate of innovation as measured by product introduction and patent generation in HP history.

We believe that open, standards-based modular building blocks are the surest way to lower acquisition costs. And that is why you have seen us—and will continue to see us—invest heavily to make sure that our product line is the most modular, the most standards-based in the industry, because we think modularity and openness gives you flexibility and choice.

You'll also see us stick to an engineering paradigm that bets on heterogeneity and a diverse technology environment . . . [Customers] are going to see us continue to invest in being the leading platform provider for NT, for UNIX and Linux platforms. Because we think all three are critical in building out an IT infrastructure.

We . . . have a standards-based building block approach to systems design in engineering—again, in everything from computing to storage.

We're focused on providing the best price/performance curve—hi-tech, low cost.

HP ships more Linux servers than anyone else in the world. Our Linux business is now a $2 billion business annually inside HP. We partner with Oracle as well as SAP on Linux. And we think we have a lead in Linux for sure in the high-performance technical computing realm. Importantly, we have the most comprehensive set of service offerings in Linux, and frankly, we think it is the service offerings as well as our technology that set us apart when we are competing on Linux opportunities. We don't see a company like Dell, for example, in the competition really at all because of the importance of the service and support offerings.

. . . We have been a leader in standards for many, many years, and have about 700 people who work in about 300 different standards organizations around the world, and we think we clearly have one of the largest and most effective standards programs in the industry. We are really focusing our standards efforts and the participation in these standards bodies in areas like improved compatibility and interoperability, because it is compatibility and interoperability that is critical to giving you the flexibility and adaptability and economic benefit that you're looking for.

We at HP are very excited about where we are today. Fundamentally, we think we have a very different set of investments and approaches to the marketplace than our competitors, and we believe that freedom of choice, adaptability, and the best return on information technology is what [customers] want and where we have an advantage.

We want to be the company that gives [customers] the best technology, at the lowest cost with the best total customer experience. That is the strategy that HP is focused on. That is the value we are delivering today in the marketplace.

IBM

IBM was seen as a "computer solutions" company and had the broadest and deepest capabilities in customer service, technical support, and systems integration of any company in the world. IBM's Global Services business group was the world's largest information technology services provider. IBM had 2002 sales of $81.2 billion and earnings of $3.6 billion versus 2001 revenues of $83.1 billion and profits of $7.7 billion. Its two biggest and best-performing businesses were software and services (see Exhibit 9). Once the world's undisputed king of computing and information processing, IBM was struggling to remain a potent contender in PCs,

exhibit 9 **IBM's Performance by Business Segment, 2001–2002 (in billions of dollars)**

Business Segment	External Revenues	Pretax Income (Loss) from Continuing Operations
2002		
Global services	$36,360	$3,657
Enterprise systems	12,646	1,561
Personal and printing systems	11,049	57
Technology	3,935	(1,057)
Software	13,074	3,556
Global financing	3,203	955
Enterprise investments	1,022	(293)
2001		
Global services	$34,956	$5,161
Enterprise systems	13,743	1,830
Personal and printing systems	11,982	(153)
Technology	5,149	177
Software	12,939	3,168
Global financing	3,407	1,143
Enterprise investments	1,118	(317)

Source: IBM press release, January 16, 2003.

servers, storage products, and other hardware-related products. Since the early 1990s, IBM had been steadily losing ground to competitors in product categories it had formerly dominated. Its recognized strengths—a potent brand name, global distribution capabilities, a position as the longtime global leader in mainframe computers, and strong capabilities in IT consulting services and systems integration—had proved insufficient in overcoming buyer resistance to IBM's premium prices. Many of its former customers had turned to lower-priced vendors—the old adage "No one ever got fired for selecting IBM products" no longer applied. IBM's revenues had been essentially flat to down for the past five years.

Believing that open architectures and common standards were inevitable in the years to come, IBM management had begun turning the company away from dependence on its proprietary products and technology, where it had made its name and reputation, and toward standardized products and technologies in the mid-1990s. Even so, no cohesive strategic theme really stood out at IBM during the 1995–2002 period beyond that of growing its revenues from services and software as the company's business in

hardware products eroded. To offset its declining share of PC and server sales, in 1998 and 1999 IBM moved to boost its R&D and manufacturing efforts to become a leading global supplier of computing components (hard drives and storage devices) and microelectronics products. It signed a long-term agreement with Dell to supply over $7 billion in components in 1999 and had increased its sales of parts and components to other PC makers as well.

IBM's Troubles in PCs IBM's market share in PCs was in a death spiral—it had lost more market share in the 1990s than any other PC maker. Once the dominant global and U.S. market leader, with a market share exceeding 50 percent in the late 1980s and early 1990s, IBM was fast becoming an also-ran in PCs, with a global market share under 6 percent in 2002. Its last stronghold in PCs was in laptop computers, where its ThinkPad line was a consistent award winner on performance, features, and reliability. The vast majority of IBM's laptop and desktop sales were to large enterprises that had IBM mainframe computers and had been long-standing IBM customers. IBM's PC group had higher costs than rivals, making it virtually impossible to match rivals on price and make a profit.

IBM distributed its PCs, workstations, and servers through reseller partners, but used its own sales force to market to large enterprises. IBM competed against rival hardware vendors by emphasizing confidence in the IBM brand and the company's long-standing strengths in software applications, IT services and support, and systems integration capabilities. IBM had responded to the direct sales inroads Dell had made in the corporate market by allowing some of its resellers to economize on costs by custom-assembling IBM PCs to buyer specifications.

Gateway

Gateway, a San Diego–based company (recently relocated from South Dakota), had 2002 revenues of $4.2 billion (down from $6.1 billion in 2001) and a net loss of $309 million (an improvement over the loss of $1.03 billion in 2001). Gateway's all-time peak revenues were $9.6 billion in 2000 and its peak-year profits were $428 million. Founder, chairman, and CEO Ted Waitt, 41, owned over 30 percent of the company. Waitt had dropped out of college in 1985 to go to work for a computer retailer in Des Moines, Iowa; after nine months, he quit to form his own company. The company, operating out of a barn on his father's cattle ranch, sold add-on parts by phone for Texas Instruments' PCs. In 1987, the company, using its own PC design, started selling fully equipped PCs at a price near that of other PC makers. Sales took off, and in 1991 Gateway topped the list of *Inc.* magazine's list of the nation's fastest-growing private companies. The company went public in 1993, achieving sales of $1.7 billion and earnings of $151 million. The company had differentiated itself from rivals with eye-catching ads; some featured black-and-white-spotted cows, while others featured company employees (including one with Waitt dressed as Robin Hood). Gateway, like Dell, built to order and sold direct.

Gateway entered the server segment in 1997. In 1999, the company became the first PC maker to bundle its own Internet service with its PCs. To promote the Gateway name in the retail marketplace, the company had opened 280 Gateway Country Stores—227 in the United States, 27 in Europe, and 26 in the Asia-Pacific region—that stocked Gateway PCs and peripheral products and that conducted classes for individuals and businesses on the use of PCs. It had also launched an online software and peripheral Web store with more than 30,000 products.

Gateway's strength had traditionally been in the consumer segment. Going into 2000, Gateway was the number one seller of PCs to consumers, but it lost its lead over the next two years to Dell Computer. In 2001–2002, Gateway's top management began a series of initiatives to reverse the company's deteriorating market position; the company had:

- Closed its retail stores in Canada, Europe, the Middle East, Africa, and the Asia-Pacific region, along with 70 underperforming U.S. retail locations.

- Combined its consumer and business sales organization into a single unit.

- Focused its sales and marketing efforts on consumers, small and medium-sized businesses, educational institutions, and government.

- Consolidated its manufacturing operations and call center operations, paving the way for a 50 percent cutback in its workforce in 2001. Manufacturing operations in Ireland and Malaysia were closed, and all production was moved to the company's two existing plants in South Dakota and Virginia. Further cutbacks to reduce the workforce from 14,000 to 11,500 employees were announced in early 2002.

- Supplemented its sell-direct distribution strategy by stocking a limited inventory of prebuilt Gateway PCs in its retail stores that customers could take home immediately.

- Improved its offering of digital cameras, music, and videos and actively marketed broadband Internet services to its customers via alliances with a number of cable broadband Internet access providers.

- Worked with third-party financing partners to provide financing for businesses and consumers to purchase gateway PCs.

- Introduced a sleek new line of desktop and notebook PCs with industry-leading features. Gateway's notebook sales in 2002 outpaced the U.S. market, growing by approximately 16 percent. Gateway's desktop PCs earned numerous awards, including *Computer Shopper*'s "Best PC Line of the Year" in 2002 for the Gateway 700 Series, *PC World*'s "Best Buy" in the office PCs value category for the Gateway 500S, and *PC Magazine*'s "Editor's Choice" in a round-up of value PCs for the Gateway 300S Value.

- Refreshed its spotted-cow box logo used since 1998.
- Expanded and improved its e-support, local support, and call centers—moves that boosted the company's already leading customer satisfaction rankings by 5 percentage points, according to Alliance Research.
- Started selling consumer electronics products made by other manufacturers in its retail stores, including digital cameras, MP3 players, and high-end plasma-screen TVs.

Going into 2003, it was unclear whether Gateway could become a strong contender in the domestic PC market. Its fourth-quarter 2002 results were disappointing: revenues of $1.06 billion (versus a best-case scenario of $1.2 billion) and shipments of only 720,000 PCs despite heavy advertising and aggressive pricing during a holiday-season quarter when its sales had typically been highest (Gateway had shipped 729,000 units in the traditionally weaker third quarter). Analysts believed that the company's retail stores were a "relatively expensive channel" that added about 10 percent to the company's cost structure.

Sun Microsystems

Sun's strength was in technical computing—it was the leader in high-end workstations and high-performance servers. But the Silicon Valley company, headed by pugnacious chairman and CEO Scott McNealy, was mired in difficulty in early 2003. Sales had nose-dived to $12.5 billion in fiscal 2002 (ending June 30) from an all-time high of $18.3 billion in fiscal 2001, and gross profit margins had dropped 20 percent. Fiscal 2002 losses were $587 million, down from record profits of $1.85 billion in fiscal 2000; in the first six months of fiscal 2003, Sun reported net losses of nearly $2.3 billion, partly due to write-offs and restructuring charges. Sun's stock price had fallen from its all-time high of $64 to around $3 per share in February 2003. According to a *Business Week* article:

A fearsome posse of competitors, from Dell Computer to Microsoft and Intel, is battering its way into Sun's core market for computer servers, selling low-cost machines at a fraction of Sun's price. A few years ago, servers powered by Microsoft Windows software and Intel chips couldn't perform in the same league

with Sun. Now they can. Worse, Linux's open-source software is making inroads into McNealy's market. It's created by legions of volunteers, and it's free—a price that's hard to beat. McNealy finds himself selling the tech equivalent of a Mercedes in a market of Honda buyers.[28]

Sun customer E*Trade Group had recently replaced 60 Sun servers costing $250,000 each with 80 Intel-powered Dell servers running Linux that cost $4,000 each.

Sun designed its own chips and wrote its own server software (called Solaris). It spent close to 18 percent of revenues on R&D, aiming at outcompeting rivals by having Sun servers and Sun software run superefficient networks better than rival brands of servers and software. It had cash and cash equivalents of close to $5 billion and had recently bought back $500 million worth of common stock, paid down its debt by $200 million (leaving it with long-term debt of $1.5 billion), and shaved about $600 million out of its supply chain (boosting its gross margins by about 5 percent). It had also begun outsourcing servers that ran on Linux, which Sun was selling at prices starting about $2,700. McNealy's goal was for Sun to have a 30 percent share of what was expected to be a $6.5 billion market for Linux-based servers in 2004. Sun's strategy was also to move bigger into services; the company had tripled the size of its service staff to 13,000 employees. In January and February 2003, Sun announced a blitz of new, high-performing server products at very competitive prices.

MICHAEL DELL'S VIEW OF DELL COMPUTER'S PROSPECTS AND CHALLENGES

In a February 2003 article in *Business 2.0,* Michael Dell said, "The best way to describe us now is as a broad computer systems and services company. We have a pretty simple system. The most important thing is to satisfy our customers. The second most important thing is to be profitable. If we don't do the first one well, the second one won't happen."[29] For

[28]"Will Sun Rise Again?" *Business Week,* November 25, 2002, p. 120.

[29]Kathryn Jones, "The Dell Way," *Business 2.0,* February 2003; posted at www.business2.com.

the most part, Michael Dell was not particularly concerned about the efforts of competitors to copy many aspects of Dell's build-to-order, sell-direct strategy. He explained why:

> The competition started copying us seven years ago. That's when we were a $1 billion business. Now we're [$36] billion. And they haven't made much progress to be honest with you. The learning curve for them is difficult. It's like going from baseball to soccer.[30]
>
> I think a lot of people have analyzed our business model, a lot of people have written about it and tried to understand it. This is an 18½ year process . . . It comes from many, many cycles of learning . . . It's very, very different than designing products to be built to stock . . . Our whole company is oriented around a very different way of operating . . . I don't, for any second, believe that they are not trying to catch up. But it is also safe to assume that Dell is not staying in the same place. You know, this past year we've driven a billion dollars of cost out of our supply chain, and certainly next year we plan to drive quite a bit of cost out as well.[31]

In a presentation at the University of Florida in the fall of 2002, Michael Dell explained how the company decided to move into new areas, usually in an effort to get a bigger share of its customer's expenditures on IT:

> We tend to look at what is the next big opportunity all the time. We can't take on too many of these at once, because it kind of overloads the system. But we believe fundamentally that if you think about the whole market, it's about an $800 billion market, all areas of technology over time go through a process of standardization or commoditization. And we try to look at those, anticipate what's happening, and develop strategies that will allow us to get into those markets. In the server market in 1995 we had a 2 percent market share, today we have over a 30 percent share, we're number 1 in the U.S. How did that happen? Well, first of all it happened because we started to have a high market share for desktops and notebooks. Then customers said, oh yes, we know Dell, those are the guys who have really good desktops and notebooks. So they have servers, yes, we'll test those, we'll test them around the periphery, maybe not in the most critical applications at first, but we'll test them here. [Then they discover] these are really good and

Dell provides great support . . . and I think to some extent we've benefited from the fact that our competitors have underestimated the importance of value, and the power of the relationship and the service that we can create with the customer.

> And, also, as a product tends to standardize there's not an elimination of the requirement for custom services, there's a reduction of it. So by offering some services, but not the services of the traditional proprietary computer company, we've been able to increase our share. And, in fact, what tends to happen is customers embrace the standards, because they know that's going to save them costs. Let me give you an example . . . about a year ago we entered into the data networking market. So we have Ethernet switches, layer 2 switches. So if you have PCs and servers, you need switches; every PC attaches to a switch, every server attaches to a switch. It's a pretty easy sale, switches go along with computer systems. We looked at this market and were able to come up with products that are priced about 2½ times less than the market leader today, Cisco, and as a result the business has grown very, very quickly. We shipped 1.8 million switch ports in a period of about a year, when most people would have said that's not going to work and come up with all kinds of reasons why we can't succeed.[32]

On another occasion, Michael Dell spoke about the size of the company's future opportunities:

> When technologies begin to standardize or commoditize, the game starts to change. Markets open up to be volume markets and this is very much where Dell has made its mark—first in the PC market in desktops and notebooks and then in the server market and the storage market and services and data networking. We continue to expand the array of products that we sell, the array of services and, of course, expand on a geographic basis.
>
> The way we think about it is that there are all of these various technologies out there . . . What we have been able to do is build a business system that takes those technological ingredients, translates them into products and services and gets them to the customer more efficiently than any company around.
>
> We only have about a 3 percent market share in the $800 billion-plus IT market, so we think . . . we've got a lot more opportunity going forward . . . It's a pretty exciting time to be in our industry and the opportunities are pretty awesome.[33]

---

[30]Comments made to students at the University of North Carolina and reported in the *Raleigh News & Observer*, November 16, 1999.

[31]Remarks by Michael Dell, Gartner Fall Symposium, Orlando, Florida, October 9, 2002; posted at www.dell.com.

[32]Ibid.

[33]Remarks by Michael Dell, MIT Sloan School of Management, September 26, 2002, and posted at www.dell.com.

Electronic Arts and the Global Video Game Industry

Arthur A. Thompson
The University of Alabama

Going into 2004, Electronic Arts (EA) was the world's leading independent developer, publisher, and marketer of video games. EA developed games for play on all the leading home video game consoles (Sony's PlayStation and PlayStation 2, Microsoft's Xbox, and Nintendo's GameCube), on handheld devices such as Nintendo's Game Boy Advance, on personal computers, and online. In 2002, more than 22 EA games sold over 1 million units, including Madden NFL Football 2003, NBA Live 2003, FIFA Soccer 2003, Harry Potter and the Chamber of Secrets, The Sims, Medal of Honor Frontline, and James Bond 007 Nightfire. EA released sequels of its popular sports titles annually. When Madden NFL Football 2004 was introduced in August 2003, it sold 2 million copies in three weeks at retail prices of $50 a copy; in the same three-week period, the new release of NCAA Football 2004 sold over 1 million copies. Players were expected to spend, conservatively, an average of 100 hours testing their skills over the course of the season and often beyond.

EA's chairman and CEO, Lawrence Probst, believed EA was on course to become the "biggest and best entertainment company in the world," eventually surpassing Disney (2002 revenues of $25.3 billion), Viacom (2002 revenues of $24.6 billion), and Time Warner (2002 revenues of $42 billion). Founded in 1982, EA earned $2.5 billion in revenues at the end of fiscal 2003 (March 31), and the company expected to post revenues of $2.9 billion in its fiscal year ending March 31, 2004. Probst saw two factors at work that gave EA tremendous growth potential in the years just ahead. One growth driver was the rapidly mushrooming number of households across the world that had high-speed Internet access, which allowed gamers to play video games over the Internet. The second growth driver was expected to come in 2005–2006 when Sony, Microsoft, and Nintendo were to launch the supercharged, next-generation versions of their game-playing platforms—the new consoles were expected to be as much as 1,000 times more powerful than the versions presently on the market. Probst and other EA executives believed that broadband connections and powerful game-playing consoles gave EA the opening it needed to take video games to heights far beyond what consumers could experience with movies and TV entertainment. Probst said, "There are a lot of potential growth drivers over the next five-, six-, seven-year period. And we think we're going to keep this business growing faster than the movie business, faster than the music business or any other form of entertainment business. So yeah, we're very bullish."[1]

In October 2003, EA formally launched EA Sports Nation, an online service that would allow tens of thousands of broadband-enabled gamers to compete against one another individually or in teams across the Internet. Sports enthusiasts could choose among such EA games as Madden NFL Football 2004, NCAA Football 2004, NASCAR Thunder, Tiger Woods PGA Tour, NBA Live 2004, NHL Hockey 2004, FIFA Soccer 2004, and MVP Baseball 2004. EA Sports Nation had tournaments, leagues, rankings, laddering systems, and stats to entice net-

[1]As quoted in Peter Lewis, "The Biggest Game in Town," *Fortune*, September 15, 2003, p. 140.

exhibit 1   **Actual and Projected Size of the Global Market for Video Games, 2002–2010 (in millions)**

	2002	2003	2007	2010
Console hardware	$ 7,187	$ 6,047	$ 6,445	$ 5,358
Console software (both sales and rentals)	14,922	16,449	13,969	13,077
Handheld hardware	1,307	1,501	1,925	1,206
Handheld software (both sales and rentals)	2,326	2,238	2,693	1,602
PC software (both sales and rentals)	3,707	3,806	3,135	2,617
Broadband	290	497	2,137	4,106
Interactive TV	133	249	1,955	4,130
Mobile phones	243	587	3,783	6,928
Total	$30,115	$31,374	$36,042	$39,024

Source: Informa Media Group news release on "Game Industry Dynamics, Data, Figures, and Forecasts," www.gii.co.jp/press/fi14850_en.shtml, accessed November 14, 2003.

work-enabled PlayStation 2 gamers to buy a sports game, log on to Sports Nation, pick an opponent, and test their skills. The pricing structure for EA Sports Nation was still being evaluated, but EA executives saw huge global revenue potential in attracting subscribers with not only the competitive challenge of online play and tournaments but also the prospect of winning cash or other attractive prizes. Probst said, "Our goal is to generate hundreds of thousands, and hopefully millions, of registered users playing EA Sports products online. We think that's pretty compelling and a pretty powerful vision."[2]

THE VIDEO GAME INDUSTRY

In 2003, the video game industry represented a $31 billion global market (see Exhibit 1), up sharply from about $10 billion in 1995. The industry consisted of makers of video game consoles, handheld players, and arcade machines; game developers who developed games for play on both personal computers (PCs) and various kinds of video games machines; retailers of video game players and video games; and companies that had Web sites for online game play. Video and computer games were an unforeseen by-product of advancing chip technology. Faster chip processing speeds and growing graphics capabilities opened the way for game developers to

put players in the midst of all kinds of action-filled situations. During the 1990s, video game developers created increasingly sophisticated, multifeatured games that allowed players to compete in a host of sports and racing events, pilot supersonic fighter jets and spacecraft to defend against all manner of enemies, and enter mystical worlds to untangle ancient webs of treachery and deceit.

Retail video game sales soared to record levels in the 1990s, with annual sales in the billions. From 1985 to 1994, Nintendo and Sega dominated the market for video game consoles, with combined market shares of around 90 percent. The two rivals sparred back and forth in an escalating battle for market leadership. Then in 1995, competitive rivalry in video games took on a new dimension when Sony entered the market with its new PlayStation. Nintendo and Sega, the longtime industry leaders, found themselves in a fierce battle with Sony, and other small-share console makers scrambled to generate enough sales to survive. There was a huge industry shakeout. By 1998, Sony emerged as the undisputed leader worldwide. In the United States, Sony's PlayStation captured a 70 percent market share, with Nintendo at 26 percent and Sega at only 4 percent. All other video console makers faded into oblivion and Sega, unable to make any headway in regaining lost market share, exited the market for video consoles in 2001 and turned its full attention to developing video games. The entry of Microsoft's Xbox in 2002 made the video console business a fierce three-way contest.

[2]As quoted in ibid., p. 138.

Total sales of PlayStation 2 were expected to reach 100 million units by 2005, making the PlayStation 3 the odds-on favorite to keep Sony as the market leader in video game hardware. But despite PlayStation 2's market dominance, Microsoft's Xbox and Nintendo were expected to gain market share and become significantly more competitive as concerned both their hardware and the number of attractive games that could be played on their equipment. Microsoft was projected to be particularly strong in Europe, a region that was less emphasized by Sony and Nintendo.

In 2003 game developers were riding the crest of a software sales wave for current-generation consoles (PlayStation 2, Xbox, and GameCube). The wave of video game sales was expected to peak in 2004 before slackening off in the run-up to the expected launch of next-generation consoles in 2005–2006. Video game industry sales were projected to reach nearly $39 billion worldwide by 2010 (Exhibit 1). Some observers were predicting that the global video game market was on track to rival the movie, music, and television industries; according to a writer for *Fortune*, "Music sales have been falling in recent years, the moviegoing experience hasn't changed that much since *Gone with the Wind*, and network TV is on the skids."[3]

The Players of Video Games

About 250 to 300 million people worldwide were very active or frequent players of video games; game enthusiasts usually owned consoles, handheld players, or PCs and spent five or more hours weekly playing video games. Perhaps another 100 million people were infrequent players, playing them occasionally on arcade machines in malls and other retail locations, on their own PCs during idle moments or as a diversion, on the consoles and handheld players of friends and acquaintances, or on personal digital assistants (PDAs) and cell phones. The majority of video game players were preteens, teenagers, and young adults (between the ages of 20 and 40). The average age of game players was rising, as people who became game players as a preteen or teenager continued to play in their adult years. And, to

exhibit 2 **Reasons People Play Video Games, 2002**

It's fun	87.3%
They're challenging	71.4
Like to play with friends/family	42.4
Lots of entertainment for the price	35.6
Like to keep up with the latest technology	18.9
Interested in the stories	17.9
Like the music and/or the celebrities involved	15.5
I do the same thing in real life	13.1

Source: 2002 survey of 1,500 households, conducted by Interactive Digital Software Association, www.idsa.com, accessed November 13, 2003.

broaden the appeal of video games for adults, game developers were creating a growing number of games with mature content. The average American was expected to spend 75 hours annually playing video games, more than double the amount spent gaming in 1997 and more than was spent watching rented movies on DVDs or videocassettes.[4]

Hard-core gamers purchased 10–15 new games annually and were also among those most attracted to playing games online. IDC, a Massachusetts-based research firm, estimated that North American households owned 75 million game consoles such as the PlayStation, Xbox, and GameCube. A study by the Pew Internet and American Life Project found that 70 percent of college students played video games at least occasionally in 2002 and that 100 percent of college students responded affirmatively when asked if they had *ever* played video games. The study said, "Computer, video, and online games are woven into the fabric of life for college students. Gaming is a part of growing up in the U.S."[5]

Still, there were drawbacks to playing video games. Not everyone had the patience to learn complex controls or wanted to spend the 20 to 30 hours it took to navigate a game successfully. Exhibit 2 presents the primary reasons people played video games, and Exhibit 3 provides game player demographics and other video game–related statistics.

---

[3]Ibid., p.135.

[4]Ibid.
[5]Ibid.

Industry Growth

A number of factors had contributed to growth of the video game industry during the 1990–2003 period:[6]

- *Broader game content*—In 2003, video gaming offered entertainment for the masses, with games involving sports, racing, action, adventure, edutainment, shooting, fighting, and a host of children's games and family entertainment games.

- *The evolution of video game consoles into multifaceted entertainment devices*—People could play DVD movies and music on game machines, expanding the entertainment value for families.

- *People who started out playing games in the 1980s were staying in the market and playing in their 30s and 40s*—Demographic research indicated that growing numbers of young adults were continuing to play video games past their teenage and college years. Sports games involving professional and college sports and NASCAR racing were appealing to adults, as were games with mature content.

- *There had been quantum leaps in the quality of both graphics and play*—Moreover, another huge leap was coming in next-generation consoles scheduled for introduction in 2005–2006. The chip designs in next-generation video game consoles featured a revolutionary new architecture that packed the processing power of a hundred 2003-style PCs onto a single chip and, further, tapped the resources of additional computers using high-speed Internet connections. The next-generation consoles, expected to retail for about $300, would have the ability to render real-life images, record TV shows, surf the Internet in 3-D, play music, and run movielike video games.

- *Growing ability on the part of video game developers to capitalize on expanding action movies into popular video games*—Games developers and Hollywood movie studios were becoming increasingly aware of the merits of working hand-in-hand on projects like a Harry Potter,

Spider-Man, Lord of the Rings, or James Bond movie that had both the action component and widespread interest (especially among teenagers) to make a good game. Releasing a game in conjunction with a hit movie could increase sales by three or four times. Sometimes, film stars recorded dialogue for video games and special scenes were filmed specifically for use in a game. Game designers would take a movie script and add to the storyline, making it more mission-rich and multifaceted than what appeared onscreen.

- *The growing capability to play games online, often in head-to-head competition with other online players*—Online gaming had allowed game designers to extend their storylines by providing new chapters, adding new missions, and introducing new characters, thus hooking enthusiasts into playing through a never-ending story. Sequels of sports games with the latest player rosters and team schedules spurred continuing interest on the part of online players. Most observers contended that online gaming gave game developers a wider vista of game-designing options than any other prior technology.

The growth in interactive entertainment was expected to continue as game-playing hardware and software continued to improve, hardware and broadband penetrated more homes, and technology continued to evolve in ways that brought more game-playing experiences into the reach of more consumers. By 2007 players were expected to be playing a yet-to-be released breed of games on a new breed of powerful game-playing consoles. Forecasters at DFC Intelligence expected the successors to PlayStation 2, Xbox, and GameCube to be the fastest-selling video game systems ever and to offer quantum leaps in graphics quality and game-playing interest. Exhibit 4 shows worldwide sales of PC and video game software for the 1996–2002 period.

Video Game Prices

The most popular video games retailed for about $50 in 2003. However, prices varied according to the games' popularity, length of time of the market, and the age and popularity of the console for which they were developed. It had been the experience of the

---

[6]Paul A. Paterson, "Synergy and Expanding Technology Drive Booming Video Industry," *TD Monthly* 2, no. 8 (August 2003), accessed at www.toydirectory.com/monthly/Aug2003 on November 15, 2003.

exhibit 3   **Video Game–Playing Statistics, U.S. Households, 2002–2003**

- An estimated 50 percent of the U.S. population, about 145 million people, played computer and video games in 2003, with the average player spending about 6.5 hours a week playing games.
- 17% of all game players in the United States in 2003 were over age 50, up from 13% in 2000. The average game player in the United States in 2003 was 29 years old.
- Boys ages 6 to 17 represented 21% of gamers in the United States and spent an average of 7.3 hours a week playing games; girls between the ages of 6 and 17 represented 12% of gamers.
- Men ages 18 and over represented 38% of all gamers.
- 40% of game players in the United States were female; women ages 18 and older made up 26% of the game-playing population in the United States.
- The average number of U.S. family members who play PC games regularly (5 or more hours per week) is 1.6, while for console games about 2 people per household play regularly.
- 31% of the most frequent game players in the United States reported playing games online in 2002, up from 24% in 2001.
- Age and gender of U.S. most frequent game players—PCs versus consoles in 2002:

	PC Players	Console Players
Age		
36 + years	40%	19%
18–35 years	26	36
Under 18 years	34	45
Gender		
Male	62%	72%
Female	38	28

- About 37% of American households either with game consoles or with PCs that are used to play games reported in 2002 they also played games on mobile devices like handheld game players, personal digital assistants (PDAs), and cell phones.
- Age and gender of U.S. buyers of consoles versus PC games in 2002:

	PC Game Buyers	Console Game Buyers
Age		
18 + years	96%	86%
Gender		
Male	45%	46%
Female	55	54

industry for game prices to decline once a generation of consoles had been in the market for a significant period of time; this was mainly due to the increasing number of game titles competing for acceptance by game players. The prices of games for older 16-bit and 32-bit consoles in 2003 were considerably lower than the prices of games for the newer 64-bit and 128-bit consoles (see Exhibit 5).

Some industry observers were predicting that rising costs would soon drive the prices of games with a triple-A rating to $59.99. According to an analyst at NPD Group, "There just doesn't seem to be negative

exhibit 3 **(concluded)**

- Best-selling video games by type of genre, 2001–2002:

Game Categories	2001 PC and Console Games	2002 PC Games	2002 Console Games
Sports	22.2%	6.3%	19.5%
Action	19.8	—	25.1
Strategy/role-playing	17.6	35.4	7.4
Racing	16.7	4.4	16.6
Fighting	5.7	0.1	6.4
Shooting	9.1	11.5	5.5
Family	3.6	9.6	—
Child	3.4	15.9	—
Adventure	—	—	5.1
Edutainment	—	—	7.6

Note: The categories were redefined between 2001 and 2002.

- Computer and video game sales by rating, 2001–2002:

	2001	2002
Everyone	62.3%	55.7%
Teen	24.6	27.6
Mature	9.9	13.2
Early Childhood	2.1	3.5

- In 2002, 16 of the top 20 best-selling console games and 18 of the top 20 best-selling PC games were rated Everyone or Teen.
- In 2001, U.S. sales equaled 141.5 million video games, 58.8 million computer games, and 25.1 million "edutainment" games, equal to an average of almost 2 games per U.S. household.

Sources: "Essential Facts about the Computer and Video Game Industry," Interactive Digital Software Association, 2002, www.idsa.com, accessed November 12, 2003; and 2003 ESA poll of 806 adults reported in August 26, 2003, press release at www.theesa.com.

reaction to game prices. Even if one publisher took the chance to lower the price of a triple-A game, it could bias the consumer that it's a lesser game." About 750 new games were expected to hit the market between mid-2003 and mid-2004. If past sales statistics held true, the top 50 to 60 games would account for 50 percent of total sales, and half of those might be able to command a $60 price if publishers took a chance on raising prices. Industry observers were predicting that overall prices for games would fall in 2004 and 2005 as more new titles were introduced and the total number of titles competing for

buyer attention grew; however, hit titles were expected to continue to command premium prices.

The Costs of Developing a New Video Game

In the early 1980s, a game for an 8-bit Nintendo game player could be developed for less than $100,000. In the early 1990s, game publishers customarily spent around $300,000 to develop a game for Nintendo's Super NES, Sega's Genesis, or PCs. In 1996, a typical

exhibit 4 **Worldwide Sales of PC and Video Games, 1996–2002**

Year	Unit Volume (in millions)	Dollar Sales (in billions)
1996	105	$3.7
1997	133	4.4
1998	181	5.5
1999	215	6.1
2000	219	6.0
2001	225	6.3
2002	255	6.9

Sources: "Essential Facts about the Computer and Video Game Industry," Interactive Digital Software Association, 2002, www.idsa.com, accessed November 12, 2003; and press release at www.theesa.com, accessed November 13, 2003.

PlayStation game cost just under $1 million to develop and retailed for $49. In 2003, development costs for a PlayStation 2 or Xbox game usually ran from $2 million to $7 million per title, and the game retailed for $49.99. However, some game titles could entail development costs upward of $30 million. Development costs were rising for several reasons:

- Games for the current 128-bit consoles required at least 40 times as many lines of code to fully exploit their capabilities as did the prior-generation 64-bit consoles.

- Costs went up when a game had to be reworked or when developers decided to push the technology envelope a bit further and add new or more elaborate features. Game developers often did not know how long it would take or what it would cost to program some games because aspects of many new games had never been done before and it took several rounds of programming to create the desired effects.

- It was taking ever bigger and more talented development teams to push the limits of each new generation of consoles. As a consequence, talented game developers were becoming a more and more valuable resource, commanding ever higher salaries and bonuses. As the industry moved to PlayStation 3 and Xbox 2, most industry observers believed that a large and capable staff of game developers would become an even more important key success factor.

- Payments for licensed content or the use of intellectual property owned by others (for rights to use certain characters or celebrities in games or to tie in with hit movies), coupled with the need for special film crews and backdrops to stage certain scenes (the Matrix game had an hour of exclusive video footage), could cost game publishers an additional $1 to $10 per game unit.

Some observers were predicting that costs to develop hit games for next-generation game consoles could *average* as high as $20 million.

Royalties Paid to Console Manufacturers Sony, Nintendo, and Microsoft, aside from creating their own games with in-house staff, licensed independent game developers to create software for use with their respective game-playing systems. The license agreements gave the platform manufacturer the right to set the fee structure that developers had to pay in order to publish games for their platforms. The customary royalty was about $8 per unit on newly released games, but the royalty payment typically decreased as game prices fell. The license agreement also gave manufacturers an assortment of controls in other areas. Typically, the game developer was required to submit a prototype for evaluation and approval that included all artwork to be used in connection with packaging and marketing of the product. The console manufacturer had final approval over all games for its consoles (sometimes limiting the number of games approved in a given time frame) and could specify the dates on which new games could be released. In many cases, console manufacturers also controlled the manufacture of the game cartridges or CDs, in which case the developer had to provide the platform manufacturer with a purchase order for the number of units to be manufactured and an irrevocable letter of credit for 100 percent of the purchase price.

All these requirements tended to increase developer lead times and costs for getting a new game to market. This was especially true when platform manufacturers opted to bring out next-generation platforms with capabilities that entailed more demanding specifications. Moreover, when next-generation platforms were introduced, platform manufacturers required a new license of developers, giving them an opportunity to alter the fee structure and impose new terms and conditions on licensees. Next-generation platforms posed two other risks to game developers. If manufacturers were delayed in introducing next-generation platforms, then the introduction of their new games was delayed as well. And if a manufac-

exhibit 5 **Average Retail Prices of Video Games, 1995–2002**

Type of Console	1995	1996	1997	1998	1999	2000	2001	2002
16-bit (1989 debut)								
Sega Genesis	$41	$29	$21	$14	$13	$10	$10	$ 7
Super Nintendo	43	41	29	22	17	11	10	9
32-bit (1995 debut)								
PlayStation	53	49	39	35	31	28	23	18
Sega Saturn	55	47	35	20	11	5	14	6
64-bit (1996 debut)								
Nintendo 64	—	65	61	51	46	42	38	28
128-bit (2000 debut)								
GameCube	—	—	—	—	—	—	50	46
Xbox	—	—	—	—	—	—	50	45
PlayStation 2	—	—	—	—	—	49	48	41

Sources: The NPD Group/NPD FunWorld, and www.msnbc.com/news.

turer's new platform met with poor reception in the marketplace, then the accompanying games of developers had shorter-than-expected life cycles.

In addition, as online capabilities emerged for video game platforms, platform manufacturers had control over the financial terms on which online game play would be offered to players. In 2003, both Microsoft and Sony provided online capabilities for Xbox and PlayStation 2, respectively. In each case, compatibility code and the consent of the platform manufacturer were required before a game developer could include online capabilities in their games for Xbox and PlayStation consoles. This tended to put the strategies and business models of Microsoft and Sony in direct competition with the strategies and business models of independent game developers, like Electronic Arts, that had their own online game-playing businesses and were promoting their PC-based video games to game enthusiasts for play online.

Marketing and Distribution Costs

Competition for shelf space and efforts to make games top sellers had prompted game publishers to boost their advertising. In 2002 industry advertising was about 65 percent higher than in 2002. In 2003 advertising budgets for video games were at record levels. EA had even scheduled ads for its Madden NFL Football game for *Monday Night Football.* With more than 500 titles for PlayStation, 200 titles

for Xbox, and 150 titles for GameCube, retailers struggled to find shelf space for even the most popular titles. Wal-Mart, for example, generally stocked only about 80–90 games, and it was the leading retailer of video game consoles, with about an 18 percent market share of the combined sales of GameCube, Xbox, and PlayStation consoles. Other key retailers in North America were Best Buy, Circuit City, Toys "R" Us, and Target. In many instances, retailers demanded hefty slotting fees to stock lesser-known or slower-selling games. The shelf life of the average video game was about five weeks, even with expensive in-store merchandising campaigns; the most popular video games had a shelf life of about 120 days.

Game publishers promoted their games in several ways:

- Television, print, radio, outdoor, and Internet ads.
- Company Web sites.
- In-store promotions, displays, and retailer-assisted cooperative advertising.
- Trade shows.
- Product sampling through demonstration software.
- Consumer contests and promotions.

Television advertising was often required to create mass-market demand for an altogether new game; a minimal TV advertising campaign for a game cost about $2 million.

exhibit 6   **Representative Value Chain for Video Games, 2002**

	PC CD-ROM	Console DVD
Retail price	$39.99	$49.99
Retailer margin	8.00	10.00
Wholesale received by publisher	$31.99	$39.99
Publisher costs		
Manufacturing/packaging	$3.00	$3.00
Hardware royalty fee (paid to console maker)	$0.00	$8.00
Licensed content royalties	$0–$6.00	$0–$10.00
Margin for game development and programming, marketing, other costs, and profit	$22.99–$28.99	$18.99–$28.99

Sources: Wedbush Morgan Securities, and www.msnbc.com/news/924871.asp.

In 2002, the top 20 best-selling video games accounted for about 22 percent of the sales of video games in North America. About 50 percent of annual video game sales occurred in the fourth quarter of the calendar year; many holiday shoppers considered video game hardware and software to be ideal gifts. Exhibit 6 shows a representative value chain for video games.

Mobile Gaming

Nintendo was the dominant market leader in handheld game devices, having sold more than 150 million Game Boys in various forms since 1989. Mobile gaming was highly popular in Japan and South Korea; the two countries represented an estimated 64 percent of the global market for mobile games. However, mobile gaming was growing rapidly in China, the United States, Britain, Germany, France, and Italy. The Game Boy business in the United States in 2003 was expected to be a $1 billon market (including sales of both hardware and software). The telecom segment of the mobile gaming market in Japan and South Korea in 2003 was estimated at $400 million. Forecasts of the size of the mobile gaming market in 2006 (including games played on cell phones as well as portable devices) varied widely, ranging from as little as $1.65 billion to as much as $38 billion. While mobile gaming had historically been a favorite pastime of preteens and teenagers, the advent of game-capable cell phones and more sophisticated handheld devices like Nintendo's Game Boy SP were expected to spur increases in mobile gaming among the young-adult population in the years ahead.

Online Gaming

The worldwide online game segment was expected to grow from $875 million in 2002 to over $5 billion in 2008.[7] Online game playing was projected to reach 35 billion hours in 2008 and include about 200 million people, distributed about equally across North America, Europe, and Asia. Forecasters expected the growth to be driven not only by PC-based subscriptions but also by the rapidly growing number of video game console systems with online capability. By 2008, the installed base of online-capable video game systems was projected to exceed 100 million worldwide. The other major factor driving online game playing was increased broadband penetration. Broadband capability in households began to rise sharply in 2002, especially in South Korea and Japan, where the growing base of broadband users was producing big gains in online game playing. Some forecasters believed online games would be the "killer application" that spurred households to upgrade their connections from modems to broadband. However, in 2003 it was still uncertain just how much online game playing would translate into revenues and profits for game developers like EA. Revenues came from annual or monthly subscription fees, "pay-to-play" fees, and onsite advertising.

While it had been demonstrated that a highly popular online video game could generate $100 million in annual revenues with a 50 percent operating profit margin, such success was the exception rather

[7]Based on research conducted by DFC Intelligence and reported in a press release, June 25, 2003, at www.dfcint.com.

than the rule. Many online game services had failed and others had built a large user base that produced little or no revenue. Moreover, there was a serious glut of online games presently on the market. In late 2003, there were close to 1.2 million PlayStation and Xbox game players using high-speed Internet connections to play online. In August and September 2003, close to 300,000 people registered to compete online with Madden NFL 2004 and NCAA Football 2004; on Sunday, September 14, the number of simultaneous online players of Madden NFL 2004 hit 7,000 and then hit progressively higher peaks as the season unfolded. Some 250,000 people were paying $10 a month to enjoy a virtual world called EverQuest (www.everquest.com); EverQuest enthusiasts were spending an average of 20 hours a week at the site in mid-2003. For its part, EA had invested close to $300 million to build its online division (called EA.com); when it launched The Sims Online site in anticipation of attracting perhaps a million people to sign up, only 10,000 of the several million buyers of the popular game were motivated to register and form Sims communities; EA had also failed with its Earth and Beyond online game site. Of EA's five "persistent state world products," which allowed players across the world to gather to play online, only the Ultima Online site was considered to be a financial success.

One of the keys to success in online gaming was easy interaction among the players—making it simple to chat with other players, heckle opponents, talk trash, or cooperate with other players to complete certain tasks and missions. Sony Online strived to evoke four core human emotions in its online games: exploration, fantasy fulfillment, social interaction, and acquisition. Gamers enjoyed being part of an online gaming community that allowed them to hang out, chat, engage in head-to-head duels, and check statistics showing their skills versus those of other players.

Microsoft's Xbox Live   Microsoft introduced a subscription-based online game-playing service dubbed Xbox Live in November 2002. About 350,000 starter kits were sold in the first 120 days, double original sales expectations. The $50 starter kits, which included a one-year subscription to Xbox Live, enabled gamers with a high-speed Internet connection to play multiplayer Xbox Live games with other gamers logged on to the Xbox Live site.

The Xbox, with a built-in hard drive and Ethernet connection, was the only video game system built from the ground up for online gaming—PlayStation 2 users had to buy network adapters for their consoles (Sony had sold about 1 million adapters for its PlayStation consoles). Xbox Live enabled gamers to find their gaming acquaintances online, talk to other players during game play through the Xbox Communicator headset, check out the latest game-paying statistics and achievement levels, download new difficulty levels and characters to their hard drives, and play online. Xbox Live offered gamers a unique ID, called a Gamertag, for use across its service; a Friends list that let gamers find their friends online and invite them to a game; and Matchmaking, which let players find opponents of similar skill levels. In a recent survey, Microsoft discovered that downloadable content was considered the most desired feature of Xbox Live by 82 percent of its users.

In late 2003 the subscription fee for Xbox Live was $49.99 for 12 months, and the price of the Xbox Starter Kit had increased to $69.99 (which included a 12-month subscription, an Xbox Communicator voice headset, and a full version of the game MechAssault). Gamers could also get a free two-month trial for Xbox Live by purchasing a specially marked Xbox Live–enabled game in retail stores (the free trial could be extended on a monthly basis for $5.99). All Xbox Live users had to enter credit card and billing information in signing up for the service.

Microsoft's strategy called for no royalties or share of subscription fees to be paid to game developers for any game played on Xbox Live. It wanted to fully control the gaming experience at Xbox Live and retain all monies collected—a policy that had prompted EA to refuse to program online play capability into any of its Xbox games, thereby preventing Xbox owners from using their consoles to play EA games on Xbox Live. EA, however, had inked a deal with Sony to make nine of its sports games compatible for online play using the PlayStation 2; Sony's online strategy was to give game makers the autonomy to establish the online environment in which the action took place for their games (even though the player was using a PlayStation 2), control the play using their own servers, and dictate subscription fees at their sites. This contrasted sharply with Microsoft's practice of keeping all revenues from online play of games via an Xbox console. Nintendo had an online policy similar to Sony's, allowing game developers to promote and manage their own online services and not to take a percentage of revenues or charge a royalty for the use of their consoles in online play.

Sales of Current-Generation Video Game Consoles

As of September 2003, Sony had sold 60 million PlayStation 2 consoles since October 2000; of these, 14.2 million were in Japan, 26.4 million were in North America, and 19.4 million were in Europe, the Middle East, Africa, and Australia. The original PlayStation had sold about 37.5 million units in its first three years on the market, and forecasters expected that PlayStation 2 sales would reach 100 million in 2005. As of July 2003, Microsoft had sold 9.4 million Xbox consoles since its November 2001 launch and expected to have an installed base of 14.5 to 16 million worldwide by June 2004. Xbox sales in North America equaled 6.2 million units (about 66 percent of the total), followed by Europe with 2.2 million units (23 percent), and the Asia-Pacific region with nearly 1 million units (11 percent). Worldwide sales of Nintendo's GameCube were approaching 20 million in the fall of 2003, but were running behind projections; to spur console sales, Nintendo cut its console price from $149 to $99 in September 2003, tripling its volume and prompting Microsoft and Sony to cut the prices of their consoles from $199 to $179.99 in November 2003. Console makers expected to sell a combined 15 million units in the U.S. market in 2003.

Since 1989, Nintendo had sold over 150 million handheld Game Boys in various versions—over 35 million of its Game Boy Advance players had been sold in 2002–2003 alone. Nearly 40 percent of those who played Game Boy Advance and the flip-top SP version were older than 18, and 20 percent were over 30.

Designs and Capability of the Next-Generation Consoles
The design for Sony's PlayStation 3 called for putting 72 microprocessors on a single chip—8 IBM PowerPC processors, each of which controlled 8 additional auxiliary processors. This would allow the PlayStation 3 to process a trillion math operations a second, the equivalent of 100 Intel Pentium 4 chips and a speed 1,000 times faster than the processing power of the PlayStation 2.

Sony envisioned that its PlayStation 3 would have the capability to simultaneously handle a wide range of electronic tasks in the home—recording a TV program, playing music, and managing home appliances, thus functioning as an in-the-home server and turning video game consoles into "a new class of beast." Microsoft envisioned much the same capability for its next-generation Xbox, and Nintendo had indicated that its new console would not lag behind Sony's on technology. There was reason to expect the capabilities of the next-generation PlayStation, Xbox, and GameCube consoles to be relatively similar because Sony, Microsoft, and Nintendo had all selected IBM to supply IBM PowerPC microprocessors for their next-generation consoles. Furthermore, programming games for these next-generation consoles was expected to be far more complicated and lengthy than for the current generation of consoles because programmers would have to keep track of all the tasks being performed by 72 processors.

Competition

The software segment of the video game industry was highly competitive, characterized by the continuous introduction of new games and updated game titles and the development of new technologies for creating and playing games. The developers of software games ranged from small companies with limited resources to large corporations with significantly greater resources for developing, publishing, and marketing video game software. Independent game developers like Electronic Arts, Activision, Take-Two Interactive, Capcom, Eidos, Acclaim Entertainment, Sega, Lucas Arts, Infogrames, THQ, Konami, Namco, Vivendi Universal, Midway Games, and 3DO competed not only with each other but also with Sony, Microsoft, and Nintendo, each of which published games for their respective consoles. Sony, Nintendo, and Microsoft licensed a number of companies to develop and publish games that operated on their consoles. Competition among game developers was based on game features and product quality, timing of game releases, access to distribution channels and retailer shelf space, brand-name recognition, marketing effectiveness, and price. Software developers also competed with other forms of entertainment (movies, television, music, and sports) for the leisure time and discretionary spending of consumers.

Small game developers were struggling. They were more capital constrained, had less predictable revenues and cash flows, lacked product diversity, and were forced to spread fixed costs over a smaller revenue base—factors that were prompting the industry to consolidate to a smaller number of larger developers. Such companies as Acclaim Entertainment, 3DO, Midway Games, and Vivendi Universal's game division had been up for sale at various times but had been unable to convince potential buyers that the value of their development teams and aging brands outweighed the risks of taking on their entire enterprise, given that they were either losing money or barely breaking even. As a result, many of the troubled game developers were either cutting operations to the bone or trying to turn their operations around with new infusions of cash from investors and renewed efforts to come up with a best-selling game. Square and Enix, two Japanese game developers, had merged in early 2003 to form what was one of the biggest game developing companies in Japan.

Sega In 2003, Sega, which had withdrawn from competing in the segment for video game consoles in 2001 to focus exclusively on developing video games, had failed to attract a buyer for its video game business; acquisition discussions had been broken off with several companies and Sega was making a major push to establish itself in sports games. Sega had teamed with ESPN to introduce a series of sports games with the ESPN label—ESPN NFL Football, ESPN NHL Hockey, and ESPN NBA Basketball. Prior to its ESPN branding approach, Sega had promoted its sports games under the 2K brand, using such titles as NFL 2K3, NBA 2K3, NCAA College Football 2K3, and so on. To differentiate its sports games from those of Electronic Arts, Sega was creating a situation in which the player would see the game through the eyes of a participant as opposed to watching the game with a bird's-eye view of the playing field. Many analysts expected that Sega's ESPN series would prove to be the primary competition for EA Sports in the sports genre. Other games in Sega's lineup included Shinobi, Super Monkey Ball, Fantasy Star Online, The House of the Dead, Bass Fishing Duel, and Panzer Dragoon.

Activision Founded in 1979 and headquartered in Santa Monica, California, Activision's mission was to be one of the largest, most profitable, most well-respected interactive entertainment companies in the world. Activision posted net revenues of $864 million for the fiscal year ended March 31, 2003, almost double the $434 million reported for fiscal 1999; Activision had a net income of $66.2 million in 2003, versus a net of $14.9 million in 1999. The company was expecting revenues close to $1 billion in the year ending March 31, 2004. Activision had operations in the United States, Canada, the United Kingdom, France, Germany, Italy, Japan, Australia, Scandinavia, and the Netherlands. Activision's strategy was grounded in three elements:

- The company developed and published games for (1) a wide range of product categories, including action, adventure, action sports, racing, role-playing, simulation, and strategy, and (2) target audiences ranging from game enthusiasts and children to mass-market consumers and "value-priced" buyers. It was concentrating on games for PlayStation 2, Xbox, GameCube, Game Boy handheld devices, and PCs. The company typically released its console products for use on multiple platforms in order to reduce the risks associated with any single platform, leverage its costs over a larger installed base, and increase unit sales.

- Activision focused its development and publishing activities principally on products that were, or had the potential to become, "franchise properties" with sustainable consumer appeal and brand recognition. It had acquired the rights to publish products based on Star Trek, various Disney films such as Toy Story 2 and Marvel Comics' properties such as Spider-Man, X-Men, Blade, Iron Man, and Fantastic Four. The company had signed long-term agreements with a number of action sports athletes in skateboarding, biking, surfing, snowboarding, and wakeboarding, and established the Activision O2 brand as the dominant brand in the action sports category.

- To try to ensure a high success rate of new product releases, Activision's management relied on a formal control process for the selection, development, production, and quality assurance of its products called the Greenlight Process. This process included in-depth reviews of each project at five intervals during their development by a team that included several of the company's highest-ranking operating managers and sales and marketing personnel. Projects that were deemed less promising were either discontinued early in the development phase or revamped before additional development costs were incurred. New games were often developed using a combination of internal and external development resources; when an external developer was used, that developer usually produced the same game for multiple platforms and also produced sequels to the original game.

Activision was modifying its acquisition strategy to focus on (1) increasing its development capacity through the acquisition of or investment in select experienced development firms and (2) expanding its intellectual property library through licenses and strategic relationships with intellectual property owners. Having completed 13 acquisitions since 1997, Activision believed that it had successfully diversified its operations, channels of distribution, development talent pool, and library of titles. But management believed that success down the road would be driven in part by the company's ability to capture greater economies of scale.

Activision's biggest competitive strength was in games based on superheroes such as Spider-Man, animated characters such as Shrek, and skateboard legend Tony Hawk. It was the market leader in action sports games; during the 1995–April 2002 period, it had number 3 and number 7 of the top 15 best-selling action sports titles. The company's franchise title was its Tony Hawk skating series, the latest version of which was Tony Hawk's Pro Skater 4. Other action sports titles included Mat Hoffman's Pro BMX 2, Kelly Slater's Pro Surfer, Shaun Murray's Pro Wakeboarder, Wreckless, True Crime: Streets of LA, Street Hoops, X-Men: Next Dimension, Tenchu 3: Wrath of Heaven, and X-Men: Wolverine's Revenge.

Activision was the third-ranked publisher of games for Nintendo's Game Boy software. For the week ending November 9, 2003, Activision's critically acclaimed first-person action game Call of Duty was the best-selling PC-based video game in North America, the United Kingdom, Scandinavia, Germany, and Australia.

Activision was scaling back its releases of new games to devote more attention to its better-selling high profile titles. Management had decided that the glut of over 500 recently released titles made it ad-

vantageous for Activision to focus its development and marketing resources on high-quality titles that stood a much better chance of winning space on retailers' shelves. However, many software publishers were also putting more emphasis on sequels to previous hits. Senior management was monitoring developments in online game play and was developing plans to enter the online segment in the near future. Robert Kotick, Activision's CEO said, "The thing I'm most excited about is prize play and cash play. When you reward people, that's going to open up a whole new universe of revenue. It's the gaming component of gaming."[8]

Acclaim Entertainment   Founded in 1987, Acclaim developed, published, marketed, and distributed games for PlayStation 2, Xbox, GameCube, Game Boy and, to a lesser extent, PC systems. It had six software development studios in the United States and the United Kingdom that developed its games, and it also contracted with independent software developers to create software products. Through its subsidiaries in North America, the United Kingdom, Germany, France, Spain, and Australia, Acclaim distributed its games directly to retailers and other outlets in North America, Europe, Australia, and New Zealand; but in Japan and other parts of the Pacific Rim, Acclaim relied on regional distributors. Acclaim had contracted to distribute a limited number of games developed by third parties, and it had a small operation that developed and published strategy guides relating to its software products and, from time to time, issued certain "special edition" comic magazines to support some of its games.

Acclaim's development time for a new game ranged from 12 to 36 months, and the average development cost for new titles ranged from $2 million to $8 million. Acclaim had spent $8 million and three years developing its Turok: Evolution (shooting) game for the PlayStation, Xbox, and GameCube platforms and spent another $8 million to market and promote the title in the marketplace. Other Acclaim "franchise" titles included All-Star Baseball, NBA Jam, Alias, and Gladiator: Sword of Vengance; among its lesser titles were three wrestling games (WWF Warzone, Legends of Wrestling, and WWF Attitude), Jeremy McGrath Supercross (motocross),

---

[8]As quoted in Lewis, "The Biggest Game in Town," p. 138.

Aggressive Inline (skating), Dave Mirra BMX XXX, and NFL QB Club. Close to 50 new titles had been released in the September 2002–November 2003 period. Most were targeted at males in the 15 to 35 age range.

Acclaim had lost money for the past two years. It reported a loss of $4.5 million on revenues of $269 million in the fiscal year ending August 31, 2002; for the seven-month period September 1, 2002, through March 31, 2003 (during which the company converted to a fiscal year ending March 31), Acclaim posted a $68 million loss on sales of almost $102 million. For the first six months of fiscal 2004 (April 2003 through September 2003), Acclaim had revenues of $74 million and a loss of $22 million. As of late fall 2003, the company was working with creditors to improve its financial condition and reduce a working capital deficit of $67 million; if sales did not improve in the 2003 holiday season, management expected to have to curtail some aspects of the company's operations starting in early 2004.

THQ   THQ was one of the world's fastest-growing video game publishers, with a diverse portfolio of game titles and a number two ranking among the independent game publishers, behind Electronic Arts. In 2003, it had more than 70 products in development across the action, racing, puzzle, wrestling, kids, action-adventure, and platform game genres. THQ's England, Germany, France, Korea, and Australia offices distributed games to retailers in more than 77 countries. The company had nearly 400 programmers, artists, and designers spread across six studios and a minority interest in wrestling game developer Yuke's Company, Ltd., of Japan. THQ's strategic priorities were to build a well-diversified product portfolio across brand, genre, and platform; establish strong technology and internal development capabilities; expand its global product development capabilities; grow its international sales; and pursue opportunities in wireless gaming. THQ's revenues and profits for the 2000–2002 period were as follows:

	2002	2001	2000
Net sales	$480,529,000	$378,992,000	$347,003,000
Net income	$ 12,994,000	$ 36,013,000	$ 18,189,000

The decline in profitability in 2002 was due to sharply higher costs for software development and for sales and marketing. For 2003, management was forecasting revenues of about $570 million and earnings of close to $28 million.

THQ had the strongest lineup of wrestling games of any game developer. It introduced over 40 new games for various platforms in 2002, including Britney's Dance Beat, 2 Rugrats titles, Jimmy Neutron vs. Jimmy Negatron, Scooby Doo! Night of 100 Frights, MX Superfly, 6 wrestling titles, 4 racing titles, and 23 Game Boy Advance titles. THQ was the leading independent publisher of games for Game Boy Advance, with roughly a 20 percent market share of all GBA games sold. GBA games accounted for about one-fourth of THQ's revenues.

Sony   Sony had revenues of $62.3 billion in 2002 ($20 billion in North America) and had 161,000 employees worldwide. The profits of Sony's video game division accounted for over 50 percent of Sony's total profits in 2001–2002, much of which came from the Sony Computer Entertainment America (SCEA) division. The head of SCEA was considered one of the most powerful executives in Hollywood. About one of three U.S. households owned a PlayStation. Sony had introduced its PlayStation 2 in Japan in March 2000, in North America in October 2000, and in Europe in November 2000. The PlayStation 2 was a 128-bit DVD-based system that was Internet and cable ready, as well as backward compatible for games published for the PlayStation.

Sony developed about 10–15 percent of the games developed for PlayStation 2. Sony game developers had created several best-selling titles—Gran Turismo (action racing), Rise to Honor (martial arts adventure), Twisted Metal (combat racing), Cool Boarders, Jet Ski X$_2$O, NFL Gameday, NBA Shootout, NCAA Gamebreaker (basketball), NHL Faceoff, World Tour Soccer, and SOCOM II: U.S. Navy SEALs (a Mature-labeled game that was the sequel to the number one–rated online game in 2002).

Sony had attracted about 25,000 European online gamers three months after launching its service in June 2003. The company's Sony Online Entertainment (SOE) division created, developed, and provided online games for the personal computer, online, and console markets. SOE's games ranged from simple card and trivia games to more strategic, tactical, and role-playing *persistent interactive worlds.* More than 13 million people had registered at SOE's award-winning Web site, The Station (www.station.com), and the division was striving to become the premier Internet gaming destination. Sony launched a multimillion-dollar marketing blitz in North America during the 2003 holiday season to expand the PlayStation 2 gaming experience among mass-market consumers, specifically targeting new users, gift-givers, and children.

Nintendo Nintendo launched its GameCube console in Japan in September 2001, in North America in November 2001, and in Europe in May 2002. The GameCube employed 128-bit technology and played games that were manufactured on a proprietary optical disk. During the six-month period from April through September 2003, Nintendo sold 890,000 GameCube consoles worldwide, well below expectations. Strong sales of Game Boy hardware and software, however, pushed Nintendo's revenues for the period up 1.6 percent, from 208 billion yen to 211 billion yen. Despite posting a loss of 2.9 billion yen for the six-month period, Nintendo said it was on track to achieve revenues of 550 billion yen and profits of 60 billion yen for its fiscal year ending March 31, 2004. Company officials hoped that the worldwide price cuts for the GameCube in September–October 2003 would enable it to meet its objective of selling 6 million GameCubes by the end of the fiscal year. About 74 percent of Nintendo's sales were outside Japan.

In 2003 Nintendo had introduced the Game Boy Advance SP, a new, foldable version of its popular Game Boy Advance with features that were appealing to adults. The makeover was intended to make the Game Boy more competitive with a raft of new handheld models coming on the market—the PlayStation Portable; Nokia's N-Gage (a cell phone that played video games); and the Zodiac, a Palm-compatible game system developed by Tapwave, a company founded by former Palm executives. Nintendo had recently reduced its royalty on Game Boy Advance games by about $3, to a range of $7 to $11, to help lower the price of Game Boy software and to give independent game developers a bigger financial incentive to create and publish new games for Game Boy Advance.

Nintendo released new versions of three of its biggest franchise games for GameCube in 2002 and 2003—Mario Sunshine, Metroid Prime, and The Legend of Zelda. Other important Nintendo games for GameCube and Game Boy were Pokémon; Super Mario Brothers; Donkey Kong; Super Smash Brothers (head-to-head fighting); Disney's Magical Quest; and the Starfox, Mario Kart, and Final Fantasy series. The most popular title played on GameCube was Resident Evil, developed by Capcom.

Industry observers believed that Nintendo's aggressive pricing of its consoles, coupled with its efforts to bundle games with its hardware and its strong relationships with game developers, would prove beneficial in boosting Nintendo's market share over the long term.

Microsoft Microsoft launched the Xbox in North America in November 2001, in Japan in February 2002, and in Europe in March 2002. While Microsoft was far from thrilled with unit sales of its Xbox consoles going into the 2003 holiday season, executives saw the industry as a marathon rather than a sprint when it came to global market leadership. The Xbox was firmly entrenched as the number two–selling console in North America and Europe in 2003, but it trailed both Sony and Nintendo in Japan, South Korea, and the rest of the Asia-Pacific region. Management expected the Xbox to narrow the gap on Sony's PlayStation and become a stronger number two when the next-generation consoles were introduced. Microsoft was using Xbox Live and the online capabilities of its Xbox console to differentiate itself from rivals and build market share. Microsoft executives saw Xbox Live as the key to its future in Japan, where sales of Xbox had not met expectations.

Microsoft had announced plans to spend $2 billion during the 2003–2007 period to build and promote Xbox Live. Xbox Live had been introduced in 14 European markets and had attracted around 100,000 European subscribers as of late 2003. Worldwide, Microsoft had an estimated 500,000 Xbox Live subscribers in late 2003 and 50 Xbox titles available for online play at Xbox Live. In early 2003 Xbox Live was hosting about 3 million game sessions weekly; more than 15.7 million hours of play had been logged in the first three months of operation.

The most popular game on Xbox was Halo: Combat Evolved, developed by Bungie, which debuted with the Xbox in November 2001 and had sold over 3 million copies. A sequel, Halo 2, originally scheduled for release in time for the 2003 holiday season, was scheduled to ship in 2004. Games that had Xbox Live capability included Microsoft's NFL Fever 2003, Counterstrike, Midtown Madness 3, MechAssault, and Whacked; Infogrames' Unreal Championship; and LucasArts' Star Wars Galaxies. So far, Microsoft's lineup of internally developed games (which also included Kung Fu Chaos, NBA Inside Drive, Brute Force, and Crimson Skies) had not proved as popular as those of Sony, Nintendo, or Electronic Arts.

In the year ending June 30, 2003, Microsoft reported consolidated revenues of $32.2 billion and net income of $10 billion, and it had cash and short-term investments of $49 billion.

ELECTRONIC ARTS

Electronic Arts began operations in 1982 in California and over the years grew from being a niche technology venture into a full-fledged entertainment company. EA maintained its headquarters in Redwood City. In 2003, it had about 4,000 employees, of whom 1,700 were outside the United States, and management had plans to add 1,200 new staff, mostly game developers. EA's revenues had more than doubled since 1999 (see Exhibit 7). The slight dip in fiscal 2001 revenues was due to the transition to the new-generation consoles in 2000–2001—many gamers postponed the purchase of new games in the months leading up to the introduction of new consoles, preferring to wait until more sophisticated games for the new consoles were released. EA reported a loss in fiscal 2001 because of heavy start-up expenditures for the EA.com segment of the company's business and low initial revenues from online operations (see Exhibit 8).

EA's near-term goal was to be the market leader of games played on the current generation of 128-bit consoles. Toward this end, EA was investing heavily in the development of tools and technologies that would facilitate the creation of new games for the existing (and future) game-playing platforms, spending $401 million for research and development (R&D) in fiscal 2003, $380.6 million in fiscal 2002, and $376.2 million in fiscal 2001. In fiscal 2004, EA planned to introduce games for six platforms: PlayStation 2, GameCube, Xbox, Game Boy Advance, PlayStation, and PCs. In the prior fiscal year, EA had introduced games for seven platforms:

PlayStation 2, GameCube, Xbox, Game Boy Advance, Game Boy Color, PlayStation, PCs, and online play. Over the past 20 years, EA had published games for 42 different platforms.

Foreign sales were expected to account for a significant and growing portion of EA's revenues. Exhibit 9 shows the geographic distribution of EA's sales in 2001, 2002, and 2003.

EA's Creative Process

EA's game design staff consisted of digital animators, programmers, and creative individuals who in many instances had backgrounds in television, the music industry, and the movie industry and were attracted by the creative opportunities in video games and EA's attractive compensation packages of high pay and stock options. Developing a game from scratch was about an 18-month process. To create a new game, small teams of EA game developers put together quick prototypes to demonstrate one small scene that represented the "creative center" of a potential game, usually focusing on the activity that would make the game fun to play.[9] If greenlighted, the team fleshed out the idea and created comiclike storyboards of every scene, much like moviemakers would illustrate a script. State-of-the-art tools were used to allow for more cost-effective product development and to efficiently convert games designed on one game platform to other platforms.

EA had two major design studios—one in Vancouver, British Columbia, and one in Los Angeles—and smaller design studios in San Francisco, Orlando, London, and Tokyo. The dispersion of design studios helped EA to design games that were specific to different cultures—for example, the London studio took the lead in designing the popular FIFA Soccer game to suit European tastes and to replicate the stadiums, signage, and team rosters. No other game software company had EA's ability to localize games or to launch games on multiple platforms in multiple countries in multiple languages. EA's Harry Potter and the Chamber of Secrets was released simultaneously in 75 countries, in 31 languages, and on seven platforms.[10]

[9]Dean Takahashi, "Electronic Arts Grows to $2.5 Billion in Annual Sales," *San Jose Mercury News*, May 5, 2003.

[10]Associated Press news release titled "Electronic Arts, A Powerhouse Well-Attuned to Public Tastes," August 18, 2003.

exhibit 7   **Summary of Electronic Arts' Financial Performance, Fiscal Years 1999–2003 (in thousands of dollars, except for per share data)**

	Fiscal Year Ending March 31				
	2003	2002	2001	2000	1999
Statement of operations data					
Net revenues	$2,482,244	$1,724,675	$1,322,273	$1,420,011	$1,221,863
Cost of goods sold	1,072,802	814,783	664,991	710,974	630,827
Gross profit	$1,409,442	$ 909,892	$ 657,282	$ 709,037	$ 591,036
Operating expenses:					
Marketing and sales	$ 332,453	$ 241,109	$ 185,336	$ 188,611	$ 163,407
General and administrative	130,859	107,059	104,041	92,418	76,219
Research and development	400,990	380,564	376,179	255,694	196,137
Amortization of intangibles	7,482	25,418	19,323	11,989	5,880
Charge for acquired in-process technology	—	—	2,719	6,539	44,115
Restructuring charges	15,102	7,485	—	—	—
Asset impairment charges	66,329	12,818	—	—	—
Total operating expenses	$ 953,215	$ 774,453	$ 687,598	$ 555,251	$ 485,758
Operating income (loss)	$ 456,227	$ 135,439	$ (30,316)	$ 153,786	$ 105,278
Interest and other income, net	5,222	12,848	16,886	16,028	13,180
Income (loss) before provision for income taxes and minority interest	$ 461,449	$ 148,287	$ (13,430)	$ 169,814	$ 118,458
Provision for income taxes	143,049	45,969	(4,163)	52,642	45,414
Income (loss) before minority interest	$ 318,400	$ 102,318	$ (9,267)	$ 117,172	$ 73,044
Minority interest in consolidated joint ventures	(1,303)	(809)	(1,815)	(421)	(172)
Net income (loss)	$ 317,097	$ 101,509	$ (11,082)	$ 116,751	$ 72,872
Net income per share—diluted	$2.17	$0.71	$ (0.08)	$0.88	$0.58
Balance sheet data at fiscal year end					
Cash and cash equivalents	$ 949,995	$ 552,826	$ 419,812	$ 246,265	$ 242,208
Short-term investments	637,623	244,110	46,680	93,539	70,614
Marketable securities	1,111	6,869	10,022	236	4,884
Working capital	1,340,261	699,561	478,701	440,021	333,256
Long-term investments	—	—	8,400	8,400	18,400
Total assets	2,359,533	1,699,374	1,378,918	1,192,312	901,873
Total liabilities	570,876	452,982	340,026	265,302	236,209
Minority interest	3,918	3,098	4,545	3,617	2,733
Total stockholders' equity	1,784,739	1,243,294	1,034,347	923,393	662,931

Source: 2003 10-K report.

exhibit 8 **EA's Financial Performance by Business Segment, Fiscal Years 2001–2003 (in thousands)**

	2003	2002	2001
Operations of "EA Core" (or non-online) business segment			
Net revenues	$2,400,669	$1,647,502	$1,280,172
Cost of goods sold	1,056,385	797,894	650,330
Gross profit	$1,344,284	$ 849,608	$ 629,842
Total operating expenses	730,747	563,146	506,427
Operating income (loss)	$ 613,537	$ 286,462	$ 123,415
Identifiable assets	$2,287,743	$1,529,422	$1,167,846
Capital expenditures	58,328	38,406	51,460
Operations of EA.com business segment			
Net revenues	$ 81,575	$ 77,173	$ 42,101
Cost of goods sold	16,417	16,889	14,661
Gross profit	$ 65,158	$ 60,284	$ 27,440
Total operating expenses	222,468	211,307	181,171
Operating income (loss)	$ (157,310)	$ (151,023)	$ (153,731)
Identifiable assets	$ 71,790	$ 169,952	$ 211,072
Capital expenditures	780	13,112	68,887

Note: EA defined its two business segments as EA Core (which included all non-online operations worldwide) and EA.com (which consisted of all online activities worldwide). Beginning in March 2003, EA consolidated the operations of EA.com into its core business operations and eliminated the distinction between the two segments.

Source: 2003 10-K report, pp. 110–12.

Every 90 days, a large group of managers and executives would gather in EA's Milestones theater to listen to game developers update their works in progress. If a game did not come across as promising, EA pulled the plug on further work. According to John Riccello, the company's chief operating officer, "We double down on things that work. We tend to stop things that don't work." Only a few new original games made it through to production and distribution each year. In fiscal 2003, a team of employees that had developed one of EA's hit Medal of Honor products was hired away by a competitor.

In the course of creating a number of its games, EA acquired intellectual property and other licensed content from sports leagues, player associations, performing artists, movie studios, music studios, and book authors. Many of its games included the like-nesses or voices of various artists, sports personalities, and cartoon characters, along with the musical compositions and performances of film stars and musicians. J. K. Rowling, the author of the Harry Potter books, had written portions of the script for EA's three Harry Potter games.

EA's policy was to make games that it could be proud of, which meant that it stayed away from games with profanity, sex, crime, and violence. While some of EA's rivals—like Take-Two Interactive, whose best-selling Grand Theft Auto: Vice City game involved doing drug deals, blowing up cars, consorting with a prostitute, and then hacking her to death—were willing to create violent or sexually suggestive games, EA had a firm policy of not creating games for mature audiences. The chief guardians of this policy were Lawrence Probst and Ruth

exhibit 9 **EA's Financial Performance by Geographic Area, Fiscal Years 2001–2003 (in thousands)**

	Fiscal Years Ending March 31		
	2003	**2002**	**2001**
North America			
Revenues from unaffiliated customers	$1,435,718	$1,093,244	$ 831,924
Operating income (loss)	216,491	8,328	(31,996)
Capital expenditures	47,955	39,259	103,048
Identifiable assets	1,764,103	1,325,939	1,034,625
Europe			
Revenues from unaffiliated customers	$ 878,904	$ 519,458	$ 386,728
Operating income (loss)	230,101	121,058	(8,914)
Capital expenditures	9,894	10,350	15,535
Identifiable assets	544,782	333,825	300,196
Japan			
Revenues from unaffiliated customers	$ 80,053	$ 58,597	$ 52,582
Operating income (loss)	4,601	3,401	7,437
Capital expenditures	384	871	660
Identifiable assets	22,800	18,175	23,733
Asia-Pacific (excluding Japan)			
Revenues from unaffiliated customers	$ 87,569	$ 53,376	$ 51,039
Operating income (loss)	4,927	2,277	2,962
Capital expenditures	875	1,038	1,104
Identifiable assets	27,848	21,435	20,364

Source: 2003 10-K report, p. 113.

Kennedy, EA's general counsel. When EA's developers were creating the DefJam Vendetta wrestling title, Probst, at the urging of Kennedy, vetoed several scenes that he and Kennedy felt were objectionable. In 1998, EA acquired Westwood Studios, which had developed a best-selling game called Thrill Kill for Sony's PlayStation; Thrill Kill was a four-player fighting game that featured beheadings, dismemberment, and lots of blood-spilling action. Several members of EA senior management, including Kennedy, did not believe that Thrill Kill belonged in the EA lineup; Probst agreed and axed the game. Web sites sprang up protesting the move, the game industry press screamed censorship, and there were even grumblings within the company. Even though the decision cost EA millions in lost revenues, Probst declared, "I don't regret it for a minute. EA will not publish games with gratuitous sex and vio-

lence."[11] But while gore and raunchy graphics were forbidden, EA did include trash talk in its sport games. During the past 20 years, EA had won over 700 awards for outstanding software in the United States and Europe.

EA's Relationships with the Three Major Console Manufacturers

Approximately 37 percent of EA's revenues in fiscal 2003 were derived from software sales for Sony's

[11]As quoted in Ashby Jones, "The Rules of the Game," *Corporate Counsel* 3, no. 7 (July 1, 2003), pp. 72 ff. (accessed December 4, 2003 at www.law.com/jsp/cc/pubarticleCC.jsp?id= 1055463668855).

exhibit 10   **EA's Revenues by Product Line, Fiscal Years 2001–2003 (in thousands)**

Revenue Source	2003	2002	2001	Percent Change 2002–2003	Percent Change 2001–2002
Games for Sony PlayStation 2	$ 910,693	$ 482,882	$ 258,988	89%	86%
Games for PCs	499,634	456,292	405,256	9	13
Games for Microsoft Xbox	219,378	78,363	—	180	n.a.
Games for Nintendo GameCube	176,656	51,740	—	241	n.a.
Games for Sony PlayStation	99,951	189,535	309,988	(47)	(39)
Games for Nintendo Game Boy Advance	79,093	43,653	—	81	n.a.
Online subscriptions	37,851	30,940	28,878	22	7
Advertising	31,988	38,024	6,175	(16)	516
Games for Nintendo Game Boy Color	26,293	38,026	—	(31)	n.a.
License, original equipment manufacture, and other	24,948	46,210	90,710	(46)	(49)
Co-publishing and distribution	375,759	269,010	222,278	40	21
Total	$2,482,244	$1,724,675	$1,322,273	44%	30%

Source: 2003 10-K report.

PlayStation 2, and it derived about 4 percent of its revenues from sales of games for the original PlayStation (see Exhibit 10). EA released 19 new titles worldwide for PlayStation 2 in fiscal 2003, compared to 18 titles in fiscal 2002; 6 titles were released for PlayStation in fiscal 2003 versus 5 in fiscal 2002. Management expected that sales of EA games for PlayStation 2 would continue to grow in fiscal 2004 but at a slower rate; sales of PlayStation games were expected to continue to decline. Under terms of an agreement in 2000, EA was authorized to develop and distribute DVD-based software for the PlayStation 2; however, the agreement called for Sony to supply PlayStation 2 DVDs for its products. Likewise, under terms of an amended 1994 agreement, EA was authorized to develop and distribute CD-based software for the PlayStation, with all PlayStation CDs being sourced from Sony. In May 2003, EA and Sony announced that EA would make many of its sports games available for Sony's PlayStation 2 online service. EA considered that its relationship with Sony was good.

EA derived about 7 percent of its 2003 revenues from GameCube software. It released 17 titles worldwide for GameCube play in 2003, versus 5 titles in 2002. Revenues from games for GameCube were expected to increase in fiscal 2004 as the installed base of GameCube consoles grew. As per a 2001 licensing agreement, EA was authorized to distribute Nintendo's proprietary optical disks containing EA game software for GameCube consoles, but Nintendo supplied EA with all the optical disks. EA management believed that it had a strong working relationship with Nintendo.

About 9 percent of EA's fiscal 2003 revenues came from sales of games for Microsoft's Xbox, up from 5 percent in fiscal 2002. The revenue gains were due to a growing installed base of Xbox consoles, plus the Xbox's being available for a full 12 months compared to only 5 months in fiscal 2002. EA introduced 16 new titles for play on the Xbox in fiscal 2003 versus 10 new games in fiscal 2002. Under terms of a licensing agreement entered into with Microsoft in late 2000, EA was authorized to develop and distribute DVD-based video games to play on the Xbox; unlike its agreements with Sony and Nintendo, it was not compelled to source its DVDs from Microsoft. However, EA's relationship with Microsoft was strained in 2003; Microsoft's policy of not allowing EA (or any other game developer) to earn any revenues from online play of Xbox games had prompted EA management, after months of back-and-forth negotiations, to refuse to program online functionality into its Xbox games. It was

exhibit 11 **Examples of Interactive Software Games Marketed Under Electronic Art's Four Major Brands**

- **EA Sports**—Madden NFL 2004, NCAA Football 2004, FIFA Soccer 2004, NBA Live 2004, NHL 2004 (hockey), MVP Baseball 2004, Rugby 2004, NCAA March Madness 2004 (basketball), Tiger Woods PGA Tour 2004, and NASCAR Thunder.
- **EA Sports Big**—Def Jam Vendetta (wrestling), SSX 3 (snowboarding), NFL Street, and NBA Street Volume 2 (basketball).
- **EA Games**—Harry Potter and the Chamber of Secrets, The Lord of the Rings: The Two Towers, James Bond 007 in Nightfire, The Sims, Superstar, Sim City 4, Need for Speed: Underground, Hot Pursuit 2, Harry Potter: Quidditch World Cup, Medal of Honor Rising Sun, Freedom Fighters, Command & Conquer Generals, Battlefield 1942: Secret Weapons of World War II.
- **Pogo**—Games marketed under this brand were electronic card games, puzzle games, and word games such as First Class Solitaire, Tumble Bees, Poppit!, Turbo 21, Word Whomp, Jungle Gin, and Sci-Fi Slots. These games, as well as many others, were available for play online at www.pogo.com, www.ea.com, and certain online services provided by America Online. At www.pogo.com, players won cash prizes and could also pay fees to enter tournaments or subscribe to Club Pogo ($4.99 per month or $29.99 per year) to become eligible for even larger prizes and awards. Club Pogo offered subscribers exclusive games with enhanced graphics, sound, and player features and a variety of ways to win big prizes and drawings.

Source: Company reports and press releases.

unclear to what extent the absence of online capability in EA's games for the Xbox would impact the sales of EA's Xbox games.

EA's Suppliers

Electronic Arts utilized four types of suppliers:

- The console makers (Sony and Nintendo) that supplied the CDs, DVDs, or optical disks on which EA then installed its video games designed for PlayStation, GameCube, and Game Boy consoles.
- Companies that pressed the CDs, DVDs, and optical disks containing its games.
- Companies that printed its game instruction booklets.
- Companies that packaged the disks and printed game instructions on the jewel cases and boxes for shipping to customers.

In many cases, EA was able to negotiate volume discounts and it was the company's practice to have multiple sources of supply for all the functions that were outsourced to suppliers. The costs to press a disk and print game instruction booklets were typically less than $1 per unit.

EA kept only a small inventory of its games on hand because (1) it could obtain additional supplies and fill retailer orders from replenished inventories within two to three weeks and (2) historically, most sales of a particular game occurred 60–90 days after initial release.

EA's Marketing and Distribution

Electronic Arts marketed its products worldwide under four brand logos: EA Sports, EA Sports Big, EA Games, and Pogo (see Exhibit 11). In fiscal 2003, EA introduced 70 new game titles under its four brands in North America, plus localized versions of its products in the rest of the world; it also distributed about 34 titles that it co-published with or distributed for other parties. In addition to releasing new versions of its popular sports titles annually, EA also released "expansion packs" for previously published games that provided additional characters, storylines, settings, and missions—for example, six expansion packs had been issued for The Sims, the best-selling PC game of 2000, 2001, and 2002. Games that were popular enough to justify sequels or expansion packs were viewed by EA as "franchise titles." The Sims, which was essentially a digital dollhouse, was EA's all-time best-selling game, achieving sales of 27 million copies in three years and luring addicted players, who included housewives and investment bankers. EA's first two Harry Potter games—both of which involved months of collaboration between EA and the producers, artists, and engineers of the movie and were released worldwide on the same day as the movie was released—had generated $500 million in revenues for EA. Sales of Harry Potter and the Chamber of Secrets, published on seven platforms, accounted for approximately 10 percent of EA's fiscal 2003 revenues, and sales of Harry Potter and the Sorcerer's Stone, published on four platforms, accounted for 12 percent of EA's fiscal 2002 revenues. Some 33 EA games had sold over 1 million copies worldwide.

The retail selling prices in North America of EA's games, excluding older titles marketed as Classics, typically ranged from $30 to $50. Classics titles had retail prices from $10 to $30. Outside North America, prices varied widely based on local market conditions. EA expected that in fiscal 2004 the premium prices of its hit titles would remain firm but that prices for its other games would be lower than in fiscal 2003, in line with the tendency for overall game prices to decline once current-generation consoles had been on the market for several years (see again Exhibit 5).

A big part of EA's marketing effort was devoted to promoting the EA Sports brand. EA saw the sports segment of the video game market as particularly attractive. Sports games were appealing to males between the ages of 16 and 40 because they had nearly photo-realistic graphics and gave game-playing sports fans the chance to carry on rivalries that were the trademark of professional and collegiate teams. Sports games were regularly endorsed by the biggest stars in professional sports, which helped spur sales (as well as providing big name sports stars with lucrative endorsement contracts). According to EA's vice president of marketing, from a marketing positioning standpoint, EA preferred to think of itself "as a sports company that makes games as opposed to a game company that makes sports games. EA Sports is as much a culture as it is a product."[12]

---

[12]As quoted in "Sports, Racing Games Are Powerhouse of Video Games World," www.Kiplinger.com, July 17, 2003.

In the past few years, EA had begun trimming its lineup of video games, eliminating many of the slow sellers and concentrating its efforts on creating "franchise" games that could achieve sales of millions of copies. In 2000 EA released 68 new titles, and in 2002 only 58 titles were released. Lawrence Probst indicated that EA's strategy was to "focus on doing fewer things and doing them better and getting more leverage out of the titles we ship." Roughly 70 percent of EA's revenues came from new releases of existing games.

Electronic Arts used a field sales organization and a group of telephone sales representatives to market its games directly to retailers; these two channels accounted for 95 percent of sales in North America. In markets where direct sales were uneconomical, EA utilized specialized and regional distributors and rack jobbers to gain retail access. Games were made available on a disk (usually a CD or DVD) or a cartridge that was packaged and sold in retail stores or through EA's online store.

In fiscal 2003, EA's games were available in approximately 80,000 retail locations worldwide, including mass-market retailers like Wal-Mart, electronics specialty stores like Best Buy, and game software specialty stores like Electronics Boutique. Over 66 percent of EA's sales in the United States were made to six retailers (Wal-Mart, Toys "R" Us, Target, Best Buy, Circuit City, and Kmart), and in Europe over 40 percent of sales were made to 10 retailers. Worldwide, Wal-Mart was EA's biggest customer, accounting for 12 percent of EA's total sales. EA's largest distribution relationship was with Sony in Japan; 60 percent of the sales of EA's PlayStation and PlayStation 2 games in Japan were made through Sony.

Because the video game business was becoming increasingly "hits driven," EA had found it necessary to boost its budgets for marketing and advertising, particularly TV advertising. Sales and marketing expenditures had increased from $163.4 million in fiscal 1999 to $332.4 million in fiscal 2003 and had averaged 13–14 percent of sales each year since 1999.

EA's business was highly seasonal. Sales were highest in the calendar year-end holiday season (about 40–50 percent of the annual total) and lowest in the April–May–June period. Orders were typically shipped upon receipt, resulting in little or no order backlog.

EA's Co-Publishing and Distribution Activities with Other Game Developers

In 2003, EA was distributing 34 co-publishing and distribution titles. Co-published titles were games conceived and developed by other game developers for which EA provided production assistance and marketing and distribution services. Some of the games were published and marketed under one of EA's three primary brands (EA Games, EA Sports, and EA Sports Big). The distribution titles were games published by another game developer and delivered to EA as ready-to-market products; EA provided only distribution services for these games.

Electronic Arts and America Online

In 1999, EA and America Online entered into a five-year agreement for EA to be AOL's exclusive provider of a broad aggregation of online games and interactive entertainment for AOL's Game Channel. EA managed all of the content of the Game Channel and had the latitude to sell its games to AOL subscribers and users. The terms of the five-year agreement resulted in AOL paying EA $21.3 million and ultimately receiving 477,350 shares of EA's common stock in return.

Nexity and the U.S. Banking Industry

John Frank Yother
The University of Alabama

David Long had to laugh at the article on his desk. Gomez, an Internet consulting firm, had written an article on the retention problems facing Internet-only banks, one of many damning articles the company had recently circulated about the future of virtual banking. Gomez was not alone in its criticism. After years of heralding online banks as the financial future, set to destroy traditional banking and the branch, consulting companies like Gomez, Jupiter, and others were recanting their previous predictions and finding virtual banks to be doomed. Brick-and-mortar banks, thought to be archaic in previous findings, were once again viewed as a necessity for customer service and quality.

Long was getting used to articles of this nature, but he found it interesting that his bank, Nexity, had defied the odds. He stepped out of his office and walked the halls of Nexity's Birmingham, Alabama, corporate headquarters, pondering the small bank's success. As bank president, he had ushered Nexity from a concept in 1999 into a company with over $500 million in assets. While most community banks of comparable size took three years to break even, Long had seen Nexity do so in 18 months. True, Nexity was a success, but was virtual banking a doomed industry, as so many consultants were saying? A large majority of traditional brick-and-mortar banks now offered online services, and the number of true virtual banks had dropped from a height of over 40 to around 25. Virtual banks, such as Nexity, had only captured 2 percent of the total U.S. banking market share.

Prepared under the supervision of Professor A. J. Strickland, The University of Alabama. Copyright © 2004 by John Frank Yother and A. J. Strickland.

David Long stopped in front of Nexity's in-house customer service center and watched as Nexity representatives fielded calls from customers. Why had Nexity succeeded while other virtual banks had failed? Long stared intently at what he believed to be the reason: exceptional service. In an age of branch renewal and the increased importance of the human touch, Nexity Bank had grown to an impressive size without ever laying eyes on the vast majority of its customers. Service, coupled with a breadth of competitively priced products, had been the bank's strength. Could Nexity's success in the banking industry last? Not satisfied with current asset size, Long walked back to his office to begin thinking of steps to continue Nexity's growth.

RECENT HISTORY OF THE BANKING INDUSTRY

The U.S. banking industry, long a fragmented and dispersed system, began to feel rapid changes in the late 1980s. The changes were due to financial legislation passed by Congress as a means to accelerate trends in making the U.S. financial system more integrated in terms of activities and products. The legislation also led to a push for consolidation throughout the industry.

The limited role banks were once allowed was due to the Glass-Steagall Act, signed into law as a response to the Great Depression. After the crash of the stock market and the failures and defaults of numerous U.S. banks, consumers, weary of the weakened institutions, began hoarding their money. Trust and confidence, keys in the banking business, were lost to mattresses and mason jars. Realizing the economic repercussions of decreasing numbers of deposits throughout the country, Congress drafted the Glass-Steagall Act. Along with the creation of the Federal Deposit Insurance Corporation (FDIC), which insured banking deposits for consumers, the Glass-Steagall Act provided a new means of confidence for consumers in placing their money in banks. The act limited the functions of banks, keeping them out of certain financial areas, like insurance, and limited the numbers of services they could provide. No longer were banks a one-stop shop for insurance, stocks, loans, and savings accounts. The separation decreased the likelihood that, in the chance of another financial crisis, the failure of one product (such as securities) would bring down the whole of the financial services industry.

The banking industry rebounded and grew rapidly after the Great Depression and World War II, and in hopes of keeping the industry from being highly concentrated, the Douglas Amendment was added to the Bank Holding Act of 1956. The act gave individual states the power to determine whether or not an out-of-state bank holding company was allowed to own and operate banks within the state. The Douglas Amendment kept banking a statewide concern for most banks throughout the 1960s and 1970s. In 1975 no state allowed out-of-state bank holding companies to buy and operate in-state banks, only 14 states allowed branching statewide, and 12 states prohibited branching in any form, keeping banking a highly fragmented industry. In the late 1970s and 1980s, states began loosening their restrictions on statewide and interstate branching. Regional pacts, like the Southeast Regional Banking Compact, began allowing banks to branch into multiple states. Seeing the trends, Congress passed the Reigle-Neal Interstate Banking and Branching Efficiency Act in 1994. The new law allowed bank holding companies to establish or acquire banks anywhere in the country, regardless of state law. Banks that wished to move into additional states had to be deemed adequately managed and capitalized by the FDIC. Reigle-Neal dramatically changed the face of banking, as banks began moving across state lines, increasing competition in an industry once protected by state law.

As banking continued to change, Congress felt the need to update the Glass-Steagall Act, limiting banks from moving into diversified product offerings. On November 12, 1999, the Gramm-Leach-Bliley Act was passed, repealing Glass-Steagall and allowing banks, securities firms, and insurance companies to affiliate with one another in a new financial holding company structure. A year before the passage of Gramm-Leach-Bliley, Citicorp and Travelers Insurance had agreed on a cross-industry merger that was dependent on Congress's passing such a law, leaving many to believe that the two companies were somewhat responsible for its passage. By July 2001, 558 financial holding companies had been created in compliance with Gramm-Leach-Bliley, and 19 of the 20 largest U.S. banks belonged to a financial holding company. The act further increased competition and merger activities that Reigle-Neal began, as superregional holding companies like Chase Manhattan and Citigroup began rapid growth.

RECENT TRENDS IN THE BANKING INDUSTRY

Consolidation

Unlike the banking systems in most other developed countries, the U.S. system was highly fragmented, even in 2003. However, since the deregulation of the 1980s and 1990s, a "merger mania" had taken place in the banking and financial services industry. Deregulation led to consolidation, which flooded once-protected markets with new rivalry. The increase in institutions within markets led not only to mergers and acquisitions but also to the failures of many banks. The Gramm-Leach-Bliley Act's diversification effects extended banking consolidation into other financial services companies, further increasing opportunities and competition for banks. Other factors also aided consolidation numbers: changes in communications and information technologies, the desire for scale economies, the need for increased geographic coverage, a more national brand recognition, higher stock prices, and increased efficiencies were but a few.[1]

Between 1980 and 2002, the number of banks in the United States dropped by nearly 50 percent, from

[1]Benton Gup, ed. *The Future of Banking* (Westport, CT: Quorum Books, 2003), p. 2.

exhibit 1 **FDIC-Insured Bank Institutions, 1980–2002**

Year	Institutions	Branches
2002	7,887	66,185
2001	8,080	65,564
2000	8,315	64,079
1999	8,581	63,684
1998	8,774	61,957
1990	12,347	50,406
1985	14,417	43,293
1980	14,434	38,738

Source: FDIC.

14,434 to 7,887 institutions (see Exhibit 1). At the height of the consolidation boom in the 1990s, there were, on average, 600 consolidations annually. While the number of banking institutions was decreasing, asset size of existing banks was increasing. According to the FDIC, there were 10 banks in 2002 with assets of over $100 billion, compared with only 3 in 1992. Also increasing were the numbers of branches. In 2002 the FDIC reported 66,185 bank branches in the United States, up 41 percent from 38,738 in 1980, implying that customers, while given fewer choices in banking institutions, increasingly desired the use of branches.

Consolidation had also led to a higher concentration in segments of the banking industry. Sixty percent of the credit card market was held by five large U.S. banking institutions, among them Citigroup, J. P. Morgan Chase, and Bank One. The nation's 30 largest banks controlled 40 percent of U.S. deposits, and 10 companies held 40 percent of mortgages.

By 2002, mergers had slowed and the number of banking institutions in the United States had declined at a rate of only around 2–3 percent annually, beginning in 1998. In 2002 and 2003, consolidation trends were once again picking up steam, as Citigroup purchased Golden State Bancorp in 2002 for $5.8 billion and Bank of America announced a planned acquisition of Fleet Boston in 2003 worth over $43 billion and having the potential to make Bank of America the second largest U.S. bank in terms of assets. These deals seemed likely to begin a copycat trend within the banking industry.

Scandal

In the late 1990s and early 21st century, the U.S. economy was rocked by one scandal after another. Corporate fraud and deceit shook consumer confidence in accounting firms, banks, and the companies they represented. Illegal dealings by companies such as Enron, WorldCom, and HealthSouth were defining business at the turn of the century. The involvement of large banks in these frauds had led to investigations and fines for many reputable institutions. Just coming to light in 2003 were the dealings of Citigroup and J. P. Morgan Chase, the country's two largest banks, with Enron, a company involved in one of the largest corporate meltdowns ever.

Citigroup and J. P. Morgan Chase had begun working with Enron in the mid-1990s, establishing a questionable means for the energy giant to raise cash and keep investors happy. Known as a prepay system, the banks established offshore entities (J. P. Morgan Chase created Mahonia, and Citigroup's entity was known as Delta) that promised a future payment to Enron for the delivery of natural gas or oil. Delta and Mahonia then would promise delivery of natural gas or oil to the lending institution. The lending institution agreed to send the same natural gas or oil back to Enron. While the transactions were supposed to be separate and were booked as such, they created a circle between Enron and the banks as interest-bearing loans, which Enron recognized as cash flows. The bogus capital inflow satisfied analysts, propped Enron's books, and kept company stock prices high at Enron. Citigroup and J. P. Morgan Chase completed $8 billion in prepay transactions with Enron over the course of six years.[2]

The banking industry was also feeling the effects of bad loans made to crumbling institutions. Citigroup was involved in loans with WorldCom, lending over $300 million to the failed long-distance service provider. J. P. Morgan Chase had lent millions to both Adelphia and Kmart. The financial services industry lost billions of dollars in bad loans in the early 21st century as banks took a $37 billion hit in combined charges. Citigroup, J. P. Morgan, and others were also accused of bad practices in not separating corporate lending and investment banking, offering underpriced loans at a loss in order to attract

[2]Bethany McLean and Peter Elkind, "Partners in Crime," *Fortune,* October 27, 2003, pp. 79–100.

high-margin investment banking. During Senate hearings investigating these allegations, Citigroup investors shaved $46 billion in market capitalization in two days and J. P. Morgan lost $12 billion.[3]

Through all of the bad dealings in the financial services industry, the trust of customers was injured, and large banks had to reestablish some relationships. More than financial, the losses suffered by the banks involved with Enron, WorldCom, and other failures were reputational. Consumer confidence was hurt, as many people questioned placing deposits in and buying services from institutions involved in fraud, deceitful lending, and illegal practices.

MARKET SIZE AND GROWTH

In 2003, the Federal Deposit Insurance Corporation (FDIC) reported 9,267 insured banking institutions in the United States (including commercial banks; savings institutions; agricultural banks; and commercial, consumer, and mortgage lenders), a 2 percent decrease from 2002 numbers. While fewer banks were operating, industry assets had increased from $8.039 trillion in 2002 to $8.923 trillion in 2003. Likewise, U.S. deposits were rising and had grown by nearly 12 percent from 2002, to $5.166 trillion. The rise in deposits and assets suggested that more consumers were placing more money into banking institutions nationwide.

Banks with over $10 billion in assets had experienced the greatest growth in deposits from 2000 to 2002, while banks with less than $100 billion had negative deposit growth over the same period. Geographically, the New York region of the Federal Reserve Banking System (New York, Pennsylvania, the District of Columbia, Delaware, Maryland, New Jersey, Virginia, and Puerto Rico) contained the nation's largest numbers of deposits, with over $1 trillion, followed by the San Francisco region (California, Oregon, Washington, Alaska, Utah, Wyoming, Hawaii, and American Samoa) with over $850 billion. By state, California, New York, and Texas contained the highest deposit levels in 2003, while Vermont, Wyoming, and Maine had the lowest.

[3]Julie Creswell, "Banks on the Hot Seat," *Fortune,* August 11, 2002.

THE TRADITIONAL BANK BRANCH

Before the proliferation of technology in the banking industry, the role of the branch was very different from the role of the modern branch. Before the 1970s, the product offerings, function, and layout of the branch were uniform from bank to bank, and branches were transactional centers, the only financial outlet for banking customers. Most U.S. banks had only one branch or office, and these buildings were gigantic, 20,000-square-foot stores with marble columns, vast offices, numerous teller lines, and many employees. Limited geographically, customers were accustomed to making the weekly drive downtown for face-to-face service at the bank. As the bank's focal point, branches were the only place for customers to borrow, save, and plan retirement. When interstate branching efforts began, banks began building more branches, expanding into new communities and states, and decreasing the size of the offices.

With the rise in banking technology, the branch began a process of change that continued through the end of the 20th century. Automated teller machines (ATMs), telephone banking, and the Internet all provided cheaper alternatives than the branch, with its high overhead and labor fees, and banks began pumping money into growing and improving these channels (see Exhibit 2). Banks sought a means to integrate their channel offerings, pushing customers to the cheapest, most convenient channel in order to save money and decrease numbers of transactions. At the same time, branches were scaled down. Banks began investing less in technology, service, and people at their branches, and the emphasis on the branch slipped.

Realizing that transactions had increased with the addition of channels and that many customers still sought face-to-face service in numerous situations, banks began a branch renewal process in 2000. Many predicted that technology would revolutionize the industry, leading to the slow death of the branch. Instead, branches were once again seen as the primary means of capturing and selling products to customers. Alternative channels were being viewed as a convenient offering for customers, with the branch as the focal point once again. Banks began reinvesting in technology, customer service, and the building

exhibit 2   **Average Channel Transaction Cost**

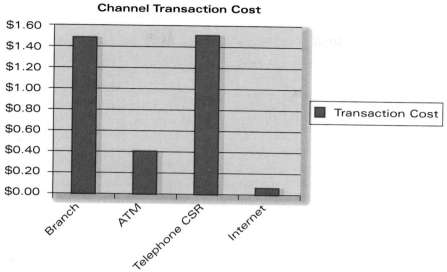

Source: Council on Financial Competition.

of knowledgeable staff, and the function of the branch returned to sales and servicing.

TECHNOLOGY AND ALTERNATIVE CHANNELS

The myth in the banking industry had always been that the newest technology would revolutionize banking, placing less pressure on the importance of the branch for retail customers, and would draw customers away to newer and cheaper channel offerings. This myth, however, had not panned out through decades of new introductions in the banking world. In fact, research had found that new technological channel introductions had only increased retail transactions, as customers began adding the numbers of channels they used to execute banking transactions. From 1996 to 2001, transactions across branches, call centers, ATMs, and the Internet increased from 23.1 billion to 30.8 billion, a rise of 33 percent.[4] As consolidation decreased the number of banking institutions, the number of branches in the United States had steadily climbed (see again Exhibit 1).

[4]Council on Financial Competition, *Essay Section I: The Unrealized Ambitions of Multi-Channel Investment.* The Advisory Board Company, 2002.

The new channel introductions *had* revolutionized the banking world in terms of convenience and availability. Once a 9-to-3 operation, banks continued to move in a 24/7 direction, giving customers the option of visiting branches for face-to-face transactions but allowing them the freedom to bank anytime they pleased.

ATMs

First seen in banks in 1969, ATMs were considered the first factor that would reduce dependencies on tellers and branches. Chemical Bank, an early adopter of ATM technology, ran an early ad campaign claiming: "On September 3, 1969, our branch will open its doors at 9:00 a.m. and we'll never close again!" By 1971 many large banks had begun installing ATMs inside and outside of their branch locations. There were 2,000 ATMs operating in the United States by 1973. The machines were online by 1976, linking directly to their home institution and providing balance inquiries, transfers, deposits, and, most important, cash withdrawals. That same year, about 7 percent of U.S. households were actively using the machines.

Until the mid-1980s, ATM networks were a marketing advantage to banks, allowing a new service, 24-hour banking, that could differentiate them from other institutions. ATMs allowed for an extension of the bank without building physical branches, and no longer were customers forced to stand in lines or be restricted by bank office hours. ATM penetration grew to include a third of all banking households. Soon, however, ATM networks became a commodity, and banks without an ATM presence were at a disadvantage.

As with any new technology, early ATM users were young and fairly wealthy, and this demographic had remained steady. In 2002, the average ATM user was 37 and had an income of $45,100. The vast majority of ATM customers had a bank account with the provider of the ATM they used most frequently, and their average cash withdrawal was $64.00.

In an age where customers were pushing for free channels, ATMs were a vital delivery system and revenue generator for banks. While other channels were often used for retention and cross-selling of products, ATMs became a means of generating profits in transaction fees, which the majority of banks had not eliminated by 2003. In 2001, U.S. banks took in $74 billion in usage fees. In 2002 the number rose to $90 billion.[5] The size of the global ATM industry was $15 billion in 2002. Revenues from transactions exceeded $10 billion, and new machine sales were $1.2 billion.

While the ATM was an important source of revenues, its usage had begun to slip in the late 1990s and early 21st century. In 1998, the 187,000 ATMs in the United States averaged 4,973 transactions per month. By 2002, the number of ATMs had climbed to 352,000, a growth of 47 percent. However, average monthly transactions had slipped by almost 50 percent, to 2,509. By 2003 there were 371,000 ATMs averaging 2,432 transactions monthly.[6] ATM use had fallen because the machines were in direct competition with debit cards, another rapidly growing channel. Also to be blamed was the shift in the economy and consumer sentiment toward a cashless society.

With the decline in ATM use and the lessening importance of cash, banks had begun investigating new means of attracting customers to ATMs and reducing the costs in existing networks. ATMs that offered stamps, movie tickets, and other products in addition to existing services had been tested. Some banks were forming network partnerships in order to squeeze profits out of ATMs. Banks with ATM networks would charge a fee to smaller banks with less extensive or no networks, allowing the small bank's customers to use the large bank's ATMs without paying a "foreign" service charge. Also being introduced was the Web-based ATM, which was more catered and personable. Along with offering standard ATM services, the Web-based ATM could take information from a consumer's banking history and tailor products and services specifically for the customer. This personalization would allow for additional cross-selling and marketing opportunities

Debit Cards

Introduced in the 1980s, debit cards did not become a well-recognized or preferred payment method until the late 1990s. By 1995, debit card transactions accounted for 2 percent of retail noncash payments. Growth since 1995 pushed that number up to 11.6 percent in 2000, and payments using debit cards were likely to continue growing into the near future.[7]

Unlike credit cards, which functioned like a loan for consumer purchases, debit cards functioned as an electronic checking system. Consumers with debit accounts drew money from their checking accounts without writing checks or paying the interest fees of credit cards. Debit cards, once rare, were being accepted by businesses that also allowed credit card purchases.

Consumers had begun accepting debit cards and the payment method had grown because of budgetary concerns and the benefit of convenience. As additional businesses began accepting debit cards as a form of payment, and with the push toward a cashless society, consumers recognized the convenience of not having to carry either cash or checkbooks. Both not having to rely on ATMs and branches to obtain cash and not having to fill out and sign checks meant a savings of time for consumers. Consumers were also less worried about overspending with debit cards versus credit cards. While credit cards allowed consumers to spend freely (up to a maximum limit), debit cards could draw only from the consumer's

[5]Ikimulisa Sockwell-Mason, "Banks Cash In on ATM's," *New York Post,* April 11, 2003.

[6]John Hackett, "Squeezing Profits Out of ATMs," *US Banker,* January 2002.

[7]Stacey Pinckerd, "Debit Reaches a Milestone," *Credit Card Management,* November 2002.

current bank account, meaning consumers were forced to spend within their means.

For customers still needing cash, debit cards turned grocery stores and retail outlets into ATMs. Cash-back features, offered at retail stores like Target and Wal-Mart and grocery stores like Publix and Albertson's, were displacing ATM usage. When consumers did not have access to their home bank's ATM, the cash-back feature reduced the costs of foreign ATM surcharges. In communities with no ATMs, cash-back was the only means, other than the branch, by which consumers could receive cash. Cash-back had been aided by the growth in the number of debit readers, which had gone from 40,000 in 1988 to 3.5 million in 2002, growing at an almost 35 percent annual rate.

Not only were debit cards convenient to consumers, but many small banks began seeing them as a means of leveling the playing field with larger banks. Historically too small to offer the programs alone, small banks could partner with Visa's or MasterCard's debit system. A portion of the fee paid by retailers for each transaction (anywhere from 15 to 50 cents) would be realized by the bank.

In a 2003 survey, Star Systems, one of the nation's leading electronic payment networks, reported a growing desire by consumers to use debit cards for purchases of under $25. The most popular items purchased with debit cards were movie tickets (24 percent), fast food (20 percent), pay phone calls (19 percent), and items from vending machines (13 percent). Small online debit purchases were also increasing as consumers became more confident in online security services such as Verified by Visa, which provided password protection for Visa credit and debit cards online.[8]

Debit cards were predicted to grow faster than any other payment method over 2004 and 2005. Between 2001 and 2003, the growth of payment by debit card was 30 percent annually, with payment by credit card growing 10 percent over the same time period. Among consumers, the cards saw the sharpest increase among Hispanics, the fastest-growing segment of the U.S. population. Hispanics' usage increased 41 percent from 2001 to 2003, while check usage was up 11 percent and cash transactions were down 22 percent. Though there were twice as many credit cards in circulation, debit card purchases were surpassing credit card purchases for the first time in 2002. In the first half of the year, the number of Visa debit purchases by consumers and small businesses was 3.04 billion, compared to 2.96 billion Visa credit card purchases.[9]

Rewards programs offered by banks were attracting customers to use debit cards. Among debit card users, 6 percent were enrolled in a rewards program. The largest of these programs were partnerships with retailers, such as Macy's and Target, who added points toward future purchases with each debit transaction. Also popular were airline miles, which, like frequent-flier miles, could reduce or pay for flights through debit transactions. Sweepstakes entries and percentages of purchases returned were also rewards systems used by debit card holders.

Call Centers and Telephone Banking

Call centers and telephone banking were necessary yet costly channels for banks to operate. Another tool of convenience for customers, call centers allowed 24-hour assistance with banking queries and problems, and also let customers hear account status. Much like an ATM, call centers allowed customers to check account balances, transfer funds, and review previous transactions. Customers could also reorder checks and ATM/debit cards, and stop payments. In 1999, one in five financial services consumers used call centers and telephone banking for problems or account updates.

Technology improvements in call centers were increasing convenience for customers and saving banks money in operations. Customers no longer had to punch commands on telephone keypads because voice recognition units, which understood patterns in the human voice, were becoming standard. The units were also able to comprehend and answer some simple questions, allowing human representatives to focus their efforts on more complex questions and cross-selling opportunities. A 2003 survey by the business intelligence firm Cutting Edge Information found that less than 10 percent of banking institutions realized profits from operating call centers, and 55–70 percent of banks operated them at a

---

[8]"Debit Payments Rise for Small Purchases, STAR Survey Finds," *Electronic Commerce News,* June 9, 2003.

[9]James Swann, "Debit Card Usage on the Rise," *Community Banker,* July 2003.

loss.[10] Much like the branch, call centers were still people intensive, and labor costs were high. To maximize efficiency and reduce losses and costs, call centers had become a cross-selling vehicle. Representatives, while aiding customers with problems, also provided information and deals on additional products. While call centers and telephone banking were free services to most customers, some banks had begun charging fees for excessive use.

Wireless Banking

As the newest channel feature at banks, wireless banking was being offered at only the largest institutions. Wireless banking let customers check balances, transfer funds, receive stock quotes, and trade using personal digital assistants (PDAs), cell phones, and pagers. Though wireless use worldwide was expected to reach 150 million people, the acceptance in the United States was low. Few cell phone users were subscribing to Internet access, and only 7.7 million phones with wireless applications had been sold in the states. Celent Technology predicted that 13.5 million Americans would be using wireless services by 2004, compared with 56 million Asians.[11]

Wireless features were not profitable to the few banks and financial service companies that provided them, but they were offered as a customer retention strategy. Technology-savvy bankers and traders who wanted the newest bells and whistles were the majority of subscribers to wireless banking and would switch banks in order to receive the service. As a costly channel used by a very small customer niche, wireless banking allowed very few companies to realize enough value to offer it.

INTERNET BANKING

History and Benefits

Internet banking was offered by two types of institutions: brick-and-mortar banks and virtual banks. Also known as traditional or branch banks, brick-and-mortar banks had a physical presence, with branch locations and ATM networks. The Internet

was seen as an additional, cheaper channel for customer use, and brick-and-mortar banks hoped to push customers to use Internet banking for simple transactions rather than continue using the more expensive branch or telephone services (see again Exhibit 2). Traditional banks understood that while Internet banking was a convenient feature at the banks, the majority of consumers still wished to occasionally use branches for face-to-face service, especially when dealing with a complicated or detailed transaction or application process. Virtual banks, also known as Internet-only or pure-play Internet banks, operated with the Internet as their primary banking platform. By not having a physical presence with branches, virtual banks looked to save overhead costs and pass savings on to price- and convenience-minded customers.

Wells Fargo, the first bank to offer Internet banking, began its transactional online banking site in 1990. Internet banking trends caught on slowly; only 16 U.S. banks had transactional Web sites in 1996. That number, however, grew to 103 in 1997, 368 in 1998, and 1,130 in 1999, mirroring the huge growth in the Internet over the same period.[12] By 2003, online banking was a common feature at the majority of banks, with over 50 percent of institutions offering the sites.

The first virtual bank was Security First Network Bank. Opened in 1995 in Atlanta, Georgia, the online-only institution was acquired three years later (during the banking consolidation boom) by the Royal Bank Financial Group of Canada. CompuBank out of Houston, Texas, received the first national charter for a virtual bank in 1997. Since then, the number of virtual banks had fluctuated, with 35 of them at the height of the Internet boom. In 2003, around 20 true Internet-only banks operated in the United States (see Exhibit 3).

Virtual banks relied heavily on the convenience they provided to grow deposits and assets. The banks were founded on the belief that Internet-savvy consumers, pressed for time and attuned with technology, would prefer banking from home or office. Internet banks did not require traveling to branches between the hours of 9 and 3 on weekdays, standing in teller lines or waiting on a sales representative, or using ATMs for transactions that could be done by personal computer. Online banks also gave customers

---

[10]"Finding Opportunity in Call Centers," *Card News,* September 3, 2003.

[11]Elisa Batista, "Wireless Banking: Bust in US," *Wired News,* July 25, 2000.

[12]Gup, *The Future of Banking,* p. 162.

exhibit 3   **U.S. Virtual Banking Institutions, 2002**

Institution	Location	Assets (in thousands)	Deposits (in thousands)
E*Trade Bank	Arlington, Virginia	$17,453,676	$ 9,157,328
ING Direct	Wilmington, Delaware	16,142,091	13,112,826
NetBank	Alpharetta, Georgia	4,280,899	2,479,421
Principal Bank	Des Moines, Iowa	1,967,342	1,826,018
BMW Bank of North America	Salt Lake City, Utah	1,149,732	156,983
National Interbank	Arlington, Texas	645,448	528,516
Nexity Bank	Birmingham, Alabama	501,167	368,523
American Bank	Allentown, Pennsylvania	472,181	336,288
First Internet Bank of Indiana	Indianapolis, Indiana	333,677	267,162
DeepGreen Bank	Seven Hills, Ohio	331,857	199,516
Nbank	Commerce, Georgia	304,096	272,708
Bank of Internet USA	San Diego, California	273,208	194,580
Stonebridge Bank	Exton, Pennsylvania	268,968	211,988
The Bancorp Bank	Wilmington, Delaware	248,709	226,755
Ascencia Bank	Louisville, Kentucky	246,023	215,591
Umbrella Bank	Chicago, Illinois	225,819	178,867
interState Net Bank	Cherry Hill, New Jersey	132,326	116,582
Earthstar Bank	Southampton, Pennsylvania	102,483	77,239

Source: FDIC.

an increased choice in institutions, as geographic limitations were erased by the Internet. Once forced to use the community or local bank, people in rural areas were able to become Citibank or E*TRADE customers with a few clicks.

Online banks provided many of the products and services of traditional branches. Customers were able to research, apply for, and open accounts online. Typical online product offerings were:

- Interest checking accounts.
- Home equity lines.
- Home equity loans.
- Annuity services.
- Savings accounts.
- Certificates of deposit.
- Money market accounts.
- ATM/debit cards.
- Mortgages.

At virtual banks, these products were typically offered at better rates than the national average—the rates could be three times better than averages (see Exhibit 4). The rates were a primary means of drawing consumers to the bank, and they could be passed

on because of overhead reduction. Without a network of expensive branches to operate, virtual banks reduced costs in occupancy (building rents, utilities, depreciation) and salaries. Traditional banks, operating anywhere from a few to thousands of branches, realized overhead costs much higher than those of virtual banks. Because of these cost savings, virtual banks could pay more interest on deposits and charge lower rates on loans, attracting price-sensitive consumers.

To compete against other virtual banks, grow, and attract customers, virtual banks needed good customer service, in-house customer data and service center operations, strong management teams, a good mix of attractively priced products, and low marketing costs.

Virtual Banking Pitfalls

In the wake of the Internet boom of the late 1990s, there were early concerns that banking customers would flock to the new virtual banks. However, a 2000 report by Mainspring Communications found that virtual banks had captured only 2 percent of the online banking market (around 760,000 of 38 million

exhibit 4 **Sample Interest Rates at E*Trade, Nexity, and Everbank versus National Averages, 2003**

	E*TRADE APYs*	Nexity APYs	Everbank APYs	National Average APYs
Checking	1.01%	.75%	2.5%	0.25%
One-year CD	1.44	2.11	1.75	1.11
Money market	1.11	1.75	1.51	0.51

*Annual percentage yields.

Sources: Bankrate.com, Etradebank.com, Nexitybank.com, and Everbank.com.

customers).[13] While the convenience and great rates were attractive to some online consumers, Internet-only banks had suffered pitfalls stunting their growth. The lack of person-to-person contact forced consumers to resolve problems over the phone or via e-mail, which could be frustrating for some. Obtaining deposit slips, easy to do at a branch, required postage and delivery time from virtual banks. Mailing deposits to the bank meant that a customer had to wait days to draw funds from accounts. Cash was also a problem, as ATMs and debit cards were the only means of obtaining cash from a virtual bank.

In some cases, overhead saved by a lack of branches was displaced by costs not seen at branching banks. Twenty-four-hour call centers, a must at all virtual banks, realized revenue losses, and while some brick-and-mortar banks could charge for overuse, virtual banks had to keep call centers a free service. Virtual banks, with little to no brand-name recognition and no branch locations to advertise the bank's presence, could incur high marketing and advertising expenses in increasing their visibility. In a five-month period in 2000, Wingspan Bank, an Internet-only bank, spent $19 million on Web advertising. In the same period, Fleet Boston Bank, a large brick-and-mortar bank with high recognition, spent only $4.6 million.

Possibly the largest issue facing virtual banks was the attraction they held for hit-and-run customers. Competitive rates offered by virtual banks, coupled with the Internet's availability of information, had fostered a spirit of bargain hunting in the banking industry. For decades brick-and-mortar banks had offered teaser rates, enticing new customers with high rates of return on saving and

checking accounts and low interest rates on mortgages and loans. The better rates were subsidized by other parts of the large organizations in hopes of selling more products and retaining the customer (eventually rates would increase/decrease to industry averages). For small virtual banks, subsidizing rates were impossible, and bargain shoppers could leave the bank after rates changed or deals ran out. Hit-and-run customers, focusing on only one product, did not represent long-term depositing.

The problems associated with virtual banks had led to a few well-profiled banking failures. Wingspan Bank, a virtual bank spun off by top-10 bank Bank One, was supposed to be the industry leader among Internet-only banks. Founded in 1999, Wingspan was never able to gain the customer base Bank One sought. At its height, Wingspan had 95,000 customers, compared to the 600,000 online customers at Bank One's own Internet site in 2000. Increased profitability and efficiency, two of Wingspan's goals, suffered, and the site folded back into Bank One in 2001. Wingspan's largest problem was its lack of brand-name recognition. Expensive marketing and advertising efforts failed, as customers did not seek out the virtual bank, and deposits did not satisfy Bank One. Another virtual failure, G&L Bank, focused on providing banking services for the gay and lesbian community. The bank was unable to grow and profit serving this niche, however, and closed in 2002 after three years of operation.

FACTORS IN CHOOSING AN ONLINE BANK

For the average banking customer, the most important factors in choosing and staying with a bank were con-

[13]Orla O'Sullivan, "Net Banks: More Dreams than Reality," *US Banker,* February 2002.

venience, product offerings, and service. Institutions that were able to provide a number of channels—including branches, ATMs, debit and credit cards, call centers, and online banking—and provide them in a way that let customers maximize efficiency while minimizing time investments were institutions likely to capture and retain customers. Banks had to be able to offer services tailored to the varied preferences of different customers, as older consumers overwhelmingly desired banking face-to-face, and younger, more affluent consumers desired mixing the branch with a number of other, faster channels.

For those using Internet-only banks over traditional brick-and-mortar institutions, the leading factors in choosing a bank were security, convenience, and rates. According to a TowerGroup report on consumer acceptance of Internet banking, the number one obstacle keeping customers from Internet-only banks was concern over security.[14] Of 3,800 respondents, 26 percent did not use Internet banking because of security issues, 22 percent lacked comfort in Internet banking, and 21 percent preferred banking face-to-face rather than using the Internet. Credit card theft and identity theft were raising concerns among consumers. Wariness regarding Internet banking in the United States and worldwide was well founded, as online security and fraud issues had been plaguing the industry. The U.S. Federal Trade Commission had found that identity theft was on the rise among U.S. consumers: 27 million identity thefts had occurred since 1998, and 10 million of those happened in 2002. Two-thirds (6.7 million) of these thefts involved account theft, such as misuse of a credit card.

A current industry security concern involved a practice known as "phishing." Banks that neglected to register domain names similar to the company's own name found that scammers were setting up deceptive Web sites and stealing customer information. In an example of phishing, Citibank customers began receiving e-mails from a site called Citicard.com, which was not registered to Citibank, asking for updates of customer information. Citibank customers, believing the site to be the home of Citibank's credit services, gave out updated personal identification numbers and credit card information. The thieves used this information to fabricate false cards. Citibank had recently begun a humorous nationwide

ad campaign dealing with the problems of identity theft in an effort to reassure customers that the bank had taken steps in reducing fraud.

Other banks had also begun combating industry security concerns. The Gramm-Leach-Bliley Act required banks to establish safeguards in protecting customers' nonpublic records and information. Safeguards included online security statements outlining the bank's steps in safeguarding customers' private information and account access. Customer authentication was the most important way to prevent security breaches in online banking, and most online banking sites also advised customers to protect themselves by not revealing passwords, changing passwords and ID numbers frequently, and reviewing account statements for unauthorized activity. TowerGroup's George Tubin said, "In order to gain the trust necessary for continued online banking adoption, banks must not only fully indemnify their customers from fraudulent activity; they must be significantly more assertive in educating consumers on how they're protected."[15] The majority of institutions had a zero liability policy, assuring consumers that any unauthorized account use would be reimbursed. Online sites used encryption, which was the scrambling of data into a code unreadable without the key used to decipher it. The highest available standard used to hide and secure customers' online information was 128-bit encryption.

While the security issue blocked some people from trying online banking, convenience was a stronger factor. With 24/7 capabilities and numerous product offerings, virtual banks were an attractive alternative to traditional banking. For existing online banking customers, the Pew Research Center found that convenience was the number one attraction for shifting to the online service, with Internet users passionate about saving time. In their findings, 79 percent of online customers under 30 said convenience was "very important" to their decision to first bank online, while 82 percent of 30–49-year-old Internet customers agreed. Time savings was also a large factor in online banking: 71 percent of online bankers said that saving time was important to their decision to bank online.[16]

[14]"Resistance Remains for Online Banking Adoption," *Community Banker,* August 2003.

[15]John Ginovsky, "E-Banking in the Comfort Zone," *ABA Bankers News,* June 24, 2003.

[16]Pew Internet and American Life Project Research, "Online Banking: A Pew Internet Project Data Memo," November 2002.

exhibit 5 **Online Banking Customer Demographics, 2002**

	Don't Do Any Banking Online	Bank (Not Bill Pay) Online	Bank and Bill Pay Online
Age (avg)	45	43	42
Income (avg)	$61,000	$69,900	$81,600
Investable assets (avg)	$225,000	$251,000	$320,300
College degree	38%	48%	53%
Male	47%	52%	55%
Weekly hours online	20	25	27
Years online	3.2	4	4.3

Source: Forrester Research.

The impressive rates offered by virtual banks were a factor drawing many consumers, both hit-and-run and long-term depositors, to virtual banks.

ONLINE BANKING DEMOGRAPHIC AND MARKET CONDITIONS

According to the Pew Research Center, by 2003, over 38 million Americans were banking online.[17] The number of online banking customers was projected to rise to over 67 million by 2007, as some 30 percent of Americans were expected to be using a bank's online services. Comfortable with technology in phases, consumers slowly embraced each new stage in online banking, first viewing account balances online, then performing transactions, and finally adopting online bill pay. The more years spent online, the more likely consumers were to use and accept new services. Of those with two to three years of online experience, 20 percent had banked online, while among those online for four or more years, 39 percent had done so. In 2002, 12 million households were paying bills online, and growth in bill pay was expected to mirror that of online banking in general.

Migrating consumers toward online bill payment was seen as one of the best ways to boost customer retention at banks. According to Wells Fargo research, once online banking users signed up for bill pay, they were 70–80 percent more likely to re-main loyal to the bank. Retention was due to convenience. After customers had set up direct deposit accounts with their bank and employer and had activated bill-pay services for their expenses, they were highly unlikely to switch banking institutions for minor inconveniences. Those using online bill-pay services were among the most profitable customers at banks, averaging almost $12,000 more in income than online consumers not using bill pay. Spending more time on the Internet and having more income and investable assets, bill-pay customers presented banks with the most opportunity for marketing and cross-selling additional services and products (see Exhibits 5 and 6).

Banking online was growing to be equally popular along racial lines in the United States. Among African American Internet users, 30 percent banked online, compared to 32 percent of white Internet users. The largest growth and enthusiasm among Internet users was with Hispanics, 33 percent of whom had done their banking online. Recognizing the potential of Hispanic customers, large U.S. banks like Citigroup and Bank of America had begun buying stakes in banks in Mexico and California in hopes of capturing the segment.

ENTRY BARRIERS

The expenses in founding a bank, whether Internet-only or brick-and-mortar, were the largest barrier to entry in the banking industry. There were three ways in which a new bank could enter the market. First, a company could buy an existing bank to form a new institution with accounts and assets. Second, investors could front capital to fund a new bank and

[17]Richard Craver, "Consumer Use of Online Banking Growing," *Knight Ridder Tribune Business News,* May 6, 2003.

exhibit 6 **Online Banking Customer Age Demographics, 2002**

Age	Likely to Bank Online
18–29	33%
30–49	36
50–64	27
65+	16

Source: Pew Internet and American Life Project.

provide adequate assets before deposits began accumulating. Third, an existing bank holding company could spin off a separate banking entity, providing investments and backing for the new bank. Staffing, locating, and building facilities; training; and marketing were early start-up concerns, and a new bank needed to raise $8–$12 million to begin operations. As deposits grew, expenses in expansion would also increase. Branch and ATM networks for brick-and-mortar banks, call centers, and online infrastructure capabilities were huge expenses.

Start-up costs for virtual banks, however, were much less expensive than for brick-and-mortar banks. Internet-only banks, without capital and overhead requirements for physical channels, needed marketing and advertising budgets large enough to attract depositors at the start-up phase. Even with high initial marketing costs, virtual banks could begin operations for millions less than brick-and-mortar banks.

A second entry barrier was loyalty to older, larger, and more established brand-name banks, such as Citigroup, J. P. Morgan Chase, Wachovia, and Bank of America. Though all of these banks had been involved in mergers, acquisitions, name changes, and some amount of recent investment problems, they were the market leaders in the financial services industry and provided the availability of services and convenience consumers desired in banks. These banks had established massive branch and ATM networks and were able to accept revenue losses in channels deemed important to retention of profitable customers. The industry leaders' involvement in providing services beyond banking also increased loyalty, as customers no longer were required to maintain accounts with a separate insurer, broker, and bank. While services such as insurance and equity offerings were available at many banks, industry lead-

ers had acquired well-established, reputable companies (such as Citigroup's acquisition of Smith Barney and Wachovia's partnership with Prudential Securities) to provide additional financial services.

The provision in the Gramm-Leach-Bliley Act allowing the formation of financial holding companies and the integration of services opened the door for insurance providers, securities firms, and others to provide banking services. Once limited to one aspect of the industry, companies were beginning to test the waters of banking, having the capital funding and brand recognition needed to survive. Gramm-Leach-Bliley allowed for the possibility of participation in the banking industry from an array of financial service providers, threatening traditional banks on all sides.

COMPETITIVE RIVALRY

Competition in the banking industry centered on wide product offering, numbers of channels and locations, and customer service. Many banks were also able to rely on their rich traditions and years of leadership in banking. While banks offered teaser rates at times in order to draw new customers, attractively priced products could be easily imitated.

Advertising in banking was done primarily by the presence of branches and ATMs. Establishing a strong physical presence in communities and cities fostered a reputation of strength and trust, and building branches grew the brand name. Other advertising practices were direct mail and billboards. Large banks were also able to conduct state, regional, or national commercial campaigns.

The most recent FDIC statistics had Citigroup as the largest U.S. bank, followed by J. P. Morgan Chase. The proposed acquisition of Fleet Boston Bank would soon give Bank of America the second position.

Citigroup

Citigroup, the world's largest financial provider, ranked first among bank holding companies in terms of both assets and earnings. Citigroup reached a banking milestone in 2002 by becoming the first U.S. bank with over $1 trillion in assets. Among financial providers, Citigroup clearly led in market share in the United States in 2003. The company's phenomenal size was due to its aggressive merger with Travelers Group in 1998. The merger, Gramm-Leach-Bliley's first large creation of a diversified bank holding company, solidified Citigroup as the largest U.S. bank holding company yearly since 1998.

Citibank, the traditional banking service of Citigroup, was founded in 1812 as the City Bank of New York. By 1894, it had become the country's largest bank. Early establishing a global presence, City Bank had moved into Asia, Europe, and India by 1902. Setting another milestone, the bank was the first U.S. financial company to reach assets of over $1 billion. Continuing to grow into the 1960s, the bank was acquired by First National City Corporation (later Citicorp), a bank holding company, and renamed Citibank. Citicorp remained the parent of Citibank until the Travelers merger, creating Citigroup, the present parent financial holding company.

Known as a cutting-edge corporation, Citigroup had pioneered many industry products and services. In 1904, City Bank of New York broke new ground by being the first bank to offer traveler's checks. In 1967 the bank introduced the "Everything" card, the bank's first credit card, which later became Master Charge (and is today's MasterCard). In 1985 Citi introduced Direct Access, linking home and office personal computers with the bank. Direct Access, long the gold standard in computer banking programs, made Citibank a provider of world-class technology in a time before the takeoff of the Internet.

While Citigroup was seen as a technology leader in the industry, the company had waited until relatively late to offer transactional services on its Web site, adding the ability to view accounts in 1997. Nevertheless, Citibank had received countless awards for its online banking services. Citibank Online was ranked number one on Gomez Inc.'s online banking scorecard for five straight quarters beginning in 2002. Forbes gave its highest honor to Citibank Online by naming the service its favorite online banking site in the Winter 2002 "Best of the Web" issue. In 2003 Gomez again honored Citibank Online, naming it number one among bank Web sites in ease of use and onsite resources and number two overall.

Citibank Online offered numerous services in an effort to give customers the widest possible array of choices. Citibank Online provided the standard functions of online bill pay, funds transfer, and online account inquiries. Other features provided free to customers were online bank statements, 24/7 customer service, and online fraud protection. Citibank

also offered somewhat unique services to customers in an effort to further build retention. Wireless alerts, sent to a computer or cell phone, told customers when checks had cleared, deposits had gone through, or accounts had reached a limit. "My Account Aggregation" linked numerous accounts, both financial and informational, Citi-affiliated and nonaffiliated, providing one easy-access page for customers. Aggregation users could see the status of checking accounts, check their e-mail, and view credit card statements from one site. My Citi, another free service, was a customizable financial home page from which to access Citibank accounts. The home page allowed not only account viewing but also bill-payment services, market activity status, portfolio tracking, and news. Customers also received exclusive offers, customized savings and deals offered to Citibank Online users (such as rebates in adding additional Citigroup services to existing accounts). Citibank recognized that once a customer had set up customizable home pages, linked numerous accounts, and begun paying bills online and receiving e-mails and alerts on account status, he or she was not likely to switch banks. In an effort to push customers to these services, Citibank offered them for free. As retention value rose, Citibank and Citigroup could cross-sell customers additional products, such as loans, equity offerings, and insurance—high-margin items overshadowing losses from Citibank's free online services.

Citigroup operated over 2,600 locations in the United States and 3,000 more offices in 100 additional countries. Citigroup extended farther globally than any other U.S. bank and owned stakes of regional banks in many countries, including Banamex, one Mexico's largest banks. In 2002, Citigroup spun off 20 percent of Travelers in order to gain capital in acquiring Golden State Bankcorp, the parent of the third largest U.S. thrift, Cal Fed. The $5.8 billion acquisition gave Citigroup a new foothold in California, a state with a young demographic, and opened doors for a larger Hispanic customer base. The bank had a network of 3,800 ATMs and reimbursed customers outside the reach of Citibank branches for four monthly ATM transactions at other banks.

With 1.9 million online customers, Citibank had fewer online accounts than both Bank of America and Wachovia, but this was due to the fact that Citibank had fewer retail customers than either bank. The bank found that 30–40 percent of its retail customers used online banking, and nearly 50 percent of online customers subscribed to online bill pay.

Possibly involved in questionable practices, Citigroup was feeling pressure from the U.S. Securities and Exchange Commission in 2003. The company was fined $400 million for issuing favorable stock ratings to companies in exchange for large investment banking contracts. An article in *Fortune* magazine's October issue reported that Citigroup, through prepay transactions, had aided Enron in cooking books and committing one of the largest-ever frauds in U.S. history.

J. P. Morgan Chase

The 2001 merger of J. P. Morgan and Chase Manhattan Bank had created one of the most diverse and far-reaching institutions in the financial services industry. Chase Manhattan, a retail-oriented powerhouse, was known for its consumer and small banking services, home and auto finance, insurance, and investments. J. P. Morgan, one the oldest and most historic financial businesses in the world, served as an investment banking and management institution, Treasury and security provider, and a large private bank. The combination of the two institutions brought together two very different functional companies in order to create a true one-stop financial services shop. Investment banking activities, one of J. P. Morgan's strongest areas, faced an industry slowdown at the time of the merger, and the company was forced to cut 10 percent of its workforce (3,000 jobs).

Much like Citibank, J. P. Morgan Chase had a relatively small base of retail customers and operated branches only in Connecticut, New Jersey, New York, and Texas. It had moved into the international banking market with operations in 52 additional countries and was planning an entrance into the large and growing Chinese market. Despite being more of an investment and financial services bank, J. P. Morgan Chase still boasted over $700 billion in assets in 2003 and had domestic deposits of nearly $200 billion, making it the second largest U.S. bank holding company.

Chase, the retail arm of J. P. Morgan Chase, was the provider of the bank's online services. Chase Bank offered three online options for customers: Chase Online, Chase Online Plus, and Chase Online for Small Businesses. Chase Online included account aggregation services, linking a number of Chase's products—such as credit card, checking and savings, auto loan, mortgage and investment accounts—all to one customizable page. Also offered were free check images, 60-day viewing of past transactions, options to download information into personal money management software (like Microsoft Money), account and wire transfers, and online bill pay. Chase Online Plus offered all of the standard Chase Online services but added e-mail, frequent-flier miles, auctions, and news information to its account aggregation page. Customers were also able to link and add non-Chase financial accounts to their home page. Chase Online for Small Businesses let customers review account activities, make payments of bills and payments to employees, transfer monies, link personal and business accounts to one site, and download account and transfer information into accounting software. Recognizing the retention value of its online services, Chase offered the three account options free to customers (small business online customers paid small monthly fees of $5 and $10 for tax and direct deposit services, respectively).

With its vast array of online options for customers, Chase Online had been chosen number one in customer confidence in the 2003 Gomez scorecard for online banking. The bank was chosen sixth for its overall score, behind both Citibank and Bank of America, banks placing far more importance on retail banking and customer service. *Forbes* had also rewarded Chase, finding its site a 2003 Best of the Web pick. *Forbes* said Chase Online had knowledgeable and courteous customer service, but the site needed to work on its confusing and clumsy navigation.

J. P. Morgan Chase, much like Citigroup, was feeling the heat of its Enron involvement in 2003. The bank lost over $1 billion in exposure over loans to the defunct company. The bank was involved in paying $135 million to settle actions stemming from the loan, a small amount for the large institution, but large enough to damage the reputation of the historic bank. Feeling losses in both commercial lending and venture capital segments stemming from involvement with Enron and other bad loans, J. P. Morgan Chase was on a push to refocus itself on consumer banking and internal growth. However, following industry trends, J. P. Morgan Chase had not ruled out the possibility of acquisitions in obtaining this growth.

Bank of America

According to Bank of America's chairman and CEO Ken Lewis, the company's vision was to be "the world's most admired company." Becoming that company required achieving key customer goals: providing "efficient, error-free service"; retaining profitable customers and rewarding them for their business; and developing "innovative new products and solutions" that changed the way financial institutions operated. With its retail emphasis, Bank of America had become the third largest U.S. bank in terms of assets, which were well over $650 billion.

To meet customer goals, Bank of America had begun a campaign to reestablish and refocus the branch as the profit center of the Charlotte, North Carolina–based bank. Long a strength of the company, Bank of America's extensive branch network was the nation's largest, with over 4,200 locations in 21 states and the District of Columbia, along with presence in 30 additional countries. Bank of America planned to open 550 new branch locations by 2005. Claiming market leadership in California, Florida, Maryland, and Washington state, Bank of America had begun establishing additional branches in California, Florida, and Texas. Hoping to attract a very large domestic Hispanic population, Bank of America bought a quarter of Grupo Financiero Santander Serfin, one of Mexico's largest and most recognizable banks, in 2002. One of the developments in the renewed branch focus was a high-tech redesign of the brick-and-mortar locations. While some banks had begun viewing the branch as archaic in the Internet age, Ken Lewis saw the potential of the branch as a means of selling more products to customers from one location. He established test branches in the Buckhead section of Atlanta in 2001 as a means of gauging the potential of the branch of the future. Each location included a greeter by the door, much like Gap retail establishments, a stock ticker on the wall, a bar location with computers for online banking and checking portfolios, and a financial planner equipped to sell mutual funds and stocks. Employees worked out of kiosks, not offices, creating a friendly, inviting atmosphere at the bank. Along with the cosmetic changes, the test branches had software capabilities to identify customers who would qualify for more premier and profitable services, prompting a sales force call and increased sales and retention. Successful in Atlanta, Bank of America had agreed in 2003 to open 15 of the new branches in Charlotte. Other locations were slated to open in Oregon, Nevada, Florida, California, Texas, Arizona, Georgia, Tennessee, Washington state, and Washington, D.C., by the end of 2003.

The renewed emphasis on the branch had not slowed growth in other key channels at Bank of America. The bank had become the nation's largest issuer of debit cards, reporting over 17 million outstanding cards and 2.1 billion yearly transactions.

Bank of America had also developed the country's largest proprietary ATM network, with over 13,250 operational ATMs nationwide. The ATMs, which together averaged 3.2 million transactions per day, were a technological advancement in which the bank took pride. Over 3,000 of the machines in the network were talking ATMs, which were developed for the blind and visually impaired. Giving spoken instructions through a headset, the talking ATMs performed all transactions of the bank's normal ATMs.

Bank of America's online emphasis was also growing. With over 4.2 million online banking subscribers in 2002, online banking at Bank of America processed 400 million transactions that year. By August 2003, over 6.63 million customers were active in online banking, an increase of nearly 50 percent. Over 1 million customers were paying bills online through Bank of America, and it was the first large bank to offer its bill-pay service for free. Seeing the profitability of online bill-pay customers, who keep larger checking account and loan balances than other customers, Bank of America promoted and helped bill pay increase by 40 percent at all banks in 2002. The number of Bank of America customers using online bill pay had jumped from 2.5 million in 2002 to 3.8 million in 2003. *Forbes* named Bank of America among the "Best of the Web" and *Global Finance* magazine ranked BankofAmerica.com the world's best consumer Internet bank.

In late 2003, Bank of America was in negotiations with Fleet Boston, a top-10 bank with nearly $200 billion in assets, for a proposed merger. The merger, which would give Bank of America a solid presence in New England, was reportedly costing Bank of America $43 billion and would increase assets to over $930 billion, surpassing J. P. Morgan Chase as the second largest U.S. financial holding company.

Wachovia

Much like its North Carolina neighbor Bank of America, Wachovia's primary concern and revenue generator was general banking, including retail, small-business, and commercial banking. In 2002, 52 percent of Wachovia's revenue was derived from general banking, and two-thirds of the bank earnings came from retail lines of business. Statistics such as these were based on Wachovia's branch and customer service focuses. With over 2,700 locations in a dozen eastern states, Wachovia held market share in deposits in Georgia, North Carolina, South Carolina, and Virginia, and was the fourth largest bank in the nation in terms of assets. The bank was also adding and testing new concept branches. In 2003 Wachovia test-marketed prototype branches with a new look: a curved roof and a floating ceiling to match lines in its logo, increasing brand and logo awareness. The branches, being tested in Georgia and Florida, included television screens showing daily financial news and had new, more efficiently designed teller lines. Wachovia planned to open an additional 100 locations through 2005, including over 12 new branches in Manhattan.

According to CEO Ken Thompson, the vision of Wachovia was "to be the best, most trusted and admired company in the financial services industry." Thompson believed that Wachovia's goals could be achieved through a passionate commitment and dedication to customers, communities, shareholders, and employees. In 2002 the bank's extended branch network reached and served the 9 million–plus Wachovia households from Connecticut to Florida. The bank's large call center capabilities processed 171 million calls annually. In 2001 and 2002 Wachovia led its peer group in the American Customer Satisfaction index, with service scores rising over 10 percent. More than other large banks, Wachovia fostered commitment to employees and their value. The bank was honored by being named one of the top 10 companies for working mothers by *Working Mother* magazine, one of 50 best companies for Latinas to work by *Latina Style*, *Essence* magazine's list of outstanding companies for black women, one of *DiversityInc.*'s top companies for diversity, and among the 100 best corporations in North America for developing human capital by *Training* magazine. Wachovia's spirit of community service was expressed by over 1 million annual hours of service by employees, gifts of $86 million in charity giving in 2002, and $19 billion in community investments in 2002, making Wachovia the number one community development lender in the United States.

Wachovia was formed by the 2001 acquisition of Wachovia Bank by East Coast powerhouse First Union Bank. The acquisition created the number one branch network and the largest market share on the East Coast. First Union Securities and ILJ Wachovia, investment banking and retail brokerages, were molded together to form Wachovia Securities, which boasted offices in 48 U.S. states and 30 countries in 2003. Continuing its securities growth, Wachovia joined forces with Prudential Financial to form a brokerage joint venture. In July 2003 Wachovia completed the legal consummation of the combination, making Wachovia Securities the third largest full-service retail brokerage firm in the United States based on client assets.

First Union's acquisition had also created one of the nation's largest online banking sites serving retail, small-business, corporate, and wealth management accounts. Some 3.1 million customers used Wachovia's online service, which processed 38 million transactions annually, making Wachovia the third largest online banking provider. Wachovia was the first top-10 bank to offer online check viewing, which, according to Chris Musto of Gomez, was one of the number one customer requests in online banking. Wachovia.com also featured balance inquiries (of checkings, savings, investments, money markets, loans, certificates of deposit, and credit cards), funds transfers, online bill pay, wireless alerts, account aggregation, and payment terminations. The bank had 280,000 online bill-pay customers, and 20,000 customers signed up for the service each month in 2002, helping to satisfy Ken Thompson's goal of reducing the bank's number of single-service users. Unlike other top-10 banks, Wachovia.com was not giving all of its online services away for free. After free trial periods, online bill pay (the number one online customer retention tool) cost $6.95 a month. Telephone bill pay cost consumers the same amount.

While Wachovia had not followed the lead of other large banks in making all online services free, it had received the same amount of accolades as those given to its peers. The Customer Respect Group ranked Wachovia.com the number one financial services Web site in June 2003. The site was ranked number one in number of visits per day among top-10 banks by Nielsen in 2003. A Greenwich Associates Study rated Wachovia number one in ease of use among banks.

Wachovia's other channel provisions were large in scope. The bank held a system of over 4,500 ATMs processing 278 million transactions yearly. A huge debit card provider, Wachovia customers were using debit cards for purchases and withdrawals 600 million times annually.

NEXITY

As David Long examined the landscape of the banking industry, he had to smile at the success Nexity Bank had achieved. In a time of consolidation and branch renewal, when other virtual banks had struggled and closed doors, Nexity Bank had survived. While banking analysts, once so enthusiastic about the potentials of Internet-only banking and the subsequent death of the branch, were recanting their previous predictions, Nexity was defying current views, building loyalty, and slowly increasing brand-name recognition.

President David Long's vision to make Nexity Bank "a leading provider of financial services" had begun in 1999, when he, along with CEO Greg Lee and two other partners formed the Nexity Financial Corporation, a bank holding company, with the intentions of opening an early virtual bank. To do so, the holding company held an initial private offering in August of 1999 and raised $22.5 million. This money was used in the acquisition of the People's State Bank of Grant, Alabama, a small community bank with $30 million in assets. The bank's name was changed to Nexity, an executive staff with a combined experience of well over 100 years was formed, offices were relocated to Birmingham, Alabama, and by February 2000, Nexity had opened for operations.

The limitations of virtual banks had allowed them only a 2 percent share of the online market. David Long was actively addressing the problems hurting online-only banks like Nexity, Netbank, and Principal:

- *Reliance on one to a few products*—Many virtual banks focused their efforts and best rates on one specific product, aiming to be the leader in mortgages, loans, or savings. Efforts like these had increased hit-and-run banking at those institutions. Nexity aimed at providing the best rates possible on all of its products, becoming a one-stop financial services shop. The broad product mix encouraged deeper relationships.
- *Differentiation and recognition*—Many banks, with inadequate marketing and a lack of focus on core principals, had never distinguished themselves from others. By coupling quality products with friendly service and availability, Nexity had made a name for itself in the virtual banking community.

Nexity sought to attack its rivals on two fronts: products and service. As the number of banks offering transactional Web sites had grown, so too had Nexity's competition. But Long realized that his stiffest rivalry came not from large brick-and-mortars but rather from other virtual banks, appealing to the same set of technology-savvy, convenience-minded customers. To gain additional market share and draw customers away from rivals, Nexity strove to keep overhead costs low, pass the savings on to customers in the form of better rates, and offer more and better products and services than other virtual banks.

Service, Nexity's primary means of differentiation, was the company's largest goal and standard. Call centers and customer service representatives, separate from headquarters at most banks, resided a few doors down the hall from Long's Birmingham office. Around-the-clock call center and e-mail operations provided customers with quick, friendly responses to inquiries and problems. Staff members were knowledgeable and friendly, and when they could not answer a query immediately, they were prompt in contacting the customer with an answer. To further emphasize Nexity's standard of service, the bank's address and phone number had been posted on every page of its Web site. Long realized that winning in the banking industry meant placing a heavy emphasis on serving the customer efficiently, politely, and quickly.

Unlike niche players in the virtual market, Nexity's strategy was to spread its geographic and demographic customer base throughout the U.S. While E*Trade Bank focused on securities traders, and G&L Bank had targeted the gay and lesbian community, Long believed that the Internet allowed marketing efforts to go beyond a limited customer group or a specific area. Nexity, through Internet-based advertising channels like online banner ads on Bankrate.com, had attracted a variety of customers from all 50 states. Web-based advertising had allowed the bank to be seen and recognized as a leader among virtual banks, receiving a top tier award from Bankrate for its high yields on money market accounts and certificates of deposit. Along with the Web, Nexity had placed re-

exhibit 7   **Nexity Bank Asset Growth, July 2000–January 2003 (in thousands)**

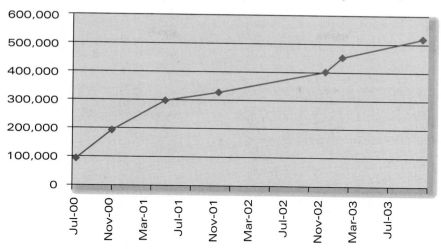

sources in direct mail marketing and had gained free advertising in print publications, like the *New York Times* and *The Wall Street Journal,* which published Bankrate's rankings.

Nexity Bank's strategy was to target these geographically and demographically diverse price- and service-minded consumers with a number of financial products. The bank offered transactions and account inquiry, online statements, online viewing of canceled checks, interest-bearing checking, savings, money market, and online bill pay accounts for free. Customers were also given competitive rates on home equity lines and loans, certificates of deposit, and annuities. A key partnership had been formed with Legg Mason Wood Walker in providing brokerage accounts to Nexity customers.

To combat the issue of security, Nexity provided reassurance with the WebTrust seal. A service of the American Institute of Certified Public Accountants and the Canadian Institute of Chartered Accountants, WebTrust was an examination and audit of business Web sites. Those passing security and privacy criteria set by WebTrust were allowed to display a seal of trust on their Web site. Realizing security to be an issue in winning customers, Long had helped pass WebTrust standards in the early phases of the bank. While few banks currently performed such a third-party Web site review, the likelihood was high that more banks would seek such a service, placing Nexity ahead of the curve.

Concerns over deposits and cash still limited the convenience of the bank. For customers without di-

rect deposit capabilities, mailing checks to the Nexity was the only means of depositing money. Waiting for deposits to post could be an inconvenience for customers. With no ATM network and no branches, cash could be received only at other banks' ATMs, or by using cash-back services with debit cards. Nexity reimbursed consumers for four monthly trips to foreign ATMs. As society moved in more of a cashless direction, David Long did not see the cash issues as a large concern.

While the numbers of virtual banks were declining and market share of online banking was small, Nexity had experienced continued asset and deposit growth over the course of its business (see Exhibits 7–11). When most comparably sized community banks took three years to break even, Long had seen Nexity do so in 18 months. The bank's current customer base was over 10,000, small in comparison to most brick-and-mortar banks but healthy among its virtual rivals. Beginning in March of 2002, Nexity had experienced six straight profitable quarters. Though industry branch renewal efforts were once again focusing on physical locations, David Long saw the future of online banking as nothing but great. In his words, Internet banking provided Nexity the opportunity to continue "delivery of financial services in the fastest growing market segment, with 500 households migrating to the Internet per hour." Long believed all of the banking industry would continue striving to capture this customer base and seeking proficiency in online banking. To David Long, the future of Nexity Bank was bright.

exhibit 8   **Nexity Bank Deposit Growth, June 2000–June 2003 (in thousands)**

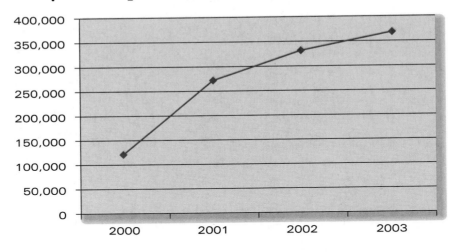

exhibit 9   **Nexity Balance Sheet, 2003 (in thousands)**

	6/30/2003	6/30/2002	6/30/2001	6/30/2000
Assets				
Cash and due from depository institutions	$ 19,966	$ 20,825	$ 3,052	$ 1,905
Securities	165,241	63,991	80,436	72,986
Federal funds sold and repurchase agreements	4,533	586	9,593	6,320
Net loans and leases	301,126	298,432	215,723	60,115
Bank premises and fixed assets	1,149	1,499	1,673	1,412
Other real estate owned	469	403	0	322
Goodwill and other intangibles	911	911	961	2,060
All other assets	7,772	4,337	4,155	2,566
Total assets	$501,167	$390,984	$315,593	$147,686
Liabilities and equity				
Liabilities				
Total deposits	$368,523	$333,150	$273,875	$123,068
Federal funds purchase and repurchase agreement	3,257	0	0	0
Other borrowed funds	85,000	20,000	10,000	67
All other liabilities	4,485	3,420	3,991	1,048
Equity				
Preferred stock	0	0	0	0
Common stock	3	3	3	3
Surplus	39,297	39,297	33,297	27,297
Undivided profits	602	−4,886	−5,573	−3,797
Total liabilities and equity	$501,167	$390,984	$315,593	$147,686

Source: FDIC.

exhibit 10   **Nexity Income Statement, 2003 (in thousands)**

	6/30/2003	6/30/2002	6/30/2001	6/30/2000
Interest income				
Domestic office loans	$ 8,411	$ 8,829	$ 6,979	$ 1,729
Lease financing receivables	357	497	563	118
Balance due from depository institutions	106	7	30	0
Securities	3,618	2,130	3,252	1,460
Trading accounts	7	1	0	0
Federal funds sold	58	62	229	299
Other interest income	98	30	25	—
Total interest income	$12,655	$11,556	$11,078	$ 3,606
Noninterest income				
Fiduciary activities	$ 0	$ 0	$ 0	$ 0
Service charges on deposit accounts	23	25	21	86
Trading account gains and fees	164	6	0	0
Additional noninterest income	176	154	125	32
Total noninterest income	$ 363	$ 185	$ 146	$ 118
Provision for loan and lease losses	$ (580)	$ (940)	$ (1,160)	$ (475)
Interest expenses				
Domestic office deposits	$ 4,219	$ 5,275	$ 6,773	$ 1,943
Federal funds purchased	2	5	13	4
Trading liabilities and other borrowed money	1,022	420	165	1
Total interest expense	$ 5,243	$ 5,700	$ 6,951	$ 1,948
Noninterest expense				
Salaries and employee benefits	$ 2,805	$ 2,582	$ 2,367	$2,085
Premises and equipment expense	577	578	453	321
Additional noninterest expense	1,558	1,394	1,876	1,840
Total noninterest expense	$ 4,940	$ 4,554	$ 4,696	$ 4,247
Pretax net operating income	$ 2,255	$ 547	$ (1,583)	$(2,946)
Securities gains	358	151	346	0
Income taxes	(152)	(0)	(4)	(86)
Income before extraordinary items	$ 2,461	$ 698	$ (1,241)	$(3,032)
Extraordinary gains	0	0	0	0
Net income	$ 2,461	$ 698	$ (1,241)	$(3,032)

Source: FDIC.

exhibit 11   **Nexity Operating Ratios, 2003**

	6/30/2003	6/30/2002	6/30/2001	6/30/2000
Return on assets	1.03%	0.38%	−0.90%	−6.41%
Return on equity	12.99	4.21	−9.83	−32.71
Yield on earning assets	5.44	6.54	8.38	8.36
Net interest margin	3.18	3.31	3.12	3.85
Noninterest income to earning assets	0.16	0.10	0.11	0.27
Noninterest expense to earning assets	2.12	2.58	3.55	9.85
Net operating income to assets	0.89	0.30	−1.16	−6.41
Efficiency ratio	63.54	75.38	108.71	230.69

Source: FDIC.

Making It Big

Joan Winn

University of Denver

Cynthia Riggs, CEO and founder of Making It Big (MIB), a manufacturer of clothing for large and supersize women, looked over her company's latest financial figures with concern. In 2001, sales had exceeded $2.3 million, an average increase of 12 percent over 10 years (see Exhibit 1). Going into the spring season, 2002 revenues had been 7 percent above 2001, but returns from the latest mail order catalog had been far lower than expected (see Exhibit 2). Cynthia didn't understand why her previously successful company was suddenly foundering.

> We are struggling to increase sales in both retail and mail order. It has been a difficult season and unexpectedly so. I think we are going to see a decrease in annual sales for the first time since 1995. This has put a crimp in our growing plans and overall morale. We were all set to move forward and instead find ourselves struggling to keep up with last fall, which after September 11 was not a pretty picture, but in fact superior to the current numbers. We just announced a wage freeze to be reevaluated at the end of the first quarter of 2003.

Looking to grow, MIB had already embarked on new approaches—expanding its mail order roster and beefing up its Web site—but they weren't panning out. "We took the steps traditionally used in mail order," Cynthia explained. "We printed more catalogs, exchanged and rented mailing lists and

The author wishes to thank Cynthia Riggs and the staff of Making It Big for their cooperation in the preparation of this case. Special thanks to Armand Gilinsky, Sonoma State University, for assistance and encouragement in this project, and to Molly Ball for editorial assistance. *All events and individuals in this case are real, but some names may have been disguised.* The original version of this case appears in the December 2004 issue of *Entrepreneurship Theory and Practice* (1042-2587). Copyright © 2004 by Baylor University.

have mailed the catalogs. The response has been far below expectations." As for the attempt to increase Web site traffic, "We worked with a very savvy guy, put together what we all thought would be a mutually beneficial project—and it bombed. It makes no sense. He was able to get more potential customers to our site, but they didn't become buyers."

Cynthia had started her business on the strength of a single inspiration—"a gift," she called it—not as a calculated plan. She sensed that the company's improvisational style was a weakness. "This is one of the shortcomings of MIB, not having a strong vision that determines the changes to come," she said. "I wouldn't say we are a boat askew on a tempestuous sea, but much of what actually happens derives from tangible events in the course of doing business," rather than an overall strategy.

And the vision, she realized, would have to come from others besides Cynthia herself. "I don't think I can grow the company alone," she said. "We are at the point where my skill set has reached its limits, and without an influx of new skills and information, nothing can really move forward the way it needs to. We need more skilled individuals who can take what we've built and propel us to the next level." A strong-willed entrepreneur whose motivations were as much personal and political as monetary, Cynthia had long been the sole driving force behind MIB. Now, she saw, she needed others' perspective and input to create a larger scheme. But who, and what?

FOUNDER'S PROFILE

Cynthia Riggs grew up in the suburbs of Los Angeles. She graduated from high school in January of 1974, a semester early, and worked to save money

exhibit 1 **Making It Big Income Statements, 1997–2001**

	1997	1998	1999	2000	2001
Sales revenues	$1,893,607	$1,921,270	$2,088,207	$2,486,893	$2,367,095
Cost of goods sold	(857,419)	(1,215,385)	(1,355,763)	(1,248,089)	(1,061,335)
Gross profit	$1,036,188	$ 705,885	$ 732,444	$1,238,804	$1,305,760
General and administrative expenses					
Advertising and marketing	33,158	26,478	17,328	136,003	112,410
Bad debts	543		2,614	304	641
Car and truck expenses	3,622	2,800	2,945	3,310	2,341
Commissions and fees	47,285	48,298	52,768	64,255	58,462
Depreciation	20,869	8,387	25,506	19,222	26,360
Employee benefit programs	24,589	35,497	36,058	32,432	36,264
Insurance	16,913	25,073	16,258	18,036	35,867
Interest expense	2,679	2,272	3,082	784	300
Legal and professional services	8,231	10,175	12,531	18,381	12,838
Office expense	9,636	14,928	9,188	8,342	17,486
Pension and profit-sharing	16,021	3,985	16,715	16,315	0
Rent					
Vehicles	—	1,266	—	1,746	—
Other business property	70,884	71,743	81,981	73,388	84,469
Repairs/maintenance	11,161	8,116	11,031	12,524	9,762
Supplies	5,971	761	1,993	2,250	2,090
Taxes and licenses	1,787	2,757	2,168	1,859	2,945
Travel, meals and entertainment					
Travel	5,130	3,399	2,902	1,976	3,523
Meals and entertainment	2,324	4,087	1,887	1,529	1,313
Nondeductible	(1,162)	(2,044)	(944)	(765)	0
Utilities	25,899	24,008	25,675	30,367	31,672
Wages	502,057	542,115	531,502	446,960	691,046
Other expenses/credits	82,309	(189,023)	(218,478)	97,688	65,030
Total expenses	$ 889,906	$ 645,078	$ 634,710	$ 986,906	$1,194,818
Pretax net profit	$ 146,282	$ 60,807	$ 97,734	$ 251,898	$ 110,942

for college. She traveled that summer and entered Sonoma State University, north of San Francisco, in the fall of 1974, majoring in humanistic psychology.

It was the height of the women's movement, and during Cynthia's first semester she joined a consciousness-raising group and took her first women's studies class: "Our Bodies, Ourselves." For a tall, big-boned girl whose mother went out of her way to make her feel like a "fat and unattractive child," the new messages she was hearing were positively liberating. "I blossomed under the tree of feminism; it made so much sense and just seemed right," she remembered. "It was validating as well as enlightening."

In 1976, Cynthia joined a women's bookstore collective called Rising Woman Books in nearby Santa Rosa. Ironically, this countercultural endeavor taught her some very capitalistic lessons. "Even though in theory everyone had equal responsibility, I was given the leadership role in running the business," she said. "I learned everything from ordering, advertising, promoting, [and] dealing with cash flow to balancing the books."

Combining the empowerment she'd gained from feminist doctrine with a dose of business savvy, Rising Woman was "truly the beginning of my entrepreneurial endeavors," Cynthia said. "It was the confidence I had developed while helping run the bookstore that enabled me to take the next step and begin my own business."

But at the time, Cynthia didn't yet see herself as an entrepreneur. She graduated from Sonoma State in 1978 and began buying and selling vintage clothing, textiles, and collectibles at flea markets in order to make ends meet until she could find a "real" job.

I had no intention of going into business. I was moving in with a lover, and we had too much of everything except money! So we went to the flea market to sell off the excess. In the course of selling, which must have taken several weeks, I started to buy from other people who had come to sell off their stuff. I kept the choice pieces for myself and began to sell the rest. It soon became a steady source of income. Eventually, I began buying from a multitude of flea markets, garage sales, rummage sales, thrift stores; ran ads in the newspaper; and built a steady business, selling primarily at the local flea market. It was a very competitive and labor-intensive business, but required no terms or financing or overhead.

With her psychology degree, Cynthia had intended to pursue a career in social work. But an ex-perience during her junior year discouraged her from following this path and made business seem more appealing by comparison. Working with juvenile delinquents in a residential rehabilitation facility had been challenging and rewarding, but her experience was soured by a critical, domineering director and bureaucratic city and county agencies.

So Cynthia was still making a living from her freelance flea-market business when, in 1980, Cheap Frills, a small retailer of used clothing in nearby Cotati, offered its name, inventory, and location for sale. With encouragement from friends, Cynthia took the opportunity to buy the name and move into its existing storefront for $4,500, gradually changing its focus to high-quality clothing and accessories, mostly vintage—a continuation of her flea-market finds. The store's first-year profits were slightly more than $15,000.

The vision of Making It Big began on a trip up the California coast one winter day in 1982, when Cynthia stopped in a small used-clothing store and discovered a selection of drawstring Army surplus pants, which were 100 percent cotton, inexpensive, and dyed in fashionable colors. Not only did they fit her, they would easily fit much larger women. Cynthia knew from her own experience that large women would love the casual style, trendy colors, and flattering fit—she remembered being taken to the "ladies' stores" as a teenager "and forced to wear black, navy, maroon and much plaid."

I set out to find the supplier, because I knew these pants would be a hot item in Cheap Frills. I dogged the owner of the used-clothing store until she told me where to purchase the pants. Initially, I could only get them already dyed, but eventually I was able to find them untreated, at true Army-surplus prices. I called them "parachute pants," and bought them in large quantities. I had them dyed in bright colors, had pockets sewn on them and traveled across the country to women's fairs and music festivals selling them. Women of all sizes and shapes bought these pants, but it was clearly the big women who benefited the most. They were thrilled that finally there was something that fit them. I sold out at every fair I attended. Ultimately, the seed money and mailing list for Making It Big emerged from sales of these pants.

Cynthia's retail business, meanwhile, was thriving but labor-intensive. "The sales [at Cheap Frills] came easy, but it took too much of my time just finding the right products to sell," she recalled. As she

exhibit 2 **Making It Big, Quarterly Summary of All Units,
January 1, 2001–September 30, 2002**

	2001			
	1st Qtr.	**2nd Qtr.**	**3rd Qtr.**	**4th Qtr.**
Sales				
Mail order—in state	$ 80,879.74	$ 99,024.44	$ 83,057.44	$ 75,736.31
Mail order—out of state	398,370.75	450,709.78	383,937.57	386,521.07
Mail order—in-state refunds	(5,150.04)	(10,326.08)	(11,441.49)	(3,362.61)
Mail order—out-of-state refunds	(30,106.01)	(62,469.11)	(46,178.68)	(21,326.37)
Retail	98,984.12	119,952.76	125,601.16	93,716.32
Houseparty sales	0.00	13,180.40	8,060.40	6,020.60
Shipping/handling—in state	4,856.56	5,699.94	4,982.13	4,898.41
Shipping/handling—out of state	26,619.86	30,157.78	25,624.73	27,883.44
Other income/discounts (includes interest-bearing accounts)	1,632.31	1,046.93	1,690.94	(1,390.67)
Net sales	$576,087.29	$646,976.84	$575,334.20	$568,696.50
Cost of goods sold				
COGS—MIB manufactured goods	163,653.34	139,131.20	183,344.30	173,455.35
COGS—clothing purchased	28,026.05	33,014.32	28,307.70	29,040.89
COGS—accessories purchased	10,567.41	5,746.44	11,898.08	10,304.23
Shipping—in state	1,485.65	2,103.25	2,942.97	2,507.75
Shipping—out of state	10,909.82	14,495.32	15,427.28	15,561.64
Catalog production and mailing	48,333.57	25,767.95	48,523.01	33,635.18
Web site and advertising	6,132.39	5,856.15	8,273.07	6,438.68
Total cost of sales	$269,108.23	$226,114.63	$298,716.41	$270,943.72
Gross profit	$306,979.06	$420,862.21	$276,617.79	$297,752.78

contemplated launching a new company to cater to large women, she realized that she would need two things: a partner, and a way to reach customers all over the country. "At this point, I knew I didn't want to start another business alone. I wanted to share the headaches, financial woes, and responsibilities with other people," she said. Through Cheap Frills, she had met Janet Sturdy, a single mother and part-time student at Sonoma State who had contacted Cynthia with vintage clothing to sell. Now she considered partnering with Janet for her proposed new venture.

Unsure how much longer she would remain in the area, Cynthia also sought greater flexibility and decided a mail order business would be the easiest way to achieve it. With that vision in mind, she began researching and developing the mail order concept.

In the spring of 1982, Cynthia began to get serious about her idea of a clothing company for big

women. She started attending apparel shows and examining what was available for plus-size women. The "standard" range of sizes made by most manufacturers of "plus size" clothing was 14 to 24; Cynthia wanted to go far beyond those sizes. After a year of extensive research, she came to the conclusion that what she was looking for did not exist, and that in order to obtain the products she needed, she would have to find someone to make the clothes for her.

She spent the next year trying to find manufacturers that would help her develop the line of clothing. This search proved fruitless. The order quantities they required were beyond the means of a start-up company that lacked a sure idea of what it could sell. Cynthia decided she would have to become a clothing manufacturer herself. The ingredients were falling into place: a partner, a catalog, and some very large clothes.

2002				
Total	**1st Qtr.**	**2nd Qtr.**	**3rd Qtr.**	**Year-to-Date**
$ 338,697.93	$ 86,837.94	$104,124.69	$ 82,531.11	$ 273,493.74
1,619,539.17	382,796.67	500,945.06	385,444.38	1,269,186.11
(30,280.22)	(6,576.79)	(14,451.26)	(18,459.66)	(39,487.71)
(160,080.17)	(37,844.26)	(57,423.08)	(58,211.48)	(153,478.82)
438,254.36	76,944.21	125,775.86	98,828.36	301,548.43
27,261.40	5,624.56	8,288.10	8,469.30	22,381.96
20,437.04	5,293.75	6,360.80	5,165.28	16,819.83
110,285.81	28,760.65	33,941.22	27,052.56	89,754.43
2,979.51	(468.83)	(99.91)	2.00	(566.74)
$2,367,122.83	$541,367.90	$707,461.48	$530,821.85	$1,779,651.23
659,584.19	204,350.52	218,481.49	153,625.69	576,457.70
118,388.96	8,045.97	15,266.79	12,816.20	36,128.96
38,516.16	8,389.41	8,394.51	1,295.09	18,079.01
9,039.62	2,869.84	4,210.89	2,842.39	9,923.12
56,394.06	17,640.31	24,134.46	19,490.31	61,265.08
156,259.71	13,759.66	35,441.88	36,992.19	86,193.73
26,700.29	31,235.85	52,254.99	59,169.84	142,660.68
$1,064,882.99	$286,291.56	$358,185.01	$286,231.71	$ 930,708.28
$1,302,239.84	$255,076.34	$349,276.47	$244,590.14	$ 848,942.95

LAUNCHING A NEW VENTURE

In the 1980s, there were few manufacturers of supersize clothing. Cynthia knew firsthand the frustration of large women whose choices were limited to poorly made polyester clothing, none of which was particularly stylish. "I had several friends who were very large women, and they couldn't find quality clothing," she explained. "Supersize women"—sizes 28 and up—"were limited in choice to the point that many of them never left their homes, went to school, or felt able to get a job. They knew that people didn't accept them, and their lack of decent clothing only enhanced this reality."

Cynthia had become involved with the National Association for the Advancement of Fat Acceptance, a national political and education organization. She believed fat people, and especially women, were oppressed and made miserable by a society that stereotyped them as "lazy, out of control, obsessive eaters, couch potatoes and the like." The supersize women Cynthia got to know showed her that this wasn't the case. So she brought to her undertaking both entrepreneurial zeal and enthusiasm for a cause. "Making It Big gave me an opportunity to combine my personal goals with my political beliefs . . . [It] evolved out of my belief that no one should be discriminated against because of his or her size. If adequate clothing would contribute to better self-esteem and make the lives of fat women easier, I felt it was worth a try."

In 1984, at the age of 28, Cynthia had $20,000 in savings and revenues of $35,000 from Cheap Frills. She figured Cheap Frills could support her as she began a new venture. Not wanting to start another company on her own, Cynthia invited Janet Sturdy to become her business partner. Having operated a cash-based business that provided a steady income, and had required no terms or start-up financing, Cynthia had no experience in establishing credit or taking on debt. Janet, like Cynthia, did not have a financial history that enabled her to obtain credit or financing. The start-up was financed by Cynthia's savings, periodic loans from her grandmother, and Janet's inheritance from her father.

Cynthia hoped that Janet's sewing abilities would be an asset, as she herself hadn't sewn anything since the seventh grade. It turned out that having the skills oneself was irrelevant. What mattered was being able to find people who knew how to make clothes. "I set out to find individuals who knew how to do what we didn't," she said. "As with most things, it was trial and error," but after a couple of years an expert seamstress who had been sewing for MIB began hiring other seamstresses to work for her and offering MIB more services. "She saw our business was growing and she saw a way to make money for herself," Cynthia said. "She eventually became our production manager, although she remained an independent contractor. She remained in that role for many years and played a major role in helping us get the business off the ground."

From her experience with the parachute pants, Cynthia decided that the way to proceed in developing a product line would be to create garment-dyed clothing—clothing manufactured in white or natural cloth then dyed to order in a variety of seasonal colors. This would serve several purposes. First and foremost, the customer could purchase her favorite item in different colors, creating multiple sales of one style. Second, the company wouldn't have to predict what would sell in what specific color and size. The inventory would be flexible; it could be carried over to the next season and still be considered a new item because of new color choices. Basically, MIB wouldn't have its money tied up in merchandise it couldn't sell. "Then began the search for fabric, notions, a pattern maker, seamstresses, the whole kit and caboodle," Cynthia recalled.

Over the course of the initial four years, Janet and Cynthia each contributed $42,500 to Making It Big. Cash flow was a constant struggle. A manufacturing business requires credit terms, usually 60 days, in order to float the production of new goods before they are ready for the market. For the first two years, everything was purchased via cash on delivery (COD). Especially when it came to fabric purchases, this procedure was a hardship that hindered both growth and opportunity. Finally, Cynthia was able to convince one of her factors (a factor is the bank that buys the fabric company's receivables) to extend the company a small line of credit. This was a turning point for the young company, a modest start toward building a credit history. It took another two years to build a financial groundwork in which terms were extended on most purchases.

"Initially, we were very focused on finding and developing the product line and learning how to become a clothing manufacturer," Cynthia said. Neither she nor Janet knew anything specifically about operating a mail order business—or even that there was anything to know. They printed 3,000 catalogs and mailed 1,400 of them to a list of names Cynthia had compiled from her parachute-pants tour. Cynthia continued to travel each summer, selling MIB clothes and successfully expanding the customer base and mailing list. "We did some advertising, not much, so it was mostly by hitting the road and word of mouth that the initial mailing list and our sales expanded," she said.

During these formative years, Cynthia said, "I was naive in every which way you could have looked at the situation." In fact, her very naïveté may have been an advantage in such an idiosyncratic, hitherto-unexplored business, as she found out when she consulted with two women from another mail order company. "They filled my head with all kinds of information, and they couldn't believe we had gotten as far as we had without following the rules of mail order," she remembered. But when MIB turned to a conventional mail order method, renting a defunct company's 5,000-name mailing list from a list broker, the mailing yielded exactly one response. The company also joined the Northern California Catalogue Club, a group of small and large businesses that provided networking, workshops, and information sessions. The club was "a good place to learn the nuts and bolts of running a catalog business," Cynthia said. But she also realized that hers was not a typical catalog business, and that the "rules" of mail order didn't necessarily apply.

"We are defiantly renegade in our marketing practices and will probably always be. This is not so much out of choice but out of necessity," Cynthia said. "Our niche market is very specific, and it is very hard to find new customers through the traditional marketing techniques. Fortunately, we have an incredibly loyal customer base." But the company needed to figure out a way to find new customers without going through the usual channels.

POSITIONING FOR GROWTH

Cheap Frills had been located in an old house on the plaza in the small town of Cotati, California. Once Making It Big got going, Cynthia and Janet took over the back of the house, which had formerly been rented out as a residence. While both women were committed in principle to their new business, they soon found that their different personal situations affected the business and strained their personal relationship. Cynthia, single and childless, was poised for action, ready to tackle any task that arose. Janet, with young children at home, did not make business her first priority.

Cynthia realized this when, in April 1998, she was injured in a car accident. Bedridden after leaving the hospital, she tried to direct production of the coming catalog, but it was soon clear that Janet couldn't do the rest without Cynthia there. Cynthia saw that "my commitment was greater then hers, as was my capacity to create this business . . . I had wanted an equal partner and, other than financially, that wasn't Janet." In October 1998, Cynthia bought out Janet, dissolved the partnership and became the business's sole proprietor.

That fall, Cynthia liquidated Cheap Frills' inventory, and MIB took over the location as an exclusive retailer of MIB clothing. The following year, MIB's administration, R&D, and mail order operations moved to a larger, 3,800-square-foot facility. The original storefront, only a mile away from the new facility, was retained as a retail outlet, which proved valuable for testing new products and liquidating overstock merchandise. In 1992, 35 percent of total sales came from the retail store; by 2002 it contributed less than 20 percent of total sales.

Cynthia regularly attended trade shows to keep up with trends and to locate new products. All the garments were designed by Cynthia, her staff, and a skilled pattern maker. Fabrics were obtained from several sources, depending on the materials desired. MIB manufactured more than 90 percent of the

exhibit 3   **MIB Product Lines**

Career wear: traditionally styled dresses, skirts, jackets, and blouses suitable for the professional work environment.

Casual sportswear: T-shirts, shorts, pants, leggings, tunics, swimsuits, jumpsuits, caftans, tank tops, turtlenecks, vests, robes, socks, hosiery, and dresses suitable for everyday wear.

Formal wear: elegant dresses, pantsuits, tunics, and dress pants in flattering styles.

Outerwear: wind breakers, sweaters, jackets, capes, wraps, and coats for both casual and formal occasions.

Accessories, including jewelry, scarves, shoes and hosiery, were provided by a variety of vendors, most of whom were located in California. Vendors were chosen on the basis of compatibility with Making It Big's existing product lines and on the basis of the vendor's ability to supply quality products on a timely basis.

products it sold and purchased the remainder from selected local vendors. Catalog design was contracted out but was overseen and developed by Cynthia and the MIB staff.

MIB contracted with a network of seamstresses in Sonoma County and San Francisco to sew precut garments in lots of 12–48 per size. Each completed garment was inspected as it was received, to ensure quality and accuracy in sizing. Customers chose from 8 to 10 colors when placing orders. Then MIB sent the garments to a dye house in quantities of nine to thirty pounds. MIB inspected each garment again during the final steam-pressing, when it was ready for delivery to the customer.

MIB offered a full line of clothing and accessories in four main categories: career wear, casual sportswear, formal wear, and outerwear (see Exhibit 3). Merchandise was sold directly to customers via a 32-page color catalog (up from 24 pages until the late 1990s), the local retail store, and, starting in 1996, a comprehensive Web site. A product's presentation in the catalog directly affected its sales. For example, the particular color in which an item was photographed would generally outsell all other color choices for that item. The catalog was structured in a "grouping" format, making it easier for the customer to find what she sought. Clothing selections were arranged by fabric groups or category, with accompanying accessories. Clothing and accessories

exhibit 4　**MIB Sales by Source, 1997-2002**

	1997	1998	1999	2000	2001	2002 at 9/30/02
Internet	$ 15,626	$ 197,090	$ 411,522	$ 561,905	$ 831,780	$ 849,184
Phone orders	1,502,682	1,312,283	1,257,326	1,470,353	1,067,204	592,551
In-store sales	375,299	411,897	419,359	454,635	465,458	323,822
Total sales	$1,893,607	$1,921,270	$2,088,207	$2,486,893	$2,364,442	$1,765,557

were carefully chosen each season according to current trends, appropriateness of a style for large sizes, and past acceptance of basic styling pieces. Best sellers would return season after season, with an occasional fabric change carried year round.

MIB had launched its Web site as a showcase for its goods in 1996, and the following year it added a shopping cart for online purchases. By 2002, nearly half of MIB's mail order sales were from online purchases (see Exhibit 4). Most purchases were made in response to the catalog mailings. Most of MIB's sales were from repeat customers. Local advertising was done via radio and newspaper. Exhibit 5 shows MIB's geographic reach.

Additional sales came from "Houseparties." Paulette, MIB's bookkeeper, explained, "Our Houseparties occur for a single day, three or four times a year. Retail merchandise is loaded into a rented truck and driven to Berkeley, where we set up shop in an old dance hall. Bay area customers are contacted via direct mail as to time and date. It's been a success for years and our customers look forward to it."

SERVING THE PLUS-SIZE APPAREL MARKET

Women's apparel was a highly competitive global industry consisting of numerous manufacturers, importers, and retailers. In the early 2000s, the "plus-size" or "extended-plus-size" market (sizes 28 through 72+) was the fastest-growing segment of the women's apparel market. U.S. retail sales for plus-size apparel alone were expected to reach $47 billion by 2005. The National Center for Health Statistics' 1999 National Health and Nutrition Examination Survey revealed that 35 percent of adult Americans were overweight, with 26 percent qualifying as obese. NPD Group, a New York market re-

search company, reported that 60 percent of American women wore size 12 or larger, and 16 percent of teenage girls were overweight. Plus-size sales accounted for one-fifth of all U.S. women's apparel spending in 2001, a figure that was predicted to increase as the population aged.

Exhibit 6 provides a profile of distribution channels for women's apparel in the United States in 1997. Over one-third of large women purchased their clothing exclusively from companies specializing in plus-size clothing. Charming Shoppes, Inc, the third-largest specialty apparel retailer in America, was the leader in plus-size women's apparel, with annual revenues exceeding $2.45 billion in 2001. Known for its Fashion Bug and Added Dimension chains, Charming Shoppes had recently acquired Lane Bryant and Catherine's Plus Sizes, bringing its retail business to 2,446 stores in 48 states in 2002. Many of the nation's best-known brands, such as Liz Claiborne, Tommy Hilfiger, and Old Navy, and department stores such as Nordstrom, Macy's, Bloomingdale's, and Saks Fifth Avenue, had recently begun to offer plus-size clothing due to the increased demand in this niche.

Despite the proliferation of independent retailers in malls and on the Internet, there was increasing consolidation and branding in the apparel industry. According to Charming Shoppes, the primary elements of competition were style, size, selection, quality, display, and price, as well as store location, design, advertising, and promotion and personalized service to the customers.[1] Charming Shoppes had recently invested $8 million on a sophisticated computer-information system to keep detailed profiles on its customers, in order to refine its direct mail and adjust inventory for maximum profitability.[2]

[1] Charming Shoppes, annual report 2002.
[2] M. Tatge, "Thinking Big," *Forbes* 169, no. 6 (March 18, 2002), pp. 82–83.

exhibit 5   **MIB Geographic Customer Profile**

Location	Percent of Sales
California	25.4%
Northwest	7.2
Southwest	4.0
Plains	2.2
Midwest	17.6
New England	6.9
Mid-Atlantic	14.2
South	19.1
Alaska and Hawaii	0.8
Canada	1.4
All other	1.1
Total buyers	100.0%

exhibit 6   **U.S. Retail Sales of Women's Apparel by Distribution Channel**

Specialty stores	22.2%
Discount stores	19.4
Department stores	19.0
Major chains	16.0
Off-price outlets	6.5
Direct mail	6.5
Factory outlets	3.7
Food/drug stores	0.7
Warehouse clubs	0.6
Total	100.0%

Source: Datamonitor Industry Market Research, 1997.

Most retailers of large-size clothing offered their goods through catalogs, and an increasing number had set up Web sites that created personal profiles for repeat customers. Nonetheless, "industry experts [claimed that] most retailers simply haven't figured out how to sell to larger customers,"[3] since fashion and fit were not always an easy combination. While shopping for clothes was a form of entertainment for many women, supersize women seldom enjoyed shopping of any sort. Large women found it hard to find clothing to fit their shape, having body proportions different from the "average size 14." "Many of these women don't shop or go out of the house very often," according to Annie Newman, editor of Size-withstyle.com, an online plus-size newsletter. Be that as it may, large women wanted to look good and wear fashionable clothes.

In 2002, there were over 2,000 manufacturers of large-size women's clothing in the United States, few of which offered clothing in the supersize range. Mast Industries, with revenues of approximately $1.5 billion (roughly $2.5 to $3.5 billion at retail), was the leading contract manufacturer of regular and large clothing, using company-owned facilities, partnerships and joint ventures worldwide. A subsidiary of The Limited, Mast Industries also produced cloth-

ing for New York & Company, Henri Bendel, Lane Bryant, Abercrombie & Fitch, Saks 5th Avenue, and Victoria's Secret.

LOOKING TOWARD THE FUTURE

In 2001, Making It Big employed five managers, a three-person research and development team (pattern maker, sample maker, sample cutter), three supervisors, 10 warehouse/fulfillment/production workers, and five customer service and office personnel. Exhibit 7 gives brief profiles of the top management team, along with brief self-assessments of their strengths and weaknesses. Cynthia owned the company and had the title of CEO, but her activities focused more on sales and money management than on strategic planning. She considered cash-flow management her area of expertise. She carefully monitored sales from the retail store, Internet, and catalog, and kept a tight rein on the company's resources.

"MIB is a very labor-intensive business and everyone works exceptionally hard, at all levels," Cynthia said. She described the search for a replacement for the company's office manager of eight years; the company went through three people before settling on JoAnn, a hardworking 60-year-old who, unlike the others, "really got what was going on."

[3]A. Wheat, "Plus-Size Prospects," *Fortune* 147, no. 7 (April 14, 2003), p. 376.

exhibit 7   **MIB Management Team as of November 2002**

Cynthia Riggs, founder and CEO

Duties: Oversees all aspects of the company, sets strategic direction.

Qualifications: B.A. (psychology) Sonoma State University (1978); Started and ran successful retail business; has been CEO of MIB for 20 years.

Strengths: Cash flow and inventory management, customer relations, and product development.

Weaknesses: Circulation and marketing, difficulty dealing with employees, expects too much from people.

Bridget, general manager

Started: July 2001

Duties: Overall operations and decision making, human resources policies and benefits, day-to-day management.

Qualifications: B.A. (psychology), Sonoma State University (1971); prior CFO and COO positions.

Strengths: Financial, computer, software, and technology.

Weaknesses: Overwhelmed by the marketing responsibilities, lack of leadership in human resources and hiring, not a "big-picture" person.

Sharon, production manager

Started: August 1992

Duties: Oversees all manufacturing, both in-house and contract work, projects and schedules fabric deliveries, hires, fires, works on photo shoot, involved in R&D.

Qualifications: A.A., Santa Rosa Junior College (1975); prior store manager, operations manager, and customer service positions. She is currently returning to school to earn her BA degree in business finance.

Strengths: Exceptional people skills, analytic skills, and loyalty.

Weaknesses: Difficulty delegating, works too many hours, tries to be "everything for everyone."

JoAnn, office manager

Started: March 2002

Duties: Administrative and office management duties, scheduling and record keeping, office-supply purchasing and invoicing, Web site and computer maintenance, telephone orders and reception, supervision, troubleshooting and problem solving, hiring and firing, and maintaining the policy and procedures manual.

Qualifications: B.A. (history), Loretto Heights College (1963); prior office manager, sales support, and retail operations manager positions.

Strengths: Good organization and leadership skills; she understands the fast pace and high expectations essential to success in this position.

Weaknesses: Difficulty delegating, takes on too much, works too many hours, admittedly "stubborn."

Cindy, retail manager

Started: February 2000

Duties: Complete responsibility for the retail store, including scheduling, organizing retail events and sales, inventory purchasing and control, and training of retail staff.

Qualifications: Heald Business School (1978); Prior general manager (retail and restaurant), sales associate, customer service representative, child care positions.

Strengths: Committed, tenacious, and determined to keep sales up.

Weaknesses: Struggles with the marketing and advertising aspects of the retail store.

Cynthia described JoAnn as enthusiastic, determined, and "a long-term and committed individual" who understood the "fast pace and high expectations" inherent to her position.

Likewise, one of MIB's longest-serving employees, the production manager, Sharon, shared Cynthia's commitment to the company and its concept. Sharon had risen through the ranks of a major department store chain to become a store's head manager when, in 1992, she stumbled upon MIB. "She wanted a change, wanted to see her children grow up, wanted to be closer to home," Cynthia said, so Sharon took a significant salary cut to become the company's first retail store manager. "She did that for about a year and was then ready to move into an area that she perceived (accurately) to be challenging, and she then earned the title of production manager," Cynthia said. "She learned the job from the ground up and developed the position to be what it is today." Cynthia said she values Sharon's loyalty to the company and her ability to take care of multiple tasks—in fact, Cynthia fears Sharon's huge load of responsibilities might eventually drive her away. "She really does too much, taking care of our entire production department," Cynthia said. "I hope I don't lose her because I don't think anyone else could handle the job—certainly not all the balls she juggles at one time." If the company weren't struggling, Cynthia said, she would like to allow Sharon to fulfill her desire of developing a new product line.

In 2001, the company hired Bridget in the position of general manager. Bridget updated MIB's computer network, changing its mail order and customer service software, installing a comprehensive accounting program, and generally improving its systems and making them more compatible.

As for Cynthia herself, she said she had started working with a business coach "to advance team building and communication among my staff." She watched the company's margins and managed cash flow in a manner she called "pretty conservative." "I don't drain the cash from the business, and we have developed excellent relationships with those that we do business with in order to call in favors when the cash flow is tight," she explained. "We have a $100,000 line of credit that we use seasonally to keep ourselves up and running. In the good times, we barely touch the line, and in the not-so-good times we are more dependent upon it." The company had no long-term debt and owned nearly all of its equipment.

The business, as Cynthia described it, was healthy but stalled. Growth was its number one goal, she says, but she was at a loss as to how to achieve it. "I don't know where to go from here, and I'm hesitant to invest in new projects or marketing ideas, given the current business climate." Given the organic way in which MIB had evolved into its current shape, Cynthia believed she needed "an experienced management team to help manage the risk that's needed to get to the next level."

THE CURRENT SETBACKS

The current decline in sales prompted Cynthia to reflect on her plans for MIB and her ability to execute those plans. She had begun the business as a partner-

ship, and the burden of being the sole decision maker was starting to take its toll. She had hired Bridget as general manager in July 2001, with the expectation that she would take over some of the daily operations and participate in personnel decisions. Cynthia was not surprised when, in October 2002, Bridget indicated that she would be leaving the following spring. Cynthia viewed this transition with a mixture of relief and concern. On the one hand, she thought Bridget was better suited to a controller or chief financial officer position than to that of general manager—Bridget, Cynthia said, did not participate in human-resources decisions and was "not a big-picture person."

On the other hand, Bridget's departure was symptomatic of one of MIB's biggest problems. "Staffing on the management level is the most challenging issue" for MIB, Cynthia said. "It has proven difficult to find and retain the right people. I know 1 expect too much from people and sometimes don't deal well with employees . . . We have a crew with an honorable work ethic. However, burnout seems inevitable."

Especially with sales slipping, Cynthia thought the company sorely needed a dedicated, trustworthy marketing director—a capacity she had always filled herself, but in which she lacked background and confidence. "I thought I had been given good advice about our new catalog and Web site, but now I'm not so sure," she said. "When marketing plans don't pan out, it proves to be both expensive and depressing. It requires more money and renewed energy to try again."

Cynthia mulled over her options. She knew that, even with 20 years as CEO of Making It Big under her belt, she still lacked essential skills. But she wasn't sure what Making It Big needed at this point—professional help, or just a few more committed, loyal employees? "Over the years, I've relied on the belief that we could teach anyone the nuances of our business if they were the 'right person' for the job," she said. "I think this was true when the business was smaller, but we have probably failed in the past few years by adhering to this idea" rather than searching for a general manager or CEO with a background in mail order sales.

And Cynthia—who never expected MIB to last 20 years when she started it—still didn't have an overall strategy to drive the company forward and was beginning to think she might not be the right person to come up with one. "When I met with my

CPA last week and tried to explain my growth goals for MIB, he reminded me that more than 90 percent of entrepreneurs can't take their business to the 'next level,' that growing a business requires a different skill set than starting one," she said. "So now I'm thinking that I should reevaluate my options. Is it time for me to relinquish control and take a back seat after all these years?"

Cynthia built her business almost single-handedly, finding a niche no one else was paying attention to, canvassing at the grassroots level and breaking all the rules—succeeding, she said, by "having a tenacious personality, youthful exuberance, and a tremendous amount of drive and desire." But now those qualities were no longer enough, and Cynthia needed a new direction. "I know that in order for growth to happen the person at the helm needs the ability to see the business with a bird's-eye view," she said. "Should I look for someone to share my commitment to the company—someone who can be a real partner in this operation? Or do I just need to renew my efforts to find a few key people to help me with marketing and strategic planning?"

Outback Steakhouse

Sarah June Gauntlett
University of Alabama

As Harry Gauntlett, joint venture partner for Outback Steakhouse, sat in his office flipping through his stores' operating results for the year, he contemplated how to keep growing revenues and profit margins in such a competitive industry. Many entered the industry, but few survived long. Outback realized it had to evolve in order to adapt to changing consumer preferences and lifestyles. From its inception, Outback had experienced tremendous growth, adding 30 to 65 new locations a year domestically and internationally.

To help drive company growth, management had diversified into a number of different restaurant formats and menus that spanned both casual and upscale dining:

- *Outback Steakhouse*—Outback offered high-quality food and service, generous portions at moderate prices, and a casual atmosphere suggestive of the Australian Outback. Although beef and steak items made up a big portion of the menu, diners at Outback could also choose from a variety of chicken, ribs, seafood, and pasta dishes.

- *Carrabba's*—Carrabba's featured a casual dinner in a warm, festive atmosphere and a variety of fresh, handmade Italian dishes cooked to order in a lively exhibition kitchen.

- *Lee Roy Selmon's*—This restaurant concept featured soul-satisfying Southern comfort cooking, served with heartwarming hospitality. Lee Roy Selmon's was the product of teaming up with NFL Hall of Famer Lee Roy Selmon and some of Mama Selmon's favorite recipes. The theme

at Lee Roy Selmon's was, "Play hard. Eat well. And don't forget to share."

- *Cheeseburger In Paradise*—This chain endeavored to bring Jimmy Buffett's famous song to life in a Key West–style structure intended to remind patrons of swaying palm trees, sea adventures, beautiful beaches, and island getaways. The menu featured a signature cheeseburger, a selection of island fare, and other fun foods, with a Tiki Bar serving up frozen favorites and cold draft beer until late in the night.

- *Bonefish Grill*—Bonefish Grill, which got its start in the Tampa Bay area, was a full-service restaurant that featured fresh fish and seafood appetizers and entrées in an attractive, slightly upscale atmosphere. Fish was flown in daily, inspected, hand cut, cooked over an oak grill, and served with a variety of toppings. Bonefish restaurants had a fun, polished atmosphere, with everyday prices.

- *Fleming's Prime Steakhouse and Wine Bar*—Fleming's featured prime cuts of meat and an extensive selection of quality wine served by the glass, with a focus on quality and creativity in a highly sophisticated and comfortable environment.

- *Roy's*—Roy's was an upscale casual restaurant featuring a contemporary Hawaiian Fusion cuisine and an "aloha" style of service. Hawaiian Fusion cuisine blended the European techniques in which renowned chef Roy Yamaguchi was trained with familiar ingredients from Asia and the Pacific. The goal of the dining experience at Roy's was to "totally please and indulge" every guest with a combination of good food and quality service.

Prepared under the supervision of Professor A. J. Strickland of The University of Alabama. Copyright © 2004 by Sarah June Gauntlett and A. J. Strickland.

exhibit 1 **Outback Steakhouse Restaurants, 2000-2002**

	Year Ended December 31		
	2002	2001	2000
Company owned	612	575	521
Domestic franchised and joint venture	118	114	103
International franchised and joint venture	54	50	40
Totals	784	739	664

Source: Outback Steakhouse, Inc., 2002 annual report.

exhibit 2 **International Locations of Outback Restaurants, 2002**

Australia	Ireland
Bahamas	Japan
Brazil	Korea
Canada	Malaysia
Cancun	Mexico
Cayman Islands	Philippines
Costa Rica	Puerto Rico
Dominican Republic	Singapore
Guam	Thailand
Hong Kong	United Kingdom
Indonesia	Venezuela

Source: Outback Steakhouse, Inc., 2002 annual report.

COMPANY BACKGROUND

On an evening in late 1987, Chris Sullivan, Bob Basham, and Tim Gannon gathered at a jazz club in Tampa, Florida, to brainstorm the name of their new restaurant venture. Their objective was to create a dining "experience" offering high-quality food and service, generous portions at moderate prices, and a casual atmosphere entrenched with an Australian theme. After several brews, the name Outback emerged as a suggestion and was unanimously agreed on. Shortly thereafter, Trudy Cooper joined the team and plans were made to open the very first Outback Steakhouse on Henderson Boulevard in Tampa, Florida. Tim Gannon, known as the "Food Guy," brought in world-renowned chef Warren Larue to design and create the menu for the new restaurant venture. Larue blended bold, distinctive spices into a unique flavor profile for each dish.

Originally, Outback's business plan consisted of four restaurants, one for each respective founder. The founders' intent was to have fun, earn a nice income, and enjoy a Florida lifestyle. The first restaurant was met with tremendous success. Word spread quickly among consumers and industry peers regarding the quality of food with its bold flavors and "no rules" service style. Unique to the restaurant industry, Outback provided the opportunity for true ownership and self-responsibility, cutting the managing partner a 10 percent share of ownership in his or her restaurant. The number of Outback Steakhouses grew rapidly after the initial opening in 1988. One restau-

rant soon became 4, then 10, 20, and by 2003, over 800 in 23 countries (see Exhibits 1 and 2).

From the beginning, Outback Steakhouse was a restaurant concept well accepted among customers, Outbackers, and industry peers. Most of the company-owned restaurants were organized as partnerships, with the company as the general partner. The company's ownership interests in partnerships and joint ventures generally ranged from 51 to 90 percent. Company-owned restaurants also included restaurants owned by consolidated ventures in which the company had less than a majority ownership. The rationale for consolidating these ventures was that Outback Steakhouse, Inc., controlled the executive committee or had control through representation on the committee by related parties. The company was responsible for 50 percent of the costs of new restaurants operated under consolidated ventures. Restaurants with no direct investment from the company operated under franchise agreements with the company, receiving a specified percentage of net income.

To keep expanding, the company brainstormed options for raising capital to grow. On June 18, 1991, Outback Steakhouse, Inc., held an initial public offering (IPO) for its common stock, selling 1,570,000 shares of stock at a price of $15.00 a share; the stock began trading on the Nasdaq. Between December 1991 and March 1999, Outback's stock split four times; in April 2000, the company moved trading from the Nasdaq to the New York Stock Exchange (NYSE). Chris Sullivan, Outback's chief executive officer, felt the move would benefit the shareholders by providing greater visibility and a broader investor base. The NYSE presented lower price volatility and smaller order execution costs that benefited investors. On October 23, 2002, the company declared its first quarterly dividend of $0.12 per share of common stock.

On October 23, 2003, Outback Steakhouse announced the restatement of its financial statements for prior periods to reflect new compensation accounting standards for its operating partner programs. The restatement resulted in an estimated reduction of net income of approximately $6.3 million for the year ended December 31, 2002. The company changed its accounting method for partnership programs from the "stock compensation" model to the minority interest model that was previously used. As a result, partnership cash flow distributions to general managers and area operating partners were treated as compensation expense instead of minority interest profit. Moreover, company purchases of partnership interests from area operating partners were treated as compensation expense instead of being recorded as an intangible asset. In mid-2002 the company initiated a program to repurchase up to 4 million shares of the company's stock and then, later, initiated a second program to repurchase shares on a regular basis to offset shares issued due to the exercise of stock options. The company funded these repurchase programs with available cash and bank credit facilities. As of year-end 2002, 5,880,000 shares of common stock had been repurchased for approximately $161,514,000. The aggressive repurchase of shares depleted cash to such an extent that Outback had net working capital of negative $13 million as of October 23, 2003. Cash at the end of the September 2003 quarter was $73 million, and the company had $43 million in short-term debt and $32 million in long-term debt. Exhibits 3, 4, and 5 show the company's restated financial statements for 2000–2002.

Carrabba's Italian Grill

To capitalize on growing popularity of casual dining, Outback Steakhouse, Inc., decided in 1993 to begin expanding its ownership of different types of restaurants, mainly through joint venture partnerships. In April 1993, Outback purchased a 50 percent interest in the cash flows of two Carrabba's Italian Grill restaurants located in Houston, Texas, and entered into a 50–50 joint venture with the founders to develop more Carrabba's restaurants.

Johnny Carrabba and Damian Mandola had founded Carrabba's. Carrabba and Mandola both possessed immense passion for Carrabba's and kept their Italian roots and traditions at the forefront of the business. Carrabba's grabbed diners' attention immediately with eye-catching rooftop gardens and a warm ambiance that featured handmade Italian dishes prepared in an exhibition-style kitchen. In addition to traditional Italian entrées, the menu featured fresh fish, seafood, wood-fired pizza, meats smothered in special seasonings, and an extensive wine list featuring wide selections of mid-range to high-end wines. Each Carrabba's location offered a chef's daily special menu, in part to allow managing partners to accommodate local tastes and preferences.

In 2000 and 2001, the Carrabba's restaurant chain beat expectations and delivered record-breaking success in same-store and company sales. In acknowledgment of changing lifestyles, Carrabba's implemented what it called Carside Carry-Out Service and planned to continue enhancing this service. Advertising had also made a positive impact on revenues. Television commercials featuring Johnny Carrabba and Damian Mandola captured their generous Italian spirit and passion for fresh, high-quality ingredients. In April 2001, Carrabba and Mandola

exhibit 3   **Statement of Operations, Outback Steakhouse, Inc., and Affiliates, 2000–2002 (in thousands)**

	2002	2001	2000
Total revenue	$2,362,106	$2,127,133	$1,906,006
Cost of revenue	1,907,663	1,734,675	1,524,617
Gross profit	$ 454,443	$ 392,458	$ 381,389
Operating expenses			
Selling, general, and administrative expenses	89,868	80,365	75,410
Nonrecurring	5,281	7,041	(2,457)
Other	69,511	69,002	58,109
Total operating expenses	$ 164,660	$ 156,408	$ 131,062
Operating income	$ 289,783	$ 236,050	$ 250,327
Total other income/expenses	(2,110)	151	4,617
Elimination of minority partners' interest	39,546	30,373	33,884
Earnings before interest and tax	$ 248,127	$ 205,828	$ 221,060
Interest expenses	—	—	2,058
Income before tax	$ 248,127	$ 205,828	$ 219,002
Income tax expense	87,341	72,451	77,872
Net income from continuing operations	$ 160,786	$ 133,377	$ 141,130
Change in accounting principle	(4,422)	—	—
Net income	$ 156,364	$ 133,377	$ 141,130

Source: Outback Steakhouse, Inc., 2002 annual report.

snagged spots on the PBS cooking show *Cucina Amore,* which aired in more than half of all TV markets. Carrabba's had a total of 123 restaurants domestically in 2002 and planned to open an additional 25 stores in 2003 (see Exhibit 6).

Bonefish Grill

To fill the niche between formal, upscale seafood restaurants and family-style seafood eateries, Outback Steakhouse, Inc., formed a joint venture partnership with Bonefish Grill. Bonefish was positioned as a casual seafood-dining concept featuring fresh, high-quality seafood served in an upbeat environment with distinctive artwork inspired by Florida's natural coastal setting. The menu featured a cosmic collection of finfish cooked over an oak-burning grill, hand-cut beef, and pasta and chicken dishes garnished with special sauces to enhance the flavor. Menu selections featured high-quality ingredients,

including hearts of palm, pine nuts, artichokes, goat cheese, and sun-dried tomatoes. Bonefish committed itself to serving fresh food by receiving, inspecting, and cutting its fish daily and preparing the fish with modern culinary techniques. It cultivated relationships with suppliers to distribute seafood daily to its restaurants. Bonefish had 15 locations by the end of 2002 and planned to develop 20 more locations in 2003. The chain possessed great growth potential, evidenced by the success and acceptance of the original four restaurants and new locations (see Exhibit 7).

Upscale Dining Segment: Fleming's Prime Steakhouse and Roy's

In 1998, Outback Steakhouse, Inc., identified the upscale casual dining industry as a new target market segment. This segment was attractive because of its

exhibit 4 **Balance Sheet, Outback Steakhouse and Affiliates, 2001–2002 (in thousands)**

	2002	2001
Assets		
Current assets		
Cash and equivalents	$ 187,578	$ 115,928
Short-term investments	20,576	20,310
Inventories	34,637	38,775
Other current assets	31,386	31,347
Total current assets	$ 274,177	$ 206,360
Property, plant, and equipment	915,022	813,065
Investments in and advances to unconsolidated affiliates, net	38,667	46,485
Intangibles	17,710	14,379
Goodwill	85,842	80,074
Other assets	58,157	77,385
Total assets	$1,389,575	$1,237,748
Liabilities and stockholders' equity		
Current liabilities		
Accounts payable	$ 54,519	$ 47,179
Short-term debt	17,464	12,763
Other current liabilities	167,138	129,791
Total current liabilities	$ 239,121	$ 189,760
Deferred income taxes	35,365	22,878
Long-term debt	14,436	13,830
Other long-term liabilities	47,677	24,500
Total liabilities	$ 336,599	$ 250,968
Stockholders' equity		
Common stock equity	237,014	221,434
Treasury stock	(86,948)	(42,004)
Retained earnings	902,910	762,414
Total stockholders' equity	$1,052,976	$ 941,844
Total liabilities and stockholders' equity	$1,389,575	$1,237,748

Source: Outback Steakhouse, Inc., 2002 annual report.

revenue potential. Therefore, Outback decided to break into this new segment through forming joint venture partnerships with two proven winners, Fleming's Prime Steakhouse & Wine Bar and Roy's.

Paul Fleming and Bill Allen, founders of Fleming's, had a long and successful track record in the restaurant industry, especially with restaurant chains such as P. F. Chang's China Bistro. Fleming's was embedded as a high-end prime steakhouse with style and contemporary features such as light-colored woods, high ceilings, and 100 quality wines by the glass.

The vast selection of upper-end wines and shape of its crystal glasses differentiated Fleming's from competitors. Fleming's offered an exceptional wine list featuring boutique vintages from California, Oregon, and Washington, augmented by selections from France, Italy, Australia, and South Africa. Fleming's served only the finest in beef certified as prime by the U.S. Department of Agriculture (USDA). USDA prime beef came from corn-fed cattle given no grazing privileges to keep the meat tender. To achieve distinctive taste, steaks were aged up

exhibit 5 **Statement of Cash Flows, Outback Steakhouse and Affiliates, 2000–2002 (in thousands)**

	2002	2001	2000
Cash flow from operating activities			
Net cash provided by operating activities	$ 338,060	$ 228,821	$ 239,546
Cash flow from investment activities			
Net cash used for investing activities	$(168,066)	$(233,662)	$(145,819)
Cash flow from financing activities			
Net cash used in financing activities	$ (98,344)	$ (10,835)	$ (54,746)
Net change in cash and equivalents	$ 71,650	$ (15,676)	$ 38,981
Cash at beginning of period	$ 115,928	$ 131,604	$ 92,623
Cash at end of period	$ 187,578	$ 115,928	$ 131,604

Source: Outback Steakhouse, Inc., 2002 annual report.

exhibit 6 **Number of Carrabba's Locations, 2000-2002**

	Year Ended December 31		
	2002	2001	2000
Company owned	94	75	60
Development joint venture	29	28	21
Total	123	103	81

Source: Outback Steakhouse, Inc., 2002 annual report.

exhibit 7 **Number of Bonefish Locations, 2000–2002**

	Year Ended December 31		
	2002	2001	2000
Company owned	11	3	—
Franchised and development joint venture	4	1	—
Total	15	4	—

Source: Outback Steakhouse, Inc., 2002 annual report.

to four weeks for flavor and texture, and then hand-cut daily and broiled at 1,600 degrees to seal the juices and flavor. The menu featured flavorful dishes ranging from fresh seafood such as ahi tuna, swordfish, and lobster tails to chicken, pork, and lamb specialties in addition to their superior prime beef. Fleming's received the *Nation's Restaurant News* "Hot New Concept" award for its innovative, successful cutting-edge restaurant concept. In 2002, Fleming's had 16 locations in such areas as Las Vegas, Newport Beach, Houston, El Segundo, Birmingham, and North Scottsdale (see Exhibit 8).

In 1999, Outback Steakhouse, Inc., formed a joint venture with Roy Yamaguchi to develop and operate Roy's restaurants worldwide (see Exhibit 9). Chef Roy Yamaguchi had won many prestigious awards, including the James Beard Award; he was also a member of the Fine Dining Hall of Fame and had garnered acclaim as the "crown jewel of East-West eateries." Roy's "Hawaiian fusion" cuisine fit nicely in the high-end seafood segment, where attention was focused heavily on the food: textures, colors, and bold flavors appealing to all the senses. Roy's dishes were complemented well by exclusive wines blended solely for Roy's by some of the finest winemakers in the world. The menu incorporated a variety of fish and seafood, beef, short ribs, pork, lamb, and chicken with blends of flavorful sauces and Asian spices. Roy's created an upscale casual dining experience featuring an exhibition-style kitchen finished in stainless steel and appointed with copper accents. Guests of Roy's were often well-traveled individuals seeking both an upscale yet casual ambiance and the convenience of reservations.

exhibit 8   **Number of Fleming's Locations**

	Year Ended December 31		
	2002	2001	2000
Company owned	16	11	5

Source: Outback Steakhouse, Inc., 2002 annual report.

exhibit 9   **Number of Roy's Locations**

	Year Ended December 31		
	2002	2001	2000
Company owned	14	11	3
Franchised and development joint venture	2	1	—
	16	12	3

Source: Outback Steakhouse, Inc., 2002 annual report.

PRINCIPLES AND BELIEFS

While Outback was growing rapidly, the founders could feel the fun and caring culture eroding at Outback as more hourly Outbackers and management came in from other restaurants. Although these workers and managers brought the positive aspect of previous experience, they also brought ingrained habits. In 1990, the four founders knew that they needed to take action quickly to uphold Outback's unique culture and business style. Thus, the four spent nine months in 1990 contemplating and verbalizing the values, beliefs, goals, keys to success, guiding principles, and direction of the company. They hoped to recapture the original flare of the corporate culture they had established in the first few restaurants. During this process, they started over from the beginning to figure out what had been lost.

When the "visioneering" process was complete in 1999, the Outback leadership team produced a tangible product called the *Principles and Beliefs (P&Bs)*. This five-and-a-half-page document quickly became the operating manifesto and gained momentum over the years. The *P&Bs* was the founders' prescribed "theory of success"; it stated the intended meaning of Outback to its stakeholders and how this meaning was to be created. Stakeholders included Outbackers, customers, purveyors, neighbors, and partners. The *P&Bs* incorporated Outback's core principles; its commitments to Outbackers (see Exhibit 10), customers, neighbors, purveyors, and partners; and its connections to exemplify that living the *P&Bs* was a source of happiness, remarkable success, and personal commitment to Outback. The leadership team recognized early that Outbackers were the faces, hearts, and hands of the company. Outbackers were the ones whom the customers saw when visiting the restaurant and the ones who established a connection with the customer. The first sentence of the *P&Bs* read: "We believe that if we take care of Our People, then the institution of Outback will take care of itself." If all elements of the *P&Bs* were followed, management believed, then Outback would be in position to achieve the five following goals:

- For Outbackers: A great place to work, have fun, and make money.
- For customers: A favorite place to eat, drink, relax, and be with friends.
- For purveyors: A great customer and source of comfort and pride.
- For neighbors: A valued corporate citizen and neighbor.
- For partners: A superior financial and emotional investment opportunity.

DAILY OPERATIONS AT OUTBACK

A typical day at an Outback Steakhouse restaurant began around nine in the morning with the arrival of the prep crew. All signature ingredients, sauces, and soups were prepared fresh daily. Food was delivered daily to the store and was immediately placed in the preparation process. Management negotiated directly with suppliers of food products to ensure uniform quality and adequate supplies. Outback used quality blends of freshly grated cheeses from Wisconsin and imported Parmesan cheese from Parma, Italy, and Gruyere from Switzerland. The crew promptly began making salad dressings. Each dressing marinated for an extended period to ensure that the proper flavor was achieved. Outback made "Aussie chips," its version of French fries, in-house

exhibit 10   **Outback Steakhouse Commitment to Outbackers**

We keep our nine commitments to Outbackers, guided by our five principles.
Our purpose is to prepare Outbackers to exercise good judgment and live
our *Principles and Beliefs.*
There are no probationary Outbackers.
Because of our *Serious Food, Concentrated Service,* and *No Rules,*
Outbackers approach our Customers with confidence and a sense of ownership while
demonstrating our principles of Hospitality and Quality. They are proud to be
Outbackers. Outback's environment requires people to be tough on results,
but kind with people.
It is an environment where managers are focused on serving Customers and supporting
their Outbackers.
Outbackers know they are valued and that situations special to them will be handled with
respect and concern.
How we take care of Outbackers is embodied in the details of our
nine commitments to them.
Clear Direction, Preparation, Involvement, Affecting One's Own Destiny,
A Fair Hearing, Sharing in the Success, Making a Commitment,
Having a Good Time, and Compassion.

to guarantee quality through an extensive rinsing process to remove excess starches and sugars. For dessert, brownies were meticulously baked daily, and chocolate and caramel sauces prepared daily as well.

Superior USDA center-cut choice steaks from Nebraska or Colorado were seasoned with Outback seasoning, a blend of various spices and 19 different peppers. To maintain quality, Outback required its beef suppliers to provide written documentation confirming that the cattle used for Outback steaks were raised and fed in compliance with U.S. government regulations designed to prevent bovine spongiform encephalopathy (known commonly as mad cow disease) in the United States. Additionally, the company prohibited suppliers to use mammal protein by-products in cattle feed. To guarantee freshness, no frozen chicken, beef, or fish was ever used. About one hour before the store opening, a line check took place, which entailed tasting all the sauces, dressings, and soups to ensure quality for the customers. The heavy emphasis on food quality meant that extra cost was always absorbed to provide serious food to customers.

OUTBACK'S STRATEGY

In 2002, Outback was a well-established brand name among consumers worldwide. Customers knew they could dine in any of Outback's 784 locations and receive a top-quality meal for a reasonable price. While continually growing, Outback reached consumers in new markets through creative television and radio advertising and sports affiliations. When Outback entered a new market, customers lined up to taste the beloved Bloomin' Onion appetizer, a deep-fried whole onion. Although beef and steak items comprised a large portion of the menu, Outback offered a variety of chicken, ribs, seafood, and pasta dishes. The company's philosophy of "No Rules, Just Right" allowed customers to personalize their dining experience through having no restrictions on how menu selections were prepared. Outback chose to differentiate themselves through generous portions of high-quality food and superior service in a casual Australian Outback atmosphere.

Marketing and Advertising

Outback spent less than half of what its competitors did on media advertising. For the six months following the September 11, 2001, terrorists attacks, Outback limited its amount of television advertising; store sales, however, remained unchanged from the prior year. During the second half of 2002, ad spending increased by 0.5 percent of sales to allow Outback to advertise on national television for the first time. With catchy and creative jingles and slogans, Outback's Curb Side Take-Away and Call Ahead Seating were heavily featured on television and radio commercials to raise awareness of the programs the company had introduced to accommodate changing lifestyles.

Outback also promoted its name through youth athletics, charitable and local events, and sports affiliations. From NCAA football to NASCAR, the name Outback was attached to many events. Starting in 1994, the Outback Bowl attracted a national ESPN audience for the New Year's Day college football bowl game. The Outback Bowl was the sixth highest-paying bowl game, with a matchup between the Big Ten and the Southeastern Conference. Outback's relationship with NASCAR consisted of an alliance with driver Dale Jarrett, in-store driver appearances, and the Outback Steakhouse Bloomin' Favorite Driver of the Race Award, which was presented at each race. Broadcaster John Madden, who had an ongoing partnership with the company, traveled to his Monday-night football games in the Outback Steakhouse Madden Cruiser, providing exposure and promotional opportunities for the company. Also, the *Bloomin' Onion I,* a.k.a. the Outback Blimp, traveled across the country providing coverage for ABC sports events including PGA Golf, the Little League World Series, and NCAA football. The blimp aided in further enhancing nationwide awareness of Outback Steakhouse.

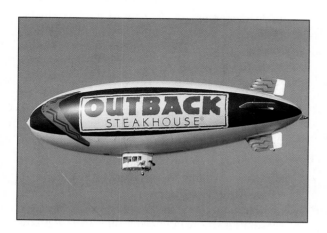

Focus on Customer and Customer Satisfaction

Outback went all-out to guarantee that customers had a positive, fun dining experience. As customers walked up to the restaurant, they were greeted by a smiling employee who opened the door especially for them. Customers who incurred a wait found many amenities to help them pass the time, such as magazines, children's toys, and free samples of Bloomin' Onion. Call Ahead Seating was implemented to help reduce wait times. Guests who called were placed on a waiting list and could thus be seated faster when they arrived at the restaurant. This initiative increased the number of customer visits.

Designed to address changing consumer preferences and lifestyles, Curb Side Take-Away became a valuable asset to the company. It worked as follows: A customer called the neighborhood Outback and was greeted by a warm, friendly take-away server, who made sure to document the color and type of car the customer would be driving. As soon as the customer arrived and parked in one of the spots specifically designated for Curb Side Take-Away, the server took the food directly out to the car. This process provided a quick, hassle-free way for customers to obtain a high-quality dinner.

Outback was convinced the items on its Commitments to Customers were key to having a competitive advantage (see Exhibit 11). The Commitments included Serious Food, Concentrated Service, and No Rules. Outbackers worked hard to personalize each customer's experience. The "No Rules, Just Right" style consisted of treating all customers as individuals and responding to their unique needs. Outbackers interacted with patrons in a friendly, energized, and extroverted manner and always gave an enthusiastic yes to all special requests. For example, it was routine for Outback to make an extraordinary effort to address the special needs of customers who might not have otherwise been comfortable dining in public, keep special dietary items on hand for regular customers, puree food for patrons who could not chew, send an Outbacker to the nearest McDonald's to buy a Happy Meal for a customer's child, and seat customers ahead of the wait when it is obvious that waiting would be a physical hardship. Overall, their philosophy was that if the company treated people "Just Right," then success was sure to follow.

Other Strategic Elements

- *A focus on dinner only*—Chris Sullivan and Bob Basham decided to open Outback just in the

exhibit 11   **Outback Steakhouse Commitment to Customers**

> We take care of our Customers.
> We totally indulge you with *Serious Food, Concentrated Service,* and *No Rules* in an environment that is welcoming, friendly, warm, energetic, and fun.
> During a wait, drinks are offered and food is shared.
> The menu is broad, the portions are generous, and the drinks poured full.
> Our serious food means freshness, flavors, attractive food, just-right temperatures.
> It is food prepared from scratch, using the finest ingredients, and to exacting standards.
> We are thick-cut steaks, fresh-cut fries, homemade croutons and salad dressings, fresh-baked brownies and meticulously prepared chocolate sauce.
> We have an intense desire to please you.
> You dictate the pace of service, from a quick meal to a relaxing evening with friends.
> We respect your privacy and tailor our service to your wants and needs.
> We delight customers one at a time ensuring everything is as you want it.
> We invite you to enjoy anything you want prepared any way you like it.
> We will please you, provide perfection your way, and enthusiastically say yes to your requests.
> We provide a hassle-free, personalized, and totally enjoyable experience.
> We do whatever it takes to deliver great food, drink, and services, are not distracted by the latest fads in the industry, and have the courage to put quality ahead of cost.

evening for two reasons. First, doing so allowed Outback to provide fresh food. Second, it allowed each Outbacker to work one shift a day. This reduced the effects of burnout and allowed Outbackers to pursue personal interests in addition to work. Outback, in fact, had the lowest labor turnover rate in the industry. Basham and Sullivan's objective in being open fewer hours was to do it better.

- *Limited seating*—The typical Outback was approximately 6,200 square feet with a seating capacity of around 220. The 220-person seating arrangement was chosen because, according to Sullivan and Basham, it was the optimum seating capacity to guarantee a quality steak. They argued that a relatively small facility was more efficient and effective than a gigantic one and decided to build more Outbacks in new locations to keep up with demand.

- *Good pay for Outbackers*—Outbackers saw substantial monetary compensation as well as intangible rewards. Outback believed in "Sharing in the Success of Outback" with all Outbackers. This was achieved through celebrations, recognizing individual Outbackers for their perfor-

mance, and other bonus incentive programs. Overall, Outbackers were paid well—a server typically earned around $125 a night working a three-table station.

- *Quality steaks and ingredients*—Outback's fine cuts of steak and bold, flavorful seasonings made customers crave and love their steaks. Every dish was meticulously prepared daily to ensure freshness and quality. Outback accepted only USDA top center-cut choice steaks from selected areas in the Midwest. Outback knew if they served a first-rate steak prepared with good seasoning, customers would be willing to wait two hours to get a seat.

- *Strong signature menu items*—The Bloomin' Onion was Outback's most-requested menu item—approximately 35 percent of all customers ordered a Bloomin' Onion when dining in the restaurant; many craved its zesty and bold seasonings. As for the drink menu, the Wallaby Darned proved to be a strong signature item unmatched by competitors. The bartenders mixed the drink daily from a special recipe including DeKuyper Peachtree Schnapps, champagne, Smirnoff vodka, and secret mixers.

- *Large portions at reasonable prices*—Outback provided a great value to its customers by serving generous portions of high-quality food at reasonable prices. The average ticket price for an adult at dinnertime was $18. Outback customers never left the restaurant hungry.

- *Fun and relaxed atmosphere*—Outback's lighting and ceiling reflected the unusual colors found in one of Australia's most popular tourist attractions, Ayers Rock. At sunset, the rock turned a burnt orange and the sky turned a deep purple. Outback invoked this scenery by painting the ceiling purple and the walls burnt orange and using pink lighting. Various Australian artifacts, such as boomerangs, surfboards, maps, and hats were hung on the walls. The floors and tables were made of a deep-colored wood with a glossy finish. Outback was designed as a place where customers from difficult walks of life could come to relax. Outback employed the use of formula facilities so that a customer could walk into any Outback Steakhouse and feel at home. Customers came to recognize the green roof with red lettering as a place to dine casually and unwind.

- *Managing partner ownership*—To attract great, qualified people and promote ownership and self-responsibility, Outback required each managing partner to purchase a 10 percent equity stake in his or her restaurant. This interest gave the partner the right to receive a percentage of his or her restaurant's annual cash flows for the duration of the contract. Additionally, managing partners signed a five-year contract, which contributed to a stable environment and a low turnover of both management and hourly Outbackers.

OUTBACK'S CULTURE

Many company policies stated the customer came first. At Outback, management realized that Outbackers came first. The founders discovered that the company had to show that it was as serious about taking care of Outbackers as it was about taking care of customers. In addition, the company recognized that Outbackers could not be asked to take care of customers if they were not being cared for themselves. The company's goal was to make work such

an enjoyable experience that all Outbackers looked forward to coming in each day. "Taking care of people" was the soul of Outback. The core belief of the six beliefs included in the *Principles and Beliefs* was "If we take care of our People—Outbackers, Customers, Purveyors, Neighbors, and Partners—the institution of Outback will take care of itself."

A prominent feature of Outback's culture was caring. Outbackers had a culture of respect and camaraderie that bred enthusiasm for helping others. One heartwarming story exemplified the nature of Outbackers: A dishwasher had his bicycle—his only means of transportation—stolen during a shift. The Outbackers at this particular location immediately collected enough money among themselves to replace the bicycle. An Outbacker was sent to a nearby store to purchase a new bicycle and had it ready, including ribbons, by the end of the shift.

Recruitment, Screening, Promotion, and Hiring

Outback maintained no internal or external recruiters and never created a human resource department but still boasted the lowest management and hourly turnover rate in the restaurant industry. Outback managers accepted all applications because they believed another dedicated, fun-loving Outbacker would always make a positive addition. They strove to hire people to create synergy that came from great diversity. After completing an application, an individual was required to take both a personality test to determine if there was a fit with Outback's culture and an analytical math test to judge how well the applicant thought on his or her feet. An external third party scored the tests to prevent bias. There was no probationary period for new Outbackers because every new employee was immediately welcomed as an integral member of the team.

Instead of requiring experience, Outback hired friendly people and provided training for work-related skills. Outback managers sought to hire people with enthusiasm, a positive outlook, and a winning attitude because they believed it was easier to add competence to friendliness than the reverse. The company defined a "Quality Hire" as an individual who performed his or her job, fit in with Outback's culture, and planned to stick around. It sought ambitious individuals whose surplus of energy drove them to achieve their goals and who understood that going the extra mile was the norm rather than exception. Each Outbacker affected his or her own destiny through a work ethic and a commitment to the *Principles and Beliefs*. Outback supported this commitment by sourcing all managers internally from hourly Outbackers. These Outbackers knew what it took to be successful the Outback way. Internal promotion also helped keep the fun-loving, generous culture alive on the management level.

Training

Every Outbacker underwent an intensive on-the-job training period as well as a classroom training program. The training period lasted for one week and included supervision by an experienced Outbacker. Classroom training programs were designed to teach Outbackers how to live the *Principles and Beliefs* and exercise good judgment. "Serious Food" seminars were conducted every month in each store to emphasize the importance of food quality to all Outbackers. The managing partner, front-of-house manager, and kitchen manager conducted miniclasses with groups of Outbackers to discuss Outback's commitment to quality food and how it was achieved. These miniclasses included tours of the kitchen, education regarding cuts of beef, tasting the food, and discussion of the Outback way for food preparation. Quarterly, each restaurant held a "Concentrated Service" meeting to revisit the purpose and implementation of the *Principles and Beliefs*.

For managers, the Better Yourself Through Education (BYTE) program was established to enhance the skills of the management team. BYTE was a 12-week, self-directed, distance-learning program consisting of 16 classes focusing on business needs. The classes encompassed business skills, communication skills, human resources, and self-management skills. The information was presented in workbook format, which took roughly 10 to 32 hours to complete. In BYTE, each managing partner served as a "working mentor" for his or her managers taking the classes. The partner assisted the manager when he or she came across difficult material or sought advice on how to handle various situations. Outback's goal for the BYTE program was to prepare its managers by giving them resources that would take them to the next level of excellence.

The Outbacker Trust

Established in 1999, the Outbacker Trust was funded primarily by voluntary contributions from Outbackers. The purpose of the program was to financially support Outbackers who were experiencing significant hardships in life. A donor of $20 or more received a collector's pin designed for that particular year. Contributions were not solicited from suppliers, customers, or friends. Requests for disbursements from the Outbacker Trust were funneled through the area joint venture partner and then presented to a trust committee in Tampa, Florida. Disbursements were granted for funeral and burial costs of loved ones; loss of housing and possessions by fire, flood, or other causes; surgery or income loss during life-threatening operations; and other life-altering challenges. Outback's philosophy for this program was as follows:

> We all travel different journeys in life, all of which are filled with different hurdles along the way. It is comforting to know that even when we are faced with the most difficult times, we are surrounded by, at the very least, our incredible family of Outbackers.

The STARS Program

Sharing the Actions, Responsibilities and Success (STARS) was instituted as a bonus program paid exclusively to hourly Outbackers to encourage them to live the *Principles and Beliefs*. The STARS program shared 25 percent of the restaurant's increase in quarterly profitability over the same quarter of the prior year. Sales had to experience an increase, and cash flow had to be up a minimum of $4,000 for the quarter. Hourly Outbackers who worked a minimum average of 10 hours a week for the quarter qualified for one share of the STARS bonus, and hourly Outbackers who worked a minimum average of 25 hours a week for the quarter qualified for two shares. Outbackers had to be employed the entire quarter to qualify. Each share of the bonus was calculated by taking the total bonus and dividing it by the total number of shares of all qualifying Outbackers. Overall, STARS gave Outbackers a sense of ownership and encouraged them to support the team in building sales and profits in their respective restaurants while putting extra money in their pockets.

Community Involvement

Outback's culture heavily emphasized community involvement. The company organized and contributed to more than 10,000 community events each year. It strove to create a source of strength in times of crisis and could always be counted on to enhance the quality of life in the neighborhoods where its restaurants were located. This was achieved through continually identifying and acting on opportunities to give back to the community and to make it a better place to live, while also having fun and conducting business. Outbackers participated in various community events and supported athletic teams, including high school and college athletic programs, community restoration efforts, and fund-raisers for charitable organizations.

A nationwide coalition of restaurants, including Outback, designated October 11, 2001, as a Dine Out for America day. This industrywide event, generated by Restaurants Unlimited, raised money to aid victims and their families affected by the September 11, 2001, terrorist attacks in New York City, Pennsylvania, and Washington, D.C. The initiative involved more than 5,000 restaurants that committed resources by designating anywhere from a percentage of proceeds to 100 percent of daily sales for that day. The proceeds directly benefited the American Red Cross and its Liberty Disaster Fund. All Outback Steakhouse, Inc., concepts contributed 100 percent of their sales, for a total of $7 million. Chris Sullivan, CEO of Outback Steakhouse, Inc., remarked, "Our restaurants have collectively been perceived as gathering places for family and friends, and our dining patrons will now have an opportunity to take an active role in reaching out to those in need during this tragic moment in world history."

In June 2002 Outback sent 15 Outbackers to Kandahar, Afghanistan, to feed over 6,000 members of the military. An additional 15 were sent in January 2003 to Kandahar and Bagram to provide food for more than 13,000 troops. Nearly 20,000 men and women of the military were served a dinner of Bloomin' Onions, Victoria's Filets, Rockhampton Rib-eyes, Grilled Shrimp on the Barbie, Aussie Chips, Jacket Potatoes, Mixed Veggies, and Cheesecake Olivia. The purpose of this effort was to show Outbackers' gratitude to and appreciation for the men and women who risked their lives to protect freedom. Later in 2003, the company implemented Mission Outback to support the U.S. military and other coalition troops in the Iraq war.

INDUSTRY OVERVIEW

The U.S. restaurant industry boasted revenues of $800 billion in 2002 with expectations to reach $1 trillion in 2003. This included revenues from related industries such as agriculture, transportation, wholesale trade, and food manufacturing. Food-and-drink revenues were projected to be $426.1 billion, with operations in 870,000 locations. On a typical day in 2003, the restaurant industry posted average sales of nearly $1.2 billion. Sales were forecasted to advance 4.5 percent in 2003 and to equal 4 percent of the U.S. gross domestic product. Between 1970 and 2002, restaurant industry sales posted a compound annual growth rate of 7.2 percent.

Excluding the government, the restaurant industry—a labor-intensive environment—was the nation's largest employer, with an estimated 11.7 million employees. The industry provided work for more than 9 percent of the workforce in the United States. One-third of all adults in the United States had worked in the industry at one point in their lives. A typical employee in food service in 1999 was a single female under 30 years of age working part-time and living in a household with two or more wage earners. Restaurant industry employment was expected to reach 13.3 million by 2012. The restaurant industry employed more minority managers than any other industry—more than two-thirds of supervisors in 2000 were women, 16 percent were African Americans, and 13 percent were Hispanic.

In 1999, the typical American household spent an average of $2,116 on food away from home, according to the National Restaurant Association's *Restaurant Spending* report, which was equivalent to $846 per person. In 1999, the U.S. Department of Agriculture estimated that the average annual per capita consumption of beef was 69.2 pounds, up slightly from 1998. More than 50 percent of all consumers visited a restaurant on their birthday, thus making birthdays the most popular occasion to dine out, followed by Mother's Day and Valentine's Day. Research had determined that more customers dined out during the month of August than any other month, while Saturday was the most popular day to dine out. Demographic characteristics dictating restaurant spending included household income, head of household's age, and household composition (see Exhibits 12, 13, and 14). The largest spenders in

exhibit 12 **Restaurant Spending by Household Income**

Annual Pretax Household Income	Average Household Spending on Food Away from Home in 1999	Average Per Capita Spending on Food Away from Home, 1999	Percent of Household Food Dollar Spent on Food Away from Home
All households	$2,116	$ 846	42.1%
$70,000+	4,398	1,419	50.4
$50,000–$69,999	2,803	967	42.9
$40,000–$49,999	2,365	910	40.6
$30,000–$39,999	2,142	857	42.3
$20,000–$29,999	1,625	650	37.6
$15,000–$19,999	1,301	591	34.0

Source: National Restaurant Association, *Restaurant Spending,* 2000.

exhibit 13 **Restaurant Spending by Age of Household Head**

Age of household head	Average Household Spending on Food Away from Home, 1999	Average Per Capita Spending on Food Away from Home, 1999	Percent of Household Food Dollar Spent on Food Away from Home
All households	$2,116	$846	42.1%
Under 25	1,526	848	45.5
25–34	2,250	776	43.8
35–44	2,572	804	42.1
45–54	2,605	965	43.8
55–64	2,136	971	42.2
65+	1,245	732	35.5

Source: National Restaurant Association, *Restaurant Spending,* 2000.

exhibit 14 **Restaurant Spending by Household Composition**

Household Composition	Average Household Spending on Food Away from Home, 1999	Average Per Capita Spending on Food Away from Home, 1999	Percent of Household Food Dollar Spent on Food Away from Home
All households	$2,116	$ 846	42.1%
Husband-wife only	2,380	1,190	44.2
Husband-wife with children	2,888	741	41.1
Households where oldest child is under 6	2,020	577	37.6
Households where oldest child is 6 to 17	3,090	754	41.4
Households where oldest child is 18+	3,129	802	42.2

Source: National Restaurant Association, *Restaurant Spending,* 2000.

the industry had a household income of over $70,000, with the household head between the ages of 45 and 54 and children older than 18.

Lone Star Steakhouse & Saloon—A Key Competitor

Lone Star Steakhouse & Saloon positioned itself in the midpriced, full-service, casual dining segment with a menu similar to that of Outback Steakhouse. Lone Star filled its restaurants with a Texas-style ambiance that included Texas artifacts and upbeat country music. Each restaurant was approximately 5,500 square feet with a seating capacity of 220 people. Planked wooden floors and dim lighting enhanced the casual atmosphere. Moreover, Lone Star limited its menu to focus on high-quality USDA choice-graded steaks, which were hand-cut daily, to create a competitive advantage. Generous "Texas-sized" portions were served for an average ticket price per customer of $10.50 for lunch and $17 for dinner in 1999.

Lone Star began operations in October 1989 in Winston-Salem, North Carolina. In March 1992, it became a public company traded on Nasdaq. Seasoned public offerings allowed the company to satisfy all debt obligations through equity financing. In 2000, Lone Star had a total of 241 locations in the United States after closing 24 underperforming stores. In 2003, Lone Star divested its Australia operations to concentrate on domestic operations. Furthermore, the company suspended development of new stores to reduce the demand for additional managers, to focus on improving operations and guest relations in current stores, and to improve the quality of management. Lone Star was met with intense competition from a variety of competitors, including locally owned, regional, and national restaurants. The company recognized that its ability to compete would depend on attraction and retention of loyal clientele, strong employees, experienced management, a continuing commitment to serve high-quality food, competitive prices, and an attractive dining atmosphere.

Issues and Conditions

Characterized by tight margins and a high failure rate, the restaurant industry was seeing increasingly intense competition. External forces, including the price and availability of commodities and consumer preferences, dictated how each restaurant conducted operations. General market conditions changed drastically after the terrorist attacks of September 11, 2001, causing the whole industry to experience soft revenue increases for nearly a year and a half. Furthermore, the fast-paced U.S. society required companies to develop efficient takeout services to accommodate working families. With fitness and health issues on the forefront of consumers' minds, restaurants had to develop new menu additions to retain health-conscious customers. In the steakhouse restaurant industry, emerging concerns over the outbreaks of mad cow disease affected sales while the media sensationalized the stories. Annually, many companies entered the industry creating an atmosphere in which each restaurant competed on the basis of food and service quality, ambiance, location, and the price–value relationship.

The restaurant industry was also subject to various federal, state, and local laws. Each restaurant was subject to licensing and regulation by a number of governmental authorities such as alcoholic beverage control and health and safety agencies. A restaurant that sold alcoholic beverages had to apply to a state authority for a license or permit. In addition, control regulations were in place for daily operations, including minimum age of patrons and employees, hours of operation, advertising, wholesale purchasing, and inventory control. To protect patrons, "dram-shop" statutes were in place that allowed a person injured by an intoxicated person to recover damages from any establishment that wrongfully served alcoholic beverages to the intoxicated person.

As Outback continued to grow, the industry competition was becoming more intense. Harry Gauntlett began to brainstorm ideas on how to make his restaurants more efficient to keep his margins high. Emerging issues were coming from all directions, and prices were rising for beef, cheese, produce, and labor. The prevalent conclusion between Gauntlett and his management team was that Outback had to adapt to changing market conditions to sustain the growth it had experienced throughout the years. The company also had to continue to indulge customers with top-quality ingredients that were perfectly prepared; employ well-trained Outbackers to

exhibit 15 **Lone Star's Statement of Income and Operating Ratios, 2000–2002 (in thousands)**

	2002	2001	2000
Total revenue	$615,715	$598,017	$575,863
Cost of revenue	509,060	519,386	512,201
Gross profit	$106,655	$ 78,631	$ 63,662
Selling, general, and administrative expenses	46,980	64,042	42,472
Nonrecurring	2,990	—	—
Operating income	56,685	14,589	21,190
Net income from continuing operations	40,065	13,256	16,130
Discontinued operations	(538)	—	—
Change in accounting principle	(318)	—	—
Net income	$ 39,209	$ 13,256	$ 16,130
Ratios			
Return on equity	9.34%	2.92%	3.68%
Return on assets	8.28%	2.57%	3.30%
Gross profit margin	17.32%	13.15%	11.06%
Net profit margin	6.37%	2.22%	2.80%
Current ratio	2.05	1.87	0.96
Debt to equity ratio	0	0	0

Source: Lone Star Steakhouse & Saloon annual reports.

provide customers with "Concentrated Service" and "No Rules" in a welcoming, friendly, warm, energetic, and fun environment; keep the physical plant updated; and live the *Principles and Beliefs* every day to remain focused on their commitments to stakeholders.

McDonald's:
Polishing the Golden Arches

Lou Marino
The University of Alabama

Katy Beth Jackson
The University of Alabama

When Ray Kroc built on the work of Dick and Maurice McDonald to form the McDonald's franchising system in 1955, he had a vision of building a restaurant chain that served a "low-priced, value-oriented product fast and efficiently in clean and pleasant surroundings."[1] In building McDonald's he probably never dreamed that it would become the world's largest burger chain, and one of the world's best-known brands, with over 30,000 stores worldwide, 46 million customers a day, and $41 billion in sales. Unfortunately, he probably also never foresaw that his beloved company would one day receive a customer service ranking that was not only the lowest among all national fast-food chains, an unenviable rank it has held since 1994, but also lower than any of the U.S. domestic airlines and, perhaps most notably, even lower than the U.S. Internal Revenue Service (based on the University of Michigan's American Customer Satisfaction Index).[2]

The fortunes of McDonald's have changed so drastically over the last two decades that David Sires of *Fortune* wrote, "If you hear of a 'Big Mac Attack' these days, it comes with chest pains. At least at McDonald's headquarters in Oak Brook, Ill., where the bad news tends to be super-sized."[3] Indeed, McDonald's posted its first ever quarterly loss—$343.8 million—in January 2003, revenue growth has been in decline, and same-store sales fell for 12 straight months prior to April 2003. The company's current situation has been attributed to a number of factors, including increased competition, poor management and marketing, and a failure to respond to the changing needs of customers and franchisees.

In the midst of these challenges, James Cantalupo came out of retirement in January 2003 to take the reins of the foundering Fortune 500 company, which he admitted was "in serious need of improvement." Cantalupo immediately announced an aggressive, broad-ranging turnaround plan designed to add customers instead of units. The purpose of this plan was to refocus McDonald's on its mission by increasing focus on internal operations, slowing store expansion (opening 640 fewer units than in 2002), enhancing the relevancy of McDonald's to its customers, and making the consumer the new boss at McDonald's.

By December 2003 McDonald's had begun to show signs of a successful turnaround, with three consecutive months of double-digit comparable sales growth. October sales were up by 10.2 percent, and November 2003 sales increased by 14.9 percent, as compared to November 2002. Analysts applauded these activities, and McDonald's stock price rose from a low of $12.50 in March 2003 to $25.28 as of December 23, 2003. While these changes have been substantial, the question remains of whether McDonald's series of missteps has allowed competitors to entrench themselves so firmly that the company will be unable to regain its prominent position in the global fast-food industry.

[1] Ray Kroc, with Robert Anderson, *Grinding It Out: The Making of McDonald's* (Chicago: H. Regnery, 1977).

[2] Grainger David, "Can McDonald's Cook Again?" *Fortune,* March 30, 2003.

[3] David Sires, "McDonald's Fallen Arches," *Fortune,* April 14, 2002.

THE FOUNDING AND DEVELOPMENT OF McDONALD'S CORPORATION

In 1937 brothers Dick and Maurice "Mac" McDonald opened a tiny drive-in east of Pasadena, California, where they worked cooking hot dogs, mixing shakes, and waiting on customers.[4] The success of this location led the brothers to open a much larger drive-in at 14th and E streets in San Bernardino, California. The new restaurant employed 20 car hops and served a menu with 25 items ranging from pork sandwiches and ribs to barbequed beef and hamburgers. The operation was wildly successful. By 1948 the brothers were wealthy beyond their expectations but were growing tired of running their operation in the face of increased competition, a labor shortage, and increasingly complex operations.

To address these issues they decided to overhaul their operations. In analyzing their sales they discovered that hamburgers accounted for 80 percent of their business. This revelation led the brothers to close their business for three months in 1948 to allow themselves to introduce a revolutionary new business model based on their new "Speedy Service System." This system featured a self-service restaurant instead of car hops, a limited menu with only nine items (a 15-cent hamburger, a cheeseburger, potato chips, pie, and five beverages), a kitchen that was redesigned to use an assembly-line layout, and an all-male staff.[5] The 15-cent price was important since it made eating out on a regular basis affordable for families, an element of the company's strategy that McDonald's still follows today. Initially the innovations were not well received, and sales fell to one-fifth of their previous level. However, the brothers believed in their business model and persisted.

By 1952 the operations were so successful that they were featured as a cover story for *Restaurant* magazine, and McDonald's signed its first franchisee, Neil Fox. Fox redesigned his own drive-in restaurant in Phoenix, Arizona, with the red-and-white tile building and Golden Arches on the sides that became the prototype for McDonald's restaurants. While Fox's operations were successful, the McDonald brothers did not aggressively pursue franchising because they were satisfied with their current income and did not want the headaches associated with building a national chain. Further, by his own admission, Dick McDonald was a "lousy franchise salesman."[6] However, the success of the McDonald brothers did not go unnoticed. They received numerous franchise inquiries and were offered financial backing by Carnation Corporation, which they turned down. By 1953 the brothers realized they were missing a significant opportunity and hired a franchise agent, William Tansey, to further their operations. Tansey, however, was forced to resign after a few months due to a heart ailment. Unfortunately, as the McDonald brothers were foundering in their franchising operations, counterfeit McDonald's began to crop up throughout California largely because of the brothers' willingness to give in-depth tours of their operations.

One of the numerous businessmen who came to observe the McDonald brothers' success firsthand was the vendor who supplied them with the Multi-mixer machines they used to mix milkshakes: a Mr. Ray Kroc. Kroc had heard about the business from his West Coast sales representative in 1953. By 1954 the store had purchased 10 Multimixers (a large operation would normally only need 2) and Kroc's curiosity was piqued. When Kroc visited the store, he was impressed with the volume of customers (about 150 at lunch), the speed of service (orders were filled in 15 seconds), the quality of the food, and the number of milkshakes sold (estimated at 20,000 a month). Initially Kroc only wanted a sales agreement to supply Multimixers to new franchisees, but he was told that he would have to wait until a new franchise agent was hired to replace William Tansey. After a week of reflection, Kroc called the McDonalds and became their exclusive franchise agent in the United States. The initial franchise deal included the brothers' retention of full control over the operations, with Kroc being prohibited from making changes in operations without their approval, as well as the establishment of a low franchise fee ($950 and 1.9 percent of sales, 1.4 percent to Kroc and 0.5 percent to the McDonald brothers). On March 2, 1955, Kroc formed the new franchising company named McDonald's System, Inc., and about six weeks later, on

---

[4]John F. Love, 1986. *McDonald's Behind the Arches* (Toronto: Bantam Books).

[5]Ibid.

[6]Ibid.

April 15, 1955, Kroc's prototype McDonald's restaurant opened for business in Des Plaines, Illinois.

By 1956, McDonald's System, Inc., had 14 restaurants with total sales of $1.2 million. In selling the franchises Kroc treated his franchisees as partners but insisted both on uniformity of operations so that customers would get the same food experience at every McDonald's and on keeping the establishments very clean. Franchisees who adhered to these policies and shared Kroc's commitment to quality, service, and cleanliness were well supported, and Kroc viewed his role as one of facilitating their success.

In 1960 Kroc and Harry Sonneborn, head of McDonald's finances, sought a $1.5 million loan to expand operations. In securing this loan, McDonald's Corporation was formed with Kroc acting as chairman of the board of directors and Sonneborn as the president and chief executive officer. (While Sonneborn was president and CEO in name, Kroc still ran the show.) Both men agreed that a top priority was negotiating a new franchise contract with the McDonald's brothers, as the current one was due to expire in a few years and Kroc was chafing under the restrictions placed on him by the McDonald bothers—he was beginning to become frustrated with what he saw as the brothers' naiveté toward business.[7] The contract was successfully renegotiated, but Kroc soon became dissatisfied again and it became apparent that for Kroc to have the level of control he felt he needed, McDonald's Corporation would have to buy out the franchise from the brothers. When Kroc made the offer, the brothers asked for $2.7 million (enough for each brother to have $1 million after taxes) and refused to include the original San Bernardino store in the deal. Both of these conditions infuriated Kroc, especially since the brothers wanted the $2.7 million immediately, not in deferred payments, and the San Bernardino store was one of the most profitable in the chain.

With the help of Sonneborn, Kroc was able to secure the necessary funding in 1961. Interestingly, Sonneborn sold the concept to investors primarily on the basis of McDonald's real estate operations and its model of buying property and leasing it to franchisees rather than on the company's fast-food operations. These real estate operations were to become a key to McDonald's business model—as the company would make more money from locating, building

and opening more stores than any other chain in the business, spurring McDonald's to open more outlets than rivals.[8] Purely out of spite, Kroc went to San Bernardino as soon as the deal was signed, and opened a location one block away from the location he was denied; he also forced the brothers to remove their name and the McDonald's golden arches from the location.

In that same year a key element of McDonald's business model, the Hamburger University training program for McDonald's franchise owners and store managers, was established. The year 1963 was a banner one for McDonald's as the company reached two significant milestones. First, McDonald's was selling 1 million hamburgers a day. Ray Kroc sold McDonald's 1 billionth hamburger to Art Linkletter on Linkletter's national television show. Second, McDonald's had its first national meetings with its franchise holders. Then, in 1965, under the leadership of Kroc and Sonneborn, McDonald's became a public company, selling shares for $22.50 each in its initial public offering. About a year later, on July 5, 1966, McDonald's was listed on the New York Stock Exchange.

McDonald's reached another first in 1967 when the first price increase in its hamburgers occurred—going from 15 cents to 18 cents. That year also saw the resignation of Sonneborn after numerous disputes with Kroc and the installment of Fred Turner in his place. Turner had been with McDonald's since the early years, joining McDonald's System, Inc., in 1956 to work with Kroc on company operations as Kroc's protégé. The year 1967 also marked McDonald's initial involvement in international expansion with a new franchise that opened in Canada on June 1, 1967. In 1968, the 1,000th restaurant was opened in Des Plaines, not far from Kroc's original location, and the Big Mac was introduced systemwide. Soon the corporation began generating sales profits on a huge scale, and in 1970 a Minnesota restaurant became the first to reach $1 million in annual sales. The company also branched out in other ways that year, as a restaurant in Hawaii was the first to serve breakfast. New ideas occurred to company executives and franchisees often, and in 1971 the first McDonald's Playland opened in California; that feature has since become a regular one in many restaurant locations. That same year, the first Japanese, German, and

---

[7]Ibid.

[8]David, "Can McDonald's Cook Again?"

Australian McDonald's opened. By the end of the 1970s McDonald's had over 5,000 restaurants.

In 1984 two important events occurred: McDonald's served its 50 billionth hamburger, earning over $10 billion in sales with a new restaurant opening somewhere in the world every 17 hours, and its founder, Ray Kroc, passed away. Over the ensuing years McDonald's continued its international expansion and even opened a new restaurant in Moscow on January 31, 1990. This opening broke the record for the most people ever served by a single restaurant as more than 30,000 people lined up to visit the new restaurant.

In 1990, Fred Turner stepped down and was replaced by Michael Quinlan. During Quinlan's tenure McDonald's began to experience a number of challenges that would plague the company for years. First, customer preferences began to change due to technological advances such as the microwave oven and increasing health consciousness that led to decreased consumption of fried food and red meat. To further complicate matters, as the number of customers began to decline, the competition increased from other quick-service restaurants as well as from nontraditional outlets for reheatable prepared foods, including grocery and convenience stores. In response to customer desires for healthier fare, McDonald's experimented with new menu items such as the McLean Deluxe hamburger, a low-fat alternative to the Big Mac that was introduced in 1992 and that failed to ever become a solid menu item; a low-fat frozen yogurt; fat-free apple bran muffins; and the salad shaker, another failed product.

Increasing competition led McDonald's to continue aggressive store expansion in the United States; to seek new outlets, including partnerships with Walt Disney and Wal-Mart; and to further focus on international expansion. Increased domestic expansion led to cannibalization in existing franchises and caused increased tension between McDonald's and it franchisees. To ease these tensions, McDonald's discontinued its Quality, Service, Value, Cleanliness (QSVC) store evaluation system.

Increased domestic competition also led to an increased focus on McDonald's international expansion efforts. On April 23, 1992, McDonald's opened a location in Beijing, China, that drew a crowd of more than 40,000 customers that quickly swamped the location's 29 cash registers. As McDonald's increased its international expansion, the menus of international locations received a more local flavor. For example, the first kosher restaurant opened in Jerusalem in 1995; it did not serve dairy products, and it closed on Saturday, the Jewish Sabbath day. By the end of 1995, McDonald's foreign store count had expanded by over 100 percent, to more than 4,700 units from only 2,000 outlets in 1987. Despite these efforts, McDonald's continued to struggle and posted its first ever quarterly decline in annual earnings. In response to this, the board of directors ousted Quinlan in early 1999 and chose Jack Greenberg over Jim Cantalupo to be the new president, CEO and chairman of the board.

Greenberg took over the reins of the embattled fast-food giant at one of the most challenging times in the company's history. Competition among the largest fast-food rivals was increasing on multiple fronts, including an intense price war, rapid product innovation, and the addition of new stores. Internally, McDonald's customer service rankings had dropped considerably, quality was beginning to become inconsistent throughout the system, and store decor in many locations was considered dated. In response to these challenges, Greenberg announced a plan that he estimated would boost profits by 10 to 15 percent. Two of the key elements of this plan were continued store expansion efforts and diversification away from the hamburger segment through the acquisition of other quick-service restaurants (QSRs), including Boston Market, Chipotle, Donato's Pizzeria, Pret a Manger, and Fazoli's.

To combat rivals' product innovations, McDonald's introduced 40 new menu items, though none of these was particularly successful, as well as a new "Made for You" cooking system designed to allow customers to order and receive their food in 90 seconds. This initiative cost McDonald's $420 million ($20 million of which was in R&D), and each franchisee between $18,000 and $100,000 in kitchen upgrades. Unfortunately, "Made for You" did not produce the desired results and led to further tension between McDonald's and its franchisees. To resolve internal issues such as inconsistent quality and service, in 2001 McDonald's reinstituted its comprehensive restaurant review operation that included Quality, Service, Cleanliness (QSC) inspections, mystery shoppers, and a toll-free number for customers to provide feedback. The company also streamlined operations, reducing the number of regions from 37 to 21 (each region had a general manager and a team reporting to him or her that included a vice president of quality, service, and cleanliness), laid off 700 corporate employees, and announced the closure of 175 underperforming overseas outlets. Finally, Greenberg announced a plan to refurbish older stores at a cost of approximately $150,000 per store. Before Greenberg could fully implement all of these plans, in the fourth quarter of 2002 McDonald's posted its first loss since going public in 1965. Critics argued that Greenberg had launched too many initiatives simultaneously and had failed to properly implement any of them. The initiatives never produced the 10 to 15 percent increases in net profit Greenberg had promised. Taking full responsibility for McDonald's poor performance, Greenberg resigned in December 2002. At this critical juncture, the company called on Jim Cantalupo to come out of retirement, which he had entered after being passed over in favor of Greenberg in 1999, to lead a company that was one of the most recognizable brands in the world serving millions of customers daily in an increasingly complex environment in more than 120 countries.

THE QUICK-SERVICE SANDWICH INDUSTRY

In 2003 sales for the U.S. consumer food-service market totaled approximately $408 billion. While there were tens of thousands of fast-food outlets in the United States, including all of the regional and local outlets, the 10 largest chains in 2003 ranked by U.S. Systemwide Foodservice Sales accounted for about 14 percent of the total sales (see Exhibit 1).

Analysts generally segment the consumer food-service market into eight categories according to the type of food served and the concept on which operations are based: sandwich, pizza, chicken, family, grill-buffet, dinner house, contract, and hotel. In 2003 the top 30 sandwich chains had U.S. systemwide sales of approximately $64 billion. Of this amount, McDonald's accounted for almost 33 percent of the sales, the top 5 chains accounted for 71.70 percent of sales, and the top 10 chains 88.88 percent. Systemwide sales for the top 17 sandwich chains are shown in Exhibit 2, market share data is provided in Exhibit 3, and the top 10 sandwich chains based on number of U.S. units in Exhibit 4.

exhibit 1 **10 Largest Chains Based on 2003 Systemwide Sales**

Chain	Sales (millions)
McDonald's	$20,305.7
Burger King	8,350.0
Wendy's	6,953.0
Aramark Global Food	5,334.0
Subway	5,230.0
Taco Bell	5,200.0
Pizza Hut	5,100.0
KFC	4,800.0
Applebee's Neighborhood Grill	3,182.6
Domino's	2,926.7
Total	$67,382.0

Source: Nation's Restaurant News.

Future growth in the sandwich segment was expected to be only around 2 percent annually for the foreseeable future.

Trends in the Quick-Service Sandwich Industry

Several trends were impacting the quick-service food industry. First, customers were increasingly focusing on value. In response to this trend most of the sandwich companies—including McDonald's, Burger King, Wendy's, Hardee's, and Jack in the Box—had implemented a version of a low-cost menu. Items on these menus were offered at the lowest possible competitive price, most commonly around 99 cents. When McDonald's was considering whether to implement a value menu in 2001, the company believed that its menu was "conceptually similar to the one that Wendy's, the nation's no. 3 burger chain, has relied on for years."[9] Wendy's introduced its value menu, with seven items, in late 1989, long before most other national chains even considered doing so; Hardee's began offering a value meal in 1996. Of the major competitors, only Sonic has refrained from following this trend; it offers regular-priced menu items but no specific "value" items.

[9]Amy Zuber, *Nation's Restaurant News* 35, no. 5 (December 10, 2001), p. 1.

exhibit 2 **Systemwide Sales in the United States, 1998–2002 (Millions)**

	2002	2001	2000	1999	1998
Top 100 chains	$152,523.8	$144,094.8	$136,512.0	$130,362.7	$122,733.7
Top 17 sandwich chains	61,049.2	58,840.3	56,559.7	54,814.5	51,736.8

exhibit 3 **Market Shares for Fast-Food Sandwich Chains, 1998–2002**

	1998		1999		2000		2001		2002	
	Rank	Market Share*	Rank	Market Share*	Rank	Market Share*	Rank	Market Share*	Rank	Market Share*
McDonald's	1	35.03%	1	34.92%	1	34.43%	1	33.74%	1	33.26%
Burger King	2	15.94	2	15.55	2	15.29	2	14.85	2	13.68
Wendy's	3	9.65	3	9.98	3	10.22	3	10.50	3	11.39
Taco Bell	4	9.66	4	9.55	4	8.97	4	8.24	5	8.52
Subway	5	5.99	5	5.88	5	6.66	5	7.54	4	8.57
Arby's	6	4.01	6	4.15	6	4.24	6	4.32	6	4.41
Dairy Queen	7	3.89	7	3.94	7	3.91	7	3.72	9	3.59
Hardee's	8	4.63	8	3.93	8	3.57	8	3.37	10	2.78
Jack in the Box	9	2.81	9	3.23	9	3.38	9	3.57	7	3.67
Sonic Drive-In	10	2.58	10	2.92	10	3.13	10	3.32	8	3.61
Carl's Jr.	11	1.52	11	1.63	11	1.76	11	1.86	11	1.67
Whataburger	12	0.93	12	0.92	12	0.98	12	1.03	12	1.09
White Castle	13	0.81	13	0.81	13	0.83	13	0.79	14	0.80
Schlotzsky's Deli	14	0.66	14	0.72	14	0.74	14	0.70	17	0.63
Blimpie Subs and Salads	15	0.75	15	0.70	15	0.68	18	0.59	Not ranked	—
Krystal	16	0.64	16	0.63	16	0.63	16	0.63	15	0.64
Del Taco	17	0.50	17	0.53	17	0.58	17	0.60	16	0.64
Quizno's	Not ranked	—	Not ranked	—	Not ranked	—	15	0.65	13	1.06

*Market shares are based on McDonald's estimates of the size of the entire market.
Source: Nation's Restaurant News.

Consistent with the increased focus on value, major competitors, especially McDonald's and Burger King, had been willing to use price cuts to attract customers. Both of those companies marketed their signature sandwiches, the Big Mac and Whopper, respectively, for only 99 cents in 2002. However, the use of price cuts as a competitive weapon had abated as McDonald's and Burger King shifted tactics in an attempt to curb deep discounts. Both chains have shifted their competitive tactics to focus on building customer loyalty by updating menu items, increasing efficiency, and improving service.

A Burger King spokesperson said, "If McDonald's wants to price its product at 99 cents, then they should do that. But the Whopper is a premium deluxe sandwich and . . . Burger King believes it is worth far more than 99 cents."[10]

While customers were focused on price, they were also concerned with quality. In addition, health-conscious consumers were increasing their demands. Although several chains had been aware of a need to offer healthier fare for years, a recent lawsuit

[10]Kim Miller, quoted in ibid.

exhibit 4 **Top 10 Sandwich Chains Ranked by Number of U.S. Units, 2002**

Chain	Units
Subway	14,522
McDonald's	13,491
Burger King	8,146
Taco Bell	6,165
Wendy's	5,549
Dairy Queen	4,870
Arby's	3,250
Sonic Drive-in	2,533
Hardee's	2,229
Jack in the Box	1,862

Source: Nation's Restaurant News.

brought by eight teens against four fast-food chains for causing obesity caused many of these restaurants to renew efforts to offer healthier menu items ranging from salads and soup to healthier hamburgers such as veggie or turkey burgers. The lawsuit was later dismissed by the court, but it had a far-reaching impact. One response to this change in customer demands was the introduction of gourmet salads. Wendy's was the first nationally franchised quick-service restaurant to sell gourmet salads, beginning in 2002, and was generally considered the market leader in that area. In fact, according to one source, "30 percent of those who have bought [Wendy's] Garden Sensations salads came just for that."[11] Since their first appearance on the market, salads had become a regular feature of most fast-food restaurants' menus because they appealed to a wide range of consumers looking for a fast, healthier alternative to burgers and fried foods. Other companies had begun offering other low-fat options: Burger King was acknowledged as the first and only chain that offered customers a veggie burger, and the slogan for a new ad campaign was "Flavor from fire-grilling . . . not from fat," while Jack in the Box was one of the only fast-food restaurants where consumers could find a turkey burger.

As an extension of this trend, several fast-food companies were testing new ideas and menu items on

[11]Gregory Richards, *Knight Ridder Tribune Business News,* October 18, 2003, p. 1.

kids' menus to determine a reaction and to show parents that they were concerned for their children's health. For example, Subway had begun replacing cookies and soft drinks in its kids' meals with fruit roll-ups and fruit juice, Wendy's was trying to substitute milk for soft drinks in kids' meals in North Carolina, and in a few select locations McDonald's was replacing french fries in Happy Meals with apple slices. Many of these hamburger chains were concerned that if they did not introduce more appealing, healthy fare, consumers would begin turning toward chains that were intrinsically healthier, such as deli sandwich chains like Subway. Indeed, by 2003, there were more Subway restaurants in the United States than McDonald's and sandwich outlets had become part of the fastest-growing segment of the quick-service restaurant industry—the "other sandwich" was growing at a rate of 12.8 percent, compared to a 2.8 percent growth rate in the hamburger segment.

Another developing trend in the industry involved broadening the customer focus to include younger, hipper consumers as well as more sophisticated customers. One way McDonald's was attempting to achieve this was by hiring Justin Timberlake and other popular singers to be the singing voices of some of its new advertisement schemes, such as the "I'm lovin' it" campaign. Many of the changes made in the area of health had a side benefit by appealing to consumers who were looking for fast food that was slightly classier and more "gourmet." Items such as grilled chicken and premium chef's salads came across as more tasteful fare than a plain hamburger and french fries. Chains that offered items other than hamburgers were also following the trend to include more gourmet offerings in their food. Several of Arby's Market Fresh sandwiches included thick-sliced pepper bacon, smoked mozzarella cheese, roasted red peppers, and baguette-type bread. The young and hip today would be the mothers and fathers of the next generation, and fast-food restaurants of all types were attempting to firmly establish a loyal customer base now for improved long-run security.

The International Quick-Service Restaurant Industry

According to Euromonitor, the global food-service industry was expected to grow by more than $200 billion between 2002 and 2006. Many of the trends

exhibit 5   **Systemwide Outlets for the Top Five Fast Food Hamburger Chains, 2002**

	Domestic Outlets	Foreign Outlets	Total Systemwide Outlets	Number of Countries
McDonald's Corporation	13,491	16,534	31,108	120
Burger King Corporation	8,146	3,309	11,455	58
Wendy's International	6,273	2,538	8,811	22
CKE Restaurants (Hardee's)	3,101	194	3,295	15
Jack in the Box	2,000	0	2,000	1

Source: Nation's Restaurant News.

affecting the domestic fast-food industry were evident in the wider international market. For example, due to their success in the United States and Canada, many companies were introducing value-priced menus overseas to test consumer reactions. Another trend was increased offerings of healthy foods and premium products in overseas markets. For example, McDonald's had introduced the McChicken Premiere, a zesty chicken breast filet served on a focaccia bun, in the United Kingdom, France, Italy, and Belgium, as well as Le 280, a premium sandwich, in France. McDonald's had had a continuous struggle recently between offering value-priced items and offering more expensive products: "We offer a variety of price and taste options designed to attract price-sensitive consumers, as well as those who are willing to pay more for premium products."[12]

McDonald's and Burger King, especially, were the earliest and most aggressive hamburger chains to begin to expand internationally (see Exhibit 5). For McDonald's the first store outside the United States opened in Canada in June 1967. That company's first store openings in new countries had consistently drawn huge crowds of people, sometimes upward of 40,000 consumers on the opening day. Burger King's first international restaurants opened in 1963 in Puerto Rico; the first European Burger King opened in 1975 in Madrid, Spain.

In foreign countries both McDonald's and Burger King had traditionally offered menu items with a distinctively local flavor. For example, in Chile, Burger King offered the Broiled Salmon Fish Sandwich, the breakfast burrito in Mexico, and other seasonal dessert items throughout Central and South America. McDonald's Le 280, offered in France, was a sandwich with a distinctive sauce designed especially to appeal to the French palate; the stores in Jerusalem offered only kosher menu items, and no dairy products.

Wendy's had also experimented with international expansion, but with slightly less success than the top two hamburger chains. Two factors that may have influenced Wendy's struggle internationally were that it was a relatively new company and that it had been much slower to begin expanding overseas. When the crisis over bovine spongiform encephalopathy (mad cow disease) occurred in Europe and the financial crisis occurred in the Far East during the 1990s, the company became hesitant to aggressively expand internationally; it even closed seven stores in the United Kingdom and all stores in Hong Kong. Furthermore, in 2001, Wendy's was forced to abandon its Argentinean operations altogether because of that country's deep financial problems. Wendy's International simply lacked a strong enough foothold in any international market to support these failing ventures. Instead, the company was forced to turn to improving domestic operations and continuing growth through acquisitions.

All of the fast-food chains had consistently reported steady international expansion and growth of sales in international markets. In fiscal year 2003, Burger King had 55 new store openings in the Latin American/Caribbean region alone. In that same fiscal year and region, Burger King reported sales of $594 million, more than 10 percent growth in system sales over the prior year. In fact, every fiscal year since 2001, Burger King had reported decreased numbers of U.S. stores but increased numbers of international locations. However, McDonald's had represented the strongest international presence and greatest amount of worldwide sales since the beginning of overseas expansion. In 2002, the U.S. sector of the company was beginning to comprise less than

[12]McDonald's company report, "Revitalization Plan," 2003.

exhibit 6   McDonald's Systemwide Restaurants by Segments, 2000–2002

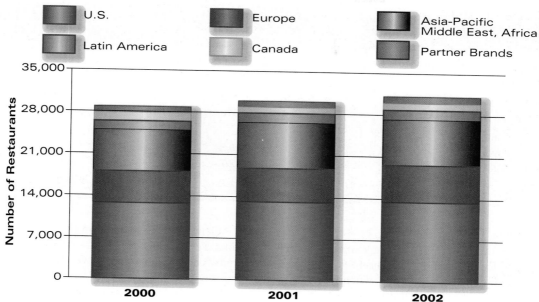

Source: www.mcdonalds.com.

half of total systemwide restaurants (see Exhibit 6); the rest of the world housed more than half of all McDonald's restaurants. Those numbers were expected to grow wider apart because the U.S. fast-food market was rapidly becoming saturated. The fast-food chains were recognizing the saturation of the industry and beginning to see the crucial importance of international expansion; growth in other countries was expected to be one of the only sources of growth for many of the top hamburger chains in future years.

McDONALD'S MAIN COMPETITORS

Burger King Corporation

Next to McDonald's, Burger King was the second largest hamburger fast-food chain in the world. Headquartered in Miami, Florida, the company had locations in 58 countries, with almost 11,400 Burger King stores across the globe, and derived 55.3 percent of its revenues from drive-through operations. Although McDonald's revenues in 2002 were significantly higher than those of Burger King—$15.4 bil-

lion and $1.72 billion, respectively—McDonald's revenues represented only a 4 percent increase over the past year, whereas Burger King's revenues had increased by almost 17 percent in the same period. In 2002, the company was put up for sale by its parent company, Diageo, because of its declining market share, and was purchased by a coalition formed by Texas Pacific Group, Bain Capital, and Goldman Sachs Capital Partners. Exhibit 7 provides information on the number of Burger King outlets and total sales from 1998 to 2003.

Founded in 1954 in Miami, Burger King offered quality food at affordable prices, much like any other fast-food hamburger chain. The Whopper was first introduced in 1957 and became an immediate success and a trademark menu item of Burger King. In advertising, the company noted both the Whopper's unique charbroiled taste and the company's policy of preparing the hamburger any way the customer wanted it. Burger King's early achievements made it a natural candidate for franchises, and so a natural competitor of McDonald's corporation, which was also being franchised and expanded during that time.

Even early on, the company sought to distinguish itself in a rapidly growing industry by providing its customers with a unique fast-food experience. One

exhibit 7   **Burger King Outlets and Sales, 1998–2003**

	Fiscal Year					
	2003	**2002**	**2001**	**2000**	**1999**	**1998**
Outlets						
United States	7,904	8,146	8,306	8,293	8,020	7,691
International	3,431	3,309	3,066	2,868	2,506	2,144
Total	11,335	11,455	11,372	11,161	10,526	9,835
Sales (in billions)						
United States	$ 7.9	$ 8.6	$ 8.5	$ 8.7	$ 8.5	$ 8.2
International	3.2	2.7	2.7	2.7	2.4	2.1
Total	$11.1	$11.3	$11.2	$11.4	$10.9	$10.3

way it achieved this was by enclosing its patio seating in 1957, thereby offering customers an indoor dining experience for the first time in fast-food history. Another example occurred in 1975, when Burger King began to install and operate drive-through windows at its restaurants. Now customers who were busy with family, jobs, and children could buy a quality meal in a hurry without ever leaving the car. Burger King's menu also offered a few items that set it apart from other fast-food restaurants. For breakfast, it offered the popular Croissan'wiches and french toast sticks, and for lunch and dinner the menu included a veggie burger and the chicken Caesar salad.

Like McDonald's and virtually every other burger chain in the world, however, Burger King was being forced to respond to a shift in consumer preferences from high-calorie burgers and fries to less fatty, more health-conscious offerings such as deli sandwiches and baked potatoes. All fast-food hamburger chains, Burger King included, were expected to be struggling for several years to come to meet new consumer health expectations without compromising the menu items on which the companies were founded.

Wendy's International, Inc.

Wendy's Old-Fashioned Hamburgers was considered the third largest fast-food hamburger business in the world, although it reported higher revenues in 2002 than did Burger King. The company as a whole generated $2.73 billion in revenues in 2002, up 14.2 percent from the previous year. With headquarters in Dublin, Ohio, the corporation operated over 9,000 restaurants in 33 countries worldwide.

General menu items were similar to those of McDonald's and Burger King—hamburgers, chicken sandwiches, and fries—but Wendy's also offered several unique products such as Frostys and Spicy Chicken Sandwiches, as well as many healthy alternatives like salads, baked potatoes, and even chili. One very important innovation contributed by Wendy's was a special value menu that consisted of about 10 items that could be purchased for 99 cents. Since its initiation in Wendy's stores, the value menu had also been implemented in McDonald's and Burger King's restaurants in order to compete with Wendy's.

Founded in 1969 in Ohio by David Thomas, Wendy's Old Fashioned Hamburgers was incorporated and in 1976 had its first public offering of 1 million shares at $28 per share. By 1981 the company had been listed on the New York Stock Exchange and had built its 2,000th restaurant. Unlike a few of its competitors, Wendy's faced difficulties with international expansion (as noted earlier in this case). Despite these failures, the corporation had grown by acquiring several smaller companies such as Tim Horton's and Baja Fresh Mexican Grill.

Wendy's possessed several strengths and weaknesses in the fast-food business. The company's Super Value Menu was definitely one of its strongest assets, although the concept had been picked up by other major companies. Also, in 2002, most fast-food chains were desperately slashing prices in a bid to go increasingly lower. However, Wendy's chose that year as a time to focus on product quality and product expansion by offering its Garden Sensations, a new selection of fresh, healthy salads. One weak point in Wendy's business plan was the lack of an easily recognizable product comparable to McDonald's Big Mac or Burger King's Whopper.

As Wendy's moved into the future without founder Dave Thomas, who passed away in 2002, it planned to add between 2,000 and 4,000 new Wendy's locations in the next decade and to focus its international expansion in Latin America. However, the company's chief executive officer and chairman, Jack Schuessler, stated that the company planned to increasingly use acquisitions of smaller brands and joint ventures as the primary driver of future growth. In selecting potential acquisition targets, Wendy's was avoiding concepts that directly competed with core Wendy's offerings and looking to the fast casual segment and to concepts that involved offering high-quality food without table service.

Hardee's

Headquartered in St. Louis, Missouri, Hardee's was the fourth largest fast-food hamburger chain and a subsidy of the parent company CKE Restaurants. There were about 2,400 Hardee's restaurants in 32 states and 11 countries, and the company brought in $1.8 billion in 2002. The company was founded in 1960 in North Carolina, and its original menu featured charbroiled hamburgers and cheeseburgers for 15 and 20 cents, respectively.

The greatest strength of the company lay in its breakfast menu, which accounted for about 35 percent of Hardee's total revenues, and its new Thickburgers, which had been well received among hamburger eaters. CKE Restaurants as a whole had experienced many difficulties in recent years due to company debt and underperformance of several of its stores, including many Hardee's restaurants. In 2000, CKE sold almost 500 Hardee's stores and began working to revamp the chain's brand image. All of the restaurant buildings were being remodeled inside and out into Star Hardee's, and the menu was being expanded to include several premium offerings such as the Angus beef Thickburger. Because of the company's recent troubles, its efforts had been focused less on low prices and hardball competition and more on the mere survival and revitalization of the company. One notable product innovation was the Six Dollar Burger. According to Andrew F. Puzder, CEO and president of Hardee's Food Systems, Inc. (Hardee's management), the success of this product had demonstrated that customers were willing to pay more for quality and exceptional taste and had led Hardee's to position itself as the "premium burger specialist among quick-service restaurants."[13] Building on this success and consumer feedback, Hardee's had eliminated 40 menu items from the lunch and dinner menus and introduced a burger line featuring one-third-pound, half-pound and three-quarter-pound hamburgers.

Jack in the Box

The Jack in the Box drive-through hamburger chain was headquartered in San Diego and operated over 1,850 restaurants in 17 states. Jack in the Box, Inc., also owned Qdoba Mexican Grills and Quick Stuff Convenience Stores. In fiscal year 2002, the company's sales totaled $2.2 billion, a 4.7 percent increase over the past year's sales of $2.1 billion. Jack in the Box was subsidized in 1968, but in 1985 its managers succeeded in buying out their business and going private. In 1992, the company went public with a stock offering of 17.2 million shares and was listed on the NYSE as JBX.

Although other fast-food chains had focused on children as well as adults for a healthy percentage of their income, Jack in the Box menu items were geared toward adult consumers only and included hamburgers, Mexican food, and specialty sandwiches. The restaurant's traditional signature items included the Jumbo Jack, the Sourdough Jack, and the Ultimate Cheeseburger, while its more innovative offerings included a teriyaki chicken bowl and a chicken fajita pita. Like most of the other competitors, Jack in the Box also offered a value menu.

The company experienced a difficult year in 2002 due to several factors. An overall weaker economy damaged the company to some extent, and larger competitors were heavily involved in cutthroat price wars. The company did not wish to engage in those price wars and instead turned to improving the quality of its product as well as to initiating efforts to attract women, despite the fact that the company regards young men as its primary focus.

Jack in the Box, like its competitors, noted the necessity in the future of broadening its product offerings in order to compete with fast-food chains as well as grocery stores, which now offered many complete, healthy, cheap meals that the consumer

[13]Company press release, "Hardee's Breaks Ranks from Competition," January 21, 2003.

could heat up at home in a few minutes. In 2003, Jack in the Box's CEO, Robert Nugent, announced that his company would undertake a fast, casual systemwide makeover intended to reduce the company's reliance on its core market of males ages 18 to 34, and attract more women and older men. According to Nugent, "The fast-food hamburger segment of the quick-serve restaurant category has been crowded and mature."[14] Nugent estimated that the renovation would take between three and five years and involve a smaller menu, simplified restaurant kitchen operations, and the introduction of "premium items." Nugent also announced a decreased emphasis on value pricing, stating, "People seeking 99-cent deals probably will go elsewhere."[15] By the end of 2003, Jack in the Box had introduced new main-course salads (Asian Chicken, Southwest Chicken, and Chick Club), roasted turkey and club sandwiches on hearth-baked rolls (Jack's Classics), a chicken taco, and a turkey burger. As customers responded favorably to these innovations, fourth-quarter sales rose 18 percent over the same period the previous year.

Sonic

Sonic Corporation, whose motto was "Service with the speed of sound," was founded by Troy Smith in 1953 in Shawnee, Oklahoma, as a hamburger and root-beer stand called Top Hat.[16] The first location to bear the Sonic name, changed from Top Hat to avoid copyright infringement, was located in Stillwater, Oklahoma in 1956; the company was headquartered in Oklahoma City. By 2003 Sonic had grown to over 2,700 locations (approximately 80 percent of which were franchises) and systemwide sales of almost $2.4 billion. Although Sonic was significantly smaller than the major players in the fast-food industry, it operated the largest American drive-in restaurant business. Sonic had been listed as one of *Forbes*'s 200 best small companies for the last 10 years, as one of *Business Week*'s Hot Growth Com-

panies in 2002 and 2003, and as one of the top franchise opportunities by *Entrepreneur* magazine.

Sonic's relatively broad menu and atmosphere attempted to emulate those of a bygone era for the consumer. Top 40 Oldies usually played over the speakers, carhops could be found serving the customers, and popular menu items included foot-long cheese coneys, toaster sandwiches, onion rings, tater tots, specialty soft drinks, and frozen shakes and malts. Sonic had a very good relationship with its franchisees, who developed many of the new menu items. In adopting new products for systemwide sales, Sonic tried to focus on items that were fun and novel. To compete with other fast-food businesses, Sonic began offering a breakfast menu in 1999 and rolled it out systemwide by the end of 2003.

Since its founding the company had experienced almost nonstop growth. The company's first public offering occurred in 1991, raising $52 million in capital that Sonic used to buy out some investors, pay off debt, and increase its working capital. The recent addition of a breakfast menu continued that trend of almost continuous growth in the fast-food industry. For the fiscal year 2004, Sonic expected earnings per share to grow between 16 and 17 percent through the addition of franchises and, to a lesser extent, company-owned drive-ins as well as by driving higher same-store sales through increased advertising designed to build brand awareness. Sonic opened 194 new drive-ins in fiscal 2003 (159 franchised and 35 company owned) and planned to open 190–200 new locations in fiscal 2004, 165–170 of these owned by franchisees. In the first quarter of fiscal 2004, which ended on November 30, 2003, systemwide same-store sales increased by 6.2 percent and net income increased by 20 percent over the same period the previous year. Sonic expected systemwide same-store sales to grow at a rate of 1–3 percent for fiscal 2004.

McDONALD'S CURRENT SITUATION

Management Team

Jim Cantalupo became chief executive officer and chairman of McDonald's Corporation on January 1, 2003. Cantalupo was a 28-year veteran of the company and had recently served as president and vice

[14]Susan Spielberg, "Jack in the Box Brand Renovation Could Aim to Tap Fast-Casual Allure," *Nation's Restaurant News* 37, no. 39 (September 29, 2003).

[15]Richard Gibson, "Jack in the Box CEO: 'We Went into the Southeast Too Quickly,'" *The Wall Street Journal,* September 17, 2003.

[16]Sherri Daye, "Sonic's First Fifty," *QSR Magazine,* September 30, 2003.

chairman of McDonald's. He first joined the company in 1974 as controller; a year later he was promoted to vice president and then senior vice president in 1981. Cantalupo also served on the board of directors of Sears, Roebuck, and Company; Illinois Tool Works, Inc.; World Business Chicago; and the Chicago Council on Foreign Relations. After stepping to the McDonald's helm, Cantalupo faced many challenges and problems, with the company suffering from recent profit losses, poor decisions, and poor management. He had begun taking steps to bring the company out of a downturn, but only time would tell whether or not his maneuvers were effective.

As chief operating officer and president of McDonald's Corporation, Charlie Bell was responsible for more than 30,000 McDonald's restaurants in over 120 countries. His immediately prior position had been as president of the European sector of the company, but he started as a regular restaurant worker in Sydney, Australia, at the age of 15. Bell's job was to be sure that the orders from the board of directors were carried out in all restaurants and countries. Matthew Paull was an executive vice president and chief financial officer of McDonald's as of 2001. Unlike the first two team members, Paull did not begin his career very early in the company; he joined in 1993, after an 18-year career with Ernst & Young. At McDonald's, Paull was responsible for all financial matters of the company and directly responsible for the reporting for information systems, accounting, facilities and systems, tax, treasury, and investor relations.

Michael Roberts was president of the U.S. sector of McDonald's Corporation. As such, he oversaw the functioning of the more than 13,000 restaurants. In 1977, Roberts joined the McDonald's team as a regional purchasing manager. He worked his way up through the ranks and also served as an advisory director to the corporation's board of directors. Russ Smyth was the president of the European segment of McDonald's Corporation; he oversaw 6,000 restaurants in over 51 countries. Beginning his career in 1984, and for the next 13 years, Smyth served in the financial arena of McDonald's; in 1987, he began to become involved in the international segment as well, with his appointment as staff director of the Europe group of the International Accounting Group. In 1988, Smyth became the first employee to receive the McDonald's President's Award, which was given to the company's top performing employees annually.

Fred Turner was senior chairman of McDonald's Corporation and a member of the board of directors. When Turner first became involved with McDonald's, he hoped to become a franchisee but instead became one of the first employees of McDonald's Corporation in 1956. By 1967, he was an executive vice president of the company. Turner became CEO of McDonald's in 1973 and then also chairman in 1977. That same year, Ray Kroc, McDonald's founder, became senior chairman; Turner had taken that position by 1990. After a long career with McDonald's, Turner was still actively involved with the company. Finally, Jim Skinner was vice chairman of McDonald's Corporation; his duties had recently been extended to include management of McDonald's Japan Limited, the company's second largest market, with more than 4,000 restaurants. Before this promotion, Skinner was president and chief operating officer of the company. Skinner's career began in 1971, when he became a restaurant manager trainee; he quickly advanced in the company and went on to hold numerous positions in the United States and international segments of the corporation.

McDonald's Business Model and Sources of Revenue

McDonald's income was provided by a variety of sources, including the company's restaurant operations (McDonald's and its partner brands), its vast real estate holdings and the retail sales of merchandise, a category that was potentially growing as a percentage of total revenue.

McDonald's restaurant operations included revenue from company-operated, franchised, and affiliated restaurant outlets in domestic as well as international markets. Over the past 10 years, franchised restaurants typically had accounted for approximately 60 percent or more of McDonald's total systemwide sales, while the company's own restaurants brought in just less than 30 percent of its sales revenue (see Exhibits 8 and 9). Globally, the combined markets in the United States and Europe accounted for the majority of the company's sales. Although the lion's share of existing McDonald's outlets were franchises, the profit of the company-owned restaurants comprised a fairly significant portion of the total income because the company kept and applied 100 percent of those profits rather than

exhibit 8 **McDonald's Systemwide Sales by Type of Outlet 1992–2002 (sales in millions)**

	1992	1993	1994	1995	1996	1997	1998	1999	2000	2001	2002
Franchised stores											
Sales	$14,474	$15,756	$17,146	$19,123	$19,969	$20,863	$22,330	$23,830	$24,463	$24,838	$25,692
Outlets	9,237	9,918	10,944	12,186	13,374	14,197	15,086	15,949	16,795	17,395	17,846
Company owned											
Sales	$5,103	$5,157	$5,793	$6,863	$7,571	$8,136	$8,895	$9,512	$10,467	$11,040	$11,500
Outlets	2,551	2,733	3,216	3,783	4,294	4,887	5,433	6,059	7,625	8.378	9,000
Affiliated stores											
Sales	$2,308	$2,674	$3,048	$3,928	$4,272	$4,639	$4,754	$5,149	$5,251	$4,752	$4,334
Outlets	1,305	1,476	1,739	2,330	3,216	3,844	3,994	4,301	4,260	4,320	4,244
Total	$21,885	$23,587	$25,987	$29,914	$31,812	$33,638	$35,979	$38,491	$40,181	$40,630	$41,526

Source: www.mcdonalds.com, December 1, 2003.

exhibit 9 **McDonald's Sales by Type of Outlet as a Percentage of Total Systemwide Sales, 1992–2002**

	1992	1993	1994	1995	1996	1997	1998	1999	2000	2001	2002
Franchised	66.13%	66.80	65.98	63.93	62.77	62.02	62.06	61.91	60.88	61.13	61.87
Company-operated	23.32	21.86	22.29	22.94	23.80	24.19	24.72	24.71	26.05	27.17	27.69
Affiliated	10.55	11.34	11.73	13.13	13.43	13.79	13.21	13.38	13.07	11.70	10.44

Source: www.mcdonalds.com, December 1, 2003.

the much smaller portion of the franchises' profits it received. The affiliated restaurants segment had begun to bring in more profits within the past few years, as McDonald's acquired Boston Market in 2000, as well as Chipotle Mexican Grill and Donato's Pizza.

Franchises continued to play a significant role in McDonald's Corporation, as they had since the very first franchise was opened in Des Plaines, Illinois, in 1955 by Ray Kroc himself. The franchising process was extensive. When an individual financially qualified for a franchise and was approved, McDonald's searched for possible locations for the proposed restaurant, and after a franchisee had undergone extensive training, McDonald's purchased the most appropriate site. The franchisee was then assigned to the property and paid rent on that land in addition to typical franchise fees. Franchisees had two options: (1) They could either purchase an existing McDonald's restaurant from the company or from another franchisee and pay a down payment equal to 25 percent of the purchase price of the building and land, or (2) they could open a brand-new McDonald's, paying a 40 percent down payment on the property. The former option was the more common one, and although there was a stated down payment of 25 percent, McDonald's typically required a person to contribute a minimum of $175,000 in personal, nonborrowed funds. After that initial payment, McDonald's did not act as a finance corporation; the franchisee was responsible for obtaining financial assistance for the remainder of the purchase price.

After the franchise was established, there were several ways in which McDonald's continued to receive an income from each restaurant. First, a monthly service fee was charged to each franchisee, determined as a percentage of total monthly sales; in 2002, the service fee was 4.0 percent. The second revenue stream was provided by the rent the company charged for the property on which each franchise was located. From early in its history, McDonald's had recognized the value of real estate, and almost from the very beginning the company's policy had been to own all property on which a McDonald's outlet was built, regardless of whether that location was franchised or company-owned. This strategy, first conceived by Harry Sonneborn, had been a key element of McDonald's strategy since. Rent income varied from property to property, but it

was estimated that McDonald's "generates more money from its rent than from its franchise fees."[17]

McDonald's real estate holdings and rent generated from these holdings had become an increasingly important component of the company's value and income. According to a *Wall Street Journal* article, "McDonald's is unique in the fast-food industry in that it owns much of its real estate, . . . giving the company more control over what it can do on the land."[18] McDonald's real estate holdings were significant in both their quantity and quality. In the vast majority of cases, McDonald's restaurants were located on prime high-traffic real estate that is highly visible and easily accessible. In fact, when McDonald's stipulated its conditions for a franchise location, requirements included a corner lot with at least 35,000 square feet of land whose entrance and exit were facilitated by a traffic light. While McDonald's did accrue a good bit of income from renting out the property to franchisees, that was certainly not the only way the company made money from its real estate—it also marketed excess land, property, and buildings on www.loopnet.com. Between rents and profits from land sales, McDonald's vast real estate holdings represented a significant portion of the company's value.

As McDonald's looked to the future, it was experimenting with several new methods of earning income. In the past, the company's initial public offerings in the United States and Japan had met with success, and if the company could grow enough, that option would be available to raise revenue in many of the other 120 countries where McDonald's had a presence. The company was also tentatively testing new methods of raising revenue, such as offering retail merchandise for sale in certain stores. There had been wide speculation about the exact nature of the products McDonald's could or would offer for sale to the public, ranging from watches to toys. Evidence that the company was moving into the age of computer technology could be found in its collaboration with Freddie Mac, a mortgage finance company, to install computers in

[17]Beverly Vasquez, "McDonald's Takes Bite from Its Land Holdings," *Denver Business Journal* 50, no. 8 (October 23–October 29, 1998), p. B9.

[18]Shirley Leung. "At McDonald's, Will 'Extension' Join the Menu?" *The Wall Street Journal,* Eastern edition, May 29, 2002, p. B1.

certain restaurants in order to provide customers with information about home ownership, courtesy of the Freddie Mac Web site. McDonald's past successes with franchises and real estate, combined with its new ventures in earning income, would allow McDonald's to remain a successful and, hopefully, profitable company for many years to come.

The recent recovery in McDonald's performance and stock price had been largely attributed to Cantalupo's implementation of the company's new strategy, known as McDonald's Plan to Win.

McDonald's Plan to Win

McDonald's Plan to Win focused on what the company had identified as its five key drivers of success: people, products, place, price, and promotion. The company expected that it would take between 12 and 16 months to implement this plan but believed that by focusing on these five key drivers the company would:

> fortify the foundation of [its] business through operations excellence and leadership marketing and lay the pipeline for long-term innovation . . . [by aligning] . . . the system around McDonald's plan to win—revitalizing the brand and becoming more relevant to a broader group of people by consistently delivering on the drivers of exceptional customer experiences allowing the company to attract new customers, encourage existing customers to visit [McDonald's] more often, build brand loyalty and, ultimately, creating enduring profitable growth for the company, the System and [its] shareholders.[19]

The first driver of exceptional customer experiences that McDonald's would focus on was people—that is, employees who were considered instrumental in delivering exceptional customer service. Accordingly, the company vowed to "do a better job of staffing our restaurants during busy periods and of training and rewarding our people to deliver outstanding service."[20] Specific initiatives the company intended to launch in this area included speeding up service by using more visual menu boards and reducing the menu, employing hospitality training to ensure the employees were friendly and focused on customer service, and using an interactive e-learning program to cost-effectively train restaurant staffs

worldwide in customer service attitudes and skills. In Latin America, McDonald's was focusing on customer service by reinstituting hostesses to help carry trays and attend to customers' service needs. McDonald's would measure its success in this area through a reduction in complaints related to service and increases in friendliness scores and speed of service.[21]

The second driver of exceptional customer experiences McDonald's chose to focus on was its products. The company planned to be responsive to changing taste preferences and the growing interest in wholesome food choices and premium products.[22] Examples of premium products included the new McGriddles sandwiches introduced in the United States and Canada, as well as the McChicken Premiere, a chicken sandwich introduced in the United Kingdom, France, Italy and Belgium. McDonald's responsiveness to changing customer preferences was reflected in new white-meat Chicken McNuggets offered in the United States and Canada, expanded Happy Meal offerings in the United Kingdom that included no-sugar-added fruit drinks, and fruit slices that could be added for an extra fee, as well as the Premium Salads being offered in the United States and the Salads Plus Menu offered in Australia that included eight products, all of which had 10 grams of fat or less. McDonald's planned to judge its success in this area through improvements in its hot and fresh food scores.

The third driver was place, which involved making McDonald's a customer destination by making its restaurants cleaner, more relevant, and more modern. Consistent with this goal the company intended to "make McDonald's a place customers seek out because it serves the food they want in a contemporary, welcoming environment they want to be in—whether dining alone, with friends or with family."[23] Improving the relevancy of the customer experience was to be achieved through initiatives such as installing wireless technology and creating wireless "hot spots" in restaurants in 28 countries, and adding coffeehouses (McCafe) in select restaurants that included premium coffee, muffins, and pastries at a value price to enhance adult appeal. To make the restaurants cleaner and more modern, McDonald's

---

[19]McDonald's Revitalization Plan, 2003, www.mcdonalds.com.
[20]Ibid.

[21]Ibid.
[22]Ibid.
[23]Ibid.

exhibit 10   **Customer Service Rankings, Fourth Quarter 2002**

Company	Quality Ranking*	Drive-Through Time†	Drive Through Accuracy†
Wendy's International	74	116.22	86.54%
KFC Corporation (Yum! Brands, Inc.)	69	172.73	88.50
Burger King Corporation	68	160.52	88.04
Taco Bell Corporation (Yum! Brands, Inc.)	67	159.12	90.14
U.S. Internal Revenue Service	62	NA	NA
McDonald's Corporation	61	156.92	84.86

*University of Michigan's American Customer Satisfaction Index (ASCI).

†"The Best Drive Thru in America '03," *QSR Magazine*, www.qsrmagazine.com.

was renovating, rebuilding, and even relocating some of its buildings; the goal was to create a fresh, sophisticated, but family-friendly atmosphere. To measure success in the place driver, McDonald's planned to use restaurants' cleanliness scores, with the goal of returning them to their all-time highs.

The fourth driver was price, with a focus on improving productivity and value. In offering value, McDonald's concentrated on offering a broad variety of products at a range of price points that would appeal to price sensitive customers, such as McDonald's dollar menu in the United States, as well as those willing to pay for premium products. Measuring the price driver involved improvements in value-for-money scores and restaurant margins.

The final driver of exceptional customer experiences was promotion, through which McDonald's hoped to build trust and brand loyalty. Initiatives to support this driver included "creating messages that reinforce [the] brand and connect with key customer segments—families and young adults . . . [while] continuing to forge bonds of trust with customers and the communities in which we do business."[24] Specific programs included the "I'm lovin' it" campaign launched worldwide in 2003; more general efforts included making McDonald's an easy choice for families by offering both premium salads and improved Happy Meals, giving Ronald McDonald a more prominent place in marketing and goodwill efforts, targeting young adults with relevant advertising featuring music from leading recording artists, using advertising media beyond television, and being a leader in social responsibility.[25] Goals in this

[24]Ibid.

[25]Ibid.

area included increasing brand awareness and increasing the number of Happy Meals sold per unit to the previous all-time high.

In conjunction with the Plan to Win was an effort to further enhance McDonald's focus on its core business. In December 2003 McDonald's announced significant changes in its partner brand activities. Specific changes included the sale of Donato's Pizzeria back to its owner, entering into a letter of intent to exit its domestic joint venture activities with Fazoli's, the discontinuation of the development of non-McDonald's brands outside of the United States, and the discontinuation of the Pret a Manger chain in Japan.

McDonald's Current Performance

Through January 1, 2003, McDonald's performance was lackluster on several metrics, including customer service rankings, employee turnover, and order-processing time. As previously mentioned, its customer service ranking was the lowest in the fast-food industry and even lower than that of the IRS (see Exhibit 10).

Several elements contributed to this poor service ranking. One factor was employee turnover. Within the fast-food industry employee turnover typically ran 300 percent a year, but McDonald's turnover rate tended to be higher than its rivals'. Another factor contributing to poor service rankings was slow service at the drive-through window; McDonald's ranked the fifth best in the industry, with an average service time of 156.92 seconds. Ahead of McDonald's were Wendy's (average time of 116.2 seconds), Chick-Fil-A

(146.38), Krystal Burger (149.57), and Checkers (153.59). McDonald's generated approximately 60 percent of it sales from its drive-through operations, but its service times were about 40.67 seconds behind rivals such as Wendy's.[26] This may seem insignificant, but each six-second increment translated into 1 percent loss in sales. Based on average franchise sales of $1.44 million, this translated into an annual loss of almost $97,000. In terms of order accuracy McDonald's also performed poorly, fulfilling only 84.41 percent (Compared to Chick-Fil-A's 97.30 percent) of the orders correctly and ranking 19th.

By implementing the strategies and tactics detailed in its Plan to Win, McDonald's intended to realize a significant improvement in performance. Short-term financial objectives included cutting capital expenditures by 40 percent in 2003, a decrease of approximately $1.2 billion. McDonald's also intended to use cash from 2003 operations to pay off debt and return some cash to shareholders through repurchase of shares and increased dividends.

Long-term financial objectives the company intended to achieve by 2005 and beyond included annual systemwide sales growth of between 3 and 5 percent, with approximately 1 to 3 percent of this growth from increased sales at existing restaurants and up to 2 percent coming from new restaurants, and growth in operating income of 6 to 7 percent and annual returns on incremental invested capital in the high teens.[27]

As McDonald's began to implement its Plan to Win, performance improvements in some areas became readily apparent. For example, by January 2, 2004, the company's stock price had reached a price of $24.79, from an all-time low of approximately $12.50 in March 2003, with some analysts predicting a price of $34.00 by the end of 2004. While this was a significant improvement, it was still well below the $40.00 per share price the stock was bringing in the late 1990s and the early 2000s. Key financial metrics are provided in Exhibits 11, 12, 13, and 14.

THE FUTURE

By January 1, 2004, McDonald's had begun to show positive progress in its turnaround strategy. The company had enjoyed 11 straight months of sales gains, with double-digit gains in October (15.1 percent) and November (10.2 percent) 2003. While this turnaround was impressive, some analysts, such as Coralie Witter, a restaurant analyst from Goldman Sachs, were withholding judgment. Witter stated, "While we expect McDonald's to maintain same-store sales momentum near-term, long-term we think it will be tough to sustain [that] growth and thus margin expansion without a substantial improvement in operations."[28] Dean T. Haskell, a securities analyst from JMP, agreed, stating, "We do not believe same-store sales growth at these double-digit rates to be sustainable."[29] Analysts' specific concerns included McDonald's ability to sustain its current level of product innovation and competitors' ability to imitate McDonald's successful new products. Analysts also questioned the extent to which McDonald's recent recovery was a reflection of the changes it had made as opposed to a reflection of a cyclical recovery in the fast-food sector and currency gains from a weak dollar. (McDonald's systemwide sales growth in October was 17.8 percent, compared to the previous October but only 10.2 percent in constant currency.)

While pleased with McDonald's recent performance, even the company's chairman and CEO, Jim Cantalupo, believed that McDonald's still had work to do. To remind his staff of this, he sent a memo to them stating, "We have come a long way in creating the kind of momentum we will need to deliver on our stated goal of sustaining increases in sales and operating income." But he said the journey was far from over and that 2004 would be a "pivotal year."[30] The most significant question that remained was whether the changes Cantalupo had made were sufficient to provide McDonald's with the core competencies necessary to build a sustainable competitive advantage in the global fast-food industry.

---

[26]David, "Can McDonald's Cook Again?"

[27]McDonald's Plan to Win, 2003.

[28]Richard Gibson, "McDonald's Is Recuperating but a Full Recovery Is a Ways Off," *The Wall Street Journal,* December 9, 2003.

[29]Ibid.

[30]Ibid.

exhibit 11 **McDonald's Condensed Consolidated Statements of Income, 1998–2003 (in millions except per share data)**

	Q3 2003	Q2 2003	Q1 2003	2002	2001	2000	1999	1998
Revenues								
Sales by company-operated restaurants	$3,351.2	$3,189.7	$2,856.1	$11,500.0	$11,041.0	$10,467.0	$9,512.5	$8,894.9
Revenues from franchised and affiliated restaurants	1,153.4	1,091.1	943.6	3,906.0	3,829.0	3,776.0	3746.8	3,526.5
Total revenues	$4,504.6	$4,280.8	$3,799.7	$15,406.0	$14,870.0	$14,243.0	$13,259.3	$12,421.4
Operating costs and expenses								
Company-operated restaurant expenses	$2,840.6	$2,744.0	$2,509.4	$9,907.0	$9,454.0	$8,750.0	$7,829.6	$5,261.6
Franchised restaurants—occupancy expenses	236.0	231.0	223.3	840.0	800.0	772.0	737.7	678.0
Selling, general, and administrative expenses	456.3	466.4	396.4	1,713.0	1,662.0	1,587.0	1,477.6	1,458.5
Other operating (income) expense, net	7.8	13.2	(4.0)	833.0	257.0	(196.0)	(105.2)	261.4
Total operating costs and expenses	$3,540.7	$3,454.6	$3,125.1	$13,293.0	$12,173.0	$10,913.0	$9,939.7	$9,659.5
Operating income	$963.9	$826.2	$674.6	$2,113.0	$2,697.0	$3,330.0	$3,319.6	$2,761.9
Interest expense	93.8	101.7	101.8	374.0	452.0	430.0	396.3	413.8
Nonoperating expense, net	47.0	16.3	25.2	77.0	52.0	18.0	39.2	40.7
Income before provision for income taxes and cumulative effect of accounting changes	$823.1	$708.2	$547.6	$1,662.0	$2,330.0	$2,882.0	$2,884.1	$2,307.4
Provision for income taxes	275.7	237.3	183.4	670.0	693.0	905.0	936.2	757.3
Income before cumulative effect of accounting changes	$547.4	$470.9	$364.2	$992.0	$1,637.0	$1,977.0	$1,947.9	$1,550.1
Cumulative effect of accounting changes, net of tax benefits of $9.4 and $17.6	—	—	(36.8)	(99.0)	—	—	—	—
Net income	$547.4	$470.9	$327.4	$893.0	$1,637.0	$1,977.0	$1,947.9	$1,550.1
Per common share								
Income before cumulative effect of accounting changes	$0.43	$0.37	$0.29	$0.78	$1.27	$1.49	$1.44	$1.14
Cumulative effect of accounting changes	—	—	(0.03)	(0.08)	—	—	—	—
Net income	$0.43	$0.37	$0.26	$0.70	$1.27	$1.49	$1.44	$1.14
Per common share—diluted								
Income before cumulative effect of accounting changes	$0.43	$0.37	$0.29	$0.77	$1.25	$1.46	$1.39	$1.1
Cumulative effect of accounting changes	—	—	(0.03)	(0.07)	—	—	—	—
Net income	$0.43	$0.37	$0.26	$0.70	$1.25	$1.46	$1.39	$1.1
Dividends declared per common share	$0.40							
Weighted average shares	1,271.5	1,272.5	1,269.6	1,273.1	1,289.7	1,323.2	1,355.3	1,365.3
Weighted average shares—diluted	1,281.0	1,277.5	1,270.3	1,281.5	1,309.3	1,356.5	1,404.2	1,405.7

Source: Company reports.

exhibit 12 **McDonald's Condensed Consolidated Balance Sheets, 1998–2003 (in millions except per share data)**

	Q3 2003	Q2 2003	Q1 2003	2002	2001	2000	1999	1998
Assets								
Current assets								
Cash and equivalents	$ 647.4	$ 520.4	$ 488.0	$ 330.4	$ 418.1	$ 421.7	$ 419.5	$ 299.2
Accounts and notes receivable	703.0	807.1	816.7	855.3	881.9	796.5	708.1	609.4
Inventories, at cost, not in excess of market	116.2	111.5	103.7	111.7	105.5	99.3	82.7	77.3
Prepaid expenses and other current assets	471.9	465.0	433.4	418.0	413.8	344.9	362.0	323.5
Total current assets	$ 1,938.5	$ 1,904.0	$ 1,841.8	$ 1,715.4	$ 1,819.3	$ 1,662.4	$ 1,572.3	$ 1,309.4
Other assets								
Investments in and advances to affiliates	$ 1,092.2	$ 1,036.4	$ 1,050.7	$ 1,037.7	$ 990.2	$ 824.2	$ 1,002.2	$ 854.1
Goodwill, net	1,763.6	1,717.6	1,652.0	1,559.8	1,320.4	1,443.4	1,261.8	973.1
Miscellaneous	1,041.2	1,102.8	1,048.7	1,074.2	1,115.1	705.9	822.4	606.2
Total other assets	$ 3,897.0	$ 3,856.8	$ 3,751.4	$ 3,671.7	$ 3,425.7	$ 2,973.5	$ 3,086.4	$ 2,433.4
Property and equipment								
Property and equipment, at cost	$27,884.2	$27,586.5	$26,689.8	$26,218.6	$24,106.0	$23,569.0	$22,450.8	$21,758.0
Accumulated depreciation and amortization	(8,485.6)	(8,254.4)	(7,873.1)	(7,635.2)	(6,816.5)	(6,521.4)	(6,126.3)	(5,716.4)
Net property and equipment	$19,398.6	$19,332.1	$18,816.7	$18,583.4	$17,289.5	$17,047.6	$16,324.5	$16,041.6
Total assets	$25,234.1	$25,092.9	$24,409.9	$23,970.5	$22,534.5	$21,683.5	$20,983.2	$19,784.4
Liabilities and shareholders' equity								
Current liabilities								
Notes and accounts payable	$ 507.0	$ 533.4	$ 488.0	$ 0.3	$ 184.9	$ 960.4	$ 1,658.8	$ 1,308.1
Dividends payable	508.0	—	—	635.8	689.5	—	—	—
Income taxes	125.1	113.0	100.7	16.3	20.4	92.2	117.2	94.2
Other taxes	209.0	212.3	194.4	191.8	180.4	195.5	160.1	143.5
Accrued interest	172.4	189.9	197.0	199.4	170.6	149.9	131.4	132.3

(continued)

exhibit 12 **(concluded)**

	Q3 2003	Q2 2003	Q1 2003	2002	2001	2000	1999	1998
Accrued restructuring and restaurant closing costs	152.5	202.8	241.6	328.5	144.2	—	—	—
Accrued payroll and other liabilities	843.6	772.6	782.7	774.7	680.7	608.4	660.0	651.0
Current maturities of long-term debt	115.8	406.9	319.1	275.5	177.6	354.5	546.8	168.0
Total current liabilities	$ 2,633.4	$ 2,430.9	$ 2,323.5	$ 2,422.3	$ 2,248.3	$ 2,360.9	$ 3,274.3	$ 2,497.1
Long-term debt	$ 9,291.7	$ 9,447.1	$ 9,686.9	$ 9,703.6	$ 8,555.5	$ 7,843.9	$ 5,632.4	$ 6,188.6
Other long-term liabilities and minority interests	668.0	620.7	598.1	560.0	629.3	489.5	538.4	492.6
Deferred income taxes	992.4	930.2	979.7	1,003.7	1,112.2	1,084.9	1,173.6	1,081.9
Shareholders' equity								
Common stock, $01 par value; authorized—3.5 billion issued—1,660.6 million	$16.6	$16.6	$16.6	$16.6	$ 16.6	$ 16.6	$ 16.6	$ 16.6
Additional paid-in capital	$ 1,808.4	$ 1,787.6	$ 1,775.5	$ 1,747.3	$ 1,591.2	$ 1,441.8	$ 1,288.3	$ 989.2
Unearned ESOP compensation	(97.9)	(98.1)	(98.2)	(98.4)	(106.7)	(115.0)	(133.3)	(148.7)
Retained earnings	20,043.3	20,003.5	19,532.3	19,204.4	18,608.3	17,259.4	15,562.8	13,879.6
Accumulated other comprehensive income (loss)	(1,018.7)	(1,067.3)	(1,442.5)	(1,601.3)	(1,708.8)	(1,287.3)	(886.8)	(522.5)
Common stock in treasury, at cost; 391.5 and 392.4 million	(9,103.1)	(8,978.3)	(8,962.0)	(8,987.7)	(8,912.2)	(8,111.1)	(6,208.5)	(4,749.5)
Total shareholders' equity	$11,648.6	$11,664.0	$10,821.7	$10,280.9	$ 9,488.4	$ 9,204.4	$ 9,639.1	$ 9,464.7
Total liabilities and shareholders' equity	$25,234.1	$25,092.9	$24,409.9	$23,970.5	$22,534.5	$21,683.5	$20,983.2	$19,784.4

Source: Company reports.

exhibit 13   **McDonald's Revenues and Operating Income by Segment, 2002–2003 (in millions)**

	Q3 2003	Q2 2003	Q1 2003	2002	2001	2000
Revenues						
United States	$1,593.5	$1,551.0	$1,316.1	$ 5,422.7	$ 5,395.6	$ 5,259.1
Europe	1,525.4	1,463.3	1,302.5	5,136.0	4,751.8	4,753.9
Asia/Pacific, Middle East and Africa	659.3	570.8	581.7	2,367.7	2,203.3	2,101.8
Latin America	221.3	212.7	186.4	813.9	971.3	949.3
Canada	213.8	196.7	151.1	633.6	608.1	615.1
Partner brands	291.3	286.3	261.9	1,031.8	939.9	563.8
Total	$4,504.6	$4,280.8	$3,799.7	$15,405.7	$14,870.0	$14,243.0
Operating income (loss)						
United States	$ 571.0	$ 503.3	$ 405.7	$ 1,673.3	$ 1,622.5	$ 1,795.7
Europe	382.6	329.8	268.4	1,021.8	1,063.2	1,180.1
Asia/Pacific, Middle East and Africa	91.4	47.9	69.4	64.3	325.0	451.2
Latin America	−20.2	2.8	2.2	−133.4	10.9	102.3
Canada	47.3	40.9	26.2	125.4	123.7	126.3
Partner brands	−0.2	−10.3	−12.9	−66.8	−66.5	−41.5
Corporate	−108.0	−88.2	−84.4	−571.7	−381.8	−284.4
Total	$ 963.9	$ 826.2	$ 674.6	$ 2,112.9	$ 2,697.0	$ 3,329.7

Source: Company reports.

exhibit 14   **McDonald's Operating Margins by Segment, 2000–2003**

	Q3 2003	Q2 2003	Q1 2003	2002	2001	2000
Company-operated						
United States	18.6%	18.5%	14.5%	15.9%	16.8%	17.0%
Europe	17.0	15.6	13.8	11.3	12.4	18.3
Asia/Pacific, Middle East and Africa	12.2	7.5	9.7	9.4	10.1	15.9
Latin America	5.7	8.0	7.8	13.7	15.6	12.4
Canada	17.1	14.4	10.9	14.4	15.1	15.4
Franchised						
United States	80.4%	80.5%	77.2%	76.7%	77.2%	78.3%
Europe	77.4	75.7	74.1	85.8	86.2	81.5
Asia/Pacific, Middle East and Africa	86.7	84.4	83.8	66.9	68.4	73.0
Latin America	64.7	64.0	66.0	79.2	80.4	80.2
Canada	79.3	78.8	75.8	78.5	79.1	79.5

Source: Company reports.

Maple Leaf Consumer Foods— Fixing Hot Dogs

Allen Morrison
The University of Western Ontario

Kelly Gervin hardly had the chance to get things straightened around in her new office. It was June 5, 2001, and Gervin had been the senior marketing director of the packaged meats group in the consumer foods division of Maple Leaf Foods (MLF) for all of four hours. She was still unpacking boxes in her office when the division's vice-president of marketing, Pat Jacobs, came flying in. He tossed a pile of papers on her desk (see Exhibits 2 to 7).

> Kelly . . . these reports I received this morning are scary. We have a serious problem in our hot dog business. Of our nine hot dog brands, five are losing significant market share and another one is down marginally. We've lost as much as 45 percent relative to last year in one category . . . and that's just the start of it! Kelly, I need you to figure out what is going on and solve this problem, and I need you to do it quickly.

Ivey

Richard Ivey School of Business
The University of Western Ontario

Scott Hill prepared this case under the supervision of Professor Allen Morrison solely to provide material for class discussion. The authors do not intend to illustrate either effective or ineffective handling of a managerial situation. The authors may have disguised certain names and other identifying information to protect confidentiality.

MAPLE LEAF FOODS

The MLF brand had been around in Canada for over 100 years. The organization had grown and evolved out of a number of mergers and amalgamations, but its origins could be traced as far back as 1836 when Grantham Mills opened a flour production and distribution facility in St. Catharines, Ontario. In 1991, U.K.-based Hillsdown Holdings PLC amalgamated with MLF through the purchase and merger of Canada Packers and Maple Leaf Mills. In 1995, McCain Capital Corporation and the Ontario Teachers' Pension Plan Board came together to acquire controlling interest of MLF. Between 1995 and 2001, new systems were introduced, operations streamlined, and several new acquisitions were completed.

By 2001, MLF was Canada's largest and most dominant food processor, generating nearly $4.8 billion in annual sales. The MLF organization and its products were also gaining significant momentum on the international scene. The company's operations focused on three core areas of business: bakery products, meat products and agribusiness. Each core business was composed of several independent operating companies (IOCs) and each IOC was run by a president who controlled the overall profitability and competitive strategy of the business. Under the direction of MLF chief executive officer (CEO), Michael McCain, IOCs were encouraged to follow a common set of values and strategic principles that emphasized the importance of brand equity, operating efficiencies, market leadership, and continuous improvement (see Exhibit 1).

exhibit 1   **Maple Leaf Foods Core 7 Principles**

Maple Leaf Foods' broad strategic direction is shaped by the Core 7 strategic principles. Continuously evolving, these seven principles are strongly grounded in the Maple Leaf culture and provide the guiding framework for the planning and execution of the company's corporate and competitive strategies.

1. Build high potential leadership.
2. Focus on markets and categories where we can lead.
3. Develop brand equity.
4. Create customer value with Six Sigma processes and products.
5. Be the lowest cost producer.
6. Execute with precision and continuous improvement.
7. Think global.

Source: Company files.

exhibit 2   **Canadian Market Share Analysis (as at June 5, 2001)**

Company	Latest 52 Weeks			
	Share in Weight	Share Point Change in Weight	$ Share	Share Point Change in $
MLF	19.3	−1.6	22.9	−2.1
Hub Larsen	5.0	−0.1	4.0	0.0
JM Schneider	22.6	2.7	28.2	2.9
Fleetwood	1.4	0.2	2.2	0.3
Freybe	0.8	0.2	1.5	0.3
Grimms	0.6	0.0	1.2	−0.1
Harvest	1.0	0.2	1.4	0.2
Fletchers	1.7	0.0	2.1	0.0
Lafleur	3.6	0.0	3.4	0.1
Lesters	0.4	−0.2	0.4	−0.1
Lilydale	0.2	−0.2	0.4	−0.1
Maple Lodge	4.2	−1.5	2.7	−0.7
Mitchells	3.9	0.8	5.0	1.1
Olymel	1.3	−0.2	1.3	−0.2
Control Label	32.3	−0.3	22.9	−0.2

Source: Company files.

The meat products group was by far the largest of the company's core groups, with 2000 sales of nearly $2.5 billion and EBITDA (earnings before interest, taxes, depreciation and amortization) of $26.5 million. The group consisted of all the company's meat and meat-related businesses and included four distinct IOCs: Maple Leaf Pork, Maple Leaf Poultry, Maple Leaf International and Maple Leaf Consumer Foods. While each IOC operated independently, ef-

forts were under way in 2001 to optimize the vertical coordination of IOCs within the broader MLF organization.

The packaged meats division, in which Kelly Gervin worked, was part of the Consumer Foods IOC. Consumer Foods had full responsibility for the production and distribution of all branded and value-added prepared meat products. This included bacon, ham, hot dogs, cottage rolls, a wide variety of deli-

exhibit 3   **Maple Leaf Foods Hot Dog Product Line (Segmentation)**

	Family (Wieners)	Adult (Franks & Sausages)
Premium (>$3.50)	• Top Dogs Singles (450g)	
Mainstream ($2.50 to $3.50)	• Top Dogs (Reg. & BBQ)	• Maple Leaf 100's
	• Lean 'n Lite (Reg. & Beef)	• Overlander
	• Beef Dogs	• Shopsy's Original Recipe
	• Shopsy's Beef	
Value ($1.89 to $2.50)	• Maple Leaf Original (& BBQ)	
	• Burns (Reg., Beef, & 6+6)	
	• Hygrade (Reg. & Beef)	
	• Shopsy's (Reg. & BBQ)	
Economy (<$1.89)	• Control Label	

Source: Company files.

exhibit 4   **Canadian Hot Dog Market Review (as of June 5, 2001)**

	Total	Family	Adult
Last 52 weeks	Category: +2.5%	Category: +0.7%	Category: +11.2%
	ML: −5.0%	ML: +0.7%	ML: −44.8%
	JMS: +18.2%	JMS: +14.5%	JMS: +35%
Last 12 weeks	Category: +3.2%	Category: +2.6%	Category: +1.0%
	ML: −8.8%	ML: −4.9%	ML: −38.4%
	JMS: +9.6%	JMS: +10.0%	JMS: +15.5%
Last 4 weeks	Category: +4.0%	Category: +3.1%	Category: −1.0%
	ML: −9.3%	ML: −6.5%	ML: −30.5%
	JMS: +10.4%	JMS: +10.6%	JMS: +16.4%

Source: Company files.

catessen products, prepared turkey products, sliced meats, cooked sausage products, frozen entrees, lard and canned meats. In 2000, Consumer Foods generated in excess of half a billion dollars in sales representing over 10 percent of MLF's overall revenues.

Excluding commodities, the MLF hot dog portfolio of products was by far the largest meat category at MLF Consumer Foods with over twice the dollar sales of any other MLF branded, value-added, or prepared meat category within the IOC. The MLF organization had been acquiring expertise in the production and distribution of hot dogs for nearly 75 years. The organization first entered the hot dog business when Canada Packers began producing hot dogs in 1927. At that time, hot dog and sausage pro-

duction was seen as a financially viable method to dispose of beef, pork, and chicken trimmings. It was this profitable opportunity to use up raw material—in combination with the increasing momentum the hot dog was gaining as a cultural icon in the marketplace—that traditionally drove the business.

In 2000, total MLF hot dog sales were approximately $50 million. Industry professionals used both dollar sales and volume by weight to measure sales performance, and these sales correlated with a total of approximately 10.5 million kilograms of hot dogs sold. In the preceding year, total MLF hot dog sales were also approximately $50 million, but volume by weight had actually been approximately 11.2 million kilograms. In Gervin's words, "Our average price per

exhibit 5   **Current Brand Share (as of June 5, 2001)**

	1998 Volume	Share	1999 Volume	Volume Variance to PY	National Share	Share Variance to PY	2000 Volume
Burns	1,071,903	1.7	1,033,266	−4%	1.5	−0.2	810,295
Hygrade	2,065,039	4.6	2,171,784	5	4.6	0	2,449,504
Lean 'n Lite	588,071	1.1	597,365	2	1.2	0.1	448,795
ML Reg./BBQ	2,917,099	4.9	2,512,953	−14	3.8	−1.1	2,087,457
ML Beef	932,830	1.7	868,634	−7	1.3	−0.4	798,928
Top Dogs		0	1,467,889		2.6	2.6	1,199,268
ML 100's	1,019,974	2.4	1,139,581	12	2.4	0	710,382
Top Dogs Singles		0			0		123,572
Overlander	394,373	0.9	470,076	19	1	0.1	416,278
Shopsys	2,058,655	3.7	2,230,319	8	3.5	−0.2	2,154,001
Total	11,047,944	21.4	12,491,867	13%	22.1	0.7	11,198,480

PY = prior year

Source: Latest 52 weeks, June 2001.

kilo was going up, but there was no question we were selling less. We were losing market share and this became our primary concern."

THE HOT DOG INDUSTRY

A good deal of disagreement exists over the origin of the hot dog. People in Frankfurt, Germany, claim they discovered the hot dog in 1487. Others argue that it was Johan Georghehner, a butcher from Coburg who travelled to Frankfurt to promote this product—which he called the "dachshund" because of its shape—in the late 1600s. Others in Vienna point to the name "wiener" as evidence of the product's Austrian roots.

In the United States, the origins of the hot dog industry can be traced to the arrival of a German immigrant by the name of Charles Feltman who opened up the first Coney Island hot dog stand in 1871. In 1893, Chris Ahe, the owner of the St. Louis Browns baseball team, started selling hot dogs in his ball park. This laid the groundwork for what would become an inseparable connection between hot dogs and the game of baseball.

The actual phrase "hot dog" was coined in 1901. It all started on a cold April day in New York City when concessionaire Harry Stevens became frus-

trated with losing money selling ice cream and soda. He ordered his assistant to go out and buy all the long, skinny sausages he could find and to sell them from portable hot-water tanks while yelling "get your red hot dachshund while they last!" Sports cartoonist Ted Dorgan became quite amused with the scene, and did a cartoon strip on it. When he had trouble spelling "dachshund," he substituted the term "dog," and the rest, as they say, is history.

The Industry Today

At the aggregate level, per capita demand for hot dogs was slightly higher in the United States than in Canada. In 2000, consumers in the United States spent nearly $1.7 billion on hot dogs in retail outlets. The average U.S. household purchased 7.65 pounds of hot dogs annually which translated to about 65 hot dogs per person per year. In 2000, total Canadian hot dog market sales were just over $220 million, which represented approximately 52.5 million kilograms of hot dogs. This translated into an annual consumption rate of about 52 hot dogs per person in Canada. Sixty-four percent of hot dogs sold in Canada were pork and meat combinations, 24 percent were all-beef hot dogs, and 12 percent were made from poultry.

Demand for hot dogs was consistently strongest during the summer months. Since the turn of the

Volume Variance to PY	National Share	Share Variance to PY	2001 LE Volume	Volume Variance to PY	National Share	Regional Share	National Share Variance to PY
−22%	1.1	(0.4)	711,491	(0.1)	0.9	3.8	−28%
13	5.1	0.5	2,630,840	0.1	5.0	22.5	16
−25	0.9	(0.3)	328,384	(0.3)	0.6		−24
−17	3.7	(0.1)	2,291,438	0.1	3.9		−1
−8	1.5	0.2	687,283	(0.1)	1.2		−7
−18	2.6	—	1,243,616	0.0	2.2		−6
−38	1.5	(0.9)	600,205	(0.2)	1.0		−45
	0.2	0.2	215,655	0.8	0.3		N/A
−11	0.8	(0.2)	365,957	(0.1)	0.6	2.9	−28
−3	3.7	0.2	2,255,999	0.1	3.5	9.2	6
−10%	20.9	(0.8)	11,330,868	0.0	19.3		−5%

century, hot dogs in buns at baseball games, summer picnics, backyard barbecues, and roadside diners had become a tradition in North American culture. Hot dog sales from May to August represented more than 44 percent of the annual total, with July—National Hot Dog Month in the United States—leading the pack. In both Canada and the United States, hot dogs were popular at barbecues and entertainment events. Four hot dogs were consumed for every 10 baseball tickets sold, so it was projected that there would be more than 26 million hot dogs consumed in major league ballparks in 2001.

Hot dog consumption preferences were subject to significant regional differences in Canada. Western Canadian consumers had the strongest demand in Canada for beef hot dogs. The Quebec market was partial to hot dogs in a specific (lower) price segment, due to the influence of "steamies" or "toasties"—hot dogs that were prepared using unique cooking methods. (In this market, lower priced hot dogs were considered adequate since any hot dog could be prepared in the preferred manner.) Atlantic Canada had the largest per capita consumer of low-fat hot dogs, due in part to the higher average age of the population versus other parts of Canada.

Hot dog consumption was consistently uniform throughout all income levels. Wealthy and low-income Canadians appeared to consume approximately the same volume of hot dogs on an annual basis. Larger families with five or more members tended to eat larger numbers of hot dogs, as did younger families where heads of households were under the age of 35. Children were heavy influencers in hot dog purchase decisions.

Despite their broad consumption, hot dogs had always been subject to considerable consumer scrutiny concerning their content and manufacture. For some time, consumers had been concerned about the presence of "mystery" meat in hot dogs. Both the Canadian and U.S. Departments of Agriculture required by law that meats used in hot dogs include only muscle meat. In addition to meeting this requirement, there was a movement in the industry to introduce all-meat, by-product-free hot dogs.

Competitive Landscape

In 2001, the competitive landscape of the hot dog industry in Canada was dominated by two organizations: MLF and Schneider Foods (JMS). Each had over 20 percent share of the national market (see Exhibit 2). Other competitors were relatively small (less than one-quarter the size of MLF and JMS) and were regionally focused.

Based in Kitchener, Ontario, JMS had over 110 years of experience in producing and distributing

exhibit 6 **Maple Leaf Consumer Foods: Hot Dog Margins**

	Projected 2001	Actual 2000
Hot dog margins by category		
Regular	$0.44	$0.56
Adult	0.16	0.37
Beef	0.24	0.27
Better for You	0.60	0.75
Average	$0.38	$0.59
Hot dog margins by brand		
Maple Leaf Regular	$0.71	$0.92
Maple Leaf 100%'s	0.31	0.47
Maple Leaf Beef Dogs	0.10	0.27
Lean 'n Lite	0.35	0.33
Top Dogs	0.60	0.78
Overlander	(0.14)	0.20
Hygrade	0.23	0.20
Burns	(0.14)	0.23
Shopsy's	0.43	0.50
Average	$0.39	$0.49

meat products throughout the Canadian marketplace. JMS also had a reputation as a tough competitor; it fought for every inch of shelf space and was tactically reactive and retaliatory. It also knew the hot dog business well and had loyal employees.

In June of 2001, JMS led the industry, possessing over 28 percent of the dollar share of the hot dog market in Canada. The company was not only the largest hot dog producer in Canada, it was the fastest growing. Between mid-2000 and mid-2001, JMS's dollar sales increased by nearly 3 percent; in contrast, MLF's overall sales declined by just over 2 percent. JMS had strong national brands that it supported with consistently effective promotional campaigns. It was also very aggressive on pricing. While MLF raised hot dog prices in both 2000 and 2001, JMS held firm to its prices and picked up market share.

In assessing JMS's performance in the Canadian hot dog market, one MLF insider commented:

> Schneider has done a great job of managing its product line from a quality perspective and overall consistency. It has done very little to its hot dog product line over the years. It has not proliferated sub-brands as we did. It did not change packaging on a regular basis as we did. It has also had great consistency in its sales

and marketing staff—as we did not. Also, Schneider has done a great job managing its trade relations.

Consumers consistently tell us that JMS means quality, heritage, and great-tasting products. This is something that Consumer Foods has to overcome!

Hot Dog Segmentation

For marketing purposes, MLF segmented the hot dog market in two ways: (1) by target consumer (adult or family), and (2) by price (premium, mainstream, and value/economy). While there were plenty of small niche players, both JMS and MLF competed in all major hot dog markets in Canada.

Target Segment   The adult segment consisted of franks and sausages. Franks had a larger diameter, slightly more course emulsion (meat blend), larger particle definition, and more spices than wieners. Also, franks were at least six inches long and by weight were usually about six per pound (2.5 ounces each). Sausages were curved and by weight were three to five per pound (three to five ounces each). Unlike franks, which were always sold precooked, sausages could be sold either uncooked or precooked. In 2001, the adult segment was growing at a rate of about 11 percent industrywide, but this segment still represented approximately only 16 percent of the total hot dog industry. In the adult segment, MLF's brands included ML 100s, Overlander, and Shopsy's Original Recipe. JMS's primary adult segment hot dog was Juicy Jumbos.

Products targeted towards the family segment were called wieners and represented 84 percent of overall industry sales. Wieners were also six inches long but had a finer emulsion than franks and by weight were generally about 12 per pound (1.3 ounces each). Across the industry, the family segment was growing at a rate of about 2 percent per year. Industry observers believed that, increasingly, consumers were trading up towards adult categories. In the family segment, JMS offered Red Hots (in Ontario) and an identical product simply called "Wieners" for the rest of Canada. MLF's brands in the family segment included Top Dogs (Regular and BBQ), Lean 'n Lite (Regular and All-Beef), Beef Dogs, and Shopsy's Beef.

Price Segment   Premium hot dogs sold at a price point greater than $3.50 per pound and contained franks and sausages. In addition, Maple Leaf

exhibit 7 **TL Wieners—National Tonnage Trends**

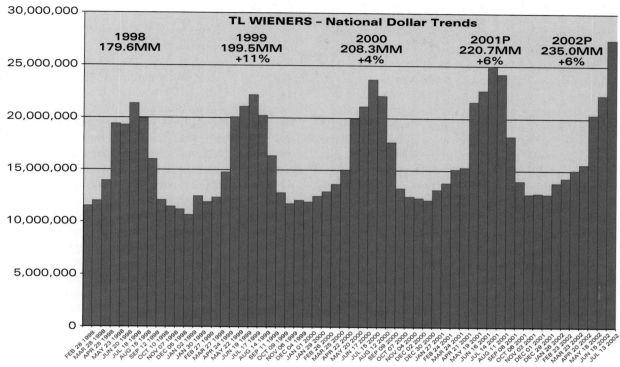

Source: Company files.

competed in this segment with Top Dogs Singles, which were premium priced to reflect the quality of their ingredients and high packaging and high labor costs. Mainstream hot dogs were the largest price segment and included all hot dogs priced between $2.50 and $3.50. MLF's Top Dogs, Lean 'n Lite, Beef Dogs, and Shopsy's Beef fit into this segment. Hot dogs in the value segment sold for between $1.89 and $2.50 per pound. MLF's products in this segment included Maple Leaf Original (Regular and Beef), Burns (Regular, Beef, and 6+6), Hygrade (Regular and Beef), and Shopsy's (Regular and BBQ). Wieners in the economy segment were priced under $1.89 per pound; MLF produced several retail brands in this segment including No-Name and Smart Choice. JMS's Red Hots and Wieners were both considered mainstream hot dogs. However, during 2001, both products were heavily discounted (to $1.99), which gave them about a 10 percent to 20 percent price advantage over MLF's value-priced products.

MLF'S CURRENT BRAND STRATEGY

In mid-2001, MLF had nine different brands competing in the Canadian marketplace. Exhibit 3 summarizes the positioning of each of the Maple Leaf hot dog brands. While MLF had strong regional brands, none of the company's brands had a strong national presence. Instead, Shopsy's brands were sold only in Ontario, Burns and Overlander brands competed only in Western Canada, and Hygrade was distributed only in Quebec.

For some time, MLF had emphasized different brands for different geographic regions within Canada. This development had resulted in strong brand equity in each of Canada's major regions. The Burns brand was strong in Western Canada. In the late 1990s, Burns lost substantial market share due to a cost-plus pricing structure which drove prices substantially higher than key competitors. MLF had recently fixed the pricing formula and had moved to reduce production costs, thereby stabilizing the brand. The Hygrade brand was a leader in the Quebec hot dog marketplace, possessing a 25 percent share in that province (8 percent nationally). The Shopsy's brand boasted an 8 percent market share in Ontario (2 percent nationally). All MLF hot dog products were produced at the company's manufacturing facility in Stoney Creek, Ontario. Despite brand distinctions and minor taste differences, there were essentially no major differences in the hot dog products within each price segment. At MLF, the senior marketing director did not have direct authority over or responsibility for manufacturing.

When interviewing for her current position, Gervin had asked about the origins of regional hot dog branding at MLF. To her surprise, no one in MLF could fully explain why the company had so many regional brands. Some believed it was the result of the company's numerous mergers and acquisitions and the desire to preserve the strength in each new brand that was acquired. Others felt the brand differences could be traced to the different consumer preferences in each region. Notwithstanding these explanations, one of the first things that Gervin noticed about the MLF hot dog portfolio was that often as many as six different MLF brands competed for shelf space in any given retail outlet at the same time.

In 1994, MLF launched Lean 'n Lite brand hot dogs. The product was introduced in an effort to meet increasing consumer demands for low-fat food products. The initial launch was very successful and produced strong profit margins for the company. However, sales for Lean 'n Lite peaked in 1997, and between 1998 and 2001, sales dropped every year. Many at MLF believed that the decline was the result of growing consumer unwillingness to compromise taste for low fat. However, this belief had not been substantiated with market research. Furthermore, the company was familiar with national consumer research that showed that 70 percent of consumers were interested in low-fat products with acceptable taste.

In 1999, MLF introduced Top Dogs as a national hot dog. The launch was in response to consumer trends that seem to emphasize healthy and natural food products and ingredients. The all-meat product was designed to appeal to both children and parents and was initially launched with vitamins and protein added. Top Dogs were the first—and only—hot dogs sold in North America that were nutritionally enhanced. The product was launched with a value price of $1.99 per package and initial consumer demand was strong. However, in the summer of 2000, the price was increased to $2.49 and sales declined noticeably. The perception was that the new price alienated many price-sensitive shoppers. Also, during this period, the formulation for Top Dogs was altered several times in an attempt to lower per unit costs. The result was a product that was priced too high and that, in the minds of many consumers, lacked good taste. By June 2001, Top Dogs had captured just 2.8 percent of the national market (4.6 percent in Western Canada, 2.6 percent in Ontario, 2.3 percent in the Maritimes, and 1.7 percent in Quebec).

Based on the initial success of Top Dogs, MLF launched Beef Dogs in 2000. The launch was designed to replace the company's existing beef hot dog product called Maple Leaf All-Beef Hot Dogs. Beef Dogs were fortified with calcium and iron. Initial taste tests were positive. However, the product's formulation came under the scrutiny of the Canadian Food Inspection Agency (CFIA), which raised concerns over the sourcing of calcium for Beef Dogs. Beef Dogs were then reformulated to incorporate a new source of calcium. Several internal taste panels concluded that the newly reformulated Beef Dogs tasted chalky and somewhat artificial. By June 2001, Beef Dog sales were down 7 percent from 2000 levels.

Kelly Gervin

Kelly Gervin had a solid professional marketing management background. Prior to joining the MLF organization, Gervin had been North American director of marketing for Moulinex, a French appliance manufacturer. She had joined Moulinex after graduating from the University of Toronto with a bachelor of science degree in microbiology. She decided to leave Moulinex after it became apparent that her opportunities for professional growth were stagnating.

Gervin first applied for a job with MLF in 1996 in response to a newspaper advertisement. Always one to embrace a challenge, she jumped at the opportunity to join an organization she could grow with. She initially accepted the position of category manager within Consumer Foods and then spent five years in sales and 18 months in purchasing where she was presented with the opportunity to take over her current position as senior marketing director. Reporting directly to the vice-president of marketing, Gervin had responsibility for overseeing all marketing decisions (product, price,[1] promotions, packaging, and marketing communications strategies) for Maple Leaf's lines of hot dogs, sliced meats, and meat snack products. While success in all categories was critical, hot dogs represented by far the largest portion of the portfolio of products over which Gervin was responsible.

Recent Developments

From 1995 through 1999, MLF went through a period of reorganization of the meats business, refocusing on vertically coordinating both its pork and poultry protein value chains. By 2000, Consumer Foods had a new president and vice-president of marketing. The president, Rick Young, had built a very successful career in sales and general management while working within the Maple Leaf Companies. The vice-president, Pat Jacobs, had just arrived at Maple Leaf Consumer Foods, having built a marketing career in the packaged goods industry. During 2000, Young focused on strengthening the management team while Jacobs concentrated on organizing a strong marketing team. As 2001 approached, it was becoming clear to Young that the team was not coming together, and he began to pay increasing attention to the marketing operations. In 2001, Young came to the conclusion that marketing needed additional changes in leadership. It was through this decision that Gervin arrived in her new role.

In Gervin's mind, the market share reports that had come to Jacobs's attention unquestionably reflected the lack of stability in the packaged meats group. Although she knew MLF's hot dog business was struggling, she was hoping that additional market analysis and customer survey data would provide her with the information needed to make appropriate decisions. On her first morning as the new marketing director, she was troubled to find many of the data she needed were simply not available. During the late 1990s, considerable research had been carried out on brands culminating with the introduction of Top Dogs. But the individual who conducted this research had since been promoted and transferred

out of the IOC. The data were now a couple of years old and had not been updated. In addition, there was essentially no consumer research relating to what drove consumers to buy MLF's hot dog products.

In addition to segment sales numbers and market share data referred to by Jacobs, Gervin found two notes of interest. One was written by the previous marketing director, suggesting that his group had been working diligently to become the low-cost producer in the value segment. On this matter, Gervin did a couple of quick calculations and realized that they weren't even close to achieving this goal. The second document of interest was a handwritten note from an unidentified source that indicated growing concerns over recent losses in market share in the adult segment. That was it.

To complicate matters, the group did not seem to have a business plan. Being new to the team, Gervin was unsure of the backgrounds, skills, and commitments of her direct reports. Also, she could sense that morale was low—not surprising, given the recent declines in market share and changes in staff. Beyond the organizational concerns, MLF hot dogs were having real problems in the marketplace. Earlier in the morning, Gervin had placed a call to a major grocery retailer to get a sense of what that customer thought of MLF's hot dog products. The retailer was surprisingly cool to Gervin and offered the following observation: "MLF has an uncompetitive product portfolio. Quite frankly, some of your hot dogs taste lousy." Gervin had no idea whether these sentiments were shared across all of MLF's retail customers, whether this retailer was dissatisfied for other reasons, or whether the retailer was, in fact, satisfied but was playing games with her to win later concessions on price or service.

In organizing a business plan, Gervin knew that she would have to work within the constraints of the broader Consumer Foods organization. As senior marketing director, she had full profit and loss accountability for hot dogs. But others in the organization were also responsible for various determinants of profit. For example, the sales team in the field—account managers, directors, and the vice-president of sales for the IOC—were in part measured by hot dog profits. Manufacturing also had a stake in the game. So, while she was responsible for profits, people outside her direct control impacted how far she could go and whether her overall approach would succeed.

---

[1]Pricing responsibility also fell under Category Management, which set price in consultation with Gervin.

Decisions

As soon as Jacobs left her office, Gervin closed the door and put her phone on voice mail. She needed time to think. There was clearly good news and bad news in what she had learned on her first day on the job. The bad news was MLF's hot dog business was a mess in almost every sense of the word, and if not handled deftly, the business could go from bad to worse. The good news was that Gervin felt the business could be turned around and that it had huge up-side potential for growth and profitability. She knew this, and she believed that Jacobs and Young also believed in the huge up-side potential in hot dogs. Reversing the negative trends and moving MLF to a leadership position in the marketplace would have positive spill-over effects on the entire Consumer Foods product line and would almost certainly capture the attention of the broader MLF organization.

As the challenges of turning the hot dog business around were becoming more and more apparent, Gervin recognized the need for short-term "fixes" and a clear strategy for the future. She pulled out a pen and scratched down two questions: (1) Which hot dog segments do we most want to be in? and (2) How are we going to grow the business in these segments?

While these were simple questions, the answers would be much more difficult. As Gervin contemplated her next steps, additional questions came to mind. Should MLF even "make" hot dogs? Gervin was aware that an increasing number of companies like Nike, IBM, and Matsushita were contracting all or part of their manufacturing over to others. Should hot dogs be any different? She also wondered whether the fact that MLF was Canada's largest supplier of pork and poultry products should influence a decision on the composition of hot dogs and their overall positioning in the marketplace. Gervin was also uncertain how the positioning of hot dogs might influence other products manufactured and sold by Consumer Foods. For example, how might an emphasis on the value segment affect the sales of branded lunch meats? Finally, she wondered what role brands should play in growing hot dog sales in a chosen segment. Should she emphasize a national brand or brands, and if so, what impact might national branding have on existing regional brands?

The more Gervin thought about the challenges she faced, the more questions came to her mind. She had no idea how to answer them, but she knew that a number of senior executives were waiting to hear what she had to say.

Krispy Kreme Doughnuts, Inc.

Arthur A. Thompson
The University of Alabama

Amit J. Shah
Frostburg State University

We think we're the Stradivarius of doughnuts.
—Scott Livengood, president, chairman, and CEO

With 319 Krispy Kreme stores in 41 states, Krispy Kreme Doughnuts in 2003 continued to rapidly build something of a cult following for its light, warm, melt-in-your-mouth doughnuts. Sales in 2003 continued their impressive climb, exceeding 7.5 million doughnuts a day. The company's business model called for 20 percent annual revenue growth, mid-single-digit comparable-store sales growth, and 25 percent annual growth in earnings per share. In the third quarter of fiscal 2004, total company revenues rose by 31.4 percent, to $169.6 million compared with the $129.1 million in the third quarter of fiscal 2003. Net income increased by 43.4 percent, to $14.5 million, during the same period.

But a number of securities analysts doubted whether Krispy Kreme's strategy and growth potential would continue to push the company's stock price upward. Shares had already increased eightfold since the company went public in April 2000. In December 2003, Krispy Kreme stock was trading at a hefty 41 times the consensus earnings estimates for fiscal 2004, a price/earnings ratio that was "justified" only if the company continued to grow by 25 percent or more annually. According to one analyst, "The odds are against this stock for long-term success." Another commented, "I think the market is overly optimistic about the long-term opportunities of the growth of the doughnut business." A third said, "Single-product concepts only have so many

years to run." Indeed, restaurants with quick-service products presently had the slowest revenue growth of any restaurant type.

COMPANY BACKGROUND

In 1933, Vernon Rudolph bought a doughnut shop in Paducah, Kentucky, from Joe LeBeau. His purchase included the company's assets, goodwill, the Krispy Kreme name, and rights to a secret yeast-raised doughnut recipe that LeBeau had created in New Orleans years earlier. Several years thereafter, Rudolph and his partner, looking for a larger market, moved their operations to Nashville, Tennessee; other members of the Rudolph family joined the enterprise, opening doughnut shops in Charleston, West Virginia, and Atlanta, Georgia. The business consisted of producing, marketing, and delivering fresh-made doughnuts to local grocery stores. Then, during the summer of 1937, Rudolph decided to quit the family business and left Nashville, taking with him a 1936 Pontiac, $200 in cash, doughnut-making equipment, and the secret recipe; after some disappointing efforts to find another location, he settled on opening the first Krispy Kreme Doughnuts shop in Winston-Salem, North Carolina. Rudolph was drawn to Winston-Salem because the city was developing into a tobacco and textiles hub in the Southeast, and he thought a doughnut shop would make a good addition to the thriving local economy. Rudolph and his two partners, who accompanied him from Nashville, used their last

$25 to rent a building across from Salem College and Academy. With no money left to buy ingredients, Rudolph convinced a local grocer to lend them what they needed, promising payment once the first doughnuts were sold. To deliver the doughnuts, he took the backseat out of the 1936 Pontiac and installed a delivery rack. On July 13, 1937, the first Krispy Kreme doughnuts were made at Rudolph's new Winston-Salem shop and delivered to grocery retailers.

Soon afterward, people began stopping by the shop to ask if they could buy hot doughnuts. There were so many requests that Rudolph decided to cut a hole in the shop's wall so that he could sell doughnuts at retail to passersby. Krispy Kreme doughnuts proved highly popular in Winston-Salem, and Rudolph's shop prospered. By the late 1950s, Krispy Kreme had 29 shops in 12 states, with each shop having the capacity to produce 500 dozen doughnuts per hour.

In the early 1950s, Vernon Rudolph met Mike Harding, who was then selling powdered milk to bakeries. Rudolph was looking for someone to help grow the business, and Harding joined the company as a partner in 1954. Starting with six employees, the two began building an equipment department and a plant for blending doughnut mixes. They believed the key to Krispy Kreme's expansion was to have control over each step of the doughnut-making process and to be able to deliver hot doughnuts to customers as soon as they emerged from the frying and sugar-glazing process. In 1960, they decided to standardize all Krispy Kreme shops with a green roof, a red-glazed brick exterior, a viewing window inside, an overhead conveyor for doughnut production, and bar stools—creating a look that became Krispy Kreme's trademark during that era.

Harding focused on operations, while Rudolph concentrated on finding promising locations for new stores and getting bank financing to support expansion into other southeastern cities and towns. Harding became Krispy Kreme's president in 1958, and he became chief executive officer when Rudolph died in 1973. Under Rudolph and then Harding, Krispy Kreme's revenues grew from less than $1 million in 1954 to $58 million by the time Harding retired in 1974. Corporate headquarters remained in Winston-Salem.

In 1976, Beatrice Foods bought Krispy Kreme and proceeded to make a series of changes. The recipe was changed, and the company's script-lettered signs were altered to produce a more modern look. As customers reacted negatively to Beatrice's changes, business declined. A group of franchisees, led by Joseph McAleer, bought the company from Beatrice in 1982 in a $22 million leveraged buyout. The new owners quickly reinstated the original recipe and the original script-lettered signs. Sales rebounded, but with double-digit interest rates in the early 1980s, it took years to pay off the buyout debt, leaving little for expansion.

To grow revenues, the company relied mainly on franchising "associate" stores, opening a few new company-owned stores—all in the southeastern United States—and boosting store volume through off-premise sales. Associate stores operated under a 15-year licensing agreement that permitted them to use the Krispy Kreme system within a specific geographic territory. They paid royalties of 3 percent of on-premise sales and 1 percent of all other branded sales (to supermarkets, convenience stores, charitable organizations selling doughnuts for fund-raising projects, and other wholesale buyers); no royalties were paid on sales of unbranded or private-label doughnuts. The primary emphasis of the associate stores and many of the company stores was on wholesaling both Krispy Kreme doughnuts and private-label doughnuts to local groceries and supermarkets. Corporate revenues rose gradually to $117 million in 1989 and then flattened for the next six years.

New Leadership and a New Strategy

In the early 1990s, with interest rates falling and much of the buyout debt paid down, the company began experimenting cautiously with expanding under Scott Livengood, the company's newly appointed president and chief operating officer. Livengood, 48, joined Krispy Kreme's human relations department in 1978 three years after graduating from the University of North Carolina at Chapel Hill with a degree in industrial relations and a minor in psychology. Believing strongly in the company's product and long-term growth potential, he rose through the management ranks, becoming president and chief operating officer in 1992, a member of the board of directors in 1994, president and CEO in 1998, and president, CEO, and chairman of the board in 1999.

Shortly after becoming president in 1992, Livengood became increasingly concerned about stagnant sales and shortcomings in the company's strategy: "The model wasn't working for us. It was more about selling in wholesale channels and less about the brand." He and other Krispy Kreme executives, mindful of the thousands of "Krispy Kreme stories" told by passionate customers over the years, concluded that the emphasis on off-premise sales did not adequately capitalize on the enthusiasm and loyalty of customers for Krispy Kreme's doughnuts. A second shortcoming was that the company's exclusive focus on southeastern U.S. markets unnecessarily handcuffed efforts to leverage the company's brand equity and product quality in the rest of the U.S. doughnut market. The available data also indicated that the standard 7,000-plus-square-foot stores were uneconomic to operate in all but very high-volume locations.

By the mid-1990s, with fewer than 100 franchised and company-owned stores and corporate sales stuck in the $110–$120 million range for six years, company executives determined that it was time for a new strategy and aggressive expansion outside the Southeast. Beginning in 1996, Krispy Kreme began implementing a new strategy to reposition the company, shifting the focus from a wholesale bakery strategy to a specialty retail strategy that promoted sales at the company's own retail outlets and emphasized the "hot doughnut experience" so often stressed in customers' Krispy Kreme stories. Doughnut sizes were also increased. The second major part of the new strategy was to expand the number of stores nationally using both area franchisees and company-owned stores. In preparing to launch the strategy, the company tested several different store sizes, eventually concluding that stores in the 2,400- to 4,200-square-foot range were better suited for the company's market repositioning and expansion plans.

The franchising part of the strategy called for the company to license territories, usually defined by metropolitan statistical areas, to select franchisees with proven experience in multi-unit food operations. Franchisees were expected to be thoroughly familiar with the local area market they were to develop and also to have the capital and organizational capability to open a prescribed number of stores in their territory within a specified period. The minimum net worth requirement for franchise area developers was $750,000 per store or $5 million, whichever was greater. Area developers paid Krispy Kreme a franchise fee of $20,000 to $40,000 for each store they opened. They also were required to pay a 4.5 percent royalty fee on all sales and to contribute 1.0 percent of revenues to a company-administered advertising and public relations fund. Franchisees were expected to strictly adhere to high standards of quality and service.

By early 2000, the company had signed on 13 area developers operating 33 Krispy Kreme stores and committed to open another 130 stores in their territories within five years. In addition, the company was operating 61 stores under its own management. Sales had zoomed to $220 million, and profits were a record $6 million.

After a decision was made to take the company public in April 2000, Krispy Kreme spent much of late 1999 and early 2000 preparing for an initial public offering (IPO) of the company's stock. The old corporate structure, Krispy Kreme Doughnut Corporation, was merged into a new company, Krispy Kreme Doughnuts, Inc. The new company planned to use the proceeds from its IPO to remodel or relocate older company-owned stores, to repay debt, to make joint venture investments in franchised stores, and to expand its capacity to make doughnut mix.

The IPO of 3.45 million shares was oversubscribed at $21 per share, and when the stock began trading in April under the ticker symbol KREM, the price quickly rose. Krispy Kreme was the second-best-performing stock among all IPO offerings in the United States in 2000. The company's stock began trading on the New York Stock Exchange in May 2001 under the symbol KKD. Exhibit 1 shows the stock chart of KKD since the IPO.

Between early 2000 and early 2004, the company increased the number of Krispy Kreme stores from 144 to over 370, boosted doughnut sales from an average of 3 million a day to an average of 7.5 million a day, and began the process of expanding internationally—opening its first factory store in Europe, located in the world-renowned department store Harrods of Knightsbridge, London (with plans for another 25 stores in Britain and Ireland by 2008), and continuing expansion in Australia, Canada, and Mexico. In 2003, Krispy Kreme captured an estimated 21 percent of the market for packaged doughnut sales, compared with 6.4 percent in 2002.

exhibit 1 **Performance of Krispy Kreme's Stock Price, April 2000–December 2003**

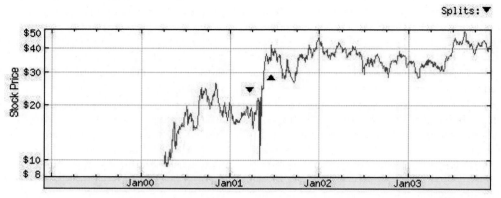

Source: www.finance.yahoo.com.

Exhibit 2 presents a summary of Krispy Kreme's financial performance and operations for fiscal years 1997–2003.

KRISPY KREME'S BUSINESS MODEL AND STRATEGY

Krispy Kreme's business model involved generating revenues and profits from three sources:

- Sales at company-owned stores.
- Royalties from franchised stores and franchise fees from new store openings.
- Sales of doughnut mixes, customized doughnut-making equipment, and coffees to franchised stores.

Exhibit 3 shows revenues, operating expenses, and operating income by business segment.

The company was drawn to franchising because it minimized capital requirements, provided an attractive royalty stream, and put responsibility for local store operations in the hands of successful franchisees who knew the ins and outs of operating multi-unit chains efficiently. Krispy Kreme had little

trouble attracting top-quality franchisees because of the attractive economics of its new stores (see Exhibit 4).

Krispy Kreme had developed a vertically integrated supply chain whereby it manufactured the mixes for its doughnuts at company plants in North Carolina and Illinois and also manufactured proprietary doughnut-making equipment for use in both company-owned and franchised stores. The sale of mixes and equipment, referred to as "KK manufacturing & distribution" by the company, generated a substantial fraction of both revenues and earnings (see again Exhibit 2).

Many of the stores built prior to 1997 were designed primarily as wholesale bakeries, and their formats and site locations differed considerably from the newer stores being located in high-density areas where there were lots of people and high traffic counts. In order to improve on-premise sales at these older stores, the company was implementing a program to either remodel them or close and relocate them to sites that could better attract on-premise sales. In new markets, the company's strategy was to focus initial efforts on on-premise sales at its stores and then leverage the interest generated in Krispy Kreme products to secure supermarket and convenience store accounts and grow packaged sales.

exhibit 2 **Summary of Krispy Kreme's Financial and Operating Performance, Fiscal Years 1997–2003 (in thousands, except per share data)**

	Fiscal Years Ending						
	Feb. 2, 1997	Feb. 1, 1998	Jan. 31, 1999	Jan. 30, 2000	Jan. 28, 2001	Feb. 3, 2002	Feb. 2, 2003
Statement of operations data							
Total revenues	$132,614	$158,743	$180,880	$220,243	$300,715	$394,354	$491,549
Operating expenses	116,658	140,207	159,941	190,003	250,690	316,946	381,489
General and administrative expenses	7,630	9,530	10,897	14,856	20,061	27,562	28,897
Depreciation and amortization expenses	3,189	3,586	4,278	4,546	6,457	7,959	12,271
Provision for restructuring	—	—	9,466	—	—	—	—
Income (loss) from operations	$ 5,137	$ 5,420	$ (3,702)	$ 10,838	$ 23,507	$ 41,887	$ 59,817
Interest expense, (income), net, and other	1,091	895	1,577	1,232	(1,698)	(2,408)	749
Income (loss) before income taxes	4,046	4,525	(5,279)	9,606	23,783	42,546	54,773
Provision (benefit) for income taxes	1,619	1,811	(2,112)	3,650	9,058	16,168	21,295
Net income (loss)	$ 2,427	$ 2,714	$ (3,167)	$ 5,956	$ 14,725	$ 26,378	$ 33,478
Net income (loss) per share:							
Basic	$ 0.17	$ 0.09	$ (0.09)	$ 0.16	$ 0.30	$ 0.49	$ 0.61
Diluted	$ 0.17	$ 0.09	$ (0.09)	$ 0.15	$ 0.27	$ 0.45	$ 0.56
Shares used in calculation of net income (loss) per share:							
Basic	14,568	29,136	32,996	37,360	49,184	53,703	55,093
Diluted	14,568	29,136	32,996	39,280	53,656	58,443	59,492
Cash dividends declared per common share	$ 0.08	$ 0.04	$ 0.04	—	—	—	—
Operating data							
Systemwide sales	$167,592	$203,439	$240,316	$318,854	$448,129	$621,665	$778,573
Number of stores at end of period							
Company-owned	61	58	61	58	63	75	99
Franchised	55	62	70	86	111	143	177
Systemwide total	116	120	131	144	174	218	276
Increase in comparable store sales							
Company-owned	n.a.	11.5%	11.1%	12.0%	22.9%	11.7%	12.8%
Franchised	n.a.	12.7%	9.7%	14.1%	17.1%	12.8%	11.8%

(continued)

exhibit 2 **(concluded)**

	Feb. 2, 1997	Feb. 1, 1998	Jan. 31, 1999	Jan. 30, 2000	Jan. 28, 2001	Feb. 3, 2002	Feb. 2, 2003
				Fiscal Years Ending			
Average weekly sales per store							
Company-owned	$39	$42	$47	$54	$69	$72	$76
Franchised	22	23	28	38	43	53	58
Balance sheet data							
Current assets	—	$ 25,792	$ 33,780	$ 41,038	$ 67,611	$101,769	$141,128
Current liabilities	—	16,641	25,672	29,586	38,168	52,533	59,687
Working capital	$ 10,148	9,151	8,108	11,452	29,443	49,236	81,441
Total assets	78,005	81,463	93,312	104,958	171,493	255,376	410,487
Long-term debt, including current maturities	20,187	20,870	21,020	22,902	—	4,643	60,489
Total shareholders' equity	$ 36,516	$ 38,265	$ 42,247	$ 47,755	$125,679	$187,667	$273,352
Cash flow data							
Net cash provided by operating activities	$ 2,652	$ 7,126	$ 11,682	$ 8,498	$ 32,112	$ 36,210	$ 51,036
Purchase of property and equipment	(9,592)	(6,708)	(12,376)	(11,335)	(25,655)	(37,310)	(83,196)
Proceeds from disposal of property and equipment	5,430	1,740	—	—	1,419	3,196	701
Net cash used for investing activities	(3,426)	(5,896)	(11,827)	(11,826)	(67,288)	(52,263)	(94,574)
Net proceeds from long-term borrowings	1,876	683	150	1,682	(19,375)	—	—
Proceeds from stock offering	—	—	4,619	—	65,637	17,202	—
Cash dividends paid	(1,159)	(1,173)	(1,180)	(1,518)	(7,005)	—	—
Net cash provided by (used for) financing activities	759	(456)	1,525	(398)	39,019	30,931	53,837
Cash and cash equivalents at end of year	2,158	2,933	4,313	3,183	7,026	21,904	32,203

Source: Company SEC filings and annual reports.

exhibit 3   **Krispy Kreme's Performance by Business Segment, Fiscal Years 1999–2003 (in thousands)**

	Fiscal Years Ending				
	Jan. 31, 1999	Jan. 30, 2000	Jan. 20, 2001	Feb. 3, 2002	Feb. 2, 2003
Revenues by business segment					
Company store operations	$145,251	$164,230	$213,677	$266,209	$319,592
Franchise operations	3,236	5,529	9,445	14,008	19,304
KK manufacturing and distribution	32,393	50,484	77,593	114,137	152,653
Total	$180,880	$220,243	$300,715	$394,354	$491,549
Operating expenses by business segment (excluding depreciation and amortization)					
Company store operations	$126,961	$142,925	$181,470	$217,419	$252,549
Franchise operations	2,731	4,012	3,642	4,896	4,877
KK manufacturing & distribution	27,913	43,066	65,578	94,631	124,088
Total	$157,605	$190,003	$250,690	$316,946	$381,489
Operating income by business segment (before depreciation and amortization)					
Company store operations	$ 18,290	$ 18,246	$ 27,370	$ 42,932	$ 58,214
Franchise operations	505	1,445	5,730	9,040	14,319
KK manufacturing & distribution	4,480	7,182	11,712	18,999	26,843
Unallocated general and administrative expenses	$ (12,020)	$ (16,035)	$ (21,305)	$ (29,084)	$ (30,484)
Total	$ 11,255	$ 10,838	$ 23,507	$ 41,887	$ 59,817
Depreciation and amortization expenses					
Company store operations	$ 2,873	$ 3,059	$ 4,838	$ 5,859	$ 8,854
Franchise operations	57	72	72	72	108
KK manufacturing & distribution	225	236	303	507	1,723
Corporate administration	1,123	1,179	1,244	1,521	1,586
Total	$ 4,278	$ 4,546	$ 6,457	$ 7,959	$ 12,271

Source: Company SEC filings and annual reports.

So far, the company had spent very little on advertising to introduce its product to new markets, relying instead on local media publicity, product giveaways, and word of mouth. In almost every instance, local newspapers had run big features headlining the opening of the first Krispy Kreme stores in their area; in some cases, local radio and TV stations had sent news crews to cover the opening and conduct on-the-scene interviews. The grand opening in Austin, Texas, was covered live by five TV crews and four radio station crews (there were 50 people in line at 11:30 PM the night before the 5:30 AM store opening). At the first San Diego store opening, there were five remote TV trucks on the scene; radio reporters were out interviewing customers camped out in their pickup trucks in the parking lot; and a nationally syndicated radio show broadcast "live" at the site. It was common for customers to form lines at the door and at the drive-through window well before the initial day's 5:30 AM grand opening, when the HOT DOUGHNUTS NOW sign was first turned on. In a number of instances, there were traffic jams at the turn in to the store—a Buffalo, New York, traffic cop said, "I've never seen anything like this . . . and I

exhibit 4   **Estimated Krispy Kreme Store Economics**

Store revenues	$3,600,000
Cash flow (after operating expenses)	960,000
Cash flow margin	27%
Owner's equity investment to construct store	$1,050,000
Cash flow return on equity investment	91%

Source: As estimated by Deutsche Banc Alex. Brown

mean it." As part of the grassroots marketing effort surrounding new-store openings, Krispy Kremes were typically given away at public events as a treat for participants—then, as one franchisee said, "the Krispy Kremes seem to work their own magic and people start to talk about them."

Krispy Kreme had originally financed its expansion strategy with the aid of long-term debt. However, the April 2000 IPO raised enough equity capital to completely pay off all long-term debt (see again Exhibit 2). When the company went public, it ceased paying dividends to shareholders; currently all earnings were being retained and reinvested in growing the business.

COMPANY OPERATIONS

Products and Product Quality

Krispy Kreme produced nearly 50 varieties of doughnuts, including specialty doughnuts offered at limited times and locations. By far the biggest seller was the company's signature "hot original glazed" doughnut made from Joe LeBeau's original yeast-based recipe. Exhibit 5 shows the company's doughnut varieties as of September 2003. Exhibit 6 indicates the nutritional content for a representative selection of Krispy Kreme doughnuts.

Company research indicated that Krispy Kreme's appeal extended across all major demographic groups, including age and income. Many customers purchased doughnuts by the dozen for their office, clubs, and family. According to one enthusiastic franchisee:

> We happen to think this is a very, very unique product which has what I can only describe as a one-of-a-kind taste. They are extremely light in weight and texture. They have this incredible glaze. When you have one

exhibit 5   **Varieties of Krispy Kreme Doughnuts**

- Original Glazed
- Chocolate Iced
- Chocolate Iced with Sprinkles
- Maple Iced
- Chocolate Iced Creme Filled
- Glazed Creme Filled
- Traditional Cake
- Apple Fritter
- Powdered Strawberry Filled
- Chocolate Iced Custard Filled
- Raspberry Filled
- Lemon Filled
- Cinnamon Apple Filled
- Powdered Blueberry Filled
- Chocolate Iced Cake
- Dulce de Leche
- Sugar Coated
- Glazed Cruller
- Powdered Cake
- Glazed Devil's Food
- Chocolate Iced Cruller
- Cinnamon Bun
- Glazed Blueberry
- Glazed Sour Cream
- Caramel Kreme Crunch

Source: www.krispykreme.com, September 22, 2003.

of the hot original doughnuts as they come off the line, there's just nothing like it.

In 2003, Krispy Kreme ranked number one in *Restaurants and Institutions'* Choice in Chains category, beating number-two-ranked Starbucks.

The company received several thousand e-mails and letters monthly from customers. By all accounts, most were from customers who were passionate about Krispy Kreme products, and there were always some from people pleading for stores to be opened in their area. Exhibit 7 presents sample comments from customers and franchisees. According to Scott Livengood:

> You have to possess nothing less than a passion for your product and your business because that's where you draw your energy. We have a great product . . . We have loyal customers, and we have great brand equity. When we meet people with a Krispy Kreme story, they always do it with a smile on their faces.

exhibit 6 **Nutritional Content of Selected Varieties of Krispy Kreme Doughnuts**

Product	Calories	Calories from Fat	Total Fat		Saturated Fat		Cholesterol (milligrams)	Sodium (milligrams)	Carbohydrates		Sugars (grams)
			Grams	% Daily Value*	Grams	% Daily Value*			Grams	% Daily Value*	
Original Glazed	200	110	12	18	3	15	5	95	22	7	10
Chocolate Iced Glazed	250	110	12	19	3	15	5	100	33	11	21
Maple Iced Glazed	240	110	12	18	3	15	5	100	32	11	20
Powdered Blueberry Filled	290	150	16	25	4	21	5	140	32	11	14
Chocolate Iced Creme Filled	350	190	21	32	5	25	5	140	39	13	23
Glazed Creme Filled	340	180	20	31	5	24	5	140	39	13	23
Traditional Cake	230	120	13	20	3	15	20	320	25	8	9
Glazed Cruller	240	130	14	22	3.5	17	15	240	26	9	14
Cinnamon Bun	260	140	16	24	4	20	5	125	28	9	13
Glazed Devil's Food	340	160	18	28	4.5	21	20	310	42	14	27

*Based on a 2,000-calorie diet.

Source: www.krispykreme.com, September 22, 2003.

exhibit 7   **Sample Comments from Krispy Kreme Customers and Franchisees**

Customer Comments:

- "I ate one and literally it brought a tear to my eye. I kid you not."
- "Oh my gosh, this is awesome. I wasn't even hungry, but now I'm going to get two dozen."
- "We got up at 3 o'clock this morning. I told them I would be late for work. I was going to the grand opening."
- "They melt in your mouth. They really do."
- "Krispy Kreme rocks."
- "It's hot, good and hot. The way a doughnut should be."
- "The doughnut's magnificent. A touch of genius."
- "I love doughnuts, but these are different. It's terrible for your weight because when you eat just one, you feel like you've barely tasted it. You want more. It's like popcorn."*
- "When you bite into one it's like biting into a sugary cloud. It's really fun to give one to someone who hasn't had one before. They bite into one and just exclaim."†

Franchisee Comments:

- "Krispy Kreme is a 'feel good' business as much as it is a doughnut business. Customers come in for an experience which makes them feel good—they enjoy our doughnuts and they enjoy the time they spend in our stores watching the doughnuts being made."
- "We're not selling doughnuts as much as we are creating an experience. The viewing window into the production room is a theater our customers can never get enough of. It's fun to watch doughnuts being made and even more fun to eat them when they're hot off the line."
- "Southern California customers have responded enthusiastically to Krispy Kreme. Many of our fans first came to Krispy Kreme not because of a previous taste experience but rather because of the 'buzz' around the brand. It was more word of mouth and publicity that brought them in to sample our doughnuts. Once they tried them, they became loyal fans who spread the word that Krispy Kreme is something special . . . We witness the excitement every day, especially when we're away from the store and wearing a hat or shirt with the Krispy Kreme logo. When people see the logo, we get the big smile and are always asked, 'When will we get one in our neighborhood?'. . . . The tremendous local publicity coupled with the amazing brand awareness nationwide has helped us make the community aware of our commitment to support local charities. Our fund-raising program, along with product donations to schools, churches, and other charitable organizations, has demonstrated our real desire to give back. This commitment also impacts our employees who understand firsthand the value of supporting the needy as well as the worthy causes in our neighborhoods."
- "In all my many years of owning and operating multiple food franchise businesses, we have never been able to please—until Krispy Kreme—such a wide range of customers in the community. It's like an old friend has come to town when we open our doors: we're welcomed with open arms. . . . Quite frankly, in my experience, publicity for Krispy Kreme is like nothing I have ever seen. It is truly unprecedented."
- "We happen to think this is a very, very unique product which has what I can only describe as a one-of-a-kind taste. They are extremely light in weight and texture. They have this incredible glaze. When you have one of the hot original doughnuts as they come off the line, there's just nothing like it."

*As quoted in "Winchell's Scrambles to Meet Krispy Kreme Challenge," *Los Angeles Times*, September 30, 1999, p. C1.
†As quoted in Greg Sukiennik, "Will Dunkin' Donuts Territory Take to Krispy Kreme?" The Associated Press State & Local Wire, April 8, 2001.
Source: Krispy Kreme's 2000 and 2001 annual reports, except for the two quotes noted above.

Coffee   Krispy Kreme had recently launched strategic initiatives to improve the caliber and appeal of its on-premise coffee and beverage offerings, aligning them more closely with the hot doughnut experience in its stores. The first move came in early 2001 when Krispy Kreme acquired Digital Java, Inc., a small Chicago-based coffee company that sourced and roasted premium quality coffees and that marketed a broad line of coffee-based and non-coffee beverages. Scott Livengood explained the reasons for the acquisition:

We believe the Krispy Kreme brand naturally extends to a coffee and beverage offering that is more closely aligned with the hot doughnut experience in our stores. Vertical integration of our coffee business provides the capability to control the sourcing and roasting of our coffee. Increasing control of our supply chain will help ensure quality standards, recipe formulation, and roast consistency. With this capability, one of our first priorities will be the research and benchmarking necessary to develop premier blends and roasts of coffee which will help make Krispy Kreme a coffee destination for a broader audience. Beyond coffee, we intend to offer a full line of beverages including espresso-based drinks and frozen beverages. We believe we can substantially increase the proportion of our business devoted to coffee specifically and beverages generally by upgrading and broadening our beverage offering.

Since the acquisition of Digital Java, coffee sales at Krispy Kreme stores had increased nearly 40 percent due to expanded product offerings and upgraded quality. In 2003, Krispy Kreme was marketing four types of coffee: Smooth, Rich, Bold, and Robust Decaf—all using coffee beans from the top 5 percent of the world's growing regions. Beverage sales accounted for about 10 percent of store sales, with coffee accounting for about half of the beverage total and the other half divided among milk, juices, soft drinks, and bottled water. In the years ahead, Krispy Kreme hoped to increase beverage sales to about 20 percent of store sales.

Store Operations

Each store was designed as a "doughnut theater" where customers could watch the doughnuts being made through a 40-foot glass window (see Exhibit 8). New stores ranged in size between 2,400 and 4,200 square feet. Stores had a drive-through window and a dining area that would seat 50 or more people—a few of the newer and larger stores had special rooms for hosting Krispy Kreme parties. Store décor was a vintage 1950s look with mint green walls and smooth metal chairs; some of the newest stores had booths (see Exhibit 9). A typical store employed about 125 people, including about 65 full-time positions. Approximately half of on-premise sales occurred in the morning hours and half in the afternoon and evening. Many stores were open 24 hours a day, with much of the doughnut making for off-premise sales being done between 6 PM and 6 AM. Production was nearly always under way during peak in-store traffic times. In several large metropolitan areas, however, the doughnut making for off-premise sales was done in a central commissary specially equipped for large-volume production, packaging, and local-area distribution.

Each doughnut took about one hour to make. After the ingredients were mixed into dough, the dough was rolled and cut. The pieces went into a 12-foot-tall machine where each piece rotated on a wire rack for 33 minutes under high humidity and a low heat of 126 degrees to allow the dough to rise. When the rising process was complete, the doughnuts moved along a conveyor to be fried on one side, flipped, fried on the other side, and drained. Following all this came inspection. Doughnuts destined to be glazed were directed through a waterfall of warm, sugary topping; the others were directed to another part of the baking section to be filled and/or frosted. Exhibit 8 depicts the mixing, rising, frying, draining, and glazing parts of the process. Depending on store size and location, a typical day's production ranged between 4,000 and 10,000 dozen doughnuts.

Each producing store featured a prominent HOT DOUGHNUTS NOW neon sign (see Exhibit 9) signaling customers that freshly made original glazed doughnuts were coming off the bakery conveyor belt and were available for immediate purchase. Generally, the signs glowed from 6 to 11 AM and then came on again during the late afternoon into the late-night hours.

Depending on the store location, Krispy Kreme's original glazed doughnuts sold for 60 to 75 cents each, or $4.29 to $5.25 per dozen; a mixed dozen usually sold for about 50 cents extra. Some stores charged a small premium for hot doughnuts coming right off the production line. Customers typically got a $1.00 per dozen discount on purchases of two or more dozen.

Stores generated revenues in three ways:

- On-premise sales of doughnuts.
- Sales of coffee and other beverages.
- Off-premise sales of branded and private-label doughnuts to local supermarkets, convenience stores, and fund-raising groups.

The company had developed a highly effective system for delivering fresh doughnuts, both packaged and unpackaged, to area supermarket chains and convenience stores. Route drivers had the capability to take customer orders and deliver products directly to retail accounts where they were typically merchandised either from Krispy Kreme branded displays or from bakery cases (as unbranded doughnuts). The popularity of Krispy Kreme's stores had prompted many area supermarkets to begin stocking a selection

exhibit 8 **Making the Doughnuts**

Mixing Ingredients   Rising   Frying and Flipping

Inspection and Draining   Drying and Entering Glazing

Exiting Glazing   Packaging

exhibit 9   **Representative Krispy Kreme Stores and Store Scenes**

of Krispy Kreme products in either branded display cases or in dozen and half-dozen packages. Krispy Kreme stores actively promoted sales to schools, churches, and civic groups for fund-raising drives.

The franchisee for Krispy Kreme stores in San Francisco had arranged to sell a four-pack of Krispy Kremes for $5 at San Francisco Giant baseball games at Pacific Bell Park—Krispy Kreme sold out of 2,100 packs by the third inning of the first game and, despite increasing supplies, sold out again after the fourth and sixth innings of the next two games; stadium vendors were supplied with 3,450 four-packs for the fourth game. The franchisee of the Las Vegas stores had a Web site that allowed customers to place orders online before 2 PM and have them delivered to their place of work by a courier service.

A Texas franchisee built a new 18,000-square-foot production and distribution center to supply Metroplex supermarkets, convenience stores, and other area retailers with Krispy Kreme 12-packs because newly opened local stores did not have the baking capacity to keep up with both on-premise and off-premise demand; there were similar franchiser-operated wholesale baking and distribution centers in Nashville, Cincinnati, Atlanta, Chicago, and Philadelphia. Several of these centers had established delivery capability to supply Krispy Kremes to retailers in outlying areas deemed too small to justify a stand-alone Krispy Kreme store.

The cost of opening a new store ranged from $1 to $2 million, depending on land costs and store size. In 2003, franchisees were required to build at least 10 stores in a specific market, and the initial franchise fee per unit was $40,000. Site selection was based on household density, proximity to both daytime employment and residential centers, and proximity to other retail traffic generators. Exhibit 10 shows data on store-opening activity. Agreements were in place for franchisees to open more than 250 new stores by 2006.

Performance of New Krispy Kreme Stores

In 2000, Krispy Kreme's first stores in 10 new geographic markets averaged $234,000 in sales the first week, attracting an average of more than 50,000 visitors and producing an average of 23,500 transactions. Sales in succeeding weeks averaged $93,400. First-week sales in new stores opened in existing marketplaces in 2000 averaged $150,000, with about 30,000 visitors—this compared favorably

with average opening-week sales of $123,000 in fiscal year 1999 and $85,600 in fiscal year 1998. Weekly sales at newly opened stores tended to moderate after several months of operation, but the company expected its newer stores to have annual sales averaging more than $3 million in their first year of operation—in fiscal 2003, sales at all of the company's 276 stores (which included those open less than a year) averaged $2.8 million.

The 2001 record opening-week revenue for a new Krispy Kreme store in a new market was $369,000. The store, located in Denver, grossed $1 million in revenues in its first 22 days of operation, commonly had lines running out the door with a one-hour wait for doughnuts, and, according to local newspaper reports, one night had 150 cars in line for the drive-through window at 1:30 AM. The 2002 opening-week sales record of $480,693 was set at the company's first Minnesota store, just outside of Minneapolis. In July 2003, the first store to open in the Massachusetts market—in Medford, outside Boston—had a record opening-day revenue of $73,813 and a record opening-week sales volume of $506,917. At the June 2003 opening of the company's first store in Australia, in the outskirts of Sydney, customers camped overnight in anticipation of the opening and others waited in line for hours to experience their first Krispy Kreme hot doughnut.

Krispy Kreme Manufacturing and Distribution

All the doughnut mix and equipment used in Krispy Kreme stores was manufactured and supplied by the company, partly as a means of ensuring consistent recipe quality and doughnut making throughout the chain and partly as a means of generating sales and profits from franchise operations. Revenues of the Krispy Kreme Manufacturing and Distribution (KKM&D) unit were 31.1 percent of total Krispy Kreme revenues, and operating income was $26,843,000 making KKM&D the second largest contributor to Krispy Kreme's overall operating income (see again Exhibit 3). The company's line of custom stainless-steel doughnut-making machines ranged in capacity from 230 to 600 dozen doughnuts per hour. The primary reason for the increase in revenues in 2003 was the opening of 49 new franchise stores. Increased doughnut sales also translated into

exhibit 10   **Store Openings, Closings, and Transfers, Fiscal Years 1998–2003**

	Company-Owned	Franchised	Total
Year ended February 1, 1998			
Beginning count	61	55	116
Opened	0	7	7
Closed	(2)	(1)	(3)
Transferred*	(1)	1	0
Ending count	58	62	120
Year ended January 31, 1999			
Beginning count	58	62	120
Opened	0	14	14
Closed	0	(3)	(3)
Transferred*	3	(3)	0
Ending count	61	70	131
Year ended January 30, 2000			
Beginning count	61	70	131
Opened	2	19	21
Closed	(5)	(3)	(8)
Transferred*	0	0	0
Ending count	58	86	144
Year ended January 28, 2001			
Beginning count	58	86	144
Opened	8	28	36
Closed	(3)	(3)	(6)
Transferred*	0	0	0
Ending count	63	111	174
Year ended February 3, 2002			
Beginning count	63	111	174
Opened	7	41	48
Closed	(2)	(2)	(4)
Transferred*	7	(7)	—
Ending count	75	143	218
Year ended February 2, 2003			
Beginning count	75	143	218
Opened	14	49	63
Closed	(3)	(2)	(5)
Transferred*	13	(13)	—
Ending count	99	177	276

*Transferred stores represent stores sold between the company and franchisees.

(continued)

exhibit 10 **(concluded)**

New Stores in New Markets, 2003		New Stores in Existing Markets, 2003	
Clearwater, FL	San Antonio, TX	Los Angeles, CA	Rochester, NY
Minneapolis, MN	Milford, CT	San Diego, CA	Greensboro, NC
Lafayette, LA	Springfield, MO	San Francisco, CA	Cincinnati, OH
Colorado Springs, CO	Amarillo, TX	Melbourne, FL	Oklahoma City, OK
Tulsa, OK	Pittsburgh, PA	Pensacola, FL	Philadelphia, PA
Spokane, WA	Tucson, AZ	Tallahassee, FL	Scranton, PA
West Palm Beach, FL	Beaumont, TX	Tampa, FL	Dallas, TX
Grand Rapids, MI	Santa Rosa, CA	Atlanta, GA	Houston, TX
Fargo, ND	Cranston, RI	Chicago, IL	Salt Lake City, UT
Boise, ID	Medford, MA	Baton Rouge, LA	Alexandria, VA
Windsor, Canada		New Orleans, LA	Seattle, WA
		Baltimore, MD	Milwaukee, WI
		St. Louis, MO	Toronto, Canada
		Buffalo, NY	

Source: Company SEC filings, annual reports, and press releases; Deutsche Banc Alex. Brown estimates.

increased revenues for KKM&D from sales of mixes, sugar, and other supplies.

Krispy Kreme had recently opened a state-of-the-art 187,000-square-foot manufacturing and distribution facility in Effingham, Illinois, dedicated to the blending and packaging of prepared doughnut mixes and to distributing mixes, equipment, and other supplies to stores in the Midwest and the western half of North America. This facility had significantly lowered Krispy Kreme's unit costs and provided triple the production capacity of the older plant in Winston-Salem.

Training

Since mid-1999, Krispy Kreme had invested enough resources in its training program to create a multimedia management training curriculum. The program included classroom instruction, computer-based and video training modules, and in-store training experiences. The online part of the training program made full use of graphics, video, and animation, as well as seven different types of test questions. Every Krispy Kreme store had access to the training over the company's intranet and the Internet; employees who registered for the course could access the modules from home using their Internet connection. Learners' test results were transferred directly to a Krispy Kreme human resources database; learners were automati-

cally redirected to lessons where their test scores indicated that they had not absorbed the material well on the first attempt. The online course was designed to achieve 90 percent mastery from 90 percent of the participants and could be updated as needed.

The course for managers had been recast into a program suitable for hourly employees. The course could also be divided into small pieces and customized to fit individual needs. In 2003, Krispy Kreme intensified its focus on leadership development by establishing the Learning Initiative Program as well as the Performance Management System. In 2003, 18 employees attended the Krispy Kreme Leadership Institute to increase their capacities in senior management areas.

Growth Potential

Krispy Kreme management believed the company was still in its infancy. The company's highest priority was on expanding into markets with over 100,000 households; management believed these markets were attractive because the dense population characteristics offered opportunities for multiple store locations, gave greater exposure to brand-building efforts, and afforded multi-unit operating economies. However, the company believed that secondary markets with fewer than 100,000 households held significant sales and profit potential—it was exploring smaller-sized store designs suitable for secondary markets. In 2002, Krispy Kreme CEO Scott Livengood stated, "We are totally committed to putting full factory stores in every town in the U.S." Krispy Kreme's management further believed the food-service and institutional channel of sales offered significant opportunity to extend the brand into colleges and universities, business and industry facilities, and sports and entertainment complexes. Management had stated that the company's strong brand name, highly differentiated product, high-volume production capability, and multichannel market penetration strategy put the company in a position to become the recognized leader in every market it entered. In fiscal year 2004, Krispy Kreme planned to open 77 new stores in domestic and international locations.

In December 2000, the company hired Donald Henshall, 38, to fill the newly created position of president of international development; Henshall was formerly managing director of new business development with the London-based Overland Group, a maker and marketer of branded footwear and apparel. Henshall's job was to refine the company's global strategy, develop the capabilities and infrastructure to support expansion outside the United States, and consider inquiries from qualified parties wanting to open Krispy Kreme stores in foreign markets. Outside of the United States, Krispy Kreme stores had opened in Canada, Australia, and most recently London. Krispy Kreme and its franchisees planned to open 39 new stores in Canada, 30 in Australia and New Zealand, 20 in Mexico, and 25 in Great Britain and Ireland in the coming years. So far, sales had been very promising at the foreign locations that had been opened, and franchise agreements were in the works for further global expansion.

As of May 2001, the company had stopped accepting franchise applications for U.S. locations, indicating that there were no open territories. By 2003, it had stopped accepting franchise applications in Canada, Mexico, Western Europe, and Australia, indicating that franchise contracts were already under way and that Krispy Kreme would be opening in these areas soon. However, it was still accepting applications from developers interested in franchised stores in Asia and Eastern Europe. According to Scott Livengood, "Krispy Kreme is a natural to become a global brand. Looking at our demographics, we appeal to a very broad customer base. We receive lots of interest on a weekly basis to expand into in-

ternational locations and we are confident our brand will be received extremely well outside the U.S."

INDUSTRY ENVIRONMENT

By some estimates, the U.S. doughnut industry was a $5 to $6 billion market in 2003. Americans consumed an estimated 10 to 12 billion doughnuts annually—over three dozen per capita. In 2002, doughnut industry sales rose by about 13 percent. According to a study done by Technomic, a marketing research specialist in foods, doughnut shops were the fastest-growing dining category in the country. There was little indication the low-carbohydrate, weight-watching craze that had swept the United States and other countries in recent years had cut much into sales; industry observers and company officials attributed this in part to doughnuts being an affordable indulgence, easy to eat on the run, and in part to the tendency of many people to treat themselves occasionally. Doughnuts were readily available almost anywhere.

The three leading doughnut chains were Krispy Kreme; Dunkin' Donuts, with worldwide 2002 sales of $2.7 billion, 5,200 outlets worldwide (3,600 in the United States), and close to a 45 percent U.S. market share based on dollar sales volume; and Tim Hortons (160 outlets and 2002 U.S. sales of $115 million, plus 2,300 Canadian outlets with 2002 sales of $536 million).

In 2002, estimated sales at outlets specializing in doughnuts rose by about 9 percent, to about $3.6 billion. Growth in packaged doughnut sales at supermarkets, convenience stores, and other retail outlets had been quite small in the past five years. The proliferation of bakery departments in supermarkets had squeezed out many locally owned doughnut shops and, to some extent, had constrained the growth of doughnut chains. Doughnuts were a popular item in supermarket bakeries, with many customers finding it more convenient to buy them when doing their regular supermarket shopping as opposed to making a special trip to local bakeries. Doughnut aficionados, however, tended to pass up doughnuts in the grocery store, preferring the freshness, quality, and variety offered by doughnut specialty shops. Most patrons of doughnut shops frequented those in their neighborhoods or normal shopping area; it was un-usual for them to make a special trip of more than a mile or two for doughnuts.

Small independent doughnut shops usually had a devoted clientele, drawn from neighborhood residents and regular commuters passing by on their way to and from work. A longtime employee at a family-owned shop in Denver said, "Our customers are very loyal to us. Probably 80 percent are regulars."[1] Owners of independent shops seemed to believe that new entry by popular chains like Krispy Kreme posed little competitive threat, arguing that the market was big enough to support both independents and franchisers, that the Krispy Kreme novelty was likely to wear off, and that unless a doughnut franchiser located a store close to their present location the impact would be minimal at worst. A store owner in Omaha said, "Our doughnut sales increased when Krispy Kreme came to town. We benefit every time they advertise because doughnuts are as popular as ever."[2]

KRISPY KREME'S CHIEF COMPETITORS

Dunkin' Donuts

Dunkin' Donuts was the largest coffee and baked-goods chain in the world, selling 4.4 million donuts and 1.8 million cups of coffee daily. The quick-service restaurant chain was owned by British-based Allied Domecq PLC, a diversified enterprise whose other businesses included the Baskin-Robbins ice cream chain, ToGo's Eateries (sandwiches), and an assortment of alcoholic beverage brands (Kahlúa, Beefeater's, Maker's Mark, Courvoisier, Tia Maria, and a host of wines). In 2003, Allied Domecq's Dunkin' Donuts chain had total sales of $3.2 billion, over 5,800 outlets in 28 countries, 3,600 U.S. outlets, and comparable store sales growth of 4.4 percent in the United States. In New England alone, Dunkin' Donuts operated 1,200 stores, including 600 in the Greater Boston area, where the chain was founded in 1950.

Despite its name Dunkin' Donuts put more emphasis on coffee and convenience than on doughnuts. According to one company executive, "People talk about our coffee first. We're food you eat on the go. We're part of your day. We're not necessarily a destination store." Roughly half of all purchases at Dunkin' Donuts included coffee without a doughnut.[3] Dunkin' Donuts menu included doughnuts (50 varieties), muffins, bagels, cinnamon buns, cookies, brownies, Munchkins doughnut holes, cream cheese sandwiches, nine flavors of fresh coffee, iced coffees, and a lemonade Coolatta. In areas where there were clusters of Dunkin' Donuts outlets, most baked items were supplied from centrally located kitchens rather than being made on-site. In 2002, Dunkin' Donuts ranked 11th in *Entrepreneur* magazine's annual Franchise Top 500.

The nutritional content of the chain's 50 doughnut varieties ranged between 200 and 340 calories, between 8 and 19 grams of fat, between 1.5 and 6 grams of saturated fat, and between 9 and 31 grams of sugars; its cinnamon buns had 540 calories, 15 grams of fat, 4 grams of saturated fat, and 42 grams of sugars. Whereas Krispy Kreme's best-selling original glazed doughnuts had 200 calories, 12 grams of fat, 3 grams of saturated fat and 10 grams of sugar, the comparable item at Dunkin' Donuts had 180 calories, 8 grams of fat, 1.5 grams of saturated fat, and 6 grams of sugar. Several Dunkin' Donuts customers in the Boston area who had recently tried Krispy Kreme doughnuts reported that Krispy Kremes had more flavor and were lighter.[4]

Dunkin' Donuts had successfully fended off competition from national bagel chains and Starbucks. When national bagel chains, promoting bagels as a healthful alternative to doughnuts, opened new stores in areas where Dunkin' Donuts had stores, the company responded by adding bagels and cream cheese sandwiches to its menu offerings. Dunkin' Donuts had countered threats from Starbucks by adding a wider variety of hot-and-cold coffee beverages—and whereas coffee drinkers had to wait for a Starbucks barista to properly craft a $3 latte, they could get coffee and a doughnut on the fly

[1]As quoted in "Dough-Down at the Mile High Corral," *Rocky Mountain News*, March 25, 2001, p. 1G.

[2]As quoted in "Hole-ly War: Omaha to Be Battleground for Duel of Titans," *Omaha World Herald*, September 7, 1999, p. 14.

[3]According to information in Hermione Malone, "Krispy Kreme to Offer Better Coffee as It Tackles New England," *Charlotte Observer*, March 16, 2001.

[4]"Time to Rate the Doughnuts: Krispy Kreme Readies to Roll into N.E. to Challenge Dunkin' Donuts," *Boston Globe*, February 21, 2001, p. D1.

at Dunkin' Donuts for less money. Quick and consistent service was a Dunkin' Donuts forte. Management further believed that the broader awareness of coffee created by the market presence of Starbucks stores had actually helped boost coffee sales at Dunkin' Donuts. In markets such as New York City and Chicago where there were both Dunkin' Donuts and Krispy Kreme stores, sales at Dunkin' Donuts had continued to rise. In commenting on the competitive threat from Krispy Kreme, a Dunkin' Donuts vice president said:

> We have a tremendous number of varieties, a tremendous level of convenience, tremendous coffee and other baked goods. I think the differentiation that Dunkin' enjoys is clear. We're not pretentious and don't take ourselves too seriously, but we know how important a cup of coffee and a donut or bagel in the morning is. Being able to deliver a great cup of coffee when someone is on their way to something else is a great advantage.[5]

Dunkin' Donuts began opening tri-brand stores in 2000 in partnership with sister businesses Baskin Robbins (for ice cream) and ToGo (for sandwiches). In 2003, the company planned to open 300 new Dunkin' Donut shops; the Fort Myers, Tampa, and Miami areas of Florida were targeted for 53 new Dunkin' Donuts restaurants. Also, in 2003, Couche-Tard, Canada's largest convenience store operator, bought control of the Dunkin' Donuts name in Quebec as well as the 104 Dunkin' Donuts outlets located there. Couche-Tard planned to double the number of outlets within five years to better compete with Tim Hortons and Krispy Kreme.

Tim Hortons

Tim Hortons, a subsidiary of Wendy's International, was one of North America's largest coffee and fresh baked-goods chains, with almost 2,300 restaurants across Canada and a steadily growing base of 166 locations in key markets within the United States. In 2002, Tim Hortons had systemwide sales of $1.7 billion. In Canada, Tim Hortons was regarded as something of an icon. The chain was named for a popular Canadian-born professional hockey player who played for the Toronto Maple Leafs, Pittsburgh Penguins, and Buffalo Sabers; Horton was born in 1930, started playing hockey when he was five years old,

and died in an auto accident while playing for the Buffalo Sabers.

The Tim Hortons division relied heavily on franchising—only 71 of the Tim Hortons outlets were company-owned. Franchisees paid a royalty of 3 to 6 percent of weekly sales to the parent company, depending on whether they leased the land and/or buildings from Tim Hortons and on certain other conditions; in addition, franchisees paid fees equal to 4 percent of monthly gross sales to fund advertising and promotional activities undertaken at the corporate level. Franchisees were also required to purchase such products as coffee, sugar, flour and shortening from a Tim Hortons subsidiary; these products were distributed from five warehouses located across Canada and were delivered to the company's Canadian restaurants primarily by its fleet of trucks and trailers. In the United States, both company and franchised stores purchased ingredients from a supplier approved by the parent company.

Tim Hortons used outside contractors to construct its restaurants. The restaurants were built to company specifications as to exterior style and interior decor. The standard Hortons restaurant being built in 2003 consisted of a freestanding production unit ranging from 1,150 to 3,030 square feet. Each included a bakery capable of supplying fresh baked goods throughout the day to several satellite Tim Hortons within a defined area. Tim Hortons locations ranged from full standard stores with in-store baking facilities, to combo units with Wendy's and Tim Hortons under one roof, to carts and kiosks in shopping malls, highway outlets, universities, airports, and hospitals. Most full standard Tim Hortons locations offered 24-hour drive-through service. Tim Hortons promoted its full-standard stores as neighborhood meeting places and was active in promoting its products for group fund-raisers and community events.

The menu at each Tim Hortons unit consisted of coffee, cappuccino, and fresh baked goods such as doughnuts, muffins, pies, croissants, tarts, cookies, cakes, and bagels. Some units also served sandwiches, soups, and fresh-baked breads. In 2002, Tim Hortons added fresh-baked baguettes to its menu. One of the chain's biggest drawing cards was its special blend of fresh-brewed coffee, which was also sold in cans for customers' use at home. About half of the purchases at Tim Hortons included coffee without a doughnut.

---

[5]As quoted in Malone, "Krispy Kreme to Offer Better Coffee."

Executives at Tim Hortons did not feel threatened by Krispy Kreme's expansion into Canada and those parts of the United States where it had stores (Michigan, New York, Ohio, Kentucky, Maine, and West Virginia). According to David House, Tim Hortons president, "We really welcome them. Anyone who draws attention to doughnuts can only help us. It is a big market and a big marketplace. I would put our doughnut up against theirs any day."[6] In Canada, Tim Hortons had a 70 percent share of the sales of coffee and baked goods in restaurants. The Tim Hortons outlets in the United States had reportedly been quite successful, and House believed that the real war for doughnut supremacy was already being waged on U.S. soil. A Canadian retailing consultant familiar with Tim Hortons and Krispy Kreme said, "This is the Canadian elephant and the U.S. mouse. Listen, if there's anything where Canadians can kick American butt, it is in doughnuts."[7] Another Canadian retailing consultant said, "It [Krispy Kreme] is an American phenomenon. These things are sickeningly sweet."[8]

Canada was reputed to have more doughnut shops per capita than any other country in the world. Aside from Tim Hortons, other chains in Canada featuring doughnuts included Dunkin' Donuts, Robin's Donuts, Country Style, and Coffee Time. Tim Hortons planned to open 40 new doughnut shops in 2004 (over 100 new stores were opened in 2003).

Winchell's Donut House

Winchell's, founded by Verne Winchell in 1948, was owned by Shato Holdings, Ltd., of Vancouver, Canada. In 2000, there were approximately 600 Winchell's units located in 10 states west of the Mississippi River, along with international franchises in Guam, Saipan, Korea, Egypt, Saudi Arabia, and New Zealand. Since then, Winchell's Doughnut House had lost steam and closed more than half of its locations. In 2003, there were only 200 or so locations. Winchell's had 110 restaurants in Southern Califor-

nia, a market that had about 1,600 doughnut shops, and it was the largest doughnut chain on the West Coast. To combat Krispy Kreme's entry into Southern California, where Winchell's had a brand awareness of 97 percent, Winchell's launched a Warm 'n Fresh program at all outlets by 2000. The program called for fresh glazed doughnuts in display cases to be replaced every 15 to 20 minutes between 6 and 9 AM daily; a flashing red light on display cases signaled that a fresh batch of glazed doughnuts was available. Winchell's was offering customers a Warm 'n Fresh doughnut between 6 and 11 AM daily.

As of September 2003, a "Winchell's dozen" of 14 doughnuts sold for $5.99 and a double dozen (28) sold for $9.99. Winchell's bakery offerings included 20 varieties of doughnuts and 14 flavors of muffins, as well as croissants, bagels (breakfast bagel sandwiches were available at select locations), éclairs, tarts, apple fritters, and bear claws. It served three varieties of its "legendary" coffees—Dark Roast Supreme, Legendary Blend, and Legendary Decaf—all using only 100 percent arabica beans (considered by many to be the finest coffee beans in the world). Other beverages included regular and frozen cappuccino, soft drinks, milk, and juices.

Winchell's corporate goal for the next five years was to triple its sales. In 2003 it was actively seeking franchisees in the Arizona, California, Colorado, New Mexico, Oregon, and Washington markets. Winchell's charged a franchise fee of $7,500; new stores cost anywhere from $125,000 to $225,000, depending on such factors as store size, location, style of decor, and landscaping. A 5 percent royalty and a 3 percent advertising fee were charged on net sales. Winchell's had begun an expansion program in 2000 in six U.S. cities where company sales were strong; the program specifically aimed at recruiting fast-food franchises to add Winchell's kiosks to their stores. Winchell's had already succeeded in getting kiosks into Subway franchises in Las Vegas and several Blimpie's Subs and Salads in Southern California. In Los Angeles, Winchell's had opened kiosks inside 11 Lucy's LaundryMat locations. Winchell's also offered co-branding partners the option to add a full-blown Winchell's World Doughnut Factory, as opposed to a Winchell's Express. But the kiosk approach failed to attract the interest of fast-food chains.

---

[6]As quoted in "Can Krispy Kreme Cut It in Canada?" *Ottawa Citizen*, December 30, 2000, p. H1.

[7]As quoted in ibid.

[8]As quoted in ibid.

LaMar's Donuts

Headquartered in Englewood, Colorado, LaMar's was a small, privately held chain that had doughnut shops in Alabama, Arizona, Colorado, Georgia, Kansas, Missouri, Nebraska, Nevada and Tennessee. Ray LaMar opened the original LaMar's Donuts in 1960 on Linwood Avenue in Kansas City and quickly turned the shop into a local institution. On a typical day, lines started forming before 6 AM and, by closing time about 11,000 donuts would be sold. Based on the doughnut shop's success and reputation, Ray and his wife, Shannon, decided in the early 1990s to franchise LaMar's. Hundreds of LaMar's devotees applied for the limited number of franchises made available in the Kansas City area; 15 were granted over a few months. Given the success of the Kansas City franchising effort, the LaMarses concluded their concept could expand beyond the confines of Kansas and Missouri and initiated a strategy to take LaMar's Donuts to the next level.

In 1997, Franchise Consortium International, headed by Joseph J. Field, purchased a majority interest in LaMar's Franchising, renamed the company LaMar's Donuts International, and began laying the groundwork for a national expansion program. In mid-2003, LaMar's had 32 corporate-owned and franchise store locations in eight states, with six stores under construction and several more in development. Its stores were typically located along neighborhood traffic routes. LaMar's was currently 11th in the doughnut industry but hoped to gain third place in world doughnut sales by 2010. Average unit sales were $500,000 in 2003, and management expected the average would increase to $750,000 in a few years. Management planned to have 1,200 stores in operation by 2013.

LaMar's utilized a secret recipe to produce "artisan quality" doughnuts that were handmade daily with all-natural ingredients and no preservatives. Day-old doughnuts were never sold at the shops but were donated at day's end to the needy. In addition to 75 varieties of doughnuts, LaMar's menu included gourmet coffee and cappuccino. LaMar's had recently partnered with Dazbog Coffee Company in Denver, Colorado, and created over a dozen customized specialty coffee blends under the LaMar's Old World Roast label. Beans were hand-picked from Costa Rica and then slow-roasted in an authentic Italian brick fire oven. Coffee products at LaMar's shops included cappuccinos, espressos, lattes, iced coffee drinks, and chai teas. Exhibit 11 shows LaMar's lineup of baked goods and nutritional information for each product.

The company used the tag line "Simply a better doughnut." Joe Fields said, "People come in and try the product and they are surprised. They are wowed, in a very different way than Krispy Kreme. They say, 'Oh my God, this is the best doughnut I've had in my life.'" The *Zagat Survey*, a well-known rater of premier dining spots nationwide, described LaMar's Donuts as "extraordinary; fit for kings." *Gourmet* magazine, in search of the country's favorite doughnut, conducted a nationwide poll; the winner was a LaMar's doughnut. LaMar's Donuts has been named Best in the Country by the *John Walsh Show,* a one-hour daily nationally syndicated television program. Several newspapers had named LaMar's doughnuts as tops in their market area.

exhibit 11 **Nutritional Content of Selected LaMar's Doughnut Products**

Product	Calories	Calories from Fat	Total Fat (grams)	Saturated Fat (grams)	Cholesterol (milligrams)	Sodium (milligrams)	Carbohydrates (grams)	Sugars (grams)
Ray's Original Glazed Donut	220	90	10	2.5	0	260	31	13g
Chocolate Iced LaMar's Bar (Unfilled)	540	200	22	6	0	440	81	49g
Cinnamon Twist	770	240	26	7	0	1190	120	32g
Old Fashioned Sour Cream Donut	420	160	18	4.5	15	380	60	40g
Cherry Filled Bizmark	550	170	19	5	0	560	88	45g
Apple Fritter	650	230	26	7	0	1020	91	13g
Cinnamon Roll	690	220	25	6	0	1020	106	30g
Raisin Nut Cinnamon Roll	850	240	27	6	0	1020	137	62g
Chocolate Iced LaMar's Bar (White Fluff Filled)	810	320	35	9	0	460	120	85g
Ray's Chocolate Glazed Donut	290	100	11	3	0	260	44	25g
White Iced Cake Donut	320	160	17	4.5	0	320	38	23g

Source: LaMar's Donuts International, Inc., 2001.

Andrea Jung and Avon Products in 2003: Accelerating the Transformation

John E. Gamble
University of South Alabama

In early 2000, Avon held the title of world's largest direct seller of beauty-related products—a title it had held for over a century. However, there were many other channels that women could use to purchase color cosmetics, hair care products, fragrances, bath products, skin care products, or jewelry. Supermarkets, drugstores, discount stores, and department stores accounted for approximately 93 percent of the industry's $140 billion global sales. With retailing becoming increasingly sophisticated and saturated with a worldwide proliferation of malls and supercenter-style discount stores, an increasing number of stand-alone specialty retailers, and the rise of business-to-consumer e-commerce, even one Avon board member asked, "Is the day of the Avon rep over?"[1]

When former CEO Charles Perrin stepped down and Andrea Jung was promoted from president to CEO of Avon Products, Inc., in November 1999, the company was in serious trouble, with annual sales growth of less than 1.5 percent and a crashing stock price during the greatest economic boom in history. Jung took on the role of Avon Lady during her first month as CEO to better understand what customers thought about the company's products and to find out what it was like to be a member of Avon's direct sales force. Jung heard customer complaints about Avon's image, poor-quality products, lack of interesting new lines, and unattractive catalogs. She also learned that at times Avon's sales representatives could not reorder popular items and very often did not receive the correct items ordered. After one month as CEO, Andrea Jung outlined a bold new vision and strategic plan for Avon that called for the company to introduce highly innovative new products, build new lines of business, transform its value chain and business processes, make the Internet a critical link in its direct selling business model, rebuild its image, enter the retail sector, and most important, update its direct sales model, developed in the late 1800s, to better fit the 21st century.

As 2003 came to a close, there was evidence that Jung's plan was producing positive results and few people had been critical of the company's performance under her leadership. Since 1999, the company's revenues had grown at a compounded annual rate of 6.5 percent, its operating margins had expanded by 10.1 percent annually, and its return on invested capital exceeded that of its nearest competitor by 11+ percentage points. In addition, the company either met or exceeded investor expectations for 14 consecutive quarters—leading to a 250 percent increase in its share price since early 2000. However, Andrea Jung was not satisfied with the company's performance; in mid-2003, she outlined a strategic plan for 2004–2007 that built on the success of her initial strategic plan and included new action items to accelerate overall growth. The new plan would

[1]"It Took a Lady to Save Avon," *Fortune*, October 15, 2001, p. 203.

expand Avon's presence in high-potential markets in Asia and Central and Eastern Europe, add new products and product lines, and target new customer groups such as the teen market. The revised strategic plan was expected to allow the company to increase revenues by 12–13 percent annually to reach $8.5 billion by 2007 and increase operating profits by nearly 3.5 points a year. Avon's financial performance for 1992–2003 and market performance for 1994–December 2003 are presented in Exhibits 1 and 2.

ANDREA JUNG: CHAIRMAN AND CEO OF AVON PRODUCTS, INC.

Andrea Jung was born in Toronto, Canada, but was raised in Wellesley, Massachusetts, as a member of a demanding family with high expectations for achievement. Andrea's father was born in Hong Kong and received a master's degree in architecture from the Massachusetts Institute of Technology after moving to the United States. Her mother was born in Shanghai and was a chemical engineer before becoming an accomplished pianist. Jung's parents expected commitment and determination from her and her younger brother from early ages. In an October 2001 interview with a *Fortune* journalist, Andrea Jung suggested that her parents' expectations for excellence contributed greatly to her successful career. She recalled an event from fourth grade when she desperately wanted a box of 120 colored pencils. Her parents offered the proposal that if Andrea were to make straight A's for school year, she could have the pencils. By Jung's own admission to the reporter, she was not a natural student and had to miss birthday parties and other activities to make the grades necessary to receive the pencils. At the end of year, Andrea delivered all A's to her parents and, in return, they took her to purchase the pencils. Jung found meaning in the life example given by her parents: "I'll never forget that. My parents ingrained in me early on that the perfect score is always something to strive for. I want to win and I want to succeed no matter what."[2]

Andrea Jung attended Princeton University and in 1979 graduated magna cum laude with a degree in

English literature before joining Bloomingdale's as a management trainee. Jung achieved early success at Bloomingdale's before moving to I. Magnin, where she became second in command before age 30. In 1992, at age 32, Jung was in charge of women's apparel for Neiman Marcus; she left two years later to marry Bloomingdale's CEO and move to Manhattan. Once in Manhattan, Jung joined Avon as president of U.S. product marketing, where she quickly impressed then-CEO James Preston. Jung made a name for herself with her decisiveness and no-nonsense style. When asked to assess whether the company should move into retail sales, Jung shocked some at Avon when she forcefully recommended that the company avoid retail sales, arguing that neither the products nor the sales agents were ready for such a move. Among her most widely recognized successes as president of marketing was her decision to eliminate the company's assortment of regional brands to be replaced with global brands. Andrea's ability to, without hesitation, make decisions that were likely to be called into question—like cutting 40 percent of the company's catalog items and dismissing the company's advertising agency—made her a standout and landed her the position of president and a spot on Avon's board before Preston's retirement. At age 40, Jung became CEO of Avon Products, Inc., and in 2001, at age 42, Andrea Jung was listed fourth on *Fortune's* ranking of the 50 most powerful women in American business. Jung was number five on the list in 2002 and third in 2003.

COMPANY HISTORY

Avon, originally known as the California Perfume Company, was founded in 1886 by a New York book salesman named David H. McConnell. McConnell entered the fragrances and cosmetics business after noting that many of the housewives who purchased books during his door-to-door sales calls weren't really interested in reading the books but mainly purchased them to receive the free bottles of perfume that he provided as a gift with each purchase. Upon opening an office in New York, McConnell immediately began to build a door-to-door sales force for his new company and hired Mrs. P. F. E. Albee as its first sales agent. Mrs. Albee not only proved to be a stellar sales agent but also helped McConnell pioneer the company's direct sales approach that by the

[2]Ibid., p. 208.

turn of the 20th century included more than 10,000 representatives. The company supported the efforts of it sales agents with a growing product line of cosmetics, fragrances, and other beauty products that were developed and produced at its newly constructed Suffern, New York, research laboratory and production facility. Also by the early 1900s, California Perfume Company had expanded its sales offices beyond New York to San Francisco, California; Luzerne, Pennsylvania; and Davenport, Iowa.

In 1914 California Perfume Company expanded beyond the United States to Canada and reached a sales milestone of 5 million units. The company's sales had grown to $2 million by 1928 when it first launched a line of beauty products under the Avon brand. McConnell branded the new line Avon as a tribute to the beauty of Stratford-upon-Avon in England, a city he had visited during his travels. The Avon products were among the company's best sellers, and California Perfume Company's name was changed to Avon Products, Inc., in 1939 by David McConnell Jr., who became president of the company after his father's death in 1937. Avon Products went public in 1946, and its sales grew at annual rates of 25 percent or more in the 1950s as the company rapidly expanded its product line; entered nearly a dozen international markets; launched its well-known "Avon Calling" advertising campaign; and, most important, expanded its network of sales representatives. Avon's direct sales model was almost tailor-made to the economic conditions and societal norms of the 1950s and 1960s since only a small percentage of women held professional careers. Avon offered the multitude of middle-class U.S. homemakers an opportunity to earn extra income by selling cosmetics to their friends and neighbors without interfering with their obligations to their families. By 1960 Avon's sales force had helped increase the company's U.S. sales to $250 million and make it the world's largest cosmetics company—a position it held until the mid-1980s, when its annual sales averaged more than $3 billion.

Even though Avon held on to its lead in the global cosmetics industry until the mid-1980s, signs of trouble began to appear during the recession of the mid-1970s as middle-income homemakers began to leave the home for the workforce. By 1980 Avon's sales began to decline as more women grew dissatisfied with part-time sales jobs and as fewer women purchased products sold door-to-door. In addition,

Avon's products held little appeal for teens and many lower-income women found Avon's products too expensive. With stalled sales growth in its core cosmetics business, Avon pursued business diversification to boost its revenues, with the acquisition of prestigious jeweler Tiffany & Company in 1979, fragrance retailers Giorgio Beverly Hills and Parfums Stern in 1987, and a variety of unrelated businesses such as magazines, retirement properties, health care products, children's toys, and menswear. The company's foray into diversification failed to produce the hoped-for level of performance, with the multitude of acquisitions all being either abandoned or divested by 1999.

Initial Steps in Revitalizing Avon

With Avon's cosmetics business achieving only modest revenue and earnings growth throughout the early and mid-1990s, the company's board developed a succession plan in late 1997 for retiring CEO James Preston that called for outsider Charles Perrin to lead Avon with the aid of two chief lieutenants, Andrea Jung and Susan Kropf. Perrin had been head of Duracell International from 1994 until its acquisition by Gillette in 1996 and had been a member of Avon's board since 1996. Jung and Kropf had both held executive positions with Avon under Preston, who was noted for fast-tracking women. The board's succession plan called for Jung to become the company's president and chief operating officer, while Kropf would become executive vice president and president of North American operations. Both Jung and Kropf were also elected board members, and Jung was identified as Perrin's eventual successor.

Among Charles Perrin's first tasks as Avon CEO was to direct a $400 million restructuring program that was drafted by outgoing CEO Preston and intended to fuel more rapid growth. The company's business process reengineering efforts freed up more than $120 million during Perrin's first year as Avon's chief manager that was used to develop new products, increase advertising, increase dividends, and buy back outstanding shares. In addition, Avon's business process redesign improved gross margins by 1.7 points and operating margins by 1.5 points by year-end 1998. Perrin's strategy also called for Avon to improve its image with consumers around the

exhibit 1 **Selected Financial and Operating Highlights, Avon Products, Inc., 1992–2003 (in millions, except per share and employee data)**

	2003	2002	2001	2000	1999	1998	1997	1996	1995	1994	1993	1992
Net sales	$6,804.6	$6,170.6	$5,957.8	$5,673.7	$5,289.1	$5,212.7	$5,079.4	$4,814.2	$4,492.1	$4,266.5	$3,844.1	$3,660.5
Other revenue	71.4	57.7	42.5	40.9	38.8	35.0	—	—	—	—	—	—
Total revenue	$6,876.0	$6,228.3	$6,000.3	$5,714.6	$5,327.9	$5,247.7	$5,079.4	$4,814.2	$4,492.1	$4,266.5	$3,844.1	$3,660.5
Operating profit	1,042.8	870.0	773.4	788.7	549.4	473.2	537.8	538	500.8	489.5	427.4	339.9
Interest expense	33.3	52.0	71.1	84.7	43.2	34.7	35.5	33.2	34.6	44.7	39.4	38.4
Income from continuing operations before taxes, minority interest and cumulative effect of accounting changes	993.5	835.6	689.7	691.0	506.6	455.9	534.9	510.4	465	433.8	394.6	290.0
Income from continuing operations before minority interest and cumulative effect of accounting changes	664.8	543.3	449.4	489.3	302.4	265.1	337	319	288.6	270.3	243.8	169.4
Income from continuing operations before cumulative effect of accounting changes	664.8	534.6	444.9	485.1	302.4	270.0	338.8	317.9	286.1	264.8	236.9	164.2
Income (loss) from discontinued operations, net	—	—	—	—	—	—	—	—	(29.6)	(23.8)	2.7	10.8
Cumulative effect of accounting changes, net	—	—	(0.3)	(6.7)	—	—	—	—	—	(45.2)	(107.5)	—
Net income	$ 664.8	$ 534.6	$ 444.6	$ 478.4	$ 302.4	$ 270.0	$ 338.8	$ 317.9	$ 256.5	$ 195.8	$ 132.1	$ 175.0
Earnings (loss) per share—basic												
Continuing operations	$ 2.82	$ 2.30	$ 1.90	$ 2.04	$ 1.18	$ 1.03	$ 1.28	$ 1.19	$ 1.05	$ 0.94	$ 0.82	$ 0.57
Discontinued operations	—	—	—	—	—	—	—	—	—	(0.09)	0.01	0.04
Cumulative effect of accounting changes	—	—	—	(0.03)	—	—	—	—	(0.11)	(0.16)	(0.37)	—
Net income	$ 2.82	$ 2.30	$ 1.90	$ 2.01	$ 1.18	$ 1.03	$ 1.28	$ 1.19	$ 0.94	$ 0.69	$ 0.46	$ 0.61

exhibit 1 **(concluded)**

	2003	2002	2001	2000	1999	1998	1997	1996	1995	1994	1993	1992
Earnings (loss) per share—diluted												
Continuing operations	$ 2.78	$ 2.20	$ 1.90	$ 2.02	$ 1.17	$ 1.02	$ 1.27	$ 1.18	$ 1.05	$ 0.93	$ 0.82	$ 0.57
Discontinued operations	—	—	—	—	—	—	—	—	(0.11)	(0.08)	0.01	0.04
Cumulative effect of accounting changes	—	—	—	(0.03)	—	—	—	—	—	(0.16)	(0.37)	—
Net income	$ 2.78	$ 2.20	$ 1.90	$ 1.99	$ 1.17	$ 1.02	$ 1.27	$ 1.18	$ 0.94	$ 0.69	$ 0.46	$ 0.61
Cash dividends per share												
Common	$ 0.84	$ 0.80	$ 0.80	$ 0.74	$ 0.72	$ 0.68	$ 0.63	$ 0.58	$ 0.53	$ 0.48	$ 0.43	$ 0.38
Balance sheet data												
Total assets	$3,562.3	$3,327.5	$3,181.0	$2,826.4	$2,528.6	$2,433.5	$2,272.9	$2,222.4	$2,052.8	$1,978.3	$1,918.7	$1,692.6
Long-term debt	$ 877.7	$ 767.0	$1,236.3	$1,108.2	$ 701.4	$ 201.0	$ 102.2	$ 104.5	$ 114.2	$ 116.5	$ 123.7	$ 177.7
Total debt	$1,121.8	$1,372.2	$1,325.1	$1,213.6	$1,007.4	$ 256.3	$ 234.3	$ 201.6	$ 161.5	$ 177.7	$ 194.1	$ 215.0
Shareholders' (deficit) equity	$ 371.3	$ (127.7)	$ (75.1)	$ (215.8)	$ (406.1)	$ 285.1	$ 285.0	$ 241.7	$ 192.7	$ 185.6	$ 314.0	$ 310.5
Number of employees	45,900	45,300	43,800	43,000	40,500	33,900	35,000	33,700	31,800	30,400	29,500	29,400

Source: Avon Products, Inc., 2000 and 2003 10-Ks.

exhibit 2 **Monthly Performance of Avon Products, Inc.'s Stock Price, 1994 to December 2003**

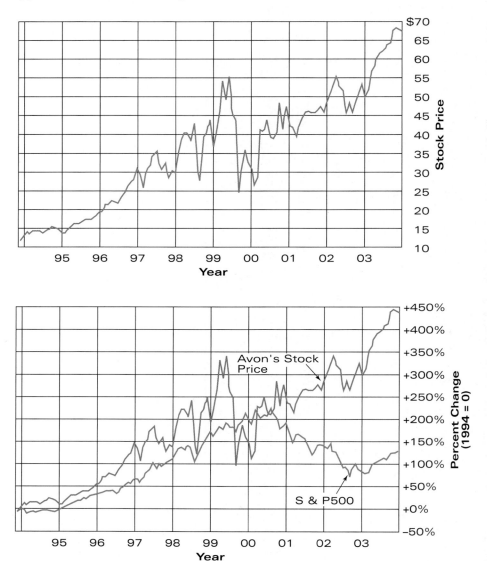

world, shorten product development times, develop new brands and products that could be marketed worldwide, and utilize technology to aid sales representatives in placing and tracking orders. In addition, Perrin believed that Avon needed to evaluate its dated direct sales model and create more lucrative income opportunities for sales representatives.

As Avon's president and chief operating officer, Andrea Jung collaborated with Perrin in the devel-

opment and execution of strategies directed at improving Avon's competitive strength in the global cosmetics, fragrances, and toiletries (CFT) industry. Specific undertakings begun in 1998 by Perrin and Jung included the establishment of Avon's Global Development Center, which eliminated duplicative local product development efforts with a coordinated global approach to develop brands that would have worldwide appeal. Avon's simultaneous launch of its

Women of Earth (WE) fragrance in 54 countries in late 1998 exceeded the initial sales of Far Away (Avon's previous sales launch leader) by 31 percent. Two other early successes of the Global Development Center included two new lines that were targeted toward younger consumers and Techniques, a premium hair care line. Avon management believed that hair care was a particularly attractive product category since personal care products accounted for 50 percent of the $140 billion retail value of the global CFT market.

The improvement of Avon's image was another strategic initiative advanced by Jung and Perrin during 1998. Market research had found that many consumers viewed Avon's products almost commodity-like in their quality and innovativeness and not in the least glamorous. Avon attacked this image with new global products, a new global advertising campaign, and the opening of its 20,000-square-foot Avon Centre in New York's Trump Tower. The Avon Centre was intended to illustrate the luxuriousness of Avon's products and included an elegantly appointed spa and salon, 5,000 square feet of meeting rooms, and select beauty products like its Avon Spa collection, which was created for exclusive use at the Avon Centre.

Avon improved its Web site under Perrin by making it easier for customers to purchase products online and began testing a Web-based ordering system for the company's sales representatives in Japan. Also, Avon allowed representatives in Japan to order more than once during a sales campaign, allowed for telephone, fax, and interactive computer voice ordering, and sped deliveries to representatives to improve sales representative satisfaction. Avon launched the pilot program in Japan to make sales representatives' jobs easier after learning of such barriers to representative success during its first-ever Representative National Convention in 1998, at which 6,000 representatives convened to learn of new products, receive sales training, and discuss areas of improvement for the company.

At the direction of Perrin and Jung, Avon also began experimenting with new ways to make the company's products available to consumers who found it inconvenient to purchase from an Avon sales representative. In 1998 the company tested Avon Beauty Centers in 40 malls across the United States. Avon Beauty Centers were freestanding kiosks where passersby could purchase the latest Avon products. The Beauty Centers were modeled after the company's 200 Avon Beauty Boutiques in Malaysia, which accounted for 68 percent of the company's sales in that country. Another major shift in strategy initiated by Perrin was the development of Avon's Leadership Opportunity program. The network marketing plan allowed representatives to receive not only commissions on their own sales but also bonuses based on the sales of their recruits and trainees. Previously, Avon used a sales force structure that included sales zone managers who recruited new sales representatives but did not receive commissions on the recruits' sales. The strategies and implementation efforts of Perrin's management team led to a 3 percent sales increase and a 17 percent earnings increase before one-time charges for 1998.

OVERVIEW OF THE GLOBAL COSMETICS, FRAGRANCE, AND TOILETRY INDUSTRY

In 2003 Avon was the world's largest direct seller of such beauty-related products as color cosmetics, hair care products, fragrances, bath products, skin care products, and jewelry. The global cosmetics, fragrance, and toiletry (CFT) industry was highly fragmented, with distribution channels beyond direct selling and multiple subcategories existing within each product category. For example, within the color cosmetics category, products like eyeliner, mascara, foundation, concealer, nail polish, and lipstick could be purchased from direct sellers like Avon or from supermarkets, drugstores, discounters, specialty retailers, and department stores. The percentage of sales accounted for by channel tended to vary widely by product category with, for example, drugstores being the largest U.S. retail sellers of cosmetics and hair care products, while discounters accounted for the greatest retail sales of fragrances. In addition, the sales growth rates for the subcategories of beauty products could also vary greatly. The market for beauty products was also segmented by consumer demographics and by geography. Teen consumers tended to look for specific product characteristics that were very different from those sought by baby boomers. Country-specific differences in consumer preferences and complexions

exhibit 3   **U.S. Sales of Cosmetics, Fragrances, and Toiletries by Retail Channel, 1996, 2000**

Channel	1996		2000		CAGR* (1996–2000)
	Dollar Value (in billions)	Percent of Total	Dollar Value (in billions)	Percent of Total	
Supermarkets	$4.6	17.9%	$5.3	16.3%	+3.6%
Drugstores	4.8	18.7	5.4	16.6	+3.0
Mass merchandisers	5.6	21.8	8.0	24.6	+9.3
Department stores	5.5	21.4	6.8	20.9	+5.4
Specialty stores	2.3	8.9	3.3	10.2	+9.4

*Compound average growth rate.
Source: Investor Update Meeting, Avon Products, Inc., May 8, 2001.

further fragmented the global CFT industry, while market penetration rate created varying growth opportunities across the world.

Exhibit 3 presents U.S. CFT sales by retail channel for 1996 and 2000. The U.S. CFT market by product category for 1996, 2000, and forecast for 2005 is shown in Exhibit 4.

Product Innovation in the Cosmetics Industry

As the global CFT industry entered the 21st century, sales increases were driven primarily by product innovation. Beginning in the mid-1990s, skin care became the fastest-growing product category in the global CFT industry, growing at annual rates approaching 15 percent. The category's growth was fueled by new product introductions that responded to a worldwide consumer focus on wellness and youthfulness. Manufacturers created skin care product formulations containing natural active ingredients like vitamins and plant extracts that moved product benefits beyond cleansing and moisturizing to anti-aging, antipollution, firming, and sebum regulation. The use of retinol, a form of vitamin A, as a skin care additive spurred most growth in sales to women over 30 since the pharmaceutical industry had demonstrated the efficacy of retinol in visibly reducing the signs of aging. By the late 1990s, almost all skin care producers offered products including retinol as an additive. Many companies also offered variants of retinol-based products that included SPF 15 sunscreens, which allowed retinol to be used during the day, or

that used sophisticated delivery systems such as liposomes, nanoparticles, and microencapsulation.

Whereas scientific research had shown vitamin A to reverse the signs of aging, vitamin C had been found to improve skin elasticity and to even out skin pigmentation, and vitamin E had become accepted as an antioxidant. Medical researchers had found that antioxidant intervention slowed basal skeletal muscle oxidation, which caused the body to age. Both Lancôme and L'Oréal had introduced lines of creams and lotions that included grape polyphenols, which had been found to be powerful antioxidants that could protect the skin against free radicals. Free radicals were created when molecules broke down and left previously paired atoms with an unpaired electron to search out bonds with other atoms. The presence of free radicals was damaging to skin and other body tissues since free radicals broke down other bonded atoms in the re-pairing process, which created the presence of new free radicals. Antioxidants were known by scientists as free-radical scavengers since they contained a free electron that could bond with and neutralize free radicals. The future direction of cosmetics and skin care research was expected to focus on improving skin hydration (since dehydration was a major contributor to premature aging of the skin) and improving skin sensitivity (since people tended to lose sensitivity as they aged).

Innovation also drove sales in cosmetics and hair care. Estée Lauder's Lightsource line of cosmetics contained not only active ingredients like amino acids and micronutrients found in skin care products but also used microcrystals to deflect light to mask wrinkles. Cover Girl and Max Factor both offered

exhibit 4 **U.S. Cosmetics, Fragrances, and Toiletries Market Sizes by Product Category, 1996, 2000, Projections for 2005**

Product Category	1996		2000		2005		CAGR* (1996–2000)
	Dollar Value (in billions)	Percent of Total	Dollar Value (in billions)	Percent of Total	Dollar Value (in billions)	Percent of Total	
Hair care	$ 6.6	25.9%	$ 8.2	25.2%	$ 8.6	21.6%	5.3%
Fragrance	4.7	18.4	5.1	15.6	6.0	15.0	1.7
Cosmetics	4.6	17.8	6.4	19.7	8.4	21.1	8.7
Skin care	4.3	16.7	6.3	19.5	9.4	23.7	10.3
Bath products and other personal care	5.4	21.2	6.5	20.1	7.4	18.6	4.6
Totals/Average	$25.7	100.0%	$32.5	100.0%	$39.8	100.0%	5.0%

*Compound average growth rate.

Source: Investor Update Meeting, Avon Products, Inc., May 8, 2001.

highly popular Outlast and Lipfinity products that contained Permatone, a semipermanent lip color that kept lipstick in place for up to eight hours. New hair care products also benefited from innovations. Products that touted aromatherapy, herbal ingredients, or other natural aspects; products that protected colored or highlighted hair; and products developed to enhance volume and body achieved the greatest sales growth. Although their beneficial effects were anecdotal rather than scientific, aromatherapy and herbal products had also led sales growth in the bath products and fragrance categories of the CFT industry. The Fragrance Foundation reported in its *Fall 2001/Winter 2002 Trends Report:* "Wellness is the growth area for all fragrance items—the association of feelings, emotions, and fragrances and how they interact with one another."[3]

Consumer Demographics and Cosmetics

Many of the innovations in skin care products, cosmetics, and hair care products were developed specifically to address the concerns of baby boomers who wished to fight the aging process. Anti-aging products accounted for most of the 2 percent annual growth in the overall CFT industry during the late 1990s and 2000–2001 and much of the growth in

[3]"Market Undergoes Sea Change," *MMR*, June 25, 2001, p. 103.

such categories as hair care, cosmetics, and skin care. However, the markets for products that focused on the needs of teens and preteens rivaled those of products developed for baby boomers, since the 23 million teenagers in the United States had an average weekly disposable income of $85. The U.S. teen and preteen market was so attractive that specialty retailers like Hotfox, Limited Too, Charlotte Russe, and Hot Topic carried only items appealing to preteens. With the help of his daughter, designer Ralph Lauren developed his Ralph fragrance line, which was targeted toward young women and was color-coded to suit the personality of the purchaser. Givenchy, Donna Karan, and Fubu also introduced fragrances specifically targeted toward teens and preteens. Skin care was a particularly attractive product category in the teen market. Product innovations also focused on the needs of women between 20 and 30 who were concerned with the oncoming effects of aging. Nivea Visage's Time Defying Fluid was targeted toward women ages 20 to 35 who were not yet ready for an antiwrinkle product but wished to take a proactive approach to delaying the first signs of aging.

African American and other consumers with dark complexions had skin care and cosmetics needs that differed substantially from those of women of European nationality or descent. Much of the product innovation directed toward reducing the effects of aging was less important to women with darker complexions since the higher melanin and oil content found in dark-colored skin naturally discouraged wrinkles. A marketing executive for Color Me Beautiful, Inc., whose cosmetics brands include Iman, Flori Roberts, Interface Cosmetics, and Patti La Belle suggested that the skin care needs of African American women had gone largely unmet since their concerns focused mainly on the availability of cosmetics pigments suitable for darker skin, skin oiliness, and hyperpigmentation caused by abrasions, blemishes, or excessive exposure to the sun. Like women with dark complexions, Asian women differed from women of European ancestry with regard to skin care, with more emphasis placed on maintaining natural or pale skin tones. The men's market had remained elusive, with few men adopting a daily skin care routine, but some manufacturers had achieved some success with cleaning and moisturizing products.

KEY RIVALS IN THE GLOBAL COSMETICS, FRAGRANCE, AND TOILETRY INDUSTRY

Even though Avon was the world's largest direct seller of cosmetics, fragrances, and toiletries in 2003, it was less than one-half the size of industry leader L'Oréal, whose 2002 sales exceeded 14.3 billion euros (€). Rivals in the CFT industry ranged from companies like L'Oréal and Avon, whose business focus was limited to a single line of business, to highly diversified companies such as Procter & Gamble and LVMH, whose business diversification included a wide variety of consumer products. Distribution strategies also varied in the industry, with many of the largest sellers like L'Oréal, Procter & Gamble, and Estée Lauder choosing to sell their products through department store, drugstore, and discounter channels, while others chose to vertically integrate into direct selling or the operation of cosmetics retail stores. The specialty retail store channel was the fastest-growing channel in the industry, with Sephora, Bath & Body Works, and Victoria's Secret Beauty accounting for the greatest share of industry retail sales growth. Specialty retailers' broad lines of cosmetics were available both in their stores dedicated to the sale of CFT products and through their catalogs and Web sites. Exhibit 5 presents the corporate and personal care revenues for 2002 and well-known products of the leading manufacturers and marketers of cosmetics, fragrances, toiletries, and other personal care products. An overview of Avon's key rivals follows.

L'Oréal

L'Oréal's history dates to 1907, when French chemist Eugene Schueller developed a safe hair dye that he sold to Parisian hairdressers. The product's ability to dye hair without damaging the hair or irritating the scalp was a welcome product innovation and one that allowed Schueller to almost immediately develop export market opportunities in Holland, Austria, Italy, Russia, the Far East, and the United States. As a chemist, Schueller sought to make this company known for quality and innovation; by 1936, he had diversified the company's product line beyond hair care products to high-quality fragrances, skin care products, and cosmetics. In the early 2000s, L'Oréal remained known for its quality products, processes, and business practices. In a review of global corporations' strategies and operations conducted by INSEAD in 2001, L'Oréal was rated the Best of the Best across such themes as mission and vision, client orientation, and innovation. In addition, the company took pride in its €468 million R&D budget, its 2,800 researchers, and its 501 patents registered in 2002 alone. L'Oréal was a leader in developing products designed to neutralize free radicals and was steering its research toward the development of products to rehydrate the skin, improve skin sensitivity, and change color characteristics with lighting.

In 2003 L'Oréal manufactured and marketed more than 500 brands and 2,000 products in more than 130 countries. The company's products were sold in the department stores around the world and, in some cases, to hair care professionals and pharmacies. L'Oréal had aggressively expanded its global reach during the 1990s by offering a wider selection of brands in countries outside Western Europe and making strategic acquisitions of brands popular outside of Europe. Approximately 50 percent of L'Oréal's sales were generated in Western Europe, with 30 percent originating in North America and the remaining 20 percent coming from other parts of the world. (See again Exhibit 5 for the company's best-known brands.)

exhibit 5　**Corporate Revenues, Global Personal Care Sales and Personal Care Brands of Leading Cosmetics, Fragrances, and Toiletry Producers**

Rank	Company	2002 Corporate Revenues (in billions)	2002 Personal Care Sales (in billions)	Personal Care Brands
1	L'Oréal	€14.3	€14.3	L'Oréal, Lancôme, Garnier, Giorgio Armani, Vichy, La Roche–Posay, Matrix, Redken, Maybelline, Ralph Lauren, Helena Rubinstein, Carson, Biotherm
2	Procter & Gamble	$43.3	$12.2	Cover Girl, Max Factor, Hugo Boss, Giorgio Beverly Hills, Head & Shoulders, Pantene Pro-V, Pert Plus, Vidal Sassoon, Olay, Clairol, Nice 'n Easy, Herbal Essences, Aussie, Infusium, Zest, Safeguard
3	Estée Lauder	$ 5.1	$5.1	Estée Lauder, Clinique, Donna Karan, Kate Spade, Tommy Hilfiger, Aramis, Bobbi Brown, Aveda, Prescriptives, Origins, M·A·C, La Mer, Michael Kors, Bumble and bumble, jane
4	Avon Products	$ 6.2	$4.1	Avon, Skin-So-Soft, Anew, Far Away, BeComing
5	LVMH	€12.1	€2.3	Christian Dior, Givenchy, Guerlain, Bliss, Fresh, Make Up For Ever, Kenzo
6	Limited Brands	$8.5	Approx. $2	Very Sexy, Garden Collection, Bath & Body Works, Dream Angels, PINK, Rapture, Body by Victoria, Breathless
7	Coty	$1.6	$1.6	Coty, Davidoff, Lancaster, Joop!, Chopard, Jil Sander, Isabella Rossellini, Vivienne Westwood, Stetson, Adidas, Aspen, Calgon, Rimmel, Yue-Sai, Jennifer Lopez, Celine Dion
8	Mary Kay	$1.6	$1.6	Mary Kay, Journey, Elige, Belara
9	Revlon	$1.1	$1.1	Revlon, Almay, Ultima II, Flex, Charlie

Source: Company Web sites.

Procter & Gamble

The Procter & Gamble Company (P&G) was begun when immigrants William Procter and James Gamble settled in Cincinnati, Ohio, in 1837 and soon thereafter married sisters. At the urging of their father-in-law, the two men, one a candle maker and the other a soap maker, created a partnership to manufacture and market their products in the Cincinnati area. The company's sales reached $1 million by 1859, but the company had yet to produce and market a national brand until 1879, when James Norris Gamble, son of the founder and a trained chemist, developed Ivory soap. Ivory quickly transformed Procter & Gamble into a national consumer products company with 30 brands and production facilities across the United States and Canada by 1890. The company added a food products division in 1911 when it introduced

Crisco and began a chemicals division to formalize its research procedures and develop new products in 1917. P&G entered the hair care business in 1934 when it developed the first detergent-based shampoo. P&G's commitment to research allowed it to continue to introduce popular-selling brands like Camay, Tide, Crest, Pampers, and Downy throughout the 1940s, 1950s, and 1960s.

P&G's presence in the CFT industry strengthened in the 1980s when the company acquired Richardson-Vicks in 1985 and Noxell in 1989. Richardson-Vicks was the producer of Oil of Olay and Pantene products, and Noxell manufactured and marketed Cover Girl, Noxema, and Clarion branded products. Procter & Gamble acquired Max Factor in 1991 and Giorgio Beverly Hills fragrances in 1994. In 2002 P&G recorded revenues of $43.3 billion through the manufacturing and marketing of more than 250 brands sold in 130 countries. In 2002, the company budgeted over $1.6 billion for research and development, had nearly 7,500 researchers, and collaborated with nearly 100 universities worldwide in the development and refinement of its consumer and pharmaceutical products. In 2003, P&G held over 29,000 patents. The company's worldwide sales of cosmetics, hair care products, and fragrances exceeded $12.2 billion in 2002. P&G cosmetics and hair care brands were primarily found in discount stores, supermarkets, and drugstores.

Estée Lauder

The Estée Lauder Company was founded in 1946 when Estée Lauder and her husband, Joseph, began to market four skin care products in New York City. The company quickly developed a reputation for quality and innovation, and in 1948 prestigious retailer Saks Fifth Avenue began carrying the Lauders' products in its New York store. In 1953 Estée Lauder extended its product line into fragrances with the introduction of Youth Dew—the first bath oil that doubled as a perfume. The company expanded internationally in 1960 when its products became available at Harrod's in London. Within the next six years, Estée Lauder's sales operations were expanded to Canada, Puerto Rico, Central America, Denmark, Italy, Spain, Switzerland, Australia, Netherlands, Belgium, France, Finland, Greece, Germany, Norway, Austria, Singapore, Thailand, and Japan.

Estée Lauder extended its product line to men's fragrances with the introduction of Aramis in 1964, and it launched Clinique, the first dermatologist-guided, allergy-tested, fragrance-free cosmetics brand, in 1968. Its Prescriptives line of cosmetics was introduced in 1979, while Origins, a line of skin care, makeup, and bath products was launched in 1990. In the 1990s, the company acquired two makeup artist brands (M·A·C and Bobbi Brown); Sassaby (the owner of the color cosmetics brand jane); and Aveda Corporation (a leader in the U.S. luxury hair care industry). Also during the 1990s, Estée Lauder acquired Stila Cosmetics (a prestige cosmetics brand) and Jo Malone (a London-based marketer of prestige skin care and fragrance products). In 2000, the company acquired a majority equity interest in New York–based Bumble and bumble (a premier hair salon) and Bumble and bumble Products (a developer, marketer and distributor of quality

hair care products). The Estée Lauder Companies also held the global license for fragrances and cosmetics for the Tommy Hilfiger, Donna Karan, and Kate Spade brands.

In 2002 the company recorded sales of $5.1 billion and its products could be found in more than 130 countries. Estée Lauder brands were usually found in department stores but could also be purchased in specialty retail stores and via the Internet at Gloss.com. The Gloss.com e-commerce site was jointly owned by Estée Lauder, Chanel, and Clarins. Estée Lauder also operated freestanding specialty stores located in prominent shopping districts where its M·A·C, Origins, and Estée Lauder branded products were showcased.

LVMH

Moët Hennessy Louis Vuitton (LVMH) was the world's leading luxury products group, with annual sales of €12.1 billion in 2002. Some of LVMH's best-known brands included Dom Pérignon, Louis Vuitton, Givenchy, Parfums Christian Dior, Christian Lacroix, TAG Heuer, and Ebel. The company's perfumes and cosmetics business recorded 2002 sales of €2.3 billion and included such well-known and innovative brands as Christian Dior, Givenchy, Kenzo, and Guerlain. The company also owned Sephora, which was the leading retail beauty chain in France and the United States and the second largest beauty chain in Europe. In 2003 Sephora operated stores in Europe, the United States, and Japan. Sephora stores carried LVMH's products and other prestigious brands of cosmetics, fragrances, and skin care products including Chanel, Dolce and Gabbana, Elizabeth Arden, Hugo Boss, Naomi Campbell, Gianni Versace, and Burberry. In 2003 Sephora.com offered the largest and most diverse selection of beauty products on the Internet, with over 11,000 products and more than 230 brands. LVMH cosmetics, fragrance, and skin care brands were also sold by prestigious retailers around the world.

Limited Brands

Limited Brands was created through the 2002 merger of The Limited, Inc., and Intimate Brands. The merger actually recombined The Limited with Victoria's Secret, which had been spun off from the company in 1995. The new company's best-known brands were The Limited, Express, Victoria's Secret, Bath & Body Works, and White Barn Candle Company, which gave the new corporation revenues of $8.5 billion in its first year as a combined company. Victoria's Secret was the largest retailer of intimate apparel in the United States, with more than 1,000 stores and sales of $2.6 billion in 2002. Bath & Body Works was the largest U.S. specialty retailer of such personal care products as bath products, skin care products, and hair care products, with more than 1,600 stores and 2002 sales of $1.8 billion. The company's White Barn Candle Company specialized in the retail sales of home fragrances and home decor and was launched in 1999. More than 120 White Barn Candle stores had been opened by 2003.

Limited Brands also operated Victoria's Secret Beauty (VSB) stores, which sold their own VSB branded lines of cosmetics, fragrances, and skin care products. Victoria's Secret Beauty was among the fastest-growing specialty retailers of cosmetics, with over 500 stores. VSB cosmetics, fragrances, skin care products, and beauty accessories could also be purchased online at Victoriassecret.com/beauty. Limited Brands did not disclose revenues from VSB stores but expected the chain to achieve $1 billion in sales by 2005 through the aggressive addition of stores, growing Internet sales, and the development of new beauty products.

Coty

In 2003 Coty was one of the world's leading manufacturers and marketers of fragrances, cosmetics and skin care products, with 2002 revenues of nearly $1.6 billion. The company was founded in Paris in 1904 by Francois Coty and was based in Germany for many years until its headquarters was moved to New York City in 1996. The privately held company distributed its products through both mass-market and prestige retail channels around the world and maintained production and sales operations in 25 countries. Coty's mass-market brands included Adidas, The Healing Garden, Stetson, and Aspen, while its moderately priced fragrance and cosmetics brands were distributed by its Paris-based Lancaster Group and included Lancaster, Davidoff, JOOP!, Isabella Rossellini, Vivienne Westwood, Jennifer Lopez, Celine Dion, and Yue-Sai.

Coty's strategy had not only yielded a number one global ranking in fragrances, with its brands appealing mainly to price-sensitive consumers, but the company's upscale brands of cosmetics had allowed it to become the market leader in several international markets. For example, the company's Astor and Rimmel London lines of cosmetics were among the top-selling brands of cosmetics in Europe. Rimmel London was introduced to the United States in 2000 and was sold exclusively by Wal-Mart in 2003.

Mary Kay Cosmetics

Mary Kay's business model resembled that of Avon more than any other cosmetics manufacturer and marketer. In 2003 Mary Kay was the second largest direct seller of cosmetics, fragrances, skin care products, and dietary supplements, with more than 200 products and 2002 revenues of $1.6 billion. The company was founded by Mary Kay Ash in 1963 with $5,000 and the help of her 20-year-old son, Richard Rogers. Ash had recently retired from a career in direct sales and, after making a list of both winning and poor management practices she had observed during her career, was moved to create a principled company for women wanting unlimited opportunity for personal and financial success. Ash led the company with its central goal of creating opportunity for women and used the Golden Rule as her guiding philosophy. She believed that members of her independent sales force should prioritize their lives with God first, family second, and career third. Ash's vision and principles allowed the company to build a sales force of more than 800,000 Independent Beauty Consultants in 37 countries and become recognized by *Fortune* as one of the "100 Best Companies to Work for in America" and one of the "10 Best Companies for Women" in 1984, 1993, and 1998. *Fortune* also listed Mary Kay among its "Most Admired Corporations" in America in 1995. By the time of her death in November 2001, Ash had become an inspiration to many women around the world. During her lifetime Mary Kay Ash published three best-selling books, received awards for aiding the financial needs of women, and was the only woman profiled in *Forbes Greatest Business Stories of All Time*.

In 2003, the company offered a full line of color cosmetics, skin care products, fragrances, and bath products that were available only through one of its 1 million Independent Beauty Consultants. Consumers could order from a Beauty Consultant during a sales call, over the phone, or by visiting Marykay. com and entering their Consultant's name and then selecting items to purchase. Visitors to the Web site who did not have a Beauty Consultant could enter their zip code and immediately make purchases that were then credited to a nearby Consultant or site visitors could have Consultants contact them for a beauty consultation.

Revlon

Revlon was established in 1932 by Charles and Joseph Revson, along with a chemist, Charles Lachman, who contributed the *L* to the Revlon name. Lachman had developed a unique nail polish that used pigments instead of dyes and was able to create a rich-looking opaque nail enamel in shades never before available. Revlon sold the new nail polish first in beauty salons and then through department stores and drugstores and recorded annual sales exceeding $1 million within six years of the company's founding. Revlon expanded beyond nail polish to cosmetics in the 1950s and entered the fragrance market in 1973 when it introduced Charlie, which became the number-one-selling fragrance in the world by 1975. Revlon's annual sales surpassed the $1 billion mark in 1977, and in the mid-1990s Revlon became the number one brand of color cosmetics in mass-market channels.

During the late 1990s Revlon encountered a wide array of problems ranging from excessively high costs to declining brand image. The company's market share peaked in 1998 at 32 percent and bottomed out at 22.3 percent during the second quarter of 2002 before improving slightly in the latter half of 2002 and 2003. Similarly, the company's revenues reached an all-time high of $2.1 billion in 1998 but declined to $1.1 billion in 2002 after the company disposed of its professional products line, exited nearly 75 international markets, and suffered market share losses in the United States. In 2003 Revlon's products were marketed in 100 countries under such well-known brand names as Revlon, ColorStay, Revlon Age Defying, Almay, and Ultima in cosmetics; Moon Drops, Eterna 27, Ultima, and Jeanne Gatineau in skin care; Charlie and Ciara in fragrances; and Flex, Outrageous, Mitchum, Colorsilk, and Jean Naté in personal care products.

ANDREA JUNG'S INITIAL STRATEGIC PLAN TO RESURRECT AVON

When Andrea Jung became Avon's new CEO in November 1999, the company's annual sales growth had slowed to less than 1.5 percent and its stock price had fallen from a high of $55 to a three-year low of $25. The strategies initiated by Charles Perrin had resulted in some initial improvement in operating ratios and yielded some modest sales growth during 1998, but in late 1999 it was clear that Avon was in need of a bold new direction. Having served 16 months as Avon CEO, Perrin resigned after concluding that his lack of experience in direct sales limited his effectiveness with the company. Avon's board took little time in turning to Andrea Jung to rejuvenate the 113-year-old beauty products company. Jung's first task as CEO was to hit the streets of her neighborhood, ringing doorbells, to better understand the desires of customers and needs of sales agents. Jung heard customers gripe about discontinued colors, mishandled orders, out-of-date catalogs, unattractive packaging, lack of innovative products, and confusing promotions. The new CEO also discovered firsthand the structural obstacles to achieving success as an Avon Lady. Policies that required sales agents to place orders only during the beginning of a campaign with no opportunity to reorder hot-selling items; procedures that required 40-page order forms to be filled out by hand and either mailed or faxed to Avon; and orders that, according to Avon's own estimates, were improperly filled more than 30 percent of the time all made it difficult for sales agents to increase their sales volumes and commissions.

In Andrea Jung's fourth week on the job, she asked Avon executives and market analysts to convene for the presentation of her turnaround plan. She called for the launch of an entirely new line of business, the development of innovative products, new packaging, new channels of distribution, a new approach to supply chain management, new sales models, and new approaches to image building. Jung promised to pay for the increased expenditures for everything from R&D to Internet-based sales support with additional process reengineering that would cut hundreds of millions in non-value-adding costs from the company's value chain. At the close of Jung's conference, few believed that she could successfully implement the ambitious plan. A Paine Webber analyst's comment that the plan "has a high probability of disappointment" was not a unique view.[4]

Jung's Vision for Avon

Andrea Jung envisioned an Avon that would be the "ultimate relationship marketer of products and services for women."[5] Jung's view of a new Avon was that of a company going far beyond selling cosmetics to becoming a trusted source for almost any type of good or service that women need. Andrea Jung's Avon would ultimately allow women to purchase not only beauty products but also goods and services unrelated to cosmetics (e.g., financial services), in whatever manner the customer found most convenient—through an Avon representative, in a store, or online. Under Jung, Avon's vision statement read, "Our vision is to be the company that best understands and satisfies the product, service and self-fulfillment needs of women globally. Our dedication to supporting women touches not only beauty – but health, fitness, self-empowerment and financial independence."

In late 1999, the company was far from what Jung envisioned. In an era in which 75 percent of American women worked and direct selling accounted for less than 7 percent of cosmetics and toiletries sold in the United States, the Avon sales model perfected by David McConnell and Mrs. P. F. E. Albee in the late 1800s seemed dated by two generations. However, with approximately 98 percent of Avon's annual sales generated by its 3.5 million sales agents, Avon could ill afford to alienate its sales force with moves that might reduce direct selling revenues. Avon's representatives were vigilant in protecting their customers and sales, and they were aggressive in reversing strategies that might increase sales for Avon but limit sales growth opportunities for sales representatives. In 1997 Avon launched a basic Web site through which a small number of

products could be purchased online, and it placed its Web address on the back of its catalogs, but Avon's sales representatives revolted, covering the Web address with their own stickers until they were successful in forcing the company to remove the Web site. Avon sales representatives were similarly displeased with any recommendation to make Avon products available for sale in department stores or malls. In addition, the company was limited by its dowdy brand image, which market research found most women viewed as "my grandmother's brand" or "not for me."[6] In addition, Avon had no products in some of the fastest-growing CFT categories and it had not introduced a hit product in decades. Other problems at Avon included distribution inefficiencies, limited income opportunity for the average sales representative, and the difficulty of selling the company's products to busy women. One Avon board member helped explain the dilemma of Avon's direct selling model: "Do you have an Avon rep? I don't . . . people like us should be able to buy the product."[7]

Upon unveiling her initial strategic plan, Jung identified the following strategic priorities to help correct Avon's competitive liabilities and set the company on a new course:

- Grow global beauty category sales through continued investment in new product development, advertising, and sampling.

- Provide representatives with greater career opportunities through sales leadership, enhanced Internet capabilities, and training.

- Reduce inventory levels while at the same time improving service to representatives.

- Improve operating margins by 50–100 basis points through business process redesign.

- Successfully launch the Avon Wellness line of nutritional supplements and vitamins.

- Begin to build a profitable retail business to fuel future growth.

- Develop e-commerce opportunities for Avon and its sales representatives.

- Pursue market opportunities in China and Eastern Europe.

---

[4]"It Took a Lady to Save Avon," p. 204.

[5]As quoted in "Avon: The New Calling," *Business Week*, September 18, 2000, p. 136.

[6]"Avon Calling," *Ad Age Global*, October 1, 2001, p. 26.

[7]"The New Calling," p. 136.

Exhibit 6 presents a list of specific objectives under Avon's major strategic priorities identified in 2000.

New Strategies to Increase Sales

Andrea Jung's strategies were intended to grow the company's revenues and market share by correcting many of the company's competitive liabilities, but not at the expense of its proven direct sales force. "If we don't include them in everything we do, then we're just another retail brand, just another Internet site, and I don't see the world needing more of those," said Jung of the importance of incorporating Avon's sales reps into new business models.[8] Jung believed that the Internet could be among Avon's best hopes for future growth and that an e-commerce business model at Avon would benefit the company's representatives. Jung initiated an eRepresentative sales concept that allowed representatives to direct customers to Avon.com to purchase products 24 hours a day, 7 days a week. However, before the company's e-commerce plans were finalized, Avon was careful to gain input from its independent sales reps through multiple surveys and focus groups.

Once implemented, Avon's eRepresentatives received commissions of 20–25 percent on Web orders shipped direct from Avon and commissions of 30–50 percent on Internet orders that they personally delivered to customers' homes. Visitors to Avon.com were given an opportunity to enter their Avon representative's 10-digit code to direct a commission to their rep, but they could also check out without requesting an eRepresentative or entering the code. Within the first nine months of the program, almost 12,000 of Avon's 500,000 sales representatives in the United States each paid $15 per month to become an eRepresentative. Jung also believed that information technology and use of the Internet could speed order processing and reduce paperwork for both sales representatives and corporate personnel. Even though 54 percent of Avon's sales representatives did not own a computer, the company hoped to get all representatives online by offering Gateway PCs plus an Internet connection for $19.95 per month.

Another opportunity for sales representatives to increase their income was the concept of Sales Leadership—an idea that had been talked of for years and was partially developed under Charles Perrin. Avon's

original direct sales model provided Avon representatives with no training and commissions only on their own sales. Individuals who came to Avon with developed sales skills or a natural ability to sell the company's products prospered, with approximately 20 percent of Avon's reps accounting for 80 percent of the company's revenues. In 1999 the annual earnings for a typical Avon sales representative in the United States was $2,400; earnings of $7,500 or more allowed agents to gain admittance into the company's President's Club. Turnover was high among representatives who had difficulty reaching an adequate sales levels, and Avon was having trouble adding new reps to replace those who dropped out. Sales Leadership allowed Avon's seasoned sales representatives to recruit new sales agents who they believed might have a knack for sales and to share in their successes. Sales Leadership also included a Beauty Advisors program that allowed sales reps to receive training in sales tactics and beauty and cosmetics tips.

Jung recognized that Avon's sales force, regardless of how well organized and trained, relied on appealing products to increase sales. As CEO, she aggressively pushed the company's plan to develop global brands, repackage existing products, and launch blockbuster products. The company's market research showed that Avon's largely working- and middle-class customers couldn't afford prestige brands like Lancôme or Estée Lauder but craved the elegance of those brands. Jung called for a redesign of the packaging of Avon's products to better match the look of upscale department store brands, launched a new "Let's Talk" advertising campaign, and signed tennis stars Venus and Serena Williams to endorsement contracts to improve the company's image. Recognizing that her earlier efforts to transition Avon's many regional brands into single global brands had produced considerable success as global brands grew from 11 percent of Avon's sales in 1993 to 70 percent of sales in 2000, Jung stressed to the company's product development teams that new lines should be marketable globally whenever possible. Most of all, Jung understood the importance of innovation to the success of new lines. She added nearly 50 percent to Avon's R&D budget during her first fiscal year as CEO and demanded that the company's researchers develop innovative new lines within two years instead of the company's usual three-plus-year product development time.

[8]Ibid.

exhibit 6 **Avon's Strategic and Financial Objectives, 2000 and 2004**

	Marketing Transformations	
	2000	2004
Active beauty product stock-keeping units (SKUs)	5,000	4,000
Breakthrough innovation frequency	3 years	2 years
Product development (average)	88 weeks	50 weeks
Campaign development	52 weeks	26 weeks

	Supply Chain Improvement	
	2000	2004
Days of inventory	119	8–10
Forecasting accuracy	Baseline	+30%
Order fill rate	68%	90%

	Sales Leadership	
	2000	2004
Leadership downlines per U.S. district	110	214
Representatives per U.S. district	322	440
Growth in active representatives	2%–3%	2%–3%
Growth in average rep earnings	—	25%–30%

	eCommerce and Internet	
	2000	2002
eRepresentative participation	13%	50%
Representative support cost savings	$3 million	+$20 million
Geographic market penetration	United States, Japan, Taiwan	20 markets

	International	
	2000	2004
Local currency sales growth	50%	20%–30%
Representative growth	25%	20%–30%
Sales outlets (China)	3,463	6,000

	Financial	
	1997–2000	2001–2004
Sales growth	9%	10%+
Beauty growth	10%	12%+
Operating margin improvement	+3.2 points	50+ basis points/year
Cash flow from operations	$350 million	$700 million
Capital expenditures	$200 million (2000)	$225 million average/year

Source: Avon Investor Presentation, Susan Kropf, president and COO, 2000.

To make products available to women who were either too busy to shop with a sales agent or preferred to shop for beauty products in retail stores, Jung pushed forward Perrin's plans to make the company's products available in malls. Even though retail sales accounted for 93 percent of the global CFT market, Avon had largely avoiding retail channels in fear of competing against its representatives. However, Jung was able to gain the support of Avon's sales reps by offering the kiosks as franchises after the test marketing had been completed. Avon opened 50 franchised mall kiosks in Jung's first year as CEO and in 2001 entered agreements with Sears and JCPenney to operate Avon Center store-within-a-store concepts that would dedicate 400 to 1,000 square feet to an entirely new Avon beComing product line. The beComing products could not be purchased from independent representatives and were priced higher than Avon's other products but they were still less expensive than department store brands like Clinique, Lancôme, or Estée Lauder.

Avon had achieved success internationally before Andrea Jung became CEO, but she wanted more aggressive growth in emerging international markets like China, Hungary, Russia, and the Czech Republic. China had been identified by Avon management as an attractive market because it held 20 percent of the world's population, its population was relatively young, and because of its large and growing market for beauty products. Avon was the first and largest international direct seller in China from 1990 until April 1998, when direct selling was banned by the Chinese government. Avon quickly found retail stores to actually process sales of Avon products while its sales reps, now banned, became sales promoters who steered customers to retail stores to maintain their sales commissions. Andrea Jung's strategy for China continued the development of sales promoters but also expanded the products into A-class department stores and hypermarts in major cities and introduced Avon products to Dealer Beauty counters in boutiques and B- and C-class department stores in smaller towns.

Jung found the emerging markets in Central and Eastern Europe attractive because of the more than 130 million women ages 15 and older living in the regions, the young average age of consumers, and the $8.2 billion market size. The company's direct selling model was well suited to these markets since there were no governmental restrictions to limit independent sales representatives. Jung's strategies for the Central and Eastern European markets focused on representative recruitment, the development of local leaders, ongoing market research, and significant spending for advertising and promotions. Avon also intended to maintain a focused product line in these markets, with limited stock-keeping units (SKUs) and 95 percent of sales coming from the sales of cosmetics, fragrances, and toiletries.

Strategy Execution and Business Results (2000–2003)

Business Process Reengineering The heart of Avon's strategy implementation efforts was its ability to eliminate non-value-adding costs from its value chain. Jung wished to allocate strategic spending of more than $100 million annually to support product development, e-commerce initiatives, better commission opportunities for independent reps, and global image building, but funding was available only if Avon's president and chief operating officer, Susan Kropf, could reconfigure the company's value chain to generate necessary cash flow. Kropf's business process reengineering (BPR) efforts reduced supply chain costs by $30 million in 2001 and $60 million in 2002 by closing five facilities, reducing the product line, and shifting to regional sourcing of certain products. Avon expected total cost savings of $225 million in 2003 and $400 million in 2004 as Kropf expanded reengineering to include product development, marketing, purchasing, and administrative activities. Avon's BPR efforts resulted in pretax charges of $97.4 million 2001 and $43.6 million in 2002 related to costs to accelerate business transformation initiatives, but were expected to improve operating margins by 250 basis points and operating cash flow by $500–$800 million by year-end 2004. Exhibit 7 provides examples of specific operating strategies and implementation efforts undertaken to accomplish Avon's strategic and financial objectives.

Sales Representatives The recruitment and retention of sales reps was a strategic objective that led to the implementation of Jung's Sales Leadership program. "If Avon stopped adding numbers of active representatives, you know, the fuel and the lifeblood of the business slows down," explained Jung when asked about the importance of growth in the number

exhibit 7 **Avon's Operating Strategies and Implementation Tactics, 2000–2003**

Marketing Transformations
- Higher-quality, more timely market intelligence
- Category-, brand-, and concept-focused marketing strategy
- Flexible product development cycles
- Comprehensive product screening
- Fewer, more highly innovative new products
- Integrated category, brand, and campaign planning
- Significantly shortened campaign planning and brochure creation
- Use of high-style, glamorous catalogs

Supply Chain Improvement
- Supplier management/sourcing savings
- The use of supply chain planning tools to reduce cost and inventory levels
- Consensus-based forecasting
- Strong links and focus between marketing and supply chain operations
- ABC planning and product segmentation
- Centralized inventory distribution hubs

Sales Leadership
- Faster growth through expanded coverage
- Improved representative earnings opportunities
- Full implementation of eRepresentative concept to Poland, Taiwan, and Japan
- Expansion of pilot eRepresentative program in Brazil, Chile, Argentina, and the United Kingdom
- Continue existing pilot eRepresentative program in Italy and Venezuela
- Redesign pilot eRepresentative program for Canada and Germany

International
- Sales Leadership and training
- Geographic expansion
- New market entries
- Expansion of outlets in China
- Establish a customer club in China
- Triple advertising to 7% of sales in China

E-commerce and Internet
- Utilization of Internet in manufacturing/sourcing (job bidding, e-auctions, international transfers)
- Internet-based customer service functions including electronic ordering, contract processing, product information, and order status
- Utilization of Internet to provide representatives with ordering information, account status, online appointments, sales training, and field reporting
- Create global Web site style guide
- Maximize and leverage existing sites in the United States, Japan, and Taiwan

Source: Avon Investor Presentation, Susan Kropf, president and COO, 2000.

of sales representatives.[9] Jung said Avon needed "double-digit growth [in the number of Avon reps] every year . . . Probably one of the biggest indicators to us of the health of the direct sales operation is how many people we are attracting."[10] Sales Leadership provided new opportunities for Avon reps since they could earn commissions on the sales of their recruits. In 2001, a Leadership Executive Unit Leader earned

[9]"It Took a Lady to Save Avon," p. 208.

[10]"Avon Calling," p. 26.

$46,500 on average, and Senior Executive Unit Leaders earned $185,000. Avon's number of reps increased by 10 percent in both 2001 and 2002, to reach 3.9 million reps worldwide in 2003.

Even though all representatives enrolled in the Sales Leadership program were required to sell products totaling at least $500 per month, some Leadership representatives spent more time recruiting and training new members than selling products. A New York Leadership rep who said she spent "Saturdays outside the supermarket trying to talk people into becoming an Avon Lady," recruited 350 new reps in 18 months and grossed more than $1.3 million in sales—one-half of which came from her recruits.[11] By 2003, 58 percent of Avon's U.S. representatives participated in the Sales Leadership program and the company had begun testing the program in 25 international markets. The company had also had 40,000 representatives sign up to become Beauty Advisors by 2003. Avon found that its Beauty Advisors typically sold 25 percent more than traditional Avon representatives.

A by-product of the Sales Leadership and Beauty Advisor programs was Avon's ability to recruit younger sales representatives. Before the two new programs the company had trouble recruiting younger reps; its greatest success had come with women over 40. The introduction of youth to Avon's sales force was important since the younger women's network of customers might be less loyal to other brands and more likely to try new products. The changing face of Avon's sales force is shown below:

Age	New Reps	Total Reps	All U.S. Women
Under 35	52%	17%	34%
35+	48%	83%	66%
Average age	35	48	46

Source: Avon Products, Inc.

E-commerce and the Internet

Jung and Kropf saw the Internet as the driver of transformation in the relationships between representatives, customers, and the company's marketing and supply chain operations. The company could use the Internet to accept bids from sourcing contractors and vendors, create global sales aids and online literature, and provide representatives with electronic ordering, contract processing, product information, and order status. Avon's Web-based ordering process eliminated paperwork for eRepresentatives and reduced Avon's internal cost of order processing from 90 cents to 30 cents per order. Avon had added most items to its U.S. Web site for online purchasing by 2001 and had established e-commerce sites in 16 international markets by 2003.

The company's Internet sales strategy achieved early success in 2000 when Avon management found that 4–6 percent of site visitors made purchases versus a purchases rate of 1–2 percent that was more typical of business-to-consumer sites. Avon management also found that eRepresentatives increased sales by 30 percent on average after linking to Avon.com. Andrea Jung suggested that the sales increases were attributable to the Web's ability to keep representatives constantly connected to customers. She also suggested that eReps experienced "higher average order productivity as the geographic borders and time differences disappear."[12]

Image Enhancement

The transformation of Avon's image called for new products, new packaging, celebrity endorsements, stylish new catalogs, and new advertising campaigns. Avon increased the company's expenditures for advertising by 50 percent, to $92.4 million, in 2000, then to $97.2 million in 2001 and to $101 million in 2002. Andrea Jung wanted Avon's advertising budget to grow from 2 percent to approximately 4 percent of total beauty sales by 2004. The company's advertising focused on its global "Let's Talk" campaign, which attempted to portray Avon as a lively, energetic, fashionable brand. The company's endorsement by the Williams sisters was seen by management as an embodiment of Avon's values of empowerment and self-fulfillment. The company also completely redesigned its catalog to better reflect the glamour associated with the cosmetics industry. Prior to the redesign, Avon's catalog had the look of an industrial products catalog, with beauty products usually depicted in photos on a plain background and only limited graphics included on the page. The new catalog, first tested in the United Kingdom in 2000, had the slick look of fashion and cosmetics ads seen in magazines like *Glamour* or

[11] "It Took a Lady to Save Avon," p. 208.

[12] "Avon Calling," p. 26.

Cosmopolitan, with copy printed in stylish fonts and products displayed by fashion models. During the test, the catalog helped Avon improve sales, average order sizes, and market share, and move from number four in the United Kingdom market to number three. Avon's redesigned catalog for the U.S. market was launched in 2002.

Changing Avon's image and developing global campaigns involved new approaches to market intelligence, marketing strategy, new product development, and marketing planning. Kropf called for (1) better-quality and more timely market intelligence on various consumer groups, channels, and competitors and (2) the development of a consumer-needs-based marketing strategy. In addition, Kropf required Avon's marketers to integrate their decisions with others in the organization, including product developers. The cross-functional product development effort called for shorter development cycles, more highly innovative products, and more frequent development of breakthrough products. Once new products were developed, Avon's marketers were to create integrated category and brand campaigns in shorter time frames so that products could go to market earlier. Market research conducted by Avon indicated that the company's efforts to enhance the Avon brand image had achieved quite a bit of success by year-end 2002. The U.S. brand image indexes of Avon and selected competitors in 2000 and 2002 were as follows:

Brand	2000	2002	Change
Cover Girl	150	130	−17 points
Revlon	126	107	−19
Maybelline	113	107	−6
Mary Kay	109	111	+2
L'Oréal	92	93	+1
Oil of Olay	92	107	+15
Avon	79	104	+25

Source: Strategic Update Meeting, Avon Products, Inc., 2003.

Product Development   Avon's R&D team responded to Andrea Jung's challenge to develop a blockbuster product within two years with the 2000 introduction of Anew Retroactive—an anti-aging skin cream. Retroactive was developed in just under one year and recorded sales of $100 million in its first year on the market—twice the first year's sales of any other previous new Avon product. Jung's emphasis on product innovation also aided Avon's move into the development of new lines of business. Avon's R&D personnel collaborated with pharmaceuticals manufacturer Roche Holding, Ltd., in the development of Avon Wellness vitamins and supplements designed to promote general health or address specific health issues such as lack of energy, poor memory, stress reduction, cardiovascular health, arthritis, bone density, and hormone regulation. Other Avon Wellness products included aromatherapy, skin care, and bath products. Avon's Wellness line exceeded sales estimates by 300 percent and achieved a 46 percent penetration rate during its first year on the market. The line achieved sales of $156 million during 2001 and $198 million in 2002. Avon's reengineered product development process and R&D expenditures of $43.1 million in 2000, $45.9 million in 2001, and $48.4 million in 2002 also resulted in the creation of its beComing line of products, Cellu-Sculpt anticellulite skin treatment, and two new fragrance brands, Incandessence (a floral scent inspired by the warmth of the sun) and Little Black Dress (a scent that was said to be timeless and perfect for almost any occasion). Exhibit 8 presents Avon's sales contribution by product line between 2001 and 2003.

International   Avon pushed its innovative new products like Anew Retroactive into such emerging markets as China, Poland, Russia, Hungary, and Slovakia; redesigned catalogs to illustrate the glamour of the Avon brand; and allocated up to 7 percent of sales to advertising in each country market to increase international sales. In China, Avon brand awareness improved from 41 percent to 53 percent, annual usage rates increased from 26 percent to 31 percent, and sales improved by 47 percent during 2000. The company's sales of beauty products in China had grown to approximately $300 million in 2003. In Central and Eastern Europe, Avon entered into new markets, implemented Sales Leadership and sales rep training, and aggressively increased spending on advertising and promotions. Avon's sales in this region grew at a compounded annual growth rate of 55 percent between 1996 and 2002, to reach $544 million. Its operating margin during 2002 on its Central and Eastern European sales was nearly 30 percent. Avon held number one market shares among CFT brands in Hungary, Poland,

exhibit 8   **Avon Products, Inc.'s Net Sales by Major Product Line Categories, 1998–2003 (in millions, except per share amounts)**

	2003	2002	2001
Beauty*	$4,487.7	$3,895.4	$3,716.5
Beauty Plus†	1,259.6	1,144.5	1,157.7
Beyond Beauty‡	1,057.3	932.7	927.9
Total net sales	$6,804.6	$6,170.6	$5,957.8

*Beauty includes cosmetics, fragrance, and toiletries.

†Beauty Plus includes fashion jewelry, accessories, apparel, and watches.

‡Beyond Beauty includes home products, gift and decorative, and candles.

Sales from Health and Wellness products and the mark. Lines are included in the above categories based on product type.

Source: Avon Products, Inc., 2003 10-K.

Russia, Ukraine, and the Czech Republic, and was the third best-selling CFT brand in Russia. Avon's net sales and operating profit by geographic region for 2000–2003 are presented in Exhibit 9.

Retail Channels   The company's Avon Centers planned for JCPenney and Sears stores was expected to be a substantial growth opportunity for the company since, in 2000, Sears and JCPenney combined had nearly 2,000 stores with total cosmetics sales of $700 million. Also, estimates indicated that 58–60 percent of all women shopped in Sears or JCPenney and preferred premium mass-market, specialty, or entry-level prestige CFT lines. This group of customers matched Avon management's target market for a new retail line of cosmetics, but one standout characteristic of Sears and JCPenney shoppers was that they tended to reject direct selling. Avon's initial agreements with Sears and JCPenney called for 195 Avon Centers in 2001 with an additional 650 store-within-a-store openings in 2002. However, Sears abandoned the plan in July 2001, just weeks before the first Avon Center opening was scheduled. Avon pushed forward with the opening of its Avon Centers in 89 JCPenney stores during 2001 and 2002 and the launch of its beComing CFT line with 400 SKUs, upscale prestige packaging, and value pricing. Avon's pricing strategy for its beComing product line, which was sold exclusively in its Avon Centers, was as follows:

Product	Core Avon	Mass Market Brands	be-Coming	Prestige Brands
Lipstick	$3–$7	$6–$9	$9.50	$12–$16
Nail polish	$2–$4	$3–$5	$6.50	$8–$12
Anti-aging treatment	$16–$24	$13–$22	$20–$40	$30–$60
Fragrance	$20	$20	$30	$45+

Source: Avon Products, Inc., Investor Update Meeting, May 8, 2001.

ACCELERATING GROWTH THROUGH AVON'S "NEXT GENERATION" STRATEGIC PLAN FOR 2004-2007

Andrea Jung had commented during a December 2001 investor conference call that her initial strategic plan included all necessary elements to accomplish Avon's objectives and meet shareholders' expectations, but she emphasized, "This turnaround is far from complete. I'm probably thinking that we need to be even bolder and faster."[13] The strategic plan

[13]"It Took a Lady to Save Avon," p. 208.

exhibit 9 **Avon Products, Inc.'s Net Sales and Operating Profit by Geographic Region, 2000–2003 (in millions, except per share amounts)**

| | 2003 | | 2002 | | 2001 | | 2000 | |
	Net Sales	Operating Profit (Loss)	Net Sales	Operating Profit (Loss)	Net Sales	Operating Profit (Loss)	Net Sales	Operating Profit (Loss)
North America								
United States	$2,217.9	$ 420.9	$2,151.2	$ 424.7	$2,024.2	$ 373.4	$1,901.7	$ 343.5
U.S. retail[a]	—	(20.7)	8.8	(25.9)	12.3	(25.9)	8.5	(4.5)
Other[b]	308.9	25.7	252.2	32.2	242.4	33.1	244.3	29.2
Total	$2,526.8	$ 425.9	$2,412.2	$ 431.0	$2,278.9	$ 380.6	$2,154.5	$ 368.2
International								
Latin America[c]	$1,747.2	$ 406.3	$1,700.1	$ 378.8	$1,898.5	$ 427.5	$1,839.9	$ 415.5
Europe	1,607.2	313.4	1,228.6	212.4	1,008.5	167.0	884.2	129.5
Pacific	923.4	156.6	829.7	133.9	773.7	112.6	803.1	117.8
Total	$4,277.8	$ 876.3	$3,758.4	$ 725.1	$3,680.7	$ 707.1	$3,527.2	$ 662.8
Total from worldwide operations	$6,804.6	$1,302.2	$6,170.6	$1,156.1	$5,959.6	$1,087.7	$5,681.7	$1,031.0
Global expenses	—	(263.3)	—	(249.8)	(1.8)	(242.8)	—	(241.1)
Contact settlement gain net of related expenses	—	—	—	—	—	25.9	—	—
Special charges, net[d]	—	(3.9)	—	(36.3)	—	(97.4)	—	—
Total	$6,804.6	$1,042.8	$6,170.6	$ 870.0	$5,957.8	$ 773.4	$5,681.7	$ 789.9

[a]Includes U.S. retail and Avon Centers.

[b]Includes Canada and Puerto Rico.

[c]Avon's operations in Mexico reported net sales for 2002, 2001, and 2000 of $661.8, $619.7, and $554.8, respectively. Avon's operations in Mexico reported operating profit for 2002, 2001, and 2000 of $163.9, $154.8, and $136.0, respectively.

[d]The 2002 and 2001 special charges of $36.3 and 97.4, respectively, were included in the consolidated statements as special charges ($34.3 in 2002 and $94.9 in 2001) and as inventory write-downs in cost of sales ($2.0 in 2002 and $2.5 in 2001).

Source: Avon Products, Inc., 2000 and 2003 10-Ks.

launched in 1999 had produced notable results by year-end 2002, including an improved image for Avon in the United States and internationally, the introduction of new blockbuster products, an increase in the number of sales reps in the United States and in key international markets, and improved financial and market performance. The company's sales had grown at a compounded annual rate of 11 percent between 2000 and 2002, its number of sales representatives had increased by 10 percent annually over the three-year period, and Avon's stock price had nearly doubled between January 2000 and January 2003.

The only notable failure of Jung's initial strategic plan was Avon's move into retail cosmetics sales. After just one year into the alliance, JCPenney and Avon agreed to abandon the Avon Center store-within-a-store cosmetics departments because of lackluster sales. JCPenney completely exited cosmetics sales but expanded its fragrances department after its alliance with Avon ended. Avon retained the beComing line and made it available exclusively through Avon Beauty Advisors. When the abandonment of the Avon Center concept was announced in January 2003, Andrea Jung stressed, "Avon remains committed to a multi-brand, multi-channel strategy and we will continue to pursue opportunities to reach new customer segments that prefer a retail shopping experience."[14]

During Jung's third year as CEO of Avon Products, Inc., she and Susan Kropf unveiled their "Next Generation" strategic plan for 2004–2007 that would accelerate the company's growth rate beyond its current 10 percent annual rate. The key components of the plan called for adding representatives at a more rapid 12 percent annual rate, expanding BPR efforts in sourcing, production, order fulfillment, and logistics to reduce costs by an additional $300 million and boost operating margins by 350 basis points by 2007, and earning the right to increase prices. Even though the company's image had improved since 2000, Avon's prices in 2003 were far below those of prestige brands such as Clinique and Estée Lauder and even below discount store brands such as Revlon and Maybelline. Jung and Kropf believed the company's increased advertising that began in 2000, its brochure enhancement that began in 2001, and its R&D in-

creases between 2001 and 2003 would allow the company to raise prices closer to those of its key mass merchant rivals beginning in 2004. For example, Avon planned to raise its $2.99 price for Creamy Powder Eyeshadow to $3.99 to more closely match Maybelline's price of $4.49 for its comparable product.

Andrea Jung also believed that Central and Eastern Europe offered tremendous growth opportunity, where she expected the company to achieve $1.5 billion in sales by 2007. Jung's plan to increase sales in this region by nearly $1 billion in less than four years included making additional market share gains in markets where it held leading positions, increasing sales of personal care and hair care products, increasing advertising from 3 percent of sales to 6 percent of sales, and establishing local production and sourcing capabilities. To support the company's push in Central and Eastern European markets, Avon began construction of a $40 million manufacturing facility near Moscow in 2003 that was expected to begin producing creams, lotions, mascara, and fragrances by mid-2004. Jung also wanted to increase sales in China to $750 million by 2007 by adding 500 franchised stores annually to its 5,500 beauty boutiques in China. Avon also intended to resume direct selling in 2005, as the Chinese government was expected to lift its direct selling ban as a condition for entry into the World Trade Organization. Japan and South Korea were other high-potential markets in Asia identified by Jung.

Sales increases in the United States were to be driven by continuing its strategies in place, increasing prices on key products, increasing advertising from $45 million in 2003 to $75 million in 2005, increasing sales of Avon Wellness products to $600 million by 2007, developing new products for the teen market, and targeting the Hispanic segment of the population. Avon management saw Hispanic consumers as an attractive segment since Hispanics were the largest and fastest-growing ethnic group in the United States. In 2003, Hispanic consumers made up 13 percent of the total U.S. population and had an annual buying power of $581 billion. By 2010, Hispanic buying power in the United States was projected to grow to $960 billion. The company's plan to increase sales to Hispanic consumers included using Spanish-language brochures, selling products developed specifically for Hispanic women, and increasing the number of Hispanic representatives. The company had added Hispanic reps

---

[14]"Avon Announces Strategic Repositioning of Its beComing Brand," *PR Newswire*, January 30, 2003.

at an annual rate of 13 percent between 1999 and 2002. The average order size for Avon's Hispanic representatives in 2002 was 12 percent greater than Avon reps in general.

Perhaps the boldest initiative in Jung's evolving strategic plan was the launch of the "mark" brand and its strategy to appeal to the demographic group of ages 16 to 24. The brand was launched in the United States during August 2003 with 300 SKUs, including color products, skin care, bath and body, fragrance, fashion jewelry, and accessories. All mark products were priced slightly higher than Avon's core products but still below key mass-market brands such as Cover Girl and Revlon. Avon had high expectations for the new brand and the company's entry into the segment, since there were more than 300 million young women ages 16–24 in the world with a combined buying power of $250 billion—$75 billion of which was spent on beauty and fashion products. A secondary target for mark was girls ages 13–15 who wished to emulate older teens. Avon estimated that less than 1 percent of its 2002 sales were to consumers in the 16–24 age group.

The name *mark* was meant to celebrate young women who were attempting to make their mark on the world. Avon would recruit its representative for mark through its existing sales force members who had daughters or other young contacts wishing to earn extra money and through an integrated recruitment strategy that included print and broadcast advertising, the Internet, events and promotions targeted to young women in colleges and high schools, shopping malls, and other youth-oriented venues. Avon had also entered into strategic alliances with NBC, Atlantic Records, the University of Phoenix, and others to get its message to young women. Representatives selling mark products could earn commissions of 40 percent on cosmetics and 25 percent on jewelry and fashion products they sold and could also earn commissions on the sales of the representatives in their Leadership networks. Avon's mark representatives were required to be at least 16 years old, and those under age 18 were required to have parental consent.

The marketing strategy for mark included celebrity endorsements, print and TV ads, grassroots marketing, and the distribution of a "magalog" to 13 million young women every four to six weeks. The "meetmark" magalog was a separate brochure/catalog for the mark product line that had the look of a beauty magazine or "hot catalog" and was sprinkled with articles of interest to young women. Meetmark would be printed in English and Spanish. Avon expected to roll out the mark line to markets in Europe and Asia during 2004.

In a December 2003 announcement to investors, Andrea Jung said she believed the company's efforts in 2000–2002 and its new strategies announced in 2003 would lead to revenue increases of 10–12 percent and an operating margin improvement of more than 100 basis points in 2004.[15]

---

[15]"Avon Expects Record Fourth Quarter Earnings of $1.03–$1.04 Per Share, Up Nearly 30%, *PR Newswire*, December 8, 2003.

eBay: In a League by Itself

Louis Marino
The University of Alabama

Patrick Kreiser
The University of Alabama

On September 20, 2000, eBay's top management surprised the financial community by announcing ambitious objectives of $3 billion in annual revenues by year-end 2005, a gross margin target above 80 percent, and target operating margins of 30–35 percent. Given that eBay's 2000 annual revenues were only $400 million, the $3 billion annual revenue target implied a compound annual growth rate of 50 percent from the end of 2000 through 2005—an objective some analysts criticized as too aggressive. Other analysts, however, wondered if the revenue target was ambitious enough, since online auction sales were forecast to reach $54.3 billion by 2007 and since eBay was far and away the dominant player in the online auction market.

But in early 2004 eBay was well on its way to meeting the 2005 goals it set for itself in 2000. In January 2004, eBay reported 2003 revenues of $2.17 billion and a gross margin of 81 percent. If the company could grow its revenues by 40 percent in 2004, it could reach its $3 billion annual revenue goal a year ahead of the 2005 target date. However, analysts

were becoming increasingly concerned about whether eBay could sustain its phenomenal growth (see Exhibit 1), given that almost one-third of all U.S. Internet users were already registered on eBay and that eBay could expect stiffening competition from other ambitious online auction sites and e-tailers as it pursued its growth initiatives.

Building on the vision of its founder, Pierre Omidyar (pronounced oh-*mid*-ee-ar), eBay was initially conceived as an online marketplace that would facilitate a person-to-person trading community based on a democratized, efficient market in which everyone could have equal access through the same medium, the Internet. Leveraging a unique business model and the growing popularity of the Internet, eBay had dominated the online auction market since its beginning in the mid-1990s and had grown its business to include over 94.9 million registered users from more than 150 countries heading into 2004. The auction site's diverse base of registered users in early 2004—which ranged from high school and college students looking to make a few extra dollars, to Fortune 500 companies such as IBM selling excess inventory, to large government agencies like the U.S.

exhibit 1 Selected Indicators of eBay's Growth, 1996–2003

	1996	1997	1998	1999	2000	2001	2002	2003
Number of registered users (in millions)	0.041	0.341	2.2	10.0	22.0	42.4	61.7	94.9
Active users (in millions)	NA	NA	NA	NA	NA	18.0	27.7	41.2
Gross merchandise sales (in millions)	$7	$95	$745	$2,800	$5,400	$9,300	$14,900	$24,000
Number of auctions listed (in millions)	0.29	4.4	33.7	129	264	423	638	971

Postal Service selling undeliverable parcels—differed greatly from its original user base of individuals and small companies.

THE GROWTH OF E-COMMERCE AND ONLINE AUCTIONS

The concepts underlying the Internet were first conceived in the 1960s, but it wasn't until the 1990s that the Internet garnered widespread use and became a part of everyday life. The *Computer Industry Almanac* estimated that by the end of 2002 there were approximately 665 million Internet users worldwide in over 150 countries and that number would grow to over 1 billion users worldwide by 2005.[1] While the top 15 countries accounted for more than 70 percent of the computers in use, slightly less than one-fourth of these Internet users (160.7 million) resided in the United States, and the United States' share as a percentage of total Internet users worldwide was falling. The highest areas of Internet usage growth were expected to be in developing countries in Asia, Latin America, and Eastern Europe with increasing access through new technologies such as Web-enabled cell phones. However, it was expected that total growth rates would not exceed 20 percent annually in the future.

Forrester Research forecast that worldwide e-commerce revenues would be $6.79 trillion in 2004 and that online retail would grow at a 19 percent annual rate between 2003 and 2008 to reach $229.9 billion, of which 25 percent, or $57.5 billion, was expected to come from online auction sales. It was also predicted that North America would account for

[1] www.c-i-a.com, press releases, April 2001 and July 2001.

51.5 percent of total e-commerce sales in 2004, with the Asia-Pacific region accounting for 24.3 percent, Western Europe accounting for 22.5 percent, and Latin America accounting for 12.1 percent of total sales. Within the business-to-consumer segment, eBay's primary area of operation, U.S. e-commerce accounted for over 65 percent of all Internet transactions in 1999 but was expected to account for only about 38 percent in 2003 and potentially less in the future, due to rapid expansion in other parts of the world. Asia was expected to grow especially rapidly following the 2001 decision to include China in the World Trade Organization. In 2002, Germany, the United Kingdom, France, and Italy accounted for 70 percent of the e-commerce revenues in Western Europe, but this share was expected to decline as business-to-business e-commerce in Europe was expected to triple from 2003 to 2006. Exhibit 2 displays the expected total growth in worldwide e-commerce between 1999 and 2004.

KEY SUCCESS FACTORS IN ONLINE RETAILING

It was relatively easy to create a Web site that functioned like a retail store; the more significant challenge was for an online retailer to generate traffic to the site in the form of both new and returning customers. To reach new customers, some online retailers partnered with search engines such as Google, MySimon, or StreetPrices that allowed customers to compare prices for a given product from many retailers. Other tactics employed to build traffic included direct e-mail, online advertising at portals and content-related sites, and some traditional advertising such as print and television advertising. For customers who found their way to a site, most online retailers endeavored to provide extensive product

exhibit 2 **Estimated Growth in Global e-Commerce 1999–2004**

	1999	2000	2001	2002	2003	2004
Estimated value of e-commerce transactions	$170 billion	$657 billion	$1.23 billion	$2.23 trillion	$3.98 trillion	$6.79 trillion

Source: Forrester Research.

information, include pictures of the merchandise, make the site easily navigable, and have enough new things happening at the site to keep customers coming back. (A site's ability to generate repeat visitors was known as *stickiness.*) For new Internet users, retailers had to help them overcome their nervousness about using the Internet itself to shop for items customers generally bought in stores. Web sites had to appease concerns about the possible theft of credit card numbers and the possible sale of personal information to marketing firms. Online retailing also had severe limitations in the case of those goods and services people wanted to see in person to verify their quality. From the retailer's perspective, there was the issue of collecting payment from buyers who wanted to use checks or money orders instead of credit cards.

ONLINE AUCTIONS

The first known auctions were held in Babylon around 500 BC. In AD 193, the entire Roman Empire was put up for auction after the emperor Pertinax was executed. Didius Julianus bid 6,250 drachmas per royal guard and was immediately named emperor of Rome. However, Julianus was executed only two months later, suggesting that he may have been the first-ever victim of the winner's curse (bidding more than the good would cost in a nonauction setting).

Auctions have endured throughout history for several reasons. First, they give sellers a convenient way to find a buyer for something they would like to dispose of. Second, auctions are an excellent way for people to collect difficult-to-find items, such as certain Beanie Babies or historical memorabilia, that have a high value to them personally. Finally, auctions are one of the "purest" markets that exist for goods, in that they bring buyers and sellers into contact to arrive at a mutually agreeable price. As technological advances led to the advent and widespread adoption of the Internet, this ancient form of trade found a new medium.

Online auctions worked in essentially the same way as traditional auctions, the only difference being that the auction process occurred over the Internet rather than at a specific geographic location with buyers and sellers physically present. There are three basic categories of online auctions:

1. Business-to-business auctions, typically involving equipment and surplus merchandise.
2. Business-to-consumer auctions, in which businesses sold goods and services to consumers via the Internet. Many such auctions involved companies interested in selling used or discontinued goods, or liquidating unwanted inventory.
3. Person-to-person auctions, which gave interested sellers and buyers the opportunity to engage in competitive bidding.

Since eBay's pioneering of the person-to-person online auction process in 1995, the number of online auction sites on the Internet had grown to well over 2,750 by the end of 2001. Forrester Research predicted that 6.5 million customers would use online auctions in 2002.

Online auction operators could generate revenue in four principal ways:

1. Charging sellers for listing their good or service.
2. Charging a commission on all sales.
3. Selling advertising on their Web sites.
4. Selling their own new or used merchandise via the online auction format.

More recently, however, online auction sites had also added a fifth revenue-generation option that allowed buyers to purchase the desired good without waiting for an auction to close:

5. Selling their own goods or allowing other sellers to offer their goods in a fixed-price format.

Most sites charged sellers either a fee or a commission and sold advertising to companies interested in promoting their goods or services to users of the auction site.

Online Auction Users

Participants in online auctions could be grouped into six categories: (1) bargain hunters, (2) hobbyist/collector buyers, (3) professional buyers, (4) casual sellers, (5) hobbyist/collector sellers and (6) corporate and power sellers.

Bargain Hunters   Bargain hunters viewed online auctions primarily as a form of entertainment; their objective usually was to find a great deal. Bargain hunters were thought to make up only 8 percent of active online users but 52 percent of eBay visitors. To attract repeat visits from bargain hunters, industry observers said, sites must appeal to them on both rational and emotional levels, satisfying their need for competitive pricing, the excitement of the search, and the desire for community.

Hobbyist and Collector Buyers   Hobbyists and collectors used auctions to search for specific goods that had a high value to them personally. They were very concerned with both price and quality. Collectors prized eBay for its wide variety of product offerings.

Professional Buyers   As the legitimacy of online auctions grew, a new type of buyer began to emerge: the professional buyer. Professional buyers covered a broad range of purchasers, from purchasing managers acquiring office supplies to antiques and gun dealers purchasing inventory. Like bargain hunters, professional buyers were looking for a way to help contain costs; and like hobbyists and collectors, some professional buyers were seeking unique items to supplement their inventory. The primary difference between professional buyers and other types, however, was their affiliation with commercial enterprises. With the growth of online auction sites dedicated to business-to-business auctions, professional buyers were becoming an increasingly important element of the online auction landscape.

Casual Sellers   Casual sellers included individuals who used eBay as a substitute for a classified ad listing or a garage sale to dispose of items they no longer wanted. While many casual sellers listed only a few items, some used eBay to raise money for some new project.

Hobbyist and Collector Sellers   Sellers who were hobbyists or collectors typically dealt in a limited category of goods and looked to eBay as a way to sell selected items in their collections to others who might want them. Items ranged from classic television collectibles, to hand-sewn dolls, to coins and stamps. The hobbyists and collectors used a range of traditional and online outlets to reach their target markets. A number of the sellers used auctions to supplement their retail operations, while others sold exclusively through online auctions and in fixed-price formats such as Half.com.

Power and Corporate Sellers   Power sellers were typically small to medium-sized businesses that favored eBay as a primary distribution channel for their goods and often sold tens of thousands of dollars' worth of goods every month on the site. One estimate suggested that while these power sellers accounted for only 4 percent of eBay's population, they were responsible for 80 percent of eBay's total business.[2] Individuals who were power sellers could often make a full-time job of the endeavor.

As with the evolution of buyers, commercial enterprises were becoming an increasingly important part of the online auction industry. These commercial enterprises generally achieved power-seller status relatively rapidly. On eBay, for example, some of the new power sellers were familiar names such as IBM, Compaq, and the U.S. Postal Service (which sells undeliverable items on eBay under the user name usps-mrc).

PIERRE OMIDYAR AND THE FOUNDING OF eBAY

Pierre Omidyar was born in Paris, France, to parents who had left Iran decades earlier. The family emigrated to the United States when Omidyar's father began a residency at Johns Hopkins University Medical Center. Omidyar attended Tufts University, where he met his future wife, Pamela Wesley, who came to Tufts from Hawaii to get a degree in biology. Upon graduating in 1988, the couple moved to California, where Omidyar, who had earned a bachelor of science degree in computer science, joined Claris, an Apple Computer subsidiary in Silicon Valley, and wrote a widely used graphics application, MacDraw. In 1991, Omidyar left Claris and cofounded Ink Development (later renamed eShop), which became a pioneer in online shopping and was eventually sold to Microsoft in 1996. In 1994 Omidyar joined General Magic as a developer services engineer and remained there until mid-1996, when he left to pursue full-time development of eBay.

Internet folklore has it that eBay was founded solely to allow Pamela to trade Pez dispensers with

[2]Claire Tristram, "'Amazoning' Amazon," www.contextmag.com, November 1999.

other collectors. While Pamela was certainly a driving force in launching the initial Web site, Pierre had long been interested in how one could establish a marketplace to bring together a fragmented market. Pierre saw eBay as a way to create a person-to-person trading community based on a democratized, efficient market where everyone could have equal access through the same medium, the Internet. Pierre set out to develop his marketplace and to meet both his and Pamela's goals. In 1995 he launched the first online auction under the name of Auctionwatch at the domain name of www.eBay.com. The name *eBay* stood for "electronic Bay area," coined because Pierre's initial concept was to attract neighbors and other interested San Francisco Bay area residents to the site to buy and sell items of mutual interest. The first auctions charged no fees to either buyers or sellers and contained mostly computer equipment (and no Pez dispensers). Pierre's fledgling venture generated $1,000 in revenue the first month and an additional $2,000 the second. Traffic grew rapidly, however, as word about the site spread in the Bay area and a community of collectors emerged, using the site to trade and chat—even some marriages resulted from exchanges in eBay chat rooms.[3]

By February, 1996 the traffic at Pierre Omidyar's site had grown so much that his Internet service provider informed him that he would have to upgrade his service. When Omidyar compensated for this by charging a listing fee for the auction, and saw no decrease in the number of items listed, he knew he was on to something. Although he was still working out of his home, Omidyar began looking for a partner and in May asked his friend Jeffrey Skoll to join him in the venture. While Skoll had never cared much about money, his Stanford master of business administration degree provided the firm with the business background that Omidyar lacked. With Omidyar as the visionary and Skoll as the strategist, the company embarked on a mission to "help people trade practically anything on earth."

Their concept for eBay was to "create a place where people could do business just like in the old days—when everyone got to know each other personally, and we all felt we were dealing on a one-to-one basis with individuals we could trust."

In eBay's early days, Omidyar and Skoll ran the operation alone, using a single computer to serve all of the pages. Omidyar served as CEO, chief financial officer, and president, while Skoll functioned as copresident and director. It was not long until Omidyar and Skoll grew the company to a size that forced them to move out of Pierre Omidyar's living room, due to the objections of Pamela, and into Skoll's living room. Shortly thereafter, the operations moved into the facilities of a Silicon Valley business incubator for a time until the company settled in its current facilities in San Jose, California. Exhibits 3 and 4 present eBay's recent financial statements.

eBAY'S TRANSITION TO PROFESSIONAL MANAGEMENT

From the beginning Pierre Omidyar intended to hire a professional manager to serve as the president of eBay: "[I would] let him or her run the company so . . . [I could] go play."[4] In 1997 both Omidyar and Skoll agreed that it was time to locate an experienced professional to function as CEO and president. In late 1997 eBay's headhunters came up with a candidate for the job: Margaret (Meg) Whitman, then general manager for Hasbro, Inc.'s preschool division. Whitman had received her bachelor of arts degree in economics from Princeton and her master of business administration from the Harvard Business School; her first job was in brand management at Procter & Gamble. Her experience also included serving as the president and CEO of FTD, the president of Stride Rite Corporation's Stride Rite Division, and as the senior vice president of marketing for the Walt Disney Company's consumer products division.

When first approached by eBay, Whitman was not especially interested in joining a company that had fewer than 40 employees and less than $6 million in revenues the previous year. It was only after repeated pleas that Whitman agreed to meet with Omidyar in Silicon Valley. After a second meeting, Whitman realized the company's enormous growth potential and agreed to give eBay a try. According to Omidyar, Meg

[3]Quentin Hardy, "The Radical Philanthropist," *Forbes,* May 1, 2000, p. 118.

[4]"Billionaires of the Web," *Business 2.0,* June 1999.

exhibit 3 **eBay's Income Statements, 1996–2002 (in thousands, except per share figures)**

	1996	1997	1998	1999	2000	2001	2002	2003
Net revenues	$32,051	$41,370	$ 86,129	$224,724	$431,424	$748,821	$1,214,100	$2,165,096
Cost of net revenues	6,803	8,404	16,094	57,588	95,453	134,816	213,876	416,058
Gross profit	$25,248	$32,966	$ 70,035	$167,136	$335,971	$614,005	$1,000,224	$1,749,038
Operating expenses:								
Sales and marketing	$13,139	$15,618	$ 35,976	$ 96,239	$166,767	$253,474	$ 349,650	$ 567,565
Product development	28	831	4,640	24,847	55,863	75,288	104,636	159,315
General and administrative	5,661	6,534	15,849	43,919	73,027	105,784	171,785	304,703
Patent litigation expense	—	—	0	0	—	2,442	—	29,965
Payroll taxes on stock options	—	—	0	0	2,337	2,442	4,015	9,590
Amortization of acquired intangibles	—	—	805	1,145	1,443	36,591	15,941	50,659
Merger-related costs	—	—	0	4,359	1,550	0	0	0
Total operating expenses	$18,828	$22,983	$ 57,270	$170,509	$300,977	$473,579	$ 646,027	$1,119,797
Income (loss) from operations	$ 6,420	$ 9,983	$ 12,765	$ (3,373)	$ 34,994	$140,426	$ 354,197	$ 629,241
Interest and other income (expense), net	(2,607)	(1,951)	1,799	23,833	46,337	41,613	49,209	37,803
Interest expense	—	—	(2,191)	(2,319)	(3,374)	(2,851)	(1,492)	(4,314)
Impairment of certain equity investments	—	—	0	0	0	(16,245)	(3,781)	(1,230)
Income before income taxes and minority interest	$ 3,813	$ 8,032	$ 12,373	$ 18,141	$ 77,957	$162,943	$ 398,133	$ 661,500
Provision for income taxes	(475)	(971)	(4,789)	(8,472)	(32,725)	(80,009)	(145,946)	(206,738)
Minority interests in consolidated companies	—	—	(311)	(102)	3,062	7,514	(2,296)	(7,578)
Net income	$ 3,338	$ 7,061	$ 7,273	$ 9,567	$ 48,294	$ 90,448	$ 249,891	$ 447,184
Net income per share:								
Basic	$ 0.39	$ 0.29	$ 0.07	$ 0.04	$ 0.19	$ 0.34	$ 0.43	$ 0.69
Diluted	0.07	0.08	0.03	0.04	0.17	0.32	0.43	0.67
Weighted average shares:								
Basic	8,490	24,428	104,128	217,674	251,776	268,971	574,992	638,288
Diluted	45,060	84,775	233,519	273,033	280,346	280,595	585,640	656,657

Source: Company financial documents.

exhibit 4 **eBay's Consolidated Balance Sheets, 1997–2003 (in thousands)**

	Year Ended December 31						
	1997	1998	1999	2000	2001	2002	2003
Assets							
Current assets:							
Cash and cash equivalents	$3,723	$ 37,285	$219,679	$ 201,873	$ 523,969	$1,109,313	$1,381,513
Short-term investments	—	40,401	181,086	354,166	199,450	89,690	340,576
Accounts receivable, net	1,024	12,425	36,538	67,163	101,703	131,453	225,871
Funds receivable	—	—	—	—	—	41,014	79,893
Other current assets	220	7,479	22,531	52,262	58,683	96,988	118,029
Total current assets	$4,967	$ 97,590	$459,834	$ 675,464	$ 883,805	$1,468,458	$2,145,882
Long-term investments	—	—	—	—	286,998	470,227	934,171
Restricted cash and investments	—	—	—	—	129,614	134,644	127,432
Property and equipment, net	652	44,062	111,806	125,161	142,349	218,028	601,785
Goodwill	—	—	—	—	187,829	1,456,024	1,719,311
Investments	—	—	373,988	—	—	—	—
Deferred tax assets	—	—	5,639	—	21,540	84,218	—
Intangible and other assets, net	—	7,884	12,675	23,299	26,394	292,845	291,553
Total assets	$5,619	$149,536	$963,942	$1,182,403	$1,678,529	$4,040,226	$5,820,134
Liabilities and stockholders' equity							
Current liabilities:							
Accounts payable	$252	$ 9,997	$ 31,538	$ 31,725	$ 33,235	$ 47,424	$ 64,633
Funds payable and amounts due to customers	—	—	—	—	—	50,396	106,568
Accrued expenses and other current liabilities	—	6,577	32,550	60,882	94,593	199,323	356,491
Deferred revenue and customer advances	128	973	5,997	12,656	15,583	18,846	28,874
Debt and leases, current portion	258	4,047	12,285	15,272	16,111	2,970	2,840
Income taxes payable	169	1,380	6,455	11,092	20,617	67,265	87,870

exhibit 4 **(concluded)**

	Year Ended December 31						
	1997	1998	1999	2000	2001	2002	2003
Deferred tax liabilities, current	—	1,682	—	5,815	—	—	—
Other current liabilities	128	5,981	7,632	—	—	—	—
Total current liabilities	$1,124	$ 24,656	$ 88,825	$ 137,442	$ 180,139	$ 386,224	$ 647,276
Debt and leases, long-term portion	305	18,361	15,018	11,404	12,008	13,798	124,476
Deferred tax liabilities, long-term	—	—	—	—	3,629	27,625	79,238
Other liabilities	157	—	—	6,549	15,864	22,874	33,494
Minority interests	—	—	—	—	37,751	33,232	39,408
Total liabilities	$1,586	$ 48,998	$111,475	$ 168,643	$ 249,391	$ 483,753	$ 923,892
Series B redeemable convertible preferred stock and Series B warrants	3,018	—	—	—	—	—	—
	1,015	100,538	852,467	1,013,760	1,429,138	3,556,473	4,896,242
Total stockholders' equity	$5,619	$149,536	$963,942	$1,182,403	$1,678,529	$4,124,444	$5,820,134

Source: Company financial documents.

Whitman's experience in global marketing with Hasbro's Teletubbies, Playskool, and Mr. Potato Head brands made her "the ideal choice to build upon eBay's leadership position in the one-to-one online trading market without sacrificing the quality and personal touch our users have grown to expect."[5] In addition to convincing Whitman to head eBay's operations, Omidyar had been instrumental in helping bring in other talented senior executives and in assembling a capable board of directors. Notable members of eBay's board of directors included Scott Cook, the founder of Intuit, a highly successful financial software company, and Fred D. Anderson, executive vice president and chief financial officer of Apple.

HOW AN eBAY AUCTION WORKED

eBay endeavored to make it very simple to buy and sell goods. In order to sell or bid on goods, users first had to register at the site. Once they registered, users selected both a user name and a password. Unregistered users were able to browse the Web site but were not permitted to bid on any goods or list any items for auction.

On the Web site, search engines helped customers determine what goods were currently available. When registered users found an item they desired, they could choose to enter a single bid or to use automatic bidding (called proxy bidding). In automatic bidding the customer entered an initial bid sufficient to make him or her the high bidder, and then the bid would be automatically increased as others bid for the same object until the auction ended and either the bidder won or another bidder surpassed the original customer's maximum specified bid. Regardless of which bidding method they chose, users could check bids at any time and either bid again, if they had been outbid, or increase their maximum amount in the automatic bid. Users could choose to receive e-mail notification if they were outbid.

Once the auction had ended, the buyer and seller were each notified of the winning bid and were given each other's e-mail address. The parties to the auction would then privately arrange for payment and delivery of the good.

[5]eBay press release, May 7, 1998.

Fees and Procedures for Sellers

Buyers on eBay were not charged a fee for bidding on items, but sellers were charged an insertion fee and a "final value" fee; they could also elect to pay additional fees to promote their listing. Listing, or insertion, fees ranged from 30 cents for auctions with opening bids, minimum values, or reserve prices of between $0.01 and $0.99, to $4.80 for auctions with opening bids, minimum values, or reserve prices of $500 and up. Final value fees ranged from 1.25 to 5 percent of the final sale price and were computed according to a graduated fee schedule in which the percentage fell as the final sales price rose. As an example, in a basic auction with no promotion, if the item had brought an opening bid of $200 and eventually sold for $1,500, the total fee paid by the seller would be $35.48—the $3.60 insertion fee plus $31.88. The $31.88 was based on a fee structure of 5 percent of the first $25 (or $1.25), 2.5 percent of the additional amount between $25.01 and $1,000 (or $24.38), and 1.25 percent of the additional amount between $1,000.01 and $1,500 (or $6.25). Auction fees varied for special categories of goods such as passenger vehicles in eBay Motors that were charged a $40 transaction fee when the first successful bid was placed and a $100 insertion fee for residential, commercial, and other real estate.

Sellers could also customize items by adding photographs and featuring their item in a gallery. Sellers could indicate a photograph in the item's description if they posted the photograph on a Web site and provided eBay with the appropriate Web address. Items could be showcased in the Gallery section with a catalog of pictures rather than text. A seller who used a photograph in his or her listing could have this photograph included in the Gallery section for 25 cents or featured there for $19.95. A Gallery option was available in all categories of eBay, but fees varied between categories and the prominence of the gallery. For example, a simple gallery listing cost 25 cents, whereas a featured gallery listing, which included a periodic listing in the featured section above the general gallery, cost $19.95. In the eBay Motors gallery, options could cost as much as $99.95.

To make doing business on eBay more attractive to potential sellers, the company introduced several features. To receive a minimum price for an auction, the seller could specify an opening bid or set a reserve price on the auction. If the bidding did not top the reserve price, the seller was under no obligation to sell the item to the highest bidder and could relist the item at no additional cost. For items with a reserve price between $0.01 and $49.99, the fee was $1.00; between $50.00 and $199.99, the fee was $2.00; and for over $200, the fee was 1 percent of the reserve price. If the seller wished, he or she could also set a Buy It Now price that allowed bidders to pay a set amount for a listed item. The fee for this service was $1.00. If the Buy It Now price was met, the auction would end immediately.

As of June 11, 2001, new sellers at eBay were required to provide both a credit card number and bank account information to register. While eBay admitted that these requirements are extreme, it argued that they helped protect everyone in the community against fraudulent sellers and ensured that sellers were of legal age and were serious about listing the item on eBay.

How Transactions Were Completed

Under the terms of eBay's user agreement, if a seller received one or more bids above the stated minimum, or reserve, price, the seller was obligated to complete the transaction, although eBay had no enforcement power beyond suspending a noncompliant buyer or seller from using the company's service. In the event the buyer and seller were unable to complete the transaction, the seller notified eBay, which then credited the seller the amount of the final value fee.

When an auction ended, the eBay system validated that the bid fell within the acceptable price range. If the sale was successful, eBay automatically notified the buyer and seller via e-mail; the buyer and seller could then either work out the transaction details independent of eBay or use eBay's checkout and payment services to complete the transaction. In its original business model, at no point during the process did eBay take possession of either the item being sold or the buyer's payment. In an effort to increase revenues, eBay expanded its offerings to facilitate buyers' payments by first offering services that accepted credit card payments and electronic funds transfers on behalf of the seller and then purchasing PayPal, the leading third-party online payment facilitator in 2003. To make selling easier, eBay also had alliances with two leading shippers, the U.S. Postal Service and United Parcel Service (UPS). Both of these shippers had centers on eBay that would allow

sellers to calculate postage and to print postage-paid labels. However, the buyer and seller still had to independently arrange shipping terms, with buyers typically paying for shipping. Items were sent directly from the buyer to the seller unless an independent escrow service was arranged to help ensure security.

To encourage sellers to use eBay's ancillary services the company offered an automated checkout service to help expedite communication, payment, and delivery between buyers and sellers.

Feedback Forum

In early 1996 eBay pioneered a feature called Feedback Forum to build trust among buyers and sellers and to facilitate the establishment of reputations within its community. Feedback Forum encouraged individuals to record comments about their trading partners. At the completion of each auction, both the buyer and seller were allowed to leave positive, negative, or neutral comments about each other. Individuals could dispute feedback left about them by annotating comments in question.

By assigning values of $+1$ for a positive comment, 0 for a neutral comment, and -1 for a negative comment, each trader earned a ranking that was attached to his or her user name. A user who had developed a positive reputation over time had a color-coded star symbol displayed next to his or her user name to indicate the amount of positive feedback. The highest ranking a trader could receive was "over 100,000," indicated by a red shooting star. Well-respected high-volume traders could have rankings well into the thousands.

Users who received a sufficiently negative net feedback rating (typically a -4) had their registrations suspended and were thus unable to bid on or list items for sale. Buyers could review a person's feedback profile before deciding to bid on an item listed by that person or before choosing payment and delivery methods. A sample user profile is shown in Exhibit 5.

The terms of eBay's user agreement prohibited actions that would undermine the integrity of the Feedback Forum, such as leaving positive feedback about oneself through other accounts or leaving multiple negative comments about someone else through other accounts. The Feedback Forum had several automated features designed to detect and prevent some forms of abuse. For example, feedback posted from the same account, positive or negative, could not affect a user's net feedback rating by more than

exhibit 5   **A Sample Feedback Forum Profile**

| home | pay | sign out | services | site map | help ⑦ |
| Browse | Search | Sell | My eBay | Community | Powered By **IBM** |

← Back to My eBay   Home > Services > Feedback Forum > **Member Profile**   Why does this page look different?

Member Profile: nuggett12 (50 ★)

Feedback Score:	**50**	Recent Ratings:				Member since: May-17-99
Positive Feedback	**100%**		Past Month	Past 6 Months	Past 12 Months	Location: United States
Members who left a positive:	50	⊕ positive	0	16	21	» ID History
Members who left a negative:	0	⊙ neutral	0	0	0	» Items for Sale
All positive feedback received:	56	⊖ negative	0	0	0	
Learn about what these numbers mean.		Bid Retractions (Past 6 months): 0				Contact Member

All Feedback Received   From Buyers   From Sellers   Left for Others

56 feedback received by nuggett12   page 1 of 3

Comment	From	Date / Time	Item #
⊙ Super transaction! Lightning FAST payment! Thanks! Come back again soon :)	Seller fussypants (fpdotcomm@aol.com) (1382 ★)	Jan-06-04 18:25	2976322019
⊙ FAST PAYMENT!! GREAT EBAY'R!! THANKS!!	Seller cheribook (cheriberri5@aol.com) (645 ★)	Dec-11-03 10:35	2207627646
⊙ Very prompt and courteous buyer, great to deal with, Thanks!	Seller network482 (sales@shopoem.com) (11742 ☆)	Nov-28-03 01:04	3057703028
⊙ Very prompt and courteous buyer, great to deal with, Thanks!	Seller network482 (sales@shopoem.com) (11742 ☆)	Nov-28-03 01:04	3058162337
⊙ very good transaction	Seller hoefker@earthlink.net (hoefker@earthlink.net) (35 ☆) **no longer a registered user**	Nov-27-03 11:48	3061637655
⊙ FAST PAY!!! EXCELLENT!!! PLEASURE TO DO BUSINESS WITH! AAAAA+++++	Seller rafaelos (lancergroup@yahoo.com) (3907 ★)	Nov-25-03 08:22	2966729737
⊙ Very prompt and courteous buyer, great to deal with, Thanks!	Seller network482 (sales@shopoem.com) (11742 ☆)	Nov-14-03 08:38	3058162328
⊙ Very prompt and courteous buyer, great to deal with, Thanks!	Seller network482 (sales@shopoem.com) (11742 ☆)	Nov-14-03 08:38	3057561133
⊙ a+	Seller mountainairvideo (firebaseutah@aol.com) (1817 ★) 🏠	Nov-10-03 11:12	243650630174
⊙ Quick payment, and easy to deal with. Fine buyer!	Seller dumbells101 (91 ★)	Oct-27-03 06:29	2863059214
⊙ A very easy and fast transaction. Couldn't ask for a better buyer.	Seller cornshedprofits (1459 ★)	Oct-05-03 03:05	243633243888
⊙ Fast payment enjoed working with you.....	Seller mmddaa@msn.com (82 ★)	Sep-21-03 20:35	3627701979
⊙ Smooth transaction!	Seller phoenix_trading_co (23518 ☆)	Sep-02-03 13:47	3044087884
⊙ Smooth transaction!	Seller phoenix_trading_co (23518 ☆)	Sep-02-03 13:42	3044088621
⊙ Great seller! Delivered promptly! Smooth transaction.	Buyer bama-tarheels (3)	Aug-25-03 11:44	2188695578
⊙ Prompt payment and good communication	Seller rjpedigo (35 ☆)	Aug-17-03 14:53	3040472706
⊙ I highly recommend this seller.	Buyer jessievanderhoff (6)	Jul-21-03 11:48	3033456370
⊙ Customer is A+! We appreciate your business and fast payment!	Seller restaurant.com (100851 ★)	Apr-14-03 13:14	2922961668
⊙ Customer is A+! We appreciate your business and fast payment!	Seller restaurant.com (100851 ★)	Apr-14-03 13:14	2922958665
⊙ Worthwhile in every way. A+	Seller genuine_oem (29204 ☆)	Feb-10-03 21:41	1949802659
⊙ EXCELLENT eBayer, GREAT customer service, DEFFINATELY do bus. with again! AAAA++	Buyer brendon800 (81 ★)	Feb-09-03 18:01	2156921953
⊙ Very understanding. I Would have great confidence buying from this seller.	Buyer longinternational (142 ☆)	Feb-01-03 18:44	2156940759
⊙ Item as described & functioning. Shipping excellent. Will do business again!	Buyer brkidsman (11 ☆)	Dec-10-02 07:25	1789511721
⊙ AN EXAMPLE OF A GOOD EBAYER _ HIGHLY RECOMMENDED _ AAAAAAA++++++	Seller shilito34 (1338 ★)	Oct-03-02 15:12	1772433194
⊙ Super quick payment and very patient. My apologies for being late...	Seller dane_mel (107 ☆)	Sep-13-02 09:00	243518255865

Source: www.ebay.com, February 4, 2004.

one point, no matter how many comments an individual made. Furthermore, a user could make comments only about his or her trading partners in completed transactions. Prior to 2004, once a feedback comment was made, it could not be altered. However, as of February 9, 2004, the system was changed in response to suggestions by community members to all users to mutually withdraw feedback about each other. Withdrawn feedback would no longer impact a user's feedback rating.

The company believed its Feedback Forum was extremely useful in overcoming users' initial hesitancy about trading over the Internet, since it reduced the uncertainty of dealing with an unknown trading partner. However, there was growing concern among sellers and bidders that feedback might be positively skewed, as many eBayers chose not to leave negative feedback for fear of unfounded retribution that could damage their carefully built reputations.

eBAY'S STRATEGY TO SUSTAIN ITS MARKET DOMINANCE

Meg Whitman assumed the helm of eBay in February 1998 and began acting as the public face of the company. In an effort to stay in touch with her customers, Whitman hosted an auction on eBay herself. She found the experience so enlightening that she required all of eBay's managers to sell on eBay. Pierre Omidyar stepped back to become chairman of eBay's board of directors and focused his time and energy on overseeing eBay's strategic direction and growth, business model and site development, and community advocacy. Jeff Skoll, who became the vice president of strategic planning and analysis, concentrated on competitive analysis, new business planning and incubation, the development of the organization's overall strategic direction, and supervision of customer support operations.

The Move to Go Public

eBay's initial public offering (IPO) took place on September 24, 1998, with a starting price of $18 per share. The IPO exceeded that price and closed the day up 160 percent at $47. The IPO generated $66 million in new capital for the company and was rec-

ognized by several investing publications. The success of the September 1998 offering led eBay to issue a follow-up offering in April 1999 that raised an additional $600 million. As a qualification to the IPOs, eBay's board of directors retained the right to issue as many as 5 million additional shares of preferred stock with no further input from the current shareholders in case of a hostile takeover attempt.

eBay's Business Model

According to eBay's Meg Whitman, the company could best be described as a dynamic, self-regulating economy. Its business model was based on creating and maintaining a person-to-person trading community in which buyers and sellers could readily and conveniently exchange information and goods. The company's role was to function as a value-added facilitator of online buyer–seller transactions by providing a supportive infrastructure that enabled buyers and sellers to come together in an efficient and effective manner. Success depended not only on the quality of eBay's infrastructure but also on the quality and quantity of buyers and sellers attracted to the site; in management's view, this entailed maintaining a compelling trading environment, a number of trust and safety programs, a cost-effective and convenient trading experience, and strong community affinity. By developing the eBay brand name and increasing the customer base, eBay endeavored to attract a sufficient number of high-quality buyers and sellers necessary to meet the organization's goals. The online auction format meant that eBay carried zero inventory and could operate a marketplace without the need for a traditional sales force.

eBay's business model was built around three profit centers: the domestic business (auction operations within the United States), international business (auction operations outside of the United States), and payments (e.g., PayPal). It was estimated that, in 2003, U.S. operations accounted for 31.7 percent of revenue growth, international's share was 34.6 percent, and the remaining 33.8 percent was from payments (see Exhibit 6).

Specific elements of eBay's business model that the company particularly recognized as key to its success included:[6]

---

[6]Company 10-K filing with the Securities and Exchange Commission, March 3, 2001, pp. 4–6.

exhibit 6 **Share of eBay Transaction Revenue Growth, 2001–2008**

	2001(a)	2002(a)	2003(e)	2004(e)	2005(e)	2006(e)	2007(e)	2008(e)
U.S.	62.8%	48.0%	31.7%	39.1%	31.7%	32.5%	32.5%	32.7%
International	32.6	36.9	34.6	35.9	41.6	42.0	38.7	38.7
Payments	4.7	15.1	33.8	25.0	26.7	25.5	28.8	28.6
	100.0%	100.0%	100.0%	100.0%	100.0%	100.0%	100.0%	100.0%

1. The fact that it was the largest online trading forum, with a critical mass of buyers, sellers, and items listed for sale.
2. Its compelling and entertaining trading environment, which had strong values, established rules, and procedures that facilitated communication and trade between buyers and sellers.
3. Established trust and safety programs such as Safeharbor. This program provided guidelines for trading, aided in resolving disputes, and warned and suspended (both temporarily and permanently) users who violated eBay's rules.
4. Cost-effective, convenient trading.
5. Strong community affinity.
6. An intuitive user interface that was easy to understand, arranged by topics, and fully automated.

In implementing its business model, eBay employed three main competitive tactics. First, it sought to build strategic partnerships in all stages of its value chain, creating an impressive portfolio of over 250 strategic alliances with companies such as America Online (AOL), Yahoo, IBM, Compaq, and Walt Disney. Second, it actively sought customer feedback and made improvements on the basis of this information. Third, it actively monitored both its external and internal environments for developing opportunities. One way eBay executives kept in touch with internal trends was by hosting online town hall meetings and by visiting cities with large local markets. The feedback gained from these meetings was used to adopt and adjust practices to keep customers satisfied.

eBay's Strategy

eBay's strategy to sustain growth rested on five key elements:[7]

[7]eBay company 10K, filed March 28, 2001.

1. *Broaden the existing trading platform* within existing product categories, across new product categories, through geographic expansion, both domestic and international, and through introduction of additional pricing formats such as fixed price sales.
2. *Foster eBay community affinity* by instilling a vibrant, loyal eBay community experience, seeking to maintain a critical mass of frequent buyers and sellers with a vested interest in the eBay community.
3. *Enhance features and functionality* by continually updating and enhancing the features and functionality of the eBay and Half.com Web sites to ensure continuous improvement in the trading experience.
4. *Expand value-added services* to include end-to-end personal trading service by offering a variety of pre- and post-trade services to enhance the user experience and make trading easier.
5. *Continue to develop U.S. and international markets* that employ the Internet to create an efficient trading platform in local, national, and international markets that can be transformed into a seamless, truly global trading platform.

Broadening the Existing Trading Platform   Efforts intended to broaden the eBay trading platform concentrated on growing the content within current categories, broadening the range of products offered according to user preferences, and developing regionally targeted offerings. Growth in existing product categories was facilitated by deepening the content within the categories through the use of content-specific chat rooms and bulletin boards as well as targeted advertising at trade shows and in industry-specific publications.

To broaden the range of products offered, eBay developed new product categories, introduced specialty sites, and developed eBay stores. Over 2,000 new categories were added between 1998 and 2000, and by 2003 eBay offered over 27,000 categories of items (greatly expanded from the original 10 categories in 1995). Ten of these categories had gross merchandise sales of over $1 billion, including eBay Motors ($7.5 billion), Consumer Electronics ($2.6 billion), Computers ($2.4 billion), Books/ Movies/Music ($2.0 billion), Clothing and Accessories ($1.8 billion), Sports ($1.8 billion), Collectibles ($1.5 billion), Toys ($1.5 billion), Home and Garden ($1.3 billion), and Jewelry and Gemstones ($1.3 billion).

Significant new product categories and specialty sites developed since eBay's early days included:

- eBay Motors, which began as a category and was developed when eBay noticed that an increasing number of automobile transactions were taking place on its site. In 2002, eBay Motors sold more than $3 billion worth of vehicles and parts and was the largest online marketplace for buying and selling autos as of mid-2003. According to Meg Whitman, "One month, we saw the miscellaneous category had a very rapid growth rate, and someone said we have to find out what's going on. It was the buying and selling of used cars. So we said, maybe what we should do is give these guys a separate category and see what happens. It worked so well that we created eBay Motors."[8] In partnership with AutoTrader.com this category was later expanded to a specialty site.

- The LiveAuctions specialty site, which allowed live bidding via the Internet for auctions occurring in brick-and-mortar auction houses around the world. Through an alliance with Icollector.com, eBay users had access to more than 300 auction houses worldwide. Auction houses that participated in this agreement were well rewarded, as more than 20 percent of their sales went to online bidders. One auction broadcast on the LiveAuctions site, held in February 2001, featured items from a rare Marilyn Monroe collection including a handwritten note from Monroe that listed her reasons for divorcing her first husband.

[8]"Q&A with eBay's Meg Whitman," *BusinessWeek E.Biz*, December 3, 2001.

- The eBay Business marketplace, launched in 2002, which allowed business-related items to be sold in one location. Items such as office technology, wholesale lots, and marketplace services were offered at this destination. By the end of 2002, over 500,000 items were listed in eBay Business each week and more than $1 billion in annualized gross merchandise sales occurred across these categories.

- eBay's Real Estate category, launched to foster eBay's emerging real estate marketplace. The offerings within this category were significantly enhanced by eBay's August 2001 acquisition of Homesdirect, which specialized in the sale of foreclosed properties owned by government agencies such as Housing and Urban Development and the Department of Veterans Affairs (formerly known as the Veterans Administration). The company estimated that a parcel of land was sold through the Real Estate category every 45 minutes during 2002.

Other notable moves to broaden the platform included the following:

- The Application Program Interface (API) and Developers Program was launched to allow other companies to use eBay's commerce engine and technology to build new sites.

- Starting in 1999, eBay launched over 60 regional sites to offer a more local flavor to eBay's offerings. These regional sites focused on the 50 largest metropolitan areas in the United States. Regional auction sites were intended to encourage the sale of items that were prohibitively expensive to ship, items that tended to have only a local appeal, and items that people preferred to view before purchasing. To supplement the regional sites, in mid-2001 eBay began offering sellers the option of having their items listed in a special seller's area in the classified sections of local newspapers. Sellers could highlight specific items, their eBay store, or their user ID in these classifieds.

- In June 2001 eBay introduced eBay stores to complement new offerings, to make it easier for sellers to build loyalty and for buyers to locate goods from specific sellers and to prevent sellers from driving bidders to the seller's own Web site. In an eBay store the entirety of a seller's auctions would be listed in one convenient location. These stores could also offer a fixed-price option from a seller and the integration of a seller's Half.com listings with their auction listings. While numerous sellers of all sizes moved to take advantage of eBay stores, the concept was especially appealing to large retailers such as IBM, Hard Rock Café, Sears, and Handspring that were moving to take advantage of eBay's reach and distribution power.

- In May 2002 eBay reached an agreement with Accenture to develop a service intended to allow large sellers to more efficiently sell their products. These sellers were able to use a wide range of tools, such as high-volume listing capabilities, expanded customer service and support, and payment and fulfillment processes.

- A fixed-price format was established through the acquisition of Half.com and allowed eBay to compete more directly with online sellers such as Amazon.com. Half.com was a fixed-price, person-to-person format that enabled buyers and sellers to trade books, CDs, movies and video games at prices starting at generally half of the retail price. Like eBay, Half.com offered a feedback system that helped buyers and sellers to build a solid reputation. eBay intended to eventually fully integrate both Half.com's listings and the feedback system into eBay's current site.

Fostering eBay Community Affinity   From its founding, eBay considered developing a loyal, vivacious trading community to be a cornerstone of its business model. This community was nurtured through open and honest communication and was built on five basic values that eBay expected its members to honor:

We believe people are basically good.

We believe everyone has something to contribute.

We believe that an honest, open environment can bring out the best in people.

We recognize and respect everyone as a unique individual.

We encourage you to treat others the way that you want to be treated.[9]

The company recognized that these values could not be imposed by fiat. According to Omidyar,

As much as we at eBay talk about the values and encourage people to live by those values, that's not going to work unless people actually adopt those values. The values are communicated not because somebody reads the Web site and says, "Hey, this is how we want to treat each other, so I'll just start treating people that way." The values are communicated because that's how they're treated when they first arrive. Each member is passing those values on to the next member. It's little things, like you receive a note that says, "Thanks for your business."[10]

Consistent with eBay's desire to stay in touch with its customers and be responsive to their needs, the company flew in 10 new sellers every few months to hold group meetings known as Voice of the Customer. The company noted that 75–80 percent of new features were originally suggested by community members.

An example of eBay values in action took place when eBay introduced a feature that referred losing bidders to similar auctions from other eBay sellers, eliciting a strong outcry from the community. Sellers demanded to know why eBay was stealing their sales, and one longtime seller went so far as to auction a rare eBay jacket so that he could use the auction as a forum to complain about "eBay's new policy of screwing the folks who built them."[11] This caught the attention of Omidyar and Whitman, who met with the seller in his home for 45 minutes. After the meeting eBay changed its policy.

Recognizing that many new users might not get the most out of their eBay experience, and hoping to introduce new entrepreneurs to the community, the company created eBay University in August 2000. The university traveled across the country to hold two-day seminars in various cities. These seminars attracted between 400 and 500 people, who each paid $25 for the experience. Courses offered ranged from freshmen-level classes that introduced buying and selling on eBay to graduate-level classes that taught the intricacies of bulk listing and competitive tactics. eBay University was so successful that the company partnered with Evoke Communications to offer an online version of the classes. While community members gained knowledge from these classes, so did eBay. The company kept careful track of ques-

---

[9]http://pages.ebay.com/help/community/values.html, January 1, 2002.

[10]"Q&A with eBay's Meg Whitman."

[11]Ibid.

tions and concerns and used them to uncover areas that needed improvement.

A second important initiative to make the eBay community more inclusive was aimed at the fastest-growing segment of the U.S. population, adults 50 and older. In an effort to bridge the digital divide for seniors, eBay launched the Digital Opportunity Program for Seniors and set a goal of training and bringing online 1 million seniors by 2005. Specific elements of this plan included partnering with SeniorNet, the leading nonprofit computer technology trainer of seniors, and donating $1 million to this organization for training and establishing 10 new training facilities by 2005, developing a volunteer program for training seniors, and creating a specific area on eBay for Senior Citizens (www.ebay.com/seniors).

To foster a sense of community among eBay users, the company employed tools and tactics designed to promote both business and personal interactions between consumers, to foster trust between bidders and sellers, and to instill a sense of security among traders. Interactions between community members were facilitated through the creation of chat rooms based on personal interests. These chat rooms allowed individuals to learn about their chosen collectibles and to exchange information about items they collected.

To manage the flow of information in the chat rooms, eBay employees went to trade shows and conventions to seek out individuals who had knowledge about and a passion for either a specific collectible or a category of goods. These enthusiasts would act as community leaders or ambassadors; they were never referred to as employees but were compensated $1,000 a month to host online discussions with experts.

Although personal communication between members fostered a sense of community, as eBay's community grew from "the size of a small village to a large city" additional measures were necessary to ensure a continued sense of trust and honesty among users.[12] One of eBay's earliest trust-building efforts was the 1996 creation of the Feedback Forum, described earlier.

Unfortunately, the Feedback Forum was not always sufficient to ensure honesty and integrity among traders. eBay estimated that far less than 1 percent of the millions of auctions completed on the site in-

volved some sort of fraud or illegal activity, but some users, like Clay Monroe, disagreed. Monroe, a Seattle-area trader of computer equipment, estimated that "ninety percent of the time everybody is on the up and up . . . [but] . . . ten percent of the time you get some jerk who wants to cheat you." Fraudulent or illegal acts perpetrated by sellers included misrepresentation of goods; trading in counterfeit goods or pirated goods that infringed on others' intellectual property rights; failure to deliver goods paid for by buyers; and shill bidding, whereby sellers would use a false bidder to artificially drive up the price of a good. Buyers could manipulate bids by placing an unrealistically high bid on a good to discourage other bidders and then withdraw their bid at the last moment to allow an ally to win the auction at a bargain price. Buyers could also fail to deliver payment on a completed auction.

Recognizing that fraudulent activities represented a significant danger to eBay's future, management took the Feedback Forum a step further in 1998 by launching the SafeHarbor program to provide guidelines for trade, provide information to help resolve user disputes, and respond to reports of misuse of the eBay service. The SafeHarbor initiative was expanded in 1999 to provide additional safeguards and to actively work with law enforcement agencies and members of the trading community to make eBay more secure. New elements of SafeHarbor included:

- Free insurance, with a $25 deductible for transactions under $200 and further protection for buyers and sellers who used PayPal.

- Cooperation with local law enforcement agencies to identify and prosecute fraudulent buyers and sellers.

- Enhancements to the Feedback Forum such as listing whether the user was a buyer or a seller in a transaction.

- A partnership with SquareTrade, an online dispute resolution service.

- A partnership with Escrow.com to promote the use of escrow services on purchases over $500.

- A new class of verified eBay users with an accompanying icon.

- Easy access to escrow services.

- Tougher policies relating to nonpaying bidders and shill bidders.

- Clarification of which items were not permissible to list for sale (such as items associated with

[12]Tristram, " 'Amazoning' Amazon."

Nazi Germany, the Ku Klux Klan, or other groups that glorified hate, racial intolerance, or racial violence).

- A strengthened antipiracy and anti-infringement program known as the Verified Rights Owner program (VeRO), and the introduction of dispute resolution services.

The use of verified buyer and seller accounts was viewed as especially significant because it allowed eBay to ensure that suspended users did not open new eBay accounts under different names. User information was verified through Atlanta-based Equifax, Inc. To further ensure that suspended users didn't register new accounts with different identities, eBay partnered with Infoglide to use a similarity search technology to examine new registrant information.

To implement these new initiatives, eBay increased the number of positions in its SafeHarbor department from 24 to 182, including full-time employees and independent contractors. It also organized the department around the functions of investigations, community watch, and fraud prevention. The investigations group was responsible for examining reported trading violations and possible misuses of eBay. The fraud prevention group mediated customer disputes over such things as the quality of the goods sold. If a written complaint of fraud was filed against a user, eBay generally suspended the alleged offender's account, pending an investigation. Despite all of these initiatives, innovative thieves were developing new ways to cheat honest bidders and sellers as quickly as eBay could identify and ban them from the system, and many eBayers still viewed this as one of the most significant threats to the eBay community.

The community watch group worked with over 100 industry-leading companies, ranging from software publishers to toy manufactures to apparel makers, to protect intellectual property rights. To ensure that illegal items were not being sold and sale items listed did not violate intellectual property rights, this SafeHarbor group automated daily keyword searches on auction content. Offending auctions were closed and the seller was notified of the violation. Repeated violations resulted in suspension of the seller's account.

As eBay expanded its categories to include Great Collections and the new automobile categories, new safeguards were introduced to meet the unique needs of these areas. In the eBay Great Collections category, the company partnered with Collector's Universe to offer authentication and grading services for specific products such as trading cards, coins, and autographs. In the automobile area, one of eBay's fastest-growing segments, eBay partnered with Saturn to provide users with access to a nationwide automobile brand and offered a free limited one-month or 1,000 mile warranty, free purchase insurance up to $20,000 with a $500 deductible, and a special escrow service (Secure Pay) designed for the needs of automotive buyers and sellers.

Expanding Value-Added Services Since its earliest days, eBay had realized that to be successful, its service had to be both easy to use and convenient to access. Recognizing this, the company continuously sought to add services to fill these needs by offering a variety of pre- and post-trade services to enhance the user experience and provide an end-to-end trading experience.

Early efforts in this direction included alliances with:

- Leading shipping services (USPS and UPS).
- Two companies that helped guarantee that buyers would get what they paid for (Tradesafe and I-Escrow).
- The world's largest franchiser of retail business, communications, and postal service centers (Mailboxes, Etc.).
- The leader in multicarrier Web-based shipping services for e-commerce (iShip.com).

To facilitate person-to-person credit card payments, eBay acquired PayPal, a company that specialized in transferring money from one cardholder to another, in October 2002. Using the newly acquired capabilities of PayPal, eBay was able to offer sellers the option of accepting credit card payments from other eBay users. At the end of 2002, PayPal was available to users in 38 countries, including the United States. eBay's objective was to make credit card payment a "seamless and integrated part of the trading experience."[13] The company expected that net revenues from the payments segment of PayPal would be approximately $300 to $310 million in 2003.

---

[13]eBay press release, May 18, 1999.

Developing U.S. and International Markets As competition increased in the online auction industry, eBay began to seek growth opportunities in international markets in an effort to create a global trading community. While international buyers and sellers had been trading on eBay for some time, there were no facilities designed especially for the needs of these community members. In entering international markets, eBay considered three options: it could build a new user community from the ground up, acquire a local organization, or form a partnership with a strong local company. In realizing its goals of international growth, eBay employed all three strategies.

In late 1998, eBay's initial efforts at international expansion into Canada and the United Kingdom relied on building new user communities. The first step in establishing these communities was creating customized home pages for users in those countries. These home pages were designed to provide content and categories locally customized to the needs of users in specific countries, while providing them with access to a global trading community. Local customization in the United Kingdom was facilitated through the use of local management, grassroots and online marketing, and participation in local events.[14] In February 1999 eBay partnered with PBL Online, a leading Internet company in Australia, to offer a customized Australian and New Zealand eBay home page. When the site went live in October, 1999 transactions were denominated in Australian dollars and, while buyers could bid on auctions anywhere in the world, they could also search for items located exclusively in Australia. Further, local chat boards were designed to facilitate interaction between Australian users, and country-specific categories, such as Australian coins and stamps as well as cricket and rugby memorabilia, were offered.

To further expand its global reach, eBay acquired Germany's largest online person-to-person trading site, Alando.de AG, in June 1999. eBay's management handled the transition of service in a manner calculated to be smooth and painless for Alando.de AG's users. While users would have to comply with eBay rules and regulations, the only significant change for Alando.de AG's 50,000 registered users was that they would have to go to a new URL to transact their business.

To establish an Asian presence, in February 2000 eBay formed a joint venture with NEC to launch eBay Japan. According to the new CEO of eBay Japan, Merle Okawara, an internationally renowned executive, NEC was pleased to help eBay in leveraging the tried-and-trusted eBay business model to provide Japanese consumers with access to a global community of active online buyers and sellers. In customizing the site to the needs of Japanese users, eBay wrote the content exclusively in Japanese and allowed users to bid in yen. The site had over 800 categories ranging from internationally popular categories (such as computers, electronics, and Asian antiques) to categories with a local flavor (such as Hello Kitty, Pokémon, and pottery). The eBay Japan site also debuted a new merchant-to-person concept known as Supershops, which allowed consumers to bid on items listed by companies.

In 2001, eBay expanded into South Korea through an acquisition of a majority ownership position in the country's largest online trading service, Internet Auction Co. Ltd., and into Belgium, Brazil, Italy, France, the Netherlands, Portugal, Spain, and Sweden through the acquisition of Europe's largest online trading platform, iBazar. Further expansion in 2001 included the development of a local site in Singapore, and an equity-based alliance with the leading online auction site for the Spanish and Portuguese-speaking communities in Latin America, MercadoLibre.com, that would give eBay access to Argentina, Chile, Colombia, Ecuador, Mexico, Uruguay, and Venezuela.

At the end of 2003 eBay had a presence in 28 countries, including Australia, Austria, Belgium, Canada, China (through an investment in the Chinese company Eachnet), France, Germany, Ireland, Italy, the Netherlands, New Zealand, Singapore, South Korea, Spain, Sweden, Switzerland, Taiwan, Great Britain, and Latin America (through an investment in MercadoLibre.com) and held the top online auction position in every country except Taiwan, where it was a close number two to Yahoo. eBay perceived this rapid international expansion as one of the keys to attaining its goal of having $3 billion in annual revenues by 2005. Growth opportunities were especially appealing in Asia (due to rapid increases in Internet access) and Europe. The company's international business grew by 165 percent in 2002, and its largest international markets were Germany (where 75 percent of eBay users were classified as

---

[14]eBay 10K, filed March 30, 2000.

active users), the United Kingdom, and South Korea. At the end of 2002, the company said:

> [We are] going to invest heavily in international expansion, to tap the huge potential that appears to be the hallmark of Germany, the UK, and Korea and so many of the other markets that we've entered. And we're going to do all of this with the same financial discipline we have always shown by staying true to our strategy of balancing returns with appropriate investment to capitalize on the company's long-term opportunities.[15]

HOW eBAY'S AUCTION SITE COMPARED WITH THOSE OF RIVALS

Auction sites varied in a number of respects: their inventory, the bidding process, extra services and fees, technical support, functionality, and sense of community. Since its inception eBay had gone to great lengths to make its Web site intuitive, easy to use by both buyers and sellers, and reliable. Efforts to ensure ease of use ranged from narrowly defining categories (to allow users to quickly locate desired products) to introducing services designed to personalize a user's eBay experience. Two specific services developed by eBay and launched in 1998 to increase personalization were My eBay and About Me. My eBay gave users centralized access to confidential, current information regarding their trading activities. From his or her My eBay page a user could view information pertaining to his or her current account balances with eBay; feedback rating; the status of any auctions in which he or she was participating, as either a buyer or a seller; and auctions in favorite categories. In October, eBay introduced the About Me service, which allowed users to create customized home pages that could be viewed by all other eBay members and could include elements from the My eBay page such as user ratings or items the user had listed for auction, as well as personal information and pictures. This service not only increased customer ease of use but also contributed to the sense of community among the traders; one seller stated that the About Me service "made it easier and more rewarding for me to do business with others."[16] New features and services

added in 2000 included new listing functions that could make an auction stand out, including Highlight and Feature Plus, as well as a feature that allowed sellers to cross-list their products in two categories, a tool to set prequalification guidelines for bidders, a new imaging and photo hosting service that made it easier for sellers to include pictures of their goods, and the introduction of the Buy It Now tool.

Throughout its history eBay had struggled to balance its explosive growth with its technological infrastructure. To counter several significant service outages the company had faced in its early days, eBay hired Maynard Webb, a premier software engineer and troubleshooter who was working at Gateway Computer. Webb took swift action, forming alliances with key vendors such as Sun, IBM, and Microsoft, and outsourcing its technology and Web site operations to Exodus Communications and Abovenet. These outsourcing agreements were intended to allow Exodus and Abovenet to "manage network capacity and provide a more robust backbone" while eBay focused on its core business.[17] While eBay still experienced minor outages when it changed or expanded services (for example, a system crash coincided with the introduction of the original 22 regional Web sites), system downtime decreased. However, the stability of the system under eBay's explosive growth and continuous introduction of new features was a continuing management concern.

In 2003 Empirix conducted a benchmark study of online auction site performance that measured key performance metrics for six leading auction sites. This study included three customer experience metrics: efficiency (how long transactions were in seconds), consistency (how much the transaction lengths varied), and reliability (how often transactions were completed successfully). Results indicated that Amazon.com had the best performance, BidVille had the shortest transaction length, and eBay's Web applications were slower and more error prone than rivals' (see Exhibit 7).

eBay's Main Competitors

eBay considered the ability to attract buyers, the volume of transactions and selection of goods, customer service, and brand recognition to be the most important competitive factors in the online auction industry.

---

[15]2002 eBay annual report.

[16]Ann Pearson, in an eBay press release dated October 15, 1998.

[17]eBay press release, October 8, 1999.

exhibit 7   **Performance Metrics for Online Auction Firms**

	Customer Experience Metrics				
	Reliability	Efficiency			Consistency
	Percent Error Rate	Average Transaction Length (seconds)	Minimum Transaction Length (seconds)	Maximum Transaction Length (seconds)	Variability of Transaction Length (seconds)
Amazon Auctions	0.52	5.68	3.39	47.1	3.6
BidVille	0.62	3.90	.05	71.1	3.77
eBay	3.97	13.20	7.34	97.5	6.01
ePier	1.02	7.29	4.7	83	5.99
uBid	11.76	5.95	3.05	185	8.39
Yahoo Auctions	2.38	10.94	2.97	112	4.37

Source: Benchmark Study of Online Auction Performance August–September 2003, www.empirix.com.

In addition to these principal factors, eBay was also attempting to compete along several other dimensions: sense of community, system reliability, reliability of delivery and payment, Web site convenience and accessibility, level of service fees, and quality of search tools.[18]

Early in eBay's history the company's main rivals could be considered classified advertisements in newspapers, garage sales, flea markets, collectibles shows, and other venues such as local auction houses and liquidators. As eBay's product mix and selling techniques evolved, the company's range of competitors did as well. The broadening of eBay's product mix beyond collectibles to include practical household items, office equipment, toys, and so on brought the company into more direct competition with brick-and-mortar retailers, import/export companies, and catalog and mail order companies. Further, with the acquisition of Half.com, the introduction of eBay stores, and the growing percentage of fixed-price and Buy It Now sales as a percentage of eBay's revenue, eBay considered itself to be competing in a broad sense with a number of other online retailers, such as Wal-Mart, Kmart, Target, Sears, JCPenney, and Office Depot. In competing with these larger sellers, eBay began to adopt some of their tools, such as the use of gift certificates. The company also felt that it was competing with a number of specialty retailers, such as Christie's (antiques), KB Toys (toys), Blockbuster (movies), Dell (computers), Foot Locker (sporting goods), Ticketmaster (tickets), and Home

Depot (tools).[19] In 2003 eBay begin experiencing competition from new sources, including portals (such as Yahoo) and search providers (such as Google and Overture) that sought to become primary launch pads for online shopping. Exhibit 8 displays eBay's customer service rankings as compared to a variety of rivals' customer service rankings.

eBay management saw traditional competitors as inefficient because their fragmented local and regional nature made it expensive and time-consuming for buyers and sellers to meet, exchange information, and complete transactions. Moreover, the competitors suffered from three other deficiencies: (1) They tended to offer limited variety and breadth of selection as compared to the millions of items available on eBay, (2) they often had high transaction costs, and (3) they were information inefficient in the sense that buyers and sellers lacked a reliable and convenient means of setting prices for sales or purchases. By the same token, eBay's management saw its online auction format as competitively superior to these rivals because (1) it facilitated buyers and sellers meeting, exchanging information, and conducting transactions; (2) it allowed buyers and sellers to bypass traditional intermediaries and trade directly, thus lowering costs; (3) it provided global reach to greater selection and a broader base of participants; (4) it permitted trading at all hours and provided continuously updated information; and (5) it fostered a sense of community among individuals with mutual interests.

[18]Ibid.

[19]eBay 10Q annual report, November 14, 2001.

exhibit 8   **Customer Service Rankings (scores out of 100)**

Sector/Company	1999	2000	2001	2002
E-commerce				
E-commerce retail	NA	78	77	83
Yahoo, Inc.	74	73	76	78
Amazon.com, Inc.	NA	84	84	88
Online Auctions Overall	NA	72	74	77
eBay	NA	80	82	82
uBid, Inc.	NA	67	69	70
Portals/search engines				
Yahoo, Inc.	74	73	76	78
Google, Inc.	NA	NA	80	82
Retail				
Overall retail	73.3	72.9	74.8	74.6
Target	74	73	77	78
Sears	71	73	76	75
Wal-Mart	72	73	75	74

Source: American Customer Satisfaction Index, www.theacsi.org.

Even with the strengthening competition, analysts estimated that eBay controlled approximately 85 percent of the consumer-to-consumer online auction market and 64 percent of total online auction revenue share. The most significant competitors to eBay's auction business included Amazon Auctions, Yahoo Auctions, and uBid. Two of the smaller competitors in the online auction industry included BidVille (an auction site with no listing fees and no final value fees) and ePier (60,000 members as of January, 2004). Both of these had closely copied eBay's look and fee structure and touted themselves as "alternatives to eBay."

Amazon.com Auctions   Amazon.com's business strategy was to "be the world's most customer-centric company where customers can find and discover anything they may want to buy online."[20] With its customer base of 35 million users in over 150 countries and a very well-known brand name, Amazon.com was considered the closest overall competitive threat to eBay, especially as eBay expanded its business model beyond its traditional auction services. Analysts estimated that Amazon.com had a 5–7 percent share of all online retail sales, but

[20]2000 Amazon annual report.

Hitwise, an Internet competitive intelligence service, found that for the week ending September 20, 2003, eBay had a 93.6 percent share of all Web traffic to auction sites while Amazon.com had only a 1.1 percent share.

Amazon was created in July 1995 as an online bookseller and had rapidly transitioned into a full-line, one-stop-shopping retailer with a product offering that included books, music, toys, electronics, tools and hardware, lawn and patio products, video games, software, and a mall of boutiques (called z-shops). Amazon.com was the Internet's number one music, video, and book retailer. One of the distinctive features customers appreciated about Amazon.com was the extensive reviews available for each item. These product reviews were written both by professionals and by regular users who had purchased a specific product. The company's 2003 net sales were estimated between $6.2 and $6.7 billion, up almost 58.9 percent from 2002. In 2002 the company showed its first income from operations—$64.1 million—and the 2003 operating revenue increased substantially from 2002 (as seen in Exhibit 9). One significant weakness analysts noted in Amazon's financials was that the company's free shipping policies, put in place to draw more customers, had a significant, negative impact on net income.

exhibit 9 Operating Results

Year	Income or (Loss) from Operations (in millions)
1996	$(6.2)
1997	(31.0)
1998	(124.5)
1999	(720.0)
2000	(863.9)
2001	(412.3)
2002	64.1
2003	400.0 (est)

By 2003 Amazon's management felt that it was in a position that would allow it to balance demands of both cost control and growth in executing a strategy intended to enhance Amazon's position as leader in retail e-commerce. As an indication of the company's success in executing its strategy, its customer base rose from 14 million to 20 million during 2000 and to 35 million by 2003. The company invested more than $300 million in infrastructure in 1999 and opened two international sites, www.amazon.co.uk (the United Kingdom) and www.amazon.de (Germany), and later added www.amazon.ca (Canada), www.amazon.co.jp (Japan) and www.amazon.fr (France). These sites, along with Amazon.com, were among the most popular online retail domains in Europe. By 2004 international sales had grown to over $2 billion from just $168 million in 1999 and accounted for 38 percent of all Internet sales.

Some analysts felt that in expanding its position both internationally and abroad Amazon had conceded the top spot in online auction to eBay and was looking to explore other avenues. Amazon often used strategic alliances to support its innovative expansion initiatives. For example, the company had agreements with Borders Books to allow customers to pick up Amazon.com book orders in-store, as well as e-commerce partnerships with Ashford.com, Drugstore.com, CarsDirect.com, and Sotheby's (a leading auction house for art, antiques, and collectibles), and opened a co-branded toy and video game store online with Toysrus.com. During 2003, the company announced an agreement with the band Pearl Jam to sell the group's music directly to fans through Amazon's Advantage program. By 2003 Amazon.com had over 550,000 active third-party sellers on its site and 350 branded sellers, most of

them selling through shops rather than auctions. These third-party sellers accounted for over 22 percent of U.S. sales. To further expand the company's reach, in September 2003 Amazon established an independent unit called A9 that was charged with creating the best shopping search tool for Amazon's use and for use by other companies and third-party Web sites. To compete with eBay's fixed-price formats, Amazon began including links on product pages that allowed customers to view identical new and used items from third-party sellers.

uBid.com   uBid's mission statement was to "be the most recognized and trusted business-to-consumer marketplace, consistently delivering exceptional value and service to its customers and supplier partners."[21] According to the company, "uBid delivers to the customer both the cost savings of an auction and the customer care of popular brand name retail e-commerce sites, making uBid a destination point for consumer share of wallet as they capitalize on the benefits of this high performance hybrid business model."[22] As such, uBid considered itself to be in direct competition with eBay, although a distant second, especially to that portion of eBay's business that was derived from large corporations and smaller companies wanting to sell their products through an auction format. The company's business model centered on offering brand-name, often refurbished and closeout, merchandise at a deep discount in a relatively broad range of categories from leading brand-name manufacturers such as Sony, Hewlett-Packard, IBM, Compaq, AMD, Minolta, and over 1,000 other suppliers. Categories included Computer and Office; Consumer Electronics; Music, Movies & Games; Jewelry & Gifts; Travel & Events; Home & Garden; Sports; Toys & Hobbies; Apparel; Collectibles; and Everything Else. The merchandise was offered in both an online auction format in which prices started at $1.00 and through uBid's fixed-price superstore. The merchandise was sourced from corporate partners and from uBid's own operations, which included a 400,000-square-foot warehouse and refurbishment center, and their current parent company Petters Group Worldwide, and from small and medium-sized companies who were members of uBid's Certified Merchant Program. Although uBid had offered

[21]www.ubid.com/about/companyinfo.asp.
[22]Ibid.

consumer-to-consumer auctions at one time, the company had discontinued this option as of 2002 due to the costs associated with policing fraud and concerns over product quality.

Founded in April 1997, uBid offered an initial public offering on the Nasdaq in December 1998. The company had experienced significantly increased revenues every year since its inception through 2000, but it had never captured the share of the auction market that its founders hoped was possible, although it at one time had a 14.7 percent share of revenues in the online auction market. In mid-2000 uBid was sold to CGMI Networks, and then it was sold again to Petters Group Worldwide in 2003. With each sale the number of workers employed by uBid fell and the product mix was changed in an attempt to find a niche market that would insulate the company from the competitive power of eBay.

Yahoo Auctions Yahoo.com, the first online navigational guide to the Web, launched Yahoo Auctions in 1998. Yahoo.com offered services to nearly 200 million users every month in North America, Europe, Asia, and Latin America. The Web site was available in 24 countries and 12 languages. Yahoo reported net revenues of $1.11 billion in 2000 (up 88 percent from 1999) and net income of $290 million. Yahoo's user base grew from 120 million to over 180 million during 2000. In December 2000 Yahoo's traffic increased to an average of 900 million page views per day (up 94 percent from 1999). Yahoo had entered into numerous alliances and marketing agreements to generate additional traffic at its site and was investing in new technology to improve the site's performance and attractiveness.

Its auction services were provided to users free of charge in the early days, and the number of auctions listed on Yahoo increased from 670,000 to 1.3 million during the second half of 1999. However, when Yahoo decided to start charging users a listing fee in January 2001, listings fell from over 2 million to about 200,000.[23] Yahoo Auctions also offered many extra services to its users. For example, the Premium Sellers Program was designed to reward the sellers that were consistently at the top of their category. These Premium Sellers were allowed enhanced promotions, premium placement, and direct access to customer support. In recognition of the fall in listings

[23]Troy Wolverton, "eBay Seeks to Sail into New Territory," CNET News.com, July 19, 2001.

due to the listing fee instituted in January, Yahoo Auctions announced a revamped performance-based pricing model for its U.S. auctions in November 2001. In this system, which was relatively similar to eBay's, listing fees were reduced and sellers were charged according to the value of an item sold. In response to this change the number of listings rose to more than 500,000 by December 7, 2001.

While Yahoo had significant reach throughout the world, including over 25 local auction sites internationally, by 2004 Yahoo Auctions had reduced its international operations from 16 countries to 7 (Brazil, Canada, Hong Kong, Japan, Mexico, Singapore, and Taiwan). In 2002 alone Yahoo conceded its auction sites in France, Germany, Italy, Spain, and the United Kingdom and Ireland and promoted eBay's sites in each of those countries via banner ads and text links. In 2003 Yahoo sold its Australian site as well. However, in 2004 Yahoo began offering auctions in China through a joint venture with a dominant Chinese Web portal, Sina, indicating that it had not completely abandoned the international auction market. Further reinforcing Yahoo's commitment to online retail, in July 2003 Yahoo acquired Overture, which was the leading provider of commercial search as of the end of the first quarter of 2003 with more than 88,000 advertisers globally as well as an extensive affiliate distribution network. Many of the sellers who advertised on Overture also advertised on eBay, and some analysts estimated that the amount of sales by merchants through the combination of Yahoo's and Overture's offerings would total between one-half to two-thirds of that available on eBay.

eBAY'S NEW CHALLENGES

Heading into 2004 eBay was the undisputed leader in the online auction industry. To reach this enviable position, eBay had to overcome a number of hurdles. Throughout its history, eBay faced each new challenge with an eye on its founding values and an ear for community members. Omidyar said, "What we do have to be cautious of, as we grow, is that our core is the personal trade, because the values are communicated person-to-person. It can be easy for a big company to start to believe that it's responsible for its success. Our success is really based on our members' success. They're the ones who have created this, and they're the ones who will create it in the future. If we lose sight of that, then we're in big trouble."[24] The company applied this perspective in response to significant customer concerns regarding the growing presence of corporate sellers on eBay.

Omidyar and Whitman recognized the importance of eBay's culture and were aware of the potential impact rapid growth and the evolution of the product line could have on this valued asset. When asked about the importance of the culture Omidyar said, "If we lose that, we've pretty much lost everything."[25] Whitman agreed with the importance of eBay's culture, but she did not see the influx of larger retailers and liquidators as a significant problem. Even as these sellers grew to account for 5 percent of eBay's total business in 2004 (from 1 percent in 2001), these large sellers received no favorable treatment. Whitman stated, "There are no special deals. I am passionate about creating this level playing field."[26] While this view was applauded by the smaller sellers, some larger sellers viewed these policies as overly restrictive.

Heading into 2004, eBay faced two fundamental challenges:

1. How could eBay continue to grow at its current pace given the maturing of its domestic market?
2. As eBay's business model evolved to include more fixed-price sales, could it transfer its competitive advantage in the online auction industry into the more general area of online retail?

Continued Growth

By virtually any measure, eBay's growth had been outstanding. However, this impressive track record, coupled with the progress they had made in reaching their stated goals had created high expectations among investors. These lofty expectations began to cause some concern among analysts as eBay's domestic core market of online auction sales began to show some warning signals. For example, in 2003 the average conversion rate (the number of auctions that were completed successfully) was approxi-

mately 51 percent, a rate that had held steady over the last two years. However, supply imbalances threatened this key metric. In many categories, as the number of sellers grew, supply was beginning to outstrip demand. One of the few categories in which demand outstripped supply was eBay Motors, which had an average of 11 bids from seven unique users for each sale. Further, almost half of eBay's registered users were from the United States and represented almost one-third of all U.S. Internet users. With the U.S. online auction market maturing and eBay maintaining the dominant market share, analysts were concerned with how much more penetration eBay could achieve.

In response to these concerns, eBay cited new trends indicating that even in the United States the company was reaching new customers and had room to grow. One of the trends eBay saw as particularly promising was the increasing use of eBay's 28,000 registered Trading Assistants and the emergence of drop-off eBay consignment services. Trading Assistants were experienced eBay sellers who, for a fee, would help users sell their items on eBay. Extending this service, drop-off consignment services began to spring up as early as 2000. These consignment services, such as AuctionDrop, QuickDrop, and Picture-It-Sold, would take physical possession of a customer's items, typically those with an eBay value of over $50, and sell them on eBay for a fee equal to between 30 and 40 percent of the item's final sale price. The company was encouraged by these activities because they reached sellers who would not normally use the Internet.

eBay also challenged the theory that the maturity of its markets was based on the company's total market penetration in key categories. For example, eBay argued that it had significant market opportunity in areas such as eBay Motors, where its $6.7 billion in gross merchandise sales accounted for less than 1 percent of the value of all vehicles sold in the United States. Based on this model, none of eBay's largest categories had a market penetration of 5 percent (see Exhibit 10).

Evolution of the Business Model

There was little concern that anyone would seriously threaten eBay in its core auction business in the near

[24]"Q&A with eBay's Pierre Omidyar," *BusinessWeek E.Biz*, December 3, 2001.

[25]"The People's Company," *BusinessWeek E.Biz*, December 3, 2001.

[26]"Queen of the Online Flea Market," Economist.com, December 30, 2003.

exhibit 10   **eBay's Largest Auction Categories, by Annualized Gross Merchandise Sales, as of Fourth Quarter 2003 (in millions)**

	Fourth-Quarter 2003	Market Penetration
Motors	$7,500	< 1%
Consumer electronics	2,600	1–4%
Computers	2,400	1–3%
Books, movies, music	2,000	~ 3%
Clothing and accessories	1,800	< 1%
Sports	1,800	2–5%
Collectibles	1,500	2–3%
Toys	1,500	~ 5%
Home and garden	1,100	< 1%

Source: Corporate reports, Lehman Brothers estimates, www.lehman.com.

future, but with the increasing use of tools such as gift certificates, the growing importance of fixed-price sales, the purchase of Half.com, and the growing popularity of Buy It Now, eBay came into more direct competition with retailers such as Amazon.com, with e-commerce solutions, and with the likes of Microsoft. Some analysts also thought that search engines such as Google that were directing customers to clients who paid to have their sites prominently featured in the search engine's results would also become a competitor in the near future, but Meg Whitman dismissed this possibility, saying, "We see Google and Yahoo search and MSN search . . . as actually enablers of our business," she said. "We think both natural search and paid search are allies of ours."[27] When asked about how the evolution of their business model influenced their sphere of competition, Whitman said,

> If we were a retailer, we'd be the 27th-largest in the world. So our sellers are competing [with retailers] for consumer dollars. If you're thinking about buying a set of golf clubs or a tennis racket or a jacket or a pair of skis, you decide whether you're going to do that at eBay, at Wal-Mart, a sporting-goods store, or

[27]Ben Berkowitz, "eBay to Experiment Again with Local Auction Sites," www.usatoday.com, February 24, 2004.

Macy's. I would define our competition more broadly than ever before.[28]

The threat of these competitors increased as fixed-price sales comprised an ever-increasing percentage of eBay's total sales and growth. By the end of 2003, fixed-price trading accounted for 28 percent of eBay's gross merchandise sales (the dollar value of merchandise sold) and was expected to experience continued growth throughout the foreseeable future.

THE FUTURE

Heading into 2004, eBay was almost certain to reach the aggressive growth targets it had set for itself in 2000—and its stock price reflected this belief (see Exhibit 11). In fact, most analysts forecast that eBay would meet these goals a year early. The main question that plagued investors was, How would the company continue its phenomenal growth rate? In considering future moves eBay had a few issues to address. First, how should it prioritize its efforts? Was additional expansion in the international markets the highest priority? If so, where? Alternatively, should eBay focus on further broadening its offerings to include more categories, more specialty sites, and more sellers? How much emphasis should be put on fixed-price options? If the company chose to continue expanding its fixed-price offerings, how could it position itself vis-à-vis established online retailers, and how could it defend itself against new, more diverse competitors such as paid search engines?

Finally, eBay was facing increasing dissatisfaction by some of its largest corporate sellers. Some corporate sellers were experiencing significant difficulty with selling a large volume of goods on the site while maintaining a sufficient profit margin. According to Walt Shill, the former chief of Return-Buy, a company that liquidated unsold merchandise for electronics retailers and manufacturers, eBay didn't have enough buyer demand to absorb significant quantities of a single good, such as a specific brand and model of a digital camera, in a short period of time, as eBay was "two inches deep and miles wide."[29] Whitman acknowledged this problem and

[28]"Meg Whitman on eBay's Self-Regulation," *Business Week Online*, August 18, 2003.

[29]Nick Wingfield, "As eBay Grows, Site Disappoints Some Big Vendors," *The Wall Street Journal*, February 26, 2004.

exhibit 11 **eBay's Stock Price Performance, March 2003–February 2004**

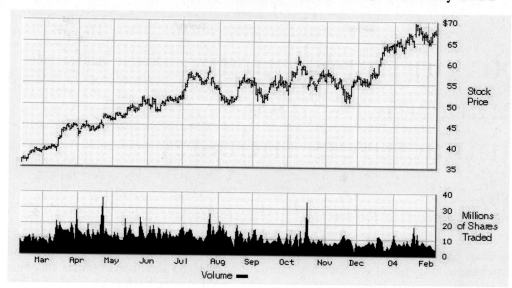

Source: www.bigcharts.com, February 9, 2004.

stated that, for sellers wishing to "move a thousand of the same computer in a day, eBay may not be one of the most effective channels."[30] This problem, coupled with eBay's fairness policy, was causing many large sellers such as Motorola and Circuit City to abandon selling on eBay and to search for additional sales outlets. According to Scott Wingo, CEO of ChannelAdvisor, a leading provider of auction and marketplace management software that was partially owned by eBay, eBay would need to reconsider its level-playing-field policy, which prohibited giving special perks or fee discounts to big sellers if it wanted to attract large businesses and keep growing at its current rate.[31]

[30]Ibid.
[31]Ibid.

When eBay posted its 2003 results in early 2004, it was apparent to most industry observers that it would easily reach its stated goals a year early. Perhaps the only significant concern among analysts and investors was whether eBay could continue its growth without stretching itself too thin, especially given Meg Whitman's philosophy, as evinced in the following statement:

> You really need to do things 100 percent. Better to do 5 things at 100 percent than 10 things at 80 percent. Because the devil in so much of this is in the detail and while we have to move very, very fast, I think you are not well served by moving incredibly rapidly and not doing things that well.[32]

[32]"What's Behind the Boom at eBay?" *Business Week Online,* May 21, 1999.

Note on the Security Management and Manufacturers Industry

Marilyn L. Taylor
University of Missouri at Kansas City

Theresa T. Coates
Rensselaer Polytechnic Institute

In the latter part of the 1990s the U.S. security management industry posed a number of opportunities and challenges for its participants. Several factors suggested that the industry would continue to experience strong growth. The factors driving the strong demand growth included lowered product costs, new technology developments, changing demographics (especially the aging of the population), and the salience of high-profile security incidents.

Among the industry's participants were firms that provided services and products as well as the firms that provided component parts. Industry entrants fell into at least five segments: (1) mass marketers; (2) installers and small systems designers; (3) large systems designers (including manufacturers and value-added resellers); (4) device manufacturers, including original equipment manufacturers (OEMs) and larger device manufacturers; and (5) high-end developers of technology and products. Each segment had a different structure and provided varying opportunities for suppliers as well as for current and potential entrants.

This industry note is drawn primarily from an industrial market research study report submitted to a private company in early 1998. The market research team based their observations on data gathered in two overlapping phases carried out in late 1997 and early 1998. These two phases were: (1) a thorough search of the 1995–97 practitioner literature as well as Internet searches and (2) interviews with approximately 30 companies located primarily on the East Coast. Permission to draw from the proprietary study was granted by the company. The bibliography provided by the consulting firm is available from the authors. The case has been published in the *Business Case Journal.* Copyright © 2003 by Marilyn L. Taylor and Theresa T. Coates.

Four technology developments appeared to provide significant opportunities for those firms that could determine how to exploit them: biometric-based security systems, radio frequency ID (RFID) systems, closed-circuit TV (CCTV), and integration of systems (i.e., "smart buildings" primarily driven by developments in computer hardware and software for linking systems). In the latter half of the 20th century's closing decade, success would come to those industry participants who best predicted the industry trends and seized the opportunities.

HISTORY OF THE INDUSTRY

The origins of the security management industry were in antiquity. Prior to the early 1800s, security depended on mechanical devices and on privately hired manpower. The first modern police force (i.e., public police) was established in 1829 when Britain's home secretary, Sir Robert Peel, set up the (London) Metropolitan Police. This police organization replaced a previously much fragmented system. The term *Bobby* referred to any member of Sir Robert's police force. The old system of private security remained in existence but was gradually restricted to functions such as guarding cash in transit, sleuthing, or making locks.

In the United States firm names such as Diebold and Mosler reflect back to heavy vaults and safes used in the banking industry.[1] The modern security alarm business began with Augustus Pope's mid-1800's patent of the first electrically operated burglar alarm. Pope's device used magnetic switches along a series circuit connected to a battery and a bell.

The beginning of electronic surveillance was credited to the Long Island resident and inventor Arthur Minasy. As a child, Minasy shoplifted marbles and tennis balls from a Woolworth store in Queens, New York. During the early 1960s, Minasy worked as consultant for the New York City police department on the growing problem of retail store pilferage. In his garage he created an electronic tag that could be attached to items and that would set off an alarm as the item passed through a security system near the door. He called the prototype Knogo (as in *no go*). The Knogo began to catch on in the 1970s. It was the first of the electronic article surveillance (EAS) innovations. EAS systems found their earliest applications in the retail industry.

Until the 1960s public safety and crime prevention were the monopoly of the public police. In the early 1970s a transformation began. In 1970 there were 1.4 public policemen for every private guard. However, in the latter part of the 1990s there were three times as many private policemen as public ones. In California the ratio was four to one. In the mid-1990s Americans spent over $90 billion a year on private security and another $40 billion through tax dollars on public police. Similar phenomena occurred in a number of other countries. In places such as Russia and South Africa, for example, there were 10 times as many private security guards as public police.

INDUSTRY GROWTH

In the latter part of the 1990s the security industry was, as one company president described it, ". . . in the middle of a revolution." The industry had become the darling of Wall Street, with some firms experiencing unparalleled growth. For example, one manufacturing executive stated that his company had

---

[1]Brief descriptions for most companies appear in the appendix to this case. Companies for which the consulting team was unable to find any information are so indicated.

seen almost 600 percent growth in the prior six years. Emerging technologies and increased software and microprocessor power marked the industry. Competitive pressure was increasing as new entrants invaded the industry. Some recent entrants were young firms based on new technologies while others were large corporate giants with competencies in electronics design and manufacture or microprocessor and software expertise. New market opportunities also characterized the security industry with the deregulation of utility companies and changes in consumer trends. More traditional segments were experiencing a shakedown as lower product prices squeezed margins and larger companies merged and flooded the market with new products. The introduction of government regulations especially on the municipal and state levels was beginning to create pressures for standards in the installation, design, and use of security devices and systems.

The security management and manufacturing industry had experienced consistent yet greater-than-expected growth over the prior three decades. In 1997 the industry generated over $100 billion in revenues/sales in North America. The industry was expected to grow at a rate of about 15 percent during the 1990s, although the various industry segments had different estimated growth rates. Industry representatives suggested that guard, or protective, services would grow at around 5 percent annually, while electronic security services were expected to expand between 8 and 10 percent annually in coming years. Margins, however, were decreasing. For example, profit margins in the alarm monitoring business had been as much as 50 percent 10 years prior. In some areas of the country margins on alarm monitoring had dropped to as low as 2 percent.

The industry consisted of a myriad of players that included a few large national companies and a multitude of smaller local firms. A map of the security device manufacturers drawn from multiple sources appears as Exhibit 1. There were so many different products and services in the security industry that customers often needed the advice of security consultants. The industry was divided into three major groups of equipment or services:

1. Protective services: guard, central security stations, and armored car services with over 3,000 firms providing guard and investigative services.

exhibit 1   **Locations of Security Device Manufacturers in the United States**

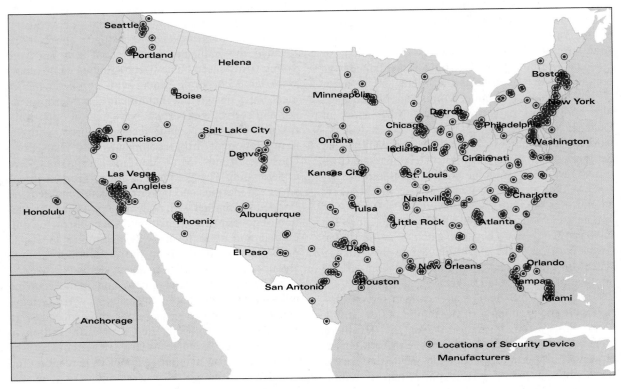

2. Deterrent equipment: often simple security tools that could significantly reduce losses.

3. Monitoring and detection equipment: electronic alarm systems and closed-circuit television security systems.

Exhibit 2 lists summary statistics for the industry.

Industry Growth Demand Drivers

Demand for security products and services was being driven by a number of factors: decreasing product costs, new technology developments, changing demographics, and security incidents. The major factor that drove the increasing demand for home security systems was the tumbling cost of products. Home security systems were once restricted to the rich. By the mid-1990s such products were in middle-class homes as well. Products once costing thousands of dollars were available for less than a hundred dollars. Some

systems cost about $20 a month, including the installation fee. In the face of declining prices for security devices and systems, residential demand was expected to remain strong.

New technology developments had also helped fuel demand. The sales of electronic security systems were growing aggressively as new microprocessors had enabled systems to be more powerful and flexible. EAS had increased its applications in stores, factories, offices, airlines, and hospitals. There was increased use of central monitoring systems in office buildings, often operated by small personal computers. Many observers expected biometrics to be increasingly used in access control and employee identification. Biometrics involved measuring some unique characteristics of an individual such as handprint, fingerprint, voice, signature, or retinal patterns. Biometric devices were used for such applications as access control and tracking employee attendance. Locks were being enhanced by inexpensive microprocessor technology. New computer software was being developed to en-

exhibit 2 **Selected Summary Statistics for the Security Industry in the United States, Mid-1990s**

Number of policemen	684,000
Number of private security officers	1.8 billion
Number of private security firms (in contrast to 70,000 in 1980)	160,000
Total revenues for private security firms (up from $20B in 1980)	$100 billion
Minimum start-up capital required for small firms	$10,000
Growth potentials	
Alarm companies, manufacturers, and distributors	12%
Contract guards	8%
Private investigators	7%
Estimated average annual revenues for firms	
Private security guard companies	$980,000
Private investigative firms	$198,000
Proprietary systems (e.g., computer security)	$272,000
Manufacturers and distributors	$5 million

hance the control of access security. Advances in the extraordinary security measures used by the U.S. Department of Defense and by the National Aeronautics and Space Administration (NASA) to protect the space shuttle were expected to filter into commercial applications.

Another driver of demand was changing demographics. The aging of the population suggested that an increasing proportion of U.S. citizens would be in a crime-vulnerable age range. These older Americans were expected to have increased overall purchasing power with which to acquire security devices and services.

Overall crime rates had peaked around 1980 in the United States and stabilized or decreased since that time. Some major cities had seen sharp decreases in crime rates. Significant increases had occurred, however, in the incidence of juvenile homicide, although some argued that the change in these rates was a result of how the police categorized incidents rather than an increase in activity. In spite of the overall decrease in crime rates, the general belief was that crime rates were increasing annually and were at an all-time high in the mid-1990s. Even newscasters expressed disbelief in statistics showing decreases in crime statistics. No one had come forth with a solid explanation for the persistence of the general belief in increasing crime rates, although television handling of crimes, especially violent crimes, was cited as one possible factor. In fact, statistics indicated that the av-

erage citizen was far more likely to die in a motor vehicle accident than to be the victim of a violent crime. Nonetheless, the belief persisted.

Security efforts had continued to increase throughout the country through the latter part of the 20th century. Airport security was very visible for a wide proportion of the population. In 1969 the Federal Aviation Administration (FAA) had initiated a task force to make recommendations regarding passenger airline security. In 1972 the FAA implemented security scanning of all passengers' carry-on luggage. Through the next decades the government continued to increase funds aimed at these efforts, and the efforts received impetus with such disasters at the bombing of Pan Am flight 103 over Lockerbie, Scotland, and the July 1996 crash of TWA flight 800.

Significant security incidents that left a number of people dead or injured and their resulting publicity further drove demand. Terrorist events such as the February 1993 World Trade Center bombing and the April 1995 federal building bombing in Oklahoma City had changed the image of the security industry and made electronic surveillance much more accepted.[2] In the two years after the 1993 World Trade Center bombing, the costs of security at the center

[2]The February 1993 World Trade bombing killed 6 people and injured 1,000 (http://ntas.mahwah.k12.nj.us/HS/EXPLTECH/ DISASTER/TwinTowr/). The Oklahoma City bombing killed 168. "Today Is Deadline for McVeigh Indictment," News (Gannett), June 12, 1995.

more than tripled, to about $24 million annually. That annual cost did not include the $60 million cost of the new security systems that came online in 1997. The 1995 Oklahoma City bombing led to increased work for security companies.

Security efforts expanded into other arenas, for example, shopping areas. As the CEO of Vicon said, "Years ago shoppers objected to electronic eyes recording their moves; today it's not only accepted, it's preferred. There are two ways to go with video surveillance—it's either visible, so people know they're being watched, or you hide it, so privacy doesn't seem intruded upon. Most clients want it out in the open."

INDUSTRY SEGMENTS

The companies providing services, products, and components within the security industry could be categorized into the following five groups: (1) mass marketers, (2) installers and small systems designers, (3) large systems designers, (4) device manufacturers, and (5) high-end technology and system developers.[3] Some companies operated in more than one group, however. Each group had distinctly different product/service offerings and served different customer segments.

Exhibit 3 maps the segments on a matrix with the segments' product/service offerings on one axis and the customer segments on the other axis. As suggested in the matrix, there were three basic categories of firms' offerings: (1) some firms manufactured security devices or products, (2) other firms provided both devices and service, and (3) still other firms sold primarily services. The firms served three types of end customers: residential, small business, and large corporate/institutional clients. The three customer categories formed a continuum of demand for increasing levels of security as well as system sophistication. Residential customers usually wanted the lowest level of security and system sophistication, whereas large corporate and institutional clients called for the highest levels of security and system

sophistication. Exhibit 4 maps the industry activity chain demonstrating the buyer–customer relationships between the segments plus suppliers of basic components and distributors. The five industry segments are described in the sections below.

Mass Marketers

The mass marketers segment of the security industry was comprised of a new set of security industry entrants. These firms sold access control systems primarily in the residential market either regionally or nationally. Their product line consisted of simple systems and devices. Mass marketers tended to sell their security devices and installation services in high volume at cost plus a low margin, and they used their low product and installation prices to sign residential consumers to long-term monitoring contracts. Mass marketers made their monitoring service profits by spreading their fixed costs over a large volume of installed security systems. According to device manufacturers, the mass marketers bought in large quantities direct from the manufacturer and looked for low price rather than quality. One manufacturing executive explained that the mass marketers bought his firm's lower-end products, that is, those that did not incorporate the newest designs or state-of-the-art technology.

In 1997 a large conglomerate electronics firm, Tyco Industries, acquired one of the larger mass marketers, ADT Inc. Although Tyco did not supply any electronic security devices, it did make components that were used in manufacturing security devices.

Installers and Small Systems Designers

Many security installers and small systems designers were more than 20 years old. They had often moved from being second- or third-generation locksmiths to companies that installed electronic security systems. A few of these companies had moved from providing fire protection devices (e.g., fire extinguishers and smoke detectors) into providing security systems design and installation. The installers and small systems designer companies tended to be local or narrow regional players. They provided access control and CCTV systems to both residential and

---

[3]The consultants also included data on the major companies that provided primarily guard services. However, since the client's technology appeared to have little application in this segment, the consultants did not address this segment in the report.

exhibit 3 **Security Device and Systems Manufacturers—Industry Segments: Buyer Type/Level of Security and Product Variety/Manufacturing Capability**

Customer Segments

Product/Service Offerings		Residential	Small Business	Large Corporate/Institutional
	Products/devices Manufacturing/ development		4a. OEMs 4b. Large device manufacturers	5. High-end technology developers
			3a. Large System Designers	
	Products/devices Manufacturing/ development and services		2. Installers and Small System Designers	3b. Value-added resellers
		1. Mass marketers		
	Services			

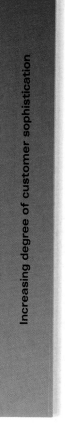

Increasing degree of customer sophistication

exhibit 4 **Industry Activity Chain**

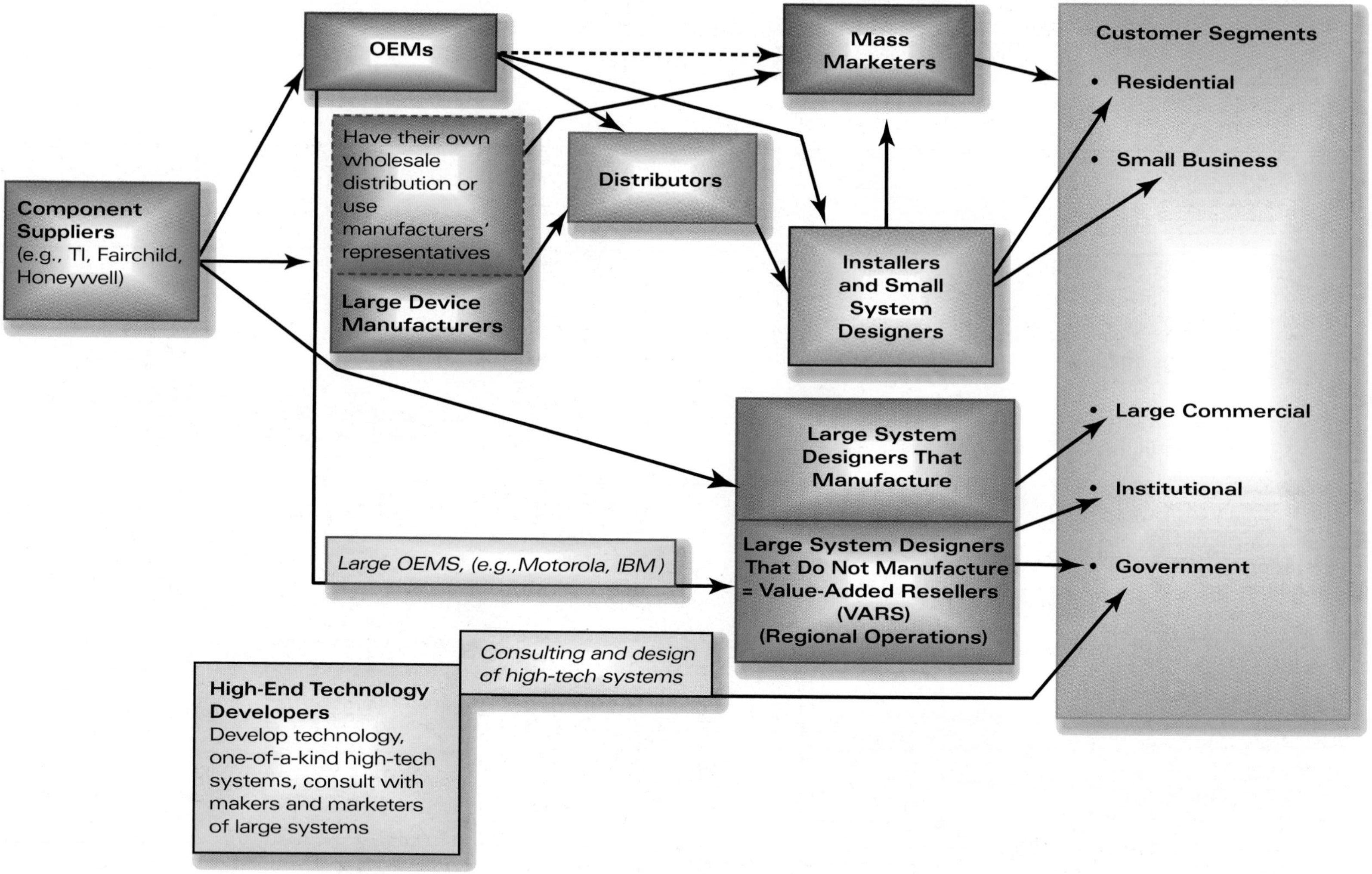

Customer Segments
- Residential
- Small Business
- Large Commercial
- Institutional
- Government

Mass Marketers

Installers and Small System Designers

Large System Designers That Manufacture

Large System Designers That Do Not Manufacture = Value-Added Resellers (VARS) (Regional Operations)

Distributors

OEMs

Have their own wholesale distribution or use manufacturers' representatives

Large Device Manufacturers

Large OEMS, (e.g.,Motorola, IBM)

Consulting and design of high-tech systems

High-End Technology Developers
Develop technology, one-of-a-kind high-tech systems, consult with makers and marketers of large systems

Component Suppliers
(e.g. TI, Fairchild, Honeywell)

C-324

small-business customers. These companies often gained clients primarily through word of mouth and the yellow pages. The firms believed they had a personal stake in the protection and security of their clients.

There were a number of factors that determined what equipment the installers and small system designers favored. The primary issue was quality. As several interviewees put it, all of the pieces "must be of a high quality." These firms felt they were selling a high degree of security; according to one company president, "When customers purchase a system they become part of our family." Managers within these companies also mentioned that they would prefer to buy American-made devices and accessories because of quality and because of their preference for reinvestment into the American economy. One company went as far as to say that his firm did not buy from a particular company because that company did not manufacture in the United States. Another significant factor in the purchase of equipment was the relationship with the distributor. Installers and small systems designers rarely bought direct from the original equipment manufacturer (OEM). Instead they bought their security devices from distributors like ADI and Alarm King. Although product variety and product integration were considerations, the firms preferred distributors that taught them new installation techniques and helped keep them abreast of systems design developments. These firms mentioned using devices manufactured by the following firms: ACS, Ademco, Central, ITI, Napco, and Detection Systems.

The group was divided about the effects of the mass marketers on the industry. Most of the installers and small systems designers felt that they were competing for residential customers. However, some firms thought that the entry of the mass marketers was raising the awareness of residential security and increasing the market potential. Firms with this latter mind-set believed that residential customers would eventually upgrade into better or more secure systems. Other firms in this group saw the mass marketer as "deteriorating the quality and value of home security systems" and giving the entire industry a negative reputation. One company president stated, "Company X gives a false sense of security to customers, besides impacting on increasing the false alarm rate."

There was a great deal of fragmentation within this group. Some of these companies were growing at tremendous rates, depending on their location and the economic conditions of the region (e.g., middle-class demographics, new housing starts, small to midsize business growth and density). Some of these firms had started to integrate forward through ownership in local building/developer/real estate agents and monitoring companies. Others had started to hire electronic specialists for wiring calibration and software maintenance and development. None of the companies seemed to realize the potential link with utilities companies or have aspirations for the scale of operations that such links would require.[4]

Where the population was dense, a few of these firms had started to install biometric systems. (See the section later in this case regarding this technology application in security systems.) Most company managers indicated that the biometric readers in a security system were expensive and that they had not installed any biometric-based systems. However, New York City installers said they had installed one to two systems. Wireless was another technology that these firms were beginning to offer customers. The customers of this segment increasingly requested linking personal computers with home and office systems as well as integrated systems in such applications as fire, access, and environment control systems. This group indicated that the greatest area of growth was CCTV installations. New keypads, miniaturization of devices, and new sensor technology were areas that interested the installers and small system designers.

Large Systems Designers (LSDs)

Large system designers (LSDs) offered systems design and installation to large corporate clients. LSDs

[4]The U.S. utility industries had been undergoing deregulation. The deregulation had led to multiple changes in industry structure and company strategies. One prominent strategy in the mid-1990s was the move several electric utility companies undertook to provide one-stop shopping for their customers' utility needs. Among the expanded set of services targeted by the utility companies was security systems and services. The utilities reasoned that they already knew the wiring layout of their residential customers' homes and business customer facilities. Thus, providing the security systems would be a horizontal product diversification.

could be divided into two subcategories: manufacturers and value-added resellers (VARs). Some of the firms in this segment had been in business for over 65 years.

Manufacturing LSDs Large system designers that manufactured sold globally to large industrial or commercial corporations. They did not sell to residential homeowners. In the past these companies had differentiated themselves by their technology capabilities and/or the market segments they served. LSDs tended to focus on specific applications such as tagging of equipment, inventory, or people. However, these firms had begun to merge under umbrella companies and were concerned with integrating systems. Two prime examples of LSDs were Knogo North America, which included the Sentry Technology group, and Sensormatic, an umbrella for companies such as Sensor Video. Firms such as Knogo often combined the ability to develop and manufacture components and devices in house for access control, CCTV, inventory monitoring and, in some cases, environmental control systems. They also designed and installed highly customized systems for very large corporate clients.

LSD firms had corporate R&D labs as well as divisional R&D activities. They often employed scientists and individuals who had patents in a variety of sciences. For example, one vice president of technology remarked that his company was looking for good physicists. Corporate R&D activities were oriented toward applications that, as one executive put it, "expand our present technologies' capabilities." Technology areas that the company executives mentioned included optics, semiconductors, and resonance frequencies. LSDs developed applications such as smart chips for tagging inventory and placing on identification cards. Company executives indicated that some R&D discoveries were allowing firms to move into other industries and applications besides security of people and property. The firms also licensed technology. Divisional R&D focused on integration and design of the proprietary devices. These firms tended to design in-house using standard components.

The LSD firms owned a variety of manufacturing facilities that incorporated both flexible and computer-aided manufacturing systems. One manufacturing executive stated that his company had moved all its manufacturing to Mexico because of the difficulties it had encountered in managing and integrating overseas manufacturing facilities. Among the difficulties the firm had encountered were language barriers and quality problems. In another company a vice president of engineering mentioned that his firm's entire manufacturing capability was located in Puerto Rico. The Puerto Rican location helped facilitate the firm's design for manufacturing philosophy and increased the dialogue between manufacturing and design. This firm sourced standard components and subassemblies from a variety of electronics firms such as Texas Instruments, Fairchild, and Honeywell. Some of these firms had in-house software development capabilities, whereas others bought existing software to run their systems.

These firms typically had large investments in their technology and manufacturing capabilities. For the most part the LSDs were less oriented to biometric systems. Instead they pursued wireless and miniaturization applications. In general this segment was characterized by strategies to consolidate, integrate backward, and increase capacity. They saw the market expanding. A vice president of one company said that his company had sold more surveillance systems in 1996 (i.e., after the 1995 Oklahoma City bombing) than it had sold in total in its prior years in business.

Value-Added Resellers The value-added resellers (VARs) were mainly large system developers and installers. They operated regionally using labeled and branded equipment to install fire, access, surveillance, and environmental control systems. These firms usually had a general system that they could modify slightly for customers. They tended to differentiate on customers and applications. For example, one firm specifically targeted university identification systems. Another firm worked with residential and commercial complexes to provide a generic system that would satisfy multiple-tenant security needs.

Usually, these firms had no in-house design or manufacturing capability. Instead they bought devices such as proximity readers, scanners, and other peripherals from large OEMs. One marketing vice president referred to the company's OEMs as the corporate giants (e.g., Motorola, Hughes, and IBM). Software was usually a minor cost, and this expertise was contracted out.

VARs were very excited about biometric technologies. They considered biometrics a big opportunity to differentiate and add value for their clients. One VAR's CEO indicated that there were some hurdles to overcome when educating the end user on how to use the systems, but that his firm was actively pursuing biometric access control applications. VARs saw the new technology as a means of increasing sales growth by redesigning and upgrading current clients' systems.

Device Manufacturers

Device manufacturers could be broken into two subgroups according to the breadth of product groups they manufactured. The first group was comprised of original equipment manufacturers (OEMs), which manufactured a narrow range of devices and/or accessories and had a narrow technology focus. The second group included manufacturers that had a broad, diverse set of product groups and technologies.

OEMs   OEMs featured a limited breadth of product line, often specializing in particular devices such as alarms, cameras, or sensors. A large proportion of this group focused on accessory items (e.g., cable, relays, wiring) and other peripherals. According to one CEO, about 60 to 70 percent of OEM products were sold as part of commercial installations. Most OEMs explained that they sold nationally and would work with any distributor. During early 1997 the segment experienced a small shakeup when one of the large OEMs acquired a distributor through which it began to sell competitors' products. This industry segment had moved away from exclusive distribution agreements. There was also a small group of OEMs that operated regionally and sold their products to regional installers and small systems designers. In general the OEMs had very limited product marketing and tended to offer lower-cost devices with no brand recognition. However, the VAR customers often ordered devices that carried their own brand names.

Although OEMs had their own proprietary designs, they designed devices around standard components. Usually the OEMs undertook design work in-house, but some OEMs had had experience with outside design and manufacturing of component/subassemblies. OEMs tended to work with low-tech (i.e., non-microprocessor-based) firms both inside and outside the industry. OEM executives expressed concern that outsourcing high-tech (i.e.,

microprocessor-based) design and manufacturing was very risky. Companies encountered several different kinds of difficulties with "imported" technology. Coordination with other companies could be problematic, and imported technology wouldn't necessarily work as envisioned. The problems could be particularly difficult with companies from outside the industry.

The OEMs' manufacturing facilities were mainly located in the United States. Some OEMs were expanding their capacity. One OEM vice president indicated that his firm had recently expanded capacity in anticipation of the increasing demand for CCTV. Other OEM executives were concerned with controlling unit costs. They were seeing more unit sales but smaller margins.

The OEMs had little internal R&D capability and usually licensed technology. Their product development sometimes involved market surveys, but usually they waited until a customer specifically asked for something before initiating design work. The OEMs' approach to market trends tended to be more reactive than proactive.

Most OEMs were not very interested in biometrics, nor were they interested in expanding their product lines. One OEM president indicated that his firm's strategy was to remain focused using the firm's current manufacturing equipment and licensed technology. Another vice president indicated that his firm was looking at different manufacturing technologies to increase efficiency.

Large Device Manufacturers (LDMs)

Large device manufacturers (LDMs) consisted of companies with large product divisions that designed and manufactured in a wide range of device categories (e.g., CCTV, fire alarm, access control, sensors, and environmental devices) for the global market of residential and small commercial security markets. This group included firms such as Digital Security Systems, Napco, Northern Video Systems Inc., Pittway Corporation, and Radionics. These companies were integrated backward and were also diversifying horizontally to become participants in every part of the security industry (e.g., burglar alarms, access control, and communications). One vice president described how his company had integrated backward to the point of doing metal pressing for plates. These firms were interested in new product lines and new business segments. Most of the companies were expanding their product ranges and market share through acquisition. The acquired companies offered both new products and proprietary technology. The firms were then able to share logistic, purchasing, information systems, manufacturing facilities, R&D, distribution, and service channels. One manufacturing vice president remarked that his company had moved the manufacturing of an acquired firm to the parent company's main compound, although other acquisitions had retained their manufacturing facilities in their original locations. The vice president also commented on how his challenge was coordinating the new locations in Italy and Chicago with the main location where R&D was located. The same company was exploring the opportunity to manufacture products in China.

The LDM firms differed in R&D capabilities. Some firms were using their technology development as means of differentiating. They focused on creating value through new technology and/or increasing the integration of their devices. One vice president of technology in such a firm declared that his firm was spending two to three times the industry standard in R&D. Other firms licensed or bought the technology and integrated it into the firm's product line. For example, one vice president of engineering stated that his firm licensed technology from Bell Labs. The firms also differed in the organization of their technology and product development activities. Firms that wanted to differentiate through technology tended to have significant R&D groups. Some had a corporate R&D department that had technology groups based on customer, technology expertise, and manufacturing expertise (e.g., wireless, circuit design, molding). Other firms had divisional R&D groups with a corporate vice president of engineering or R&D to coordinate the divisional groups.

In developing product designs the LDM firms bought standard components from suppliers, and all outsourced liquid crystal display (LCD) and other display components. There was very little outsourcing of design and manufacturing of end products or subassemblies. In some firms there was strong concern for coordinating product development efforts within the diverse product offerings. For example, development of product control panels had to integrate with all of the company's product groups. One vice president of engineering described the LDMs as having developed three tiers of product aimed at different customers. The first tier included simple, low-cost, low-technology products aimed at the mass marketers. The second tier provided a product of higher quality and technology content that serviced the needs of the small installer and some VARs. The third tier promoted higher technology and quality for LSDs and specifically VARs. These firms either distributed their products through independent manufacturers' representatives or had a wholesale distribution network.

LDM firms saw the residential segment and CCTV technology and products as the fastest-growing segments. Europe was considered a market with significant potential, and some firms were making investments in manufacturing facilities abroad. One executive stated that his firm would possibly acquire a European manufacturer in order to overcome EEC barriers to the market and then transfer its proprietary designs and manufacturing know-how from the U.S. corporate parent to the European subsidiary.

There was a dichotomy in this segment over the viability of biometrics. Some executives mentioned the inherent cost and felt that biometrics was a technology that could not be aimed at the mass market. Other executives thought it was a technology that had potential in numerous applications; they were having biometric firms come in and talk to their engineers and designers. Technologies that executives felt would impact the market in the near term included radio frequency (RF) or wireless, voice recognition, and miniaturization. The executives said higher-end products would become more sophisticated, with graphic user interfaces and more systems integration in control panels.

Another dichotomy within this group was over the issue of government regulation and the development of the standards within the industry. LDMs did not agree about the role that government should play in the design and use of security devices. The variety of responses from executives ranged from excitement (e.g., "Government legislation will be good for the industry") to anger (e.g., "Government will be biased and raise the costs of manufacturing") to indifference.

High End

This segment consisted mainly of technology developers that licensed technology to other companies. Firms in this segment often acted as consultants to advise about security systems. They would design one-of-a-kind high-tech security systems for large corporations. Typically they outsourced the manufacturing of their devices and were involved in the installation process on a consultative basis. Clients for these companies included government agencies, the U.S. Department of Defense, and large research and financial institutions. Some of these developers were starting to look at broader commercial applications for their technologies as well as partnerships with manufacturers.

TECHNOLOGY DEVELOPMENTS

Among the major technology developments were (1) biometric-based security systems, (2) access control and radio frequency ID (RFID) systems, (3) closed circuit television (CCTV), and (4) integration of security systems with other control systems. Each of these technologies provided opportunities and challenges for the various industry segments.

Biometric Security Systems

Biometrics, narrowly defined, was the statistical analysis of biological characteristics. But the word had come to refer more broadly to a whole family of "James Bond technologies." Eyes, hands, fingers, voice, face, typing pattern, handwriting style, or other distinguishing biological and behavioral measures could be used to control access to physical premises and computers. Biometrics could verify, in most cases, whether the individuals requesting access were who they claimed to be. Every biometric system performed somewhat similarly. Each began by capturing an image of a physical trait from an individual, converting the image into a mathematical code, and making a template associated with the individual's name. When someone sought access under that name again, the system would compare that individual's biometrics with the template and decide whether to grant access.

Biometric companies anticipated increasing demand for biometrics to guard computers, homes, credit and ATM cards, cars, and other valuables. According to one CEO, "The market is a lot bigger and will develop faster than many people would think.

Last year [1996], $1.45 billion was spent on facilities for access control alone. The cost of biometrics is getting down to the point where we could get a good share of that market. And there are computers. We think more than one in 100 will be secured with some form of biometric application before 1998 is out." Many of the biometrics firms expected an explosion in demand. Firms such as BAC and Intelitrak were positioning themselves to exploit the opportunity. Indeed, both BAC and Intelitrak claimed that interest in their new systems was high.

There were advantages and disadvantages to biometric systems. Among the old technology disadvantages were that (1) a password could be cracked and (2) swiped cards could be stolen. However, biometric technologies were relatively foolproof alternatives given current client-server, Internet, and physical security challenges. Some described biometrics as an ideal tool for identification. At $200 million a year in sales, the technology was already widely used in private industry, government, and the military for access control to buildings and computer networks.

However, biometrics was not a panacea. Like other security measures, biometrics came in strong and weak versions. Biometric security systems worked well when the biometric readers were secure from tampering and a person wanting access had to present his eye, hand, finger, face, voice, or handwriting sample directly to the reader or scanner. The president of a consulting firm specializing in cryptology and computer security observed, ". . . When biometrics are used remotely, they are very easy to steal . . . It is hard to steal a [physical] fingerprint. Once it goes digital, though, it can be intercepted. You can think of new passwords. But once your fingerprints have been compromised, you can't get new ones." There was considerable value in integrating biometrics with other security devices, like smart cards. These cards were credit-card-sized devices using an embedded computer chip loaded with encrypted IDs. The cards controlled access to computers and locations. They could be programmed to self-destruct if the wrong password was entered too many times. Encoding fingerprints on a smart card provided an added layer of security should a smart card be stolen and its loss not reported.

Every form of biometric systems had weaknesses. Fingerprint equipment had a negative association with criminal activity. In addition, the image quality of a fingerprint could be adversely affected by a multitude of factors including dirt, dry or cracked skin, age, gender, ethnic background, and the way a user interacted with the scanner. Biometrics had racial and occupational biases. People who worked with their hands, like brickmasons or carpenters, often had worn fingerprint minutiae that were difficult to scan in fingerprint systems. Certain ethnic groups like Asians had small, fine-lined fingerprints that could present scanning problems. Because of accidents or hard physical work, some people didn't have good fingerprints. About 3 percent of people using a hand-scanning system, for instance, were rejected and had to be sent to an alternate verification system (e.g., a different line in a bank) for access security clearance. Firms such as Printrak competed in this segment.

Voice systems suffered problems with interference and background noise. Some voice systems had proved susceptible to computer voice replication. Voice scans were subjected to changes in crowded conditions or with speaker conditions, including illness or the consumption of medication or alcohol. Twins could fool face-recognition systems.

Some individuals resisted the biometric technologies. For example, the act of looking into a retinal scanner or speaking into a microphone at a checkout counter was disturbing for some people. Thus, many companies that used some form of access control were counting on fingerprint scanning or other minutiae reading to become the technology of choice in biometric applications. To date consumers perceived fingerprints to be less invasive and safer than laser scans of the eyes.

Biometrics Demand Drivers and Deterrents

A number of issues were driving demand for biometrics at the same time that a number of factors were deterring its acceptance. There was considerable debate over what demand in the near term (i.e., three to five years) would look like. Some users certainly expected strong demand over the medium term (i.e., 5 to 10 years). However, there were also a number of naysayers.

Fraud was a major factor fueling the demand for biometric applications. In 1996 credit card fraud cost U.S. Visa and MasterCard issuers over $750 million. That figure did not include American Express, retail cards, and other credit cards. A MasterCard spokesperson said, "Biometrics is one of the security features we have identified as something we could add to our fraud prevention programs. If you can cut that [i.e., losses] even in half with technology like biometrics, that is a significant change."

Bank fraud was also increasing annually. Passwords and personal identification numbers (PINs) were susceptible to fraud. As a result, financial institutions were looking for new ways to protect customers and their money by developing mechanical and electronic systems to identify individuals through unique biological characteristics in the place of or in addition to PINs.

Demand had also increased because the technology was becoming much more reliable, accessible, and user friendly. Companies were finding that the price of hardware and equipment was dropping rapidly. Reader and scanner prices were expected to drop below $1,000 before the end of the decade.

Biometrics Industry Growth

The total sales of biometric hardware, excluding sales to law enforcement and integration revenue, amounted to $16.2 million in 1996. Sales were projected to hit $50 million in 1999, with as many as 50,000 units shipped. Cost and effectiveness were expected to be key factors in the battle emerging in the biometric segment.

The biometrics industry as a whole had yet to emerge as a viable business. Ron Smith, CEO of BAC, indicated that he believed there was a tremendous amount of volatility within the segment. Currently, there were a variety of competing technologies and systems. A host of new biometric technology companies had formed. Some of the more traditional security device manufacturers had begun to initiate talks with the new companies.

Access Control and Radio Frequency ID (RFID)

Access control referred to any number of technologies that screened individuals prior to entry or use of physical areas, computers, and even copying machines. The technology applied to access, egress, and movement tracking (e.g., of equipment, inventory, newborn infants, and Alzheimer's patients). Access control technologies included push-button locks (i.e., with a multidigit code) and keypads, as well as smart card, Wiegand, magnetic stripe, barium ferrite, proximity, and biometric readers.

Growth in overall demand for industrial access readers and systems was moderate indicating a mature market. However, a significant portion of demand appeared to be dependent on integration with human resource applications and environmental control systems. In addition, replacement demand and technology upgrades continued to fuel growth. In 1996 access control demand was over $1.45 billion in sales. There was a significant increase in demand for new installations in upscale residential markets where more homeowners were expected to install increasingly sophisticated locks and access systems. Demand for products to be incorporated in systems for lower-priced homes and the do-it-yourself market was expected to be price-sensitive.

During the latter part of the 1990s industry participants expected two significant issues for the access control reader. The first issue was the "hot" coming technology of biometrics. The second issue was radio frequency identification (RFID). The focus was on whether security systems would require a swipe card or use a proximity card that carried its own battery and carrier signal. Security system readers that required physical insertion risked dysfunction due to grime and dirt. Thus for many applications RFID was preferred.

RFID technology was used in more than just access control. Wires that transported the communications from access control devices or CCTV surveillance could be cut, leaving the premises with momentary loss of protection. Wireless transmission required greater technical sophistication to jam and offered greater flexibility for the user. RFID was also used in magnetic tagging systems that controlled access and egress of inventory (e.g., in retail stores), equipment, and persons. Demand was skyrocketing for RFID applications. This wireless technology was used in CCTV systems, remote video monitoring, and burglar alarm systems. Wireless systems offered several advantages, including lower installation costs and increased flexibility. Wireless identification systems had their origins in the retail security environment but in the latter part of the 1990s were being applied extensively in other settings. These technologies allowed security systems to track and locate people, vehicles, library books, and other assets.

A third issue was integration. A major issue for access control in companies was integration, that is, manufacturing or designing systems involving a broader spectrum of capabilities such as CCTV, access, and environmental control. Manufacturers were acquiring or merging with other companies in order to broaden their product lines. Some of the integration was coming at the manufacturing level in the industry stream. However, systems designers continued to effect a great deal of the integration.

Closed-Circuit TV: The All-Seeing Eye

CCTV's role in automating security systems also continued to grow. The president of a small firm noted that the role of CCTV in automating security systems was growing by an exponential degree. "Everyone wants multiplexers to view scenes and be able to record them quickly and then bring those images back," he said. CCTV's role was especially growing by leaps and bounds as part of the identification process. Another industry participant noted, "It used to be that the ID card was the most important [means of IDing. However,] CCTV is bypassing the smart card that can be altered. Now the latest technology is facial recognition that can be linked into certain databases to see what the person looks like and who he really is. This is where automation truly comes into play." Imaging identification, CCTV surveillance, and communications systems including audio verification burglar systems, video transmission in paging systems, and emergency telephone systems were all bringing sound *and* pictures into security monitoring systems. Video transmission could bring real-time motion pictures into a command-and-control area from numerous remote sites hundreds, even thousands, of miles away. The systems also allowed a central security operation to control remote cameras and videotaping equipment. The addition of motion detection made the multimedia systems even more automated since they could capture and send images and alarms without human intervention to and from any place on earth.

School campuses, shopping areas, town squares, parks and recreation areas, housing projects, dangerous intersections, and other similar locations were increasingly using CCTV systems for public surveillance. Temporary CCTV surveillance systems could be installed at special events, such as summer concerts. Such installations helped law-enforcement professionals in their crime-prevention efforts and were a manpower-saving way of managing traffic and safety activities. The director of communications for the Security Industry Association, an organization

exhibit 5   **Examples of CCTV Installations**

- A 1996 SIA report documented the use of CCTV in public surveillance in 15 U.S. cities. Cities and other entities with CCTV applications include Oak Park, Oak Brook, the Village of Winnetka, Chicago's elevated train system, the city of Toledo, and the state of Ohio's public court systems. This report promised a later update detailing CCTV use in another 30 cities.

- Pinole, California (a community of 18,000 located near San Francisco), received extensive federal government funds that were used to install color cameras at three areas: a senior citizens' recreation center in a high-crime, high-vandalism area near a park, a bridge across the Interstate 80 freeway, and the Pinole Crossing Shopping Center. The primary objectives were to deter crime, identify and apprehend offenders, and capture incidents on tape. According to the Pinole Police Department, the issue of privacy never came up in meetings with civic groups, community leaders, and elected officials.

- The village of Rosemont, Illinois (near Chicago), had used CCTV for public surveillance for many years. The village owned and operated many public sites, including the Rosemont Convention Center, Rosemont Theater, Rosemont Horizon and other municipal properties that were frequented by large numbers of residents and tourists. Rosemont's installations included fixed and movable black-and-white cameras that were monitored at the police department's 911 communications center. Signs advised of the presence of surveillance cameras. Lieutenant Joseph Peterson of the Rosemont Police Department said, "With the cameras, we can respond quickly and effectively. The cameras are a crime deterrent and aid in positive identification if there is an incident. The first system [was] installed at the Convention Center . . . [It] was primarily to monitor all access points, docks, lobbies, walkways, etc., and enhance manpower resources. It also provides protection in that we can respond immediately if we believe there's criminal intent. In addition, it establishes the fact that the village is taking a proactive approach to security, providing a safe environment for residents and visitors. It's actually a real selling point for conventions." Peterson indicated that privacy issues were never raised.

- The United States was not the only country in which CCTV surveillance was being used. For example, one such application in Swa-Zulu-Natal came out of Premier Dr. Baldwyn Sipho's commitment to extend policing to all communities. Elected premier in March 1997, Dr. Sipho described his approach to keeping his commitment: "More visible security was a key move—mobile police, foot patrols, car watches, monitoring of public areas by cameras . . . The vast majority of people are in favour of law enforcement, it's the criminals who resent it."

that represented security equipment manufacturers and distributors, commented on the issue: "Public surveillance is definitely a growing trend. It's a cost-effective way to fight crime and also supplement police manpower." (Examples of public surveillance CCTV installations appear in Exhibit 5.)

The use of CCTV in education facilities was also growing. For example, the director of security and maintenance for the school district in Lake Grove, New York, described his school's system as follows:

> The primary purpose of CCTV is to deter, controlling access . . . [It] allows us to concentrate on other security areas . . . The CCTV program is expected to work well with card-access systems in controlling district-wide access . . . In total we have 60 cameras, 15 time-lapse video recorders, 15 quad splitters, 27 television monitors, and 300 video recording tapes, along with thousands of feet of cable, fittings, enclosures, and hardware . . . Our system offers the district versatility, since the software is selective in its programming. With over 1,500 staff members, I can program a number of individual and distinct clearance levels. Teach-

ing, security, and custodial staff are issued clearance codes that fit their locations, and days and hours of employment. The software also permits the programmer to issue temporary security clearance (e.g., for the summer season).

Integrated Systems and Environmental Controls

The integration of security systems with environmental control applications such as fire alarms and climate control was becoming more important to commercial and industrial buildings. More and more customers were asking for an integrated system controlled by a central location and software interface. Customers were asking for seamless, hassle-free offerings especially as more companies outsourced their security services. Integrated systems provided greater efficiencies through decreased duplicate information databases and data entry. Some estimated that about 18 percent of businesses might be using integrated systems in their security programs, and the growth rate appeared to be 20 percent a year. Industry players were acquiring and merging to put together broad product lines. In other instances various partnership arrangements, such as marketing agreements, were company strategies for providing such integration. Security manufacturers were responding to this demand by acquiring smaller environmental control companies. The technologies and manufacturing expertise involved were very similar to those used in access control and CCTV devices. Continuous increases in PC hardware and software technology power permitted integration of increasingly complex and far-flung systems. Other enabling technology was in the form of device-to-device and device-to-host communications.

The applications involved in integration included protective services that required fire prevention, environmental control systems, emergency power supplies, flooding protection, and security systems. Security systems used included access control systems, CCTV, metal detection, and guard tour systems. Building intelligence was also a part of the integration trend. These applications included automatic temperature controls to meet occupant comfort needs and efficient energy use. Lighting control helped minimize energy consumption or provided lighting at predetermined times. Building security might consist of electronically opened door locks linked to a central security computer, card access control system, voice-activated alarms, and bolt-position monitors. These "smart building" control plans might also include connections to facility management systems including heating, ventilation, and air-conditioning (HVAC), demand-side energy management, water-level monitoring, elevator control, and process controls.

The Future

Past growth trends indicated a bright future for this industry. However, there were uncertainties. Different segments offered differing opportunities and challenges, as did the various "hot" technologies. In addition, the industry structure was changing as current entrants completed mergers and acquisitions and as other firms entered the industry.

Current industry members would have to choose their strategic moves carefully, and new entrants would have to think through the risks associated with the technologies and market segments they chose to address. Existing competitors had to consider whether their objectives could be met by focusing on their current market segments, geographical locales, and product lines or whether they needed to expand their market domains via merger/acquisition or aggressive internal entry into new market segments. Potential new entrants would have to weigh carefully their own capabilities and how these matched the perceived opportunities in each industry segment.

appendix | Directory of Selected Companies in the Security Management and Manufacturers Industry

Note: The companies in this directory were selected from a somewhat larger directory of companies provided in the consulting report. Information was drawn principally from publicly available sources listed at the conclusion of this directory. Information is provided in the following sequence: name of company, location, parent or subsidiary (if associated with another company), year established, sales and net income in 1996 (or, if so indicated, another year), primary business, other miscellaneous information. The industry segment as categorized by consultants appears in brackets at the conclusion of the entry—the numbers reflect the classification in Exhibit 3. Companies for which consultants found no information are indicated by *NA* (i.e., not available).

ACS NA.

Access Control Technologies (ACT), Hackensack, NJ, 1989. Sales, profits, and employees: NA. Service provider to over 400 customers in four eastern states. Established to provide quality products manufactured by premier name-brand institutions possessing substantial engineering and support systems and services with emphasis on access control. Service lines expanded to evolve ACT into a highly technical company with extensive experience in computer hardware and software. Provides access control, CCTV, video imaging, and alarm monitoring. Web site: www.accesscontroline.com/profile.htm. Private company. [2 or 3b]

ADI (See Ademco)

Ademco, Syosset, NY, 1984. $102M, profits NA, employees 500. World's largest manufacturer of burglar and fire alarm products. Subsidiary of Pittway formed in 1929. Product line includes burglary controls, fire/burglary systems, fire systems, keypads, wireless devices, motion detectors, glass break detectors, sirens/sounders, and long-range radios. Wireless devices include key and two-way keypads that allow the user to remotely control the security system as well as operate lights and appliances. Web site: www.ademco.com. [4b]

ADT, Inc., Boca Raton, FL, year established NA. $1.7B, profits NA. Subsidiary of Tyco since 1997. Leading installer and servicer of electronic security systems. Provides 1.8M industrial, commercial, and residential customers with four service areas: building alarm systems, CCTV, fire alarm sprinkler systems, and access control. Is the largest provider of electronic security services in North America and United Kingdom. Residential customers number 1.1M with 85% in United States. [1]

AES Corp. (AKA[1] Intellinet), Peabody, MA, 1974. $5M (about 25% int'l), profits NA, 27 employees w/ no change from prior year. Manufacturer of intrusion detection and control equipment, home security systems, and RF telemetry systems. Products are sold to the security and process control industries. [4a or b]

American Medical Alert Corp, Oceanside, NY. $7.3M (includes int'l), profits and employees NA. Manufacturer and monitoring of emergency medical response/alert systems known as Voice of Help, home security system, audio verification products and two-way voice communication products. Products are sold to hospitals, long-term facilities, and consumers. E-mail: vohsoo@aol.com. [4a—Medical Specialty Applications]

AmeriNet, St. Louis, MO, year established NA. Sales, profits, and employees NA. Will provide three kinds of security devices systems designed to comply with federal guidelines: (*a*) monitor patient wandering, (*b*) infant and child security, and (*c*) fall prevention. Target customers: acute care hospitals and other long-term care facilities. [4a—Medical Specialty Applications]

Ameritech, Chicago, IL, year established NA. Sales, profits, and employees NA. Bought security division of Republic Industries. The Republic security unit had 3,000 employees and 310,000 subscribers in the Southeast, Middle Atlantic, Midwest, and Rocky Mountain States. Purchase increased Ameritech's SecurityLink customer base to 876,000 (55% increase). SecurityLink becomes second to Tyco Industries' ADT LTD. [1]

Astro-Guard Industries, Inc., San Marcos, CA, 1979. $540K (w/10% int'l), profits and employees NA. Manufacturer of teletext decoders and home security alarms sold to multiple industries. [4a]

---

[1]AKA = Also known as.

Baker Industries, Inc. (Subsidiary of Borg-Warner Corp.), Parsippany, NJ, year established NA. $8.4M (2.5% int'l), profits NA, 75,000 employees w/ 15% increase from prior year. Is the holding company for Borg-Warner units involved in alarms and security services. [1]

Biometric Sensing Corp. (See The National Registry, Inc.)

BIT Integration Technology, Inc., Markham, Ontario, Canada, year established NA. Sales, profits, and employees NA. A systems integration company that announced sales of its smart-card technology to a Chinese province. Technology includes computer networks and software. [3a]

Borg-Warner Security Corp. (NYSE: BOR), Chicago, IL (year established NA). $1.7B (including int'l); $18.9M, 73,000 employees. Company is the largest U.S. provider of security to government and business customers. Offers complete range of service lines including electronic and physical security solutions including guard, alarm, armored transport, and courier services. Services provided under Wells Fargo, Burns, and Globe to over 13,000 customers from approximately 319 locations in the United States, Canada, Colombia, and the United Kingdom. Subsidiaries include Baker Industries, Inc., Fargo Pyro Technologies, and Wells Fargo Alarm Services. [1 & 3]

Brinks Home Security, Inc. (Subsidiary of Pittston Company NYSE: PZS), Darien, CT, founded 1859 and changed ownership in 1956. $164M, profits NA, employees 11,000. Pittston was founded 1930 and includes business lines of freight forwarding, domestic freight forwarding, coal mining, armored car services, air courier services, burglar alarm maintenance, and monitoring. Pittston has $2.9B in sales. [1]

C&K Systems, Inc. (PKA[2]: Intellisense, Inc., Unit of C&K Components, Inc.), Folsom, CA, 1985. $10–$25M w/ >25% int'l, profits NA, 196 employees w/no change from prior year. Manufacturer of burglar alarm control panels, infrared detection space protection equipment, glass break detection equipment, motion sensor equipment, microwave burglar detection, equipment and dual-reed magnetic contacts (double-sided magnets attached to doors or windows and connected to wires that monitor the opening and closing of the same). Manufacturer of business and home security systems. [4b?]

Cardkey Systems, Inc. (unit of Amtech Corp., TX), Simi Valley, CA, 1946. $117M (parent) w/ >25% int'l, profits and employees NA. Designer of electronic access control and facility management security systems. Web site: www.cardkey.com. [4b]

CEDCO, Inc., Louisville, KY, year established NA. Sales, profits, employees NA. Manufactures MedCall, a security and medical emergency device as well as other alarm systems. [Specialty Medical Applications]

Central Could not find any information.

Checkpoint Systems, Inc., Thorofare, NJ, 1969. $292M including int'l, profits NA, 2,400 employees w/ 6% reduction from prior year. Manufacturer of electronic article surveillance equipment and accessories. EAS equipment uses radio transmissions to monitor the exits of retail outlets for articles that have not been paid for. Tags are attached to the merchandise. Technology appears to be free of interactions with pacemakers. Also manufactures surveillance gates and turnstiles. Subsidiary: Checkpoint Systems, Inc./Access Control Products Division with $9M sales. Manufactures electronic access control systems and cards. [4b]

---

[2]PKA = Previously known as.

Computer Sentry Software, Inc., location, date founded, sales, profits, and employees NA. Company agreed to partner with ADT in computer security. Firms makes CyberAngel software which sits on a laptop. User must type a password onto a blank screen. If password is not entered, a silent alarm will go off. Cost is $25 for software and $60/year for monitoring fee. [4b]

Continental Instruments (see also Sensormatic), Edgewood, NY, 1960. Sales less than 1% of Sensormatics revenues, profits, and employees NA. Is an access control vendor that was a management buyout (MBO) in April 1997. Sensormatic purchased in 1989. Manufactures, sells, and supports a line of card access products to dealers only. Had installed operating base of 25,000 large systems and 145,000 smaller systems. Has an older DOS-based card access system and with MBO was challenged to promote its Windows 95–compatible software. [4a or b]

Chugai Boyeki America Corp., Commack, NY, year established NA. $25–$50M including int'l, profits NA, 5 employees w/ 8% growth over last year and 7% projected. Manufacturer of machine vision system components and CCTV lenses and cameras. Products sold to multiple industries. [4a?]

DADCO Mfg. Corp., Deer Park, NY, 1963. $1.0M w/ <10% int'l, profits NA, 8 employees with 20% reduction from last year and 25% growth expected next year. Manufacturer of commercial and industrial security monitoring equipment and on-site paging equipment. Used for monitoring entries, exits, and industrial equipment. Products are sold to alarm installers and government agencies. [4a?]

Detection Device Systems, Inc., Hayward, CA, 1985. $10–$25M w/ no int'l, profits and employees NA. Manufacturer and designer of electronic security systems for prisons and municipalities. [3 or 4]

De La Rue/LeFebure/Brandt Corp. (Unit of De La Rue Plc, Switzerland), Cedar Rapids, IA, 1892. $360M w/ <10% int'l, profits NA, 1,800 employees w/ 5% growth over last year. Manufacturer of currency and coin handling equipment, motor banking systems, and physical and electronic security systems sold to financial institutions, retail, gaming, and vending organizations. Revenue mainly from computer hardware. [4b]

Detection Systems, Inc. (Nasdaq: DETC), Fairport, NY, 1968. $42M including int'l, 1994: $30.9M w/ 1.2M profits, 340 employees. On cutting edge of security and fire detection industry. Also has personal security handheld devices attached to a keychain which can send distress signals and set off sirens and strobes in the area. Manufactures electronic detection, control, and signaling equipment including electronic intrusion detectors, fire detectors, microprocessor-based alarm control systems, and emergency call systems. See U.S. high-tech operating unit Radionics, Inc. [4a]

Detex, New Braufels, TX, year established NA. Sales, profits, and employees NA. Has application-reporting software for guard tour program used for fire applications. [4a?—Software provider]

Diebold, Ohio, year established NA. Sales, profits, and employees NA. Company originally focused on safes, vaults, and other security devices for banks. In 1980s moved to automated teller machines, credit authorization terminals, electronics funds transfer equipment and electronic alarm systems. Has expertise in computers, video systems, and communications. [4a or b]

Digital Biometrics, Inc., Minnetonka, MN, 1985. $9M w/ <2.5% int'l. Manufacturer of computer based inkless live-scan fingerprint systems that use electro-optical imaging to capture a fingerprint and create a digital image called TENPRINTER and a portable unit called SQUID. Products are sold to law enforcement industry. [4a—Biometrics]

Digital Monitoring Products, Inc., Springfield, MO, year established NA. Sales, profits, and employees NA. Manufacturer of control panels and keypads for the electronic security and fire alarm industry. Agreed in 1996 to acquire a minority interest in Integrated Security Technologies. Transaction gave DMP marketing rights to IST's Integra product line. [4a]

Digital Security Systems Could not find any information.

Dynaflo, Syosset, NY, year established NA. Sales, profits, employees NA. Began making electronic bracelets to keep track of adult patients in 1990 and entered infant security market in 1995. Dynaflo systems cost about $30K. [4a—Specialty medical applications]

Dynamark Security Centers, Inc., Hagerstown, MD, 1975. $12.1M, profits NA, employees 85. Provides burglar alarm maintenance and monitoring, protective devices, security, security control equipment and systems, franchises. [2]

ELMO (PKA: ELMO Mfg. Corp.), New Hyde Park, NY, 1921. Owned by non-U.S. firm. $25–$50M, profits NA, 37 employees with no change from last year and none projected. Manufacturer of electronic imaging equipment including CCTV cameras, overhead slide conference room and pedestal projectors, and file to video converters. Products are sold to multiple industries. [4]

Fingermatrix, Inc. (FINX), Dobbs Ferry, NY, 1976. Sales and profits unknown, 19 employees with 18% growth from last year. Researcher and developer of booking stations and access control systems and fingerprint scanner equipment sold to law enforcement agencies. Primary revenues are from computer hardware. [4a—Biometrics]

Firetector, Syosset, Long Island, NY. Sales, profits, and employees NA. Designs, manufactures, and services a variety of fire control/life safety, security and communication profits, and systems for commercial, industrial, retail, residential, and transit. [3a]

Honeywell, division: Home and Building Control division ranked no. 4 in 1997 *Security Device Manufacturers'* top 100 with estimated 300K subscribers. $223M, profits and employees NA. In November 1997 entered into contract with Columbia Gas System (one of the nation's largest gas firm, with more than 7M customers) Reston, VA, to sell a set of control products and services that would provide customers systems to control energy usage, monitors and controls for indoor air quality, lighting controls, commercial grade security and access control systems, utilities management, and energy procurement services. [1]

Identacard Systems, Inc., Lancaster, PA, 1970. Sales and profits NA, employees 200. Has photo identification and access control systems, security identification badges, and video imaging systems. [4a]

ILCO Unican Corp., Winston-Salem, NC, 1984. $10–$25M w/ no int'l, profits and employees NA. R&D Division is in St. Charles, IL. R&D focuses on access control systems. Another division is Simplex Access Controls, which manufactures push-button mechanical locks for computer room doors. High-tech unit is Simplex Access Controls/Safelock Division, Winston-Salem, NC, 1962, $20M, profits NA, 150 employees with no change from last year and none predicted. Owned by Unican Security Systems Ltd., Canada. Manufacturer of push-button mechanical safe deposit locks. Products are sold to banks. [4b]

Integrated Security Systems, Inc. (Nasdaq: ISSI), Irvine, TX, date established NA. $7.6M, profits and employees NA. Has four subsidiaries. Is a developer, manufacturer, and national supplier for total security solutions for industrial and commercial marketplaces. Also a leading supplier of automatic gates and lane changers to the U.S. road and bridge industry. [3a]

IriSCAN, Inc., Mount Laurel, NJ, 1990. $1M with internal >25%. Developer and marketer of biometric identification technology that is based upon the recognition of patterns in the iris of the eye. Products are sold to health care, security, financial, computer, and access control industries. [Biometrics]

Knogo North America (traded AMEX; combined with Sentry Technology, which see), Hauppauge, NY, established 1960s by Arthur Minasy. $19M (1995), profits $1.7M (1995), 125 employees. Designs, manufactures, and services EAS and CCTV systems in the United States and Canada. Original systems were bulky plastic tags. Current technology is a flexible fine wire, Knogo Electro-Thred, which uses low-frequency magnetics and measures 1.5 inches long, 3/10 inch wide, 25/100 inch deep. User and application labor costs are 3–7 cents per item. Applications include computers, libraries, blanket/linens in airports and hospitals. Merged in 1997 with Video Sentry Corp. of Minneapolis to form Sentry Technology. [4b]

Mosler, Hamilton, OH, established last century and was especially known for safes for banks. $24–49M, profits NA, 250 employees. Involved in electronic security and surveillance systems. In recent years has had to close plants in Buffalo and Cincinnati. [4b]

Napco Security Systems, Inc. (Nasdaq: NSSC), Amityville, NY, 1969. $53M w/ int'l <25%; profits and employees NA. One of the nation's leading manufacturers of electronic security equipment including fire, smoke, and heat detection equipment; intrusion detection and control equipment; and home security systems. Sells through wholesale distributors, large central stations, and selected OEMs, primarily in the United States and Canada. Products are used in residential, commercial, institutional, and industrial installations. [4b]

The National Registry, Inc. (AKA: NRI, PMW, Biometric Sensing Corp.), Tampa, FL, 1991. $2M (1994: $.40M). No int'l, profits NA; 45 employees with 200% growth from last year and 77% projected for next year. Developer of biometric software and manufacturer of turnkey electronic identification systems using biometric identification technology. Products and services sold to state and local governments, financial services, health care, network security, and other commercial industries. Bulk of revenue is from software. [4a—Biometrics]

Northern Video Systems, Inc. Could not find any information.

Pittway Corp., Chicago, IL, 1925. $945M, profits NA, 6,000 employees. Involved in burglar alarm apparatus, fire alarm apparatus, fire detection systems, fire extinguishers, periodicals, publishing, magazines, publishing and printing, trade journals, direct mail advertising services, mailing services. See subsidiary Ademco. [4b]

Printrak International, Inc., Anaheim, CA, date established NA. $66M ($46M 1995) w/ int'l >25%, profits NA, 300 employees with 25% growth from prior year and no change projected for next year. Manufacturer of automated fingerprint identification systems. Products sold to law enforcement and social services industries. Bulk of revenue is from sales of computer hardware. [4a—Biometrics]

Protection One merged with electric utility Western Resources to form a security unit with 670,000 customers. This was the number 2 position in the security services business until the 1997 Ameritech acquisition of Republic Industries' security services unit. [1]

Radionics, Inc., (Unit of Detection Systems, Inc.), Salinas, CA, date established NA. $42M parent sales including int'l, profits and employees NA. Manufactures and markets electronic security communications systems. Are sold nationwide for commercial and residential use. Also manufactures ReadyKey access control systems. Web site: www.radionicsinc.com. [3a]

SAC Technologies, Inc. (SACM), Edina, MN, 1994. $10M w/ int'l <25%, profits and employees NA. Manufacturer of fingerprint identification equipment sold to multiple industries. Most revenue from computer hardware. [4a—Biometrics]

Senior Technologies, Inc. (AKA: WanderGuard, Inc.). 1974. $16M with int'l <10%, profits NA, 120 employees with 20% growth from last year and 8% projected next year. Manufacturer of personal response and fall monitoring systems and personal alarms. Products are sold to senior living industry, nursing homes, and home care industry. Web site: www.seniortechnologies.com. Privately held company. [4a—Specialty medical applications]

Sensor Engineering Co. (subsidiary of Techlin, Inc., CT), Hamden, CT, 1975. $10–$25M, profits NA, 100–249 employees. Manufacturer of encoded cards, readers, hubs, and access control components. The readers read the magnetized strip on items such as bankcards and allow entrance into ATMs and other locations. Products are sold to multiple industries. [4a]

Sensormatic Electronics, Boca Raton, FL, 1967. Sales, profits, and employees NA. Manufacturer of radio frequency, microwafer and magnetic EAS, CCTV, and card access systems. Has high-tech units involved in video security and teleconference equipment and building access/entry software. Products included Sensortip II labels, an electromagnetic antishoplifting technology. For example manufacturer of computer circuit boards embedded the labels into the boards during the initial manufacturing process. Public company. **Sensormatic Electronics Corp./Industrial Division,** Costa Mesa, CA, 1967. Sales, profits, employees NA. Manufactures business security systems including access control, CCTV and alarm systems. Provides full security systems integration services. **Sensormatic Video Products Division,** San Diego, CA, year established NA. $100–$200M, profits NA, 160 employees with 6% growth from last year and 12% projected. Manufacturer of video security and teleconferencing equipment sold to multiple industries. **Sensormatic Electronics, Corp.,** Deerfield Beach, FL, 1967. $1.0B w/ int'l >25%, profits NA, 700–800 employees in South Florida and 6,600 worldwide. Makes electronic antitheft devices including EAS equipment, antishoplifting, CCTV, and card access systems. In 1995 suffered significant losses and downsized workforce 10%. Sold Continental Instruments in early 1995. Also has software house. [4b]

Sensor Video Unit of Sensormatic Electronics.

Sentry Technology Corporation, Hauppauge, NY, year established not known. $23M w/ int'l <2.5%, profits and employees NA. Formed from combination of Knogo and Video Sentry in 1997. Product SentryVision is third-generation CCTV released in 1996 from Knogo North American Video Sentry. System eliminates blind spots because pan, tilt, and zoom cameras move on a tracking system. Has new MiniView line of miniature board camera housings. Permits seeing over shelving and down the aisle in retail operations or large distribution centers. Has outdoor video intrusion detection system. Used by retailers, hospitals, libraries, nursing homes, and industry for protection against shoplifting, robbery, and employee theft. [4b]

Simplex (FKA Simplex Time Recorder Co. See also: ILCO Unican Corp. FKA Simplex Access Controls), Gardner, MA, 1888. $400M w/ int'l <25%, profits unknown, 3,000 employees with no change from last year and none predicted for next year. Leading supplier of fire alarm and detection as well as just in time, attendance, and workforce management solutions. Engaged in time, date, and numbering stamps, attendance and job cost recorders, time control systems, fire alarm and security systems. Manufacturer of microprocessor-based fire alarm systems, time systems, and security systems. The fire alarm system is comprised of both hardware and software and is used in commercial buildings. 1997 announcement that Philips Communication and Security Systems will collaborate on development of advanced communications and security systems for institutional, commercial and industrial marketplace applications. Philips has been a long-standing Simplex supplier of CCTV, access control, paging, public address equipment, and other products. Has 140 company-owned sales and service offices in North America with certified engineers and trained technicians—is the industry's strongest distribution and customer support network. Web site: www. simplexnet.com [4a and/or b]

Simplex Access Controls/Safelock Division (Unit of Unican Security Systems Ltd. of Canada), Winston-Salem, NC, 1962. $20M, profits NA, 150 employees with no change from last year and none predicted for next year. Manufacturer of push-button mechanical safe deposit locks sold to banks. [4b]

Sytron, Inc., Broomfield, CO, year of establishment NA. Sales, profits, employees NA. Integrated security systems company that designs and manufactures security, fire access control products and systems for airports, government facilities, banks, and corporate and industrial sites. In 1997 issued two announcements: (*a*) introduction of its Universal Reader, which can be combined with mag stripe and/or keypad and will read HID, Motorola Indala, Casi Rusco, and Westinghouse proximity technologies, and (*b*) acquired fire alarm product related assets from an NV firm including inventory, intellectual property, and existing customer base of more than 30 sites. [3a]

Texas Instruments, Dallas, TX, in 1997 firm began to penetrate retail sales mainstream with its TIRIS RFID technology. One application is a keyring tag. Mobil has developed the keyring tag called Speedpass, which connects with a reader inside the fuel dispenser and accepts the customer's preferred credit card automatically. [4a]

Thermo-Electron Corporation (NYSE), Waltham, MA, date of establishment NA. $2.2B (1995), profits and employees NA. Thermedics is the fourth subsidiary to be spun off by Thermo-Electron Corporation, Inc. (1995 revenues of $175M and traded ASE). Thermo-Electron Corporation has 19 publicly held subsidiaries. Subsidiaries include Thermedics, Inc., and Thermedics Detection, Inc. **Thermedics Detection, Inc.,** Woburn, MA, date established NA. $175M (1995), profits and employees NA. Manufacturer of detection equipment including bomb, narcotics, and chromatography detection equipment. Has subsidiary with a high-tech unit involved in moisture detection equipment. Thermedics' primary bomb detection system is EGIS, which is widely used in non-U.S. airports to check for explosives in checked luggage. System includes a trace detector that, unlike X-ray system usually used in airports, takes samples of the air to analyze for traces of explosives. In late 1996 announced SecurScan trace detector used to test for traces of explosives on passengers and their carry-on baggage. The 1997 presidential budget included $144M for improved U.S. airport security systems. Company plans public offering next year. **Thermedics, Inc.,** Woburn, MA. $292M w/ >25% int'l, profits NA, 2,088 employees. Company is a manufacturer of biomaterials and biomedical products including drug detection equipment, process quality assurance equipment, electromagnetic compatibility test equipment and transport security systems for airport security. Products are sold to medical, research, and airport security industries. [4a and perhaps 5]

Talon Medical, San Antonio, TX, year established NA. Sales, profits, and employees NA. A new company with a system for the infant security market. Product is KidMatch with computer chips embedded in the plastic hospital ID bracelets worn by baby, mother, and father. Nurses use a touch probe, a handheld device, to match the baby to the parent. Inventor specializes in medical devices. [4a—Specialty medical applications]

Tyco International Ltd. (1997 merger of Tyco Industries and ADT, Ltd.), Exeter, NH, year established NA. $5B w/ int'l >25%, profits NA, 75,000 employees in 50 countries. Diversified manufacturer of industrial and commercial products. Worldwide manufacturer with strong leadership positions in disposable medical products, packaging materials, flow control products, electrical and electronic components. Bulk of revenue derived from activity in subassembly activities. ADT activities became part of Tyco's Fire and Safety Services group. Tyco operated in over 300 offices in 50 countries. ADT had 230 offices in 10 countries. Is the world's largest manufacturer and provider of fire and safety systems and services. Other U.S. high-tech operating units: Grinnell Corp., Grinnell Fire Protection Systems, Sentry Medical Products, Inc., Simplex Technologies, Inc. [4b]

Unican Security Systems Ltd., Montreal, Quebec, Canada, year established NA. $140M (Canadian), profits and employees NA. Leading global supplier of electronic access control products for hospitality and commercial sectors as well as mechanical and electronic security products for safes and vaults. World's leading supplier of key blanks, key cutting equipment, and mechanical push-button locks. Subsidiaries: Ilk Unican France and U.S. high-tech operating units: Ilk Unican Corp./Simplex Access Controls Division, ILCO Unican Corp/Research and Development Division, Simplex Access Controls/Safelock Division. [3a and 4b]

Ultra-Scan Corporation, Amherst, NY, 1989. $5–$10M w/ int'l >25%, profits NA, 20 employees with no change from last year and 50% projected for next year. Manufacturer of ultrasonic live scan fingerprint readers for use in PI systems. Products sold to multiple industries. Bulk of revenues from computer hardware. [4a]

Vicon Industries, Inc., Melville, NY, 1967 (public in 1969 AMEX). $10.5M, $102K (1995: $16K), 225 employees on Long Island. Leading manufacturer of video surveillance systems. Markets include commercial/industrial (50%) and financial/transportation (e.g., banks and traffic/road surveillance). Vicon and Knogo are two of Long Island's largest manufacturers of ES equipment. 1996 marketing agreement. Vicon to be the exclusive supplier of closed-circuit video systems to Knogo. First diversification beyond EAS systems for Knogo. [4b]

Video Sentry, Minneapolis, MN, 1990. Sales, profits, and employees NA. Travelling CCTV surveillance systems. Has a cable-free design that allows cameras to move freely and rapidly through a tinted enclosure that conceals the camera's location while transmitting a continuous video signal. Division, Sentry Vision, provides loss prevention surveillance in retail stores and distribution centers. Merged with Knogo North America in 1997 to form Sentry Technology. [3a]

Wells Fargo, King of Prussia, PA, year established NA. $350M with no international revenues, profits and employees NA. Manufacturer of security/safety equipment that detects and monitors smoke, fire, water, air conditioners, CCTV, water towers, evaporation, humidity, security guards, computer rooms, and other areas. Has produced security systems for Pentagon and NATO. Manufactures a state of the art monitoring computer. Subsidiary of Borg-Warner Corp., IL, a Unit of Baker Industries, Inc. [4b]

Sources from which information was drawn: *American Business Directory (published by each state), Business Periodicals Index, Corptech Directory of Technology, D&B Million Dollar Directory, Dun and Bradstreet, Harris Manufacturers Directory, Sorkins Directory, Regional Business Directory 1998 (Kansas and Missouri east of Columbia),* and *Ward's Business Directory.*

Pivot International—Pursuing Growth

Marilyn L. Taylor
University of Missouri at Kansas City

Theresa T. Coates
Rensselaer Polytechnic Institute

J. Kirkland (Kirk) Douglass, president of Pivot International, picked up the preliminary report on the security device and systems manufacturers industry he had just received. (See the appendix to this case for excerpts.) Douglass had engaged an industrial marketing research firm to undertake the industry study earlier in the year. It was two weeks before the late-March 1998 International Security Conference (ISC) in Las Vegas. Douglass wondered whether the security device and systems industry was really the appropriate one to fuel Pivot's growth or whether he should look elsewhere—for example, in the medical equipment, other sports equipment, or training aids industries. However, the present work by the industrial marketing firm had taken three months and considerable expense. He wondered whether a delay and additional expense were warranted to consider other industries.

Pivot International was a contract industrial design[1] and manufacturing firm located in a suburb of greater Kansas City. Its customers were manufacturers and assemblers in the fitness equipment industry. For these customers Pivot had primarily designed and manufactured display and control units using liquid crystal display (LCD) technology. Pivot's customers attached the display units to the fitness equipment sold under the customer firm's brand.

On Douglass's desk were copies of the marketing materials he intended to use at the conference. He planned to take five of his engineering staff members to the conference. One member was a company engineer who was pursuing an advanced degree in engineering management and who had attended the 1997 summer ISC in New York. At the engineer's recommendation, Pivot had secured a booth at the March 1998 exhibition. To date, Pivot had no customers among the manufacturing firms in the security industry. Douglass expected that more aggressive follow-up efforts with contacts identified at the 1998 conference would yield customers. If the security device and systems industry was growing as rapidly as the market research report indicated, he wondered how he should market to this industry and what kinds of firms he should target in order to position Pivot as a custom design and contract manufacturing firm for the security device and systems manufacturers.

Earlier versions of this case were presented at the North American Case Research Association 1998 Workshop and at the Midwest Academy of Management Case Critique Colloquium in Fall 2000. The authors express appreciation to the reviewers at these two meetings and also to the *Business Case Journal* reviewers for their helpful suggestions. The case has been published in the *Business Case Journal*. Copyright © 2003 by Marilyn L. Taylor and Theresa T. Coates.

[1]Industrial design included design of appearance of the equipment with attention to functionality and aesthetics. It could also include packaging, including graphic design. Equipment design issues included ease of use for the end consumer and manufacturing process considerations.

COMPANY HISTORY

Founding and Purchase by Allegheny

A Kansas City native had founded Pivot International—then called Applied Resources, Inc.—as a contract design firm in the early 1970s. Kirk Douglass described the founder as "one of the brightest and most creative product designers I have ever seen

. . . a great salesman [and] one of the fastest thinking people on his feet that I have ever encountered." By 1984 Applied Resources' activities included the design and manufacture of a broad range of products, including anesthesia monitoring equipment, controllers for low-end X-ray equipment, control systems for fire suppression equipment, wireless electric blanket controllers, and one of the first electronic monitors for fitness equipment. None of the products were proprietary; rather, Applied Resources designed the products to meet the specifications of its customers and undertook contract manufacturing as requested. Patents were held by the company's customer firms or component suppliers.

In 1984 Allegheny International, a large multibusiness conglomerate, purchased the company. Douglass described the beginning of his career at Applied Resources as follows:

> I had started my career at Butler Manufacturing Company. Butler is headquartered here in Kansas City and is the dominant manufacturer in preengineered buildings. I worked in both engineering and sales for Butler. I then went on to head Quartz Crystals, a smaller firm in Kansas City that manufactures quartz crystals for the electronics industry. I joined Applied Resources in 1985 to add business strength to the organization. You will note that all the firms that I have worked for are either family firms or, as with Applied Resources, headed by the founder and entrepreneur.
>
> At the time Allegheny owned Vita Master, a manufacturer of consumer fitness products. That division was in North Carolina. Allegheny had actually purchased Applied Resources to protect Applied Resources as a source of new product development for the various Allegheny divisions. Shortly after I came on board, we opened the Applied Resources office in Taipei, Taiwan. The purpose of the [Taiwan] office was to source parts, produce tooling, and manage sub-contract manufacturing in the Far East. The price-technology issues in the low end of the market virtually dictated that we look for manufacturing opportunities in Asia. There are many sub-contractors in Asia, and Taiwan is a world center for both tool and die operations and electronic assembly.
>
> Frankly, I am glad that Allegheny owned Applied Resources at the time because we made many expensive mistakes as we sought to establish our overseas base!

Allegheny had also purchased Sunbeam, a well-recognized brand name in electronic consumer products. Subsequently, severe problems at Sunbeam

forced Allegheny to divest itself of a number of its divisions and other producing assets, including Applied Resources.

A PPG Subsidiary

In 1987 Allegheny sold Applied Resources to PPG Industries, Inc.[2] PPG's three main businesses were paint, glass, and inorganic chemicals. These were mature slow-growth markets in which the company had strong presence and technological leadership. However, there were limited opportunities for growth for PPG in these lines of business. PPG's senior executives worked on a strategic plan with Stanford Research Institute (SRI). As a result of the planning process, the PPG senior executives decided that "systems and instruments" should be the "fourth leg" of the company. PPG implemented the strategy by acquiring divisions of other companies, including Honeywell's New York–based medical division and Litton's medical division in Freiburg, Germany. These two acquired companies, together with Applied Resources, became PPG's Biomedical Systems Division. As before, Applied Resources provided supplementary design and manufacturing capabilities for other PPG product divisions.

Douglass described the period with PPG as follows:

> In 1987 PPG asked me to divest the former Allegheny group of all its nonmedical businesses. I did so. However, in that process I determined that the application of electronics to the fitness industry was about to take off and I recommended that PPG retain that business and grow it. I was told that PPG would accept the fitness industry as the "low end" of the medical business and therefore within the mission statement of PPG Biomedical. I was made business unit manager of the Health and Fitness (H&F) Business Unit, which was a unit within PPG's biomedical group.
>
> I grew the business from $250,000 in 1988 to over $10 million in 1993. At the time the biomedical division had sales of approximately $200 million. So, we were a very small entity indeed within the biomedical division.

Applied Resources supplied contract design and manufacturing of electronic components, in particu-

---

[2]Established in 1883, Pittsburgh Plate Glass Company uses the abbreviation PPG Industries, Inc., as its corporate name.

lar, digital display readouts for health and fitness manufacturers.

From 1985 to 1987, the value of the New Taiwan dollar (NT$) rapidly increased. In addition, labor was not readily available in Taiwan. These two factors led Applied Resources to move production from Taiwan to the Philippines. The new subcontractor was TTI, a Philippines manufacturing company wholly owned by Emilio Ching. Douglass described how he found TTI:

> We went around looking for other places to subcontract our production. We were seasonal and unemployment in Taiwan was about 1 percent. We needed to be able to react quickly to opportunities, and the situation in Taiwan simply didn't allow us to flexibly enlarge the labor force to respond to an opportunity. We looked everywhere in Asia—in the Philippines, Thailand, Korea, Hong Kong, and China.

The Buyout from PPG

In the early 1990s the H&F unit within PPG Biomedical was healthy. However, the Biomedical Systems Division as a whole had lost a great deal of money over the seven-year period from 1987 to 1993. Kirk Douglass gave the following account of what happened next:

> In early 1993, the CEO of PPG, who was responsible for the "fourth leg" strategy, retired and a new CEO came in from outside. The new CEO used his honeymoon period to correct a number of problems, of which Biomedical was at the top of the list. In October 1997 PPG announced the biomedical division was for sale. Initially PPG thought they would sell H&F as part of the biomedical group. However, none of the buyers interested in Biomedical were interested in H&F. Therefore, we had an opportunity to negotiate a buyout of H&F.
>
> Mr. Ching approached me and said, "Let's buy it. I will provide bridge financing until you can put a bank line in place." So he became a majority stockholder and I a minority shareholder. The sales price of $7 million was agreed to August 31, 1994, and the transaction completed November 8, 1994. The resulting company was Pivot International.

As part of the sale, Douglass became president of Pivot International. Douglass described his role in the buyout as follows:

> The buyout process did put me in a potential conflict of interest considering my fiduciary responsibility to

PPG. However, PPG was glad to sell the division profitably and relatively easily. Understand that Pivot was only a fleabit to PPG.

> Mr. Ching and I have gotten along very well. He comes over here, and I also go to Taipei and the Philippines regularly. Mr. Ching is an investor, although he owned the Philippines manufacturing plant prior to purchasing Pivot. He owns a number of businesses and expects me to drive significant growth in Pivot.
>
> Mr. Ching was a friend of a friend. Mr. Ching is an *investor*. He is a self-made man. He started selling hardware to contractors. Then he became a general contractor and subsequently moved to the role of developer. He has a visceral sense about how to make money. He hit the land boom in the Philippines just right at a time when an investor could double his money very quickly. In addition, he made other investments, including a small electronics manufacturing firm.

The company, renamed Pivot International, was incorporated in Kansas. Pivot's wholly owned subsidiary, Applied Resources, Ltd., was a Taiwanese corporation. Emilio Ching owned most of the Pivot International stock, while Kirk Douglass had a minority position. TTI, Pivot's manufacturing partner, was a separate Philippines corporation. The Ching family owned all of the TTI stock.

In December 1994, Pivot provided contract design, tool and die development, and manufacturing capabilities to approximately 10 firms in the fitness manufacturers and assemblers industry. Sales to one customer, DP, accounted for about 50 percent of Pivot's revenue. All of Pivot's customers were in the high-volume, low-cost segment of the fitness business. PPG had confined Pivot to this business segment. Douglass described the situation:

> Outside the narrow confines of the fitness [manufacturers] community Pivot was entirely unknown. We were also unknown in the Kansas City community, our own home base. We had no capability brochures or product flyers. Our work consisted of selling custom designed LCD[3] readouts to fitness equipment manufacturers or assemblers. It was a small industry where everybody already knew us. Our competition was entirely foreign manufacturers who operated out of either Taiwan or Hong Kong. No other firms

---

[3]Liquid crystal display. The alternate technology was light-emitting diodes (LED), which provided a brighter image in an electronic display unit but used more current.

exhibit 1   **Income Statements for Pivot International, 1994–1997 (in thousands)**

	1997 $	1997 %	1996 $	1996 %	1995 $	1995 %	1994 $	1994 %
Sales revenues*	$15,668	100.0%	$12,334	100.0%	$19,565	100.0%	$17,999	100.0%
Operating expenses	15,457	98.7	12,951	105.0	18,039	92.2	16,739	93.9
Operating profit	211	1.3	(617)	(5.0)	1,526	7.8	1,260	7.0
Interest	32	0.2	79	0.6	22	0.1	9	0.1
Profit before taxes	179	1.1	(696)	(5.6)	1,504	7.7	1,251	7.0
Taxes†	0	0.0	0	0.0	559	2.9	436	2.4
Net income	$179	1.1	$(696)	(5.6)	$945	4.8	$815	4.9

Comparative Industry Data‡	SIC#3625	SIC#8711
Net sales	100.0%	100.0%
Gross profit margin	35.0	na
Operating expenses	28.4	95.6
Operating profit	6.6	4.4
All other expenses (net)	1.3	0.6
Profit before taxes	4.4	3.7

*About 97% of all manufacturing for Pivot International was carried out by Teletech Telesystems, Inc., Passy City, Philippines which was 100% owned by Edwin Ching.

†Tax carryforward from 1996.

‡Based on data from Robert Morris Associates, 1997 edition. RMA publishes comparative financial data on industries on a yearly basis. SIC#3625 refers to a subcategory of Manufacturing Industries—Machinery, Equipment & Components, except Computer Equipment specifically Relays & Industrial Controls including manufacturing relays, motor starters and controllers, control accessories, and other industrial controls. Does not include automatic temperature controls or industrial process instruments. SIC# 8711 refers to the subcategories of Services Industries—Engineering, Architectural & Surveying Services (and includes SIC codes 8712 and 8713).

provided the breadth of services that we did, that is, contract design, or tool and die development, or manufacturing, or combinations. For our customers we provided primarily electronic display units using custom microprocessors with embedded code.

Pivot personnel worked closely with the company's clients to develop designs and product prototypes in Lenexa. Through the Taiwan office, the company could design and develop tooling and molds for manufacturing the plastic or metal casings for the LCD readout devices. Pivot purchased most of its raw materials through the Taiwan office. Products were manufactured in the Philippine plant.

Turmoil in the Fitness Industry

Douglass wanted to move the company beyond its reliance on the fitness industry original equipment manufacturers (OEMs). Tremendous turnover in fit-

ness equipment manufacturers had occurred. Primary causes of the turbulence were the entry of large-scale mass merchandisers (such as Wal-Mart, Kmart, and Target) and the effect of infomercials. Douglass explained the effect of the mass merchandisers:

In 1995 we peaked at just under $20 million in sales. [See Exhibits 1 and 2 for Pivot's Income Statements and Balance Sheets.] Then the low end of the fitness industry just fell apart. Two years after the buyout, 70 percent of our customers went bankrupt. DP, which had been 50 percent of our business, was one of the companies that failed. I talked to their CFO during this period. What happened to DP was this—DP sold a treadmill to Wal-Mart at $139. At that price DP covered its variable costs, but barely anything else. The final straw, though, was when Wal-Mart sent back 25 percent of the product. That put DP over the edge into bankruptcy. In essence, the company lost control of their operations as the mass merchandisers insisted on lower and lower costs "or else"!

exhibit 2 **Comparative Balance Sheets, Pivot International, December 31, 1996 and 1997 (in thousands)**

	1997		1996	
	$	%	$	%
Assets				
Cash	$ 212,128	3.7%	$ 184,691	2.7%
Accounts receivable	3,285,638	57.4	4,886,056	70.1
Inventory	592,828	10.4	537,680	7.7
Other current assets	1,095,597	19.1	938,883	13.5
Total current assets	5,186,191	90.6	6,547,310	94.0
Fixtures and equipment	353,555	6.2	370,609	5.3
Other fixed assets	184,196	3.2	49,353	0.7
Total assets	$5,723,942	100.0%	$6,967,272	100.0%
Liabilities and owners' equity				
Accounts payable*	$2,598,335	45.4%	$2,758,474	39.6%
Notes payable	0	0.0	826,287	11.9
Accruals	300,228	5.2	735,809	10.6
Total current liabilities	2,898,563	50.6	4,320,570	62.0
Long-term debt and deferred taxes	0	0.0		0.0
Retained earnings	(75,097)	(1.3)	(253,774)	(3.6)
Owners' equity	2,900,476	50.7	2,900,476	41.6
Total liabilities and owners' equity	$5,723,942	100.0%	$6,967,272	100.0%

Comparative Industry Data		
	RMA 1997 SIC#3625	RMA 1996 SIC#8711
Cash and equivalents	7.2%	6.3%
Trade receivables	30.5	55.8
Inventory	29.6	5.0
All other current assets	1.6	6.9
Total current assets	68.9	74.0
Fixed assets	23.3	16.6
Intangibles and other	7.8	9.5
Total assets	100.0%	100.0%
Notes payable	8.7	14.2
Trade payables	13.2	11.5
All other current assets	18.4	19.7
Total current assets	40.4	45.4
Long-term debt	11.0	6.8
All other noncurrent liabilities	6.4	7.3
Net worth	42.2	40.5
Total liabilities and net worth	100.0%	100.0%

*Accounts payable: top 10 industries accounted for about $900 including: Wholesale electronic parts = $775K; Wholesale computer/software $1K; Nonclassifiable $20K; Wholesale electrical equipment $3K; Computer mfg. $5K; Help supply service $4K, Trucking nonlocal $3K; Electric services $1K; Semiconductor mfgs $55K; Air courier service $10K.

Infomercials created a different difficulty, as Douglass explained:

> One of seven infomercials is a hit. When an infomercial hits, it creates instantaneous demand. The manufacturer gears up for that level of demand. Then, all of a sudden, the market interest moves on to other products. The manufacturer cannot so readily ramp down, and the company is left holding not only the higher fixed costs of expanded capacity but probably considerable inventory as well. I've seen companies producing 5,000 units per week drop off to zero in two to three weeks. Meanwhile the supply train of up to 26 weeks of inventory was already on its way and could not be canceled. It is a vicious cycle. In addition to these difficulties our SKUs proliferated and complexity increased. Where once we had produced 250,000 units a year of a relatively simple product, suddenly we were asked to produce 25,000 units a year of 10 *different* units of generally greater complexity. Our engineering overhead skyrocketed.

Douglass gave three specific examples of the problems created for companies:

- Nordic Track had negative worth as a result of the battering it took in the market.
- Sales of Health Rider, another brand name in the fitness industry, had grown from $0 to $200 million. The company's growth came, as Douglass put it, ". . . solely through infomercials." After two years of tremendous success, the volume of infomercial responses suddenly declined from 15,000 units per week to very few units per week. The company declared bankruptcy and did not restart.
- Fitness Master supplied products to the infomercial industry. Among the company's products was the Jane Fonda Treadmill. Fitness Master's primary customer went bankrupt. The customer left Fitness Master holding $4 million of accounts receivables. Fitness Master closed.

Changes in Strategy

The effect on Pivot of the fitness industry's turmoil was almost as dramatic. Douglass explained:

> So there we were—completely unknown other than to the fitness equipment manufacturers—and we were watching our market go down the drain. It sounds like a formula for [company] burial . . . Here's what we did:
>
> - We took good care of the customers that did survive the shakeout.

- We moved upscale in the fitness industry. That way, we got a higher dollar per unit with customers that were not dependent on the mass merchandisers.
- We also recognized that we had capabilities in design and manufacturing that were applicable to businesses outside of the fitness industry, and we resolved to market ourselves to those industries.

To counter the difficulties of the fitness industry, Pivot increasingly targeted manufacturers of upscale fitness equipment (i.e., equipment retailing for $1,000 or more). For these customers Pivot helped design and often manufactured various electronic monitors and the motor controllers. As Douglass put it, "We have a competitive advantage in product design and in the interface between product development and manufacturing abroad. We are a low-cost manufacturer and we have a reputation for good quality which we have worked over the years at maintaining."

Douglass described the change in marketing strategy as follows:

> We developed a capabilities brochure and a mailing campaign and began to market ourselves to other companies. We have defined the new Pivot International as:
>
> - A contract product developer and manufacturing house. Our company provides turnkey product development and manufacturing services to companies interested in outsourcing some or all of these functions.
> - Our company provides the benefits of U.S.-based design with the economies of Far East purchasing and manufacturing.
> - Compare us to an engineering or industrial design company. An engineering/design firm wants to make money by charging their customer by the hour for development. If the engineering/design firm can take longer, so much the better. [In contrast] Pivot makes money by shipping product as soon as possible and cutting time to delivery to the market. Our interests are aligned with those of our customers.
> - We can charge less for engineering and design services because of our manufacturing base. We try to capture our costs, to make a profit on design activities. That means we are generally not interested in taking on design work that does not lead to manufacturing.
> - We are fast. The process from design through manufacturing is carefully coordinated by one of Pivot's product managers so that things are done

in parallel and the design staff provides manufacturing with a product that can in fact be made.

Pivot considered targeting several other vertical markets, including the security device manufacturers market. For the security management market, Pivot was particularly interested in the closed-circuit television monitoring and surveillance and the access control segments. Both segments required the component product design and manufacturing capabilities that Pivot could supply. Pivot could provide such components as LCD displays and motor controllers. Eventually the company hoped to develop some proprietary products of component parts for new markets.

PIVOT'S OPERATIONS AND CAPABILITIES

The U.S.-Taiwan-Philippines Facilities

The company's operations included the U.S. design firm, its Taiwanese tool and die subsidiary, and the Philippines manufacturing facility. The design office was located in an upscale suburb of the greater Kansas City area. Kansas City was the fifth largest engineering center in the United States thanks to two very large engineering design firms. However, most of the Kansas City firms were involved in design and building of facilities such as power plants and other commercial facilities. Pivot's Kansas City facility company personnel built electronic models and prototypes. The Kansas City facility had very little capacity for manufacturing per se.

The Taiwan facility focused on tool and die development for plastic and metal parts. In addition, the Taipei office constantly searched the world, with special emphasis on Pacific Rim countries, for parts that offered customers maximized performance at minimized cost.

Pivot's manufacturing facilities were located in the Philippines. The Manila facility included 62,000 square feet.[4] Although legally a separate company, the Manila facility was operated as an integral part of Pivot. In contrast, competitors often partnered with third-party suppliers to undertake the contract manufacturing. Pivot committed to "warranty the quality and performance of every product we manufacture." Pivot had also developed considerable ex-

pertise in logistics so that it could promise "precise shipping practices that guarantee timely delivery by air or sea." The company's commitment to customers guaranteed careful attention to keeping customers fully informed with regard to design and manufacturing progress and promised meeting deadlines.

Kirk Douglass described the relationship among the three parts of the corporation as follows:

> We run as one operating whole. Lenexa and Taiwan are legally one company. The Philippines plant is a separate entity wholly owned by Mr. Ching; however we operate all three as one unit. In short, we have the whole thing in one package. As a result we get to market faster and cleaner. Our designers [in Lenexa] talk to our engineers [in Taiwan] and both talk to the factory [in the Philippines]. Our project managers coordinate the entire process and are in constant communication with our customer. As a result, we offer the whole seamless process and thus considerable advantage to our customers.

Pivot described itself as providing "the convenience of U.S.-based project management and product development, the efficiency of high-volume overseas buying power, and the economy of off-shore manufacturing . . . all from one source." Its services included project management, offshore manufacturing, product design, mechanical design, electronic design, and worldwide shipping, as well as warranty and service activities.

Employing its facilities and capabilities at three locations, Pivot could provide plastic and metal component part assemblies, engineering, quality assurance, through-hole technology, surface-mount technology, PCB[5] assembly, and chip on board (COB)[6] capabilities, MRPII,[7] prototyping and concepts, a full 3-D solids CAD[8] platform, electronic engineering, mechanical, electronic and industrial design capabilities, and graphics and packaging. Pivot's electronic design capabilities included software development as well as LCD, circuit, and IC customer designs. Pivot had strong vendor alliances with leading microcontroller manufacturers[9] that led to shorter lead times and lower costs.

[4]44,000 square feet is an acre.

[5]Printed circuit board.

[6]Integrated circuit chips mounted on an integrated circuit board. The chip was usually manufactured by Texas instruments or Intel and contained the intelligence for the equipment.

[7]Advanced Materials Requisition Planning software system.

[8]Computer-assisted design. 3-D modeling required additional training and higher-powered computers.

[9]I.e., chip manufacturers.

Pivot's Project Managers

Pivot's project managers were primarily engineers because, as Douglass put it,

> Most of our projects have engineering aspects. The project manager has to be sensitive to the potential engineering problems and communicate them throughout the organization as early in the process as possible. There has to be a constant dialogue. We like to say that we work on projects 24 hours a day. When our people here in Lenexa [Kansas] go home at night, they leave an e-mail for the staff in Taipei [Taiwan]. About the time our personnel here are leaving, our people in Taipei are arriving in our facility there—and vice versa.
>
> At the same time, someone is also talking to the factory in the Philippines about manufacturing issues. Labor costs are low in the Philippines, so we can manufacture differently there than we would in a place where labor is more expensive. Taiwan does the document package.[10] The document package transmits the project to the factory. We expedite and focus on rapid time to market. Thus we don't handle things sequentially. Because we are coordinating across the three stages, that is, (a) design here in Lenexa, (b) tool and die development and parts procurement in Taiwan, and (c) manufacturing in the Philippines, we get ahead of the game in terms of parts. For example, if we know that a part takes a long time to procure, we might have already ordered it before we send the document package to the Philippines.

Customer Applications

Most of the firm's output was custom LCDs for a variety of products especially in the higher end of the physical fitness market. The new capabilities brochure depicted several projects the firm had undertaken recently. These included products that had been designed and manufactured as well as products that had been manufactured only:

- A readout display unit that displayed time, speed, calorie burn rate, distance, and pulse rate on one LCD display. The unit was designed for the manufacturer of the brand Pulse.
- A unit with seven LCD displays, dedicated to time, speed, distances, calories, pulse, effort, and program. This unit was designed for Nordic

[10]A document package for an electronic part or product was analogous to a blueprint for a building.

Track and was described as "high design value with fast turn—18 weeks from concept to delivery. Among its features was "quick assembly."

- Two products that had no LCD display and that had been manufactured in the Philippines: (1) a cordless telephone that was described as "manufactured for the wireless telecommunications industry," and (2) a handheld control device with a custom keypad that was described as "manufactured for the European market and designed for high-volume production; among its features was high reliability."

Another customer was Schwinn, a manufacturer of bicycles. Schwinn attached an LCD readout meter made by Pivot to three of its bike models. Douglass described the three stages—industrial design, engineering, and manufacturing—that Pivot undertook for Schwinn:

> Schwinn came to us and wanted us to do the following:
>
> (1) Industrial design. So we sat down and made up hand sketches. Then we made solid model. Basically in this stage the critical questions were "What does it have to do?" and "What should it look like?"
> (2) Engineering. In this stage we were thinking about how big the LCD readout display had to be in order to fit certain components inside the casing that Schwinn indicated it wanted. We designed an LCD readout display for this product, in other words, a custom LCD.

Ultimately, Pivot developed the tools and dies in Taiwan and manufactured the readout meter in the Philippines. Douglass described the Schwinn LCD readout meter:

> It does readout and display of various pieces of data for the bike user. We provided it in different colors. The year after we did the original project we undertook a slight modification. The newer version does not have a control function, but we are talking to Schwinn people about that possibility.
>
> Here's the model of the original. You can see it's designed essentially in four layers including the top and bottom of the plastic casing. The second layer has the chip and display panel. The third layer has the various connections.

The capabilities brochure described the Schwinn LCD readout as follows: a "Family line monitor with cost-effective tooling and low-cost electronic assembly. Plastic case tooled with same inserts. High design value with fast turn—18 weeks from concept to delivery. Features custom LCDs, keys, and COB."

PIVOT PERSONNEL

Pivot International's Kansas City–based facility employed 48 engineers and other professionals. Pivot had recently hired some very strong electronic and mechanical engineers and designers to complement the existing engineering staff. Eighteen months prior, the facility had had only 32 professionals. The company used AutoCAD, a well-established computer-aided design software program that had the leading market share throughout the world for many of its applications. In recent years Pivot had moved to reply on Solidworks and ProE platforms, two other software systems that had better solid modeling capabilities. There were another 30 individuals in the Taipei office working on product integration as well as tool and die engineering in plastics, metal, and other materials. The Taipei group also concentrated on sourcing components in various Asian countries. The Manila manufacturing facility could undertake through-hole assemblies, surface-mount assemblies, and full electronic mechanical (plastic and metal) assemblies as well as finished products including retail packaging.

J. Kirkland Douglass, president of the Lenexa division of the company, was a 1996 graduate of Yale, with a bachelor of science degree in electrical engineering, and a 1968 alumnus of the Carnegie-Mellon MBA program. Among his professors were Bill Cooper, a founding member of the Operations Research Society; Herbert Simon, an organizational theorist and later Nobel Prize winner; and Igor Ansoff, an early and highly respected theorist in the field of strategic management. Douglass talked about the challenge his professors brought to his education:

> I have always appreciated my MBA experience. I was one of Carnegie's early MBA graduates and lucky to be exposed to minds like Dr. Ansoff. That experience was a critical part of my development. Dr. Ansoff was a major contributor to the early development of the field of strategic management, and he is also considered a futurist, that is, a scholar who is very concerned about forward predictions of the state of industries, environments, technology, and the like. These aspects of my education made me want to keep my horizons sufficiently broad so that I could retain my functional specialty in finance yet never lose sight of the strategic implications. . . . It was that kind of thinking and background that led ultimately to my being able to play the role I did in the Pivot buyout and continue to have the fun I have running this firm. My wife asks frequently if I will ever slow down and then she will laugh and say that the day I do is the day I no longer exist. As long as I am having fun, and I am, I want to stay with it.

MARKETING AT PIVOT INTERNATIONAL

Pivot had focused for the early part of its history on relationship marketing. The firm was well known by design and manufacturing personnel in the fitness industry firms. Marketing within the industry had consisted of establishing and maintaining relationships with appropriate personnel in firms.

In preparation for more aggressive marketing to firms where Pivot's capabilities were not known, Kirk Douglass had developed a set of advertising materials. He wrote the copy and hired a copy editor to do the wordsmithing. Douglass also hired a local artist to execute a set of thematic postcards. The seven oversized postcards could be either sent as postcards or enclosed as inserts with other materials. (See Exhibit 3 for one of the postcards.) The company had already won two awards for its advertising materials.

The company planned to use its materials in highly directed mailings aimed at specific industries. Douglass explained his approach to marketing:

> The nature of our business is to become a backup product development and manufacturing resource for companies that want to outsource these functions. Once we develop a relationship, the total dollar volume of business with a single customer can and should become significant. This means we have a small number of customers, each of which does a large volume of business. Under these circumstances, we can only absorb a few new customers in a given year. The worst thing we could do would be to advertise on a broad scale and get several hundred responses. We would not know what to do with them. Instead, we need to develop a marketing program that is directed to a smaller group of likely prospects with the idea of generating responses from 10 or 15 of them in a year. From that group, we would hope to close two or three more customers.

exhibit 3   **Pivot's Postcards**

The set of seven postcards all had a circus theme. The pictures on the front were printed in full-color while the backs were in black and white.

Front of Postcard	Back of Postcard

Text on the back of the postcard:

Get Overseas Manufacturing Without Risking Your Neck

Trying your hand in overseas manufacturing can be frightening—unless you are working with Pivot International. With branches strategically located in Kansas City, Manila, and Taipei, we provide the convenience of U.S.-based project management and product development, the efficiency of high-volume buying power, and the economy of off-shore manufacturing . . . all from a single source. Don't lose your head. Call today.

THE OPPORTUNITY IN THE SECURITY DEVICE AND SYSTEMS MANUFACTURERS INDUSTRY

In thinking about expansion and diversifying Pivot's markets, Kirk Douglass had identified the security device and systems manufacturers industry as a possible target. The upcoming International Security Conference was one of several major conferences that brought the device and systems manufacturers together with the security personnel from companies and law enforcement agencies. Over 400 exhibitors were listed in the preconference materials. These included:

- Service providers such as ADT, Guardian Monitoring, and Protection One.

- Security systems and device manufacturers such as AES, AIT Advance Information Technologies, Cardkey Systems, Clark Security Products—Closed Circuit Television, Detex, and Identicard Systems.

- Other suppliers to the industry such as B&B Battery (USA).

Pivot had secured a booth at the conference. Douglass planned to lead a team of six people from the company to work the conference. Douglass especially planned to circulate through the booths to make contacts for follow-up during the postconference period.

PIVOT'S COMPETITORS

Pivot had few competitors that provided the full range of design, tool and die, purchasing, and manufacturing services as one integrated package. According to Kirk Douglass,

We don't appear to have many competitors. Our biggest competitor is usually the internal operations of our customer. However, we have seen a few similar companies in the literature:

- There was a recent *Fast Company* article that described an industrial design company in Silicon Valley that has used our strategy very successfully. That firm has expanded into engineering and has developed some sort of relationship with a Far East manufacturer so that they can provide production service. The company designed the Palm Pilot and has about $80 million in revenues.
- There is also an LA company that is smaller and does not have production capability, but it is actively promoting outsourcing of product development.
- There are a number of contract manufacturers in the industry—some of them quite large. Solotron is an example of a large contract manufacturing company. Solotron manufactures for companies like Hewlett Packard.

You will also find companies that do industrial design or other companies that do contract manufacturing. However, seldom does a company do both as Pivot does. Customers that go to a firm that does one or the other have to work on coordination issues between two or more companies to get a finished component part like an LCD readout display or control unit.

Douglass summarized his company's current position as follows:

We're well positioned to help companies in several industries undertake the design, development, and manufacture of consumer, industrial, and medical products through the use of U.S.-based design and cost-effective Far East sourcing of components and manufacturing. We have full services in industrial design, mechanical engineering, electronic software and hardware design, manufacturing, and product warranty support. Now all we have to do is crack a market beyond the fitness OEMs.

However, we get business in large chunks. The right customer can represent $5 million of revenue in 18 months. I want every customer's billings to be under 20 percent of our business.

As a minority shareholder, Douglass felt that that $50 million would be an appropriate revenue target:

Then we can take the company public or some other arrangement such as an ESOP.[11] It could remain a privately held corporation. However, at our current $20 million revenue, I don't view us as stable. We are too dependent on too few customers. That's why I would feel more comfortable at $50 million. I've got about a five-year target for getting to the $50 million.

[11]Employee stock ownership plan.

appendix|A Excerpts from the Industrial Marketing Research Firm's Preliminary Report to the Company Regarding the Security Device and Systems Manufacturers' Industry

Below is a summary of our preliminary observations about the security device manufacturers' industry; technologies and applications; potential customers for Pivot; and the interviews we conducted with executives in nearly 30 firms in the northeastern United States. Also attached is a summary of the relationships among the various segments of the Security Device and Systems Manufacturers' Industry (See Exhibit A-1) as well as a summary of the characteristics of the segments that may be of interest to Pivot (See Exhibit A-2). The full report will follow at next week.

exhibit a-1 **Industry Activity Chain**

C-354

exhibit a-2 **Summary Characteristics of Selected Segments of the Security Device and Systems Manufacturers Industry**

Residential

Small Business

Large Commercial

Institutional

Government

#1. Mass Marketers
- General Description: Relatively new entrants selling high volume
- Scope: Regional/national
- Customers: Primarily residential
- Offering:
  - Simple systems & devices
  - $ from service contracts
  - Low price (not quality)
  - Not so often newest technology
- Source: Buy from manufacturers
- Industry change: 1997 Tyco acquired ADT

#2. Installers & Small System Designers
- General Description: Often 20 yrs old; 2nd & 3rd generation locksmiths or fire protection migrants
- Scope: Local or narrow regional small companies some growing very rapidly
- Offering:
  - Access control & CCTV
  - Stress quality (customers are "family")
- Customers: residential & sm business
- Source: prefer US made from distributors (e.g., ADI, Alarm King)
- Examples: Ademco, Napco, Detection Systems
- Industry Observations:
  - Mass Marketer effect: divided opinion
  - Forward integration into building, real estate, monitoring
  - Where population dense some biometrics
  - Customers want integration w/PC home & office

#3. Large System Designers (LSDs)
a) Manufacture:
- General Description: Often 65 yrs old; have corp. & divisional R&D; large investment in mfg (some offshore) and technology
- Scope: Global
- Offering: Access control, CCTV, Inventory Monitoring, Environmental Control, Focus on specific applications, e.g., tag equipment; customized large systems
- Customers: Large commercial customers
- Source: Standard components from e.g., Texas Instruments, Fairchild, Honeywell; license some technology; may develop or buy software
- Examples: Knogo and Sensormatic
- Industry Observations: Begun to merge for vertical integration backward, expand capacity, & broader product line, e.g., Knogo and Sensormatic
b) Don't manufacture (Value Added Resellers—VARs)
- General Description: Often 65 yrs old; have corp. & divisional R&D
- Scope: Regional
- Offering: Labelled and branded equipment in fire, access, surveillance, & environmental controls; usually general system that can be modified
- Customers: Differentiated on customers & applications (Differentiated & Focus Strategy)
- Source: Large OEMs, e.g., Motorola, Hughes, & IBM; software contracted out
- Examples: None given
- Industry Observations: excited about biometrics as a value added to new and existing systems

#5. High-End Technology Developers
- General Description: Technology developers
- Scope:
- Customers: Large corporations; government (e.g., DOD); research and financial institutions
- Offering: Technology, one-of-a-kind designs, or consulting/design services
- Source: Outsources mfg and not usually involved in actual installation
- Industry change: Beginning to look at commercial application of technologies and/or partnerships with manufacturers

#4. Device Manufacturers
a) OEMs
- General Description: Low tech (non-micro-processor based); wary of newer technologies
- Scope: National; some regional focus (sell to installers & SSDs)
- Offering: Limited product line, e.g., specialize in alarms, cameras, sensors, accessory items; lower cost with no brand recognition; may brand for VAR; some proprietary designs
- Customers: Sold into those putting in commercial installations; distributors
- Source: Standard components
- Examples: None given
- Industry Changes: moved away from exclusive distributors; recent example of OEM acquiring a distributor
b) Large Device Manufacturers
- General Description:
- Scope: Global; see Europe as having significant potential
- Offering: Wide range of device categories (CCTV, fire alarm, access control, sensors, environmental); may have three tiers of products: low cost/simple/lower tech to high tech/quality
- Distribution: wholesale network or mfgrs reps
- R&D Capabilities: Vary, some with corp. & div. R&D labs; sometimes differentiate on tech; may license from national sources, e.g., Bell Labs
- Customers: Residential & small business security markets
- Source: standard components; outsource LDC and display
- Examples: Digital Security Systems, Napco, Northern Video Systems, Inc., Pittway Corp., Radionics
- Industry Observations: Had integrated backwards and were diversifying horizontally; interested in new products and segments; generally acquire rather than internal development

C-355

a. Industry Observations

- Overall the security industry had about $100 billion in revenues last year and is expected to grow at about 15 percent per year during the rest of the 1990s and into the next decade. Growth varies significantly in various segments.

- Both technology-based security (e.g., access control and CCTV) and "plain," "old-fashioned" guard service are experiencing continuing demand increases. Service providers are growing most slowly. Guard service is growing at about 5 percent, and electronic security services at about 8–10 percent. Margins have been dropping, especially in the service segments.

- The industry is highly fragmented, although certain segments, such as the manufacturers and service providers, are consolidating through acquisition.

- Players evidence a considerable variety of strategies.

- Companies listed as "manufacturers" are often not manufacturers. Rather, they are system assemblers that function as system designers. These firms may also install and service the systems.

- Security systems assemblers/designers sometimes label equipment with their own brand name.

- Demand overall is spurred by a number of factors, including:
  - Perceptions of the crime rate (e.g., some crime is actually declining, but visibility of crime is not declining; there is concern about the apparent nonselectivity of crime).
  - The aging of the population.
  - Growth in upscale housing.
  - The perception that public policing may be declining.

- Technology developments are spurring demand in certain segments (e.g., biometrics) and regulatory changes are responsible for increased demand in other segments (e.g., medical applications).

- Consolidation and changes in the utility industry will spur demand, as security becomes one of the components in a package of "utilities" marketed to customers along with electricity, telecommunications, and other services.

b. Technologies and Applications

Technologies and applications include access control/RFID[1]/false alarms; biometrics; access and egress applications, CCTV, and system integration.

Access Control

- The "old" technologies include personal identification numbers, magnetic-stripe cards, and Weigand wires.

- An important technology for access control is RFID. RFID readers are known as proximity readers.
  - RFID is the coming technology for such applications as inventory control.

---

[1] Radio frequency identification; that is, the ability to sense a piece of identification from a distance. The identification piece could be a card that could transmit a radio frequency that the sensor would match to frequency codes that had clearance for entry.

- RFID solves the problem that devices requiring insertion (e.g., cards—or, for that matter, a hand) are subject to malfunction due to dirt and grime.
- However, RFID has the drawback that the cards, tokens, and tags used to trigger access can be lost and thus wind up in nonauthorized hands, thus compromising security.

- Access control is often concerned with access and also *egress* detection.
- Technologies include sound, motion, heat, and microwave detection.
- Applications include:
  - Deterrence of theft by individuals internal and external to organizations (thus monitoring the location of equipment and inventory are important applications)
  - Safety including that of older individuals (e.g., Alzheimer's patients) and newborns in hospitals.
- False alarms continue to be a problem for the industry:
  - Security systems users are less concerned about this issue than police departments because the police departments have historically had to absorb the costs of answering false alarms.
  - However, municipalities are generally tightening regulations by: i) requiring paid yearly registration of all systems, ii) threatening nonresponse to alarms from nonregistered systems, iii) reducing the number of "free" responses; and iv) increasing the fee for excessive false alarms.
  - Most false alarms appear to occur during arm/disarm procedures.
  - No one appears to have a good solution for this problem.
- A critical issue for access control overall is integration, i.e., the linking of surveillance, access, fire alarms, and climate control systems. For example, some companies link access control with employee time card systems and surveillance of employee movements.

Biometrics

- The "hot" item in 1997 was certainly biometrics (however)
- There is considerable uncertainty on how quickly this market will become robust.
- Biometrics is a coming technology platform for access control.
- Biometric technologies are based on a number of different biometric measures, including finger/thumbprint, handscan, voice recognition, handwriting, typing/keying patterns, and eye.
- One major deterrent to adoption is cost of the readers; however, prices for some types will quickly drop to under $1,000.
- Another major deterrent to adoption is user reluctance to participate. (E.g., will employees and patrons be willing to have their eye "shot" by a camera to match with the pattern of iris scan metrics in the computer?)
- Our observation is that enough "ordinary" applications are coming into place that biometrics will be accepted (e.g., handscan at the YMCA in RedWing, Minnesota).
- There are several companies in Minnesota and Texas that are the forefront in this sector.
- Several companies appear to have promise, but most tend to be small and some are unstable.

CCTV

- The Oklahoma bombing has focused attention on external surveillance of grounds, buildings, and lobbies. CCTV surveillance has had more extensive use in Europe than in the United States and Japan. However, the pattern in the United States is changing.
- Systems essentially consist of:
  - Cameras (stationary and moving; important issues include resolution and breadth of camera scan).
  - Trajectories for moving the cameras (important issues: speed of movement and turnaround; 360-degree focus capability).
  - Wire or wireless links with video and computer monitoring (either on premise or in any distant location).
  - Computer software and hardware.
- Cameras: Some of the security device manufacturers manufacture their own cameras.
- Monitors: There is increased demand for color monitors.
- CCTV does not have much application in residential security systems primarily because of price.
- There is increasing use of CCTV in:
  - Employee surveillance. (Questions included: Are the employees working? Did they truly have the accident as claimed or was it feigned?)
  - Public places (e.g., parks).
  - Upscale housing security systems (e.g., for intrusion detection, premise surveillance, front door security, and nanny monitoring).
- A critical issue for CCTV is integration (i.e., the linking of systems for multiple purposes). Some systems are installed that do not currently have CCTV but do have the ability to be readily upgraded for the same.

System Integration

- As noted, integration is an important issue for both access control and CCTV. The old term was *smart buildings*. The newer terms appear to be *total facilities/building/management control*.
- The important issues are the software needed to control the systems; the choice of telephone versus wireless links; and the constellation of applications. For example, the swipe of an access card at the parking garage could turn on the lights in the employee's work area, adjust heating to the person's preference, alert other systems or individuals to the user's needs, and monitor the individual's movements through the parking garage and building.
- Both the technologies and the user demand for a broader array of integrated applications are one factor in the consolidation of the industry.
- Thus, integration of systems is a significant reason why companies are acquiring others to enlarge their product lines.

c. Potential Customers for Pivot

- We have a source that will help identify potential companies that Pivot could target as customers.
- We have identified a number of those companies.
- Most of these companies are in the Northeast (especially in New York, New Jersey, and Massachusetts) or California; there are also several companies in Texas that may be of interest.
- We concentrated our efforts, as per our prior discussion, on New York but have identified companies in other states.
- One of the greatest concentrations appears to be in the Long Island area.
- Several players have applications in the medical field where issues such as newborn security are salient.
- Medical applications:
  - As suggested above, there are a number of applications in the medical field that could intersect the interests we heard Kirk Douglass express in the security industry and that your lead engineering marketing person identified in the medical field.
  - An important issue to note is that health care provider facilities (e.g., inner-city service providers; nursing homes) and hospitals are being subjected to increasing regulatory demands regarding security especially in such places as maternity/nursery, pediatrics, and emergency rooms.
  - With regard to elder care, state regulations differ with regard to the ability of facilities to control patient movement through locked doors or bracelet/anklet monitoring of movement and location.

d. Observations from the Interviews

- The East Coast office has completed a number of interviews with companies located in the Northeast. These companies included systems designers/installers and device manufacturers. We did not talk to component manufacturers.
- The interviews corroborate many of the observations above, including the emphasis on access control/CCTV integration, the uncertainty about biometrics, and the variety of strategic choices among the players.
- As indicated previously, the head of the East Coast office has coordinated exhibition display booths for her company (fairly sophisticated software) and is developing several insights from the interviews that may be helpful as you prepare for the Las Vegas meeting.

case 20

Bayer AG: Children's ASPIRIN

Lauranne Buchanan
Thunderbird—The American Graduate School of International Management

Christopher K. Merker
Thunderbird—The American Graduate School of International Management

INTRODUCTION

Joachim Zander, director of brand equity and modernity expansion in the Global Strategy Group of Bayer's Consumer Care Division, looked up from articles he had been reading on the latest medical study on Reye's Syndrome (RS). The study was published in the esteemed *New England Journal of Medicine*, a journal written primarily by and for the American medical community. One of the articles had a headline that read, "Children's Reye's Syndrome Now Rare."[1] He rubbed his eyes as he thought to himself, "This is surely the final nail in the coffin of Children's ASPIRIN."[2]

Bayer's Children's ASPIRIN business had been declining ever since the early '80s when the US medical community alleged a link between the consumption of children's aspirin and the occurrence of a dangerous condition in children known as Reye's Syndrome. Though the link was never proven, Bayer

THE AMERICAN GRADUATE SCHOOL
OF INTERNATIONAL MANAGEMENT

[1]*The Associated Press,* May 5, 1999, at 16:58 EDT, Copyright 1999, File: h0505165.900; see also Belay, Bresee, Holman, Khan, Shahriari, Schonberger, "Reye's Syndrome in the United States from 1981 through 1997," *New England Journal of Medicine,* May 6, 1999, Vol. 340, No. 18, pp. 1377–1382.

[2]ASPIRIN is a brand name owned by Bayer in many countries; therefore to avoid confusion, this case will refer to the brand name as ASPIRIN (upper case) and to the substance aspirin as ASA or aspirin (lower case).

acted responsibly to the public relations crisis by self-imposing a worldwide ban on all promotion and advertisement of Children's ASPIRIN in 1988. In the years that followed, Bayer had not fully reconsidered its strategy for Children's ASPIRIN, nor had it considered introducing other analgesic products for children.

For years, Zander had wanted to conduct a brand audit to determine the future of ASPIRIN in the children's segment. But the project always fell behind something more pressing; given this new wave of publicity, it seemed like the time for the audit was now or never. Zander had recently hired a new intern, Chris Merker, from Thunderbird, The American Graduate School of International Management, and Merker was interested in conducting a study of the product market. Dividing up the work would make the task of examining and assessing the world market more manageable.

As Zander reflected on Children's ASPIRIN, his mind turned to other developments in the overall aspirin market and how it related to the little 100 mg. tablet. Concurrent with the decline within the children's segment, there had been new discoveries opening other business opportunities. In 1985, the medical profession revealed that aspirin is effective in the prevention of heart attacks and strokes. As the prevention market developed, Zander and other managers at Bayer realized that an increasing percentage of Children's ASPIRIN sales went to prevention. This was due, in part, to its lower cost but also to the lower dosage recommended for prevention (81–100 mg. compared to 325–500 mg. in adult aspirin). The percentage of sales of Children's ASPIRIN accounted for by the prevention market, however, was unclear.

From worldwide sales data, it appeared that Children's ASPIRIN was growing. Total sales of Children's ASPIRIN had increased at a compounded annual growth rate (CAGR) of 13.34% over the five-year period from 1994 through 1998. Yet the growth in sales could have been driven completely by the growth in the prevention market.

With the new Thunderbird intern on his staff, Zander was determined to get to the bottom of the issues surrounding Children's ASPIRIN. He wondered to himself, "How much of these sales are attributable to the children's market and how much to prevention? And, what are the implications not only for the Consumer Care (CC) Division of Bayer, but for Pharma, the division which handles other prevention brands?"

BACKGROUND
Industry Dynamics

Throughout the 1990s, the pharmaceutical industry underwent several major changes. One of these changes was a strategic movement away from the concentration of dollars on Research & Development (R&D) within the value chain to greater attention and resources being devoted to marketing and advertising. Another change was the way marketing dollars were allocated. Historically, the sales force had been the center of the marketing program, and they had focused on direct selling to doctors, the gatekeepers of prescription drugs.

As government regulations, particularly in the US, loosened within the area of direct-to-consumer (DTC) advertising, more of the marketing dollars shifted to advertising. In DTC ads, consumers are made aware of a drug product available only by prescription and are told to "ask their doctor about" the drug. As marketing research established the effectiveness of these ads, more and more firms turned to DTC advertising as a source of sustainable competitive advantage. These trends were expected to continue:

> . . . pharmaceutical makers launched new advertising programs to raise awareness of products among consumers. In 1994, the amount spent on drug advertising was about $240 million, a 50% increase over 1993 expenditures. Expenditures were forecast to double by 1997. By 1995, manufacturers advertised more than two dozen prescription drugs on television,

radio, and printed material. A 1995 survey indicated that 10% of consumers had some knowledge about 13 of the 17 most heavily advertised drugs. In contrast, only one drug received a similar response rate in 1989. Survey results also indicated that 99% of physicians surveyed—as opposed to 84% in 1989—would prescribe or consider prescribing a specific drug if a patient asked for it by name.[3]

Not only does creating awareness of a pharmaceutical generate additional sales, but it also prepares the market for transfer of the ethical drug to over-the-counter (OTC) status.[4] Converting ethical drugs to OTCs is a strategy to increase market share and sales over the product life cycle of the drug. This strategy is one means of prolonging—and possibly increasing—sales revenues of the drug as generic copycats arrive on the market upon patent expiration. The value of the brand to the consumer differentiates otherwise identical and competing products.

DTC advertising, deemed by many authorities as inappropriate, is more prevalent in the US than in other parts of the world such as Europe. Europe historically has taken a much more conservative approach with regard to advertising claims in general. For example, comparative advertising was permitted by EU law for the first time in the spring of 2000, while it had been permissible for decades in the US. A study commissioned by Bayer in the late 1990s indicated that DTC advertising in Europe would not occur for at least five to ten years. Nonetheless, a combination of direct selling to doctors and direct advertising to consumers is expected to become the predominant global strategy of pharmaceutical companies in both ethical and OTC categories in the future. The official regulatory status of products is expected to become less important, blurring the lines between ethical and OTC drugs.

The Company

Bayer is a pharmaceutical and chemical company headquartered in Leverkusen, Germany with about 20 different business units that research, develop, and

---

[3]McGahan, Coxe, Keller, and McGuire, "The Pharmaceutical Industry in the 1990s," Harvard Business School Case 9-796-058 (1995), pp. 9–10.

[4]Ethical drugs are drugs sold only with a doctor's prescription; over-the-counter (OTC) status means that a drug may be sold without a doctor's prescription.

exhibit 1 **ASPIRIN Milestones**

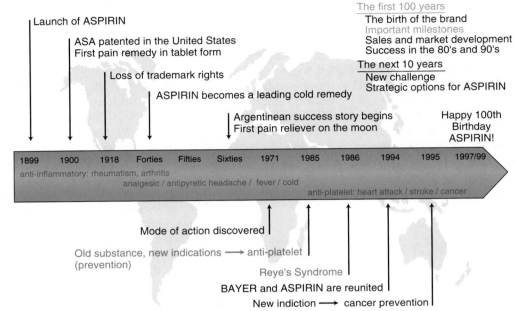

CCJZA/Daten/ASPIRIN/NicholasHallSept1999.Master.pptpage1

manufacture products in the life sciences, polymers and specialty chemicals areas. Employing 120,400 people worldwide, the group has operations in nearly all countries of the globe and a portfolio of about 10,000 products. With annual worldwide sales of DM 54.9 billion and an operating result of DM 6.15 billion (1998), it is considered a world leader in its sector.[5]

The jewel at the very center of the Bayer crown is the brand ASPIRIN, and it is without question the most successful over-the-counter drug in history. In fact 1999 marked the 100th anniversary of ASPIRIN (see Exhibit 1 for a timeline of ASPIRIN milestones over the last 100 years). Felix Hoffman, a Bayer chemist, invented the drug in 1897, and the drug was brought to market two years later. The brand AS-PIRIN is still the number two analgesic drug in the world with net sales in 1998 of DM1.1 billion (US$654.8 million). Only Tylenol exceeds ASPIRIN in sales, but 95% of Tylenol's sales are in the US; in the rest of the world, Bayer is still number one (see Exhibit 2 for sales and market development).

Consumer Care is the division of Bayer charged with the management of ASPIRIN and other OTCs, as well as other consumer products. In 1998, Pharma, Bayer's pharmaceutical division, was given control of the ASPIRIN prevention business since aspirin is typically prescribed by doctors for this indication.[6]

The ASPIRIN Family

ASPIRIN is a family of well-known brands and products, which includes Children's ASPIRIN, AS-PIRINProtect®, ASPIRIN Direct®, ASPIRIN+C®, and many others. All are geared for specific uses such as cough and cold, headache and pain, stroke and heart attack prevention. Many have unique delivery systems such as granules, effervescent tablets, and chewable forms. Of the US$654.8 million in total worldwide net sales of all ASPIRIN products in 1998, US$37.5 million (5.8%) came from the sale of Children's ASPIRIN.

[5]All facts and figures, unless otherwise stated, are provided by Bayer AG.

[6]A drug's indication simply means what the drug is used/prescribed for. The indication will typically be printed on the drug's packaging label, and is in almost all cases closely controlled by the government.

exhibit 2   Market Development

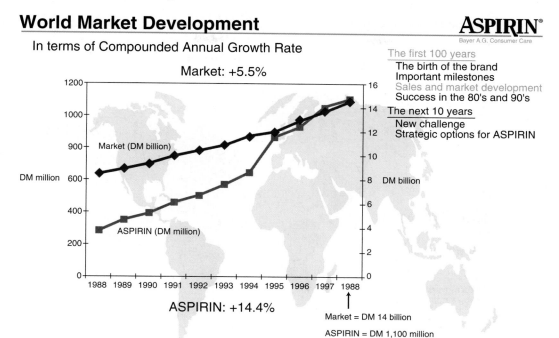

World Market Development

ASPIRIN®
Bayer A.G. Consumer Care

In terms of Compounded Annual Growth Rate

Market: +5.5%

The first 100 years
The birth of the brand
Important milestones
Sales and market development
Success in the 80's and 90's

The next 10 years
New challenge
Strategic options for ASPIRIN

ASPIRIN: +14.4%

Market = DM 14 billion

ASPIRIN = DM 1,100 million

CCJZA/Daten/ASPIRIN/NicholasHallSept1999.Master.pptpage1

Brand

Originally, the brand name ASPIRIN was coined by Bayer as the tradename for acetylsalicylic acid (ASA). Bayer continues to hold a trademark on the brand name in many countries of the world, but has lost that right in several key countries like the United States (see Exhibit 3 for more information on where Bayer sells aspirin and continues to hold a trademark). The Bayer trademark was lost initially in the US at the end of World War I to Sterling Drug, Inc. as the result of the US government's retaliatory practice of confiscating and then auctioning off the property of German companies with holdings in the United States.[7] It wasn't until 1994, 76 years after the expropriation of the trademark Bayer ASPIRIN, that Bayer Group finally reacquired the brand (with a few other Sterling Drug OTC businesses in North America such as Phillip's Milk of Magnesia®) for US$1 billion.

Despite regaining the name Bayer, Bayer Group cannot recoup the trademark on aspirin in the United States. In 1920, the US Patent Office cancelled the exclusive right of Sterling Drug, Inc., which held the Bayer ASPIRIN trademark, to sell ASA exclusively under the name ASPIRIN. A judge later supported this decision arguing that people knew ASA by the term "aspirin," and therefore any company should be permitted to sell the product under what had become the generic name.[8] There are significant economic implications of losing the right to market ASA exclusively under the name ASPIRIN, and Bayer has fared better in countries where it still retains that right.

In terms of Children's ASPIRIN, some OTC marketers at Bayer believe that a children's product is essential to the overall brand in two ways. One, it conveys a message of safety to the consumer; and, two, it fosters brand loyalty in future adult ASPIRIN customers.

---

[7]For more information about the history of the trademark, see Mann and Plummer's fascinating and comprehensive history of aspirin in *The Aspirin Wars: Money, Medicine and 100 Years of Rampant Competition,* pp. 32–38.

[8]Ibid., p. 66.

exhibit 3 **Market Presence**

Market Presence

ASPIRIN is sold in 90 countries around the world

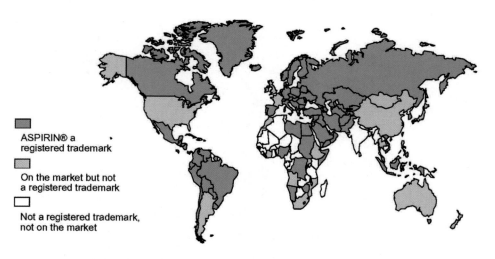

ASPIRIN® a
registered trademark

On the market but not
a registered trademark

Not a registered trademark,
not on the market

CCJZA/Daten/ASPIRIN/NicholasHallSept1999.Master.pptpage4

REYE'S SYNDROME

History

In June 1986, the US Food and Drug Administration (FDA) mandated that all manufacturers of aspirin include this warning in their labeling:[9]

> Children and teenagers should not use this medicine for chicken pox or flu symptoms before a doctor is consulted about Reye's Syndrome, a rare but serious illness.[10]

In 1963, the Australian pathologist Reye described a very rare disease in children, the exact cause of which remains unknown. Reyes' Syndrome (RS) is an acute, noninflammatory disease of the brain and liver, usually seen following a viral infection. Some of the symptoms include frequent vomiting, seizures, episodes of disorientation, and coma. The disease can result in death.

In the late 1970s, epidemiologists began to review studies of RS that were conducted over two decades. They acted on a suspicion that aspirin could have been a contributing factor in the cause of the disease. The source of that suspicion was that most of the children in the initial RS studies were given aspirin—a known antipyretic (fever reducer)—to reduce fever in the early stages of a viral infection, which preceded the onset of RS. The ruling by the FDA was the culmination of the series of epidemiological studies conducted in the United States that alleged a connection between aspirin and the occurrence of Reye's Syndrome in children.

Since the ruling, the occurrence of RS has declined. Many in the US medical community argue that this has been a direct result of the information campaign launched in the US by the Center for Disease Control (CDC) and the FDA labeling requirement. This view is widely accepted, as indicated by

[9]The label will contain the brand name, directions and indications, ingredient information, and any possible warnings on usage, such as conflicts with other drugs or, as in the case of Reye's Syndrome, any potential side effects of the drug. In most cases, labeling is strictly controlled by the government. Governments are typically involved in every step of the development and marketing of a new drug. Consequently, a large percentage of an R&D budget for developing a new drug is allocated toward regulatory affairs.

[10]See the back of any bottle of aspirin sold in the US.

an article in the popular press citing research published in the prestigious medical journal, the *New England Journal of Medicine:*

> Reye's Syndrome, a rare but deadly disorder usually caused by giving aspirin to children with flu or chickenpox, has almost disappeared, thanks to a public education campaign and changes in treatment, a study found . . . In 1980, when the connection between aspirin and Reye's Syndrome was discovered, the CDC began warning doctors and parents not to give aspirin to children with viral infections . . . the study appears in Thursday's *New England Journal of Medicine.*[11]

Dissenting medical opinion and, of course, manufacturers of aspirin, claim that the evidence linking aspirin to RS lacks scientific validity. (See Appendix A for a rebuttal Bayer made to the *New England Journal of Medicine* study cited above; the rebuttal was circulated widely to the international press.)

To support this position, they cite empirical evidence from countries like Argentina, where children's consumption of aspirin remains strong, yet the occurrence of Reye's Syndrome is very low. The same is true in the seven major markets for Children's ASPIRIN, including Spain, Italy, Turkey, and several Latin American countries.

These groups also suggest that it is improvements in diagnostics that have made RS a much rarer condition, i.e. what in the past looked like RS might not have been RS at all, and thus not the result of taking aspirin for a viral infection. In other words, there has been no real decrease in the disease known as RS; rather there has been a decline in what is diagnosed as RS.

Finally, this side argues that there are many other factors present in genes or within the environment that could be responsible for causing RS, and that evidence isolating aspirin as a primary, contributing factor is still lacking. The reason alternative causes of the disease have not been identified and ruled out is that the biochemistry involved in explaining RS, which is a metabolic disorder, is extremely complex.

Unfortunately, the debate and the hundreds of studies, white papers and articles written on RS have done little to resolve these issues. But in this case,

perception is everything. The debate within the health sciences that has gone on for over 20 years has had no impact on the conclusion reached by the public or by an influential medical community (specifically in the US) that there is a high risk in using aspirin to medicate children.

The regulation of aspirin for children is not without its downside. At a minimum, it limits consumer choice in the market and discourages both innovation and price declines associated with a competitive market. More importantly, however, it has reduced the use of aspirin among young consumers who could have benefited from the product for other indications.

Regulatory Issues, Public Opinion, and Bayer's Response

Initially, with allegations that aspirin caused death in children, the Bayer company was obviously greatly concerned about the threat to children. But they also wondered what it would mean for the future of the business. Some of the managers believed that the future viability of the entire brand was in question.

The first regulation came in 1984 when the German food and drug authority, the Bundesgesundheitsamt (BGA), mandated a warning on the label of all children's aspirin products. The warning indicated that, while there was a correlation between aspirin and RS, a direct relationship had not been established. In 1989, a revised BGA ruling dropped the disclaimer that the relationship had not been established. Bayer fully complied with both rulings just as it did in the United States with the FDA's 1986 decision.

In compliance with FDA standards, Bayer placed warnings on labels of Children's ASPIRIN worldwide, regardless of whether it was required by the host country's government. In 1988, Bayer took the additional step of invoking a worldwide ban on all advertising or promotion of ASPIRIN for children. In many ways, this was an extraordinary measure since Bayer AG, like many German companies, has a loose affiliation with its subsidiaries, and rarely engages in worldwide policymaking. Most subsidiaries are independent entities and operate as such. Nonetheless, virtually all affiliates complied with the ban.

Bayer's policy of no promotion and advertising was developed, in part, to satisfy its constituency of customers, policymakers, and shareholders at home. Bayer had already pulled ASPIRINJunior® to satisfy

[11]*The Associated Press,* May 5, 1999, at 16:58 EDT, Copyright 1999, File: h0505165.900; see also Belay, Bresee, Holman, Khan, Shahriari, Schonberger, "Reye's Syndrome in the United States from 1981 through 1997," *New England Journal of Medicine,* May 6, 1999, Vol. 340, No. 18, pp. 1377–1382.

exhibit 4   **Effect of Reye's Syndrome on Sales of ASPIRIN (all products)**

Has Reye's Syndrome negatively impacted the overall sales performance of the ASPIRIN brand ?

CC-EU-NB/MR

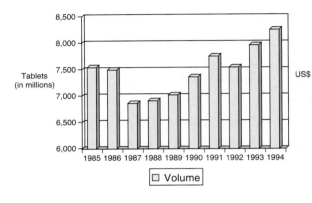

Tablets (in millions) — Volume

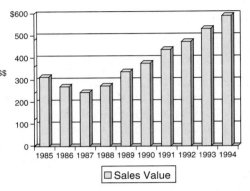

US$ — Sales Value

the German public. It could not continue promoting the product in developing markets without being accused of exploiting consumers and taking advantage of the ambivalence of their government's regulatory bodies.

Despite these measures, Children's ASPIRIN remains a viable brand in many markets in southern Europe, e.g., Spain, Italy, Turkey, and in Latin America. In these countries, it is still prescribed by doctors and purchased by consumers. In Argentina, for example, where Bayer has an extremely strong brand presence, ASPIRINETAS continues to be the number one seller in the children's segment. Children's ASPIRIN is, therefore, managed in countries like Argentina as a cash cow. With virtually no monies set aside for advertising and promotion, the profit margins on the 100 mg. tablet are naturally higher.

Throughout the rest of the world, the publicity surrounding the association of aspirin with RS, the lack of any advertising and promotional support from Bayer, and aggressive competitive reaction lead to a dramatic decline in market share. For decades the number one children's analgesic, in 1998 Children's ASPIRIN accounted for 2.3% of total world market share for children's analgesics, which was valued at approximately US$865 million annually.[12]

While the Children's ASPIRIN business declined in many countries, the overall sales performance of the ASPIRIN brand (all products) continued to grow. During the crisis, there was a drop in the sales of all ASPIRIN products, but this can be attributed to other factors including huge price increases in Latin America and inadequate promotion in Asia and Africa. In fact, directly following the Reye's Syndrome crisis, ASPIRIN rebounded and experienced the highest growth rates in years (see Exhibit 4 for sales and volume performance of ASPIRIN during and after the crisis).

PREVENTION

At the same time that Bayer faced the crisis over Children's ASPIRIN and RS, there was some good news for Bayer. In October 1985, eight months before FDA imposed its labeling requirement for the children's indication, Margaret Heckler, then-US Secretary of Health and Human Services, held up a bottle of Bayer ASPIRIN at a press conference. She announced to the world that scientific studies had shown that first-time heart attack sufferers taking an aspirin a day could significantly reduce their chances of having a second heart attack.[13] In the battle against

[12]IMS, Inc.; PADDS database (Bayer and IMS); IRI, Inc.; Bayer subsidiaries.

[13]*The Aspirin Wars*, p. 309.

exhibit 5 **ASPIRIN's Three Distinct Indications and Three Distinct Markets**

Therapeutic Quality	Indication	Product Markets OTC/Ethical	Competing Brands/ Substances	ASPIRIN's Market Share Worldwide
Analgesic Anti-inflammatory Antipyretic	Pain	Adult and children analgesics (OTC)	Tylenol/ acetaminophen (paracetamol) Advil/ibuprofen	8.2%
	Cough and cold	Cough, cold, anti-flu (OTC)	Nyquil, Contact, Theraflu, Robitussin	4.2
Anti-platelet	Prevention— heart attack	Anti-platelets and anti-coagulants (ethical)	Platet Cleartab, Heparin	9.1

one of the leading causes of death in the developed world, the significance of this medical breakthrough could not be over-emphasized. It was wonderful news to scores of people at risk, for it meant that thousands of lives could be saved annually.

As a drug, aspirin not only has the properties of an analgesic or painkiller, it is also an antipyretic (anti-fever), an anti-inflammatory and an anti-platelet (see Exhibit 5). The first three qualities make it a headache, cold, and flu medication, but it is the fourth quality that makes ASPIRIN a preventive medication.

Interestingly, the anti-platelet effects of aspirin occur at a surprisingly low dosage: 30–50 mg. or so, and Children's ASPIRIN is one of the lowest dose aspirin products on the market. It also happens to be the cheapest among the ASPIRIN family of products. The significance of these two characteristics gave Children's ASPIRIN a new market, as doctors around the world started recommending and prescribing Children's ASPIRIN to their middle-aged patients as a means of prevention.

Bayer and their competitors have capitalized on the anti-platelet quality of aspirin by developing a whole battery of sophisticated—and more expensive—dosage and delivery systems intended for the at-risk-of-a-heart-attack user. Some, such as Bayer CardioASPIRIN®, are designed for persons with sensitive stomachs and are coated for enteric digestion. The tablet of aspirin is encased by a high-tech outer layer that allows the tablet to be digested and absorbed in the intestines rather than in the stomach. Others, such as ADIRO®, are microencapsulated and feature sustained release of the active ingredient over time, ensuring bioavailability and mucosa protection.

But for customers who don't require any special features of the medication, a lower dosage is all that's needed, and Children's ASPIRIN fills that role well. Almost half of all Children's ASPIRIN sales in 1998 were to prevention users, and the proportion was expected to increase rapidly.

A TALE OF TWO MARKETS

With the history of the Children's ASPIRIN brand in mind, Zander and Merker wondered how much prevention demand was driving the 13.34% CAGR in total sales. To answer this question, they began polling the country managers in the major market countries: Spain, Italy, Turkey, Argentina, Venezuela, Chile, Colombia, Brazil, Guatemala, Honduras, Nicaragua, Panama, Costa Rica, and El Salvador. They wanted to know the split in sales of Children's ASPIRIN between children and the adult prevention market. Country managers had a very good feel for the numbers, and they were able to go back five years to describe the development of the split in their respective countries of business. Exhibit 6 shows the splits in terms of total worldwide sales from 1994 to 1998 and with a five-year forecast through 2003. (White represents the prevention portion of sales, and gray, the children portion.)

In 1998, total sales of Children's ASPIRIN were US$20.8 million and US$16.8 million in the children's and prevention markets, respectively. Sales forecasted to the children's market decline to US$12.3 million by 2003.

The results further indicated that prevention customers had been rapidly replacing children customers over the five years from 1994 through 1998.

exhibit 6   **Sales Forecast**

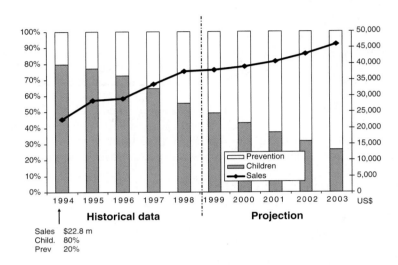

Sales Forecast: Children's ASPIRIN

CC-EU-NB/MR

By 2003 children's usage will fall to 26.6%

Historical data | Projection

Sales $22.8 m
Child. 80%
Prev 20%

Forecasts indicated that by 2003 approximately 27% of Children's ASPIRIN sales would be for children and 73% for prevention customers, effectively reversing the 80% / 20% split, respectively, from 1994.

From this, Zander and Merker realized that Children's ASPIRIN was naturally evolving into a low-cost, low-dosage prevention product. And it looked as if the combination of the rapid growth in the prevention market and the decline of the children's market would be the death of the Children's ASPIRIN brand.

This raised the following questions in their minds:

- What was the point of keeping Children's ASPIRIN on the market at all if the majority of sales went to prevention customers? Or, was Children's ASPIRIN meeting an implicit market demand that would be lost to competitors if Bayer left the market?

- And what impact was Children's ASPIRIN having on CardioASPIRIN® and ADIRO®, the preventive products managed by Pharma, Consumer Care's sister division? Was Children's ASPIRIN

cannibalizing these brands, and if so, to what extent?

Based on these questions, Zander and Merker summarized the two possible directions Bayer could take in protecting and developing its prevention business:

1. Retract Children's ASPIRIN, pulling it off the market altogether and concentrating on pursuing the prevention market with the current high-end, enteric-coated CardioASPIRIN® and microencapsulated ADIRO® products.[14]

    Pulling the product off the market altogether would take care of the risk of cannibalizing Pharma's products. And it could lead to higher sales of CardioASPIRIN®, assuming the strength of the Bayer ASPIRIN brand ensured a commitment from doctors and customers to the high-end CardioASPIRIN® products, even though they

[14]Financials on ADIRO were not included in the team's analysis because its share of the prevention business was not deemed significant. Therefore, the team chose to analyze prevention only in terms of CardioASPIRIN®'s projected performance.

were twice as expensive. If not, it could replace the risk of cannibalization with one of losing the entire low-end prevention business to a competitor.

2. Reintroduce Children's ASPIRIN worldwide as a prevention product and rename it under the brand ASPIRIN 100®.

    This would require repackaging, relabeling, and reindicating the brand. While the new brand might accelerate the cannibalization of Pharma's sales, it could also attract users from competitive brands.

Whatever the outcome, the decision had to be balanced with respect to the growth (38% CAGR for five years of Children's ASPIRIN sales to prevention customers) of a product whose customers were not even being targeted.

Zander and Merker discussed the implications of each decision in an effort to develop some assumptions to model the outcomes of each.

Zander: If we retract Children's ASPIRIN to solve our cannibalization problem, we could at best keep 75% of our current prevention customers of Children's ASPIRIN and transfer them to our high-end products. We may transfer more than 75%, but to be conservative in our approach, let's assume we lose 25% to the competition.

Merker: But, don't we also run the risk of losing the low-end prevention business altogether, if that's what we see developing before us: a market for low-end prevention aspirin? Won't a competitor come in and offer a low-cost 100 mg. aspirin geared toward prevention?

Zander: Maybe, so let's look at this in terms of best and worst possible outcomes, with a middle scenario assuming that we keep 50% of the prevention customers, and transfer them to the higher end.

Merker: Now, let's consider what might happen if instead of retracting the product, we, instead, give into this low-end demand, and we reintroduce Children's ASPIRIN as ASPIRIN 100® completely geared toward the prevention customer. We exit the children's market, but we keep essentially the same product on the market, just under a different name.

Zander: In that case, I see two scenarios. Under the first scenario, we essentially create attention for ourselves and the market reacts. As a result, Pharma's high-end product, CardioASPIRIN®, loses 10% of its sales due to our cheaper alternative. However, we also appropriate incremental sales of 10% from the competition. Beyond that, by keeping the product on the market, though in a new form, we are able to keep 20% of the children's ASPIRIN customers.

    Under the second scenario, I envision that the market does the opposite and reacts very little to our product change. Thus, Pharma doesn't lose any volume, and Consumer Care is unable to gain any incremental volume from the competition. Either way, we still keep 20% of the children's ASPIRIN customers.

The decisions and their assumptions are summarized in Exhibit 7. Also refer to Exhibits 8 through 10 to understand the quantitative forecasts modeled under each scenario.

Of course, the implied third option was to do nothing, but with the numbers looking as they did, how could Bayer not take any action?

EVALUATING THE OPTIONS

1. Given the respective scenarios and the projections described in the exhibits for each option, evaluate and choose the alternative that best optimizes Bayer's prevention *and* children's businesses. Explain.

2. Do you agree with the quantitative assumptions used to develop the forecasts? Why or why not?

3. What other nonquantitative factors should be considered as part of this decision, such as brand or strategic implications? Is this simply an economic decision or are there other factors not captured by the numbers that should be considered before deciding on a course of action?

exhibit 7   **Market Development**

Decision Structure

CC-EU-NB/MR

STAY IN   GET OUT   ← Decisions

| Business-as usual | Market Pullout |

Options →

| Retract | Reintroduce |

Possible →
Outcomes

Best
Transfer 75% of current prev. customers to high-end

Middle
Transfer 50% of current prev. customers, lose the other 50%

Worst
Transfer 0% of current prev. customers. Lose low-end prevention business to competition

Reactive Market
• Pharma loses 10% due to cheaper CC alternative
• CC gets 10% incremental prevention volume from competition
• CC keeps 20% of children users

Nonreactive Market
• Pharma does not lose any volume
• CC cannot get incremental volume
• CC still keeps 20% of children users

---

exhibit 8   **Children's ASPIRIN Business Forecast, 1998* (US$ in 000s)**

	1998 (Actual)	1999	2000	2001	2002	2003	Cumulative
Children's ASPIRIN (based on current business model)							
Children's share of sales (forecast)	55%	49%	43%	37%	32%	27%	
Sales forecast (combined sales from children and prevention)	$37,547	$37,989	$39,016	$40,664	$42,980	$46,021	$244,216
Children sales	20,761	18,685	16,816	15,135	13,621	12,259	97,277
Prevention sales	16,786	19,304	22,199	25,529	29,359	33,762	146,939
Net margin	$11,264	$11,397	$11,705	$12,199	$12,894	$13,806	$ 73,265
Margins							
Children's ASPIRIN	30%						
CardioASPIRIN®	20%						

*All numbers are disguised.

exhibit 9 **Option One: Retract ($US in 000s)***

	1998 (Actual)	1999	2000	2001	2002	2003	Cumulative
Incremental business transferred to Pharma							
Best case—total	$18,881	$21,713	$24,970	$28,716	$33,023	$37,977	$165,281
Net margin	3,776	4,343	4,994	5,743	6,605	7,595	33,056
Middle case—total	12,587	14,476	16,647	19,144	22,016	25,318	110,187
Net margin	2,517	2,895	3,329	3,829	4,403	5,064	22,037
Worst case—total	6,294	7,238	8,323	9,572	11,008	12,659	55,094
Net margin	1,259	1,448	1,665	1,914	2,202	2,532	11,019
Net effect (incremental sales—sales forecast, based on current business model)							
Sales gain/loss Bayer (CC/Ph)							
Best	−$18,666	−$16,275	−$14,045	−$11,948	−$9,957	−$8,045	−$78,936
Middle	−24,959	−23,513	−22,369	−21,520	−20,964	−20,704	−134,029
Worst	−31,253	−30,751	−30,692	−31,092	−31,972	−33,363	−189,123
Net effect (incremental margins—margin forecast, current business model)							
Net margin gain/loss Bayer (CC/Ph)							
Best	−$7,488	−$7,054	−$6,711	−$6,456	−$6,289	−$6,211	−$40,209
Middle	−8,747	−8,501	−8,375	−8,370	−8,491	−8,743	−51,227
Worst	−10,005	−9,949	−10,040	−10,285	−10,692	−11,275	−62,246

*All numbers are disguised.

exhibit 10a **Option Two: Reintroduce, Reactive Market ($US in 000s)***

Scenario I

Pharma loses 10% volume due to cheaper CC alternative	10%	
CC gets 10% incremental prevention volume from competition	10%	
CC can keep 20% of children users	20%	

		1998 (Actual)	1999	2000	2001	2002	2003	Cumulative
Pharma (forecast based on current business model)	Sales	$21,104	$27,230	$34,265	$37,272	$40,335	$42,150	$202,356
	Margin	4,221	5,446	6,853	7,454	8,067	8,430	40,471
Pharma (forecast, scenario assumptions)	Sales	18,993	24,507	30,838	33,544	36,302	37,935	182,120
	Margin	3,799	4,901	6,168	6,709	7,260	7,587	36,424
Pharma gain / loss (net effect)	Sales	−2,110	−2,723	−3,426	−3,727	−4,034	−4,215	−20,236
	Margin	−422	−545	−685	−745	−807	−843	−4,047
CC (forecast, current business model)	Sales	37,541	37,989	39,016	40,664	42,980	46,021	244,210
	Margin	11,262	11,397	11,705	12,199	12,894	13,806	73,263
CC (forecast, scenario assumptions)	Sales	22,613	24,971	27,782	31,109	35,019	39,590	181,085
	Margin	4,523	4,994	5,556	6,222	7,004	7,918	36,217
CC gain / loss (net effect)	Sales	−14,928	−13,018	−11,233	−9,555	−7,961	−6,431	−63,126
	Margin	−6,740	−6,402	−6,148	−5,977	−5,890	−5,888	−37,046
CC & Pharma gain / loss (net effect)	Sales	−17,038	−15,741	−14,660	−13,282	−11,995	−10,646	−83,361
	Margin	−7,162	−6,947	−6,833	−6,723	−6,697	−6,731	−41,093

*All numbers are disguised.

exhibit 10b　**Option Two: Reintroduce, Nonreactive Market ($US in 000s)***

Scenario II								
Pharma doesn't lose volume due to cheaper CC alternative			0%					
CC doesn't get incremental prevention volume from competition			0%					
CC can keep 20% of children users			20%					

		1998 (Actual)	1999	2000	2001	2002	2003	Cumulative
Pharma (forecast based on current business model)	Sales	$21,104	$27,230	$34,265	$37,272	$40,335	$42,150	$202,356
	Margin	4,221	5,446	6,853	7,454	8,067	8,430	40,471
CC (forecast, current business model)	Sales	37,541	37,989	39,016	40,664	42,980	46,021	244,210
	Margin	11,262	11,397	11,705	12,199	12,894	13,806	73,263
CC prevention (forecast, prevention portion only)	Sales	16,783	19,304	22,199	25,529	29,359	33,762	146,936
CC +20% of children users	Sales	4,152	3,737	3,363	3,027	2,724	2,452	19,455
CC total	Sales	20,935	23,041	25,563	28,556	32,083	36,214	166,391
	Margin	4,187	4,608	5,113	5,711	6,417	7,243	33,278
CC gain / loss (net effect)	Sales	−16,606	−14,948	−13,453	−12,108	−10,897	−9,807	−77,819
	Margin	−3,321	−2,990	−2,691	−2,422	−2,179	−1,961	−15,564

*All numbers are disguised.

appendix | A

Gisela Latta, M.D.　　　May 20, 1999
CC-EU-PDC-Med

Medical Comment on the Publication
by Belay, Breese, Holman, Khan, Shahriari, and Schonberger:
"Reye's syndrome in the United States from 1981 through 1997"
(*New England Journal of Medicine* 340:1377–82, 1999)

In the aforementioned paper, the authors, all from the Division of Viral and Rickettsial Diseases, National Center for Infectious Disease, Center for Disease Control and Prevention (CDC), Atlanta, present an analysis of national surveillance data collected from December 1981 through November 1997 on the incidence of Reye's Syndrome (RS) in the USA. The surveillance system was based on voluntary reporting by practicing physicians and hospital personnel with the use of a standard case-report form.

Belay and colleagues focus on the decline of RS and correlate this observation with the reduction in the use of acetylsalicylic acid (ASA) in children. They claim that some reports of a possible relation between RS and ASA were causal for the decline from 555 cases of RS in 1980 to no more than 36 cases per year since 1987. A close look at the literature cited as proof for this statement reveals that just one of the five publications derives from 1980, the others were published in 1982, 1985, and 1987! It appears more than improbable that these few papers published in scientific journals were sufficient for not only drawing public attention to this subject but even influence the attitude of parents concerning the use of anti-pyretic drugs for their children. Should this be the reason for the substantial reduction of RS in the following years (1981: 297 cases, 1982: 213, 1983: 198, 1984: 204, 1985: 93, 1986: 101, 1987: 36,

1988: 25, 1989: 25) ? As another point, the authors mention the "surgeon general's advisory" in 1982 (see figure 1, p. 1379). The official warning of RS on ASA products, however, the most important source of information for consumers, was only demanded by the FDA in 1986!

So what could really be the cause for the decline of RS in these years? One important answer is the discovery of so-called "inborn errors of metabolism," hereditary enzyme defects of infants and small children resulting in symptoms very similar to RS. The existence of these metabolic diseases is just mentioned in the text by Belay et al., but they do not say that this increase in diagnostic possibilities due to progress in medical and biochemical research occurred at the same time as the decline of RS as well: the more inborn errors of metabolism were discovered (today nearly thirty entities can be differentiated!), the fewer "true" cases of RS were diagnosed!

According to the CDC's definition, RS is an "exclusion diagnosis": only if all other possible explanations for the clinical symptoms have been ruled out, the diagnosis "RS" is correct! Has this always been the case? A reappraisal of diagnosis in 49 presumptive cases of RS suggests the opposite (Gauthier et al., 1989): the original diagnosis was considered certain in 1 case (2%), probable in 11 (22%), unlikely in 21 (43%), and excluded in 15 (31%)! However, this study derives from Canada, not the US! Belay et al. do not express any doubts about the validity of the data their assumptions are based on. There were certainly no such things like selection bias, recall bias, data collection bias, or categorization bias.

In this publication, the authors report that antecedent illness was reported in 93% of children and detectable blood salicylate levels in 82%. However, do "detectable" salicylate blood levels prove any causal relationship between the drug and the disease? In a study of 130 biopsy-proven cases of RS, Partin et al. (1982) measured serum salicylate concentrations; they came to the conclusion that "it is impossible to determine from this data whether salicylates are involved in the etiology of or in determining the outcome of Reye's disease. Increased concentrations of salicylates at admission could be the result of excessive dosage because of a greater severity of the prodromal illness; or to diminished excretion because of impaired hepatic metabolism." Even if the authors' statement were correct, then RS occurred in 18% of all cases in spite of the absence of ASA! Moreover in other countries, this percentage is much higher: 73% in South Africa, 80% in Germany, and 89% in Hong Kong; in a report from the Mayo Clinic, again 80% of the patients had not been given ASA (Smith, 1996). In Australia, not ASA but paracetamol/acetaminophen was found to be linked to RS (Orlowski, 1987).

To summarize, there is nothing new in this publication: it is just the repetition of well-known prejudices! Belay and co-workers only create the appearance of accuracy but they do not question the validity of the data they handle. Moreover, as the authors do not mention any argument in favor of ASA (as e.g. the time point when the inborn errors of metabolism were discovered!), it becomes obvious that for the CDC, ASA is still the culprit causing RS—although this has never been proven in any study!

However, from an international perspective, things look different. Professor David Stumpf from the Northwestern University Medical School, Chicago, wrote in 1995: "In the United States, epidemiological studies noted an association of Reye's syndrome with aspirin. This led to promulgation of professional and government guidelines that essentially eliminated the use of aspirin in children. Most Americans believe that the subsequent decline in Reye's syndrome is related to this change in practice pattern. However, the experiences in other countries suggest otherwise. In Japan there was no change in aspirin use. In Australia and India, aspirin was not in wide general use. Yet the decline in Reye's syndrome was equally dramatic in America, Japan and Australia. Clearly other factors were involved in the disappearance of Reye's syndrome."

Nothing further . . .

Gisela Latta, M.D.

Literature:

Gauthier M, Guay J, Lacroix J, Lortie A:
Reye's syndrome—A reappraisal of diagnosis in 49 presumptive cases.
AJDC 143:1181–1185, 1989

Orlowski JP, Campbell P, Goldstein S:
Reye's syndrome: a case control study of medication use and associated viruses in Australia.
Cleveland Clin J Med 57:323–329, 1990

Partin JS, Partin JC, Schubert WK, Hammond JG:
Serum salicylate concentrations in Reye's disease—A study of 130 biopsy-proven cases.
Lancet I:191–194, 1982

Smith TCG:
Reye's syndrome and the use of aspirin.
Scot Med J 41:4–9, 1996

Stumpf DA:
Reye syndrome: an international perspective.
Brain & Development 17:77–78, 1995

appendix | B

Joachim Zander

Education
10/1976–02/1980   University of Cologne
                                 Business Economics; focus: Marketing

Work Experience
01/1982–05/1986   Marketing Controller
                                 Bayer; Business Group: Pharma
                                 Leverkusen, Germany
06/1986–06/1989   Financial Controller
                                 Bayer—Miles; Business Group: Biotechnology
                                 Paris, France

07/1989–04/1990	Product Manager Bayer; Business Group: Selfmedication Leverkusen, Germany
05/1990–12/1995	Head of International Brand Management ASPIRIN Bayer; Business Group: Consumer Care Leverkusen, Germany
01/1996–12/1997	Regional Country Management Southeast Asia Bayer; Business Group: Consumer Care; Region: Asia/South America Leverkusen, Germany
01/1998–02/1999	Team Leader within the Global Strategy Group Analgesics Bayer; Business Group: Consumer Care Leverkusen, Germany
03/1999–present	Head of New Business and Marketing Research Bayer; Business Group: Consumer Care; Region: Europe Leverkusen, Germany

Extracurricular Activities
Travelling throughout the world; wine tasting; jogging

Harley-Davidson

John E. Gamble
University of South Alabama

Roger Schäfer
University of South Alabama

Harley-Davidson's management had much to be proud of as the company wrapped up its Open Road Tour centennial celebration, which had begun in July 2002 in Atlanta, Georgia, and ended on the 2003 Memorial Day weekend in Harley's hometown of Milwaukee, Wisconsin. The 14-month Open Road Tour was a tremendous success, drawing large crowds of Harley owners in each of its five stops in North America and additional stops in Australia, Japan, Spain, and Germany. Each stop along the tour included exhibits of historic motorcycles; performances by dozens of bands as diverse as Lynyrd Skynyrd, Earl Scruggs, and Nickelback; and hundreds of thousands of Harley enthusiasts who came together to celebrate the company's products. The Ride Home finale brought 700,000 biker-guests from four points in the United States to Milwaukee for a four-day party that included concerts, factory tours, and a parade of 10,000 motorcycles through downtown Milwaukee. The company also used the Open Road Tour as a platform to support its association with the Muscular Dystrophy Association (MDA)—raising $7 million for the MDA in the process. Photos from the Open Road Tour are presented in Exhibit 1, along with a photo of the company's new V-Rod model.

Also in its centennial year, Harley-Davidson was named to *Fortune*'s list of "100 Best Companies to Work For" and was judged third in automotive quality behind Rolls-Royce and Mercedes-Benz by Harris Interactive, a worldwide market research and consulting firm best known for the Harris Poll. Consumer loyalty to Harley-Davidson motorcycles was unmatched by almost any other company. As a Canadian Harley dealer explained, "You know you've got strong brand loyalty when your customers tattoo your logo on their arm."[1] The company's revenues had grown at a compounded annual rate of 16.6 percent since 1994 to reach $4.6 billion in 2003—marking the 18th consecutive year of record revenues and earnings. In 2003, the company sold more than 290,000 motorcycles, giving it a commanding share of the 651+ cubic centimeter (cc) motorcycle market in the United States and the leading share of the market in the Asia/Pacific region. The consistent growth had allowed Harley-Davidson's share price to appreciate by more than 15,000 percent since the company's initial public offering in 1986.

In January 2004, the company's CEO, Jeffrey Bleustein, commented on the centennial year and the company's prospects for growth as it entered its second century:

> We had a phenomenal year full of memorable once-in-a-lifetime experiences surrounding our 100th Anniversary. As we begin our 101st year, we expect to grow the business further with our proven ability to deliver a continuous stream of exciting new motorcycles, related products, and services. We have set a new goal for the company to be able to satisfy a yearly demand of 400,000 Harley-Davidson motorcycles in 2007. By offering innovative products and services, and by driving productivity gains in all facets of our business, we are confident that we can deliver an earnings growth rate in the mid-teens for the foreseeable future.[2]

However, not everyone was as bullish on Harley-Davidson's future. Analysts pointed out that the company had achieved its record growth during the 1990s

[1]As quoted in "Analyst Says Harley's Success Had Been to Drive into Buyers' Hearts," *Canadian Press Newswire,* July 14, 2003.

[2]As quoted in a January 21, 2004, press release.

exhibit 1   **Photos from Harley-Davidson's Open Road Tour and Its VRSC V-Rod**

and early 2000s primarily through the appeal of its image with baby boomers in the United States. Some questioned how much longer boomers would choose to spend recreational time touring the country by motorcycle and attending motorcycle rallies. The company had yet to develop a motorcycle that appealed in large numbers to motorcycle riders in their 20s or cy-

clists in Europe who both preferred performance-oriented bikes rather than cruisers or touring motor-cycles. Another concern of analysts watching the company was Harley-Davidson's short-term oversup-ply of certain models brought about by the 14-month production run for its 100th anniversary models. The effect of the extended production period shortened the waiting list for most models from over a year to a few months and left some models on showroom floors for immediate purchase. The combined effects of a market focus on a narrow demographic group, the difficulty experienced in gaining market share in Europe, and short-term forecasting problems led to a sell-off of Harley-Davidson shares going into 2004. Exhibit 2 presents a summary of Harley-Davidson's financial and operating performance for 1994–2003. Its market performance for 1994 through January 2004 is presented in Exhibit 3.

COMPANY HISTORY

Harley-Davidson's history began in 1903 when 20-year-old Arthur Davidson convinced his father to build a small shed in their backyard where Davidson and 21-year-old William Harley could try their hand at building a motorcycle. Various types of motorized bicycles had been built since 1885, but the 1901 development of a motorcycle with an integrated engine by a French company inspired Davidson and Harley to develop their own motorcycle. The two next-door neighbors built a two-horsepower engine that they fit onto a modified bicycle frame. At first the motorcycle could not pull itself and a rider up a steep hill, but after some additional tinkering, the first Harley-Davidson motorcycle could run as fast as 25 miles per hour. Milwaukee residents were amazed as Harley and Davidson rode the motorcycle down local streets, and by the end of the year they were able to produce and sell three of their motorcycles. Walter Davidson joined his brother and William Harley during the year to help assemble and race the company's motorcycles. In 1905 a Harley-Davidson motorcycle won a 15-mile race in Chicago with a time of 19:02, and by 1907 the company had developed quite a reputation in motorcycle racing with numerous wins in Milwaukee-area races. In 1907 another Davidson brother, William, joined the company and the company began adding dealers. Harley-Davidson's dealers helped the company sell 150 motorcycles in 1907.

In 1909, to keep its edge in racing, Harley-Davidson developed a more powerful seven-horsepower motorcycle engine that turned out to define the look of the company's motorcycles. The engine's twin cylinders joined at a 45-degree angle became a trademark Harley-Davidson design characteristic and created a distinctive "potato-potato-potato" sound.

Harley designed his V-twin engine with two pistons connected to a single crankpin, whereas later designs used crankpins for each piston. The single-crankpin design has been called inferior because it causes the pistons to come into firing positions at uneven intervals, which produces an uneven cadence in sound and excessive vibrations. Nevertheless, the vibrations and distinctive rumble of a Harley engine were accepted by the market in the early 1900s and continued to appeal to motorcyclists in the early 2000s.

The stronger engine allowed the company not only to produce 17,000 motorcycles for the U.S. military during World War I but also to become the largest motorcycle producer in the world by 1920, with 2,000 dealers in 67 countries. A number of features that make up Harley-Davidson's image originated during the 1920s, including the teardrop gas tank, its "Hog" nickname, and its "Flathead" engine design. By relying on exports and sales to police departments and the U.S. military, Harley-Davidson became one of two U.S. motorcycle companies (the other being Indian) to survive the Great Depression. The 1930s saw Harley-Davidson win more races and develop additional elements of its differentiated image, including the art deco eagle design painted on its gas tanks, three-tone paint, and the "Knucklehead" engine rocker boxes. Harley-Davidson's 1936 EL model, or Knucklehead, became its first highly styled motorcycle and formed the foundation of style elements that remained present in the highly demanded 2004 Softail Fat Boy. The company suspended production of civilian motorcycles in 1941 to produce almost 90,000 motorcycles for the U.S. military during World War II.

The recreational motorcycle market grew dramatically after World War II, as ex-GIs purchased motorcycles and led enthusiasm for riding. Harley-Davidson introduced new models for enthusiasts, including the Hydra-Glide in 1949, the K-model in 1952, the Sportster in 1957, and the Duo-Glide in 1958. The combination of racing success—Harley-Davidson riders won 18 of 24 races and set six new racing records in 1950 alone—and innovative new Harley-Davidson models led to Indian's demise in 1953. Harley-Davidson would remain the sole U.S. manufacturer of motorcycles until 1998, when the Indian brand was revived.

Harley-Davidson continued to win races throughout the 1960s, but its reputation began to erode soon after its acquisition by American Machine and Foundry Company (AMF) in 1969. Harley-Davidson *exhibit 2* **Summary of Harley-Davidson's Financial Performance, 1994–2003 (in thousands, except per share amounts)**

	2003	2002	2001	2000	1999	1998	1997	1996	1995	1994
Income statement data										
Net sales	$4,624,274	$4,090,970	$3,406,786	$2,943,346	$2,482,738	$2,087,670	$1,762,569	$1,531,227	$1,350,466	$1,158,887
Cost of goods sold	2,958,708	2,673,129	2,253,815	1,979,572	1,666,863	1,414,034	1,176,352	1,041,133	939,067	800,548
Gross profit	$1,665,566	$1,417,841	$1,152,971	$ 963,774	$ 815,875	$ 673,636	$ 586,217	$ 490,094	$ 411,399	$ 358,339
Operating income from financial services	167,873	104,227	61,273	37,178	27,685	20,211	12,355	7,801	3,620	—
Selling, administrative and engineering	(684,175)	(639,366)	(551,743)	(485,980)	(427,701)	(360,231)	(328,569)	(269,449)	(234,223)	(204,777)
Income from operations	$1,149,264	$ 882,702	$ 662,501	$ 514,972	$ 415,859	$ 333,616	$ 270,003	$ 228,446	$ 180,796	$ 153,562
Gain on sale of credit card business	—	—	—	18,915	—	—	—	—	—	—
Interest income, net	23,088	16,541	17,478	17,583	8,014	3,828	7,871	3,309	96	1,682
Other income (expense), net	(6,317)	(13,416)	(6,524)	(2,914)	(3,080)	(1,215)	(1,572)	(4,133)	(4,903)	1,196
Income from continuing operations before provision for income taxes and accounting changes	$1,166,035	$ 885,827	$ 673,445	$ 548,556	$ 420,793	$ 336,229	$ 276,302	$ 227,622	$ 175,989	$ 156,440
Provision for income taxes	405,107	305,610	235,709	200,843	153,592	122,729	102,232	84,213	64,939	60,219
Income from continuing operations before accounting changes	$ 760,928	$ 580,217	$ 437,746	$ 347,713	$ 267,201	$ 213,500	$ 174,070	$ 143,409	$ 111,050	$ 96,221
Income (loss) from discontinued operations, net of tax	—	—	—	—	—	—	—	22,619	1,430	8,051
Income before accounting changes	$ 760,928	$ 580,217	$ 437,746	$ 347,713	$ 267,201	$ 213,500	$ 174,070	$ 166,028	$ 112,480	$ 104,272
Cumulative effect of accounting changes, net of tax	—	—	—	—	—	—	—	—	—	—
Net income (loss)	$ 760,928	$ 580,217	$ 437,746	$ 347,713	$ 267,201	$ 213,500	$ 174,070	$ 166,028	$ 112,480	$ 104,272

(continues)

exhibit 2 **(concluded)**

	2003	2002	2001	2000	1999	1998	1997	1996	1995	1994
Weighted average common shares:										
Basic	302,271	302,297	302,506	302,691	304,748	304,454	151,650	150,683	149,972	150,440
Diluted	304,470	305,158	306,248	307,470	309,714	309,406	153,948	152,925	151,900	153,365
Earnings per common share from continuing operations:										
Basic	$2.52	$1.92	$1.45	$1.15	$0.88	$0.70	$1.15	$0.95	$0.74	$0.64
Diluted	$2.50	$1.90	$1.43	$1.13	$0.86	$0.69	$1.13	$0.94	$0.73	$0.63
Dividends paid	$0.195	$0.135	$0.115	$0.098	$0.088	$0.078	$0.135	$0.110	$0.090	$0.070
Balance sheet data										
Working capital	$1,773,354	$1,076,534	$ 949,154	$ 799,521	$ 430,840	$ 376,448	$ 342,333	$ 362,031	$ 288,783	$ 189,358
Current finance receivables, net	1,001,990	855,771	656,421	530,859	440,951	360,341	293,329	183,808	169,615	—
Long-term finance receivables, net	735,859	589,809	379,335	234,091	354,888	319,427	249,346	154,264	43,829	—
Total assets	4,923,088	3,861,217	3,118,495	2,436,404	2,112,077	1,920,209	1,598,901	1,299,985	980,670	676,663
Short-term finance debt	324,305	382,579	217,051	89,509	181,163	146,742	90,638	8,065	—	—
Long-term finance debt	670,000	380,000	380,000	355,000	280,000	280,000	280,000	250,000	164,330	—
Total debt	994,305	762,579	597,051	444,509	461,163	426,742	391,572	285,767	185,228	10,452
Shareholders' equity	$2,957,692	$2,232,915	$1,756,283	$1,405,655	$1,161,080	$1,029,911	$ 826,668	$ 662,720	$ 494,569	$ 433,232

Source: Harley-Davidson, Inc., 2003, 2002, and 1998 10-Ks.

exhibit 3   **Monthly Performance of Harley-Davidson, Inc.'s Stock Price, 1994 to January 2004**

(a) Trend in Harley-Davidson, Inc.'s Common Stock Price

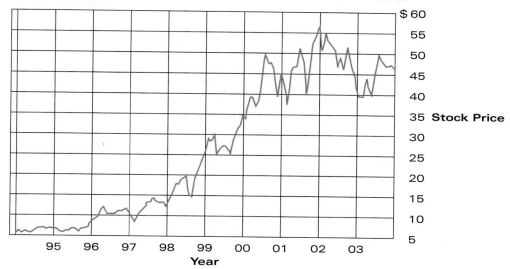

(b) Performance of Harley-Davidson, Inc.'s Stock Price Versus the S&P 500 Index

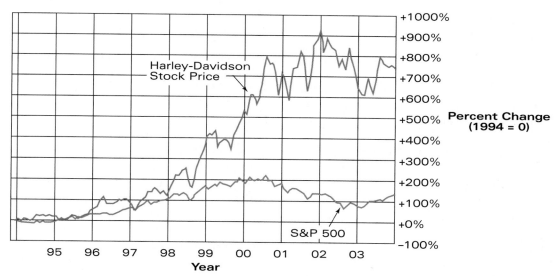

under AMF was known for its leaking engines, unreliable performance, and poor customer service. At one point during AMF's ownership of the company, more than one-half of its bikes had to be repaired before leaving the factory. The company attempted to offset its declining sales of road bikes with the introduction of dirt bikes and snowmobiles in the early 1970s, but by the late 1970s AMF lost faith in the acquisition and

slated it for divestiture. When no buyers for the company emerged, 13 executives engineered a leveraged buyout of Harley-Davidson in 1981. Harley-Davidson struggled under a heavy debt load and came within four hours of bankruptcy in 1985, before then-CEO Richard Teerlink was able to convince new creditors to step in and restructure Harley with less costly financing terms. Teerlink also launched a restructuring program that updated manufacturing methods, improved quality, and expanded the model line. U.S. tariffs imposed on 651+ cc Japanese motorcycles also aided Harley-Davidson in gaining financial strength and competitiveness in the heavyweight segment of the U.S. motorcycle industry.

Harley-Davidson completed an initial public offering in 1985 and petitioned the International Trade Commission to terminate tariffs on Japanese heavyweight motorcycles in 1987 when its market share in the U.S. heavyweight category had improved to 25 percent from 16 percent in 1985. The company purchased Wisconsin-based Buell Motorcycle in 1998, a performance brand using Harley-Davidson engines that began as a venture between Erik Buell and Harley-Davidson in 1992. Harley-Davidson opened its 358,000-square-foot Kansas City, Missouri, plant in 1998 to produce Sportster, Dyna Glide, and V-Rod models and built an assembly plant in Brazil in 1999 to aid in its Latin American expansion. The new capacity allowed Harley-Davidson to set production records each year during the early 2000s to reach 290,000 units by year-end 2003.

OVERVIEW OF THE MOTORCYCLE INDUSTRY

Demand for motorcycles in developed countries such as the United States, Germany, France, Spain, and Great Britain grew dramatically after World War II as veterans who enjoyed riding motorcycles during the war purchased their own bikes upon return to civilian life. Groups of enthusiasts began to form motorcycle clubs through which they socialized and participated in rallies and races. Two of the earliest motorcycle rallies in the United States were the Daytona Bike Week in Florida and the Sturgis Rally in South Dakota. The first Daytona 200, held during Bike Week, was run in 1937 on a 3.2-mile beach and road course. The first Sturgis race took place in 1938 when nine participants raced a half-mile track and performed such stunts as jumping ramps and crashing through plywood walls. These two and other such events grew dramatically in popularity beginning in the 1970s; the Daytona Bike Week and the Sturgis Rally each drew over 200,000 bikers in 2003. The Sturgis Rally was said to be among the most raucous motorcycle rallies in the United States—

plenty of public drunkenness and lewd behavior accompanied the seven days of races. Such behavior was common enough that the rally Web site (www.sturgis.com) listed the fines and bonds associated with such offenses as indecent exposure, disorderly conduct, possession of open containers in public, and possession of controlled substances.

The rowdy and rebellious image of bikers can be traced to some of the motorcycle clubs that began after World War II. The outlaw image of cyclists first developed in 1947 when *Life* magazine photographers captured images of an impromptu rally at Hollister, California, by a motorcycle group calling themselves the Boozefighters. The group became quite rowdy during their motorcycling exhibition, but *Life* reporters embellished the story significantly, claiming the Boozefighters descended on the town and proceeded to terrorize its residents by drag-racing down the main street, tossing beer bottles, and riding motorcycles through the front doors of the town's saloon. The imagery of the drunken Fourth of July attack on the town became etched deeper into the minds of the world when the story became the subject of *The Wild One,* a 1954 movie starring Marlon Brando. When asked by a local resident what he was rebelling against, Brando's character Johnny replied, "Whaddya got?"[3]

If the general public came to dislike bikers because of incidents like the one in Hollister and because of the Hollywood treatment of the event, Hells Angels made many people fearful of bikers and put motorcycle gangs under the close scrutiny of law enforcement at local, state, and federal levels. The Hells Angels Motorcycle Club was established in 1948 in Fontana, California, by a group of young cyclists who had read of the Hollister rampage and wished to start their own outlaw biker group. The club, which took its name and symbols from various World War II flying units, became notorious during the 1960s when it became linked to drug trafficking and other organized crime activities. Sonny Barger, a founder of the Oakland, California, chapter in the late 1950s, became the United States' most infamous biker after organizing a disastrous security effort for the 1969 Rolling Stones concert in Altamont, at which one concertgoer was stabbed to death by Hells Angels members. Barger, who after the event was

---

[3]As quoted in "Wings of Desire," *The Independent,* August 27, 2003.

convicted of attempted murder, possession of narcotics with intent to sell, and assault with a deadly weapon, commented in a 2000 interview with BBC that he had pressed a pistol into Rolling Stones guitarist Keith Richards' ribs and ordered him to continue to play after threatening to end his band's show because of Hells Angels' rough tactics with the fans.[4]

Hells Angels and rival motorcycle clubs like the Pagans, Banditos, and Outlaws, rode only Harleys, which hurt Harley-Davidson's image with the public in the 1960s and beyond. Honda successfully exploited Harley's outlaw image with the slogan "You meet the nicest people on a Honda" to become the largest seller of motorcycles in the United States during the late 1960s and early 1970s.[5] The Hells Angels image spilled over to the entire industry and contributed to declines in motorcycle demand in the United States and Europe before a new Hollywood film resurrected interest in motorcycles. When it premiered in 1969, *Easy Rider* portrayed bikers as less villainous rebels and appealed greatly to young people in the United States and Europe. The movie eventually gained cult status and helped charge a demand for motorcycles that continued through 2003. The red-white-and-blue 1951 Harley "Captain America" chopper ridden in the movie by Peter Fonda's Wyatt character helped Harley-Davidson break the outlaw image and come to represent less malevolent rebellion.

Industry Conditions in 2003

In 2003, there were more than 950,000 motorcycles sold in the United States and 28 million in operation worldwide. The industry was expected to grow by approximately 5 percent annually through 2007, with light motorcycles, mopeds, and scooters accounting for most of the expected growth. A rising income level in such emerging markets as China, India, and Southeast Asia was the primary force expected to drive industry growth. Demand growth for the heavyweight motorcycle category had outpaced smaller motorcycles in the United States during the 1990s and into 2003, but analysts projected that demand for larger motorcycles would decline as the population aged and became less able to travel on two-wheelers.

[4]As quoted in "Born to Raise Hell," *BBC News Online,* August 14, 2000.

[5]"Wheel Life Experiences," *Whole Pop Magazine Online.*

In 2002, demand for heavyweight motorcycles in the United States grew by 17 percent compared to an industrywide growth rate of 10 percent.

The industry was segmented into various groups according to engine size and vehicle style. Mopeds, scooters, and some small motorcycles were equipped with engines having displacements of 50 cc or less. These motorbikes were best suited for urban areas where streets were narrow and parking was limited or for developing countries in which personal incomes were limited and consumers could make only small investments in transportation. Motorcycles used for basic transportation or for motocross events were typically equipped with engines ranging from 125 to 650 cc. Larger street bikes required more power and usually had engines over 650 cc. Large motorcycles with engine displacements greater than 651 cc accounted for the largest portion of demand in North America and Europe as riders increasingly chose motorcycles with more horsepower and better performance. Exhibit 4 presents registrations of 651+ cc motorcycles in the United States, Europe, and Asia/Pacific for 1998–2003. Even though it had fewer registrations of 651+ cc motorcycles than the United States, Europe was the world's largest market for motorcycles, with 1.1 million registrations of 125+ cc motorcycles in 2002. Registrations of motorcycles with engine displacements greater than 125 cc in the largest European markets are presented in Exhibit 5.

Segmentation within the 651+ cc Category

Motorcycles in the 651+ cc segment were referred to as heavyweights and were grouped into four categories: standard, performance, custom, and touring. Standard heavyweight motorcycles were designed for low-cost transportation and lacked many of the features and accessories of more expensive classes of heavyweights. Performance bikes had streamlined styling, low-profile fairings, and seat and handlebar configurations that required the rider to lean forward; they were characterized by responsive handling, rapid acceleration, and high top-end speeds. Custom motorcycles ranged from motorcycles with a custom paint scheme to highly personalized bikes painted with murals or other designs, chrome frames and other components, and accessories not found on stock motorcycles. Among the more unusual custom

exhibit 4 **Market Shares of the Leading Producers of Motorcycles by Geographic Region for the Heavyweight Segment, 1998–2003 (Engine Displacement of 651+ cc)**

	2003	2002	2001	2000	1999	1998
New U.S. registrations (thousands of units)						
Harley-Davidson	228.4	209.3	177.4	155.1	134.5	109.1
Buell	3.5	2.9	2.6	4.2	3.9	3.2
Total company new registrations	231.9	212.2	180.0	159.3	138.4	112.3
Total market new registrations	461.2	442.3	394.3	340.0	275.6	227.1
Percentage market share						
Harley-Davidson	49.5%	47.5%	45.0%	45.6%	48.8%	48.1%
Buell	0.8	0.7	0.7	1.2	1.4	1.4
Total	50.3%	48.2%	45.7%	46.8%	50.2%	49.5%
Honda	18.4	19.8%	20.5%	18.5%	16.4%	20.3%
Suzuki	9.8	9.6	10.8	9.3	9.4	10
Kawasaki	6.7	6.9	8	9	10.3	10.1
Yamaha	8.5	8.9	7.9	8.4	7	4.2
Other	6.3	6.6	7.1	8	6.7	5.9
Total	100.0%	100.0%	100.0%	100.0%	100.0%	100.0%
New European registrations (thousands of units)						
Total market new registrations	323.1	303.5	292.1	293.4	306.7	270.2
Total Harley-Davidson new registrations	26.3	20.1	19.6	19.9	17.8	15.7
Percentage market share						
Total Harley-Davidson	8.1%	6.6%	6.7%	6.8%	5.8%	5.8%
Honda	16.7	21.0	17.4	21.8	22.2	24.1
Yamaha	16.0	17.7	16.4	17.3	18.0	16.3
BMW	15.3	15.1	15.1	13.0	13.0	13.4
Suzuki	15.5	14.8	16.5	14.3	15.4	17.2
Other	28.4	24.8	27.9	26.8	25.6	23.2
Total	100.0%	100.0%	100.0%	100.0%	100.0%	100.0%
New Asia/Pacific registrations (thousands of units)						
Total market new registrations	58.9	63.9	62.1	62.7	63.1	69.2
Total Harley-Davidson new registrations	15.2	13.0	12.7	12.2	11.6	10.3
Percentage market share						
Total Harley-Davidson	25.8%	21.3%	20.4%	19.5%	18.5%	14.8%
Honda	17.8	19.1	17.3	20.4	22.4	28.0
Kawasaki	13.8	15.8	15.6	18.9	19.0	22.1
Yamaha	11.4	13.6	15.8	17.0	19.0	16.0
Suzuki	10.7	10.1	12.8	10.4	9.3	7.9
Other	20.5	20.1	18.1	13.8	11.8	11.2
Total	100.0%	100.0%	100.0%	100.0%	100.0%	100.0%

Source: Harley-Davidson, Inc., 10-Ks and annual reports.

exhibit 5 **Registrations of New Motorcycles in Major European Markets, 1998–2002 (Engine Displacement of 125+ cc)**

Country	1998	1999	2000	2001	2002
Germany	175,937	187,192	170,636	158,270	145,369
Italy	79,400	103,800	122,085	126,400	129,261
France	88,500	109,105	103,900	106,802	113,852
Great Britain	84,500	98,186	93,634	91,543	93,557
Spain	35,600	39,200	38,052	31,829	35,252

Sources: Association des Constructerus Européens de Motocycle, Brussels; Industrie-Verband Motorrad Deutschland e.V.

styles was the chopper, limited only by designers' imaginations but typically featuring extended forks, high handlebars, a narrow front tire, and a rigid "hardtail" frame design that lacked rear shocks and was stretched longer than that of normal motorcycles. Another notable feature of custom choppers was that they were almost always built from stock Harley-Davidson motorcycles, sometimes retaining only the engine.

Custom bikes were the largest segment of the U.S. heavyweight market for motorcycles and had become a curiosity for noncyclists in the United States. The Discovery Channel regularly aired two programs dedicated to the topic of choppers and other custom vehicles. The names of two custom motorcycle shops, West Coast Choppers (WCC) and Orange County Choppers, frequently made the Internet search engine Lycos's list of 50 most-searched terms. Jesse James, a descendant of the famous American Old West outlaw and owner of West Coast Choppers, also made Lycos's list of most-searched terms. WCC charged between $60,000 and $150,000 for its custom motorcycles, which were usually sold to celebrities such as movie stars, professional athletes, and rock musicians.

Touring bikes were set apart from other categories by creature comforts and accessories that included large fairings, storage compartments, CD players, cruise control, and other features typically found on cars rather than on motorcycles. Touring bikes were popular in the United States since many baby boomers wished to enjoy biking in comfort. Comfortable saddles, upright riding positions, and other features found on touring bikes were especially welcomed by those who took cross-country or other long-distance journeys. Custom and touring motorcycles were less popular outside the United States

since cyclists in other countries were more likely to travel only short distances and did not necessarily identify with the individualist or outlaw image associated with heavyweights in the United States. The largest segment of the heavyweight motorcycle category outside the United States was the performance bike category since most riders in other countries preferred sleek styling and were more interested in speed and handling rather than comfort and tradition. In addition, motorcyclists in Europe and Asia tended to choose performance bikes over motorcycles in the custom and touring category because of the high relative prices of such motorcycles. Exhibit 6 presents a regional comparison of motorcycle registrations by heavyweight category for 1998 through 2002.

Competition in the Global Motorcycle Industry

Rivalry in the motorcycle industry centered on performance, styling, breadth of product line, image and reputation, quality of after-the-sale service, and price. Most motorcycle manufacturers had good reputations for performance and styling, with the greatest variance between brands occurring in pricing, variety of models, and quality of dealer service. Most cyclists preferred not to purchase specific brands, even if they were attracted to specific models, if the company's dealers did not have trained mechanics or had a reputation for shoddy workmanship or poor parts availability. There was also a great degree of price variability in the industry with comparable models of Japanese motorcycles typically carrying retail prices far below that of U.S.- or European-made motorcycles.

exhibit 6   **Regional Comparison of the 651+ cc Motorcycle Market by Segment, 1998–2002 (percent of units registered)***

	1998	1999	2000	2001	2002
United States					
Custom	58.4%	57.7%	56.6%	58.9%	60.3%
Touring	20.4	21.7	21.1	20.3	20.2
Performance	19.4	18.9	20.4	19.1	17.3
Standard	1.8	1.8	2.0	1.7	2.2
	100.0%	100.0%	100.0%	100.0%	100.0%
Europe					
Custom	22.8%	20.2%	17.6%	17.8%	13.8%
Touring	5.3	5.5	5.2	5.2	4.8
Performance	59.8	58.0	61.7	59.8	61.2
Standard	12.1	16.3	15.5	17.2	20.2
	100.0%	100.0%	100.0%	100.0%	100.0%
Asia/Pacific					
Custom	18.3%	28.6%	26.7%	23.9%	n/a
Touring	3.9	4.7	3.7	7.2	n/a
Performance	76.1	64.5	66.2	65.5	n/a
Standard	1.7	2.2	3.5	3.4	n/a
	100.0%	100.0%	100.0%	100.0%	n/a

*Category definitions:

Custom: Characterized by "American styling." Often personalized by accessorizing.

Touring: Designed primarily for long trips, with an emphasis on comfort, cargo capacity, and reliability. Often have features such as two-way radios (for communication with passenger), stereo, and cruise control.

Performance: Characterized by quick acceleration, top speed, and handling. Commonly referred to as "sport bikes."

Standard: A basic, no-frills motorcycle with an emphasis on low price.

Source: Harley-Davidson, Inc., 2003 and 2002 10-K reports.

Exhibits 7 and 8 illustrate the difficulty U.S. and European manufacturers had experienced in attracting price-sensitive buyers in Europe. The Japanese producers were able to offer high-performance motorcycles at prices below those of Harley-Davidson, Ducati, Triumph, or Moto Guzzi. BMW had achieved considerable success in Europe, especially in Germany, because of exceptional performance and reputation, a strong dealer network, and regional loyalty to the brand.

Motorcycle manufacturers, like automobile manufacturers, maintained relationships with suppliers to produce or assemble components such as upholstery, tires, engine parts, brake parts, wiring harnesses, shocks, and rims. Almost without exception, the manufacturer designed and manufactured its engines and frames. Design and assembly of motorcycles took place in the manufacturer's home country, and completed motorcycles were exported to country markets where dealer networks had been established.

Consumers typically evaluated brands by talking to other cyclists, reading product reviews, perusing company Web sites, noting ads in print and other media, and noting a manufacturer's performance in competitive events. Typically, consumers had some ability to negotiate prices with dealers, but most did prefer to buy from dealers with good service departments, large parts inventories, and attractive financing programs. Similarly, strong motorcycle dealers preferred to represent manufacturers with good reputations and strong consumer demand, responsive customer service and parts delivery, formal training programs for service technicians, and financing divisions that offered competitive rates and programs.

exhibit 7   **Market Shares of the Leading Sellers of Motorcycles in Germany, 2001–2003 (Engine Displacement of 125+ cc)**

Brand	2001	2002	2003*
Suzuki	21.7%	20.3%	19.2%
BMW	16.0	18.1	18.8
Honda	16.8	17.3	15.6
Yamaha	16.3	16.0	16.1
Kawasaki	11.1	10.7	10.8
KTM	3.1	3.8	4.4
Harley-Davidson	3.6	3.7	4.2
Ducati	2.8	2.8	2.9
Triumph	2.5	1.8	2.0
Aprilia	1.7	1.5	1.4
Moto Guzzi	0.6	0.7	0.9
Buell	0.4	0.3	0.7
MV/Cagiva	1.2	0.8	0.6
MZ	0.5	0.4	0.3
Sachs	0.3	0.2	0.2
Other	1.4	1.6	1.9
Total	100.0%	100.0%	100.0%

*Based on registrations occurring between January and November 2003.
Sources: Kraftfahrtbundesamt; Industrie-Verband Motorrad Deutschland e.V.

Consumers purchased motorcycles for various reasons. Some individuals, especially in developing countries, were looking for low-cost transportation. Lightweight motorcycles, mopeds, and scooters were priced inexpensively compared to cars and used far less gasoline. However, most riders also owned a car and used motorcycles for fair-weather transportation. In the United States and Europe, most consumers preferred to travel by motorcycle on weekends or other times they were not working. Some in Europe did choose to commute to and from work on motorcycles when weather permitted because of limited parking available in large European cities and the high cost of fuel. Many motorcycle owners, particularly those in the United States, looked at riding as a form of recreation and had given up other sports or hobbies to spend time touring on motorcycles. Many middle-aged bikers in the United States had purchased motorcycles after giving up sports and activities requiring more athleticism or endurance.

Regulation and Legal Challenges

The motorcycle industry was subject to laws and regulations in all countries in which motorcycles were operated. The European Parliament and the European Council included motorcycles in their agreement to reduce exhaust-gas values during their March 2002 meeting. The agreement required producers of motorcycles and scooters to reduce pollutants by 60 percent for all new cycles produced after April 2003. A further 60 percent reduction would be required for motorcycles produced after January 2006. Demand for motorcycles in Europe was impacted to a great degree by the implementation of the euro in 2002; prices of motorcycles increased substantially in some countries when the currency exchange took effect. For instance, because Germany's currency was much stronger than that of many other European Union countries, prices of most products and services increased in Germany after the change to the euro since the euro attempted to equalize the differences between currencies. The difficulty in obtaining a driver's license for motorcycles in some European countries also affected demand for motorcycles. Germany required separate automobile and motorcycle licenses for anyone born after 1980, and France required those applying for motorcycle licenses to have first held an automobile license for two years. Austria's licensing laws were the most restrictive—requiring applicants to first hold an automobile license for five years and to complete six training sessions prior to obtaining a motorcycle license. Motorcycles that produced excessive noise were also under attack in most European countries.

In the United States, motorcycle producers were subject to certification by the Environmental Protection Agency (EPA) for compliance with emission and noise standards, and agencies in some states imposed more stringent noise and emission standards. The California Air Resources Board (CARB) had outlined new tailpipe emission standards that would go into effect in 2004 and 2008. The EPA developed new emission standards that would go into effect in 2006 and 2010 to match national standards with

exhibit 8 **Best-Selling Motorcycle Models in Germany, November 2003**

Rank	Brand	Model	Manufacturers' Recommended Price (USD)	Year-to-Date 2003 Registrations	Heavyweight Classification
1	BMW	R 1150 GS	$14,500	6,100	Performance
2	Suzuki	GSF 1200 (KL)	7,399	3,963	Performance
3	Suzuki	SV 650	6,299	3,433	Standard
4	BMW	F 650 GS	8,190	3,304	Standard
5	Yamaha	FZS 600	6,499	3,230	Standard
6	Suzuki	GSF 600	6,299	3,175	Performance
7	Suzuki	GSX-R 1000	10,599	2,830	Performance
8	Kawasaki	Z1000	8,499	2,813	Performance
9	BMW	R 1150 RT	16,290	2,505	Touring
10	BMW	R 1150 R	9,990	2,469	Performance

Sources: Kraftfahrtbundesamt; Company Web sites.

those in California. Motorcycle producers in the United States were also required to meet the product safety standards imposed by the National Highway Traffic Safety Administration (NHTSA).

Also in the United States, many motorcyclists found that their health insurance providers excluded coverage for any injuries sustained while on a motorcycle. The American Motorcyclists Association (AMA) had successfully petitioned the U.S. Senate to pass a bill in October 2003 that would prohibit insurance companies from denying coverage to someone hurt while riding a motorcycle, snowmobile, or all-terrain vehicle. Insurance companies had based their policies on NHTSA statistics that found motorcycling to be much more dangerous than traveling by car. While traffic fatalities per 100 million vehicle miles traveled hit a historic low in 2002, motorcycle fatalities had increased for a fifth consecutive year to reach 3,244 deaths. There were 42,815 traffic fatalities in 2002 involving occupants of automobiles. Fatalities involving motorcyclists ages 50 and older increased by 26 percent during 2002—a higher rate of increase than any other age demographic. Legislatures in states where helmets were optional had attempted to force motorcyclists who chose not to wear helmets to become mandatory organ donors. However, the AMA and its membership had successfully stopped all such attempts to pass mandatory organ donor laws.

HARLEY-DAVIDSON'S STRATEGY FOR COMPETING IN THE MOTORCYCLE INDUSTRY

Harley-Davidson was reincorporated in 1981 after it was purchased by 13 of its managers through a leveraged buyout (LBO). The management team's main focus at the time was to preserve jobs, but managers soon realized that the company would need to be rebuilt from the ground up to survive. The company's market share in the United States had fallen to 3 percent, primarily because its products were unreliable and had poorer performance relative to less-expensive Japanese motorcycles. In addition, its network of dealers ran greasy, run-down shops that many people didn't feel comfortable visiting. Upon assessing the company's situation, the management team concluded that a strong allegiance to the Harley brand by many bikers was the company's only resource strength. However, when management began to meet with customers, they found that long time Harley riders felt cheated by the company and were angry about the lack of attention to product quality and customer service under AMF ownership. Some of the most loyal Harley riders refused to call models produced in the 1970s Harleys, preferring to label them as AMFs. After the LBO, Harley management tried to win over previous customers by attending any function at which motorcyclists congregated. The company's director of communications commented in a 2003 interview with a trade publication, "At first we found that our customers didn't like us, and they didn't trust us."[6] However, the distrust subsided when Harley owners saw their suggestions being implemented by the company.

Harley-Davidson's turnaround strategy including improving product quality by adopting Japanese management practices, abandoning a reliance on advertising in favor of promotions at motorcycle rallies, and improving its dealer network to broaden its appeal to new customers. After hearing complaints about dealers from Harley riders at rallies and other bike events, Harley-Davidson conducted a pilot program with two dealers in Milwaukee that called for the dealers to build clean, attractive stores to showcase Harley's improved motorcycles and display apparel and other merchandise that cyclists might wish to purchase. The two dealerships recaptured their investments within 18 months, while other dealers struggled. The pilot program led to new or remodeled dealerships across the Harley-Davidson network and helped the company enter into a new product category. Harley showrooms offered a large assortment of clothing items and such accessories as helmets, boots, leather jackets, and T-shirts in addition to new motorcycles. In 2003 Harley-Davidson introduced 1,200 new clothing items and licensed its name to more than 100 manufacturers making everything from Harley-Davidson Edition Ford F-150 pickups to Harley Barbie dolls. Apparel and accessories were so important to the company and its dealers that in 2003 every dealership had a fitting room.

Cultivating Loyalty through HOG Membership

After Harley-Davidson's product quality issues had been resolved, the company focused on cultivating the mystique of Harley ownership. The company formed Harley Owners Groups (HOGs) in 1983 to provide Harley owners with local clubs where they could socialize and ride with other owners. Harley-Davidson established HOGs in cities where dealers were located but did not interfere with HOGs' operations or try to use the organization in a self-serving way. The company's primary interest in setting up the chapters was to give motorcycle buyers a sense of community. Management understood that once new owners came to feel they belonged to the Harley community, they would bring new buyers to the company without any encouragement from Harley-Davidson.

The company provided each new Harley buyer with a free membership to a HOG, through which they could not only meet other area bikers but also learn the ins and outs of the biker world. HOGs also organized rides, raised money for charities, and participated in nationwide HOG events. Owners were required to renew their free memberships each year to ensure that only active participants would be on chapter rolls. The HOG organization started with 33,000 members in 1983 and had grown to 793,000 members in 1,200 chapters in 2003. The company sponsored about 100 HOG rallies in 2003, with thousands of additional events organized by local chapters.

Harley's Image and Appeal with Baby Boomers

Even though Harley-Davidson sold many motorcycles to construction workers, mechanics, and other blue-collar workers, Harley riders included a great many accountants, lawyers, bankers, and corporate executives. In 2003, Harley-Davidson's typical customer was 46-year-old male earning $78,000 a year. The company had successfully added upscale consumers to its list of customers without alienating the traditional biker. Some of the more traditional bikers did complain about the new breed of "bean counter" Harley owners, sometimes calling them "rubbers"— rich urban bikers. Such concern had been calmed to some degree by William G. Davidson's continuing involvement with the company. "Willie G." was the grandson of the company's cofounder and, as chief designer, had designed every motorcycle for the company since the 1960s. Willie G. was an "old-school" biker himself and rationalized the company's alliance with upscale baby boomers with comments

[6] As quoted in "Will Your Customers Tattoo Your Logo?" *Trailer/Body Builders,* March 1, 2003, p. 5.

such as "There's a lot of beaners, but they're out on the motorcycles, which is a beautiful thing."[7]

Part of the appeal of HOG membership was that new motorcyclists could experience freedom of the open road, much like a Hells Angel might, if only during occasional weekends when the weather was nice. Some middle-aged professionals purchased Harleys because riding was an opportunity to recreate and relax without being reminded of their daily responsibilities. Belonging to a HOG or other riding group was different from joining a country club or other club dominated by upper-income families. The CEO of a Fortune 500 company explained, "Nobody cares what anybody else does. We share a common bond of freedom on a bike"; he also claimed after a few hours of riding, he forgets he's a CEO.[8] Another affluent Harley owner suggested that Harley owners from all walks of life shared the brotherhood of the open road: "It doesn't matter if you make $10,000 a year or $300,000."[9] Others suggested that Harley ownership gave them an identity and provided them with a close group of friends in an increasingly anonymous culture.

However, other Harley owners were lured to the appeal of Harley-Davidson's outlaw image. The editor of *AARP Magazine* believed that baby boomers purchased Harleys because of a desire to feel "forever young."[10] The *AARP Magazine* editor said that riding a Harley helped take boomers back to a time when they had less responsibility. "You saw 'Easy Rider.' As a kid, you had a bit of a wild period in the '70s and you associate the motorcycle with that. But you got married. You had kids and a career. Now you can afford this. It's a safe way to live out a midlife crisis. It's a lot safer than running off with a stewardess."[11] In fact, many of Harley-Davidson's competitors have claimed that Harley sells lifestyles, not motorcycles. Harley-Davidson's CEO, Jeffrey Bleustein, commented on the appeal of the company's motorcycles by stating, "Harley-Davidson stands for freedom, adventure, individual expression and being a little on the edge, a little bit naughty. People are drawn to the brand for those reasons."[12]

The desire to pose as a Hells Angel, Peter Fonda's Wyatt character, or Marlon Brando's Johnny helped Harley-Davidson sell more than 290,000 motorcycles and over $200 million in general merchandise in 2003. Many of Harley-Davidson's 1,400 dealers dedicated as much as 75 percent of their floor space to apparel and accessories, with most suggesting that between 25 and 40 percent of their annual earnings came from the sale of leather jackets, chaps, boots, caps, helmets, and other accessories. One dealer offered her opinion of what drove merchandise sales by commenting, "Today's consumer tends to be a little more affluent, and they want the total look."[13] The dealer also said that approximately 5 percent of the dealership's apparel sales were to nonbike owners who wanted the biker image. Even though some high-income baby boomers wanted to be mistaken from a distance for Hells Angels' "1 percenters"—the most rebellious 1 percent of the population—for most it was all show. When looking out at the thousands of leather-clad bikers attending Harley-Davidson's 2003 Memorial Day centennial celebration in Milwaukee, a Harley owner said, "The truth is, this is mostly professional people . . . People want to create an image. Everybody has an alter side, an alter ego. And this is a chance to have that."[14]

Another Harley owner who had ridden his Heritage Softail from his home in Sioux Falls, South Dakota, to attend the centennial event commented on his expectations for revelry during the four-day celebration by pointing out, "Bikers like to party pretty big. It's still a long way to go before you forget the image of the Hells Angels."[15] However, most weekend bikers were quite different from the image they emulated. Hells Angels continued to be linked to organized crime into 2003, with nine Hells Angels members being convicted in September 2003 of drug trafficking and murdering at least 160 people, most

[7]As quoted in "Will Harley-Davidson Hit the Wall?" *Fortune,* July 22, 2002.

[8]As quoted in "Even Corporate CEOs Buy into the Harley-Davidson Mystique," *Milwaukee Journal Sentinel,* August 24, 2003.

[9]As quoted in "Harley-Davidson Goes Highbrow at Annual Columbia, S.C., H.O.G. Rally," *The State,* September 26, 2003.

[10]As quoted in "Even Corporate CEOs Buy into the Harley-Davidson Mystique."

[11]Ibid.

[12]As quoted in "Milwaukee-Based Harley-Davidson Rides into Future with Baby Boomers Aboard," *Milwaukee News-Sentinel,* August 5, 2003.

[13]As quoted in "Harley-Davidson Fans Sport Motorcycle Style," *Detroit Free Press,* August 28, 2003.

[14]As quoted in "Bikers Go Mainstream 100 Years On," *Global News Wire,* September 11, 2003.

[15]Ibid.

of whom were from rival gangs.[16] Similarly, Hells Angels organizations in Europe had been linked to drug trafficking and dozens of murders.[17] Fifty-seven Hells Angels in the United States were arrested in December 2003 for crimes such as theft of motorcycles, narcotics trafficking, and firearms and explosives trafficking following a two-year investigation of the motorcycle club by the Bureau of Alcohol, Tobacco, Firearms and Explosives.[18]

Harley-Davidson balanced its need to promote freedom and rebellion, while distancing the company from criminal behavior. Its Web site pointed out that "the vast majority of riders throughout the history of Harley-Davidson were law-abiding citizens," and the company archivist proposed, "Even those who felt a certain alienation from society were not lawless anarchists, but people who saw the motorcycle as a way to express both their freedom and their identity."[19] When looking at the rows of Harleys glistening in the sun in front of his Southern California roadside café, the longtime proprietor of one of the biggest biker shrines in the United States commented, "There used to be some mean bastards on those bikes. I guess the world has changed."[20] A Harley-Davidson dealer commented that dealers considered hard-core bikers 1 percenters because they made up less than 1 percent of a dealer's annual sales. The dealer found that very affluent buyers made up about 10 percent of sales, with the remainder of customers making between $40,000 and $100,000 a year.[21]

Harley-Davidson's Product Line

Unlike Honda and Yamaha, Harley-Davidson did not produce scooters and mopeds or motorcycles with engine displacements less than 651 cc. In addition, Harley-Davidson did not produce dirt bikes and

performance bikes like those offered by Kawasaki and Suzuki. Of the world's major motorcycle producers, BMW offered a product line that most closely resembled Harley-Davidson's traditional line of bikes, although BMW also offered a large number of performance bikes. In 2004, Harley-Davidson's touring and custom motorcycles were grouped into five families: Sportster, Dyna Glide, Softail, Touring, and the VRSC V-Rod. Sportsters, Dyna Glide, and VRSC models were manufactured in the company's Kansas City, Missouri, plant, while Softail and Touring models were manufactured in York, Pennsylvania. Harley-Davidson considered Sportsters, Dyna Glide, and VRSC models custom bikes, while Softails and Touring models fell into the touring industry classification. Sportsters and Dyna Glides each came in four model variations, while Softails came in six variations and touring bikes came in seven basic configurations. The VRSC V-Rod came in two basic styles. Harley-Davidson produced three models of its Buell performance bikes in its East Troy, Wisconsin, plant. In 2004, Harley-Davidson Sportsters carried retail prices ranging from $6,495 to $8,675; Dyna Glide models sold at price points between $11,995 and $16,580; VRSC V-Rods sold for $16,895 to $17,995; Softails were offered for $13,675 and $17,580; and the Road King and Electra Glide touring models sold at prices between $16,995 and $20,405. Consumers could also order custom Harleys through the company's Custom Vehicle Operations (CVO) unit, started in 1999. Customization and accessories added to CVO models could add as much as $10,000 to the retail price of Harley-Davidson motorcycles. Images of Harley-Davidson's five product families and CVO models can be viewed at www.harley-davidson.com.

Honda, Kawasaki, Suzuki, and Yamaha had all introduced touring models that were very close replicas of Harley Sportsters, Dyna Glides, Road Kings, and Electra Glides. The Japanese producers had even copied Harley's signature V-Twin engine and had tuned their dual crankpin designs in an attempt to copy the distinctive sound of a Harley-Davidson engine. However, even with prices of up to 50 percent less on comparable models, none of the Japanese producers had been able to capture substantial market share from Harley-Davidson in the United States or in their home markets. Indian Motorcycle Corporation had experienced similar difficulties gaining adequate market share in the U.S. heavyweight segment

[16]"Nine Montreal Hells Angels Sentenced to 10 to 15 Years in Prison," *CNEWS,* September 23, 2003.

[17]"Hells Angels: Easy Riders or Criminal Gang?" *BBC News,* January 2, 2004.

[18]"Feds Raid Hells Angels' Clubhouses," *CBSNews.com,* December 4, 2003.

[19]As quoted in "Wings of Desire," *Global News Wire,* August 27, 2003.

[20]Ibid.

[21]Interview with Mobile, Alabama, Harley-Davidson dealership personnel.

and ceased its operations for a second time in September 2003.

Harley-Davidson's difficulties in luring buyers in the performance segment of the industry was similar to challenges that Japanese motorcycle producers had encountered in their attempts to gain market share in the custom and touring categories of the U.S. heavyweight motorcycle segment. Harley-Davidson had co-developed and later purchased Buell to have a product that might appeal to motorcyclists in the United States in their 20s who did not identify with the *Easy Rider* or Hells Angels images or who did not find Harley-Davidson's traditional styling appealing. Harley management also believed that Buell's performance street-racer-style bikes could help it gain market share in Europe, where performance bikes were highly popular. The Buell brand competed exclusively in the performance category against models offered by Honda, Yamaha, Kawasaki, Suzuki, and lesser-known European brands such as Moto Guzzi, Duccati, and Triumph. Buell prices began at $4,595 for its Blast model to better compete with Japanese motorcycles on price as well as performance and styling. Buell's Lightning and Firebolt models were larger, faster motorcycles and retailed between $9,000 and $11,000. The VSRC V-Rod—with its liquid-cooled, Porsche-designed engine—was also designed to appeal to buyers in the performance segment of the industry, both in the United States and Europe.

As of 2004, Harley-Davidson had not gained a significant share of the performance motorcycle segment in the United States or Europe. Some industry analysts criticized Harley-Davidson's dealers for the lackluster sales of V-Rod and Buell models since most dealers did little to develop employees' sales techniques. Demand for Harleys had exceeded supply since the early 1990s and most dealers' sales activities were limited to taking orders and maintaining a waiting list. In addition, most Harley-Davidson dealers had been able to charge $2,000 to $4,000 over the suggested retail price for new Harley-Davidson motorcycles, although most dealers had begun to sell Harleys at sticker price in 2003. The number of Harley-Davidson and Buell motorcycles shipped annually between 1998 and 2003 is presented in Exhibit 9. Harley-Davidson's revenues by product group are shown in the following table:

Harley-Davidson Revenues by Product Group (in millions)

	2003	2002	2001
Harley-Davidson motorcycles	$3,621.5	$3,161.0	$2,671.3
Buell motorcycles	76.1	66.9	61.7
Total motorcycles	$3,697.6	$3,227.9	$2,733.0
Motorcycle parts and accessories	712.8	629.2	509.6
General merchandise	211.4	231.5	163.9
Other	2.5	2.4	0.3
Net revenue	$4,624.3	$4,091.0	$3,406.8

Source: Harley-Davidson, Inc., 2002 and 2003 annual reports.

Distribution and Sales in North America, Europe and Asia/Pacific

Harley-Davidson's dealers were responsible for operating showrooms that allowed customers to examine and test-ride motorcycles; for stocking parts and accessories that existing owners might need; for operating service departments; and for selling biking merchandise such as apparel, boots, helmets, and various Harley-Davidson branded gift items. Some Harley owners felt such strong connections to the brand that they either gave or asked for Harley gifts for birthdays, weddings, and anniversaries. Some Harley owners had even been married at Harley-Davidson dealerships or at HOG rallies. Harley-Davidson dealers were also responsible for distributing newsletters and promoting rallies for local HOGs. The 10,000-member Buell Riders Adventure Group (BRAG) was also supported by Harley-Davidson dealers.

Harley mechanics and other dealership personnel were trained at the Harley-Davidson University (HDU) in Milwaukee, where they took courses in such subjects as retail management, inventory control, merchandising, customer service, diagnostics, maintenance, and engine service techniques. More than 17,000 dealership employees took courses at the company's university in 2002. Harley-Davidson also provided in-dealership courses through its Web-based distance learning program. In 2002, HDU held

exhibit 9 **Annual Shipments of Harley-Davidson and Buell Motorcycles, 1998–2003**

	2003	2002	2001	2000	1999	1998
Harley-Davidson						
Sportster	57,165	51,171	50,814	46,213	41,870	33,892
Custom*	151,405	141,769	118,303	100,875	87,806	77,434
Touring	82,577	70,713	65,344	57,504	47,511	39,492
	291,147	263,653	234,461	204,592	177,187	150,818
Domestic	237,656	212,833	186,915	158,817	135,614	110,902
International	53,491	50,820	47,546	45,775	41,573	39,916
	291,147	263,653	234,461	204,592	177,187	150,818
Buell						
Buell (excluding Blast)	8,784	6,887	6,436	5,043	7,767	6,334
Buell Blast	1,190	4,056	3,489	5,416	—	—
	9,974	10,943	9,925	10,189	7,767	6,334

*Custom includes Softail, Dyna Glide, and VRSC.

Source: 2002 and 2003 Harley-Davidson, Inc., annual reports

665 instructor-led classes and 115 online classes; 96 percent of the company's dealers participated in HDU courses that year.

The company also held demo rides in various locations throughout the United States, and many Harley dealers offered daily rentals for novices to decide if they really wanted a motorcycle. Some dealers also rented motorcycles for longer periods of time for individuals who wished to take long-distance trips. Harley-Davidson motorcycles could also be rented from third parties like EagleRider—the world's largest renter of Harleys, with 29 locations in the United States and Europe. Harley-Davidson's Riders Edge motorcycle training courses were also offered by quite a few dealers in North America, Europe, and Asia/Pacific. The company had found that inexperienced riders and women were much more likely to purchase motorcycles after taking a training course. Harley-Davidson management believed that the 25-hour Riders Edge program had contributed to the company's increased sales to women, which had increased from 2 percent of total sales prior to the adoption of the program to 9 percent in 2003.

In 2003, Harley-Davidson motorcycles were sold by 644 independently owned and operated deal-erships across the United States. Buell motorcycles were also sold by 436 of these dealers. There were no Buell-only dealerships, and 81 percent of Harley dealers in the United States sold Harley motorcycles exclusively. The company also sold apparel and merchandise in about 50 nontraditional retail locations such as malls, airports, and tourist locations. The company's apparel was also available seasonally in about 20 temporary locations in the United States where there was significant tourist traffic. The company also had three nontraditional merchandise outlets in Canada, where it had 76 independent dealers and one Buell dealership. Thirty-two of its Canadian Harley dealers also sold Buell motorcycles.

Harley-Davidson had 161 independent dealers in Japan, 50 dealers and three distributors in the Australian/New Zealand market, and 7 other dealers scattered in smaller East and Southeast Asian markets. Only 73 of Harley-Davidson's Asia/Pacific dealers also sold Buell motorcycles. The company also had two dealers that sold Buell but not Harley-Davidson motorcycles. Harley-Davidson motorcycles were sold in 17 Latin American countries by 32 dealerships. The company did not have a dealer for its Buell motorcycles in Latin America, but had

exhibit 10   **Harley-Davidson's Net Revenues and Long-Lived Assets by Business Group and Geographic Region, 2000–2003**

	2003	2002	2001	2000
Motorcycles net revenue				
United States	$3,807,707	$3,416,432	$2,809,763	$2,357,972
Europe	419,052	337,463	301,729	285,372
Japan	173,547	143,298	141,181	148,684
Canada	134,319	121,257	96,928	93,352
Other foreign countries	89,649	72,520	57,185	57,966
	$4,624,274	$4,090,970	$3,406,786	$2,943,346
Financial services income				
United States	$ 260,551	$ 199,380	$ 172,593	$ 132,684
Europe	8,834	4,524	1,214	655
Canada	10,074	7,596	7,738	6,796
	$ 279,459	$ 211,500	$ 181,545	$ 140,135
Long-lived assets				
United States	$1,400,772	$1,151,702	$1,021,946	$ 856,746
Other foreign countries	41,804	36,138	33,234	27,844
	$1,442,576	$1,187,840	$1,055,180	$ 884,590

Source: Harley-Davidson, Inc., 2002 and 2003 10-Ks.

13 retail stores carrying only apparel and merchandise in the region.

The company's European distribution division based in the United Kingdom served 32 countries in Europe, the Middle East, and Africa. The European region had 436 independent dealers, with 313 choosing to also carry Buell motorcycles. Buell motorcycles were also sold in Europe by 10 dealers that were not Harley dealers. Harley-Davidson also had 26 nontraditional merchandise retail locations in Europe.

Exhibit 10 presents the company's revenues by geographic region along with the division of assets in the United States and abroad and a breakdown of financial services revenues by region. The company's financial services unit provided retail financing to consumers and wholesale financial services to dealers including inventory floor plans, real estate loans, computer loans, and showroom remodeling loans.

CHALLENGES CONFRONTING HARLEY-DAVIDSON AS IT ENTERS ITS SECOND CENTURY

As Harley-Davidson entered its second century in 2004, the company celebrated not only a successful centennial that brought more than 700,000 of Harley's most loyal customers to Milwaukee but also a successful year with record shipments, revenues, and earnings. New capacity had allowed the company's shipments to increase to more than 290,000 units, which drove annual revenues to $4.6 billion and net earnings to nearly $761 million. The company's planned 350,000-square-foot expansion of its York, Pennsylvania, plant would allow the company to increase production to 400,000 units by 2007.

However, there was some concern that the company may not need the additional capacity. Some market analysts had begun to believe Harley-Davidson's stock was approaching its apex because of the aging of its primary baby boomer customer group. Between 1993 and 2003, the average age of the company's customers had increased from 38 to 46. The average age of purchasers of other brands of motorcycles in 2003 was 38. Some analysts suspected that, within the next 5 to 10 years, fewer baby boomers would be interested in riding motorcycles and Harley's sales might begin to decline. Generation X buyers were not a large enough group to keep Harley's sales at the 2003 level, which would cause the company to rely on Generation Y (or echo boomer) consumers. However, most Generation Y motorcyclists had little interest in the company's motorcycles and did not identify with the *Easy Rider* or outlaw biker images that were said to appeal to baby boomers. The company's V-Rod motorcycle had won numerous awards for its styling and performance, but its $17,000-plus price tag kept most 20-year-olds away from Harley showrooms. Similarly, Buell motorcycles were critically acclaimed in terms of performance and styling but had been unable to draw performance-minded consumers in the United States or Europe away from Japanese street-racing-style bikes to any significant degree.

Europe was the largest market for motorcycles overall, and the second largest market for heavyweight motorcycles, but Harley-Davidson had struggled in building share in the region. In some ways the company's 6+ percent market share in Europe was impressive since only 4.8 percent of motorcycles purchased in 2002 were touring cycles and custom cycles accounted for only 13.8 percent of motorcycles sold in Europe during 2002. The V-Rod's greatest success was in Europe, but neither the V-Rod nor any other Harley-Davidson model had become one of the top 10 best-selling models in any major European market.

There was also some concern that Harley-Davidson's 14-month production run had caused an unfavorable short-term production problem since the company's waiting list, which required a two-year wait in the late 1990s, had fallen to about 90 days beginning in mid-2003. The overavailability of 2003 models had caused Harley-Davidson's management to adopt a 0 percent down payment financing program that began at midyear 2003 and would run through February 2004. When asked about the program during a television interview, Harley-Davidson's CEO, Jeffery Bleustein, justified the program, noting that "it's not zero percent financing, as many people understood it to be, it's zero dollars down, and normal financing. The idea there was to get the attention of some of the people who aren't riding Harleys and are used to a world of other motorcycles where there's always a financing program of some sort going on. We just wanted to get their attention."[22] By year-end 2003, dealer inventories had declined to about 2,000 units and many dealers again began charging premiums over list price, but not the $2,000–$4,000 premiums charged in prior years.

---

[22] As quoted in a CNNfn interview conducted on "The Money Gang," June 11, 2003.

case 22

Hero Honda Motors (India) Ltd.: Is It *Honda* that Made It a *Hero*?

Kannan Ramaswamy
Thunderbird—The American Graduate School of International Management

Rahul Sankhe
Thunderbird—The American Graduate School of International Management

Hero Honda Rides Splendor to Become World's No. 1

India has finally got a world leader in manufacturing with "no problem." Hero Honda Motors Ltd. (HHM) has attained the distinction of being the largest two-wheeler company in the world in volume terms. With a new factory on the anvil, it is gearing itself for Operation One Billion, targeting $1 billion revenues in 2002–03. "Next year, we will enter the (dollar) billionaire's club (in revenues). After Operation Million for volumes in 2001–02, our slogan for the next year is Operation One Billion," said Mr. Pawan Munjal, Director & CEO, HHM. The distinction of being the largest two-wheeler company in the world came in calendar 2001, with sales rocketing past the one million mark in the first nine months of the current fiscal year. This performance was in conjunction with Splendor, launched in 1995, becoming the world's largest-selling bike.

—*Business Standard,* January 2002

Things could not have possibly looked any better for Mr. Brijmohan Lal Munjal, the Chairman and Managing Director of Hero Honda Motors (HHM). Quarter after quarter, and year over year, HHM had continued to grow, delivering superb performance in India's two-wheeler marketplace. The company had come from nowhere to whiz past Bajaj Auto Ltd., the traditional leader of the pack in two-wheelers. Mr. Munjal had not only earned the crowning title of heading the largest two-wheeler company in the world, but also the personal glory of having presided over one of the most successful joint ventures in the country. Having built a storied legacy, he could rest easy. Or could he?

The spectacular track record of the company was being threatened by predatory moves made by its Japanese partner, Honda Motor Company. The first dark clouds appeared on the horizon in August 1999. Honda Motor Company Ltd. (HMC), HHM's joint venture partner, announced that it would be setting up a 100% subsidiary, Honda Motorcycle & Scooter India (HMSI) to initially make scooters and later, motorcycles as well. HHM's stock plummeted by 30% on the day of the announcement. It was apparent that the investors were no longer optimistic about the company's ability to continue its sterling performance record, especially in the face of competition from Honda. Was this a portent of things to come? Adding another dimension to an arena already fraught with significant complexity, reports from the marketplace clearly showed increasing intensity of rivalry. Not only were domestic rivals getting better equipped to challenge HHM for supremacy, there were foreign interlopers as well who seemed determined on giving HHM a run for its money. It was definitely not a time to rest on past laurels.

THUNDERBIRD
THE AMERICAN GRADUATE SCHOOL
OF INTERNATIONAL MANAGEMENT

THE TWO-WHEELER INDUSTRY IN INDIA

History and Background

India had the largest population of two-wheelers (around 41.6m vehicles) in the world.[1] They accounted for almost 70% of the country's automobile market in volume terms. India was the second largest manufacturer of two-wheelers in the world. Exhibit 1 provides comparative financial and operating statistics for the major two-wheeler manufacturers in India.

The birth of the Indian two-wheeler industry can be traced to the small beginnings that it made in the early 1950s when Automobile Products of India (API) started manufacturing scooters in the country. Although API initially dominated the scooter market with its Lambrettas, Bajaj Auto Ltd., a company that later became a legend in the global scooter industry, overtook it fairly quickly. Although a number of government and private enterprises also entered the scooter segment, almost all of them had disappeared from the market by the turn of the century. Bajaj Auto Ltd. stood the test of time perhaps due to its initial association with Piaggio of Italy (manufacturer of Vespa) that provided the technological know-how for the venture.

The *license raj* that existed prior to economic liberalization (1940s–1980s) in India did not allow foreign companies to enter the market, making it an ideal breeding ground for local players. Local players were subject to a very stringent capacity licensing process, and imports were tightly controlled. This regulatory maze created a seller's market, with customers often forced to wait 12 years just to buy a scooter from companies such as Bajaj. In 1980 Bajaj had a waiting list that was equal to about thirteen times its annual output, and by 1990 this list had doubled. Clearly, there was no incentive to implement proactive strategies to woo the customer. In a 1980 interview with a local magazine, Mr. Rahul Bajaj, the CEO of Bajaj Auto, observed, "My marketing department? I don't require it. I have a dispatch department. I don't have to go from house to house

[1]Two-wheelers include all motorized vehicles using a two-wheel chassis (e.g., motorcycles, scooters, and mopeds).

to sell." The motorcycle segment was no different; with only three manufacturers—Royal Enfield, Ideal Jawa, and Escorts—there was hardly any significant competition for the customer. While this segment was dominated by Enfield's 350cc Bullet, the only motorcycle with a four-stroke engine at the time, Jawa and Escorts also had a fair share of the middle and lower end of the market.

The winds of change began to take hold in the mid-'80s when the Indian government started permitting foreign companies to enter the Indian market through minority joint ventures. Under these relaxed regulations, the two-wheeler market witnessed a veritable boom with four Indo-Japanese joint ventures; namely, Hero Honda, TVS Suzuki, Bajaj Kawasaki, and Kinetic Honda all lining up to target the Indian consumer market for motorcycles. The simultaneous entry of four players into this underserved market helped boost motorcycle revenues to stratospheric heights. For the first time, the market dynamics changed in favor of the Japanese players in both two-stroke and four-stroke vehicles, and the Indian manufacturers who had held sway for such an extended period of time were suddenly cornered. The entry of these new foreign companies transformed the very essence of competition from the supply side to the demand side. Confronted with a larger array of choices, the consumers were regaining their influence over the products that they bought. In keeping up with these higher customer expectations, the industry accelerated the launch of new models, and every company was trying to outdo the other in terms of styling, price, and fuel efficiency. The technological expertise that the foreign companies brought to the marketplace helped increase the overall quality and reliability of the products quite significantly. The old-guard companies soon found themselves under pressure to improve their offerings and bring their products on par with their global counterparts.

The Indian Consumer

Two-wheelers had become the standard mode of transportation in many of India's large urban centers. Increasing urbanization, saturation of cities, and lack of adequate roads helped to propel demand for two-wheelers. The two-wheeler was typically a prized

exhibit 1   **Comparative Financial and Operating Statistics for the Major Two-Wheeler Manufacturers in India**

	Kinetic Honda					Hero Honda		
	1990	1993	1996	1999	2001	1990	1993	1996
Sales (gross)	132.1	157.7	315.2	321.1	423.1	149.8	301.5	632.7
Sales (net)	110.4	126.8	257.6	264.9	350.8	149.3	300.3	630.8
Cost of goods sold	77.6	124.2	235.4	238.2	291.2	134.0	266.8	515.5
R&D expenditure	0.0	0.0	1.5	0.2	4.1	0.0	0.0	2.0
Advertising and sales expenditure	0.9	2.6	6.2	13.4	32.7	4.0	9.5	28.1
Capital expenditure	0.6	2.4	9.3	2.2	10.1	10.7	10.4	30.6
Imports (imported materials)	22.7	15.2	54.6	44.7	19.8	18.0	35.7	68.8
Imported materials (% of COGS)	0.3	0.1	0.2	0.2	0.1	0.1	0.1	0.1
Current assets	20.3	44.3	69.8	88.6	98.0	34.1	93.2	146.2
Current liabilities	15.4	24.1	55.6	63.1	72.7	57.1	59.3	145.6
PBDIT (operating profit)	10.7	5.6	11.5	16.4	34.6	12.4	32.4	59.7
Net income (PAT)	4.4	0.4	5.2	3.5	15.6	−0.2	16.7	26.8
Return on sales	0.0	0.0	0.0	0.0	0.0	0.0	0.1	0.0
Return on investment (ROI)	0.3	0.1	0.1	0.1	0.2	0.1	0.2	0.2
Return on average equity	1.0	0.0	0.1	0.1	0.3	0.0	0.4	0.3
Total debt	16.9	17.0	22.0	40.1	21.8	50.8	63.3	50.0
Net fixed assets	17.7	20.2	29.2	46.9	52.1	60.2	67.0	103.9
ROCE (% pre-tax)	40.3	16.0	27.3	23.3	45.7	46.8	34.7	55.5

possession in the average Indian household. It was normally used to transport both people and goods, substituting for a car that was prohibitively expensive. While a two-wheeler normally cost around Rs. 40,000 [1 U.S. $ = 49 Rupees (Rs.)], an entry-level car was priced around Rs. 300,000. Two-wheelers had long road lives, and were often used for even 15 years, passed down from one generation to the next. However, in global terms the market was far from mature. Industry watchers reported that India had a penetration rate of 10% as of the late 1990s (107 two-wheelers for every 1,000 adults), far below the penetration rates of other developing countries. It was clear that the manufacturers had a lot of ground to cover.

There were indeed visible signs that the companies were gearing up to address this growing market. While the production and sales of motorcycles grew substantially (CAGR of 22% between 1996 and 2001), the performance of the other two segments of two-wheelers was poor. Scooter production grew by only 0.5%, while the production of mopeds fell by 29% during 2001–02.

THE LEGEND OF HERO HONDA

The Hero Group

The Munjals, owners of the Hero Group and promoters of HHM, had made a modest beginning as suppliers of bicycle components in the early '40s. Currently, the group's bicycle company, Hero Cycles, manufactured over 16,000 bicycles a day and had sold over 86 million bicycles in aggregate as of 2002. It had been acknowledged as the world's largest bicycle manufacturer in 1986 when it overtook the U.S. manufacturer, Huffy. Despite the lack of significant process automation, the company had been able to achieve among the highest levels of employee productivity and efficiency on a global basis. Although a publicly traded company, the family was extensively involved in day-to-day management of operations, as well as setting strategic direction.

Much of the company's strategy was anchored to the fundamental principle of providing products of

Hero Honda		TVS Suzuki					Bajaj Auto				
1999	2001	1990	1993	1996	1999	2001	1990	1993	1996	1999	2001
1536.4	3177.2	143.1	186.1	618.3	1018.6	1821.0	1018.1	1246.0	2742.9	3604.7	3628.7
1532.8	3171.2	141.6	182.9	606.1	1000.2	1781.6	814.7	1011.3	2309.9	3039.0	3052.9
1240.9	2533.5	120.5	150.9	484.9	770.3	1517.6	686.7	891.5	1687.2	2203.8	2598.4
3.5	5.1	0.0	0.8	6.1	15.5	16.1	4.5	9.2	22.7	31.4	61.0
54.4	122.3	4.5	6.7	25.4	76.8	119.0	13.2	26.6	105.0	198.6	245.5
106.2	121.2	11.5	2.3	53.0	85.0	74.2	75.7	59.9	297.5	229.8	367.9
235.6	420.6	19.4	10.3	50.3	99.4	179.3	111.8	64.1	215.6	255.3	338.4
0.2	0.2	0.2	0.1	0.1	0.1	0.1	0.2	0.1	0.1	0.1	0.1
326.1	663.8	49.1	58.5	144.2	257.6	363.2	364.2	505.8	1425.0	2964.1	2608.7
308.7	460.1	76.9	77.8	150.9	160.3	322.3	315.1	350.1	871.3	1570.5	1547.4
220.4	459.6	9.9	18.2	74.8	144.8	149.0	181.3	186.3	666.9	836.6	474.4
120.1	250.1	−5.5	3.8	35.2	68.5	63.1	58.1	32.8	405.9	481.6	298.9
0.1	0.1	0.0	0.0	0.1	0.1	0.0	0.1	0.0	0.1	0.1	0.1
0.3	0.4	0.1	0.2	0.3	0.3	0.2	0.3	0.2	0.3	0.2	0.1
0.5	0.5	−0.4	0.3	0.5	0.4	0.2	0.2	0.1	0.3	0.2	0.1
78.2	69.2	36.5	41.5	33.5	142.4	225.2	159.6	164.4	197.2	351.2	527.3
308.6	453.9	54.1	51.0	97.6	187.5	436.1	301.4	291.9	559.7	921.8	1362.4
122.3	78.6	64.3	52.2	86.8	61.2	29.8	51.4	38.4	46.8	31.1	14.2

superior value at reasonable prices to the consumer. This basic belief was reflected in the company's approach to product innovation, quality, and reliability. Over time, the group had nurtured an excellent network of dealers to serve India's expansive markets. This network was not just focused on the high-density urban centers, but also encompassed rural outlying regions that typically did not attract the attention of large manufacturers. The company truly believed in its mission of bringing transportation to the masses.

Over the years, the Hero Group had entered multiple business areas, largely related to the transportation industry. The group evolved into a fairly integrated set of operations that spanned multiple areas of raw material processing, such as steel rolling, to the manufacture of subassemblies and components. Many of these ventures were owned and controlled by members of the Munjal family or operated by very close friends and associates. Thus, the company had seemingly established control over all facets of production and marketing. Exhibit 2 shows the portfolio of Hero Group businesses.

Honda Motor Company of Japan

Honda Motor Company had surprisingly similar origins like its counterpart in India. Founded in 1946 as the Honda Technical Institute by Mr. Soichiro Honda, the company produced its first bicycle engine a year later. There had been no looking back from that time on as the company grew to dominate the global automotive market, with over 100 plants in 33 countries selling 11 million product units as of 2002. The engine was the centerpiece of Honda's global expansion. It had parlayed this expertise into a wide range of products such as lawnmowers, generators, scooters, motorcycles, and cars.

Honda called its global strategy "glocalization" to signify its approach of building plants locally to meet local demand. Within this web of localized operations, the company had been able to leverage synergies in R&D and manufacturing by regionalizing its operations, consolidating local strategy at the regional level. It had worked quite well. The reach of

exhibit 2   **Portfolio of Hero Group Businesses**

Business			
Bicycles	Hero Cycles Limited Established in 1956 **Product:** Bicycles	Hero Cycles Limited (Unit II) Established in 1988 **Product:** Bicycles	Gujarat Cycles Limited Established in 1988 **Product:** Bicycles
Business Auto two-wheelers	Hero Honda Motors Limited Established in 1983 New Delhi **Product:** Motorcycles **Collaborator:** Honda Motor Co. Ltd., Japan	Majestic Auto Limited Established in 1978 **Product:** Mopeds and fitness equipment	Hero Motors (A division of Majestic Auto Limited) Established in 1988 **Product:** Mini-motorcycles **Collaborator**: Steyr Daimler Puch, Austria **Product:** Scooters **Collaborators**: Malguti, Italy
Business Bicycle and auto components	Rockman Cycle Industries Limited Established in 1960 **Products:** Automotive and bicycle chains; steel and aluminum hubs	Highway Cycle Industries Limited Established in 1971 **Products:** Freewheels and special machine tools	Munjal Showa Limited Established in 1985 **Product:** Shock absorbers **Collaborator:** Showa Manufacturing Co., Japan
Business Castings and steel	Munjal Castings Established in 1981 **Product:** Nonferrous castings	Sunbeam Castings Established in 1987 **Product:** Nonferrous castings	Hero Cycles–Cold Rolling Division Established in 1990 **Product:** Cold rolled steel sheets and coils
Business Services	Hero Exports Established in 1993 **Product:** International trading company dealing in commodities and engineering items	Hero Corporate Services Established in 1995 **Product:** Corporate services in finance, HRD, IT, and strategic planning	Munjal Sales Corporation Established in 1975 **Product:** Sole selling agents of bicycles and bicycles parts for India

wholly owned subsidiaries was augmented through astute management of select joint ventures, although not a preferred mode of entry for the company. In many cases, the company was motivated to enter into joint ventures either because of regulatory constraints or because of a desire to access local market knowledge that was not easily available.

Forging a Partnership with Honda Motor Company

Given the impending liberalization of India's markets, HMC had come looking for suitors. Initial plans called for entry both into the two-wheeler market and the electric generator market. HMC identified a short list of Indian companies that it felt would make good partners. Topping the list in the two-wheeler category was Bajaj Auto, a company that traced its reputation to the storied history of Piaggio of Italy and the chic-yet-egalitarian brand of transportation it offered through its series of Vespas. When that first choice did not work out for HMC, it moved on to its second choice, the Firodia group, an automotive products conglomerate based in the prosperous western Indian state of Maharashtra. Kinetic Engineering Ltd. (KEL), the group's flagship company, manufactured the first mopeds in India. Hugely popular in the late '70s and early '80s, KEL had a 44% share of the Indian moped market and about 15% of the entire two-wheeler market. It seemed to hold much promise at the time, and thus attracted the attention of HMC. KEL and HMC entered into a 50/50 joint venture, Kinetic Honda Motors Ltd., with the express objective of launching a line of scooters in India. It was widely reported that KEL was offered a choice between scooters and motorcycles and chose scooters based on prevailing trends that favored scooters. Honda was already close to signing on another partner for its other venture in power products, and hence its bid for a motorcycle JV was all that was left in play.

HMC came to the Hero group as the last choice for its motorcycle venture. The market for motorcycles was not booming in any sense of the term in the early '80s. Many Indian consumers still believed that motorcycles were more accident prone and less safe for Indian roads. The market had been largely carved among three Indian firms with various levels of old imported technology. It was against this backdrop that the Hero group sought to throw its hat into the ring as a means of consolidating its position in the two-wheeler market. Since it had a flourishing bicycle business and a fairly strong moped business as well, the Munjals felt that entering into a joint venture with a company that enjoyed a worldwide reputation would help them achieve their goal of dominating the two-wheeler market in India. It was indeed a golden opportunity for Mr. Brijmohan Lal Munjal to achieve the distinction of "beating Bajaj," a seldom-vocalized desire that he had harbored.

The Deal Is Done

The negotiations between HMC and the Hero group had by all accounts gone quite smoothly. Although there had been some lingering resentment that HMC had come to Hero as a last resort, Mr. Brijmohan Lal Munjal had tried to maintain the enthusiasm amongst the members of the Munjal family, emphasizing the benefits of the alliance they were about to enter. The negotiations culminated in an agreement that was signed in June 1984 creating a joint venture firm called Hero Honda Motors Ltd.

Honda agreed to provide technical know-how to HHM and assist in setting up manufacturing facilities. This included providing the design specifications and responsibility for future R&D efforts relating to the product lines that the company would offer. For these services, HHM agreed to pay Honda a lump-sum fee of $500,000 and a 4% royalty on the net ex-factory sale price of the product. Both partners held 26% of the equity with another 26% sold to the public and the rest held by financial institutions. HHM became a public company listed on the Bombay Stock Exchange (BSE).[2]

A 13-member board was formed to oversee the governance of the company. Honda had four key appointees including the Joint Managing Director, a particularly powerful position in Indian companies. The Hero group was represented by four family members and appointed the chairman of the company. Honda brought in its staff of technical experts to run the engineering and quality support functions. Hero brought in local talent to manage all other functions including marketing, finance, and HR. A seven-member top management team drawn almost exclusively from local ranks took charge of the daily operations of the venture. Both partners agreed to review the terms and relevance of the agreement in 1994 when the current joint venture arrangement would lapse. Time was short, and it was clear that HHM would have to act very quickly to build a foothold in the motorcycle business.

Rubber Hits the Road

The manufacturing plant which was established in Dharuhera in the state of Haryana started manufacturing the CD-100 model motorcycle in 1985. The CD-100 was powered by India's first four-stroke engine, the unique selling point that put Hero Honda in the driver's seat in the marketplace. Soon, the CD-100 set the standards for fuel efficiency, pollution control, and quality. Perhaps the most appealing characteristic of the CD-100 was its fuel efficiency (approximately 80 km/litre), an attribute highly valued by the Indian consumer. As the CD-100 was the only one with a four-stroke engine at the time, it became a runaway success. Interestingly, it was Mr. Munjal who persuaded HMC to launch the 100cc vehicle instead of the 70cc version that HMC had originally planned to offer. Given his long experience with the manufacture of bicycles and mopeds, he really understood the intricacies of the Indian marketplace very well. "Our bicycle and moped manufacturing background gave us insights into the

---

[2]Bombay Stock Exchange is one of the two biggest stock exchanges in India. http://www.bseindia.com

customer psyche that the running cost of the vehicle had to be low," he recalled in a press interview focusing on the rationale behind the CD-100. The organization had since spearheaded many "firsts" for the auto sector in India, being the first two-wheeler manufacturer to implement an ERP across the functions, and the first to implement initiatives such as six-sigma.

Under the stewardship of Mr. Munjal, HHM had grown consistently, earning the title of the world's largest motorcycle manufacturer after having churned out 1.3 million vehicles in 2001. Its motorcycle volumes nearly quadrupled during the period 1997–2001, a feat unparalleled in the Indian two-wheeler industry. While the motorcycle market grew at an average 21.74% per annum between 1997 and 2001, Hero Honda averaged a growth rate of 35.46% a year. In 2001–02, it again doubled volumes from 0.76 million in 1999–2000 to 1.3 million. However, there were several significant bumps on the road along the way.

The CD-100 had captivated the Indian consumer when it was first launched, but the uniqueness soon wore off. Exhibit 3 illustrates some of the product offerings from HHM. Competitors such as TVS-Suzuki and Bajaj-Kawasaki were introducing feature-rich models that were vying for the attention of customers. Many of these vehicles boasted comparable fuel efficiency and some were priced much lower than the CD-100. However, Mr. Munjal was boxed in by the relationship with HMC. His dependence on Honda for all product innovation inputs hobbled HHM's ability to respond to emerging changes in the market. Honda had decided to consolidate all its R&D activities worldwide in three countries, and India was not one of them. Therefore, Hero Honda was forced to wait its turn before getting any changes vetted by Honda's R&D. New product designs did not materialize as fast as the market demands dictated. It was quite difficult to sustain customer interest when all HHM could do was to release newer models that were only variations of the CD-100 platform. This was particularly costly for the company, since it did not have any new products, when competitors were releasing new products to ride the boom in demand from 1993 to 1996, when industry sales grew at a cumulative average rate of 31% per year.

HHM managed to dampen some of the negative impact of these years through astute marketing and by leveraging its knowledge of customers and mar-

exhibit 3   **Some Offerings from the Hero Honda Stable**

kets. It had built an expansive network of dealers who were extremely loyal to the company. Much of this network was culled from Hero Group's bicycle operations. The company instituted modern programs and incentives to motivate its dealer network. The best dealers were chosen to visit the Japanese operations of Honda each year. They formed an extended family and HHM was perceived as being very supportive of its dealers. As of 2000, the company had close to 400 dealers across the country. It was this well-penetrated dealer network that allowed the firm to actively market its products in rural India, a significant departure from other firms that concentrated solely on the urban market. The challenge of rural marketing would have been quite difficult without intimate knowledge of the dramatic differences, not only between the urban and rural consumer, but also the various shades of gray that differentiated rural consumers in one region from another.

The dealers were strongly supported through major advertising campaigns. HHM retained the best advertising agencies to execute its campaigns. Its "fill it, shut it, forget it" campaign promoting the maintenance-free nature of its motorcycles was a major hit with the Indian public. These campaigns also leveraged the Honda name to maximum advantage. Capitalizing on Honda's reputation for the quality of its engines, HHM ran advertisements that proclaimed, "It is the Honda that makes it a Hero." Exhibit 4 provides an illustration from this advertising campaign.

Hero Honda was among the first manufacturers to understand the impact of product differentiation and market segmentation on sales revenues. While the differentiated positioning brought price premiums, the customer got a much more fuel-efficient and reliable product in exchange. The mantra of fuel economy formed the core of all HHM's product launches. On a single platform (CD-100 series), it devised three models catering to different market segments. The CD-100 bike was an excellent pick for the rural and semi-urban customer for whom cost was critical consideration. The CD-100 SS was a basic model for the urban market. Splendor catered to the middle-class, office-going segment. Since all these products came from a single platform, product development costs were spread over higher volumes, and after-sales service quality was maintained, thereby reducing costs and increasing margins.

The influence of the Hero group was quite visible in the way the supply chain was organized at HHM. The company had built an extensive network of primary and secondary suppliers for components and subassemblies. Since the Indian government had stipulated that the joint venture must indigenize production within a fairly short period of time, develop-ing the supplier network was deemed crucial. By 1996, over 95% of the motorcycle was manufactured from locally procured parts, a rate of localization that even Honda at times thought would be difficult to achieve. However, the Munjals realized that it was not only in the interests of the Indian government to indigenize but also in their own interests, since they would otherwise be held hostage to the rupee-yen exchange rate which had historically been unfavorable to Indian firms relying on imported components. The Munjal family had set up a range of firms to supply components, not just to HHM, but also to other buyers. These operations ranged from the manufacture of shock absorbers and wheel rims, to aluminum castings and plastic products. Munjal family interests ran seven of its crucial supplier firms. HMC had also helped establish some of these ventures, and HHM had a controlling shareholding in Munjal Showa, for shock absorbers, and Sunbeam Castings and Munjal Castings, both of which supplied castings.

Honda did not seem to be concerned about the rate at which foreign sources were replaced with Indian suppliers. However, HHM shareholders had expressed some concerns. The preferred provider network of suppliers was filled with either Hero family companies or firms that were run by promoters who were closely aligned with Munjal family interests, and this posed a potential conflict of interest. Since HHM was a publicly traded company, it was felt that the profitability impact of outsourcing to allied firms would affect shareholder returns. The flip side of this sourcing approach was the reliability of the network and its ability to respond quickly to environmental change. There was very little inventory in process or waste due to supply chain bottlenecks, which resulted in better margins. Of course, this also ensured that many among the Munjal family were gainfully engaged.

Renegotiating the Venture in 1994

As 1994 rolled around, the sentiments amongst the Munjal family were mixed but largely negative. Some felt that while Hero had ploughed a lot into making HHM a success, HMC had not contributed as much. There was a lack of new product innovation and much uncertainty surrounded the negotiations at that time. Even routine design changes were taking

exhibit 4   **Advertisement of Hero Honda**

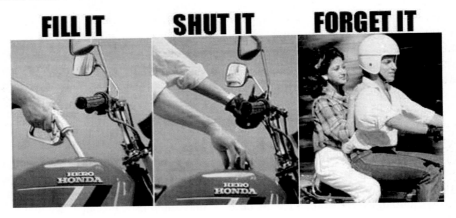

too long, and HMC's R&D engineers did not appear cooperative on this count at all. The impending negotiations paralyzed HHM, and it had to sit on the sidelines while its competitors roared past. Archrival Bajaj had introduced a new four-stroke engine for its motorcycle line and usurped the lead that HHM had carefully nurtured. In the meantime, HMC had negotiated new ventures with other Indian partners for manufacturing automobiles and power equipment. Mr. Munjal would have liked very much to have been part of the automobile venture, but did not allow this disappointment to color the relationship.

Perhaps in protecting its own destiny, Hero had been evaluating alternative product lines and market approaches right from 1986. It entered into a collaboration agreement with Steyr Daimler Puch, an

exhibit 5   **Hero Honda Stock Performance Chart, Feb., 2000–April, 2002**

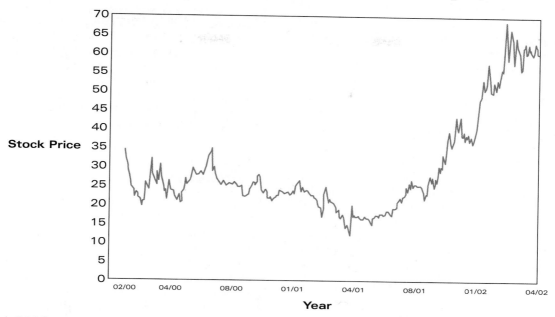

Source: indiainfoline.com.

Austrian subsidiary of Daimler A.G., to manufacture motorcycles in the 50cc–65cc range. This business was organized under the Hero Motors banner and targeted both Indian and foreign markets. Hero Motors was successful in exporting completely knocked-down (CKD) kits for assembly in Spain, Iran, Mauritius, Vietnam, Bangladesh, and Egypt. Bolstered by these initial successes, Hero Motors even entered into discussions with BMW of Germany to manufacture 650cc bikes. Although these talks eventually fizzled out, they could hardly have inspired any trust or confidence at Honda headquarters.

It was 1995 by the time the joint venture agreement was renegotiated and extended until 2004. HHM was able to negotiate far more attractive terms from HMC with respect to royalties. They were able to persuade HMC to accept a paltry Rs. 200 per vehicle in 1995. Licenses to manufacture future models were dealt with on a case-by-case basis using a mix of lump sum payments and royalties. By 1999, the proportion of royalty payments to sales revenues had declined considerably from a high of 4% at founding to about 0.5%. Honda displayed new willingness to share its R&D and product suites in a more timely fashion. Subsequent to the 1995 contract renewal, Honda licensed HHM to manufacture Street, a model that was based on Honda's recent global hit called the Dream, which had sold over 25 million worldwide. In addition to the reduced royalties and fast-track transfer of technology, HMC agreed to increase the extent of components and sub-assemblies purchased from Hero's supplier network.

With the emergence of significant competition from similarly positioned offerings from Bajaj and TVS-Suzuki, Hero Honda had become more aggressive in terms of its marketing with new product launches and market segmentation. The company had announced new product launches (two every year) to continue this effort. This phenomenal rate of new product introductions was, of course, solely dependent on HMC's continuing its R&D support, since HHM had not explored setting up R&D facilities in India. HHM had also undertaken significant expansion of its distribution network.

The going was good for HHM, and the financial results followed. The company had reported flawless quarter-on-quarter growth for 18 consecutive quarters between 1997 and 2001. Hero Honda's quarterly sales during the period grew 303.28% and its net profit jumped from Rs. 16.28 crore[3] to Rs. 98.34 crore. HHM hardly required any incremental working capital over the seven-year period following the renegotiation. In fact, its working capital was lower in 2001 than in 1994 by Rs. 1160m, despite sales having grown by approximately 7X during this period. Return on average capital employed (ROACE) at 65% was among the highest in the country. Hero Honda was among the few Indian companies that enjoyed the distinction of generating a positive economic spread for an extended period of time. Between 1995 and 2001, the economic spread (difference between WACC and ROIC) expanded from 16.5% to 65.4%. This performance had not been lost on the investors who helped the share rise among the ranks of established blue chips. Exhibit 5 (page C-405) charts the performance of HHM shares. However, just as things appeared to be set for a smooth sailing, storm clouds appeared.

STORM CLOUDS AND SILVER LININGS

Competition began to intensify in the late '90s as many of the foreign joint ventures in the Indian motorcycle industry reached maturity. Players such as Kawasaki and Yamaha were helping their local companies mount a credible assault on Hero Honda. Closer to home, HHM partner HMC was forced to dissolve Kinetic Honda Ltd., the venture it set up with Kinetic Engineering to manufacture scooters. This left a void in HMC's product suite in India and it was poised to enter the scooter market on its own. Both of these developments were cause for significant alarm.

The Competition Revs Up

The competitors for HHM were Kawasaki-Bajaj, TVS-Suzuki, and Yamaha Motors, a familiar bevy of powerhouses from Japan. Exhibit 6 shows the key competitors by two-wheeler category in the Indian marketplace. Refer to Exhibit 7 for recent sales and production figures for these players in the two-wheeler market.

[3]1 Crore = 10 million

exhibit 6

Subsegment	Major Players
Motorcycles	Hero Honda, Bajaj Auto, Yamaha Motors Escorts, TVS Suzuki, Eicher
Scooters	Bajaj Auto, LML, Kinetic Motor Co., Maharastra Scooters, TVS Suzuki
Mopeds	TVS Suzuki, Kinetic Engineering, Majestic Auto, Bajaj Auto

Bajaj Auto

Bajaj Auto Limited was one of India's largest two- and three-wheeler (three-wheelers, also known as auto-rickshaws, are unique to the South Asian region) manufacturer. The Bajaj group came into existence in 1945 and got a start by importing scooters and three-wheelers from Italy for sale in India. In 1960, it struck a technical know-how agreement with Piaggio of Italy, and the company became a public corporation the same year. Scooter production commenced in 1961 and three-wheeler production was followed in 1962. The Piaggio collaboration expired in 1991. Since then, the company's scooters and three-wheelers were sold under the brand name of Bajaj. As of 2001, Bajaj had become a market leader in scooters with annual production in excess of 1.34 million units. It offered products in all segments such as mopeds, scooters, motorcycles, and three-wheelers.

Subsequent to the opening up of the two-wheeler sector to foreign technology and equity participation in the mid '80s, Bajaj Auto entered into a technical collaboration agreement with Kawasaki of Japan. It started production of Kawasaki 100cc motorcycles in 1986. Bajaj became a key manufacturing base for Kawasaki and accounted for 60% of the latter's global sales. The company had chalked out a strategy for co-existence with Kawasaki, wherein Bajaj would concentrate on developing products in the price range of Rs 30,000–60,000 and Kawasaki would offer a wider choice of products priced from Rs 35,000 up to Rs 250,000. Though the company planned to introduce some high-tech motorcycles from the Kawasaki range, it was fighting an uphill battle trying to shed its image of a "screwdriver" company (assembler as opposed to manufacturer) by developing its own range of motorcycles.

exhibit 7 **Comparative Sales and Production Figures for Two-Wheeler Manufacturers, (April 2001 to February 2002)**

	Production		Sales	
	Number	% Change	Number	% Change
Motorcycles	2,666,456	33.7	2,650,822	36.4
Hero Honda	1,288,933	37.7	1,289,838	38.3
Bajaj Auto	654,051	29.2	649,920	32.9
TVS Motor Co.	399,151	20.0	395,494	22.8
Yamaha Motor	212,954	29.6	210,568	40.0
LML	40,380	15.6	42,115	44.6
Kinetic Engg	48,992		40,937	
Eicher	21,995	10.6	21,950	11.7
Scooters	808,185	0.5	808,768	−1.6
Bajaj Auto	347,997	10.0	347,785	7.0
TVS Motor Co.	136,070	2.3	135,432	1.8
LML	119,163	−24.6	121,857	−23.3
Kinetic Motor Co.	103,253	−7.8	103,292	−10.7
Mah Scooters	54,532	−35.9	53,601	−39.8
Honda Motorcycle	47,170		46,801	
Mopeds	454,680	−29.2	451,784	−28.8
TVS Motor Co.	246,317	−28.6	247,136	−27.6
Kinetic Engg	96,606	−31.8	91,467	−32.5
Majestic Auto	75,997	−23.7	77,014	−24.3
Bajaj Auto	35,760	−36.4	36,167	−35.2

TVS-Suzuki

A leading producer of automotive components, the TVS group was formed as a transport company in 1911. Originally incorporated in 1982 as Indian Motorcycles Pvt. Ltd to produce motorcycles in collaboration with Suzuki, Japan, the company later went public under the banner Ind-Suzuki Motorcycles Limited, which was later renamed TVS-Suzuki Limited. The perfect blend between the best design engineers and the latest technology made TVS-Suzuki one of the leading two-wheeler manufacturers in the country.

However, the relationship between Suzuki and TVS was far from amicable. A divorce was in the cards for nearly a decade. In August 2001, TVS bought out the 25.97% stake of the Japanese partner in August 2001, increasing its equity holding to 32%. The parting also meant that Suzuki would not be allowed to enter India for a 30-month period. The decision to buy out Suzuki was prompted by the fact that the partners felt it was in their own long-term interests to pursue their own interests separately rather than through the joint venture.

The TVS Group wanted to promote the TVS brand, grow their revenues, and develop products indigenously. Further, they wanted to export TVS-made vehicles to the rest of the world, a proposition Suzuki Motors opposed. From Suzuki's point of view, its contribution to the joint venture was shrinking. With the exception of the two-stroke Suzuki Max 100R, an evolution of the original Ind-Suzuki, none of the company's fast-selling two-wheelers had a major Suzuki contribution. TVS-Suzuki's bread-and-butter product, the moped, was fully Indian. The hugely successful TVS Scooty was also a non-Suzuki product. It was only in two-stroke motorbikes that TVS-Suzuki had to rely on the Japanese parent. However, with the decline of two-stroke motorcycles in India, and with the recent launch of the all-Indian TVS Victor, it was clear that the Indian partner could do without the Japanese collaborator.

As per the terms of the joint venture agreement, there was to be a 30-month licensing arrangement, during which time the joint venture would continue to pay royalties to Suzuki. After this period, TVS was free to sell the four licensed vehicles (Samurai, Max 100, Max 100R, and Fiero) as TVS vehicles. As it turned out, TVS had localized production ahead of schedule and voted to terminate the agreement before the 30-month period could lapse.

Escorts-Yamaha (EYML)

EYML was a joint venture between Escorts Ltd., the flagship company of the Escorts Group, and the global giant, Yamaha Motors Co. Ltd of Japan. Ever since signing the first technical assistance agreement between the two companies in 1985, Yamaha Motor Company Limited (YMC) and Escorts Limited had built a cooperative relationship dedicated to the manufacture and sales of Yamaha-brand motorcycles. In November 1995, the two companies established the joint venture company, Escorts Yamaha Motors Limited, based on a 50-50 capital investment. In June 2000, that investment ratio was changed to 74% for YMC and 26% for Escorts Limited, and YMC assumed managerial control of the company with the name being changed to Yamaha Motors Escorts Limited (YMEL). It then undertook numerous measures to build the company's motorcycle manufacturing and marketing operations. In June 2001, an agreement was reached between YMC and Escorts Ltd. under which YMC acquired the remaining 26% of the stock held by Escorts. The stated aims of this move to make YMEL a 100% YMC subsidiary were to increase the overall speed of managerial and business decisions, to improve product development capabilities and production efficiency, while also strengthening the marketing organization.

Kinetic Honda Ltd.

Kinetic Engineering Ltd. (KEL), one of the leading manufacturers and exporters of two-wheelers for over 20 years, came into existence in 1970. It manufactured scooters, motorcycles, and mopeds that were all well known for their fuel economy and quality. KEL was the beneficiary of Honda's advances when the Japanese company first came to India shopping for partners. They set up a 50-50 joint venture called Kinetic Honda Ltd. (KHL) to manufacture and market scooters. Unfortunately, the terms of the agreement specified that KHL could not enter the motorcycle business. KHL seemed to be doing an excellent job in cornering the market and was within striking distance of a leadership spot in the race for market share. When the two-wheeler business began to boom in the early 1990s, Honda wanted to take charge, an idea that was welcomed by the Indian partner. KEL felt that such a move might motivate Honda to bring in new products more quickly to India. Strangely, Honda began to lose interest in the venture and decided to turn off the spigot, putting the brakes on R&D spending, which was a paltry 0.31% of sales when Indian competitors were spending 1.5%. It also decelerated its advertising spending significantly when the competition was blitzing the consumer with new campaigns. All these actions hurt the sustainability of the company, and soon the personal relationship started to sour and culminated in a KEL buyout of Honda's interests. This effectively released Honda to pursue its own agenda in the scooters segment.

Other Challengers

In addition to domestic competition, another competitive threat took shape in the form of cheap Chinese imports when import restrictions were lifted in 2001. A relatively unknown company named Monto Motors in Alwar (Rajasthan[4]) was the first to import Semi-Knocked-Down (SKD) kits from one of the top motorcycle manufacturers in China. A 72cc motorbike from China cost the customer Rs. 27,000 on road, a 125cc would cost Rs. 33,000, and a 250cc motorbike would cost Rs. 36,000. The Indian models seemed frightfully expensive in comparison. In early 2002, a moped cost around Rs. 22,000, a 100cc motorbike cost around Rs. 45,000, and a 125cc motorcycle cost around Rs. 50,000. The domestic two-wheeler industry was bound to feel the pinch, especially in the mid and lower price segments of the motorcycle, scooter, and moped segments.

The Other Shoe Drops

HMC, having extricated itself from the KHL venture, announced plans to set up a new company, Honda Motor Scooters India Ltd., for the sole pur-

[4]Rajasthan is one of the states in West India.

pose of manufacturing scooters for the Indian market. At that time, it also announced that it intended to enter the motorcycle market in 2004, ominously the very year when the HHM joint venture agreement would come up for its next revalidation. This announcement shocked the top brass at Hero Group. Mr. Munjal put on a brave face and announced that Honda had made its plans public only after Hero signed off on its plans. This led to further speculation as to why Mr. Munjal would give his blessings to a venture that would place the destiny of HHM in peril.

HMSI was indeed a troubling development for the Munjal family and the shareholders of HHM. However, Mr. Munjal was looking for the silver lining in what was apparently a huge storm cloud brewing. He announced that HHM had negotiated three key concessions from Honda. First, Honda agreed to delay entry into the motorcycles segment until 2004. It also agreed to form a four-person committee with two members from HHM to examine any new motorcycles that it would release post-2004. Lastly, it offered an opportunity to HHM to share in the equity as a minority holder in HMSI. These assurances were followed by a visit by Mr. Yoshino, the CEO of Honda from Japan, for the launch of Honda's first scooter in India. At the launch ceremony, he addressed the simmering problems that were perceived by HHM and its investors. He observed, "By 2003 the two companies will together be selling 25% of the world's projected seven million market for two-wheelers."[5] The President and CEO of HMSI, Mr. Takiguchi painted a similar scenario in his interview with a leading news magazine. He said, "The discussion in 2004 will not be on whether to continue with the joint venture. We will sit and discuss about the products which both the companies—Hero Honda and HMSI—should build on."[6] However, in the same breath, he also observed, "Our strategy will be to offer motorcycles which keep up with the overall market trend in the post-2004 scenario."[7] It was anybody's guess what that statement truly meant.

Honda was already bolstering its dealership network and had plans to set up over 100 dealerships by the end of 2002. It was also spending Rs. 1 billion to set up a manufacturing plant that would double HMSI's existing capacity.[8] Given the rate of growth of scooters that was in the 4% range, it was difficult to imagine how Honda would be able to use the capacity effectively without stepping onto HHM's turf.

Mr. Munjal seemed to be reassured about the situation, however. After Mr. Yoshino's visit, he proclaimed, "His visit has made a lot of difference to the outlook at Hero Honda."[9]

ARE THERE ROAD HAZARDS AHEAD?

Mr. Munjal sifted through the various options he had in front of him. While the investors were sated with the flurry of announcements and reassurances for now, what would the future hold for HHM? How should the company arm itself for the post-2004 marketplace? How would the competitors, especially the Japanese companies, respond to the uncertainties that faced HHM? What if HMSI, despite all its assurances, saw the potential marketplace in 2004 and decided to push HHM to the periphery and engineer a frontal assault on the motorcycle business? Would HMC go back to its old ways of withholding R&D now that it had plans to make motorcycles in India post-2004? The joint venture had been in existence for a very long period of time by international standards. Perhaps its time had come. Would HHM have to be dismantled in the same way its competitors in India had been? These were troubling questions, but nevertheless very critical ones. Charting the future strategy of HHM would undoubtedly require clear answers to all these questions. These were indeed the best of times and the worst of times for HHM.

bibliography

http://www.herohonda.com/web/index.htm
www.yamaha-motor.co.jp
http://www.indiainfoline.com
www.securities.com
http://www.expressindia.com/ie/daily/19980823/23550444.html
http://www.businessworldindia.com/archive/7Jan99/corpo3(1420).html

[5]*Business Standard*, Entrepreneur of the Year issue, 2001.
[6]Hindu, *Businessline*, June 19, 2001.
[7]Ibid.

[8]moneycentral.com, July 25, 2002.
[9]*Business Standard*, Entrepreneur of the Year issue, 2001.

Transcript of interview with Ms. Sulajja Firodia Motwani, Joint Managing Director of Kinetic Engineering, February 22, 2002

Business World, January 28, 2002

Report on TVS Motor Company Limited—ICICI Securities, January 18, 2002

Business Line, Sunday, Sept 30, 2001

Business Line (International Edition), Tuesday, June 19, 2001

Reports on Hero Honda Motors Limited:
HSBC, March 28, 2002
HSBC, September 21, 2001
Merrill Lynch, June 20, 2001
CSFB (Hong Kong), July 6, 2000
Probity, December 16, 1998
Dresdner Kleinwort Benson Research, May 8, 1998
Morgan Stanley, May 31, 1996
Reports on Automotive Sector in India
LKP Shares & Securities Limited, February 2002
Scope Marketing, September 2001

Puma AG

Lutz Kaufmann

The WHU Otto Beisheim Graduate School of Management

On Monday, January 27, 2003, at 8:30 AM Jochen Zeitz, CEO and chairman of the German sports company Puma AG in Herzogenaurach, Bavaria, carefully read the cover pages of several international newspapers. He was very satisfied as he saw the picture of Serena Williams with the Puma logo highly visible after having won her fourth consecutive Grand Slam title in the Women's Tennis Association series. Zeitz remembered that 10 years ago—before he took over the job as CEO—the Puma brand had severe image problems; people were ashamed to wear shoes or clothes with a Puma label. Fortunately, things had changed. Within a single decade, Puma had turned into one of the most admired sports brands and offered highly desired lifestyle products, worn by celebrities and trendsetters worldwide. Since the revival and overwhelming success of Puma's brand, the international media and business world had gotten interested: If Puma's managers had been successful with the turnaround, how would they address the obvious challenges in the future? How could the Puma cat run even faster?

COMPANY BACKGROUND

In 1924, two brothers Adalbert (Adi) and Rudolf (Rudi) Dassler founded the Dassler Schuhfabrik (shoe factory) in Herzogenaurach, a small village in Bavaria. Their company, Gebrüder Dassler OHG, gained international recognition in the developing market for sport shoes after Jesse Owens won four

gold medals at the 1936 Berlin Olympic Games wearing Dassler shoes.

By World War II, disputes within the family had led to the end of the brothers' successful partnership. They separated and never spoke to each other again. Adi kept the Dassler Schuhfabrik on the lower side of the Aurach River and renamed it Adidas, while Rudi founded the Puma Schuhfabrik Rudolf Dassler on the other side of the Aurach. Nearly 40 employees remained with Adi, and 7 joined Rudi. Most probably by mere coincidence, in 2003 the companies still had this same ratio of employees, 5:1; the same ratio held for the companies' respective sales volumes. This everlasting rivalry only strengthened employee loyalty: Once Puma, always Puma; and once Adidas, always Adidas. This competition was nicely exemplified by the fact that there was not a single dealer in Herzogenaurach offering shoes or textiles from both brands.

Puma's Rise and Fall

By sponsoring some of the world's most famous soccer players—including Pelé, Diego Maradona, Johan Cruyff, Rudi Väller, and the Herzogenaurach-born Lothar Matthäus—Puma established itself as one of the most important suppliers of soccer shoes and accessories. Through its cooperation with Boris Becker, the youngest Wimbledon champion ever, Puma became the world market leader in tennis rackets in the 1980s and for the first time pulled ahead of Adidas in tennis footwear.

Despite the success of the sponsored athletes, Armin, Rudi Dassler's son, compromised the Puma brand and its value. He wanted to address customers from every social class, from the welfare recipient to the millionaire. "Thereafter, many Puma shoes were delivered to department stores and sold 'dirt-cheap'" on rummage tables, remembered Helmut Fischer, a marketing manager at Puma. Individuals from the upper class were no longer willing to wear the brand. Additionally, new collections failed, as U.S.-based competitors Nike and Reebok successfully entered the European market. Puma went public in 1986, and the Dassler family sold most of its shares to the Swedish investor group Proventus. In 1988, liquidity problems made it obvious that Puma was struggling. Puma was lacking a leader.

The Comeback

Searching for a new leader with strong capabilities in marketing, strategy, and finance, investors finally found promising newcomer Jochen Zeitz in 1993. Zeitz had studied international business administration and worked in the marketing division of Colgate-Palmolive before joining Puma's marketing department in 1990. He was promoted to the Head of Marketing in 1991. At the age of 30 he became CEO and chairman of the board, and the youngest ever chairman heading a company listed on the German Stock Exchange.

Together with Martin Gaensler, who was in charge of supply chain management and strategy implementation and who later became vice chairman, Zeitz applied a two-phase plan: The first phase aimed at making Puma profitable in order to build a strong financial foundation. On the one hand, changes centered on the company's accounting practices. Many products had previously been sold at low margin prices, generating "unhealthy" sales. Their costs were attributed to total sales regardless of product categories, thus hiding profitable products among the company's accounting records. Zeitz introduced profit centers and distribution-oriented controlling to identify products and adjust profit margins. Additionally, the company decreased working capital and accounts receivable. On the other hand, the organization was restructured to be more cost-efficient and half of the employees were laid off. Following the model of Nike and Adidas, Puma completely outsourced production to Asia and Turkey. The company could now focus on its core competencies: marketing, brand management, and product management.

These changes enabled Puma to meet market needs more efficiently and to save a substantial amount of money. Despite this drastic action plan, employees and unions were entirely behind the restructuring since they realized that something needed to be done to turn the company around. Against all odds, Zeitz turned Puma back to profitability. The restructuring phase ended in 1997, when the company announced record earnings of 37 million euros (€), positive cash flows, and a payoff of debts.

After these positive results, both investors and banks widely supported phase two of Zeitz's plan: to transform Puma into an attractive sports brand. The main idea of the second phase consisted of positioning Puma as a high-value brand in both sport and lifestyle sales categories. At the time, Puma was still a low-value brand, and the transformation would be very costly. Luckily, Zeitz convinced the Israeli film producer Arnon Milchan to invest in Puma in 1997 through his holding company Monarchy Enterprise (see Exhibit 1). With his New Regency film company, which had produced blockbusters like *Pretty Woman* and *L.A. Confidential,* Milchan was among the world's most influential filmmakers. Producing several films a year, he understood what it meant to build a brand from scratch, and he recognized that huge investments were required to do so. With the help of Tri-Star founder David Matalon and the president and chief operating officer of News Corporation, Peter Chernin, Zeitz won over other entertainment professionals to serve as members of the supervisory board of Puma (see Exhibit 2). From then on, Puma products appeared in several Hollywood productions. Additionally, Zeitz regained ownership of the American Puma licenses. For 2002, Puma posted record sales of €910 million and earnings of €85 million (see Exhibit 1). Thus, Zeitz announced the completion of the second phase and the beginning of a third.

Company Structure

Puma described its structure as "virtualized." It had a global management structure with several headquarters supported by a strong information technology infrastructure. The management headquarters were located in Germany, the United States, and Hong Kong. Puma's seven corporate functions—consisting of product, product supply, brand, growth, structure, brand value, and culture—were dispersed among these core competence centers. Production was completely outsourced. Additionally, there were

exhibit 1   **Financial Comparison of Puma and Selected Public Listed Companies, 1999–2002**

Puma Aktiengesellschaft Rudolf Dassler Sport (in millions of euros)

	1999	2000	2001	2002
Net sales	€373	€462	€598	€910
Gross profit	142	176	251	397
Royalty and commissions	24	29	37	45
Marketing and retail expenses	61	67	87	125
Product development	15	18	20	24
Other expenses	68	91	114	155
EBITDA	21	30	67	138
Depreciation	5	7	8	13
EBIT	16	23	59	125
Interest expenses	2	2	2	1
EBT	14	21	58	125
Taxes	6	7	17	40
Minority interests expenses	(1)	—	1	0
Extraordinary income	—	3	—	—
Net income	9	17	40	85
Equity value (March 2003)	€1,010			

Assets	€526		Liabilities and equity	€526
Cash and cash equivalents	114		Financial liabilities	19
Inventories	168		Accounts payable	118
Accounts receivables	136		Other current liabilities	47
Other current assets	8		Total current liabilities	€184
Total current assets	€425		Pension accruals	18
Property, plant and equipment	57		Other accruals	71
Goodwill	14		Long-term borrowings	—
Other intangible assets	5		Total long-term liabilities	89
Other assets	25		Minority interests	0
Total long-term assets	100		Shareholders' equity	252

Source: Company information, Onvista.

Nike, Inc. (in millions of dollars)

	1999	2000	2001	2002
Net sales	$8,777	$8,995	$9,489	$9,893
Gross profit	3,283	3,591	3,704	3,888
EBITDA	975	1,143	1,136	1,294
EBIT	746	964	980	1,065
Net income	451	579	590	668
Equity value (March 2003)	$8,148			

(continues)

exhibit 1   **(continued)**

Nike, Inc. *(in millions of dollars)*

Assets	$6,443	Liabilities and equity	$6,443
Cash and cash equivalents	576	Financial liabilities	681
Inventories	1,374	Accounts payable	504
Accounts receivables	1,807	Shareholders' equity	3,839
Property, plant and equipment	1,615	Others	1,419
Others	1,072		

Source: Company information, Reuters.

Adidas-Salomon AG *(in millions of euros)*

	1999	2000	2001	2002
Net sales	€5,345	€5,835	€6,112	€6,523
Gross profit	2,352	2,528	2,601	2,819
EBITDA	584	555	605	619
EBIT	482	437	474	477
Net income	228	182	208	229
Equity value (March 2003)	€3,575			

Assets	€4,261	Liabilities and equity	€4,261
Cash and cash equivalents	76	Financial liabilities	1,574
Inventories	1,190	Accounts payable	669
Accounts receivables	1,560	Shareholders' equity	1,081
Property, plant and equipment	366	Others	938
Others	1,070		

Source: Company information, Onvista.

Reebok International Ltd. *(in millions of dollars)*

	1999	2000	2001	2002
Net sales	$2,900	$2,865	$2,993	$3,128
Gross profit	1,116	1,116	1,086	1,170
EBITDA	118	204	211	243
EBIT	69	158	174	210
Net income	11	81	103	126
Equity value (March 2003)	$1,911			

Assets	$1,543	Liabilities and equity	$1,543
Cash and cash equivalents	413	Financial liabilities	363
Inventories	362	Accounts payable	127
Accounts receivables	383	Shareholders' equity	720
Property, plant and equipment	134	Others	333
Others	251		

Source: Company information, Reuters.

exhibit 1 **(continued)**

Fila Holding SpA (in millions of euros)

	1999	2000	2001	2002
Net sales	€907	€1,004	€977	€860
Gross profit	360	393	345	350
EBITDA	15	—	(20)	—
EBIT	(10)	(25)	(47)	20
Net income	(59)	(72)	(140)	81
Equity value (March 2003)	€31			

Assets	€532	Liabilities and equity	€532
Cash and cash equivalents	—	Financial liabilities	190
Inventories	161	Accounts payable	—
Accounts receivables	183	Shareholders' equity	107
Property, plant, and equipment	120	Others	236
Others	68		

Source: Company information, Onvista.

Selected Fashion and Lifestyle Companies

Company	Fiscal Year	Currency (in millions)	Equity Value	Sales	Gross Profit	EBITDA	EBIT	Net Income
LVMH SA	2001	Euro	20,695	12,229	7,575	1,596	1,560	(455)
Gucci Group NV	2001	U.S. dollar	9,273	2,285	1,596	355	239	278
Escada AG	2002	Euro	53	773	505	55	25	4
Hugo Boss AG	2001	Euro	901	1,095	535	183	152	107
Cie Financière Richemont AG	2002	Euro	7,926	3,860	2,478	482	300	151
Pinault Printemps Redoute SA	2002	Euro	6,683	27,735	10,590	2,282	1,827	1,589

Source: Company information, Onvista, Reuters, FY 2002.

Historic Exchange Rates: U.S. Dollar:Euro

	$:€
1999	0.9392
2000	1.0850
2001	1.1170
2002	1.0611
Q1 2003	0.9318

Source: Interbank exchange rates, 365 days average for 1999–2002, 97 days average for 2003, Oanda.

(continues)

exhibit 1 **(concluded)**

Relative Stock Market Performance

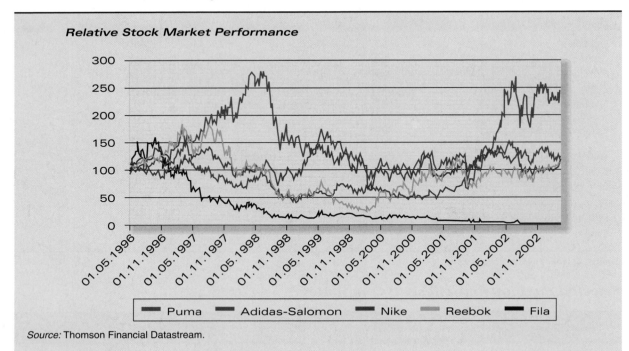

Relative Stock Market Performance

Legend: Puma — Adidas-Salomon — Nike — Reebok — Fila

Source: Thomson Financial Datastream.

Shareholders' Structure of Puma AG

Shareholders	Shares in %
Monarchy Enterprise Holding B.V.	39.38%
Morgan Stanley & Co. International Ltd.	5.48
Fidelity Investments	5.02
Others	50.12

Source: Company information, April 2003.

regional hubs, leading to the following geographical divisions: Germany, responsible for Western Europe; the United States, for the Americas; Austria, for Eastern Europe, Africa, and the Middle East; Hong Kong, for Asia; Australia, for the Pacific region; and Japan as an independent region. These hubs were created to oversee Puma distributors and licensees, as well as some subsidiaries located within the respective regions. This structure placed Puma in a dynamic position to capture regional differences and enabled the company to fine-tune and incorporate those differences into its global brand initiatives.

The management team was very international. Less then 20 percent of the employees were of German nationality. In contrast to Nike or Reebok, there

was no one culture that dominated. This was why Puma considered itself as a multinational company, not a German one.

Products and Events

The Puma product lines addressed the needs of various athletes (see Exhibit 3). To facilitate the customer's orientation, the company categorized its products according to different types of sports. The two biggest product lines were Pumafootball and Pumarunning. These featured footwear and apparel, with Pumafootball also including diverse accessories. Without a doubt, the most famous product was the Puma King Football shoe. In the late 1960s

exhibit 2   **Puma's Supervisory Board**

Werner Hofer, Germany
Chairman
Lawyer, Germany
Member of other supervisory boards:
- H&M Hennes & Mauritz AB, Sweden
- Electrolux Deutschland GmbH, Germany
- AEG Hausgeräte GmbH, Germany
- ISPAT Europe Group S.A., Luxembourg
- ISPAT Germany GmbH, Germany
- ISPAT Hamburger Stahlwerke GmbH, Germany
- ISPAT Stahlwerk Ruhrort GmbH

Arnon Milchan, Israel
Producer, United States
Member of other supervisory boards:
- Monarchy Enterprises Holdings BV, Netherlands

David Matalon, United States
President of New Regency Productions, Inc., United States
Member of other supervisory boards:
- Monarchy Enterprises Holdings BV, Netherlands
- Regency Entertainment USA Corp., United States
- Restless Records Corp., United States

Peter Chernin, United States
President and COO of News Corp. Ltd., United States/Australia
Member of other supervisory boards:
- The News Corporation Ltd., Australia
- Monarchy Enterprises Holdings BV, Netherlands
- Fox Entertainment Group, Inc., United States
- E*Trade Group, Inc., United States

Thore Ohlsson, Sweden
Deputy chairman
President of Elimexo AB, Sweden
Member of other supervisory boards:
- Boss Media AB, Sweden
- Bastex AB, Sweden
- Elite Hotels AB, Sweden
- Proventus AB, Sweden
- Tretorn AB, Sweden
- T. Frick AB, Sweden
- Trianon AB, Sweden

Mikael Kamras, Sweden
President of Proventus AB, Sweden
Member of other supervisory boards:
- SSRS Holding AB, Sweden
- Von Roll Holding AG, Switzerland
- Nessuah Zannex Ltd., Israel
- Microdug AG, Switzerland

Inge Baumann, Germany
Employees' representative

Katharina Wojaczek, Germany
Employees' representative

Horst Zyder, Germany
Employees' representative

Source: Company information, March 2003.

exhibit 3   **Puma's Product Pipeline (Spring 2003)**

Cropped woven pants

Nuala Nylon coat

Boxter

Curato

TrainerJack

Puma Avanti

King ss soccer shirt

Puma King Pro

Retro logo tee

exhibit 3 **(concluded)**

H-Street

Jamaica collection

Serena tennis dress

this shoe had been worn by soccer legends such as Eusebio and Pelé. Since then, the shoe had been developed, refined, and improved so that, 30 years later, the Puma King was still one of the best soccer shoes on the market.

Additionally, in 2000, Puma introduced the Action Sports line, dedicated to emerging sports such as BMX, skateboarding, and downhill mountain biking; Nuala, a lifestyle brand for women's clothing; and, finally, the Platinum series, offering casual luxury footwear. Customers' growing demand for sports footwear and fashion apparel in the 1970s and 1980s was satisfied with the Originals Edition. These new product lines were each expected to account for about 10 percent of revenues.

In the soccer market, Puma had to respond to the needs of both young kids playing on the local soccer pitch and national soccer teams competing on a professional level. The latter especially required a high level of quality. Due to its extensive expertise and numerous innovations, Puma was widely accepted by professionals. One example of Puma's innovation was "cell technology," which introduced the first foam-free midsole. Individually designed products convinced many famous athletes to wear Puma products. For example, the Cameroon national soccer team enjoyed Puma's newly developed and innovative sleeveless jerseys, and Jamaican running professionals trusted the company's apparel and footwear brands. Having such charismatic sportspeople as customers created a new atmosphere for Puma that combined professional sporting goals and the joy of participating in sports.

Contributing to Puma's brand revival were not only well-known products but also several outstanding events. In 1994, the first Puma Street Soccer Cup attracted many amateurs, in particular the young soccer fans. In 2003, Puma organized the 4SOME Competition across different European countries, spurring teams of four women to excel in biking, running, swimming, and soccer.

OVERVIEW OF THE ATHLETIC FOOTWEAR AND APPAREL MARKET IN 2003

People around the world participated in sports, either to relax from their everyday worklife or to pursue highly ambitious athletic goals. Athletes could be of both genders, of almost every age group, and from any social level. A huge variety of different sports were practiced worldwide. As the variation necessitated different core competencies, many different companies emerged over time, leading to a highly fragmented global market. Market leaders such as Nike, Adidas, and Reebok shared about 27 percent of total sales within the global sports market (footwear and accessories), which reached a sales volume of about $58 billion in 2000 (see Exhibits 4 and 5).

The most commonly used product categorizations consisted of footwear, apparel, and accessories/equipment. The apparel category consisted of

exhibit 4 **Worldwide Market Shares in Apparel Market (in millions of dollars)**

	United States			International			Total		
	Sales	Share	Change	Sales	Share	Change	Sales	Share	Change
Nike	$ 1,293	7.6%	8.8%	$ 1,526	6.2%	-10.6%	$ 2,819	6.8%	-2.6%
Adidas-Salomon	474	2.8	4.2	1,605	6.6	-3.9	2,079	5.0	-2.2
Russell	1,080	6.3	-3.2	80	0.3	-27.9	1,160	2.8	-5.5
Reebok	395	2.3	68.8	578	2.4	-5.2	973	2.3	-15.3
VF Knitwear	620	3.6	1.6	150	0.6	6.4	770	1.9	-2.5
Quiksilver	380	2.2	18.4	289	1.2	26.2	669	1.6	-21.6
Columbia	458	2.7	23.8	178	0.7	14.8	636	1.5	-21.1
Champion/Jogbra	315	1.8	6.8	265	1.1	0.0	580	1.4	3.6
Speedo	236	1.4	2.2	260	1.1	-3.0	496	1.2	-0.6
Fruit of the Loom	354	2.1	-23.7	137	0.6	12.3	491	1.2	-16.2
Umbro	—	0.0	-100.0	471	1.9	16.3	471	1.1	10.8
Fila	136	0.8	24.8	325	1.3	-10.7	461	1.1	-2.5
Descente	15	0.1	-6.3	413	1.7	-13.6	428	1.0	-13.4
Goldwin	—	0.0	0.0	426	1.7	-5.5	426	1.0	-5.5
Mizuno	7	0.0	133.3	368	1.5	-23.5	375	0.9	-22.5
Puma	**27**	**0.2**	**-12.9**	**308**	**1.3**	**2.0**	**335**	**0.8**	**0.6**
Gildan Sportswear	270	1.6	7.6	56	0.2	7.7	326	0.8	7.6
Asics	21	0.1	23.5	286	1.2	-12.8	307	0.7	-11.0
Ellesse	4	0.0	-20.0	300	1.2	-28.1	304	0.7	-28.0
Timberland	129	0.8	40.2	143	0.6	-5.3	272	0.7	11.9
Billabong	99	0.6	17.9	125	0.5	38.9	224	0.5	28.7
Subtotal	$ 6,313	37.1%	6.8%	$ 8,289	48.7%	-5.8%	$14,602	35.2%	-0.7%
Other Performance	300	1.8	0.0	365	1.5	0.0	665	1.6	0.0
Other Bodywear	350	2.1	-12.5	325	1.3	0.0	675	1.6	-6.9
Other Branded	250	1.5	-37.5	1,350	5.5	-12.9	1,600	3.9	-17.9
Other Beach/Swimwear	2,150	12.6	-8.5	2,750	11.3	-10.6	4,900	11.8	-9.7
Other Ski/Outdoor	600	3.5	-7.7	1,200	4.9	-14.3	1,800	4.3	-12.2
Other Licensed	450	2.6	-18.2	625	2.6	-7.4	1,075	2.6	-12.2
Other Tennis	125	0.7	0.0	225	0.9	0.0	350	0.8	0.0
Other Fleece/Knitwear	1,500	8.8	-16.7	3,000	12.3	-7.7	4,500	10.9	-10.9
Other Activewear	5,000	29.3	-3.8	6,300	25.8	-5.3	11,300	27.3	-4.6
Total	$17,038	100.0%	-3.7%	$24,429	100.0%	-7.2%	$41,467	100.0%	-5.8%

Source: Sporting Goods Intelligence (2002), FY 2001.

exhibit 5   **Worldwide Market Shares in Footwear Market (in millions of dollars)**

Company	United States	International	Licensed	Total	Market Share	Change
Nike	$3,327	$2,363	$ —	$5,690	34.6%	4.6%
Adidas	811	1,380	250	2,441	14.8	−1.4
Reebok	926	494	226	1,646	10.0	2.8
New Balance	750	140	210	1,100	6.7	23.6
Asics	148	437	—	585	3.6	6.4
Fila	114	304	45	463	2.8	−11.5
Puma	**57**	**193**	**135**	**385**	**2.3**	**10.6**
Converse	144	65	148	357	2.2	−6.1
Vans	216	94	—	310	1.9	33.0
Keds	190	15	55	260	1.6	−5.5
American SG	195	40	25	260	1.6	15.6
K-Swiss	197	24	—	221	1.3	−22.5
Mizuno	15	160	38	213	1.3	15.8
Brooks	58	13	95	166	1.0	−14.9
Foot-Joy	129	22	9	160	1.0	10.3
Hi-Tec	44	98	6	148	0.9	−2.6
Saucony	125	20	—	145	0.9	9.8
Diadory	15	71	28	114	0.7	14.0
Airwalk	60	15	30	105	0.6	0.0
Tommy Hilfiger	—	—	104	104	0.6	−11.9
Subtotal	$7,521	$5,948	$1,404	$14,873	90.5%	3.6%
Others	281	1,209	76	1,566	9.5	−10.7
Total	$7,802	$7,157	$1,480	$16,439	100.0%	2.0%

Source: Sporting Goods Intelligence (2001), FY 2000.

textile products such as T-shirts, pants, and caps. The accessories/equipment category included bags, watches, glasses, and perfumes, as well as golf clubs, hockey sticks, and skis. Although for large sportswear companies approximately 60 percent of total sales were generated by footwear divisions, experts predicted future growth mainly in the apparel and accessories categories. This had already been the case in recent years for companies like Nike and Reebok. However, analysts came to a different conclusion when looking at specific geographic regions. With the trend holding for the Americas and Asia, Europe still was a fast-growing footwear market.

A high level of diversity within potential target groups made it increasingly difficult to recognize major trends in the sports market. Naturally, product customization for different genders and ages had played a significant role in the past. Another major trend was the orientation toward high-value and lifestyle-oriented products. This also explained why the major luxury goods producers such as LVMH, Hugo Boss, and Prada introduced their own sportswear collections.

While traditional market segments, such as running, soccer, and basketball were in mature stages, several niches offered attractive growth rates to both incumbent and new market players. One significant niche in the 1990s had been the skateboarding market, in which Adidas and Puma successfully competed with focused players such as Vans and Airwalk. These efforts added to the revival of Puma's brand. Other examples of highly attractive niches were golf sports, sports equipment for outdoor activities, and snowboarding.

Major Competitors

Puma's major competitors were Adidas, Nike, Reebok, Fila, Prada Sport, and Diesel.

Adidas-Salomon AG   After the separation with his brother Rudolf, Adalbert Dassler decided to rename the Gebrüder Dassler OHG company Adidas in 1948. The headquarters were still located in Herzogenaurach, Bavaria. As one of the first professional sports equipment manufacturers, Adidas (whose shoes bore the brand's signature stripes) became famous all over the world. The founder's death in 1972 led to difficult times for the company, which resulted in the sale of its majority holding to different investors. By the end of the 1980s, Adidas had already lost its dominant position in the worldwide sports market to Nike and Reebok. It was only after French manager Robert Louis Dreyfus took over control as CEO in 1993 that Adidas regained profitability. Dreyfus increased brand awareness and sales, and acquired French Salomon SA, a leading manufacturer of ski apparel and golf and outdoor equipment. In 2001, Herbert Hainer officially succeeded Dreyfus as CEO. In 2002, Adidas was the world's second largest sports equipment manufacturer, with approximately $6.5 billion in sales and 13,400 employees (see Exhibit 1).

Adidas was present in nearly every country in the world. Production sites were on every continent except Australia, with administration, design, and marketing concentrated in Germany and France. Parts of its production were outsourced to subcontractors, located mainly in Asia. The main supplier was Hong Kong–based shoe manufacturer Yue-Yuen, which manufactured millions of shoes yearly for Adidas as well as for both Reebok and Nike.

Its product range under various brands made Adidas the only other supplier, besides Nike, that covered all sports. However, the company's main strengths were its soccer line. Furthermore, it had a very strong standing in the ski and tennis market. Its brand portfolio included Adidas (general brand, used for all sports); Salomon (outdoor, ski); TaylorMade (golf); Mavic (biking); Arcteryx (outdoor); Bonfire (snowboard); Cliché (skateboard); and Maxfli (golf).

From the beginning, Adidas pursued a more general market approach than Puma. It was a brand for the family, satisfying a broad range of needs. But it completely missed market changes in the 1980s, when sports brands were becoming more dynamic and consumer tastes diversified into new—and more exciting—sports. Only in November 2000, did Adidas decide to concentrate its sponsoring activities on huge sports events, famous teams, and individual athletes. This included the FIFA World Cup, the UEFA Champions League, and the French national soccer team as well as David Beckham, Kobe Bryant, Tim Henman, and Anna Kournikova. In special cases, Adidas even invested in sports teams. For example, it acquired a 10 percent stake in the German soccer club FC Bayern München for €75 million, to underline its long-term strategic partnership. Furthermore, Adidas was very strong in youth sports development, enabling the company to improve its long-term brand awareness. In order to continuously improve brand perception and design, Adidas started adding lifestyle products to its portfolio in the late 1990s. A number of classic products were relaunched, and famous designers were invited to deliver visions for future Adidas product lines. However, sales of sports-related goods still accounted for the majority of Adidas's revenues.

Nike, Inc.   Nike was incorporated in 1964 by Bill Bowerman and Phil Knight as Blue Ribbon Sports in the latter's family basement. Supported in its early stages by the Bank of Tokyo and Japanese designer Nissho Iwai, Knight was able to expand his business with sound financial backing, and he soon introduced its new name, Nike, as well as the "swoosh" logo, which later became world famous. Nike quickly outsourced parts of its production to China and concentrated its skills on product design, marketing, and distribution. After a phase of impressive growth, Nike became the world's largest sports equipment manufacturer in the late 1980s and had kept this position since then. In 2003, Nike, now located in Eugene, Oregon, employed some 22,700 people and generated sales around $9.9 billion (see Exhibit 1).

By 2000, Nike had outsourced almost all production to third parties, mainly to Mexico, Canada, and East Asia. All major administrative activities were then concentrated in the United States. Regional headquarters for Europe, Africa, and Asia decided sales strategies but had no influence on design, product changes, or innovations. R&D and the production of electronic components were subcontracted to Panasonic, S3 Rio Division, and Philips. The companies share licenses for these technologies.

In 2003, Nike was still focused on its core brand but decided to acquire Cole Haan (casual luxury footwear), Hurley International (teen lifestyle brand), and Bauer (hockey equipment) and to build up Jordan/Jumpan23 (basketball). The majority of Nike's sales were generated in traditional American sports such as basketball and baseball. However, the brand was also extremely strong in the running and golf markets. Since the late 1990s, Nike had tried to compete with Adidas in the global soccer markets.

While Nike's origins were in track and field, the company changed its focus in the early 1990s and diversified its product portfolio. It decided to target young people ages 20 to 30 with an enthusiastic sports feeling. Nike's well-known slogan "Just do it" perfectly targeted this group. Its marketing strategy focused on sponsoring huge events, popular teams, and outstanding individual athletes, such as the Brazilian national soccer team, Michael Jordan, the U.S. "Dream Team," Andre Agassi, and Tiger Woods. Enormous sums were consequently spent on marketing. For example, a five-year, $100 million sponsoring agreement was signed with Tiger Woods. A 13-year €500 million contract was signed with the soccer club Manchester United. Furthermore, huge image campaigns were launched regularly to increase brand awareness. Through the introduction of specialized sub-brands, such as Tiger or ACG, Nike attempted to give its products a more exclusive and competent image. The aim was to approach a wider range of customers. A new marketing strategy involved multiplayer computer games targeting the younger generation. Additionally, in 2001, Nike started the Web-based NikeID service offering clients an option to customize their Nike products.

With a revenue share of 10.9 percent, Foot Locker was Nike's biggest retailer in 2002. Furthermore, in opening the first NikeTown in 1990, Nike started distribution through company-owned dealerships. By 2003, many of the 17 NikeTowns had posted losses, which were generally accepted by headquarters because these flagship stores represented a main tool for supporting Nike's image. About 100 such franchise-owned stores were expected to follow in Europe through 2007.

Reebok International Ltd.

Joseph William Foster founded Reebok in 1895 in the United States as J. W. Foster and Sons. Only in 1958 did grandsons of Foster rename the company Reebok. Despite its long tradition, Reebok became a major player on the international sports market only in the 1980s but eventually became the world's largest sports-item manufacturer between 1986 and 1988. Reebok early identified the footwear industry as a key market, in which it focused on the aerobics industry, women's sportswear, and specially designed street and casual footwear. A key event was the company's 1985 IPO, after which Reebok began to expand aggressively into overseas markets. With sales around $3 billion in 2001, Reebok was recognized as the world's third largest player in the sports market (see Exhibit 1).

The company had only a U.S. division and an international division but was nevertheless present in more than 140 countries. R&D was concentrated in China, Korea, and Taiwan, while most of the company's production was outsourced to independent manufacturers outside the United States, mainly in China, Indonesia, and Thailand. However, finishing for most of the products was done by the company itself in the United States. The company distributed finished goods via traditional retailers. In contrast to its main competitors Nike and Adidas, Reebok lacked a strong distribution network in Europe, especially in France. Reebok initially concentrated on generating sales via gym club trainers, who would receive royalties for each pair of Reebok shoes sold within their fitness center.

In addition to products under own labels, Reebok had multiple licensing agreements. One example was the licensing agreement with the National Basketball Association (NBA) and the National Football League (NFL), in the course of which Reebok gained wider brand awareness and attractive income opportunities. Furthermore, its brand portfolio included Ralph Lauren footwear, Rockport, and the Greg Norman Collection.

Reebok's female sports shoe Freestyle was introduced in 1983 and subsequently sold more than 100 million pairs, making it the most successful shoe in the world. The brand's small Union Jack logo and fine leather helped to transform an ordinary sports shoe into a sneaker with high perceived value. In 1992, Reebok significantly changed its marketing strategy, beginning a transition toward American football, baseball, basketball, and soccer as well as track and field. The company sponsored sports events and popular athletes, like the tennis stars Venus Williams and Andy Roddick. Reebok also increased brand presence in the NBA and NFL and through popular TV shows such as *Survivor*. Further partnerships, like a new shoe line featuring music artist Jay-Z, aimed at improving Reebok's popularity. By introducing new materials (e.g., kangaroo leather), Reebok tried to regain the innovation leadership in the industry. Despite these efforts, the company was often regarded as a fitness and exercise equipment manufacturer.

Fila Holding SpA   Fila was established in 1911 in Biella, Italy, as a textile manufacturer specializing in knitwear production. Only in 1973 did Fila enter the world of sports, namely tennis, after having established its brand name in Italy. After several changes in the company's shareholder structure, Fila was renamed Fila Holding SpA in 1993, and 46.6 percent of its shares were then placed on the New York Stock Exchange. The remaining shares stayed with the Fila Holding di Partecipazione. Following a period of unsatisfying performance, the company appointed Marco Isaia as CEO in February 2002. By 2002, Fila reported sales of $860 million (see Exhibit 1).

Distribution was handled by third-party retailers in nearly 50 countries worldwide, except for two Fila Sport Life stores in Milan and London. The company planned to expand these direct distribution channels. While the company's administrative headquarters were still concentrated in Italy, R&D efforts were also undertaken in Boston, Massachusetts. These efforts mainly consisted of biomedical research and new product development, involving top professionals like Alberto Tomba, Reinhold Messner, and Gelindo Bordin.

Fila offered a product portfolio of activewear, sportswear, and athletic footwear under its major brands Fila, Ciesse, and Enyce. However, Fila focused mainly on running, basketball, and fitness, as well as on apparel for all purposes.

Fila's key sponsorships included being the official supplier of apparel and footwear to the Ferrari racing team in the Formula One tournament. Another significant sponsorship was that of Grant Hill, a famous NBA player. Fila tried to position itself in both the high-performing sports equipment market and the original style segment dating from the 1970s and the 1980s.

Prada SpA/Prada Sports   In 1913, Prada was founded in Milan, Italy, as a family luxury leather goods company by Mario Prada. But only after his granddaughter took over the reins from her mother in 1978 did the company gain international recognition. In 1985, Miuccia Prada succeeded in positioning the brand in the luxury apparel market with a newly designed line of unlabeled, finely woven black nylon handbags. Their high price made her products even more desirable. Numerous supermodels and celebrities of the fashion scene wore Prada. More successful products followed, such as the introduction of the less expensive Miu Miu line in the fashion of the 1960s and 1970s. Miuccia Prada's decision to empower her husband, Patrizio Bertelli, with the company's financials and to then make him CEO in 1992 proved to be wise. In 2002, Prada generated net sales of $1.2 billion. Additionally, Prada acquired a number of famous fashion companies, such as Jil Sander, Church's, and parts of Helmut Lang. Although Prada had planned its IPO since 1999 in order to reduce bank liabilities, going public was delayed several times due to falling stock markets.

As of 2003, Prada had also implemented a sportive line called Prada Sport, which complemented Prada's women wear, shoes, and accessories with its focus on activewear such as waterproof jackets and sunglasses. According to Miuccia Prada, this move was inevitable. She believed that in the future people would be dressing up formally only on special occasions and wearing sportswear in their everyday life. Unlike some competitors, like Pierre Cardin, Prada controlled most parts of its value chain, and stressed design and marketing, and supported the idea of providing more than a brand name for licensing.

Diesel SpA   The brand Diesel was established in the 1970s and by 2002 had become an innovative international design company, manufacturing jeans and casual clothing as well as accessories. The individual who powered the company's growth was Renzo Rosso. In 1978 Rosso joined forces with several other manufacturers in Northern Italy to form the Genius Group, which created a number of brands still widely known, such as Katherine Hamnett, Goldie, Martin Guy, and of course Diesel. In 1985, Rosso took over complete control of Diesel by buying out the other partners. Thereafter, the company began a period of remarkable growth and expansion. From the beginning, Rosso believed in addressing the world with one product and one language. One of his first steps was building a solid and vast distribution platform stretching across five continents. From 1991 on, the company's sales increased significantly. A 38-year-old

exhibit 6 **Product Mix and R&D Expenses Comparison***

Products	Adidas	Nike	Reebok	Puma	Fila
Footwear	44%	61%	70%	64%	45%
Accessories	21	8	—	7	—
Apparel	35	38	30	28	53

*Approximately 5% of Nike's revenues are generated through other brands, for which there were no details available.
Source: Company information, FY 2002.

Region	Adidas Total	Nike Footwear	Nike Apparel	Equipment	Reebok Total	Puma Total	Fila Footwear	Fila Apparel
Europe/Africa	49%	16%	10%	2%	33%	69%	18%	19%
Asia	18	7	4	1	10	8	13	18
The Americas	33	36	15	5	58	24	14	16

Source: Company information, FY 2002.

Company	Currency (in millions)	R&D Expenses 2002	% of Revenues	R&D Expenses 2001	% of Revenues
Puma	Euro	24	2.6%	20	3.3%
Nike	U.S. dollar	280	2.8	250	2.6
Reebok	U.S. dollar	45	1.4	42	1.4
Fila	Euro	15	1.7	20	2.0
Adidas	Euro	85	1.3	86	1.4

Source: Company information, own estimates, FY 2002 and FY 2001.

Swede, Johann Lindeberg, took responsibility for the international marketing strategy. He developed the unconventional advertisements that contributed to the image and success of Diesel. Diesel's ads made the brand famous all over the world.

Despite globalization, Diesel's headquarters were still located in Molvena, Italy, from where the company managed 12 subsidiaries across Europe, Asia, and the Americas. Most of Diesel's production was outsourced to small and medium-sized companies. Jeans production was exclusively based in Italy. All international logistics operations (wholesale and retail) were centrally managed and carefully controlled. Diesel employed over 1,300 people worldwide.

In 2002, Diesel was a global company with annual sales of $330 million, of which 85 percent was generated outside of Italy. Renzo Rosso considered the company's outlook to be promising: "I could explode the volume of revenues easily. But we are controlling growth . . . Diesel is the only example of a casualwear or sportswear company that became a luxury brand. We sell jeans from $100 to $300 a pair.

Even when we entered the U.S. market with a price tag of $89, people thought we were crazy and overpriced. The market changed."

PUMA'S VALUE CHAIN

The major components of Puma's value chain were R&D; sourcing, procurement, and logistics; brand management; distribution and retail activities; and collaboration with strategic partners and allies.

Research and Development

Research and development (R&D) played an important role in Puma's corporate strategy. In 2001 and 2002, about 2.5 to 3.5 percent of Puma's revenues were invested in this part of the value chain (see Exhibit 6). This figure was supposed to remain stable during the coming years, and was subject to further increases. Because Puma wanted its products to combine functionality and stylish appearance, product development consisted of R&D and design. Over the past few years, the company had begun to cooperate with famous designers from different cultural backgrounds. New projects were developed under the supervision of modern trendsetters such as Yasuhiro Mihara and designer Jil Sander. Mihara's 2002 collection, for instance, was strongly influenced by the sport of kickboxing. According to Puma's brand strategy, the company launched the New Collection, which blended the elements of sport, lifestyle, and fashion.

Puma tried to be innovative in each part of the production process. To develop the new Shudoh shoe, the company worked with engineering teams of Jordan Grand Prix Racing to learn about new materials, like carbon fiber. These materials were then built into Puma soles. Innovation was strong in Puma's marketing strategy. The company tried to attract customers by both design and functionality in new collections like Nuala and Platinum. Nuala was made of fine fabrics that could still meet the strains of activities like working, traveling, or exercising. Another trend in Puma's design was the retro look. Some products from the 1970s and 1980s collections were relaunched after adding modern elements such as fit or colorway. Other products were taken as an inspiration for the design of new retro-look products. Puma based its latest collections on different hard designs like worker boots, but it transformed and modernized them. In 2002 Puma seemed to be influenced by many different styles. Staying in touch with the most famous influential figures in the music, film, and lifestyle businesses, the company was continuously improving its innovative looks.

Sourcing, Procurement, and Logistics

Puma completely outsourced the production and raw material procurement for its footwear because the labor-intensive production in Germany or other European countries was too expensive and the availability of raw materials was superior elsewhere, especially in Asia. Eighty percent of all production took place in Asia, mainly in Vietnam. Because textiles were more subject to fashion trends, they had to be produced closer to the European and North American market; thus, they were manufactured in Turkey and Mexico. This outsourcing allowed Puma to reduce its working capital, especially inventory, to about 21 percent. Additionally, in 2002, the related costs increased only underproportionally in respect to sales volume.

A business model like that of Inditex, a Spanish fashion company, was not feasible for Puma. Inditex's Zara brand was known for its expertise in quick response, needing only three weeks from the design stage to the delivery to customer. Inditex was highly vertically integrated—managing sourcing, production, and retailing itself. All operations were located in Spain, which drastically cut lead times and allowed quick reaction to customers' needs. Puma could only implement the first component of the strategy, the raw material sourcing. This would allow Puma to shorten the production and enable full quality control of input factors.

Puma selected its production partners according to three criteria: quality, price, and environmental/social factors. It had no long-term contracts with suppliers. Nonetheless most partners worked 10 to 15 years with Puma and were considered strategic partners. These long-term relationships were terminated only in cases of violation of these criteria, or in exceptional circumstances. For example, after the terrorist attacks of September 11, 2001, and the war in Afghanistan, geopolitical uncertainties led Puma to shift its production from Pakistan to China.

One of Puma's major suppliers was Yue Yuen Inc., the world's largest manufacturer of branded footwear. Yue Yuen produced shoes for some of the biggest names in sportswear, including Nike, Reebok, and Adidas. About 75 percent of its sales came from sports shoes. With about 100 footwear and apparel stores in China and manufacturing subsidiaries in Indonesia and Vietnam, Yue Yuen employed about 200,000 people. The company's sales grew to $1.9 billion in 2002, with a net income of $229 million. Yue Yuen's largest competitors were Kingmaker and Pegasus.

By 2002, about 70 percent of Puma's logistics were outsourced. Logistics was not considered to be one of Puma's core competencies and could be done more efficiently by specialized companies. For its apparel and footwear merchandise, sourcing, procurement, and logistics costs accounted for around 62 percent of Puma's revenues. Accessories provided a 44.8 percent gross margin.

Brand Management

A major reason for Puma's turnaround was the new positioning of the brand itself. Especially in the

1980s, Puma had developed an unpopular image; almost no one wanted to wear the jumping cat. This induced a heavy price decline, which only exacerbated the situation. But Jochen Zeitz found investors who understood, just as he did, not only the difficulty and financial implication but also the importance of building a new brand image. The process of repositioning the brand was going to last several years. The key was to make Puma desirable again. From 1997 on, the company made many efforts to ensure that Puma became, according to Zeitz, a "strong and dynamic brand with a huge potential." By 2003, Puma's popularity was so high that international superstars like Madonna were proud to wear Puma products without any compensation. Puma products were exposed in exclusive boutiques next to luxury brands such as Gucci and Prada. This revitalization of the brand was exceptional. Although Adidas also had severe image problems in the 1980s and 1990s, it had never become as disreputable as Puma, as it had never lost specialized sport dealers in its distribution network.

To ensure its ongoing success, Puma searched for charismatic personalities who could proliferate the desired brand perception, recognition, and awareness even further. But it was essential that these representatives stood for exactly what Puma wanted to communicate. In 2000, the model and yoga fan Christy Turlington created her own Puma collection under the name of Nuala, derived from the Puma-coined word *Nutopia*—a place of utopic dreams, full of fresh air, laughter, relaxation and revitalization. Nuala products were exclusively for women and designed to express their wish of being independent, athletic, and attractive at the same time.

Sponsorship played a major role in Puma's brand management. Unlike competitors, Puma aimed not solely to display its label but also to communicate its philosophy. An example was the company's sponsorship of the Jamaican running team. Everybody loved Jamaican athletes because they always played the role of the underdog. For example, they were never really expected to win the 1998 soccer world championship or the Olympic bobsled competition. Many people associated Jamaica with the joy of living, sunshine, and the athletic spirit. Jamaicans were just different from other athletes. This was perfect for Puma's purposes, which were to communicate how much fun and how unique it was to participate in sports while using Puma products. Similarly, sponsorship of the national soccer team of Cameroon showed that Puma understood the needs of its customers. Very often, the Cameroon team had to play under extreme temperatures, and Puma's newly designed sleeveless jerseys perfectly met the players' wishes. In early 2003 Puma announced more sponsorship, namely for the Italian national soccer team.

Puma also equipped several racing teams from the Formula One circuit. The move into motor sports had previously been tried in the 1970s and 1980s, but since 2000 the company had made much more effort to become a major motor sportswear supplier. At the beginning of 2003, Puma provided five teams with shoes and apparel: Toyota, Jaguar, Sauber, Minardi, and Jordan. The company's willingness to enter this sports category was underlined by the official supply of sportswear for the FIA World Rally Championship, the Ford Rally division, and freestyle motocross champion Travis Pastrana.

Because Puma did not have the same financial resources as its bigger competitors Nike and Adidas, it was important for the company to make the best possible use of what was available. Linford Christie, one of the world's most famous short-distance sprinters, participated in a race and later appeared on a press conference during the Atlanta 1996 Olympic Games wearing contact lenses with the Puma cat symbol. Even though Christie did not win the race, the attention of the fans and the media focused on Puma. Zeitz emphasized, "Such successes are the results of the endless creativity of our workforce, which we maximize through our open-minded corporate culture. We prefer quality over quantity and rely on innovation, also for our publicity."

Moving toward lifestyle products was fundamental for the new positioning of Puma. On the one hand, the company had to answer and follow upcoming trends quickly, and on the other hand, it had to create trends. Certainly one outstanding trend in the early 2000s that Puma significantly influenced was the revival of the sports look of the 1970s and 1980s. These products were designed in cooperation with fashion celebrity Jil Sander, who was searching for a sports shoe for her presentations. The Puma classic King was reintroduced with street styling in the Avanti. Other companies such as Prada, Gucci, Versace, Dolce & Gabbana, Hugo Boss, Nike, Adidas, and Reebok also observed this convergence of sports and fashion products. A new market segment of lifestyle sportswear was created.

According to Zeitz, Puma had a significant advantage in the lifestyle sportswear segment over competitors from the fashion industry. While it was easier for a sports company like Puma to build up fashion know-how with the help of designers, it was hard for fashion companies to gain knowledge and credibility in sports apparel and equipment. This knowledge was usually the result of years of experience. Another reason why Puma was well prepared for this trend was Zeitz's understanding of fashion as "the new combination of elements of the past." Moreover, Puma had an enormous store of old product variations, its so-called heritage, out of which it could easily pick samples for a potential product re-launch, without having to design from scratch. Products based on old models accounted for 10 percent of sales. Thus, it was crucial to be a first-mover or fast-follower: "Nike was late and is now pumping lots of resources in this market to make up for their tardiness."

It was also very important to find the right timing for launching a new product line. Because the popularity of sports usually followed a cyclical pattern, the demand for the corresponding products varied. Cycles differed from sport to sport, but a general rule of thumb predicted that cycles lasted for approximately 12 to 15 years, with 5 to 8 years of popularity. Consequently, there was a lower demand for 4 to 10 years. This showed that an investment in a new product line had to be well planned. In the best-case scenario, Puma had to enter a sports market two years before its revival in order to maximize profits. These two years gave Puma enough time to prepare for the upcoming demand. As the first-mover, the company could gain essential market experience and give the customer the impression of always having been present in this market, fostering a professional image. In 2003, for example, Puma entered the cricket market. It started in Australia and South Africa, where cricket was one of the most practiced sports. Eventually, cricket was expected to gain more popularity around the world. In this case Puma's experience would be key in entering other national markets quickly.

However, even the best brand positioning would not help if customers were not aware of it. Although Puma undertook numerous sponsoring activities, the company knew it also had to carry out advertising activities. Initially, Puma chose the music television channel MTV, which was known for having a rather young audience who tried to differentiate themselves from or even rebel against ordinary social standards and the average community. For example, funny TV commercials that dealt with a Jamaican who shared the wish of all Jamaican people to wear Puma shoes

were broadcast several times a day. The same was true for the 4SOME competition, which was often announced on MTV. Furthermore, Puma benefited massively from generous product placement of its shareholder New Regency, which placed Puma in several successful Hollywood movies, such as *Dare-Devil, Unfaithful, Life or Something Like It,* and *High Crimes.* However, Puma only selected movies that communicated the same message as the company.

Additionally, Puma created a Web presence that fit its image. The home page displayed different advertisements from the Jamaica line. Interactive stories transported the reader into a manager's thoughts during his 96-hour business trip around the world wearing Puma casual and business attire. Another project promoted on the Internet was the "top winner thrift." A collection of 510 unique and individual shoes was created and sold at premium prices all over the world. These shoes consisted of a mixture of recycled cloth from such items as jeans and ties. With the purchase of one of these shoes the buyer was allowed to enter an exclusive community on the Web. During the promotion of the Regency film *DareDevil,* Puma linked a pop-up to its home page, which displayed a quiz game. Participants could win Puma and "DareDevil" products.

Puma had become very popular during the last few years, inducing increased sales. But could popularity endanger the brand's exclusiveness? If the number of Puma customers steadily grew, could the brand name and desirability rapidly go down? For customers, wearing Puma was a way to differentiate themselves from others. What would happen if this was not possible anymore? Puma's managers did not seem to fear this threat. According to them, the critical size at which overpopularity might become a problem had not yet been reached. Nike, although already a huge company, had succeeded in remaining popular. Jochen Zeitz saw Nike's decisive factor as numerous innovations. According to him, a brand's desirability depended mainly on innovations and on the ability to continuously arouse customer attention. Thus, any brand, regardless of its size, had to cope with the challenge of keeping its uniqueness. Nevertheless, there was still a size beyond which it was very difficult to grow and yet keep the brand attractiveness on a high level. Puma, however, was on the right track. It was considered as rebellious and stylish, two desirable attributes, especially compared to its competitors. Nike was perceived more as a cool company with reliable products for everyone. Adidas stood for technical expertise and family products. Reebok had no specific characteristics.

Distribution and Retail

Puma outsourced up to 70 percent of its distribution logistics. For the remaining 30 percent, there were two possibilities of handling distribution: building up a system or acquiring one from competitors. A typical example for buying a distribution network was the takeover of Tretorn, a specialized Swedish sports brand. Building up a distribution network for the small Scandinavian market would have been too expensive, but generally Puma preferred to develop its own network in Europe.

In retail, Puma relied on carefully selected partners, which fit its corporate message. Few of the company's partners were traditional sports dealers. Some product lines such as Nuala or Platinum were even sold in shops together with luxury brands like Prada and Escada.

Sport retailers rarely operated globally. The only worldwide operating partners were Foot Locker and Intersport. In Germany the most important retailer was Intersport, with a market share of 29.7 percent; in France, Decathlon with 29.9 percent; and in Britain, JJB Sports with 22.6 percent (see Exhibit 7). Due to low transportation costs among the different countries, there was no price discrimination. Only in the United States did low retailing costs allow for a more competitive pricing.

Puma's so-called concept stores had been introduced a few years ago and represented an additional direct distribution channel. Contrary to competitors' "temples," Puma stores had more than simply a representative function: They had to be profitable as well. By the end of 2002, Puma was running 15 stores, which were expected to account for 10 percent of net sales by 2006.

In some countries, especially in Asia, the risk for Puma was too high. To avoid these uncertainties, the company licensed to local companies that produced and sold under the Puma label.

Partnerships and Alliances

Since the end of the 1990s, analysts had repeatedly predicted probable mergers, acquisitions, or joint ventures between Puma and other companies. Among these companies, Kappa, Lotto, Roots, Helly Hansen, and Quiksilver were often mentioned, partly because of their geographic focus and complementary brand positioning in regard to Puma. In fact, however, Puma only once participated in the industry's consolidation. It acquired the Swedish company Tretorn, Europe's third largest manufacturer of tennis balls, from Proventus for €23 million in July 2001. Tretorn then contributed about €45 million in sales. One reason for Puma's acquisition of Tretorn was the latter's great positioning for outdoor wear in Scandinavia. It had a sophisticated and broad distribution system in the Scandinavian market and, according to Zeitz, a very skilled management team. Following this acquisition, Puma was able to efficiently allocate overhead costs for its distribution functions in Sweden, Denmark, and Norway. Other single merger and acquisition activities in the sports market were the acquisition of Salomon by Adidas in 1997, the takeover of Canstar Sports and Hurley International by Nike in 1995 and 2002, and the acquisition of Avia and Ellesse International by Reebok in 1987.

However, compared to the fashion industry, the number and volume of merger and acquisition activities in sports apparel were relatively low. In the fashion industry, luxury and lifestyle goods giants like LVMH, PinaultPrintempsRedoute, Gucci, and Richemont emerged within a short time and gained market control. In addition to potential synergies, these companies realized the opportunity of broad product portfolios. Thus, LVMH not only possessed a wide range of world-renowned brands (Moët & Chandon, Louis Vuitton, Kenzo, Givenchy, Donna Karan) but was also forward-integrated, owning Sephora, a perfume retailer, and controlling duty-free shops on a worldwide scale. Stock markets rewarded these strategies by allowing high company valuations to this industry (see Exhibit 1).

For the sports apparel industry Zeitz saw the possibility for many smaller, regional companies to be profitable. He did not believe that, in the short run, companies needed a critical mass to survive. Thus, Puma did not see any benefit that an acquired company could develop within the Puma organization at the moment. Synergies on the cost side were hard to realize, especially if the target company had also outsourced most of its production.

Zeitz believed in Puma's historic brand credibility, which could be applied to a whole variety of sports. He believed that the Puma brand was far stronger and more flexible than the brands of some

exhibit 7   **European and Worldwide Market Shares of Retailers in the Sports Equipment Industry**

Country	Retailers	Euros (in millions)	Market Share
Austria	Intersport	603	44.7%
	Sport Eybl & Sport Experts (part of Intersport)	387	28.7
	Sport2000	254	18.8
	Hervis	200	14.8
	Kästner & Oehler	100	7.4
	Market size	*1,350*	
Belgium	Decathlon	53	8.0%
	Disport	50	7.6
	Fair Play	49	7.4
	Makro	40	6.1
	Intersport	32	4.8
	GoSport	27	4.1
	Market size	*660*	
Denmark	Sport Masters	120	21.1%
	Intersport	120	21.1
	Market size	*570*	
Finland	Kesport/Intersport	211	26.2%
	Sportia	87	10.8
	Citymarket	77	9.6
	Prisma	50	6.2
	Top-Sport	42	5.2
	Sport Group Finland/Elmo	24	3.0
	Market size	*805*	
France	Decathlon	2,300	29.9%
	Rallye (GoSport & Courir)	710	9.2
	Intersport	690	9.0
	Sport2000	305	4.0
	Technicien du Sport	240	3.1
	Market size	*7,680*	
Germany	Intersport	2,300	29.7%
	Sport2000	1,270	16.4
	KarstadtQuelle	1,200	15.5
	Metro	720	9.3
	Sport-Scheck (part of Intersport)	312	4.0
	Sport Voswinkel (part of Intersport)	70	0.9
	Market size	*7,740*	
Holland	Intres Sport	229	15.5%
	Fair Play	150	10.1
	Euretco Sport	135	9.1
	Market size	*1,480*	

exhibit 7   **(continued)**

Country	Retailers	Euros (in millions)	Market Share
Italy	Intersport	510	11.2%
	Gisalfa (part of Intersport)	330	7.2
	Giacomelli	239	5.2
	Selezione Sport	230	5.0
	Longoni (part of Selezione)	132	2.9
	Decathlon	120	2.6
	Market size	*4,570*	
Norway	G-Sport	300	34.1%
	Intersport	170	19.3
	MX Sport	82	9.3
	Market size	*880*	
Spain	El Corte Inglés	384	13.5%
	Décathlon	250	8.8
	Intersport	245	8.6
	Detall Sport	173	6.1
	Sport Disseny	112	3.9
	Market size	*2,840*	
Sweden	Intersport	298	19.5%
	Stadium	298	19.5
	Team Sportia	182	11.9
	Market size	*1,530*	
Switzerland	Intersport	385	19.3%
	Migros & Globus	304	15.2
	Ochsner	165	8.3
	Manor Group	146	7.3
	Market size	*2,000*	
United Kingdom	JJB Sports	1,190	22.6%
	Blacks	552	10.5
	Sports Soccer	520	9.9
	JD Sports	395	7.5
	All:sports	238	4.5
	Intersport	190	3.6
	Market size	*5,270*	
Total market size		*37,375*	

Source: Sporting Goods Intelligence (2002), FY 2001.

Largest Sports Equipment Retailers Worldwide

Buying Groups	Country	2000	1999
Intersport	Switzerland	5,622	6,181
Sport2000	Germany	2,712	2,801

(continues)

exhibit 7 **(concluded)**

Retailers	Country	2000	1999
Venators	United States	4,233	3,726
Decathlon	France	2,304	2,318
The Sports Authority	United States	1,498	1,493
Alpen	Japan	1,465	1,276
L. L. Bean	United States	1,100	1,030
Karstadt	Germany	1,014	1,094
JJB Sports	United Kingdom	1,005	993
Bass Pro Shops	United States	960	950
Canadian Tire	Canada	929	966
Dick's Sporting Goods	United States	900	675
Cabela's	United States	800	750
Rallye	France	789	776
Joshuya	Japan	610	618
Gart Sports	United States	751	681
R.E.I.	United States	698	621
The Finish Line	United States	664	586
Academy Sports	United States	612	600
Pacific Sunwear	United States	590	437
Footaction USA	United States	588	643
Xebio	Japan	587	598
Big 5 Sporting Goods	United States	572	514
Blacks	United Kingdom	449	337
Victoria	Japan	446	453
Forzani	Canada	434	379
Modell's	United States	425	380
Galyan's	United States	422	328
Sport Soccer	United Kingdom	368	317
El Corte Ingles	Spain	363	378
Allsports	United Kingdom	350	246
Himaraya	Japan	341	324
Subtotal		26,267	24,487
Total		32,761	30,811

Source: Sporting Goods Intelligence (2001), in USD m, FY 2000.

of its large competitors. But he also realized that there was an upper boundary, above which it was very difficult to continue organic growth. He was undecided but felt that the large player Nike would soon have reached that line. This could be the trigger for fierce industry consolidation. In fact, there had been rumors recently about a takeover of Benetton's SportsSystem division by Puma.

Recent developments and the expected market changes would force the Puma cat to run even faster.

Should the company continue its organic growth strategy? If so, how could this be done most efficiently? What would be the natural restrictions in terms of size and market maturity? How far could the Puma brand be stretched while at the same time improving overall brand perception? These were only some of the questions Zeitz had to consider when thinking about Puma's future. He knew that there were many feasible options and he had many ideas . . .

The Globalization of Beringer Blass Wine Estates

Armand Gilinsky, Jr.
Sonoma State University

Richard Castaldi
San Francisco State University

Raymond H. Lopez
Pace University

In late September 2002, Walt Klenz was deciding whether Beringer Blass Wine Estates should pursue internal growth via development of its current premium wine brands or external growth via acquisitions of new brands. Klenz was ending his first year as Beringer Blass's managing director and 12th year as Beringer's president.

Two years earlier, he had overseen a merger between the Australia-based Foster's Brewing Group and California-based Beringer Wine Estates, a move that had triggered a wave of similar consolidation transactions around the world of premium wines. Rumors abounded in the industry that larger rivals such as E. & J. Gallo, Constellation, and Diageo were actively seeking acquisitions of premium wineries to increase global market share.

As Klenz (pronounced *cleanse*) prepared his notes for a presentation called "Globalization of the Wine Industry" to over 300 attendees at an annual wine industry conference in Napa, California, he privately wondered how he was going to guide Beringer Blass toward globalization in the future.

The authors gratefully acknowledge a Business and International Education (BIE) grant from the U.S. Department of Education and a matching grant from the College of Business at San Francisco State University in partial support of this research. We also gratefully acknowledge the financial support of the Wine Business Program at Sonoma State University, which made possible the contributions of student researchers Elizabeth Rice and Garrett Savage.

BERINGER'S HISTORY

In 1875 two German emigrants, Jacob and Frederick Beringer, purchased property in St. Helena, California, for $14,500. During the following year, Jacob began working his new vineyards and started construction of a stone winery building. He employed Chinese laborers to build limestone-lined aging tunnels for his product. In 1880, Frederick opened a store and a wine cellar to accommodate the sale of wine in New York. The Beringer brothers commenced an education and marketing program to introduce Napa Valley wine to the East Coast market. Their specialty, even in those early years, was premium table wines.

Beringer family members continuously owned the winery until 1971, when they sold it to the Nestlé Company, which renamed the Beringer subsidiary Wine World Estates. Over the next 25 years, Nestlé hired management to implement an expansion strategy that included purchase and development of extensive acreage positions in prime growing regions of Napa, Sonoma, Lake, Santa Barbara, and San Luis Obispo Counties in California. Ownership of these vineyards enabled Wine World to control a source of premium-quality wine grapes at an attractive cost.

In a series of sweeping moves, Wine World's winemaker, Myron Nightingale, overhauled operations, retooled the winery, acquired new vineyard properties, negotiated long-term leases for additional vineyard capacity, and refocused production on the development and sale of world-class wines. Michael Moone became CEO in 1984 to oversee the operations of Wine World. Moone pursued expansion via both acquisitions and start-ups of new brands. Chateau Souverain, located in the Sonoma Valley, was acquired in 1986. Also in that year, Wine World launched a new brand, Napa Ridge. In 1988, Wine World's Estrella River Winery in Paso Robles was refurbished and renamed Meridian Vineyards. Results of these initiatives began to bear fruit by the late 1980s. New private reserve wines won accolades throughout the industry, and overall wine quality rose rapidly. Wine World had thus begun the process of redefining itself as a top-quality producer, slowly but steadily shedding its prior image as a company that made "ordinary wines." In 1990, Moone relinquished his CEO position to Walter Klenz. Klenz had been hired by Nestlé and joined Wine World in 1976, first working in marketing and then in financial operations.

THE LEVERAGED BUYOUT

In early 1996, Michael Moone reentered the market with a private company named Silverado Partners. Moone and dealmaker David Bonderman, who headed the El Paso–based Texas Pacific Group (TPG), engineered a leveraged buyout of Wine World Estates. TPG acquired all the then-outstanding common stock of Beringer Wine Estates Company. The total purchase price was approximately $371 million, which included net cash paid of $258 million, short-term mezzanine financing provided by the seller of $96 million, and acquisition costs of $17 million. The deal resulted in the business going back to its roots, with the new name of Beringer Wine Estates.

In addition to paying down acquisition debt, one of the most important goals of venture-capital-sponsored leveraged buyouts was an "exit strategy" to realize positive returns on investment. The principals of TPG had chosen the Beringer operations and completed their acquisition with this goal in mind. In addition to having a strong brand recognition in the product marketplace, the company expected that, when a public sale of shares was eventually completed, the stock would be well received by investors, especially those familiar with the wine industry.

On April 1, 1996, Beringer acquired the net assets of Chateau St. Jean from Suntory International Corporation. Net cash paid to the seller amounted to

$29.3 million, with acquisition costs of $1.9 million, for a total purchase price of $31.2 million. In order to pay for this acquisition, the company issued 945,000 Class B common shares for a net proceeds of $4.725 million. Subsequently, in September 1996, the company issued 11,980 Class A shares and 224,380 Class B shares to investors, resulting in net proceeds of $825,000.

On February 28, 1997, Beringer acquired Stags' Leap Winery, Inc., from Stags' Leap Associates and various individuals. Net cash paid to the sellers amounted to $19.2 million, with a note due to the seller aggregating $2.85 million. The total purchase price amounted to $23.2 million, which included transaction expenses of $1.15 million.

Beringer's strategies at the time included internal growth through brand development and external growth through mergers and/or acquisitions. A publicly traded company would create the greatest financial flexibility in order to accomplish its goals as well as to provide liquidity for its owners. This meant preparing Beringer for life as a public company. Management information systems needed to be enhanced; accounting, reporting, and control systems needed to be put into place; and Beringer needed to keep its records on a quarterly basis, in order to comply with Securities and Exchange Commission (SEC) requirements. Doug Walker had been hired in 1996 to implement many of these systems, but the final piece of the puzzle was the hiring of a chief financial officer, whose job was to coordinate the financial and reporting activities as well as to develop a plan for future operations.

THE INITIAL PUBLIC OFFERING

Early in June 1997, Peter F. Scott was hired as a senior vice president for finance and operations. Scott had spent seven years with Kendall-Jackson Winery, most recently as senior vice president of finance and administration. He had also spent six years as a management consultant and eight years with a nationally known public accounting firm. Scott was pleased to learn of Beringer's planned initial public offering (IPO) and from the outset become intimately involved with its preparation.[1]

---

[1] Scott was subsequently appointed chief financial officer of Foster's Group in November 2003.

In a 2001 interview, Klenz described the rationale behind taking Beringer public:

> We made a conscious decision to proceed with the IPO based on our feeling that, in the wine industry you need to be either very big or very small—you can't be a "tweener." Becoming big provided economies of scale and the ability to have a critical mass of products and volume for distributors—and access to them. The major pluses for an IPO included improving our balance sheet, providing us with an opportunity to grow even faster via acquisitions, and establishing first-mover advantage on the way to becoming a big premium winery. Now we could compete with the top four or five wineries in the world, rather than 300–400 other small wineries. It also enabled us to provide for employee ownership, not to mention the liquidity to "monetize" their ownership down the road.[2]

As of 1997, however, only three American wine businesses, Canandaigua (New York), Chalone Wine Group (Napa), and Robert Mondavi Corporation (Napa), were publicly traded. Klenz had been inspired by their success as public companies:

> Were we selling 25 percent of our company to the public too cheap? Some people on our team did argue, "Why not wait one or two years and sell at $40 per share rather than the $26 per share IPO price." Yet October 1997 was in the middle of a hot market for company IPOs, and we couldn't control for external market factors. We didn't know how long the window would stay open for IPOs, especially for relatively small companies like Beringer Wine Estates. Financial people—Wall Street—were at the time interested in the high growth story in the premium wine segment. The wine industry had recently experienced sustained double-digit growth for over a decade, unique in beverages. We felt that mid-teen growth rates in sales were sustainable throughout the future. We also offered downside protection in terms of real sales, real inventories, real consumers, and real assets, including real estate.[3]

Despite the sell-off in the U.S. financial markets and dampened trading conditions due to the worsening Asian financial crisis in the late summer of 1997, Beringer continued on course toward its IPO. Beringer was initially listed on the Nasdaq[4] on October 29, 1997, at $26 per share.

According to Klenz, the stock offering turned out to be oversubscribed, despite some last-minute jitters in the U.S. stock markets, attributed to the financial crisis in Asia:

> We waited 24 hours past the original IPO date due to a collapse in the Asian financial markets. Only two IPOs were done that day, which was unusual as nearly 20 IPOs were done per day at that time. Our IPO deal, as it turned out, was eight times oversubscribed. We raised $135 million net from the IPO. That gave us currency that we attempted to use over the next couple of years to do a couple of major acquisition deals—which, as it later turned out, we were unsuccessful at doing.[5]

CONTINUED DIVERSIFICATION OF THE PORTFOLIO OF WINE BRANDS

In April 1998, Beringer's stock price reached an all-time high of $55 per share. Beringer had by then become one of the most popular wine companies in the world, with six award-winning wines and one exporting company. Its Beringer Estates–branded wines were among the fastest-growing in the premium wine segment.

Over the next two years Beringer developed a portfolio of brands to compete across different price segments of the wine business. This led to a rumored bid to acquire privately held Kendall-Jackson Estates in 2000; however, terms of the deal could not be agreed on by both parties. Kendall-Jackson, based in Sonoma County, California, also rebuffed friendly takeover offers from Diageo, Brown-Forman, and Allied Domecq. Meanwhile, plans were under way to diversify Beringer's product line at the low end of the market, previously dominated by its White Zinfandel, by introducing new varietal wines to its portfolio such as a White Merlot and a Red Zinfandel.[6]

Klenz recalled:

> Our diversification challenge at this time was to build a company across two major price points: mass-market premium and ultrapremium. The mass-market

---

[2]Interview with casewriters on April 23, 2001.
[3]Ibid.
[4]As Nasdaq ticker symbol BERW.

[5]Interview with casewriters, April 23, 2001.
[6]In 1983, laws in the United States had taken effect controlling what wineries could put on their labels. A *varietal wine* meant one variety of grape—the name of a single grape could be used if not less than 75 percent of the wine was derived from grapes of that variety, the entire 75 percent of which was grown in the labeled appellation of origin.

exhibit 1   **Beringer Wine Estates, Financial and Operating Highlights, 1995–1999 (all data in millions)**

	Fiscal Year Ended June 30				
	1999	**1998**	**1997**	**1996**	**1995**
Net revenue	$376.2	$318.4	$269.5	$231.7	$202.0
Adjusted gross profit	194.6	163.7	134.9	116.1	100.7
Adjusted operating income	83.0	70.5	56.3	43.9	34.8
Adjusted net income	39.3	29.5	15.1	15.6	16.8
Volume (9-liter case equivalent)	6.8	6.1	5.4	5.0	4.6
Total assets	$644.3	$543.6	$467.2	$438.7	$289.9
Total debt	$328.0	$277.2	$319.1	$289.2	N/A

N/A = not available

Source: Beringer Wine Estates, 1999 annual report.

premium segment, wines selling for $5–$10, was a very competitive market and for this segment we needed scale economies. The ultrapremium segment, wines selling for $20–$40, was represented by our Stag's Leap, Chateau St. Jean, and St. Clement winery acquisition in 1999. We hoped to build a large portfolio of ultrapremium wines. This would give us an enormous benefit with the wine trade (not the consumer), in that we could become a "one-stop shop" for wholesalers and distributors. Being a big wine company would provide access to international markets.[7]

Klenz intended to expand Beringer's distribution into international markets. By the early 21st century, exports to Europe, Canada, and Asia were forecast to represent approximately 10 percent of Beringer's operating income. (See Exhibit 1 for Beringer's financial and operating highlights from 1995 to 1999.)

THE FOSTER'S DEAL

Over the past six years, Foster's had transformed itself from an Australia-centric brewing company into a "global premium branded beer and wine company." While during the 1990s beer and wine consumption around the world had been declining by 1–2 percent a year, consumption of premium wines (those costing over $5 a bottle) had been rising

steadily—by over 5 percent a year—in selected markets such as Britain and America.[8] In 1996, Foster's, Australia's biggest brewer, bought its first wine company, Mildara Blass of Australia. Since then it had acquired more than 20 wine producers—the largest being Beringer of St. Helena, California.

On August 29, 2000, Foster's Brewing Group announced a friendly merger agreement to buy Beringer Wine Estates for $1.5 billion, comprising $1.2 billion in cash for 100 percent of Beringer's outstanding stock and the assumption of $300 million in debt.[9] Foster's completed the acquisition of Beringer Wine Estates in October 2000, which was subsequently merged with Foster's existing wine business, Mildara Blass, and renamed Beringer Blass Wine Estates. According to a Beringer Blass press release, "Our new name signals our future direction, which is to maximize our combined strengths in high-return, high-growth wine markets worldwide."

In September 2001, Foster's bought Napa Valley producer Etude Wines and 51 percent of New Zealand's Matua Valley Wines. By 2002, Beringer Blass claimed to be the second most profitable wine producer in the world, after E. & J. Gallo of California. Wine now accounted for 40 percent of Foster's profits.

---

[7]Interview with casewriters, April 23, 2001.

[8]L. Himelstein, "This Merlot's for You," *Business Week,* September 30, 2002, pp. 66–68.

[9]All amounts in U.S. dollars, unless otherwise stated. Exchange rate: Australian $1 = U.S.$0.56.

exhibit 2 **The Three-Tier Distribution System for Wine in the United States**

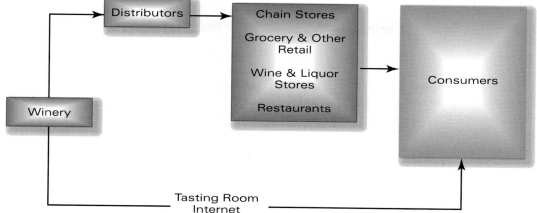

The deal offered both shareholder value and synergy, according to Klenz:

> Globalization was already a key aspect of our diversification strategy, but could we afford to do it by ourselves using internally generated funds? The U.S. was the largest premium wine market in the world and by far the most profitable in the world. We'd already become the low-cost producer in the wine industry. That part was easy to replicate elsewhere, but gaining access to distribution channels was a different proposition. Synergy in our industry meant having trade credibility, and trade credibility meant having access to distribution channels around the world. It was difficult to build this access. It was better to buy access. When Foster's approached us, we thought this deal would give them access to distribution here in the U.S. and us access to distribution in Europe and Asia. Foster's got geographical diversification, financial diversification (lowering its currency risk), and product diversification. We got the high multiple and deeper pockets to pursue globalization.[10]

The merger resulted in the creation of the largest premium wine company in the world, with combined revenue of nearly $886 million in fiscal year 2000. At the time, its Mildara Blass operating unit possessed 25 percent of Australia's superpremium wine market segment (over A$10.00 per bottle, or about $5.00–$6.00), and its main export markets were the United States, the United Kingdom, and Europe. With its purchase of Beringer, Foster's hoped to lever-

age its U.S. distribution channels for Australian wines as well as its Australian distribution channels for California wines. Foster's Brewing Group was renamed Foster's Group, reflecting its desire to shed its former image as a brewing company.

DISTRIBUTION CHANNELS

As was the case with other producers of alcoholic beverages, Beringer Blass's wine was sold in the United States through a three-tier distribution system. See Exhibit 2 for a diagram depicting the three-tier distribution system. Wineries or importers (the first tier) sold wine to wholesalers and distributors (the second tier), who provided legal fulfillment of wine products to local retail businesses (the third tier) within a certain state. Wine was a controlled substance, and laws in each state differed regarding how it could be sold. Typically, wine passed through the second tier via wholesalers and distributors, making direct shipping to retailers or selling wine through the Internet and wine-buying clubs difficult or impossible in all but 13 states. Three major distributors, Southern Wine & Spirits, Charmer/Sunbelt, and National, dominated alcoholic beverage distribution. Three other dominant distributors included Glazer and Republic (in Texas) and Young's Market (in California). According to *Impact Databank*, these distributors together controlled nearly

---

[10]Interview with casewriters, April 2001.

50–60 percent of all wine distributed in the United States. Over the past decade nearly 1,000 smaller distributors had become marginalized or acquired due to the advantages of scale and scope afforded to the three largest distributors. Similar consolidation was under way in the third tier, primarily on the retail ("off-premises") side.

The third tier of the distribution system consisted of retail and nonretail outlets. According to *Adams Wine Handbook,* supermarkets, convenience stores, club stores, mail order and Internet retailers, specialty stores, and wine clubs accounted for 78 percent of total sales volume.[11] In the United States, supermarkets alone accounted for 41 percent of retail wine sales and the largest chains—including discount retailers such as Costco, Wal-Mart, and Trader Joe's—were very influential in wine distribution. They had become dominant in food and drink retailing and made one-stop shopping an appealing concept for consumers. Furthermore, supermarkets and discount retailers had considerable bargaining leverage with wholesalers. The role of specialty stores—independent wine shops—in wine distribution diminished due to the increasing power of supermarkets. Specialty stores' share of retail wine sales was about 23 percent in the United States. Nevertheless, specialty stores were unlikely to disappear soon because they provided superior knowledge of wine and customer service. Specialty stores tended to carry specialty brands and limited production labels, attracting wine connoisseurs and enthusiasts. "On-premises" sales, via nonretail outlets such as restaurants, hotels, and airlines, accounted for the remaining 22 percent of wine volume in the United States, according to *Adams Wine Handbook.*

BERINGER BLASS'S WINE BUSINESS STRATEGY

Following the merger, Beringer Blass's new mission statement declared a "focus on becoming the most valuable premium wine company in the world by providing a quality wine experience to every customer in every market." Exhibit 3 presents Beringer Blass's mission statement and strategy.

The integration of the Beringer and Blass international operations into a unified operating unit commenced in 2001. Related to the challenge of building

a global wine business was identifying and leveraging the capabilities previously developed by the two wine businesses, in essence redefining them as multicountry "centers of excellence." Broadly speaking, a center of excellence could be defined as an organizational unit that embodied a distinctive set of capabilities that were recognized as an important source of value creation, with the intention that its capabilities be leveraged by and/or disseminated to the other parts of the firm.[12] With increased value creation in mind, Beringer Blass began its strategic reorganization plan. This plan entailed the creation of distinct operating divisions to recognize a consumer-based, trade channel, and product mix focus: premium wine, luxury wine, on-premise sales, and consumer direct sales. According to Foster's 2001 annual report, "Initial synergies were expected by 2002."

Beringer Blass's wine business strategy consisted of using three separate channels in its efforts to become a major international wine producer: wine trade, clubs, and services:

1. *Wine trade.* Beringer's wine trade strategy was to make and market to institutional (on-premises) and retail (off-premises) customers the world's leading portfolio of international premium wine brands. In September 2001, Beringer Blass completed the $35 million buyout of Italian producer Castello di Gabbiano and the purchase of California's Etude Wines. On September 4, 2002, Beringer agreed to purchase the Carmenet brand of wines from Chalone Wine Group in Napa, California, for $5.4 million. Top priority was placed on increasing export sales of Beringer Blass's portfolio brands, particularly to the United Kingdom, by combining Mildara Blass and Beringer Blass's existing networks of international distributors. Beringer Blass set up expanded sales offices in each of its major markets (the United States, Europe, and the Pacific Rim), targeting five-star hotels, up-market restaurants, and premium liquor outlets. Signaling its strong commitment to further developing its European wine business, on February 20, 2002, Beringer Blass

---

[11]*Adams Wine Handbook* (New York: Adams Business Media, 1999).

[12]Adapted from T. S. Frost, J. M. Birkinshaw, and P. C. Ensign, "Centers of Excellence in Multinational Corporations," *Strategic Management Journal* 23 (2002), pp. 997–1018. This paper examines the conditions under which centers of excellence emerge in foreign subsidiaries of multinational firms and their impact on firm performance. The authors conclude that achieving internal recognition as a center of excellence and the resultant impact on firm performance are largely a function of parent company investment.

exhibit 3   **Beringer Blass Wine Estates' Mission and Strategy, 2002**

Mission

Our mission at Beringer Blass Wine Estates is to be clearly recognised as the "most valuable" premium wine company in the world, by providing a quality wine experience to every customer in each market and segment in which we operate.

Strategy

Focus on premium end of the global wine market

We differentiate ourselves from competitors by focusing on the premium end of the global wine market.

Our Wine Trade business makes and markets an outstanding international portfolio of premium regional varietal wines. Our approach is to offer a balanced, multi-brand, multi-price-point portfolio, ensuring that the brand values and reputations of our icon wines are preserved and leveraged throughout the entire brand range. This balanced approach creates value and affords a natural hedge against economic trends. In addition, our continuing, defined program of new product development maintains vitality in the portfolio, providing growth opportunities over and above the organic growth of our base brands.

Recognising that fine wines consumers value distinctiveness and diversity, we actively cultivate and promote the unique heritage and style of each of our wineries around the world, with individual wine brands being championed by individual winemakers. We also tailor our portfolio and marketing investment to local market demand and opportunities wherever we operate. For our flagship international retail wines (including Wolf Blass, Beringer Vineyards, Black Opal and Greg Norman Estates), brand management is led from the primary market, with our global brand development panel setting overall brand priorities and protecting brand integrity across all markets.

Targeting premium wine consumers who want the conveniences and other benefits of buying direct, our Wine Clubs seek to differentiate themselves from competitors by offering exclusive quality wines, outstanding customer services and comprehensive member benefits such as personal cellar management software, wine cellaring services and wine accessories.

Many of our Wine Clubs across the world are highly awarded wine producers in their own right, and increasingly the Wine Clubs channel is leveraging its ability to supply wines from across the world to enhance member offers.

Supplying wine producers, our Wine Services channel also focuses on the premium end of the market. Growth is driven by the increasing trend among premium wine producers to differentiate their brands through more sophisticated packaging material and higher quality contract bottling services.

Global Presence

Global distribution strength is the second plank of our strategy.

No other table wine company in the world has better market depth than Beringer Blass across the key premium wine markets of North America, Australia and Europe.

We have a decentralised approach to global distribution, locating managers within their region of responsibility to ensure that business decisions are based on local market conditions and individual customer requirements. Our Trade sales offices are located in the USA, Australia, United Kingdom, Switzerland, Canada, New Zealand, Singapore, Hong Kong and Japan.

Our clubs operate in Australia, New Zealand, Germany, Netherlands, France, Belgium, UK, USA and Japan.

Our Wine Services businesses operate in Australia, New Zealand and France.

Unique multiple-channel approach

We are unique among the world's major wine producers in operating three separate business channels—Trade, Clubs and Services.

- Our Wine Trade strategy is to make and market the world's leading portfolio of international premium wine brands.
- Our Wine Clubs channel aims to reinforce and further develop its position as the world's leading consumer-direct merchant for premium wine and wine-related products.
- In Wine Services, our goal is to be the leading supplier of premium packaging and warehousing services to the wines industry, globally.

With relatively low capital requirements, our Clubs and Services businesses achieve strong capital returns, giving us greater strength and flexibility for the company's continuing overall growth in the world's premium wines markets.

In the more capital-intensive Trade business, our investment is targeted to premium vineyards and wineries, which supply and produce our high-end wines. For some entry-level wines in our portfolio, we limit our capital exposure by purchasing and processing fruit externally, under the close supervision of our winemakers.

Source: www.beringerblass.com/about/index.asp, accessed November 15, 2002.

appointed John Philips to the newly created position of managing director for Europe, the Middle East, and Africa. Philips had previously been president of Diageo's UDV/Guinness Wine Group. "John's appointment is consistent with our strategy of establishing strong geographic bases from which we can drive our trade business forward throughout the world," commented Klenz.[13]

2. *Wine clubs.* Beringer's wine club strategy aimed to reinforce and further develop the company's position as the world's leading consumer-direct merchant for premium wine and wine-related products. Wine clubs, such as the Australian Wine Club in the United Kingdom and Wine Buzz in Japan, were set up across the world to cater to premium wine consumers. The clubs offered members access to quality wines, outstanding customer service and other benefits such as cellar management software and wine accessories. Its wine clubs served more than 1 million customers worldwide and were positioned to become one of the world's leading direct wine merchants. On July 4, 2001, Beringer Blass acquired International Wine Accessories (IWA) to assist in keeping accessories' costs down for its wine club members. These accessories included wine glasses, bottle openers, and decanters. The purchase price was $18 million (A$35 million), and earnings per share were expected to be positive from day one. The acquisition:

- Provided a lower cost base for Beringer Blass's wine clubs to achieve positioning as a one-stop shop for wine and wine-related products in all countries.

- Created significant opportunities to cross-market to IWA's quality database of wine accessory buyers.

- Enabled Beringer Blass to review opportunities to offer Australian and European wine trade customers a significant sales opportunity in high-end wine merchandise. (In the United States, almost one-quarter of IWA's sales revenue was generated from the retail wine trade, ranging from wine shops to hotels and restaurants.)

- Served Beringer Blass's aim to continuously upgrade its Australian cellar doors by improving the range and standard of wine merchandise available for sale to visitors. Offering a substantial range of wine-related merchandise was a focal point for the company's highly successful Californian "cellar door program."[14]

3. *Wine service.* Beringer's goal for the wine service business was to be the leading supplier of premium packaging and warehousing services to the wine industry on a global level. In September 2001, Beringer Blass purchased Tarac Bottlers for $A15.5 million ($8.7 million), enabling it to become the world's largest contract wine bottler. In that same month, Beringer Blass also formed partnerships with François Frères, the world's second largest cooperage. A cooperage was a manufacturer of barrels used in the aging of wine. The joint venture was expected to more than double Beringer Blass's oak barrel sales to 37,000 annually and to create the potential to increase its oak barrel production in both Australia and the United States.

AWARDS AND HONORS

According to Foster's 2001 annual report, Beringer Blass's wines won numerous awards in 2001. At the international wine and spirits competitions at Vin-Expo in Bordeaux, France, Beringer Blass was awarded the Schenker Trophy for Best Australian Wine Producer for its Annie's Lane, Jamieson's Run, Wolf Blass, and Saltram brands. Australian subsidiary Wolf Blass was named winner of the Maurice O'Shea Award, the most prestigious in the Australian wine industry, for the introduction of new winemaking techniques, marketing strategies, and development of new export markets.

Beringer Blass's California and imported wines won over 300 medals in U.S. competitions, including 63 gold or best-of-class medals. Three California wineries, Beringer Vineyards, Stags' Leap, and

---

[13]"Beringer Blass Wine Estates Appoints New Managing Director, Europe—John Philips Tapped for New Position," press release, www.beringerwineestates.com/investors/fr_newsrelease.html, February 20, 2002.

[14]Australian Associated Press, "Beringer Blass Continues Bolt-On Acquisition Strategy with Wine Clubs' Purchase," July 4, 2001.

exhibit 4   **Beringer Blass Wine Estates' Segment Data, Fiscal Years 2001 and 2002 (in A$ millions)**

	Revenue			Earnings Before Interest, Tax, and Amortization (EBITA)		
	2002*	2001*	% Change	2002*	2001*	% Change
Results by division						
Wine trade	A$1,326.2	A$1,015.3	30.6%	A$401.0	A$294.8	36.0%
Wine clubs	398.1	346.3	15.0	54.9	59.4	−7.6
Wine services	246.8	178.4	38.3	30.7	19.9	54.3
Less: Intradivision sales	(37.3)	(27.1)				
Total	A$1,933.8	A$1,512.9	27.8%	A$486.6	A$374.1	30.1%
Wine trade division, by geographic region						
North America				A$316.6	A$215.0	47.4%
Asia Pacific				67.9	65.0	4.1
UK/Europe				16.5	14.8	11.6
Total				A$401.0	A$294.8	36.0%

*Year ended June 30.

Source: Foster's Group 2002 financial report.

Chateau St. Jean, were included in *Wine & Spirits* magazine's top 50 on-premise wine brands. Two luxury portfolio California wines, Beringer Vineyards' '96 Private Reserve Cabernet and Chateau St. Jean's '97 Cinq Cépages, received tasting scores of 90 or above from *Wine Spectator* and *Wine Advocate*, influential U.S. trade publications. Chateau St. Jean's '97 Cinq Cépages was named as the outstanding wine of the year by *Wine Spectator* in 2001.

RECENT FINANCIAL PERFORMANCE

In fiscal year 2001, sales for the combined wine division more than doubled to A$1,359.7 million ($761.4 million), reflecting nine months of Beringer's contribution to Foster's wine business sales (A$667.7 million, or $373.4 million). Earnings before interest, taxes, and amortization (EBITA) for the combined operations were A$342.1 million ($191.6 million), up 121.7 percent. Excluding Beringer, EBITA for the wine division increased to A$176.2 million ($98.7 million), a 14.2 percent improvement over fiscal year

2000. EBITA for the Australian wine trade business, comprising domestic and export sales, increased by 11 percent to A$107.7 million ($60.3 million). Improved earnings for the Australian wine operations were driven by increased outsourcing, lower production costs, gross margin improvement, the rationalization of underperforming brands, and better inventory management. International EBITA growth was driven by increases in volumes of 20 percent. Notably, case shipments of wine increased by more than 20 percent in the United States, Canada, and the United Kingdom. Return on capital employed (ROCE) for the newly combined Beringer and Mildara Blass wine operation was between 13 and 15 percent; with the acquisition premium taken into account, combined returns dropped to slightly below 9 percent.

In fiscal year 2002, Beringer Blass's EBITA contribution was A$486.6 million ($272.5 million), up 30.1 percent over FY 2001 (FY 2001 EBITA included only nine months of Beringer contributions). Global volumes increased by 25.8 percent to nearly 17 million nine-liter cases shipped. Exhibit 4 shows year-on-year comparisons of Beringer's financial results in fiscal year 2001 and fiscal year 2002. On a divisional basis, wine trade EBITA rose by 36 percent over fiscal year 2001 to A\$401.0 million (\$224.6 million). Wine clubs EBITA fell by 7.6 percent to A\$54.9 million (\$27.5 million). Wine services EBITA rose by 54.3 percent to A\$30.7 million (\$17.2 million). According to company reports, Foster's ROCE increased 30 basis points to 13.4 percent, about 280 basis points above the group's weighted average cost of capital. The restructuring of Beringer's global wine trade businesses was completed, and regional businesses were now in place in the three key world wine markets: North America, Asia Pacific, and United Kingdom/Europe.

On May 1, 2001, Beringer Blass introduced a new brand called Stone Cellars, featuring Cabernet/Shiraz, Chardonnay, and Merlot, and selling in the \$6.00–\$8.00 (A\$11.50–A\$15.30) bracket. Beringer Blass aimed for case sales of 1 million in the first year. Notably, Stone Cellars achieved sales volumes of nearly 1 million cases in the first 15 months following its introduction into the North American and UK/European markets.

Exhibit 5 shows Foster's historical and projected financial statements from 1997–2005. Exhibit 6 lists Beringer Blass's portfolio wine brands in 2002. Exhibit 7 lists Beringer Blass's key vineyard holdings in 2002.

MARKETS AND COMPETITION

Beringer Blass competed with two major types of businesses: stand-alone wineries and large multi-business conglomerates that had wine divisions. Beringer's primary stand-alone winery competitors in the United States included publicly traded Robert Mondavi and the privately held E. & J. Gallo, Kendall-Jackson, and a host of small- to medium-sized wineries primarily based in Northern California. Large diversified competitors included Allied Domecq, Brown-Forman (Wine Estates division), Constellation Brands (Canandaigua division), Diageo (Chateau & Estates division), Fortune Brands, Louis Vuitton Moët Hennesey (LVMH), and UST (formerly known as U.S. Tobacco). Recent comparative financial data for several publicly traded wine industry rivals are shown in Exhibit 8. Stand-alone wine competitors, their key brand holdings, and estimated case sales are shown in Exhibit 9.

Beringer Blass faced intense global competition in the premium and ultra-premium wine segments. Rival beverage conglomerates such as Allied Domecq, Brown-Forman, Constellation, and Diageo sought to build wine portfolios through acquisitions and partnership arrangements. Beringer Blass's conglomerate competitors had historically expanded their wine portfolios through acquisitions of independent wineries as well as purchases of majority interests in the beverage divisions of other conglomerates. From 2000 to 2002, several conglomerates began divesting those subsidiaries that diverted resources from their core beverage businesses, notably Diageo's and Allied Domecq's sales of their food operations, capped by Diageo's \$1.5 billion sale of its Burger King fast-food subsidiary to an investment group in December 2002.[15]

The beverage conglomerates' redeployment of assets and investment dollars into wine brands was also driven by predictions that premium-brand wine consumption would continue to grow faster than consumption of other alcoholic beverages such as beer and spirits, despite the challenges of economic uncertainty, consolidation, and oversupply of grapes.[16] According to Chris Carson, the chief executive of BRL Hardy (Europe):

> With the advent of brands there is more profit being made and there are several companies in the world making attractive returns on investments at the sort of level that is interesting to the spirits companies. They are looking for a 15% return and there are several wine companies at that level. We are now one of the key players . . . I think what will emerge is half a dozen very strong global wine businesses. Whether they will tuck in with Diageo, Lion Nathan, Allied Domecq and Fortune Brands, or be stand-alone operators such as Gallo and Constellation [formerly Canandaigua] remains to be seen.[17]

Other wine industry experts predicted that an accelerating trend of worldwide consolidation in the

---

[15]"Diageo Agrees to the Sale of Burger King," *Business Wire,* December 13, 2002. Interestingly, the group that purchased Burger King from Diageo included Texas Pacific Group (TPG). TPG was the same leveraged buyout firm that had purchased Wine World Estates from Nestlé in 1996.

[16]"Turning to the Bottle," *Marketing Week,* November 21, 2001, p. 25.

[17]"Wine: In for the Kill," *The Grocer,* March 10, 2001, p. 35.

exhibit 5 **Foster's Group, Selected Financial Highlights and Projections, 1997–2005**

	2005e	2004e	2003e	2002	2001	2000	1999	1998	1997
Profit and Loss Statement (in A$ millions)									
Sales revenue	A$5,468.0	A$5,118.0	A$4,797.0	A$4,572.0	A$4,079.0	A$3,408.0	A$3,012.0	A$3,058.0	A$2,780.0
EBITDA	1,409.2	1,328.4	1,246.7	1,210.4	1,041.6	759.5	708.5	641.6	505.9
EBITDA margin	25.8%	26.0%	26.0%	26.5%	25.5%	22.3%	23.5%	21.0%	18.2%
Depreciation and amortization	(235.2)	(227.4)	(219.8)	(224.5)	(175.0)	(108.9)	(122.0)	(106.8)	(79.1)
EBIT	1,174.3	1,101.3	1,027.2	986.2	866.9	650.8	586.7	535.0	427.0
EBIT margin	21.5%	21.5%	21.4%	21.6%	21.3%	19.1%	19.5%	17.5%	15.4%
Net interest expense	(155.2)	(160.6)	(165.8)	(182.4)	(172.1)	(65.0)	(61.1)	(111.4)	(90.1)
Profit before tax	1,019.3	940.9	861.6	804.0	695.0	586.0	525.8	423.8	337.0
Tax expense	(317.3)	(291.0)	(262.2)	(240.6)	(199.7)	(154.5)	(158.2)	(150.8)	(70.9)
Minority interests	(7.0)	(6.4)	(5.8)	(5.5)	(4.1)	(3.4)	(2.0)	2.6	2.5
Net profit after tax	695.0	643.5	593.6	557.9	491.2	428.1	365.6	275.6	268.6
Abs and extras (after tax)	—	—	—	3.5	(25.5)	—	4.0	171.4	(17.8)
Reported profit	A$ 695.0	A$ 643.5	A$ 593.6	A$ 561.4	A$ 465.7	A$ 428.1	A$ 369.6	A$ 447.0	A$ 250.8
% of revenues	12.7%	12.6%	12.4%	12.3%	11.4%	12.6%	12.3%	14.6%	9.0%

	2005e	2004e	2003e	2002	2001	2000	1999	1998	1997
Segment Analysis (in A$ millions)									
EBITA									
Australian brewing	A$485.3	A$467.3	A$450.1	A$430.5	A$410.8	A$391.8	A$387.6	A$369.6	A$324.7
International brewing ex-Asia	50.3	44.9	40.1	35.8	30.8	19.3	11.0	2.1	(3.2)
Asian brewing	3.3	1.4	(1.1)	(4.4)	(5.4)	(12.7)	(24.2)	(42.2)	(19.0)
Spirits	9.6	9.2	8.8	10.7	15.4	—	—	—	—
Gaming clubs (ALH)	135.6	127.7	119.7	114.4	105.9	111.3	82.7	55.2	43.0
Wine trade	457.4	412.2	373.0	356.8	269.1	88.9	83.0	66.8	61.9
Wine clubs	66.4	62.6	58.7	54.9	59.4	55.6	40.5	17.4	—
Wine services	41.5	37.9	34.6	30.7	19.9	11.1	9.0	8.2	—
EBITA margins (selected divisions)									
Australian brewing	29.1%	28.7%	28.3%	27.6%	26.5%	26.4%	26.8%	26.0%	24.3%
Wine trade	26.8%	26.8%	26.8%	26.9%	26.5%	28.8%	32.2%	27.2%	28.6%
Wine clubs	13.9%	14.0%	13.9%	13.8%	17.2%	19.8%	17.7%	16.2%	—

(continues)

exhibit 5 (continued)

	2005e	2004e	2003e	2002	2001	2000	1999	1998	1997
Per Share Data									
Average diluted shares outstanding	2,146	2,119	2,081	2,040	1,910	1,724	1,750	1,803	2,017
Reported EPS (fully diluted)	A$0.324	A$0.304	A$0.285	A$0.274	A$0.257	A$0.249	A$0.211	A$0.158	A$0.137
Growth rate in EPS (%)	6.7%	6.4%	4.4%	6.3%	3.5%	17.8%	34.0%	14.6%	−9.0%
Dividends per share	A$0.20	A$0.19	A$0.18	A$0.17	A$0.16	A$0.15	A$0.13	A$0.11	A$0.11
Dividend payout (%)	62.0%	62.0%	62.0%	62.0%	60.0%	58.0%	62.0%	70.0%	80.0%

	2005e	2004e	2003e	2002	2001	2000	1999	1998	1997
Balance Sheet (in A$ millions)									
Cash and deposits	A$277	A$277	A$277	A$277	A$543	A$508	A$165	A$300	A$120
Inventories	1,916	1,736	1,547	1,679	1,565	718	485	415	307
Debtors	1,301	1,214	1,123	1,187	942	337	329	292	279
Other assets	643	597	554	518	555	269	202	316	1,205
Property, plant, and equipment	3,535	3,448	3,360	3,267	3,351	1,937	2,200	1,715	1,699
Elders finance group	—	—	—	—	—	—	253	216	322
Intangibles	2,439	2,487	2,535	2,584	2,669	1,333	1,275	1,166	1,013
Total assets	10,111	9,759	9,396	9,512	9,625	5,102	4,909	4,420	4,945
Creditors	1,203	1,175	1,146	1,166	1,079	518	503	490	309
Provisions	793	780	764	748	655	517	378	504	483
Borrowings	3,131	3,151	3,251	3,385	4,081	1,759	1,171	907	1,255
Total liabilities	5,127	5,106	5,161	5,299	5,815	2,794	2,052	1,901	2,047
Shareholders' funds	4,984	4,653	4,235	4,213	3,810	2,308	2,857	2,519	2,898

exhibit 5 (concluded)

Cash Flow Statement (in A$ millions)

	2005e	2004e	2003e	2002	2001	2000	1999	1998	1997
EBITDA	A$1,409	A$1,328	A$1,247	A$1,210	A$1,042	A$760	A$709	A$642	A$506
Change in working capital	(239)	(252)	(192)	(212)	(162)	(16)	(53)	(222)	(28)
Net interest paid	(155)	(161)	(166)	(182)	(172)	(65)	(61)	(111)	(90)
Tax paid	(317)	(291)	(262)	(241)	(200)	(155)	(158)	(151)	(71)
SGARA revenues reversed out	(76)	(86)	(93)	(136)	(72)	(33)	—	—	—
Other (additional provisions)	19	19	19	33	(39)	(3)	(113)	(68)	(27)
Net operating cash flow	641	558	553	472	397	488	323	89	290
Capital expenditures	(285)	(285)	(285)	(285)	(323)	(210)	(196)	(158)	(196)
Asset sales	41	41	41	81	33	13	39	—	18
Acquisitions	—	—	(54)	(130)	(3,049)	(264)	(491)	(519)	(105)
Elders finance group net recoveries	—	—	18	35	35	134	72	44	60
Divestitures/other	23	24	73	330	(300)	(50)	25	1,639	208
Investing cash flow	(221)	(220)	(207)	31	(3,604)	(377)	(551)	1,006	(15)
New equity issues	—	—	(41)	96	1,025	(112)	(70)	(626)	—
Dividends paid	(416)	(387)	(360)	(319)	(256)	(240)	7	(188)	(216)
Dividends reinvestment program	8	149	180	165	150	—	—	—	—
Equity cash flows	(408)	(238)	(180)	(154)	(106)	(240)	7	(188)	(216)
Change in net cash	A$12	A$100	A$166	A$349	A$(3,313)	A$(129)	A$(221)	A$907	A$59

Sources: Company reports and Salomon Smith Barney estimates, November 13, 2002.

exhibit 6   **Key Brands Marketed by Beringer Blass Wine Estates**

California	Australian/Asia-Pacific	Europe
Beringer	Wolf Blass	Gabbiano
Carmenet (acquired 9/02)	Black Opal	Campanile
Chateau St. Jean	Jamiesons Run	
Chateau Souverain	Yellowglen (Sparkling)	
Meridian	Annie's Lane	
St. Clement	Matua Valley (New Zealand)	
Stags' Leap Winery	The Rothbury Estate	
Etude	Greg Norman Estate	

Source: www.beringerblass.com/about/index.asp, accessed November 15, 2002.

exhibit 7   **Key Vineyard Holdings of Beringer Blass Wine Estates**

Country	Hectares	Acres	% Developing	Key Regions
United States (California)	5,000	12,300	19	Napa Valley, Sonoma County, Central Coast, Lake County
Australia	3,500	8,700	14	75% of plantings in South Australia's premium regions, including Coonawarra, Wrattonbully, Barossa Valley, Clare Valley, Langhorne Creek and McLaren Vale
New Zealand	250	650		Auckland, Gisborne, Hawkes Bay and Wairarapa in the North Island and Marlborough in the South Island
Italy	50	100		Tuscany's Chianti Classico zone
Total	8,800	21,750		

NOTE: The group controls a total of 8,800 hectares (21,750 acres) of vineyard plantings in Australia, New Zealand, California, and Europe.

Source: www.beringerblass.com/about/index.asp, accessed November 15, 2002.

producer, distributor, and trade segments for premium wines would be more than offset by several factors. These factors included the continuing increase in the number of small wineries, a fundamental increase in consumer demand, the increasing affluence of the wine-buying public, and the results of decade-long efforts directed toward improving quality in production, sales, and service.[18]

[18]A. Arno, "Globalization of the Wine Industry," *Wine Business Monthly* 9, no. 4 (May 2002).

THE GLOBALIZATION CHALLENGE

From 2000 to 2002, several prominent American-based wineries and beverage conglomerates such as Constellation Brands' Canandaigua division (with BRL Hardy), Brown-Forman Wine Estates (with McPherson and Chateau Tahbilk), Kendall-Jackson (with Yangarra Park), and Mondavi (with Southcorp) set up joint ventures with other "New World" wineries from Australia. Traditional "Old World" producers were located in Europe: Austria, France, Italy,

exhibit 8 **Comparative Financial Data for Publicly Traded Australian and International Wine Companies, 2000–2002**

	BRL Hardy	Foster's Group	Southcorp	Allied Domecq	Diageo	Constellation Brands	Robert Mondavi
Country	Australia	Australia	Australia	United Kingdom	United Kingdom	United States	United States
Year-end	December	June	June	August	June	February	June
Ticker symbol	BRL	FGL	SRP	ALLD	DGE	STZ	MOND
Stock price, October 2002	A$7.68	A$4.72	A$5.35	£3.93	£7.39	U.S.$24.82	U.S.$31.39
Market cap. October 2002	A$1,345m	A$9,881m	A$3,955m	£4,150m	£23,744m	U.S.$2,184m	U.S.$497m
P/E ratio							
2000	18.0x	18.6x	15.6x	14.3x	19.9x	23.7x	12.4x
2001	16.9	17.6	19.6	12.7	27.3	19.1	10.6
2002	15.5	16.8	18.6	12.4	17.0	15.8	13.1
Core EPS growth							
2000	19.4%	15.3%	10.8%	(32.2)%	8.5%	35.3%	17.1%
2001	6.4	5.2	(20.2)	13.1	15.1	20.3	16.1
2002	9.2	5.3	5.2	2.6	1.6	17.5	(18.6)
EBIT margins							
2000	16.2%	18.1%	18.8%	18.0%	18.1%	10.0%	17.8%
2001	16.1	21.3	28.7	12.8	18.9	11.2	18.0
2002	15.9	21.6	16.4	16.6	20.3	12.1	19.0
ROI							
2000	15.0%	18.3%	13.7%	34.7%	19.3%	14.6%	11.8%
2001	13.2	16.4	10.8	24.2	20.1	16.2	12.2
2002	12.3	13.8	9.9	19.1	18.4	n/a	n/a
Dividend yield							
2000	2.3%	3.1%	3.9%	2.8%	2.8%	—	—
2001	2.6	3.3	3.9	3.1	3.0	—	—
2002	2.9	3.6	4.1	3.4	3.2	—	—

n/a = not available

Sources: Company reports and Salomon Smith Barney estimates, October 25, 2002.

exhibit 9 **Wine Companies: Key Brands and Estimated Cases Shipped, 2002**

Company	Headquarters	Estimated annual worldwide consumption	Key brands/ Number of cases	Key wineries/brands outside the United States
Allied Domecq PLC	London, England Healdsburg, CA (Allied Domecq Wines USA)	24 million cases	Atlas Peak—40,000 Callaway Coastal Vineyards—340,000 Clos du Bois—1,600,000 William Hill—115,000 Mumm Cuvee Napa—200,000	Argentina—Bodegas, Balbi, Graffigna France—Perrier Jouet, Champagne Mumm New Zealand—Brancott Vineyards, Montana Wines Portugal—Cockburn's Port Spain—Marques de Arienzo, Bodegas y Bebidas, Harveys Bristol Cream Sherry
Beringer Blass	Australia (Foster's) St. Helena, CA (Beringer)	17 million cases	Beringer Vineyards—3,500,000 Carmenet, Sonoma—(in transition) Chateau St. Jean—300,000 Chateau Souverain—150,000 Etude Wines—9,000 Meridian Vineyards—1,250,000 Stags' Leap Winery—60,000 St. Clement—30,000 Windsor—300,000	Australia—Greg Norman Estates, Wolf Blass, Yellow Glen Italy—Castello di Gabbiano, Travaglini
Brown-Forman	Louisville, KY Healdsburg, CA (Brown-Forman Wine Estates)	9–10 million cases	Fetzer (incl. Bel Arbor & Bonterra)—3,600,000 Jekel Vineyards—150,000 Sonoma-Cutrer—95,000	Australia—Chateau Tahbilk, Geoff Merrill, Owens Estate France—Michel Picard Italy—Bolla, Fontina Candida
Canandaigua	Freeport, NY (Constellation Brands)	45 million cases	Batavia Wine Cellars—1,800,000 Canandaigua Winery—7,000,000 Columbia Winery—160,000 Franciscan Vineyards—130,000 Mission Bell Winery—18,900,000 Ravenswood—535,000 Turner Road—7,300,000 Widmer Wine Cellars—2,500,000	Australia—Alice Wine

exhibit 9 **(continued)**

Company	Headquarters	Estimated annual worldwide consumption	Key brands/ Number of cases	Key wineries/brands outside the United States
Diageo PLC	London, England Napa, CA (Diageo Chateau & Estates)	*	Barton & Guestier (U.S. sales only)—750,000 Beaulieu Vineyards—400,000 BV Coastal—1,100,000 Blossom Hill—4,000,000 The Monterey Vineyard—300,000 Painted Hills—50,000 Sterling Vineyards—380,000	
E. & J. Gallo	Modesto, CA Healdsburg, CA (Gallo of Sonoma)	65 million cases 2 million in premium wine	Louis M. Martini—150,000 Mirassou Vineyards—105,000 Gallo of Sonoma—* Turning Leaf—* Indigo Hills—* Gossamer Bay—* Peter Vella—*	
JFJ Bronco	Ceres, CA	4–5 million cases	Forest Glen—* Napa Ridge—* Napa Creek—300,000 Rutherford Vintners—* Charles Shaw—*	
Kendall-Jackson	Healdsburg, CA	*	Kendall-Jackson Vineyards and Winery—400,000 La Crema—150,000 Cardinale—* Edmeades—12,000	Argentina—Tapiz Australia—Yangarra Park Chile—Calina Italy—Villa Arcena

(continues)

exhibit 9 (concluded)

Company	Headquarters	Estimated annual worldwide consumption	Key brands/ Number of cases	Key wineries/brands outside the United States
Robert Mondavi	Napa, CA	*	Arrowood—30,000 Byron Vineyards and Winery—28,200 Robert Mondavi Napa—268,000 Robert Mondavi Private Selection—1,400,000 Opus One—30,000 Woodbridge—7,100,000	Chile—Caliterra Italy—Luce, Danzante
Southcorp	Australia	13.9 million cases	Lindemans—6,000,000 Penfolds—2,800,000 Rosemount—5,000,000 Wynns Coonawarra Estate—100,000	
Vincor	Canada	8 million cases	Hawthorne Mountain—36,000 Hogue Cellars—450,000 Inniskillin Wines—130,000 Jackson-Triggs Niagara Estate—100,000 R. H. Phillips—600,000 Sumac Ridge Estate—55,000	
The Wine Group	San Francisco, CA	20–22 million cases	Colony—* Concannon—80,000 Corbett Canyon—* Franzia—* Glen Ellen—* Lejon—* M. G. Vallejo—* Mogen David—* Summit—*	Argentina—Altamonte Australia—Austin Vale Italy—Casarsa, Marasutti

*Unknown.

Source: L. Walker, "Who Owns What?" *Wines & Vines* 84, no. 1 (San Rafael, CA: The Hiaring Companies, January 2003), p. 34.

Germany, Portugal, and Spain. The purposes of these joint ventures were to enable California wineries to increase market share; create synergy with distribution channels, marketing, and sales; diversify production sources and growing seasons; and reduce costs.[19]

Imports of Australian wines to the United States rose dramatically from 1997 to 2001. (See Exhibit 10 for recent statistics on the top five markets for Australia's wine exports.) Of note, Southcorp's Lindemans and Rosemount Estates wines held the number one and two positions among the fastest-growing wine brands in the United States in 2001. (See Exhibit 11 for a profile of Southcorp.) Additionally, two Australian imports, Pernod Ricard's Jacob's Creek and Canandaigua's Alice White, were ranked among the top 10 fastest-growing U.S. wine brands in 2001. Three other Australian brands (Greg Norman Estates, McPherson, and Stonehaven) were considered by the industry to be rising stars, ranked by recent volume growth. (See Exhibit 12 for 1997–2001 rankings of wine brands in the United States.)

Since 1992, trade imbalances in wine had grown as a result of a strengthening dollar as well as the rising value of imported wines. U.S. wine producers' exports softened in 2000 and 2001. Exhibit 13 presents bottled U.S. table wine exports by country in 2001 and 2002. Exhibit 14 presents U.S. wine balance of trade statistics from 1984 to 2001.

Around the world, changes in consumer perception about wine, an oversupply of wines, and an economic recession combined to depress sales of premium wines. The market had moved from connoisseur elite French and Eurocentric wines (such as Bordeaux, Burgundy, and Champagne) to generic or varietal types (such as Chardonnay, Chenin Blanc, Cabernet Sauvignon, Pinot Noir, and Merlot). Despite their growth in the decade just past, California wines continued to lose market share to imports.

The long cycle of growth for the premium wine segment of the industry during the 1990s had resulted in the expansion of grape-growing acreage at a faster rate than the growth of demand. Yet supplies of wine grapes had only recently begun to grow rapidly due to the characteristics of vine development. It normally took five to six years for newly planted grapevines to mature and start to produce quality grapes. Premium varietal wines typically required further aging prior to bottling, from one year for Chardonnay to up to three years for Cabernet Sauvignon. The wine supply chain had globalized, as grapes could now be purchased almost anywhere and in season (that is, from growing regions in the Southern Hemisphere). By the turn of the century, imports of quality premium wines from New World growing regions such as Australia, Argentina, and Chile were competing quite successfully with California wines' share of an increasingly price-conscious market.[20]

Vic Motto, of Motto Kryla, Fisher, a wine industry consultant, commented on these trends:

> Globalization has created a world market with a trend towards worldwide normalization of taste and stylistic standards. Global communication networks have also created the potential for small brands to access the same consumers as large ones. However, no one has succeeded in building a global brand—yet.[21]

Statistics on worldwide wine consumption, trended from 1990 to 2002, are shown in Exhibits 15 and 16. Exhibit 17 presents worldwide production statistics by country. In response, the U.S. wine industry created a globalization task force to address the challenge of growing the U.S. producers' share in worldwide wine markets. (See Exhibit 18 for the task force's position paper.) David Freed, a co-founder of Beringer Wine Estates after its leveraged buyout from Nestlé, headed up the industry's globalization task force. In his introduction of Klenz as keynote speaker to the Wine Industry Symposium, Freed commented:

> [Wine producers] in California have to recognize that we're not the low-cost producers. We cannot compete in a global marketplace based upon price. So, if we can't compete on price, then it seems we have to compete on value. Value can either be perceived value, for example, the value attached to a strong brand like Sony in electronics or Nike in tennis shoes, or the price/value of the product/deliverable.[22]

[19]F. Prial, "A Surplus of Grapes Is a Boon for Buyers," *New York Times,* September 25, 2002, p. D4.

[20]W. Echikson et al., "Wine War," *Business Week,* September 3, 2001, pp. 54–60.

[21]"World Wine Market Keynote Highlights Impact of Globalization on U.S. Wine Market," *PR Newswire,* June 21, 2002.

[22]D. Freed, Wine Industry Symposium, Napa, California, September 18, 2002.

exhibit 10 **Australian Wine Exports: Top Five Markets, by Volume, Fiscal Years 1999–2005e**

	United Kingdom	United States	New Zealand	Canada	Germany	Rest of World	World
Volume shipments (in thousands of liters)							
1998/99	102,374	37,383	21,320	9,229	5,857	40,063	216,226
1999/00	139,689	50,030	20,119	12,597	9,393	55,739	287,567
2000/01	164,992	67,661	21,351	14,962	11,805	58,195	338,966
2001/02	202,354	94,910	25,145	18,687	11,919	64,252	417,267
2002/03E	232,707	118,637	27,156	22,425	13,707	69,592	484,224
2003/04E	260,632	144,737	28,514	24,667	17,819	75,008	551,377
2004/05E	286,695	170,970	29,940	27,134	23,165	80,709	618,613
Volume growth							
1999/00	36.4%	33.8%	−5.6%	36.5%	60.4%	39.1%	33.0%
2000/01	18.1	35.2	6.1	18.8	25.7	4.4	17.9
2001/02	22.6	40.3	17.8	24.9	1.0	10.4	23.1
2002/03E	15.0	25.0	8.0	20.0	15.0	8.3	16.0
2003/04E	12.0	22.0	5.0	10.0	30.0	7.8	13.9
2004/05E	10.0	18.1	5.0	10.0	30.0	7.6	12.2
CAGR 1999–2002	21.3%	32.5%	8.2%	19.5%	33.0%	n/a	20.4%
CAGR 2002–2005E	12.3%	21.7%	6.0%	13.2%	24.8%	7.9%	14.0%
Average value/liter							
1998/99	A$4.36	A$5.77	A$2.83	A$5.51	A$4.25	n/a	A$4.58
1999/00	4.23	6.33	3.25	5.85	4.35	n/a	4.70
2000/01	4.18	6.17	3.61	6.10	4.24	n/a	4.76
2001/02	4.16	6.14	3.37	6.61	4.03	n/a	4.79
2002/03E	4.08	5.65	3.44	6.87	4.03	n/a	4.69
2003/04E	4.00	5.42	3.51	7.01	4.11	n/a	4.65
2004/05E	3.92	5.31	3.51	7.01	4.19	n/a	4.58
CAGR 1999–2002	2.6%	4.4%	6.4%	8.1%	0.9%	n/a	5.3%
CAGR 2002–2005E	−2.0%	−4.7%	1.4%	2.0%	1.3%	n/a	−1.5%

n/a = not available

Sources: Australian Wine Export Council, and Salomon Smith Barney estimates, November 11, 2002.

FUTURE GROWTH STRATEGIES

Leaning on the lectern and delivering what instantly became known in the industry as a controversial presentation, Klenz propounded that a truly global premium wine business might:[23]

- Become roughly three times the current size of Beringer Blass.
- Produce 50 million cases of wine each year.
- Generate $3 billion in annual revenues.
- Hold a 20 percent market share of the global "commercial premium" segment.[24]

[23] W. Klenz, "The Globalization of Beringer Blass Wine Estates," speech to Wine Industry Symposium, Napa, California, September 18, 2002.

[24] This segment consisted of bottles of wine priced at $5–$6 and $10–$12, or brands priced to produce profits that could attain mass distribution and mass exposure in key retail channels.

exhibit 11 **Southcorp Wines: A Profile**

Australia-based Southcorp Wines was the world's largest premium branded wine company and the maker of three leading international premium brands—Penfold's, Rosemount, and Lindemans. Over the past 35 years, Southcorp had evolved into a major global wine producer via organic growth and through a series of corporate transactions, culminating in its March 2001 merger with Rosemount Estate, Australia's premier family-owned winery.

- Southcorp produced more than 22 million cases and 18 brands of wine each year, accounting for nearly one-third of Australian domestic wine production and wine exports.
- Southcorp accounted for 65% of the total of Australian wines sold in the United States. A total of 9.6 million cases of its global brands were sold worldwide in 2001/02, comprising more than half of the 18.5 million cases of all Southcorp brands sold worldwide.
- Southcorp operated 12 wineries across the major wine-producing regions in New South Wales, Victoria, South Australia, and West Australia, as well as one winery in France.
- Southcorp's 2001/02 net profit increased 45% to U.S.$170 million from U.S.$117.6 million in the prior year, partially reflecting the one-time gain on sale of its water heater business. Excluding that sale, net profits were U.S.$95.5 million.
- Southcorp's joint venture with U.S. winemaker Robert Mondavi was expected to launch a new range of superpremium wines (priced in the $13–$15 range) in February 2003, with prestige reserve wines in the $60–$80 range expected to be released in late 2003.
- At an investor's conference in New York on October 2, 2002, Southcorp presented its strategy of focusing on three core brands (Penfolds, Lindemans, and Rosemount) and forecast growth of its core earnings per share (EPS) of +10% for fiscal year 2003 and 17% for fiscal year 2004.

Southcorp's International Sales Growth, 1994–2001 (in millions)

| | Fiscal Year Ending June 30 | | | | | | | |
	1994	1995	1996	1997	1998	1999	2000	2001
Europe	A$66	A$74	A$90	A$108	A$142	A$159	A$217	A$291
United States/Canada	27	35	47	71	104	122	156	311
Asia	12	16	18	21	27	32	35	40
Total exports	A$105	A$125	A$155	A$200	A$273	A$313	A$408	A$642

Sources: L. Walker, "International Management Style: A Conversation with Southcorp's John Gay," *Wines & Vines,* October 2002, pp. 16–21; and Salomon Smith Barney Estimates, October 25, 2002.

- Rival the size of some of its trade customers, like Kroger's and Safeway.[25]
- Achieve a market capitalization of $8 to $10 billion or greater.

"A truly global wine business would be equivalent in size to every spirits company with the obvious exception of Diageo [about $17 billion in sales in 2002] and equal to or bigger than most beer companies besides Heineken and Anheuser-Busch," Klenz told the stunned wine business conference attendees.

[25]These supermarket chains had market capitalizations of $12 and $14 billion, respectively, in 2002.

Klenz ended his speech by saying:

Nobody has a global wine company as I define it, but we are developing a blue print for how to do that going forward. I actually believe it's gonna happen—somebody's gonna do it. But are we [Beringer Blass] ready for another set of consolidation transactions? We also need to balance between global values, that is, building a brand that is common to all markets, while adapting to what every local market needs. How do we develop a series of core global brands at different price points, create a globally-oriented organizational culture, revamp our product line to make it more accessible to a new generation of wine consumers, and build internal communications systems to support an increasingly complex production/

exhibit 12 **Fastest-Growing U.S. Wine Brands, by Volume of Cases Shipped, 1997–2001**

	Appellation of Origin	Supplier	Thousands of 9-Liter Cases					2000–2001 % Change	1997–2001 CAGR
			1997	1998	1999	2000	2001		
Fast-track brands (top 10, ranked by 2001 case sales)*									
Lindemans	Australia	Southcorp	959	1,145	1,421	1,414	1,597	12.9%	13.6%
Rosemount Estate	Australia	Southcorp	540	760	920	1,251	1,492	19.3	28.9
Clos du Bois	California	Allied Domecq	750	890	1,092	1,192	1,325	11.2	15.3
Robert Mondavi—Coastal	California	Robert Mondavi	649	805	914	1,142	1,265	10.8	18.2
Cavit	Italy	Palm Bay Imports	275	375	475	575	780	35.7	29.8
Luna di Luna	Italy	A. V. Imports	265	202	412	535	665	24.3	25.9
Jacob's Creek	Australia	Pernod Ricard	186	207	272	423	573	35.5	32.5
Pepperwood Gove	California	Cecchetti Sebastiani	104	180	272	302	365	20.9	36.9
Alice White	Australia	Canandaigua Wine	16	77	136	221	260	17.6	100.8
Camelot	California	Kendall-Jackson	10	29	61	114	192	68.4	109.3
Rising stars (top 10, ranked by 2001 case sales)†									
Arbor Mist	California	Canandaigua Wine	—	1,280	3,500	4,050	4,230	4.4%	nmf
Foxhorn	California	The Wine Group	—	—	755	1,026	1,245	21.3	nmf
Sterling Vintner's Collection	California	Diageo Chateau & Estates	—	—	—	80	190	137.5	nmf
Greg Norman Estates	Australia	Mildara Blass	—	—	15	138	160	15.9	nmf
McPherson	Australia	Brown-Forman Wine Estates	—	—	21	106	141	33.0	nmf
Sycamore Lane	California	Trinchero Family Estates	—	11	43	62	140	125.8	nmf
Belmondo	Italy	A. V. Imports	—	15	90	103	121	17.5	nmf
Stonehaven	Australia	Banfi Vintners	—	—	—	100	110	10.0	nmf
Trinchero	California	Trinchero Family Estates	—	—	29	75	103	37.3	nmf
Monterra	California	Delicato Family Vineyards	—	25	43	70	88	25.7	nmf

exhibit 12 (concluded)

Established growth brands (top 10, ranked by 2001 case sales)‡	Appellation of Origin	Supplier	Thousands of 9-Liter Cases					2000–2001 % Change	1997–2001 CAGR
			1997	1998	1999	2000	2001		
Almaden	California	Canandaigua Wine	7,600	7,660	9,200	9,380	9,730	3.7%	6.4%
Woodbridge	California	Robert Mondavi	4,239	4,702	5,504	6,376	6,563	2.9	11.5
Beringer	California	Beringer Blass Wine Estates	4,000	4,473	4,920	5,850	6,000	2.6	10.7
Boone's	California	E. & J. Gallo Winery	2,600	3,000	4,000	4,500	4,650	3.3	11.6
Peter Vella	California	E. & J. Gallo Winery	3,400	3,800	3,800	4,200	4,350	3.6	3.4
Turning Leaf	California	E. & J. Gallo Winery	1,800	2,300	2,500	2,750	3,025	10.0	13.9
Beaulieu Vineyard	California	Diageo Chateau & Estates	770	860	944	1,243	1,325	6.6	14.5
Burlwood	California	E. & J. Gallo Winery	550	650	800	1,200	1,300	8.3	24.0
Casarsa	California	Gary Raden & Sons	1,050	1,150	1,208	1,210	1,275	5.4	5.0
Meridien	California	Beringer Blass Wine Estates	630	842	1,030	1,150	1,200	4.3	17.5

*Brands at least five full years of age that exceeded 100,000 nine-liter cases in 2001, with double-digit growth over each of the past four years.

†Brands less than five full years of age that have exhibited substantial growth over the past few years.

‡Top-selling brands that have grown moderately or substantially over the past four years.

nmf = not meaningful figure

Source: Adapted by casewriters from Richard Brandes, *Beverage Dynamics* 114, no. 2 (March 2002), pp. 14–24.

exhibit 13   **Bottled U.S. Table Wine Exports: Top Five Markets, by Total Value and Volume, Fiscal Years 2000 and 2001**

	United Kingdom	Canada	Netherlands	Japan	Belgium	Rest of World	World
Volume shipments (liters 000)							
2000	60,047	24,929	30,932	26,883	4,422	53,152	200,365
2001	77,642	23,446	32,762	21,476	8,767	41,940	206,033
Variance 2001 vs. 2000	17,595	(1,483)	1,830	(5,407)	4,345	(11,212)	5,668
Percent change	29.3%	−5.9%	5.9%	−20.1%	98.3%	−21.1%	2.8%
Value of shipments ($000)							
2000	$131,389	$73,399	$73,200	$43,925	$8,486	$106,783	$437,182
2001	154,508	66,883	65,671	38,037	15,900	79,290	420,289
$ change, 2001 vs. 2000	$23,119	$(6,516)	$(7,529)	$(5,888)	$7,414	$(27,493)	$(16,893)
Percent change	17.6%	−8.9%	−10.3%	−13.4%	87.4%	−25.7%	−3.9%
Average value/liter (U.S. $)							
2000	$2.19	$2.94	$2.37	$1.63	$1.92	—	$2.18
2001	1.99	2.85	2.00	1.77	1.81	—	2.04
Variance 2001 vs. 2000	(0.20)	(0.09)	(0.37)	0.14	(0.11)		(0.14)
Percent change	−9.1%	−3.1%	−15.6%	8.6%	−5.7%		−6.4%

Sources: California Wine Export Program, January 2003, from statistics compiled by the U.S. Department of Commerce, Stat-USA.

marketing interface? We're still struggling with these issues, though we have made some progress. We still have a long way to go to become the first global wine business.[26]

[26]As quoted in C. Penn, "Walt Klenz on Developing a Global Wine Business," *Wine Business Monthly* 9, no. 10 (October 31, 2002), p. 31.

Nevertheless, an emerging glut of wine due to bountiful grape harvests, worldwide political instability, and economic uncertainty combined to increase Beringer Blass's operating risk in late 2002. In light of these adverse conditions, Klenz and his fellow 3,800 employees worldwide needed a strategy to retain its first-mover advantage in the race to become the first global wine business.

exhibit 14   U.S. Wine Balance of Trade: 1984–2001

Year	Exports Value ($ million)	Exports Volume (liters 000)	Imports Value ($ million)	Imports Volume (liters 000)	Balance of Trade Value ($ million)	Balance of Trade Volume (liters 000)
1984	$ 25	23,002	$ 954	539,738	$ (929)	(516,736)
1985	28	23,869	1,010	518,108	(982)	(494,239)
1986	35	27,493	1,030	411,969	(995)	(384,476)
1987	61	44,995	1,017	364,981	(956)	(319,986)
1988	85	64,184	954	307,077	(869)	(242,893)
1989	98	83,031	937	287,911	(839)	(204,880)
1990	126	99,719	923	254,544	(797)	(154,825)
1991	146	117,448	819	232,096	(673)	(114,648)
1992	194	145,746	759	176,819	(565)	(31,073)
1993	231	142,320	1,006	252,559	(775)	(110,239)
1994	195	133,383	1,084	280,294	(889)	(146,911)
1995	242	146,895	1,209	291,560	(967)	(144,665)
1996	327	177,099	1,478	364,891	(1,151)	(187,792)
1997	426	228,585	1,759	462,662	(1,333)	(234,077)
1998	537	272,311	1,916	420,723	(1,379)	(148,412)
1999	561	291,420	2,244	424,458	(1,683)	(133,038)
2000	548	295,555	2,319	495,731	(1,771)	(200,176)
2001	542	305,935	2,344	532,698	(1,802)	(226,763)
Compound Annual Growth Rates						
1984–2001	20%	16%	5%	0%	nmf	nmf
1984–1996	24%	19%	4%	−3%	nmf	nmf
1996–2001	11%	12%	10%	8%	nmf	nmf

nmf = not meaningful figure

Note: Includes both bulk wine and bottled wine.

Sources: California Wine Export Program, January 2003, from statistics compiled by the U.S. Department of Commerce, Stat-USA.

exhibit 15 **Per Capita Wine Consumption in the Top 15 Countries, Ranked by Volume, 1990, 1995, and 2000–2002**

Country	Population, Year 2000	Consumption (Liters Per Capita)[a]					Average Annual Compound Growth Rate		Percent Change[b]		Volume Rank
		1990	1995	2000	2001	2002	1990–1995	1995–2000	2000–2001	2001–2002	
France	59,329,691	72.56	62.94	55.54	56.68	55.05	−2.8%	−2.5%	2.1%	−2.9%	1
Portugal	10,048,232	50.73	60.51	50.12	49.79	49.22	3.6	−3.7	−0.7	−1.1	10
Italy	57,634,691	62.07	62.13	49.89	48.87	48.16	0.0	−4.3	−2.0	−1.5	2
Spain	39,996,671	42.08	38.76	36.33	35.07	35.07	−1.6	−1.3	−3.5	0.0	5
Argentina	36,955,182	54.46	38.81	33.73	32.11	31.60	−6.6	−2.8	−4.8	−1.6	7
Germany[c]	82,797,408	20.53	22.75	23.85	23.97	23.87	2.1	0.9	0.5	−0.4	4
Australia	19,357,594	18.06	18.25	20.32	20.48	21.19	0.2	2.2	0.8	3.5	12
Romania	22,411,121	25.77	29.11	23.24	21.00	21.16	2.5	−4.4	−9.6	0.8	11
United Kingdom	59,508,382	10.95	12.38	16.32	17.36	20.87	2.5	5.7	6.4	20.2	6
Netherlands	15,892,237	16.08	14.01	19.38	19.46	19.67	−2.7	6.7	0.4	1.1	15
South Africa	43,421,021	9.93	10.31	8.99	9.03	8.79	0.8	−2.7	0.4	−2.7	13
United States	275,562,673	6.26	6.40	7.25	7.28	7.64	0.4	2.5	0.4	4.9	3
Russia[d]	146,001,176	13.53	4.22	3.99	4.01	4.04	−20.8	−1.1	0.5	0.7	9
Brazil	172,860,370	1.95	1.94	1.95	2.09	2.06	−0.1	0.1	7.2	−1.4	14
China	1,261,832,482	0.03	0.32	0.43	0.45	0.49	60.5	6.1	4.7	8.9	8
Average—top 15		27.00	25.52	23.42	23.18	23.26	−1.1%	−1.7%	−1.0%	0.4%	
Rest of world	3,784,338,702	1.23	1.22	1.20	1.19	1.16	−0.2%	−0.3%	−0.8%	−2.5%	
World average		4.39	3.90	3.61	3.58	3.57	−2.3%	−1.5%	−0.8%	−0.3%	

[a]Based on total population.

[b]Based on unrounded data.

[c]1990 includes West Germany only.

[d]1990 includes the entire (former) Soviet Union.

Sources: Wine Institute, 2003, www.wineinstitute.org/communications/statistics/keyfacts_worldwineconsumption02.htm; data also extracted from *Impact Databank 2003* (New York: M. Shanken Publications, 2003), p. 504.

exhibit 16 **Share of World Wine Consumption, Top 15 Countries, Ranked by 2002 Share**

Rank	Country	World Share[a]					Share Point Change[b]			
		1990	1995	2000	2001	2002	1990–1995	1995–2000	2000–2001	2001–2002
1	France	17.8%	16.5%	15.0%	15.3%	14.8%	−1.3%	−1.5%	0.3%	−0.5%
2	Italy	15.3	16.1	13.1	12.8	12.5	0.8	−3.0	−0.3	−0.3
3	United States	6.9	7.7	9.4	9.5	9.9	0.8	1.7	0.1	0.4
4	Germany[c]	7.1	8.4	8.9	8.9	8.8	1.3	0.5	0.0	−0.1
5	Spain	7.2	6.9	6.6	6.4	6.3	−0.3	−0.3	−0.2	−0.1
	Total top 5	54.3%	55.6%	53.0%	52.9%	52.3%	1.3%	−2.6%	−0.1%	−0.6%
6	United Kingdom	2.7	3.3	4.4	4.7	5.6	0.6	1.1	0.3	0.9
7	Argentina	7.7	6.1	5.7	5.5	5.4	−1.6	−0.4	−0.2	−0.1
8	China	0.2	1.8	2.5	2.6	2.8	1.6	0.7	0.1	0.2
9	Russia[d]	8.7	2.8	2.6	2.6	2.6	−5.9	−0.2	0.0	0.0
10	Portugal	2.2	2.7	2.3	2.3	2.2	0.5	−0.4	0.0	−0.1
	Total top 10	75.8%	72.3%	70.5%	70.6%	70.9%	−3.5%	−1.8%	0.1%	0.3%
11	Romania	2.6	3.0	2.4	2.1	2.1	0.4	−0.6	−0.3	0.0
12	Australia	1.3	1.5	1.8	1.8	1.9	0.2	0.3	0.0	0.1
13	South Africa	1.5	1.7	1.8	1.8	1.7	0.2	0.1	0.0	−0.1
14	Brazil	1.2	1.4	1.5	1.6	1.6	0.2	0.1	0.1	0.0
15	Netherlands	1.0	1.0	1.4	1.4	1.4	0.0	0.4	0.0	0.0
	Total top 15	83.4%	80.9%	79.4%	79.3%	79.6%	−2.5%	−1.5%	−0.1%	0.3%
	Rest of world	16.6%	19.1%	20.6%	20.7%	20.4%	2.5%	1.5%	0.1%	−0.3%
	Total world	100.0%	100.0%	100.0%	100.0%	100.0%				

[a]Based on total population.
[b]Based on unrounded data.
[c]1990 includes West Germany only.
[d]1990 includes the entire (former) Soviet Union.
Source: Impact Databank 2003 (New York: M. Shanken Publications, 2003), p. 505.

exhibit 17   **World Wine Production by Country in Hectoliters (000), 1996–2000**

Country*	Hectoliters†				Average 1996–1999	2000	% Change 2000 vs. 1996–99
	1996	1997	1998	1999			
France	57,047	53,561	52,671	60,435	55,929	57,541	2.9%
Italy	58,772	50,894	54,188	56,454	55,077	51,620	−6.3
Spain	31,000	33,218	31,175	33,723	32,279	41,692	29.2
United States	18,840	21,606	20,504	19,050	20,000	23,300	16.5
Argentina	12,681	13,500	12,673	15,888	13,686	12,538	−8.4
Germany	8,642	8,495	10,834	12,123	10,024	9,852	−1.7
Australia	6,734	6,174	7,415	8,511	7,209	8,064	11.9
South Africa	8,739	8,115	7,703	7,968	8,131	6,949	−14.5
Portugal	9,712	6,124	3,750	7,859	6,861	6,694	−2.4
Chile	3,824	4,549	5,475	4,807	4,664	6,419	37.6
China	3,000	3,200	3,550	5,200	3,738	5,750	53.8
Romania	7,663	6,688	5,002	6,054	6,352	5,456	−14.1
Brazil	3,128	2,743	2,782	3,190	2,961	3,704	25.1
Greece	4,109	3,987	3,826	3,680	3,901	3,558	−8.8
Hungary	4,188	4,472	4,334	3,339	4,083	3,000	−26.5
Total, top 15 producing countries	238,079	227,326	225,882	248,281	234,892	246,137	4.8%
Rest of world	32,452	34,133	30,517	28,890	31,498	29,755	−5.5%
Total world production	270,531	261,459	256,399	277,171	266,390	275,892	3.6%

*Ranked by production in year 2000.

†Conversion: After adding three zeros to the figures to get hectoliters, multiply hectoliters times 26.418 to convert to gallons.

Source: Wine Institute, 2003, www.wineinstitute.org/communications/statistics/keyfacts_worldwineproduction02.htm.

exhibit 18   **How the U.S. Wine Industry Defines Success in Global Markets**

WineVision
American Wine in the 21st Century

GLOBAL TASK FORCE

Meeting Notes
Napa Marriott Inn
October 25, 2002
10:30 a.m.–1:30 p.m.

Our definition of becoming successful globally includes:

- Having a defined position for American wines and conveying it consistently in the global market
- Having a world presence—not just a few global markets
- Achieving a 20% increase in global sales by 2006
- Developing (possibly) a California brand
- Helping smaller wineries enter the global market
- Thinking strategically and doing things to be in the global market long term
- Creating regional associations to provide global encouragement and support
- Targeting specific markets, understanding the desires of their consumers and ultimately having a significant presence in the targeted markets

Source: David Freed, WineVision Globalization Task Force.

Land O'Lakes, Inc.

Michael A. Boland
Kansas State University

David Barton
Kansas State University

Vincent Amanor-Boadu
Kansas State University

In early 2003, Jack Gherty, president and CEO of Land O'Lakes Inc., a leading U.S. producer of dairy foods and provider of agricultural services, called his senior executives together to discuss the company's future. Faced with intensely competitive pressures in these sectors since 1998, Land O'Lakes had used mergers and acquisitions, joint ventures, and asset sales to grow the business. In a letter to member-owners at the 2003 annual meeting, Gherty and the company's chairman, Jim Fife, wrote:

> In recent years, we have achieved significant growth . . . moving from a regional cooperative to a national, farmer-owned system with competitive size and scale in our core Feed and Agronomy businesses; to achieve appropriate strategic growth in Seed; and build a national dairy procurement and processing system to support our national brand and marketing system in Dairy Foods . . . Land O'Lakes continues to focus on channeling our investments into those critical core businesses which will help us compete, win and deliver value to members and customers—and repositioning under-performing, non-strategic assets which do not meet these standards.

Unexpected challenges in recent years had included price declines in various farm industries—dairy, feed, layers (chickens that lay eggs), and swine—and increased competitive pressures in the farm input supply industry. Gherty was getting ready for a strategic planning session with his senior executives. Land O'Lakes had undergone many changes in the past five years; in particular, its portfolio of businesses had changed considerably as the cooperative grew from its midwestern roots to having plants in California and Pennsylvania. Gherty believed that:

> size and scale [are] important. I think if you put it on the back of a postcard what you would see us doing is very simply saying, "Deliver the promises in our feed, seed, and agronomy business, deliver the earnings, return on investments, improve the balance sheet, and then grow our value added dairy foods business."

The main issue facing Gherty and his management team was the need to evaluate Land O'Lakes' diversified portfolio of businesses and find ways to improve future corporate performance. It had become highly leveraged in recent years due to mergers and acquisitions, which had helped Land O'Lakes achieve size and scale in many of its businesses.

JACK GHERTY

Jack Gherty grew up on a family dairy and livestock farm in western Wisconsin. He began his career as an attorney for Land O'Lakes in 1970, after completing graduate degrees in law and industrial relations at the University of Wisconsin. Before joining Land O'Lakes, he also worked as a volunteer with Volunteers in Service to America (VISTA), serving on Chicago's South Side. He was named assistant to the president of Land O'Lakes in 1979. In 1981, he became a group vice president and chief administrative officer, and in 1989 he was named president and CEO.

Copyright © 2004 by Michael A. Boland, Vincent Amanor-Boadu, and David Barton. All rights reserved. The case authors gratefully appreciate the comments and suggestions of Land O'Lakes employees, including Paul Christ, Jack Gherty, Jane Politiski, and Kevin Schluender.

Gherty used several roles as CEO to encourage good strategy execution among his managers. He was a strong believer in exercising ethics leadership. For example, one time Land O'Lakes was using a well-known speaker at its annual meeting who was very popular but also had a habit of telling off-color jokes. Gherty let the speaker know that such jokes were unacceptable at the meeting, going so far as to say that if such jokes were told, he would have the microphone unplugged.

Gherty often said that his experiences on a farm had taught him that there were things that one didn't think about but that were pretty instrumental in molding who you were—especially service and practicing a strong work ethic. On a dairy farm, that meant seven days a week, morning and night. He learned that farm families balanced work, family, and community. Gherty had married in his mid-30s and had young children when he became CEO. His attendance at their school events and other functions sent a strong signal to the organization that family was important.

People described Gherty as a situational leader, someone who had the flexibility to adopt different management styles. The challenge with this approach was the impact that it had on team members. Gherty once got some feedback that people were sometimes intimidated and confused by his manner. One moment he would be the sociable neighbor next door; the next, he might be in a controller position. To address this response, he spent an hour and a half at an officers' meeting discussing his management style to help people at Land O'Lakes understand him better.

LAND O'LAKES' VISION, MISSION, AND OBJECTIVES

After Land O'Lakes first tackled the development of its vision and mission statement, Jack Gherty recounted some of the circumstances and requirements:

> Whatever the mission is, it needs to be short enough so that people at least can remember the essence of it. And ours ended up being "to be a market- and customer-driven cooperative, committed to optimizing our members' dairy, crop, and livestock production." The "market- and customer-driven" was a little bit of a cultural response to the fact that we were a co-

operative and cooperatives tend to be inward looking. It was in the mission to get those words "market- and customer-driven" right up front. The word "cooperative" is our purpose or reason for being. When we go out to the world, we don't wear it on our sleeves, but in our mission, we are not embarrassed to say we are a cooperative. We spent a lot of time on the word "optimizing." We wanted no fuzziness, no cobwebs relative to the accountability of this organization to believe that performance is important, so we said "optimizing."

Exhibit 1 presents the company vision, mission, values, and organizational beliefs as of 2003.

Land O'Lakes as a Cooperative

As a cooperative, Land O'Lakes was owned by the patrons who used its products and services. These patrons included dairy producers that supplied fluid milk to Land O'Lakes and farmers that used its products such as animal feed and services such as crop nutrient application. There were over 11,000 producers and 1,300 local cooperatives that owned Land O'Lakes. Jack Gherty knew that strategic planning was very important for farm cooperatives because their owners were dependent on them to provide them with crop inputs and services and to market their products. He observed:

> One thing that makes managing a cooperative more satisfying is that the ultimate ownership of a cooperative is farmers, ranchers, and local cooperatives. When you think about the rural values and what they stand for, to be in a leadership position and try to make a difference in improving their life or their income is something that is fairly unique. Our shareholders are not invisible. That makes cooperatives very different.

Governance Issues

Land O'Lakes was governed by 24 directors—the dairy members nominated 12 directors from among the dairy members, and the agricultural services members nominated 12 directors from among the agricultural members. The nomination of directors was conducted within each group by region. The number of directors nominated from each region was based on the total amount of business conducted with the cooperative by that region's members. Directors were elected to four-year terms at the annual meeting by voting members in a manner similar to a

exhibit 1   **Land O'Lakes Vision, Mission, Values, and Organizational Beliefs, 2003**

Vision

Our vision is to be one of the best food and agricultural companies in the world by being: Our customers' first choice; our employees' first choice; responsible to our owners; and a leader in our communities. We are committed to doing more than meeting our customers' needs. We strive to delight our customers by anticipating and exceeding their expectations through an innovative and creative workforce. We recognize employees as our most important asset and we focus on making Land O'Lakes their first choice for work. We believe in respecting diversity and in encouraging teamwork, involvement, development, and empowerment of all employees. We aim to create greater shareholder value while fulfilling our responsibilities as a cooperative. Finally, we recognize our responsibilities to the communities in which we operate. We are proactive in dedicating resources to build a better quality of life, operate in an ethical and environmentally sensitive manner and live by our values.

Mission

We are a market- and customer-driven cooperative committed to optimizing the value of our members' dairy, crop, and livestock production.

Values

The Land O'Lakes heritage is rich in rural values, family, and respect for the land. Our cooperative roots run deep. With determination and pride, we will continue our commitment to serve farmers, rural America, and our customers. Our values reflect who we are and what we firmly believe in:

- *People:* We believe in people—in valuing and recognizing a workforce of diverse individuals as the key to our success.
- *Performance:* We believe in setting high standards—defining clear goals and rewarding initiative that turns ideas into action and goals into reality.
- *Customer Commitment:* We believe the customer is fundamental to our success—working together to meet their needs is the basis for all that we do.
- *Quality:* We believe Land O'Lakes stands for quality—striving to make our best better.
- *Integrity:* We believe in honesty—respecting each individual, fairness, and open communication.

Organizational Beliefs

The breadth of the Land O'Lakes system must be leveraged where it creates competitive advantage. This means that:

- We must continue to grow to have the size and scale necessary to compete on behalf of our owners. In each of our core businesses, our competitors and customers continue to drive toward increased size, scale, and market shares. If our farmer-owned system is to remain competitive, we must continue to pursue appropriate, strategic growth.
- Resources are finite and our growth must be consistent with proactive management of our portfolio.
- Generating industry-competitive results is critical to success.
- Exceptional people will be essential to success.

Source: Company documents.

typical corporation. Membership was divided into eight dairy regions and five agricultural supply regions. At present, 19 of the directors were producers and 5 were managers of local farm supply cooperatives. Board meetings were held monthly for almost two days (including travel time). The board and Jack Gherty operated according to a traditional structure in which the CEO proposed a vision and mission to the board; the proposal was then debated and either approved or modified in an agreed-upon manner.

Strategic and Financial Objectives

Land O'Lakes had several strategic objectives, including being the leader in the U.S. butter category. As leader, Land O'Lakes wanted to have the highest quality, the most innovative products, and the most well known brand. Its roots as a company were in butter manufacturing, and this was an important symbol of the company. Land O'Lakes was the first to use sweet cream in its butter. It also wanted to be a market share leader in other categories like deli cheese, dried milk replacer for calves, and alfalfa seed. It had been the first to develop a dried milk replacer for calves and was the first to develop alfalfa with multiple leaves that increased hay yields. Finally, it wanted to have the highest market share in feed and crop nutrient distribution.

Jack Gherty did not publicly announce specific financial objectives but used return on invested capital and return on equity as two measures of financial performance. In 2002, he and his management team wanted to achieve $255 million in earnings before interest, tax, depreciation and amortization (EBITDA), pay down debt by $80 million, and limit capital expenditures to between $90 and $100 million.

LAND O'LAKES' BUSINESS ORGANIZATION

Headquartered in Arden Hills, Minnesota, Land O'Lakes was a national food and agricultural cooperative, founded in 1921 through the federation of 320 Minnesota cooperative creameries. It operated 200 processing, manufacturing, warehousing, and distribution facilities throughout the United States and employed about 8,000 people. In its 81 years, the company had grown into one of the nation's largest agrifood companies, with more than $5.8 billion (not including joint ventures) in net sales revenue in 2002. It had more than 11,000 producer-members and 1,300 local community cooperatives members who actively participated in its governance through a 24-member elected board of directors.

Land O'Lakes' business was divided into two main segments: dairy foods and agricultural services. The dairy foods group was divided into two broad segments:

- *Value-added,* focusing on retail, deli, specialty, and food-service products.
- *Industrial,* focusing on procurement and manufacturing activities, along with the sale of bulk cheeses, dried cheese, and whey products (used for processed foods, sports drinks, and nutritional supplements) to industrial and high-volume customers (e.g., mozzarella sales to large pizza chains and manufacturers).

Examples of Land O'Lakes' products, some with the familiar Indian maiden logo, are shown in Exhibit 2.

Dairy value-added and dairy industrial products accounted for 44 percent and 56 percent of dairy product sales, respectively, in 2001. These were broken down into retail customers (35 percent), fluid milk (27 percent), commodity (19 percent), ingredients (10 percent), and food service (9 percent). By the end of 2003, Land O'Lakes had 12 plants manufacturing butter, spreads, nonfat dry milk (NFDM), cheese, and whey (see Exhibit 3).

Butter, deli cheese, and food-service offerings remained Land O'Lakes' principal retail products. Deli cheese was sold through the Land O'Lakes, Alpine Lace, and New Yorker brands. Partnering opportunities included providing the butter for certain flavors of General Mills Pop Secret popcorn and the butter flavor for Frito-Lay Rold-Gold pretzels. Land O'Lakes and Dean Foods also were partners in a strategic alliance that combined the strength of Dean Foods' position in the dairy case with the strength of the Land O'Lakes brand, which had a 96 percent brand awareness. The agricultural services business encompassed five principal business units: LOL Farmland Feed LLC, Layers, Swine, Seed, and a 50 percent ownership in Agriliance, LLC.

Land O'Lakes had an international division that conducted education and training in dairy processing, agribusiness management, and other operations. Employees and producers could volunteer for these programs, which were operating in more than a dozen countries in 2003. Land O'Lakes sold products overseas in more than 50 countries and had licensing agreements in other countries. Internal sales were very small but did provide unique opportunities for the company's members and employees to work in a developing country for a few weeks.

THE BUSINESS ENVIRONMENT FACING LAND O'LAKES' U.S. DAIRY OPERATIONS

Dairy Product Consumption

Consumer preferences had shifted over time due to increasing awareness about the relationship between

exhibit 2   **Examples of Land O'Lakes Branded Dairy Food and Agricultural Services Products**

diet and health. The implications of this shift for dairy products depended on consumer perceptions about their impacts on health. Dairy products were typically grouped into several broad categories: beverages (milk and milk-based beverages), hard and frozen products (ice cream and frozen yogurt), butter and cheese, and soft products (yogurt and fluid cream). Sales of hard and frozen and soft products tended to be demand driven, while those of butter and cheese tended to be supply driven because the latter were made from the residual butterfat from fluid milk.

Dairy Processing

The U.S. dairy processing industry had undergone significant structural changes over the last two decades. The shifts had occurred in both the number of plants and the location distribution of plants. The total number of plants processing cheese decreased between 1980 and 1999 by almost 49 percent, from 737 to 376.[1] A similar trend was seen for plants processing butter, whose numbers fell by 68 percent over the same period; the number of plants processing NFDM fell by 58 percent. There was only a 16 percent reduction in the number of plants making processed cheese, decreasing from 62 to 52 plants between 1980 and 1999.

The location of plants also changed. For example, California's share of butter and cheese plants increased by 55 percent and 183 percent, respectively,

[1]D. Blayney, "The Changing Landscape of U.S. Milk Production." Statistical Bulletin No. SB978. U.S. Department of Agriculture, Economic Research Service, June 2002.

exhibit 3   **Location of Land O'Lakes Dairy Processing Plants in the United States, March 2003**

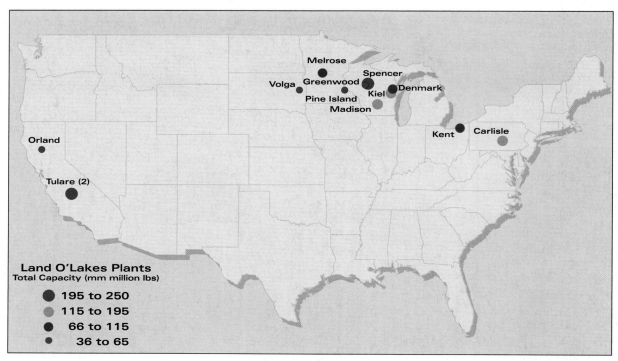

Note: The Volga plant was scheduled to be closed in late 2003, and Land O'Lakes planned to market the cheese output of a plant in Lake Norden, South Dakota. The Cheese and Protein International Tulare plant was scheduled to double its size by the end of 2004.

between 1980 and 1999, while Wisconsin's shares decreased by 2 percent and 26 percent, respectively. There were slight increases in plant numbers in New York and Pennsylvania over this period.

The reduction in plant numbers was a result of consolidation of processing capacity and, in the case of cheese, an expansion in production capacity. Total cheese production increased by about 107 percent, from 4 billion pounds to about 8.3 billion pounds between 1980 and 2000.[2] Butter production, however, increased by only 10 percent within the same period. This reflected the differences in increased demand for cheese and the decreased supply of butterfat available for butter (the residual claimant on butterfat).

The annual volatility in wholesale prices for butter and cheese had increased over the years but wholesale prices for butter had declined by 19 percent while cheese prices had increased by 14 percent between 1986 and 2001.[3] The price volatility had increased due to market-driven forces and changes in agricultural policy beginning in 1995. The 1996 Farm Bill Act consolidated and reformed federal milk marketing orders. It established 11 federal milk marketing orders (reduced from 33 in 1996), introduced new methods for determining class prices into effect, and made some of the language of the orders more uniform. It also reduced the price supports on milk.

---

[2]L. Southard, "Livestock, Dairy, and Poultry Outlook," U.S. Department of Agriculture, Economic Research Service report LDP-M-102 (http://jan.mannlib.cornell.edu/reports/erssor/ livestock/ldp-mbb/2002/ldp-m102f.pdf), December 2002. Accessed June 2, 2003.

[3]E. Jesse, B. Barham, and B. Jones, "Wisconsin and U.S. Dairy Trends," Chapter 2 in *Rethinking Dairyland*, Department of Agricultural and Applied Economics, University of Wisconsin, Paper No. 78B, September 2002.

Milk Production

Although milk was produced in all 50 states in the United States, the distribution of production was concentrated in five states—California, Wisconsin, New York, Pennsylvania, and Minnesota—which together accounted for about 53 percent of total U.S. milk production in 2002. In absolute terms, California was the leader in growth. Total milk production between 1980 and 2000 increased by 30 percent from 128.4 billion pounds to 167.6 billion pounds. Also during this period, the average production per milking cow in the United States increased by 53 percent from 11,891 pounds to 18,201 pounds. These productivity improvements had resulted from better genetics and herd management skills.

Wisconsin and Minnesota had many advantages in dairy production. There was a large infrastructure of many cheese plants, university research and outreach programs, ideal locations for grain and forage production, state government programs, and historically strong support for dairy production. These states, however, also had disadvantages, including small average herd size, lower milk production per cow, a declining supply of labor, a lack of consistent-quality forage (i.e., lack of consistent protein for use in total mixed rations), and a lack of equity capital to expand production to take advantage of economies of size.[4]

Greater competition between processors for milk in Wisconsin due to excess cheese plant capacity in recent years and declining milk production, coupled with marketing orders and other factors, meant that Wisconsin producers received premiums for their milk relative to dairy producers in California and other states. Cheese processors such as Land O'Lakes needed to reduce their costs or face capacity rationalization.

Given the consumption trend and plant consolidation trends at the processing level, it was obvious that similar consolidation trends had occurred at the milk production level of the U.S. dairy supply chain. However, this high attrition level had been compensated by increases in both size of operations and cow

[4]W. Dobson and P. Christ, "Structural Change in the U.S. Dairy Industry: Growth in Scale, Regional Shifts in Milk Production and Processing, and Internationalism," Department of Agricultural and Applied Economics, University of Wisconsin, Staff Paper 438 (www.aae.wisc.edu/www/pub/sps/stpap438.pdf), December 2000. Accessed June 2, 2003.

productivity. The share of these larger herds in the industry had increased rapidly. For example, operations consisting of 200 or more head accounted for 31.8 percent of milking cows in 1993 and 79.3 percent of operations by 2000. That is, 10.2 percent of operations accounted for 79.3 percent of milking cows in 2000. Size was not the only issue. Productivity as measured by pounds of milk per cow per annum was also greater on these large dairies. For example, in 1996 the average pounds of milk per cow in California, New York, and Wisconsin were 19,161; 16,396; and 15,442, respectively. In 2001, these members were 17,527; 17,182; and 20,913, respectively.

Industrial Organization in the Dairy Industry

Two types of firms operated in the U.S. dairy industry: proprietary or investor-oriented companies and cooperatives or patron-oriented companies. The number of proprietary companies and cooperatives had decreased, and the size of these firms, on average, had increased. Proprietary companies had moved toward the fluid milk, cheese, and frozen products, while cooperatives had taken on major roles in processing butter and cheese products. Cooperatives also were mainly responsible for the assembly and marketing of raw bulk milk to other processors. Cooperatives were the first handlers of about 87 percent of raw milk in 2000.

There were two types of dairy cooperatives: bargaining-only and manufacturing/processing. The bargaining-only cooperatives negotiated prices and terms of trade for their members' milk and did not handle, own, or process the milk. They required less capital to operate and handled relatively smaller volumes of milk. Manufacturing/processing cooperatives arranged prices and marketed some of their members' milk through their own processing and manufacturing facilities. These firms assembled milk, processed products, and bargained for prices too. Due to larger marketing expenses and higher capital requirements, members of manufacturing/processing cooperatives might see lower prices than those in the bargaining-only cooperative. However, members of the former also might see higher patronage refunds than those received by bargaining-only cooperatives.

exhibit 4   **Dairy Foods** **Magazine's List of Top 25 Dairy Processors Based on 2001 Sales**

Rank	Company	Sales (in billions)	Plants	Products
1	Dean Foods	$9.70	113	Milk, juice, cultured, novelties, ice cream
2	Kraft Foods North America[a]	4.11	18	Cheese, yogurt, cultured
3	Land O'Lakes, Inc.	3.06	13	Cheese, butter, cultured
4	National Dairy Holdings LP[b]	2.40	33	Milk, cultured, frozen, cheese, ice cream
5	Saputo Inc.	2.28	16	Cheese, novelties, milk, cultured, dry
6	Kroger Co. Dairy Operations	1.90	18	Milk, ice cream, novelties, cultured, cheese
7	DFA	1.70	27	Cheese, milk, dried products,
8	Parmalat Canada	1.40	29	Cheese, cultured, milk, juice, ingredients
9	Leprino Foods	1.50	11	Cheese (Mozzarella)
10	Schreiber Foods Inc.	1.50	12	Cheese, butter
11	Dreyer's Ice Cream[c]	1.40	5	Ice cream, novelties
12	Foremost Farms	1.33	23	Cheese, cultured, milk, whey products, juice
13	WestFarm Foods	1.30	11	Milk, cheese, cultured, ice cream, novelties
14	Agropur Cooperative	1.20	20	Cheese, butter, milk, yogurt
15	Good Humor—Breyers Ice Cream[d]	1.19	6	Ice cream, novelties
16	Prairie Farms Dairy Inc.	1.10	17	Milk, ice cream, novelties, cultured
17	California Dairies Inc.	1.10	6	Milk, cheese, butter, powder, condensed
18	Associated Milk Producers	1.00	14	Cheese, butter, powder, whey
19	Con Agra Foods	1.00	14	Cheese, ice cream, whipped topping
20	Yoplait–Colombo[e]	0.95	3	Cultured
21	Lactalis USA / Sorrento Lactalis[f]	0.90	6	Cheese
22	Great Lakes Cheese Co.	0.84	6	Cheese
23	Safeway Dairy Division	0.81	17	Milk, cultured, ice cream, novelties
24	HP Hood Inc.[g]	0.80	7	Milk, ice cream, novelties, cultured
25	Superbrand[h]	0.73	6	Ice cream, cultured, milk

[a]Philip Morris owns 84 percent.
[b]DFA owns 50 percent.
[c]Nestlé owns 67 percent.
[d]Unilever is the parent company.
[e]General Mills is the parent company.
[f]Groupe Lactalis (France) is the parent company.
[g]Catamount Holdings LP is the parent company.
[h]Winn-Dixie is the parent company.

Source: "The Dairy 100," Dairy Foods (www.dairyfoods.com/spec_features/top100/2002/0802_dairy100_list_1.htm), August 2002. Accessed June 2, 2003.

Land O'Lakes' Major Competitors

Competition had greatly changed in recent years, as several firms had grown large enough to compete in various markets in the United States. Historically, the dairy processing industry was fragmented due to issues related to local supply of milk. One reason often cited for the recent consolidation was the response to similar consolidation at retail supermarkets that might prefer to deal with the same supplier. There were at least six national dairy: Suiza Foods, Dean Foods, Land O'Lakes, Dairy Farmers of America (DFA), Kraft, and Leprino Foods.

Land O'Lakes operated in many different segments and faced a variety of competitors in those segments (see Exhibit 4). For example, in retail nonbutter spreads, Land O'Lakes competed against

exhibit 5   **U.S. Market Share for the Top 10 Competitors in Butter, Sour Cream, Cheese, and Skim/Low Fat Milk**

	Sales (in millions)[a]	Market Share
Butter (excludes sales to Wal-Mart)		
Private label	$ 560.7	46.0 percent
Land O'Lakes	378.3	31.1
Challenge Dry Products	58.8	4.8
Kraft	28.7	2.4
Tillamook County Creamery	24.2	2.0
Kellers Creamery	19.7	1.6
Hotel Bar Foods	17.2	1.4
Crystal Farms	17.0	1.4
Cabot Creamery	12.5	1.0
Darigold	11.6	1.0
Others	89.3	7.3
Category total	$1,218.0	100.0 percent
Sour cream (excludes sales to Wal-Mart)		
Private label	$ 214.3	31.6 percent
Kraft	106.3	15.7
Daisy Brand Inc.	90.1	13.3
Knudsen Corp.	67.7	10.0
Dean Foods	19.0	2.8
Friendship Dairies	13.7	2.0
Land O'Lakes	10.9	1.6
Gandy's Dry Inc.	8.2	1.2
Tillamook County Creamery	8.0	1.2
Darigold	7.5	1.1
Others	132.6	19.5
Category total	$ 678.3	100.0 percent
Natural cheese, not shredded (excludes sales to Wal-Mart)		
Private label	$1,001.0	36.3 percent
Kraft	294.0	10.7
Tillamook	168.0	6.1
Kraft Cracker Barrel	96.0	3.5
Sargento	69.0	2.5
Precious	59.0	2.1
Frigo Cheese Heads	58.0	2.1
Athenos	55.0	2.0
Land O'Lakes	53.0	1.9
Polly O	46.0	1.7
Others	856.0	31.1
Category total	$2,755.0	100.0 percent

(continues)

large food processors such as Unilever and Con Agra. In the retail cheese segment, Kraft was a direct competitor. Furthermore, store brands or private-label brands were also competitors in every retail dairy foods segment (see Exhibit 5). Food-service competitors included Kraft and Schreiber Foods. Foremost

exhibit 5 **(concluded)**

	Sales (in millions)[a]	Market Share
Skim/lowfat milk (excludes Wal-Mart)		
Private label	$4,310.0	64.5 percent
Kemps	113.0	1.7
Lactaid 100	104.0	1.6
Dean's	95.0	1.4
Mayfield	74.0	1.1
Prairie Farms	67.0	1.0
Land O'Lakes	65.0	1.0
Hiland	58.0	0.9
Horizon Organic	56.0	0.8
Garelick Farms	54.0	0.8
Others	1,689.0	25.3
Category total	$6,685.0	100.0 percent

[a]Sales for the butter and sour cream categories are for the 52 weeks ending April 20, 2003; sales for the natural cheese category are for the 52 weeks ending December 1, 2002; and sales for the skim/lowfat milk category are for the 52 weeks ending September 8, 2002.

Source: Information Resources, Inc., as published in *Dairy Foods* (www.dairyfoods.com/articles/2002/1102/NPM_market_trends.htm) November 2002. Accessed June 2, 2003.

Farms, DFA, Leprino, and the Canadian-based Saputo were competitors in industrial cheese.

BUSINESS ENVIRONMENT FACING LAND O'LAKES' U.S. AGRICULTURAL SERVICES OPERATIONS

Feed Manufacturing

Feed historically was the largest purchased item for U.S. farmers. U.S. Department of Agriculture's Economic Research Service estimates were that feed expenses accounted for 48.1 percent of total expenditures on farm inputs in 2001, excluding livestock. The purchase of Purina Mills in 2001 elevated Land O'Lakes to the first position in the U.S. feed manufacturing industry, which produced 55.74 million pounds of feed in 2001 (see Exhibit 6). It also provided significant market share in lifestyle feed products (i.e., feed for horses), where margins were significantly higher than in commercial animal production.

LOL Farmland Feed LLC was formed in 2000 as a joint venture between Land O'Lakes and Farmland Industries. Land O'Lakes brought its former farm feed and supply businesses and joint ventures to the LOL Farmland Feed initiative; it owned 69 percent of the new company upon its formation and had 100 feed mills across the United States. Purina Mills was merged into LOL Farmland Feed, increasing its expected annual sales to $2.5 billion with a capacity of 16 million tons. Land O'Lakes thus owned 92 percent of the feed venture with two popular brands, Land O'Lakes and Purina.

LOL Farmland Feed produced complete feeds that were a balanced mixture of grains, proteins, nutrients, and vitamins. The feeds were sold as ground meal, in pellets, or in extruded pieces. The lifestyle animal feed was sold as a complete feed through the trademarked Purina Chow and the nine-square "checkerboard" logo. Supplements were also used by commercial livestock producers, typically mixed together with homegrown grain for livestock rations. Premixes were concentrated additives for use in com-

exhibit 6   **Leading U.S. Commercial and Integrated Feed Manufacturers, 2001 (1,000 tons per year)**

| Firm | Capacity | Number of Feed Mills | Percentage of Locations That Sell | | | | States Served |
			Complete	Pelleted	Bulk	Dealer-Sold	
Land O'Lakes	14,275	100	64%	54%	71%	52%	39
Tyson	12,000	40	100	78	100	0	n.a.
Cargill	10,000	79	80	80	80	65	49
ADM	3,200	45	57	57	67	59	42
Perdue	3,016	12	100	100	67	59	42
Gold Kist	3,000	12	91	91	100	0	5
J. D. Heiskell	2,800	6	5	5	95	5	n.a.
Westway	2,004	22	0	0	97	80	48
Kent	2,000	23	5	45	58	98	28
Southern States	1,747	14	86	40	65	62	6
PM Ag Products	1,700	24	0	0	100	20	50

Source: "The Top Feed Companies," *Feed Management*, January 2002.

bination with bulk grain and a protein source, such as soybean meal, and were sold to commercial animal producers and to other feed mill operators for mixing with bulk grains and proteins. Milk replacers were sold to commercial livestock producers to meet the nutritional needs of young animals. Finally, ingredient merchandising was performed that had led to significant cost savings for its feed mills and cooperatives.

Barriers to entry in U.S. feed manufacturing were low, and the industry was very fragmented. Lifestyle animal products were typically purchased on trademarked names, and Land O'Lakes employed production specialists who helped make recommendations about feed selection and nutrition. These specialists were important sources of information and served as a link between the producer, the local cooperative, and Land O'Lakes.

Swine Production

Land O'Lakes had a relatively small swine business unit that owned approximately 65,000 sows at owned and leased facilities. In comparison, the leader, Smithfield Foods, owned about 744,000 sows. There were almost 6 million sows in total in the United States. The dramatic volatility in the live hog market in 1998, 1999, and 2000, when selling prices were well below production costs, resulted in large losses.

Layers (MoArk LLC)

In January 2000, Land O'Lakes formed MoArk LLC, a joint venture of which it owned 50 percent, with Osborne Investments, LLC, to produce and market eggs and egg products. MoArk produced and marketed shell eggs and egg products that were sold at retail and wholesale levels for consumer and industrial use throughout the United States. In 2002, MoArk marketed and produced about 740 million dozen eggs annually, which made it a top-three company. The United States produced 7.2 billion dozen eggs in 2002. MoArk recently launched a high-quality, all-natural shell egg product marketed under the Land O'Lakes brand name in a Northeast market.

Seed Division

The seed division of Land O'Lakes marketed the proprietary Croplan Genetics brand, along with third-party and private-label offerings. It was the fourth largest seed company in the United States. With the seed industry, Land O'Lakes' principal competitors were the top companies in the industry: DuPont (Pioneer), Monsanto, and Syngenta. DuPont, clearly the leader, had sales of $2.029 billion in 2002. Monsanto was the second largest company in the industry, with almost $1.6 billion in sales in 2002, followed by

Syngenta, with $937 million in 2002 seed sales. Land O'Lakes had $407 million in seed sales in 2002. Because of the intense concentration in the industry, Land O'Lakes was among the top-four seed companies in the United States, ranking first in market share of alfalfa genetics seed. A significant distinguishing factor was that Land O'Lakes and Pioneer were the only two major seed companies that provided agronomic services to producers.

Many of the crops (e.g., corn and soybeans) planted by Land O'Lakes members had been bioengineered for tolerance to certain herbicides and pesticides. Croplan's agreements with Monsanto and Syngenta enabled it to have access to these input traits. Many of Land O'Lakes' members used their crops such as alfalfa and corn as feed inputs into dairy and meat production. Thus, Croplan's research and development focused on developing output traits that would improve a crop's feed value.

Agronomy

Agriliance was primarily a marketing and distribution alliance between Land O'Lakes and United Country Brands (owned by Farmland Industries and CHS Cooperatives) and was the leading crop input marketing organization in the United States. Land O'Lakes held 50 percent ownership of Agriliance. Agriliance provided crop protection, including herbicides and pesticides, and crop nutrients such as fertilizers and micronutrients.

Agriliance held nearly 30 percent of the U.S. market for crop nutrients and 25 percent of the market for crop protection products. Agriliance had warehouses and distribution facilities located throughout the United States with retail units in the Southeast. Formed in 2000, it was owned by United Country Brands and Land O'Lakes. The company provided various services, including soil testing, adjuvant and herbicide formulation, and application.

Its primary competitors were national crop nutrient distributors such as Cargill, IMC, PCS, Agrium, and Royster Clark; national crop protection product distributors such as UAP, Helena, and Wilbur-Ellis; and regional brokers and distributors. Consolidation was under way as distributors sought to expand capabilities and increase efficiencies. Wholesale agronomy customers tended to purchase products according to a distributor's ability to provide ready

access to them at critical times prior to and during the growing season.

Agriliance not only had a distribution network that enabled it to efficiently distribute products to customers but also had trained agronomists who provided advice to farmers on both agronomy and crop seed products to optimize their crop production. Agriliance's trained agronomists were a critical strength for Land O'Lakes. These individuals worked closely with the local cooperative agronomy operations and were a critical link between Land O'Lakes, the local cooperative, and its members. A goal was to build close relationships with producers that could result in new long-term business for Land O'Lakes products. In addition, the agronomists provided technology advice on topics such as precision agriculture in much the way that land-grant university county extension agents did for producers.

THE BUILDING OF LAND O'LAKES' BUSINESS PORTFOLIO

Recent Portfolio Restructuring

Exhibits 7 and 8 show that mergers, acquisitions, and joint ventures played an important role in the growth of Land O'Lakes. The cooperative's divestitures are shown in Exhibit 9. These strategic moves had a direct impact on the changes in Land O'Lakes' financial performance.

Land O'Lakes had collaborated with Dean Foods on several ventures. For example, the two companies formed the Dairy Marketing Alliance in 2000, with Dean Foods taking Land O'Lakes' fluid milk operations and creating value-added fluid and cultured dairy products. Land O'Lakes sold five milk-processing plants to Dean Foods; in exchange, Dean Foods gained the licensing rights to market milk, yogurt, sour cream, and cottage cheese under the Land O'Lakes brand. The two firms also formed a joint venture to develop and sell convenience-oriented dairy products, including the Grip n' Go line of single-serve milk bottles. The Cheese and Protein International LLC was formed with Mitsui & Company of Japan and included a mozzarella and whey plant in Tulare, California.

exhibit 7   **Mergers, Acquisitions, and Joint Ventures Made by Land O'Lakes in Dairy Manufacturing, 1981 to 2001**

Year	Merger, Acquisition, or Joint Venture
1981	Lake to Lake Dairy Cooperative—merger (Wisconsin)
1986	Lakeside Dairy—acquisition (South Dakota)
1997	Atlantic Dairy Cooperative—merger (Pennsylvania)
1997	Alpine Lace—acquisition
1998	Dairyman's Cooperative Creamery Association—merger (California)
1999	Swiss Valley Farms—joint venture (Iowa, Illinois)
2000	Beatrice cheese plant (California)—acquisition
2000	Madison Dairy Produce Company—acquisition, $59.3 million
2001	Kraft Foods cheese plant (Melrose, MN)—acquisition
2001	Alto Dairy Cooperative—joint venture

exhibit 8   **Mergers, Acquisitions, and Joint Ventures Made by Land O'Lakes in Farm Supply (Feed, Seed, and Agronomy Products), 1970 to 2001**

Year	Merger, Acquisition, or Joint Venture
1970	Farmers Regional Cooperative (Felco)—merger (Iowa, Minnesota)
1982	Midland Cooperatives—merger (Wisconsin, Minnesota)
1987	Cenex (now CHS Cooperatives)—agronomy joint venture
1998	Countrymark Co-op—acquisition (Indiana)
1998	GROWMARK—joint venture (Illinois, Wisconsin)
1999	CHS Cooperatives and Farmland Feed—joint venture, $91.7 million
1999	Terra—acquisition of eastern U.S. assets, $70.7 million
2000	Agro Distribution—joint venture with CHS Cooperatives
2000	Advanta Seeds and AgriBioTech—seed company acquisitions
2001	Purina Mills—acquisition, $540.5 million
2001	Agriliance—joint venture (with United Country Brands), $79.5 million
2001	Novartis—joint venture (specialty seeds)

exhibit 9   **Business Assets Divestitures by Land O'Lakes, 2000 to 2002**

Year	Assets Divested
2000	Fluid dairy assets (to Dean Foods), $112.2 million
2000	Swine business (North Carolina)
2002	Seed coating business (Idaho)
2002	Seed inoculation business (Brazil)
2002	Dairy operations (Poland)
2002	Feed operations in Mexico

The Dairy Marketing Alliance was dissolved in July 2002 with the expansion of the relationship between Dean Foods and Land O'Lakes in which Dean Foods used Land O'Lakes' brand name nationally on a range of value-added fluid milk and cultured dairy products and on all basic fluid dairy products. The new agreement granted perpetual, royalty-bearing national licensing rights of the Land O'Lakes brand directly to Dean Foods, and it expanded the qualifying products to include value-added products such as fortified nutritional milks, aseptic products, infant formula, and soy beverages.

Two proposed mergers did not take place. The first proposed merger was a unification of Land O'Lakes, Inc., and four regional milk marketing co-operatives in Maryland, Virginia, Arkansas, and Texas. This would have created a new Eastern Fluid Milk Marketing Division of Land O'Lakes and would have operated under the established Advantage Dairy Group identity. A second merger, proposed in the late 1980s, would have combined Land O'Lakes, CHS Cooperatives, and Farmland Industries into one regional cooperative. Talks were ultimately called off.

There were various reasons why the mergers were called off. Membership concerns regarding the benefits of the mergers was cited. Some Maryland and Virginia members were uncertain about the benefits of the merger but did want to include their joint-venture milk marketing relationship through Advantage Dairy Group. The merger of the three big midwestern regional cooperatives was called off primarily because of members' uncertainty about the benefits of unification and their desire for separate organizations.

In 2000, Land O'Lakes completed acquisitions that totaled $101.4 million in cash outlays, and divested assets that totaled $184.1 million. In 2001, Land O'Lakes acquired Purina Mills, Inc., in a $359 million cash transaction (net of cash acquired) that included $247 million for stock and acquisition costs and $112 million in debt retirement (see Exhibit 10). In 2002, Land O'Lakes divested assets that totaled $22.4 million. Land O'Lakes incurred restructuring and impairment costs due to consolidation and closing of facilities that totaled $54.2 million in 2000, $3.7 million in 2001, and $31.4 million in 2002. Exhibit 11 shows the investments that Land O'Lakes had in joint ventures and interregional cooperatives in 2002.

Financial Performance

The mergers, acquisitions and joint ventures had stretched Land O'Lakes' balance sheet in recent years (see data presented in Exhibit 12). The Purina acquisition that had been made in part using debt also contributed to the stress.

A more revealing view of Land O'Lakes' financial performance is given by the financial data for its business segments in Exhibit 13. Dairy foods had seen an increase in sales and assets through its portfolio restructuring. Animal feed had achieved the largest increase in sales and assets. A vitamin price-fixing lawsuit had also been settled in Land O'Lakes' favor, resulting in a one-time $152.1 million gain in earnings in its feed segment in 2002.

THE CURRENT SITUATION

Land O'Lakes had been badly hurt by downturns in its swine and fertilizer segments. Similar downturns had contributed to the bankruptcy of two other large regional cooperatives, Farmland Industries and Agway. In September 2002, the financial community pointed out that Land O'Lakes' debt was trading below par shortly after it released its quarterly earnings report in July 2002. The markets judged the company's performance/outlook as neutral to not good.

There was agreement among industry watchers that both the dairy and agricultural services businesses were going to remain under considerable pressure. Land O'Lakes was faced with the challenge of managing its debt load, sustaining growth, and maintaining member enthusiasm. Although Jack Gherty and his staff had focused on two principal strategic approaches in the two business units—brand extension and joint ventures in the dairy business, and acquisitions and joint ventures in the agricultural services business—there was concern as to whether Land O'Lakes could participate in any further acquisitions given its current debt situation.

Given the strong competitive threat in the dairy products market from Kraft and other players, it appeared Land O'Lakes needed to assess the growth arenas for Dean Foods as it worked on the relationship. Land O'Lakes had just opened a cheese and dairy protein ingredient plant in Tulare, California, a

exhibit 10 **Purina Mills, Inc., Operating Data, 1996–2000 (in millions)**

	1996	1997	1998	1999	2000
Operating data					
Net sales	$1,212.2	$1,128.4	$998.7	$ 881.9	$839.8
Cost of products sold	1,035.9	913.0	811.5	706.9	665.2
Gross profit	$ 176.3	$ 215.4	$187.2	$ 175.0	$174.6
Other costs and expenses:					
Marketing and distribution	84.7	87.3	90.6	91.5	86.8
General and administrative	31.4	55.7	87.5	65.4	49.1
Research and development	7.0	7.2	6.8	6.0	5.7
	$ 123.1	$ 150.2	$184.9	$ 162.9	$141.6
Provision for asset write-offs	14.0	4.4	—	19.7	—
Restructuring expenses	—	—	—	18.1	28.4
Provision for intangible assets impairment	—	—	—	161.6	—
Provision for loss guarantees	—	—	14.2	—	—
Other expense (income)—net	(10.5)	(3.5)	4.6	0.7	(30.2)
Amortization of intangibles	19.5	20.6	18.4	15.1	22.4
	$ 146.1	$ 171.7	$222.1	$ 378.1	$162.2
Operating income (loss)	30.2	43.7	(34.9)	(203.1)	12.4
Interest expense	43.6	41.5	47.6	48.7	16.7
Income (loss) before income taxes	$ (13.4)	$ 2.2	$ (82.5)	$(251.8)	$ (4.3)
Provision (benefit) for income taxes	(3.4)	1.7	(29.6)	29.0	3.0
Income (loss) before extraordinary item and revaluation	(10.0)	0.5	(52.9)	(280.8)	(7.3)
Extraordinary item-gain on extinguishments of debt, net of tax	—	—	—	—	159.3
Revaluation of assets and liabilities pursuant to the adoption of "fresh-start" reporting	—	—	—	—	2.5
Net income (loss)	$ (10.0)	$ 0.5	$ (52.9)	$(280.8)	$154.5
Other data					
Total depreciation and amortization	$ 50.4	$ 50.0	$ 50.2	$ 48.0	$ 52.9
Capital expenditures	23.9	30.4	29.8	21.0	25.5
Cash provided (used)—operations	58.3	70.0	19.8	(32.0)	54.7
Cash provided (used)—investing	(22.1)	(29.3)	(28.6)	(23.3)	(4.7)
Cash provided (used)—financing	(32.2)	(38.5)	22.7	61.6	(60.4)

Source: Land O'Lakes.

joint venture with Mitsui & Company. For now, it seemed that its production-base assets would allow it to grow through such joint venture initiatives.

Like other food companies such as General Mills, Land O'Lakes had restructured its portfolio by relying heavily on debt. Future profitability was tied to the cost savings forecast by achieving size and scale. The challenge facing Jack Gherty and his management team was to craft and execute the right corporate strategy. As Jack put it:

Well, Land O'Lakes has had a lot of growth in the last five to seven years. Quite frankly, right now, as we look at our businesses, we try to look at them in the context of a portfolio of businesses. When I do that I

exhibit 11   **Investments in Joint Ventures and Interregional Cooperatives by Land O'Lakes as of December 31, 2002**

Joint Venture/Entity in Which Investments Were Made	Industry	Amount Invested (in millions)
CF Industries	Fertilizer and crop nutrients	$249.50
Agriliance LLC	Crop protection and nutrients	91.63
MoArk LLC	Egg production and processing	44.68
Ag Processing, Inc.	Soybean meal and oil production	37.85
Advanced Food Products LLC	Asceptic products	27.42
CoBank	Lending	22.06
Melrose Dairy Proteins, LLC	Dairy proteins	6.58
Universal Cooperatives	Tires, batteries, and accessories	6.47
Prairie Farms Dairy, Inc.	Dairy	5.09
Other		54.31
Total		$545.59

Source: Land O'Lakes.

exhibit 12   **Financial Performance Summary, Land O'Lakes, 1993 to 2002 (in millions)**

	1993	1994	1995	1996	1997	1998	1999	2000	2001	2002
Operations data										
Net sales	$2,733	$2,859	$3,014	$3,486	$4,195	$5,174	$5,616	$5,673	$5,865	$5,847
Net earnings	47	75	121	119	95	69	21	103	71	99
Allocated patronage refunds	41	66	104	101	84	76	35	142	71	97
Cash returned to members	40	41	46	53	59	40	49	54	47	38
Tax expense (benefit)						1.5	0.1	−12.9	−5.4	−2.2
Balance sheet data and financial position										
Working capital	$ 151	$ 151	$ 185	$ 199	$ 228	$ 305	$ 362	$ 324	$ 445	$ 209
Investments	129	152	184	240	242	397	460	466	568	546
Plant and equipment	165	180	205	218	283	450	462	489	675	686
Total assets	866	943	1,149	1,235	1,566	2,292	2,700	2,473	3,091	3,246
Long-term debt (including capital securities)	160	155	180	212	297	547	683	663	1,147	1,007
Equities	326	353	417	480	539	781	769	805	837	912

Source: Land O'Lakes records.

exhibit 13 **Selected Financial Data for Land O'Lakes Business Segments, 1998–2002 (in millions)**

	1998	1999	2000	2001	2002
Net sales					
Dairy foods	$3,266.6	$3,291.1	$3,098.2	$3,463.9	$2,899.1
Animal feed	824.3	931.2	1,182.2	1,864	2,444.7
Crop seed	145.3	190.8	365.5	413.6	406.9
Swine	62.5	82.7	102	109.9	83.2
Agronomy	774.7	1,023.3	857	n.a.	n.a.[a]
Other	100.8	96.7	67.9	13.5	13
Operating profit					
Dairy foods	$99.8	$36.8	$115.4	$109.9	$66.2
Animal feed	34.4	33.9	41.8	83.7	243.5[b]
Crop seed	9.9	8.4	18.6	17.6	7.7
Swine	−17.7	−12.6	6.8	13.3	−11.3
Agronomy	24.3	17.6	27.5	−9.9	4.8
Other	7.2	3.8	4	1.2	3.6
Total assets					
Dairy foods	n.r.[c]	$741.3	$715.3	$730.4	$815.2
Animal feed	n.r.	231.5	446.2	981.2	1301.3
Crop seed	n.r.	220.6	335.3	379.9	446.5
Swine	n.r.	102.9	96.0	77.9	69.8
Agronomy	n.r.	497.7	417.6	411.7	416.0
Other	n.r.	906.1	463.0	510.2	197.6
Depreciation and amortization					
Dairy foods	$37.1	$47.4	$42.8	$42.5	$36.8
Animal feed	10.8	14.7	18.6	31.7	46.6
Crop seed	0.9	2.7	5.6	5	3
Swine	4.7	7.9	6.2	5.6	3.8
Agronomy	0.8	3.4	4.6	6.3	6.1
Other	7.1	5.6	5.8	6.2	10.5
Interest					
Dairy foods	$17.2	$30.3	$29.4	$20.0	$20.1
Animal feed	4.3	3.9	4.3	13.8	28.3
Crop seed	0.8	2.0	6.4	6.3	2.7
Swine	0.3	4.9	6.5	6.2	5.4
Agronomy	4.1	4.9	6.1	8.1	9.5
Other	0.5	−1.4	−0.3	1.3	2.8
Capital expenditures					
Dairy foods	$55.5	$63.3	$60.3	$37.7	$32.3
Animal feed	14.4	17.4	21.5	24.9	26
Crop seed	2.4	4.8	3.5	2.7	0.6
Swine	22.6	14	9.6	7.3	3.1
Agronomy	n.a.	n.a.	n.a.	n.a.	n.a.
Other	8.2	9.8	9.4	11.3	25.4

[a]Not available as these were transferred to Agriliance in 2001.
[b]Includes $152.1 million gain from legal settlement.
[c]n.r. = not reported.
Source: Land O'Lakes financial records.

see that we have four core businesses: feed, agronomy, seed, and dairy foods. The first three are agricultural input businesses. The challenge to any branded food company is to bring innovation into their product lines and that's the only way that you bring life and vitality on an ongoing basis to your branded businesses. When we look at our size and scale relative to other food companies, we're a relatively small food company. We could look at it in one sense and say, "Well, just in terms of dollar sales, you're the 23rd largest food company in the United States."

Other References

M. A. Boland, and J. Katz, "Jack Gherty: CEO of Land O'Lakes," *Academy of Management Executive* 17, no. 3 (August 2003), pp. 24–30.

A. Baker, E. Allen, and W. Chambers, "Feed Situation and Outlook Yearbook." U.S. Department of Agriculture, Economic Research Service, FDS-2003. (www.ers. usda.gov/publications/so/view.asp?f = field/fds-bb/), April 2003. Accessed June 2, 2003.

Other Information

Land O'Lakes also has a consumer Web site (www.landolakes.com) and a corporate Web site (www.landolakesinc.com) with extensive information on the company and links to its businesses. Three Web links that contain useful information on cooperatives include the U.S. Department of Agriculture's Rural Business Cooperative Services (www.rurdev.usda.gov/rbs/pub/newpub.htm), the National Cooperative Business Association (www.ncba.org), and the University of Wisconsin Center for Cooperatives (www.wisc.edu/uwcc). Instructors who do not have access to the Internet may call the Arthur Capper Cooperative Center at Kansas State University for information on cooperatives (785-532-1522). The authors of the case would like to thank Paul Christ, Jack Gherty, Dave Karpinski, and Jane Politiski at Land O'Lakes for their help in writing the case.

Unilever's Path to Growth Strategy: Is It Working?

Arthur A. Thompson
The University of Alabama

Throughout 2003, Niall FitzGerald and Antony Burgmans, Unilever's co-chairmen, expressed confidence that the company's five-year Path to Growth strategy was on track. The two co-chairmen had fashioned the strategy initiative in early 2000, following several years of sluggish performance, to rejuvenate the company and restructure its wide-ranging portfolio of food, home, and personal care businesses, which included some 1,600 brands and sales and marketing efforts in 88 countries across the world. Prior to the launch of the Path to Growth strategy, company critics characterized Unilever as burdened by lack of a coherent corporate strategy and an array of lesser-known, low-volume brands; comparatively few Unilever brands had global standing or qualified as "power" brands in 1999. In emerging-country markets, where there was the greatest potential to grow sales of food and household products, Unilever's performance was said to be lackluster.

The key elements of Unilever's Path to Growth strategy involved cutting the size of the company's portfolio from 1,600 brands down to 400 "core" brands, concentrating R&D and advertising on the company's leading brands, divesting underperforming brands and businesses, relying more on product innovation to boost internal growth, and making new acquisitions. The key strategic targets were to achieve top-line sales growth of 5–6 percent annually and to increase operating profit margins from 11 percent to over 16 percent—both to be accomplished by year-end 2004. FitzGerald and Burgmans expected the Path to Growth strategy to produce double-digit earnings per share growth and better position

Unilever in the global food and household products industry against such giants as Nestlé, Procter & Gamble, Kraft, Group Danone, Campbell Soup, and General Mills. Moreover, focusing on key brands was expected to allow Unilever to concentrate its advertising and marketing efforts on higher-margin businesses and to build brand value, thus gaining increased pricing power with supermarket retailers.

The five-year initiative was expected to cost a total of some 5 billion euros (€), entail closing or selling 100 factories and laying off some 25,000 employees (10 percent of Unilever's workforce) so as to consolidate production at fewer plants, and ultimately produce annual savings of €3.9 billion through better strategic fits, a streamlined supply chain, and greater operating efficiencies. In addition, Unilever executives believed that the Path to Growth initiative would rectify the company's lagging sales per employee relative to other food companies—Unilever had sales per employee of around $160,000 in 2000, compared with $205,000 for Nestlé, $360,000 for Procter & Gamble, $458,000 for Kellogg's, and $605,000 for General Mills.

Following the announcement of its Path to Growth strategy in February 2000, which was met with considerable skepticism on the part of industry analysts, Unilever undertook a series of actions over the next 12 months. By March 2001 the company had:

- Made 20 new acquisitions worldwide, including SlimFast diet foods; Ben & Jerry's ice cream; Bestfoods (whose major brands included Hellmann's mayonnaise, Skippy peanut butter, Mazola corn oil and margarines, and Knorr packaged soup mixes—Bestfoods had 1999 sales of $8.6 billion across 110 countries); Corporacion Jaboneria Nacional (an Ecuadorian company that had strong market positions in detergents, toilet soaps, skin creams, dental care, margarine, and edible oils and sales of approximately €114 million); Grupo Cressida (a leading consumer products company in Central America); and Amora-Maille (a French maker of mustards, mayonnaises, ketchups, pickles, vinegars, spices, and cooking sauces with 1999 sales of about $365 million).

- Cut the company's brand portfolio from 1,600 brands to 970. To reach the 2004 corporate goal of focusing on about 400 core brands, Unilever's brand reduction strategy called for letting certain brands wither and decline without active promotion and support, selling those brands that no longer fit in with Unilever's future strategy, and discontinuing the rest. An additional 250–300 brands had been targeted for pruning by 2002, and yet another 200 designated for "merger and migration" into the product families of the top 400 brands. According to Niall FitzGerald, "This [migration] is a complex process. No one else has [done it] on this scale. It is easy to change a name—the marketing challenge is to bring the consumer with you."[1]

- Launched 20 internal initiatives to deliver additional sales of €1.5 billion on an annualized basis.

- Divested 27 businesses, including the company's Elizabeth Arden cosmetics business; the Elizabeth Taylor and White Shoulders fragrances brands; the company's European bakery business, the Bestfoods Baking Company (a U.S. bakery business inherited from the acquisition of Bestfoods); most of its European dry soups and sauces businesses, and an assortment of small businesses that produced and marketed lesser-known European grocery brands. The European dry soups and sauces businesses that Unilever divested (via a sale to Campbell Soup Company) had combined sales of €435 million in 2000 and had grown at 1 percent annually over the last three years. (The divestiture was undertaken to alleviate market power concerns in packaged soups expressed by the European Commission

and gain the commission's approval of Unilever's acquisition of Bestfoods—the Knorr packaged soup business that was part of the Bestfoods acquisition had global sales of $3 billion.)

- Reorganized the company into two roughly equal-sized global divisions, one including all of the company's food products and the other including all of its household and personal care products.

- Started two new businesses—Cha, a chain of tea houses, and Myhome, a laundry and home-cleaning service test-marketed in Britain in 2000 and in the United States and India in 2001.

In the fall of 2003, some three and a half years after launching the Path to Growth strategy, FitzGerald and Burgmans claimed that Unilever's operating results showed "significant progress" toward delivering top-line growth of 5–6 percent and operating margins of 16 percent or more. In their report on third-quarter 2003 results, Unilever's two co-chairmen cited several accomplishments to indicate that Unilever was "on track or ahead on all key elements" of the five-year plan:

- Unilever's leading brands (which included Dove soaps and shampoos; Knorr soups; Lipton teas; Hellman's mayonnaise; Bertolli's olive oil; Ragú sauces; Country Crock margarine; SlimFast; and Heart, Breyers, and Ben & Jerry's ice creams) accounted for almost 92 percent of the company's nearly €50 billion in revenues (up from 75 percent of total revenues in 1999) and sales of leading brands had grown 5.4 percent over the past 12 months.

- The company's businesses and brand lineup had been reshaped and enhanced through acquisitions and the divestiture of 110 businesses (proceeds from the sales of these businesses had generated over €6.8 billion).

- The company's restructuring of its businesses and brands had produced savings of €3.4 billion out of the €3.9 billion total targeted by year-end 2004.

- Net debt had been reduced from €26.5 billion at the end of 2000 to €16 billion and was expected to fall further to €12–€15 billion by year-end 2004.

- Annual free cash flow of €4 billion was up by €1 billion since 1999.

[1] As quoted in "Unilever Unveils 'Big Hit' Innovations, Brand Cull Progress," *Euromarketing via E-mail* 4, no. 3 (February 9, 2001).

Nonetheless, there were several troubling signs at Unilever in late 2003. Whereas Nestlé's revenues had grown by 5.5 percent in the first half of 2003, Unilever's revenues were up by only 1.7 percent (after stripping out the effects of fluctuating exchange rates). On two occasions in 2003 Unilever had cut its revenue growth forecasts—indicating on its second announcement in the fall of 2003 that companywide revenues for 2003 would likely increase by less than 2 percent over 2002. Management said a sharp deceleration of growth in sales in frozen foods, household care, fine fragrances, and SlimFast had restrained the growth of its leading brands in the third quarter of 2003 to just 3.2 percent and that full-year 2003 growth in sales of leading brands would be below 3 percent. Several analysts indicated that the Path to Growth strategy lacked the punch to produce 5–6 percent revenue growth. One analyst said, "Clearly their program has failed. The worst-case scenario is happening."[2] Another said, "Management needs to give up on the top-line [sales revenue] targets and do some more restructuring."[3]

Exhibit 1 shows Unilever's product and brand portfolio in late 2003. Exhibit 2 shows the 2003 slowdown in the sales growth of Unilever's leading brands.

COMPANY BACKGROUND

Unilever was created in 1930 through the merger of Margarine Unie, a Dutch margarine company, and British-based Lever Brothers, a soap and detergent company. Margarine Unie had grown through mergers with other margarine companies in the 1920s. Lever Brothers was founded in 1885 by William Hesketh Lever, who originally built the business by establishing soap factories around the world. In 1917, Lever Brothers began to diversify into foods, acquiring fish, ice cream, and canned foods businesses. At the time of their merger, the two companies were purchasing raw materials from many of the same suppliers, both were involved in large-scale marketing of household products, and both used

similar distribution channels. Between them, they had operations in over 40 countries.

Searching for Focus and Identity

Over the next decades, Unilever continued acquiring companies and brands, gradually moving into more food and household products categories in more and more countries. Still, as late as the mid-1970s, more than half of Unilever's profits came from its West African plantations, which produced bulk vegetable oils for margarine and washing powders. In the 1970s and early 1980s, Unilever diversified beyond food and household products into specialty chemicals, advertising, packaging, market research, and a UK-based franchise for Caterpillar heavy equipment. The specialty chemicals business transformed products from some of the company's plantations into ingredients for food and household products; Unilever also had shipping lines that transported Unilever products. However, during the late 1980s and 1990s, the specialty chemicals, advertising, packaging, shipping, and market research businesses were divested in an attempt to shed the company's image as a conglomerate and focus resources on the company's core businesses.

Unilever's broad-based product and geographic diversification in foods, personal care products, and household products spawned a complex management structure that gave considerable decision-making power to country managers to set their own priorities and to tailor products to local tastes. From time to time, executives at Unilever's headquarters had launched new initiatives and reorganization plans aimed at giving the company more focus as a multinational marketer of food, personal care, and household products. Still, in 2000 when the Path to Growth strategy was launched, the company had 1,600 brands of food, personal care, and household products, with 1999 sales of €41.2 billion and operations in 88 countries.

In 2003, Unilever had pared its brand portfolio to 500–600 brands and reported 2002 sales of about €48.8 billion. A number of Unilever brands had either the highest or second highest share in their respective markets. Unilever was one of the world's five largest food and household products companies and had been ranked among the top 60 of *Fortune's*

[2]Deborah Ball, "Unilever Cuts Its Growth Target Again," *The Wall Street Journal*, October 21, 2003, p. A3.
[3]Ibid., p. A7.

exhibit 1   **Unilever's Business and Product Line Portfolio in Late 2003**

Unilever Foods Group		
Product Category	**Brands**	**Comments**
Margarines, spreads, and cooking oils	I Can't Believe It's Not Butter, Country Crock, Imperial, Take Control, Promise, Brummel & Brown, Rama, Flora/Becel, Dorina, Doriana, and Blue Band spreads and cooking products; Bertolli olive oils; Skippy peanut butter	The world leader in margarine and related spreads and olive oil, with sales in more than 100 countries. Rama was the world's largest margarine brand; Country Crock was the number one U.S. margarine, and Doriana and Dorina were leading margarine brands in Latin America. The Rama, Country Crock, Blue Band, and Flora/Becel brands had 2002 sales of €2.4 billion. Bertolli was the world's leading brand of olive oil, with 2002 revenues of €500 million. Unilever had significant oil plantations in the Democratic Republic of Congo, Côte d'Ivoire, Ghana, and Malaysia.
Frozen foods	Birds Eye (sold in the United Kingdom), Findus (sold in Italy), and Iglo (sold in most other European countries)	Unilever was the biggest marketer of frozen foods in Europe; this product category had an inconsistent growth record but produced a 30% return on capital employed.
Ice cream and frozen novelties	Heart, Breyers, Ben & Jerry's, Magnum, Solero, Wall's, Langnese, Ola, Streets, Cornetto, Carte de'Or, Kibon, Viennetta, Popsicle, Klondike, and Good-Humor ice cream products	Unilever was the world leader in sales of ice cream, with global revenues of €5 billion, a 17% global market share, and sales in over 90 countries. The Heart family of ice cream brands had sales of €3.5 billion across 40 countries; the Breyers and Ben & Jerry's brands generated €1.5 billion in sales.
Tea-based beverages	Lipton, Lipton Ice Tea and Lipton Brisk (ready-to-drink teas), Brooke Bond, and Beseda teas	Lipton was the world's most popular tea brand and the third largest beverage brand worldwide based on volume; Lipton products were sold in 110 countries. Unilever had extensive tea plantations in India, Tanzania, and Kenya that supplied tea for its own brands and the tea market in general.
Culinary products	Knorr soups, Hellman's mayonnaise; Ragú and Five Brothers pasta sauces; Colman's, Amora, and Maille mustards and condiments; Lawry's seasonings; Wishbone and Calvé salad dressings; Calvé peanut butter; Slotts and Klocken mustards, ketchup, and seasonings; Sizzle & Stir sauces	Knorr was Unilever's biggest selling brand with sales of over €2.3 billion; Hellman's was Unilever's third biggest selling brand. Ragú was Unilever's third biggest selling brand in the culinary products group; Amora was the best-selling mustard brand in France.
Health and wellness	SlimFast, AdeS (a soy-based beverage), Maizena	SlimFast was the number one weight management brand in the United States.

Global 500 largest corporations since 1995. According to Niall FitzGerald, "We're not a manufacturing company any more. We're a brand marketing group that happens to make some of its products."[4]

Exhibit 3 provides a summary of Unilever's financial performance for the 1992-2002 period.

[4]As quoted in *The Financial Times*, February 23, 2000, p. 27.

Organization and Management

To preserve the company's Dutch and British heritage, Unilever maintained two headquarters—one in Rotterdam and one in London—and operated under two co-chairmen. The company's headquarters group in Rotterdam, headed by Antony Burgmans, was in

exhibit 1 **(concluded)**

Unilever Home and Personal Care Group (operations in 60-plus countries)		
Product Category	**Brands**	**Comments**
Prestige fragrances	Calvin Klein, Eternity, Escape, Chloé, Cerruti, Valentino, Obsession, Lagerfeld, Nautica, Vera Wang, and BCBG	Unilever's prestige fragrances division was one of the largest fragrance businesses in the world.
Deodorants and toiletry products	Rexona/Sure, Axe/Lynx, Dove, Degree, Brut, Suave, and Impulse	Rexona/Sure was the world's number one deodorant brand.
Hair care	ThermaSilk, Sunsilk, Seda, Finesse, Suave, Caress, Dove, Salon Selectives, Timotei, and Organics shampoos; AquaNet and Rave hair care products	
Oral care and oral products	Aim, Pepsodent, Mentadent, and Close-up (Asia-Pacific, United States), Signal (Europe), Zhongua (China) toothpastes; Signal and Mentadent chewing gums	
Soaps, lotions, and skin care products	Dove, Lux, Degree, Caress, Lever 2000, Lifebuoy, and Shield's soap bars; Pond's, Vaseline, and Fair & Lovely skin care products; Hazeline shampoos and skin care products (sold in China); Q-tips cotton swabs and balls	Dove was the world's number one brand of soap.
Laundry detergents and fabric conditioners	Wisk, Oxo, Omo, Surf, Ala, Persil, All, Radiant, and Skip detergents; Snuggle, Cajoline, and Comfort fabric conditioners	Unilever was a distant number two to Procter & Gamble in North America, a close number 2 behind P&G in Europe, and the clear leader in the developing and emerging country markets with an estimated 55 percent share. The Omo, Surf, and Radiant brands all had annual sales in the €1–€2 billion range.
Household care and cleaning products	Domestos surface cleaners, Cif household cleaners, Sunlight dish detergents, and Solvol (a heavy-duty hand cleaner marketed in Australia and New Zealand)	Domestos was marketed in 43 countries, and Cif was marketed in 53 countries.

Source: Compiled by the case researcher from a variety of company sources.

charge of food products, while the London headquarters group, under Niall FitzGerald, was in charge of personal care and household products. FitzGerald had been chairman of the London-based portion of Unilever since 1996 and was said to have been instrumental in reorganizing Unilever's 1,600-brand portfolio around 14 groups as opposed to the former 57 groups. Company observers regarded FitzGerald as one of the most able and innovative Unilever chairmen in decades. Officially, the two co-chairmen had equal status and responsibilities. Each had offices in both Rotterdam and London, shuttling between the two headquarters' locations every couple of weeks. They kept in contact via phone daily.

To complement its unique dual headquarters, dual chairperson approach, the company had a dual holding company structure whereby Unilever's ownership was divided into two classes—some shareholders owned Unilever NV stock (based largely on food products), which traded on the Dutch stock exchange, and some shareholders owned Unilever PLC stock (based largely on personal care and household products), which traded on the Financial Times and the London Stock Exchange (London FTSE) and was included as part of the FTSE 100 Index. Since Unilever stock was also traded on the New York Stock Exchange, the company reported its financial results in euros, British pounds, and U.S. dollars. The

exhibit 2   **Growth in Sales of Unilever's Leading Brands, by Category, 2000–2003**

	Growth Rate in Sales of Leading Brands				
Category	2000	2001	2002	January–September 2003	July–September 2003
Margarines, spreads, oils, and cooking products	(1.5)%	5.5%	4.3%	(0.4)%	(0.7)%
Frozen foods	3.0	0.3	0.9	(0.2)	0.3
Ice cream	1.2	2.9	4.0	4.0	5.5
Tea-based beverages	4.5	3.3	3.3	4.9	11.5
Soups, dressings, and culinary products	6.0	4.2	5.1	3.4	2.0
Health and wellness	17.0	25.4	9.1	(14.5)	(23.5)
Total foods	1.9%	4.1%	4.4%	1.7%	1.8%
Personal care	7.5%	9.0%	10.8%	8.6%	9.6%
Fragrances	2.8	(7.2)	1.3	(8.0)	(25.8)
Laundry	3.2	5.3	1.9	1.3	2.3
Other household products	2.0	7.1	2.6	(3.6)	1.2
Total home and personal care	5.3%	6.5%	6.7%	4.8%	5.1%
Overall Unilever average	3.8%	5.3%	5.4%	3.1%	3.2%

Source: Unilever press release, October 29, 2003.

two companies, Unilever NV and Unilever PLC, operated as nearly as practicable as a single entity; a series of intercompany agreements ensured that the position of shareholders in both companies was virtually the same as having shares in a single company.

Unilever's food businesses had traditionally been organized around countries, with each country having its own factories engaged in making products for mostly national and sometimes regional geographic markets. Some countries had multiple brands of the same product—for example, in 2001 American shoppers could choose from six Unilever brands of margarine (Promise, Imperial, Country Crock, Brummel & Brown, Take Control, and I Can't Believe It's Not Butter!); in the United Kingdom there were nine Unilever margarine brands, although only three were supported by advertising. The strategy in margarine was to cater to a wide range of tastes—from a German preference for lighter-colored spreads to British preferences for spreads with a higher fat content to American tastes for flavorful and healthier spreads.

Longtime company analysts regarded Unilever management as a slow-moving, unwieldy, and inherently conservative Anglo-Dutch bureaucracy—one that operated in a staid manner resembling the civil service approach of government agencies. As one analyst put it, "Historically, Unilever has been a very inbred business. People used to join the company from college and leave it when they were carried out in a box. It was a cradle-to-grave company."[5] In 2001 about 90 percent of the company's managers were locally recruited and trained.

To stimulate more innovation and entrepreneurial thinking, Unilever had begun stepping up efforts to attract talented managers from outside the company. In addition, Unilever had revised its incentive compensation system. In the old system, the top 300–400 managers could earn an annual bonus worth up to 40 percent of their salaries, with the average bonus rate being 15 to 25 percent. Under the recently introduced system, outstanding managers who hit exacting growth and earnings targets could earn up to 100 percent bonuses. A further move was to alter the award of stock options from giving equal

[5]Quote attributed to David Lang, consumer industry analyst at brokerage firm Investec Henderson Crosthwaite, in an article by John Thornhill in the *Financial Times*, London Edition, August 5, 2000, p. 12.

exhibit 3 **Selected Financial and Operating Highlights for Unilever, 1992–2002**

	1992	1994	1996	1998	2000	2001	2002
Sales revenues (in millions)	€34,746	€37,478	€39,840	€40,639	€48,066	€52,206	€48,760
Operating profit, BEIA* (in millions)	3,099	3,266	3,693	4,323	5,794	7,269	7,260
Operating profit margins, BEIA*							
By product area							
Foods	8.7%	7.9%	8.0%	9.6%	11.6%	14.4%	14.8%
Personal care	9.9	11.0	11.6	12.8	16.2	18.0	18.2
Home care and cleaning	7.8	7.7	8.2	10.2	8.9	8.5	11.1
By geographic area							
Europe	8.9%	8.5%	9.3%	11.4%	12.7%	14.7%	15.3%
North America	8.0	8.5	9.2	10.9	12.8	14.2	16.1
Africa, Middle East, Turkey	10.5	9.6	9.2	8.8	10.0	11.0	11.0
Asia and Pacific	9.4	8.9	8.6	8.8	11.2	13.4	14.2
Latin America	10.0	9.7	10.4	10.6	10.8	13.2	13.9
Overall	8.9%	8.7%	9.3%	10.6%	12.0%	13.9%	14.9%
Research and development expenditures (in millions)	€ 649	€ 686	€ 714	€ 830	€ 1,187	€1,178	€1,166
Expenditures for advertising and promotions (in millions)	3,846	4,224	4,499	5,188	6,545	6,648	6,839
Capital expenditures (in millions)	1,560	1,804	1,389	1,329	1,356	1,513	1,298
Cost of new acquisitions (in millions)	543	789	1,892	361	24,728	120	53
Funds received from divestitures (in millions)	713	165	541	736	586	3,233	1,703
Number of acquisitions/divestitures	43	40	50	44	47	34	38
Average number of employees	287,000	304,000	306,000	267,000	261,000	279,000	258,000

*BEIA = Before exceptional items and amortization of goodwill and intangibles.

Source: Unilever records posted at www.unilever.com, accessed December 30, 2003.

amounts to all managers at a particular level (based on the company's overall performance) to making awards of shares based on individual performance.

INDUSTRY ENVIRONMENT

The food and household products industry was composed of many subsectors, each with differing growth expectations, profit margins, competitive intensity, and business risks. Industry participants were constantly challenged to respond to changing consumer preferences and to fend off maneuvers from rival firms to gain market share. Competitive success started with creating a portfolio of attractive products and brands; from there success depended largely on product line growth through acquisitions (it was generally considered cheaper to buy a successful brand than to build and grow a new one from scratch) and on the ability to continually grow sales of existing brands and improve profit margins. Advertising was considered a key to increasing unit volume and helping drive consumers toward higher margin products; sustained volume growth also usually entailed gaining increased international exposure for a company's brands. Improving a company's profit margins included not only shifting sales to products with higher margins but also boosting efficiency and driving down unit costs.

In 2000, there was a wave of megamergers involving high-profile food and household products companies (see Exhibit 4). Three factors were driving consolidation pressures in the food industry—slower growth rates in the food sector, rapid consolidation among retail grocery chains (which enhanced the buying power of the major supermarket chains and enhanced their ability to demand and receive lucrative "slotting fees" for allocating manufacturers favorable shelf space on their grocery aisles), and fierce competition between branded food manufacturers and private-label manufacturers.

Growth prospects for many food companies had been bleak for several years, and the trend was expected to continue. In the United States, for example, sales of food and household products were, on average, growing 1–2 percent annually, just slightly higher than the 1 percent population growth. More women working outside the home, decreasing house-

hold sizes, and greater numbers of single-person and one-parent households were causing a shift of food and beverage dollars from at-home outlays to away-from-home outlays. The growth rate for food and household products across the industrialized countries of Europe was in the 2 percent range, with many of the same growth-slowing factors at work as in the United States. Food industry growth rates in emerging or less-developed countries were more attractive—in the 3–4 percent range—prompting most growth-minded food companies to focus their efforts on markets in Latin America, Asia, Eastern Europe, and Africa, where about 85 percent of the world's population was concentrated. The household and personal care business (excluding food products) was a €21 billion market, with sales of €5 billion in North America, €6 billion in Europe, €5 billion in the Asia-Pacific region, €3 billion in Latin America, and €2 billion in Africa and the Middle East.

Since 1985 the share of private-label food and beverages sold in the United States had risen steadily, accounting for roughly 25 percent of total grocery sales in 2000, up from 19 percent in 1992. Growing shopper confidence in the leading supermarket chains and other food retailers like Wal-Mart (which was selling a full line of grocery and household items at its Supercenters and had become the largest supermarket retailer in the world during the past five years) had opened the way for retail chains to effectively market their own house-brand versions of name-brand products, provided the house brand was priced attractively below the competing name brands. Indeed, with the aid of checkout scanners and computerized inventory systems, retailers knew as well or better (and more quickly) than manufacturers what customers were buying and what price differential it took to induce shoppers to switch from name brands to private-label brands. These developments tilted the balance of power firmly toward retailers. Thus competition between private-label goods and name-brand goods in supermarkets was escalating rapidly, since retailers' margins on private-label goods often exceeded those on name-brand goods. The battle for market share between private-label and name-brand goods was expected to continue as private-label manufacturers improved their capabilities to match the quality of name-brand products while also gaining the scale economies afforded by a growing market share.

Most food and household products manufacturers were trying to counteract the bargaining power of

exhibit 4 **Selected Major Acquisitions in the Food and Household Products Industry, 2000–2002**

Companies Involved	Value of Deal	Principal Products and Brands of Acquiring Company	Brand/Products Acquired
2002 transactions			
Nestlé acquired a majority ownership of Dreyer's Grand Ice Cream, Inc.	$2.4 billion in stock	• Chocolates, candies, candy bars (Nestlé Crunch, KitKat, Smarties, Butterfinger, Lifesaver, Milkybar, Baci, Lion, Rolo, Aero, Wonderball, Wonka, PowerBar) • Dairy (Carnation, Coffee-Mate, Yoco, LC1, Munch Bunch, Gloria, Bären Marke) • Beverages (Nescafé, Nesquik, Nestea, Juicy Juice, Milo) • Bottled water (San Pellegrino, Perrier, Poland Spring, Contrex, Panna, Vittel, 24 others) • Prepared foods (Stouffer's, Maggi, Buitoni, Lean Cuisine, Herta, Libby's) • Ice cream (Dreyer's, Extreme, Maxibon, 3 others) • Pet care (Friskies, Fancy Feast, Alpo, Mighty Dog, Purina, Tidy Cat, Felix, 8 others) • Baby foods (Alete, Beba, 8 others)	• Dreyer's ice creams and sherbets
Del Monte Foods acquired the pet foods, tuna, soup, and infant feeding businesses of the H. J. Heinz Company	$2.8 billion in stock	• Del Monte canned fruits and vegetables • Contadina canned tomato products • S&W canned fruits and vegetables	• Heinz steak sauces and other condiments • Ore Ida potatoes • Wyler's bouillon and soup mixes • Weight Watchers dinners • StarKist tuna • Pet Foods (9 Lives, Kibbles and Bits, Meaty Bone, Skippy) • Baby foods (Heinz, Nature's Goodness, Plasmon, Farley's, tinytums)
Nestlé acquired Chef America	$2.6 billion in cash	See above	• Chef America frozen stuffed sandwiches
Associated British Foods PLC acquired 19 brands from Unilever	$360 million in cash	• Silver Spoon sweeteners (United Kingdom) • Allinsons, Kingsmill, Ryvita, and Speedibake breads (United Kingdom) • Ovomaltine malt beverage (Europe, China, Thailand) • Twinings and Jackson of Piccadilly teas	• Mazola cooking oil • Argo and Kingsford's cornstarches • Karo and Golden Griddle syrups • Henri's salad dressing • A number of related Canadian brands

(continues)

exhibit 4 (continued)

Companies Involved	Value of Deal	Principal Products and Brands of Acquiring Company	Brand/Products Acquired
2001 transactions			
Sara Lee acquired The Earthgrains Company	$1.8 billion in cash	• Sara Lee deli lunch meats, sliced and packaged meats, fresh and frozen bakery products, and frozen foods • Coffee and coffee systems (Douwe Egberts and Superior) • Meats (Hillshire Farms, Aoste, Bryan, Ball Park, Jimmy Dean) • Kiwi shoe products • Apparel (Champion, Playtex, Hanes, DIM, Wonderbra, Loveable, Bali, Just My Size, Nurdie, L'eggs)	• Earth Grains, IronKids, Rainbo, Colonial, and Grant's Farms breads
Nestlé acquired Ralston Purina Company	$10.3 billion in cash	See list of Nestlé brands earlier in table	• Ralston Purina pet food and pet care brands—Purina Dog Chow, Purina Puppy Chow, Felix, Purina One, T Bonz, Beggin' Strips, Pro Plan, Puppy Chow, Tidy Cats, Tender Vittles
2000 transactions			
General Mills acquired the Pillsbury unit of Diageo (a UK-based company with a wide-ranging portfolio of wines and alcoholic beverage brands and the then parent of Burger King and Pillsbury)	$10.5 billion in cash	• Wheaties, Cheerios, Total, Lucky Charms, Trix, Chex, Golden Grahams, and Kix cereals • Betty Crocker desserts and side dishes, Gold Medal flours, Bisquick, and Hamburger Helper • Lloyd's barbeque meats • Yoplait and Colombo yogurts • Pop Secret, Chex Mix, Nature Valley, and Bugles snack foods	• Pillsbury and Martha White flours, baking mixes, and baking products, and Hungry Jack pancake mix • Häagen-Dazs ice cream and frozen yogurt • Green Giant frozen and canned vegetables • Old El Paso Mexican foods • Totinos and Jenos pizzas • Progresso soups
Phillip Morris (the parent of Kraft Foods prior to Kraft's 2001 IPO) acquired Nabisco	$19 billion in cash, stock, and debt	• Kraft cheeses, mayonnaise, salad dressings, barbeque sauces, and dinners • Post cereals • Jell-O • Kraft, Velveeta; Cheez Whiz; Cracker Barrel, and Hoffman's cheeses • Maxwell House, Yuban, and Sanka coffees • Minute rice • Claussen pickles • Louis Rich and Oscar Mayer meats • Others: Shake 'N Bake, Breakstone, Cool Whip, Planters nuts, Kool-Aid, Stove Top, Altoids, Tobler and Toblerone chocolates	• Nabisco cookies, crackers, and snacks • Grey Poupon French mustards

exhibit 4 (concluded)

Companies Involved	Value of Deal	Principal Products and Brands of Acquiring Company	Brand /Products Acquired
Kellogg's acquired Keebler	$4.4 billion	• Kellogg's cereals • Eggo, Nutri-Grain, Pop-Tarts • Kashi cereal and breakfast bars • Rice Krispies Treats • Snack'Ums	• Keebler and Murray cookies • Keebler snack foods (Cheez-It, Wheatables, Toasteds, Munch'ems, Harvest Bakery, Snax Stix) • Krispy and Zesta saltine crackers, Club crackers, Hi Ho crackers • Ready Crust pie shells
ConAgra acquired International Home Foods	$2.9 billion	• Armour, Banquet, Butterball, Eckrich meats • Blue Bonnet and Parkay margarines • Chun King and La Choy Chinese foods • Orville Redenbacher's and Act II popcorns • Peter Pan and County Line cheeses • Morton prepared foods • Fleischmann's, Egg Beaters • Healthy Choice foods • Hunt's ketchup, tomatoes, and tomato sauces	• Chef Boyardee sauces • Pam cooking spray • Louis Kemp/Bumblebee seafood products • Libbey's canned meats • Gulden's mustard
PepsiCo acquired Quaker Oats	$12.4 billion in cash and stock	• Pepsi and Mountain Dew soft drinks • Frito-Lay snack foods • Tropicana juices	• Gatorade • Quaker Oats cereals • Rice a Roni • Aunt Jemima mixes and syrups • Near East food products • Golden Grain-Mission pastas
Cadbury Schweppes acquired the Snapple Beverage Group from Triarc, Inc.	$1.45 billion	• Schweppes and Canada Dry tonics, sodas, and ginger ales; 7Up, Dr Pepper, and A&W soft drinks; Mott's and Clamato juices; Cadbury chocolates and confectionery items; and Trebor, Pascall, Cadbury Éclair, and Bassett candies	• Snapple ready-to-drink teas and beverages

large supermarket chains and the growth of private-label sales by building a diverse lineup of strong brands—the thesis being that retailers, fearful of irritating shoppers by not carrying well-known brands, would be forced to stock all of the manufacturer's name-brand products and, in many cases, award them favorable shelf space. At the same time, because they faced pressures on profit margins in negotiating with retailers and combating the competition from both name-brand and private-label rivals, manufacturers were trying to squeeze out costs, weed out weak brands, focus their efforts on those items they believed they could develop into global brands, and reduce the number of versions of a product they manufactured wherever local market conditions allowed (to help gain scale economies in production).

Exhibit 5 provides a brief profile of Unilever's main competitors. Other competitors included Sara Lee, H. J. Heinz, Kellogg's, and well over 100 regional and local food products companies around the world. Many of the leading food products companies had a food-service division that marketed company products to restaurants, cafeterias, and institutions (such as schools, hospitals, college student centers, private country clubs, corporate facilities) to gain access to the growing food-away-from-home market.

UNILEVER'S BUSINESSES AND BRAND PORTFOLIO

Analysts familiar with the household products business and with Unilever were skeptical that there were meaningful strategic and resource fits between food products and household/personal care products. Some saw Unilever's reorganization into a foods group and a home and personal care group as a possible precursor to the breakup of Unilever, an outcome denied by Unilever executives.

The foods division, known as Unilever Bestfoods following the 2000 acquisition and integration of Bestfoods, was organized around six product categories: spreads, culinary, and cooking products; savory (soups and sauces) and dressings; beverages; health and wellness; frozen foods; and ice cream. The foods division, which had consistently generated 50–52 percent of Unilever's corporate-wide revenues from 1992 to 2000, accounted for 55 percent of revenues in 2001 and 56 percent in 2002—chiefly

because of the Bestfoods acquisition. The Home and Personal Care (HPC) division consisted of eight categories: deodorants, hair care, household care, laundry, mass skin care, oral care, personal wash, and fragrances and cosmetics. HPC generated about 43 percent of Unilever's corporatewide revenues.

Unilever Bestfoods and HPC were each headed by a director who had global profit responsibility and executive authority for aligning brand strategy with operations worldwide.[6] Underneath the division heads were directors for each product category and regional presidents who were responsible for profitability in their respective regions. Both divisions had an executive committee—composed of the division director (acting as chairperson), the directors for each product category, and the regional presidents—that was responsible for the overall results and performance of Unilever. Most research and new product development activities were integrated into the divisional structure, but the company formed a small number of "global innovation centers" to interlink with R&D at the division level and the company's worldwide brand innovation organization. Unilever's local companies were to remain as the key interface with customers and consumers, responding to local market needs. Unilever executives saw the formation of two global divisions as having three benefits:

- Improving the company's focus on foods and HPC activities regionally and globally.
- Accelerating decision making and execution through tighter alignment of brand strategy with operations.
- Strengthening innovation capability through more effective integration of R&D into the divisional structure and the creation of global innovation centers.

Some analysts had criticized Unilever for paying too much for several of its acquisitions. For example, Unilever paid a purchase price of €715 million to acquire Amora Maille (equal to 16.6 times Amora Maille's 1999 operating earnings of €43 million)—a price well above the earnings multiples commanded by other food businesses and an amount said to be double what the present owners paid to acquire Amora Maille from Group Danone in 1997. Unilever

[6]Company press release describing the realignment of the senior management structure at Unilever, August 3, 2000.

exhibit 5 **Profile of Selected Unilever Competitors**

Company (Headquarters)	Sales (in billions)	Profits (in billions)	Scope of Operations and Key Facts
Nestlé (Swiss)	2002: SFr89.2 2001: SFr84.7 2000: SFr81.4 1999: SFr74.7 1998: SFr71.7 1997: SFr70.0 1996: SFr60.5	2002: SFr7.56 2001: SFr6.81 2000: SFr5.76 1999: SFr4.72 1998: SFr4.20 1997: SFr4.18 1996: SFr3.59	World's largest food company with sales in almost every country of the world; 508 factories; 254,000 employees.
Procter & Gamble (U.S.)	2003: $43.4 2002: $40.2 2001: $39.2 2000: $40.0 1999: $38.1 1998: $37.2 1997: $35.8 1996: $35.3	2003: $5.19 2002: $4.35 2001: $2.92 2000: $3.54 1999: $3.76 1998: $3.78 1997: $3.42 1996: $3.05	Sales in over 140 countries; on-the-ground-operations in more than 70 countries, 98,000 employees; and 300 brands (13 with sales of over $1 billion). P&G believed it was the global sales leader in its four core product categories: fabric care, hair care, feminine care, and baby care products. P&G had 5 global business units: ● Fabric and home care—2003 sales of $12.6 billion and 32 key brands, including Tide, Ariel, Downy, Lenor, Dawn, Fairy, and Joy. ● Beauty care—2003 sales of $12.2 billion and 38 key brands, including Pantene, Olay, Head & Shoulders, Clairol, Secret, and Tampax. ● Baby and family care—2003 sales of $9.9 billion of such brands as Pampers, Luvs, Kandoo, Charmin, Bounty, Tempo, and Puffs. ● Health care—2003 sales of $5.8 billion; key brands include Crest, Pepto-Bismol, Vicks, Metamucil, and 2 pet health and nutrition brands (Iams and Eukanuba). ● Snacks and beverages—2003 sales of $3.2 billion; brands included Pringles, Folgers, Millstone, Sunny Delight, Punica, and Torengos. Tide's market share was over 4 times larger than its nearest competitor; Ariel laundry detergent was sold in 115 countries (with the highest or second highest share in 25 countries). Tide and Ariel had combined sales greater than any other P&G brand.
Kraft Foods (U.S.)	2002: $29.7 2001: $29.2 2000: $26.5 1999: $26.8 1998: $27.3 1997: $27.7 1996: $27.9	2002: $3.89 2001: $1.89 2002: $6.28* 2001: $6.04* 2000: $4.62* 1999: $4.25* 1998: $4.18* 1997: $4.20* 1996: $3.36*	Kraft had 60 major brands in its business lineup, sales in over 150 countries, 218 manufacturing plants (118 outside the U.S.), 5 R&D technology centers, 109,000 employees, and operating units in 68 countries. Kraft brands held the number one share position in 21 of the top 25 categories in the U.S. In international markets, Kraft brands were number one based on unit volume in one or more countries in 10 product categories. Kraft was committed to innovation, with more than $1.1 billion of 2002 revenue generated from new products. In 2003, Kraft planned to launch more than 100 new products.

(continues)

exhibit 5 (concluded)

Company (Headquarters)	Sales (in billions)	Profits (in billions)	Scope of Operations and Key Facts
Groupe Danone (France)	2002: €13.4 2001: €14.5 2000: €14.3 1999: €12.9 1998: €13.5 1997: €12.8 1996: €12.1	2002: €1.28 2001: €0.13 2000: €0.72 1999: €0.60 1998: €0.56 1997: €0.51 1996: €0.32	Sales in 120 countries (38% outside the European Union); 148 production plants, 86,000 employees. Four brands represented more than 50% of sales: • Danone yogurts (the world leader in yogurt with a 15.1 global share). • LU (the world's second largest cereal biscuit and snack crackers brand). • Evian and Volvic bottled waters (2 of the 4 biggest bottled water brands worldwide). Other key brands include Actimel and Galbani in dairy products; Brio Fountain, and Fontvella in bottled waters; Prince and Tiger in biscuits and crackers; Lea & Perrins; and Amoy Asian products.
Campbell's Soup (U.S.)	2003: $6.7 2002: $6.1 2001: $5.8 2000: $6.3 1999: $6.4 1998: $6.7 1997: $8.0 1996: $7.7	2003: $0.60 2002: $0.52 2001: $0.65 2000: $0.71 1999: $0.72 1998: $0.66 1997: $0.71 1996: $0.80	Campbell's products were sold in 120 countries and included such brands/products as Campbell's soups, tomato juice, and Super Bakes; Batchelors, Erasco, Leibig, McDonnells, and Oxo soups (Europe); Homepride sauces (Europe); Franco American and Prego in culinary foods and sauces, Pepperidge Farm, Swanson canned meats and soups; Pace salsas, and Godiva chocolates. Campbell's was the number one wet soup brand in the world; Arnott's was the market leader in biscuits and crackers in Australia and was the number two brand in New Zealand.
General Mills/ Pillsbury (U.S.)	2003: $10.5 2002: $7.9 2001: $5.5 2000: $6.7 1999: $6.2 1998: $6.0 1997: $5.6 1996: $5.4	2003: $0.92 2002: $0.46 2001: $0.66 2000: $0.61 1999: $0.54 1998: $0.42 1997: $0.44 1996: $0.48	General Mills/Pillsbury products were manufactured in 17 countries and distributed in over 100 countries. However, about 95% of sales were in the United States. The company's internationally recognized products were Häagen-Dazs ice creams, Old El Paso Mexican foods, Green Giant vegetables, Pillsbury dough products and mixes, Betty Crocker mixes, and Bugles snacks.

*Operating earnings—Philip Morris (the former parent of Kraft) did not report net income separately for its business divisions.

Source: Compiled by the case researcher from company Web sites and company documents.

exhibit 6   **Selected Financial Performance Statistics for SlimFast, 1997 through the First Quarter of 2000 (dollars in millions)**

	1997	1998	1999	Q1 2000
Sales revenues	$390	$505	$611	$194*
Advertising and promotional expenditures	87	102	142	n.a.
Earnings before interest, taxes, depreciation, and amortization (EBITDA)	78	117	133	
Earnings before interest and taxes (EBIT)—operating profits	76	112	125	39†
EBIT % (operating profit margin)	19.4%	22.2%	20.5%	20.1%

*Up 21% over Q1 1999.

†Up 28% over Q1 1999.

Source: www.unilever.com, April 17, 2001.

paid 14.1 times earnings before interest, taxes, depreciation, and amortization (EBITDA) for Best-foods—a record high for a foods company and above the 12.8 times EBITDA that Philip Morris/Kraft paid for Nabisco and the 12.1 times EBITDA that PepsiCo paid for Tropicana in 1999. Unilever defended its price for Amora Maille, saying it was justified based on the superior growth prospects the business would deliver relative to other grocery products and on the 19.3 times earnings before interest and taxes (EBIT) that PepsiCo paid for Tropicana in 1999.

THE SLIMFAST ACQUISITION

Two months after announcing the new Path to Growth strategy in February 2000, Unilever negotiated an agreement to acquire SlimFast diet foods for $2.3 billion cash. SlimFast, a privately held company headquartered in Miami, Florida, was the U.S. market leader in the $1.3 billion North American weight management and nutritional supplement industry, with a 45 percent market share. The company's nearest competitor had a market share of just over 25 percent. SlimFast had sales of $611 million in 1999, up 20 percent over 1998 (see Exhibit 6); the company's net assets totaled $160 million at the time of acquisition. SlimFast's ready-to-drink selections (72 percent of total sales), powders (16 percent), and bars (12 percent) all had the leading positions in their category segments. An estimated 2 million U.S. consumers used SlimFast products daily, and an additional 5 million used SlimFast products occasionally. About 94 percent of SlimFast's sales were in North America. Studies showed the SlimFast brand name had an unaided 89 percent recognition rate among U.S. consumers. SlimFast produced a portion of its products at a company-owned manufacturing facility in Tennessee and sourced the remainder from contract suppliers. It had a strong sales and distribution network, having been successful in gaining shelf space in most supermarkets and drugstores, and had spent over $400 million on advertising and promotion during the past four years.

SlimFast products were made from "natural ingredients" supplemented with added vitamins and minerals to provide a strong nutritional profile—no appetite suppressants were used. Promotional efforts centered on the themes of good health, balanced nutrition, great taste, and convenient product formats (ready-to-drink products, powders, and bars). SlimFast had conducted extensive clinical trials to validate the performance of its products. The company had a strong physician education program and enjoyed good relationships with the U.S. Food and Drug Administration (FDA) and other regulatory agencies.

Unilever was attracted to SlimFast because the company was growing by about 20 percent annually and because people all across the world were increasingly interested in living a longer, healthier, and more vital life. Market research indicated that in the United States, Germany, and the United Kingdom nutrition was the number one dietary concern and that weight was number three. In the United States, Western Europe, Australia, and the largest cities in the rest of the world, between 40 and 55 percent of the population were overweight and 15 to 25 percent were obese. According to the World Health Organization, the number of people who were either overweight or obese was increasing at an alarming rate.

Unilever management saw opportunities to use the company's global distribution capabilities to introduce SlimFast in Europe, Australia, and cities in developing countries, perhaps doubling SlimFast's sales within two or three years. According to independent market research, the world market for diet products and nutritional foods was about $31.7 billion annually and was growing annually at 11.3 percent. Unilever executives believed that SlimFast products would appeal to weight-conscious Europeans; according to co-chairman Antony Burgmans, "Europe at the moment is underdeveloped. We are in a perfect position to boost the presence of this brand."[7] Company projections at the time of the acquisition indicated that SlimFast would begin to contribute positively to Unilever's cash flows in 2002 and to earnings in 2003. Unilever believed that SlimFast had a strong management team.

But Unilever's SlimFast acquisition, which looked so promising in 2000–2001, showed signs of being in deep trouble in 2003. Sales growth of SlimFast products slowed to about 9 percent in 2002, and then unit volume plummeted in 2003, chiefly due to growing consumer infatuation with low-carbohydrate diets and a mushrooming number of new diet and nutrition bars that competed directly against SlimFast products and that had gained highly visible shelf space in supermarkets, convenience stores, and drugstore chains. SlimFast's revenues, which were €1 billion in 2002, were down 23 percent in the first nine months of 2003.

THE BEN & JERRY'S ACQUISITION

After considering offers from Unilever, Diageo (at the time the parent company of archrival Häagen-Dazs), Nestlé, Roncadin (an Italian company), and Dreyer's (a rival maker of superpremium ice cream products and a longtime distributor of Ben & Jerry's products), the board of directors of Ben & Jerry's

[7]As quoted in an article by Mark Bendeich, "Unilever Buys U.S. Health Foods Firm for $2.3 Billion," April 12, 2000, and posted at www.economictimes.com.

Homemade, Inc., in April 2000 agreed to accept Unilever's offer of $43.60 a share for all of the company's 7.48 million shares, resulting in an acquisition price of $326 million. The $43.60 price represented a premium of 23 percent over the closing price the day prior to the announcement of the agreement and was well above the $15.80–$20.00 range the stock traded in prior to the five buyout offers becoming public knowledge in December 1999. Exhibit 7 shows Ben & Jerry's financial highlights for years prior to the acquisition. The Ben & Jerry's acquisition put Unilever in the high-end superpremium segment of the ice cream market for the first time and made Unilever the world's largest marketer of ice cream products.

Company Background

Ben & Jerry's began active operations in 1978 when Ben Cohen and Jerry Greenfield, two former hippies with counterculture lifestyles and very liberal political beliefs, opened a scoop shop in a renovated gas station in Burlington, Vermont. Soon thereafter, the cofounders decided to package their ice cream in pint cartons and wholesale them to area groceries and mom-and-pop stores—their sales slogan became "Vermont's Finest All Natural Ice Cream" and the carton design featured a picture of the cofounders on the lid and unique hand-style lettering to project a "homemade" impression. The cartons were inscribed with a sales pitch by Ben and Jerry:

> This carton contains some of the finest ice cream available anywhere. We know because we're the guys who made it. We start with lots of fresh Vermont cream and the finest flavorings available. We never use any fillers or artificial ingredients of any kind. With our specially modified equipment, we stir less air into the ice cream, creating a denser, richer, creamier product of uncompromising high quality. It costs more and it's worth it.

A *Time* magazine article on the superpremium ice cream craze appeared in August 1981 with the opening sentence, "What you must understand is that Ben & Jerry's in Burlington, Vermont, makes the best ice cream in the world." Sales at Ben & Jerry's took off, rising to $10 million in 1985 and to $78 million in 1990. By 1994 Ben & Jerry's products were distributed in all 50 states, the company had 100 scoop shops, and it was marketing 29 flavors in pint cartons and 45 flavors in bulk cartons.

exhibit 7 **Financial Performance Summary, Ben & Jerry's Homemade, Inc., 1994-1999 (in thousands, except per share data)**

	1999	1998	1997	1996	1995	1994
Income statement data						
Net sales	$237,043	$209,203	$174,206	$167,155	$155,333	$148,802
Cost of sales	145,291	136,225	114,284	115,212	109,125	109,760
Gross profit	$ 91,752	$ 72,978	$ 59,922	$ 51,943	$ 46,208	$ 39,042
Selling, general, and administrative expenses	78,623	63,895	53,520	45,531	36,362	36,253
Special charges*	8,602	—	—	—	—	6,779
Other income (expense)—net	681	693	(118)	(77)	(441)	228
Income (loss) before income taxes	5,208	9,776	6,284	6,335	9,405	(3,762)
Income taxes	1,823	3,534	2,388	2,409	3,457	(1,869)
Net income (loss)	$ 3,385	$ 6,242	$ 3,896	$ 3,926	$ 5,948	$ (1,869)
Net income (loss) per share—diluted	$ 0.46	$ 0.84	$ 0.53	$ 0.54	$ 0.82	$ (0.26)
Shares outstanding—diluted	7,405	7,463	7,334	7,230	7,222	7,148
Balance sheet data						
Working capital	$ 42,805	$ 48,381	$ 51,412	$ 50,055	$ 51,023	$ 37,456
Total assets	150,602	149,501	146,471	136,665	131,074	120,296
Long-term debt and capital lease obligations	16,669	20,491	25,676	31,087	31,977	32,419
Stockholders' equity†	89,391	90,908	86,919	82,685	78,531	72,502

*The special charge in 2000 concerned a writedown of Springfield plant assets and employee severance costs associated with outsource novelty ice cream products. The 1994 charge stemmed from early replacement of certain software and equipment installed at the plant in St. Albans, Vermont, and included a portion of the previously capitalized interest and project management costs.

†No cash dividends had been declared or paid since the company's formation in 1978. Earnings were retained and reinvested in growing the business.

Source: Company annual reports.

Products and Operations in 2000

At the time it was acquired by Unilever, Ben & Jerry's produced and marketed over 50 super-premium ice cream flavors, ice cream novelties, low-fat ice cream flavors, low-fat frozen yogurts, and sorbets, using Vermont dairy products and high-quality, all-natural ingredients. Like other super-premium ice creams, Ben & Jerry's products were high in calories (about 300 per serving), had a fat content equal to 40 to 55 percent of the recommended daily allowance for saturated fat per serving, and were high in cholesterol content (20 to 25 percent of the recommended daily allowance). About 35 of the flavors were packaged in pint cartons for sale in supermarkets, grocery stores, and convenience stores; the rest were packaged in bulk tubs for sale in about 200 franchised and company-owned Ben & Jerry's scoop shops, restaurants, and food-service accounts. To stimulate buyer interest, the company came up with attention-getting names for its flavors: Chunky Monkey, Bovinity Divinity, Cherry Garcia, Chubby Hubby, Double Trouble, Totally Nuts, and Coffee Olé. Many of the flavors contained sizable chunks of cookies or candies, a standout attribute of the company's products. Retail prices for a pint of Ben & Jerry's were around $3.25 in May 2001.

At year-end 1999, Ben & Jerry's had 164 franchised scoop shops, 8 PartnerShop franchises (not-for-profit organizations that operated scoop shops), 19 Featuring Franchises (scoop shops within airports, stadiums, college campus facilities, and similar venues), 12 Scoop Station franchises (prefabricated units that operated within other large retail establishments), and 9 company-owned scoop shops (4 in Vermont, 2 in Las Vegas, and 3 in Paris, France). Internationally, there were 9 franchised Ben & Jerry's scoop shops in Israel, 4 in Canada, 3 in the Netherlands, 1 in Lebanon, and 1 in Peru. The company began exporting from its Vermont plants to Japan in 1997, selling single serve containers through an exclusive arrangement with 7-Eleven Japan. In 1999, it established a wholly owned subsidiary in Japan for the purpose of importing, marketing, and distributing its products through Japanese retail grocery stores. Beginning in January 2000, Ben & Jerry's imported all products into Japan through an agreement with a Japanese trading company.

Distribution   Ben & Jerry's products were distributed throughout the United States and in several foreign countries. Company trucks, along with several local distributors, handled deliveries to retailers in Vermont and upstate New York. In the rest of the United States, Ben & Jerry's relied on distribution services provided by other ice cream manufacturers and marketers. It was the distributor's job to sell retailers on stocking a brand, deliver supplies to each retail location, and stock the freezer cases with the agreed-on flavors and number of facings. Until 1998, Ben & Jerry's used two primary distributors, Sut's Premium Ice Cream for much of New England and Dreyer's Grand Ice Cream for states in the Midwest and West. To round out its national coverage, the company had a number of other distributors that serviced limited market areas. In 1994, distribution through Dreyer's accounted for 52 percent of Ben & Jerry's net sales. The arrangement with Dreyer's was somewhat rocky, and in 1998 Ben & Jerry's began redesigning its distribution network to gain more company control. Under the redesign, Ben & Jerry's increased direct sales calls by its own sales force to all grocery and convenience store chains and set up a network where no distributor had a majority percentage of the company's sales. Starting in 1999, much of the distribution responsibility in certain territories was assigned to Ice Cream Partners (a joint venture of Nestlé and Pillsbury, the parent of Häagen-Dazs); the balance of U.S. deliveries was assigned to Dreyer's and several other regional distributors, but Dreyer's territory was smaller than before and entailed Ben & Jerry's receiving a higher price than formerly for products distributed through Dreyer's.

Manufacturing   Ben & Jerry's operated three manufacturing plants, two shifts a day, five to seven days per week, depending on demand requirements. Superpremium ice cream and frozen yogurt products packed in pint cartons were manufactured at the company's Waterbury, Vermont, plant. The company's Springfield, Vermont, plant was used for the production of ice cream novelties and ice cream, frozen yogurt, low-fat ice cream, and sorbets packaged in bulk, pints, quarts, and half-gallons. The St. Albans, Vermont, plant manufactured superpremium ice cream, frozen yogurt, frozen smoothies, and sorbet in pints, 12-ounce, and single-serve containers. Beginning in October 1999, in order to reduce costs and improve its profit margins, the company ceased production of ice cream novelties at its Springfield plant and began outsourcing its requirements from third-party co-packers.

Competitors

Ben & Jerry's two principal competitors were Dreyer's/Edy's (which had introduced its Dreamery and Godiva superpremium brands in 1999) and Häagen-Dazs (part of Pillsbury, which was formerly a subsidiary of Diageo but which was acquired by General Mills in 2000—see Exhibit 4). Other significant frozen dessert competitors were Colombo frozen yogurts (a General Mills brand), Healthy Choice ice creams (a ConAgra brand), Breyers ice creams and frozen yogurts (Unilever), Kemps ice cream and frozen yogurts (a brand of Marigold Foods), and Starbucks (whose coffee ice cream flavors were distributed by Dreyer's). In the ice cream novelty segment, Ben & Jerry's products (S'Mores, Phish Sticks, Vanilla Heath Bar Crunch pops, Cookie Dough pops, Cherry Garcia frozen yogurt pops, and several others) competed with Häagen-Dazs, Dove bars (made by a division of Mars, Inc.), Good Humor bars (a Unilever brand), an assortment of Nestlé products, and many private-label brands.

Häagen-Dazs was considered the global market leader in the superpremium segment, followed by Ben & Jerry's. Ben & Jerry's had only a negligible market share in ice cream novelties and a low single-digit share of the frozen yogurt segment. Whereas close to 90 percent of Ben & Jerry's sales were in the United States, Häagen-Dazs was represented in substantially more foreign markets, including markets in

Europe, Japan, and other Pacific Rim countries. Like Ben & Jerry's, Häagen-Dazs marketed several ice cream flavors using pieces of cookies and candies as ingredients.

Management and Culture

Since 1988 Ben & Jerry's had formalized its business philosophy by adopting and pursuing a three-part mission statement:

- *Product mission*: To make, distribute, and sell the finest-quality all-natural ice cream and related products in a wide variety of innovative flavors made from Vermont dairy products.
- *Economic mission*: To operate the company on a sound financial basis of profitable growth, increasing value for our shareholders, and creating career opportunities and financial rewards for our employees.
- *Social mission*: To operate the company in a way that actively recognizes the central role that business plays in the structure of society by initiating innovative ways to improve the quality of life of a broad community—local, national, and international.

Pursuing the Company Mission The three parts of the mission were deemed equally important, and management strived to integrate their pursuit in its day-to-day business decision making. Starting in 1988, the company's annual report had contained a "social report" on the company's performance during the year, with emphasis on workplace policies and practices, concern for the environment, and the social mission accomplishments. To support its social mission activities, Ben & Jerry's had a policy of allocating 7.5 percent of pretax income (equal to $1.1 million in 1999) to support various social causes through the Ben & Jerry's Foundation, corporate grants made by the company's Director of Social Mission Development, and employee community action teams. In addition, the company made a practice of sourcing some of its ingredients from companies that gave jobs to disadvantaged individuals who would otherwise be unemployed, and it strived to operate in an environmentally friendly manner, frequently partnering with environmentally and socially conscious organizations that were trying to make the world a healthier and more humane place. Over the

years, Ben & Jerry's had been actively involved with hundreds of grassroots organizations working for progressive social change, such as Greenpeace, the Children's Defense Fund, National Association of Child Advocates, the Coalition for Environmentally Responsible Economies, the Environmental Working Group, and the Institute for Sustainable Communities. It had contributed to efforts to save the rain forests in Brazil. One day each year, the company hosted a Free Cone Day at its scoop shops as a way of thanking customers for their patronage.

Ben & Jerry's had selected Vermont communities with high unemployment rates for all three of its plants. It had created a blueberry ice cream so it could buy blueberries exclusively from a tribe of Maine Indians and help support their economy. In 1991, Ben & Jerry's had entered into an agreement with St. Albans Cooperative Creamery (a group of Vermont dairy farmers) to pay not less than a specified minimum price for its dairy products in order to bring prices up to levels the company deemed fair and equitable. In 1994, this agreement was amended to include, as a condition of paying the premium price, assurance that the milk and cream purchased by the company would not come from cows that had been treated with recombinant bovine growth hormone (rBGH), a synthetic growth hormone approved by the FDA. The company quit selling a handmade brownie-and-ice-cream sandwich upon discovering that workers' hands were developing repetitive strain injuries. In 1999, Ben & Jerry's became the first U.S. ice cream company to convert a significant portion of its pint containers to a more environmentally friendly unbleached paperboard (bleaching paper with chlorine to make it whiter was said to be one of the largest causes of toxic water pollution in the United States).

Company Culture The work environment at Ben & Jerry's was characterized by informality, casual dress, attempts to make the atmosphere fun and pleasurable, and frequent communications between employees and management. Ben Cohen was noted for not owning a suit. Efforts were made to treat employees with fairness and respect; employee opinions were sought out and given serious consideration. Rank and hierarchy were viewed with distaste, and until the late 1990s executive salaries were capped at no more than seven times the pay for entry-level jobs. Compensation levels were above average, compared to pay scales in the Vermont communities where Ben & Jerry's operated. Ben & Jerry's had instituted a very liberal benefits package for its nearly 850 employees that included health benefits for the gay or lesbian partners of employees, parental leave for fathers as well as mothers, leave for the parents of newly adopted children, $1,500 contributions toward adoption costs, on-site cholesterol and blood pressure screening, smoking cessation classes, tuition reimbursement for three classes a year, a profit-sharing plan, a 401(k) plan, an employee stock purchase plan that allowed employees to buy shares at 15 percent below the current market price, a housing loan program, a sabbatical leave program, free health club access, and free ice cream. Nonetheless, there had been occasions on which vocal employees had expressed dissatisfaction with various aspects of their jobs; the periodic meetings management held to discuss issues and concerns with employees had often provoked hot debates.

Ben & Jerry's had long prided itself on treating workers so fairly that they did not need and would not want to be represented by a union. But in late 1998 the company became embroiled in a union controversy at its St. Albans plant, where the International Brotherhood of Electrical Workers (IBEW) was trying to organize a group of 19 maintenance workers. Management refused the IBEW's request to recognize the union voluntarily. Company lawyers, appearing before the National Labor Relations Board, opposed the IBEW organizing attempt, arguing that the vote should be held among all workers at the plant, not just among the 19 maintenance workers. Production workers, who made up the majority of the plant's workforce, did not support the union's organizing effort as strongly. In early 1999, following an NLRB ruling that the maintenance workers at the St. Albans plant were an appropriate bargaining unit, the 19 maintenance workers voted narrowly for representation by the IBEW. Even though the 19 workers constituted less than 3 percent of the company's full-time workforce, top management at Ben & Jerry's was concerned that the voting outcome raised questions about the quality of employer–employee relations at Ben & Jerry's.

Management Changes   When Ben Cohen, the creative driving force in the company from the beginning, decided to step down as CEO in 1994, the search for a replacement included an essay contest in which anyone wishing to be considered for the CEO position was asked to state in 100 words or less "why I want to be a great CEO for Ben & Jerry's." Robert Holland, a former consultant at McKinsey & Company, was selected to become the company's CEO in February 1995; he helped transition the company from a founder-led to a professional management structure and begin the company's ventures into international markets. Holland resigned in October 1996, partly because of growing disagreements with the founders over how the company was being operated; he was replaced by Perry Odak, who had held senior management positions at Armour-Dial, Atari, Jovan, Dellwood Foods (a dairy products company), and, most recently, at U.S. Repeating Arms Company (the maker of Winchester firearms) and Browning, a manufacturer of firearms and other sporting goods.

Company Image and Events Leading Up to the Acquisition   Ben & Jerry's counterculture values, unconventional policies, and passionate commitment to social causes were widely known and, in many respects, had emerged as the company's biggest brand asset. Frequent and usually favorable stories in the New England and national press describing Ben & Jerry's proactive approach to "caring capitalism" had fostered public awareness of the company and helped mold a very positive image of the company and its business philosophy. Indeed, substantial numbers of the company's customers patronized Ben & Jerry's ice cream products because they were suspicious of giant corporations, shared many of the same values and beliefs about how a company ought to conduct its business, and wanted to support Ben & Jerry's efforts and good deeds. So strong was the anti-big-business feeling of some customers, employees, and shareholders that, when the press reported that Ben & Jerry's was considering various acquisition offers, there were protest rallies at company facilities in Vermont and a Save Ben & Jerry's Web site sprang up for followers to express their displeasure and to help mount a public relations campaign to block a sale. Hundreds of messages were posted at the site—one message said, "My friend and I will not buy Ben & Jerry's again if you sell out. It would not taste the same." Most messages conveyed concerns that Ben & Jerry's would lose its character and social values, ceasing to be a model for other businesses to emulate. Vermont's governor told Reuters, "This company has really come to symbolize Vermont to the country and the world. It would be a shame if it were sucked into the corporate homogenization that's taking over the planet."[8]

Reportedly, neither Ben Cohen nor Jerry Greenfield was enthusiastic about selling the company; both had publicly expressed their desires for the company to remain independent. But the company's languishing stock price and the attractive offers of interested buyers forced the board of directors to consider being acquired. To counter an offer of $38 per share from Dreyer's, Ben Cohen had entered into negotiations with Meadowbrook Lane Capital (one of the company's large shareholders) and others to take the company private. This fell through when Unilever made its offer of $43.60 per share. In agreeing to accept Unilever's price, Cohen netted over $39 million for his controlling interest in the company, while Odak received over $16 million and Greenfield got $9.6 million. A substantial fraction of Ben & Jerry's 11,000 shareholders were Vermont (or former Vermont) residents.

Developments Following the Acquisition

To win approval for the acquisition from Ben & Jerry's cofounders and the board, Unilever agreed to keep the company's headquarters in Vermont, to operate it separately from Unilever for a period of time, to maintain employment at current levels for at least two years, to hold employee benefits at current levels for at least five years, and to contribute 7.5 percent of pretax income annually to the Ben & Jerry's Foundation. (Historically, the foundation had been managed by a nine-member employee board of directors that considered proposals relating to children and families, disadvantaged groups, and the environment.) Unilever further agreed to form an independent 11-member board of directors for Ben & Jerry's to monitor how well these conditions were being met, with eight of the board members to be named by Ben & Jerry's management, one by Unilever, and two by Meadowbrook Lane Capital. Ben Cohen and Jerry Greenfield were also to continue to have active roles in management.

[8]Article by Mike Mills in *The Vermont Post*, December 9, 1999.

In a joint statement announcing the acquisition, Unilever's co-chairmen said, "Ben & Jerry's is an incredibly strong brand name with a unique consumer message. We are determined to nurture its commitment to community values." Ben Cohen said, "The best and highest use for Ben & Jerry's is to try to influence what goes on at Unilever. It's a gargantuan task. Who knows how far we'll get? Who knows how successful we'll be?"

In November 2000, Unilever announced that Yves Couette had been appointed CEO of Ben & Jerry's, to succeed Perry Odak. Couette, a native of France, was one of the top executives in Unilever's ice cream group and had worked in the United States, Mexico, Indonesia, and the United Kingdom. Couette had recently been managing director of Unilever's ice cream business in Mexico, where he had turned Unilever's Helados Holanda business into a solid success with distinctive local brands and scoop shops. In commenting on his appointment, Couette said,

> Ben & Jerry's is a unique company, with highly professional and committed people from whom I look forward to learning and connecting to Unilever's world-class knowledge of ice cream. In addition, I am determined to deliver on Ben & Jerry's social mission commitment.

Perry Odak remained with the company until January 2001 to assist Yves Couette in the transition.

Unilever's Global Ice Cream Business in 2003
In late 2003, Unilever had the largest and most profitable ice cream business of any company in the world. In Europe Unilever had a 26 percent overall market share—and its lead over the number two competitor, Nestlé (with a 2002 share of 13 percent), was increasing. Top executives of Unilever's ice cream business were confident of achieving 5–6 percent annual revenue growth and saw ice cream as on the Path to Growth. Since acquiring Ben & Jerry's, Unilever had moved to:

- Grow the sales of its ice cream businesses from €4.3 to €5.0 billion.
- Unify the marketing of its 10 ice cream brands outside the United States under a single "heart" logo—in an effort to create an ice cream "powerbrand."
- Boost profitability in ice cream by exiting sales in 12 countries, consolidating production into 36

factories (down from 53 in 1999), and reducing headcount by almost 8,800 employees.

Sales of ice cream worldwide were an estimated €55.4 billion in 2002, growing at 2.5 percent annually. North America was the biggest geographic market, with 2002 sales of €23 billion. Ice cream sales in Latin America were up 9.2 percent in 2002, the highest growth rate of any region in the world. Out-of-home consumption of ice cream accounted for about €37 billion of total sales in 2002 but was growing by only about 1.7 percent annually; 2002 ice cream consumption in the in-home segment grew by 5.2 percent in North America, 13.5 percent in Latin America, and about 2.5 percent in the rest of the world. Unilever management saw the global ice cream market as fragmented; in Europe there were some 200 brands of ice cream, many of which had different identities in different country markets.

THE BESTFOODS ACQUISITION

At the time of its acquisition by Unilever in mid-2000, Bestfoods was a global company engaged in manufacturing and marketing consumer foods. The company had offices and manufacturing operations in 60 countries and marketed its products in 110 countries. About 60 percent of Bestfoods' $8.6 billion in sales in 1999 came from outside the United States. Bestfoods employed approximately 44,000 people, of whom about 28,000 were at non-U.S. locations. Food industry analysts considered Bestfoods to be one of the best managed American food companies, and it was one of the 10 largest U.S.-based food products companies.

Exhibit 8 shows Bestfoods' lineup of products and brands in mid-2000. During the decade of the 1990s, Bestfoods had grown revenues at a 7.8 percent annual rate, operating earnings at a 10.5 percent annual rate, and earnings per share at a 12.1 percent annual rate; the company had increased its dividends for 14 consecutive years. Growth had slowed during the 1997–1999 period, however. In 1999, Bestfoods' sales were up 2.7 percent over 1998, unit volumes were up 4.1 percent, and operating income was up 9.0 percent (see Exhibit 9). Bestfoods' corporate strategy in 2000 had four core elements:

- *Globalization of the company's core consumer businesses*—the Knorr product line, salad dressings, and food-service operations.
- *Continual improvement in cost-effectiveness.*
- *Seeking out and exploiting new market opportunities* (via both new product introductions and extending sales of existing products to additional country markets).
- *Using free cash flow to make strategic acquisitions.* Since the 1980s, Bestfoods had made over 60 acquisitions to expand its lineup of products and brands and to position the company in new geographic markets.

Exhibits 10 and 11 show Bestfoods' performance and market positions in various country markets at the time it was acquired.

After several weeks of back-and-forth negotiations and increases in Unilever's offer price from the $61–$64 per share range to $66 per share to $72 per share and finally to $73 per share, Bestfoods in June 2000 agreed to be acquired by Unilever for what amounted to $20.3 billion in cash (equivalent to €23.6 billion), plus assumption of Bestfoods net debt (which amounted to $3.1 billion as of June 30, 2000). The $73 per share buyout agreement represented a price 44 percent higher than the nearly $51 price at which Bestfoods' shares were trading before Unilever's overtures became public and represented about a 20 percent premium over the $59–$62 range, in which Bestfoods shares were trading in late 1999. Bestfoods was by far the largest acquisition ever undertaken by Unilever and the largest combination of food companies in 12 years.

Unilever management believed that combining and integrating the operations of Bestfoods and Unilever would "result in pre-tax cost savings of approximately $750 million annually through combined purchase savings, greater efficiencies in operations and business processes, synergy in distribution and marketing, streamlining of general and administrative functions, and increased economies of scale." In addition, management said that the complementary nature of Unilever's and Bestfoods' product portfolios and geographic market coverage better positioned the combined company for faster revenue growth through:

- Creating a "more robust" combined business in the U.S. market.

exhibit 8   **Bestfoods' Products and Brands, June 2000**

Products/Brands	Comments
Hellmann's mayonnaise and salad dressings; Bestfoods, Lady's Choice, and Lesieur mayonnaise and salad dressings; Dijonnaise creamy mustard; and Henri's and Western salad dressings	Worldwide sales of about $2 billion, with the leading market share in mayonnaise in North America, Latin America, and many countries of Asia and Europe. In parts of the United States, Hellmann's products were marketed under the Bestfoods brand; Lesieur mayonnaise products were marketed in France and had the second highest market share in that country.
Knorr dry soups, sauces, bouillons, and related products	Worldwide sales of about $3 billion. Knorr products were sold in virtually all of the 110 countries where Bestfoods had a market presence. It was the number two soup brand, behind Campbell's.
Mazola corn and canola oils and Mazola margarine; Mazola No-Stick and Pro Chef cooking sprays; RightBlend oils	Marketed in 35 countries
Skippy peanut butter	One of the leading brands in the United States and also strong in parts of Asia
Karo and Golden Griddle syrups	
Argo, Kingsford's, Canada, Benson's, and Maizena corn starches	The Maizena brand of corn starch and other basic nutritional foods was marketed primarily in Latin America.
Mueller's pastas	
Rit dyes and laundry products	
Entemann's bakery goods; Thomas' English muffins; Arnold, Brownberry, Oroweat, and Freihofer's breads; and Boboli pizza crusts	The Bestfoods Baking division was the largest baker of fresh premium products in the United States; Entemann's was the number one brand of fresh bakery-style cakes and pastries in the United States; Boboli had a 57 percent share of the market for fresh pizza crusts; Bestfoods total sweet baked goods share was 19.2 percent in 1998.
Glaxose-D energy drinks	A newly acquired business in Pakistan
Globus dressings, condiments, and liquid sauces	A newly acquired brand in Hungary
Alsa and Ambrosia ready-to-eat desserts, dessert mixes, and baking aids	Marketed primarily in Europe; sales of about $280 million in 1999
AdeS soy beverages	Marketed throughout Latin America
Captain Cook salt	A packaged salt business in India
Bestfoods (in the United States) and Caterplan (outside the United States) food services	Provided food-service packs of company products, specially formulated products, and menu-planning and other unique services to support restaurants, cafeterias, and institutions in the growing global market for food prepared and consumed away from home—geographic coverage in virtually all of the countries where Bestfoods operated. The food-service division had worldwide sales of $1.4 billion in 1999.
Others: Pfanni potato products (Germany); Pot Noodle instant hot snacks (United Kingdom); Telma soups and instant foods products (Israel); Bovril bouillons; Marmite spread; Santa Rosa jams; Sahara pita breads; Goracy Kubek instant soups (Poland); Delikat seasonings (Central Europe); and Molinos de la Plata mayonnaise, ketchup, and mustard (Argentina)	

exhibit 9   **Selected Financial Statistics for Bestfoods, 1997–1999 (in millions, except for per share amounts)**

	1999	1998	1997
Selected income statement data			
Net sales	$8,637	$8,413	$8,438
Cost of sales	4,546	4,562	4,693
Gross profit	$4,091	$3,851	$3,745
Marketing expenses	996	976	978
Selling, general, and administrative expenses	1,765	1,655	1,659
Operating income	$1,330	$1,187	$ 866
Financing costs	183	166	162
Income from continuing operations before income taxes	1,147	1,021	704
Provision for income taxes	384	352	250
Net income	$ 717	$ 640	$ 429
Earnings per share of common stock (diluted)	$ 2.48	$ 2.09	$ 1.15
Selected balance sheet data			
Inventories	$ 792	$ 827	$ 818
Current assets	2,204	2,405	2,188
Plant, property, and equipment	1,964	1,965	1,941
Intangible assets, including goodwill associated with acquiring businesses at costs exceeding net assets	1,811	1,854	1,742
Total assets	$6,232	$6,435	$6,100
Current liabilities	2,368	2,312	2,347
Long-term debt	1,842	2,053	1,818
Total stockholders' equity	$ 938	$ 981	$1,042
Selected cash flow data			
Net cash flows from operating activities	$1,110	$ 819	$ 915
Capital expenditures	278	304	321
Payments for acquired businesses	225	121	298
Net cash flows used for investing activities	477	264	732
Repayment of long-term debt	153	94	99
Dividends paid on common and preferred stock	295	277	256
Net cash flows used for financing activities	697	440	267

Source: Company annual reports, 1998 and 1999.

- Maximizing the complementary strengths of Unilever and Bestfoods in Europe.
- Building on the strength of Bestfoods in Latin America to accelerate the growth of Unilever's brands.
- Using Unilever's distribution network strengths in the Asia-Pacific region to grow the sales of Bestfoods' brands.
- Utilizing Bestfoods' food-service channel to gain increased sales for Unilever's portfolio of spreads, teas, and culinary products.

According to a statement issued by Antony Burgmans and Niall FitzGerald, the Bestfoods acquisition would give Unilever "a portfolio of powerful worldwide and regional brands with strong growth prospects." Knorr, with $3 billion

exhibit 10   **Summary of Bestfoods Worldwide Business Results, 1997–1999**

1999 Sales and Operations, by Geographic Region				
Geographic Region	Sales Revenues (in millions)	Fixed Assets (in millions)	Areas of Operation, 1999	Number of Plants, 1999
Europe, Africa/ Middle East	1999 $3,598 1998 3,490 1997 3,539	1999 $1,568 1998 1,809 1997 1,637	Operations in 33 countries of Europe, Africa, and Middle East	59
North America	1999 $3,594 1998 3,452 1997 3,412	1999 $1,682 1998 1,507 1997 1,547	Operations in the United States, Canada, and the Caribbean	36
Latin America	1999 $1,071 1998 1,149 1997 1,105	1999 $ 277 1998 284 1997 291	Operations in 16 countries	19
Asia	1999 $ 374 1998 322 1997 382	1999 $ 124 1998 120 1997 101	Operations in 12 countries, including joint ventures in 7 countries	18

1999 Sales by Product Group				
Product Group	Region	Sales (in millions)	% Change	Volumes
Knorr soups, sauces, bouillons, and related products	Europe	$2,091	+4.2%	+9.8%
	North America	470	+10.3	10.3
	Latin America	342	−9.0	−7.6
	Asia	185	+17.0	+25.0
	Total	$3,088	+4.1%	6.8%
Dressings	Europe	$ 464	+2.7%	+7.9%
	North America	1,001	+4.8	5.4
	Latin America	443	−5.7	+1.7
	Asia	96	+14.0	+10.2
	Total	2,004	+2.2%	5.4%
Baking	United States	$1,697		
Starches	Worldwide	$ 569		
Bread spreads	Worldwide	$ 406		
Desserts	Worldwide	$ 280		
All other sales	Worldwide	$ 593		
Bestfoods and Caterplan food services	Worldwide	$1,400 (distributed across several of the product groups above)	+8.4%	Included in the appropriate product groups above

in annual sales, would become Unilever's biggest food brand.

To finance the $21.4 billion Bestfoods acquisition, Unilever arranged for a $20 billion line of credit from several banks, with annual interest costs that analysts expected to exceed $1 billion. It was anticipated that Unilever would ultimately finance the transaction with longer-term debt securities having a currency profile paralleling the geographic composition of the business.

exhibit 11　Market Positions of Bestfoods Products, by Country, 1999

1 Leader in Market Share
2 Second in Market Share
• Present in the Market

	Soups*	Sauces*	Bouillons	Meal Kits*	Potato Products	Pasta/Pasta Dishes	Mayonnaise	Pourable Dressings	Corn Oil	Foodservice†	Peanut Butter	Starches	Desserts (Ambient)	Premium Baking
North America, Caribbean														
Canada	2	2	1				1		1	•	2	1		
Dominican Republic	2		2				•		•	•		1		
United States	•	•	2	•	•	•	1	•	1	•	2	1	•	1
Europe														
Austria	1	1	1	1	1				1	•		1		
Belgium	1	1	1	1						•		1		
Bulgaria	•	•	•		•					•				
Czech Republic	2	2	2	2	•		1	1		•				
Denmark	1	1	1	1	2			2	1			1	•	
Finland	1	1	1	2					1			2		
France	1	2	2				2	2		•		1	1	
Germany	2	2	2	2	1		•		1	•		1	•	
Greece	1	1	1		2	1	1	1		•		2	2	
Hungary	1	1	1	2	1		2			•			•	
Ireland	1	1	1	1	1	•	1	2	•	•		2	1	
Italy	1	•	2		1		•		•	•		1		
Netherlands	2	1	2	2	•				•	•		2		
Norway	•	2	•						•	•		1		
Poland	1	1	1	1	1		2			•			•	
Portugal	1	•	1		2		1	2		•		1	2	
Romania	1		1							•			•	
Russia	2	1	2		1		•		•	•	•			
Slovak Republic	2	•	•	•	•		1			•				
Slovenia														
Spain	2	•	2	•		•	•	•		•		1	2	
Sweden	1	2	1	1				•	1	•	1	1		
Switzerland	1	1	1	1	1		•		•	•		1	•	
United Kingdom	•	•	2	•		•	1	2	1	•		1	1	
Africa/Middle East														
Egypt														
Israel	1	2	2	1	•	•	1		1	•	1		2	
Jordan	2		2							•				
Kenya	1		2							•	•	2	1	
Morocco	1	•	1							•		1	1	
Saudi Arabia							2		2	•	•	•		
South Africa	1	2	1	1			•	1	•	•	•	1	•	
Tunisia	1	•	1				•			•		2	•	
Turkey	1	2	•							•		1	•	

exhibit 11 **(concluded)**

1 Leader in Market Share / 2 Second in Market Share / • Present in the Market	Soups*	Sauces*	Bouillons	Meal Kits*	Potato Products	Pasta/Pasta Dishes	Mayonnaise	Pourable Dressings	Corn Oil	Foodservice†	Peanut Butter	Starches	Desserts (Ambient)	Premium Baking
Latin America														
Argentina	1		1		1	1	1	1	2	•		1		
Bolivia	•		•				2			•		1		
Brazil	2		1			2	1	1	1	•		1		
Chile	•		•		2		1	1	1	•		1	•	
Colombia	•	2	2	2	•		1	•	•	•		1	1	
Costa Rica	2	1	•		•		1	1	1	•	•	1	•	
Ecuador	2	•	•	2			•		1	•		•		
El Salvador	•	•	•				•	•	1	•		1		
Guatemala	•	•	•		•		•	1	1	•	•	1		
Honduras		•					•		1			2		
Mexico	1	•	1	1		1	2	•	2	•		1	•	
Panama	•	•	•				•	•	•	•		1		
Paraguay	2		2		2	•	1		2	•		1		
Peru	2	•	2		2	2	1	2	1	•		1		
Uruguay	1		1		1	•	1		2	•		1		
Venezuela	2	•	2	1			•	•		•		1		
Asia														
China	•	•	•				•			•	•	•	•	•
Hong Kong	•	•	1			•	2			•	•	1	1	1
India	1			1									1	1
Indonesia	1	•	•				2	2	1	•	1			
Japan	1	•	1	•			2	2	1	•	•			
Malaysia	1	•	2				1	1	1	•	1	1	2	
Pakistan	1	•	1	•			2		1	•		1	1	
Philippines	1	•	1		1		1	•	•	•	1	•	1	
Singapore	1		1				2	2	•	•	1	1	1	
Sri Lanka	2	1	2						2	•				
Taiwan	1		1				2	•	•	•	1			
Thailand	1	1	1	2		1	1		1	•	1	•	•	
Vietnam	2		1				•			•				

*Dehydrated products only.

†Bestfoods food-service (catering) products hold leading share positions in many of the categories in which they compete.

Source: Company annual report, 1999.

In February 2001, Unilever announced the sale of the Bestfoods Baking Company to George Weston, a Canadian food and supermarkets group, for $1.76 billion in cash. Unilever had announced its intention to divest Bestfoods Baking Company two weeks after closing its merger with Bestfoods on October 4, 2000, noting that the characteristics of the baking business did not fit other Unilever products and that bakery products was a category no longer in existence at Unilever. Bestfoods Baking was entirely U.S.-based, with 19 plants across the country, a strong management team, 12,000 employees, and one of the best distribution systems for delivering fresh-baked products directly to retail stores. In 1999, Bestfoods Baking had sales of $1.7 billion (up 2.3 percent over 1998) and an operating profit margin of 8 percent (good for the baking business).

In April 2002 Unilever announced an agreement to sell 19 former Bestfoods brands sold across North America to ACH Food Companies, a subsidiary of Associated British Foods, for €406 million ($360 million) in cash. The brands had combined sales of €350 million (U.S.$310 million) in 2001 and included Mazola cooking oil products, Argo and Kingsford's corn starches, Karo and Golden Griddle syrups, and Henri's salad dressing sold in the United States, Puerto Rico, and Canada, plus such Canadian brands as Benson's and Canada corn starches, St. Lawrence/St. Laurent corn oil, Crown and Bee Hive corn syrups, Old Colony maple syrup, and Old Tyme pancake syrup. The deal also included a cornstarch manufacturing facility in Argo, Illinois. Approximately 200 Unilever Bestfoods employees were transferred to ACH Food Companies.

By year-end 2003, Unilever management believed that it had successfully integrated the operations of Bestfoods with those of Unilever. Businesses of the two companies had been merged in 63 countries across 5 regions of the world, pro-ducing €790 million in cost-saving synergies and efficiencies and leading to increased operating margins (15.7 percent for the first nine months of 2003 versus 14.8 percent in 2002 and 14.4 percent in 2001). Unilever's entire food division was operating under the name Unilever Bestfoods (UBF).

UNILEVER IN 2003

Despite the obvious progress that Unilever had made as of the fall of 2003 in executing its Path to Growth strategy—most notably boosting its operating margins to over 15 percent (in striking distance of the 16+ percent target), the company's third-quarter 2003 report of a growth slowdown in the sales of its leading brands (Exhibit 2) raised questions among investors and analysts of whether the company's current lineup of businesses and brands could deliver 5–6 percent growth in revenues in the years to come. Did Unilever really have a "world-beating brand portfolio and unrivaled geographic coverage" as Niall FitzGerald and Antony Burgmans had claimed in the months following the company's acquisitions of SlimFast, Ben & Jerry's, and Bestfoods? Was the 2003 drop-off in the sales growth of leading brands just temporary or a sign of things to come? What options did Unilever have for addressing the underperforming parts of its business? How much confidence should be placed in the claim by FitzGerald and Burgmans that "higher levels of leading brands growth will resume"? What should be made of their statement that "good progress in the vast majority of our business is not yet sufficient to offset the weaknesses in a limited number of under-performing businesses"?

Exhibits 12, 13, and 14 present highlights of Unilever's performance for the first nine months of 2003, as compared to the first nine months of 2002.

exhibit 12   **Summary of Unilever's Financial Performance Based on Constant Exchange Rates, First Nine Months, 2003 versus 2002 (in millions)**

	First Nine Months		
	2003	2002	Percent Change
Income statement data			
Revenues	€35,559	€36,008	(1.25)%
Operating profit (BEIA*)	5,519	5,434	1.56
Operating profit	4,412	4,306	2.46
Net earnings	2,032	1,884	7.86
Balance sheet data			
Cash and short-term investments	€ 3,027	€ 4,476	(32.37)%
Net debt	14,363	18,846	(23.79)
Shareholders' equity	6,400	6,196	3.29

*BEIA = Before exceptional items and amortization of goodwill and intangibles.
Source: Unilever press release, October 29, 2003, accessed at www.unilever.com, January 9, 2004.

exhibit 13   **Unilever's Financial Performance by Geographic Area at Constant Exchange Rates, First Nine Months, 2003 versus 2002 (euros in millions)**

Geographic Area Performance	First Nine Months, 2003	First Nine Months, 2002	Percent Change
Revenues			
Europe	€14,273	€14,832	(4)%
North America	8,822	9,502	(7)%
Africa, Middle East, Turkey	2,516	2,373	6%
Asia and Pacific	6,000	5,781	4%
Latin America	4,164	3,899	7%
Total	€35,775	€36,387	(2)%
Operating profit—BEIA*			
Europe	€ 2,452	€ 2,183	12%
North America	1,310	1,550	(16)%
Africa, Middle East, Turkey	331	287	15%
Asia and Pacific	858	847	1%
Latin America	568	567	0%
Total	€ 5,519	€ 5,434	2%
Operating margin—BEIA*			
Europe	17.2%	14.7%	
North America	14.8%	16.3%	
Africa, Middle East, Turkey	13.1%	12.1%	
Asia and Pacific	14.3%	14.6%	
Latin America	13.6%	14.5%	
Total	15.4%	14.9%	

*BEIA = Before exceptional items and amortization of goodwill and intangibles.
Source: Unilever press release, October 29, 2003, accessed at www.unilever.com, January 9, 2004.

exhibit 14   **Unilever's Financial Performance by Business Segment at Constant Exchange Rates, First Nine Months, 2003 versus 2002 (euros in millions)**

Business Segment Performance	First Nine Months, 2003	First Nine Months, 2002	Percent Change
Revenues			
Foods	€20,059	€20,569	(2)%
Soups and dressings	6,892	6,654	1
Spreads and cooking products	3,954	4,521	(13)
Health and wellness and beverages	3,078	3,170	(3)
Ice cream and frozen foods	6,135	6,024	2
Home care and professional cleaning	6,000	6,529	(8)
Personal care	9,449	8,931	6
Other operations	267	358	(25)
Total	€35,557	€36,387	(2)%
Operating profit—BEIA*			
Foods	€ 3,154	€ 2,925	7%
Soups and dressings	1,084	967	12
Spreads and cooking products	627	676	(7)
Health and wellness and beverages	420	427	(1)
Ice cream and frozen foods	1,023	865	18
Home care and professional cleaning	752	766	(2)
Personal care	1,617	1,714	(6)
Other operations	(4)	19	(123)
Total	€ 5,519	€ 5,434	2%
Operating profit margin—BEIA*			
Foods	15.7%	14.3%	
Soups and dressings	15.7	14.1	
Spreads and cooking products	15.9	14.9	
Health and wellness and beverages	13.6	13.4	
Ice cream and frozen foods	16.7	14.4	
Home care and professional cleaning	12.5	11.7	
Personal care	17.1	19.2	
Other operations	(1.6)	5.4	
Overall	15.4	14.9	

*BEIA = Before exceptional items and amortization of goodwill and intangibles.

Source: Unilever press release, October 29, 2003, accessed at www.unilever.com, January 9, 2004.

LVMH's Diversification Strategy into Luxury Goods

John E. Gamble
University of South Alabama

In 2002, Moët Hennessy Louis Vuitton (LVMH) was the world's largest luxury products company, with annual sales of 12.2 billion euros (€) and a business portfolio that included some of the most prestigious brand names in wines and champagnes, fashion, watches and jewelry, and perfumes and cosmetics. The French conglomerate's business portfolio also included two prestigious Parisian department stores, two chains of duty-free shops, a retail cosmetics chain, e-commerce businesses, and a variety of French media properties. Even though no one "needed" LVMH's products—a magnum of its 1985 Dom Pérignon Rose champagne retailed for $925, its Givenchy gowns could exceed $15,000, and the finest TAG Heuer watch carried a retail price of about $58,000—the company's products were desired by millions across the world. CEO Bernard Arnault suggested that desire for the company's products "in some way, fulfills a fantasy. You feel as if you must buy it, in fact, or else you won't be in the moment. You will be left behind."[1]

The company's business portfolio began to take shape in 1987 when Louis Vuitton, known worldwide for its purses and luggage, merged with the maker of Moët & Chandon champagne and Hennessy cognac. LVMH's present lineup of star luxury brands was forged by Bernard Arnault, who became CEO of the company in 1989 and promptly set about acquiring such names as Christian Dior, Fendi, Donna Karan, Givenchy, Celine, Christian Lacroix, and Marc Jacobs in fashion and leather goods; TAG Heuer and Ebel in watches; and Le Bon Marché and Sephora in retailing. By 2002 Arnault had assembled a portfolio of nearly 50 luxury brands, which he categorized as a collection of star brands and rising stars—brands that Arnault believed "speak to the ages" but, at the same time, feel intensely modern.[2] Arnault suggested that star brands were not only timeless and modern but also highly profitable and rapidly growing. He portrayed star brands as illogical since, in most cases, the quality of timelessness was in conflict with innovation, and rapid growth usually was at odds with high profits. When asked about the managerial challenges of developing star brands, Arnault stated, "Mastering the paradox of star brands is very difficult and rare—fortunately. In my opinion, there are fewer than ten star brands in the luxury world."[3]

Arnault believed LVMH's collection of star brands such as Moët & Chandon, Krug, Louis Vuitton, Givenchy, and Parfums Christian Dior and its rising stars like Donna Karan, Christian Lacroix, and Kenzo would lead to long-term corporate advantage since star brands had staying power. "The brand is built, if you wish, for eternity. It has been around for a long time; it has become an institution. Dom Pérignon is a perfect example. I can guarantee that people will be drinking it in the next century. It was

Reprinted by permission of *Harvard Business Review.* From "The Perfect Paradox of Star Brands: An Interview with Bernard Arnault of LVMH," by Bernard Arnault and Suzy Wetlaufer, 79, no. 9 (October 2001), p. 116. Copyright 2001 by the Harvard Business School Publishing Corporation; all rights reserved.

[1]Quoted in "The Perfect Paradox of Star Brands: An Interview with Bernard Arnault of LVMH," *Harvard Business Review,* 79, no. 9 (October 2001), p. 116.

[2]Ibid.
[3]Ibid.

created 250 years ago, but it will be relevant and desired for another century and beyond that."[4]

Arnault's rapidly growing portfolio had allowed LVMH to grow from approximately €2.5 billion in 1990 to €12.2 billion in 2001. However, the company's sales growth slowed in late 2001 and early 2002 as the effects of the September 11, 2001, terrorist attacks on New York City and Washington, D.C., and a lingering global recession contributed to a worldwide decline in the purchase of luxury goods. In addition, LVMH management issued three profit warnings during its fourth quarter 2001 prior to announcing a net income of €10 million for fiscal 2001. As LVMH's stock price reflected the company's slowing sales growth and weak profitability, its investors began to call for Arnault to evaluate the company's portfolio for possible restructuring. A summary of LVMH's financial performance between 1993 and 2001 is presented in Exhibit 1. A time line of its brands is presented in Exhibit 2.

COMPANY HISTORY

LVMH's history as an enterprise is traced to 1743 when Moët & Chandon was established in the Champagne Province in northeastern France. Moët & Chandon not only became among France's premier brands of champagne but was also sought after outside of France, with exports accounting for a large percentage of its sales by the 20th century. The company first diversified in 1968 when it acquired Parfums Christian Dior and a 1971 merger between Moët & Chandon and Champagne Mercier combined France's two best-selling brands of champagne. The company changed its name to Moët-Hennessy when it again merged in 1971; this time with Jas Hennessy & Company, the world's second largest producer of cognac.

The company diversified further in 1987 as the French government launched into an era of privatization to promote economic growth and reduce the country's excessively high unemployment rate. The families who controlled Moët-Hennessy and leather goods designer Louis Vuitton saw a merger between their two companies as their best strategy to prevent the companies from becoming takeover targets of large international corporations making investments

in France. The $4 billion merger that created LVMH allowed the heirs of the two companies' founders to retain control of the new entity with a combined ownership of 50 percent of outstanding shares. The new ownership structure also placed Hennessy heir and chairman Alain Chevalier in the position of chairman of LVMH, while Vuitton family member and company president Henry Racamier became LVMH's director general.

The new company became France's 40th largest company, with total revenues in 1987 of FF 13.1 billion ($2.1 billion) and a portfolio of such well-known luxury brands as Veuve Clicquot, Moët & Chandon, and Dom Pérignon champagnes; Canard-Duchíne wines; Hennessy cognac; Christian Dior and Givenchy perfumes and cosmetics; Georges Delbard (France's leading grower of roses); and Louis Vuitton leather handbags and luggage. On the day the merger was consummated, LVMH chairman Alain Chevalier also signed an international distribution agreement with British brewer Guinness PLC to improve the distribution of the company's champagne and cognac brands in Asia and the United States. The joint venture with Guinness called for both firms to acquire interlocking interests of about 10 percent of each company's shares and accounted for nearly one-fourth of LVMH and Guinness profits within the joint venture's first year.

The success of the LVMH-Guinness joint venture led Alain Chevalier to propose that Guinness purchase an additional 10 percent interest in LVMH to further protect the company from possible foreign raiders. The growing relative importance of the company's wine, champagne, and spirits businesses and the proposal for increased ownership of LVMH shares by Guinness became worrisome to Racamier and other Vuitton family members who believed the company's core business should center on fashion and leather goods. To fortify the company's focus on haute couture, Racamier in mid-1988 asked Bernard Arnault (the owner of the Christian Dior, Celine, and Christian Lacroix brands) to purchase shares of LVMH and join forces with Vuitton heirs in their disagreement with Chevalier.

Thirty-nine-year-old Bernard Arnault had only recently become known among France's business elite, since only four years before he was building condominiums in Florida for his family's modest real estate and construction firm. Arnault returned to France in 1984 and purchased nearly bankrupt

[4]Ibid.

exbibit 1 **Summary of LVMH's Financial Performance, 1993–2001 (in millions of euros, except per share amounts)**

	2001	2000	1999	1998*	1997*	1996*	1995*	1994*	1993*
Net sales	€12,229	€11,581	€8,547	€6,936	€7,322	€4,748	€4,539	€4,264	€3,630
Income from operations	1,560	1,959	1,547	1,184	1,269	1,071	1,111	1,037	856
Operating margin	12.8%	16.9%	18.1%	17.1%	17.3%	22.6%	24.5%	24.3%	23.6%
Net income before amortization of goodwill and unusual items	€ 334	€ 846	€ 738	€ 525	€ 742	€ 679	€ 640	€ 559	€ 453
Net income	€ 10	€ 722	€ 693	€ 267	€ 690	€ 563	€ 617	€ 979	€ 545
Earnings per share before amortization of goodwill and unusual items	€ 0.68	€ 1.75	€ 1.53	€ 1.07	€ 1.52	€ 1.39	€ 1.31	€ 1.16	€ 0.99
Net income per share	€ 0.02	€ 1.49	€ 1.44	€ 0.55	€ 1.41	€ 1.16	€ 1.26	€ 2.03	€ 1.18
Dividend per share including tax credit	€ 1.13	€ 1.13	€ 1.02	€0.927	€0.927	€0.828	€0.782	€0.711	€0.542
Cash flow from operations	€ 919	€1,214	€1,051	€ 571	€1,163	€ 851	€ 904	€ 935	€ 700
Capital expenditures	984	857	574	381	310	n.a.	n.a.		
Stockholders' equity	8,701	8,512	7,781	6,316	6,179	5,486	4725	4,625	3,567
Long-term debt	5,402	3,498	3,085	1,425	1,382	675	573	794	1,180

n.a. = Not available.

*French franc to euro conversion rate at 6.5595.

Source: LVMH annual reports.

exhibit 2   **History of LVMH Brands**

16th Century	
1593	Château d'Yquem champagne

18th Century	
1729	Ruinart champagne
1743	Moët & Chandon champagne
1763	Hine cognac
1765	Hennessy cognac
1772	Veuve Clicquot champagne
1780	Chaumet watches and jewelry

19th Century	
1828	Guerlain perfumes
1843	Krug champagne
1846	Loewe leather goods
1852	Le Bon Marché department store
1854	Louis Vuitton leather goods
1858	Mercier champagne
1860	Heuer watches
1865	Zenith watches
1868	Canard Duchêne champagne
1870	La Cote Desfossés publications
1870	La Samaritaine department store
1895	Berluti leather goods

20th Century	
1911	Ebel watches
1925	Fendi fashion and furs
1925	Omas writing instruments
1930	Acqua di Parma perfumes
1936	Dom Pérignon champagne
1936	Fred fashion
1945	Celine fashion
1947	Parfums Christian Dior perfumes
1948	Emilio Pucci fashion
1952	Connaissance des Arts magazine
1952	Givenchy fashion

1957	Parfums Givenchy perfumes
1960	DFS duty free shoppers
1963	Miami Cruiseline Services duty free shoppers
1970	Etude Tajan fine art auction house
1970	Kenzo fashion
1972	Mount Adam wine
1973	Domaine Chandon champagne
1973	Sephora cosmetics retailing
1974	Investir magazine
1976	Cape Mentelle wine
1979	Art & Auction magazine
1983	Radio Classique radio network
1984	Donna Karan fashion
1984	Marc Jacobs fashion
1984	Newton wine
1984	Thomas Pink fashion
1985	Benedom–CD Montres watches
1985	Cloudy Bay wine
1985	La Tribune de l'Economie magazine
1987	Christian Lacroix fashion
1987	Kenzo Parfums perfumes
1987	Laflachère toiletries/household items
1989	Make Up For Ever cosmetics
1991	Fresh cosmetics
1991	StefanoBi leather goods
1995	Hard Candy cosmetics
1995	BeneFit Cosmetics
1996	Bliss cosmetics and spas
1996	Urban Decay cosmetics
1997	Chandon Estates wine
2000	eLuxury Internet luxury retailer

21st Century	
2001	LVMH/De Beers joint venture diamond retail stores

Source: LVMH Web site.

Agache-Willot-Boussac—a state-owned conglomerate of retailing, fashion, and manufacturing. The French government sold Arnault the business at far below book value in expectation that privatization would bring an entrepreneurial spirit to the company's collection of businesses and ultimately expand employment by Agache-Willot-Boussac. Arnault saw his mission differently than the French government and sold the assets of Agache-Willot-Boussac's poor-performing businesses and retained its profitable businesses, of which Christian Dior was the most notable. Within three years of the company's acquisition by Arnault, Agache-Willot-Boussac (renamed Financiere Agache by Arnault) had earned $112 million on revenues of $1.9 billion. In 1987, Arnault leveraged Financiere Agache's cash flow from operations and liquidated assets to expand its presence in the fashion industry with the purchase of Celine, a fashion and leather goods company, and the launch of a new fashion brand headed by France's hottest young designer, Christian Lacroix.

After meeting with LVMH's director general, Henry Racamier, Arnault also met with the company's chairman, Alain Chevalier, before forming a joint venture with Guinness PLC to purchase 37 percent of LVMH's shares. Guinness was receptive to Arnault's proposal to form the joint venture since it assured the British company's management that its highly profitable distribution agreement with LVMH would remain intact, despite the feud between the Hennessy and Vuitton clans. Financiere Agache held a 60 percent interest in the joint venture, while Guinness held 40 percent. The controlling interest in the Guinness-Agache joint venture made Bernard Arnault the largest shareholder of LVMH by November 1988 and gave him a blocking minority of shares. After becoming LVMH's largest shareholder and asked of his intentions to bring about management changes at the company, Bernard Arnault commented that he approved of Chevalier's strategies, but added: "His problem is that he is not a major shareholder. In the businesses I manage, I'm the principal shareholder; and that helps me control the situation."[5]

Bernard Arnault became LVMH's president in January 1989 and chairman in mid-1990 after prevailing in an 18-month legal battle with Henry Racamier, who had petitioned the court to invalidate a portion of Arnault's stake in LVMH. Upon becoming chairman, Arnault launched an aggressive plan to transform LVMH into France's largest company. Arnault dismissed LVMH's top management, folded Agache's brands and assets into LVMH, and began making rapid acquisitions to expand the company's portfolio of luxury brands. Many French executives resented Arnault's business tactics and questioned his motives in becoming the head of LVMH. An ex-LVMH officer called Arnault "an asset shuffler, a raider, a French Donald Trump," and after a meeting with Arnault, the chairman of Yves Saint Laurent characterized the LVMH chief as "friendly—like a bird of prey that might want to devour you."[6] Bernard Arnault dismissed such criticism by asserting, "I'm going to run LVMH for the long term. We'll become an even stronger No. 1. My image will change."[7]

LVMH UNDER BERNARD ARNAULT

When Bernard Arnault became president of LVMH in January 1989, the company was the world's leading luxury products group with revenues of FF 16.4 billion (approximately €2.5 billion) and net income of FF 2.0 billion (approximately €300 million) in 1988. The company's business portfolio included champagnes and wines, cognac and spirits, luggage, leather goods and accessories, perfumes and beauty products, and horticulture. The 1988 revenue and operating income contributions and capital expenditures for each business unit are presented in the following table. The table also presents each business unit's percentage of sales to countries outside of France.

	Champagne and Wines	Cognac and Spirits	Luggage, Leather Goods and Accessories	Perfumes and Beauty Products	Horticulture
Sales (in millions)	FF 4,876	FF 4,083	FF 3,530	FF 3,735	FF 218
% from outside France	72%	98%	84%	74%	40%
Income from operations (in millions)	FF 1,042	FF 1,348	FF 1,458	FF 594	FF (202)
Capital expenditures (in millions)	FF 272	FF 114	FF 214	FF 170	N/A

N/A = Not available.
Source: LVMH 1988 annual report.

[5]Quoted in "Pivotal Figure Emerges in Moët-Vuitton Feud," *New York Times,* September 19, 1988, p. D1.

[6]Both quotes from "Bernard Arnault Is Building a Huge Empire—But Can He Manage It?" *Business Week,* July 30, 1990, p. 48.
[7]Ibid.

LVMH's champagne and wines business unit was the global leader in premium champagnes, with some of the oldest and most prestigious brands in the world. Dom Pérignon was arguably the world's best-known brand of champagne, Ruinart was the world's oldest champagne company, and Mercier was France's best-selling brand of champagne. Moët & Chandon, Canard-Duchêne, Veuve Clicquot Ponsardin, and Henriot rounded out LVMH's portfolio of centuries-old champagne brands. LVMH's champagne and wine division also included the respected Napa Valley sparkling wine producer Domaine Chandon. LVMH's cognac and spirits business, like its champagne and wine business unit, possessed two of the most prestigious brands worldwide with Hennessy and Hine—both founded in the mid-1700s and consistently recognized by connoisseurs for quality.

Louis Vuitton accounted for the largest share of LVMH's luggage, leather goods, and accessories division's sales, with market leading positions in luggage and travel accessories worldwide. Louis Vuitton's luggage had been popular since the mid-1800s, when Vuitton's monogrammed products first became available to affluent travelers who visited his Paris store. In 1988 Louis Vuitton leather products were available in 118 fine department stores in Europe, the United States, and Asia. Loewe was a prestigious Spanish brand that earned the distinction of Supplier to the Royal Household in 1905 and had since become noted for fine ready-to-wear leather and textile apparel, handbags, and travel accessories. Loewe also marketed a fragrance line in 1988.

LVMH's perfumes and beauty products division was composed of three different houses: Parfums Christian Dior was internationally renowned for its quality, innovation, and prestige and was the leading prestige brand of fragrance in France; the brand was also among the fastest growing in the United States and held the number one position in Western Europe. Parfums Givenchy was among the most successful prestige brands in the United States and had extended its product line to include cosmetics in 1988. RoC specialized in hypoallergenic cosmetics and was endorsed by dermatologists in Europe and the United States. RoC was the number one hypoallergenic cosmetic brand in Europe and was expected to increase sales both in Europe and the United States as LVMH expanded its distribution beyond pharmacy channels.

LVMH's horticulture group held a majority interest in Georges Delbard—one of the world's most respected producers of high-quality rose bushes and fruit trees. The company utilized a direct sales force to market its plants to horticulture professions and operated 12 Jardineries Delbard retail stores to make its products available to consumers in France.

LVMH's Rapid Growth under Bernard Arnault

LVMH's rapid portfolio diversification began shortly after Arnault gained a controlling percentage of company shares when it acquired Givenchy Couture haute couture, men's and women's ready-to-wear fashions, and accessories in November 1988. LVMH's management had been working to unite its Parfums Givenchy with Givenchy Couture since 1987 and agreed on terms with Hubert de Givenchy just prior to Arnault's becoming president of LVMH in January 1989. In 1990 Arnault purchased an additional interest in Loewe and purchased all assets of Pommery—the largest vineyard in the Champagne Province and producer of champagnes since 1860. Arnault's most ambitious target during 1990 was Guinness PLC. Arnault increased LVMH's share in Guinness from about 12 percent to 24 percent in what was suggested by outsiders as an attempt to make LVMH the world's largest alcoholic beverage seller with more than $5.5 billion in sales and a vast international distribution network.

Arnault abandoned his quest to gain a controlling stake in Guinness in 1994 when Guinness management agreed to a stock swap between LVMH and the British brewer that netted LVMH $1.9 billion in cash. Arnault had initiated a few small acquisitions of fashion and spirits businesses between 1990 and 1994, but the $1.9 billion cash infusion that resulted from the company's Guinness stock swap allowed Arnault to pursue his pledge to shareholders that LVMH was going to buy more luxury companies in cosmetics, perfume, fashion, and retailing.[8] Arnault initially focused on L'Oréal, a leading manufacturer and marketer of cosmetics with 1993 sales of $6 billion, and French drug manufacturer Sanofi, which bought Yves Saint Laurent in 1993. However, neither company was acquired by LVMH. Arnault brought additional fashion and fragrance brands to the company's portfolio and diversified outside of lux-

[8]Quoted in "Arnault Is Shopping," *Business Week,* February 7, 1994, p. 44.

ury goods with the purchase of three of France's leading financial and business publications—*Investir, La Tribune Desfosses,* and *L'Agefi.* Arnault also used the company's cash reserves to expand the number of company-owned retail stores where its Louis Vuitton and Loewe leather goods and Celine, Christian Dior, and Givenchy haute couture and ready-to-wear fashions could be found.

Bernard Arnault believed that LVMH control of the retail channels where its products were sold was critical to the success of luxury brands. The use of company-owned retail locations allowed LVMH not only to make certain its products were of the highest quality and most elegant but also to ensure that its products were sold by retailers offering the highest level of customer service. Arnault believed that ultimately the finer points of retailing impacted the overall image of luxury products as much as the products' attributes. This belief drove the company's moves into vertical integration into the operation of Louis Vuitton, Christian Dior, and other designer-label stores in Paris, New York, Beverly Hills, and other locations and also led to the $2.5 billion acquisition of Duty Free Shoppers (DFS) in 1996. San Francisco–based DFS operated a chain of 180 duty-free boutiques in Asia and various international airports. Arnault saw DFS as an ideal acquisition candidate since the chain specialized in the sale of luxury goods to affluent international travelers and since its stores were concentrated in Asia. Asia was among LVMH's best geographic markets, accounting for as much as two-thirds of the sales of such products as Louis Vuitton luggage.

Arnault expanded further into retailing in 1997 with the acquisition of French cosmetics retailer Sephora and the purchase of a 30 percent interest in Douglas International, a German beauty-goods retailer with 190 stores in Europe and the United States. LVMH also expanded its line of fine champagnes in 1997 with the acquisition of Château d'Yquem—a brand produced with such care and under such exacting standards that each vine yielded just one glass of champagne. Arnault again made an attempt to have LVMH become the world's largest wine and spirits producer and distributor when he spent $2.3 billion in 1997 to purchase 11 percent of Grand Metropolitan PLC—a British food conglomerate with $1.5 billion in annual wine and spirits sales. Arnault used the ownership position in Grand Met to insert himself into merger negotiations that were under way between Guinness and Grand Met. Arnault proposed an alternate merger scenario that would combine Guinness, Grand Met, and LVMH and make LVMH the controlling entity with a 35 percent stake in the three-way merger. Guinness and Grand Met shareholders rejected the proposal but provided Arnault with a $400 million payoff to allow the two-way merger to proceed, an 11 percent interest in the new company, and a seat on its board of directors.

Arnault expanded LVMH's retailing operations beyond specialty retailing in 1998 with the acquisition of famous Parisian department stores La Belle Jardiniere and Le Bon Marché. Arnault also added Laflachère—France's leading producer of hygiene, beauty, and household cleaning products—and Marie-Jeanne Godard, a fine fragrance line, to LVMH's portfolio in 1998, but his boldest acquisition spree occurred during 1999 and 2000. During that two-year period, Arnault created a new watch and jewelry division with the purchase of TAG Heuer, Ebel, Chaumet, and Zenith; pushed the company into makeup-artist-quality cosmetics with the purchase of Bliss, BeneFit, Hard Candy, Make Up for Ever, Fresh, and Urban Decay; and entered the fine art and collectible auction industry with the acquisition of famous auction houses Phillips, de Pury & Luxembourg, and L'Etude Tajan.

Arnault's buying binge broadened the company's media operations via the addition of a French radio network and magazines targeted to music aficionados and art connoisseurs. Other business additions included (*a*) New World wine producers located in the United States and Australia; (*b*) new retail outlets in the form of an Italian cosmetics retailing chain and Miami Cruiseline Services, which offered duty-free shopping aboard 100 cruise ships sailing in the Caribbean and elsewhere; (*c*) an enhanced line of champagnes with Krug, the producer of some of the world's most expensive champagnes; and (*d*) the fashion houses of Emilio Pucci, Thomas Pink, and Fendi.

Arnault had attempted to add Gucci to the company's impressive lineup of designer brands by purchasing more than 34 percent of the Italian fashion label's shares but was thwarted by rival French conglomerate Pinault-Printemps-Redout (PPR) when it acquired 42 percent of Gucci shares. The battle for control of Gucci pitted France's two wealthiest men, LVMH's Arnault and PPR's Francois Pinault, against each other in a battle that would eventually be won by Pinault but would provide LVMH with more than $1.8 billion for its stake in Gucci. LVMH's most notable acquisitions in 2001 included Donna Karan International and La Samaritaine, the largest department store in Paris. A complete list of LVMH's acquisitions and divestitures is presented in Exhibit 3.

LVMH'S APPROACH TO BUILDING SHAREHOLDER VALUE IN LUXURY PRODUCTS BUSINESSES

LVMH's corporate strategy under Bernard Arnault included diversification into a wide variety of luxury products. The company's wines, champagnes, haute couture and ready-to-wear fashions, cosmetics, fragrances, writing instruments, watches, and jewelry were among the most innovative, prestigious, elegant, and expensive produced. The company's retailing division focused on the sale of luxury items—whether LVMH products or brands offered by rival producers. The company's media division, for the most part, published periodicals of interest to the financial and art communities and its auction house specialized in the sale of fine art. LVMH's broad collection of businesses was grouped into six business units. Exhibit 4 presents LVMH's business portfolio in 2002.

Wine and Spirits

The production of extraordinary class wine and champagne required considerable attention to detail and decades-long commitment to quality. For example, Château d'Yquem's vineyards were cultivated over generations and were made up of vines grown from individually selected seeds. Also, on nine occasions during the 20th century the winery rejected an entire harvest, viewing all grapes from the season as unworthy of the brand. Wine production also required technical expertise to develop techniques to improve the immune systems of vines to prevent grape diseases and the skills of master blenders, who selected combinations of grapes that would result in exceptional vintages. Not any less important was the

time required to produce fine wines and champagnes, some of which were aged for several years prior to distribution. Distribution from production facilities to retail outlets was typically handled by either a subsidiary, a joint venture, or a third party.

In 2002 LVMH was the world's leading champagne producer, with a 22 percent global market share and a 2001 sales volume of 49.8 million bottles. The company was also number one in the global cognac market, with a 36 percent market share and a 2001 sales volume of 40.1 million bottles. Eighty-nine percent of LVMH's wine and spirits were sold outside of France. LVMH's still wine sales were becoming stronger as Newton's California wines and MountAdam's Australian wines benefited from Moët Hennessy's international distribution network and began to gain praise from connoisseurs beyond their domestic markets. The company's champagne sales declined by 7 percent in 2001 as retailers continued to reduce inventories built up prior to 1999's millennium celebrations and as demand for champagne in the United States fell by 29 percent after the September 11, 2001, terrorist attacks on Washington, D.C., and New York City. The sales of Hennessy and Hine expanded by 6 percent as the cognac market continued to grow in the United States and Asia.

Fashion and Leather Goods

The fashion and leather industry entailed the recruitment of highly talented and creative designers who were able to create a line of apparel or accessories that appealed to some segment of consumers. Designers had a great deal of leeway with the direction of their designs since individual tastes and preferences varied considerably among consumers. For example, whereas Ralph Lauren designs tended to reflect elements of men's and women's fashion that had been popular for decades, other designers such as LVMH's John Galliano (chief designer at Christian Dior) had caught the attention of the fashion world with a line of women's wear created from newspaper. Other important elements of creating high-end apparel and leather goods included the selection of fabrics or leather and the quality of construction. LVMH's Louis Vuitton products were all hand-assembled by craftsmen who had trained for years perfecting their talents. Apparel and leather goods were distributed to either third-party retailers or company-owned retail locations.

exhibit 3   **LVMH Acquisitions and Divestitures, 1987–2002**

	LVMH Acquisitions		
Year	**Company Acquired**	**Principal Business**	**Acquisition Cost**
1987	Hine	Cognac production	Not disclosed
1988	Givenchy	Haute couture, ready-to-wear fashions	FF 225 million
1990	11.4% of Guinness PLC (United Kingdom)	Brewing and spirits production and distribution	FF 8.2 billion
	10.75% of Loewe SA (Spain)	Leather goods, fashion	Not disclosed
	Pommery	Champagne production	Not disclosed
1991	67.5% of Asbach Brandy (Germany)	Brandy production	Not disclosed
	Morris E Curiel Distributing (Venezuela)	Beer distributing	Not disclosed
	Pampero (Venezuela)	Spirits production	Not disclosed
	70% of Union Cervecera (Spain)	Brewing	Not disclosed
1993	Christian Lacroix	Haute couture, ready-to-wear fashions	FF 80 million
	Kenzo	Haute couture, ready-to-wear fashions/ fragrances	FF 483 million
	55% of Desfosses International	Media production, magazines, radio	FF 126 million
1994	Outstanding 50% of *Investir*	Financial magazine	Not disclosed
	49.99% of Djedi Holding (Guerlain)	Fragrances	Not disclosed
1995	An additional 41% of Fred Joaillier	Haute couture, ready-to-wear fashions	Not disclosed
	44% of Desfosses International	Media production, magazines, radio	Not disclosed
1996	An additional 76% of Loewe SA (Spain)	Leather goods, fashion	€120 million
	Outstanding interest in Djedi Holding (Guerlain)	Fragrances	Not disclosed
	Outstanding 41% of Djedi Holding (Guerlain)	Fragrances	Not disclosed
	54% of Celine SA	Haute couture, ready-to-wear fashions	Not disclosed
	Remaining interest in Fred Joaillier	Haute couture, ready-to-wear fashions	Not disclosed
	58.75% of DFS (USA)	Duty-free retail shops in Asia/Pacific, airports	$2.6 billion
	Remaining 46% of Celine	Haute couture, ready-to-wear fashions	Not disclosed
1997	51% of Château d'Yquem	Champagne production	Not disclosed
	Sephora	Cosmetics retailing	FF 1.6 billion
	30% stake in Douglas International (Germany)	Cosmetics retailing	Not disclosed
1998	An additional 37% of Château d'Yquem	Champagne production	FF 111 million
	Marie-Jeanne Godard	Fragrances	€118 million
	Le Bon Marché	Department store in Paris	1,343,150 shares
	99% of La Belle Jardiniere	Retailer in Paris	Not disclosed
	Interest in Cie Financiere Laflachere	Household items, toiletries	Not disclosed
1999	Krug	Champagne production	FF 1 billion
	Increased interest to 52% in Cie Financiere Laflachere	Household items, toiletries	Not disclosed
	Increased interest in Gucci from 4.8% to 34.4%	Haute couture, ready-to-wear fashions	FF 7 billion
	70% of Bliss (USA)	Cosmetics production, health spas	Not disclosed
	BeneFit (USA)	Cosmetics production	Not disclosed
	Increased interest to 64% in Château d'Yquem	Champagne production	Not disclosed

(continued)

exhibit 3 **(concluded)**

LVMH Acquisitions		
Year	**Company Acquired** / **Principal Business**	**Acquisition Cost**

Year	Company Acquired	Principal Business	Acquisition Cost
	Hard Candy (USA)	Cosmetics production	Not disclosed
	TAG Heuer (Switzerland)	Watch design and assembly	SFr 1.15 billion
	70% of Thomas Pink (United Kingdom)	Haute couture, ready-to-wear fashions	£42 million
	Ebel (Switzerland)	Watch design and assembly	Not disclosed
	Chaumet	Watch design and assembly	Not disclosed
	Majority interest in Make Up For Ever (USA)	Cosmetics producer	Not disclosed
	Zenith (Switzerland)	Watch design and assembly, mechanism production	Not disclosed
	Radio Classique & SID Editions	French radio stations, media	Not disclosed
	5% of Oxygen Media (USA)	U.S. television and Internet media	Not disclosed
	72.5% interest in Phillips, de Pury & Luxembourg	Fine art auctioning	€90 million
2000	Miami Cruiseline Services (USA)	Duty free cruiseline retailing	€361 million
	67% of Emilio Pucci (Italy)	Haute couture, ready-to-wear fashions	Not disclosed
	Urban Decay (USA)	Cosmetics production	Not disclosed
	Omas (Italy)	Writing instrument production	Not disclosed
	25.50% of Fendi (Italy)	Haute couture, ready-to-wear fashions, furs	€295 million
	65% of Fresh Inc (USA)	Cosmetics production	Not disclosed
	Control of Boidi (Italy)	Cosmetics retailing	Not disclosed
	60% of Newton Vineyards (USA)	Winery and vineyards	$45 million
	An additional 5% of Oxygen Media (USA)	U.S. television and Internet media	Not disclosed
	MountAdam Vineyards (Australia)	Winery and vineyards	Included w/Newton
	L'Etude Tajan	Fine art auctioning	Not disclosed
	Micromania	Videogame retailing	Not disclosed
	Art & Auction, Connaissance des Arts	Art magazines	Not disclosed
2001	Majority interest in La Samaritaine	Parisian department store	Not disclosed
	Donna Karan International (USA)	Haute couture, ready-to-wear fashions	$243 million
	Morellato (Italy)	Watch bracelet producer	Not disclosed
	50% interest in Acqua di Parma (Italy)	Fragrances	Not disclosed

LVMH Divestitures		

Year	Company Divested	Principal Business	Sales Price
1993	RoC Group	Cosmetics producer	FF 1,314 million
1997	9.43% of Guinness PLC	Brewing and spirits producer and distributor	FF 7,989 million
	50% of Christian Dior Perfumes Inc (USA)	Fragrances	Not disclosed
	Delbard Group	Roses and fruit tree producer	Not disclosed
1999	Simi Winery (USA)	Winery	Not disclosed
2001	34.4% interest in Gucci	Haute couture, ready-to-wear fashions	$806.5 million
2002	Pommery	Champagne producer	€230 million
	45% interest in Phillips, de Pury & Luxembourg	Fine art auctioning	Not disclosed

Source: Extel Financial Limited Annual Card, April 24, 2002.

exhibit 4 **LVMH's Business Portfolio in 2002**

Wines and Spirits	Fashion and Leather Goods	Perfumes and Cosmetics	Watches and Jewelry	Selective Retailing	Media and Other Businesses
Moët & Chandon	Louis Vuitton	Parfums Christian Dior	TAG Heuer	Duty Free Shoppers (DFS)	*L'Etrude Tajan*
Dom Pérignon	Loewe	Guerlain	Ebel	Miami Cruiseline	Advertising agency
Veuve Clicquot	Celine	Parfums Givenchy	Zenith	Sephora	Press agency
Krug	Berlucci	Kenzo Parfums	Benedom—CD Montres	Le Bon Marché	Radio Classique
Mercier	Kenzo	Bliss	Fred	La Samaritaine	*La Tribune*
Ruinart	Givenchy	Hard Candy	Chaumet		*Investir*
Canard-Duchêne	Christian Lacroix	BeneFit Cosmetics	Omas		*Jazzman*
Château d'Yquem	Marc Jacobs	Urban Decay	LVMH/De Beers		*Le Monde de la Musique*
Chandon Estates	Fendi	Fresh	joint venture		*Défis*
Cloudy Bay	StefanoBi	Make Up For Ever			*SID Editions*
Cape Mentelle	Emilio Pucci	Laflachère			*Salon des Entrepreneurs*
Hennessy	Thomas Pink	Acqua di Parma			5 news-related Internet sites
Hine	Donna Karan				*Connaissance des Arts*
Newton					*Art and Auction*
MountAdam					Sephora.com
					eLUXURY.com

Source: LVMH Web site.

LVMH's Louis Vuitton was the world's leading luxury brand and the foundation of LVMH's Fashion and Leather Goods division, which had increased both sales and operating income by more than 100 percent between 1998 and 2001. LVMH's Fashion and Leather Goods division also included such prestigious brands as Kenzo, Christian Lacroix, Marc Jacobs, Berlucci, Thomas Pink, Donna Karan, Emilio Pucci, Givenchy, Celine, and Fendi. In 2001, Louis Vuitton grew by 9 percent, while the entire division grew by 13 percent. The group outpaced its key rivals by a notable margin as Prada Group's sales increased by 5 percent (the sales of the Prada brand grew by 1 percent), Hermes' sales grew by 6 percent, and Groupe Gucci's sales increased by 1 percent, while the Gucci brand grew by 4 percent. France accounted for 11 percent of the division's sales.

Perfumes and Cosmetics

Success in the global cosmetics, fragrance, and toiletry (CFT) industry was largely attributable to the ability of producers to develop new combinations of chemicals and natural ingredients to create innovative and unique fragrances and develop cosmetics that boasted product benefits beyond cleansing and moisturizing to anti-aging, antipollution, firming, and sebum regulation. The industry was highly fragmented, with various distribution channels and multiple subcategories existing within each product category. For example, within the color cosmetics category, products like eyeliner, mascara, foundation, concealer, nail polish, and lipstick could be purchased from supermarkets, drugstores, discounters, specialty retailers, department stores, or direct sellers such as Mary Kay or Avon. In addition, the sales growth rates for the subcategories of beauty products could also vary greatly. For example, between 2000 and 2001, the U.S. sales of eye shadow increased by nearly 14 percent, while the sales of foundation declined by 2 percent. The market for beauty products was also segmented by consumer demographics and by geography. Teen consumers tended to look for specific product characteristics that were very different from what was expected by baby boomers. Country-specific differences in consumer preferences and complexions further fragmented the global CFT industry, while market penetration rate created varying growth opportunities across the world.

LVMH's perfumes and cosmetics business led the European luxury segment and had outpaced industry growth by 18.0 percent in 1999, 17.5 percent in 2000, and 5.0 percent in 2001 to reach sales of 2.2 billion euros at year-end 2001. The company's growth was attributed to its strong brands, new product introductions that included Flower by Kenzo, J'adore by Christian Dior, Hot Couture by Givenchy, and Michael by Michael Kors; the addition of new American cosmetics brands such as BeneFit, Fresh, Urban Decay, and Make Up For Ever; and the success of its Sephora retail cosmetics operations. Sephora's network of stores located in Europe, the United States, and Japan carried LVMH's perfumes and cosmetics brands, which were also sold by prestigious retailers around the world. The division also included Laflachère—France's leading brand of hygiene, beauty, and household cleaning products. Even though LVHM's perfumes and cosmetics division had recorded impressive growth rates, its sales ranked it seventh in the industry and were only about one-sixth that of industry leader L'Oréal. Approximately 80 percent of the division's sales were outside of France.

Watches and Jewelry

The watch and jewelry industry was much like the fashion and CFT industries in that it was highly fragmented with multiple product categories and wide-ranging price points. The upscale segment of the industry also reflected the fashion industry's demand for quality and creative or distinctive designs. The producers of many exquisite timepieces such as Rolex, Cartier, and Patek Phillipe maintained long-established lines known not only for style but also for craftsmanship and accuracy. Most manufacturers of upmarket watches also added new models from time to time that were consistent with the company's tradition, history, and style. Watch production involved the development and production of the movement (although many watch manufacturers purchased movements from third-party suppliers), case design and fabrication, and assembly. Watches were rarely sold by manufacturers directly to consumers but rather were usually distributed to independent jewelers or large upscale department stores.

LVMH's watch and jewelry division was established in 1999 with the acquisitions of TAG Heuer, Ebel, Chaumet, Benedom-Christian Dior, and Zenith. The Omas line of Italian pens was added in 2000. The company's most popular watches included TAG Heuer's Kirium F1 and Monza lines, Christian Dior's

Chris 47, and Ebel Beluga and Classic Wave. Zenith was the only Swiss watchmaker to produce chronographs without outsourcing the movement. The automatic chronograph movement utilized in its El Primero also equipped the Rolex Daytona and other fine Swiss chronographs. New watch and jewelry lines by Ebel, Christian Dior Watches, Chaumet, and Fred were scheduled for release in 2002.

The division experienced a sales decline of 11 percent during 2001 as it withdrew from contract manufacturing for third-party brands. LVMH acquired the supplier of its TAG Heuer watch bracelets and opened a TAG Heuer boutique in London in 2001. The division also opened new Fred jewelry stores in Paris, London, and Tokyo during 2001. LVMH planned to open an Omas shop in Milan and its first De Beers jewelry store during 2002. The first De Beers store would be located in London and was to be part of a worldwide chain of jewelry stores that would be operated as a joint venture between LVMH and De Beers Centenary AG, the world's largest producers of diamonds. Only 7 percent of LVMH's sales of watches and jewelry originated from France.

Selective Retailing

LVMH's selective retailing division was made up of DFS and Miami Cruiseline duty-free stores, Le Bon Marché and La Samaritaine department stores, and Sephora cosmetics stores. The division also operated upscale Galleria shopping malls located in downtown areas of major air destinations in the Asia-Pacific region and the United States. LVMH's Gallerias featured DFS stores, Sephora, and designer boutiques such as Louis Vuitton, Hermes, Chanel, Prada, Fendi, Celine, Bulgari, and Tiffany. LVMH opened two new Gallerias in 2001—one located in Hawaii and the other in Hollywood, California.

Le Bon Marché was Paris's most exclusive department store, and La Samaritaine—the city's largest department store—was being repositioned with an emphasis on upscale fashion and accessories. Sephora was the leading retail beauty chain in France and the United States, and the second largest beauty chain in Europe. In 2001 Sephora operated more than 225 stores in Europe and more than 80 stores in the United States, all of which carried LVMH's products and other prestigious brands of cosmetics, fragrances, and skin care products, including Chanel, Dolce and Gabbana, Elizabeth Arden, Hugo Boss, Naomi Campbell, Gianni Versace, and Burberry. Sephora had operated

seven stores in Japan, but withdrew from that market and from Germany in 2001. A change in strategy initiated in 2001 called for the chain to focus on country markets where it could achieve profitable growth, such as the United States, Italy, France, and Greece. LVMH believed that developing countries such as Poland and Romania also presented profitable growth opportunities for Sephora.

The division's 2001 sales grew by 6 percent even though the sales of DFS fell by 10 percent after tourism in the Asia-Pacific region fell by more than 50 percent after the September 11, 2001, terrorist attacks on the United States. Sephora's sales increased 23 percent during 2001 with its strongest performance coming in the United States, Portugal, Italy, France, and the United Kingdom. Exhibit 5 depicts LVMH's global network of company-owned fashion, watch and jewelry, and selective retail stores by geographic region.

Other Businesses

LVMH also maintained a business unit made up of media, art auction, and e-commerce businesses. Media operations included six print publications sold in France, two art-related publications marketed to the international art market, business newsletters, and a French radio network. The division's other media businesses included an advertising sales company, an audiovisual press agency, and four news-related Internet sites. The most prominent businesses of LVMH's media sector were *Investir*, France's leading online and print daily investment publication; Radio Classique's network of radio stations across France, which attracted 600,000 listeners a day; *Connaissance des Arts* and *Art & Auction*, which were benchmark art publications with monthly circulations of 40,000 and 17,500, respectively; and *Jazzman* and *Le Monde de la Musique*, two leading French music publications.

The company held an interest in Phillips, de Pury & Luxembourg, the world's third largest auction house specializing in fine art and antiquities, and owned L'Etrude Tajan, the leading fine art auction house in France. The group's eLUXURY Web site was launched in June 2000 and offered more than 50 of the world's most exclusive brands, including LVMH's Louis Vuitton, Dior, Fred, Guerlain, and Celine and a number of non-LVMH luxury brands. Sephora.com offered the largest and most diverse selection of beauty products on the Internet with over 11,000 products and more than 230 brands. The division's

exhibit 5   **LVMH's Global Network of Retail Stores, 2000 and 2001**

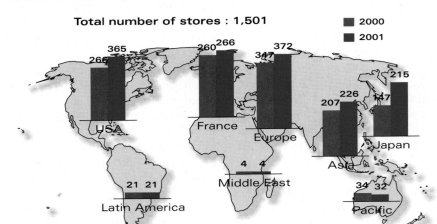

Source: LVMH 2001 Annual Results Presentation.

operating loss of 372 million euros in 2001 was largely attributable to Internet development costs and expansion costs at Phillips, de Pury & Luxembourg.

LVMH's performance by business group for 1999–2001 is presented in Exhibit 6.

LVMH's Corporate Strategy

Although much of LVMH's growth was attributable to the acquisition of new businesses, Arnault placed an emphasis on internal growth by exploiting common strategies and capturing strategic-fit benefits across the portfolio. Arnault based the company's strategies on a set of core values that were essential to the success of each business unit. Arnault demanded that each of the corporation's businesses demonstrate commitment to creativity, innovation, and product excellence. The long-term success of LVMH's brands, in Arnault's view, was largely a function of artistic creativity, technological innovation, and the closest attention to every detail of the production process. Innovation and creativity contributed to internal growth among LVMH's businesses, with new products accounting for more than 18 percent of Louis Vuitton's 2001 sales and more than 20 percent of LVMH's cosmetics and fragrance sales in 2001. LVMH management believed that by 2005 more than 10 percent of the company's champagne sales would be generated by 15 new cuvées introduced in 1998.

The image and reputation of the company's products were seen as equal to the creativity and craftsmanship employed during the development and production of LVMH luxury goods since image was a product dimension that defied logic but caused consumers to have strong desires for a particular brand. Arnault believed that image was priceless and irreplaceable, and that it required stringent management control over every element of a brand's image, including advertisements, corporate announcements, and speeches by management and designers.

The final element of LVMH's corporate strategy—control over the distribution and sale of its products—allowed its divisions to listen to customer needs, better understand their tastes, and anticipate their desires. LVMH's ownership of more than 1,500 retail locations in developed countries throughout the world also allowed the company to refine its brands' images with controlled store aesthetics, a consistent retailing approach, and irreproachable customer service.

Bernard Arnault discussed LVMH's strategic approach to managing its portfolio of star brands in an October 2001 *Harvard Business Review* interview:

Product Quality
The problem is that the quality of timelessness takes years to develop, even decades. You cannot just decree it. A brand has to pay its dues—it has to come to stand for something in the eyes of the world. But you can, as

exhibit 6   **LVMH's Performance by Business Group, 1999–2001 (in millions of euros)**

	2001	2000	1999
Sales			
Wine and spirits	€ 2,232	€ 2,336	€2,240
Fashion and leather goods	3,612	3,202	2,295
Perfumes and cosmetics	2,231	2,072	1,703
Watches and jewelry	548	614	135
Selective retailing	3,475	3,287	2,162
Other businesses and eliminations	131	70	12
Total	€12,229	€11,581	€8,547
Operating profit			
Wine and spirits	€ 676	€ 716	€ 655
Fashion and leather goods	1,274	1,169	826
Perfumes and cosmetics	149	184	146
Watches and jewelry	27	59	5
Selective retailing	(194)	(2)	(2)
Other businesses and eliminations	(372)	(167)	(83)
Total	€ 1,560	€ 1,959	€1,547
Capital expenditures			
Wine and spirits	€ 61	€ 66	€ 52
Fashion and leather goods	210	194	155
Perfumes and cosmetics	90	83	68
Watches and jewelry	26	16	9
Selective retailing	205	294	266
Other businesses and eliminations	392	204	24
Total	€ 984	€ 857	€ 574

Source: LVMH 2001 annual report.

a manager, enhance timelessness—that is, create the impression of timelessness sooner rather than later. And you do that with uncompromising quality.

A lot of companies talk about quality, but if you want your brand to be timeless, you have to be a fanatic about it. Before we launch a Louis Vuitton suitcase, for example, we put it in a torture machine, where it is opened and closed five times per minute for three weeks. And that is not all—it is thrown, and shaken, and crushed. You would laugh if you saw what we do, but that is how you build something that becomes an heirloom. By the way, we put some of our competitors' products through the same tests, and they come out like bouillie—the mush babies eat.

Quality also comes from hiring very dedicated people and then keeping them for a long time. We try to keep the people at the brands, especially the artisans—the seamstresses and other people who make

the products—because they have the brand in their bones—its history, its meaning. At the stores, too, many of the salespeople have the brand in their bones. Most companies clean house when they acquire a new brand. We don't do that because we have found it hurts quality terribly. When you clean house, you usher out the people who respect the brand the most and who contribute to its longevity, its timelessness, its authenticity.

Innovation

Fashion, of course, comes from innovation—the creativity of the designers. That is sometimes harder to guarantee than quality, which you can actually build in to a product, but just as important. The hard truth is, you must be old and new at once. In a star brand you honor your past and invent your future at the same time. It is a subtle balance.

If you think and act like a typical manager around creative people—with rules, policies, data on customer preferences, and so forth—you will quickly kill their talent. Our whole business is based on giving our artists and designers complete freedom to invent without limits.

Our philosophy is quite simple, really. If you look over a creative person's shoulder, he will stop doing great work. Wouldn't you, if some manager were watching your every move, clutching a calculator in his hand? So that is why LVMH is, as a company, so decentralized. Each brand very much runs itself, headed by its own artistic director. Central headquarters in Paris is very small, especially for a company with 54,000 employees and 1,300 stores around the world. There are only 250 of us, and I assure you, we do not lurk around every corner, questioning every creative decision.

The most successful creative people want to see their creations in the street. They don't invent just to invent. Yes, they come up with many exciting ideas, and many of these ideas shock; they look crazy at first, completely crazy. But the true artists that make LVMH a success, they don't want the process to end there. They want people to wear their dresses, or spray their perfume, or carry the luggage they have designed.

The responsibility of the manager in a company dependent on innovation, then, very much becomes picking the right creative people—the ones who want to see their designs on the street. And that desire inside them is something that you, as a leader of a company, can only sense. After all, most artists don't go around proclaiming, "I want to be a commercial success." They would actually hate to say that. And frankly, if you asked them, they would say they don't actually care one way or another if people buy their products. But they do care. It's just buried in their DNA, and as a manager, you have to be able to see it there. I know you are going to ask, "How can I see into a person's DNA, to know if he is an artist with commercial instincts?" So I will answer, it just takes experience. Years of practice—trial and error—and you learn.

And just as important, to allow creativity to happen, a company has to be filled with managers who have a certain love of artists and designers—or whatever kind of creative person you have in your company, if you deeply appreciate and love what creative people do and how they think, which is usually in unpredictable and irrational ways, then you can start to understand them. And finally, you can see inside their minds and DNA.

Image

Without growth, it is not a star brand, as far as I am concerned. In 2000, Louis Vuitton, which is by far the largest luxury brand in the world, had 40% growth in sales, which makes it a superstar, no? Growth shows the shareholders that you have struck the right balance between timelessness and fashion and that you have been able to charge a premium price because of that correct balance.

Now, growth is not just a function of high price. You also grow when you move into new markets, such as those in developing countries. But mainly, growth is a function of high desire. Customers must want the product. That sounds simple, I am sure, but to get advertising right is very, very difficult—it's difficult to get advertising to represent the true brand. Most companies think it is enough to use advertising to present a picture of the product. That's not enough. You need to project the image of the brand itself.

The latest Dior ad campaign is a perfect example of how to do this right. [A Parfums Christian Dior J'adore advertisement is presented in Exhibit 7.] You would know this was an ad for a Dior product even without the name of the company there. You cannot mistake it for anything else. You know this is Dior because the model projects the image of the brand—very sexy and modern, very feminine and energetic.

The last thing you should do is assign advertising to your marketing department. If you do that, you lose the proximity between the designers and the message to the marketplace. At LVMH, we keep the advertising right inside the design team. With the Dior campaign, John Galliano (chief designer) himself did the makeup on the model. He posed her. The only thing Galliano did not do himself was snap the photo.

Craftsmanship and the Production Process

It is true that the front end of a star brand—the innovation, supporting the creative process, the advertising, and so on—is very, very expensive. High profitability comes at the back end of the process, and behind the scenes.

It comes in the atelier—the factory. Our products have unbelievably high quality; they have to. But their production is organized in such a way that we also have unbelievably high productivity. The atelier is a place of amazing discipline and rigor. Every single motion, every step of every process, is carefully planned with the most modern and complete engineering technology. It's not unlike how cars are made in the most modern factories. We analyze how to make each part of the product, where to buy each component, where to find the best leather at the best price, what treatment it should receive. A single purse can have up to 1,000 manufacturing tasks, and we plan each and every one. In that way, the LVMH production process is the exact opposite of its creative process, which is so freewheeling and chaotic.

exhibit 7   **Advertisement for Parfums Christian Dior J'adore**

Source: Parfums Christian Dior Web site.

If you walk into a Vuitton factory, you will see very few machines. Almost every piece is made by hand. Usually, piecework is the most inefficient operating system in the world, but for us it is different because we give our craftsmen and craftswomen fantastic training. They are trained for months before they touch the products, and then, every task they do has been studied and refined for many years, so we know precisely how to arrange the atelier. No motion is wasted there. And that allows us to offer a very high quality product at a cost that makes our business very profitable.

The one catch to this system is that it takes time. You cannot rush the training of the artisans or the planning of the atelier to make a product at maximum efficiency. When we come up with a new purse, for instance, it takes months to plan a process for producing it so that it will be profitable. So sometimes customers have to wait because output is so limited. Which is why you get long lines outside your stores. And actually, that is not such a bad thing sometimes, because those lines have a way of increasing demand even further. But the main reason for the lines of customers is the combination of exceptional quality and craftsmanship at a good price.

Risk Tolerance

We don't like failures. We try to avoid them. That is why, with many of our new products, we make a limited number. We do not put the entire company at risk by introducing all new products all the time. In any given year, in fact, only 15% of our business comes from the new; the rest comes from traditional, proven products—the classics.

Vuitton is a perfect example. This year, Marc Jacobs came up with the graffiti design, and it was a big departure for the line. Did you see it? It is beautiful and crazy, right? It does not look like Vuitton at first glance; who would have thought of that on suitcases? But we only had that on several items—for which, by the way, there is now a waiting list worldwide. The rest of the products were Vuitton that you could have bought last year, or five years ago, or ten years from now. They are legacy pieces.

We will use the same approach with the new Dior handbag. It is very exciting, very expensive. You will see it in all the ads and want to buy it. I assure you we will be out of stock fast. But it is very expensive: $1,800. We will make only several thousand of them. The rest of the line will reflect some ideas of that new purse—the same shape—but will be less radical in terms of fabrics and design. We will make more of those and sell them for less. That way, we can have our creativity but also minimize risk.

Of course, with some businesses, you cannot avoid risk, and sometimes you do not succeed. And so you learn. With still other businesses, you cannot say they are outright failures or learning experiences, just that their success is taking time. That is the case with Christian Lacroix.

At the beginning, we thought, "Okay, we have a genius here with Christian Lacroix," but we learned that genius is not enough to succeed. It was something of a shock, to be honest, to discover that even great talent could not launch a brand from zero. A brand must have a heritage; there are no shortcuts.

The fact is, star brands take time to grow. Take some of the small makeup companies we have acquired recently, like Bliss and Urban Decay. When we bought them, they were little start-ups run by their founders—very simple businesses, but with a lot of originality in the products. So now we know we must nurture them until they have some history. But even if it takes ten or 15 years for them to become stars, that has been an amazing investment, right?

Capturing Synergies between Business Units

LVMH management had identified a variety of opportunities for its portfolio of businesses to share best practices, leverage competencies and skills, and combine common activities to reduce expenses. In 1999, the company created its training institute, LVMH House, in London to allow managers from different businesses, job classifications, or geographic regions to discuss such issues as leadership, technological innovation, design innovation, and operating efficiency and share their personal knowledge and experiences. By year-end 2001, more than 600 LVMH managers had attended LVMH House forums. The interactions between managers from different divisions had spawned continuing discussions of strategy and operations via the company's intranet and had initiated several intercompany projects.

Much of LVMH's Internet strategy resulted from forums held at LVMH House between May and October 2001. The theme of forum sessions focused on business-to-business, business-to-enterprise, and business-to-consumer opportunities and resulted in the formulation of strategies used in the development of LVMH's 50-plus brand Web sites and e-commerce activities at ThomasPink.com, eLUXURY.com, and

Sephora.com. The forums also helped the company implement online information exchange systems between some LVMH businesses and their suppliers and distributors. The company had successfully instituted the e-procurement of office supplies at Moët & Chandon and had created a common internal communications system called LVMH pl@net that allowed its businesses to share information through company intranets.

Among the most important competencies that LVMH management had hoped to transfer between businesses was its approach to customer relationship management. LVMH management believed that its ability to develop richer, deeper ties with a targeted group of customers was essential to building customer loyalty for its prestigious luxury brands. Relationship management entailed maintaining personal communications with customers through mail, e-mail, Internet sites, or in-store systems to transform an initial impulse purchase into more frequent purchases for larger amounts. LVMH's president of Parfums Christian Dior suggested, "The better you know your customers, the better you can define messages and actions that will trigger their desire to purchase products."[9]

Customer relationship management also allowed LVMH to pursue cross-selling opportunities between product lines. A Louis Vuitton executive explained, "A customer who bought a trendy leather goods item like a Monogram Graffiti bag is likely to be interested in our ready-to-wear lines, and should be on the list to receive special communications on our latest collection."[10] In 2001, Parfums Christian Dior had conducted joint promotions with Christian Dior Couture in major department stores to introduce fragrance customers to Dior fashions. LVMH's Moët & Chandon also conducted joint promotions with the company's fashion businesses to promote its name among established purchasers of LVMH fashions by creating the Moët & Chandon Fashion Awards and the Moët Fashion Debut.

LVMH had achieved cost savings through the development of a common research and development group for its variety of fragrance and cosmetics brands. Beginning in 2000, LVMH Laboratories' 220 researchers developed beauty care, makeup, and

[9]Quoted in "Focus on Customer Relationship Management," www.lvmh.com.
[10]Quoted in "Special Report: Internet at the Heart of Customer Relationship Management," www.lvmh.com.

fragrance solutions for Dior, Guerlain, and Givenchy and conducted development work for Kenzo Parfums and its U.S. cosmetics brands (BeneFit, Bliss, Urban Decay, Hard Candy, and Fresh). The development of LVMH Laboratories not only allowed competencies and resources to be shared between the company's cosmetics and fragrance brands but also created a single office responsible for toxicology research and regulatory affairs.

LVMH also began implementing a common supply chain management system in its perfumes and cosmetics business in 2001 that would allow its brands to manage orders, production, purchasing, accounting, finance, and inventories. The new enterprise resource planning (ERP) system had been partially employed at Parfums Christian Dior and was expected to lead eventually to substantial improvements in margins and cash flow, out-of-stock rates, obsolescence costs, and product freshness and availability since the CFT industry required product lines that might include thousands of products. Efficient inventory management was also critical to success in the CFT industry since items were very expensive and fragile and since retailers demanded quick renewal rates.

LVMH IN 2002: LUXURY PRODUCTS AND GLOBAL ECONOMIC UNCERTAINTY

LVMH's slowing sales growth and declining profitability was, in some part, a function of declining demand for luxury goods. Its dilemma was not unlike that of other luxury goods producers like Prada, Richemont, Gucci, and Bulgari, which had all issued profit warnings in 2001. Beginning in 2000, most developed countries had experienced some economic slowdown, which was compounded by the effects of the September 11, 2001, terrorist attacks on the United States. The threat of terrorism had contributed to a decline in international travel during late 2001 and had created an emotional climate where champagne, designer fashions, and expensive timepieces seemed less important than during the boom years of the late 1990s. For example, the global sales of champagne declined by 20 percent during 2001 and the men's apparel industry declined 7 percent—falling from $60.9 billion in 2000 to

$54.7 billion in 2001. The chief executive of Richemont, owner of Cartier, Dunhill, and Montblanc brands, explained the state of the luxury goods industry by suggesting, "We sell the feelgood factor and there are few people in the world that feel good, especially after 11 September."[11]

Some analysts and investors believed that LVMH's problems ran deeper than a cyclical move away from spending on big-ticket luxury items. Arnault had been criticized for his purchase of Phillips, de Pury & Luxembourg in 1999 and his subsequent attempts to unseat incumbents Sotheby's and Christie's as the world's two leaders among fine art auctioning. Some believed the move was part of an ongoing personal rivalry between Arnault and Pinault-Printemps-Redoute chairman Francois Pinault, who had purchased Christie's in 1998. Arnault had attempted to acquire Sotheby's after Pinault's acquisition of Christie's but was unable to agree on a price.

Under Arnault, Phillips, de Pury & Luxembourg undertook aggressive strategies to make a name for itself in the art auction industry such as offering generous guarantees to win prestigious consignments. However, Phillips's auctions frequently failed to meet the guarantees, leaving the art auction house liable for the shortfall. It was estimated that Phillips, de Pury & Luxembourg lost $80 million on one auction alone. Phillips's management justified the guarantees, claiming that the tactics would allow the auction house to build market share. However, analysts questioned the overall strategy to overtake either Sotheby's or Christie's, arguing that there was not room in the fine art market for three auction houses since there were only about 50 private collectors who bought works of art for $20 million or more. Among others, a J. P. Morgan analyst claimed, "The deal didn't make any sense to begin with. Auction houses are not luxury goods, so why bother with that?"[12] LVMH's art auction house recorded a net loss of approximately $150 million in fiscal 2001.

Analysts and investors also questioned the company's acquisition of Donna Karan, claiming the brand did not meet Arnault's star brand criteria. Donna Karan became known worldwide during the late 1980s as her sophisticated business suits became

[11]Quoted in "Fading Feelgood Factor Leaves Luxury Labels Tarnished," *Independent*, November 18, 2001, p. B5.

[12]Quoted in "Luxury Conglomerate Sells Its Art Auction House," *New York Times*, February 20, 2002, p. C1.

a hit with executive women and her DKNY casual wear obtained a dedicated following among urban women for after-business attire. However, beginning in 1996, Donna Karan International began to lose favor with upscale consumers as Karan's designs strayed from her traditional roots into a hodgepodge of unrelated styles. Donna Karan also pushed the company into financial distress as she spent lavishly on a New York flagship store and designs that never made it to the runway. The brand was tarnished further when Donna Karan signed licensing agreements that allowed Haggar to produce and distribute Donna Karan branded men's slacks and Van Heusen to produce and sell Donna Karan shirts. In addition, Donna Karan lost prestigious retail accounts like Neiman Marcus when DKNY liquidated its growing inventories to discounter T. J. Maxx. Arnault justified the acquisition, claiming that "what appealed to us is the fact that [Donna Karan] is one of the best-known brand names in the world."[13]

Investors also called for Arnault to examine the worth of LVMH's selective retailing businesses. DFS and Sephora had each lost approximately $100 million during 2001, and the company's department stores in Paris required considerable capital investments and carried brands outside of LVMH's portfolio. A Merrill Lynch analyst suggested that LVMH "should focus on high-end luxury brands and not pour more money into low-margin and capital-intensive retailing."[14] LVMH's head of its perfume and cosmetics business supported concerns of investors by stating, "The fact that LVMH owns DFS and Sephora is entirely neutral to my business. To be successful they have to treat competitors as they treat me. There is no synergy from having these two businesses."[15]

Bernard Arnault began restructuring LVMH's portfolio during the first six months of 2002, divesting more than €800 million worth of assets that included a portion of its stake in Phillips, de Pury & Luxembourg; Pommery Champagne; and certain real estate properties. LVMH's sale of Pommery Champagne for approximately €230 million allowed it to retain the world's fifth largest champagne producer's 470 hectares of vineyards. The sales price of Phillips, de Pury & Luxembourg was not disclosed but was suggested by insiders to be less than LVMH's original €90 million investment. Arnault dismissed reports claiming that the company was considering the sale of DFS, Miami Cruiseline, Le Bon Marché, La Samaritaine, and Sephora by stating, "I do not plan to sell them in this current market—so they are not for sale"; he acknowledged, however, that "these retailing businesses are loss-making. We do not like businesses that lose money, but we know why they are losing money and we will fix them."[16] Arnault also denied reports that LVMH was considering the sale of Loewe.

With Arnault controlling 48 percent of LVMH shares and a majority of shareholder votes, many analysts believed that portfolio restructuring would come slowly at LVMH. A Merrill Lynch luxury goods analyst likened Arnault's penchant for acquisitions to that of a collector of fine art (which Bernard Arnault was) observing, "Arnault has rarely sold anything."[17] An ABN Ambro analyst characterized Arnault as "not a man who likes to admit he has been wrong on a number of occasions . . . so the disposal process may be slow."[18] Arnault hinted that he might divest LVMH's selective retailing businesses in the future when he stated that "retailing is not a core business for LVMH" and suggested that the company would not "expand further in retailing beyond our existing plans."[19] There was also some belief that, rather than retrench, Arnault might like to expand the portfolio further, with Giorgio Armani, Tiffany & Company, and Bulgari named as potential acquisition candidates.

LVMH's stock performance between 1994 and May 2002 is tracked in Exhibit 8. The company's consolidated statements of income and balance sheets for 1999 through 2001 are presented in Exhibits 9 and 10, respectively. The company's first-quarter 2002 sales of wines and spirits increased 19

---

[13]Quoted in *The Business,* April 7, 2002.

[14]Quoted in "A Veteran Dealmaker Chews Over His Core," *Financial Times,* November 21, 2001, p. 16.

[15]Ibid.

[16]Quoted in "Retailing Is 'Non-Core' for LVMH, Says Arnault," *Financial Times,* November 21, 2001, p. 30.

[17]Ibid.

[18]Quoted in "LVMH's Auction House Sale Reflects Troubles," *Daily Deal,* February 21, 2001.

[19]Quoted in "A Veteran Dealmaker Chews Over His Core."

exhibit 8   **Market Performance of LVMH's Common Stock, by Quarter, 1994–May 2002**

(a) Trend in LVMH's Common Stock Price

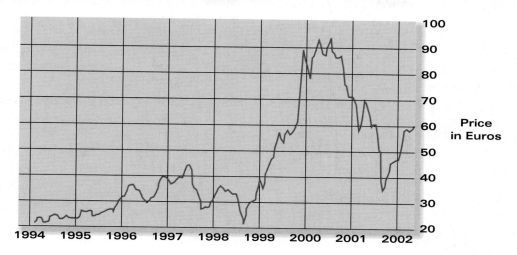

(b) Performance of LVMH's Stock Price versus the Paris Stock Exchange

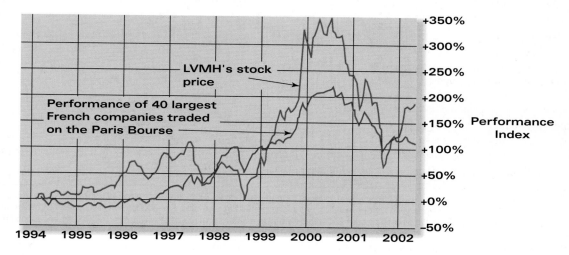

percent over those of first quarter 2001. Its first-quarter 2002 fashion and leather goods sales increased 22 percent over the same period in 2001, while the sales of its selective retailing division declined by 5 percent. The company's sales of watches, jewelry, perfumes, and cosmetics remained nearly unchanged between the first quarter of 2001 and the first quarter of 2002.

exhibit 9 **LVMH's Statements of Income, 1999–2001 (in millions of euros, except per share amounts)**

	2001	2000	1999
Net sales	€12,229	€11,581	€8,547
Cost of sales	4,654	4,221	3,132
Gross margin	7,575	7,360	5,415
Marketing and selling expenses	4,568	4,206	2,964
General and administrative expenses	1,447	1,195	904
Income from operations	1,560	1,959	1,547
Financial expense—net	459	421	227
Dividends from nonconsolidated investments	21	45	97
Other income or expense—net*	(455)	109	18
Income before income taxes	667	1,692	1,435
Income taxes	192	633	554
Income (loss) from investments accounted for using the equity method	(42)	(34)	(6)
Net income before amortization of goodwill, minority interests, and unusual items	433	1,025	875
Amortization of goodwill	168	141	102
Net income before minority interests and unusual items	265	884	773
Minority interests	(99)	(179)	(137)
Net income before unusual items	166	705	636
Unusual items†	(156)	17	57
Net income	€ 10	€ 722	€ 693
Earnings per share before amortization of goodwill, minority interests, and unusual items	€ 0.89	€ 2.11	€ 1.81
Fully diluted earnings per share before amortization of goodwill, minority interests, and unusual items	€ 0.89	€ 2.11	€ 1.81
Earnings per share	€ 0.02	€ 1.49	€ 1.43
Fully diluted earnings per share	€ 0.02	€ 1.49	€ 1.43
Average number of common shares outstanding during the year	488,064,659	484,800,930	483,157,146
Number of common shares and share equivalents after dilution	488,072,374	484,886,474	483,445,278

*Other income and expenses include the results linked to LVMH's treasury shares; in 2001, this item included 39 million euros of realized capital gains and a 343 million euro provision for depreciation of the shares held at year-end. For 2000, LVMH recorded 115 million euros of capital gains from the sales of its treasury shares. In 2001, this item also includes various asset write-offs, notably for unconsolidated equity investments.

†Unusual items include €864 million of proceeds from Gucci, which include €774 million in capital gains from the disposal of these shares and €90 million for an exceptional dividend received in the fourth quarter. Unusual charges included €446 million in restructuring provisions, €385 million of which was for Selective Retailing in order to lower the break-even point of these companies, which are very sensitive to economic fluctuations. Exceptional asset depreciation totaling €480 million was also recorded. This figure includes €323 million for DFS goodwill, €83 million on the Bouygues equity stake and €60 million on the Group's unconsolidated equity investments in the new technologies business. Lastly, the balance includes notably a charge for the sale of LVMH's controlling stake in Phillips, de Pury & Luxembourg to its current principals at December 31, 2001, including a full write-off of goodwill. Unusual items are disclosed net of a €71 million positive tax effect. The €57 million unusual income item for 1999 reflects the €315 million gain realized as a result of the Diageo share buy-back program, to which LVMH tendered 143 million shares. This was partly offset by indirect charges related to the acquisition of equity interests; by a provision related to the residual interest in Diageo; by reorganization costs related to Fashion activities and logistics; and by asset depreciations, primarily related to intangible assets.

Source: LVMH 2001 annual report.

exhibit 10   **LVMH's Balance Sheets, 1999–2001 (in millions of euros)**

	2001	2000	1999
Assets			
Current assets			
Cash and cash equivalents	€ 795	€ 695	€ 546
Short-term investments	622	1,326	183
Treasury shares	1,046	1,289	853
Trade accounts receivable	1,538	1,638	1,442
Deferred income taxes	544	266	273
Inventories	3,655	3,382	2,943
Prepaid expenses and other current assets	1,352	1,596	1,500
Total current assets	9,552	10,192	7,740
Investments and other assets circulant			
Investments accounted for using the equity method	77	21	10
Unconsolidated investments and other investments	1,386	1,892	3,959
Treasury shares	318	156	210
Other noncurrent assets	467	307	251
Property, plant and equipment, net	4,208	3,367	2,856
Brands & other intangible assets, net	4,308	3,415	2,527
Goodwill, net	3,516	3,842	3,181
Total, other assets	14,280	13,000	12,994
Total assets	€23,832	€23,192	€20,734
Liabilities and stockholders' equity			
Current liabilities			
Short-term borrowings	€ 3,765	€ 5,333	€ 4,439
Accounts payable	1,401	1,305	1,087
Accrued expenses and other current liabilities	2,622	2,371	2,548
Income taxes	—	318	139
Current portion of long-term debt	238	235	161
Total current liabilities	8,026	9,562	8,374
Net deferred income taxes	169	110	167
Long-term liabilities			
Long-term debt, less current portion	5,402	3,498	3,085
Other long-term liabilities	1,250	1,164	921
Repackaged notes	284	346	406
Total long-term liabilities	6,936	5,008	4,412
Minority interests in subsidiaries	1,800	1,481	1,077
Stockholders' equity			
Common stock	147	147	147
Additional paid-in capital and retained earnings	6,894	7,017	6,679
Cumulative translation adjustment	(140)	(133)	(122)
Total stockholders' equity	6,901	7,031	6,704
Stockholders' equity and minority interests	8,701	8,512	7,781
Total liabilities and stockholders' equity	€23,832	€23,192	€20,734

Source: LVMH 2001 annual report.

case 28

Robin Hood

Joseph Lampel
New York University

It was in the spring of the second year of his insurrection against the High Sheriff of Nottingham that Robin Hood took a walk in Sherwood Forest. As he walked he pondered the progress of the campaign, the disposition of his forces, the Sheriff's recent moves, and the options that confronted him.

The revolt against the Sheriff had begun as a personal crusade. It erupted out of Robin's conflict with the Sheriff and his administration. However, alone Robin Hood could do little. He therefore sought allies, men with grievances and a deep sense of justice. Later he welcomed all who came, asking few questions and demanding only a willingness to serve. Strength, he believed, lay in numbers.

He spent the first year forging the group into a disciplined band, united in enmity against the Sheriff and willing to live outside the law. The band's organization was simple. Robin ruled supreme, making all important decisions. He delegated specific tasks to his lieutenants. Will Scarlett was in charge of intelligence and scouting. His main job was to shadow the Sheriff and his men, always alert to their next move. He also collected information on the travel plans of rich merchants and tax collectors. Little John kept discipline among the men and saw to it that their archery was at the high peak that their profession demanded. Scarlock took care of the finances, converting loot to cash, paying shares of the take, and finding suitable hiding places for the surplus. Finally, Much the Miller's son had the difficult task of provisioning the ever-increasing band of Merrymen.

The increasing size of the band was a source of satisfaction for Robin, but also a source of concern. The fame of his Merrymen was spreading, and new recruits were pouring in from every corner of England. As the band grew larger, their small bivouac became a major encampment. Between raids the men milled about, talking and playing games. Vigilance was in decline, and discipline was becoming harder to enforce. "Why," Robin reflected, "I don't know half the men I run into these days."

The growing band was also beginning to exceed the food capacity of the forest. Game was becoming scarce, and supplies had to be obtained from outlying villages. The cost of buying food was beginning to drain the band's financial reserves at the very moment when revenues were in decline. Travelers, especially those with the most to lose, were now giving the forest a wide berth. This was costly and inconvenient to them, but it was preferable to having all their goods confiscated.

Robin believed that the time had come for the Merrymen to change their policy of outright confiscation of goods to one of a fixed transit tax. His lieutenants strongly resisted this idea. They were proud of the Merrymen's famous motto: "Rob the rich and give to the poor." "The farmers and the townspeople," they argued, "are our most important allies. How can we tax them, and still hope for their help in our fight against the Sheriff?"

Robin wondered how long the Merrymen could keep to the ways and methods of their early days. The Sheriff was growing stronger and becoming better organized. He now had the money and the men and was beginning to harass the band, probing for its weaknesses. The tide of events was beginning to turn against the Merrymen. Robin felt that the campaign must be decisively concluded before the Sheriff had a chance to deliver a mortal blow. "But how," he wondered, "could this be done?"

Robin had often entertained the possibility of killing the Sheriff, but the chances for this seemed increasingly remote. Besides, killing the Sheriff might satisfy his personal thirst for revenge, but it would not improve the situation. Robin had hoped that the perpetual state of unrest, and the Sheriff's failure to collect taxes, would lead to his removal from office. Instead, the Sheriff used his political connections to obtain reinforcement. He had powerful friends at court and was well regarded by the regent, Prince John.

Prince John was vicious and volatile. He was consumed by his unpopularity among the people, who wanted the imprisoned King Richard back. He also lived in constant fear of the barons, who had first given him the regency but were now beginning to dispute his claim to the throne. Several of these barons had set out to collect the ransom that would release King Richard the Lionheart from his jail in Austria. Robin was invited to join the conspiracy in return for future amnesty. It was a dangerous proposition. Provincial banditry was one thing, court intrigue another. Prince John had spies everywhere, and he was known for his vindictiveness. If the conspirators' plan failed, the pursuit would be relentless, and retributions swift.

The sound of the supper horn startled Robin from his thoughts. There was the smell of roasting venison in the air. Nothing was resolved or settled. Robin headed for camp promising himself that he would give these problems his utmost attention after tomorrow's raid.

Procter & Gamble: Organization 2005 and Beyond

Ravi Madapati
ICFAI Knowledge Center

In September 1998 Procter & Gamble (P&G) announced a corporate restructuring program called Organization 2005. The set of far-reaching initiatives involved comprehensive changes in organizational structure, work processes, and culture to make employees stretch themselves and speed up innovation. Organization 2005 also sought to leverage P&G's global presence. The program was intended to boost sales and profits by introducing new products, closing plants, and eliminating jobs. Spearheaded by Durk Jager, who became P&G's CEO in 1999, this initiative was to be a six-year, $1.9 billion effort. Jager believed that rapid restructuring was necessary to create new growth opportunities for P&G. While launching the program he expressed his optimism:

> Success is defined first and foremost in terms of growth. Unless a company grows at an acceptable rate—year in, year out—it can't sustain its organization. Success also means growing profitably. Otherwise, it can't produce the resources and capability to invest, take risks, or seize new opportunities. The program we lay out here today is designed to deliver that growth, at a consistently higher level. Just come back in a couple of years and take a look. I believe that the best way to accelerate growth is to innovate bigger and move faster consistently and across the entire company.[1]

Jager indicated that the cultural changes he planned to introduce would create an environment that produced bolder goals and plans, bigger innovations and greater speed. As part of the exercise, Jager redesigned the reward system to strengthen the link between executive compensation and results.

BUSINESS SEGMENTS

P&G was one of the best-known consumer goods companies in the world. For the year ended June 30, 2002, P&G reported revenues of $40.2 billion. The company was in the Fortune Global 50 list. It owned several well-known brands that were sold in over 140 countries to nearly 5 billion consumers (see Exhibit 1). P&G had operations in North America, Europe, the Middle East, Africa, Asia, and Latin America. Exhibits 2 and 3 highlight the company's recent financial performance.

P&G had five main business segments: Fabric and Home Care; Baby, Feminine, and Family Care; Beauty Care; Health Care; and Food and Beverage:

- Fabric and Homecare was the most important segment, accounting for nearly a third of P&G's total sales. The division dealt with cleaning products for clothes, surfaces, and dishes. Key brands included Bold and Tide laundry detergents, and Cascade dishwasher powder.

- The Baby, Feminine, and Family Care segment produced tissues and paper towels, feminine protection products, diapers, and baby wipes. Well-known brands in this category were Bounty paper towels and Tampax tampons.

- Beauty Care products included deodorants such as Old Spice, Sure, Cover Girl, and Max Factor

[1]"Organization 2005 Drive for Accelerated Growth Enters Next Phase," P&G press release, June 9, 1999.

exhibit 1 **P&G Brands around the World**

Region	Shaving Products	Skin Care	Cleansing	Cosmetics
United States	Noxema Old Spice	Noxema Olay	Camay Ivory Moisture Care Olay Safeguard Zest	Cover Girl Max Factor Olay
Latin America	Old Spice	Noxema Olay	Camay Ivory Olay Old Spice Safeguard Zest	Cover Girl Max Factor
Europe, Middle East, Africa	Old Spice	Noxema Olay Roge Cavailles	Infasil Ivory Safeguard Zest	Cover Girl Ellen Betrix Max Factor
Asia		Olay	Camay Ivory Muse Safeguard Zest	Cover Girl Max Factor SK-II

Source: Collected from various sources.

cosmetics. The segment also produced fragrances, shaving products, and shampoos such as the Head & Shoulders and Pantene brands.

- Health Care products ranged from prescription drugs to toothpastes such as Crest, over-the-counter remedies such as Pepto-Bismol, and pet foods.
- Food and Beverage produced cooking oil, Pringles snacks, and peanut butter. It also offered drinks like Sunny Delight and Folgers coffee.

Exhibits 4 and 5 show recent earnings growth of these five groups, and Exhibit 6 presents each group's sales, profitability, and major brands.

CORPORATE HISTORY

William Procter and James Gamble founded P&G as a partnership in 1837 in Cincinnati, Ohio, by merging Procter's candle-making company with Gamble's soap business. The company grew to $1 million in sales by 1859. P&G's initial foray into branding was the Moon and Stars, a trademark that appeared on all company products starting in the early 1860s. In 1887, P&G became one of the first companies in the United States to offer a profit-sharing program for its employees. In 1924, P&G was one of the first companies to create a market research department to study consumer preferences and behavior. The company's marketing organization and brand management system began to evolve in the early 1930s. In 1933, P&G's Oxydol soap powder sponsored a serial radio program.

P&G had been a late globalizer. But after World War II, P&G began its international expansion in earnest. In 1948, it established an overseas division while setting up its first Latin American subsidiary in Mexico. P&G entered Europe in 1954, Saudi Arabia in 1961, and Japan in 1973. By 1980, P&G was operating in 23 countries and reporting over $10 billion in annual sales. By the mid-1990s, over half of the company's sales came from outside the United States. As its global expansion progressed, P&G

exhibit 2 **Summary of P&G's Financial Performance, 1997–2001**

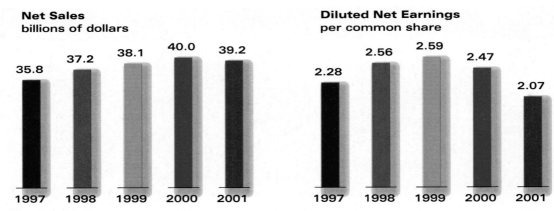

Net Sales
billions of dollars

| 1997 | 1998 | 1999 | 2000 | 2001 |
| 35.8 | 37.2 | 38.1 | 40.0 | 39.2 |

Diluted Net Earnings
per common share

| 1997 | 1998 | 1999 | 2000 | 2001 |
| 2.28 | 2.56 | 2.59 | 2.47 | 2.07 |

Source: P&G annual report, 2002.

exhibit 3 **P&G's Performance in 2002**

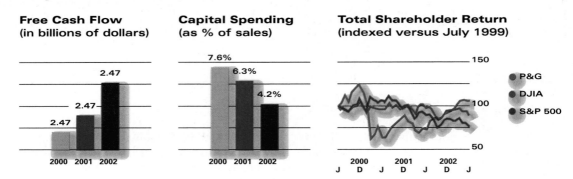

Free Cash Flow
(in billions of dollars)

| 2000 | 2001 | 2002 |
| 2.47 | 2.47 | 2.47 |

Capital Spending
(as % of sales)

| 2000 | 2001 | 2002 |
| 7.6% | 6.3% | 4.2% |

Total Shareholder Return
(indexed versus July 1999)

- P&G
- DJIA
- S&P 500

Source: P&G annual report, 2002.

exhibit 4 **P&G's Earnings Growth from Different Segments**

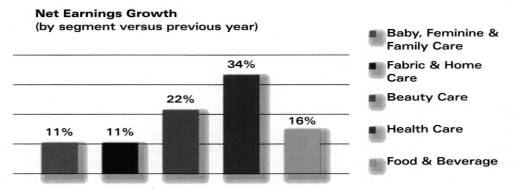

Net Earnings Growth
(by segment versus previous year)

- Baby, Feminine & Family Care — 11%
- Fabric & Home Care — 11%
- Beauty Care — 22%
- Health Care — 34%
- Food & Beverage — 16%

Source: P&G annual report, 2002.

exhibit 5   **P&G Net Sales and Net Earnings by Segment**

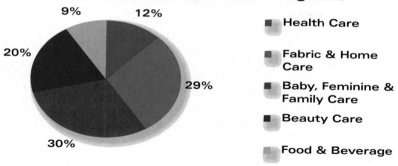

2002 Net Sales by Business Segment

- Health Care
- Fabric & Home Care
- Baby, Feminine & Family Care
- Beauty Care
- Food & Beverage

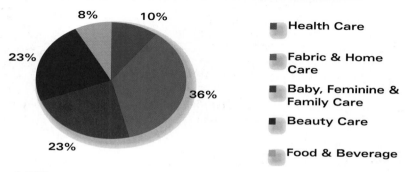

2002 Net Earnings by Business Segment

- Health Care
- Fabric & Home Care
- Baby, Feminine & Family Care
- Beauty Care
- Food & Beverage

Source: P&G annual report, 2002.

continued to modify its structure and internal processes to maximize global leverage. Various initiatives were launched to facilitate exchange of knowledge and best practices across the company.

Exhibits 7 and 8 provide additional background on the company.

ORGANIZATION 2005

In 1998, P&G's earnings per share (EPS) fell below the 14 to 15 percent that Wall Street had gotten used to. Revenue growth, which had varied between 1.4 and 5.5 percent between 1995 and 1999, was also well below P&G's internal target of 7 percent. Revenue growth was slowing down, particularly in developed markets, due to the maturity of the company's established brands. Half the brands were generating

the bulk of the growth while the rest were lagging behind. In a retail world increasingly populated by private-label goods, P&G's premium products were having difficulty competing. More nimble competitors were beating P&G to the market by launching new products, by executing marketing plans better, and by increasing innovation speeds. There was also speculation that P&G's profitability was being eroded by the increasing dominance of retailers like Wal-Mart. With a turnover of about $160 billion in 1999, Wal-Mart was a particularly formidable player.

P&G's innovation track record had also been disappointing. New brands had the ability to add billions of dollars in incremental revenue, but P&G had not launched a major new brand in almost a decade.

The need to reinvigorate growth led P&G to conceive Organization 2005. The goal of the program was to improve P&G's competitive position and generate

exhibit 6   **P&G's Business Lineup in 2002**

Baby, Feminine, and Family Care	
Sales*	$12 billion (flat)
Profits[†]	$1.9 billion (up 10%)
$Billion brands	Always, Pampers, Charmin, Bounty
New developments	Brand extensions Bounty napkins, Charmin Fresh Mates, and Tampax Compak were all performing well. Ailing feminine brands moved to Beauty Care in July 2002.

Fabric and Home Care	
Sales*	$11.8 billion (up 1%)
Profits[†]	$2.7 billion (up 12%)
$Billion brands	Tide, Ariel, Downy
New developments	Swiffer WetJet revolutionized cleaning in 2000 with disposable mop-and-cleanser-in-one. New scents like Tide Clean Breeze and Downy Clean Breeze helped freshen old brands.

Beauty Care	
Sales*	$8 billion (up 10%)
Profits[†]	$1.6 billion (up 13%)
$Billion brands	Pantene
New developments	Hugo Boss fragrance sales grew 47% in latest quarter. Ohm by Olay, P&G's first line of body care products, arrived in July 2002. Sales of Olay were likely to exceed $1 billion in 2003.

Health and Oral Care	
Sales*	$5 billion (up 14%)
Profits[†]	$742 million (up 27%)
$Billion brands	Crest, Iams
New developments	Acquired in 1999, Iams pet food sales tripled with new products like Eukanuba Dental Diet (using Crest know-how). Heartburn drug Prilosec is going o-t-c this year, pending FDA approval.

Food and Beverage	
Sales*	$3.9 billion (down 5%)
Profits[†]	$596 million (up 9%)
$Billion brands	Folgers, Pringles
New developments	The company dumped Crisco and Jif but was trying to save Sunny Delight. A bright spot was tortilla chips, with sales up 33% since November 2001 following the introduction of Pringles sibling Torengos.

*Sales: Estimated for fiscal year ending June 30, 2002.
[†]Profits: Pretax estimate for fiscal 2002.
Source: Luisa Kroll, "A Fresh Face," *Forbes,* July 8, 2002.

exhibit 7 **P&G's Simplification Drive in the 1990s**

Standardizing	Product formulas and packages
Reducing trade promotions	Fewer discounts and rebates
Easing up on coupons	Issuing fewer coupons
Getting rid of marginal brands and cutting product lines	Cutting extra sizes, flavors and other variants to make it easier for customers to find what they were looking for
Reapplying strategies that work	Extending successful strategies to other parts of the world.

Source: A. V. Vedpuriswar, *The Global CEO: Lessons from the World's Leading Corporations* (New Delhi: Vision Books, 2001).

exhibit 8 **P&G: Chronology of Recent Events**

September 9, 1998	P&G taps Durk Jager as CEO
June 9, 1999	P&G says it will lay off 15,000 workers as part of Organization 2005 program
July 29, 1999	P&G posts fiscal fourth-quarter profits well below those of the prior year
January 19, 2000	Warner-Lambert, American Home Products disclose they are in merger talks with P&G
January 23, 2000	P&G investors sell stock, causing a 10% drop in the share price
January 25, 2000	Stock price falls more than $2 after the company warns of lower-than-expected third-quarter results
March 7, 2000	P&G warns that it expects third-quarter profits to be down 10% to 11% from a year ago.

operating efficiencies through more ambitious goals, nurturing greater innovation, and reducing time-to-market. This was to be accomplished by substantially redesigning the company's organizational structure, work processes, culture, and pay structures.

P&G estimated that Organization 2005 would accelerate annual sales growth to 6–8 percent and annual earnings growth to 13–15 percent.

Organization 2005 envisaged the transformation of P&G's organizational structure from one based on geography to one based on global product lines. The program had five key elements:

1. *Global business units (GBUs):* P&G moved from four business units based on geographical regions to seven GBUs based on global product lines. By putting the responsibility for strategy and profit on brands, instead of geographic regions, P&G hoped to spur greater innovation and speed.

2. *Market development organizations (MDOs):* P&G established eight MDOs whose objective was to tailor global marketing programs to local markets.

3. *Global business services (GBS):* Overhead functions such as human resources, accounting, order management, and information technology were consolidated from separate geographic regions to one corporate organization—the GBS—that would serve all GBUs.

4. *Corporate functions:* Most of the corporate staff were transferred to one of the new business units.

5. *Company culture:* P&G redesigned reward systems and training programs to improve result orientation among employees.

Organization 2005 involved substantial costs. Of the approximately $1.9 billion in costs, approximately $400 million were planned for 1999, approximately $1.0 billion over the next two fiscal years, and the balance during fiscal years 2002–2004. However, these costs were expected to be more than offset by savings from the program. The company expected to increase its after-tax profits by approximately $600–$700 million annually by fiscal year 2003–04 and $900 million by fiscal 2004. P&G would eliminate 10,000 positions through fiscal 2001, with a further 5,000 cuts after 2001. Approximately 42 percent of the total workforce reduction would occur in Europe, the Middle East, and Africa; 29 percent in North America; 16 percent in Latin America; and 13 percent in Asia.

Despite the substantial retrenchment, Durk Jager remained confident that employee morale would not

exhibit 9   **Organization 2005: The Costs of Restructuring, 2001–2003 (in millions)**

| | Years Ended June 30 | | |
	2002	2001	2000
Separations	$393	$ 341	$153
Accelerated depreciation	135	276	386
Asset write-downs	208	731	64
Other	222	502	211
Total (before tax)	958	1,850	814
Total (after tax)	706	1,475	688

Source: P&G annual report, 2002.

exhibit 10   **Organization 2005 Program Impact**

	Total	Fiscal Years 1998, 1999–2000, 2001	Fiscal Years 2001, 2002–2003, 2004
Estimated costs (after-tax)	$1.9 billion	$1.4 billion	$0.5 billion
Estimated job impact	15,000	10,000	5,000

| Estimated Job Impact by Item | | | |
	Product Supply	GBS	Other
Job impact	6,700	3,900	4,400

| Estimated Job Impact by Region | | |
	Job Impact	Expressed as %
Europe, Middle East, Africa	6,250	42
North America	4,300	29
Latin America	2,450	16
Asia	2,000	13
Total	15,000	100%

Source: P&G annual report, 1999.

be affected. He believed that Organization 2005 was about accelerating growth, not cutting jobs:

> These job reductions are principally an outgrowth of changes, such as standardizing global manufacturing platforms, to drive innovation and faster speed to market, as always, we have considered these decisions very carefully with deep concern for the impact on our people. We would carry out the changes with maximum respect and attention to the welfare and future of our employees.[2]

P&G announced it would make full use of normal attrition and retirements, hiring reductions, reloca-

[2]Ibid.

tions, job retraining, and voluntary separations to help reduce the number of potential involuntary separations. In cases of involuntary separations, P&G would offer employees financial assistance to help them in their new careers. Exhibits 9 and 10 provide additional information on P&G's Organization 2005 initiative.

JAGER'S RESIGNATION

Soon after it was introduced, Organization 2005 ran into various problems. After reaching $117 per share

exhibit 11 **Procter & Gamble's Share Price, 1999–2002**

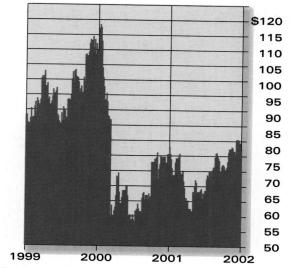

Source: www.aol.com.

in January 2000, P&G's stock price fell below $90 per share in February. On March 7, 2000, P&G warned that its earnings would drop by 10 to 11 percent rather than rise 7 to 9 percent as previously expected. Among the reasons P&G cited for the drop in earnings were higher raw materials costs, lower realization, and increasing competition from many generic brands that produced cheaper versions of many of its core products. The news sent the company's stock to its lowest level since the mid-1990s. The stock price plunged to less than $60 per share, wiping out $40 billion in market value in one day (see Exhibit 11). Then in April 2000, P&G posted an 18 percent decline in third-quarter profit, its first decline in eight years. It also announced that fourth-quarter results would fall short of estimates. Jager accepted responsibility for the company's problems and resigned. But he maintained:

> I am proud of the vision we set out to achieve with Organization 2005, and we've made important progress. It's unfortunate our progress in stepping up top-line sales growth resulted in earnings disappointments.[3]

Analysts speculated on the reasons behind Jager's failure. It was said Jager had tried to put too much pressure on P&G managers to bring products to mar-

[3]"P&G CEO Quits Amid Woes," *CNN Money,* June 8, 2000.

ket faster. Major moves such as the dual acquisition of Warner-Lambert and American Home Products had turned out to be futile—none improved P&G's performance. Jager's exhortations also did not fit well with P&G's cautious corporate culture. His plan had been too aggressive. He had introduced new products recklessly in the hope of finding the next billion-dollar product. He had also decided arbitrarily that P&G would sell its products under the same name all around the world—so in Germany, the name of P&G's dishwashing liquid suddenly changed from Fairy to Dawn, the name under which it sold in the United States; but since Dawn was unknown in Germany, sales plummeted.

There had also been problems related to people. Managers had become critical of Jager's confrontational style. As employees felt they were being pushed, there was significant disenchantment. In Europe, about 2,000 people were suddenly transferred to Geneva. About 200 employees were asked to relocate from various parts of Asia to Singapore. Besides transfers, the program had also led to various behavioral problems. As a result of the Organization 2005 program, some food and beverage managers, based in Cincinnati, were asked to report to a president in Caracas, Venezuela. Managers in the laundry and household cleaning business reported to Brussels.

ORGANIZATION 2005 UNDER LAFLEY

Alan George Lafley, a 23-year P&G veteran, replaced Jager as president and CEO in mid-2000 when the company's stock price was $57. Lafley announced he would improve operations and profitability and rebuild the management team. The heads of P&G's operating businesses and corporate functions hailed from 13 different countries. The new faces included Deb Henretta, head of global baby care; Jim Stengel, global marketing officer; and Fabrizio Freda, head of the global snacks business. Overall, the average age of the Global Leadership Council (GLC) was only 49, compared to 54 three years earlier (see Exhibit 12). Unlike Jager, who focused on taking new initiatives in underdeveloped markets, Lafley decided to concentrate more on big countries and big products. He decided to increase sales of Tide and Pampers in Western

exhibit 12 **Procter & Gamble's Global Leadership Council, June 1999 and June 2002**

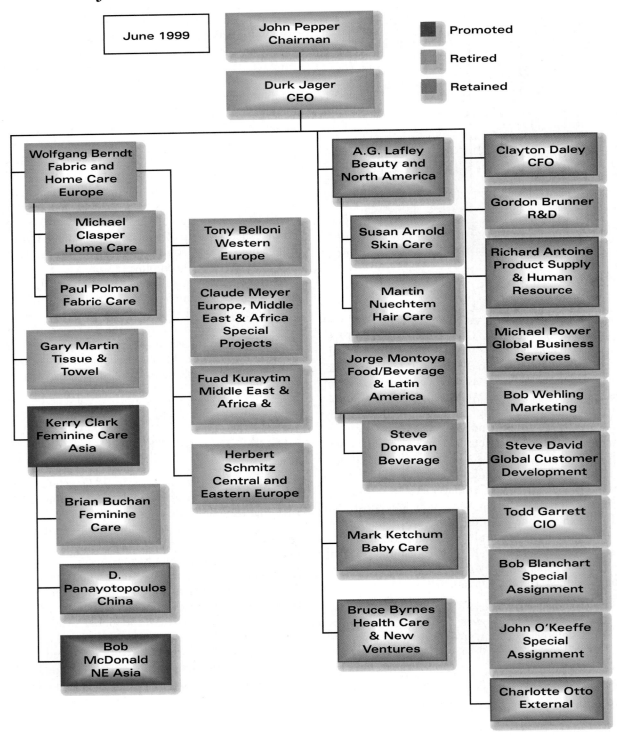

exhibit 12   **(concluded)**

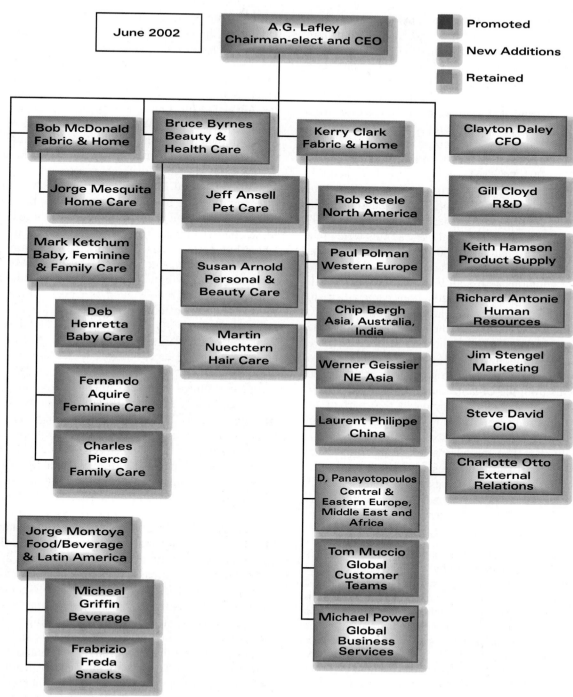

Europe before developing new products in Poland. The new CEO gave top priority to P&G's best-selling brands, which generated over $1 billion in sales. He announced they would get the bulk of P&G's resources, manpower, and financial backing.

Lafley also announced plans to improve the company's competitiveness and revitalize long-term growth through initiatives that seemed to be an expansion and acceleration of Organization 2005. This would be achieved by streamlining P&G's cost structure by further reducing overhead and manufacturing costs. The company expected savings on this count to be approximately $600–$700 million annually by fiscal year 2003–04. These savings would be in addition to those projected in the original Organization 2005 program. During 2000, Lafley reduced staffing by about 9,600 jobs worldwide, or 9 percent of P&G's workforce. About 40 percent of these cuts were in the United States, and about 60 percent were overseas. Two-thirds of the reductions came from nonmanufacturing functions across all levels of the company. In manufacturing functions, reductions came as a result of both plant closures and rationalization.

P&G also completed the remaining 7,800 separations that were part of the Organization 2005 restructuring announced in 1999. The combination of separations from the new program and remaining separations from the Organization 2005 program totaled 17,400. The company anticipated that part of the workforce reduction would have to be made through involuntary separations, but it intended to minimize that number. The company also continued to review its businesses and new investments with the goal of achieving sharper focus on its core businesses. While no decisions had been reached, the company believed it could incur additional restructuring costs as a result of this strategic review. Lafley said:

> The cost benefits of strengthened competitiveness and improved productivity are significant, but this is not just a cost-cutting program. No one ever cost-saves their way to sustainable growth, We will invest these savings in getting our consumer value and pricing right, continuing to invest in innovation on core businesses and the most promising new businesses, and continuing to provide strong marketing and sales support for our brands. All of these actions are necessary to deliver P&G's long-term financial goals.[4]

[4]"Procter & Gamble Announces Next Step in Overall Plan to Restore Competitiveness and Growth," P&G press release, March 22, 2001.

To boost growth, Lafley introduced several new products. Big brands like Tampax (tampons) rolled out new extensions in 2002. P&G started shipping its new Ohm by Olay line of body care products, which was the company's first skin care foray and which used natural products like ginger and jasmine, and also included new technologies such as body mist. Research-oriented units like P&G Pharmaceuticals continued to invest in new products. Sales of the unit's flagship brand, the Actonel osteoporosis drug, approached $400 million in 2002. In baby care, Pampers rolled out its Baby Stages line in Europe and North America. In laundry, Tide and Downy were offered in different fragrances.

Lafley singled out progress in oral care, baby care, and dish care businesses as one of the best outcomes of the restructuring initiatives. All these businesses had struggled and lost market share in the 1990s but posted sales and market share gains in 2002. P&G's fabric and home care business posted 9 percent sales growth in 2002 on unexpectedly strong gains in cases of brands such as Cheer, which recently had been offered in reduced pack size and price to combat a similar move by rival Unilever's Wisk. Sales in P&G's baby and family care businesses grew by 5 percent despite increasing competition from players like Kimberly-Clark. In 2002 the company dropped numerous brands—including Jif, Crisco, and Clearasil—that did not fit with its global strategy. By early 2003 P&G had finished reviewing its portfolio of brands. The sales growth of 6 percent in 2003 had been the biggest gain since 1996. Another accomplishment for Lafley was enabling Crest to return as the number one oral care brand in the United States, a position it had lost to Colgate in 1998.

Lafley believed that a key enabler for Organization 2005 was information technology (IT). The company's IT spending reached $1 billion in 2002 and continued to increase. Organization 2005 incorporated several IT initiatives, including collaborative technology to facilitate planning and marketing, business-to-consumer e-commerce, Web-enabling P&G's supply chain, and a data standards and data warehouse project that delivered timely data to desktops worldwide. The company decentralized its 3,600-person IT department so that 97 percent of those employees now worked in P&G's individual product, market, and business teams or were part of global business services, which supported shared services such as infrastructure to P&G units. The remaining 3 percent worked in corporate IT. Lafley said, "I have made a lot of symbolic, very physical changes so people understand we are in the business of leading change."[5]

THE FUTURE

P&G expected to conclude its Organization 2005 initiative by June 2003. After the ouster of Jager, Lafley had shifted the focus from new initiatives to advancing the market share of big brands in developed markets. Lafley believed that, overall, Organization 2005 had brought much-needed discipline to P&G's global marketing efforts. But he felt a lot of work remained in convincing people that the program had a broad application. Lafley believed that P&G could innovate and cut costs while growing profits by double-digit margins every year. But Lafley realized the same basic question that had prompted Jager to start Organization 2005 still remained: With already-dominant market positions in mature markets, how much more growth could P&G really generate? With company's stock price trading in the $80–$95 range throughout most of 2002, what more could be done to boost the company's performance prospects?

---

[5]A. G. Lafley, "The Best and the Worst Managers," *Business Week,* Special Report, January 11, 2003.

bibliography

Arndt, Michael, and Robert McNatt. "A Veggie Cleaner to Shine Up P&G Stock." *Business Week,* April 17, 2000.

Barrett, Amy, and Louis Lavelle. "It's Getting Lonely at the Top." *Business Week,* November 13, 2000.

"The Best and the Worst Managers." *Business Week,* Special Report, January 11, 2003.

"Beverages." *Forbes,* May 21, 2001.

Brooker, Katrina, and Julie Schlosser. "The Un-CEO." *Fortune,* November 16, 2002.

Brown, Eryn. "Loving P&G, Leaving a Dot-Com." *Fortune,* May 29, 2000.

"The Color of Money." *The Economist,* March 8, 2003.

Foust, Dean. "Wiped Out." *Business Week,* February 24, 2003.

"Jager's Gamble." *The Economist,* October 28, 1999.

Kroll, Luisa. "A Fresh Face." *Forbes,* July 8, 2002.

Mackenzie, Susan. "The Procter & Gamble Company: Accounting for Organization 2005." Harvard Business School Case, February 2002.

McCoy, Michael. "Product Report, Soaps & Detergents." *Chemical & Engineering News,* January 15, 2001.

"Mr. Lafley's Makeover." *The Economist,* March 20, 2003.

Neuborne, Ellen, and Robert Berner. "Warm and Fuzzy Won't Save P&G." *Business Week,* February 26, 2000.

"P&G CEO Quits Amid Woes." *CNN Money,* June 8, 2000.

P&G press releases and annual reports from the company Web site (www.pg.com).

Peale, Cliff. "How A. G. Lafley Turned Procter Around." *Cincinnati Enquirer,* June 2002.

———. "The Lafley Method: Face the Facts, Think Like a Consumer." *Cincinnati Enquirer,* June 2002.

———. "UpNext, Innovation and Cost Cutting." *Cincinnati Enquirer,* June 2002.

"Procter's Gamble." *The Economist,* June 10, 1999.

Serwer, Andy. "P&G's Covert Operation." *Fortune,* November 17, 2001.

Swibel, Matthew. "Spin Cycle." *Forbes,* March 2, 2001.

Vedpuriswar, A. V. *The Global CEO: Lessons from World's Leading Corporations.* New Delhi: Vision Books, 2001.

The Global Leadership of Carlos Ghosn at Nissan

John P. Millikin

Thunderbird—The American Graduate School of International Management

Dean Fu

Thunderbird—The American Graduate School of International Management

I did not try to learn too much about Japan before coming, because I didn't want to have too many preconceived ideas. I wanted to discover Japan by being in Japan with Japanese people.[1]

Well, I think I am a practical person. I know I may fail at any moment. In my opinion, it was extremely helpful to be practical [at Nissan], not to be arrogant, and to realize that I could fail at any moment.

—Carlos Ghosn, 2002[2]

INTRODUCTION

Nissan had been incurring losses for seven of the prior eight years when, in March 1999, Carlos Ghosn (pronounced GOHN) took over as the first non-Japanese Chief Operating Officer of Nissan. Many industry analysts anticipated a culture clash between the French leadership style and his new Japanese employees. For these analysts, the decision

THUNDERBIRD
THE AMERICAN GRADUATE SCHOOL
OF INTERNATIONAL MANAGEMENT

[1]"Decision-Making and Coordination Structures of the Alliance," 20 October 1999, http://www.nissanglobal.com.

[2]"Nissan President Carlos Ghosn Talks about His Company's Recovery," *Nikkei Business,* 20 May 2002, http://nb.nikkeibp.co.jp/Article/1142.

to bring Ghosn in came at the worst possible time because the financial situation at Nissan had become critical. The continuing losses were resulting in debts (approximately $22 billion) that were shaking the confidence of suppliers and financiers alike. Furthermore, the Nissan brand was weakening in the minds of consumers due to a product portfolio that consisted of models far older than competitors. In fact, only four of the company's 43 models turned a profit. With little liquid capital available for new product development, there was no indication that Nissan would see increases in either margin or volume of sales to overcome the losses. The next leader of Nissan was either going to turn Nissan around within two to three years, or the company faced the prospect of going out of business.

Realizing the immediacy of the task at hand, Ghosn boldly pledged to step down if Nissan did not show a profit by March 2001, just two years after he assumed duties. But it only took eighteen months (October 2000) for him to shock critics and supporters alike when Nissan began to operate profitably under his leadership.

BACKGROUND OF CARLOS GHOSN

Born in Brazil in 1954 to French and Brazilian parents, both of Lebanese heritage, Carlos Ghosn received his university education in Paris. Following graduation at age 24, Ghosn joined the French firm, Compagnie Générale des Etablissements Michelin. After a few years of rapid advancement to become COO of Michelin's Brazilian subsidiary, he learned to manage large operations under adverse conditions such as the runaway inflation rates in Brazil at that time. Similarly, as the head of Michelin North America, Ghosn faced the pressures of a recession while putting together a merger with Uniroyal Goodrich. Despite his successes in his 18 years with Michelin, Ghosn realized that he would never be promoted to company president because Michelin was a family-run company. Therefore, in 1996 he decided to resign and join Renault S.A., accepting a position as the Executive Vice President of Advanced Research & Development, Manufacturing, and Purchasing.

Ghosn led the turnaround initiative at Renault in the aftermath of its failed merger with Volvo. Because he was so focused on increasing margins by improving cost efficiencies, he earned the nickname "Le Cost-Killer" among Renault's top brass and middle management personnel. Three years later, when Renault formed a strategic alliance with Nissan, Ghosn was asked to take over the role of Nissan COO in order to turn the company around in a hurry, just as he had done earlier in his career with Michelin South America. For Ghosn this would be the fourth continent he would work on, which combined with the five languages he spoke, illustrates his capacity for global leadership.

BACKGROUND OF NISSAN

In 1933, a company called Jidosha-Seizo Kabushiki-Kaisha (which means "Automobile Manufacturing Co., Ltd." in English) was established in Japan. It was a combination of several earlier automotive ventures and the Datsun brand which it acquired from Tobata Casting Co., Ltd. Shortly thereafter in 1934, the company name was changed to Nissan Motor Co., Ltd. After the Second World War, Nissan grew steadily, expanding its operations globally. It became especially successful in North America with a lineup of smaller gasoline efficient cars and small pickup trucks as well as a sports coupe, the Datsun 280Z. Along with other Japanese manufacturers, Nissan was successfully competing on quality, reliability

and fuel efficiency. By 1991, Nissan was operating very profitably, producing four of the top ten cars in the world.

Nissan management throughout the 1990s, however, had displayed a tendency to emphasize short-term market share growth, rather than profitability or long-term strategic success. Nissan was very well known for its advanced engineering and technology, plant productivity, and quality management. During the previous decade, Nissan's designs had not reflected customer opinion because they assumed that most customers preferred to buy good quality cars rather than stylish, innovative cars. Instead of reinvesting in new product designs as other competitors did, Nissan managers seemed content to continue to harvest the success of proven designs. They tended to put retained earnings into equity of other companies, often suppliers, and into real-estate investments, as part of the Japanese business custom of *keiretsu* investing. Through these equity stakes in other companies, Ghosn's predecessors (and Japanese business leaders in general) believed that loyalty and cooperation were fostered between members of the value chain within their *keiretsu*. By 1999, Nissan had tied up over $4 billion in the stock shares of hundreds of different companies as part of this *keiretsu* philosophy. These investments, however, were not reflected in Nissan's purchasing costs, which remained between 20-25% higher than Renault's. These *keiretsu* investments would not have been so catastrophic if the Asian financial crisis had not resulted in a devaluation of the yen from 100 to 90 yen = 1 US dollar. As a result, both Moody's and Standard & Poor's announced in February 1999 that if Nissan could not get any financial support from another automobile company, then each of them would lower Nissan's credit rating to "junk" status from "investment grade."

Clearly, Nissan was in need of a strategic partner that could lend both financing and new management ideas to foster a turnaround. In addition, Nissan sought to expand into other regions where it had less presence. In March 1999, Nissan President and Chief Executive Officer Yoshikazu Hanawa found such an alliance opportunity with Renault, which assumed a 36.8% stake in Nissan, allowing Nissan to invest $5.4 billion and retain its investment grade status. Hanawa was also able to get Renault's top management to agree to three important principles during negotiations:

1. Nissan would maintain its company name.
2. The Nissan CEO would continue to be selected by the Nissan Board of Directors.
3. Nissan would take the principal responsibility of implementing a revival plan.

It was actually Hanawa who first made the request to Louis Schweitzer, CEO of Renault, to send Carlos Ghosn to Nissan to be in charge of all internal administration and operations activities.

Why would Renault agree to all of these conditions in this bailout of Nissan? Renault was also looking for a partner, one that would reduce its dependence on the European market and enhance its global position. In 1997 85% of Renault's revenue was earned in Europe, 32.8% of which came from its domestic (French) market. Renault also had high market share in Latin America, especially Brazil. On the other hand, Nissan had the second largest market share in Japan and a strong market share in North America. Nissan lacked, however, market share and distribution facilities in Latin America. By creating the new alliance, Nissan and Renault expected to balance their market portfolios and become more competitive. Renault wanted a partner that was savvy and established in the North American and Asian markets. Furthermore, the merger of Daimler and Chrysler in May 1998 gave Renault a sense of urgency about finding a partner to compete more effectively on a global scale. As a result, Renault and Nissan agreed to a Global Alliance Agreement on March 27, 1999, with Carlos Ghosn designated to join Nissan as COO.

ADDRESSING NATIONAL CULTURE ISSUES

When Ghosn went to Japan, he knew that industry analysts were reasonable in doubting whether a non-Japanese COO could overcome Japanese cultural obstacles, as well as effectively transform a bureaucratic corporate culture. Ghosn was going to have to address several Japanese cultural norms in order to transform the company back into a successful one.

The following are some of the issues he faced.

Consensus Decision Making and Its Relationship to Career Advancement

Since the war, the Japanese business culture for decades had been producing leaders who were very good at reaching consensus and working cooperatively within a department (a derivative of the *mura-shakai* consensus based society system). Thus, the conventional wisdom in Japan was that conscientiousness and cooperation were the key elements to maintaining operational efficiency and group harmony. This paradigm often resulted in delays to the decision-making process in an effort to achieve consensus.

As an unintended consequence of the emphasis on conscientiousness, Japanese professionals tended to avoid making mistakes at all costs in order to protect their career growth. This can result in frequent informal informational meetings and coalitions (called *nemawashi*) that occur between professional departments prior to a decision-making meeting. Through these informal contacts, participants try to poll the opinions of other participants beforehand in order to test which positions have the strongest support so that their position is aligned with the position most likely to be influential. Then, at the time for a meeting with their superiors, participants tender their aligned positions one by one to the ultimate decision maker with the feeling that if the decision maker agrees to the consensus, then no one individual can be identified later for originating a faulty position if that decision results in failure. Rules and conformity replace process.

In Japan, age, education level, and number of years of service to an organization are key factors determining how an employee moves up the career ladder. Due to a cultural tenet called *Nennkou-Jyoretu*, placing power in the hands of the most knowledgeable and experienced, promotions are normally based on seniority and education. In practice, the only things that usually thwart these time- and education-based promotions are performance errors that reflect poorly on the team and any behavior that causes disharmony among team members. When something goes wrong, the most senior person accepts responsibility while accountability at lower levels is diffused.

This part of Japanese culture had been useful to reinforce control over operations and enhance quality and productivity. During the postwar period of the company's growth, it contributed to great working relationships among everyday team members at Nissan, but these norms, by the mid 1990s, were actually impeding the company's decision making. Specifically, these cultural norms severely hampered risk-taking and slowed decision making at all levels. Existing teams of employees routinely spent much time on concepts and details, without much sense of urgency for taking new action, due in part to the risks involved with actions that could result in failure. This mindset contributed to a certain degree of complacency with market position and internal systems at Nissan, undermining the company's competitiveness.

In a related cultural issue, as employees became increasingly aware that Nissan was not performing well, the Japanese culture of protecting career advancement led to finger pointing rather than acceptance of responsibility. Sales managers blamed product planning. Product planning blamed engineering. Engineering blamed manufacturing and so on.

When Ghosn first arrived in Japan, he was surprised to learn that, while most of the employees sensed that there was indeed a problem within the company, they nearly always believed that their respective departments were operating optimally. The consensus was that other departments and other employees were creating the company's problems. Ghosn also learned that many of the employees of the company did not have a sense of crisis about the possibility of bankruptcy at Nissan because of the Japanese business tradition, which implied that large troubled employers would always be bailed out by the government of Japan. This view was based on the long standing partnership between the government and the major businesses to ensure employment and expand exports to world markets. The businesses for their part were committed to providing lifetime employment to their workers.

ADDRESSING CORPORATE CULTURE ISSUES

Not only were there Japanese cultural norms for Ghosn to contend with, but there were procedural norms at Nissan, both formal and informal, which were holding the company back. First, once decisions were made at Nissan, the follow-up during implementation was often not effective. This was not usually the case in other Japanese companies. Second, top management had developed tunnel vision regarding its strategic focus on regaining market share, as opposed to restoring margin per unit sold. This was in part due to a focus on what was best for maintaining the company's size and its employees, i.e. more units to produce, rather than what was best for customers (newer, better products to meet market demands) or for investors (higher earnings and higher stock value). Additionally, in an unusual break from Japanese business culture, there were communication problems between the layers of the organization. Staffs seemed relatively uninformed of key corporate business decisions, while top management seemed out of touch with what policy execution issues were present at the middle and lower management levels.

Ghosn realized that Nissan's fundamental problem was the lack of vision from management and the persistent problem of ignoring the voice of Nissan's customers.[3] Furthermore, he identified the following problems at Nissan:

1. Lack of a clear profit orientation.

2. Insufficient focus on customers and too much focus on competitors.

3. Lack of a sense of urgency.

4. No shared vision or common long term plan.

5. Lack of cross-functional, cross-border, cross-cultural lines of work.[4]

[3] ルネッサンス 「再生への挑戦」 p. 155, Carlos Ghosn (2001) (August 10, 2002).
[4] 日産ゴーン 『成算ありやなしや』 p. 26, 小学館文庫 (2000) (August 8, 2002).

CARLOS GHOSN'S PHILOSOPHIES OF MANAGEMENT

Despite all of his doubters, Ghosn embraced the cultural differences between the Japanese and himself, believing fervently that cultural conflict, if paced and channeled correctly, could provide opportunity for rapid innovation. He felt that by accepting and building on strengths of the different cultures, all employees, including Ghosn himself, would be given a chance to grow personally through the consideration of different perspectives. The key, he reiterated many times, was that no one leader should try to impose his/her culture on another person who was not ready to try the culture with an open mind and heart. In this vein, Carlos Ghosn came to Japan knowing that if he were to start imposing reforms by using the authority of his company position, rather than work through the Japanese culture, then the turnaround he sought would likely backfire.

What he did bring with him was three overriding principles of management that transcended all cultures. And he used these as a backdrop to give employees structure as to their efforts of determining the proper reforms. These three principles are as follows:

1. Transparency—an organization can only be effective if followers believe that what the leaders think, say, and do are all the same thing.
2. Execution is 95% of the job. Strategy is only 5%—organizational prosperity is tied directly to measurably improving quality, costs, and customer satisfaction.
3. Communication of company direction and priorities—this is the only way to get truly unified effort and buy-in. It works even when the company is facing layoffs.

THE FIRST MONTHS IN JAPAN AND THE CROSS-FUNCTIONAL TEAMS

When you get a clear strategy and communicate your priorities, it's a pleasure working in Japan. The Japan-

ese are so organized and know how to make the best of things. They respect leadership.
—Ghosn[5]

Even though Ghosn expected that his attitude toward cultural respect and opportunism would lead to success, Ghosn was pleasantly surprised by how quickly Nissan employees accepted and participated in the change of their management processes. In fact, he has credited all of the success in his programs and policies (described below) to the willingness of the Nissan employees at all levels to change their mindsets and embrace new ideas.

Perhaps it was the way he started that set the foundation among the employees. He was the first manager to actually walk around the entire company and meet every employee in person, shaking hands and introducing himself. In addition, Ghosn initiated long discussions with several hundred managers in order to discuss their ideas for turning Nissan around. This began to address the problems within the vertical layers of management by bringing the highest leader of the company in touch with some of the execution issues facing middle and lower management. It also sent a signal to other executives that they needed to be doing the same thing.

But he did not stop there. After these interviews, he decided that the employees were quite energetic, as shown by their recommendations and opinions. With this in mind, Ghosn opted to develop a program for transformation which relied on the Nissan people to make recommendations, instead of hiring outside consultants. He began to organize Cross-Functional Teams to make decisions for radical change. Part of his interest in doing this in-house was to address the motivation and horizontal communication issues that he encountered throughout the organization. He felt that if the employees could accomplish the revival by their own hands, then confidence in the company as a whole and motivation would again flourish. In a sense he was making it clear that he was also putting his own future in their hands because he had publicly stated several times that the Nissan company had the right employees to achieve profitability again in less than two years.

Before the strategic alliance occurred between Renault and Nissan, Renault had made an agreement

[5]Middleton, John. *ExpressExec.com,* http://www.expressexec. wiley.com/ee/ee07.01.07/sect0.html, Acquired on Internet, 7 August 2002.

with Hanawa to remain sensitive to Nissan's culture at all times, and Ghosn was intent on following through on that commitment. First and foremost, when he chose expatriates to accompany him from Renault to Nissan, he screened carefully to ensure that those expatriates would have his same cultural attitudes toward respecting Nissan and the Japanese culture. And, after completing his rounds of talking with plant employees, he chose not to use his new-found understanding of the problems to impose a revival plan. Instead, Ghosn mobilized existing Nissan managers by setting up nine Cross-Functional Teams (CFTs) of approximately 10 members each in the first month. Through these CFTs, he was allowing the company to develop a new corporate culture from the best elements of Japan's national culture.

He knew that the CFTs would be a powerful tool for getting line managers to see beyond the functional or regional boundaries that defined their direct responsibilities. In Japan, the trouble was that employees working in functional or regional departments tend not to ask themselves as many hard questions as they should. Working together in CFTs helped managers to think in new ways and challenge existing practices.

Thus, Ghosn established the nine CFTs within one month of his arrival at Nissan. The CFTs had responsibility for the following areas: Business Development, Purchasing, Manufacturing and Logistics, Research and Development, Sales and Marketing, General and Administrative, Finance and Cost, Phase-out of Products and Parts, Complexity Management, and Organizational Structure.

Ghosn had the teams review the company's operations for three months and come up with recommendations for returning Nissan to profitability and for uncovering opportunities for future growth. Even though the teams had no decision making power, they reported to Nissan's nine-member executive committee and had access to all company information. The teams consisted of around ten members who were drawn from the company's middle management.

Ten people could not cover broad issues in depth. To overcome this each CFT formed a set of sub-teams. These sub-teams also consisted of ten members and focused on particular issues faced by the broad teams. CFTs used a system reporting to two supervisors. These leaders were drawn from the executive committee and ensured that the teams were given access to all the information that they needed.

To prevent a single function's perspective from dominating, team had two senior voices that would balance each other.

One of the regular members acted as a pilot who took responsibility for driving the agenda and discussion. The pilot and leaders selected the other members. The pilots usually had frontline experience as managers.

The CFTs also prescribed some harsh medicine in the form of plant closures and employee reductions. The CFTs would remain an integral part of Nissan's management structure. They continue to brief the CEO; however the team's missions have changed somewhat. They are to carefully watch the on-going revival plan and try to find further areas for improvement.

Since the members of the teams were often mid-level managers who rarely saw beyond their own functional responsibilities, this new coordination had high impact on participants. Specifically, it allowed them to understand how the standard measures of success for their own departments were meaningless to Nissan unless they were framed in a way that connected to other departments to result in customer attraction and retention. In many cases, these mid-level managers enjoyed learning about the business from a bird's eye perspective and felt fully engaged in the change process, giving them a sense of responsibility and ownership about turning Nissan around.

As Ghosn explained in a speech in May 2002, "The trouble is that people working in functional or regional teams tend not to ask themselves as many hard questions as they should. By contrast, working together in cross-functional teams helps managers to think in new ways and challenge existing practices. The teams also provide a mechanism for explaining the necessity for change and for projecting difficult messages across the entire company."[6]

Ghosn did have one great stroke of luck that helped him reinforce the need for change. At approximately the same time as he was arriving in Japan, Yamaichi, the major financial house in Japan, went bankrupt and was not bailed out by the Japanese government. Before that, Japanese employees, including Nissan's, did not worry about corporate problems because the government was always saving

[6]Ghosn, Carlos, "Saving the Business without Losing the Company," *Harvard Business Review,* Vol. 80, No. 1, January 2002.

the day. This recent turn of events helped to develop a sense of urgency among Nissan employees. Ghosn, to his credit, used the Yamaichi example whenever he could to continue to motivate his employees, repeating that their fate would be no different if they did not put all of their effort into figuring out, and then executing, the best way to turn Nissan around.

REFORMS IN FULL SWING

Within the first six months, the fruit of the CFTs and the increased sense of urgency were apparent. Management (especially Ghosn) was increasingly perceived as transparent among all levels of employees, which Ghosn attributed to his respect for protecting Nissan's identity. In addition, decisions were being made faster; and there was increased communication and understanding about what was important to management. There was, however, very little implementation yet, only planning. Having received from the CFTs the recommendations, which included plant closures and reduced headcount, Ghosn created and communicated what he called the Nissan Revival Plan (or NRP) in October of 1999. From that point forward he stressed implementation and follow-up, rather than planning and reexamining decisions. Other CFTs were formed, but the bulk of his efforts lay in ensuring high-quality execution of the decisions that were laid out in the plan.

Ghosn's main focus areas included: (1) development of new automobiles and markets, (2) improvement of Nissan's brand image, (3) reinvestment in research and development, and (4) cost reduction.

Reducing Redundancies

To achieve these results, the closing of five factories and the reduction of 21,000 jobs (14% of Nissan's workforce) were planned. Job cuts would occur in manufacturing, management, and the dealer network.[7] Since Japanese business culture had tended to have lifelong employment as a principle, Ghosn endured strong criticism from the media, including being labeled as a *gaijin,* a foreigner. In addition, Ghosn fired several managers who did not meet targets, regardless of the circumstances. Many industry ana-

lysts cited his demotion of Vice President of Sales and Marketing in Japan, Mr. Hiroshi Moriyama, as unacceptable and reckless. They contended that falling revenues and dissipated market share were due to Nissan's aging product line rather than to Moriyama's performance. In addition to the media and industry analysts, the government also expressed concern about the layoffs, but Prime Minister Keizo Obuchi responded by offering subsidies and programs to help the affected workers.[8]

Keiretsu Partnerships

As one of the biggest changes of the NRP, Nissan broke away from the Japanese cultural norm of *keiretsu* investments. However Nissan maintained customer-supplier relationships with those former *keiretsu* partners. As it turned out, Nissan regained billions in tied up capital to use for debt servicing and new product development without losing any significant pricing advantages. In fact, because Ghosn put such an emphasis on reducing purchasing costs, Nissan actually began to substantially lower its costs after the *keiretsu* investments were sold.

Reorganization

Another major component of the NRP was the restructuring of the organization toward permanent cross-functional departments, which each serviced one product line. As a result, the staffs gained better visibility of the entire business process and began to focus on total business success and customer satisfaction, as opposed to misleading performance goals that could be taken out of context. In addition, Ghosn also eliminated all advisor and coordinator positions that carried no responsibilities and put those personnel in positions with direct operational responsibility. Employees were disciplined much more strongly for inaccurate or poor data than misjudgment, thereby stimulating risk-taking behavior and personal accountability. Ghosn also made it clear, however, that engineers were not to reduce product cycle times or do anything that would negatively impact product quality or reliability. He

---

[7]"Nissan's Napoleon," *Worldlink,* 11 July 2002, http://www.worldlink.co.uk.

[8]Barr, C. W. "Get Used to It: Japanese Steel Themselves for Downsizing. Mitsubishi and Nippon Telephone Have Added 30,000 Layoffs to Nissan's 21,000 Announced Oct. 19," *Christian Science Monitor,* Nov. 12, 1999.

repeated this often to drive home the point that the way to restore the power of the Nissan brand was through each individual customer's experience.

For higher-level staff, Ghosn created a matrix organization to improve transparency and communication. Within this matrix, he assigned each staff member two responsibilities: functional (e.g., marketing, engineering) and regional (e.g., domestic, North America). The result was that each staff member would have two bosses, thereby building awareness of both functional and regional issues. Ghosn also put an emphasis on cross-functional department members having very clear lines of responsibility and high standards of accountability. Every report, both oral and written, was to be 100% accurate. Ghosn is quoted as saying, "Right from the beginning, I made it clear that every number had to be thoroughly checked. I did not accept any report that was less than totally clear and verifiable, and I expected people to personally commit to every observation or claim they made."[9]

Performance Evaluations and Employee Advancement

Ghosn also put focus on performance by introducing a performance based incentive system. These incentives included cash incentives and stock options for achievements that could be linked directly to successful operating profits and revenue. This was a large departure from the traditional Japanese compensation system, in which managers usually received no stock options or bonuses. Under Ghosn's compensation system, the highest achievers got the highest rewards. And promotions were no longer limited to age, length of service, or educational level. For example, a female factory worker who had only a high school diploma was promoted to be a manufacturing manager based on her strong abilities to perform the work, relating promotion and salary increase to the ability to perform challenging or demanding tasks. The promotion of some younger leaders over older, longer-serving employees caused some problems regarding lack of cooperation. But just as Ghosn saw cultural differences as growth opportunities, he thought these tests of authority were growth experiences for young managers.

[9]Ghosn, Carlos. "Saving the Business without Losing the Company," *Harvard Business Review*, Vol. 80, No. 1, January 2002.

THE FIRST THREE YEARS

The NRP was achieved in March 2002, one year ahead of schedule.[10] One success was a 20% reduction in purchasing costs. This was a result of achieving a purchase price from *kereitsu* suppliers that matched the prices offered by Renault's suppliers. In addition, the supplier base shrunk by 40% and the service suppliers decreased by 60%.[11]

Prior to NRP, seven plants produced automobiles based on 24 platforms. After NRP, four plants produced automobiles based on 15 platforms.[12]

THE NEAR FUTURE—IMPLEMENTATION OF NISSAN 180

On May 9, 2002, Ghosn stated in a speech for an annual business review, "The Nissan Revival Plan is over. Two years after the start of its implementation, all the official commitments we took have been overachieved one full year ahead of schedule . . . Nissan is now ready to grow." He went on in the speech to set out the goals for a new plan, one he called "Nissan 180" which would focus on profitable growth. All new goals were to be accomplished by April 1, 2005. The one in "Nissan 180" represents an additional 1,000,000 car sales for Nissan worldwide; the eight, an 8% operating profitability with no changes in accounting standards; and the zero represented zero automotive debt. In addition, the plan called for an increase of global market share from 4.7% presently to 6.1%, a further reduction of purchasing costs by 15%, and a significant increase in customer satisfaction and sales satisfaction ratings. In 2002, midcareer hires (400) outnumbered college recruits (280). Because hiring outside managers might create animosity among managers within Nissan, this practice reflects a sharp change in hiring decisions. "We're moving to a system where it doesn't matter if you've been in the company ten

[10]2002 News, "Nissan Announced NRP Will Conclude One Year Earlier than Planned," http://www.nissan-global.com.

[11]Nissan 180, "Fiscal Year 01 Business Review," http://www.nissan-global.com.

[12]Nissan 180, "Fiscal Year 01 Business Review," http://www.nissan-global.com.

years or 40 years . . . If you contribute, there will be opportunity and reward," said Kuniyuki Watanabe, Nissan's Senior Vice President for Human Resources.[13]

Not only was Ghosn aggressively launching the Nissan 180 program to transition out of the Nissan Revival Plan program, but he was also pushing a new, customer-focused initiative called "Quality 3-3-3." He said that this program focuses on three categories of quality: product attractiveness, product initial quality and reliability, and sales & service quality.

CHALLENGES FOR GHOSN AND NISSAN

As Ghosn contemplates the future, he knows that the transformation has really just begun. How could the

[13]Raskin, Andy. "*Voulez-Vous* Completely Overhaul This Big, Slow Company and Start Making Some Cars People Actually Want *Avec Moi?*" *Business 2.0,* January 2002.

momentum and the energy that his employees exhibited be maintained now that they had all reached the goals that were seemingly Herculean just over two years ago? Would there be a letdown of effort and results by Nissan employees, or would Ghosn be able to mobilize them to get to the next level of profitable growth and reestablishment of brand power and market share?

He was aware that current succession plans called for him to return to Renault as its new CEO, replacing Louis Schweitzer in 2005. Before this could happen, Ghosn would be challenged to find an adequate replacement who could take Nissan to new heights of accomplishment as planned. Could the new approaches that had been so successful become part of the Nissan culture without his continued guidance? Would the success of the NRP spoil the sense of urgency that helped reinforce the need for change allowing Nissan to slip back into old habits? How could he find someone to carry forward the need to create a sustainable pattern of customer focus and profitable growth?

appendix | 1   Summary of Results of NRP

The turnaround at Nissan was phenomenal, with the following statistics:

- From seven out of eight years of operating losses to profitability within the first 12 months. Since 1999, Nissan has shown four consecutive semi-annual operating profits, and the year 2001 was marked by the best-ever, full-year earnings at Nissan. The current operating margin is 7.9%, over 3% greater than committed to in the NRP.

- Net automotive debt is the lowest it has been in 24 years (down from $10.5 billion to $4.35 billion).

- The company developed eight new car models to be launched by late 2002/early 2003, including the award-winning, revamped Altima, and the new 350Z.

- Supplier costs were reduced by 20%, as per the NRP, mainly through sourcing and other strategies to minimize exchange rate issues, as well as the reduction of the number of parts suppliers by 40% and the number of service providers by 60%.

- Five plants have been closed, according to the NRP.

- Headcount was reduced by 21,000, according to the NRP, mainly through natural turnover, retirements, pre-retirement programs, and by selling off non-core businesses to other companies.

- The number of car models that were profitable increased to 18 of 36 models from 4 of 43 models.

appendix|2   Nissan and Renault Profile

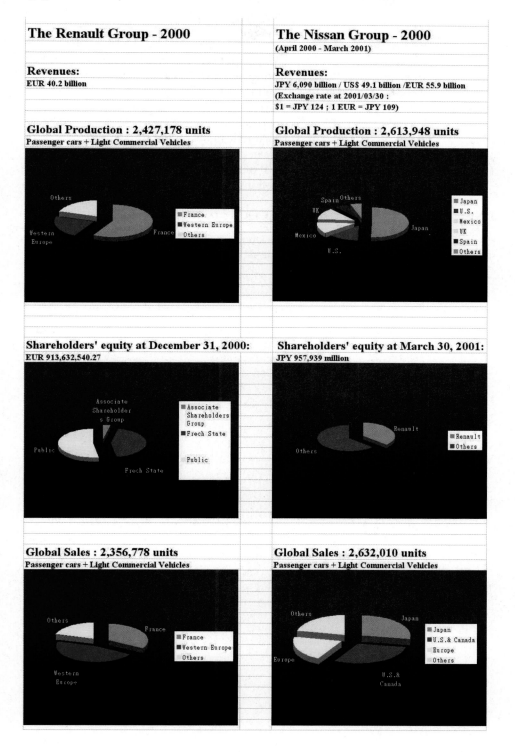

The Renault Group - 2000

Revenues:
EUR 40.2 billion

Global Production : 2,427,178 units
Passenger cars + Light Commercial Vehicles

Shareholders' equity at December 31, 2000:
EUR 913,632,540.27

Global Sales : 2,356,778 units
Passenger cars + Light Commercial Vehicles

The Nissan Group - 2000
(April 2000 - March 2001)

Revenues:
JPY 6,090 billion / US$ 49.1 billion /EUR 55.9 billion
(Exchange rate at 2001/03/30 :
$1 = JPY 124 ; 1 EUR = JPY 109)

Global Production : 2,613,948 units
Passenger cars + Light Commercial Vehicles

Shareholders' equity at March 30, 2001:
JPY 957,939 million

Global Sales : 2,632,010 units
Passenger cars + Light Commercial Vehicles

appendix|3   Carlos Ghosn's Background*

1954	Born in Brazil, March 9
1974	Receives chemical engineering degree from École Polytechnique, Paris
1978	Graduates from École des Mines de Paris. Joins Michelin
1981	Becomes plant manager at Le Puy plant, France
1984	Becomes head of R&D
1985	Becomes COO of South American operations. Turns company around
1989	President and COO of North American operations
1990	Named CEO of North American operations
1996	Joins Renault as Executive VP of advanced R&D, car engineering and development, power train operations, manufacturing, and purchasing. Gains nickname, "Le Cost-Killer"
1999	Named Nissan president and COO

*http://www.google.co.jp/search?q=cache:NNR0tavWLwAC:www.ai-online.com/articles/0302cover-story.asp+carlos+Ghosn,+background&hl=ja&ie=UTF-8

Wal-Mart Stores, Inc.: A New Set of Challenges

Arthur A. Thompson
The University of Alabama

In early 2004, Wal-Mart's president and CEO, H. Lee Scott, was bullish not only about Wal-Mart's growth prospects but also its ability to deal with critics who were challenging the company's seemingly virtuous business model of relentlessly wringing cost efficiencies out of its supply chain and providing customers with everyday low prices. Scott and other members of Wal-Mart's highly regarded management team, as well as members of founder Sam Walton's family, could look with justifiable pride on the company's remarkable journey from humble beginnings in the 1960s as a folksy discount retailer in the boondocks of Arkansas to what in 2004 was a $260 billion retailing juggernaut in the early stages of globalizing its operations from its headquarters in Bentonville, Arkansas (which was now served by two daily nonstop flights to New York's LaGuardia Airport). Wal-Mart's growth over the past four decades was unprecedented:

	1962	1970	1980
Sales	$1.4 million	$31 million	$1.2 billion
Profits	$112,000	$1.2 million	$41 million
Stores	9	32	276

	1990	2000	2004
Sales	$26 billion	$191 billion	$256 billion
Profits	$1 billion	$6.3 billion	$9.0 billion
Stores	1,528	4,188	4,906

Copyright © 2003 by Arthur A. Thompson.

Just as unprecedented was Wal-Mart's impact on general merchandise retailing and the attraction its stores had to shoppers. During 2003, about 140 million people in 11 countries shopped Wal-Mart's almost 4,700 stores every week. More than half of American shoppers visited a Wal-Mart at least once a month, and one-third went once a week—in 2002 an estimated 82 percent of American households made at least one purchase at Wal-Mart.[1] Since the early 1990s, the company had gone from dabbling in supermarket sales to taking the number one spot in grocery retailing worldwide. In the United States, Wal-Mart was the biggest employer in 21 states, and it employed 1.4 million people worldwide, far more than any other company.[2] It was the largest retailer in Canada and Mexico, as well as in the United States and the world as a whole. On November 28, 2003, Wal-Mart set a one-day sales record of $1.52 billion in the United States and over $1.6 billion worldwide—figures bigger than the gross domestic products of 36 countries.

Wal-Mart's performance and prominence in the retailing industry had resulted in numerous awards. By the turn of the century, it had been named "Retailer of the Century" by *Discount Store News,* made the *Fortune* magazine lists of "Most Admired Companies in America" and "100 Best Companies to Work for in America," and been included on the *Financial Times*' "Most Respected in the World" list.

[1] Anthony Bianco and Wendy Zellner, "Is Wal-Mart Too Powerful?" *Business Week,* October 6, 2003, p. 102.

[2] Jerry Useem, "One Nation Under Wal-Mart," *Fortune,* March 3, 2003, p. 66.

In 2000, Wal-Mart was ranked fifth on *Fortune*'s list of the "Global Most Admired Companies." In 2002, Wal-Mart became number one on the Fortune 500 list of the largest companies in America and also on Fortune's Global 500 list. Wal-Mart topped Fortune's 2003 list of "Most Admired Companies in America" and was recognized as the "Largest Corporate Cash Giver" by *Forbes* magazine based on the *Chronicle of Philanthropy*'s survey of sales and cash donations for 2002—Wal-Mart's cash contributions to some 80,000 organizations increased in 2002 to $136 million, up 17 percent from 2001; in addition, customers and associates raised another $70 million at Wal-Mart's stores and clubs. Wal-Mart received the 2002 Ron Brown Award, the highest presidential award recognizing outstanding achievement in employee relations and community initiatives. In 2003, American Veterans Awards gave Wal-Mart its "Corporate Patriotism Award."

Wal-Mart's success had made the Walton family (Sam Walton's heirs and living relatives) the wealthiest in the world—in 2003, five Walton family members controlled about 1.75 billion shares of Wal-Mart stock worth about $93 billion. Increases in the value of Wal-Mart's stock over the years had made hundreds of Wal-Mart employees, retirees, and shareholders millionaires or multimillionaires. Since 1970, when Wal-Mart shares were first issued to the public, the company's stock had split 11 times. A $1,650 investment in Wal-Mart stock in 1970 (100 shares purchased at the initial offer price of $16.50) equated to 204,800 shares worth $10.8 million as of December 2003.

COMPANY BACKGROUND

Sam Walton graduated from the University of Missouri in 1940 with a degree in economics and took a job as a management trainee at J. C. Penney Company. His career with Penney's ended with a call to military duty in World War II. When the war was over, Walton decided to purchase a franchise and open a Ben Franklin retail variety store in Newport, Arkansas, rather than return to Penney's. Five years later, when the lease on the Newport building was

lost, Walton decided to relocate his business in Bentonville, Arkansas, where he bought a building and opened Walton's 5 & 10 as a Ben Franklin–affiliated store. By 1960 Walton was the largest Ben Franklin franchisee, with nine stores.

In 1961 Walton started to become concerned about the long-term competitive threat to variety stores posed by the emerging popularity of giant supermarkets and discounters. An avid pilot, he took off in his plane on a cross-country tour to study the changes in stores and retailing trends, then put together a plan for a discount store of his own. Walton went to Chicago to try to interest Ben Franklin executives in expanding into discount retailing; when they turned him down, he decided to go forward on his own because he believed deeply in the retailing concept of offering significant price discounts to expand sales volumes and increase overall profits. The first Wal-Mart Discount City opened July 2, 1962, in Rogers, Arkansas. The store was successful, and Walton quickly began to look for opportunities to open stores in other small towns and to attract talented people with retailing experience to help him grow the business. Although he started out as a seat-of-the-pants merchant, he had great instincts, was quick to learn from other retailers' successes and failures, and was adept at garnering ideas for improvements from employees and promptly trying them out. Sam Walton incorporated his business as Wal-Mart Stores in 1969. When the company went public in 1970 and sold 300,000 shares at $16.50 each to help finance its rapid growth, it had 38 stores and sales of $44.2 million. In 1979, with 276 stores, 21,000 employees, and operations in 11 states, Wal-Mart became the first company to reach $1 billion in sales in such a short time.

As the company grew, Sam Walton proved to be an effective and visionary leader. His folksy demeanor and his talent for motivating people, combined with a very hands-on management style and an obvious talent for discount retailing, produced a culture and a set of values and beliefs that kept Wal-Mart on a path of continuous innovation and rapid expansion. Moreover, Wal-Mart's success and Walton's personable style of leadership generated numerous stories in the media that cast the company and its founder in a positive light. As Wal-Mart emerged as the premier discount retailer in the

United States in the 1980s, an uncommonly large cross-section of the American public came to know who Sam Walton was and to associate his name with Wal-Mart. Sam Walton's folksy personality, unpretentious manner, and interest in people and their feelings caused people inside and outside the company to hold him in high esteem. Regarded by many as "the entrepreneur of the century" and "a genuine American folk hero," he enjoyed a reputation of being not only a community-spirited man who was concerned for his employees but also a devoted family man who epitomized the American dream and demonstrated the virtues of hard work.

Just before Sam Walton's death in 1992, his vision was for Wal-Mart to become a $125 billion company by 2000. But his handpicked successor, David D. Glass, beat that target by almost 2 years. Under Glass's leadership (1988–2000), Wal-Mart's sales grew at an average annual compound rate of 19 percent, pushing revenues up from $20.6 billion to $165 billion. When David Glass retired in January 2000, H. Lee Scott was chosen as Wal-Mart's third president and CEO. In the four years that Scott had been CEO, Wal-Mart's sales had grown over $100 billion, matching the company's growth in its first 35 years. Even though there were Wal-Mart stores in all 50 states and 10 foreign countries in 2004, Scott and other senior executives believed there were sufficient domestic and foreign growth opportunities to permit the company to grow at double-digit rates for the foreseeable future and propel Wal-Mart's revenues past $500 billion by 2010.

Exhibit 1 provides a summary of Wal-Mart's financial and operating performance for the 1993–2004 fiscal years.

Yet, while a report by the prominent Boston Consulting Group said, "The world has never known a company with such ambition, capability, and momentum," in 2003 there were growing signs that the continued growth and influence of the "Beast of Bentonville" was breeding a backlash among competing retailers, organized labor, community activists, and so-called cultural progressives. Wal-Mart was drawing increasing flak from organized labor about the company's low wages and anti-union posture. It was confronting some 6,000 lawsuits on a variety of issues, including one claiming that it discriminated against female employees.

WAL-MART'S STRATEGY

The hallmarks of Wal-Mart's strategy were multiple store formats, low everyday prices, wide selection, a big percentage of name-brand merchandise, a customer-friendly store environment, low operating costs, innovative merchandising, a strong emphasis on customer satisfaction, disciplined expansion into new geographic markets, and in many case using acquisitions to enter foreign markets. On the outside of every Wal-Mart store in big letters was the message "We Sell for Less." The company's advertising tag line reinforced the low-price theme: "Always low prices. Always." Major merchandise lines included housewares, consumer electronics, sporting goods, lawn and garden items, health and beauty aids, apparel, home fashions, paint, bed and bath goods, hardware, jewelry, automotive repair and maintenance, toys and games, and groceries.

Multiple Store Formats

In 2004, Wal-Mart was seeking to meet customers' needs with four different retail concepts: Wal-Mart discount stores, Supercenters, neighborhood markets, and Sam's Clubs:

- *Discount stores*—These stores ranged from 40,000 to 125,000 square feet, employed an average of 150 people, and offered as many as 80,000 different items, including family apparel, automotive products, health and beauty aids, home furnishings, electronics, hardware, toys, sporting goods, lawn and garden items, pet supplies, jewelry, housewares, prescription drugs, and packaged grocery items. Discount stores had sales in the $30 to $50 million range, depending on store size and location.

- *Supercenters*—Supercenters, which Wal-Mart started opening in 1988 to meet a demand for one-stop family shopping, joined the concept of a general merchandise discount store with that of a full-line supermarket. They ranged from 109,000 to 220,000 square feet, employed between 200 and 550 associates, had about 36 general merchandise departments, and offered up to 150,000 different items, at least 30,000 of which were grocery products. In addition to the value-priced merchandise offered at discount stores

exhibit 1   **Financial and Operating Summary, Wal-Mart Stores, Fiscal Years 1993–2004 (in billions, except earnings per share data)**

	Fiscal Year Ending January 31					
	2004	2003	2002	2001	2000	1993
Financial and operating data						
Net sales	$256.3	$244.5	$217.8	$191.3	$165.0	$55.5
Net sales increase	12%	12%	14%	16%	20%	26%
Domestic comparable store sales increase*	5%	5%	6%	5%	8%	11%
Cost of sales	198.7	191.8	171.6	150.3	129.7	44.2
Operating, selling, general and administrative expenses	44.9	41.0	36.2	31.6	27.0	8.3
Interest costs, net	0.8	0.9	1.2	1.2	0.8	0.3
Net income	$ 9.0	$ 8.0	$ 6.7	$ 6.3	$ 5.4	$ 2.0
Earnings per share of common stock (diluted)	$2.07	$1.81	$1.49	$1.40	$1.20	$0.44
Balance sheet data						
Current assets	$ 34.2	$30.5	$27.9	$26.6	$24.4	$10.2
Net property, plant, equipment, and capital leases	55.2	51.9	45.8	40.9	36.0	9.8
Total assets	104.9	94.7	83.5	78.1	70.3	20.6
Current liabilities	37.4	32.6	27.3	28.9	25.8	6.8
Long-term debt	17.5	16.6	15.7	12.5	13.7	3.1
Long-term obligations under capital leases	3.0	3.0	3.0	3.2	3.0	1.8
Shareholders' equity	43.6	39.3	35.1	31.3	25.8	8.6
Financial ratios						
Current ratio	0.9	0.9	1.0	0.9	0.9	1.5
Return on assets	8.6%	9.2%	8.5%	8.7%	9.5%	11.1%
Return on shareholders' equity	20.6%	21.6%	20.1%	22.0%	22.9%	25.3%
Other year-end data						
Number of domestic Wal-Mart Discount stores	1,478	1,568	1,647	1,736	1,801	1,848
Number of domestic Wal-Mart Supercenters	1,471	1,258	1,066	888	721	34
Number of domestic Sam's Clubs	538	525	500	475	463	256
Number of domestic Neighborhood Markets	64	49	31	19	7	—
Number of international stores	1,355	1,288	1,170	1,070	1,004	10

*Defined as sales at stores open a full year that have not been expanded or relocated in the past 12 months.

Source: Wal-Mart annual reports for 2003 and 2004.

and a large supermarket section with 30,000+ items, Supercenters contained such specialty shops as vision centers, tire and lube expresses, a fast-food restaurant, portrait studios, one-hour photo centers, hair salons, banking, and employ-

ment agencies. Typical Supercenters had annual sales in the $80–$100 million range.

- *Sam's Clubs*—A store format that Wal-Mart launched in 1983, Sam's was a cash-and-carry, members-only warehouse that carried about

4,000 frequently used, mostly brand-name items in bulk quantities along with some big-ticket merchandise. The product lineup included fresh, frozen, and canned food products, candy and snack items, office supplies, janitorial and household cleaning supplies and paper products, apparel, CDs and DVDs, and an assortment of big-ticket items (TVs, tires, large and small appliances, watches, jewelry, computers, camcorders, and other electronic equipment). Stores were approximately 110,000 to 130,000 square feet in size, with most goods displayed in the original cartons stacked in wooden racks or on wooden pallets. Many items stocked were sold in bulk quantity (five-gallon containers, bundles of a dozen or more, and economy-sized boxes). Prices tended to be 10–15 percent below the prices of the company's discount stores and Supercenters since merchandising costs and store operation costs were lower. Sam's was intended to serve small businesses, churches and other religious organizations, beauty salons and barber shops, motels, restaurants, offices, local schools, families, and individuals looking for great prices on large-volume quantities or big-ticket items. Annual member fees were $30 for businesses and $35 for individuals—there were 46 million members in 2003. Sam's stores employed about 125 people each and had annual sales averaging $63 million. A number of Sam's stores were located adjacent to a Supercenter or discount store.

- *Neighborhood markets*—Neighborhood markets—the company newest store format, launched in 1998—were designed to appeal to customers who just needed groceries, pharmaceuticals and general merchandise. They were always located in markets with Wal-Mart Supercenters so as to be readily accessible to Wal-Mart's food distribution network. Neighborhood Markets ranged from 42,000 to 55,000 square feet, employed 80–100 people each, and featured fresh produce, deli foods, fresh meat and dairy items, health and beauty aids, one-hour photo and traditional photo developing services, drive-through pharmacies, stationery and paper goods, pet supplies, and household supplies—about 28,000 items in total.

Domestically, during 2004 Wal-Mart planned to open approximately 50 to 55 new discount stores, 220 to 230 new Supercenters, 25 to 30 new neigh-borhood markets, and 35 to 40 new Sam's Clubs. Relocations or expansions of existing discount stores accounted for approximately 140 of the new Supercenters, and approximately 20 of the Sam's Clubs were relocations or expansions.

Internationally, Wal-Mart planned to open 130 to 140 units in the 10 countries where it already had stores; of these, 30 were expected to be relocations or expansions. In 2004 Wal-Mart expected to spend $18 million to open three new stores in eastern China, an area where French retailer Carrefour (the world's second largest retailer behind Wal-Mart) and Germany's Metro AG had stores; Wal-Mart had opened 31 stores in 15 cities across the country since 1996.

Exhibit 2 shows the number of Wal-Mart stores in each state and country. There were still many locations in the United States that were underserved by Wal-Mart stores. Inner-city sections of New York City had no Wal-Mart stores of any kind because ample space with plenty of parking was unavailable at a reasonable price. Wal-Mart's first Supercenter in all of California opened in 2003 at a three-story location in downtown Los Angeles that had escalators sized for shopping carts. There were no Supercenters in New Jersey, Rhode Island, Vermont, or Hawaii, and only 1 in Massachusetts and 2 in Connecticut (versus 155 in Texas, 87 in Florida, 58 in Missouri, 52 in North Carolina, 49 in Alabama, and 47 in Louisiana).

Wal-Mart's various domestic and international stores were served by 108 regional general merchandise and food distribution centers. Five additional distribution centers averaging over 1 million square feet of space were planned for 2004.

Wal-Mart's Geographic Expansion Strategy

One of the most distinctive features of Wal-Mart's domestic strategy was the manner in which it expanded outward into new geographic areas. Whereas many chain retailers achieved regional and national coverage quickly by entering the largest metropolitan centers before trying to penetrate less-populated markets, Wal-Mart always expanded into adjoining geographic areas, saturating each area with stores before moving into new territory. New stores were usually clustered within 200 miles of an existing distribution center so that daily deliveries could be made cost-effectively; new distribution centers were added as

exhibit 2   **Wal-Mart's Store Count, January 2003**

State	Discount Stores	Supercenters	Sam's Clubs	Neighborhood Markets
Alabama	34	49	9	2
Alaska	6	0	3	0
Arizona	24	17	10	0
Arkansas	35	43	4	6
California	133	0	30	0
Colorado	17	29	14	0
Connecticut	27	2	3	0
Delaware	3	3	1	0
Florida	66	87	37	1
Georgia	42	61	20	0
Hawaii	6	0	1	0
Idaho	5	11	1	0
Illinois	81	33	27	0
Indiana	42	42	14	0
Iowa	27	24	7	0
Kansas	29	23	6	0
Kentucky	34	41	5	0
Louisiana	35	47	12	0
Maine	12	9	3	0
Maryland	32	5	13	0
Massachusetts	41	1	3	0
Michigan	48	14	22	0
Minnesota	34	9	12	0
Mississippi	21	41	5	1
Missouri	56	58	14	0
Montana	5	6	1	0
Nebraska	10	11	3	0
Nevada	11	7	5	0
New Hampshire	19	6	4	0
New Jersey	30	0	8	0
New Mexico	6	18	5	0
New York	52	22	18	0
North Carolina	47	52	17	0
North Dakota	8	0	2	0
Ohio	70	28	26	0
Oklahoma	41	40	7	12
Oregon	24	3	0	0
Pennsylvania	50	43	20	0
Rhode Island	8	0	1	0
South Carolina	22	37	9	0
South Dakota	6	4	2	0
Tennessee	33	57	15	2
Texas	117	155	68	24

(continues)

exhibit 2 **(concluded)**

State	Discount Stores	Supercenters	Sam's Clubs	Neighborhood Markets
Utah	6	15	7	1
Vermont	4	0	0	0
Virginia	21	52	13	0
Washington	29	6	2	0
West Virginia	8	20	3	0
Wisconsin	49	20	11	0
Wyoming	2	7	2	0
U.S. totals	1,568	1,258	525	49
International/Worldwide				
Argentina	0	11	0	0
Brazil	0	12	8	2[a]
Canada	213	0	0	0
China	0	20	4	2
Germany	0	94	0	0
S. Korea	0	15	0	0
Mexico	472[b]	75	50	0
Puerto Rico	9	1	9	33[c]
United Kingdom	248[d]	10	0	0
International totals	942	238	71	37
Grand totals	2,510	1,496	596	86

[a]Brazil includes Todo Dias.
[b]Mexico includes 118 Bodegas, 50 Suburbias, 44 Superamas, 260 Vips.
[c]Puerto Rico includes 33 Amigos.
[d]United Kingdom includes 248 ASDA Stores.

needed to support store expansion into additional areas. In the United States, the really unique feature of Wal-Mart's geographic strategy had involved opening stores in small towns surrounding a targeted metropolitan area before moving into the metropolitan area itself—an approach Sam Walton had termed "backward expansion." Wal-Mart management believed that any town with a shopping-area population of 15,000 or more was big enough to support a Wal-Mart Discount Store and that towns of 25,000 could support a Supercenter. Once stores were opened in towns around the most populous city, Wal-Mart would locate one or more stores in the metropolitan area and begin major market advertising.

By clustering new stores in a relatively small geographic area, Wal-Mart could spread advertising expenses for breaking into a new market across all the area stores, a tactic the company used to keep its advertising costs under 1 percent of sales (compared to 2 or 3 percent for other discount chains). Don Soderquist, Wal-Mart's retired senior vice chairman, explained why the company preferred its backward expansion strategy:

> Our strategy is to go into smaller markets first before we hit major metro areas because you've got a smaller population base to convince over. So you begin to get the acceptance in smaller markets and the word begins to travel around and people begin to travel further and further to get to your stores.[3]

In the small towns Wal-Mart entered, it was not unusual for a number of local businesses that carried merchandise similar to Wal-Mart's lines to fail within a year or two of Wal-Mart's arrival. Wal-Mart's low

[3]*Discount Store News,* December 18, 1989, p. 162.

prices tended to attract customers away from apparel shops, general stores, pharmacies, sporting goods stores, shoe stores, hardware stores, supermarkets, and convenience stores operated by local merchants. The "Wal-Mart effect" in small communities was so potent that it had spawned sometimes fierce local resistance to the entry of a new Wal-Mart among both local merchants and area residents wanting to preserve the economic vitality of their downtown areas and protect against the invasion of what they considered to be an unsightly Wal-Mart store and parking lot. Consulting firms formed that specialized in advising local retailers on how to survive the opening of a Wal-Mart.

For the past several years, Wal-Mart had been driving hard to expand its geographic base of stores outside the United States through a combination of new store construction and acquisition. Acquisition of general merchandise or supermarket chains had been a part of Wal-Mart's entry and/or store expansion strategy in Canada, Mexico, Brazil, Japan, Puerto Rico, China, and Great Britain. International sales accounted for 16.7 percent of total sales in fiscal 2003, and the percentage was expected to rise in the coming years. Wal-Mart stores in China had some of the highest traffic counts of any stores in the world. Wal-Mart's entry into Japan via minority ownership of Japan's fifth largest supermarket chain, Seiyu, had stirred a retailing revolution among Japanese retailers to improve their merchandising, cut their costs, lower their prices, and streamline their supply chains. Prior to buying a minority stake in Seiyu in 2002 (with an option to increase its ownership to 67 percent by 2007), Wal-Mart had studied the Japanese market for four years. It planned to spend most of 2003–2004 getting Seiyu stores and its Japanese supply chain ready for a full-scale assault on penetrating the Japanese market with a lineup of both supermarket and general merchandise products. Sales at Wal-Mart's nearly 1,300 international stores averaged about $31 million per store in fiscal 2003; the company's international division had 2003 total sales of $40.7 billion (up 15 percent) and operating profits of $2.0 billion (up almost 56 percent).

But as Wal-Mart grew more global, management intended to "remain local" in terms of the goods it carried and in some of the ways it operated. Most store managers and senior managers in its foreign operations were natives of the countries where Wal-Mart operated; many had begun their careers as hourly employees. Wal-Mart did, however, have a program that allowed stores in different areas to exchange best practices.

Everyday Low Prices

While Wal-Mart did not invent the concept of everyday low pricing, it had done a better job than any other discount retailer in executing the strategy. The company was widely seen by consumers as being the lowest-priced general merchandise retailer in its market. Recent studies showed that prices of its grocery items were 8 to 27 percent below those of such leading supermarket chain competitors as Kroger (which used the City Market brand in the states west of the Mississippi), Safeway, and Albertson's, after making allowances for specials and loyalty cards. In-store services were also bargain-priced—customers could wire money for a flat $12.95 (versus a fee of $50 to wire $1,000 at Western Union) and could purchase money orders for 46 cents (versus 90 cents charged by the U.S. Postal Service). Wal-Mart touted its low prices on its storefronts ("We Sell for Less"), in advertising, on signs inside its stores, and on the logos of its shopping bags. Some economists believed that Wal-Mart's everyday low prices had reduced inflationary pressures economywide, allowing all U.S. consumers to benefit from the Wal-Mart effect. The well-known financier Warren Buffet said, "You add it all up and they have contributed to the financial well-being of the American public more than any other institution I can think of."[4]

Merchandising Innovations

Wal-Mart was unusually active in testing and experimenting with new merchandising techniques. From the beginning, Sam Walton had been quick to imitate good ideas and merchandising practices employed by other retailers. According to the founder of Kmart, Sam Walton "not only copied our concepts; he strengthened them. Sam just took the ball and ran with it."[5] Wal-Mart prided itself on its "low threshold for change," and much of management's time was spent talking to vendors, employees, and customers to get ideas for how Wal-Mart could improve.

[4]As quoted in Useem, "One Nation Under Wal-Mart," p. 68.
[5]As quoted in Bill Saporito, "What Sam Walton Taught America," *Fortune*, May 4, 1992, p. 105.

Suggestions were actively solicited from employees. Most any reasonable idea was tried; if it worked well in stores where it was first tested, then it was quickly implemented in other stores. Experiments in store layout, merchandise displays, store color schemes, merchandise selection (whether to add more upscale lines or shift to a different mix of items), and sales promotion techniques were always under way. Wal-Mart was regarded as an industry leader in testing, adapting, and applying a wide range of cutting-edge merchandising approaches. In 2003 Wal-Mart was testing the merits of an in-store candy department featuring an assortment mainly targeted to children, with bulk candy from Brach's, Jelly Belly, and M&M, plus a wide range of novelty and licensed items and coin-operated kiddie rides.

Advertising

Wal-Mart relied less on advertising than most other discount chains did. The company distributed only one or two circulars per month and ran occasional TV ads, relying primarily on word of mouth to communicate its marketing message. Wal-Mart's advertising expenditures ran about 0.3 percent of sales revenues, versus 1.5 percent for Kmart and 2.3 percent for Target. Wal-Mart spent $676 million on advertising in fiscal 2003, $618 million in fiscal 2002, and $574 million in fiscal 2001. Wal-Mart's spending for radio and TV advertising was said to be so low that it didn't register on national ratings scales. Most Wal-Mart broadcast ads appeared on local TV and local cable channels. Wal-Mart did no advertising for its Sam's Club stores. The company often allowed charities to use its parking lots for their fund-raising activities.

Distribution

Over the years, Wal-Mart's management had turned the company's centralized distribution systems into a competitive edge—the company's low distribution costs and cost-effective supply chain management practices were a big reason why its prices were low. Wal-Mart got an early jump on competitors in distribution efficiency because of its rural store locations. Whereas other discount retailers relied on manufacturers and distributors to ship directly to their mostly metropolitan-area stores, Wal-Mart found that its rapid growth during the 1970s was straining suppli-

ers' ability to use independent trucking firms to make frequent and timely deliveries to its growing number of rural store locations. To improve the delivery of merchandise to its stores, the company in 1980 began to build its own centralized distribution centers and to supply stores from these centers with daily deliveries by its own truck fleet. Wal-Mart added new distribution centers when new outlying stores could no longer be reliably and economically supported from an existing center.

THE COMPETITIVE ENVIRONMENT

Discount retailing was an intensely competitive business. Competition among discount retailers centered on pricing, store location, variations in store format and merchandise mix, store size, shopping atmosphere, and image with shoppers. Wal-Mart's primary competitors were Kmart and Target in general merchandise retailing and in superstores that also included a full-line supermarket Super Target stores and Super Kmart stores. Wal-Mart also competed against category retailers like Best Buy and Circuit City in electronics; Toys "R" Us in toys; Goody's in apparel; Bed, Bath, and Beyond in household goods; and Kroger, Albertson's, and Safeway in groceries.

Surveys of households comparing Wal-Mart with Kmart and Target indicated that Wal-Mart had a strong competitive advantage. According to *Discount Store News:*

> When asked to compare Wal-Mart with Kmart and Target, the consensus of households is that Wal-Mart is as good or better. For example, of the households with a Wal-Mart in the area, 59 percent said that Wal-Mart is better than Kmart and Target; 33 percent said it was the same. Only 4 percent rated Wal-Mart worse than Kmart and Target . . . When asked why Wal-Mart is better, 55 percent of the respondents with a Wal-Mart in their area said lower/better prices . . . Variety/selection and good quality were the other top reasons cited by consumers when asked why Wal-Mart is better. Thirty percent said variety; 18 percent said good quality.[6]

The two largest competitors in the warehouse club segment were Costco and Sam's Clubs; BJ's

---

[6]*Discount Store News,* December 18, 1989, p. 168.

Wholesale Club, a smaller East Coast chain, was the only other major U.S. player in this segment.[7] For the year ended August 31, 2003, Costco had U.S. sales of $34.4 billion at 312 stores versus $32.9 billion at 532 stores for Sam's. The average Costco store generated annual revenues of $112 million, almost double the $63 million average at Sam's. Costco catered to affluent households with upscale tastes and located its stores in mostly urban areas. Costco's 42 million members averaged 11.4 store visits annually and spent an average of $94 per visit, which compared favorably with averages of 8.5 visits and expenditures of $78 at Sam's. Costco was the nation's biggest retailer of fine wines ($600 million annually) and roasted chickens (55,000 rotisserie chickens a day). While its product line included food and household items, sporting goods, vitamins, and various other merchandise, its big attraction was big-ticket luxury items (diamonds and plasma TVs) and the latest gadgets at bargain prices (Costco capped its markups at 14 percent). Costco had beaten Sam's in being the first to sell fresh meat and produce (1986 versus 1989), to introduce private-label items (1995 versus 1998), and to sell gasoline (1995 versus 1997). Costco offered its workers good wages and fringe benefits (full-time hourly workers made about $40,000 after four years).

Wal-Mart's rapid climb to become the largest supermarket retailer had triggered heated price competition in the aisles of most supermarkets. Wal-Mart's three major rivals—Kroger, Albertson's, and Safeway—along with a host of smaller regional supermarket chains, were scrambling to cut costs, narrow the price gap with Wal-Mart, and otherwise differentiate themselves so as to retain their customer base and grow revenues. Continuing increases in the number of Wal-Mart Supercenters meant that the majority of rival supermarkets would be within 10 miles of a Supercenter by 2010. Wal-Mart had recently concluded that it took fewer area residents to support a Supercenter than the company had thought; management believed that Supercenters in urban areas could be as little as four miles apart and still attract sufficient store traffic. Kroger had announced plans to cut its costs by $500 million by January 31, 2004, to put it in better position to match Wal-Mart's lower prices

on grocery items. Supermarket industry observers were speculating that either Albertson's (which was already closing underperforming stores and struggling to maintain current revenues) or Safeway (which had its hands full trying to digest a series of acquisitions of regional supermarket chains) would not survive a coming shakeout among the weaker supermarket competitors.

WAL-MART'S APPROACHES TO STRATEGY EXECUTION

To implement and execute its strategy, Wal-Mart put heavy emphasis on getting the lowest possible prices from its suppliers, forging close working relationships with key suppliers in order to capture win–win cost savings throughout its supply chain, keeping its internal operations lean and efficient, paying attention to even the tiniest details in store layouts and merchandising, making efficient use of state-of-the-art technology, and nurturing a culture that thrived on hard work, constant improvement, and pleasing customers, especially passing cost savings on to customers in the form of low prices.

Wal-Mart's Use of Cutting-Edge Technology

Wal-Mart began using computers to maintain inventory control on an item basis in its distribution centers and stores in 1974. Wal-Mart began testing point-of-sale scanners in 1981 and then committed to systemwide use of scanning bar codes in 1983—a move that improved checkout times by 25–30 percent. In 1984, Wal-Mart developed a computer-assisted merchandising system that allowed each store to tailor the product mix to its own market circumstances and sales patterns. Between 1985 and 1987 Wal-Mart installed the nation's largest private satellite communication network, which allowed two-way voice and data transmission between headquarters, the distribution centers, and the stores and one-way video transmission from Bentonville's corporate offices to distribution centers and to the stores; the system was less expensive than the previously used telephone network. The video system was

---

[7]The information in this paragraph is drawn from John Helyar, "The Only Company Wal-Mart Fears," *Fortune,* November 24, 2003, pp. 158–66.

used regularly by company officials to speak directly to all employees at once.

In 1989 Wal-Mart established direct satellite links with about 1,700 vendors supplying close to 80 percent of the goods sold by Wal-Mart; these links allowed the use of electronic purchase orders and instant data exchanges. Wal-Mart also used the satellite system's capabilities to develop a credit card authorization procedure that took five seconds, on average, to authorize a purchase, speeding up credit checkout by 25 percent compared to the prior manual system. In the early 1990s, through pioneering collaboration with Procter & Gamble, Wal-Mart instituted an automated reordering system that notified suppliers as their items moved through store checkout lanes; this allowed suppliers to track sales and inventories of their products (so they could plan production and schedule shipments accordingly).

Throughout the 1990s Wal-Mart continued to invest in information technology and online systems, usually being a first-mover among retailers in upgrading and improving its capabilities as new technology was introduced. By 2003 the company had developed and deployed sophisticated information technology systems and online capability that not only gave it real-time access to detailed figures on most any aspect of its operations but also made it a leader in cost-effective supply chain management. It could track the movement of goods through its entire value chain—from the sale of items at the cash register backward to stock on store shelves, in-store backup inventory, distribution center inventory, and shipments en route. Moreover, Wal-Mart collaborated with its suppliers to develop data-sharing capabilities aimed at streamlining the supply of its stores, avoiding both stockouts and excess inventories, identifying slow-selling items that might warrant replacement, and spotting ways to squeeze costs out of the supply chain. The company's Retail Link system allowed suppliers to track their wares through Wal-Mart's value chain, get hourly sales figures for each item, and monitor gross margins on each of their products (Wal-Mart's actual selling price less what it paid the supplier).

In mid-2003 Wal-Mart informed its suppliers that they would have to convert to electronic product code (EPC) technology based on radio frequency identification (RFID) systems by 2005. EPCs involved a new product numbering standard that went beyond identifying products. Every single item that rolled off a manufacturing line was embedded with an electronic tag containing a unique number. EPCs offered users significant time savings and enhanced their ability to update online databases—identifying where and when a case or pallet of goods arrived, for example—in supply chain logistics applications. EPC tags could be read by RFID scanners when brought into range of a tag reader—unlike bar codes, they did not have to be directly in the line of sight of the scanner. Wal-Mart's management expected EPC scanning would eventually be built into warehouse bin locations and store shelves, allowing the company to locate and track items throughout the supply chain in real time. With EPC and RFID capability, every single can of soup or DVD or screwdriver in Wal-Mart's supply chain network or on its store shelves could then be traced back to where and when it was made, where and when it arrived at the store, and where and when it was sold (or turned up missing). Further, EPCs linked to an online database provided a secure way of sharing product-specific information with supply chain partners. Wal-Mart management believed that EPC technology, in conjunction with the expanding production of RFID-capable printers/encoders, had the potential to revolutionize the supply chain by providing more accurate information about product movement, stock rotation, and inventory levels; it was also seen as a significant tool for preventing theft and dealing with product recalls. An IBM study indicated that EPC tagging would reduce stockouts by 33 percent, while an Accenture study showed that EPC/RFID technology could boost worker productivity by 5 percent and shrink working capital and fixed capital requirements by 5 to 30 percent.

The attention Wal-Mart management placed on using cutting-edge technology and the astuteness with which it deployed this technology along its value chain to enhance store operations and continuously drive down costs had, over the years, resulted in Wal-Mart's being widely regarded as having the most cost-effective, data-rich information technology systems of any major retailer in the world. So powerful had Wal-Mart's influence been on retail supply chain efficiency that its competitors (and many other retailers as well) had found it essential to follow Wal-Mart's lead and pursue "Wal-Martification" of their retail supply chains.[8]

[8]Paul Lightfoot, "Wal-Martification," *Operations and Fulfillment,* June 1, 2003, posted at www.opsandfulfillment.com.

exhibit 3 **The Scale of Wal-Mart's Purchases from Selected Suppliers and Its Market Shares in Selected Product Categories**

Supplier	Percent of Total Sales to Wal-Mart	Product Category	Wal-Mart's U.S. Market Share*
Tandy Brands Accessories	39%	Dog food	36%
Dial	28	Disposable diapers	32
Del Monte Foods	24	Photographic film	30
Clorox	23	Shampoo	30
Revlon	20–23	Paper towels	30
RJR Tobacco	20	Toothpaste	26
Procter & Gamble	17	Pain remedies	21
		CDs, DVDs, and videos	15–20
		Single-copy sales of magazines	15
Although sales percentages were not available, Wal-Mart was also the biggest customer of Disney, Campbell Soup, Kraft, and Gillette.		Although market shares were not available, Wal-Mart was also the biggest seller of toys, guns, diamonds, detergent, video games, socks, and bedding.	

*Based on sales through food, drug, and mass merchandisers.

Sources: Jerry Useem, "One Nation Under Wal-Mart," *Fortune,* March 3, 2003, p. 66; and Anthony Bianco and Wendy Zellner, "Is Wal-Mart Too Powerful?" *Business Week,* October 6, 2003, p. 102.

Relationships with Suppliers

Wal-Mart was far and away the biggest customer of virtually all of its suppliers (see Exhibit 3). Wal-Mart's scale of operation allowed it to bargain hard with suppliers and get their bottom prices. It looked for suppliers who were dominant in their category (thus providing strong brand-name recognition), who could grow with the company, who had full product lines (so that Wal-Mart buyers could both cherry-pick and get some sort of limited exclusivity on the products the company chose to carry), who had the long-term commitment to R&D to bring new and better products to retail shelves, and who had the ability to become more efficient in producing and delivering what it supplied.

Procurement personnel spent a lot of time meeting with vendors and understanding their cost structure. By making the negotiation process transparent, Wal-Mart buyers soon learned whether a vendor was doing all it could to cut down its costs and quote Wal-Mart an attractively low price. Wal-Mart's purchasing agents were dedicated to getting the lowest prices they could, and they did not accept invitations to be wined or dined by suppliers. The marketing vice president of a major vendor told *Fortune* magazine:

They are very, very focused people, and they use their buying power more forcefully than anybody else in America. All the normal mating rituals are verboten. Their highest priority is making sure everybody at all times in all cases knows who's in charge, and it's Wal-Mart. They talk softly, but they have piranha hearts, and if you aren't totally prepared when you go in there, you'll have your ass handed to you.[9]

All vendors were expected to offer their best price without exception; one consultant that helped manufacturers sell to retailers observed, "No one would dare come in with a half-ass price."[10]

Even though Wal-Mart was tough in negotiating for absolute rock-bottom prices, the price quotes it got were still typically high enough to allow suppliers to earn a profit. Being a Wal-Mart supplier generally meant having a stable and dependable enough sales base to operate production facilities in a cost-effective manner. Moreover, once Wal-Mart decided to source from a vendor, then it worked closely with the vendor to find *mutually beneficial* ways to squeeze costs out of the supply chain. Every aspect of a supplier's operation got scrutinized—how products got developed, what they were made of, how

[9]As quoted in *Fortune,* January 30, 1989, p. 53.

[10]As quoted in Useem, "One Nation Under Wal-Mart," p. 68.

costs might be reduced, what data Wal-Mart could supply that would be useful, how sharing of data online could prove beneficial, and so on. Nearly always, as they went through the process with Wal-Mart personnel, suppliers saw ways to prune costs or otherwise streamline operations in ways that enhanced their profit margins. In 1989 Wal-Mart became the first major retailer to embark on a program urging vendors to develop products and packaging that would not harm the environment. In addition, Wal-Mart expected its vendors to contribute ideas about how to make its stores more fun insofar as their products were concerned. The maker of Power Rangers products, for example, had created the world's largest inflatable structure—a 5,000-cubic-foot moon—which toured Wal-Mart parking lots.[11] Coca-Cola had routed its Los-Angeles-to-Atlanta Olympic Torch Run past as many Wal-Mart stores as possible. Those suppliers that were selected as "category managers" for such product groupings as lingerie or pet food or school supplies were expected to educate Wal-Mart on everything that was happening in their respective product category.

Some 200 vendors had established offices in Bentonville to work closely with Wal-Mart on a continuing basis—most were in an area referred to locally as "Vendorville." Vendors were encouraged to voice any problems in their relationship with Wal-Mart and to become involved in Wal-Mart's future plans. Top-priority projects ranged from using more recyclable packaging to working with Wal-Mart on merchandise displays and product mix to tweaking the just-in-time ordering and delivery system to instituting automatic reordering arrangements to coming up with new products with high customer appeal. Most recently, one of Wal-Mart's priorities was working with vendors to figure out how to localize the items carried in particular stores and thereby accommodate varying tastes and preferences of shoppers in different areas where Wal-Mart had stores. Most vendor personnel based in Bentonville spent considerable time focusing on which items in their product line were best for Wal-Mart, where they ought to be placed in the stores, how they could be better displayed, what new products ought to be introduced, and which ones ought to be rotated out.

A 2003 survey conducted by Cannondale Associates found that manufacturers believed Wal-Mart was the overall best retailer with which to do business—the fifth straight year in which Wal-Mart was ranked number one.[12] Target was ranked second, and Costco was ranked seventh. The criteria for the ranking included such factors as clearest company strategy, best store branding, best buying teams, most innovative consumer marketing/merchandising, best supply chain management practices, best overall business fundamentals, and best practice management of individual product categories. One retailing consultant said, "I think most [suppliers] would say Wal-Mart is their most profitable account."[13] While this might seem surprising because of Wal-Mart's enormous bargaining clout, the potentially greater profitability of selling to Wal-Mart stemmed from the practices of most other retailers to demand that suppliers pay sometimes steep slotting fees to win shelf space and their frequent insistence on supplier payment of such extras as in-store displays, damage allowances, handling charges, penalties for late deliveries, rebates of one kind or another, allowances for advertising, and special allowances on slow-moving merchandise that had to be cleared out with deep price discounts; further, most major retailers expected to be courted with Super Bowl tickets, trips to the Masters golf tournament, fancy dinners at conventions and trade shows, or other perks in return for their business. All of these extras represented costs that suppliers had to build into their prices. At Wal-Mart everything was boiled down to one price number, and no "funny-money" extras ever entered into the deal.[14]

Most suppliers viewed Wal-Mart's single bottom-line price and its expectation of close coordination as a win–win proposition, not only because of the benefits of cutting out all the funny-money costs and solidifying their relationship with a major customer but also because what they learned from the collaborative efforts and mutual data-sharing often had considerable benefit in the rest of their operations. Many suppliers, including Procter & Gamble, liked Wal-Mart's supply chain business model so well that they had pushed their other customers to adopt similar practices.[15]

[11]Ibid., p. 74.

[12]Reported in a *DSN Retailing Today Online* editorial by Tony Lisanti, November 10, 2003.

[13]As quoted in Useem, "One Nation Under Wal-Mart," p. 74.

[14]Ibid.

[15]Ibid.

Wal-Mart's Standards for Suppliers   In
the 1990s Wal-Mart began establishing standards for
its suppliers, with particular emphasis on foreign
suppliers that had a history of problematic wages
and working conditions. Management believed that
suppliers' practices regarding workers' hours; child
labor; discrimination based on race, religion, or
other factors; workplace safety, and compliance with
local laws and regulations could be attributed to Wal-
Mart and could affect its reputation with customers
and shareholders. To mitigate the potential for being
adversely affected by the manner in which its suppliers conducted their business, Wal-Mart had established a set of supplier standards and set up an
internal group to see that suppliers were conforming
to the published ethical standards and business practices of Wal-Mart itself.

The company's supplier standards had been
through a number of changes as the concerns of Wal-
Mart management evolved over time. Suppliers' factories were monitored regularly, and in February
2003 Wal-Mart took direct control of foreign factory
audits. Wal-Mart had factory certification teams
based in offices in Dubai, Singapore, India, and
China; the offices were staffed with more than 100
Wal-Mart employees dedicated to monitoring foreign factory compliance with the company's supplier
standards. All suppliers were asked to sign a document certifying their compliance with the standards
and were required to post a version of the supplier
standards in both English and the local language in
each production facility servicing Wal-Mart.

Distribution Center Operations

Throughout the 1980s and 1990s, Wal-Mart had pursued a host of efficiency-increasing actions at its distribution centers. The company had been a global
leader in automating its distribution centers and expediting the transfer of incoming shipments from
manufacturers to its fleet of delivery trucks, which
made daily deliveries to surrounding stores. Prior to
automation, bulk cases received from manufacturers
had to be opened by distribution center employees
and perhaps stored in bins, then picked and repacked
in quantities needed for specific stores, and finally
loaded onto trucks for delivery to Wal-Mart stores—
a manual process that was error-prone and sometimes slow. Using state-of-the-art technology,
Wal-Mart had automated many of the labor-intensive

tasks, gradually creating an ever-more-sophisticated
and cost-efficient system of conveyors, bar-coding,
and handheld computers, along with other devices
with the capability to quickly sort incoming shipments from manufacturers into smaller, store-
specific quantities and route them to waiting trucks
to be sent to stores to replenish sold merchandise.
Often, incoming goods from manufacturers being
unloaded at one section of the warehouse were immediately sorted into store-specific amounts and
conveyed directly onto waiting Wal-Mart trucks
headed for those particular stores—a large portion of
the incoming inventory was in a Wal-Mart distribution center an average of only 12 hours. Distribution
center employees had access to real-time information regarding the inventory levels of all items in the
center and used the different bar codes for pallets,
bins, and shelves to pick up items for store orders.
Handheld computers also enabled the packaging department to get accurate information about which
items to pack for which store and what loading dock
to convey them to.

Truck Fleet Operations

Wal-Mart operated a fleet of 3,500+ company-
owned trucks to get goods from its 100+ distribution centers to its almost 5,000 stores. Wal-Mart
hired only experienced drivers who had driven more
than 300,000 accident-free miles with no major traffic violations. Distribution centers had facilities
where drivers could shower, sleep, eat, or attend to
personal business while waiting for their truck to be
loaded. A truck dispatch coordinator scheduled the
dispatch of all trucks according to the available time
of drivers and estimated driving time between the
distribution center and the designated store. Drivers
were expected to pull their trucks up to the store
dock at the scheduled time (usually late afternoon or
early evening) even if they arrived early; trucks were
unloaded by store personnel during nighttime hours,
with a two-hour gap between each new truck delivery (if more than one was scheduled for the same
night).

In instances where it was economical, Wal-Mart
trucks were dispatched directly to a manufacturer's
facilities, picked up goods for one or more stores,
and delivered them directly, bypassing the distribution center entirely. Manufacturers that supplied certain high-volume items or even a number of different

items sometimes delivered their products in truck-load lots directly to some or many of Wal-Mart's stores.

Store Construction and Maintenance

Wal-Mart management worked at getting more mileage out of its capital expenditures for new stores, store renovations, and store fixtures. Ideas and suggestions were solicited from vendors regarding store layout, the design of fixtures, and space needed for effective displays. Managers had open-air offices that could be furnished economically, and store designs featured a maximum of display space that could be rearranged and refurbished easily. Wal-Mart claimed that the design and aisle width at its new Supercenters would accommodate 100 million shoppers a week. Because Wal-Mart insisted on a high degree of uniformity in the new stores it built, the architectural firm Wal-Mart employed was able to use computer modeling techniques to turn out complete specifications for 12 or more new stores a week. Moreover, the stores were designed to permit quick, inexpensive construction as well as to allow for low-cost maintenance and renovation. All stores were renovated and redecorated at least once every seven years. If a given store location was rendered obsolete by the construction of new roads or the opening of new shopping locations, then the old store was abandoned in favor of a new store at a more desirable site. In 2003, Wal-Mart stores were being expanded or relocated at the rate of 100–200 annually.

In keeping with the low-cost theme for facilities, Wal-Mart's distribution centers and corporate offices were also built economically and furnished simply. The offices of top executives were modest and unpretentious. The lighting, heating, and air-conditioning controls at all Wal-Mart stores were connected via computer to Bentonville headquarters, allowing cost-saving energy management practices to be implemented centrally and freeing store managers from the time and worry of trying to hold down utility costs. Wal-Mart mass-produced a lot of its displays in-house, not only saving money but also cutting the time needed to roll out a new display concept to as little as 30 days. The company also had a group that disposed of used fixtures and equipment

via auctions at the store sites where the surplus existed—a calendar of upcoming auctions was posted on the company's Web site.

Wal-Mart's Approach to Providing Superior Customer Service

Wal-Mart tried to put some organization muscle behind its pledge of "Satisfaction Guaranteed" and do things that would make customers' shopping experience at Wal-Mart pleasant. Store managers challenged store associates to practice what Sam Walton called "aggressive hospitality." A "greeter" was stationed at store entrances to welcome customers with a smile, thank them for shopping at Wal-Mart, assist them in getting a shopping cart, and answer questions about where items were located. Clerks and checkout workers were trained to be courteous and helpful and to exhibit a "friendly, folksy attitude." All store associates were called on to display the "10-foot attitude" and commit to a pledge of friendliness: "I solemnly promise and declare that every customer that comes within ten feet of me, I will smile, look them in the eye, and greet them." Wal-Mart's management stressed five themes in training and supervising store personnel:

1. Think like a customer.
2. Sell what customers want to buy.
3. Provide a genuine value to the customer.
4. Make sure the customer has a good time.
5. Exceed the customer's expectations.

In all stores, efforts were made to present merchandise in easy-to-shop shelving and displays. Floors in the apparel section were carpeted to make the department feel homier and to make shopping seem easier on customers' feet. Store layouts were constantly scrutinized to improve shopping convenience and make it easier for customers to find items. Store employees wore blue vests to make it easier for customers to pick them out from a distance. Fluorescent lighting was recessed into the ceiling to create a softer impression than exposed fluorescent lighting strips. Yet nothing about the decor conflicted with Wal-Mart's low-price image; retailing consultants considered Wal-Mart to be very adept at sending out an effective mix of signals concerning customer service, low prices, quality merchandise, and friendliness. Wal-Mart's management believed that the effort the company put into making its stores more user-friendly and inviting caused shoppers to view Wal-Mart in a more positive light. A reporter for *Discount Store News* observed:

> The fact is that everything Wal-Mart does from store design to bar coding to lighting to greeters—regardless of how simple or complex—is implemented only after carefully considering the impact on the customer. Virtually nothing is done without the guarantee that it benefits the customer in some way . . . As a result Wal-Mart has been able to build loyalty and trust among its customers that is unparalleled among other retail giants.[16]

The Culture at Wal-Mart in 2003

Wal-Mart's culture in 2003 continued to be deeply rooted in Sam Walton's business philosophy and leadership style. Mr. Sam, as he had been fondly called, had been not only Wal-Mart's founder and patriarch but also its spiritual leader—and still was in many respects. Four key core values and business principles underpinned Sam Walton's approach to managing:[17]

- Treat employees as partners, sharing both the good and bad about the company so that they will strive to excel and participate in the rewards. (Wal-Mart fostered the concept of partnership by referring to all employees as "associates," a term Sam Walton had insisted on from the company's beginnings because it denoted a partnerlike relationship.)

- Build for the future, rather than just immediate gains, by continuing to study the changing concepts that are a mark of the retailing industry and be ready to test and experiment with new ideas.

- Recognize that the road to success includes failing, which is part of the learning process rather than a personal or corporate defect or failing. Always challenge the obvious.

- Involve associates at all levels in the total decision-making process.

[16]*Discount Store News,* December 18, 1989, p. 161.
[17]Sam Walton with John Huey, *Sam Walton: Made in America* (New York: Doubleday, 1992), p. 12.

Sam Walton practiced these principles diligently in his own actions and insisted that other Wal-Mart managers do the same. Up until his health failed badly in 1991, he spent several days a week visiting the stores, gauging the moods of shoppers, listening to employees discuss what was on their minds, learning what was or was not selling, gathering ideas about how things could be done better, complimenting workers on their efforts, and challenging them to come up with good ideas.

The values, beliefs, and practices that Sam Walton instilled in Wal-Mart's culture and that still carried over in 2003 were reflected in statements made in his autobiography:

> Everytime Wal-Mart spends one dollar foolishly, it comes right out of our customer's pockets. Everytime we save a dollar, that puts us one more step ahead of the competition—which is where we always plan to be.

> One person seeking glory doesn't accomplish much; at Wal-Mart, everything we've done has been the result of people pulling together to meet one common goal.

> I have always been driven to buck the system, to innovate, to take things beyond where they've been.

> We paid absolutely no attention whatsoever to the way things were supposed to be done, you know, the way the rules of retail said it had to be done.

> My role has been to pick good people and give them the maximum authority and responsibility.

> I'm more of a manager by walking and flying around, and in the process I stick my fingers into everything I can to see how it's coming along . . . My appreciation for numbers has kept me close to our operational statements, and to all the other information we have pouring in from so many different places.

> The more you share profit with your associates—whether it's in salaries or incentives or bonuses or stock discounts—the more profit will accrue to your company. Why? Because the way management treats the associates is exactly how the associates will then treat the customers. And if the associates treat the customers well, the customers will return again and again.

> The real challenge in a business like ours is to become what we call servant leaders. And when they do, the team—the manager and the associates—can accomplish anything.

There's no better way to keep someone doing things the right way than by letting him or her know how much you appreciate their performance.

I like my numbers as quickly as I can get them. The quicker we get that information, the quicker we can act on it.

The bigger we get as a company, the more important it becomes for us to shift responsibility and authority toward the front lines, toward that department manager who's stocking the shelves and talking to the customer.

We give our department heads the opportunity to become real merchants at a very early stage of the game . . . we make our department heads the managers of their own businesses . . . We share everything with them: the costs of their goods, the freight costs, the profit margins. We let them see how their store ranks with every other store in the company on a constant, running basis, and we give them incentives to want to win.

We're always looking for new ways to encourage our associates out in the stores to push their ideas up through the system . . . Great ideas come from everywhere if you just listen and look for them. You never know who's going to have a great idea.

A lot of bureaucracy is really the product of some empire builder's ego . . . We don't need any of that at Wal-Mart. If you're not serving the customers, or supporting the folks who do, we don't need you.

I believe in always having goals, and always setting them high . . . The folks at Wal-Mart have always had goals in front of them. In fact, we have sometimes built real scoreboards on the stage at Saturday morning meetings.

You can't just keep doing what works one time, because everything around you is always changing. To succeed, you have to stay out in front of that change.[18]

Walton's success flowed from his cheerleading management style, his ability to instill the principles and management philosophies he preached into Wal-Mart's culture, the close watch he kept on costs, his relentless insistence on continuous improvement, and his habit of staying in close touch with both consumer and associates. It was common practice for Walton to lead cheers at annual shareholder meetings, store visits, managers' meetings, and company events. His favorite was the Wal-Mart cheer:

> Give me a W!
> Give me an A!
> Give me an L!
> Give me a Squiggly!
>   (Here, everybody sort of does the twist.)
> Give me an M!
> Give me an A!
> Give me an R!
> Give me a T!
> What's that spell?
> Wal-Mart!
> Whose Wal-Mart is it?
> My Wal-Mart!
> Who's number one?
> The Customer! Always!

In 2003, the Wal-Mart cheer was still a core part of the Wal-Mart culture and was used throughout the company at meetings of store employees, managers, and corporate gatherings in Bentonville to create a "whistle while you work" atmosphere, loosen everyone up, inject fun and enthusiasm, and get sessions started on a stimulating note. While the cheer seemed corny to outsiders, once they saw the cheer in action at Wal-Mart they came to realize its cultural power and significance. And much of Sam Walton's cultural legacy remained intact in 2003, most especially among the company's top decision makers and longtime managers. As a *Fortune* writer put it:

> Spend enough time inside the company—where nothing backs up a point better than a quotation from Walton scripture—and it's easy to get the impression that the founder is orchestrating his creation from the beyond.[19]

The Three Basic Beliefs Underlying the Wal-Mart Culture in 2003
Wal-Mart top management stressed three basic beliefs that Sam Walton had preached since 1962:

1. *Treat individuals with respect and dignity*— Management consistently drummed the theme that dedicated, hardworking, ordinary people who teamed together and who treated each other with respect and dignity could accomplish extraordinary things. Throughout company literature, comments could be found referring to Wal-Mart's "concern for the individual." Such expres-

---

[18]Ibid., pp. 10, 12, 47, 63, 115, 128, 135, 140, 213, 226–229, 233, 246, 249–254, and 256.

[19]Useem, "One Nation Under Wal-Mart," p. 72.

sions as "Our people make the difference," "We care about people," and "People helping People" were used repeatedly by Wal-Mart executives and store managers to create and nurture a family-oriented atmosphere among store associates.

2. *Service to customers*—Management stressed that the company was nothing without its customers. Management emphasized that, to satisfy customers and keep them coming back again and again, the company had to build their trust in its pricing philosophy—Wal-Mart customers had to always find the lowest prices with the best possible service. One of the standard Wal-Mart mantras preached to all associates was that the customer was boss. Associates in stores were urged to observe the rule regarding the "10-foot attitude."

3. *Strive for excellence*—The concept of striving for excellence stemmed from Sam Walton's conviction that prices were seldom as low as they needed to be and that product quality was seldom as high as customers deserved. The thesis at Wal-Mart was that new ideas and ambitious goals made the company reach further and try harder—the process of finding new and innovative ways to push boundaries and constantly improve made the company better at what it did and contributed to higher levels of customer satisfaction. Wal-Mart managers at all levels spent much time and effort motivating associates to offer ideas for improvement and to function as partners. It was reiterated again and again that every cost counted and that every worker had a responsibility to be involved.

These three beliefs were supplemented by several supporting cultural themes and practices:

- Go all-out to exceed customers' expectations and make sure that customers have a good time shopping at Wal-Mart. Every associate repeatedly heard "The customer is boss and the future depends on you."

- Practice Sam Walton's 10 rules for building a business. Management had distilled much of Sam Walton's business philosophy into 10 rules (see Exhibit 4); these were reiterated to associates and used at meetings to guide decision making and the crafting and executing of Wal-Mart's strategy.

- Observe the Sundown Rule: Answer requests by sundown on the day they are received. Management believed this working principle had to be taken seriously in a busy world in which people's job performance depended on cooperation from others.

Wal-Mart's culture had unusually deep roots at the headquarters complex in Bentonville. The numerous journalists and business executives who had been to Bentonville and spent much time at Wal-Mart's corporate offices uniformly reported being impressed with the breadth, depth, and pervasive power of the company's culture. Jack Welch, former CEO of General Electric and a potent culture builder in his own right, noted that "the place vibrated" with cultural energy. There was little evidence that the culture in Bentonville was any weaker in 2003 than it had been 12 years earlier when Sam Walton personally led the culture-building, culture-nurturing effort.

But Wal-Mart executives nonetheless were currently facing a formidable challenge in sustaining the culture in the company's distribution centers and especially in its stores. Annual turnover rates in Wal-Mart's stores were running about 45 percent in 2002–2003 and had run as high as 70 percent in 1999 when the economy was booming and the labor market was tight. Such high rates of turnover among the company's worldwide workforce of 1.4 million, coupled with the fact that Wal-Mart would need to add another 800,000 new employees from 2004 to 2008 (including 47,000 management positions) to staff its new stores and distribution centers, made keeping the culture intact outside Bentonville a Herculean task. No other company in all of business history had been confronted with cultural indoctrination of so many new employees in so many locations in such a relatively short time.

Soliciting Ideas from Associates

Associates at all levels were expected to be an integral part of the process of making the company better. Wal-Mart store managers usually spent a portion of each day walking around the store checking on how well things were going in each department, listening to associates' comments, soliciting suggestions, discussing how improvements could be made, and praising associates who were doing a good job.

exhibit 4   **Sam Walton's 10 Rules for Building a Business**

Rule 1: Commit to your business. Believe in it more than anybody else. I think I overcame every single one of my personal shortcomings by the sheer passion I brought to my work. I don't know if you're born with this kind of passion, or if you can learn it. But I do know you need it. If you love your work, you'll be out there every day trying to do it the best you possibly can, and pretty soon everybody around will catch the passion from you—like a fever.

Rule 2: Share your profits with all your Associates, and treat them as partners. In turn, they will treat you as a partner, and together you will all perform beyond your wildest expectations. Remain a corporation and retain control if you like, but behave as a servant leader in a partnership. Encourage your Associates to hold a stake in the company. Offer discounted stock, and grant them stock for their retirement. It's the single best thing we ever did.

Rule 3: Motivate your partners. Money and ownership alone aren't enough. Constantly, day-by-day, think of new and more interesting ways to motivate and challenge your partners. Set high goals, encourage competition, and then keep score. Make bets with outrageous payoffs. If things get stale, cross-pollinate; have managers switch jobs with one another to stay challenged. Keep everybody guessing as to what your next trick is going to be. Don't become too predictable.

Rule 4: Communicate everything you possibly can to your partners. The more they know, the more they'll understand. The more they understand, the more they'll care. Once they care, there's no stopping them. If you don't trust your Associates to know what's going on, they'll know you don't really consider them partners. Information is power, and the gain you get from empowering your Associates more than offsets the risk of informing your competitors.

Rule 5: Appreciate everything your Associates do for the business. A paycheck and a stock option will buy one kind of loyalty. But all of us like to be told how much somebody appreciates what we do for them. We like to hear it often, and especially when we have done something we're really proud of. Nothing else can quite substitute for a few well-chosen, well-timed, sincere words of praise. They're absolutely free—and worth a fortune.

Rule 6: Celebrate your successes. Find some humor in your failures. Don't take yourself so seriously. Loosen up, and everybody around you will loosen up. Have fun. Show enthusiasm—always. When all else fails, put on a costume and sing a silly song. Then make everybody else sing with you. Don't do a hula on Wall Street. It's been done. Think up your own stunt. All of this is more important, and more fun, than you think, and it really fools the competition. "Why should we take those cornballs at Wal-Mart seriously?"

Rule 7: Listen to everyone in your company. And figure out ways to get them talking. The folks on the front lines—the ones who actually talk to the customer—are the only ones who really know what's going on out there. You'd better find out what they know. This really is what total quality is all about. To push responsibility down in your organization, and to force good ideas to bubble up within it, you must listen to what your Associates are trying to tell you.

Rule 8: Exceed your customers' expectations. If you do, they'll come back over and over. Give them what they want—and a little more. Let them know you appreciate them. Make good on all your mistakes, and don't make excuses—apologize. Stand behind everything you do. The two most important words I ever wrote were on that first Wal-Mart sign, "Satisfaction Guaranteed." They're still up there, and they have made all the difference.

Rule 9: Control your expenses better than your competition. This is where you can always find the competitive advantage. For 25 years running—long before Wal-Mart was known as the nation's largest retailer—we ranked No. 1 in our industry for the lowest ratio of expenses to sales. You can make a lot of different mistakes and still recover if you run an efficient operation. Or you can be brilliant and still go out of business if you're too inefficient.

Rule 10: Swim upstream. Go the other way. Ignore the conventional wisdom. If everybody else is doing it one way, there's a good chance you can find your niche by going in exactly the opposite direction. But be prepared for a lot of folks to wave you down and tell you you're headed the wrong way. I guess in all my years, what I heard more often than anything was: a town of less than 50,000 population cannot support a discount store for very long.

Source: www.walmartstores.com, accessed December 18, 2003.

Store managers frequently asked associates what needed to be done better in their department and what could be changed to improve store operations. Associates who believed that a policy or procedure detracted from operations were encouraged to challenge and change it. Task forces to evaluate ideas and plan out future actions to implement them were common, and it was not unusual for the person who developed the idea to be appointed the leader of the group. An assistant store manager explained the importance of getting employees to suggest ways to boost sales:

We are encouraged to be merchants. If a sales clerk, a checker or a stockman believes he can sell an item and wants to promote it, he is encouraged to go for it. That associate can buy the merchandise, feature it, and maintain it as long as he can sell it.[20]

That same assistant store manager, when he accidentally ordered four times as many Moon Pies for an in-store promotion as intended, was challenged by the store manager to be creative and figure out a way to sell the extra inventory. The assistant manager's solution was to create the first World Championship Moon Pie Eating Contest, held in the store's parking lot in the small town of Oneonta, Alabama. The promotion and contest drew thousands of spectators and was so successful that it became an annual store event.

Listening to employees was a very important part of each manager's job. All of Wal-Mart's top executives relied on a concept known as management by walking around; they visited stores, distribution centers, and support facilities regularly, staying on top of what was happening and listening to what employees had to say about how things were going. Senior managers at Wal-Mart's Bentonville headquarters believed that visiting stores and listening to associates was time well spent because a number of the company's best ideas had come from Wal-Mart associates—Wal-Mart's use of people greeters at store entrances was one of those ideas.

Compensation and Incentives

New hourly associates at U.S. Wal-Mart stores were paid anywhere from $1 to $6 above the minimum wage, depending on the type of job, and could expect to receive a raise within the first year at one or both of the semiannual job evaluations. Typically, at least one raise was guaranteed in the first year if Wal-Mart planned to keep the individual on the staff. The other raise depended on how well the associate worked and improved during the year. At the store level, only the store manager was salaried; all other associates, including the department managers, were considered hourly employees. A 2003 study by *Forbes* found that Wal-Mart employees earned an average hourly wage of $7.50, which translated to an

annual income of $18,000. Store clerks generally earned the least—one study showed that sales clerks earned an average of $8.23 an hour and $13,861 annually in 2001.[21] Workers that unloaded trucks and stocked store shelves could earn anywhere from $25,000 to $50,000.

Part-time jobs were most common among sales clerks and checkout personnel in the stores where customer traffic varied appreciably during days of the week and months of the year. New full-time and part-time associates became eligible for health care benefits after a six-month wait and a one-year exclusion for preexisting conditions. As of 2003, about 60 percent of the roughly 800,000 U.S. Wal-Mart associates signed up for coverage (compared with an average of 72 percent for the whole retailing industry); many Wal-Mart associates did not sign up for health care coverage because another household member already had family coverage at his or her place of employment. Worker premiums for coverage were as little as $13 every two weeks with an annual deductible of $1,000, but associates could opt for plans with a higher premium and a lower deductible.[22] The health care benefit package covered 100 percent of most major medical expenses above $1,750 in employee out-of-pocket expenses and entailed no lifetime cap on medical cost coverage (a feature offered by fewer than 50 percent of U.S. employers). The company's health benefits also included dental coverage, short- and long-term disability, an illness protection plan, and business travel accident insurance. But to help control its health care costs for associates, Wal-Mart's plan did not pay for flu shots, eye exams, child vaccinations, chiropractic services, and certain other treatments allowed in the plans of many companies; further, Wal-Mart did not pay any health care costs for retirees. Due to Wal-Mart management's recent efforts to control costs for health care benefits, the company's health care costs compared very favorably with those of other organizations:[23]

[20]*Discount Store News,* December 18, 1989, p. 83.

[21]According to documents filed in a lawsuit against the company and cited in Bianco and Zellner, "Is Wal-Mart Too Powerful?" p. 102.

[22]Bernard Wysocki Jr. and Ann Zimmerman, "Wal-Mart Cost-Cutting Finds a Big Target in Health Benefits," *The Wall Street Journal,* September 30, 2003, p. A16.

[23]Ibid., p. A1.

	Average Cost per Eligible Employee	
	2001	2002
U.S. employees of a cross-section of large, medium, and small companies	$4,924	$5,646
Employees of wholesale/retail stores	4,300	4,834
Wal-Mart employees (estimated)	3,000	3,500

Wal-Mart's package of fringe benefits for full-time employees (and some part-time employees) also included:

- Vacation and personal time.
- Holiday pay.
- Jury duty pay.
- Medical and bereavement leave.
- Military leave.
- Maternity/paternity leave.
- Confidential counseling services for associates and their families.
- Child care discounts for associates with children (through four national providers).
- GED reimbursement/scholarships for associates and their spouses.

Wal-Mart associates received 10 percent off selected merchandise and Sam's Club associates received a Sam's Club membership card at no cost.

According to management, some 60 percent of associates indicated that a major reason they joined Wal-Mart was the benefits. In addition to compensation and fringe benefits, Wal-Mart had installed an extensive system of incentives that allowed associates to share monetarily in the company's success.

The Profit-Sharing Plan Wal-Mart maintained a profit-sharing plan for full- and part-time associates; individuals were eligible after one year and 1,000 hours of service. Annual contributions to the plan were tied to the company's profitability and were made at the sole discretion of management and the board of directors. Employees could contribute up to 15 percent of their earnings to their 401(k) accounts. Wal-Mart's contribution to each associate's profit-sharing account became vested at the rate of 20 percent per year beginning the third year of participation in the plan. After seven years of continuous employment the company's contribution became fully vested; however, if the associate left the company prior to that time, the unvested portions were redistributed to all remaining employees. The plan was funded entirely by Wal-Mart, and most of the profit-sharing contributions were invested in Wal-Mart's common stock. The company had contributed more than $2.7 billion toward associates' profit-sharing and 401(k) accounts since 1972. Company contributions to the plan totaled $98.3 million in 1991, $129.6 million in 1992, and $166 million in 1993 but had risen significantly over the last decade—annual contributions to 401(k) and profit-sharing worldwide amounted to $663 million in fiscal 2003, $555 million in fiscal 2002, and $486 million in fiscal 2001. Associates could begin withdrawals from their account upon retirement or disability, with the balance paid to family members upon death.

Stock Purchase and Stock Option Plans
A stock purchase plan was adopted in 1972 to allow eligible employees a means of purchasing shares of common stock through regular payroll deduction or annual lump-sum contribution. Prior to 1990, the yearly maximum under this program was $1,500 per eligible employee; starting in 1990 the maximum was increased to $1,800 annually. The company contributed an amount equal to 15 percent of each participating associate's contribution. Longtime employees who had started participating in the early years of the program had accumulated stock worth over $100,000. About one-fourth of Wal-Mart's employees participated in the stock purchase plan in 1993, but this percentage had since declined because many new employees opted not to participate.

In addition to regular stock purchases, certain employees qualified to participate in stock option plans; options expired 10 years from the date of the grant and could be exercised in nine annual installments. In 2003 there were over 59 million shares reserved for issuance under stock option plans. The value of options granted in recent years was substantial: $96 million (1990), $128 million (1991), $143 million (1992), and $235 million (1993).

Sales Contests and Other Incentive Programs Associate incentive plans were in place in every store, club, distribution center, and support facility. Associates received bonuses for "good ideas," such as how to reduce shoplifting or how to improve merchandising. Wal-Mart instituted a shrinkage bonus in 1980. If a store held losses from theft and damage below the corporate goal, every associate in that store was eligible to receive up to $200. As a result, Wal-Mart's shrinkage ran about 1 percent, compared to an industry average of 2 percent. One of Wal-Mart's most successful incentive programs involved in-store sales contests that allowed departments within the store to do a special promotion and pricing on items they themselves wanted to feature. Management believed these contests boosted sales, breathed new life into an otherwise slow-selling item, and helped keep associates thinking about how to help bolster sales. In 1999 (the most recent year for which data were available), Wal-Mart paid $500 million in incentive bonuses based on store and individual performance to 525,000 full- and part-time employees.

On the basis of data provided by Wal-Mart associates, *Fortune* had included Wal-Mart on its list of the "100 Best Companies to Work For" for four of the six years from 1998 to 2003. Wal-Mart was the largest U.S. employer of African Americans and Hispanics.

However, in 2003, Wal-Mart was faced with a federal lawsuit filed by six female employees claiming that the company discriminated against women in pay, promotions, training, and job assignments—plaintiffs' attorneys were seeking class-action status for the lawsuit on behalf of all past and present female workers at Wal-Mart's U.S. stores and wholesale clubs. According to data from various sources, while two-thirds of Wal-Mart's hourly employees were women, less than 15 percent held store manager positions. There were also indications of pay gaps between male and female employees. The differences increased up the corporate ladder for the same positions, beginning with full-time hourly women employees making 6.2 percent less than their male counterparts, and female senior vice presidents making 50 percent less than men in the same position. According to a study conducted by the plaintiffs as part of their discrimination lawsuit and based on an analysis of Wal-Mart's payroll data, female workers at Wal-Mart between 1996 and 2001 earned 4.5 to 5.6 percent less than men doing similar jobs and with similar experience levels. The pay gap allegedly widened higher up the management ladder. The study found that male management trainees made an average of $23,175 a year, compared with $22,371 for women trainees. At the senior vice president level, the average male made $419,435 a year, whereas the four female senior vice presidents earned an average of $279,772.

Training

Top management was committed to providing all associates state-of-the-art training resources and development time to help achieve career objectives. The company had a number of training tools in place, including classroom courses, computer-based learning, distance learning, corporate intranet sites, mentor programs, satellite broadcasts, and skills assessments. In November 1985 the Walton Institute of Retailing was opened in affiliation with the University of Arkansas. Within a year of its inception every Wal-Mart manager from the stores, the distribution facilities, and the general office were expected to take part in special programs at the Walton Institute to strengthen and develop the company's managerial capabilities.

Management Training   Wal-Mart store managers were hired in one of three ways. Hourly associates could move up through the ranks from sales to department manager to manager of the check lanes into store management training—more than 65 percent of Wal-Mart's managers had started out as hourly associates. Second, people with outstanding merchandising skills at other retail companies were recruited to join the ranks of Wal-Mart managers. And third, Wal-Mart recruited college graduates to enter the company's training program. Store management trainees went through an intensive on-the-job training program of almost 20 weeks and then were given responsibility for an area of the store. Trainees who progressed satisfactorily and showed leadership and job knowledge were promoted to an assistant manager, which included further training in various aspects of retailing and store operations. Given Wal-Mart's continued store growth, above-average trainees could progress to store manager within five years. Through bonuses for sales increases above projected amounts and company stock options, the highest-performing store managers earned well into six figures annually.

Associate Training   Wal-Mart did not provide a specialized training course for its hourly associates. Upon hiring, an associate was immediately placed in a position for on-the-job-training. From time to time, training films were shown in associates' meetings. Store managers and department managers were expected to train and supervise the associates under them in whatever ways were needed. As one associate put it, "Mostly you learn by doing. They tell you a lot; but you learn your job every day."

Respect for the individual, one of the company's three core values, was reinforced throughout the training process for both managers and associates. Wal-Mart had been ranked among *Training* magazine's "Top Training 100" companies in 2001 and 2002.

Meetings and Rapid Response

The company used meetings both as a communication device and as a culture-building exercise. In Bentonville, there were Friday merchandising meetings and Saturday-morning meetings at 7:30 AM to review the week. The weekly merchandising meeting included buyers and merchandising staff headquartered in Bentonville and various regional managers who directed store operations.

David Glass, Wal-Mart's former CEO explained the purpose of the Friday merchandise meetings:

> In retailing, there has always been a traditional, head-to-head confrontation between operations and merchandising. You know, the operations guys say, "Why in the world would anybody buy this? It's a dog, and we'll never sell it." Then the merchandising folks say, "There's nothing wrong with that item. If you guys were smart enough to display it well and promote it properly, it would blow out the doors." So we sit all these folks down together every Friday at the same table and just have at it.
>
> We get into some of the doggonedest, knock-down drag-outs you have ever seen. But we have a rule. We never leave an item hanging. We will make a decision in that meeting even if it's wrong, and sometimes it is. But when the people come out of that room, you would be hard-pressed to tell which ones oppose it and which ones are for it. And once we've made that decision on Friday, we expect it to be acted on in all the stores on Saturday. What we guard against around here is people saying, "Let's think about it." We make a decision. Then we act on it.[24]

At the Saturday-morning meetings—a Wal-Mart tradition since 1961, top officers, merchandising and regional managers, and other Bentonville headquarters' staff—about 100 people in all—gathered to exchange ideas on how well things were going and talk about any problems relating to the week's sales, store performance, special promotion items, store construction, distribution centers, transportation, supply chain activities, and so on. As with the Friday merchandise meetings, decisions were made about what actions needed to be taken.

The store meetings and the Friday/Saturday meetings in Bentonville, along with the in-the-field visits by Wal-Mart management, created a strong bias for action. A *Fortune* reporter observed, "Managers suck in information from Monday to Thursday, exchange ideas on Friday and Saturday, and implement decisions in the stores on Monday."[25]

WAL-MART'S FUTURE: MOUNTING FLAK FROM SEVERAL DIRECTIONS

Sam Walton had engineered the development and rapid ascendancy of Wal-Mart to the forefront of the retailing industry—the discount stores and Sam's Clubs were strategic moves that he directed. His handpicked successor, David Glass, had directed the hugely successful move into Supercenters and grocery retailing, as well as presiding over the company's growth into the world's largest retailing enterprise; the neighborhood market store format also came into being during his tenure as CEO. H. Lee Scott, Wal-Mart's third CEO, had the challenge of globalizing Wal-Mart operations and continuing the long-term process of saturating the U.S. market with Supercenters and adding other types of stores in those areas that were underserved.

But as 2003 unfolded, it was apparent that Scott had to deal with a growing number of issues and obstacles that were being thrown in Wal-Mart's path, some of which were embarrassing or threatening. Not only was the company faced with over 6,000 active lawsuits, ranging from antitrust and consumer issues to torts claims (like a customer suffering

---

[24]Walton with Huey, *Sam Walton,* pp. 225–26.

[25]Saporito, "What Sam Walton Taught America," p. 105.

injury from falling in a store or being in a collision with a Wal-Mart truck). A couple of the lawsuits had potentially serious consequences—like the one alleging the company discriminated against women, which had potential to turn into the largest sex-bias class action ever, and a second alleging that associates were forced to work unpaid overtime. But Wal-Mart was also getting flak from other quarters, forcing management to devote more time and attention to putting out brushfires than to growing and operating the business (as had been the case during the David Glass era):

- Wal-Mart had to temporarily stop selling guns at its 118 stores across California following what California's attorney general said were hundreds of violations of state laws. Investigations by California authorities revealed that six Wal-Mart stores had released guns before the required 10-day waiting period, failed to verify the identity of buyers properly, sold illegally to felons, and committed other violations. Wal-Mart cooperated with governmental officials and agreed to immediately suspend firearms sales until corrective action could be taken and store associates properly trained on state firearms laws.

- In New York, Wal-Mart had run afoul of the state's 1988 toy weapons law. The toy guns Wal-Mart sold had an orange cap at the end of the barrel but otherwise looked real, thus violating New York laws banning toy guns with realistic colors such as black or aluminum and not complying with New York's requirement that toy guns have unremovable orange stripes along the barrel. Investigators from the state attorney general's office shopped 10 Wal-Marts in New York state from Buffalo to Long Island and purchased toy guns that violated the law at each of them. The president of New York's State Police Investigators Union said, "Without clear markings, it is extremely difficult to tell the difference between a toy gun and a real weapon." Wal-Mart acknowledged that its toy guns did not have all of the state-required markings, but the company maintained that it need only comply with federal law, which requires an orange cap on the end of the barrel. Wal-Mart had sold more than 42,000 toy guns in the state during the past two and a half years. If the state of New York prevailed in its halt of toy gun sales at Wal-Mart, it could seek damages equal to $1,000 for each illegal toy gun sold since April 1, 1997.

- Immigration authorities were investigating certain Wal-Mart managers for knowingly hiring janitorial contractors who were using illegal immigrants to clean stores. In a series of predawn raids on October 23, 2003, federal agents had arrested nearly 250 illegal immigrants after cleaning shifts at 61 Wal-Mart stores in 21 states; agents also searched a manager's office at Wal-Mart's Bentonville headquarters and took 18 boxes of documents relating to cleaning contractors dating back to March 2000.[26] Federal officials reportedly had wiretaps showing that Wal-Mart officials knew its contractors were furnishing illegal cleaning crews. Several weeks later, Wal-Mart was notified that it had been included in a federal grand jury probe of the contractors. Wal-Mart, however, was indignant about the charges, saying that Wal-Mart managers at many levels knew about the problem of illegal workers in its stores and had been cooperating with federal authorities in the investigations for almost three years. Wal-Mart indicated that it had helped federal investigators tape conversations between some of its store managers and employees of the cleaning contractors suspected of using illegal immigrants; that it revised its written contracts with cleaning contractors in 2002 to include language that janitorial contractors were complying with all federal, state, and local employment laws (because of the information developed in 2001); and that it had begun bringing all janitorial work in-house rather than outsourcing such services in 2003 because outsourcing was more expensive—in October 2003 fewer than 700 Wal-Mart stores used outside cleaning contractors, down from almost half in 2000.

- United Food and Commercial Workers (UFCW) was exerting all the pressure it could to force Wal-Mart to raise its wages and benefits for associates to levels that would be comparable to union wages and benefits at unionized supermarket chains. A UFCW spokeswoman in Southern California, where union members

[26]Ann Zimmerman, "After Huge Raid on Illegals, Wal-Mart Fires Back at U.S.," *The Wall Street Journal,* December 19, 2003, pp. A1, A10.

were striking supermarket chains to protest efforts to trim health care costs, said:

> Their productivity is becoming a model for taking advantage of workers, and our society is doomed if we think the answer is to lower our standards to Wal-Mart's level. What we need to do is to raise Wal-Mart to the standard we have set using the supermarket industry as an example so that Wal-Mart does not destroy our society community by community.[27]

Wal-Mart's labor costs were said to be 20 percent less than those at unionized supermarkets.[28] In Dallas, 20 supermarkets had closed once Wal-Mart had saturated the area with its Supercenters. According to one source, for every Wal-Mart Supercenter opened in the next five years, two other supermarkets would be forced to close, thus casting some doubt on whether Wal-Mart's entry into a community resulted in a net increase in jobs and tax revenues.[29] One trade publication estimated that Wal-Mart's plans to open more than 1,000 Supercenters in the United States in the 2004–2008 period would boost Wal-Mart's grocery and related revenues from $82 billion to $162 billion, thus increasing its market share in groceries from 19 percent to 35 percent and its share of pharmacy and drugstore-related sales from 15 percent to 25 percent.[30]

• Opponents of "big-box" retailers had battled against Wal-Mart's efforts to locate new stores in such states as Vermont and California. Oakland officials had recently voted to limit stores with full-service supermarkets to 100,000 square feet or 2.5 acres—a move deliberately aimed at blocking Wal-Mart's plan to open 187,000-square-foot Supercenters in the Oakland area. In Contra Costa County, near San Francisco, county supervisors enacted an ordinance prohibiting any retail outlet larger than 90,000 square feet from devoting more than 5 percent of its floor space to food or other non-

taxable goods—Wal-Mart gathered enough signatures to force a referendum in March 2004, but the referendum lost due mainly to certain tactics Wal-Mart employed as opposed to citizens' rejection of Wal-Mart Supercenters.[31] Restrictive zoning codes, vocal opponents of big-box retailers (most of whom were desirous of protecting local businesses from the competition of Wal-Mart's everyday low prices), high land costs in urbanized areas, and combative labor unions were major reasons why in 2003 Wal-Mart had more stores in rural and less urbanized areas compared to major metropolitan areas. Saturating major metropolitan areas with Supercenters, Sam's Clubs, and neighborhood markets was crucial to Wal-Mart's strategy of sustaining its double-digit growth rate in the United States.

• An article by newspaper reporter Jon Talton in the August 17, 2003 issue of Phoenix's *Arizona Republic* slammed Wal-Mart on several fronts:

> Fair play is a heartland value. But Wal-Mart is known for clear-cutting the retail landscape. Competing national stores won't even consider locating within three miles of a Wal-Mart Supercenter, and local retailers go out of business. Suppliers are bullied for "everyday low prices," with the result being that many have been forced from business.
>
> Speaking of fair, you're the nation's largest employer, with a million "associates." But relatively few work 40-hour weeks, and a union cashier at Safeway or Albertson's can make twice as much as one of your checkers. Nor is it easy for someone making seven bucks an hour to afford your "pay-for-it-yourself" benefits.

• Wal-Mart had been criticized for refusing to stock CDs or DVDs with parental warning stickers (mostly profanity-laced hip-hop music) and for either pulling certain racy magazines (*Maxim, Stuff,* and *FHM*) from its shelves or obscuring their covers. Critics contended that Wal-Mart made no effort to survey shoppers about how they felt about such products but rather that it responded in ad hoc fashion to complaints lodged by a relative handful of customers and by conservative outside groups.[32] Wal-Mart had also

[27]As quoted in Lorrie Grant, "Retail Giant Wal-Mart Faces Challenges on Many Fronts," *USA Today,* November 11, 2003, p. B2.

[28]Bianco and Zellner, "Is Wal-Mart Too Powerful?" p. 103.

[29]Ibid.

[30]Ibid., p. 108.

[31]Ibid.

[32]Ibid., pp. 104, 106.

been the only one of the top 10 drugstore chains to refuse to stock Preven, a morning-after contraceptive introduced in 1999, because company executives did not want its pharmacists have to grapple with the moral dilemma of abortion.

- In Colorado, the UFCW accused Wal-Mart of harassing workers to keep them from joining its local in Denver and elsewhere. According to the complaint filed with the National Labor Relations Board, Wal-Mart managers at a Denver store threatened, intimidated, and illegally monitored employees who were organizing. Similar complaints had previously been filed in Florida and Texas. A Wal-Mart spokesman denied the charge concerning the Denver store and noted that similar complaints at other locations had been dismissed without a hearing. Even so, Wal-Mart, which had an official policy of being strongly opposed to unionization, had seen the number of complaints about its efforts to prevent unionization grow in recent years—so far, 17 complaints had been filed in 12 states.

A Web site Walmartwatch.com had sprung up to collect and publicize reports of misbehavior and wrongful conduct on the part of Wal-Mart management and the company's growing economic power and influence. A union-affiliated Web site (www.nlcnet.org), run by the National Labor Committee, was also disseminating anti–Wal-Mart information.

H. Lee Scott was understandably concerned about the raft of issues that threatened to mar Wal-Mart's reputation and raise questions about the company's efforts to secure the lowest prices for its customers. He recognized that the company's size and market standing made it an attractive target for critics; as he put it, "In the part we were judged by our aspirations. Now, we're going to be judged by our exceptions."[33] Scott had launched his own investigations into the sex-bias claims and the use of illegal workers and vowed that there would be zero tolerance on Wal-Mart's part for misbehavior:

> Wal-Mart does not and will not tolerate illegal workers in any capacity. Whatever we find, we would be shocked if a Wal-Mart executive were ever involved in the hiring of illegal workers.
>
> What we can't do is give people the fuel to attack us. I have a responsibility that is twofold: to make sure we're not doing the wrong thing, and to make sure that we are trying to communicate that this is a quality company.[34]

However, despite concerns in some quarters over Wal-Mart's growing size and economic influence, Scott believed the company could grow to be two or three times its present size.

[33]Useem, "One Nation Under Wal-Mart," p. 78.
[34]Grant, "Retail Giant Wal-Mart Faces Challenges on Many Fronts," p. B1.

Kmart: Striving for a Comeback

John E. Gamble
University of South Alabama

In March 2003 Kmart Corporation was entering what its management hoped would be the last two months of bankruptcy protection that had allowed it to continue its operations even though it had been delinquent on obligations of more than $4.7 billion owed to creditors, vendors, and leaseholders. The bankruptcy, which was filed in January 2002, was the largest bankruptcy in U.S. retailing history and was the culmination of decades of poor strategy execution that resulted in an overall deterioration of Kmart's competitive position in the discount retail industry and a roller-coaster earnings history.

Specific problems that contributed to Kmart's bankruptcy were poor supply chain management, poor customer service, frequent stockouts of popular items, excessive inventory of slow-selling items, poor store housekeeping, unsound pricing strategies, and too many deteriorating stores built in the 1960s and 1970s. To make matters worse, as Kmart committed blunder after blunder in strategy execution during the 1980s and 1990s, Wal-Mart's distribution efficiency was becoming the global benchmark across all industries and the department store operator Dayton Hudson was perfecting its strategy for its Target stores that made designer-inspired apparel and housewares available at discount prices. Kmart's problems and competitive liabilities had long been obvious not only to industry insiders but also to the company's board of directors, employees, and customers, but the problems had been unresolved throughout a series of five executive regime changes dating to the late 1980s—three of which had occurred between June 2000 and January 2003.

Kmart's most recent CEO, Julian Day, who was installed in January 2003, began his tenure with the company in March 2002, when as chief operating officer he aided outgoing CEO James Adamson in the implementation of Kmart's restructuring plan. The reorganization plan, which focused on improving the company's weak competitive position and restoring financial solvency, included the closure of 600 stores and elimination of 52,000 employees, the restructuring of Kmart's supply chain, the elimination of slow-moving inventory, and the development of new private-label soft goods licensed from Disney and Joe Boxer that might compete with more expensive branded apparel. Upon his acceptance of the new position, Day stated the company would emerge from bankruptcy by April 30, 2003, and was poised to be a contender in the U.S. discount retail industry as it had achieved "a discernible shift in the company's internal culture, . . . repositioned itself as a high/low retailer of exclusive proprietary brands, . . . and restructured the store base and distribution network to protect and strengthen Kmart's competitive position in key markets."[1]

When the company closed out its fiscal 2002 books on January 31, 2003, the plan had yet to achieve any great successes with Kmart Corporation recording a net loss of $3.2 billion for the year and experiencing a sales decline of 18.5 percent during the fourth quarter of 2002 while rivals Wal-Mart and Target achieved sales growth of 12.3 percent and 9.0 percent, respectively, during the quarter. In addition, Kmart's sales per square foot (a key performance measure in retailing) of $212 during 2002 trailed Wal-Mart's sales per square foot of $404 and Target's sales per square foot of $263 by an unacceptable margin. Exhibit 1 presents a summary of Kmart's financial performance between 1992 and 2002. The company's common shares were delisted by the New York Stock Exchange in December 2002.

---

[1]Quoted in Kmart Corporation press release, January 19, 2003.

exhibit 1 **Selected Financial and Operating Statistics, Kmart Corporation, 1992–2002 (dollars in millions, except per share data)**

	2002	2001	2000	1999	1998	1997	1996	1995	1994	1993	1992
Summary of operations											
Total sales	$30,762	$36,151	$37,028	$35,925	$33,674	$32,183	$31,437	$31,713	$29,563	$28,039	$26,470
Cost of sales, buying and occupancy	26,258	29,853	29,732	28,161	26,357	25,167	24,390	24,675	22,331	20,732	19,087
Selling, general and administrative expenses	6,544	7,588	7,366	6,569	6,288	6,174	6,274	6,876	6,651	6,241	5,830
Restructuring, impairment and other charges	705	1,091	—	—	19	114	—	—	—	—	—
Interest expense, net	155	344	287	280	293	363	453	434	479	467	411
Continuing income (loss) before income taxes, preferred dividend, and reorganization items	(2,900)	(2,725)	(370)	959	755	407	330	(313)	102	(306)	1,142
Chapter 11 reorganization items, net	(362)	183	—	—	—	—	—	—	—	—	—
Net income (loss) from continuing operations	(3,262)	(2,612)	(268)	594	491	242	231	−230	96	(179)	745
Discontinued operations, net	43	166	—	(230)	—	—	(451)	(341)	200	(795)	196
Net income (loss)	($ 3,219)	($ 2,446)	($ 268)	$ 364	$ 491	$ 242	($ 220)	($ 571)	$ 296	($ 974)	$ 941
Per share of common stock											
Basic:											
Continuing income (loss)	($6.44)	($5.29)	($0.53)	$ 1.21	$ 1.00	$ 0.50	$ 0.48	($0.51)	$ 0.19	($0.41)	$ 1.63
Discontinued operations	$0.08	$0.34	$ —	($0.47)	$ —	$ —	($0.93)	($0.74)	$ 0.44	($1.74)	$ 0.43
Net income (loss)	($6.36)	($4.95)	($0.53)	$0.74	$ 1.00	$ 0.50	($0.45)	($1.24)	$ 0.65	($2.13)	$ 2.06
Book value	($0.59)	$6.42	$12.09	$12.73	$11.84	$10.89	$10.51	$10.99	$13.15	$13.39	$16.64
Financial data											
Total assets	$11,238	$14,183	$14,815	$15,192	$14,238	$13,614	$14,286	$15,033	$16,085	$15,875	$16,769
Liabilities subject to compromise	7,969	8,093	—	—	—	—	—	—	—	—	—
Long-term debt	—	330	2,084	1,759	1,538	1,725	2,121	3,922	1,989	2,209	2,995
Long-term capital lease obligations	623	857	943	1,014	1,091	1,179	1,478	1,586	1,666	1,609	1,612
Capital expenditures	252	1,385	1,089	1,277	981	678	343	540	1,021	793	1,187
Depreciation and amortization	737	824	777	770	671	660	654	685	639	650	566
Basic weighted average shares outstanding (millions)	506	494	483	492	492	487	486	460	457	457	456
Number of stores	1,829	2,114	2,105	2,171	2,161	2,136	2,261	2,310	2,481	2,486	2,435
U.S. Kmart store sales per comparable selling square footage	$ 212	$ 235	$ 236	$ 233	$ 222	$ 211	$ 201	$ 195	$ 181	$ 160	$ 152
U.S. Kmart total selling square footage (millions)	139	154	153	155	154	151	156	160	166	182	181

Source: Kmart Corporation annual reports.

COMPANY HISTORY AND BACKGROUND

Kmart's roots in the discount retail industry can be traced to 1899 when Sebastian S. Kresge opened a five-and-dime store in downtown Detroit, Michigan. Kresge's 5- and 10-cent pricing strategy appealed to turn-of-the-century working families and allowed him to expand the S. S. Kresge Company chain to 85 stores with $10 million in sales by 1912. Kresge was known for his bold and innovative strategies, which included expansion into Canada in 1929, the development of a mall-based store concept in the first suburban shopping center in 1937, the use of newspaper advertising circulars in the 1940s, and the introduction of checkout lines in the 1950s. When Sebastian Kresge retired as CEO of the company in 1959, his successor, Harry Cunningham, began to investigate new store concepts that included a wider variety of household items and apparel than what was found in five-and-dimes. Cunningham opened the first Kmart full-line discount store in Garden City, Michigan, in 1962. The new store concept was an instant hit with consumers, and Cunningham responded by opening an average of about three new Kmart stores each month over the next four years. At the time of Sebastian Kresge's death in 1966, the S. S. Kresge Company operated 753 Kresge variety stores and 162 Kmart full-line discount stores with combined annual sales of over $1 billion.

Throughout the remainder of the 1960s and 1970s, Kresge management continued to increase the number of Kmart stores and replaced existing Kresge stores with Kmart stores. In 1976, the S. S. Kresge Company opened 271 stores and thus became the only retailer to ever open 17 million square feet of retailing space in one year. By year-end 1976, Kresge operated 1,206 Kmart stores and 441 Kresge five-and-dime stores. The company changed its name to Kmart Corporation in early 1977 since its Kmart stores had generated nearly 95 percent of the company's 1976 domestic revenues. In 1981 the company opened its 2,000th Kmart location.

During the 1980s and early 1990s Kmart management diversified the company into additional retailing businesses rather than rely only on new Kmart store openings to generate revenue growth. In 1984 Kmart acquired Builders Square (a chain of warehouse-style home centers) and Walden Book Company, which operated Waldenbooks stores in all 50 states. PayLess Drug Stores, Inc., and Bargain Harold's Discount Outlets (a Canadian retailer) were acquired in 1985. In 1988 three start-up businesses—American Fare hypermarts (giant stores carrying a huge variety of household, apparel, and supermarket merchandise), Pace Membership warehouse clubs, and Office Square warehouse-style office supply stores—were added to the corporation's portfolio of retail businesses.

The Sports Authority (a 10-store chain of sporting goods superstores) was acquired in 1990 to complement and strengthen Kmart's own Sports Giant stores started in 1989; the Sports Giant stores were subsequently renamed and integrated into the Sports Authority chain. Kmart also acquired a 22 percent interest in OfficeMax office supply superstores in 1990 and increased its interest in the business to over 90 percent in 1991. In 1992, Kmart management acquired Borders, Inc. (a chain of 22 book superstores in the midwestern and northeastern United States); purchased a chain of 13 discount stores in the Czech Republic and Slovakia; acquired Bizmart (a 105-store chain of office supply stores); and announced that it would open up to 100 Kmart stores in Mexico in a 50–50 joint venture with Mexican retailer El Puerto de Liverpool. The company also entered into a joint venture with Metro Limited to open discount stores in Singapore in 1994.

The following year, Kmart's board brought in new executive management after concluding that the company's diversification moves had done little to improve revenues and had actually damaged earnings by distracting management's attention from the company's core discount store business. With its sales growing at an annual rate of only 7.7 percent between 1980 and 1990, Kmart Corporation lost its position as the world's largest discount chain in 1990 to Wal-Mart. Kmart's position had weakened further by 1995, following annual sales rate growth of only 1.2 percent between 1990 and 1995. Wal-Mart's sales, by comparison, had grown at annual rates of 34.8 percent and 23.5 percent over the same respective periods. Exhibit 2 presents a financial comparison of Kmart Corporation, Target, and Wal-Mart Stores for selected years between 1980 and 2002.

exhibit 2 **Comparative Financial Performance of Target, Kmart, and Wal-Mart, 1980, 1990, 1995–2002**

Year	Sales* (in millions of dollars)			Operating Profit* (in millions of dollars)			Operating Profit as a Percent of Sales			Net Income* (in millions of dollars)			Net Income as a Percentage of Sales		
	Target	Kmart	Wal-Mart	Target	Kmart	Wal-Mart	Target	Kmart	Wal-Mart	Target†	Kmart	Wal-Mart	Target†	Kmart	Wal-Mart
1980	$ 1,531	$14,118	$ 1,643	$ 91	n.a	n.a	5.9%	n.a	n.a.	n.a.	$ 429	$ 56	n.a.	3.0%	3.4%
1990	8,175	29,775	32,602	466	1,151	2,212	5.7	3.9%	6.8%	n.a.	756	1,291	n.a.	2.5	4.0
1995	15,807	31,713	93,627	721	162	5,247	4.6	0.5	5.6	n.a.	(571)	2,740	n.a.	−1.8	2.9
1996	17,853	31,437	104,859	1,048	773	5,722	5.9	2.5	5.5	n.a.	(220)	3,056	n.a.	−0.7	2.9
1997	20,368	32,183	117,558	1,287	728	6,503	6.3	2.3	5.5	n.a.	242	3,526	n.a.	0.8	3.0
1998	23,014	33,674	137,634	1,578	1,010	8,120	6.9	3.0	5.9	n.a.	491	4,430	n.a.	1.5	3.2
1999	26,080	35,925	165,013	2,022	1,239	10,105	7.8	3.4	6.1	n.a.	364	5,377	n.a.	1.0	3.3
2000	29,278	37,028	191,329	2,223	(83)	11,490	7.6	−0.2	6.0	n.a.	(268)	6,295	n.a.	−0.7	3.3
2001	32,588	36,151	217,799	2,546	(2,381)	12,077	7.8	−6.6	5.5	n.a.	(2,446)	6,671	n.a.	−6.8	3.1
2002	36,917	30,762	246,525	3,088	(2,745)	13,644	8.4	−8.9	5.5	n.a.	(3,219)	8,039	n.a.	−10.5	3.3

n.a. = not available.

*The fiscal year end for all three retailers occurs on or near January 31 of each year. In Wal-Mart's case, data for the period January 31, 1979, through January 31, 1980, are reported in Wal-Mart's annual report as 1980 results. Because the company's fiscal year results really cover 11 months of the previous calendar year, this exhibit shows Wal-Mart's 1996 fiscal results in the 1995 row, its 1997 fiscal results in the 1996 row, and so on. This adjustment makes Wal-Mart's figures correspond more to the same time frame as the calendar year data for Kmart and Target, which both report results as if the 11-month period dictated the year rather than the closing month.

†Net income is not reported for Target Corporation's Target stores. The company's retail chains include Mervyn's, Marshall Field's, and Target. The company does not make net income figures available for its different chains.

Source: Company annual reports.

KMART UNDER JOSEPH ANTONINI, 1987–1995

Kmart's strategy of growth via diversification into a variety of retail businesses was initiated by Bernard Fauber, the company's chief executive officer from 1980 to 1987. However, most of Kmart's acquisitions were orchestrated by Joseph Antonini, who succeeded Fauber as Kmart's chairman, CEO, and president in 1987. Both Fauber and Antonini believed that entry into specialty retail stores would provide the company with greater growth opportunities than would be possible with only the Kmart chain of discount stores. The move to expand Kmart's scope of retail operations was intended to position the company in such fast-growing product categories as drugstore merchandise, office supplies, books, building materials, and sporting goods. Antonini also believed it made good strategic sense for Kmart to be involved in warehouse clubs and hypermarts because such stores were simply a larger-scale and slightly modified retailing format of the traditional discount stores that Kmart was already operating. Antonini saw the purchase of the discount stores in the Czech Republic and Slovakia and the joint ventures in Mexico and Singapore as valuable ways to begin positioning Kmart more aggressively in international retail markets.

Antonini's second strategic initiative to stimulate revenue growth focused on a $3.5 billion "renewal" program in 1991 to modernize, expand, or relocate Kmart's 2,435 discount stores. Most of these stores were built during the company's dramatic growth period in the 1960s and 1970s and had undergone little or no remodeling or renovation since they were constructed. Antonini wanted to increase the size of Kmart stores from a typical 80,000 square feet to about 100,000 square feet so that a wider variety of merchandise could be offered to consumers. The modernized Kmart stores provided brighter lighting, wider aisles, more modern and colorful interior signs, and more attractive merchandise displays. In 1992 he announced that the company would launch as many as 500 Super Kmart Centers that, like American Fare, would include both a discount store and a grocery store in a 160,000–180,000-square-foot building. By 1994 the sales of the renovated and new Super Kmart Centers were 23 percent above the sales of the chain's older, unrefurbished stores.

Antonini also initiated efforts to increase the volume of apparel sold in Kmart stores. He believed that increased sales of high-margin apparel would provide the stores with better operating margins and allow the company to offer lower everyday pricing on nonapparel items, like household items and health and beauty products. The company improved the styling and quality of its private-label apparel and began to include more natural fibers and less polyester in its garments. Kmart used endorsements from Jaclyn Smith and Kathy Ireland to create private-label branded lines of apparel to appeal to fashion-conscious and designer-conscious shoppers. Antonini also added national brands of apparel and footwear like Wrangler, Hanes, L.A. Gear, and Brittania to the company's merchandise mix.

Attempts to Cure Kmart's Longstanding Inventory Management Problems

Joseph Antonini also believed that the company needed to correct its long-running inability to maintain proper inventory levels in its stores. Kmart had been confronted with this problem for years, but the company had never really been able to resolve it. Most Kmart stores either frequently stocked out of popular items and/or were burdened with excess stocks of slow-moving items that eventually had to be marked down significantly. Antonini believed that Kmart's decentralized buying and merchandising process was at the root of the company's poor inventory management practices. Typically, Kmart buyers negotiated purchases with manufacturers, distribution people shipped products to stores, advertising specialists coordinated the company's advertising, and a separate marketing staff was responsible for promotions. Additionally, the company's store managers were authorized to purchase merchandise specific to their geographic locale and to place special ads in local area newspapers.

Antonini and Kmart's chief information officer, David Carlson, implemented a number of state-of-the-art information systems to correct the inventory management problems in the company's 2,000+ stores. In 1990 Kmart launched a GTE Spacenet satellite-based network that linked individual Kmart stores with the Kmart corporate office in Troy, Michigan, and some suppliers. The system allowed

Kmart management to eliminate its traditional decentralized inventory management process and adopt a centralized process that was intended to reduce escalating inventory costs while meeting local preferences and price sensitivities. The GTE Spacenet communication system allowed management to implement its Central Merchandising Automated Replenishment (CMAR) system that was jointly developed by Kmart's information systems staff and Electronic Data Systems, a leading supplier of data processing services. The CMAR system allowed Kmart's corporate office to keep track of every sale in each store. All scanner data were transmitted via a local area network to a Unix server in the back room of each individual store. At the end of every day, the server transmitted sales data to the corporate headquarters via the GTE Spacenet satellite.

The next morning Kmart product category managers studied the sales data from each store; later in the day they placed orders with vendors to replenish each store's inventory. Vendors that were members of Kmart's Partners in Merchandise Flow program were allowed to monitor the scanner data themselves and ship to Kmart distribution centers when they determined it was necessary to maintain Kmart's desired inventory levels. The distribution centers used a cross-docking system that helped keep inventory levels at the distribution center to a minimum. A senior executive at Kmart explained how centralized category management allowed the company to reduce expenses and keep products that consumers wanted on the shelves:

> Category management has been very successful for us. It's shifted our entire focus to the front door. Years ago we were busy with shipments—looking at what was coming in the back door from our suppliers. Today we have a front-door focus in that we are focusing on the consumer and what the register tape tells us she's taking out the front door. We've seen dramatic improvements in turnover. In fact, we used to call our distribution centers "warehouses" because products would come in and sometimes just sit there. Now they are truly distribution centers with goods flowing in and right out, often within a day or two.[2]

Kmart identified about 1,500 hard-line categories and several hundred soft-line categories and selected managers to make all buying and merchan-

dising decisions—including pricing, assortments, and promotions—for their assigned category of products. Each category manager used the scanner data available from CMAR and demographic profiles and consumer purchasing behavior data provided by third parties such as Nielsen Marketing Research to make their purchasing decisions. Each category manager was required to develop a sales plan, a gross margin plan, and a turnover plan that was presented to the senior marketing executives at the beginning of the financial year.

Kmart spent about $160 million annually to create and implement information systems like CMAR technology and other state-of-the art computer systems during Antonini's tenure as Kmart's top executive. The company implemented electronic data interchange (EDI) systems with some suppliers that attempted to reduce the company's dependence on paper-based transaction processing. The company also developed the ShopperTrack system, which used backroom computers and ceiling-mounted sensors to monitor how many customers were in each department throughout the day. The system used the tracking data to project store and department customer counts at 15-minute intervals. Store managers were instructed to use this information to schedule employee staffing at the store's checkout stations and merchandise departments.

Difficulties in Implementing and Executing Antonini's Strategy

At the outset, both Wall Street and Kmart investors reacted favorably to Antonini's moves to diversify the corporation into a number of attractive discount retail segments, to renovate and enlarge Kmart stores, to improve merchandise selection, quality and availability, and to improve information systems. The consensus was that these moves would allow the company to grow faster and to compete more effectively against its major rivals. However, as efforts to implement the strategy continued to unfold, events made it increasingly clear that Kmart was being outmaneuvered by its rivals; Wal-Mart, in particular, was leaving Kmart far behind (see Exhibit 2). Kmart's sales per store continued to run near $180 per square foot in 1994, despite the merchandising efforts initiated by Antonini and other Kmart execu-

[2]Quoted in "Kmart's Category Approach," *Discount Merchandiser,* May 1994, p. 118.

tives. Also, Kmart's pricing continued to average 10 to 15 percent above its chief competitors, as Kmart sought to boost its subpar store margins and make up for the higher selling, general, and administrative expenses brought on by relatively low sales volumes per square foot of selling space.

Moreover, while Fauber and Antonini built Kmart's retailing portfolio far beyond its core discount store base, Kmart management never was able to transform any of its acquisitions into enterprises able to compete successfully against key segment rivals in terms of sales, net income, or efficient inventory management. In almost every retailing business that Kmart diversified into, it trailed the industry leader by a considerable distance. Sales volumes at Builders Square stores were only one-third of those at industry leader Home Depot. The company's Pace warehouse clubs never were able to match the selection and pricing of Sam's Clubs and, in the end, many of Pace's store locations were eventually sold to Wal-Mart.

Knowledgeable retail analysts attributed the failure of Kmart's American Fare stores in part to poor store design and poor store management. PayLess Drugs, Waldenbooks, and OfficeMax were all weak-performing businesses under Kmart's management, posting either operating losses or minimal operating profits.

Joseph Antonini attributed some of Kmart's difficulties in the apparel segment of its core retail discount business to rapidly shifting market conditions rather than weak strategy on Kmart's part. For example, although the Kathy Ireland and Jaclyn Smith apparel lines were successfully positioned as national brands in the minds of shoppers, as the company had planned, the initial success proved short-lived. By 1994, sales of the two apparel lines were sagging because of changing buyer preferences. Antonini, whose background and experience had been largely in apparel and soft lines, explained the reasons for the downturn: "Substantial shifts are taking place. For example, clothes just don't mean as much as they did five years ago, focus groups tell us. Designer names are not driving shoppers to stores, but in many ways have the opposite effect. Today, Mom is usually the last family member to get a new outfit. She is sacrificing for her family."[3] Antonini, in a 1994 Forbes in-

terview, said that the U.S. economy played a role in undermining some of Kmart's merchandising efforts: "The economy is hurting, disposable income is down, and people are spending money only on essential products. The fringe items—and I consider apparel to be a fringe item—aren't selling anywhere across the country like they used to."[4]

Antonini's expectation that sales of higher-margin apparel items would allow the company to offer lower prices on thousands of other items sold in Kmart stores didn't pan out either. As it turned out, Kmart was at a cost disadvantage relative to Wal-Mart and was not able to meet Wal-Mart's pricing on many items. In addition, Wal-Mart management was intent on being the low-price leader and chose not to allow competitors to price popular items below what Wal-Mart charged. A Wal-Mart executive gave the following explanation of the importance of the company's five-point operating cost advantage in setting its pricing strategy: "It's very simple. We're not going to be undersold. What that means is, that in an all-out price war, [our competitors] will go broke 5% before we will."[5]

When asked about Wal-Mart's meteoric climb to the top of the full-line discount industry, Antonini stated that Wal-Mart managers, whom he at times referred to as "snake oil salesmen,"[6] came across as successful largely because Wal-Mart was new to the industry and consumers were inclined to try out a new store. In 1994 he commented, "They have enjoyed the advantage of being the new show in town in many of our markets."[7] Antonini suggested that Wal-Mart's newcomer advantage was very similar to the new retail shopping excitement that Kmart was able to create during its period of rapid growth in the 1960s and 1970s.

Kmart's Image with Consumers   Surveys of U.S. discount store shoppers commissioned by *Chain Store Age Executive* found three consistent negative images that customers attributed to Kmart: out-of-stock merchandise, poor housekeeping, and indifferent service. Additionally, the consumers sur-

[3]Quoted in "Antonini: On Changes in the Marketplace," *Discount Merchandiser*, December 1994, p. 12.

[4]Quoted in "The Best-Laid Plans . . . ," *Forbes*, January 3, 1994, p. 44.

[5]Quoted in "The High Cost of Second Best," *Fortune*, July 26, 1993, p. 99.

[6]Quoted in ibid.

[7]Quoted in "Kmart's Agenda for Recovery." *Discount Merchandiser*, July 1994, p. 14.

veyed found Wal-Mart's locations more convenient and believed that Wal-Mart offered better pricing and product selection than Kmart. Antonini's store renovation and remodeling strategy was directed at eliminating Wal-Mart's pricing and selection advantage. However, in 1995—the company's fourth year into its renovation, relocation, and remodeling strategy—sales per square foot at Kmart remained flat at around $195, resulting in selling, general, and administrative expense ratios that were far above Wal-Mart's because the typical Wal-Mart store had sales per square foot of over $370. The higher expense ratios kept Kmart's bottom-line performance from materially improving.

Kmart's Store Renovation and Renewal Program

Wall Street analysts were very critical of Kmart's efforts to upgrade its stores. Many investors were displeased with Kmart management's use of the proceeds of a $1 billion equity issue in 1991. At the time the new shares of stock were sold, management had indicated that the capital was to be used to renovate and refurbish older Kmart stores and build new Super Kmart Centers. As it turned out, a big portion of the money spent in its "renewal" program went into acquiring new specialty retail stores rather than renovating older Kmart stores. Wall Street analysts made the following comments about Kmart's store renewal efforts.

> They aren't doing full renovations, just repainting or putting in new linoleum instead of gutting the stores entirely and redesigning them. And that has hurt them. It's back to the old Kmart culture where it's better to spend money on new stores and expand the chain.
>
> Even Betty Crocker got a new hairdo. I just drove by a Kmart store sign and it looked like a Howard Johnson should be next to it, circa 1957. They have a long way to go before getting rid of the popcorn smell when you walk in the door.[8]

Some shareholders and industry analysts suggested that the lack of management commitment to the store renewal program was a result of the company's past strategies. Kmart had achieved great success during the 1960s and 1970s as a result of its rapid addition of stores. The company's stock jumped from $0.50 per share when the first Kmart store was opened in 1962 to $32 in 1972. Some in-

vestors believed that the era of store growth at Kmart helped mold a managerial mind-set that favored putting more emphasis on store expansion than on proper management of existing stores and on merchandising efforts to boost annual sales at each existing store.

Continuing Inventory Problems

Even though Kmart had invested far more than its industry rivals on developing systems and procedures to correct its inventory-related problems, the problems still existed. Kmart stores still were faced with frequent stockouts of merchandise, and some of Kmart's vendors had criticized Kmart's buying procedures, stating that the corporate office frequently placed orders for merchandise and then later canceled the orders. A Kmart executive explained the difficulties of implementing its centralized merchandising strategy:

> Bringing this decision-making power to the desktop is a hurdle. Category management evolved with computer systems, but it's still a challenge to get these high-powered PCs on everyone's desktops and to have them linked together via local area networks. Furthermore, some buyers may not be computer literate or used to dealing with scanner and syndicated data. So it can be an educational process as well as a hardware installation process. Most of our buyers started out as store managers, so to them it's attractive to think, "Oh, I'll call my old store to see how this product is doing." We have to get them additionally looking at and relying on this internal computer data, syndicated third party data, and quantitative information. It also takes a certain kind of person, someone who knows merchandising, who knows computer processing, who knows about financing, who knows a little about advertising—someone who knows enough about everything, as opposed to being a specialist in just one area. The information and the software available are just tools. You still need an experienced person who can tie it all together.[9]

In a January 28, 2002, interview published in *Crain's Detroit Business,* David Carlson, Kmart's chief information officer between 1984 and 1995, provided further understanding of why Antonini's efforts to cure Kmart's inventory management problems failed:

> One of the core problems was that there was just way too much merchandise, and the stores didn't have adequate volume to justify the assortment. I produced reports that showed our inventory turns in the fishing

[8]Quoted in "Attention Bottom Fishers," *Financial World,* March 28, 1995, p. 31.

[9]Ibid., pp. 119–20.

rod category were abysmal. But the merchants were never able to move in the right direction of editing what was carried in the stores to ensure higher-moving items were in stock. The number of items just kept growing. Too often customers would go to Kmart and stores would be out of stock, or shelves would be full of the wrong products. If headquarters said you had to carry 13 toasters, you carried 13 toasters. Never mind the fact that the bottom-five were each selling one or less a year.

Customer Service Problems   Some Kmart stores were plagued with unresponsive customer service. A 1994 *Forbes* article cited customer complaints of indifferent Kmart employees who, when asked for a specific item in the store, would wave their hand in a general direction. One disgruntled shopper complained, "At the superstores in Farmington Hills or Southfield, the help is surly and uncooperative and you can never find the products that you need and have to have."[10]

FLOYD HALL'S TURNAROUND EFFORTS, 1995–2000

Kmart's board of directors appointed Floyd Hall as the company's new chairman, chief executive officer, and president in June 1995. Hall, who was recruited from Grand Union Supermarkets, had engineered Target's growth during the 1980s and had more recently gotten Grand Union back on track. Floyd Hall accepted the position with the intention of turning around Kmart within three years and then moving on to other ventures. He said, "I'm just trying to build a team . . . get a good succession plan and new policies and practices in place."[11] Hall and the board quickly assembled a new top-level management team—with 12 new vice presidents in marketing, product development, strategic planning, finance, administration, merchandising, information systems, and other key areas. The 12 new vice presidents had an average of 27 years of retail experience. When Hall asked his new management team to review and evaluate

Kmart's competitive position, he found that Kmart trailed Wal-Mart by a considerable distance on every key performance indicator. Wal-Mart's customers averaged 32 store visits per year, while Kmart's customers averaged 15 visits per year. Kmart's sales per square foot in 1994 were $185, compared to Wal-Mart's $379 and Target's $282. Only 19 percent of Kmart shoppers considered themselves loyal to the chain, while 46 percent of Wal-Mart shoppers considered themselves loyal Wal-Mart shoppers. Hall stated, "The most devastating news I saw in all the research was that 49% of Wal-Mart's shoppers drive past a Kmart to get to Wal-Mart."[12]

Hall believed that Kmart must be fixed "department by department" and that management must not try to "put a Band-Aid on our problems. This requires surgery."[13] Hall's first priority was to close nearly 400 Kmart stores and divest all noncore businesses from the company's portfolio between 1995 and 1997. Hall also initiated over $900 million in cost reductions during 1995 and 1996 by consolidating the company's Canadian operations with its U.S. operations, clearing out $700 million in old inventory, and using the company's volume buying power to reduce the cost of benefits for its 300,000 employees.

Some of the portfolio restructuring actually had taken place in the months just before Antonini's departure. Kmart sold PayLess Drug Stores in 1993 and spun off OfficeMax and Sports Authority as independent, stand-alone companies in late 1994. The initial public offerings of stock in OfficeMax and in Sports Authority were completed in December 1994, with Kmart retaining a 25 percent equity ownership in OfficeMax and a 30 percent equity ownership in Sports Authority. In addition, the company's 21.5 percent interest in Cole Myer, an Australian retailer, was sold in 1994.

In 1995 and 1996, Hall and Kmart's new management team sold the company's Czech and Slovak stores for $115 million; completed public offerings of stock to divest the company's remaining interests in OfficeMax and Sports Authority (netting the company an after-tax gain of $155 million); sold the assets of the Kmart auto centers to Penske for $84 million; completed a public stock offering of Borders Bookstores group (which resulted in an after-tax loss

---

[10]Quoted in "The Antonini Transcript," *Discount Store News,* April 17, 1995, p. 12.

[11]Quoted in "Kmart Is Down for the Count," *Fortune,* January 15, 1996, p. 103.

[12]Ibid., p. 102.

[13]Quoted in "Kmart: Who's in Charge Here?" *Business Week,* December 4, 1995, p. 107.

of $185 million); and sold the Rite Aid drugstore chain for $257 million. The company also discontinued its joint ventures in Singapore and Mexico in 1996 and divested its 162-store Builders Square home improvement chain for a mere $10 million in 1997.

A Near Bankruptcy as Floyd Hall Begins a Turnaround

Floyd Hall and the other members of Kmart's top management team were confronted with a potentially devastating financial crisis during the last half of 1995 that was a result of Kmart's poor cash flow and the financial decisions made by previous Kmart management. As was common with most retailers, Kmart management had a long-standing preference of financing new store construction off the company's balance sheet. Groups of newly constructed stores were sold to pension funds, insurance companies, and other such organizations, who then leased the stores back to Kmart on long-term lease agreements. This was a hidden financial obligation, since long-term lease payment obligations were not required, under accounting rules then prevailing, to be shown as a long-term liability on Kmart's balance sheet; the company had only to report current-year lease payments as an operating expense on its annual income statement.

In the early 1990s, Kmart's financial officers had agreed to special "put provisions" in a number of Kmart's store leasing agreements in exchange for better lease terms from the financing organizations. The put provisions stipulated that if Kmart's bond rating was downgraded to junk-bond status, then Kmart would immediately be obligated to buy back the leased stores from the lease owner. Kmart's contingent liability under the put provisions amounted to about $600 million. In July 1995—just one month after Hall became Kmart's CEO—Kmart was placed on credit watch by various credit rating agencies as an indication that they were considering downgrading Kmart's bond rating. The credit watch placement prevented Kmart from borrowing on 30–60-day commercial paper over the October–November period to pay suppliers for shipping the volume of goods needed to build its Christmas inventory. In order to have ample inventories for the Christmas season, Kmart was forced to activate a $2 billion backup revolving line of credit, adding interest costs and fur-

ther straining Kmart's already precariously thin profit margins and cash flows. To make matters worse, the covenants of Kmart's $2 billion revolving line of credit stated that if the leaseholders exercised their put options, any borrowings under the line of credit would immediately become due and payable. Kmart's accounts payable to its vendors already exceeded $3.5 billion for its purchases for Christmas inventory. The potential for Kmart to be faced with obligations to its vendors and creditors totaling $6 billion, compounded by swirling rumors, drove the company's stock price down to $5¾ per share—50 percent of its book value.

As Wall Street rumors predicted, Kmart's long-term debt was downgraded to junk bond status in January 1996. Hall and Kmart financial officers had already visited with the leaseholders in late December of 1995 and negotiated an agreement for them not to immediately exercise the put options and demand payment. With temporary agreements in place, Hall and Kmart financial executives used the company's available cash to pay vendors in a manner sufficiently timely to ensure continued shipments of merchandise. As Kmart paid its suppliers, management continued talks with the 70 banks that funded Kmart's line of credit. Kmart's creditors agreed to allow the company to suspend principal payments on its debt for 18 months while Hall and Kmart's financial officers negotiated a new financing proposal with a consortium of banks led by Chemical Bank. Chemical Bank agreed to put a consortium of lenders together to provide Kmart with $3.7 billion to refinance its obligations under the revolving line of credit and the leased-store debt associated with put options—contingent on the company's ability to raise $750 million through an equity issue. The close call with bankruptcy came to an end in June 1996, when Kmart issued $1 billion in convertible preferred shares and signed a new $3.7 billion financing agreement with Chemical Bank.

Attracting Customers to Kmart

Floyd Hall and his new management team developed a combination of new strategies and improved implementation techniques to better compete with low-cost leader Wal-Mart and rapidly growing Target.

A New Merchandising and Distribution Strategy   Kmart had been confronted with serious inventory management problems as far back as the early 1980s, and the new management team saw inventory management as the single biggest problem that had to be corrected. A big part of the solution, they believed, lay in eliminating many slow-selling items and unpopular brands and reducing the number of vendors. Under Antonini's centralized merchandising strategy, Kmart carried one or two national brands, an assortment of second- and third-tier brands, and some private-label brands. The new top management team found that many of the second- and third-tier brands cluttered store shelves and frequently did not sell without deep markdowns. Kmart's new merchandising executives eliminated some second-tier brands and most third-tier brands and began to develop its private-label brands to fill the gaps in its merchandise mix left by the removal of the lesser-known brands.

Kmart also completely redesigned the Martha Stewart Everyday bed and bath collection and relaunched the brand in 1997. The Martha Stewart private-label line of linens, towels, and other bed and bath products had been created during the Antonini era; however, under Antonini, the brand had not done particularly well because of inadequate promotion and a limited product line. The reintroduced Martha Stewart bed and bath collection included a wider variety of products—linens, bath towels, beach towels, draperies, pillows, blankets, lawn and garden products, baby products, and paint.

Company management took a series of steps to improve its working relationships with suppliers, to correct stockouts, and to reduce its distribution costs. Kmart began a Collaborative Forecasting and Replenishment program with vendors that shared Kmart's customer and product information with its suppliers over the Internet. The company also upgraded its IBM Inventory Forecasting and Replenishment Modules system to shorten its replenishment cycle by a full day. Kmart's chief information officer, Donald Norman, said that the company had reduced the amount of time to replenish some merchandise from 40 hours to 18 hours.

Improving Kmart's Store Productivity and Relative Cost Position

Despite the efforts of Kmart executives, at year-end 1996 Kmart's store productivity still trailed Wal-Mart's by a wide margin. Kmart had sales of $201 per square foot of retail space, compared to sales of $379 per square foot for Wal-Mart. While Kmart's new superstores achieved higher sales volumes than the company's older stores, they did not attract customers in sufficient volume to come close to matching sales per square foot at Wal-Mart. Kmart executives saw increased store traffic as the key to improving store productivity and lowering prices.

Hall developed and rolled out a redesign of existing stores that was intended to attract more customers to Kmart stores. The company tested its high-frequency Pantry concept during 1995 in selected stores and announced in 1997 that it would expand the Pantry concept to as many as 1,800 stores during the next three years. The Pantry concept was a redesign of existing stores that took items typically found in a convenience store and placed them in the front of Kmart stores. Merchandise that was already sold in Kmart stores—diapers, paper towels, bread, milk, dog food, beverages, snack foods, and so on—was gathered and placed in one department, then supplemented by additional dry grocery items. Kmart rearranged remaining store merchandise so that frequently purchased items like small appliances and soft lines (underwear, T-shirts, socks, and fleece products) were placed near the Pantry area. The cost to convert an existing Kmart store to the new Pantry concept was $600,000 versus $10 million for a new 100,000-square-foot Kmart store or $20 million for a new 180,000-square-foot Super Kmart Center.

Changes in Structure, Communications, Culture, and Rewards

Concerned that the attitudes and performance of Kmart store managers and associates were adversely impacting shopper visits and loyalty, Hall brought all Kmart store managers together in 1996 for the company's first-ever store managers' meeting. At the meeting, the executive team explained the company's mission and strategy and what individual store managers' roles were in implementing the strategy. The executive team also made it clear that they intended to end Kmart's historically insular, turf-wary organizational culture and adopt a more team-oriented atmosphere at both corporate headquarters and in the stores. The company also announced its new management development program to help the company develop future store-level and corporate-level managers from within its ranks.

Kmart corporate management also unveiled a new organizational structure during the conference that reduced the number of stores that each district manager was responsible for from 28 to 14. This reduction was intended to allow district managers to have the time necessary to visit every store in their districts more frequently and to provide better coaching to store managers. Within the stores, associates no longer had at-large responsibility but instead were assigned to departments. Kmart executives believed that giving associates defined areas of responsibility would create a feeling of ownership within their department and encourage employees to offer better service.

A new incentive compensation plan for store managers was developed to replace Kmart's old managerial pay plan. Previously, Kmart managers were paid a salary plus a bonus based on store sales. Under the new compensation plan, store managers were eligible for both bonuses and stock options. The new bonus plan tied 50 percent of a store manager's bonus to meeting the store's budget objectives for the year and 50 percent to the store's customer satisfaction rating. The customer satisfaction rating was determined by the results of independent mystery shoppers who visited each store 28 times per year.

Hall's Success in Getting Kmart on Track   By 1999, Floyd Hall's turnaround efforts were showing signs of success: More than 1,600 Kmart stores had been remodeled with wider aisles, brighter lighting, and lower shelving; the Martha Stewart line accounted for $1 billion per year in sales; and operating expenses had fallen by more than $500 million. Hall was also able to put together a string of three consecutive profitable years. The company's sales per square foot of $233 at year-end 1999 approached Target's sales per square foot of $253, though it still trailed Wal-Mart's sales per square foot of $360. However, many consumers still found Kmart's customer service unacceptable; the company's distribution system still had many bottlenecks; shelves still lacked best-selling items; stores had too much inventory of items consumers rarely needed; and, most important, the company found itself unattractively positioned between Wal-Mart's low prices and Target's more upscale merchandising. Even though Floyd Hall had expected to serve as Kmart's CEO for only three years, he remained CEO until May 2000, when he was succeeded by former CVS executive Charles Conaway.

CHARLES CONAWAY AND KMART'S BANKRUPTCY, JUNE 2000–MARCH 2002

Charles Conaway was selected as Hall's replacement in June 2000 by Kmart's board of directors, based largely on the 39-year-old Conaway's performance while president and chief operating officer of the rapidly growing drugstore chain CVS Corporation. Kmart board member James Adamson commented, "Floyd got us to Point B, now Chuck has got to get us beyond."[14] Some analysts questioned the hiring of Conaway, noting that even though he was known as an operations whiz at CVS, he had not managed a chain as large as the 2,100-store Kmart and had no experience with soft goods such as apparel. Conaway moved decisively after he was installed as Kmart's new CEO. His first official action was to replace Hall's top management team with a group of 40-ish retail veterans who became known at Kmart headquarters as "the frat boys."[15] Conaway also replaced many higher-level managers outside the corporate office with 500 outsiders from companies such as Wal-Mart, Coca-Cola, and Sears. Conaway expanded the number of district managers from 150 to 275—reducing the number of stores in each territory from 14 to 8. Conaway also expanded the number of geographic regions from six to eight and added 25 regional managers—a new level of management between district managers and senior regional vice presidents. Conaway believed that the smaller districts and additional management oversight would improve Kmart's poor customer service.

Conaway's Strategy and Execution Approaches to Revitalize Kmart

Conaway and members of Conaway's new management team crafted a strategy that addressed the discount chain's poor inventory management, muddled marketing strategy, and pricing disadvantage relative

---

[14]Quoted in "A Kmart Special: Better Service," *Business Week,* September 4, 2000, p. 80.
[15]"Kmart's Last Chance," *Business Week,* March 11, 2002, online edition.

to Wal-Mart. Conaway's team tackled the company's poor image by closing 78 of the company's poorest-performing and most run-down stores, revising the company's advertising campaign to cut more than $200 million in annual advertising expenditures and eliminate its newspaper circulars used since the 1940s, improving the company's e-commerce capabilities, and improving its merchandise quality.

Conaway adopted the marketing slogan "Kmart: The authority for moms, home, and kids" and placed greater emphasis on private-label brands such as Kathy Ireland and Jaclyn Smith women's wear, Martha Stewart Everyday home collection, Sesame Street kids' wear, and Route 66 jeans in attempt to differentiate Kmart from Wal-Mart and Target. Conaway also entered into a new seven-year contract with Martha Stewart Living that called for the company to launch a new line of Martha Stewart products every six months. The original line and its extensions proved successful, with Martha Stewart products accounting for $1.5 billion in sales by year-end 2002. Analysts were less satisfied with the company tag line; many believed it failed to convey meaning to consumers and believed that the Kathy Ireland, Jaclyn Smith, Sesame Street, and Route 66 private-label brands did not come close to either Kmart's own Martha Stewart line or Target's exclusive brands such as Mossimo in terms of quality or style.

Conaway also wanted Kmart customers to be able to purchase standard and differentiated products sold in Kmart stores over the Internet. Under Conaway the company expanded its e-commerce capabilities beyond its Kmart.com Web site through the development of a BlueLight.com venture with Softbank. Kmart committed $55 million to the e-commerce venture, which initially began as a free Internet service for Kmart customers and evolved into a discount e-tailing site where consumers could purchase any of 100,000 items typically found in Kmart stores. Kmart eventually paid its venture partner $84 million in cash and stock to gain control of BlueLight.com.

Kmart's boldest strategies under Conaway involved a $1.7 billion investment in new information technology systems to improve Kmart's supply chain management and a Blue Light Always plan to beat Wal-Mart on price on 38,000 stock-keeping units (SKUs). Kmart's Play to Win information technology initiative was designed to resolve Kmart's supply chain problems. When Conaway became the company's CEO, Kmart's in-stock rating stood just below 90 percent, while more than 99 percent of Wal-Mart's products were always in stock. Conaway also learned that Kmart had 15,000 trailers of unsold merchandise sitting outside stores because there was no space available for the merchandise inside. In addition, Kmart's 4.39 inventory turns per year were just over one-half of Wal-Mart's 7.29 turns. The president of a retail industry consulting firm, commenting on Kmart's poor inventory management and its 15,000 trailers of overflow merchandise, said, "Trucks and trailers are supposed to move product. They are not supposed to be a warehouse on wheels."[16]

The Play to Win program was designed to improve supply chain management by keeping track of what was selling in stores, store inventory levels, warehouse inventory levels, and shipments en route to stores. Kmart contracted with i2 Technologies, a highly regarded systems designer, but had great difficulty in implementing the supply chain technology program since the software had integration problems with Kmart's existing computing systems and because of the vast amount of data to process. For example, Kmart's 2,100 stores might stock more than 70,000 items each—creating 140 million possible data points to track. Analysts claimed that Conaway's $1.7 billion plan failed, in part, because it attempted to do too much too soon, but they did commend him for eliminating $700 million in inventory, including Kmart's 15,000 trailers of overflow merchandise, during his brief stay with the company. A former Kmart executive suggested that Kmart's inventory management program also failed because, even under Conaway, point-of-sale data available through the system were ignored by Kmart's buying department, with purchasing decisions based on which vendors were willing to pay the largest slotting fees rather than what products Kmart shoppers wanted. Conaway also invested $200 million for new Internet-enabled IBM SurePOS point-of-sales systems in all 2,100 stores to speed customer checkout and built two new distribution centers to improve productivity and the flow of goods to over one-half of Kmart's stores. The company incurred a $195 restructuring charge related to the relocation of its distribution centers.

[16]Quoted in "Kmart Misses Mark Amid Tech Field," *Investor's Business Daily,* April 25, 2002, p. A10.

Kmart's Blue Light Always plan was developed by Conaway's most notable and influential hire, Mark Schwartz—his choice for chief operating officer. Schwarz was a former Wal-Mart executive who had been second in command of Wal-Mart's Supercenters operations at one time but who also had other responsibilities at Wal-Mart, including managing an unrelated real estate investment firm that filed for bankruptcy in 1996 and was dissolved under his leadership. Schwartz left Wal-Mart in 1998, not long after the failure of the real estate firm, to become head of Hechinger Company, a home improvement chain that was in need of a turnaround. Under Schwartz, Hechinger built up excessive inventory, ran out of cash, and filed for bankruptcy within weeks of Schwartz's departure for Big V Supermarkets, which was also looking for a turnaround. Big V also filed for bankruptcy just weeks after Schwartz left to become Kmart's chief operating officer.

Many industry analysts believed that Schwartz's Blue Light Always pricing strategy, which attempted to beat Wal-Mart on price every day on 38,000 SKUs (and ultimately underprice Wal-Mart on 50,000 items), was the biggest reason for Kmart's slide into bankruptcy as compared to any of the other management gaffes. Analysts noted that no matter how much Kmart was willing to cut price, Wal-Mart, which was light-years ahead of Kmart in terms of efficiency, could cut more. Some observed that Kmart declaring a price war against Wal-Mart was comparable to Luxembourg declaring war against the United States. Similarly, they were unimpressed with the idea of revising the Blue Light Special concept. A business professor with Northwestern University's Kellogg School of Management commented, "The underlying principle behind a Blue Light Special was 'you are going to be surprised in a positive way when you walk in the store.' You don't know what you'll see, but you will see something. It may have worked in 1965, but in 1995 or 2000 consumers are too busy, so they don't go to the store to be surprised."[17]

Kmart's Slide into Bankruptcy

Kmart's Blue Light Always pricing strategy and Schwartz's decision to build $8.3 billion worth of inventory for the Christmas shopping season led to the company's January 22, 2002, bankruptcy after Kmart had a disastrous holiday season in which sales declined by 1 percent during the month of December 2001, while Wal-Mart's sales increased by 8 percent and Target's sales increased by 0.6 percent. With sales failing to materialize, many of Kmart's suppliers went unpaid after the holiday season concluded. Kmart's food supplier, Fleming Companies, stopped its shipments of food items to Kmart stores the day before Kmart's bankruptcy after it failed to receive its weekly payment from Kmart for approximately $78 million worth of food. Although Kmart management attempted to avert bankruptcy by putting together an emergency financial package to pay its creditors and suppliers, lenders balked and a last-minute bailout in early 2002 failed to materialize.

Kmart Corporation's bankruptcy filing enabled it to restructure payments on $4.7 billion in debt and keep shipments of inventory coming from suppliers since bankruptcy courts give vendors who continue to ship goods first priority in repayment status. On the day of the bankruptcy filing, Charles Conaway commented, "After considering a wide range of alternatives, it became clear that this course of action was the only way to truly resolve the company's most challenging problems."[18] In the quarter prior to Kmart's bankruptcy filing, the company's sales per square foot reached $243—an improvement, but well below Wal-Mart's sales per square foot of $410. In addition, its selling, general, and administrative (SG&A) expenses as a percentage of sales were 22.7 percent, compared to Wal-Mart's SG&A-to-sales ratio of 17.3 percent, and its prices averaged 3.8 percent higher than Wal-Mart's pricing on comparable products despite its efforts to underprice Wal-Mart with its Blue Light Always campaign. Exhibit 3 presents Kmart's statements of operations for fiscal 1999 through fiscal 2002. Its balance sheets and cash flow statements are presented in Exhibits 4 and 5, respectively. Exhibit 6 presents a listing of Kmart's contractual obligations and other commercial commitments at fiscal year-end 2001.

---

[17]Quoted in "Kmart Struggles to Escape Oblivion," *The Business,* January 27, 2002, p. 17.

[18]Quoted in "Kmart Lays Out Plans to Trim Its Size, Boost Efficiency, in Bankruptcy Filing," *The Wall Street Journal Online,* January 22, 2002.

exhibit 3   **Consolidated Statement of Operations for Kmart Corporation, Fiscal 2000–2003 (dollars in millions, except per share data)**

	Fiscal Year Ended January			
	2003	2002	2001	2000
Sales	$30,762	$36,151	$37,028	$35,925
Cost of sales, buying, and occupancy	26,258	29,853	29,732	28,161
Gross margin	4,504	6,298	7,296	7,764
Selling, general and administrative expenses	6,544	7,588	7,366	6,569
Equity (loss) income in unconsolidated subsidiaries	34	—	(13)	44
Restructuring, impairment and other charges	739	1,091	—	—
Continuing (loss) income before interest, reorganization items, income taxes and dividends on convertible preferred securities of subsidiary trust	(2,745)	(2,381)	(83)	1,239
Interest expense, net (contractual interest for fiscal year 2001 was $352)	155	344	287	280
Reorganization items, net	386	(183)	—	—
(Benefit from) provision for income taxes	(24)	—	(148)	315
Dividends on convertible preferred securities of subsidiary trust, net of income taxes of $0, $25 and $27, respectively (contractual dividend for fiscal year 2001 was $72, net of tax)	—	70	46	50
Net (loss) income from continuing operations	(3,262)	(2,612)	(2)	594
Discontinued operations, net of income taxes	43	166	—	(230)
Net (loss) income	($3,219)	($2,446)	($ 268)	$ 364
Basic earnings (loss) per common share				
Net (loss) income from continuing operations	($6.44)	($5.29)	($0.53)	$1.21
Discontinued operations	$0.08	$0.34	—	($0.47)
Net (loss) income	($6.36)	($4.95)	($0.53)	$0.74
Diluted (loss) earnings per common share				
Net (loss) income from continuing operations	($6.44)	($5.29)	($0.53)	$1.15
Discontinued operations	$0.08	$0.34	—	($0.41)
Net (loss) income	($6.36)	($4.95)	($0.53)	$0.74
Basic weighted average shares (millions)	506.4	494.1	482.8	491.7
Diluted weighted average share (millions)	506.4	494.1	482.8	561.7

Source: 2001 Kmart Corporation revised 10K report and 2002 Kmart Corporation 10K report.

exhibit 4   **Kmart's Consolidated Balance Sheets, Fiscal Years 2001–2003 (dollars in millions)**

| | As of January 29, 2003, January 30, 2002, and January 31, 2001 | | |
	2003	2002	2001
Assets			
Current assets			
Cash and cash equivalents	$ 613	$ 1,245	$ 401
Merchandise inventories	4,825	5,796	6,350
Other current assets	664	800	925
Total current assets	6,102	7,841	7,676
Property and equipment, net	4,892	6,093	6,522
Other assets and deferred charges	244	249	617
Total assets	$11,238	$14,183	$14,815
Liabilities and shareholders' equity			
Current liabilities			
Long-term debt due within one year	$ —	$ —	$ 68
Accounts payable	1,248	89	2,190
Accrued payroll and other liabilities	710	420	1,691
Taxes other than income taxes	162	143	187
Total current liabilities	2,120	652	4,136
Long-term debt and notes payable	—	330	2,084
Capital lease obligations	623	857	943
Other long-term liabilities	181	132	883
Total liabilities not subject to compromise	$ 2,924	$ 1,971	$ 8,046
Liabilities subject to compromise	$ 7,969	$ 8,093	—
Company obligated mandatorily redeemable convertible preferred securities of a subsidiary trust holding solely 7¾% convertible junior subordinated debentures of Kmart (redemption value of $898 and $898, respectively)	$ 646	$ 889	$ 887
Common stock, $1 par value, 1,500,000,000 shares authorized; 503,294,515 and 486,509,736 shares issued, respectively	519	503	487
Capital in excess of par value	1,922	1,695	1,578
Retained earnings	(2,742)	1,032	3,817
Total liabilities and shareholders' equity	$11,238	$14,183	$14,815

Source: 2001 Kmart Corporation revised 10K report and 2002 Kmart Corporation 10K report.

exhibit 5   **Kmart's Consolidated Statements of Cash Flows, Fiscal Years 2000–2003 (dollars in millions)**

	Years Ended January 29, 2003, January 30, 2002, January 31, 2001, and January 26, 2000			
	2003	**2002**	**2001**	**2000**
Cash flows from operating activities				
Net (loss) income	($3,219)	($2,446)	($ 268)	$ 364
Adjustments to reconcile net income (loss) to net cash provided by operating activities:				
Discontinued operations	(43)	(166)	—	230
Inventory writedown	1,291	163	—	—
Restructuring, impairment and other charges	739	1,091	728	—
Reorganization items, net	386	(183)	—	—
Depreciation and amortization	737	824	777	770
Equity loss (income) in unconsolidated subsidiaries	(34)	—	13	(44)
Dividends received from Meldisco	45	51	44	38
Decrease (increase) in inventories	(168)	560	335	(544)
Increase (decrease) in accounts payable	401	1,046	(137)	169
Deferred income taxes and taxes payable	23	(55)	(204)	258
Changes in other assets	161	295	29	(127)
Changes in other liabilities	67	(23)	14	133
Cash used for store closings	(134)	(230)	(217)	(80)
Net cash provided by operating activities	252	927	1,114	1,084
Net cash used for reorganization items	135	(6)	—	—
Cash flows from investing activities				
Capital expenditures	(252)	(1,385)	(1,089)	(1,277)
Investment in BlueLight.com	—	(45)	(55)	—
Acquisition of Caldor leases	—	—	—	(86)
Net cash used for investing activities	(252)	(1,430)	(1,144)	(1,363)
Cash flows from financing activities				
Net borrowings on DIP credit facility	(330)	330	—	—
Proceeds from issuance of debt	—	1,494	400	300
Payments on debt	(31)	(320)	(73)	(90)
Debt issuance costs	(42)	(49)	(3)	(3)
Payments on capital lease obligations	(94)	(86)	(78)	(77)
Payments of dividends on preferred securities of subsidiary trust	—	(72)	(73)	(80)
Purchase of convertible preferred securities of subsidiary trust	—	—	(84)	—
Issuance of common shares	—	56	53	63
Purchase of common shares	—	—	(55)	(200)
Net cash provided by (used for) financing activities	(497)	1,353	87	(87)
Net change in cash and cash equivalents	(632)	844	57	(366)
Cash and cash equivalents, beginning of year	1,245	401	344	710
Cash and cash equivalents, end of year	$ 613	$1,245	$ 401	$ 344

Source: 2001 Kmart Corporation revised 10K report and 2002 Kmart Corporation 10K report.

exhibit 6　**Kmart's Contractual Obligations and Other Commercial Commitments at Fiscal Year-End 2001**

Contractual Obligations	Payments Due by Period				
	Within 1 Year	Within 2–3 Years	Within 4–5 Years	After 5 Years	Total
Long-term debt	$1,151	$ 714	$ 728	$1,083	$ 3,676
Capital lease obligations	234	433	344	1,232	2,243
Operating leases	728	1,374	1,177	6,355	9,634
Other long-term obligations	143	248	165	90	646
Total contractual cash obligations	$2,256	$2,769	$2,414	$8,760	$16,199

Other Commercial Commitments	Amount of Commitment Expiration Per Period				
	Within 1 Year	Within 2–3 Years	Within 4–5 Years	After 5 Years	Total
Trade lines of credit	$162	$ —	$ —	$ —	$162
Standby letters of credit	98	—	—	—	98
Guarantees	49	102	125	365	641
Total commercial commitments	$309	$102	$125	$365	$901

Source: 2001 Kmart Corporation revised 10K report.

KMART'S RESTRUCTURING PROGRAM AND PLANNED EMERGENCE FROM BANKRUPTCY, MARCH 2002–APRIL 2003

Five days prior to Kmart's January 22, 2002, bankruptcy filing, its board of directors promoted board member James Adamson to the position of chairman of the board, a position previously held by CEO Charles Conaway. Adamson had been a member of Kmart's board of directors since 1996 and was among those enthralled by the youthful Conaway during the selection process for Floyd Hall's replacement. Adamson was the retired chairman and CEO of Advantica Restaurant Group, which operated the Denny's, Coco's, and Carrows restaurant chains. Adamson had also held executive positions with Revco, Target, and B. Dalton Booksellers prior to joining Kmart's board. Kmart's board named Adamson to the additional position of CEO when Charles Conaway resigned in March 2002.

Kmart's board believed that Adamson was a good choice to head up Kmart during its bankruptcy because of his retailing experience and his experience operating under bankruptcy protection. While Adamson was its chairman and CEO, Advantica filed for bankruptcy protection and successfully emerged from Chapter 11 a year later. Adamson's restructuring plan for Kmart included the following components, some of which had been initiated by Charles Conaway prior to his exit from the company:

- An announcement in March 2002 that the company would close 284 stores and eliminate 22,000 jobs before year-end. The terminations and store closings would result in a charge against earnings of $1.3 billion.

- Liquidation of $758 million in inventory in the closed stores, some of which was transferred from remaining stores.

- Reduction of annual overhead expenses by $130 million.

- Utilization of a $2 billion debtor-in-possession financing that would be used to supplement Kmart's cash flow during its reorganization.

- Development of a new advertising phrase, "The Stuff of Life." The company hoped to win customer loyalty by claiming to be the "store that understands what really matters in life."[19] The campaign was supported by an advertising budget of $20–$30 million and artistic 30-second television spots directed by filmmaker Spike Lee.

- Sale of BlueLight.com for $8.4 million to an Internet service provider. BlueLight.com had incurred undisclosed millions in losses and sold products to fewer than 1 percent of its visitors during the fourth quarter of 2001. Kmart continued to make products available to consumers over the Internet at Kmart.com after the sale.

- Development of a prototype store that had futuristic icons, wider aisles, lower shelves, and brighter lighting. Martha Stewart Everyday, Joe Boxer, Disney, and Sesame Street products were located in dedicated sections rather than spread about the store.

- An announcement in January 2003 that the company would close an additional 316 stores and eliminate 25,000 more jobs. The store closings were expected to result in the liquidation of an additional $1.5 billion in inventory for closed and remaining stores.

LEGAL WORRIES FOR KMART'S BOARD AND FORMER MANAGEMENT IN EARLY 2003

Three days after Kmart filed for bankruptcy, an anonymous letter from a Kmart employee addressed to the Securities and Exchange Commission (SEC), Kmart's auditors (PricewaterhouseCoopers), and the company's board of directors initiated investigations into Kmart's accounting practices. The investigations were led by the SEC, the U.S. Attorney's Office for Eastern Michigan, and the company's board of directors. The letter was followed by more than a dozen additional letters from different Kmart employees, all of whom suggested that Kmart executives told finance department employees to deviate from standard accounting practices and that those executives

also made misleading or deceptive statements to investors. As a result of Kmart's internal investigation, its financial statements for fiscal 1999 through the first two quarters of 2002 were restated because of the improper recording of vendor allowances that provided discounts or rebates to Kmart based on certain sales volumes of merchandise supplied by vendors. In numerous instances, Kmart recorded the discounts even though the sales volumes necessary to receive the allowances were not achieved. The audit had the effect of increasing Kmart's 2001 expenses by approximately $100 million. After Kmart had completed its audit and the letter campaign continued, James Adamson sent an e-mail to all employees asking them to end the letter campaign and report potential violations of the company's Code of Conduct through proper channels.

The letter-writing campaign also brought oversight attention to $28.9 million in retention loans granted to Charles Conaway and other top executives just days prior to Kmart's bankruptcy. The loans, which did not require a repayment, were questioned by investigators since the individual loan amounts were unusually high (e.g., Charles Conaway received a $5 million retention loan, Mark Schwartz received a $3 million loan, and a manager who had been with the company only two months received a loan for $1.75 million) and since Kmart suppliers had gone unpaid for goods shipped to and sold by Kmart. Conaway and his top management team also received generous severance packages—Conaway received severance pay of $4 million when he left the company in March 2002.

James Adamson launched a stewardship review of Kmart's outgoing management team in May 2002—agreeing to pay Conaway's severance package but suspending the severance pay of several members of Conaway's team. Kmart also suspended $2 million in annual special retirement benefits for 20 former executives in June 2002. Some critics of Conaway questioned the veracity of Adamson's review since his own employment contract with Kmart granted him a $2.5 million "inducement payment" to take the job of Kmart's CEO and provided such perks as weekly private plane service between his residences in Detroit, New York, and Florida; limousine service in Michigan and New York; and temporary accommodations in a $320-per-night hotel near Kmart's headquarters. In addition, Adamson was the chairman of Kmart's board of directors' audit committee

---

[19]Quoted in "Kmart Pitches Family Values in New TV Spots by Spike Lee," *The Wall Street Journal Online*, February 25, 2002.

in 2000 and 2001, which was the period under examination for accounting irregularities.

Adamson stepped down as Kmart's CEO on January 19, 2003. Julian Day was selected to lead the company through the remaining months of bankruptcy. The investigation initiated by Kmart's board disclosed the following findings on January 27, 2003:

- Former officers were grossly derelict in performing their duties.
- Former managers failed to provide the board with important information concerning Kmart's retention loan program.
- Former senior executives authorized the purchase of $850 million in additional inventory for the Christmas 2002 shopping season that Kmart didn't need.
- In September 2001, former executives created "Project Slow It Down," in which the company avoided payments to vendors and told vendors who asked about payments that the invoices had been paid.
- Former officers hired unqualified employees and provided them with extraordinary compensation packages.

On February 27, 2003, the U.S. Justice Department filed criminal indictments against two former Kmart executives—Joseph A. Hofmeister, a divisional vice president of merchandising within Kmart's drugstore operations, and Enio Montini, a senior vice president and general merchandise manager for Kmart's drugstore division. Legal experts believed that the Justice Department had indicted the two relatively low-level managers to help gain their cooperation in investigating the actions of higher-ranking Kmart managers.

The Portman Ritz-Carlton Shanghai: Asia's Best Employer

Matthew Chang
International Institute for Management Development

Ellie Weldon
International Institute for Management Development

We Are Ladies and Gentlemen Serving Ladies and Gentlemen.
—Ritz-Carlton motto

We strive to find the right people for the right roles, treat them with respect, provide them with opportunities and constant teaching, but we also have great expectations.
—Mark J. DeCocinis, General Manager, The Portman Ritz-Carlton Shanghai

In an emerging market like China, the greatest challenge in establishing a first class workforce is their short-term mentality. The ongoing tug of war between professionalism and indifference requires employers to be patient with people's old habits and create an environment that will initiate and preserve lasting changes in employees.
—Michelle D. Wan, Director of Communications, The Portman Ritz-Carlton Shanghai

In September 2001 the Portman Ritz-Carlton Shanghai took top honors in the first regionwide survey of the Best Employers in Asia. The survey was conducted by Hewitt Associates in partnership with the *Asian Wall Street Journal* and *Far Eastern Economic Review*. More than 92,000 employees working in 355 companies took part in the survey.

The success of the Portman Ritz-Carlton in Shanghai was surprising for two reasons. First, the hotel had been open for only a short time. Second,

and more important, the Shanghai labor market was notorious for high employee turnover resulting from high demand for but short supply of Westernized, English-speaking Chinese workers. As a result, the good employees had many opportunities and it was difficult to retain the best.

THE HOTEL INDUSTRY IN SHANGHAI

In 1979, after 50 years of war and revolution, Deng Xiaoping announced China's new open door policy to attract Western investment to fuel China's growth. At this time, the Shanghai municipal government began an ambitious drive to reclaim its historical place as China's center of international finance and commerce and one of the world's most vibrant cities. Companies from around the world were eager to participate in Shanghai's growth. During the 1990s over 70 percent of the Fortune Global 500 companies established a presence in Shanghai, and foreign businesspeople flocked to the city. The local government also promoted tourism and the number of foreign tourists increased.

These tourists and foreign businesspeople created a huge demand for hotels meeting international standards of quality. However, the city had only a handful of aging hotels, some dating back to colonial days and all suffering from misuse and neglect.

The Sheraton Huating Hotel, the first hotel to meet international standards, opened under Western management in 1986. By the end of 1997 there were 8 internationally recognized five-star hotels and over 20 four-star hotels in the city. Most of them were managed by major international hotel groups, and they enjoyed an average occupancy rate of 71 percent and a gross profit margin of 50 percent.

THE PORTMAN RITZ-CARLTON SHANGHAI

Company Background

Ritz-Carlton was one of the elite names in the hotel industry. Its sterling reputation was based on its comfort, luxury and—most of all—impeccable service. The Ritz-Carlton tradition began when Swiss hotelier César Ritz, in partnership with renowned French chef Auguste Escoffier, opened the Ritz Hotel in Paris in 1898 and, later, the Carlton Hotel in London. Ritz's name became synonymous with opulence, and his philosophy of service and management redefined the luxury hotel experience in Europe. When he died in 1918, his wife, Marie, continued the tradition.

In 1927 the first Ritz-Carlton hotel opened in Boston. For over 55 years, this elegant hotel was the only one operating under the Ritz-Carlton name. Then, in 1983, the Ritz-Carlton Hotel Company, LLC, was formed to manage hotels under the Ritz-Carlton service mark. Some 15 years later, the Ritz-Carlton Hotel Company was 100 percent owned by Marriott International, with headquarters in Atlanta, Georgia. The company did not own any hotels itself but managed 45 hotels worldwide, all in the "premier" segment of the hotel industry. A premier hotel offered its guests two essentials: (1) the comfort and style of the hotel's physical facilities, and (2) the quality and variety of its guest services.

The Portman Ritz-Carlton Shanghai

On January 1, 1998, the Ritz-Carlton group entered the Chinese market when it took over the operation of the Portman Shangri-La Hotel in Shanghai. The 564-room Portman Shangri-La was located in the Shanghai American Center, which was built in 1990. The principal investors in the American Center were the Portman Group, based in Atlanta, Georgia, and American International Group, the insurance giant based in New York City. When the Ritz-Carlton Group took over the management of the hotel, it was renamed the Portman Ritz-Carlton. In 1997 the Portman Shangri-La Hotel had a 75 percent occupancy rate and was profitable (specific figures were not made available).

THE JANUARY 1998 TAKEOVER

In mid-1997 general manager Mark DeCocinis had come to Shanghai with an experienced Ritz-Carlton transition team to prepare for the handover. The challenge facing the new Portman Ritz-Carlton management was daunting. There would be no shakedown period before the doors opened to the public, and the Shanghai hotel market, by then well developed, was beginning to experience a downturn precipitated by the spreading Asian financial crisis that had begun in the summer of 1997.

Looking back on the handover, DeCocinis recalled:

> It was one of the rare instances that a hotel did an instant switch. Literally at midnight on January 1, the hotel went from being a Shangri-La property to a Ritz-Carlton without any interruption of service.

Even though the Portman Shangri-La was regarded as one of Shanghai's premier hotels, DeCocinis felt that it fell far below the standards of a Ritz-Carlton hotel. First, the physical infrastructure of the hotel was lacking. DeCocinis explained:

> The property was eight years old and had experienced high occupancy rates. For whatever reason, the previous management did not reinvest in the hotel at all. Perhaps it had something to do with their new property opening across town a few months later. So we knew from the start that a major renovation was imminent and very necessary.

However, DeCocinis was not worried about this because he had the budget to bring it up to Ritz-Carlton standards. Some projects would take time, but DeCocinis also saw the opportunity to make some immediate small changes that would have a noticeable impact, such as replacing all the china used in the hotel with premium-brand products.

Second, DeCocinis was worried about the level of service his staff could provide:

> The legend and strength of the Ritz-Carlton brand lie in our truly impeccable service. Our guests have certain expectations from a Ritz-Carlton property. The problem we faced was that the staff that came with the hotel did not even know that such a level of service existed.

When Ritz-Carlton took over, the Portman Shangri-La had 1,067 employees, with an average age of mid to late 20s. Although DeCocinis thought the hotel staff was too large, he and his team decided to give all of the locals working there an opportunity to find their place in the new Portman Ritz-Carlton. Ritz-Carlton did not, however, retain the expatriates working for the Shangri-La Group.

The employees had a rather diffident attitude—with more new hotels opening in the Shanghai market, there was no shortage of job opportunities for those with experience in the industry. Nevertheless, most of the local employees chose to continue working at the hotel after Ritz-Carlton took over and waited to find out what, if any, changes would come. They could always change jobs later.

Since it was clear that more experience with Ritz-Carlton standards would be required for a successful transition, veteran Ritz-Carlton managers from other Ritz-Carlton operations and from the parent Marriott Group assumed all the top management positions (i.e., division and department level managerial positions). The decision to bring in expatriates raised some concern that local employees would feel that their ability to advance was limited and that turnover would therefore increase. The nonmanagerial staff, the first-line supervisors, and their managers were all local Chinese. (See Exhibit 1 for an outline of the Portman Ritz-Carlton Shanghai's organization structure.)

The Challenge: The Classic Foreign Employer/Chinese Employee Relationship

To succeed, DeCocinis felt he must overcome the problematic relationship with the hotel's employees that many foreign employers experienced in China.

exhibit 1 **The Portman Ritz-Carlton Shanghai Organization Structure**

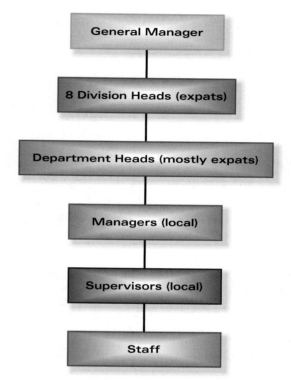

Source: Company information.

In many cases there was no cultural affinity between the foreign employer and local employees, and their values were also different. Moreover, young Chinese workers seemed to be primarily motivated by money and, with their English-language skills, they were also in demand. As a result, they changed jobs frequently, often for just a small increase in wages. A senior expatriate manager explained the prevailing mind-set:

> There was a common belief that since all local employees were motivated by the level of pay, an employer would only need to make sure they were paid adequately according to market conditions. Hence companies invested in little else, like continuous training and long-term development. The problem was made worse when the employers accepted this kind of practice. That kind of short-term mentality was the fundamental issue that contributed to the crazy job-hopping trend within foreign invested companies, including ours.

exhibit 2   **Three-Level Pyramid Representing Essence of the Hotel's Business**

ON THE ROAD TO BECOMING ASIA'S BEST EMPLOYER

Breaking the Mold: Recasting the Foreign Employer/Chinese Employee Relationship

Knowing that Ritz-Carlton had a long-term interest in China, DeCocinis saw the need to build a superior-quality workforce based on loyalty to the company grounded in a shared commitment to the highest standards of service. He was convinced that this was the only way to ensure quality and consistency in guest services, even if it meant investing money in training, which might affect the bottom line in the short term.

DeCocinis and his team came up with a three-level pyramid (Exhibit 2) to describe the essence of their business. Employee satisfaction formed the foundation, on which guest satisfaction rested. Together, they supported financial performance. The idea was that satisfied, motivated employees were necessary to achieve top-rate guest services, which in turn were necessary to establish and keep a loyal clientele and to achieve profitable financial performance over the long term.

DeCocinis was quick to point out, however:

> Happy employees don't necessarily mean the highest paid employees. We set out to show them there are many aspects to true happiness. Monetary reward is only one of them. Pride, respect, and opportunities are fantastic elements of satisfaction. They had been missing out.

Becoming Ladies and Gentlemen

When the hotel started operating under the Portman Ritz-Carlton name, DeCocinis announced to the employees that the new management's first initiative would be the complete redesign and renovation of the employee dining room. He commented:

> The state of the employee dining room was absolutely appalling. It was hard to imagine how employees could have a strong sense of self-respect in such an environment. People stayed on to see if Ritz-Carlton would be different, really different. We used the employee dining room to demonstrate our commitment to the Ritz-Carlton value: "We *are* ladies and gentlemen serving ladies and gentlemen."

With the opening of the new employee dining room, the management provided a comfortable dining facility but, more important, also created respectable and civilized surroundings that employees could be proud of.

As a senior manager commented:

China has a sensitive problem. Many Westerners feel that there is a lack of manners and a professional attitude in modern China. For instance, people tend to speak quite loudly in public and often they rush into the elevator as soon as the door opens without letting people inside get out. This is part of an accepted daily routine, which makes it more difficult to address. Professionalism, or lack of it, is another big headache. People's attitude to their jobs often involves doing the minimum to earn the salary. That is why covering for colleagues or going the extra mile are often foreign concepts. When we took over the hotel, we were determined to change that.

The new management team did not, however, expect to accomplish this overnight. They knew they would have to be patient with people's old habits. Such a change would have to come willingly and with practice. Some of the senior managers tried to make things easier for their staff by suggesting they incorporate good habits into the rest of their lives so that they would become automatic. Michelle Wan, director of communications, for example, encouraged her staff to answer their private telephone with the same personable and polite greeting they had been trained to use at work. She recalled:

We were trying to leave a lasting impression on people. Our hope was to extend the civil environment beyond the workplace. Only when the employees felt accustomed to the new way of life would they truly appreciate the working environment we'd created.

Management sought to instill in their employees a sense of professionalism and pride in providing the high level of service expected at a Ritz-Carlton hotel. Professionalism began with respect from the employer but, equally, employees had to view it as an essential element of the job description, not an optional extra that earned rewards. According to DeCocinis:

We wanted our employees to know that everyone within the organization would be treated with real and equal respect. But there would be expectations of everyone's professional conduct. Being professional means you can choose to leave if you are not satisfied with the job or company, or for any other reason. But if you choose not to leave, happy or not, you must perform your duty with full dedication.

As he explained the pyramid concept to the Portman Ritz-Carlton employees, DeCocinis made it clear that he would always be available to them. He set up a monthly "general manager's breakfast," to which selected employees from different departments would be invited to discuss any issues that concerned them. The objective was twofold. One was to recognize promising talent and excellent performance on the job. The other was to ensure an open communication channel between staff and management so that potential problems could be dealt with as they arose and not only when they had become serious. Subjects varied from logistical problems, such as handling check-in during lobby renovation, to employee concerns, such as the comfort of the uniform. Management was open to discussion and responded quickly to employee suggestions.

Once employees could see that top management respected them, the managers thought it would be appropriate to empower the workers with trust and responsibility. The most notable action was to authorize every employee to settle a customer complaint or dissatisfaction up to $2,000 without management approval.

A senior manager acknowledged:

This was an awesome responsibility and a tremendous source of self-respect and pride to the employees. There have been some rare cases of overcompensating the guests, but these were mostly due to inexperience. In such cases, the management team did not penalize the employees; rather we trained them and explained how to handle such situations properly. So the next time, they would do it right.

Acutely aware of the importance of employee pride, DeCocinis made a strong effort to turn the hotel into a model corporate citizen. The company often cosponsored or contributed to major charity events. And DeCocinis himself even became something of a local celebrity, with his eye-catching three-wheel motorcycle, a rare replica of the 1938 BMW R-71. Seeing their own place of work associated with noble causes and their high-profile boss roaring down the city's expressway giving local TV crews a joy ride had a positive effect on the employees. Surveys indicated that they were pleased to work for such a responsible and cool organization.

Human Investment

Although the Portman Ritz-Carlton started with a full complement of staff—indeed, with more employees than necessary—management realized that, given the expected turnover in the Shanghai job market, it would need to recruit new people. From the start, the hotel established a comprehensive human resource program with the goal of bringing suitable local recruits into the organization and providing them with continuous professional development.

During job interviews, in addition to looking at the usual technical qualifications, the Portman Ritz-Carlton also screened candidates' psychological profiles. Superior language skills and other technical training would not be enough to guarantee a job—the company also looked for sincerity, personality, and evidence of, or potential for, good teamwork. Wan explained:

> Technical capabilities can be learned on the job, but a person's drive and motivation and ability to work as a team may not. So in the hiring process, we are much more concerned about a candidate's "soft skills."

Another element of the process was DeCocinis's insistence on interviewing every candidate personally before the final decision to hire. According to him, not only did having a single decision maker ensure consistency and fairness in hiring but it also sent a message to new recruits that top management cared and would keep dialogue open with all employees. In addition, the Portman Ritz-Carlton conducted an annual employee satisfaction survey and two individual employee reviews per year, all designed to provide open feedback between management and employees.

Compensation for all employees at the Portman Ritz-Carlton Shanghai consisted of a base salary, with bonuses for both team and individual performance at year-end. In addition, employees in the top 5 percent based on performance as determined in the semiannual performance reviews received an extra bonus.

The hotel guaranteed at least 100 training hours per year for all of its employees. At junior staff levels, the emphasis was on language proficiency and

exhibit 3 **Key Performance Ratios**

	1999	2000	2001
Employee satisfaction rate	70%	85%	96%
Guest satisfaction rate	91	92	96
Net profit improvement	—	18	25

information technology literacy. For middle-level managers—to counter the perception that there was a glass ceiling for local hires—training frequently included exchanges with sister properties in other countries such as Singapore or the United States. Senior managers believed that the main differentiating factor between local talent and expatriates was not competence but experience. Their long-term objective was to replace as many expatriates as possible with local hires, and they believed that the best way to achieve this was by broadening the horizons of promising locally hired middle managers.

Making Progress

By the end of 2001, four years after the Ritz-Carlton takeover, everything seemed to be moving in the right direction. DeCocinis's pyramid had yielded solid results (see Exhibit 3). The employee satisfaction rating had improved dramatically from 1998 to 2001. Over the same period, both guest satisfaction and profit growth also increased.

The company managed to improve efficiency significantly, reducing the overall number of employees to 800, from 1,067 at the beginning. DeCocinis explained:

> We never lost sight of reducing wastage in manpower. Our investment in employees has allowed us to achieve that.

The attrition rate for 2001 was 21 percent, much lower than the local industry average. The figure included regular dismissals of employees who had been given opportunities but failed to meet expectations. At the end of the year, 300 of the employees who had stayed on after the takeover in 1998 were still there. Grooming of local management talent had also begun to bear fruit—the number of expatriate managers had declined to 27, from 40 in 1998.

exhibit 4 **Major Awards, Portman Ritz-Carlton, Shanghai**

1998	Best Hotel in Shanghai—Finance Asia, Institutional Investor
1999	Best Business Hotel in China—Bloomberg TV/Business Asia
2000	Best Business Hotel in China—Bloomberg TV/Business Asia
2001	Best Conference Hotel
	Best Business Hotel in China
	Best Overall Business Hotel in Asia—Bloomberg TV/Business Asia
	Best Employer in China
	Best Employer in Asia—*Asian Wall Street Journal, Far Eastern Economic Review,* and Hewitt Associates

Source: Company information.

exhibit 5 **The Top 20 Best Employers in Asia, 2001**

Rank	Company
1.	The Portman Ritz-Carlton, Shanghai
2.	Agilent Technologies (Singapore)
3.	The Ritz-Carlton Millenia Singapore
4.	Western Digital (Malaysia)
5.	Elegant Textile Industry, Indonesia
6.	Federal Express Services (Malaysia)
7.	Tricon Restaurants International, Thailand
8.	The Ritz-Carlton, Hong Kong
9.	AMD (Thailand)
10.	Navion (Shanghai) Software Development
11.	Tenaga Nasional, Malaysia
12.	Ford Lio Ho Motor, Taiwan
13.	Intel Malaysia
14.	Four Seasons Hotel Singapore
15.	Agilent Technologies (Malaysia)
16.	Jollibee Foods, Philippines
17.	H&CB, South Korea
18.	Shanghai Hormel Foods
19.	Crown Motors, Hong Kong
20.	Hewlett-Packard Korea

Source: Survey conducted by *Asia Wall Street Journal, Far Eastern Economic Review,* and Hewitt Associates.

The net outcome of the transformation was enthusiastic reaction from international media and independent survey groups. The Portman Ritz-Carlton was awarded Best Hotel in Shanghai in 1998, then Best Business Hotel in China in 1999 and 2000, and ultimately Best Overall Business Hotel in Asia and Asia's Best Employer in 2001 (see Exhibits 4 and 5).

January 2002

By the end of 2001 the Portman Ritz-Carlton Shanghai could be said to be the most desirable place to stay in Shanghai. President George W. Bush, like his predecessor, Bill Clinton, stayed there in October 2001. The ensuing international exposure may have helped the hotel to achieve its highest-ever monthly occupancy rate the following month. DeCocinis was, of course, pleased with these results, but past successes do not ensure future profits, especially in a tightening market.

After the terrorist attacks on the World Trade Center in New York and the Pentagon in Washington, D.C., on September 11, 2001, international business travel saw an immediate sharp decline. For a hotel such as the Portman Ritz-Carlton, which catered mostly to business travelers, a decline in occupancy was inevitable—and it was immediate. To make matters worse, the decline in business travel happened just as the Shanghai hotel market added capacity. Before September 11, the hotel had not viewed large groups like Hilton and Sheraton as direct competitors, because the Portman Ritz-Carlton attracted a more sophisticated and demanding clientele. However, the post–September 11 decline challenged this assumption. Moreover, there was a greater threat in the form of two new direct competitors: The St. Regis had admitted its first guests in July 2001, and the first Four Seasons hotel in China was scheduled to open its doors in February 2002. From his office window, DeCocinis could see the almost-completed building just three blocks away.

But it was not only the loss of clientele that concerned DeCocinis. As a result of his own success in developing professional and service-oriented local employees, he had good reason to worry that his new competitors would aggressively recruit his staff. Although they were well paid, his competitors might offer them more. Would the job satisfaction created at the Portman Ritz-Carlton stand up to increased competitive pressures? What could DeCocinis do to make sure that it did?

Enjoying coffee served in a fine Wedgwood china cup, DeCocinis debated what to do next. Should he lower the accommodation rates, which had consistently been the highest in the city, to keep his occupancy rate up? Should he raise salaries before his competitors tried to lure his staff away? And most important of all, what could he now use to motivate his staff to keep going after such a meteoric rise to the top?

Continental Airlines in 2003: Sustaining the Turnaround

Arthur A. Thompson
The University of Alabama

In 1994, Continental Airlines was a troubled company. While it was the fifth largest commercial airline in the United States, with revenues of $6 billion, Continental had reported a net loss every year since 1985. Strained finances had forced Continental to seek Chapter 11 bankruptcy protection in 1983 and again in 1990; it had taken the company until April 1993 to get in good enough shape to emerge from its 1990 bankruptcy filing. Since 1983, nine different CEOs had tried unsuccessfully to fix Continental, initiating numerous internal reorganizations, revitalization and turnaround efforts, and strategy shifts. During Continental's bankruptcy proceedings in 1990–93, wages and salaries had been cut and management had tried to rid the company of unions. Turnover and use of sick time were quite high; on-the-job injuries were far above the industry average. There was considerable infighting among employee groups and departments. When problems occurred, finger-pointing often overwhelmed efforts at constructive problem solving and employees ran for cover, insisting they had followed procedures. Continental's ticket agents and gate personnel spent many stressful hours dealing with dissatisfied and angry passengers—some of Continental's airport personnel, when they were off duty or on break, removed the Continental insignia from their uniforms to avoid having to answer uncomfortable questions from coworkers or customers.[1]

When Gordon Bethune agreed to become Continental's president and chief operating officer (COO) in February 1994 and take on the challenge of improving the company's operations, Continental ranked last among the 10 largest U.S. commercial airlines in on-time arrivals (the percentage of flights that arrived within 15 minutes of the scheduled time). It also had the highest number of mishandled baggage reports per 1,000 passengers and by far the highest number of complaints per 100,000 passengers. Complaints filed with the Department of Transportation by Continental passengers about various aspects of their experiences on Continental flights were 30 percent higher than the ninth-ranking airline and three times the industry average. Bethune recognized the terrible conditions that existed:

> This was a crummy place to work. The culture at Continental, after years of layoffs and wage freezes and wage cuts and broken promises, was one of backbiting, mistrust, fear, and loathing. People, to put it mildly, were not happy to come to work. They were surly to customers, surly to each other, and ashamed of their company . . .
>
> In a company where cost-cutting was revered, departments fought one another to the death over scarce resources. In a company where management strategies—and management teams—changed overnight, employees schemed above all else to protect themselves, at the cost of their co-workers if necessary. Interdepartmental communication was almost nonexistent.
>
> Everybody was screwing over everybody—no wonder the planes were late and the baggage was lost. The product was crummy. The fundamental reasons for that had nothing to do with flying planes correctly or being able to clean and fix them. It had to do with

[1]Gordon Bethune with Scott Huler, *From Worst to First: Behind the Scenes of Continental's Remarkable Comeback* (New York: John Wiley & Sons, 1998), p. 6.

an environment where nobody could get their jobs done.

> . . . The organization itself was so dysfunctional that it couldn't have implemented the best idea in the world.[2]

Despite his early confidence that he could rectify many of Continental's operating difficulties, Bethune soon found himself disenchanted and frustrated in his role as president and COO because Continental's CEO refused to go along with Bethune's plans to get Continental's operations on track unless the actions he wanted to initiate would also reduce costs. In late October 1994, with the company headed for another money-losing year and a looming financial crisis, Continental's board of directors determined that a change had to be made at the top. Initially, the board decided that it would give the present CEO a six-month leave of absence and let Bethune run the company from his position as president and COO. However, the CEO decided to step down immediately. Continental's board made Bethune the company's temporary CEO and asked him to present a plan for turning Continental around at the board's regularly scheduled meeting in 10 days.

GORDON BETHUNE'S GO FORWARD PLAN

Gordon Bethune's first act when he temporarily took over on October 24, 1994, was to prop open the doors to Continental's executive suite, which heretofore had been locked and monitored by security cameras. He wanted people to enter freely at any time rather than having to show an ID to gain admission, and he wanted to begin to change the atmosphere in the executive suite. Next, he began working on the plan he would present to the board. He requested help from Greg Brenneman, a Bain & Company vice president with expertise in turning companies around; Brenneman had been working with Continental for several months on an assortment of ways to revamp Continental's maintenance operations (which had the highest cost but the lowest dispatch reliability in the industry), and his efforts had produced some good results. Brenneman and Bethune came up with what

[2]Ibid., pp. 6, 14–15.

they called the Go Forward Plan. It had four parts—a market plan to fly profitable routes, a financial plan to put the company into the black in 1995, a product plan to improve Continental's offering to customers, and a people plan to transform the company's culture. All four parts of the Go Forward Plan were to be implemented simultaneously.

The Market Plan: Fly to Win

The guiding principle behind the Fly to Win market plan was for Continental to stop doing those things that were losing money or causing the company to lose money and to concentrate on Continental's market strengths. Six strategic initiatives formed the backbone of Bethune's market plan:

1. *Substantially revising Continental's route schedule to focus on hub-and-spoke operations rather than point-to-point routes.* More flights were targeted for spoke destinations out of Continental's Newark, Houston, and Cleveland hubs that held promise of generating enough passenger traffic to generate a profit. Spoke destinations and point-to-point routes where Continental had too many flights with too few passengers and fares too low to make a profit were to be abandoned. The analysis conducted by Bethune and Brenneman revealed that the company was losing money on 18 percent of its routes, many of which were low-fare point-to-point routes for which Continental had a relatively small market share.

2. *Drastic cutbacks in the flight schedule for Continental Lite, the company's low-fare/no-frills operation that was modeled after Southwest Airlines.* Analysis indicated that about one-third of Continental Lite's routes were responsible for about 70 percent of Continental's losses. Continental Lite had been created by replacing the first-class seats with coach seats in 100 of Continental's smaller Boeing jets, painting the name Continental Lite on planes to identify the product, setting up point-to-point routes that management thought were underserved, offering a number of flights on each route, not serving meals on flights of less than two and a half hours, and flying planes from early morning to late at night to generate as much revenue per

plane as feasible. But Continental Lite had failed to catch on with Continental's customer base. Bethune's diagnosis was that Continental customers were not interested in the Continental Lite product, preferring to pay full fares for full-service flights—especially on longer flights and flights spanning normal meal hours. Moreover, Continental Lite's costs were too high relative to the revenues being generated by its low-fare approach—Bethune did not believe that Continental Lite's costs could be cut far enough to make its operation profitable and, at the same time, make the Continental Lite product attractive to air travelers.

3. *Raising fares on some of Continental's routes.*

4. *Closing the company's money-losing Greensboro, North Carolina, hub.* The relatively new Greensboro hub was not generating enough traffic from the various spoke locations to justify trying to continue to win additional market share in the Southeast, where Delta and US Airways had a strong presence. (Hub operations in Denver had been abandoned several years earlier.)

5. *Eliminating Continental's big Airbus 300 planes from the fleet.* The planned flight frequency and destination cuts meant that Continental would have too much seat capacity. Taking the Airbus 300 planes out of circulation (which on many flights were only 50–60 percent full) eliminated most of Continental's excess seat capacity—and with the next-biggest planes flying these same routes at close to capacity, the revenues generated by the Airbus 300 flights were retained. Moreover, Continental's Airbus 300 aircraft were expensive to operate, required special maintenance procedures, and entailed lease payments of up to $200,000 a month. Bethune and Brenneman proposed disposing of all Airbus 300 planes in Continental's fleet, thereby removing the necessity of a special parts inventory, special facilities and people, and special procedures to manage that one particular aircraft.

6. *Launching a concerted marketing campaign to win back customers that it had lost, especially business travelers.* Continental's cost-cutting efforts in prior years had entailed reducing the commissions paid to travel agents (who at the time handled 80 percent of all flight reserva-

tions); stripping popular features from its OnePass frequent flyer program; and eliminating perks (first-class seats, upgrades, coupons for free drinks) that travel agents could offer corporate customers as inducements to choose Continental flights. Bethune believed that such actions had alienated Continental customers, prompting many business travelers to switch much of their air travel to rival carriers. And he believed Continental's poor on-time performance and customer satisfaction ratings, along with lower commissions, had alienated travel agents, causing them to steer customers to other carriers. To try to win back the confidence and business of travel agents, Bethune proposed going hat in hand to all the major travel agents, apologizing for prior mistakes, promising that Continental's on-time performance and passenger satisfaction levels were going to improve dramatically, reestablishing higher commissions, and giving them a package of incentives they could use to induce their corporate clients to book more flights on Continental. To try to win back business travelers, Bethune planned to restore the features of the award-winning OnePass frequent flyer program that prior management had dismantled.

The Financial Plan: Fund the Future

In October 1994, Continental was strapped for cash and burdened by debt—it owed considerable money on its aircraft fleet, and it had a $2 billion debt hangover from the Chapter 11 proceedings in 1993. Bethune and Brenneman concluded that it was critical for the company's survival to have a credible financial plan for making a profit in 1995. They put together a package of proposed changes involving renegotiation of aircraft lease payments, refinancing some of Continental's debt at lower interest rates, postponing some debt repayments, and raising fares on certain routes. These moves, they projected, held a realistic chance of generating a profit of $45 million in 1995 (a substantial improvement over the $200 million in losses that Continental would likely show for 1994) and would produce sufficient cash flows for Continental to avoid another financial crisis.

The Product Plan: Make Reliability a Reality

The Make Reliability a Reality piece of Bethune's Go Forward Plan aimed at quantum improvements in Continental's on-time performance, baggage handling, and overall flying experience—doing the very things that would please customers and make them inclined to fly Continental again. The centerpiece of Bethune's product plan was to focus employees' attention on on-time performance by rewarding them with a $65 bonus each month that Continental was in the top five U.S. airlines in percentage of flights arriving on-time—as measured and reported monthly by the U.S. Department of Transportation, which considered a flight to be on time if it arrived at the gate within 15 minutes of the scheduled time.

The People Plan: Working Together

Bethune believed that the most important component of the Go Forward Plan was to radically change Continental's corporate culture. He was convinced that a successful turnaround at Continental hinged on getting Continental's employees pulling together and creating a positive work environment. Bethune explained his thinking:

> The environment was so bad that regardless of marketing strategies, financial plans, and reliability incentives, there weren't going to be any improvements in Continental's operations until we stopped treating people the way we had been treating them and got them to start working together. You just can't be successful in any kind of business without teamwork.
>
> So part of our plan—and it was vague at this point, even though over the long term it was by far the most important part of the plan—was to make it a corporate goal to change how people treated each other: to find ways to measure and reward cooperation rather than infighting, to encourage and reward trust and confidence.

Bethune's Meeting with the Board

Bethune presented the Go Forward Plan to Continental's board, indicating that it represented a joint effort with Greg Brenneman.[3] After the presentation, which was generally well received, the board deliberated whether to appoint Bethune as permanent CEO. Board members initially indicated their preference was to establish an "office of the chairman," with Bethune remaining as president and COO. Bethune thought that was a mistake, arguing that the turnaround effort he proposed required the clear and unequivocal authority of a leader who was designated CEO and enjoyed the full support of the board of directors. Many board members were unconvinced by Bethune's plea that a strong leader/CEO was essential to implement a turnaround plan, and they were not entirely sure that the company was in as dire straits as Bethune indicated. The board asked Bethune to excuse himself while they reconsidered the matter. After an hour and a half, the chairman of the board recalled Bethune to the meeting and indicated that a majority of the board had decided to appoint Bethune as CEO. Although disappointed that the board had not enthusiastically embraced his Go Forward Plan and then immediately and unanimously elected him as CEO, Bethune was nonetheless gratified for the chance to try to turn Continental around.

THE IMPLEMENTATION AND EVOLUTION OF BETHUNE'S GO FORWARD PLAN, 1995–2001

At the outset, Bethune recognized that Continental's employees would view his actions with suspicion and that he would therefore need to build credibility with them. He judged that employees weren't going to rally around the Go Forward Plan without some good reason to trust that he was different and that his administration was going to do a far better job of really fixing what was wrong with the company than the nine prior executive regimes. Bethune also realized that as CEO at Continental he would need to draw on many of his prior experiences. He was a licensed airline pilot, qualified to fly Boeing 757 and 767 jets. He had an airframe and powerplant mechanic's license. He had been a maintenance facility manager

[3]Ibid., pp. 26–28.

at both Braniff and Western Airlines, and a senior vice president for operations at Piedmont Airlines in the 1980s (before Piedmont was acquired and became a part of US Airways). His operations background at Boeing had made him familiar with the aircraft side of commercial airline business and somewhat knowledgeable about the strategies of various airlines and the executives who ran them.

Bethune's Early Days as Continental's CEO

The same day he took over as CEO, Gordon Bethune announced the closing of the company's Los Angeles maintenance operations, where approximately 1,800 people were employed. With Continental moving to concentrate its flight operations at the Newark, Houston, and Cleveland hubs, a big maintenance facility in Los Angeles was no longer economic.

Bethune asked Greg Brenneman to remain as a consultant to the company and a close adviser. In May 1995 Bethune named Brenneman Continental's chief operating officer. As Continental's new COO, Brenneman played a key role in helping implement and execute the Go Forward Plan. In September 1996, Brenneman took on the additional title of president, with Bethune functioning as chairman and CEO.

After dispensing with all the security and opening the executive suite, Bethune instituted open houses for employees at the Houston headquarters on the last working day of each month. Employees were invited to tour the executive offices on the 20th floor, visit with Bethune and other executives, and help themselves to food and drinks. Casual-dress Fridays were instituted across the company for all employees except those dealing directly with customers, partly to make Continental managers and executives more approachable. Bethune mandated a no-smoking rule in all company facilities—and he extended the ban on smoking to include all North American and South American flights (over the objections of Continental's marketing people, who contended that such a ban would irritate smoking passengers). The smoking ban was later extended to all of Continental's European flights and then worldwide, with little apparent negative effect. At executive meetings, Bethune began sitting at the middle of the long table in the executive conference room rather than at the head. He insisted that meetings begin and end on schedule.

One of his most dramatic actions involved gathering a few Continental employees, along with some of the manuals containing the company's regulations and procedures, going out to the parking lot outside the Houston headquarters, and having the employees set fire to the manuals. Employees in the field were told that they were expected to use their best judgment to solve problems and deal with issues, rather than following the rigid procedures described in the manual. A task force of employees was created to go over the entire manual and come up with guidelines that would help employees make good decisions and take appropriate actions—the idea was that Houston headquarters was there to help but not to dictate to the nth degree. Bethune wanted the message to employees to be: "Use these guidelines, think things through, and unless you do something completely out of bounds, you don't have to worry about hearing from Houston. Houston wants you to do your job. Houston wants to leave you alone unless you need help. And believe it or not, if you need help, Houston wants to help you."[4]

As of late 1994, Continental's aircraft fleet was not painted uniformly; at the company's hubs, differently painted Continental planes were usually lined up at the gates. While in earlier years Continental had tried to create a new image with a completely new paint scheme for all its aircraft, only about half the fleet had been repainted because of executive pressures to cut costs. Believing that professional, identical-looking planes would send a message to employees and customers that Continental was running a better operation, Bethune issued an order that every one of Continental's planes was to receive a fresh paint job by July 1, 1995—there were to be no exceptions. People in Continental's fleet operations said this was too short a time frame in which to get 200 planes repainted; Bethune refused to relent:

> I did something I rarely do: I made a threat. I said, "Yes you can, and you know why?" Because I have a Beretta at home with a 15-round magazine, and if you don't get those planes painted by July 1 I'm going to come in here and empty the clip. You're wonderful

[4]Ibid., pp. 37–38.

people and I love you, but you're going to get those airplanes painted or I'm going to shoot every last one of you.[5]

The last Continental plane was painted on June 30, just in time to meet Bethune's deadline.

Meanwhile, Bethune and other Continental executives spread the word among employees that the Go Forward Plan was management's blueprint—there were meetings with employees at virtually every site in the company to introduce the plan and explain how it addressed all of Continental's problems. Many employees had already heard about the open houses and open-door policy, the burning of the manual, and other initiatives, but management wanted to present the plan personally and answer whatever questions employees had. The meetings did not always go smoothly; a number of employees voiced doubt and skepticism, openly expressing their mistrust of what management was telling them. One pilot told Bethune, "You're the tenth guy I've seen, and you sound good, but let me tell you, this goddamn place is broken. There ain't nobody going to fix it, including you. So it doesn't matter what you say, this place is going to fail."[6] Bethune took issue with pilot, saying in part:

I don't know about you, but I don't know of any self-respecting pilot, regardless of what predicament the airplane is in—it's on fire, it's upside down, it's spinning around, whatever—who stops trying to fly the airplane before it hits the ground. You don't ever give up and say, screw it, it's over, I can't do anything . . . Listen, I'm the captain of this company now. This is what we are going to do. I'm flying, it's my leg. If you don't like the way I'm working, the jetway is still attached. You can step off if you want to. But I am going to fly this company where it's going.[7]

Bethune's response to the pilot mirrored his concept of what a leader did and what a leader's role was. Bethune explained further:

My definition of a leader is pretty simple. The leader is the person who looks at the big picture and says, "Okay, everybody, go west."

Now west is precisely a compass heading of 270 degrees, but anywhere from about 240 to 300 degrees is heading generally west. So if I say go west, and one

person is heading out at about 295 degrees, that's okay with me . . . I don't want to precisely determine how you interpret it when I say, hey, let's go west. You see things a certain way, and what's happening in your department and what's happening to you today may affect what has to happen when I say go west.

On the other hand, the guy who's going 090 degrees, which is due east, is a problem. You have to catch him and readjust his thinking so he's going the right way. If he won't be readjusted, I say no way buster: You either head west or get out of here. Maybe he needs to go to a company headed east . . .

I'm not saying that everybody has to be marching in lockstep—in fact, that's exactly what we *don't* want. We want people doing their jobs with a minimum of interference from their bosses. That's why we burned the manual . . .

Your real job as boss—my real job as chief executive—is to let people do their jobs. It's to assemble the right team, set the big-picture direction, communicate that, and then get out of the way . . . You have to trust people to do their jobs. That's the strongest leadership there is.[8]

At a meeting with employees in Denver in late 1995, Bethune encountered another vocal employee who reacted to his presentation of the Go Forward Plan and the turnaround actions that were under way by saying, "It sounds fine, but I still don't believe it. We've had too many new programs here and I don't believe it."[9] Bethune tried to reason with the employee, explaining why and how things were on the mend at Continental and what role the Working Together initiatives would play. The employee still did not buy what Bethune was saying, at which time Bethune told him what he told the pilot in Newark—that the jetway was still attached and that if he didn't like the direction the company was headed, maybe he should get off the plane. The employee turned and walked out the door; the audience of employees applauded his exit.

Executing the Fly to Win Market Plan

Under Bethune, Continental marketing executives began treating travel agencies as partners and worked with them closely, creating programs whereby agencies that sold a certain volume of tickets or hit other

---

[5]Ibid., p. 39.
[6]Ibid., p. 41.
[7]Ibid., pp. 41–42.

[8]Ibid., pp. 42–43.
[9]Ibid., p. 142.

sales targets specified by Continental would be paid an incentive above the normal commission rate. Programs involving upgrades to first class and discounts for certain travel volumes were created for travel agents to use in marketing Continental to large corporations. In some cases, new destinations were added when feedback from travel agencies indicated that such destinations would be attractive to their corporate clients. Continental wanted to move its business from what Greg Brenneman called the backpack-and-flip-flop crowd to the coat-and-tie crowd or at least the Patagonia backpack crowd, believing that such travelers were usually willing to pay higher fares in order not to take chances with their comfort and convenience. To assist travel agencies in marketing Continental to business travelers, Continental sent letters to corporate CEOs, middle managers, and sales representatives who flew frequently, apologizing for the company's poor performance in past years, laying out the customer-related features of the Go Forward Plan, and asking them to give flying Continental a try. Continental executives made personal calls on the executives of companies that already were doing a lot of business with Continental to thank them for their business, and they made calls on corporate executives of companies where they thought Continental might be able to win a bigger share of the air travel budget.

To help lure Houston-area business travelers back to Continental, Gordon Bethune held a party at his house for 100 of the company's high-mileage frequent fliers—spouses were invited, too. At the party, Bethune announced that the company had made mistakes in the past and wanted another chance at proving it could be relied on to provide good service. Each attendee was presented a leather ticket case. Continental executives circulated through the crowd, thanking people for coming, asking forgiveness for past sins, and explaining what the company was doing to earn their business.

To grow the business during the 1995–2001 period, Continental gradually added more destinations from its hubs and added more flights to existing destinations. Expansion was particularly aggressive in international markets, with service being added to Hong Kong, Tokyo, Rome, Milan, Tel Aviv, several other European cities, the Caribbean, Guam, South America, Central America, and Mexico. By mid-2001, Continental had over 2,000 flights going to nearly 90 international and 130 domestic destinations; it served more international destinations than any other carrier. Guam evolved into a fourth, albeit much smaller, hub for a number of Continental flights operating in the Asia-Pacific region. Newark was the primary gateway for flights to Europe (15 cities) and the Middle East; the Houston hub was the primary gateway for flights to Mexico (20 cities), Central America (every country), and South America (6 cities). The Cleveland hub had international flights to Montreal, Toronto, San Juan, and Cancun. In 2000, Continental announced plans to expand its service to 30 European cities within the next three to five years, and it was exploring adding more destinations in the Middle East. Management believed that it could benefit from TWA's decision to cease all transatlantic services from New York—TWA had long been a force in Europe and the Middle East.

The company's Web site (www.continental.com) was used as an increasingly important distribution channel for marketing tickets to individuals and businesses; in 2000, Continental expanded e-ticketing to about 95 percent of its destinations. Also in 2000, Continental partnered with United, Delta, American, and Northwest to create a comprehensive travel planning Web site called Orbitz (www.orbitz.com), which offered airline tickets, hotel reservations, car rentals, and other services. Continental's Web site recorded $600 million in ticket sales in 2002, compared with $487 million in 2001 and $320 million in 2000.

Continental Express Soon after the company decided in 1996 to phase out Continental Lite entirely, management decided to create a feeder operation for its hubs called Continental Express. Continental Express operated as a separate subsidiary with its own president. By year-end 2002, Continental Express had expanded its operations to include 950 daily flights, with regional jet service to 110 cities in the United States, Mexico, and Canada. Continental management believed that Continental Express flights allowed more frequent service to small cities than could be provided economically with larger conventional jets and contributed to higher load factors on Continental's regular jet service by feeding passengers into Continental's three major hubs to connect to regular Continental flights.

Bethune's Row 5 Test One of the challenges Bethune faced was in deciding what constituted "better" service and "better" performance. In his view, Fly to Win meant that Continental had to fly where people wanted to go, stop doing things that lost money, find out what things customers wanted and provide them, and compete effectively against rivals. He was willing for Continental to do things that added cost, provided they added so much value that passengers were willing to pay for them and the costs could therefore be incorporated in fare prices. When Continental people came up with proposals to spend money to increase the technological sophistication of Continental planes or make other operating changes that had cost-increasing implications, Bethune insisted on applying what he called the Row 5 Test—which involved asking whether a hypothetical passenger sitting in row 5 on a Continental plane would be willing to pay 50 cents or a dollar more in order to have the proposed benefit.[10] Bethune argued, for example, that if the floors on Continental's aircraft maintenance facilities were so clean you could eat off them, then Continental was probably paying too much attention to keeping the floors clean. He wanted Continental to focus on doing the things that created value for the customer—add only those costs that added customer value. In Bethune's view, defining success and good performance in customers' terms meant clean, safe, reliable service from well-managed hubs; convenient flight schedules to places customers wanted to go; the kinds of amenities that made a customer's travel experience more pleasant; and frequent flyer benefits that represented real rewards.

Executing the Fund the Future Financial Plan

Despite Continental's having recently emerged from Chapter 11 bankruptcy proceedings in April 1993, Gordon Bethune and Greg Brenneman believed that there was substantial risk of a third bankruptcy unless the company moved decisively in late 1994 and early 1995 to get its finances in order. Aggressive implementation of Continental's initial Fund the Future plan to renegotiate aircraft lease payments, refinance some of Continental's debt at lower interest rates (saving about $25 million in annual interest payments), stretch out debt repayments on loans from three years to seven or eight years, and raise

fares on selected routes relieved much of the near-term potential for a financial crisis. Whereas in 1994 Continental incurred $202 million in interest costs, by 1996 interest expenses had been reduced to $117 million. Three other actions helped Continental deal with its 1994–95 cash crunch:

1. When Continental determined it could not afford the new planes it had on order at Boeing and decided to cancel its order, Continental's financial predicament was such that Bethune felt compelled to telephone his close friend Ron Woodard, the president of Boeing, asking him to return Continental's $70 million nonrefundable deposit because Continental needed the cash in the worst way. Woodard suspected that Continental was in dire straits and despite his reluctance to go against company policy and refund a deposit (aircraft manufacturers used deposits to help finance initial manufacturing of planes on order), Woodard agreed to send Continental a partial $29 million refund. Bethune accepted the offer, indicating that, if possible, Boeing should wire the funds immediately; Woodard laughed but agreed to Bethune's plea.[11]

2. Excess parts inventories were sold and maintenance contracts were renegotiated.

3. Cash outlays for operating expenses were reduced by entering into code-sharing agreements with other airlines to achieve joint operating economies. Code sharing typically involved two airline partners operating a single flight to a particular destination but having that flight listed in the separate flight schedules of each partner; one of the partner's planes and crews would be used to operate flight, but both partners could book passengers on the flight to that location, share in the revenues generated, and achieve a better load factor on that flight than they might achieve operating two independent flights. Often, code-sharing partners also cooperated in other mutually beneficial ways. For instance, in Phoenix and Las Vegas, where it only had two or three flights coming in daily, Continental partnered with America West to handle the ground work on Continental's flights; in Orlando and Tampa, where Continental had a greater presence than America West, Continental personnel

---

[10]Ibid., pp. 64–69.

[11]Ibid., pp. 84–85.

handled the ground work for America West's flights. Each airline thus gained the savings of not having to staff gates that were used for only a few flights a day. During the 1996–2002 period, Continental expanded its code-sharing efforts, entering into agreements with such domestic carriers as Northwest Airlines, Delta Airlines, Hawaiian Airlines, Alaska Airlines, American Eagle, and Horizon Airlines and such international carriers as Air Europa, Air France, Virgin Airways, Air China, and KLM Royal Dutch Airlines.

Upset by what he considered untrustworthy information coming from the finance department, Bethune moved to install much stronger financial systems. A new chief financial officer, Larry Kellner, was brought in to overhaul the company's financial systems and generate better information for decision making. Under Kellner's guidance, Continental developed systems that allowed management to have dependable and regularly updated estimates of revenues, costs, profits, and cash flows; every morning by 10 AM, executives had a report of the previous day's credit card receipts. Not long thereafter, the system was upgraded to include the capability to produce a 40-item daily forecast that included credit card receipts, fuel costs, maintenance costs, revenue per available seat mile, cost per available seat mile, profit per available seat mile per type of aircraft, profit at each hub, and profit on each route from each hub. According to Bethune, "The measurements became more and more accurate, which meant we could make better and better decisions with increasingly current numbers."[12] For instance, the new financial systems revealed that Continental's European flights were unusually profitable; management used this information to add more European flights and to increase the fares on some of its international routes. It also learned which routes and flights were losing money, thus providing a basis for revising Continental's flight schedules—employees in locations where service was discontinued (or where code sharing was implemented) were offered jobs in other parts of the company whenever possible. Kellner also began the practice of hedging Continental's jet fuel purchases to give the company an insurance policy against unexpected increases in

fuel costs—in 1995, fuel hedges saved Continental an estimated $3 million as fuel prices rose.

During the 1996–98 period, Continental initiated efforts to lower training and maintenance costs by reducing the number of different types of aircraft comprising its fleet. The company achieved its goal of having only 5 different types of aircraft by the end of 1999, as compared to 10 in 1994. Further maintenance savings were realized as the company took delivery on new Boeing aircraft in 1997 and 1998, reducing the average age of its fleet. New aircraft were financed by long-term borrowing and leasing arrangements.

In July 1997, Continental launched a three-year program to bring employee wages and salaries up to industry standards; the program was completed on schedule in July 2000. At this point, Continental launched another three-year program to bring employee benefits to industry standards by 2003; the program to improve benefits involved increases in vacations, paid holidays, increases in matching contributions to 401(k) programs, and past service retirement credits for most senior employees.

Exhibit 1 provides a summary of Continental's financial and operating performance for the 1993–2002 period. Continental had paid no dividends on its common stock and had no current intention to do so. Starting in 1998, Continental began a stock repurchase program under which it had purchased a total of 28.1 million shares at a cost of approximately $1.2 billion through December 2002. Throughout much of the 1998–2002 period, most of Continental's assets were pledged as collateral on its borrowings or were otherwise encumbered; the company operated its aircraft under leasing agreements and also had operating leases for its airport and terminal facilities—the obligations for its leases were not included in the company's consolidated balance sheets. Going into 2003, Continental had about $1 billion in unencumbered assets, consisting mostly of spare parts inventories and equity in its Continental Express subsidiary.

The Alliance with Northwest Airlines

In 1998, Northwest Airlines purchased an 8.7-million-share block of Continental's common stock, sufficient to give it voting control of Continental. This formed the basis for a long-term global alliance between Continental and Northwest that provided for each carrier to place its flight code on a large number

[12]Ibid., p. 88.

exhibit 1 **Financial and Operating Summary, Continental Airlines, 1993–2002**

	2002	2001	2000	1999	1998	1997	1995	1993
Financial data								
(in millions, except for per share data)								
Operating revenues	$8,402	$8,969	$9,899	$8,639	$7,927	$7,194	$5,825	$5,767
Total operating expenses	8,714	8,825	9,170	8,024	7,226	6,478	5,440	5,786
Operating income	(312)	144	729	615	701	716	385	(19)
Net income	(451)	(95)	342	455	383	385	224	(39)[a]
Basic earnings per share	$(7.02)	$(1.72)	$5.62	$6.54	$6.34	$6.65	$4.07	$(1.17)[a]
Diluted earnings per share	$(7.02)	$(1.72)	$5.45	$6.20	$5.02	$4.99	$3.37	$(1.17)[a]
Operating data								
Revenue passengers (000s)	41,016	44,238	46,896	45,540	43,625	41,210	37,575	38,628
Revenue passenger miles (millions)[b]	59,349	61,140	64,161	60,022	53,910	47,906	40,023	42,324
Available seat miles (millions)[c]	80,122	84,485	86,100	81,946	74,727	67,576	61,006	67,011
Passenger load factor[d]	74.1%	72.4%	74.5%	73.2%	72.1%	70.9%	65.6%	63.2%
Breakeven passenger load factor[e]	79.2%	74.9%	66.3%	64.7%	61.6%	60.1%	60.8%	63.3%
Passenger revenue per available seat mile	8.61¢	8.98¢	9.84¢	9.12¢	9.23¢	9.29¢	8.20¢	7.17¢
Total revenue per available seat mile	9.52¢	9.78¢	10.67¢	9.86¢	9.95¢	10.06¢	n.a.	n.a.
Operating cost per available seat mile	9.22¢	9.58¢	9.68¢	8.99¢	8.89¢	9.04¢	8.36¢	7.90¢
Average price per gallon of fuel	74.01¢	82.48¢	88.54¢	50.78¢	51.20¢	67.36¢	55.02¢	59.26¢
Average fare per revenue passenger	$168.25	$171.59	$180.66	$164.11	$158.02	$152.40	n.a.	n.a.
Actual aircraft in service at end of period (not including Continental Express)	366	352	371	363	363	337	309	316
Average age of jet aircraft fleet (years)	n.a.	5.2	6.7	7.4	7.6	10.7	14.4	n.a.

[a]Covers only the period April 28, 1993, through December 31, 1993, after Continental emerged from Chapter 11 bankruptcy proceedings that began in 1990; results prior to April 28 are not meaningful due to recapitalization of company and other matters pertaining to the bankruptcy proceedings.

[b]The number of scheduled miles flown by revenue passengers.

[c]The number of seats available for passengers multiplied by the number of scheduled miles those seats are flown.

[d]Revenue passenger miles divided by available seat miles.

[e]The percentage of seats that must be occupied by revenue passengers in order for the airline to break even on an income before income-tax basis, excluding nonrecurring charges, non-operating items, and other special items.

Source: Company press release, January 15, 2003; 1999 and 2001 company 10K reports; 2001 annual report.

of flights of the other and for sharing of executive lounges in certain airports as well as reciprocal frequent flyer benefits. The alliance also provided for joint marketing activities, while preserving the separate identities of the two carriers. However, the alliance soon came under fire from the U.S. Department of Justice, which filed an antitrust suit charging that Northwest's controlling ownership in Continental violated Section 7 of the Clayton Act and Section 1 of the Sherman Act and had the effect of reducing actual and potential competition in various ways and in a number of geographic markets.

Both Northwest and Continental decided to contest the lawsuit. During the 1998–2000 period, while the litigation was working itself through the court process, Continental and Northwest proceeded to implement the terms of their alliance agreement.

In January 2001, in a successful effort to end the litigation, Continental paid Northwest $450 million in cash to repurchase 6.7 million of the 8.7 million shares of Continental common stock that Northwest owned, making Continental independent of any one outside entity's control for the first time since the company had been formed. Gordon Bethune declared January 22, 2001 as Independence Day at Continental and marked the occasion by paying a $100 cash bonus to Continental's 54,300 employees around the world and holding celebrations at company facilities featuring apple pie and Coca-Cola.

However, as part of the share repurchase deal, Continental and Northwest agreed to extend until 2025 their master alliance agreement, which called for code sharing, reciprocal frequent flyer programs, shared executive lounge access, and various joint marketing agreements. At the time Continental began implementing its global alliance with Northwest Airlines in November 1998, management anticipated that the alliance would be fully implemented by the end of 2001 and would produce an increase of approximately $225 million in additional operating income for Continental. Due to implementation delays in establishing common technical platforms and jointly implementing alliances with other carriers, management subsequently revised that projection to $160 million for 2001 and projected that the full benefit would be achieved during the next few years. Due primarily to the effects on the industry of the September 11, 2001, terrorist attacks, the actual incremental contribution for 2001 was $140 million. In

2002 management was unclear whether the full projected benefit would be achieved.

Executing the Make Reliability a Reality Product Plan

Boosting On-Time Performance   Because surveys of air travelers consistently showed that on-time arrival was the single most important determinant of customer satisfaction, Bethune opted to use on-time percentage as the chief indicator of how well Continental was performing. The decision to pay employees a $65 bonus for achieving good on-time performance was the result of a company analysis showing that Continental was spending about $5 million monthly taking care of passengers who had missed connecting flights because of late incoming flights—some passengers had to be provided meals and/or housed overnight, and some had to be reticketed to the flights of other carriers. Plus, it took time on the part of ticket agents to handle all these arrangements, adding to staffing costs. Bethune determined that Continental would come out ahead if the company took half of the $5 million and gave it to employees in the form of a monthly incentive to achieve good on-time performance ($2.5 million divided by just under 40,000 Continental employees was roughly $65); Continental managers were not eligible for the $65 bonus because the company already has a performance-based bonus plan for managers.

The $65 bonus plan was announced in January 1995; that month Continental's on-time percentage was 71 percent, a ranking of 7th among the top 10 airlines—not good enough for the bonus (which required a ranking in the top 5) but better than the 61 percent on-time arrivals the prior January. In February, 80 percent of Continental's flights arrived on time, good for a fourth-place ranking; Continental cut a special $65 check and sent it to all employees (withholding taxes on the $65 bonus were taken out of the regular paychecks). In March 1995, Continental ranked first in on-time performance, with 83 percent on-time arrivals. In April, Continental was first again. Continental's on-time performance suffered in May, June, and July because pilots initiated a work slowdown as leverage in their contract negotiations then under way with the company. But following the contractual agreement with the pilots' union, Continental's on-time percentage improved to second best in the industry in August and September, third best in October, and fourth best in November.

Given these results, Bethune decided to raise the bar for paying bonuses for on-time performance. The new standard, scheduled to start in January 1996, was that Continental had to finish third or higher for employees to receive a bonus, but the bonus payment was upped to $100. When Continental came in first in on-time performance in December 1995, the month before the new $100 bonus was to go into effect, Bethune decided that all employees should be paid $100 (rather than $65) for their December 1995 performance. In 1997 Continental management began noticing that although Continental's monthly on-time percentages were at respectably high levels (sometimes at record levels) there were a number of months when the company did not rank third or higher—partly because other airlines had launched campaigns to improve their own on-time percentages. Continental adjusted the bonus requirements to either rank in the top three nationwide in on-time arrivals or have an on-time arrival percentage above 80 percent—Bethune figured that an on-time arrival percentage above 80 percent represented good performance and merited paying employees a $100 bonus even if Continental was only fourth best in a given month. The bonus standards were altered again in 2000; a $100 bonus was paid when Continental finished first in on-time performance among the major U.S. carriers, and a $65 bonus was paid when it finished second or third or had an on-time percentage above 80 percent. In 2000, Continental gave on-time bonus checks to employees 11 out of 12 months, totaling $39 million. During the 1995–2000 period, Continental paid employees a total of $157 million in on-time bonuses.

To further promote better on-time performance, Continental revised the routes of aircraft flying into airports where flights were often delayed. For example, at the congested Newark hub (where at certain times of the day it was not unusual for planes to sit on the runway for 15 to 30 minutes waiting for clearance to take off even if the weather was good) most planes departing Newark at congested times were assigned out-and-back routes between Newark and particular spoke destinations rather than, say, being routed to Washington and then on to Houston and Denver. Thus, if a particular Continental flight was regularly delayed out of Newark because of congestion, it would affect passengers traveling to the spoke destination and would hurt that route's on-time performance, but a delay leaving Newark would not spill over to create frequent delays for passengers at Washington, Houston, and Denver, resulting in three flights with poor on-time performances. Continental had on-time arrival percentages of 80.7 percent in 2001 and 83.5 percent (a record) in 2002.

Improving Baggage Handling   When the on-time bonus was instituted in 1995, the number of lost bags went up at first—partly because flight crews elected not to wait on slow-arriving baggage in order to get planes away from the gates on time and help promote on-time arrivals. Continental executives elected not to institute a bonus payment for getting passengers' baggage on the planes, believing it was employees' jobs to get the bags on the planes. Bethune explained:

> We had to get the word out that if the number of baggage complaints was increasing, that wasn't going to make it. We didn't want on-time flights without bags, or without people, or with dirty aisles. On-time meant the whole system was working on time, not just part of it. So we explained this to our employees, and baggage started making it onto the planes.[13]

In the following months, Continental's baggage handling improved—during one period, Continental ranked among the top three airlines in fewest number of baggage complaints for 30 out of 31 months. Moreover, management stressed that the on-time arrival percentage was being used as a metric for measuring the reliability of the company's whole operation. They emphasized that "making reliability a reality" meant Continental's planes should not only arrive on time but also depart on time with a full supply of meals, all passengers, and all their bags.

Other Product Enhancements   To reduce the time it took Continental reservation agents to answer phone calls and handle the task of making a reservation, Continental increased its call capacity by adding more agents and upgrading its reservation systems software. Calls involving flight status and other standard questions that did not require speaking directly to a reservations agent were directed to an automated system.

---

[13]Ibid., p. 107.

In-flight services were improved according to surveys of customer preferences. Continental began serving Coca-Cola instead of Pepsi and increased the variety of beers that were available. First-class passengers were given priority baggage handling. New and tastier meals were developed, with Bethune and Brenneman personally testing and approving each of the new offerings. In-flight phones were installed in most of Continental's planes by the end of 1997. Music was played as passengers boarded planes. In 2000, Continental spent $12 million on bigger overhead bins to accommodate larger carry-on bags and provide more storage space for carry-ons.

Executing the Working Together Plan

When the rigid procedures manual was burned and replaced with general guidelines, many Continental executives feared that employees would give away the store in spending money to satisfy stranded or disgruntled passengers or to buy new airplane parts when existing ones could be repaired. But Bethune wanted employees to have more discretion and be able to use their best judgment, believing that management actions to give employees more free rein to do their jobs would build bridges of trust between management and employees. He further believed that, once the company began making money and the profit-sharing plan with employees kicked in, the vast majority of Continental employees would think twice about giving away the store. He was willing to take the risk that some employees would probably be too generous. During the 1995–2000 period, Continental paid employees $545 million in profit-sharing bonuses—the amount for 2000 (paid in February 2001) was $98 million.

To help employees better understand what was expected, the company created checklists for pilots regarding takeoffs and landings, for maintenance technicians regarding engine maintenance, for flight crews regarding proper provisioning, for crews regarding plane cleanups, and so on. The idea was that if certain jobs were broken down into a series of steps that get the job done, then it would be easier for people to do the jobs they signed on for and easier to keep them focused on the tasks at hand.

Open Communications and Teamwork
A toll-free voice-mail number directly to Bethune's

office was set up for employees to use when they got particularly frustrated or felt a need to talk directly to the CEO—on a normal day, Bethune tended to get a couple of calls; on days when something unusual happened or major policy changes were announced, he might get 20 to 25 calls.[14] To make sure that employees could get help when they got into trouble or something wasn't fixed properly, an 800 line was set up for them to call whenever they encountered a technical operations problem—an operational response team was on duty seven days a week to provide assistance. There was a hotline employees could call for information about pay, benefits, and their 401(k) program. To keep employees up-to-date on company developments, there was a daily update from corporate headquarters distributed via the company intranet and e-mail, a weekly three-minute voice-mail message from Gordon Bethune giving his take on any new developments at the company, a monthly employee newsletter called *Continental Times,* and a company publication called the *Continental Quarterly* that was mailed to employees' homes. Bethune and the company's head of corporate communications decided in 1995 to install some 600 bulletin boards in employee break rooms, high-traffic hallways, and common rooms and post a daily newsletter on the same area of each bulletin board by late afternoon; in 1997, streaming LED display message boards were installed in crew break rooms and office hallways to provide employees with constantly updated breaking news, the latest daily on-time flight percentages, Continental's stock price, and airport weather reports. Bethune made a point of leveling with employees, keeping them fully informed, and giving straight answers to questions—in contrast to prior management's practice of telling employees as little as possible. The four elements of the Go Forward Plan—Fly to Win, Fund the Future, Make Reliability a Reality, and Working Together—were always discussed in the same order at employee meetings, in company publications, and on bulletin-board postings; the agenda at the biweekly management committee meetings was also structured according to the four elements of the Go Forward plan.

The monthly open houses at Houston headquarters were expanded to include employee meetings twice a year at the three hub locations and other

[14]Ibid., p. 115.

Continental facilities with sizable workforces. Bethune wanted all Continental employees to feel like they could get to top-level executives and ask whatever questions were on their minds. One question Bethune got was from an employee at the Newark hub who asked why it made sense to give all employees a $65 bonus for good on-time performance when the jobs of many Continental employees did not directly affect on-time performance. Bethune, holding up his watch, responded, "Which part of this watch don't you think we need?"[15] The employee had no answer and sat down; Bethune believed his question about the watch made his point about the importance of teamwork, the value that each employee contributed, and why it made sense for all Continental employees to win or lose together. Bethune pushed the theme that each Continental employee was a part of what was happening at Continental, that Continental's people *were* the company, and that the Working Together Plan was about making Continental a place where people were happy to come to work. Bethune was fond of saying that he had never heard of a successful company that didn't have a good product and where people didn't enjoy coming to work. And he liked to say that running an airline was the biggest team sport in the world.

The Culture-Changing Effort

In Bethune's view, the keys to changing Continental's corporate culture were for management to act differently, for the company to treat its people differently, and for management to look closely at what it was like for Continental employees to come to work every day and deliberately set out to change the things that made the work environment unpleasant or that made employees unhappy.

The manual burning, the new guidelines that gave employees more rein to do their jobs, and management's emphasis on teamwork were all deliberate steps that management took to signal employees that the Working Together initiative truly represented a new day at Continental. The final part of the Working Together plan that Continental executives implemented was to insist that Continental people treat each other with dignity and respect—the goal was for every worker to treat coworkers like a customer or family member. Bethune believed prior management had created a lot of scar tissue and mistrust that

needed to be eradicated. "Dignity and Respect" became the company's slogan for 1996.

In early 1995, high-level executives ranked all managerial and supervisory employees on a scale of 1 to 4 with regard to the quality of their work and whether they were team players, with 1 being good and 4 indicating deficient work quality and/or shortcomings in people management skills. During the first nine months of 1995, executives talked to supervisors about their performance, giving them a chance to get on board and measure up to expectations. The ratings were fluid, changing as supervisors changed their behavior. In October 1995, when it became clear that the company had too many managers, especially middle managers, Continental decided to dismiss all managers and supervisors who had a 4 rating.

Within the executive ranks, there was a big but gradual turnover. Of the 61 vice presidents at Continental when Bethune took over, about half either left on their own accord for other jobs or were let go for reasons of ineffective management or failing to be team players. Some of those who departed were not happy with the direction Bethune wanted to take the company, and some were not pleased with certain aspects of the programs of change that he instituted. Bethune recruited a number of outsiders for top positions at Continental, hiring several people with whom he had worked at Piedmont Airlines and identifying others by asking trusted acquaintances. In 1998, several Delta Airlines executives told Bethune that Continental had the best management team of any airline. To retain its key executives, Continental adopted a very attractive salary and bonus package. Just as employees got monthly bonuses for on-time performance and had a performance-based profit-sharing plan that paid them up to 15 percent of pretax profits, Continental executives got bonuses based partly on Continental's overall performance and partly on the achievement of individual goals. Bethune preached teamwork among senior executives, warning them that he took a very dim view of power plays, backstabbing, jockeying for position, and departments that failed to work cooperatively with other departments.

A technique that Gordon Bethune liked to use to build trust was to reward people early and unexpectedly. In mid-1996, Continental was doing so well that it was clear the company would hit its performance targets for the whole year. Bethune decided to have bonus checks cut for 50 percent of the full 1996

[15]Ibid., p. 126.

bonus amounts and to give the checks to Continental's managers at the company's midyear managers' meeting. When he came in to give his luncheon address, Bethune asked the 350 executives there (who had been assigned seats) to stand and turn over their chairs—a bonus check was taped to the bottom of each chair. He told the group, "This is because you've done such an outstanding job—because Continental is going to make its plan this year. Here's the money the company owes you for that success."[16] He got a standing ovation. According to Bethune, "The managers left that meeting like it was halftime of a championship game. They had come in expecting the usual corporate rah-rah and they left with a check for half of their bonus, which they weren't expecting for another six months."[17]

Another visible action was Bethune's mandate for departments to work cooperatively, specifically in the areas of scheduling, flight operations, and aircraft maintenance. Prior to Bethune's joining Continental, marketing and scheduling personnel would work out a flight and route schedule which they thought would attract the most passengers and yield the biggest load factors; then they handed the schedule off to operations to figure out which planes to assign to fly which routes and when and where maintenance on each plane would be done. Often the schedule that was drawn up created all kinds of problems and inefficiencies in flight operations and maintenance—and neither department was inclined to work with the other to resolve the difficulties. Bethune required people in marketing, scheduling, flight operations, and aircraft maintenance to form a team to arrive at a schedule that was workable from all perspectives.

Starting in 1996, Continental began a program to reward employees for perfect attendance. Employees with perfect attendance for a six-month period (either January–June or July–December) were awarded a $50 gift certificate and entered into drawings for fully equipped Eddie Bauer Ford Explorers, with the company paying all sales and gift taxes, title fees, and license fees. Since the program had been initiated, the company had given away more than 110 vehicles. For the July–December 2001 period, there were 16,207 eligible employees with perfect attendance records and Explorers were awarded to 8 em-

exhibit 2   **Comparative Labor Costs, Major U.S. Airlines, Third Quarter 2002**

Airline	Labor Cost per Available Seat Mile (in cents)
American Airlines	4.62¢
United Airlines	4.60
Delta Airlines	4.56
U.S. Airways	4.55
Alaska Air	4.32
Northwest Airlines	3.90
Continental Airlines	3.53
Southwest Airlines	2.90
America West	2.16

Source: The Wall Street Journal, December 10, 2002, p. B1.

ployees; in 2001, Explorers were awarded to 20 employees. Continental's human resources department estimated that the perfect attendance incentives had saved the company close to $25 million.

Management believed that employee morale at Continental was the highest in the airline industry. Continental's calendar was dotted each year with company picnics, ice cream parties, barbecues, and fried chicken dinners. According to one top executive, "Three to four celebrations a year cost us $20 per employee. Compare that to our payroll and you can't find it. But those are the things people remember."[18] Voluntary turnover rates for Continental's employees were 6.7 percent in 1998, 6.1 percent in 1999, and 5.3 percent in 2000. In 2001–2002, roughly 33 percent of Continental's operating costs were for labor and 44 percent of the company's employees were represented by unions. In 2002, Continental's mechanics and related employee groups ratified a new four-year collective bargaining agreement between the company and the International Brotherhood of Teamsters by a 73 percent majority. Management operated on the principle that employee compensation and fringe benefits should be "fair to employees and fair to the company." Exhibit 2 shows comparative labor costs for the major U.S. commercial airlines during the third quarter of 2002.

[16]Ibid., p. 241.
[17]Ibid., pp. 241–42.

[18]Quoted in "Happy Skies of Continental," *Continental*, July 2001, p. 53.

At every Continental facility he visited, Bethune preached the importance of teamwork, likening the company to a watch in which each piece had to do its job to make the whole thing work and in which if even the smallest piece failed, the whole watch could fail. In 1998, Bethune wrote:

> If you want to make the most sweeping statement you can about the change at Continental since I came on board, it's that now everybody's on the same team and everyone knows it. Everyone knows what the goal is and what his or her part is and how it relates to the goal. Everyone knows what the reward is for making the goal and what happens if we fail.
>
> We're all working from the same plays, the same playbook—plays everyone's had a chance to buy into, plays the people who will be running them had a chance to help design, plays everyone believes in, plays everyone believes can win.[19]

Bethune was a firm advocate of the management principle that what gets measured is what gets managed. It was his philosophy that a company could not just run on autopilot and stay good; it had to keep getting better and better at what it did. He regularly urged Continental employees to thrash the competition. Bethune talked with every class of flight attendants at the end of their training. He was well regarded by employees. During a ceremony at which the Ford Explorer winners were presented their keys by Gordon Bethune and Greg Brenneman, one employee commented, "I started the week we went into bankruptcy 10 years ago. It is now 300 times better. What helps a lot is Gordon and Greg. Their personalities enthuse everybody. They're funny. I love listening to them speak."[20]

Exhibit 3 shows how Continental's operating costs compared with those of other major U.S. airlines during the 1995–2002 period.

Executive Changes at the Top

In May 2001, Greg Brenneman at the age of 39 resigned as Continental's president, COO, and director, electing to devote full-time to his own firm, TurnWorks, Inc., which specialized in helping start-up companies and firms going through major transitions; in announcing his resignation, Brenneman indicated he would donate $500,000 to endow two charities that helped Continental employees. Larry Kellner, formerly Continental's chief financial officer (CFO) and one of Gordon Bethune's first executive hires in early 1995, was elevated to the position of president; Kellner had the distinction in 2000 of having become the first three-time winner of the CFO Excellence Awards named annually by *CFO* magazine. C. D. McLean, former executive vice president of operations, was named Continental's chief operating officer.

Recognition and Awards

Since 1996, Continental had been the recipient of numerous awards. Continental Airlines was named Airline of the Year in 1996 and 2001 by *Air Transport World,* a leading aviation industry trade magazine; the magazine cited Continental's employee-friendly culture and said that Continental had the best labor relations of any major U.S. hub-and-spoke carrier. It also noted that Continental had "superior passenger service," especially where business travelers were concerned. OAG, publisher of *OAG Pocket Flight Guides,* in 2001 named Continental as Best Trans-Atlantic Airline and Best Airline Based in North America. J. D. Power had named Continental as tops in customer satisfaction for five of the past six years and was ranked the nation's number one airline in customer satisfaction for long-haul and short-haul flights by *Frequent Flyer* magazine in 2002. Continental was named as the second most admired U.S. airline in 2000, 2001, and 2002 by *Fortune* magazine, trailing Southwest Airlines in all three years. Continental had received numerous awards for its BusinessFirst premium cabin (from *Conde Nast Traveler, OAG, Smart Money,* and *Entrepreneur* magazines) and for its OnePass frequent flier program (from *InsideFlyer's* Freddie Awards). Continental had been named to the list of the 100 Best Companies to Work For in America for five years (1998–2002) and been included on *Hispanic* magazine's list of the "Corporate 100 Providing the Most Opportunities for Latinos" for five consecutive years. *Worth* magazine, in its April 2001 issue, named Gordon Bethune one of the 50 best CEOs, the third consecutive year he

---

[19]Bethune, *From Worst to First,* p. 181.

[20]Quoted in "Happy Skies of Continental," p. 52.

had appeared in *Worth*'s rankings. In June 2001, *Aviation Week & Space Technology* gave Continental its highest rating for "outstanding management."

CRISIS CONDITIONS AT CONTINENTAL SUDDENLY REAPPEAR

Going into September 2001, Continental and Continental Express were flying over 2,500 flights daily. Continental had reported 25 consecutive profitable quarters. But four days after the September 11 terrorist attacks on the World Trade Center and the Pentagon, Gordon Bethune announced that Continental Airlines would immediately reduce its long-term flight schedule by approximately 20 percent on a systemwide available-seat-mile basis and would furlough approximately 12,000 of its current 56,000 employees in connection with its flight cutbacks. On Monday, September 17, 2001, Continental announced that it would not be able to make $70 million in debt payments due that day but said it would be able to make the payments within the 10-day grace period to prevent defaulting.

Bethune indicated that even if Continental cut costs by 20 percent, the company would incur losses of $200 million per month at the presently depressed levels of passenger traffic. If passenger traffic and revenue did not snap back quickly, Bethune said, Continental might have to seek bankruptcy protection by early November. Bethune joined top executives at several other airlines in calling on the federal government to enact a major assistance package to help the airline industry cope with the sudden downturn in passenger traffic and the added costs of FAA-mandated airport security regulations regarding baggage handling; passenger screening at security checkpoints; and tighter security screening of caterers, cleaning crews, and flight crews. New security measures were expected to slow passengers moving through terminals, increase the time to process baggage and turn planes at the gates, and otherwise slow down hub operations.

Most of the flight reductions implemented by Continental in the aftermath of September 11 involved cutting the number of flights between particular locations, but the flight schedule reduction also resulted in Continental's discontinuing service to 10 cities/airports and abandoning plans to initiate service to Montego Bay and Kingston, Jamaica, as planned in late 2001. The Denver Reservations Center was closed, along with the flight attendant base in Los Angeles and several maintenance facilities. To further save on maintenance costs, Continental grounded 14 Continental Express turboprops, all of the company's DC-10s, and 31 other aircraft.

Layoffs at Other Airlines

Meanwhile, other airlines in the United States and around the world were also hastily rearranging their flight schedules to protect their financial positions and respond to air travel reductions, figuring out how best to implement tighter security regulations, and canceling orders or delaying deliveries of new aircraft. Many airlines had announced workforce reductions:

- American Airlines—a workforce reduction of 20,000 employees.
- United Airlines—a workforce reduction of 20,000 employees.
- US Airways—a workforce reduction of 11,000 employees and anticipated pay cuts.
- British Airways—a workforce reduction of 7,000 employees.
- America West Airlines—a workforce reduction of 2,000 employees.
- Virgin Atlantic—a workforce reduction of 1,200 employees.
- American Trans Air—a workforce reduction of 1,500 employees.
- Midwest Express—a workforce reduction of 450 employees.
- Frontier Airlines—a workforce reduction of 440 employees.
- Mesaba—undetermined furloughs and significant pay cuts.
- KLM—a workforce reduction of 10 percent.

With layoffs of 30,000 employees at Boeing and another 12,000 at Honeywell (all related to cutbacks in the production of commercial aircraft), close to

exhibit 3 **Comparative Operating Cost Statistics, Major U.S. Airlines, 1995– Second Quarter Ending June 30, 2002 (in cents per average seat mile)**

Carrier	Year	Food	Salaries and Benefits	Aircraft Fuel and Oil	Commissions
American	1995	0.41¢	3.70¢	1.01¢	0.80¢
	2000	0.44	4.18	1.48	0.60
	2001	0.44	4.55	1.57	0.47
	2002*	0.40	4.97	1.33	0.35
Alaska	1995	0.31¢	2.60¢	1.07¢	0.55¢
	2000	0.29	3.53	1.76	0.38
	2001	0.31	3.81	1.45	0.35
	2002*	0.32	3.83	1.21	0.30
Continental	**1995**	**0.22¢**	**2.45¢**	**1.11¢**	**0.74¢**
	1996	**0.23**	**2.65**	**1.29**	**0.76**
	1997	**0.25**	**2.80**	**1.34**	**0.76**
	1998	**0.26**	**3.05**	**1.02**	**0.69**
	1999	**0.28**	**3.10**	**0.97**	**0.63**
	2000	**0.28**	**3.30**	**1.62**	**0.54**
	2001	**0.27**	**3.44**	**1.39**	**0.37**
	2002*	**0.26**	**3.52**	**1.10**	**0.28**
Delta	1995	0.26¢	3.25¢	1.11¢	0.85¢
	2000	0.27	3.73	1.27	0.42
	2001	0.28	4.10	1.20	0.36
	2002*	0.25	4.37	1.10	0.28
America West	1995	0.19¢	2.08¢	0.96¢	0.64¢
	2000	0.12	2.21	1.54	0.32
	2001	0.10	2.42	1.35	0.28
	2002*	0.06	2.36	1.09	0.19
Northwest	1995	0.28¢	3.47¢	1.24¢	0.93¢
	2000	0.29	3.65	1.80	0.61
	2001	0.27	4.15	1.73	0.45
	2002*	0.24	4.18	1.40	0.36
Southwest	1995	0.02¢	2.56¢	1.01¢	0.39¢
	2000	0.03	2.99	1.38	0.30
	2001	0.03	3.01	1.29	0.18
	2002*	0.03	3.02	1.17	0.10
United	1995	0.37¢	3.34¢	1.06¢	0.93¢
	2000	0.38	4.16	1.43	0.59
	2001	0.37	4.73	1.50	0.43
	2002*	0.35	4.87	1.21	0.32
US Airways	1995	0.25¢	4.93¢	1.04¢	0.90¢
	2000	0.28	5.35	1.72	0.51
	2001	0.28	5.62	1.56	0.39
	2002*	0.21	5.93	1.20	0.25

*Based on data for first six months of 2002 only.

Source: U.S. Department of Transportation, Bureau of Transportation Statistics, Office of Airline Information, Form 41B, Form 41P, Form T100.

Landing Fees	Advertising	Other Operating and Maintenance Expenses	Total Operating Expenses	Rent and Leasing Fees
0.15¢	0.15¢	3.23¢	9.45¢	0.73¢
0.17	0.13	3.49	10.49	0.74
0.19	0.13	4.53	11.89	0.78
0.22	0.11	3.75	11.12	0.87
0.15¢	0.12¢	3.10¢	7.89¢	1.17¢
0.18	0.38	3.72	10.25	1.08
0.25	0.21	3.78	10.17	1.07
0.21	0.10	3.98	9.95	1.02
0.18¢	**0.16¢**	**3.82¢**	**8.67¢**	**1.20¢**
0.20	**0.13**	**4.05**	**9.31**	**1.18**
0.20	**0.15**	**3.77**	**9.27**	**1.12**
0.18	**0.14**	**4.08**	**9.41**	**1.16**
0.18	**0.14**	**4.21**	**9.51**	**1.22**
0.18	**0.07**	**4.21**	**10.20**	**1.23**
0.21	**0.02**	**4.52**	**10.23**	**1.32**
0.25	**0.00**	**5.18**	**10.57**	**1.42**
0.20¢	0.13¢	3.06¢	8.86¢	0.81¢
0.16	0.08	3.51	9.43	0.72
0.16	0.11	3.81	10.02	0.76
0.18	0.10	4.03	10.30	0.81
0.16¢	0.19¢	3.07¢	7.29¢	1.30¢
0.13	0.09	4.17	8.57	1.58
0.15	0.06	4.50	8.86	1.72
0.16	0.08	4.67	8.61	1.56
0.27¢	0.16¢	2.80¢	9.15¢	0.70¢
0.24	0.13	3.24	9.96	0.67
0.27	0.11	3.55	10.52	0.70
0.27	0.10	3.60	10.15	0.77
0.23¢	0.27¢	2.61¢	7.09¢	0.71¢
0.22	0.26	2.55	7.72	0.55
0.22	0.24	2.51	7.48	0.54
0.24	0.22	2.58	7.36	0.55
0.21¢	0.13¢	2.84¢	8.89¢	0.94¢
0.20	0.20	3.64	10.60	0.88
0.22	0.13	4.64	12.02	0.90
0.22	0.11	4.27	11.35	1.07
0.19¢	0.11¢	4.18¢	11.61¢	1.16¢
0.20	0.08	5.73	13.88	1.11
0.20	0.08	6.00	14.13	1.31
0.23	0.06	6.57	14.45	1.30

120,000 employees were affected by the flight cutbacks and cost-saving measures being initiated across the airline industry.

The Federal Government's Rescue Package

In the days following the attacks, at the urging of the Bush administration and most U.S. airline executives, Congress passed an airline bailout bill (the Air Transportation Safety and System Stabilization Act) designed to keep the U.S. airline industry solvent until travel rebounded. The act gave airlines $5 billion in direct payments (to compensate air carriers for losses resulting from the terrorist attacks) and provided for up to $10 billion in loan guarantees to assist airlines in covering negative cash flows and making debt payments even if they had weak balance sheets. Continental received $417 million in cash in the third and fourth quarters of 2001 as a result of the $5 billion emergency relief package passed by Congress. Continental viewed its ability to apply for loan guarantees as an important safety net, but its heavily leveraged status left it with few unencumbered assets to pledge in applying for government loan guarantees.

A Financial Crisis in the U.S. Airline Industry

In 2001, the major commercial airlines in the United States reported combined losses of $7.8 billion. All except Southwest Airlines reported losses for the third and fourth quarters of 2001. Continental reported a $3 million profit for the third quarter; however, except for special charges of $85 million and a federal grant of $243 million pursuant to the Air Transportation Safety and System Stabilization Act, Continental would have reported a loss of $97 million. American Airlines posted the largest quarterly operating loss in its history for the three months ending September 30. Northwest reported a third-quarter operating loss of $155 million and indicated that it incurred $250 million in operating losses during the September 11–30 period; in October 2001, despite a modest traffic rebound, Northwest indicated that it was burning through $6 to $8 million of cash a day due to fare discounts aimed at attracting traffic, fewer passengers carried, and slightly higher

costs per mile. US Airways reported a third-quarter net loss of $766 million, which took into account special charges and a $331 million grant the airline received as part of the Air Transportation Safety and System Stabilization Act (ATSSSA); without the federal grant, US Airways would have lost $1.1 billion in the third quarter. United Airlines reported 2001 losses of $3 billion.

The financial crisis spilled over deep into 2002 as traffic failed to return to pre–September 11 levels. All major U.S. airlines except Southwest lost money in each of the first three quarters of 2002. During 2002, United spent close to $7 million a day more than it collected in revenues and filed for Chapter 11 bankruptcy protection in December 2002. US Airways filed for bankruptcy protection in August 2002. Losses at American Airlines totaled $2 billion for the first nine months of 2002, equal to more than $7 million a day. Combined losses of the major U.S. commercial airlines were about $11 billion in 2002, with only Southwest Airlines reporting a profit for 2002. In March 2003 analysts predicted that the major U.S. airlines would lose $7–$12 billion in 2003, depending on the length of the war in Iraq. United Airlines lost $12 million a day in January 2003.

Continental Reacts to the Crisis

On September 26, 2001, Gordon Bethune announced that he and Larry Kellner, Continental's president, would not accept any salary or bonus for the remainder of 2001.

In September 2001, Continental incurred a traffic decrease worldwide of 31.0 percent compared to September 2000, with domestic traffic being down 32.3 percent versus 29.0 percent for international flights. Traffic on Continental's flights improved during the first two weeks of October 2001, with the domestic load factor rising to 71.3 percent and the systemwide load factor increasing to 65.6 percent.

Starting in October 1, 2001, Continental began a program to award double miles to its frequent flyers for travel between October 2 and November 15; it also reduced fares for business travel on most domestic routes for the remainder of 2001. To encourage both business and leisure travel, the company began a reduced fare promotion to select destinations in Mexico, Central and South America, and

Europe—passengers could save an additional 10 percent on the sale fares (and frequent flyers got an additional 1,000 bonus miles) by booking their travel at the company's Web site.

Continental had installed crossbar or deadbolt cockpit door restraints in all of its aircraft by October 23, ahead of the Federal Aviation Administration's targeted November deadline. Management expected to install even stronger doors in all its aircraft over the upcoming months, as manufacturers completed the production of newly designed doors with greatly enhanced cockpit security features.

Continental's full-year 2001 financial and operating results are shown in Exhibit 1. The company ended 2001 with $1.1 billion in cash and had around $1 billion in unencumbered assets that it could pledge as collateral on additional borrowing.

CONTINENTAL AIRLINES IN 2002 AND 2003

During 2002, Continental reinstated 6,000 of the 12,000 positions that it had cut in late 2001 and added back about half of the capacity that it had removed in the weeks following September 11. The company took delivery of 20 of the 48 new Boeing jets originally scheduled for delivery in 2002; currently, it had no financing in place for 67 additional aircraft scheduled for delivery during 2003–2008. The company's strategy was to let its flight schedule and employment levels be driven by the market.

Also during 2002, Continental opened its new international arrivals facility at the Newark Liberty International Airport that housed customs, immigration, and other government services for arriving international passengers on Continental flights; this $80 million facility was the last major milestone in $1.4 billion of customer improvements that management believed made Continental's Newark hub the premier airport facility in the New York City region. In addition, construction on Continental's new $324 million Terminal E expansion at Bush Intercontinental Airport in Houston continued; when completed, the project would add 20 gates and offer travelers a world-class facility. Also, to enhance the comfort of international passengers on long-haul flights, Continental completed installation of new BusinessFirst sleeper seats throughout its fleet of 18 Boeing 777

aircraft; the new seats featured increased seat width, a 170-degree recline from seat cushion to seat back, and six and a half feet of sleeping space in the fully extended position.

Continental launched its redesigned Web site in the third quarter of 2002, enabling customers to book OnePass reward travel online for the first time. The redesigned site also made it easier for customers to check fares, flight availability, and status; purchase tickets; and access OnePass frequent flier account information.

Continental had outstanding operational performance in 2002, breaking 9 of 11 operational records during the year. For 2002, Continental reported a record on-time arrival rate of 83.5 percent and a record completion factor of 99.7 percent, going 103 days without a single flight cancellation. Exhibit 4 shows how Continental's operating performance compared with other airlines on four key measures during the 1998–2002 period.

In August 2002 Continental began implementing more than 100 changes to generate more revenues and reduce its expenses; the objective was to achieve pretax gains amounting to $80 million in 2002 and $400 million when fully implemented. These initiatives included the following:

- Removing 11 additional aircraft from the fleet (in addition to 49 that had already been grounded since September 2001) and permanently grounding the company's entire fleet of DC-10-80 leased aircraft—an action that reduced the number of different aircraft in the fleet from five to four and entailed write-offs of $52 million. (Earlier in 2002, Continental had finalized an agreement with Boeing to defer the deliveries of aircraft on order to 2003 and beyond.)

- Reducing its domestic capacity by 4.3 percent, to levels about 17 percent below those in August 2001. This decrease was in addition to seat-capacity reductions of about 6.5 percent that had already been implemented in 2002. However, capacity on TransAtlantic and Pacific flights was being increased by about 6 percent. By the end of 2003, management expected to reduce the number of aircraft in service from 366 to 357 and to cut the number of grounded aircraft from 25 to 15 (the company had 51 planes in storage at the end of 2001).

exhibit 4 **On-Time Flights, Mishandled Baggage, Oversales, and Passenger Complaints for Major U.S. Airlines, 1998–2002**

Percentage of Scheduled Flights Arriving Within 15 Minutes of the Scheduled Time					
Carrier	Jan.–Sept. 2002	2001	2000	1999	1998
Alaska Airlines	75.8%	69.0%	68.1%	71.0%	72.0%
America West	78.5	74.8	65.5	69.5	68.5
American	78.9	75.9	72.9	73.5	80.1
Continental*	78.7	80.7	78.1	76.6	77.3
Delta	77.5	78.0	75.3	78.0	79.6
Northwest	79.7	79.7	77.4	79.9	70.6
Southwest	82.3	81.7	75.2	80.0	80.8
TWA†		80.8	76.9	80.9	78.3
United	75.5	73.5	61.4	74.4	73.8
US Airways	78.4	78.2	72.3	71.4	78.9

Mishandled Baggage Reports per 1,000 Passengers					
Carrier	Jan.–Sept. 2002	2001	2000	1999	1998
Alaska Airlines	2.68	3.00	3.48	5.75	7.27
America West	3.47	4.22	6.62	4.52	3.88
American	4.32	4.60	5.50	5.21	4.40
Continental*	3.06	4.29	5.35	4.42	4.06
Delta	3.61	4.11	4.49	4.39	4.27
Northwest	4.79	4.19	5.24	4.81	6.63
Southwest	3.54	4.77	5.00	4.22	4.53
TWA†	—	6.35	6.06	5.38	5.39
United	3.69	5.07	6.57	7.01	7.79
US Airways	3.01	3.86	4.76	5.08	4.09

- Instituting a hiring freeze, encouraging early retirements, and counting on voluntary leaves and attrition to avoid additional employee layoffs.

- Eliminating most travel agent commissions. The company was aggressively promoting its Web site to passengers and urging that they make their reservations on their company's newly designed Web site.

- Charging a fee of $20 on all paper tickets that were issued and rigidly enforcing all fare rules that resulted in collecting additional fares and fees from passengers. E-tickets as a percentage of total sales had climbed from 44 percent in September 1999 to 64 percent in September 2001 to 87 percent in September 2002.

- Taking delivery of new and more fuel-efficient planes.

- Rebidding of supplier contracts.

- Installing the world's largest e-ticket check-in network, with more than 675 kiosks in more than 113 airports and cities. As of December 2002, 70 percent of Continental's passengers with e-tickets were using the self-service check-in kiosks, about double the percentage in 2001.

In announcing Continental's belt-tightening moves, Gordon Bethune said, "Unless market conditions improve quickly, we'll be forced to make further changes in all aspects of our operations." The company's chief financial officer indicated that the actions currently being initiated would "not be

exhibit 4 **(concluded)**

Involuntary Denied Boardings per 10,000 Passengers Due to Oversold Flights					
Carrier	Jan.–Sept. 2002	2001	2000	1999	1998
Alaska Airlines	1.24	1.36	1.53	0.99	1.49
America West	0.21	0.38	1.27	1.38	1.12
American	0.22	0.36	0.44	0.42	0.42
Continental*	0.93	1.51	1.44	0.28	0.13
Delta	0.87	0.77	0.34	1.98	1.24
Northwest	0.53	0.45	0.43	0.20	0.33
Southwest	1.06	1.50	1.84	1.40	1.84
TWA†		1.83	2.76	0.88	1.69
United	0.65	0.92	1.64	0.69	0.59
US Airways	0.26	0.34	0.67	0.57	0.23

Complaints per 100,000 Passengers Boarded					
Carrier	Jan.–Sept. 2002	2001	2000	1999	1998
Alaska Airlines	1.02	1.27	2.04	1.64	0.54
America West	1.88	3.72	7.51	3.72	2.11
American	1.41	2.51	3.54	3.49	1.14
Continental*	1.46	2.23	2.84	2.62	1.02
Delta	1.51	2.16	2.01	1.81	0.79
Northwest	1.60	1.97	2.61	2.92	2.21
Southwest	0.37	0.38	0.47	0.40	0.25
TWA†		2.54	3.47	3.44	1.29
United	1.90	3.24	5.3	2.65	1.28
US Airways	1.24	1.87	2.59	3.13	0.84

*Figures for Continental include Continental Express flights.
†Acquired by American Airlines in 2001; TWA data for 2002 included in American Airlines statistics.
Source: Office of Aviation Enforcement and Proceedings, *Air Travel Consumer Report,* multiple issues.

sufficient to return the company to profitability in the present environment."

Through the first three quarters of 2002, Continental had made little progress in reducing its operating costs per available seat mile—were it not for lower market prices for aircraft fuel, Continental's operating costs would have been as high in 2002 as they were in the previous year (see Exhibit 5).

The Spin-Off of Continental Express

In 2002, Continental went forward with plans to sell part of its ownership of Continental Express through an initial public offering of 10 million shares of stock and the subsequent sale of an additional 20 million shares. Continental realized $447 million from the proceeds of the stock sales; it then used $147 million of the proceeds to repay a portion of ExpressJet's debt to Continental and $150 million to fund a portion of its obligations to the Continental pension plan for its employees. The remainder was used to help cover the company's continuing negative cash flows from operations and fund Continental's ongoing capital expenditures.

Following the sale of 30 million ExpressJet shares, Continental Airlines' ownership of ExpressJet fell to about 53.1 percent. Continental Airlines did not intend to remain a stockholder of ExpressJet over the long term, instead planning to sell all or

exhibit 5 **Continental's Operating Expenses per Available Seat Mile, Nine Months Ending September 30, 2001 versus 2002**

	Operating Expense per Available Seat Mile (in cents)	
	Nine Months Ending September 30, 2002	Nine Months Ending September 30, 2001
Wages, salaries, and related costs	3.27¢	3.21¢
Aircraft fuel	1.08	1.40
Aircraft leasing fees	0.91	0.86
Other rents, leases, and landing fees	0.69	0.57
Maintenance, materials, and repairs	0.46	0.54
Depreciation and amortization	0.49	0.46
Reservations and sales	0.42	0.48
Passenger services	0.36	0.39
Commissions	0.27	0.42
Other	1.25	1.22
Total operating expenses	9.20¢	9.55¢

Source: Company 10Q filing, September 30, 2002.

most of its remaining shares during late 2002 or 2003, subject to market conditions.

Continental Express planned to add 48 regional jets to its fleet in 2003, giving it a total of 236 jets. Passenger revenues for Continental Express in the last quarter of 2002 were 33.8 percent higher than for the same period in 2001; revenue passenger miles in 2002 were 16.6 percent higher than in 2001.

Continental's Financial Performance in 2002

Continental reported 2002 revenues of $8.4 billion, versus $8.97 billion for 2001; net losses were $451 million, versus a loss of $95 million in 2001. The company's liquidity continued to be shaky as the company reported third-quarter current assets of $2.3 billion and current liabilities of $3.0 billion. Moreover, Continental remained highly leveraged, with long-term debt and capital lease obligations of $5.1 billion and stockholders' equity of $1.4 billion as of September 30, 2002. In the third quarter of 2002, Continental received its last cash payment under the Air Transportation Safety and System Stabilization Act; total receipts under the act in 2002 were $51 million (versus $417 million in 2001).

In October 2002, Continental management had forecast that cash operating expenses would exceed

revenues by an average of $1.5 million daily during the fourth quarter of 2002; counting principal payments on debt and capital expenditures, management had predicted negative cash flows averaging close to $3.0 million per day during the last three months of 2002. To bolster its cash position, Continental in December 2002 issued $200 million in five-year notes that were secured by a designated pool of spare parts and an insurance policy. But unexpected higher revenues from holiday travel allowed Continental to end 2002 with $1.34 billion in cash and short-term investments, about $200 million more than had been anticipated. Passenger revenues in the fourth quarter of 2002 were 13 percent higher than in the last quarter of 2001.

As of late 2002, Continental had 30 owned out-of-service aircraft with a fair market value of $97 million; in addition the company had 48 leased out-of-service aircraft, 2 of which had been subleased. Management was exploring sublease opportunities for the remaining 46 leased out-of-service planes.

Exhibit 6 summarizes Continental's expected cash outflows stemming from its long-term debt, capital and operating leases, future aircraft purchase and operating lease commitments, and other contractual obligations.

As it began 2003, Continental was the world's seventh largest airline, with more than 2,000 daily

exhibit 6 **Continental's Future Contractual Obligations, 2003 and Beyond (in millions)**

Type of Contractual Obligation	Continental's Cash Outflows Due to Contractual Obligations					
	2003	2004	2005	2006	Later Years	Totals
Long-term debt	$ 410	$ 329	$ 563	$ 417	$ 2,209	$ 4,256
Capital lease obligations	40	38	39	41	243	446
Convertible preferred securities	—	—	—	—	250	250
Aircraft operating leases	880	843	821	715	7,089	11,271
Nonaircraft operating leases	556	616	656	656	2,259	5,132
Aircraft purchase commitments	158	641	597	397	516	3,438
Future operating lease commitments	72	116	197	202	2,986	3,591
Total	$2,116	$2,583	$2,873	$2,428	$15,552	$28,384

Source: 2001 10K report.

departures, 131 domestic and 93 international destinations, and the broadest global route network of any U.S. airline. According to *Conde Nast Traveler* magazine's annual survey of business travelers, Continental outperformed its U.S. rivals in premium-class comfort, reliability, and value on trans-Atlantic and trans-Pacific flights; on domestic trips, Continental's first-class service received the highest ranking among major carriers and was rated the greatest "value for cost." According to Gordon Bethune, "Our goals are simple—they are our customers' goals. We continue to deliver a high-quality product each and every day, getting our customers where they want to go, on time and with their bags, while providing preflight and inflight service that is globally recognized for consistency and excellence."

Southwest Airlines: Culture, Values, and Operating Practices

Arthur A. Thompson
The University of Alabama

John E. Gamble
The University of South Alabama

When the September 11 terrorist attacks triggered close to a 20 percent falloff in airline traffic in the fourth quarter of 2001, the commercial airline industry in the United States went into a crisis mode—companies began borrowing money to cover cash drains of $3 to $8 million daily, cutting flights, laying off employees, deferring or canceling the delivery of new aircraft on order, speculating on how much to cut fares to induce passengers to fly and on how long traffic might stay depressed, figuring out what it would take to avoid bankruptcy, and scrambling to institute a host of security measures. Roughly 100,000 of the industry's approximately 500,000 airline employees were laid off. Even after the federal government came through with emergency cash grants of over $1 billion, the major U.S. carriers lost a combined $7.8 billion in 2001, of which $3.3 billion came in the fourth quarter.

At Southwest Airlines, the crisis was dealt with far differently—no flights were cut and no employees were laid off. Because management's philosophy, for the past two decades, had been to manage Southwest in good times so that both the company and its employees could prosper through bad times, Southwest was in a strong position when the industry got hammered in the aftermath of September 11. It had the lowest operating costs of any U.S. airline, it had $1 billion in cash, and it had the strongest balance sheet and credit rating of any U.S. airline (allowing

management to quickly borrow an additional $1.1 billion and give the company a buffer to pay all its bills and absorb any cash drains). Despite all the costs associated with implementing a raft of new security measures and the downturn in passenger traffic, Southwest reported a profit of $63.5 million for the fourth quarter of 2001 and a profit of $511.1 million for the full year—it was the only U.S. airline to operate in the black in either period.

And, unlike its rivals, Southwest continued to operate profitably throughout 2002 even though passenger traffic nationwide remained below levels prior to September 11. During 2002, Southwest proceeded to add almost 40 new daily flights and was able to boost its market share by about 2 percent. Southwest was profitable in 2002. Its eight biggest U.S. rivals, however, posted losses of more than $11 billion in 2002, with both US Airways and United Airlines filing for bankruptcy.

COMPANY BACKGROUND

In late 1966, Rollin King, a San Antonio, Texas, entrepreneur who owned a small commuter air service, marched into Herb Kelleher's law office with a plan to start a low-cost/low-fare airline that would shuttle passengers between San Antonio, Dallas, and Houston.[1] Over the years, King had heard many Texas

[1] Kevin and Jackie Freiberg, *NUTS! Southwest Airlines' Crazy Recipe for Business and Personal Success* (New York: Broadway Books, 1998), p.15.

businesspeople complain about the length of time that it took to drive between the three cities and the expense of flying the airlines currently serving them. His business concept for the airline was simple: Attract passengers by flying convenient schedules, get passengers to their destination on time, make sure they have a good experience, and charge fares competitive with travel by automobile. Though skeptical that King's business idea was viable, Kelleher dug into the possibilities during the next few weeks and concluded that a new airline was feasible; he agreed to handle the necessary legal work and also to invest $10,000 of his own funds in the venture.

In 1967, Kelleher filed papers to incorporate the new airline and submitted an application to the Texas Aeronautics Commission for the new company to begin serving Dallas, Houston, and San Antonio.[2] But rival airlines in Texas pulled every string they could to block the new airline from commencing operations, precipitating a contentious four-year parade of legal and regulatory proceedings. Herb Kelleher led the fight on the company's behalf, eventually prevailing in June 1971 after winning two appeals to the Texas Supreme Court and a favorable ruling from the U.S. Supreme Court. Kelleher recalled, "The constant proceedings had gradually come to enrage me. There was no merit to our competitors' legal assertions. They were simply trying to use their superior economic power to squeeze us dry so we would collapse before we ever got into business. I was bound and determined to show that Southwest Airlines was going to survive and was going into operation."[3]

In January 1971, Lamar Muse was brought in as CEO to get operations under way. Muse was an aggressive and self-confident airline veteran who knew the business well and who had the entrepreneurial skills to tackle the challenges of building the airline from scratch and then competing head-on with the major carriers. Through private investors and an initial public offering of stock in June 1971, Muse raised $7 million in new capital to purchase planes and equipment and provide cash for start-up. Boeing agreed to supply three new 737s from its inventory, discounting its price from $5 million to $4 million and financing 90 percent of the $12 million deal.

Because the airline industry was in the throes of a slump in the early 1970s, Muse was able to recruit a talented senior staff that included a number of veteran executives from other carriers. He particularly sought out people who were innovative, wouldn't shirk from doing things differently or unconventionally, and were motivated by the challenge of building an airline from scratch. Muse wanted his executive team to be willing to think like mavericks and not be lulled into instituting practices at Southwest that were largely imitative of how they were done at other airlines. According to Rollin King, "It was our one opportunity to do it right . . . We all understood that this was our opportunity to decide how to do it our way. Our philosophy was, and still is, we do whatever we have to do to get the job done."[4]

Southwest's Struggle to Gain a Market Foothold

In June 1971, Southwest initiated its first flights with a schedule that soon included 6 round-trips between Dallas and San Antonio and 12 round-trips between Houston and Dallas. The introductory $20 one-way fares to fly the Golden Triangle, well below the $27 and $28 fares charged by rivals, attracted disappointingly small numbers of passengers—some days the total for all 18 flights would be less than 250 people. Southwest's financial resources were stretched so thin that the company bought fuel for several months on Lamar Muse's personal credit card. The company was short of ground equipment, and most of what it had was used and in worn condition. Money for parts and tools was so tight that, on occasion, company personnel got on the phone with acquaintances at rival airlines operating at the terminal and arranged to borrow what was needed. Nonetheless, morale and enthusiasm remained high; company personnel displayed can-do attitudes and adeptness at getting by on whatever resources were available.

To try to gain market visibility and drum up more passengers, Southwest decided it had to do more than just run ads in the media:

- Management decided to have flight hostesses dress in colorful hot pants and white knee-high boots with high heels. Recruiting ads for Southwest's first group of hostesses read, "Attention,

[2]Ibid., pp. 16–18.
[3]Katrina Brooker, "The Chairman of the Board Looks Back," *Fortune,* May 28, 2001, p. 66.

[4]Freiberg and Freiberg, *NUTS!,* p. 41.

Raquel Welch: You can have a job if you measure up." Two thousand applicants responded, and those selected for interviews were asked to come dressed in hot pants to show off their legs—the company wanted to hire long-legged beauties with sparkling personalities. Over 30 of Southwest's first graduating class of 40 flight attendants consisted of young women who were cheerleaders and majorettes in high school and thus had experience performing in front of people while skimpily dressed.

- A second attention-getting action was to give passengers free alcoholic beverages during daytime flights. Most passengers on these flights were business travelers. Management's thinking was that many passengers did not drink during the daytime and that with most flights being less than an hour's duration it would be cheaper to simply give the drinks away rather than collect the money.

- Taking a cue from being based at Dallas Love Field, Southwest began using the tag line "Now There's Somebody Else Up There Who Loves You." The routes between Houston, Dallas, and San Antonio became known as the Love Triangle. Southwest's planes were referred to as Love Birds, drinks became Love Potions, peanuts were called Love Bites, drink coupons were Love Stamps, and tickets were printed on Love Machines. The "love" campaign set the tone for Southwest's approach to its customers and company efforts to make flying Southwest an enjoyable, fun, and differentiating experience. (Later, when the company went public, it chose LUV as its stock-trading symbol.)

- In order to add more flights without buying more planes, the head of Southwest's ground operations came up with a plan for ground crews to off-load passengers and baggage, refuel the plane, clean the cabin, restock the galley, on-load passengers and baggage, do the necessary preflight checks and paperwork, and push away from the gate in 10 minutes. The 10-minute turn became one of Southwest's signatures during the 1970s and 1980s. (In later years, as passenger volume grew and many flights were filled to capacity, the turnaround time gradually expanded to 25 minutes—because it took more time to unload and load 125 passengers, as compared to a half-full plane with just 60–65 passengers. Even so, the 25-minute average turnaround times at Southwest in 2002 were still shorter than the 40–60-minute turnarounds typical at other major airlines.)

- In late November 1971, Lamar Muse came up with the idea of offering a $10 fare to passengers on the Friday-night Houston–Dallas flight. Even with no advertising, the 112-seat flight sold out. This led Muse to realize that Southwest was serving two quite distinct types of travelers in the Golden Triangle market: (1) business travelers who were more time-sensitive than price-sensitive and wanted weekday flights at times suitable for conducting business and (2) price-sensitive leisure travelers who wanted lower fares and had more flexibility about when to fly.[5] He came up with a two-tier on-peak and off-peak pricing structure in which all seats on weekday flights departing before 7 PM were priced at $26 and all seats on other flights were priced at $13. Passenger traffic increased significantly—and systemwide on-peak and off-peak pricing soon became standard across the whole airline industry.

- In 1972, the company decided to move its flights in Houston from the newly opened Houston Intercontinental Airport (where it was losing money and where it took 45 minutes to get downtown) to the abandoned Houston Hobby Airport, located much closer to downtown Houston. Although Southwest was the only carrier to fly into Houston Hobby, the results were spectacular—business travelers who flew to Houston frequently from Dallas and San Antonio found the Houston Hobby location far more convenient than the Intercontinental Airport location, and passenger traffic doubled almost immediately.

- In early 1973, in an attempt to fill empty seats on its San Antonio–Dallas flights, Southwest cut its regular $26 fare to $13 for all seats, all days, and all times. When Braniff International, at that time one of Southwest's major rivals, announced $13 fares of its own, Southwest retaliated with a two-page ad, run in the Dallas newspapers, headlining "Nobody is going to shoot Southwest Airlines out of the sky for a lousy $13" and con-

[5]Ibid., p. 31.

taining copy saying Braniff was trying to run Southwest out of business. The ad announced that Southwest would not only match Braniff's $13 fare but also give passengers the choice of buying a regular-priced ticket for $26 and receiving a complimentary fifth of Chivas Regal scotch, Crown Royal Canadian whiskey, or Smirnoff vodka (or, for nondrinkers, a leather ice bucket). Over 75 percent of Southwest's Dallas–Houston passengers opted for the $26 fare, although the percentage dropped as the two-month promotion wore on and corporate controllers began insisting that company employees use the $13 fare. The local and national media picked up the story of Southwest's offer, proclaiming the battle to be a David-versus-Goliath struggle in which the upstart Southwest did not stand much of a chance against the much larger and more well-established Braniff; grassroots sentiment in Texas swung to Southwest's side.

Southwest reported its first-ever annual profit in 1973.

More Legal and Regulatory Hurdles

During the rest of the 1970s, Southwest found itself embroiled in another round of legal and regulatory battles. One involved Southwest's refusal to move its flights from Dallas Love Field, located 10 minutes from downtown, out to the newly opened Dallas–Fort Worth (DFW) Regional Airport, which was 30 minutes from downtown Dallas. Local officials were furious because they were counting on fees from Southwest's flights in and out of DFW to help service the debt on the bonds issued to finance the airport's construction. Southwest's position was that it was not required to move because it had not agreed to do so, nor had it been ordered to do so, by the Texas Aeronautics Commission—moreover, the company's headquarters were located at Love Field. The courts eventually ruled Southwest's operations could remain at Love Field.

A second battle ensued when rival airlines protested Southwest's application to begin serving several smaller cities in Texas; their protest was based on arguments that these markets were already well served and that Southwest's entry would result in costly overcapacity. Southwest countered that its low fares would allow more people to fly and grow the market. Again, Southwest prevailed and its views about low fares expanding the market proved accurate. In the year before Southwest initiated service, 123,000 passengers flew from Harlingen Airport in the Rio Grande Valley to Houston, Dallas, or San Antonio; in the 11 months following Southwest's initial flights, 325,000 passengers flew to the same three cities.

Believing that Braniff and Texas International were deliberately engaging in tactics to harass Southwest's operations, Southwest convinced the U.S. government to investigate what it considered predatory tactics by its chief rivals. In February 1975, Braniff and Texas International were indicted by a federal grand jury for conspiring to put Southwest out of business—a violation of the Sherman Antitrust Act. The two airlines pleaded "no contest" to the charges, signed cease-and-desist agreements, and were fined a modest $100,000 each.

When Congress passed the Airline Deregulation Act in 1978, Southwest applied to the Civil Aeronautics Board (now the Federal Aviation Agency) to fly between Houston and New Orleans. The application was vehemently opposed by local government officials and airlines operating out of DFW because of the potential for passenger traffic to be siphoned away from that airport. The opponents solicited the aid of Fort Worth congressman Jim Wright, the majority leader of the U.S. House of Representatives, who took the matter to the floor of the House of Representatives; a rash of lobbying and maneuvering ensued. What emerged came to be known as the Wright Amendment of 1979: No airline may provide nonstop or through-plane service from Dallas Love Field to any city in any state except for locations in states bordering Texas. The amendment, which was still in effect at the start of 2003, meant that Southwest could not advertise, publish schedules or fares, or check baggage for travel from Dallas Love Field to any city it served outside Texas, Louisiana, Arkansas, Oklahoma, and New Mexico.

Battles to Survive and the Warrior Mentality

The legal, regulatory, and competitive battles that Southwest fought in its early years produced a strong esprit de corps among Southwest personnel and a drive to survive and prosper despite the odds. With newspaper and TV stories regularly reporting Southwest's difficulties, employees were fully aware that the airline's existence was constantly on the line. Had the company been forced to move from Love Field, it would most likely have gone under, an outcome that employees, Southwest's rivals, and local government officials understood well. According to Southwest's president, Colleen Barrett, the obstacles thrown in Southwest's path by competitors and local officials were instrumental in building Herb Kelleher's passion for Southwest Airlines and ingraining a combative, can-do spirit into the corporate culture:

> They would put twelve to fifteen lawyers on a case and on our side there was Herb. They almost wore him to the ground. But the more arrogant they were, the more determined Herb got that this airline was going to go into the air—and stay there.
>
> The warrior mentality, the very fight to survive, is truly what created our culture.[6]

The Start of the Herb Kelleher Era

When Lamar Muse resigned in 1978, Southwest's board wanted Herb Kelleher to take over as chairman and CEO. But Kelleher enjoyed practicing law and, while he agreed to become chairman of the board, he insisted that someone else be CEO. Southwest's board appointed Howard Putnam, a group vice president of marketing services at United Airlines, as Southwest's president and CEO in July 1978. Putnam asked Kelleher to become more involved in Southwest's day-to-day operations, and over the next three years Kelleher got to know many of the company's personnel and observe them in action. Putnam announced his resignation in the fall of 1981 to become president and chief operating officer at Braniff International. This time, Southwest's board succeeded in persuading Kelleher to take on the additional duties of CEO and president.

When Herb Kelleher took over in 1981, Southwest had 27 planes, $270 million in revenues, 2,100 employees, and flights to 14 cities. Over the next two decades, Southwest Airlines prospered, racking up many industry firsts and expanding geographically

(see Exhibit 1). Going into 2003, Southwest was the fourth largest U.S. commercial airline in terms of passengers flown and the sixth largest in terms of revenues. It had revenues in excess of $5 billion annually and 35,000 employees, and it operated 370 jets to 59 airports in 58 cities in 30 states. Southwest had been profitable every year since 1973—in an industry noted for its vulnerability to economic cycles and feast-or-famine profitability. During 1990–1994—when the airline industry had five straight money-losing years, laid off 120,000 employees, and lost a cumulative $13 billion—Southwest earned a profit every quarter of every year.

Exhibit 2 provides a five-year summary of Southwest's financial and operating performance. Exhibits 3 and 4 provide industrywide data on airline travel for the 1995–2002 period.

HERB KELLEHER

Herb Kelleher majored in philosophy at Wesleyan University in Middletown, Connecticut, graduating with honors. He earned his law degree at New York University, again graduating with honors and also serving as a member of the law review. After graduation, he clerked for a New Jersey Supreme Court justice for two years and then joined a law firm in Newark. Upon marrying a woman from Texas and becoming enamored with Texas, he moved to San Antonio, where he became a successful lawyer and came to represent Rollin King's small aviation company.

When Herb Kelleher took on the role of Southwest's CEO in 1981, he made a point of visiting with maintenance personnel to check on how well the planes were running and of talking with the flight attendants. Kelleher did not do much managing from his office, preferring instead to be out among the troops as much as he could. His style was to listen, observe, and offer encouragement. Kelleher attended most graduation ceremonies of flight attendants from "Southwest University," and he often appeared to help load bags on "Black Wednesday," the busy travel day before Thanksgiving. He knew the names of thousands of Southwest employees, who held him in the highest regard. When he attended a Southwest employee function, he was swarmed like a celebrity.

Kelleher had an affinity for bold-print Hawaiian shirts, owned a tricked-out motorcycle, and made no

[6]Ibid., pp. 26–27.

exhibit 1   **Milestones at Southwest Airlines, 1983–2002**

1983	Three additional Boeing 737s are purchased; Southwest flies over 9.5 million passengers.
1984	Southwest is ranked first in customer satisfaction among the U.S. airlines for the fourth straight year.
1985	Service begins to St. Louis and Chicago Midway airports. Southwest names the Ronald McDonald House as its primary charity—the tie-in was the result of an effort by a Southwest pilot who lost a daughter to leukemia and who believed that Ronald McDonald Houses were a worthy way to demonstrate Southwest's community spirit.
1986	Southwest flies over 13 million passengers.
1988	Southwest becomes the first U.S. airline to win the Triple Crown (best on-time record, fewest reports of mishandled baggage, and fewest complaints per 100,000 passengers) for a single month.
1990	Revenues reach $1 billion; Southwest is the only major U.S. airline to record both an operating profit and a net profit.
1992	Southwest wins its first annual Triple Crown for best on-time record, best baggage handling, and fewest customer complaints; for the second year running, Southwest is the only major U.S. airline to record both an operating profit and a net profit.
1993	Southwest begins operations on the East Coast and wins its second annual Triple Crown; revenues exceed $2 billion, and profits exceed $100 million. For the third consecutive year, Southwest is the only major U.S. airline to record both an operating profit and a net profit.
1994	Southwest leads the industry by introducing ticketless travel in four cities; Southwest wins its third Triple Crown and acquires Morris Air, based in Salt Lake City.
1995	Ticketless travel becomes available systemwide; Southwest wins fourth consecutive Triple Crown.
1996	Service to Florida begins; Southwest wins fifth consecutive Triple Crown; Southwest and its employees contribute almost $740,000 to help support Ronald McDonald Houses, including $34,000 in cash donations from the company and $302,500 in free air travel for families staying at Ronald McDonald Houses in cities served by Southwest.
1997	Service begins to Southwest's 50th city; over 50 million people fly Southwest.
1998	Southwest is named by *Fortune* as the best company to work for in America.
1999	Service is added to three more cities.
2000	The number of passengers on Southwest flights exceeds 60 million, and revenues surpass the $5 billion mark; the company records its 28th consecutive year of profitability and ninth consecutive year of increased profits; Southwest becomes the fourth largest U.S. airline in terms of passengers carried.
2001	Southwest is profitable for the 30th consecutive year and the only U.S. airline to report a profit for 2001; a record 64.5 million passengers fly Southwest.
2002	Southwest is ranked second among companies across all industry groups, and first in the airline industry in *Fortune*'s 2002 list of America's Most Admired Companies.

secret of his love for drinking Wild Turkey whiskey and smoking. He loved to make jokes and engage in pranks and corporate antics, prompting some people to refer to him as the "clown prince" of the airline industry. He once appeared at a company gathering dressed in an Elvis costume and had arm-wrestled a South Carolina company executive at a public event in Dallas for rights to use "Just Plane Smart" as an advertising slogan.[7] Kelleher was well known inside and outside the company for his combativeness, particularly when it came to beating back competitors. On one occasion he reportedly told a group of veteran employees, "If someone says they're going to smack us in the face—knock them out, stomp them out, boot them in the ditch, cover them over, and move on to the next thing. That's the Southwest spirit at work."[8] On another occasion he said, "I love battles. I think it's part of the Irish in me. It's like what Patton said, 'War is hell and I love it so.' That's how I feel. I've never gotten tired of fighting."[9]

While Southwest was deliberately combative and flamboyant in some aspects of its operations,

[7]Ibid., pp. 246–47.

[8]Quoted in the *Dallas Morning News,* March 20, 2001.

[9]Quoted in Katrina Brooks, "The Chairman of the Board Looks Back," *Fortune,* May 28, 2001, p. 64.

exhibit 2   **Summary of Southwest Airlines' Financial and Operating Performance, 1998–2002 (in thousands except per share amounts)**

	2002	2001	2000	1999	1998
Financial data					
Operating revenues	$5,521,771	$5,555,174	$5,649,560	$4,735,587	$4,163,980
Operating expenses	5,104,433	4,924,052	4,628,415	3,954,011	3,480,369
Operating income	417,338	631,122	1,021,145	781,576	683,611
Other expenses (income), net	24,656	(196,537)	3,781	7,965	(21,501)
Income before income taxes	392,682	827,659	1,017,364	773,611	705,112
Provision for income taxes	151,713	316,512	392,140	299,233	271,681
Net income	$ 240,969	$ 511,147	$625,224	$474,378	$433,431
Net income per share, basic	$0.31	$0.67	$0.84	$0.63	$0.58
Net income per share, diluted	$0.30	$0.63	$0.79	$0.59	$0.55
Cash dividends per share	$0.0180	$0.0180	$0.0147	$0.0143	$0.0126
Total assets at period-end	$8,953,750	$8,997,141	$6,669,572	$5,653,703	$4,715,996
Cash and cash equivalents at end of year	$1,815,352	$2,279,861	$522,995	$418,819	$378,511
Current assets at end of year	$2,231,960	$2,520,219	$831,536	$632,595	$574,155
Current liabilities at end of year	$1,433,828	$2,239,185	$1,298,403	$962,056	$850,653
Long-term obligations at end of year	$1,552,781	$1,327,158	$760,992	$871,717	$623,309
Stockholders' equity at end of year	$4,421,617	$4,014,053	$3,451,320	$2,835,788	$2,397,918
Operating data					
Revenue passengers carried	63,045,988	64,446,773	63,678,261	57,500,213	52,586,400
Revenue passenger miles (000s)	45,391,903	44,493,916	42,215,162	36,479,322	31,419,110
Available seat miles (000s)	68,886,546	65,295,290	59,909,965	52,855,467	47,543,515
Load factor*	65.9%	68.1%	70.5%	69.0%	66.1%
Average passenger haul (miles)	720	690	663	634	597
Trips flown	947,331	940,426	903,754	846,823	806,822
Average passenger fare	$84.72	$83.46	$85.87	$79.35	$76.26
Passenger revenue per mile	11.77¢	12.09¢	12.95¢	12.51¢	12.76¢
Operating revenue per seat mile	8.02¢	8.51¢	9.43¢	8.96¢	8.76¢
Operating expenses per seat mile	7.41¢	7.54¢	7.73¢	7.48¢	7.32¢
Number of employees at year-end	33,705	31,580	29,274	27,653	25,844
Size of fleet at year-end†	375	355	344	312	280

*Revenue passenger miles divided by available seat miles.
†Includes leased aircraft.
Source: 2001 10K report and company press releases.

when it came to the financial side of the business Kelleher insisted on fiscal conservatism, a strong balance sheet, comparatively low levels of debt, and zealous attention to bottom-line profitability. While believing strongly in being prepared for adversity, Kelleher had an aversion to formal strategic plans, saying, "Reality is chaotic; planning is ordered and logical. The meticulous nit-picking that goes on in most strategic planning processes creates a mental straitjacket that becomes disabling in an industry where things change radically from one day to the next." Kelleher wanted Southwest managers to think ahead, have contingency plans, and be ready to act when it appeared that the future held significant risks or when new conditions suddenly appeared and demanded prompt responses.

Kelleher was a strong believer in the principle that employees—not customers—come first:

exhibit 3   **Commercial Airline Revenues, Scheduled Revenue Passenger Miles, and Overall Load Factor for Major U.S. Airline Carriers, 1995–2002**

Year	Total Revenues	Scheduled Revenue Passenger Miles*	Operating Profit	Load Factor[†]
1995	$73.5 billion	509.6 billion	$4.92 billion	67.3%
1996	78.5	534.7	5.27	69.8
1997	83.5	570.0	7.52	70.8
1998	84.6	583.0	7.47	71.3
1999	89.6	616.8	6.00	71.4
2000	98.1	651.8	5.50	72.8
2001	85.4	606.7	(10.2)	70.3
2002	75.4	585.0	(9.6)	72.0

*Scheduled revenue passenger miles is the total number of miles flown by all passengers on all scheduled flights.
[†]Load factor is the total number of passengers boarded as a percentage of total seats available.
Source: Airline Quarterly Financial Review, Majors, Department of Transportation, Office of Aviation Analysis, Fourth Quarters 1995–2002.

exhibit 4   **Operating Revenues of the Major U.S. Commercial Airlines, 1996–2002 (in millions of dollars)**

Airline	2002	2001	2000	1999	1998	1997	1996
American	$15,870.6	$15,638.8	$18,117.1	$16,085.5	$16,298.8	$15,855.8	$15,125.7
United[a]	13,915.6	16,087.4	19,331.3	17,966.7	17,517.5	17,335.2	16,316.7
Delta	12,410.4	13,211.2	15,320.9	14,901.4	14,629.8	14,203.9	13,317.7
Northwest	9,151.6	9,591.8	10,956.6	9,868.1	8,706.7	9,983.7	9,751.4
US Airways[b]	6,914.9	8,253.4	9,181.2	8,460.4	8,555.7	8,501.5	7,704.1
Continental	7,407.9	8,199.7	9,449.2	8,381.5	7,907.7	7,089.9	6,264.4
Southwest	5,521.8	5,555.2	5,649.6	4,735.6	4,164.0	3,817.0	3,407.4
TWA[c]	—	2,632.8	3,584.6	3,308.7	3,259.1	3,330.3	3,554.4
America West	2,021.0	2,305.5	2,309.3	2,164.0	1,983.0	1,887.1	1,751.8
Alaska	1,832.4	1,763.1	1,762.6	1,695.6	1,581.3	1,457.4	1,306.6

[a]Filed for Chapter 11 bankruptcy protection in December 2002.
[b]Filed for Chapter 11 bankruptcy protection in August 2002.
[c]Acquired by American Airlines in 2001; data for 2002 included in figures for American Airlines.
Source: Airline Quarterly Financial Review, Majors, Department of Transportation, Office of Aviation Analysis, Fourth Quarters 1995–2001 and Second Quarter 2002.

You have to treat your employees like your customers. When you treat them right, then they will treat your outside customers right. That has been a very powerful competitive weapon for us. You've got to take the time to listen to people's ideas. If you just tell somebody no, that's an act of power and, in my opinion, an abuse of power. You don't want to constrain people in their thinking.[10]

Another indication of the importance that Kelleher placed on employees was the message he penned in 1990 and had prominently displayed in the lobby of Southwest's headquarters in Dallas:

The people of Southwest Airlines are "the creators" of what we have become—and of what we will be.

Our people transformed an idea into a legend. That legend will continue to grow only so long as it is nourished—by our people's indomitable spirit, boundless energy, immense goodwill, and burning desire to excel.

[10]Ibid., p. 72.

Our thanks—and our love—to the people of Southwest Airlines for creating a marvelous family and a wondrous airline.

SOUTHWEST AIRLINES' STRATEGY

From day one, Southwest had pursued a low-cost/low-price/no-frills strategy. Its signature low fares made air travel affordable to a wide segment of the U.S. population—giving substance to its tag line "The Freedom to Fly." Southwest was a shrewd practitioner of the concept of price elasticity, proving in one market after another that the revenue gains from increased ticket sales and the volume of passenger traffic would more than compensate for the revenue erosion from reduced fares. When Southwest entered the Florida market with an introductory $17 fare from Tampa to Fort Lauderdale, the number of annual passengers flying the Tampa–Fort Lauderdale route jumped 50 percent, to more than 330,000. In Manchester, New Hampshire, passenger counts went from 1.1 million in 1997, the year prior to Southwest's entry, to 3.5 million in 2000 and average one-way fares dropped from just over $300 to $129. Success in stimulating higher passenger traffic at airports across the United States via low fares and frequent flights had been dubbed the "Southwest effect" by personnel at the U.S. Department of Transportation.

The company designed its routes to stress flying between pairs of cities ranging anywhere from 150 to as much as 700 miles apart where there was high traffic potential and Southwest could offer a sizable number of flights. As a general rule, Southwest did not initiate service to an airport unless it envisioned the potential for originating at least eight flights a day there. Southwest's point-to-point route system, as opposed to the hub-and-spoke route systems of its rivals, minimized connections, delays, and total trip time—its emphasis on nonstop flights between about 350 pairs of cities allowed about 77 percent of Southwest's passengers to fly nonstop to their destination. Southwest's average aircraft trip in 2002 was 540 miles long and lasted approximately 1.5 hours. Exhibit 5 shows the cities and airports Southwest served in late 2002. Southwest was the dominant carrier at four airports (Baltimore/Washington, Las Vegas, Kansas City, and Chicago Midway) and the

leading carrier in intrastate air travel in California, Texas, and Florida.

Southwest's Drive to Achieve Low Operating Costs

Southwest management fully understood that low fares necessitated zealous pursuit of low operating costs. The company had over the years instituted a number of practices to keep its costs below those of rival carriers:

- The company operated only one type of aircraft—Boeing 737s—to minimize the size of spare parts inventories, simplify the training of maintenance and repair personnel, improve the proficiency and speed with which maintenance routines could be done, and simplify the task of scheduling planes for particular flights. Furthermore, as the launch customer for Boeing's 737-300, 737-500, and 737-700 models, Southwest acquired its new aircraft at favorable prices. See Exhibit 6 for statistics on Southwest's aircraft fleet.

- Southwest encouraged customers to make reservations and purchase tickets at the company's Web site, thus bypassing the need to pay commissions to travel agents for handling the ticketing process and reducing the number of personnel needed to staff Southwest's nine reservation centers. Selling a ticket on its Web site cost Southwest roughly $1, versus $6–$8 for a ticket booked through a travel agent and $3–$4 for a ticket booked through its own internal reservation system. In January 2001, Southwest cut the commissions paid to travel agents to 8 percent of the price of an electronic ticket and 5 percent of the price of a paper ticket (down from 10 percent paid on both), with a commission cap of $60 for a round-trip ticket (either electronic or paper)—management estimated that the move would save the company $40 million in 2001. In 2000 about 30 percent of Southwest's revenue came from ticket sales through travel agents (versus 40 percent in 1998), and by year-end 2002 over 50 percent of ticket sales were occurring at the company's Web site. Ticketless travel accounted for more than 85 percent of all sales in 2002, which significantly reduced paperwork and back-office processing.

exhibit 5   **Airports and Cities Served by Southwest Airlines, Fall 2002**

Southwest's Top 10 Airports			
	Daily Departures	Number of Gates	Nonstop Cities Served
Phoenix	181	21	38
Las Vegas	171	19	42
Houston (Hobby)	141	15	24
Baltimore/Washington	139	17	33
Chicago (Midway)	130	14	29
Dallas (Love Field)	130	14	13
Oakland	123	13	19
Los Angeles	118	12	19
Nashville	86	10	28
San Diego	80	9	14

Other Airports Served by Southwest Airlines			
Albany	El Paso	Lubbock	Raleigh-Durham
Albuquerque	Fort Lauderdale	Manchester, NH	Reno/Tahoe
Amarillo	Harlingen/South Padre Island	Midland/Odessa	Sacramento
Austin	Hartford/Springfield	New Orleans	St. Louis
Birmingham	Houston (Hobby and Bush Intercontinental)	Norfolk	Salt Lake City
Boise	Indianapolis	Oklahoma City	San Antonio
Buffalo	Long Island/Islip	Omaha	San Jose
Burbank	Jackson, MS	Ontario, Canada	Seattle
Cleveland	Jacksonville	Orange County, CA	Spokane
Columbus, OH	Kansas City	Orlando	Tampa
Corpus Christi	Little Rock	Portland, OR	Tucson
Detroit (Metro)	Louisville	Providence	Tulsa
			West Palm Beach

Source: Southwest Airlines.

- The company tried to steer clear of congested airports, stressing instead serving airports relatively near major metropolitan areas and in medium-sized cities. This helped produce better-than-average on-time performance and reduce the fuel costs associated with planes sitting in line on crowded taxiways or circling airports waiting for clearance to land; plus, it allowed the company to avoid paying the higher landing fees and terminal gate costs at such high-traffic airports such as Atlanta's Hartsfield International, Chicago's O'Hare, Denver International, and Dallas–Fort Worth (DFW), where landing-slots were controlled and rationed to those airlines willing to pay the high fees. In several cases, Southwest was able to compete on the perimeters of several big metropolitan areas by flying into nearby airports with less congested air space. For example, Southwest drew some Boston-area passengers away from Boston's Logan International by initiating service into nearby Providence, Rhode Island, and Manchester, New Hampshire; similarly, it initiated flights into Islip, Long Island, which siphoned some passengers away from New York's LaGuardia and Kennedy International airports. Southwest's preference for less congested airports also helped minimize total travel time for passengers—driving to the airport, parking, ticketing, boarding, and flight time.

- Southwest's point-to-point scheduling of flights was more cost-efficient than the hub-and-spoke

exhibit 6   **Southwest's Aircraft Fleet as of Fall 2002**

Type of Aircraft	Number	Seats	Comments
Boeing 737-200	27	122	
Boeing 737-300	194	137	Southwest was Boeing's launch customer for this model.
Boeing 737-500	25	122	Southwest was Boeing's launch customer for this model.
Boeing 737-700	124	137	Southwest was Boeing's launch customer for this model.

Other Facts

Average age of aircraft fleet—close to 9 years
Average aircraft trip length—540 miles; average duration—96 minutes
Average aircraft utilization in 2002—7.2 flights per day and about 12 hours of flight time
Fleet size—1990: 106; 1995: 224; 2000: 344; 2002: 370
Firm orders for new aircraft—2003: 21; 2004: 23; 2005: 24; 2006: 22; 2007: 25

systems used by rival airlines. Hub-and-spoke systems involved passengers on many different flights coming in from spoke locations (or perhaps another hub) to a central hub airport within a short span of time and then connecting with an outgoing flight to their destination—a spoke location or another hub. Most flights arrived and departed a hub across a two-hour window, creating big peak–valley swings in airport personnel workloads and gate utilization—airport personnel and gate areas were very busy when hub operations were in full swing and then were underutilized in the interval awaiting the next round of inbound/outbound flights. In contrast, Southwest's point-to-point routes permitted scheduling aircraft so as to minimize the time aircraft were at the gate—currently approximately 25 minutes—thereby reducing the number of aircraft and gate facilities that would otherwise be required. Furthermore, with a relatively even flow of incoming/outgoing flights and gate traffic, Southwest could staff its terminal operations to handle a fairly steady workload across a day, whereas hub-and-spoke operators had to staff their operations to serve peak-period requirements.

- To economize on the amount of time it took terminal personnel to check passengers in and to simplify the whole task of making reservations, Southwest dispensed with the practice of assigning each passenger a reserved seat. Instead, for many years, passengers were given color-coded plastic cards with numbers on them when they checked in at the boarding gate. Passengers then boarded in groups of 30, according to the color and number on their card, sitting in whatever seat was open when they got on the plane—a procedure described by some as a "cattle call." Passengers who were particular about where they sat had to arrive at the gate early to get a low number on their boarding cards and then had to push up to the front when it was their group's turn to board. In 2002, Southwest streamlined the system further by simply printing a big, bold A, B, or C on the boarding pass when the passenger checked in at the ticket counter; passengers then boarded in groups according to the letter on their boarding pass.

- Southwest flight attendants were responsible for cleaning up trash left by deplaning passengers and otherwise getting the plane presentable for passengers to board for the next flight. (Other carriers had cleaning crews come on board to perform this function.)

- Southwest did not have a first-class section on any of its planes and had no fancy clubs for its frequent flyers to relax in at terminals. No meals were served on flights, even long ones; passengers were offered beverages and snacks—in 2002, Southwest provided passengers with 162.4 million packages of peanuts, 51.3 million packages of other snacks, 9.9 million alcoholic beverages, and 44.5 million cans of nonalcoholic beverages. Serving no meals made reprovisioning planes simple and quick.

- Southwest offered passengers no baggage transfer services to other carriers—passengers with checked baggage who were connecting to other carriers to reach their destination were responsible for picking up their luggage at Southwest's baggage claim and then getting it to the check-in facilities of the connecting carrier. (Southwest booked tickets involving its own flights only; customers connecting to flights on other carriers had to book their connecting tickets through either travel agents or the connecting airline.)

- In mid-2001 Southwest implemented use of new software that significantly decreased the time required to generate optimal crew schedules and help improve on-time performance.

- Starting in 2001, Southwest began converting from cloth to leather seats; the team of Southwest employees who investigated the economics of the conversion concluded that an all-leather interior would be durable and easy to maintain, thus more than justifying the high initial costs.

Southwest's operating costs as a percentage of its revenues were consistently the lowest in the industry (see Exhibit 7). Exhibit 8 shows a detailed breakdown of Southwest's operating costs for the period 1995–2002.

Southwest's Focus on Customers and Customer Satisfaction

Southwest went all out to make sure passengers had a positive, fun flying experience. Gate personnel were cheery and witty, sometimes entertaining those in the gate area with trivia questions or contests such as "Who has the biggest hole in his or her sock?" Casually dressed flight attendants greeted passengers coming onto planes and offered friendly advice to customers looking for open seats. Flight attendants were encouraged to let their personalities show, to joke with passengers, and even to play gags. On some flights, attendants played harmonicas and sang announcements to passengers on takeoff and landing. On one flight while passengers were boarding, an attendant with bunny ears popped out of an overhead bin exclaiming "Surprise!" The entertainment repertoires varied from flight crew to flight crew.

While Southwest had built up quite a reputation presenting a happy face to passengers and displaying a fun-loving attitude, the company had on occasion encouraged some of its not-so-pleasant customers to patronize other carriers. One woman who flew Southwest frequently became known as "Pen Pal" because she wrote in a complaint after almost every flight; her complaints were eventually bumped up to Herb Kelleher, who quickly penned a short note: "Dear Mrs. Crabapple, We will miss you. Love Herb."[11] Kelleher made a point of sending congratulatory notes to those employees customers singled out in complimentary letters; complaint letters were seen as learning opportunities for employees and reasons to consider making adjustments. Colleen Barrett, Southwest's president, had articulated the company's policy some years earlier:

> No Employee will ever be punished for using good judgment and good old common sense when trying to accommodate a Customer—no matter what our rules are. Let's start leaning towards our Customers again—not away from them. Let's start encouraging our line employees to be a little more flexible and to take that extra minute to accommodate special needs. Let's start encouraging our Supervisors to give our Customers the benefit of the doubt.[12]

Southwest was convinced that conveying the Southwest spirit to customers was the key to competitive advantage; as one Southwest manager put it, "Our fares can be matched; our airplanes and routes can be copied. But we pride ourselves on our customer service."[13]

Marketing and Promotion

Southwest was continually on the lookout for novel ways to tell its story, make its distinctive persona come alive, and strike a chord in the minds of air travelers. Many of its ads and billboards were deliberately unconventional and attention-getting so as to create and reinforce the company's maverick, fun-loving, and combative image. Others promoted the company's performance as "The Low-Fare Airline"

[11]Freiberg and Freiberg, *NUTS!*, pp. 269–70.
[12]Ibid., p. 288.
[13]Brenda Paik Sunoo, "How Fun Flies at Southwest Airlines," *Personnel Journal* 74, no. 6 (June 1995), p. 70.

exhibit 7 **Comparative Operating Cost Statistics, Major U.S. Airlines, 1995– Second Quarter Ending June 30, 2002 (in cents per average seat mile)**

Carrier	Year	Food	Salaries and Benefits	Aircraft Fuel and Oil	Commissions
American	1995	0.41¢	3.70¢	1.01¢	0.80¢
	2000	0.44	4.18	1.48	0.60
	2001	0.44	4.55	1.57	0.47
	2002*	0.40	4.97	1.33	0.35
Alaska	1995	0.31¢	2.60¢	1.07¢	0.55¢
	2000	0.29	3.53	1.76	0.38
	2001	0.31	3.81	1.45	0.35
	2002*	0.32	3.83	1.21	0.30
Continental	1995	0.22¢	2.45¢	1.11¢	0.74¢
	2000	0.28	3.30	1.62	0.54
	2001	0.27	3.44	1.39	0.37
	2002*	0.26	3.52	1.10	0.28
Delta	1995	0.26¢	3.25¢	1.11¢	0.85¢
	2000	0.27	3.73	1.27	0.42
	2001	0.28	4.10	1.20	0.36
	2002*	0.25	4.37	1.10	0.28
America West	1995	0.19¢	2.08¢	0.96¢	0.64¢
	2000	0.12	2.21	1.54	0.32
	2001	0.10	2.42	1.35	0.28
	2002*	0.06	2.36	1.09	0.19
Northwest	1995	0.28¢	3.47¢	1.24¢	0.93¢
	2000	0.29	3.65	1.80	0.61
	2001	0.27	4.15	1.73	0.45
	2002*	0.24	4.18	1.40	0.36
Southwest	**1995**	**0.02¢**	**2.56¢**	**1.01¢**	**0.39¢**
	2000	**0.03**	**2.99**	**1.38**	**0.30**
	2001	**0.03**	**3.01**	**1.29**	**0.18**
	2002*	**0.03**	**3.02**	**1.17**	**0.10**
United	1995	0.37¢	3.34¢	1.06¢	0.93¢
	2000	0.38	4.16	1.43	0.59
	2001	0.37	4.73	1.50	0.43
	2002*	0.35	4.87	1.21	0.32
US Airways	1995	0.25¢	4.93¢	1.04¢	0.90¢
	2000	0.28	5.35	1.72	0.51
	2001	0.28	5.62	1.56	0.39
	2002*	0.21	5.93	1.20	0.25

*Based on data for first six months of 2002 only.

Note: The big increases in the "other operating and maintenance expenses" category for 2001 and 2002 at several airlines (most notably United and US Airways) reflect special charges for the grounding and early retirement of aircraft and for employee severance expenses that were incurred in the aftermath of the September 11, 2001, terrorist attacks.

Source: U.S. Department of Transportation, Bureau of Transportation Statistics, Office of Airline Information, Form 41B, Form 41P, Form T100.

Landing Fees	Advertising	Other Operating and Maintenance Expenses	Total Operating Expenses	Rent and Leasing Fees
0.15¢	0.15¢	3.23¢	9.45¢	0.73¢
0.17	0.13	3.49	10.49	0.74
0.19	0.13	4.53	11.89	0.78
0.22	0.11	3.75	11.12	0.87
0.15¢	0.12¢	3.10¢	7.89¢	1.17¢
0.18	0.38	3.72	10.25	1.08
0.25	0.21	3.78	10.17	1.07
0.21	0.10	3.98	9.95	1.02
0.18¢	0.16¢	3.82¢	8.67¢	1.20¢
0.18	0.07	4.21	10.20	1.23
0.21	0.02	4.52	10.23	1.32
0.25	0.00	5.18	10.57	1.42
0.20¢	0.13¢	3.06¢	8.86¢	0.81¢
0.16	0.08	3.51	9.43	0.72
0.16	0.11	3.81	10.02	0.76
0.18	0.10	4.03	10.30	0.81
0.16¢	0.19¢	3.07¢	7.29¢	1.30¢
0.13	0.09	4.17	8.57	1.58
0.15	0.06	4.50	8.86	1.72
0.16	0.08	4.67	8.61	1.56
0.27¢	0.16¢	2.80¢	9.15¢	0.70¢
0.24	0.13	3.24	9.96	0.67
0.27	0.11	3.55	10.52	0.70
0.27	0.10	3.60	10.15	0.77
0.23¢	**0.27¢**	**2.61¢**	**7.09¢**	**0.71¢**
0.22	**0.26**	**2.55**	**7.72**	**0.55**
0.22	**0.24**	**2.51**	**7.48**	**0.54**
0.24	**0.22**	**2.58**	**7.36**	**0.55**
0.21¢	0.13¢	2.84¢	8.89¢	0.94¢
0.20	0.20	3.64	10.60	0.88
0.22	0.13	4.64	12.02	0.90
0.22	0.11	4.27	11.35	1.07
0.19¢	0.11¢ ·	4.18¢	11.61¢	1.16¢
0.20	0.08	5.73	13.88	1.11
0.20	0.08	6.00	14.13	1.31
0.23	0.06	6.57	14.45	1.30

exhibit 8   **Trends in Southwest Airlines' Operating Expenses per Average Seat Mile, 1995–2002**

Expense Category	2002	2001	2000	1999	1998	1997	1996	1995
Salaries, wages, and benefits	2.56¢	2.51¢	2.41¢	2.39¢	2.35¢	2.26¢	2.22¢	2.17¢
Employee retirement plans	.33	.33	.40	.36	.35	.30	.23	.23
Fuel and oil	1.11	1.18	1.34	.93	.82	1.11	1.19	1.01
Maintenance materials and repairs	.57	.61	.63	.70	.64	.58	.62	.60
Agency commissions	.08	.16	.27	.30	.33	.35	.35	.34
Aircraft rentals	.27	.29	.33	.38	.43	.45	.47	.47
Landing fees and other rentals	.50	.48	.44	.46	.45	.46	.46	.44
Depreciation	.52	.49	.47	.47	.47	.44	.45	.43
Other expenses	1.48	1.49	1.44	1.49	1.48	1.45	1.51	1.38
Total	7.41¢	7.54¢	7.73¢	7.48¢	7.32¢	7.40¢	7.50¢	7.07¢

Note: Figures in this exhibit differ slightly from those for Southwest in Exhibit 7 due to an assortment of differences in Southwest's internal accounting for its expenses and the Department of Transportation's expense category definitions and reporting for all commercial airlines.
Source: Company annual reports and 10-K reports.

or "The All-Time On-Time Airline"; still others highlighted its Triple Crown awards. Exhibit 9 provides four sample ads. One of the company's billboard campaigns touted the frequency of the company's flights with such phrases as "Austin Auften," "Phoenix Phrequently," and "L.A. A.S.A.P." Each holiday season since 1985, Southwest had run a "Christmas card" ad on TV featuring children and their families from the Ronald McDonald Houses and Southwest employees.

From time to time Southwest ran special fare promotions. To celebrate its 30th anniversary in 2001, Southwest announced special $30 one-way fares to 30 destinations from 35 cities for travel between June 25 and October 26; Southwest's car rental and hotel partners participated in the promotion, offering $30-a-day rentals, $30-off discounts, and $30-a-day hotel rooms at some locations. The 30-year celebration also included decorations in gate areas, prize giveaways, and employees playing games in the gate areas so that customers could share in the "Southwest Spirit." Along with most other airlines in 2002, Southwest featured a series of special fare promotions to stimulate ticket sales and fill up otherwise empty seats.

In 2002 Southwest began changing the look of its planes, updating its somewhat drab gold/orange/red scheme to a much fresher and brighter canyon blue/red/gold/ orange scheme (see Exhibit 10).

Other Strategy Elements

Southwest's strategy included several other components:

- *A fare structure that was consistently the simplest and most straightforward of any of the major U.S. airlines.* All of Southwest's different fare options could easily be perused at the company's Web site, and the company's restrictions on tickets were more lenient than those of its rivals.

- *Gradual expansion into new geographic markets.* Southwest generally added one or two new cities to its route schedule annually, preferring to saturate the market for daily flights to the cities/airports it currently served before entering new markets. In selecting new cities, Southwest looked for city pairs that could generate substantial amounts of both business and leisure traffic. Management believed that lots of flights were appealing to business travelers looking for convenient flight times and the ability to catch a later flight if they unexpectedly ran late.

- *Adding flights in areas where rivals were cutting back service.* When rivals cut back flights to cities that Southwest served, Southwest often moved in with more flights of its own, believing its lower fares would attract more passengers. When Midway Airlines ceased operations in

exhibit 9   **Four Sample Southwest Ads**

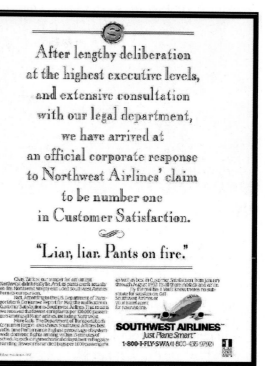

exhibit 10   **Southwest's New Look**

Old

New

November 1990, Southwest moved in overnight and quickly instituted flights to Chicago's Midway Airport. When American Airlines closed its hubs in Nashville and San Jose, Southwest immediately increased the number of its flights into and out of both locations. During the first half of 2002, as air traffic showed some signs of picking up, Southwest was a first-mover in adding flights on routes where rivals had cut their offerings following the September 11, 2001, terrorist attacks.

- *An attractive frequent flier program.* Southwest's Rapid Rewards members received a free round-trip ticket, good for travel anywhere on Southwest's system for up to one year, after purchasing and flying eight round-trips. There were no restrictions on the number of free Rapid Rewards seats on a particular flight and very few blackout dates around holidays. Southwest was considered to have the most generous frequent flier program in the industry, winning awards for best award redemption, best bonus promotion, and best customer service among all frequent flier programs.

- *Adding longer nonstop flights to the route system.* Although over 85 percent of Southwest's flights involved actual in-air flight times of less than 90 minutes, the company was judiciously adding nonstop flights to more distant destinations at those airports where its classic low fares could generate sufficient passenger traffic to achieve high enough load factors and revenues to be profitable. Most of the flights that the company added in 2002 were longer than 750 miles.

- *Putting strong emphasis on safety, high-quality maintenance, and reliable operations.* In the 31 years it had been flying, Southwest had never had a plane crash. Southwest had one of the most extensive and thorough maintenance programs in the commercial airline industry. The company's state-of-the-art flight dispatch system helped minimize weather and operational delays.

According to Southwest management, the company's strategy of low-cost, no-frills flights and reliable, friendly service delivered "more value for less money" to customers rather than "less value for less money." Kelleher said, "Everybody values a very good service provided at a very reasonable price."[14]

SOUTHWEST'S PEOPLE MANAGEMENT PRACTICES AND CULTURE

Whereas the litany at many companies was that customers come first, at Southwest the operative principle was that "employees come first and customers come second." The importance placed on employees

[14]Statement made in a 1993 Harvard Business School video and quoted in Roger Hallowell, "Southwest Airlines: A Case Study Linking Employee Needs Satisfaction and Organizational Capabilities to Competitive Advantage," *Human Resource Management* 35, no. 4 (Winter 1996), p. 517.

reflected management's belief that delivering superior service required employees who not only were passionate about their jobs but also knew the company was genuinely concerned for their well-being and committed to providing them with job security. Southwest's thesis was simple: Keep employees happy—then they will keep customers happy.

What Southwest management thought about the importance of Southwest's people and their role is reflected in the following excerpt from the company's 2000 annual report:

> Our people are warm, caring and compassionate, and willing to do whatever it takes to bring the Freedom to Fly to their fellow Americans. They take pride in doing well for themselves by doing good for others. They have built a unique and powerful culture that demonstrates that the only way to accomplish our mission to make air travel affordable for others, while ensuring ample profitability, job security, and plentiful Profitsharing for ourselves, is to keep our costs low and Customer Service quality high.
>
> At Southwest, our People are our greatest assets, which is why we devote so much time and energy to hiring great People with winning attitudes. Because we are well known as an excellent place to work with great career opportunities and a secure future, lots of People want to work for Southwest . . . Once hired, we provide a nurturing and supportive work environment that gives our Employees the freedom to be creative, have fun, and make a positive difference. Although we offer competitive compensation packages, it's our Employees' sense of ownership, pride in team accomplishments, and enhanced job satisfaction that keep our Culture and Southwest Spirit alive and why we continue to produce winning seasons.

The company changed the personnel department's name to the People Department in 1989.

Recruiting, Screening, and Hiring

Southwest hired employees for attitude and trained them for skills. Kelleher explained:

> We can train people to do things where skills are concerned. But there is one capability we do not have and that is to change a person's attitude. So we prefer an unskilled person with a good attitude . . . [to] a highly skilled person with a bad attitude.[15]

Management believed that delivering superior service came from having employees who genuinely believed that customers were important and that treating them warmly and courteously was the right thing to do, not from training employees to *act* like customers are important. The belief at Southwest was that superior, hospitable service and a fun-loving spirit flowed from the heart and soul of employees who themselves were fun-loving and spirited, who liked their jobs and the company they worked for, and who were also confident and empowered to do their jobs as they saw fit (rather than being governed by strict rules and procedures).

Southwest recruited employees by means of newspaper ads, career fairs, and Internet job listings; a number of candidates applied because of Southwest's *Fortune* listings as one of the best companies to work for in America and because they were impressed by their experiences as a customer on Southwest flights. Recruitment ads were designed to capture the attention of people thought to possess Southwest's "personality profile." For instance, one ad showed Herb Kelleher impersonating Elvis Presley and read as follows:

> Work In A Place Where Elvis Has Been Spotted. The qualifications? It helps to be outgoing. Maybe even a bit off center. And be prepared to stay for a while. After all, we have the lowest employee turnover rate in the industry. If this sounds good to you, just phone our jobline or send your resume. Attention Elvis.[16]

All job applications were processed through the People Department.

Screening Candidates   In hiring for jobs that involved personal contact with passengers, the company looked for people-oriented applicants who were extroverted and had a good sense of humor. It tried to identify candidates with a knack for reading people's emotions and responding in a genuinely caring, empathetic manner. Southwest wanted employees to deliver the kind of service that showed they truly enjoyed meeting people, being around passengers, and doing their job, as opposed to delivering the kind of service that came across as being forced or taught. According to Kelleher, "We are interested in people who externalize, who focus on other people, who are motivated to help other people. We are

---

[15]Quoted in James Campbell Quick, "Crafting an Organizational Structure: Herb's Hand at Southwest Airlines," *Organizational Dynamics* 21, no. 2 (Autumn 1992), p. 51.

[16]Southwest Airlines; and Sunoo, "How Fun Flies at Southwest Airlines," pp. 64–65.

not interested in navel gazers."[17] Southwest was drawn to candidates who, in addition to having a "whistle while you work" attitude, appeared likely to exercise initiative, work harmoniously with fellow employees, and be community spirited.

Southwest did not use personality tests to screen candidates, nor did it ask candidates what they would or should do in certain hypothetical situations. Rather, the hiring staff at Southwest analyzed each job category to determine the specific behaviors, knowledge, and motivations that job holders needed and then tried to find candidates with the desired traits—a process called targeted selection. A trait common to all job categories was teamwork; a trait deemed critical for pilots and flight attendants was judgment. In exploring an applicant's aptitude for teamwork, interviewers often asked applicants to tell them about a time in a prior job when they went out of their way to help a coworker or to explain how they had handled conflict with a coworker. Another frequent question was "What was your most embarrassing moment?" Southwest believed that having applicants talk about their past behaviors provided good clues about their future behaviors.

To test for unselfishness, Southwest interviewing teams typically gave a group of potential employees ample time to prepare five-minute presentations about themselves; during the presentations, which took place in an informal conversational setting, interviewers watched the audience to see who was absorbed in polishing their own presentations and who was listening attentively, enjoying the stories being told, and applauding the efforts of the presenters. Those who were emotionally engaged in hearing the presenters and giving encouragement were deemed more apt to be team players than those who were focused on looking good themselves. All applicants for flight attendant positions were put through such a presentation exercise before an interview panel consisting of customers, experienced flight attendants, and members of the People Department. Flight attendant candidates who got through the group presentation interviews then had to complete a three-on-one interview conducted by a recruiter, a supervisor from the hiring section of the People Department, and a Southwest flight attendant; following this interview, the three-person panel tried to reach a consensus on whether to recommend or drop the candidate.

In 2002, the company reviewed 243,657 résumés and hired 5,042 new employees.

Training

Apart from the Federal Aviation Administration's mandated training for certain employees, training activities at Southwest were designed and conducted by Southwest's University for People, a part of the company's People Department. The curriculum included courses for new recruits, employees, and leadership training programs for both new and experienced managers. Leadership courses emphasized a management style based on coaching and encouraging, rather than supervising or enforcing rules and regulations. All employees who came into contact with customers, including pilots, received customer care training. There were also courses on safety, communications, stress management, career development, performance appraisal, decision making, and employee relations. From time to time supervisors and executives attended courses on corporate culture that were intended to help instill, ingrain, and nurture such cultural themes as teamwork, trust, harmony, and diversity.

Depending on the influx of new employees, orientation courses were conducted two to five times a week for between 20 and 100 new recruits. The orientation program included videos on Southwest's history, an overview of the airline industry and the competitive challenges that Southwest faced, and an introduction to Southwest's culture and management practices. One of the program's highlights was a video called the *Southwest Shuffle,* which featured hundreds of Southwest employees rapping about the fun they had on their jobs. Orientation programs at the Dallas headquarters typically included exercises designed to demonstrate the role of creativity and teamwork and a scavenger hunt in which new hires were given a time line with specific dates in Southwest's history and were asked to fill in the missing details by viewing the memorabilia decorating the corridors and getting information from people working in various offices. Much of the indoctrination of new employees into the company's culture was done by coworkers and the employee's supervisor. Southwest made active use of a one-year probationary employment period to help ensure that new employees fit in with its culture and adequately embraced the company's cultural values.

[17]Quick, "Crafting an Organizational Structure," p. 52.

One of Southwest's supervisory training programs involved three teams; one member of each team was blindfolded and asked to throw a ball into a bucket. Unknown to the throwers, the other members on one team could say nothing about where the bucket was, members of the second team were instructed to say only "Good job" or "Keep trying," and the third group was allowed to give its thrower detailed information about where the bucket was. Not surprisingly, the third group's thrower had the most success—an outcome that was intended to demonstrate the value of good coaching on the part of supervisors and good listening on the part of supervisees.

Promotion

Approximately 80 to 90 percent of Southwest's supervisory positions were filled internally, reflecting management's belief that people who had "been there and done that" would be the ones most likely to appreciate and understand the demands that people under them were experiencing—and also most likely to enjoy the respect of their peers and higher-level managers. Employees could either apply for supervisory positions or be recommended by their present supervisor. New appointees for low-level management positions attended a three-day "Leading with Integrity" class aimed at developing leadership and communication skills. Employees being considered for managerial positions of large operations (Up and Coming Leaders) received training in every department of the company over a six-month period in which they continued to perform their current job. At the end of the six-month period, candidates were provided with 360-degree feedback from department heads, peers, and subordinates; representatives of the People Department analyzed the feedback in deciding on the specific assignment of each candidate.[18]

Compensation

Southwest's pay scales were at levels close to the industry average and its benefit packages were good relative to other airlines. According to a 1997–98 survey, Southwest's pilots earned, on average, about 10 percent above the industry average; however, they flew an average of 85 hours per month versus an industry average of 80.2 hours.

[18]Sunoo, "How Fun Flies at Southwest Airlines," p. 72.

Southwest introduced a profit-sharing plan for senior employees in 1973, the first such plan in the airline industry. By the mid-1990s the plan had been extended to cover most Southwest employees. As of 2001, Southwest had 12 different stock option programs for various employee groups, a 401(k) employee savings plan that included company-matching contributions, and a profit-sharing plan that covered virtually all employees and consisted of a money purchase defined contribution plan and an employee stock purchase plan. Company contributions to employee 410(k) and profit-sharing plans totaled $167.1 million in 1998, $192.0 million in 1999, $241.5 million in 2000, $214.6 million in 2001, and $155.6 million in 2002. In recent years, these payments had represented 8 to 12 percent of base pay. Employees participating in stock purchases via payroll deduction bought 1 million shares in 2000; 1 million shares in 2001; and 1.4 million shares in 2002—at prices equal to 90 percent of the market value at each payroll period. Southwest employees owned about 10 percent of Southwest's outstanding shares and held options to buy some 138 million additional shares over the next 10 years.

Employee Relations

About 80 percent of Southwest's 35,000 employees belonged to a union, making it one of the most highly unionized U.S. airlines. The Teamsters Union represented Southwest's airline mechanics, stock clerks, and aircraft cleaners; the Transport Workers Union (TWU) represented flight attendants; Local 555 of the TWU represented baggage handlers, ground crews, and provisioning employees; and the International Association of Machinists represented the customer service and reservation employees. There was one in-house union—the Southwest Airline Pilots Association, which represented pilots. Despite having sometimes spirited disagreements over particular issues, Southwest's relationships with the unions representing its employee groups were for the most part harmonious and nonadversarial—the company had experienced only one brief strike by machinists in the early 1980s.

Management encouraged union members and negotiators to research their pressing issues and to conduct employee surveys before each contract negotiation. Southwest's contracts with the unions representing its employees were relatively free of restrictive work rules and narrow job classifications that might impede worker productivity. All of the contracts allowed any qualified employee to perform any function—thus, pilots, ticket agents, and gate personnel could help load and unload baggage when needed and flight attendants could pick up trash and make flight cabins more presentable for passengers boarding the next flight.

In 2000–2001 the company had contentious negotiations with Local 555 of the TWU (representing about 5,300 Southwest employees) over a new wage and benefits package; the previous contract had become open for renegotiation in December 1999, and a tentative agreement reached at the end of 2000 was rejected by 64 percent of the union members who voted. A memo from Kelleher to TWU representatives said, "The cost and structure of the TWU 555 negotiating committee's proposal would seriously undermine the competitive strength of Southwest Airlines; endanger our ability to grow; threaten the value of our employees' profit-sharing; require us to contract out work in order to remain competitive; and threaten our 29-year history of job security for our employees." In a union newsletter in early 2001, the president of the TWU said, "We asked for a decent living wage and benefits to support our families, and were told of how unworthy and how greedy we were." The ongoing dispute resulted in informational picket lines in March 2001 at several Southwest locations, the first picketing since 1980. Later in 2001, with the help of the National Mediation Board, Southwest and the TWU reached an agreement covering Southwest's ramp, operations, and provisioning employees.

Prior to September 11, 2001, Southwest's pilots were somewhat restive about their base pay relative to pilots at other U.S. airlines. The maximum pay for Southwest's 3,700-plus pilots (before profit-sharing bonuses) was $148,000, versus maximums of $290,000 for United's pilots; $262,000 for Delta's pilots; $206,000 for American's pilots; and $199,000 for Continental's pilots.[19] Moreover, some veteran Southwest employees were grumbling about staff shortages in certain locations (to hold down labor costs) and cracks in the company's close-knit family culture due to the influx of so many new employees over the past several years. A number of employees who had accepted lower pay because of Southwest's underdog status were said to feel entitled to "big airline" pay now that Southwest had emerged as a major U.S. carrier.[20]

The No-Layoff Policy

Southwest Airlines had never laid off or furloughed any of its employees since the company began operations in 1971. The company's no-layoff policy was seen as integral both to how the company treated its employees and to management efforts to sustain and nurture the culture. According to Kelleher,

> Nothing kills your company's culture like layoffs. Nobody has ever been furloughed here, and that is unprecedented in the airline industry. It's been a huge strength of ours. It's certainly helped negotiate our union contracts . . . We could have furloughed at various times and been more profitable, but I always thought that was shortsighted. You want to show your people you value them and you're not going to hurt them just to get a little more money in the short term. Not furloughing people breeds loyalty. It breeds a sense of security. It breeds a sense of trust.[21]

Southwest had built up considerable goodwill with its unions over the years by avoiding layoffs.

Management Style

At Southwest, management strived to do things in a manner that would make Southwest employees proud of the company and its workforce practices. Managers were expected to spend at least one-third of their time out of the office, walking around the facilities under their supervision, observing firsthand what was going on, listening to employees and being responsive to their concerns. A former director of people development at Southwest told of a conversation he had with one of Southwest's terminal managers:

> While I was out in the field visiting one of our stations, one of our managers mentioned to me that he wanted to put up a suggestion box. I responded by saying, "Sure—why don't you put up a suggestion box right here on this wall and then admit you are a

[19]Shawn Tully, "From Bad to Worse," *Fortune,* October 15, 2001, p. 124.

[20]Melanie Trottman, "Amid Crippled Rivals, Southwest Tries to Spread Its Wings," *The Wall Street Journal,* October 11, 2001, p. A10.

[21]Brooks, "The Chairman of the Board Looks Back," p. 72.

failure as a manager?" Our theory is, if you have to put up a box so people can write down their ideas and toss them in, it means you are not doing what you are supposed to be doing. You are supposed to be setting your people up to be winners. To do that, you should be there listening to them and available to them in person, not via a suggestion box. For the most part, I think we have a very good sense of this at Southwest. I think that most people employed here know that they can call any one of our vice presidents on the telephone and get heard, almost immediately.

The suggestion box gives managers an out; it relinquishes their responsibility to be accessible to their people, and that's when we have gotten in trouble at Southwest—when we can no longer be responsive to our flight attendants or customer service agents, when they can't gain access to somebody who can give them resources and answers.[22]

Company executives were very approachable, insisting on being called by their first names. At new employee orientations, people were told, "We do not call the company chairman Mr. Kelleher; we call him Herb." Managers and executives had an open-door policy, actively listening to employee concerns, opinions, and suggestions for reducing costs and improving efficiency.

Employee-led initiatives were common. Southwest's pilots had been instrumental in developing new protocols for takeoffs and landings that conserved fuel. Another frontline employee had suggested not putting the company logos on trash bags, saving an estimated $250,000 annually. Rather than buy 800 computers for a new reservations center in Albuquerque, company employees determined that they could buy the parts and assemble the PCs themselves for half the price of a new PC, saving the company $1 million. It was Southwest clerks who came up with the idea of doing away with paper tickets and shifting to e-tickets.

There were only four layers of management between a frontline supervisor and the CEO. Southwest's employees enjoyed substantial authority and decision-making power. According to Kelleher:

We've tried to create an environment where people are able to, in effect, bypass even the fairly lean structures that we have so that they don't have to convene a meeting of the sages in order to get something done. In many cases, they can just go ahead and do it

on their own. They can take individual responsibility for it and know they will not be crucified if it doesn't work out. Our leanness requires people to be comfortable in making their own decisions and undertaking their own efforts.[23]

From time to time, there were candid meetings of frontline employees and managers where operating problems and issues between or among workers and departments were acknowledged, openly discussed, and resolved.[24] Informal problem avoidance and rapid problem resolution were seen as managerial virtues.

Southwest's Core Values

Two core values—LUV and fun—permeated the work environment at Southwest. LUV was much more than the company's ticker symbol or a recurring theme in Southwest's advertising campaigns. Over the years, *LUV* grew into Southwest's code word for treating individuals—fellow employees and customers—with dignity and respect and demonstrating a caring, loving attitude. The word *LUV* and red hearts commonly appeared on banners and posters at company facilities, as reminders of the compassion that was expected toward customers and other employees. Practicing the Golden Rule, internally and externally, was expected of all employees. Employees who had to struggle to live up to these expectations were subjected to considerable peer pressure and usually were asked to seek employment elsewhere if they did not soon leave of their own volition.

Fun at Southwest meant exactly what the word implies. Fun occurred throughout the company in the form of the generally entertaining behavior of employees in performing their jobs, the ongoing pranks and jokes, and frequent company-sponsored parties and celebrations. On holidays, employees were encouraged to dress in costumes. There were charity benefit games, chili cook-offs, Halloween parties, new Ronald McDonald House dedications, and other special events of one kind or another at one location or another almost every week. According to one manager, "We're kind of a big family here, and family members have fun together."

---

[22]Freiberg and Freiberg, *NUTS!*, p. 273.

[23]Ibid., p. 76.
[24]Hallowell, "Southwest Airlines: A Case Study," p. 524.

The Culture Committee

Southwest formed a Culture Committee in 1990 to promote "Positively Outrageous Service" and devise tributes, contests, and celebrations intended to nurture and perpetuate the "Southwest Spirit." The committee, chaired by Colleen Barrett, was composed of up to 100 employees representing a cross-section of departments and locations; members served a two-year term. Members, chosen for their zeal in exhibiting the Southwest Spirit and their commitment to Southwest's mission and values, functioned as cultural ambassadors, missionaries, and storytellers. The committee had four all-day meetings annually; ad hoc subcommittees, formed throughout the year, met more frequently. Over the years, the committee had sponsored and supported hundreds of ways to promote and ingrain the Southwest Spirit, with members showing up at a facility to serve pizza or ice cream to employees or to remodel and decorate an employee break room. Kelleher indicated, "We're not big on committees at Southwest, but of the committees we do have, the Culture Committee is the most important."[25]

Efforts to Nurture the Southwest Culture

Apart from the Culture Committee, Southwest reinforced its core values and culture via such efforts as a CoHearts mentoring program; a Day in the Field program, in which employees spent time working in another area of the company's operations; a Helping Hands program, in which volunteers from around the system traveled to work two weekend shifts at other Southwest facilities that were temporarily short-handed or experiencing heavy workloads; and periodic Culture Exchange meetings to celebrate the Southwest Spirit and company milestones. Almost every event at Southwest was videotaped, which provided footage for creating such multipurpose videos as *Keepin' the Spirit Alive* that could be used in training courses and shown at company events all over the system. Many of the committee's activities revolved around promoting the use of red hearts and the word *LUV* to embody the spirit of Southwest employees caring about each other and Southwest's customers. The concepts of LUV and fun were spotlighted in all of the company's training manuals and videos. There was an annual "Heroes of the Heart Award."

Southwest's monthly newsletter, *LUV Lines,* often spotlighted the experiences and deeds of particular employees, reprinted letters of praise from customers, and reported company celebrations of milestones. A quarterly news video, *As the Plane Turns*, was sent to all facilities to keep employees up-to-date on company happenings, provide clips of special events, and share messages from customers, employees, and executives. The company had published a book for employees describing "outrageous" acts of service. Sometimes important information was circulated to employees in "fun" packages such as Cracker Jack boxes.

Southwest executives believed that the company's growth was primarily a function of the rate at which it could hire and train people to fit into its culture and mirror the Southwest Spirit. With about 150 cities annually petitioning Southwest to initiate service to their airports, management believed that the company's growth was not constrained by a lack of market opportunities to expand into other geographic locations. About 15,000 of Southwest's 35,000 employees had been hired since 1995.

Employee Productivity

Management was convinced that the company's strategy, culture, esprit de corps, and people management practices fostered high labor productivity and contributed to Southwest's low labor costs compared to other airlines (see again Exhibit 7). When a Southwest flight pulled up to the gate, ground crews, gate personnel, and flight attendants hustled to perform all the tasks requisite to turn the plane quickly—employees took pride in doing their part to achieve good on-time performance. Southwest's average turnaround times were about two-thirds the industry average. One study found that Southwest had an average of 2.2 station personnel per 1,000 passengers in 1994 versus an industry average of about 4.2.[26] According to the Air Transport Association, labor costs were the airlines' biggest cost component, accounting for 38 percent of operating costs in 2002; the average airline employee had an estimated cost of $75,200 in 2002, including pension, payroll taxes,

---

[25]Freiberg and Freiberg, *NUTS!,* p. 165.

[26]J. H. Gittell, "Cross-Functional Coordination and Human Resource Systems: Evidence from the Airline Industry," doctoral dissertation, Massachusetts Institute of Technology, cited in Hallowell, "Southwest Airlines: A Case Study," p. 527.

health care, and insurance benefits. In 2000, Southwest's labor productivity compared favorably with the average of its eight biggest U.S. rivals:

Productivity Measure	Southwest	Average of Southwest's Eight Largest U.S. Rivals
Passengers enplaned per employee	2,145	1,119
Employees per plane	83.4	121.7

Awards, Recognition, and Operating Performance Comparisons

Southwest's strategy and approaches to conducting its business had resulted in numerous awards over the years. Southwest ranked number one in customer satisfaction among U.S. major airlines every year from 1991 though 2000. In *Fortune* magazine surveys, Southwest had been ranked as the most admired airline in the world every year since 1997. In 1998, *Fortune* named Southwest number 1 in its listing of the 100 best companies to work for in America; Southwest was ranked number 4 in 1999, number 2 in 2000, and number 4 in 2001—the company elected not to go through the screening process for the awards given out in early 2002. Southwest's Web site had won top awards from both *Business Week* and *PC Magazine.* In 2001, *Business Ethics* included Southwest Airlines on its "100 Best Corporate Citizens" list.

Exhibit 11 provides comparative statistics on Southwest's performance versus that of other major commercial airlines during the 1998–2002 period.

SOUTHWEST'S NEW LEADERSHIP TEAM

In June 2001 Southwest Airlines, responding to anxious investor concerns about the company's leadership succession plans, began an orderly transfer of power and responsibilities from its longtime CEO and cofounder, Herb Kelleher, age 70, to two of his most trusted protégés. James F. Parker, 54, Southwest's general counsel, was elevated to CEO. Colleen

Barrett, 56, Southwest's executive vice president of customers and self-described keeper of Southwest's pep-rally corporate culture, became president and chief operating officer. Kelleher stayed on as chairman of Southwest's board of directors and the head of the board's executive committee and continued to be in charge of strategy, expansion to new cities and aircraft scheduling, and governmental and industry affairs; his contract called for him to remain in those roles through December 2003 at an annual salary of $450,000, plus bonuses and stock options. Many observers and longtime employees did not expect Kelleher to ever fully remove himself from management of the company as long as his health held up—Kelleher had undergone treatment for prostate cancer in 1999.

James Parker

Southwest's new CEO, James Parker, had an association with Herb Kelleher going back 23 years to the time when they were colleagues at Kelleher's old law firm. Parker moved over to Southwest from the law firm in February 1986. Parker's profile inside the company as Southwest's vice president and general counsel had been relatively low, but he was Southwest's chief labor negotiator and much of the credit for Southwest's good relations with employee unions belonged to him. Prior to his appointment as CEO, Parker had been a member of the company's executive planning committee; his experiences ranged from properties and facilities to technical services team to the company's alliances with vendors and partners. Parker and Kelleher were said to think much alike, and Parker was regarded as having a good sense of humor, although he did not have as colorful and flamboyant a personality as Kelleher. Parker was seen as an honest, straight-arrow kind of person who had a strong grasp of Southwest's culture and market niche and who could be nice or tough, depending on the situation. When his appointment was announced, Parker said:

> There is going to be no change of course insofar as Southwest is concerned. We have a very experienced leadership team. We've all worked together for a long time. There will be evolutionary changes in Southwest, just as there have always been in our history. We're going to stay true to our business model of being a low-cost, low-fare airline.[27]

[27]Quoted in the *Seattle Times,* March 20, 2001, p. C3.

exhibit 11   **On-Time Flights, Mishandled Baggage, Oversales, and Passenger Complaints for Major U.S. Airlines, 1998–2002**

Percentage of Scheduled Flights Arriving within 15 Minutes of the Scheduled Time					
Carrier	**Jan.–Sept. 2002**	**2001**	**2000**	**1999**	**1998**
Alaska Airlines	75.8%	69.0%	68.1%	71.0%	72.0%
America West	78.5	74.8	65.5	69.5	68.5
American	78.9	75.9	72.9	73.5	80.1
Continental	78.7	80.7	78.1	76.6	77.3
Delta	77.5	78.0	75.3	78.0	79.6
Northwest	79.7	79.7	77.4	79.9	70.6
Southwest	82.3	81.7	75.2	80.0	80.8
TWA*	—	80.8	76.9	80.9	78.3
United	75.5	73.5	61.4	74.4	73.8
US Airways	78.4	78.2	72.3	71.4	78.9

Mishandled Baggage Reports per 1,000 Passengers					
Carrier	**Jan.–Sept. 2002**	**2001**	**2000**	**1999**	**1998**
Alaska Airlines	2.68	3.00	3.48	5.75	7.27
America West	3.47	4.22	6.62	4.52	3.88
American	4.32	4.60	5.50	5.21	4.40
Continental	3.06	4.29	5.35	4.42	4.06
Delta	3.61	4.11	4.49	4.39	4.27
Northwest	4.79	4.19	5.24	4.81	6.63
Southwest	3.54	4.77	5.00	4.22	4.53
TWA*	—	6.35	6.06	5.38	5.39
United	3.69	5.07	6.57	7.01	7.79
US Airways	3.01	3.86	4.76	5.08	4.09

Colleen Barrett

Barrett began working with Kelleher as his legal secretary in 1967 and had been with Southwest since 1978. As executive vice president of customers, Barrett had a high profile among Southwest employees and spent most of her time on culture building, morale building, and customer service. She and Kelleher were regarded as Southwest's guiding lights, and some analysts said she was essentially functioning as the company's chief operating officer prior to her formal appointment. Much of the credit for the company's strong record of customer service and its strong culture belonged to Barrett.

Barrett had been the driving force behind lining the hallways at Southwest's headquarters with photos of company events and trying to create a family atmosphere at the company. Believing it was important to make employees feel cared about and important, Barrett had put together a network of contacts across the company to help her stay in touch with what was happening with employees and their families. When network members learned about events that were worthy of acknowledgment, word quickly got to Barrett—the information went into a database and an appropriate greeting card or gift was sent. Barrett had a remarkable ability to give individualized gifts that connected her to the recipient.[28]

Barrett was the first woman appointed as president and chief operating office of a major U.S. air-

[28]Freiberg and Freiberg, *NUTS!*, p. 163.

exhibit 11   **(continued)**

Involuntary Denied Boardings per 10,000 Passengers Due to Oversold Flights					
Carrier	Jan.–Sept. 2002	2001	2000	1999	1998
Alaska Airlines	1.24	1.36	1.53	0.99	1.49
America West	0.21	0.38	1.27	1.38	1.12
American	0.22	0.36	0.44	0.42	0.42
Continental	0.93	1.51	1.44	0.28	0.13
Delta	0.87	0.77	0.34	1.98	1.24
Northwest	0.53	0.45	0.43	0.20	0.33
Southwest	1.06	1.50	1.84	1.40	1.84
TWA*	—	1.83	2.76	0.88	1.69
United	0.65	0.92	1.64	0.69	0.59
US Airways	0.26	0.34	0.67	0.57	0.23

Complaints per 100,000 Passengers Boarded					
Carrier	Jan.–Sept. 2002	2001	2000	1999	1998
Alaska Airlines	1.02	1.27	2.04	1.64	0.54
America West	1.88	3.72	7.51	3.72	2.11
American	1.41	2.51	3.54	3.49	1.14
Continental	1.46	2.23	2.84	2.62	1.02
Delta	1.51	2.16	2.01	1.81	0.79
Northwest	1.60	1.97	2.61	2.92	2.21
Southwest	0.37	0.38	0.47	0.40	0.25
TWA*	—	2.54	3.47	3.44	1.29
United	1.90	3.24	5.3	2.65	1.28
US Airways	1.24	1.87	2.59	3.13	0.84

*Acquired by American Airlines in 2001; TWA data for 2002 included in American Airlines statistics.
Source: Office of Aviation Enforcement and Proceedings, *Air Travel Consumer Report*, multiple issues.

line. In October 2001, *Fortune* included Colleen Barrett on its list of the 50 most powerful women in American business (she was ranked number 20).

CRISIS CONDITIONS STRIKE THE AIRLINE INDUSTRY: THE AFTERMATH OF SEPTEMBER 11

In the days and weeks following the terrorist attacks on the World Trade Center and the Pentagon on September 11, 2001, the commercial air travel system in the United States was suddenly and unexpectedly in shambles. The unprecedented three-day shutdown of flights, the sudden erosion of passenger traffic, and strict new security measures threw major airlines into a financial crunch of huge proportions and triggered a struggle to revamp flight schedules and respond to sharply lower passenger travel. During the three days that flights were suspended by the Federal Aviation Administration, airlines burned through an estimated $220 million a day in cash to cover ongoing expenses.

On the first day of trading after the terrorist attacks, investor worries about almost empty flights, higher costs from added security measures, and a clouded financial future for the whole airline industry caused airline stock prices to plunge. With about $26.1 billion in debt as of 2001; billions more in capital lease obligations for planes that had been leased rather than purchased; and ongoing costs for labor, terminal facilities, and maintenance, U.S. commercial airlines typically had to fill close to 65 percent of the available seats in order to reach breakeven. For the four weeks immediately following the attacks, load factors at most airlines were in the 40–60 percent range. Most airlines responded by cutting the number of flights by about 20 percent, grounding the unneeded planes, and laying off employees.

Many airline executives expressed concerns about an impending liquidity crunch, rapid burns of cash on hand, and the potential for a number of carriers to end up in bankruptcy without some kind of relief from the federal government. Industry analysts speculated that losses for U.S. airlines in the wake of the terrorist attacks could reach $7 billion in 2001 and that slack demand for air travel could last well into 2002. Congress responded by passing a $15 billion aid package that (1) provided $5 billion in cash grants to help airlines cover losses and negative cash flows stemming from traffic declines and (2) allowed airlines to apply for $10 billion in loan guarantees to bolster their balance sheets and provide needed liquidity.

During the last three months of 2001, airlines scrambled to revise their flight schedules to better match the reduced traffic patterns. Delta, American, and TWA cut 40 percent of their international flights out of New York's Kennedy International, suspending all service to a number of destinations until March 2002. Late-night domestic flights and domestic flights on weak performing routes bore the brunt of the flight cutbacks. Some routes served by full-size jets were converted to commuter jet service. United Airlines announced that it would cease operating its Shuttle by United service on the West Coast, which overlapped with Southwest in such markets as Las Vegas, Oakland, and Los Angeles. US Airways announced that it would close down its low-fare MetroJet subsidiary, which operated on the East Coast and overlapped with Southwest's service in Providence and Baltimore (one of Southwest's fastest-growing locations). US Airways also announced that it would eliminate 51 of its 75 mainline jet flights from Baltimore, including all nonstop flights to Florida. Delta Airlines announced that it would cut the operations of its low-fare operation,

Delta Express, by 50 percent; Delta Express served three locations also served by Southwest—Orlando, Tampa, and Hartford. In Orlando, Delta Express said it would cut back from 49 daily flights to 21 (Southwest operated 52 daily nonstop flights out of Orlando to 24 cities).

Southwest's Situation

Southwest, however, continued to fly its full schedule of 2,772 flights even though its load factors for the four weeks ending October 14, 2001, were 38.5 percent, 52.4 percent, 62.5 percent, and 67.0 percent—for the period July 1, 2001, until the attacks, Southwest's load factor was 74.6 percent. The company initiated new service to Norfolk, Virginia, on October 7, as planned. Southwest's primary responses involved a temporary freeze on hiring until January 2002, deferring nonessential capital spending and nonessential operating costs, and negotiating a revised delivery schedule for the 132 Boeing 737 jets it had on order.

In January 2002, Southwest Airlines reported its 29th consecutive year of profitability, with annual net income of $511.1 million ($0.63 per diluted share), compared to 2000 net income (excluding the cumulative effect of a change in accounting principle) of $625.2 million ($0.79 per diluted share)—a decline of 18 percent. Southwest's 2001 net income included a special pretax gain of $235 million from a federal grant received pursuant to the Air Transportation Safety and System Stabilization Act and special pretax charges of $48 million arising from the terrorist attacks on September 11, 2001. Excluding the special gain, special charges, and related profit-sharing and income tax effects, the company's 2001 net income was $412.9 million, or $0.51 per diluted share.

Then in early 2002 Southwest announced that it would begin expanding its flight schedule during the February–June 2002 period; the new schedule included the addition of 21 new daily nonstop flights, many of which were on long-distance routes that Southwest had not previously served with nonstop flights. Later in 2002, Southwest announced the addition of 10 more new long-distance, nonstop flights. Many of the newly added flights were round-trip flights between points in the Northeast and Florida and Texas and between two of Southwest's most important airports, Baltimore/Washington and Chicago

Midway, and points west—Las Vegas, Phoenix, Oakland, Seattle, and Los Angeles.

Chicago Midway was targeted by Southwest as a particularly lucrative place for expanded flights. Southwest's share of flight departures from Chicago (both O'Hare and Midway) was much higher in April 2002 than in April 2001:

	April 2001	April 2002
Chicago–Tampa		
Southwest	20%	27%
United	50	38
American	30	27
Chicago–Seattle		
Southwest	0	9
United	60	51
American	34	29
Chicago–Phoenix		
Southwest	9	17
United	27	22
American	27	25

*Percentages include all flights from both O'Hare and Midway; Southwest flights all were into and out of Midway.

Jim Parker, Southwest's CEO and vice chairman, said, "We are approaching growth opportunities conservatively, but we know our customers have been anxious for this new nonstop service. Although the airline is still in the recovery process, we cannot forget the wishes of our customers to continue to bring low fares and affordable travel to more people with more convenient flights." Parker indicated that Southwest's employees had been working feverishly on initiatives to make the airport experience more convenient in the new environment of heightened security.

Introductory fares for the flights on the new routes were in the range of $89–$99 each way. The fares were well below the fares on comparable flights of rival airlines. On the high-traffic Chicago–Los Angeles route, an unrestricted, fly-anytime fare or a last-minute fare (no advance purchase) on United and American ran $2,480. To try to rebuild traffic during 2002, Southwest had fare sales in January, March, April, July, August, October, and December; it had also instituted some special vacation fares to resort destinations like Las Vegas and California's Disneyland. But as 2002 drew to an end, passenger traffic on Southwest's flights (see Exhibit 2) and on those of rival airlines remained below pre–September 11 levels. In December 2002, Southwest announced another round of fare sales for January–April 2003.

Southwest's Financially Troubled Rivals

The financial picture at rival airlines was grim. Every passenger airline in the United States except Southwest lost money in 2002. US Airways filed for Chapter 11 bankruptcy in August 2002; it was trying to persuade its unions to agree to deeper wage and salary cuts in order to qualify for a $900 million federal loan and to secure $500 million in interim financing from the Retirement Systems of Alabama, which had recently purchased a 37.5 percent ownership stake. US Airways management had indicated that the company was abandoning its growth strategy and would focus instead on providing regional service with smaller jets primarily on the East Coast and in the Caribbean.

United Airlines filed for Chapter 11 bankruptcy in December 2002 and was in dire straits. United's costs per available seat mile in the third quarter of 2002 were $0.11, the highest in the industry, and its labor costs were $0.046, the second highest in the industry. While management had called on its union and nonunion employees to agree to wage and salary cuts totaling $9 billion over six years, the unions so far had pledged to give up only $5.2 billion over five years—United's employees owned 55 percent of the company's stock; however, under the bankruptcy laws, the union agreements could be declared null and void (United management was expected to take such a step if necessary to establish financial solvency). Federal officials had turned down United's request for a $1.8 billion loan, indicating the company's business plan for getting the company back on solid financial footing was unsound and contained unreasonably optimistic revenue projections. A number of observers had predicted that if United did not get its financial house in order by April 2003, the company would have to be liquidated because it would run out of cash—the company had lost nearly $4 billion in the past two years, was in default on a $920 million loan, and was bleeding millions in cash every day. Most industry observers believed that, in order to survive, United would have to scale back its operations significantly—since September 11, it had already cut its daily flights by 25 percent and laid off about 20,000 employees.

American Airlines, with the highest labor costs in the industry ($0.0462 per available seat mile), was negotiating work rule changes with its unions to try to boost labor productivity and had requested all employees to forgo any pay raise in 2003—management was trying to achieve $3–$4 billion in annual cost savings to bring American's costs more in line with those of Southwest and other lower-cost airlines. American's pilots were among the best paid in the industry and flew an average of 700 hours per year, well under the federal limit of 1,000 hours annually; they worked an average of 14 days a month. In 2002, American spent about $2.5 billion to pay for the salaries and benefits of its 10,000 pilots; the company's total payroll for its 109,000 employees was about $8.4 billion. Productivity improvements of 20 percent would save American about $500 million annually.

Benziger Family Winery

Murray Silverman
San Francisco State University

Tom Lanphar
California Department of Toxic Substances Control

Matt Atkinson, ranch manager at Benziger Family Winery (BFW), was overseeing the development of the winery's environmental management system (EMS). Matt was working with Chris Benziger, partner and national sales manager, to ensure that development of the EMS was consistent with BFW's operational and strategic direction. It was February 2003 and Matt and Chris had already invested countless hours in the EMS, which was being developed with assistance from the California Environmental Protection Agency (Cal/EPA). Through its EMS winery pilot project, Cal/EPA hoped to design an EMS template that eventually could be made available to other wineries. Furthermore, Cal/EPA was attempting to develop a template that was consistent with ISO 14001, an internationally recognized standard for environmental management systems. Cal/EPA had selected BFW in June 2000 as one of two pilot wineries because of the winery's proactive commitment to environmental policies and the significant environmental advances it had already made.

Matt believed that considerable progress had been made on the company's EMS. With Cal/EPA's assistance, BFW had developed a formal environmental policy, identified and prioritized its environmental impacts, and established objectives and targets. However, there were still many steps to be carried out in establishing a full-fledged EMS. Further development would require time-consuming efforts in writing standardized operating procedures and in establishing document control and record-keeping procedures. Also, because Matt and Chris

Copyright © 2003 by Murray Silverman and Tom Lanphar. The authors gratefully acknowledge a Business and International Education (BIE) grant from the U.S. Department of Education and a matching grant from the College of Business at San Francisco State University in support of this case research.

had been the primary participants developing the system, the rest of the organization would have to become involved and staff training would be required. In light of the financial investments and time that would be required from management and employees, Matt and Chris had to decide whether to aggressively pursue ISO 14001 certification. The alternative was to continue to develop an EMS as time and resources permitted, leaving open the possibility of eventually pursuing ISO 14001 certification.

BENZIGER FAMILY WINERY'S HISTORY

Mike Benziger, general partner and founder of Benziger Family Winery, grew up working in his father's wine import business in New York City. His dream was to grow his own grapes and make his own wine. Mike was the oldest of Helen and Bruno Benziger's seven children. Bruno worked for 23 years in the wine import business, starting out with his father, Joseph, who founded the Park-Benziger Import Company in 1933 in New York City. Mike and his siblings worked in the family business, selling and delivering wine throughout the city's five boroughs. After graduating college in 1973, Mike relocated to Europe with his wife, Mary; the couple worked in vineyards and cellars as they moved from region to region. In 1975, Mike took a cellar position with Stony Ridge Winery in California, where as assistant winemaker he took a giant leap forward in appreciating the craft end of the business, sparking his continuing passion for the creation of truly great wine.

As their desire to start their own winery grew more insistent, Mike and Mary spent their free time searching for the ideal site. While driving through the charming little northern California town of Glen Ellen, on a sudden impulse Mike turned into a narrow road winding up the mountain. One particular plot of land, the 85-acre Sonoma Mountain Ranch, a hanging volcanic valley spread across the side of the mountain, was the site he had been seeking. In October of 1981, Mike convinced the reluctant owner to sell and, borrowing a substantial amount from his father, initiated an all-consuming adventure for three generations of the Benziger family.

Soon after, Mike's father, Bruno Benziger, sold his share of Park-Benziger and moved to the Sonoma Mountain Ranch. Mike's younger brothers, Bob and Joe, sold their successful wine shop in upscale Scarsdale, New York, and followed closely behind their parents. Joe studied enology and viticulture at Santa Rosa Junior College and the University of California at Davis. As winemaker, Joe supervised every aspect of the production of all Benziger wines from fermentation to bottling. Bob helped build the wine distribution network and eventually took charge of business development. Brother Jerry arrived in 1981 and settled into winemaking.

The three youngest Benzigers were also involved in the family business. Mike's sister Patsy developed and ran the Benziger Family Winery Apprenticeship Program, perpetuating the family tradition by arranging for the Benziger children and the children of employees to spend six weeks working in each of the winery's departments during their high school and college years. Chris earned a degree in marketing from the University of San Francisco and was the national sales manager. Kathy, the youngest of Bruno and Helen's seven children, earned a degree in management from Sonoma State University. She was in charge of sales in the eastern region of the United States. Tim Wallace, Patsy's husband, a Harvard Business School graduate, was president and chief operating officer. He was in charge of all aspects of sales and marketing, finance and administration, and the hospitality and wine-tasting function. Mike Benziger supervised the vineyard and wine production. The winery employed 49 people full-time, and 29 people were either part-time or seasonal workers.

BFW was a medium-sized winery producing 180,000 cases of ultrapremium wine per year, with annual revenues of about $15 million. Superpremium wines ($8–$14 a bottle) accounted for 60 per-

cent of case volume, ultrapremium wines ($15–$25 a bottle) accounted for 30 percent, and luxury wines (over $25 a bottle) accounted for the remaining 10 percent. BFW was about to launch a new brand, Tribute, that would be an estate wine (grown from grapes in the company's own vineyards) selling in the range of $50–$60 a bottle. Eventually, the company hoped to sell 4,000 cases of Tribute annually. Currently, BFW exported 10 percent of its total case volume and was targeting 20 percent as a long-term goal. Most of its exports were to Canada and Europe. European markets expressed a significant amount of interest in biodynamic and organic wines, and BFW therefore planned to target Tribute exports to the European market.

BENZIGER'S ENVIRONMENTAL INITIATIVES

BFW was a recognized leader in environmentally responsible winemaking. Its environmental practices extended to both its vineyards and wine production. In 1999, BFW was one of the initial wineries certified by the Sonoma County Green Business Program (SCGBP), on the basis of its proactive environmental programs within its winery operations. In April 2000, BFW won Cal/EPA's Department of Pesticide Regulation's Integrated Pest Management Innovators Award.

The Sonoma Mountain Ranch site held a remarkable diversity of soils. Twenty-one distinct types of soil were identified and grouped by the Benzigers into "flavor blocks." The variety of soil types related to one of the key elements of BFW's philosophy—farming for flavors, a method of carefully tailoring viticultural techniques to soil type, exposure, and climate in order to produce fruit of optimal complexity, concentration, and intensity. Sixty-five acres of vines were planted at the ranch, and another 20-acre parcel was planted with vines in nearby Sonoma Valley.

At the root of the Benziger family's environmental stewardship was a goal to "produce world-class wines that had a sense of place"—that is, wines that contained the unique personality and character of the place where the grapes were grown. The Benzigers' approach was to farm in concert with nature and not in opposition to it. According to Mike Benziger, chemical pesticides and fertilizers reduced the unique and natural characteristics of a vineyard and its grapes. Restoring the biologic capital of a vineyard (the ability of nature to provide services such as pest control, fertilizing, and moisture retention) enhanced the unique qualities of the wine. To achieve the natural conditions they sought in their vineyards, the Benziger family practiced biodynamic farming. While similar to organic agriculture in that chemicals were eliminated, biodynamic farming went further in that it attempted to respond to the earth's natural energies and cycles. The Benziger family's two Sonoma County vineyards were certified in 2000 by the Demeter Association, the international organization that monitored and approved biodynamic practices. Chris Benziger estimated that biodynamic farming increased grape-growing costs by about 10 percent. According to BFW's Web site (www.benziger.com), the principles of biodynamic farming included:

- Promoting the unique environment of a given site by minimizing outside influences and by utilizing only farm-produced composts and manure for soil preparation. At BFW, compost developed by combining waste from the winery with manure from a local dairy was spread over the vineyard, increasing both soil fertility and vitality. The resulting increase in the diversity of soil organisms eliminated the need for soil fumigants. The soil's water-holding capacity was also increased, reducing irrigation needs.

- Using no chemically synthesized fertilizers, pesticides, herbicides, fungicides, or fumigants, and no hormones, antibiotics, growth regulators, or genetically modified organisms. Reliance on these synthetics reduced the vine's natural ability to absorb nutrients from the soil, leaving it susceptible to disease.

- Employing a series of eight herbal preparations that were applied to the soil to promote soil vitality through increased microbiologic activity and diversity (these were considered as vitamins for the plants and soil). The more nutrient-rich and biologically diverse the soils, the more character imparted to the wine.

- Using cover crops and companion plants to maximize the health of the vineyard environment. BFW's cover crops, planted between vineyard rows, served to reduce soil erosion, fertilize soil through nitrogen fixation, and attract beneficial insects. Also, BFW had set aside areas in the vineyard for plants that attracted beneficial insects (insectaries).

BFW's vineyards supplied only a small proportion of the winery's grapes; the balance of the grapes was bought from more than 60 growers. To improve quality and to teach them the techniques, costs, and benefits associated with sustainable agricultural practices, BFW educated its growers in the farming methods employed in its own vineyards. It conducted a quarterly series of "hot topic" seminars demonstrating practices such as canopy management, irrigation, and weed control. According to Matt Atkinson, the message was: "The quality of your grapes will improve if you follow our practices."

Environmental practices at BFW also extended into the winery, as reflected by BFW's being certified by the Sonoma County Green Business Program (SCGBP). The SCGBP provided technical assistance to businesses in the areas of compliance, resource conservation, and pollution prevention. The SCGBP certified that a business was in full environmental compliance and met the Green Business standard for beyond-compliance environmental practices in the areas of energy and water conservation, solid waste reduction, and pollution prevention. As part of the Green Business certification process, BFW demonstrated a 2-million-gallon-per-year water savings through recycling all wastewater generated by the winery. Its wastewater was biologically treated in a series of ponds and wetlands and supplied 75 percent of the winery's vineyard irrigation needs. Significant reductions in solid waste were also shown. Forty-one percent of the winery's waste stream was recycled. To reduce energy costs associated with wine storage, BFW constructed a set of wine caves in its vineyard hillside. This 22,000-square-foot facility maintained a natural temperature of 63 degrees Fahrenheit, significantly reducing the energy requirements for storing the company's wines.

ENVIRONMENTAL PRACTICES IN THE WINE INDUSTRY

The U.S. wine industry ranked fourth in the world in terms of volume of wine produced and consisted of approximately 1,500 wineries. The industry, however,

exhibit 1   **Typical Environmental Impacts in Vineyards and Wineries**

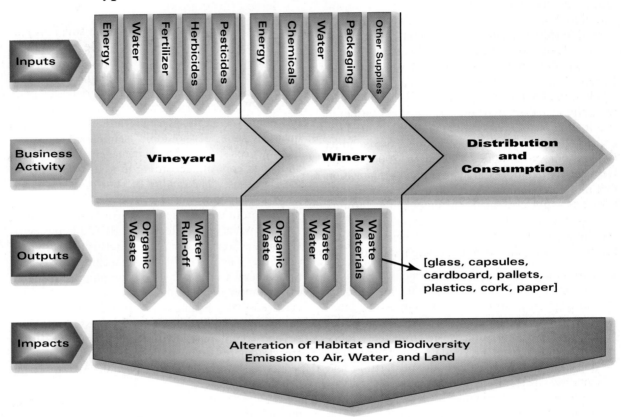

was highly concentrated, with the top 10 wineries accounting for 70 percent of U.S. production by volume. Wine was grown and produced in every state except Alaska, but the U.S. wine industry was dominated by California, whose 800+ wineries accounted for more than 90 percent of the wine produced and exported by U.S. wineries. The Pacific Northwest (Washington, Oregon, and Idaho) had over 200 wineries that were developing an excellent reputation for quality wines. An estimated 245 million cases of wine, representing over 6,500 brands, were consumed in the United States in 2002; some 23 brands sold at least 2 million cases each and represented about 40 percent of total consumption.

The supply chain for the wine industry started with wine-grape growers and proceeded to wineries, where the grapes were crushed, fermented, clarified, stabilized, and aged. Eventually, the wines were bottled and shipped through the distribution channels to wholesalers, then to retailers who sold to the end consumer. A very small proportion of the wine circumvented the traditional distribution channels and was sold directly from the winery to the end consumer. While some smaller wineries grew all their own wine grapes, most wineries purchased some of their grapes from independent growers. There were a large number of independent wine-grape growers who sold their grapes under contract to specific wineries or on the open market.

Exhibit 1 displays the chief environmental impacts associated with a typical winery. Environmental impacts associated with growing wine grapes were agricultural, while those in the wineries were related to food processing. A comprehensive listing of all the potential environmental impacts associated with vineyard and winery operations would be too extensive to be listed here, but the most significant include the following:

- Vineyard inputs included fertilizers (both synthetic and natural), pesticides, water for irrigation, and energy to power equipment in the field. While there were natural pesticides and pest control approaches, a majority of vineyards used synthetic chemical pesticides in the form of insecticides, herbicides, and fungicides. According to California's 1998 "Annual Pesticide Use Report," there were over 34 million pounds of pesticides applied to wine grapes, using 298 different chemicals. These chemicals, while varying in terms of level of toxicity, were detrimental to air, water, and soil quality. They also had harmful impacts on vineyard workers, neighbors, and animals sharing the local habitat. A major issue with synthetic fertilizers was their potential to contaminate local water supplies due to inappropriate or excessive application. Water shortages could also be an issue in many geographic areas. Energy issues associated with the use of fossil fuels related to greenhouse gas emissions, depletion of natural resources, and air quality impacts. There was also significant consumption of energy in producing the commonly utilized synthetic nitrogen fertilizers.

- Winery inputs included energy (cooling during the fermentation process, maintaining storage temperature, pumping, running equipment, etc.); water (barrels and vats needed to be constantly cleaned and rinsed, as did all other equipment, to ensure a minimum level of bacteria that might interfere with the controlled processes in the winery); chemicals (cleansers, diatomaceous earth, sulfur gas, refrigerants, etc.); and packaging materials (including glass, corks, wood pallets, glues, cardboard, metal, and plastic foil). Winery operational water issues related to the treatment of waste water containing organic matter, nitrates, and phosphorous. Chemical issues varied according to the chemical but could include spills and various air, soil, and water quality impacts. Packaging materials impacted natural resource stocks and posed landfill issues.

Wineries varied considerably in their efforts and effectiveness in dealing with their environmental impacts. A small percentage of wineries and growers had certified some or all of their vineyards as organic. To be organically certified, a winery could use no synthetic fertilizers or pesticides. A vineyard could be certified organic following a three-year transition period. In 2002, approximately 10,000 acres of wine grapes in California were certified organic, out of a total of 434,000 acres. In the early 1980s, Frey Winery became the first winery to produce organic wines. By 2000, Frey was selling 40,000 cases a year of organic wine. Fetzer Winery was also an early industry leader in attempting to mitigate its environmental impacts. It certified the vineyards it owned as organic in 1986 and since then had also engaged in a series of practices that reduced the environmental impacts of its winery operations and administration. These practices included energy efficiency initiatives (building an energy-efficient administration building with thick rammed-earth walls, installing photovoltaic panels to supplement electricity requirements, and building earthen berms around its warehouse to reduce energy requirements for cooling), winery wastewater treatment using reed-bed ponds and recycling the cleansed water for irrigation, elimination of chlorine use, establishment of a comprehensive companywide recycling program, and establishment of an in-house barrel restoration program.

Wine industry associations were playing an important role in moving the industry to become more environmentally sustainable. A number of regional associations had been supporting a pesticide reduction approach called integrated pest management (IPM). If pesticides were used, they were selectively applied on the basis of data from close monitoring of pest infestations. Preemptive applications of broad-spectrum pesticides throughout the vineyard were discouraged. IPM practitioners limited pesticide use to applications that were economically rational. In 1998, the industry created a national initiative called WineVision, whose agenda included a Sustainability Task Force. A WineVision goal was to be a wine industry leader internationally in sustainable practices. One task force was a joint effort by the California Association of Winegrape Growers (CAWG) and the Wine Institute to create a code of sustainable practices for the industry. The purposes of the code were to "establish voluntary high standards of sustainable practices to be followed and maintained by the entire wine community" and to "promote farming and winemaking practices that are sensitive to the environment, responsive to the needs and interests of society-at-large, and are economically feasible in practice."

WINERY ENVIRONMENTAL PRACTICES AND MARKETPLACE ADVANTAGE

There were many opportunities for wineries to attain marketplace recognition and advantage via their environmental practices. These advantages were typically secondary considerations for the U.S. wine consumer. A wine's quality, price point, and reputation were primary considerations, and thus the environmental attributes could play a role in consumers' choices among comparable offerings. Wineries could promote specific environmental aspects of their grape-growing practices, such as organic or biodynamic certification. Or they could publicize their water, energy, or other initiatives in their winery operations. These practices and initiatives could become a point of differentiation in the tasting-room selling process, in sales calls, and during wine-tasting events. The label on the wine bottle could extol environmental aspects or certifications. The winery's literature and Web site could promote the environmental dimension. Most important, wineries were always seeking good public relations (PR) through articles in industry magazines and other publications. New environmental initiatives could often generate free PR.

In 2001, wines made from organic grapes and labeled as such constituted 1 percent of the U.S. wine market, representing a retail value of $190 million. That segment of the industry was growing by 20 percent annually. In California, approximately one-third of the wineries farmed their own vineyards organically. They did so because they believed it enhanced the quality of their wine. However, only one in four of those wineries were certified organic—and only a few of those claimed credit for being certified on their label.

Wineries had two main reasons for not promoting their organic practices. First, the initial organic wines that came on the market in the 1980s were not considered comparable to traditional wines at similar price points, and the reputation of organic wines had suffered ever since. Part of the problem was that sulfur dioxide, a preservative in the winemaking process, was not added to the organic wines. Unless the wine was bottled according to certain procedures and maintained within a certain temperature range during distribution and subsequent storage, too low a sulfite level could result in a significant deterioration in quality. Second, there had been confusion in the U.S. market regarding the definition of organic wine. Until 2002, wines could not be called organic because there was no official, standard definition of the term. The U.S. Department of Agriculture had recently defined a standard for organic wine, but because this standard included a requirement that there be no added sulfites, most wines did not qualify. Wineries could label their wines as "made with organic grapes" so long as the grapes were certified organic and sulfite levels did not exceed 100 parts per million. Still, potential confusion among consumers, coupled with the poor reputation of organic wine's quality, meant that promoting wine grapes as organic could be detrimental in U.S. markets.

While organic certification did not seem to provide much in the way of competitive advantage in U.S. markets, export markets were a different matter. Wine consumers throughout the European Union sought organic foods in general and valued organic wines. The considerable success of Fetzer's Bonterra brand in the United Kingdom could be attributed in part to the organic grapes used in making the wine. Similarly, Japanese distributors importing wines made from certified organic grapes promoted that aspect in their highly environmentally sensitive country.

BFW did not explicitly advertise or label the biodynamic or environmental aspects of its wines. However, there was a small but growing number of distributors and retailers interested in BFW's environmental accomplishments, and Chris Benziger did not hesitate to use those selling points in his sales calls when the opportunity presented itself. According to Chris, one of BFW's primary distributors frequently emphasized the winery's biodynamic practices as a selling point, and Chris was seeing more wine consumers at tastings and auctions buying BFW wines because of the winery's environmental practices. BFW's brochures and Web site featured those practices, the winery's tasting-room personnel were trained to explain them, and winery tours highlighted them.

exhibit 2 **Elements of an Environmental Management System (EMS)**

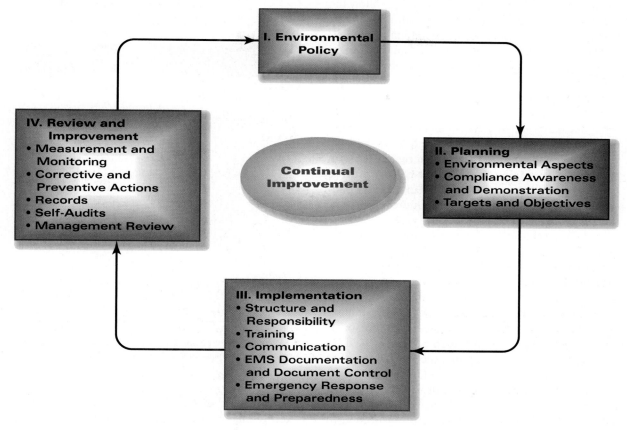

CALIFORNIA EPA'S EMS PILOT PROGRAM

The years following the formation of the U.S. Environmental Protection Agency in 1970 were characterized primarily by a command-and-control approach to regulating business organizations. The 1990s witnessed federal and state agencies experimenting with a range of more flexible options to reduce environmental risks, including market incentives and voluntary programs. In 1998, the California Environmental Protection Agency (Cal/EPA) established an Innovation Initiative and joined with the U.S. EPA, nongovernmental organizations (NGOs), business, academia, and other state EPAs as a member of the Multi-State Working Group (MSWG) to study the environmental benefits of environmental manage-

ment systems (EMSs) as a tool for enhancing environmental protection and achieving sustainable development. The MSWG participants and observers included all 50 states, several of which were actively engaged in approximately 50 EMS pilot projects. The EMS pilot project goal was to evaluate the potential of EMSs to achieve environmental results within and beyond the limitations of the existing regulatory system.

An EMS was a managerial process designed to help an organization meet environmental objectives and demonstrate improved environmental performance (see Exhibit 2). It entailed a continuous cycle of planning, implementing, reviewing, and improving. An EMS could be informal, with minimal documentation; this was a common approach in small companies. Or it could be formal and fully documented, an approach often taken by larger organizations that had many high-risk issues to manage. Many organizations had an EMS whose primary purpose was to allow the organization to stay in compliance with regulations. However, an EMS could be designed to take an organization well beyond compliance, allowing it to proactively minimize its significant environmental aspects. This type of proactive EMS was what the regulators and a wide range of other stakeholders were seeking. However, prior to the development of the ISO 14000 series standards, outside stakeholders could not assess the adequacy of an organization's EMS. ISO 14000 was an attempt to develop a widely accepted, uniform approach to certifying that a company's or facility's EMS was an organizationally integrated, beyond-compliance system to continually improve environmental performance.

The International Organization for Standardization (ISO) was widely recognized and accepted in the global business community. Facilities certified to ISO 9001 could assure their customers that their quality management systems met the standards and guidelines established by the ISO. While pursuing certification was voluntary, more and more businesses were requiring that their suppliers be ISO 9001 certified. Following the success of the ISO 9000 standards, ISO began to develop the ISO 14000 series of guidelines and standards to aid companies dealing with environmental issues. In order to be ISO 14001 certified, a company/facility needed to have an EMS that met ISO guidelines.

ISO 14001 was the basic EMS standard within ISO 14000 to which firms certified. Meeting ISO 14001 standards could be time-consuming and costly. The initial costs included both system development costs and ISO registration fees. If an external consultant was used, the cash outlay could easily exceed $100,000. If the system was developed internally, staff time requirements would be substantial, but costs would be reduced. Other costs would include ongoing system maintenance costs. These costs would come in the form of staff time devoted to overseeing the system, planning and monitoring it, entering data, training workers, and so on. Among the many potential benefits that could be realized from an ISO 14001–certified EMS system were (1) enhanced public image among external stakeholders, (2) systematization of existing environmental activities, (3) competitive advantage in markets where consumers were sensitive to environmental product attributes, (4) cost savings due to waste reduction

exhibit 3   **Top 15 Countries in Terms of Number of ISO 14001 Registrations**

Country	Number of ISO 14001 Certifications
Japan	2,124
Germany	1,400
United Kingdom	947
Sweden	645
Taiwan	506
United States	480
Korea	463
Netherlands	443
Switzerland	370
Denmark	350
Australia	300
France	285
Spain	234
Austria	200
Finland	191

Source: Reinhard Peglau, *Worldwide Statistics on EMAS-Registered Companies and ISO 14001 Certified Organizations* (Berlin: Federal Environmental Agency, June 1999).

and avoidance of environmental liabilities, (5) relaxed regulatory oversight, and (6) improved environmental performance.

The number of ISO-certified companies in the 15 countries with the most registrations is shown in Exhibit 3. By June 1999, there were 480 companies in the United States with ISO 14001 certifications, none of which were wineries. A number of wineries outside the United States had been certified. In 1998, a New Zealand winery was the first winery to be ISO 14001 certified. By 2001, Allied Domecq, with global wine holdings and among the 20 largest U.S. wineries, had been actively pursuing ISO 14001 certification for its production facilities. Its wine brands included Clos du Bois, Callaway Coastal, Atlas Peak, William Hill, and Buena Vista from California; Balbi and Graffigna from Argentina; Marques de Arienzo, Siglo, Campo Viejo, Tarsus, and Aura from Spain; and Montana from New Zealand. It had achieved ISO 14001 certification at 28 sites globally, representing more than 80 percent of its production volume, but had not yet certified a U.S. facility.

The Cal/EPA EMS winery pilot project involved two wineries in Sonoma County, Benziger Family Winery and Davis Bynum Winery. Cal/EPA selected Davis Bynum and BFW in June 2000 as pilot wineries after receiving stakeholder suggestions to include agriculture in the EMS project. Wineries were considered because of their importance in California's economy and their environmental impacts—especially in the areas of water quality and availability, pesticide use, habitat loss, and urban encroachment. Another consideration was the effort of the wine industry to become environmentally responsible. Both the grape-growing and winemaking operations were included in the pilot project.

The Cal/EPA project manager was Tom Lanphar, senior hazardous substances scientist for the Department of Toxic Substances Control. The pilot project with the Sonoma wineries had as its objectives to determine (1) whether and how the use of an EMS by a regulated entity increased public health and environmental protection over current requirements, and (2) whether and how the use of an EMS provided the public greater information on the nature and extent of public health and environmental effects than information provided by current regulatory requirements. Lanphar believed that BFW and Davis Bynum were the only smaller wineries actively developing EMSs that were consistent with ISO 14001 certifications.

DEVELOPMENT AND IMPLEMENTATION OF BENZIGER FAMILY WINERY'S EMS

Chris Benziger and Matt Atkinson had several motivations for participating in the pilot project and developing an EMS at BFW. Prior to the pilot program, their environmental initiatives were not part of a systematic planning process. Thus, they saw an EMS as a logical next step in organizing their existing environmental programs into a comprehensive system that would provide (1) better understanding of their environmental impacts, (2) systematic planning for meeting their environmental responsibilities, and (3) monitoring and follow-up. The potential for cost-saving initiatives and improvements in wine quality

further motivated them. And they hoped to use the EMS as an educational tool for their employees and suppliers. Finally, they viewed this as an opportunity for BFW to be among the first U.S. wineries to be ISO 14001 certified, enhancing their reputation as an environmental leader in the wine industry.

The technical assistance being provided by Cal/EPA through the EMS winery pilot project was substantial. The pilot project extended through December of 2001. During the one-and-a-half-year period of the project, there were meetings every two weeks that included Tom Lanphar from the EPA, Matt Atkinson from BFW, and representatives from Davis Bynum Winery. Also, Chris Benziger attended many of these meetings. The purpose of these meetings was to walk through the process of developing each winery's EMS. In addition, Cal/EPA and the U.S. EPA sponsored five all-day workshops that were open to the businesses in all of the EMS pilot projects. The first of these workshops was an overview of EMSs. Another was designed to assist in the development of an environmental policy statement consistent with ISO 14000. In addition to the workshops, Cal/EPA organized a series of stakeholder meetings that included the winery representatives, local industry associations, activists, and other wineries.

On the basis of its experiences in working with the two pilot wineries, Cal/EPA was developing a template in the form of a manual that any winery could use in developing an EMS. One part of this template was a Gap Analysis form, an EMS checklist consistent with ISO 14000 requirements (see Exhibit 4). Other sections of the template would include procedures and examples to assist wineries in completing the various steps listed in the Gap Analysis.

One of the first steps involved in developing an EMS was to write or update the organization's environmental policy. Prior to the pilot project, BFW did not have a formal environmental policy. Matt attended a Cal/EPA and U.S. EPA workshop that focused in large part on environmental policies. Following the workshop, he and Chris drafted an environmental policy. They shared the draft and received helpful feedback at a Cal/EPA-sponsored stakeholder meeting. The final environmental policy statement (Exhibit 5) was then shared with BFW employees at a staff meeting. BFW planned to post the statement on its Web site.

To assist with identifying significant environmental impacts, Cal/EPA developed (1) the Vineyard

exhibit 4   **EMS Gap Analysis for Benziger Family Winery, February 2003**

A Gap Analysis compares current methods for managing environmental responsibilities with the required elements of the ISO 14001 EMS standard. The purpose of a Gap Analysis is to help a firm understand the differences between its current system and the required elements of an ISO 14001 EMS. The following outlines the main elements of an EMS consistent with ISO 14001 and the current status of Benziger Family Winery's EMS.

	Yes	No
Environmental Policy		
Do you have an environmental policy?	X	
Benziger has developed an environmental policy that includes commitments to continual improvement, the prevention of pollution, and staying in compliance with relevant environmental regulations.		
Environmental Aspects	Yes	No
Have you conducted an analysis of the environmental impacts of your activities, products or services?	X	
Using the Aspects Register developed by Cal/EPA, environmental impacts had been prioritized according to a systematic procedure.		
Legal and Other Requirements	Yes	No
Do you have a procedure to identify legal and other environmental requirements that are applicable to your activities, products or services?		X
The ranch manager is responsible for identifying legal and other environmental requirements; no formal procedure is written. Ranch manager will write one. Estimated time to complete: 2 hours.		
Objectives and Targets	Yes	No
Do you have documented environmental objectives and targets?	X	
Objective and targets have been developed and documented based on significant environmental aspects and legal requirements.		
Environmental Management Programs: Action Plans	Yes	No
Have you established programs for achieving objectives and programs?	X	
Action plans (environmental management programs) have been written and identify responsibilities, resources needed, and time frame for implementation and completion.		
Structure and Responsibility	Yes	No
Has top management appointed specific management representative(s) to have the responsibility for ensuring that the environmental management system is established, implemented, and maintained?	X	
The ranch manager has been given the responsibility for ensuring the EMS is established, implemented and maintained. More specific responsibilities still must be defined.		

(continues)

exhibit 4 **(continued)**

Structure and Responsibility	Yes	No
Are other personnel roles and responsibilities defined, documented, and communicated in order to facilitate effective environmental management, and are adequate resources (human, technical, and financial) provided for implementation and control of the environmental management system? Responsibility matrix has been produced; however, specific names must still be defined. Ranch manager will complete. Estimated time: 4 hours.		X

Training, Awareness and Competence	Yes	No
Are all personnel whose work may create a significant environmental impact trained to minimize potential impacts? Training of personnel does occur on a regular basis to meet regulatory requirements; however, additional training needs based on EMS aspects and impacts are still being planned based on training matrix in the EMS. Ranch manager and department managers and supervisors are responsible. Estimated time: Planning and writing training programs: 8 hours. Training given on continual basis.		X

Communication	Yes	No
Do you have procedures for informing personnel about the elements of your EMS? Communication plan is still in development. Environmental Committee (department managers) will complete procedure. Estimated time: 6 hours.		X

EMS Documentation	Yes	No
Are the core elements of your EMS and their interaction documented in either paper or electronic form? An EMS binder has been created to maintain relevant documents; however, binder does not contain all necessary documents for a completed EMS. Ranch manager is responsible. Estimated time: 40 hours.		X

Document Control	Yes	No
Have you established document control procedures that ensure that documents are created and maintained in a proper and consistent manner? Procedure is in the process of being developed. Ranch manager is responsible. Estimated time: 1 hour.		X

Operational Control	Yes	No
Have you identified operations, activities, goods, and services that are associated with significant environmental aspects and impacts of your organization? Procedure for identifying significant environmental aspects and impacts link these with operations, activities, goods or services.	X	

(continues)

exhibit 4 **(continued)**

Operational Control	Yes	No
Do you have established documented procedures for operations and activities that cover situations which might result in adverse environmental impacts or deviations from your environmental policy or objectives and targets?		X
The need for developing standard operation procedures (SOPs) is included within objectives and targets. Some SOPs have been created. Three more SOPs need writing. Relevant department manager and ranch manager are responsible. Estimated time for completion: 24 hours per SOP for total of 72 hours.		

Emergency Preparedness and Response	Yes	No
Do procedures exist for identifying the potential for and response to accidents and emergency situations and for preventing and mitigation of the environmental impacts that may be associated with emergencies?	X	
Plan currently exists. An updated plan is in process of final approval. Company president, ranch manager, and executive secretary are responsible. Estimated time for completion: 4 hours.		

Monitoring and Measurement	Yes	No
Do documented procedures exist to regularly monitor and measure the key characteristics of operations having a significant impact on the environment? Do these procedures require the recording of information to track performance and conformance with objectives and targets?		X
Draft procedure exists. Ranch manager is responsible. Estimated time for completion: 2 hours.		

Nonconformance and Corrective and Preventative Action	Yes	No
Do you have procedures for defining responsibility and authority for handling nonconformances and for taking action to mitigate any impacts?		X
Draft procedure exists. Ranch manager is responsible. Estimated time for completion: 2 hours.		

Records	Yes	No
Do you have procedures for the identification, maintenance, and disposition of environmental records, including training and audit results?		X
Draft procedure exists. Ranch manager is responsible. Estimated time for completion: 2 hours.		

EMS Audit	Yes	No
Do you have a program and procedures for periodic EMS audits? Can the audits determine whether your EMS conforms to the ISO 14001 standard?		X
This topic is yet to be discussed by the environmental committee. Estimated time: unknown.		
Do you have procedures that establish the audit scope, frequency, methods, responsibilities, and requirements for conducting audits and reporting results?		X
Procedures will be written once the environmental committee makes decisions about audit protocols.		

(continues)

exhibit 4 **(concluded)**

Management Review	Yes	No
Does your top management regularly review the EMS to ensure its suitability, adequacy, and effectiveness? EMS estimated completion date is fall of 2003 and first management review is scheduled for winter of 2003.		X

exhibit 5 **Benziger Family Winery Environmental Policy**

Benziger Family Winery is committed to identifying and promoting the most environmentally safe and sustainable business and farming practices.

We believe that sound environmental policy will lead to an increase in product quality as well as the social well-being of our employees and community.

We will:

- Continually monitor and improve environmental performance through an EMS.
- Appoint an environmental committee to propose annual targets and objectives for management approval.
- Integrate environmental consideration across all business functions (vineyard, winemaking, purchasing, etc.).
- Comply fully with the letter and spirit of environmental laws and regulations.
- Seek to prevent pollution before it is produced and reduce the amount of waste at our facilities.
- Recycle whenever possible and use environmentally preferred materials.
- Communicate this policy throughout the company and provide appropriate training and educate employees to be environmentally responsible on the job and at home.
- Manage our natural resources in an environmentally sensitive manner and use energy efficiently throughout our operations.
- Continuously work to improve our adherence to these principals and report to our stakeholders.
- Make this policy available to our customers, our community members, and the general public.

Operations and Winery Operations Aspects Register, a comprehensive description of possible environmental impacts in a winery's vineyard and winemaking operations, and (2) a Procedure for Identifying and Evaluating Environmental Aspects and Impacts. The procedure had the winery first identify its environmental impacts using the Aspects Register, then it provided a method of assigning points to each impact according to whether the impact was regulated (0 = not regulated, 2 = regulated); the level of environmental harm the winery experienced in relation to that impact (0 = low, 1 = moderate, and 2 = high); and whether it was covered in the winery's environmental policy (0 = not covered, 2 = covered). One more point was added if there were other environmental concerns.

Using this procedure, Matt and Chris developed a list of BFW's significant environmental vineyard and winery impacts (see Exhibit 6). They circulated this list of BFW's significant aspects to other managers in the winery and asked for validation and input on what they might have missed. Managers from winery operations, sales and marketing, administration, and hospitality/wine tasting reviewed and approved the list without any additions or suggested changes. BFW's most significant impacts in the vineyard were stormwater containment, spillage/leakage, and fuel consumption. In the winery, the most significant impacts included fuel consumption, spillage/leakage, mercury-containing lights and ballast, and use of refrigerants. Stormwater was an issue because of the potential for erosion and the

exhibit 6   **Significant Vineyard Aspects of Benziger Family Winery (Scale: 1 = excellent; 10 = poor)**

Aspect	Score
Stormwater	7
Use of electricity	5
Removing water from aquifer	5
Use of plastic	2
Use of water	5
Waste plastic	2
Use of sulphur	4
Use of fences and barriers	2
Spillage or leakage (solvent, plastic, metal, construction materials)	7
Air emissions	4
Fuel consumption	7
Noise	2
Landfill disposal (wood, plastic, metal, construction materials)	2
Use of electricity	5
Noise	2
Fuel consumption	7
Use of propylene glycol	2
Use of refrigerants	6
Generation of CO_2	2
Air emissions	4
Use of wood	3
Use of diatomaceous earth	6
Use of sulphur	4
Use of glass	3
Use of corks	3
Use of glues	2
Use of paper	3
Use of cardboard	3
Use of metal and plastic foil	3
Use of plastic	3
Use of water	5
Waste electric equipment	2
Use of Styrofoam	3
Mercury-containing lights and ballasts	6
Use of paint	6

washing of sediment into local streams. Spillage and leakage were issues, especially in relation to diesel oil, glycol refrigerants, and cleaning agents. Fuel consumption was an issue not only because it generated pollution but also because BFW's environmen-tal policy specifically called for "managing our natural resources" and "using energy efficiently."

Following prioritization of significant environmental impacts, objectives and targets were developed at the end of 2001 (see Exhibit 7). Cal/EPA provided an Objectives and Targets Procedure along with technical assistance. In setting objectives, Cal/EPA suggested considering the winery's environmental policy; impacts; applicable legal requirements; stakeholder views; technological options; and financial, operational, and other business requirements. Targets were to be quantitative, realistic, measurable, and linked to environmental aspects. Matt and Chris felt that BFW already had an adequate approach to stormwater containment. They thought that their objectives should advance their progress in developing a full-fledged EMS. Thus, a number of formal objectives were developed in terms of completing standard operating procedures. In terms of energy efficiency, Mike Benziger wanted to see significant reduction in energy use and pushed for a 20 percent reduction in electrical consumption by the end of 2002.

ISSUES IN DEVELOPING BENZIGER FAMILY WINERY'S EMS

By the beginning of 2002, Cal/EPA's pilot program had officially ended, although Tom Lanphar continued to provide assistance on an informal basis. During 2002, progress was made on many of the objectives and targets listed in Exhibit 7. Water use was monitored in 2002, creating a baseline for future reduction targets. Proposals were being reviewed for a photovoltaic system that would partially reduce dependence on the electrical grid. Standard operating procedures for the safe handling and use of dietamaceous earth were developed. (Dietamaceous earth was used in the winemaking process and presented a respiratory risk to employees.)

In February of 2003, Tom and Matt met and filled out the Gap Analysis, indicating what had been accomplished and what steps would be required to complete the EMS. There were many steps remaining in the development of an EMS that was in conformance with ISO 14001 standards. These steps included training personnel, developing and implementing a plan to communicate and inform employees about the EMS, keeping records, developing

exhibit 7   **Objectives and Targets for Benziger Winery and Vineyard Operations**

Objective	Target	Status	Regulated Meets	Regulated Beyond	Non Regulated
1. Reduce electrical consumption by 20 percent	20 percent by 12/02	In process			X
2. Monitor water use to establish 2002 baseline, set performance target in 2003	By 12/02	In process			X
3. Minimize dependency on nonrenewable electrical energy sources by generating 5 percent of needs	Generate 5% of energy needs by 12/02	In process			X
4. Write standard operating procedure (SOP) for safe handling and disposal of hazardous materials	By 09/02	In process			X
5. Write SOP for safe handling and disposal of diatomaceous earth	By 12/02	In process			X
6. Develop Environmentally Preferred Purchasing policy and program for more efficient use of resources.	By 07/02	In process			X
7. Write SOP for refrigerant handling to prevent accidental discharge	By 12/02	In process			X

procedures and establishing measurement and monitoring capabilities. Approximately 150 hours would be required to complete development of the EMS. At least 100 hours of Matt's time would be required, and because other demands on his time were significant and hard to predict, completion of his EMS tasks could take six to nine months. However, the time required could be longer depending on the level of cooperation and support forthcoming from the managers and employees who needed to be involved in the development of the EMS.

Later in 2003, Tom Lanphar met with Matt Atkinson and Chris Benziger to discuss BFW's EMS. Chris stated, "Pursuit of ISO 14001 certification was the right thing to do . . . The winery was committed to its ultimate development." If BFW was able to complete the required steps on the Gap Analysis, Tom estimated that the cost to then become certified would be approximately $20,000. This would include pre-audit assistance from a consultant at $1,000 a day for five days and certification costs of $15,000.

However, Matt and Chris identified a number of challenges facing them. Externally, the wine industry was facing an unprecedented economic squeeze due to a glut of wine grapes and increasing interna-tional competition. This meant that time and money for system development would be extremely tight. Tim Wallace, BFW's president, was supportive of winery's environmental agenda but wanted any decision regarding investments in EMS development to make "good business sense." Second, there were internal impediments. Buy-in from all of the managers was not complete. It would not be easy to convince all of the managers that the payoff from an ISO 14000 system justified the investment in employee time that would be required to complete the EMS. The EMS was seen as "Matt's thing." As a result, it had been difficult for Chris and Matt to get managers to participate in developing and implementing the system. There was an Environmental Committee composed of just Chris and Matt, but they knew they had to broaden the committee's membership and engender organizational support if the EMS was ultimately to be successful. Third, the marketability and PR value of a winery's environmental pedigrees was intangible. While there was certainly a strong demand for organic wines and eco-labels in Europe, it was unclear as to when this would translate into mainstream demand in the U.S. domestic market.

Andy Decker and the Ethics of Downloading Music from the Internet

Janet Rovenpor
Manhattan College

The absolute transformation of everything that we ever thought about music will take place within 10 years, and nothing is going to be able to stop it. I see absolutely no point in pretending that it's not going to happen. I'm fully confident that copyright, for instance, will no longer exist in 10 years, and authorship and intellectual property is in for such a bashing. . . . Music itself is going to become like running water or electricity. —David Bowie[1]

Andy Decker, a college freshman, sat at his desk in his dormitory room. It was the middle of January and the semester had just begun. He was thinking of home. In a week, it would be his sister's 10th birthday. He did not have much time. He would have to come up with an idea for a gift soon. He switched on his computer and navigated to eBay. A new silver ladybug bracelet was up for auction with a starting price of $7.99. The auction was to end in seven days. Not enough time. Besides, he would have to get his mother to place a bid

and pay with her credit card. He thought for a moment. Why not put together a customized mix of his sister's favorite songs? He could download, burn, label, shrink-wrap, and UPS the gift within two hours at the most.

Andy connected to the latest version of Kazaa's file-sharing program. He searched for Jessica Simpson's song "Irresistible" and found 15 available MP3 files, 4 of which were of "excellent" integrity. He closed a number of annoying advertisements, including one inviting him to play Blackjack at www.casino.com. He was about to close an instant message box that had popped up on his screen when something caught his eye. The word *illegal* jumped out. He read the message carefully: "Distributing or downloading copyrighted music on the Internet without permission from the copyright owner is IL-LEGAL. When you break the law, you risk penalties. There is a simple way to avoid that risk: Don't steal music, either by offering it to others to copy or downloading it on a 'file-sharing' system like this." Andy noted that the message was sent by the Recording Industry Association of America (RIAA).

Time-out. Andy was not sure that he should proceed. He had never done anything illegal before. In his compact disc (CD) collection at home, he owned most of the albums with the eight song tracks he had planned to download. He purchased them at Tower Records with the money he had earned delivering newspapers. He merely wanted to download and burn the same songs onto a single CD, starting with

[1]As quoted in J. Pareles, "David Bowie, 21st-century Entrepreneur," *New York Times,* June 9, 2002. Retrieved August 27, 2003, from ABI/INFORM (Proquest) database.

his sister's most favorite song and ending with his sister's least favorite song. Besides, everyone downloaded music from the Internet.

Andy's roommate, Tom, called for lights out. Andy reluctantly logged off and shut down his computer. The issue of copyright infringement was still on his mind. He would decide in the morning what the best course of action might be.

ANDY'S OPTIONS

Over a glass of orange juice the next morning, Andy sat back and considered his options. First, he could purchase a CD online from Amazon.com (Jessica Simpson's album *Irresistible* sold for $12.99). He could get the CD gift-wrapped and attach a personal note. Andy was not, however, implementing his original idea, which was to send a customized mix of tunes compiled from several albums. Second, Andy could try to search for music that might appeal to his sister that had entered into the public domain. He realized that his quest, however, might not be too successful. From previous surfing experiences, Andy knew that while he could listen to Roger McGuinn, from the folk-rock band the Byrds, sing "Turn, Turn, Turn" or "Mr. Tambourine Man," he did not have permission to distribute, copy, or record any of the files. Most U. S. sound recordings would only begin to enter the public domain in the year 2043.[2]

Third, Andy could sign up for a legitimate subscription service such as Emusic, operated by Vivendi Universal, for $9.95 a month. He could legally download and copy songs that were listed on the site. Royalties were paid to the record label every time a recording was downloaded. But he was concerned that he might not be satisfied with the selection of music available from such services. Fourth, Andy could just follow the crowd and go forward with his original plan to make his own custom CD with music files downloaded from the Internet. Could his actions result in disciplinary action taken by his college or, even worse, in a lawsuit by the RIAA? Andy concluded that he needed more information. He would seek the advice of his resident hall assistant.

THE RESIDENT HALL ASSISTANT'S ADVICE

On the way to his first class, Andy caught up to Patrick, his resident hall assistant, who was a few feet ahead of him. Patrick advised him not to download songs from Kazaa. First, it was like stealing a book from a bookstore. Second, various types of computer worms and viruses were passed from user to user on file-sharing networks. Instead, Patrick recommended a new legitimate service just introduced by Apple Computer, called iTunes Music Store. The service offered songs from all five major music companies, paying them 65 cents on average for each track it sold. Members did not pay monthly subscription fees. They could listen to a 30-second preview of a song and download a high-quality copy for 99 cents. Each song was encrypted with a digital key so that it could be played on only three authorized computers. This prevented the song from being distributed on person-to-person (P2P) file-sharing networks.[3]

There was, however, one problem with what Patrick suggested. Always a problem! A Windows-based version of iTunes would not be available for another several months. Andy would have to search high and low for an Apple Macintosh computer on campus. Maybe those free-spirited students in the School of Arts would have one!

TECHNOLOGICAL PROGRESS AND MUSIC DOWNLOADING

Technology has always had an impact on how music is played and enjoyed. The invention of the printing press in 1450 gave birth to the sheet music publishing industry, which dominated mainstream music until World War II. A popular composition, like Charles Harris's "After the Ball," might have sold approximately 2 million copies in sheet music form and achieved sales of $5 million. With the arrival of Emile Berliner's gramophone in 1888, the possibility

[2]S. Fishman, *The Public Domain: How to Find Copyright-Free Writings, Music, Art & More* (Berkeley, CA: Nolo, 2000).

[3]D. Leonard, "Songs in the Key of Steve," *Fortune* 147, (no. 9) (May 12, 2003), pp. 52–62. Retrieved May 23, 2003, from ABI/INFORM (Proquest) database.

of making an unlimited number of audio copies of a song from a single master was entertained for the first time. Folk tunes that had been previously malleable, changing every time the performer sang them, became fixed and exactly repeatable. Musicians shortened their pieces because early recording equipment could capture music that lasted for only four and a half minutes. Radio broadcasting gave popular music an edge over classical music while advances in satellite transmission enabled fans to enjoy live concerts on their television sets.[4]

The subsequent convergence of several technologies contributed to the tremendous interest in the free distribution and reproduction of music. First, CD manufacturing improved the sound of recordings and created a durable and easy-to-use format. Second, computers originally used for mathematical calculations and database management became multimedia. Stereo sound systems and CD-burning software and hardware were added as accessories. Perfect copies of music could be produced and enjoyed. Recordings became fluid: The sequence of tunes could be rearranged, the lyrics could be substituted with other lyrics, and the sound could be fine-tuned to better suit the acoustics in one's living room.[5] Finally, the emergence of the Internet and its ubiquity provided opportunities for new applications, including P2P file-sharing software. (See Exhibit 1 for a time line tracing the file-sharing revolution.)

Such technological advances made the downloading of music from the Internet a popular leisure-time activity in 2003. It was common for students to get together in their dorm rooms and make copies of each other's downloaded music files. Lucila Crena, a freshman at Emory University, downloaded Christmas carols one night in early December and estimated that she had 1,200 songs on her hard drive.[6] Liz Whippy, a sophomore at Pitzer College, boasted that she had not purchased a new CD in at least four

years.[7] A survey by the Pew Internet and American Life Project found that 60 percent of college student Internet users had downloaded music files compared to 28 percent of the overall population.[8]

Part of the problem was that music piracy was not viewed as an ethical issue. A national survey conducted by Edison Media Research found that 74 percent of teenagers (12–17 years old) did not see anything wrong with downloading music for free.[9] Many students did not accept the analogy that downloading music was similar to stealing a CD from a store. The music was merely being copied; no one was deprived of his or her personal property. Teens expressed a number of reasons for why they felt that sharing music was appropriate. Some argued that they were only downloading a song that they already owned on CD or a song from an expensive album that they would not have purchased anyway. Others said that they were just sampling tunes to see if they would want to purchase the entire album later. Why take a chance on a newly released album when it cost between $13 and $17?

Students maintained that they ended up buying more music when they could sample it first. Still other students felt that they were entitled to the free downloads to compensate for the many years during which they paid high prices for CDs. Recording companies were seen as being greedy, charging $20 per CD when the costs of duplication were minimal. Moreover, only a small percentage of the retail price of a CD went to the artist.

Despite these rationalizations, courts of law said that individuals who digitally transferred files of copyright-protected songs and stored them on the hard drives of their computers were breaking the law. Here were some pertinent facts:

1. Napster, the first service to enable the exchange of music online, was shut down in 2001. The

[4]R. Garofalo, "From Music Publishing to MP3: Music and Industry in the Twentieth Century," *American Music* 17, (no. 3) (1999), pp. 318–353. Retrieved May 31, 2003, from ABI/INFORM (Proquest) database; and K. Kelly, "Where Music Will Be Coming From," *New York Times Magazine,* March 17, 2002, pp. 29–31.

[5]Ibid.

[6]P. Kloer, "Questions of Law and Morality Sharpen as Tens of Millions Continue to Download Music," *Atlanta Journal-Constitution,* December 22, 2002, p. LS1. Retrieved May 20, 2003, from ABI/INFORM (Proquest) database.

[7]R. Trounson, "Pirated Files Clog College Networks," *Los Angeles Times,* December 2, 2002. Retrieved August 27, 2003, from www.chicagotribune.com/technology/local/chi-021202college,0,3286066.

[8]S. Jones, "The Internet Goes to College: How Students Are Living in the Future with Today's Technology," Pew Internet and American Life Project, September 15, 2002. Retrieved May 31, 2003 from www.pewinternet.org/reports/pdfs/PIP_College_Report.pdf.

[9]Edison Media Research, "The National Record Buyers Study II," June 10, 2002. Retrieved May 27, 2003, from www.edisonresearch.com/recordbuyersiipress.htm.

exhibit 1   **P2P File-Sharing Services Challenge the Music Industry: A Chronology of Events**

May 1999	Napster, a P2P file-sharing service allowing users to exchange music for free, was founded by Shawn Fanning and Sean Parker.
December 1999	The Recording Industry Association of America (RIAA) filed a lawsuit against Napster on behalf of five major U.S. recording companies. Napster was accused of copyright infringement and encouraging the illegal copying and distribution of music.
April 2000	Swedish programmer Nikas Zennstrom and his partner, Janus Friis, established Kazaa. The Amsterdam-based company planned to market its proprietary P2P file-sharing technology.
February 2001	The Ninth U.S. Circuit Court of Appeals ruled that Napster was fully aware that users illegally traded music. Napster's offer of $1 billion to the RIAA for the rights to its corporate members' music was rejected.
March 2001	Napster began the process of blocking copyrighted music from its site.
April 2001	StreamCast Networks, founded by Steven Griffin and Darrel Smith, released its P2P file-sharing software called Morpheus. Grokster, another P2P file-sharing service, run by Wayne Rosso, also opened for business.
July 2001	A judge ordered Napster offline until it could prove to be entirely free of illegal music.
October 2001	A group of recording and movie picture companies filed a lawsuit against Kazaa, Morpheus, and Grokster for contributing to copyright infringement and financially benefiting from it.
End of 2001	Recording companies reported a 5% decline in worldwide sales of CDs.
January 2002	Sharman Networks Ltd., an Australian firm, purchased the assets of Kazaa BV from its original owners.
January 2002	U.S. District Court judge John Bates ordered the online division of Verizon Communications to give the RIAA the name of a Verizon customer who downloaded 600 songs a day using Kazaa. Verizon appealed.
April 2002	A federal judge ordered Verizon Internet Services to reveal the names of two subscribers accused of music piracy.
June 2002	Napster filed for Chapter 11 bankruptcy.
June 2002	Audiogalaxy, a P2P file-sharing service, reached a financial settlement with the RIAA and the National Music Publishers Association (NMPA). It also agreed to operate a "filter-in" system requiring artists to consent to have their work swapped online. The service would then pay a fee to the music publishers and the recording companies.
September 2002	A coalition of music professionals called Music United for Strong Internet Copyright (MUSIC), launched an advertising campaign asking consumers to "just say no" to piracy. Among the artists who spoke out were Britney Spears, Luciano Pavarotti, and Sean Combs.
October 2002	The RIAA sent letters to Fortune 1,000 companies regarding the legal liabilities they could face if employees illegally traded music on corporate computer networks. Similar letters were also sent to 2,300 college and university presidents.
November 2002	The U.S. Naval Academy seized 100 computers from students suspected of downloading unauthorized copies of songs from the Internet.
December 2002	A federal judge issued a temporary restraining order against P2P file-sharing service Aimster (now known as Madster) founded by Johnny Deep. The service was forced to immediately shut down all its computers and terminate its Internet connections.
End of 2002	Recording companies experienced an 11% decline in worldwide sales of CDs. Approximately 1.7 billion blank CDs were sold in 2002, up 40% from 2001.
April 2003	U.S. District Court judge Stephen Wilson in Los Angeles ruled that the P2P file-sharing services operating Grokster and Morpheus were not breaking copyright laws by making their software available. Unlike Napster, these services did not run a centralized file-sharing network. If the services were to be shut down, users could still continue to share files. The Kazaa case was still pending.
April 2003	Apple Computer Incorporated launched its iTunes Music Store, which sold legal copies of songs for 99 cents and entire albums for $9.99.

(continues)

exhibit 1 **(concluded)**

May 2003	Four college students at Princeton University, Rensselaer Polytechnic Institute, and Michigan Technological University agreed to pay as much as $17,500 each to settle lawsuits filed by the music industry for operating file-sharing services on college computer networks. The services enabled students to illegally exchange copyright-protected music.
June 2003	Earthstation 5, a P2P-based technology company headquartered in the Gaza Strip, launched its file-sharing software. It promised users anonymity by breaking up the music files into tiny parts, which were transmitted and reassembled when they reached a user's computer. EDonkey2000 made similar claims.
July 2003	A federal appeals court in Chicago upheld an injunction that forced Aimster to shut down.
July 2003	The RIAA filed more than 900 subpoenas with Internet service providers and university administrators requesting the names and addresses of individuals sharing music files. It promised to file lawsuits against these individuals by the end of August.
July 2003	Several P2P file-sharing services announced upgrades to their software that would make it more difficult to uncover the identities of its users.
September 2003	Vivendi Universal SA's Universal Music Group lowered the suggested retail price to $12.98 and the wholesale price to $9.09 for most CDs.
September 2003	The RIAA filed copyright infringement lawsuits against 261 individual file sharers. It offered an amnesty program to individuals not under investigation for copyright infringement. If they signed an affidavit promising to delete illegal copies of songs from their computer and never to trade copyrighted works again, they would not be sued.

Court of Appeals for the Ninth Circuit held that "the individuals who posted the file names on the Napster system violated the copyright holders' right of distribution and that the individuals who downloaded the files violated the copyright holders' right of reproduction."[10]

2. The doctrine of "fair use" recognized that in some limited cases it might be acceptable to violate the exclusive rights of copyright holders. The use of parts of copyrighted works was allowed for news reporting, scholarship, teaching, and critique. Courts considered four factors to determine fair use: the purpose and character of the use, the nature of the copyrighted work, the amount and substantiality of the portion used in relation to the work as a whole, and the effect of the use on the potential for or value of the work.

The Ninth Circuit found that the uploading and downloading of music was not consistent with the doctrine of fair use because the music files that were being copied remained the same; they did not assume a new purpose or a different character and because the files contained creative (rather than factual or historical) works.

Use of the copyrighted songs was deemed commercial because Napster users got something for free that they would ordinarily have been required to purchase. Entire songs were copied, not just parts of songs.[11]

3. MP3.com purchased thousands of CDs and copied them to its servers without the permission of the copyright holders. Its service allowed users to listen to music from any computer connected to the Internet as long as they could prove that they owned the original CDs. Users had to insert the CDs one by one into their computer's CD-ROM drive for initial verification. MP3.com was nevertheless found liable for copyright infringement.[12]

4. A U.S. District Court judge ordered Verizon Internet Services to provide the names and addresses of two subscribers; one was accused of downloading 600 songs from Kazaa; the second was accused of downloading 800 songs from Kazaa.[13]

---

[11]Ibid., pp. 154–55.

[12]Ibid.

[13]D. C. Chmielewski, "Verizon Ordered to Identify Two Customers Accused of Internet Piracy," *Knight Ridder Tribune Business News,* April 25, 2003. Retrieved May 23, 2003, from ABI/INFORM (Proquest) database.

[10]As cited in M. Landau, "Digital Downloads, Access Codes, and US Copyright Law," *International Review of Law, Computers and Technology* 16, no. 2 (2002), p. 153.

5. The U.S. Naval Academy seized 100 computers from students suspected of downloading unauthorized copies of music files from the Internet. The students had violated federal copyright laws as well as the academy's own code of ethics. They faced loss of leave time, court-martial, or expulsion.[14]

6. Four college students agreed to pay fines ranging from $12,000 to $17,500 each to settle lawsuits filed by the RIAA. The students had set up search engines on campus computer networks so that term papers, photographs, and MP3 music files residing on students' computers could be shared.[15]

7. Nielsen SoundScan reported that CD sales fell by 11 percent in 2002. At the same time, the Consumer Electronics Association predicted that sales of blank CDs would rise by more that 40 percent in 2002.[16]

8. In a study done for her economics thesis, a Princeton University student found that 46 percent of the students surveyed said that they would be willing to pay for a legal online music service while 27 percent said they would not.[17]

Students were not the only stakeholders involved in the heated debate on the ethics of downloading copyright protected music. College administrators found that the frequent downloading of songs, movies, and games overloaded campus computer networks, making it harder for professors to use the Internet for research and teaching. Recording artists, some of whom struggled to make a decent living, were cheated out of royalties they deserved. P2P file-sharing businesses claimed that they were not responsible for the illegal conduct of their members and reminded the public that there were legitimate uses of their services. Recording companies saw revenues from CDs decline sharply. Vivendi's Universal Music Group dropped its wholesale price for

CDs from $12.02 to $9.09. In the first signs of industry consolidation, the EMI Group lined up financing in a bid to acquire Time Warner's music division while Bertelsmann AG and Sony Corporation agreed in principle to combine their music operations.

ROLES AND RESPONSIBILITIES OF COLLEGE ADMINISTRATORS

College administrators were reluctantly drawn into the controversy surrounding the downloading of music by students. They performed a delicate balancing act: They valued students' right to privacy but felt obliged to comply with the Digital Millennium Copyright Act (DMCA). In October 2002, the RIAA and its partners sent 2,300 letters to college presidents directing them to treat online piracy as they would the theft of a textbook (see Exhibit 2). In February 2003, the RIAA intensified its efforts by sending "notice and take-down orders" calling on schools (and businesses) to remove infringing material from their computer networks.

By July 2003, the RIAA issued over 900 subpoenas to Internet service providers (including Verizon and Comcast) and colleges (including Boston College and the Massachusetts Institute of Technology) in an effort to gather the names and addresses of individuals suspected of illegally downloading music. The DMCA gave colleges immunity from prosecution if they revealed the names of students who had violated copyright laws. Yet many administrators did not want to give out information about students to outsiders because of the potential for abuse. They did not like the idea of spying on students or monitoring how they used their computers.

Some administrators were upset that although their colleges had cooperated with the RIAA in good faith, the RIAA had started suing students for copyright infringement anyway. Tracy Mitrano, director of a computer policy and law program at Cornell University, believed that colleges had done a lot to comply with the DMCA and that at the very least the RIAA could have paid a courtesy call or provided advance information to colleges whose students were

[14]A. Harmon, "100 Computers of U.S. Midshipmen Seized," *New York Times,* November 26, 2002. Retrieved November 26, 2002, from www.nytimes.com/2002/11/26/technology/26MUSI.html?todaysheadlines=&page.

[15]J. Graham, "Colleges Aggressively Cracking Down on Downloads of Music," *USA Today,* April 28, 2003, p. D1. Retrieved May 19, 2003, from ABI/INFORM (Proquest) database.

[16]Kloer, "Questions of Law."

[17]Graham, "Colleges Aggressively Cracking Down."

exhibit 2   **Letter Sent by Recording Industry Association of America to 2,300 University Presidents, October 2002**

October 3, 2002

[UNIVERSITY]
[TITLE FIRST LAST NAME]
[ADDRESS]
[CITY], [ST] [ZIP]

Dear [University/College President]:

We are writing to you as representatives of America's creative community on an urgent matter regarding copyright infringement by some university students.

We are concerned that an increasing and significant number of students are using university networks to engage in online piracy of copyrighted creative works. The educational purpose for which these networks were built is demeaned by such illegal behavior and is inconsistent with the ethical principles underlying the university community. We believe there must be a substantial effort, both disciplined and continuous, to bring this piracy under control. Because this issue pertains to various interests within a university community, we ask that you forward copies of this letter to your General Counsel/Chief Legal Officer, as well as your Director of Information Technology/Information Systems, your Chief Financial Officer, and your Dean of Student Affairs.

In the past few years, Peer to Peer (P2P) network use has dramatically grown. P2P technology is not only exciting — it may fundamentally change the way digital works are legitimately distributed. However, student trafficking in music, movies, software, video games and other copyrighted material without authorization on P2P networks not only raises issues of copyright infringement, it is an invitation to invasions of student privacy, viruses and numerous potential security threats to the university's network. A number of forward-looking educational institutions have led the way and have adopted informational and corrective policies aimed at preventing such infringing activity. We applaud these initiatives and would like to support this movement by working with colleges and universities to help establish Codes of Conduct and other procedures to stop theft of creative content.

Copyright Infringement is Theft

The students and other users of your school's network who upload and download infringing copyrighted works without permission of the owners are violating Federal copyright law. "Theft" is a harsh word, but that it is, pure and simple. As Deputy Assistant Attorney General John Malcolm recently stated, "Stealing is stealing is stealing, whether it's done with sleight of hand by sticking something in a pocket or it's done with the click of a mouse." It is no different from walking into the campus bookstore and in a clandestine manner walking out with a textbook without paying for it.

(continues)

exhibit 2 **(continued)**

Sheldon E. Steinbach, General Counsel of the American Council on Education, said of such illegal file "sharing" activities:

> "Why is this issue important to higher education institutions? First, educational institutions are in the business of forming students' minds. A fundamental part of this formation is teaching about ethics, personal responsibility, and respect for the rule of law. Colleges and universities should not be in the business of condoning or promoting unlawful activities."

Additional education about the law with regard to uploading and downloading movies, music, software, games, etc., is essential. Students must know that if they pirate copyrighted works they are subject to legal liability. A number of colleges and universities have already taken positive steps by putting in place codes of online conduct. They include such schools as the University of North Carolina, Drake University, and the University of Michigan.

Increasing Bandwidth Use Associated with P2P

Not only is piracy of copyrighted works illegal, it can take up a significant percentage of a university's costly bandwidth. A recent article in the *Chronicle of Higher Education* reported that one university discovered P2P uploading accounted for 75% of its entire bandwidth. In that case, 75% of that university's bandwidth was being used primarily by individuals outside of the university. When students run P2P applications and offer files for upload, much of the bandwidth drain is likely to be users outside of the university downloading files from students. One student offering a dozen infringing files on P2P may be serving those files up to hundreds, if not thousands, of users around the world. The non-university users downloading these illegal files take bandwidth away from students and members of the university community intending to use the network for educational purposes.

Many universities use bandwidth management tools to reduce bandwidth demands from illegal and improper use of the university networks. These tools can be used to take such steps as monitoring for inappropriate use, metering the bandwidth available to each student, setting caps on upload speeds, and blocking access to infringing P2P services. The Sergeant at Arms of the United States Senate has recently announced it would block the Senate's network users from accessing P2P networks. Other government, corporate, and educational institutions have put in place measures to prevent illegal use of P2P services. There are a number of companies that offer these bandwidth management tools, and we have attached a list of some of those companies for your information. Of course, P2P technology is exciting and holds great promise as a means of legitimately distributing works — it is the misuse of this technology by entities such as KaZaa, Grokster and Morpheus that causes problems for digital networks.

Security and Privacy Risks from P2P

P2P also poses serious network security and student privacy risks. For example, it has been widely reported that KaZaa, one of the most popular P2P applications, has software imbedded that allows a third party company to take over a portion of the user's computer and bandwidth. P2P software is also susceptible to worms and viruses

(continues)

exhibit 2 **(continued)**

specifically designed to exploit P2P applications. Many P2P users are not fully aware that their most personal documents may be available for millions of users to download.

★ ★ ★ ★ ★ ★ ★ ★ ★ ★ ★ ★

This is a serious challenge that calls for immediate, concrete action. As a president of an educational institution and a leader in the university community, we ask for your leadership in addressing student piracy on your network. Specifically, we urge you to adopt and implement policies that:

- Inform students of their moral and legal responsibilities to respect the rights of copyright owners
- Specify what practices are, and are not, acceptable on your school's network
- Monitor compliance
- Impose effective remedies against violators

We have attached a list of Internet links to selected university Codes of Conduct to demonstrate some of the positive steps already being taken in the university community to address the issues implicated by misuse of university networks. The Internet poses challenges to all institutions with digital networks, and we believe that these colleges and universities have done a commendable job in responding to these emerging challenges.

We appreciate your taking careful account of these serious matters and hope that you will take the time to share with us your comments and observations. We stand ready to be of assistance in any way you might find helpful and look forward to working with you on this project of mutual interest.

Hilary Rosen
Chairman and CEO,
Recording Industry Association of America

Jack Valenti
President and CEO,
Motion Picture Association of America

Edward P. Murphy
President and CEO,
National Music Publishers' Association

Rick Carnes
President,
The Songwriters Guild of America

(continues)

exhibit 2 **(concluded)**

ATTACHMENT

Selected University Acceptable Use Policies

Drake University
http://www.drake.edu/it/cio/AcceptableUse.html
http://www.drake.edu/it/cio/Copyright.html

The University of North Carolina at Chapel Hill
http://www.unc.edu/policy/copyinfringe.html
http://www.unc.edu/policy/copyright_primer.html

University of Michigan
http://www.umich.edu/~policies/responsible-use.html
http://www.umich.edu/~policies/digital-media.html

Companies That Offer Bandwidth Management

Allot Communications
http://www.allot.com/

NetReality
http://www.net-reality.com/

Packeteer, Inc.
http://www.packeteer.com/

Palisade Systems, Inc.
http://www.palisadesys.com

You may contact signatories of this letter at:

RIAA	**MPAA**	**NMPA**	**SGA**
1330 Connecticut Ave, NW	1600 Eye Street, NW	475 Park Avenue South	1500 Harbor Blvd.
Suite 300	Washington, DC 20006	29th Floor	Weehawken, NJ 07086
Washington, DC 20036	www.mpaa.org	New York, NY 10016	www.songwriters.org
www.riaa.org		www.nmpa.org	

Source: http://acenet.edu/washington/letters/2002/10October/universityletter.pdf.

sued.[18] There was also concern that higher education budgets, which were already tight, would go toward monitoring student Internet usage instead of toward technology upgrades. An atmosphere of suspicion and mistrust might be created on campus.

Administrators tried to play an appropriate role. To encourage students to stop downloading music, some held information sessions during freshman orientation. Others gave warnings to students and temporarily took away Internet access from repeat violators (the penalty at Harvard University was one year). Still others, like the University of Wyoming, hired computer consultants who monitored data flows across the network and generated a report of which songs, movies, and software were being downloaded illegally. Access to P2P file-sharing services could be blocked altogether. The drawback to this solution was that there were legitimate uses of materials available on file-sharing networks (e.g., for research and teaching). Creativity and experimentation might be suppressed. Furthermore, anytime a technological solution was implemented, ways could be found to get around it. P2P services reportedly found ways to disguise transferred files to look like normal hypertext Internet traffic. Absolute blockage might not be technologically practicable without also blocking "good traffic."

THE POSITION OF RECORDING ARTISTS

Several well-known singers, songwriters, and musicians got together and formed a group called Music United for Strong Internet Copyright (MUSIC). The group received funding from the RIAA. In a series of advertisements in the media and in personal pleas on their Web site (www.musicunited.org), artists asked fans not to download copyrighted music. The songwriter Troy Verges for example, posted the following message: "Go to your job every day next week and work. When payday rolls around, tell your boss you only want half of your check. That's what illegal downloading does to artists, musicians, songwriters, and everyone that supports them. It's wrong." Singer Stephan Jenkins said, "Burning CDs

is like an arranged marriage and the artists are the shot-gun brides. When nobody asks your permission, things tend to go bad." Madonna apparently allowed her voice to be used in a fake music file that appeared to be a song from her new album, *American Life,* and the file was circulated on file-sharing networks. Instead of hearing the song, users who downloaded the file heard Madonna asking them what they thought they were doing.

STRATEGIES OF P2P FILE-SHARING NETWORKS

The most popular P2P file-sharing services were Kazaa, Grokster, and Morpheus. Together, the three services had 70 million active users, compared to Napster's peak of 20 million users.[19] Members exchanged music, photographs, film clips, software, and text files. Not all of the transferable files contained copyrighted materials. Some files might have included original artwork, stories, or music created by members. Policy statements and end-user license agreements available on network sites warned individuals not to use the software to transmit, access, or communicate data that infringed on patents, trademarks, or copyrights. The networks made money primarily by selling advertising space on their sites.

Users first downloaded software from the music service's Web site. To find a song, users clicked on a search button and typed in the name of the song or the artist. In contrast to Napster, the new generation of file-sharing services did not use a centralized computer database to keep track of the user files that were available for download at a given time. They used new programming protocols like Gnutella, which enabled users to search the music libraries residing on the personal computers of other users who were logged on to the network. A user's computer sent out a search request to the computers within the network to which it was connected. If a match was found, the file could be directly transferred from that computer to the user's computer.[20] Sometimes, com-

---

[18]S. Carlson, "Recording Industry Sues 4 Students for Allegedly Trading Songs within College Networks," *Chronicle of Higher Education,* April 18, 2002, p. 41. Retrieved May 21, 2003, from LexisNexis Academic database.

[19]M. Warner, "The New Napsters," *Fortune* 146, no. 3 (August 1, 2002), pp. 115–16. Retrieved May 23, 2003, from ABI/INFORM (Proquest) database.

[20]J. Fry, "Selling Strategies—Music: The Music Man—What Comes After Napster? Vincent Falco May Have the Answer," *The Wall Street Journal,* September 16, 2002, p. A1. Retrieved October 27, 2002, from ABI/INFORM (Proquest) database.

puter viruses were passed from user to user. The worst virus transmitted through the Kazaa network, called Fizzer, appeared on May 8, 2003.[21]

Kazaa, Morpheus, and Grokster did not distribute music; they merely provided the software that enabled the exchange of files among members. A federal court judge ruled that the users, and not the networks offering the software, were responsible for copyright infringement. The RIAA appealed the decision. Meanwhile, the networks were able to stay in business and were able to attract additional investors and advertisers now that the viability of their businesses models was more certain.[22]

While P2P file-sharing services provided some useful and legal services for their subscribers, other less socially redeeming features were prevalent. The content of the files being exchanged as well as the advertising strategies used by the networks could have a negative impact on their primary users—teenagers. According to an Ipsos-Reid survey, 19 percent of Americans 12 years and older said that they had downloaded an audio file from a file-sharing network; more than half of people between 12 and 17 years old said they had done so.[23] Yet it was possible that young people were being exposed to age-inappropriate materials. In particular, parents may not have wanted their teenagers to download files with pornographic images or receive advertisements inviting them to visit online gambling sites.

A study by the U.S. General Accounting Office (GAO) found that 56 percent of the files on Kazaa included some form of pornography while 8 percent depicted child pornography. Its researchers looked for titles containing the names Britney, Olsen Twins and Pokemon. Screening software that blocks pornography from regular Web sites did not work on file-sharing programs.[24]

In a survey of 100 popular Web sites, the U.S. Federal Trade Commission found that minors had easy access to online gambling sites and were exposed to ads for online gambling on nongambling sites. Many sites had inadequate or hard-to-find warnings about underage gambling restrictions and had no effective mechanism to block minors from entering.[25] On P2P services, young people also gained access to games like Run Over the Jogger and Get a Prize (the prize being a free laser pointer).

Other controversial activities involved the use of software to track user movements on the Internet so that file-sharing networks could send users targeted advertisements, diverting sales commissions from rightful online vendors. Users often unknowingly installed "adware" or "spyware" on their computers when saying yes to licensing agreements. Kazaa came with the Cydoor advertising program, and Grokster was bundled with Gator eWallet. Kazaa had a partnership with Brilliant Digital Entertainment, which enabled it to use student computers and university bandwidth for commercial purposes (e.g., to send out Internet advertisements or to sell computer storage space).[26]

Another problem was the diversion of sales commissions. Users installing Morpheus's file-sharing software, for example, were asked whether or not they wanted to support the service by shopping through an online affiliate program. Users who agreed had their computers electronically marked. If the user decided to shop online for, say, a book, and got referred to Amazon.com from, say, Alloy.com, then Morpheus's software intercepted the transaction and substituted its affiliate number for the number of Alloy.com's site. Amazon.com sent a referral payment to the music service instead of to Alloy.com. Morpheus claimed that such diversions were unintentional, and it fixed the problem. Other services did not apologize.[27]

[21]R. Richmond, "New Computer Virus Circles Globe," *The Wall Street Journal,* May 13, 2003, p. D3. Retrieved May 23, 2003, from ABI/INFORM (Proquest) database.

[22]A. W. Mathews and N. Wingfield, "Entertainment Industry Loses File-Sharing Case—Two Companies Are Cleared to Distribute Software Used to Copy Music and Movies," *The Wall Street Journal,* April 28, 2003, p. A1. Retrieved May 23, 2003, from ABI/INFORM (Proquest) database.

[23]Ibid.

[24]B. Holland, "Government Studies Say P2P Sites Are Porn Havens," *Billboard* 115, no. 14 (April 5, 2003), p. 4. Retrieved May 23, 2003, from ABI/INFORM (Proquest) database.

[25]S. Tartar, "U.S. Marketers Continue Targeting Youths," *Knight Ridder Tribune Business News,* July 16, 2002, p. 1. Retrieved May 24, 2003, from ABI/INFORM (Proquest) database.

[26]S. Carlson, "KaZaA's Sneaky Software Worries Colleges," *Chronicle of Higher Education,* April 26, 2002. Retrieved May 24, 2003, from ABI/INFORM (Proquest) database.

[27]J. Schwartz and B. Tedeschi, "New Software Quietly Diverts Sales Commissions," *New York Times,* September 27, 2002, pp. C1, C4.

THE INTERESTS OF THE RIAA

The RIAA, a trade association, represented the interests of the U.S. recording industry. Among its members were the five largest recording companies: Vivendi's Universal Music Group, AOL Time Warner's Warner Music Group, Sony Music Entertainment, Bertelsmann's BMG unit, and EMI Group. RIAA members created, manufactured, and/or distributed approximately 90 percent of all legitimate sound recordings in the United States (www.riaa.com/About-Who.cfm).

Attributing the decline of CD sales in 2001 and 2002 to digital technologies that enabled consumers to download music and burn it onto blank CDs, the RIAA attacked music piracy on a number of different fronts. It sued P2P file-sharing services such as Napster, Kazaa, and Morpheus in an effort to get the courts to shut them down. It sued college students who set up file-sharing services on campus computer networks. It sent out letters to universities and large companies threatening them with legal action if they harbored copyrighted work on their networks. The RIAA's response was reactive and alienated the public to some degree.

Not everyone agreed that the decline in CD sales could be attributed solely to music piracy.[28] Four other factors were also likely causes. First, the economic slowdown made consumers more careful regarding how they spent money. Second, sales soared in the last decade because music lovers were replacing audiocassettes and LP records with higher-quality CDs, but by 2003 that conversion process had been completed. Third, other forms of entertainment—DVDs, movies, and computer games—competed for consumer attention. Fourth, fewer new titles were being released and lower numbers of talented artists were being discovered.

Public perceptions of the RIAA and its members were not favorable. Relationships between the recording companies and their artists had never been good. Recording artists complained that chronic ac-counting errors made by music companies prevented them from getting their due share of royalty payments. Don Engel, a lawyer, complained that industry accounting practices were "intentionally fraudulent" and resulted in underpayments of royalties by 10 to 40 percent.[29] Artists also lobbied for shorter contracts and better health care and pension benefits.

Relationships between recording companies, retailers, and consumers did not fare well either. During the mid-1990s, recording companies threatened retailers such as Best Buy and Wal-Mart with the withholding of funds for promotional use if they advertised CDs below certain minimum prices. The Federal Trade Commission concluded that, as a result of this practice, consumers overpaid for music by as much as $480 million.[30] To settle a class-action lawsuit, consumers who purchased music between January 1, 1995, and December 22, 2000, were eligible for awards of up to $20 per person from a fund of $67.4 million established by music companies and retailers.

Concern was raised over the tactics employed by the RIAA to deter people from swapping music on the free P2P networks. The association had hired software developers to post files that consisted of static, silence, and loops of a song's chorus ("file spoofing") and to insert instructions in a file that triggered a Web browser to take the user to a commercial music site ("redirection"). It had also developed software to overload a computer that shared pirated files with a flood of download requests ("interdiction"), send viruses, disable a computer for a certain amount of time, and search a hard drive with the intent of deleting music files.[31]

In addition, the RIAA began aggressively filing lawsuits against file sharers from all walks of life. The RIAA's message, as it appeared in July 2003 in

[28]J. Black, "Big Music's Broken Record," *Business Week Online,* February 13, 2003. Retrieved May 21, 2003 from www.businessweek.com:/print/technology/content/feb2003/tc20030213_9095_tc078. See also D. Hinckley, "Music Business' Blues Have Many Roots," *Daily News,* March 12, 2002. Retrieved May 28, 2003, from ABI/INFORM (Proquest) database.

[29]E. Gundersen, "Rights Issue Rocks the Music World: Artists Take on Record Goliaths over Royalties, Health Insurance, Payola," *USA Today,* September 16, 2002, p. D1. Retrieved May 22, 2003, from EBSCO Host database.

[30]J. Ordonez, "The Record Industry Owes You $20—For Music Buyers, a Deadline Is Approaching to File Claims in a Big CD Price-Fixing Case," *The Wall Street Journal,* February 5, 2003. Retrieved May 20 2003, from ABI/INFORM (Proquest) database.

[31]A. R. Sorkin, "Software Bullet Is Sought to Kill Musical Piracy," *New York Times,* May 4, 2003, p. 1. Retrieved May 20, 2003, from ABI/INFORM (Proquest) database.

the *New York Times* and *Entertainment Weekly,* read: "Next time you or your kids 'share' music on the Internet, you may also want to download a list of attorneys."[32] The public reeled when it learned that a 12-year-old honor student in Manhattan, Brianna La-Hara, and a 66-year-old sculptor and retired schoolteacher in a suburb of Boston, Sarah Ward, were the targets of lawsuits. LaHarra's mother quickly settled the case for $2,000, while Ward convinced the RIAA to drop the lawsuit because she had never traded music and her Apple Macintosh computer was not even capable of running Kazaa's file-sharing program.[33] Other file sharers, however, admitted that they had downloaded copyright protected music from the Internet. They knew the activity was illegal but did not seriously consider the consequences. As a gesture of goodwill, the RIAA offered an amnesty program. Individuals not under investigation for copyright infringement who signed an affidavit promising to delete illegal copies of music files from their computers would not be sued.

A study by the financial advisory firm KPMG estimated that media companies could lose $8 to $10 billion in revenues annually from file-sharing piracy, but KMPG doubted whether file-sharing could be prevented.[34] The firm suggested that media companies change their business models and find ways to profit from digital music instead of spending so much time combating piracy. So far, efforts made by recording companies had fallen short. Of 40 media companies surveyed, only 43 percent made some content available in digital form while another 43 percent made most of their content available in digital form; 57 percent of the companies did not even have a process to determine the value of their intellectual property.

MARKET OPPORTUNITIES IN THE MUSIC INDUSTRY

In 2003, consumers witnessed the beginnings of significant change in the music industry (see Exhibit 3). Recording companies began to cut costs, lay off employees, restructure their operations, and seek merger partners. Retail music stores, including the 513 stores operated by Wherehouse Entertainment, which filed for Chapter 11 bankruptcy protection, struggled to survive. A few musicians and bands (e.g., the Rolling Stones) who were previously opposed to digital music opportunities agreed to make their songs available for download from legitimate online music services.

College administrators conceived of creative solutions to music piracy on campus. They believed that recording companies should develop a service that allowed schools to pay a flat license fee for the downloading of songs. In a similar fashion, licenses were granted for usage of software and access to journals. A slight increase in student tuition would cover the costs of the licenses. This was proposed by Charles Phelps, provost of the University of Rochester, and Graham Phelps, president of Penn State University.[35]

P2P file-sharing services had an opportunity to diversify their offerings and promote legitimate uses of their software. Garageband.com, for example, brought together emerging musicians and music lovers. Listeners rated anonymously streamed songs from the service's registered artists. The artists benefited from thoughtful and unbiased critique as they worked to further their careers. Garageband.com planned to provide a digital download service that would find fresh tracks that matched members' tastes.

To make the transition from rogue operations to respected businesses, P2P file-sharing services needed to exert more control over the content of the files being shared. Many services had appropriate policies but did not enforced them. Kazaa, for example, stated in its policy that its software was not to be used to communicate any data that were unlawful, harmful, threatening, abusive, defamatory, vulgar or

---

[32]A. Harmon, "Subpoenas Sent to File Sharers Prompt Anger and Remorse," *New York Times,* July 28, 2003, p. C1. Retrieved September 1, 2003, from ABI/INFORM (Proquest) database.

[33]N. Wingfield and N. Baker, "RIAA Targets Are Surprised by Piracy Suits," *The Wall Street Journal,* September 10, 2003, p. B1; and J. Schwartz, "She Says She's No Music Pirate. No Snoop Fan, Either," *New York Times,* September 25, 2003, p. C1.

[34]"KMPG Study Faults Entertainment Companies' Focus on Piracy," Silicon Valley.com, September 24, 2002. Retrieved May 27, 2003, from www.siliconvalley.com/mld/siliconvalley/news/editorial/4144.

[35]Graham, "Colleges Aggressively Cracking Down."

exhibit 3   **Useful Web Sites Related to Downloading Music Found on the Internet**

www.musicunited.org	Operated by a coalition of songwriters, recording artists, musicians, record companies, and the Recording Industry Association of America (RIAA), the Music United site provided a list of legal online music stores as well as pages on the law and on what the artists said. Criminal penalties for copying and distributing copyrighted music without permission ran up to five years in prison and/or $250,000 in fines.
www.riaa.com	The RIAA was a trade association comprised of recording companies. Its mission was to protect intellectual property rights worldwide and the First Amendment rights of artists; conduct consumer, industry, and technical research; monitor and review state and federal laws, regulations, and policies. There were four specific categories of music piracy: pirate recordings (unauthorized duplication of only the sound of legitimate recordings, as opposed to all the packaging); counterfeit recordings (unauthorized recordings of the sound as well as the duplication of original artwork, label, and packaging); bootleg recordings (unauthorized recordings of live concerts or musical broadcasts on radio and television); and online piracy (unauthorized uploading of a copyrighted sound recording and making it available to the public).
www.loc.gov/copyright	The Web site of the U.S. Copyright Office explained what a copyright is, what works are protected, what the laws are, and how to register a work.
www.alliancefordigitalprogress.org	The Alliance for Digital Progress consisted of consumer groups, think tanks, and businesses launched to oppose government designed and mandated technology to solve the problem of digital piracy. The group was opposed to the Consumer Broadband and Digital Television Promotion Act introduced by Senator Fritz Hollings in 2002. The bill would require electronics manufacturers to install software that blocks illegal copying of movies and music on computers and CD and DVD players.
www.epic.org	The Electronic Privacy Information Center was a nonprofit research center that focused on the right to privacy. It felt that colleges should not monitor students' computer use.

obscene. Nonetheless, pornographic materials were exchanged among members. Auction sites like eBay removed auction listings for banned items (e.g., sales of firearms), and some Internet service providers like AOL monitored public chat rooms and sanctioned individuals using obscene language, yet most file-sharing services did not strictly enforce their policies.

Industry experts believed that recording companies and artists would eventually need to change with the times. Kevin Kelly had some ideas.[36] He believed that consumers would pay for music that was authenticated, was personalized, and came with added value. Individuals did not, for example, have enough hours in their lifetime to listen to all the available music. They were likely to pay a profes-

sional to recommend, edit, and present the music in a convenient and fun way. They might pay to view live streaming video of their favorite band's concert while the musicians were onstage in, say, Tokyo. Limited editions of CDs would be loaded with music, lyrics, autographs, and artwork. Music lovers were also likely to pay for extra frills. When fans legally bought Bon Jovi's CD *Bounce,* they received a unique serial number enabling them to register online and receive such exclusives as prioritized concert ticket purchases and unreleased music. The band Daft Punk also sold CDs with unique numbers enabling customers to download MP3 singles of remixes and live recordings of a song.[37]

[36]Kelly, "Where Music Will Be Coming From."

[37]M. Chait, "Are Media Companies Missing the Boat?" *InternetNews,* September 25, 2002. Retrieved May 27, 2003, from www.internetnews.com/bus-news/print.php/1470191.

INDEXES

ORGANIZATION

Note: Page numbers in *italics* indicate material in illustrations; page numbers followed by *t* indicate material in tables; page numbers followed by *n* indicate footnotes; page numbers preceded by C–indicate material in Cases.

NAME INDEX

Note: Page numbers in *italics* indicate material in illustrations; page numbers followed by *t* indicate material in tables; page numbers followed by *n* indicate footnotes; page numbers preceded by C– indicate cases; page numbers preceded by EN– indicate endnotes.

SUBJECT INDEX

Note: Page numbers in *italics* indicate illustrations; page numbers followed by *t* indicate material in tables.

ENDNOTES

Chapter 1

[1]For a discussion of the different ways that companies can position themselves in the marketplace, see Michael E. Porter, "What Is Strategy?" *Harvard Business Review* 74, no. 6 (November–December 1996), pp. 65–67.

[2]See Henry Mintzberg and J. A. Waters, "Of Strategies, Deliberate and Emergent," *Strategic Management Journal* 6 (1985), pp. 257–72; Costas Markides, "Strategy as Balance: From 'Either-Or' to 'And,'" *Business Strategy Review* 12, no. 3 (September 2001), pp. 1–10; Henry Mintzberg, Bruce Ahlstrand, and Joseph Lampel, *Strategy Safari: A Guided Tour through the Wilds of Strategic Management* (New York: Free Press, 1998), Chapters 2, 5, and 7; and C. K. Prahalad and Gary Hamel, "The Core Competence of the Corporation," *Harvard Business Review* 70, no. 3 (May–June 1990), pp. 79–93.

[3]For an excellent treatment of the strategic challenges posed by high velocity changes, see Shona L. Brown and Kathleen M. Eisenhardt, *Competing on the Edge: Strategy as Structured Chaos* (Boston: Harvard Business School Press, 1998), Chapter 1.

[4]For a fuller discussion of strategy as an entrepreneurial process, see Mintzberg, Ahlstrand, and Lampel, *Strategy Safari,* Chapter 5. Also, see Bruce Barringer and Allen C. Bluedorn, "The Relationship Between Corporate Entrepreneurship and Strategic Management," *Strategic Management Journal* 20 (1999), pp. 421–44; and Jeffrey G. Covin and Morgan P. Miles, "Corporate Entrepreneurship and the Pursuit of Competitive Advantage," *Entrepreneurship: Theory and Practice* 23, no. 3 (Spring 1999), pp. 47–63.

[5]Joseph L. Badaracco, "The Discipline of Building Character," *Harvard Business Review* 76, no. 2 (March–April 1998), pp. 115–24.

[6]Joan Magretta, "Why Business Models Matter," *Harvard Business Review* 80, no. 5 (May 2002), p. 87.

Chapter 2

[1]For a more in-depth discussion of the challenges of developing a well-conceived vision, as well as some good examples, see Hugh Davidson, *The Committed Enterprise: How to Make Vision and Values Work* (Oxford: Butterworth Heinemann, 2002), Chapter 2; James C. Collins and Jerry I. Porras, "Building Your Company's Vision," *Harvard Business Review* 74, no. 5 (September–October 1996), pp. 65–77; and W. Chan Kim and Renée Mauborgne, "Charting Your Company's Future," *Harvard Business Review* 80, no. 6 (June 2002), pp. 77–83.

[2]Davidson, *The Committed Enterprise* pp. 20, 54.

[3]Ibid. pp. 36, 54.

[4]As quoted in Charles H. House and Raymond L. Price, "The Return Map: Tracking Product Teams," *Harvard Business Review* 60, no. 1 (January–February 1991), p. 93.

[5]The concept of strategic intent is described in more detail in Gary Hamel and C. K. Prahalad, "Strategic Intent," *Harvard Business Review* 89, no. 3 (May–June 1989), pp. 63–76; this section draws on their pioneering discussion. See also, Michael A. Hitt, Beverly B. Tyler, Camilla Hardee, and Daewoo Park, "Understanding Strategic Intent in the Global Marketplace," *Academy of Management Executive* 9, no. 2 (May 1995), pp. 12–19.

[6]The strategy-making, strategy-implementing roles of middle managers are thoroughly discussed and documented in Steven W. Floyd and Bill Wooldridge, *The Strategic Middle Manager* (San Francisco: Jossey-Bass, 1996), Chapters 2 and 3.

[7]"Strategic Planning," *Business Week* (August 26, 1996), pp. 51–52.

[8]For more discussion of this point, see Orit Gadiesh and James L. Gilbert, "Transforming Corner-Office Strategy into Frontline Action," *Harvard Business Review* 79, no. 5 (May 2001), pp. 72–79; and Kathleen M. Eisenhardt and Donald N. Sull, "Strategy as Simple Rules," *Harvard Business Review* 79, no. 1 (January 2001,) pp. 106–16.

[9]For an excellent discussion of why a strategic plan needs to be more than a list of bullet points and should in fact tell an engaging, insightful, stage-setting story that lays out the industry and competitive situation as well as the vision, objectives, and strategy, see Gordon Shaw, Robert Brown, and Philip Bromiley, "Strategic Stories: How 3M Is Rewriting Business Planning," *Harvard Business Review* 76, no. 3 (May–June 1998), pp. 41–50.

[10]For a discussion of what it takes for the corporate governance system to function properly, see Cynthia A. Montgomery and Rhonda Kaufman, "The Board's Missing Link," *Harvard Business Review* 81, no. 3 (March 2003), pp. 86–93. See also Gordon Donaldson, "A New Tool for Boards: The Strategic Audit," *Harvard Business Review* 73, no. 4 (July–August 1995), pp. 99–107.

Chapter 3

[1]There are a large number of studies of the size of the cost reductions associated with experience; the median cost reduction associated with a doubling of cumulative production volume is approximately 15%, but there is a wide variation from industry to industry. For a good discussion of the economies of experience and learning, see Pankaj Ghemawat, "Building Strategy on the Experience Curve," *Harvard Business Review* 64, no. 2 (March–April 1985), pp. 143–149.

[2]The five-forces model of competition is the creation of Professor Michael Porter of the Harvard Business School. For his original presentation of the model, see Michael E. Porter, "How Competitive Forces Shape Strategy," *Harvard Business Review* 57, no. 2 (March–April 1979), pp. 137–45. A more thorough discussion can be found in Michael E. Porter, *Competitive Strategy: Techniques for Analyzing Industries and Competitors* (New York: Free Press, 1980), chapter 1.

[3]These indicators of what to look for in evaluating the intensity of rivalry are based on Porter, *Competitive Strategy,* pp. 17–21.

[4]Porter, *Competitive Strategy,* pp. 7–17.

[5]When profits are sufficiently attractive, entry barriers are unlikely to be an effective entry deterrent. At most, they limit the pool of candidate entrants to enterprises with the requisite competencies and resources and with the creativity to fashion a strategy for competing with incumbent firms. For a good discussion of this point, see George S. Yip, "Gateways to Entry," *Harvard Business Review* 60, no. 5 (September–October 1982), pp. 85–93.

[6]Michael Porter, "How Competitive Forces Shape Strategy, *Harvard Business Review* 57, no. 2 (March–April 1979), p. 140, and Porter, *Competitive Strategy,* pp. 14–15.

[7]Porter, "How Competitive Forces Shape Strategy," p. 142 and Porter, *Competitive Strategy,* pp. 23–24.

[8]Porter, *Competitive Strategy,* p. 10.

[9]Porter, *Competitive Strategy,* pp. 27–28.

[10]Porter, *Competitive Strategy,* pp. 24–27.

[11]For a more extended discussion of the problems with the life-cycle hypothesis, see Porter, *Competitive Strategy,* pp. 157–62.

[12]Porter, *Competitive Strategy,* p. 162.

[13]Most of the candidate driving forces discussed here are drawn from Porter, *Competitive Strategy,* pp. 164–83.

[14]Porter, *Competitive Strategy,* chapter 7.

[15]Ibid., pp.129–30.

[16]For an excellent discussion of how to identify the factors that define strategic groups, see Mary Ellen Gordon and George R. Milne, "Selecting the Dimensions that Define Strategic Groups: A Novel Market-Driven Approach," *Journal of Managerial Issues* 11, no. 2 (Summer 1999), pp. 213–33.

[17]Porter, *Competitive Strategy,* pp. 152–54.

[18]Ibid., pp. 130, 132–38, and 154–55.

[19]Strategic groups act as good reference points for predicting the evolution of an industry's competitive structure. See Avi Fiegenbaum and Howard Thomas, "Strategic Groups as Reference Groups: Theory, Modeling and Empirical Examination of Industry and Competitive Strategy," *Strategic Management Journal* 16 (1995), pp. 461–76. For a study of how strategic group analysis helps identify the variables that lead to sustainable competitive advantage, see S. Ade Olusoga, Michael P. Mokwa, and Charles H. Noble, "Strategic Groups, Mobility Barriers, and Competitive Advantage," *Journal of Business Research* 33 (1995), pp. 153–64.

[20]For a discussion of legal ways of gathering competitive intelligence on rival companies, see Larry Kahaner, *Competitive Intelligence* (New York: Simon & Schuster, 1996).

[21]Kahaner, Competitive Intelligence, pp. 84–85.

Chapter 4

[1]Many business organizations are coming to view cutting-edge knowledge and intellectual resources as a valuable competitive asset and have concluded that explicitly managing these assets is an essential part of their strategy. See Michael H. Zack, "Developing a Knowledge Strategy," *California Management Review* 41, no. 3 (Spring 1999), pp. 125–45; and Shaker A. Zahra, Anders P. Nielsen, and William C. Bogner, "Corporate Entrepreneurship, Knowledge, and Competence Development," *Entrepreneurship Theory and Practice* (Spring 1999), pp. 169–89.

[2]In the past decade, there's been considerable research into the role a company's resources and competitive capabilities play in crafting strategy and in determining company profitability. The findings and conclusions have coalesced into what is called the resource-based view of the firm. Among the most insightful articles are Birger Wernerfelt, "A Resource-Based View of the Firm," *Strategic Management Journal* (September–October 1984), pp. 171–80; Jay Barney, "Firm Resources and Sustained Competitive Advantage," *Journal of Management* 17, no. 1 (1991), pp. 99–120; Margaret A. Peteraf, "The Cornerstones of Competitive Advantage: A Resource-Based View," *Strategic Management Journal* (March 1993), pp. 179–91; Birger Wernerfelt, "The Resource-Based View of the Firm: Ten Years After," *Strategic Management Journal* 16

(1995), pp. 171–74; Jay B. Barney, "Looking Inside for Competitive Advantage," *Academy of Management Executive* 9, no. 4 (November 1995), pp. 49–61; and Christopher A. Bartlett and Sumantra Ghoshal, "Building Competitive Advantage through People," *MIT Sloan Management Review* 43, no. 2 (Winter 2002), pp. 34–41.

[3]For a discussion of how to measure the competitive power of a company's resource base, see Nick Bontis, Nicola C. Dragonetti, Kristine Jacobsen, and Goran Roos, "The Knowledge Toolbox: A Review of the Tools Available to Measure and Manage Intangible Resources," *European Management Journal* 17, no. 4 (August 1999), pp. 391–401.

[4]For a more extensive discussion of how to identify and evaluate the competitive power of a company's capabilities, see David W. Birchall and George Tovstiga, "The Strategic Potential of a Firm's Knowledge Portfolio," *Journal of General Management* 25, no. 1 (Autumn 1999), pp. 1–16; also see David Teece, "Capturing Value from Knowledge Assets: The New Economy, Markets for Know-How, and Intangible Assets," *California Management Review* 40, no. 3 (Spring 1998), pp. 55–79.

[5]See David J. Collis and Cynthia A. Montgomery, "Competing on Resources: Strategy in the 1990s," *Harvard Business Review* 73, no. 4 (July–August 1995), pp. 120–23.

[6]See Jack W. Duncan, Peter Ginter, and Linda E. Swayne, "Competitive Advantage and Internal Organizational Assessment," *Academy of Management Executive* 12, no. 3 (August 1998), pp. 6–16.

[7]Value chains and strategic cost analysis are described at greater length in Michael E. Porter, *Competitive Advantage* (New York: Free Press, 1985), Chapters 2 and 3; Robin Cooper and Robert S. Kaplan, "Measure Costs Right: Make the Right Decisions," *Harvard Business Review* 66, no. 5 (September–October, 1988), pp. 96–103; and John K. Shank and Vijay Govindarajan, *Strategic Cost Management* (New York: Free Press, 1993), especially Chapters 2–6, 10.

[8]M. Hegert and D. Morris, "Accounting Data for Value Chain Analysis," *Strategic Management Journal* 10 (1989), p. 183.

[9]Porter, *Competitive Advantage,* p. 36.

[10]Ibid., p. 34.

[11]Hegert and Morris, "Accounting Data for Value Chain Analysis," p. 180.

[12]For more on how and why the clustering of suppliers and other support organizations matter to a company's costs and competitiveness, see Michael E. Porter, "Clusters and the New Economics of Competition," *Harvard Business Review* 76, no. 6 (November–December 1998), pp. 77–90.

[13]For discussions of the accounting challenges in calculating the costs of value chain activities, see Shank and Govindarajan, *Strategic Cost Management,* pp. 62–72 and Chapter 5; and

Hegert and Morris, "Accounting Data for Value Chain Analysis," pp. 175–88.

[14]Porter, *Competitive Advantage,* p. 45.

[15]For a discussion of activity-based cost accounting, see Cooper and Kaplan, "Measure Costs Right," pp. 96–103; Shank and Govindarajan, *Strategic Cost Management,* Chapter 11; and Joseph A. Ness and Thomas G. Cucuzza, "Tapping the Full Potential of ABC," *Harvard Business Review* 73, no. 4 (July–August 1995), pp. 130–38.

[16]Shank and Govindarajan, *Strategic Cost Management,* p. 62.

[17]For more details, see Gregory H. Watson, *Strategic Benchmarking: How to Rate Your Company's Performance Against the World's Best* (New York: John Wiley, 1993); and Robert C. Camp, *Benchmarking: The Search for Industry Best Practices That Lead to Superior Performance* (Milwaukee: ASQC Quality Press, 1989). See also Alexandra Biesada, "Strategic Benchmarking," *Financial World* (September 29, 1992), pp. 30–38.

[18]Jeremy Main, "How to Steal the Best Ideas Around," *Fortune* (October 19, 1992), pp. 102–3.

[19]Shank and Govindarajan, *Strategic Cost Management,* p. 50.

[20]Porter, *Competitive Advantage,* Chapter 3.

[21]James Brian Quinn, *Intelligent Enterprise* (New York: Free Press, 1993), p. 54.

[22]Ibid., p. 34.

Chapter 5

[1]The classification scheme is an adaptation of one presented in Michael E. Porter, *Competitive Strategy: Techniques for Analyzing Industries and Competitors* (New York: Free Press, 1980), Chapter 2, especially pp. 35–39 and 44–46.

[2]Michael E. Porter, *Competitive Advantage,* (New York: Free Press, 1985), p. 97.

[3]The items and explanations in this listing are condensed from ibid., pp. 70–107.

[4]Ibid., p. 109.

[5]Ibid., pp. 135–38.

[6]For a more detailed discussion, see George Stalk, Philip Evans, and Lawrence E. Schulman, "Competing on Capabilities: The New Rules of Corporate Strategy," *Harvard Business Review* 70, no. 2 (March–April 1992), pp. 57–69.

[7]Porter, *Competitive Advantage,* pp. 160–62.

[8]Gary Hamel, "Strategy as Revolution," *Harvard Business Review* 74, no. 4 (July–August 1996), p. 72. For an interesting and entertaining presentation of Trader Joe's mission, strategy, and operating practices, see the information the company has posted at www.traderjoes.com.

[9]This discussion draws from Porter, *Competitive Strategy,* pp. 138–42. Porter's insights here

are particularly important to formulating differentiating strategies because of the relevance of intangibles and signals.

Chapter 6

[1]Yves L. Doz and Gary Hamel, *Alliance Advantage: The Art of Creating Value through Partnering* (Boston: Harvard Business School Press, 1998), pp. xiii, xiv.

[2]Salvatore Parise and Lisa Sasson, "Leveraging Knowledge Management across Strategic Alliances," *Ivey Business Journal* (March–April 2002), p. 42.

[3]Michael E. Porter, *The Competitive Advantage of Nations* (New York: Free Press, 1990), p. 66. For a discussion of how to realize the advantages of strategic partnerships, see Nancy J. Kaplan and Jonathan Hurd, "Realizing the Promise of Partnerships," *Journal of Business Strategy* 23, no. 3 (May–June 2002), pp. 38–42.

[4]Doz and Hamel, *Alliance Advantage,* pp. 16–18.

[5]For an excellent review of the strategic objectives of various types of mergers and acquisitions and the managerial challenges that different kinds of mergers and acquisition present, see Joseph L. Bower, "Not All M&As Are Alike—and That Matters," *Harvard Business Review* 79, no. 3 (March 2001), pp. 93–101.

[6]See Kathryn R. Harrigan, "Matching Vertical Integration Strategies to Competitive Conditions," *Strategic Management Journal* 7, no. 6 (November–December 1986), pp. 535–56; for a more extensive discussion of the advantages and disadvantages of vertical integration, see John Stuckey and David White, "When and When *Not* to Vertically Integrate," *Sloan Management Review* (Spring 1993), pp. 71–83.

[7]Robert H. Hayes, Gary P. Pisano, and David M. Upton, *Strategic Operations: Competing Through Capabilities* (New York: Free Press, 1996), pp. 419–22.

[8]For more details, see James Brian Quinn, "Strategic Outsourcing: Leveraging Knowledge Capabilities," *Sloan Management Review* 40, no. 4 (Summer 1999), pp. 9–21.

[9]"The Internet Age," *Business Week,* October 4, 1999, p. 104.

[10]Ian C. MacMillan, "How Long Can You Sustain a Competitive Advantage?" in *The Strategic Planning Management Reader,* ed. Liam Fahey (Englewood Cliffs, NJ: Prentice Hall, 1989), pp. 23–24.

[11]Ian C. MacMillan, "Controlling Competitive Dynamics by Taking Strategic Initiative," *The Academy of Management Executive* 2, no. 2 (May 1988), p. 111.

[12]Philip Kotler and Ravi Singh, "Marketing Warfare in the 1980s," *The Journal of Business Strategy* 1, no. 3 (Winter 1981), pp. 30–41; Philip Kotler, *Marketing Management,* 5th ed. (Englewood Cliffs, NJ: Prentice Hall,

1984), pp. 401–6; and Ian MacMillan, "Preemptive Strategies," *Journal of Business Strategy* 14, no. 2 (Fall 1983), pp. 16–26.

[13]Kotler, *Marketing Management,* p. 402.

[14]Ibid., p. 403.

[15]Ian C. MacMillan, Alexander B. van Putten, and Rita Gunther McGrath, "Global Gamesmanship," *Harvard Business Review* 81, no. 5 (May 2003), pp. 66–67.

[16]For a discussion of the use of surprise, see William E. Rothschild, "Surprise and the Competitive Advantage," *Journal of Business Strategy* 4, no. 3 (Winter 1984), pp. 10–18.

[17]MacMillan, van Putten, and McGrath, "Global Gamesmanship," p. 66.

[18]For an interesting discussion of the use of end-run offensives in the battle between Netscape and Microsoft over Internet browsers, see David B. Yoffie and Michael A. Cusumano, "Judo Strategy: The Competitive Dynamics of Internet Time," *Harvard Business Review* 77, no. 1 (January–February 1999), pp. 70–81.

[19]For an interesting study of how small firms can successfully employ guerrilla-style tactics, see Ming-Jer Chen and Donald C. Hambrick, "Speed, Stealth, and Selective Attack: How Small Firms Differ from Large Firms in Competitive Behavior," *Academy of Management Journal* 38, no. 2 (April 1995), pp. 453–82.

[20]For more details, see Ian MacMillan, "How Business Strategists Can Use Guerrilla Warfare Tactics," *Journal of Business Strategy* 1, no. 2 (Fall 1980), pp. 63–65; Kathryn R. Harrigan, *Strategic Flexibility* (Lexington, MA: Lexington Books, 1985), pp. 30–45; and Liam Fahey, "Guerrilla Strategy: The Hit-and-Run Attack," in *The Strategic Management Planning Reader,* ed. Liam Fahey (Englewood Cliffs, NJ: Prentice Hall, 1989), pp. 194–97.

[21]The use of preemptive moves is treated comprehensively in MacMillan, "Preemptive Strategies," pp. 16–26.

[22]Kotler, *Marketing Management,* p. 400,

[23]Porter, *Competitive Advantage,* p. 518.

[24]Ibid., pp. 489–94.

[25]Ibid., pp. 495–497. The list here is selective; Porter offers a greater number of options.

[26]For a more extensive discussion of how the Internet impacts strategy, see Michael E. Porter, "Strategy and the Internet." *Harvard Business Review* 79, no. 3 (March 2001), pp. 63–78.

[27]Porter, *Competitive Strategy,* pp. 232–33.

[28]For research evidence on the effects of pioneering versus following, see Jeffrey G. Covin, Dennis P. Slevin, and Michael B. Heeley, "Pioneers and Followers: Competitive Tactics, Environment, and Growth," *Journal of Business Venturing* 15, no. 2 (March 1999), pp. 175–210.

[29]Gary Hamel, "Smart Mover, Dumb Mover," *Fortune,* September 3, 2001, p. 195.

[30]Ibid., p. 192.

Chapter 7

[1]For an insightful discussion of how much significance these kinds of demographic and market differences have, see C. K. Prahalad and Kenneth Lieberthal, "The End of Corporate Imperialism," *Harvard Business Review* 76, no. 4 (July–August 1999), pp. 68–79.

[2]Michael E. Porter, *The Competitive Advantage of Nations* (New York: Free Press, 1990), pp. 53–54.

[3]Ibid., p. 61.

[4]For more details on the merits of and opportunities for cross-border transfer of successful strategy experiments, see C. A. Bartlett and S. Ghoshal, *Managing Across Borders: The Transnational Solution,* 2nd ed. (Boston: Harvard Business School Press, 1998), pp. 79–80 and Chapter 9.

[5]H. Kurt Christensen, "Corporate Strategy: Managing a Set of Businesses," in *The Portable MBA in Strategy,* ed. Liam Fahey and Robert M. Randall (New York: Wiley, 2001), p. 42.

[6]Porter, *The Competitive Advantage of Nations*, p. 54.

[7]C. K. Prahalad and Yves L. Doz, *The Multinational Mission* (New York: Free Press, 1987), p. 60.

[8]Porter, *The Competitive Advantage of Nations*, p. 57.

[9]Ian C. MacMillan, Alexander B. van Putten, and Rita Gunther McGrath, "Global Gamesmanship," *Harvard Business Review* 81, no. 5 (May 2003), pp. 63–68.

[10]Porter, *The Competitive Advantage of Nations*, p. 66; see also Yves L. Doz and Gary Hamel, *Alliance Advantage* (Boston, MA: Harvard Business School Press, 1998), especially Chapters 2–4.

[11]Christensen, "Corporate Strategy," p. 43.

[12]For an excellent discussion of company experiences with alliances and partnerships, see Doz and Hamel, *Alliance Advantage,* Chapters 2–7, and Rosabeth Moss Kanter, "Collaborative Advantage: The Art of the Alliance," *Harvard Business Review* 72, no. 4 (July–August 1994), pp. 96–108.

[13]Jeremy Main, "Making Global Alliances Work," *Fortune,* December 19, 1990, p. 125.

[14]Details of the disagreements are reported in Shawn Tully, "The Alliance from Hell," *Fortune,* June 24, 1996, pp. 64–72.

[15]Doz and Hamel, *Alliance Advantage,* Chapters 4–8.

[16]Much of this section is based on Prahalad and Lieberthal, "The End of Corporate Imperialism," pp. 68–79, and David J. Arnold and John A. Quelch, "New Strategies in Emerging Markets," *Sloan Management Review* 40, no. 1 (Fall 1998), pp. 7–20.

[17]Arnold and Quelch, "New Strategies in Emerging Market," p. 7.

[18]Prahalad and Lieberthal, "The End of Corporate Imperialism," pp. 72–73.

[19]Niraj Dawar and Tony Frost, "Competing with Giants: Survival Strategies for Local Companies in Emerging Markets," *Harvard Business Review* 77, no. 2 (March–April, 1999), pp. 122–23. See also Gutiz Ger, "Localizing in the Global Village: Local Firms Competing in Global Markets," *California Management Review* 41, no. 4 (Summer 1999), pp. 64–84.

[20]Dawar and Frost, "Competing with Giants," p. 124.

[21]Ibid., p. 125.

[22]Ibid., p. 126.

Chapter 8

[1]Michael E. Porter, *Competitive Strategy* (New York: Free Press, 1980), pp. 216–23.

[2]Charles W. Hofer and Dan Schendel, *Strategy Formulation: Analytical Concepts* (St. Paul, MN: West Publishing, 1978), pp. 164–65.

[3]Phillip Kotler, *Marketing Management,* 5th ed. (Englewood Cliffs, NJ: Prentice Hall, 1984), p. 366; and Porter, *Competitive Strategy,* Chapter 10.

[4]Hofer and Schendel, *Strategy Formulation,* pp. 164–65.

[5]The strategic issues companies must address in fast-changing market environments are thoroughly explored in Gary Hamel and Liisa Välikangas, "The Quest for Resilence," *Harvard Business Review* 81, no. 9 (September 2003), pp. 52–63, and Richard A. D'Aveni, *Hyper-Competition: Managing the Dynamics of Strategic Maneuvering* (New York: Free Press, 1994). See also Richard A. D'Aveni, "Coping with Hypercompetition: Utilizing the New 7S's Framework," *Academy of Management Executive* 9, no. 3 (August 1995), pp. 45–56; and Bala Chakravarthy, "A New Strategy Framework for Coping with Turbulence," *Sloan Management Review* (Winter 1997), pp. 69–82.

[6]Shona L. Brown and Kathleen M. Eisenhardt, *Competing on the Edge: Strategy as Structured Chaos* (Boston: Harvard Business School Press, 1998), pp. 4–5.

[7]Ibid., p. 4.

[8]For insight into building competitive advantage through R&D and technological innovation, see Shaker A. Zahra, Sarah Nash, and Deborah J. Bickford, "Transforming Technological Pioneering into Competitive Advantage," *Academy of Management Executive* 9, no. 1 (February 1995), pp. 32–41.

[9]Brown and Eisenhardt, *Competing on the Edge,* pp. 14–15. See also Kathleen M. Eisenhardt and Shona L. Brown, "Time Pacing: Competing in Markets That Won't Stand Still," *Harvard Business Review* 76, no. 2 (March–April 1998), pp. 59–69.

[10]Porter, *Competitive Strategy,* pp. 238–40.

[11]The following discussion draws on ibid., pp. 241–46.

[12]R. G. Hamermesh and S. B. Silk, "How to Compete in Stagnant Industries," *Harvard Business Review* 57, no. 5 (September–October 1979), p. 161.

[13]Ibid., p. 162.

[14]Ibid., p. 165.

[15]This section is summarized from Porter, *Competitive Strategy,* Chapter 9.

[16]Eric D. Beinhocker, "Robust Adaptive Strategies," *Sloan Management Review* 40, no. 3 (Spring 1999), p. 101.

[17]Gary Hamel, "Bringing Silicon Valley Inside," *Harvard Business Review* 77, no. 5 (September–October 1999), p. 73.

[18]Beinhocker, "Robust Adaptive Strategies," p. 101.

[19]Kotler, *Marketing Management,* Chapter 23; Michael E. Porter, *Competitive Advantage* (New York: Free Press, 1985), Chapter 14; and Ian C. MacMillan, "Seizing Competitive Initiative," *Journal of Business Strategy* 2, no. 4 (Spring 1982), pp. 43–57. For a perspective on what industry leaders can do when confronted with revolutionary market changes, see Richard D'Aveni, "The Empire Strikes Back: Counterrevolutionary Strategies for Industry Leaders," *Harvard Business Review* 80, no. 11 (November 2002), pp. 66–74.

[20]The value of being a frequent first-mover and leading change is documented in Walter J. Ferrier, Ken G. Smith, and Curtis M. Grimm, "The Role of Competitive Action in Market Share Erosion and Industry Dethronement: A Study of Industry Leaders and Challengers," *Academy of Management Journal* 42, no. 4 (August 1999), pp. 372–88.

[21]Hamermesh, Anderson, and Harris, "Strategies for Low Market Share Businesses," p. 102.

[22]Porter, *Competitive Advantage,* p. 514.

[23]William K. Hall, "Survival Strategies in a Hostile Environment," *Harvard Business Review* 58, no. 5 (September–October 1980), pp. 75–85. See also Frederick M. Zimmerman, *The Turnaround Experience: Real-World Lessons in Revitalizing Corporations* (New York: McGraw-Hill, 1991), and Gary J. Castrogiovanni, B. R. Baliga, and Roland E. Kidwell, "Curing Sick Businesses: Changing CEOs in Turnaround Efforts," *Academy of Management Executive* 6, no. 3 (August 1992), pp. 26–41.

[24]Leigh Gallagher, "Avoiding the Pitfalls of Orphan Stocks," www.forbes.com, April 24, 2003.

[25]Phillip Kotler, "Harvesting Strategies for Weak Products," *Business Horizons* 21, no. 5 (August 1978), pp. 17–18.

Chapter 9

[1]For a further discussion of when diversification makes good strategic sense, see Constantinos C. Markides, "To Diversify or Not to Diversify," *Harvard Business Review* 75, no. 6 (November–December 1997), pp. 93–99.

[2]Michael E. Porter, "From Competitive Advantage to Corporate Strategy," *Harvard Business Review* 45, no. 3 (May–June 1987), pp. 46–49.

[3]Michael E. Porter, *Competitive Strategy: Techniques for Analyzing Industries and Competitors* (New York: Free Press, 1980), pp. 354–55.

[4]Ibid., pp. 344–45.

[5]Yves L. Doz and Gary Hamel, *Alliance Advantage: The Art of Creating Value through Partnering.* (Boston: Harvard Business School Press, 1998), Chapters 1 and 2.

[6]Ibid., p. 46.

[7]Porter, *Competitive Strategy,* p. 340.

[8]Doz and Hamel, *Alliance Advantage,* p. 48.

[9]Michael E. Porter, *Competitive Advantage* (New York: Free Press, 1985), pp. 318–19, 357–53; and Porter, "From Competitive Advantage to Corporate Strategy,: pp. 53–57. For an empirical study confirming that strategic fits are capable of enhancing performance (provided the resulting resource strengths are competitively valuable and difficult to duplicate by rivals), see Constantinos C. Markides and Peter J. Williamson, "Corporate Diversification and Organization Structure: A Resource-Based View," *Academy of Management Journal* 39, no. 2 (April 1996), pp. 340–67.

[10]For a discussion of the strategic significance of cross-business coordination of value chain activities and insight into how the process works, see Jeanne M. Liedtka, "Collaboration across Lines of Business for Competitive Advantage," *Academy of Management Executive* 10, no. 2 (May 1996), pp. 2034.

[11]"Beyond Knowledge Management: How Companies Mobilize Experience," *Financial Times,* February 8, 1999, p. 5.

[12]For a discussion of what is involved in actually capturing strategic fit benefits, see Kathleen M. Eisenhardt and D. Charles Galunic, "Coevolving: At Last, a Way to Make Synergies Work," *Harvard Business Review* 78, no. 1 (January–February 2000), pp. 91–101. Adeptness at capturing cross-business strategic fits positively impacts performance; see Constantinos C. Markides and Peter J. Williamson, "Related Diversification, Core Competences and Corporate Performance," *Strategic Management Journal* 15 (Summer 1994), pp. 149–65.

[13]Peter Drucker, *Management: Tasks, Responsibilities, Practices* (New York: Harper & Row, 1974), pp. 692–93.

[14]While arguments that unrelated diversification are a superior way to diversify financial risk have logical appeal, there is research showing that related diversification is less risky from a financial perspective than is unrelated diversification; see Michael Lubatkin and Sayan Chatterjee, "Extending Modern Portfolio Theory into the Domain of Corporate

Diversification: Does It Apply?" *Academy of Management Journal* 37, no. 1 (February 1994), pp. 109–36.

[15]For a review of the experiences of companies that have pursued unrelated diversification successfully, see Patricia L. Anslinger and Thomas E. Copeland, "Growth through Acquisitions: A Fresh Look," *Harvard Business Review* 74, no. 1 (January–February 1996), pp. 126–35.

[16]Of course, management may be willing to assume the risk that trouble will not strike before it has had time to learn the business well enough to bail it out of almost any difficulty. But there is research that shows this is very risky from a financial perspective; see, for example, Lubatkin and Chatterjee, "Extending Modern Portfolio Theory," pp. 120–32.

[17]For an excellent discussion of what to look for in assessing these fits, see Andrew Campbell, Michael Gould, and Marcus Alexander, "Corporate Strategy: The Quest for Parenting Advantage," *Harvard Business Review* 73, no. 2 (March–April 1995), pp. 120–32.

[18]Ibid, p. 128.

[19]Ibid, p. 123.

[20]A good discussion of the importance of having adequate resources, and also the importance of upgrading corporate resources and capabilities, can be found in David J. Collis and Cynthia A. Montgomery, "Competing on Resources: Strategy in the 90s," *Harvard Business Review* 73, no. 4 (July–August 1995, pp. 118–28).

[21]Ibid., pp. 121–22.

[22]Drucker, *Management*, p. 709.

[23]See, for example, Constantinos C. Markides, "Diversification, Restructuring, and Economic Performance," *Strategic Management Journal* 16 (February 1995), pp. 101–18.

[24]For a discussion of why divestiture needs to be a standard part of any company diversification strategy, see Lee Dranikoff, Tim Koller, and Antoon Schneider, "Divestiture: Strategy's Missing Link," *Harvard Business Review* 80, no. 5 (May 2002), pp. 74–83.

[25]Drucker, *Management*, p. 94.

[26]See David J. Collis and Cynthia A. Montgomery, "Creating Corporate Advantage," *Harvard Business Review* 76, no. 3 (May–June 1998), pp. 72–80.

[27]Drucker, *Management*, p. 719.

[28]Evidence that restructuring strategies tend to result in higher levels of performance is contained in Markides, "Diversification, Restructuring and Economic Performance," pp. 101–18.

[29]Dranikoff, Koller, and Schneider, "Divestiture," p. 76.

[30]C. K. Prahalad and Yves L. Doz, *The Multinational Mission* (New York: Free Press, 1987), p. 2.

[31]Ibid., p. 15.

[32]Ibid., pp. 62–63.

[33]For a fascinating discussion of the chess match in strategy that can unfold when two DMNC's go head-in-head in a global marketplace, see Ian C. MacMillan, Alexander B. van Putten, and Rita Gunther McGrath, "Global Gamesmanship," *Harvard Business Review* 81, no. 5 (May 2003, pp. 62–71).

Chapter 10

[1]James E. Post, Anne T. Lawrence, and James Weber, *Business and Society: Corporate Strategy, Public Policy, Ethics,* 10th ed. (Burr Ridge, IL: McGraw-Hill Irwin, 2002), p. 103.

[2]Archie B. Carroll, "Models of Management Morality for the New Millennium," *Business Ethics Quarterly* 11, no. 2 (April 2001), pp. 367–69.

[3]Ibid., pp. 369–70.

[4]For more details see Ronald R. Sims and Johannes Brinkmann, "Enron Ethics (Or: Culture Matters More than Codes)," *Journal of Business Ethics* 45, no. 3 (July 2003), pp. 244–46.

[5]As reported in Gardiner Harris, "At Bristol-Myers, Ex-Executives Tell of Numbers Games," *The Wall Street Journal,* December 12, 2002, pp. A1, A13.

[6]Ibid, p. A13.

[7]The following account is based largely on the discussion and analysis in Sims and Brinkmann, "Enron Ethics," pp. 245–52.

[8]George A. Steiner and John F. Steiner, *Business, Government, and Society: A Managerial Perspective* (Burr Ridge: McGraw-Hill/Irwin, 2003), p. 213.

[9]Stephen J. Carroll and Martin J. Gannon, *Ethical Dimensions of International Management* (Thousand Oaks, CA: Sage, 1997), p. 9.

[10]See John J. Hannifin, "Morality and the Market in China: Some Contemporary Views," *Business Ethics Quarterly* 12, no. 1 (January 2002), pp. 6–9.

[11]For more documentation of cross-country differences in what is considered ethical, see Robert D. Hirsch, Branko Bucar, and Sevgi Oztark, "A Cross-Cultural Comparison of Business Ethics: Cases of Russia, Slovenia, Turkey, and United States," *Cross Cultural Management* 10, no. 1 (2003), pp. 3–28; P. Maria Joseph Christie, Ik-Whan G. Kwan, Philipp A. Stoeberl, and Raymond Baumhart, "A Cross-Cultural Comparison of Ethical Attitudes of Business Managers: India, Korea, and the United States," *Journal of Business Ethics* 46, no. 3 (September 2003), pp. 263–87; and Turgut Guvenli and Rajib Sanyal, "Ethical Concerns in International Business: Are Some Issues More Important than Others?" *Business and Society Review* 107, no. 2 (June 2002, pp. 195–206).

[12]Ibid. However, for a view that the most important moral standards are universal, see Mark S. Schwartz, "A Code of Ethics for Corporate Codes of Ethics," *Journal of Business Ethics* 41, nos. 1–2 (November–December 2002), pp. 27–43.

[13]Based on a report in M. J. Satchell, "Deadly Trade in Toxics," *U.S. News and World Report,* March 7, 1994, p. 64, and cited in Thomas Donaldson and Thomas W. Dunfee, "When Ethics Travel: The Promise and Peril of Global Business Ethics," *California Management Review* 41, no. 4 (Summer 1999), p. 46.

[14]For more discussion of this point, see Schwartz, "A Code of Ethics for Corporate Codes of Ethics," pp. 29–30.

[15]Donaldson and Dundee, "When Ethics Travel," p. 53.

[16]John Reed and Erik Portanger, "Bribery, Corruption Are Rampant in Eastern Europe, Survey Finds," *The Wall Street Journal,* November 9, 1999, p. A21.

[17]Donaldson and Dundee, "When Ethics Travel," p. 59.

[18]P. M. Nichols, "Outlawing Transnational Bribery through the World Trade Organization," *Law and Policy in International Business* 28, no. 2 (1997), pp. 321–22.

[19]Donaldson and Dunfee, "When Ethics Travel," pp. 55–56.

[20]Gedeon J. Rossouw and Leon J. van Vuuren, "Modes of Managing Morality: A Descriptive Model of Strategies for Managing Ethics," *Journal of Business Ethics* 46, no. 4 (September 2003), pp. 389–400.

[21]Sarah Roberts, Justin Keeble, and David Brown, "The Business Case for Corporate Citizenship," a study for the World Economic Forum, www.weforum.org/corporatecitizenship, accessed October 14, 2003, p. 3.

[22]Business Roundtable, "Statement on Corporate Responsibility," New York< October 1981, p. 9.

[23]N. Craig Smith, "Corporate Responsibility: Whether and How," *California Management Review* 45, no. 4 (Summer 2003), p. 63.

[24]World Business Council for Sustainable Development, "Corporate Social Responsibility: Making Good Business Sense," www.wbscd.ch, January 2000 (accessed October 10, 2003), p. 7. For a discussion on how companies are connecting the social initiatives to their core values, see David Hess, Nikolai Rogovsky, and Thomas W. Dunfee, "The Next Wave of Corporate Community Involvement: Corporate Social Initiatives," *California Management Review* 44, no. 2 (Winter 2002), pp. 110–25.

[25]Susan Ariel Aaronson, "Corporate Responsibility in the Global Village: The British Role Model and the American Laggard," *Business and Society Review* 108, no. 3 (September 2003), p. 323.

[26]www.chick-fil-a-.com, accessed October 16, 2003; and Archie B. Carroll, "The Four Faces of Corporate Citizenship," *Business and Society Review* 100/101 (September 1998), p. 6.

[27]Smith, "Corporate Responsibility," p. 63; see also World Economic Forum, "Findings of a Survey on Global Corporate Leadership," www.weforum.org/corporatecitizenship, accessed October 11, 2003.

[28]Roberts, Keeble, and Brown, "The Business Case for Corporate Citizenship," p. 6.

[29]Ibid., p. 3.

[30]Wallace N. Davidson, Abuzar El-Jelly, and Dan L. Worrell, "Influencing Managers to Change Unpopular Corporate Behavior through Boycotts and Divestitures: A Stock Market Test," *Business and Society* 34, no. 2 (1995), pp. 171–96.

[31]Tom McCawley, "Racing to Improve Its Reputation: Nike Has Fought to Shed Its Image as an Exploiter of Third-World Labor Yet It Is Still a Target of Activists," *Financial Times,* December 2000, p. 14; and Smith, "Corporate Social Responsibility," p. 61.

[32]Based on data in Amy Aronson, "Corporate Diversity, Integration, and Market Penetration," *Business Week,* October 20, 2003, pp. 138 ff.

[33]Smith, "Corporate Social Responsibility," p. 62.

[34]See Social Investment Forum, *2001 Report on Socially Responsible Investing Trends in the United States* (Washington, DC: Social Investment Forum, 2001).

[35]Smith, "Corporate Social Responsibility," p. 63.

[36]See James C. Collins and Jerry I. Porras, *Built to Last: Successful Habits of Visionary Companies,* 3rd ed. (London: HarperBusiness, 2002); Roberts, Keeble, and Brown, "The Business Case for Corporate Citizenship," p. 4; and Smith, "Corporate Social Responsibility," p. 63.

[37]Roberts, Keeble, and Brown, "The Business Case for Corporate Citizenship," p. 4.

[38]Smith, "Corporate Social Responsibility," p. 65; Lee E. Preston and Douglas P. O'Bannon, "The Corporate Social-Financial Performance Relationship," *Business and Society* 36, no. 4 (December 1997), pp. 419–29; Ronald M. Roman, Sefa Hayibor, and Bradley R. Agie, "The Relationship between Social and Financial Performance: Repainting a Portrait," *Business and Society,* 38, no. 1 (March 1999), pp. 109–25; and Joshua D. Margolis and James P. Walsh, *People and Profits* (Mahwah, NJ: Erlbaum, 2001).

[39]Smith, "Corporate Social Responsibility," p. 71.

[40]Business Roundtable, "Statement on Corporate Governance," Washington, DC, September 1997, p. 3.

[41]Henry Mintzberg, Robert Simons, and Kunal Basu, "Beyond Selfishness," *MIT Sloan Management Review* 44, no. 1 (Fall 2002), p. 69.

[42]For a good discussion of the debate between maximizing shareholder value and balancing stakeholder interests, see. H. Jeff Smith, "The Shareholders versus Stakeholders Debate," *MIT Sloan Management Review* 44, no. 4 (Summer 2003), pp. 85–91.

[43]Smith, "Corporate Social Responsibility," p. 70.

[44]Based on information in Edna Gundersen, "Rights Issue Rocks the Music World," *USA Today,* September 16, 2002, pp. D1, D2.

[45]Based on information in Ann Zimmerman, "Grocery Supplier Squeezes Suppliers at Bill-Paying Time," *The Wall Street Journal,* September 5, 2002, pp. A1, A10.

Chapter 11

[1]As quoted in Steven W. Floyd and Bill Wooldridge, "Managing Strategic Consensus: The Foundation of Effective Implementation," *Academy of Management Executive* 6, no. 4 (November 1992), p. 27.

[2]For an excellent and very pragmatic discussion of this point, see Larry Bossidy and Ram Charan, *Execution: The Discipline of Getting Things Done* (New York : Crown Business, 2002), Chapter 1.

[3]For an insightful discussion of how important staffing an organization with the right people is, see Christopher A. Bartlett and Sumantra Ghoshal, "Building Competitive Advantage through People," *MIT Sloan Management Review* 43, no. 2 (Winter 2002), pp. 34–41.

[4]John Byrne, "The Search for the Young and Gifted," *Business Week,* October 4, 1999, p. 108.

[5]James Brian Quinn, *Intelligent Enterprise* (New York: Free Press, 1992), pp. 52–53, 55, 73–74, 76. See also Christine Soo, Timothy Devinney, David Midgley, and Anne Deering, "Knowledge Management: Philosophy, Processes, and Pitfalls," *California Management Review* 44, no. 4 (Summer 2002), pp. 129–51; and Julian Birkinshaw, "Why Is Knowledge Management So Difficult?" *Business Strategy Review* 12, no. 1 (March 2001), pp. 11–18.

[6]Robert H. Hayes, Gary P. Pisano, and David M. Upton, *Strategic Operations: Competing through Capabilities* (New York: Free Press, 1996), pp. 503–7. Also, see Jonas Ridderstrale, "Cashing in on Corporate Competencies," *Business Strategy Review* 14, no. 1 (Spring 2003), pp. 27–38.

[7]Peter F. Drucker, *Management: Tasks, Responsibilities, Practices* (New York: Harper & Row, 1974), pp. 530, 535.

[8]For a more extensive discussion of the reasons for building cooperative, collaborative alliances and partnerships with other companies, see James F. Moore, *The Death of Competition* (New York: HarperBusiness, 1996), especially Chapter 3; James Brian Quinn and Frederick G. Hilmer, "Strategic Outsourcing," *Sloan Management Review* 35, no. 4 (Summer 1994), pp. 43–55; and James Brian Quinn, "Strategic Outsourcing: Leveraging Knowledge Capabilities," *Sloan Management Review* 40, no. 4 (Summer 1999), pp. 9–22.

[9]Quinn, *Intelligent Enterprise,* p. 43.

[10]Ibid., pp. 33, 89; Quinn and Hilmer, "Strategic Outsourcing," pp. 43–55; and Quinn, "Strategic Outsourcing," pp. 9–22. See also Jussi Heikkil and Carlos Cordon, "Outsourcing: A Core or Non-Core Strategic Management Decision," *Strategic Change* 11, no. 3 (June–July 2002), pp. 183–93. For a discussion of why outsourcing initiatives fall short of expectations, see Jérome Barthélémy, "The Seven Deadly Sins of Outsourcing," *Academy of Management Executive* 17, no. 2 (May 2003), pp. 87–98.

[11]Quinn, "Strategic Outsourcing," p. 17.

[12]Quinn, *Intelligent Enterprise,* pp. 39–40.

[13]The importance of matching organization design and structure to the particular needs of strategy was first brought to the forefront in a landmark study of 70 large corporations conducted by Professor Alfred Chandler of Harvard University. Chandler's research revealed that changes in an organization's strategy bring about new administrative problems that, in turn, require a new or refashioned structure for the new strategy to be successfully implemented. He found that structure tends to follow the growth strategy of the firm—but often not until inefficiency and internal operating problems provoke a structural adjustment. The experiences of these firms followed a consistent sequential pattern: new strategy creation, emergence of new administrative problems, a decline in profitability and performance, a shift to a more appropriate organizational structure, and then recovery to more profitable levels and improved strategy execution. That managers should reassess their company's internal organization whenever strategy changes is pretty much common sense. A new or different strategy is likely to entail new or different key activities, competences, or capabilities, and therefore to require new or different internal organizational arrangements. For more details, see Alfred Chandler, *Strategy and Structure* (Cambridge, MA: MIT Press, 1962).

[14]There are many ways a company can organize around functions other than those just cited. A technical instruments manufacturer may be organized around research and development, engineering, production, technical services, quality control, marketing, personnel, and finance and accounting. A hotel may have a functional organization based on front-desk operations, housekeeping, building maintenance, food service, convention services and special events, guest services, personnel and training, and accounting. A discount retailer may organize around such functional units as purchasing, warehousing and distribution, store operations, advertising, merchandising and promotion, customer service, and corporate administrative services. Likewise, process organization assumes a form that matches a company's processes.

[15]Michael Hammer and James Champy, *Reengineering the Corporation* (New York: Harper-Business, 1993), pp. 26–27.

[16]Although functional organization incorporates Adam Smith's division-of-labor principle (every person/department involved has specific responsibility for performing a clearly defined task) and allows for tight management control (everyone in the process is accountable to a functional department head for efficiency and adherence to procedures), *no one oversees the whole process and its result.* Hammer and Champy, *Reengineering the Corporation,* pp. 26–27.

[17]Gene Hall, Jim Rosenthal, and Judy Wade, "How to Make Reengineering Really Work," *Harvard Business Review* 71, no. 6 (November–December 1993), pp. 119–31.

[18]For more information on business process reengineering and how well it has worked in various companies, see James Brian Quinn, *Intelligent Enterprise* (New York: Free Press, 1992), p. 162; Gene Hall, Jim Rosenthal, and Judy Wade, "How to Make Reengineering Really Work," *Harvard Business Review* 71, no. 6 (November–December 1993), pp. 119–31; Ann Majchrzak and Qianwei Wang, "Breaking the Functional Mind-Set in Process Organizations," *Harvard Business Review* 74, no. 5 (September–October 1996), pp. 93–99; and Iain Somerville and John Edward Mroz, "New Competences for a New World," in *The Organization of the Future,* ed. Frances Hesselbein, Marshall Goldsmith, and Richard Beckard (San Francisco: Jossey-Bass, 1997), p. 71.

[19]Somerville and Mroz, "New Competences for a New World," p. 70.

[20]Exercising adequate control over empowered employees is a serious issue. For example, a prominent Wall Street securities firm lost $350 million when a trader allegedly booked fictitious profits; Sears took a $60 million write-off after admitting that employees in its automobile service departments recommended unnecessary repairs to customers. For a discussion of the problems and possible solutions, see Robert Simons, "Control in an Age of Empowerment," *Harvard Business Review* 73 (March–April 1995), pp. 80–88.

[21]For a discussion of the importance of cross-business coordination, see Jeanne M. Liedtka, "Collaboration across Lines of Business for Competitive Advantage," *Academy of Management Executive* 10, no. 2 (May 1996), pp. 20–34.

[22]Rosabeth Moss Kanter, "Collaborative Advantage: The Art of the Alliance," *Harvard Business Review* 72, no. 4 (July–August 1994), pp. 105–6.

[23]For an excellent review of ways to effectively manage the relationship between alliance partners, see Ibid., pp. 96–108.

Chapter 12

[1]For a discussion of the value of benchmarking in implementing strategy, see Yoshinobu Ohinata, "Benchmarking: The Japanese Experience," *Long-Range Planning* 27, no. 4 (August 1994), pp. 48–53.

[2]Darrell K. Rigby, "What's Today's Special at the Consultant's Café?" *Fortune,* September 7, 1998, p. 163.

[3]For some of the seminal discussions of what TQM is and how it works, written by ardent enthusiasts of the technique, see M. Walton, *The Deming Management Method* (New York: Pedigree, 1986); J. Juran, *Juran on Quality by Design* (New York: Free Press, 1992); Philip Crosby, *Quality Is Free: The Act of Making Quality Certain* (New York: McGraw-Hill, 1979); and S. George, *The Baldrige Quality System* (New York: Wiley, 1992).

[4]For a discussion of the shift in work environment and culture that TQM entails, see Robert T. Amsden, Thomas W. Ferratt, and Davida M. Amsden, "TQM: Core Paradigm Changes," *Business Horizons* 39, no. 6 (November–December 1996), pp. 6–14.

[5]Based on information posted at www.isixsigma.com, November 4, 2002.

[6]Kennedy Smith "Six Sigma for the Service Sector," *Quality Digest Magazine*, May 2003, posted at www.qualitydigest.com, accessed September 28, 2003.

[7]Del Jones, "Taking the Six Sigma Approach," *USA Today*, October 31, 2002, p. 5B.

[8]Kennedy Smith, "Six Sigma for the Service Sector," *Quality Digest Magazine*, May 2003, posted at www.qualitydigest.com, accessed September 28, 2003.

[9]Ibid.

[10]Jones, "Taking the Six Sigma Approach," p. 5B.

[11]See, for example, Gene Hall, Jim Rosenthal, and Judy Wade, "How to Make Reengineering Really Work," *Harvard Business Review* 71, no. 6 (November–December 1993), pp. 119–31.

[12]Judy D. Olian and Sara L. Rynes, "Making Total Quality Work: Aligning Organizational Processes, Performance Measures, and Stakeholders," *Human Resource Management* 30, no. 3 (Fall 1991), pp. 310–311; and Paul S. Goodman and Eric D. Darr, "Exchanging Best Practices Information through Computer-Aided Systems," *Academy of Management Executive* 10, no. 2 (May 1996), p. 7.

[13]Thomas C. Powell, "Total Quality Management as Competitive Advantage," *Strategic Management Journal* 16 (1995), pp. 15–37. See also Richard M. Hodgetts, "Quality Lessons from America's Baldrige Winners," *Business Horizons* 37, no. 4 (July–August 1994), pp. 74–79; and Richard Reed, David J. Lemak, and Joseph C. Montgomery, "Beyond Process: TQM Content and Firm Performance," *Academy of Management Review* 21, no. 1 (January 1996), pp. 173–202.

[14]Based on information at www.otiselevator.com, November 7, 2002; and James Brian Quinn, *Intelligent Enterprise* (New York: Free Press, 1992), p. 186.

[15]Stephan H. Haeckel and Richard L. Nolan, "Managing by Wire," *Harvard Business Review* 75, no. 5 (September–October 1993), p. 129.

[16]Quinn, *Intelligent Enterprise*, p. 181.

[17]Fred Vogelstein, "Winning the Amazon Way," *Fortune*, May 26, 2003, pp. 70, 74.

[18]Such systems speed organizational learning by providing fast, efficient communication, creating an organizational memory for collecting and retaining best-practice information, and permitting people all across the organization to exchange information and updated solutions. See Goodman and Darr, "Exchanging Best Practices Information through Computer-Aided Systems," pp. 7–17.

[19]Vogelstein, "Winning the Amazon Way," p. 64.

[20]For a discussion of the need for putting appropriate boundaries on the actions of empowered employees and possible control and monitoring systems that can be used, see Robert Simons, "Control in an Age of Empowerment," *Harvard Business Review* 73 (March–April 1995), pp. 80–88.

[21]Ibid. See also, David C. Band and Gerald Scanlan, "Strategic Control through Core Competencies," *Long Range Planning* 28, no. 2 (April 1995), pp. 102–14.

[22]Jeffrey Pfeffer and John F. Veiga, "Putting People First for Organizational Success," *Academy of Management Executive* 13, no. 2 (May 1999), pp. 41–42.

[23]Ibid., pp. 37–45; Linda K. Stroh and Paula M. Caliguiri, "Increasing Global Competitiveness through Effective People Management," *Journal of World Business* 33, no. 1 (Spring 1998), pp. 1–16; and articles in *Fortune* on the 100 best companies to work for (1998, 1999, 2000, and 2001).

[24]Quoted in John P. Kotter and James L. Heskett, *Corporate Culture and Performance* (New York: Free Press, 1992), p. 91.

[25]For a provocative discussion of why incentives and rewards are actually counterproductive, see Alfie Kohn, "Why Incentive Plans Cannot Work," *Harvard Business Review* 71, no. 6 (September–October 1993), pp. 54–63.

[26]See Steven Kerr, "On the Folly of Rewarding A While Hoping for B," *Academy of Management Executive* 9, no. 1 (February 1995), pp. 7–14; Kerr, "Risky Business: The New Pay Game," pp. 93–96; and Doran Twer, "Linking Pay to Business Objectives," *Journal of Business Strategy* 15, no. 4 (July–August 1994), pp. 15–18. For a discussion of executive compensation, see Francis T. Hannafey,

"Economic and Moral Criteria of Executive Compensation," *Business and Society Review* 108, no. 3 (September 2003), pp. 408–15.

[27]Kerr, "Risky Business: The New Pay Game," p. 96.

Chapter 13

[1]John P. Kotter and James L. Heskett, *Corporate Culture and Performance* (New York: Free Press, 1992), p. 7. See also Robert Goffee and Gareth Jones, *The Character of a Corporation* (New York: HarperCollins, 1998).

[2]Kotter and Heskett, *Corporate Culture and Performance,* pp. 7–8.

[3]Ibid., p. 5.

[4]John Alexander and Meena S. Wilson, "Leading across Cultures: Five Vital Capabilities," in *The Organization of the Future,* ed. Frances Hesselbein, Marshall Goldsmith, and Richard Beckard (San Francisco: Jossey-Bass, 1997), pp. 291–92.

[5]Kotter and Heskett, *Corporate Culture and Performance,* p. 5.

[6]Avan R. Jassawalla and Hemant C. Sashittal, "Cultures that Support Product-Innovation Processes," *Academy of Management Executive* 16, no. 3 (August 2002), pp. 42–54.

[7]Kotter and Heskett, *Corporate Culture and Performance,* pp. 15–16. Also, see Jennifer A. Chatham and Sandra E. Cha, "Leading by Leveraging Culture," *California Management Review* 45, no. 4 (Summer 2003), pp. 20–34.

[8]Terrence E. Deal and Allen A. Kennedy, *Corporate Cultures* (Reading, MA: Addison-Wesley, 1982), p. 22. See also Terrence E. Deal and Allen A. Kennedy, *The New Corporate Cultures: Revitalizing the Workplace after Downsizing, Mergers, and Reengineering* (Cambridge, MA: Perseus, 1999).

[9]Vijay Sathe, *Culture and Related Corporate Realities* (Homewood, IL: Richard D. Irwin, 1985).

[10]Kotter and Heskett, *Corporate Culture and Performance,* Chapter 6.

[11]Ibid., p. 68.

[12]This section draws heavily on the discussion of Kotter and Heskett, *Corporate Culture and Performance,* Chapter 4.

[13]There's no inherent reason why new strategic initiatives should conflict with core values and business principles. While conflict is always possible, most strategy makers lean toward choosing strategic initiatives that are compatible with the company's character and culture and that don't go against ingrained values and beliefs. After all, the company's culture is usually something that strategy makers have had a hand in building and perpetuating, so they are not often anxious to undermine core values and business principles without serious soul-searching and compelling business reasons.

[14]Kotter and Heskett, *Corporate Culture and Performance,* p. 52.

[15]Ibid., pp. 84, 144, 148.

[16]Judy D. Olian and Sara L. Rynes, "Making Total Quality Work: Aligning Organizational Processes, Performance Measures, and Stakeholders," *Human Resource Management* 30, no. 3 (Fall 1991), p.324.

[17]For several perspectives on the role and importance of core values and ethical behavior, see Joseph L. Badaracco, *Defining Moments: When Managers Must Choose between Right and Wrong* (Boston: Harvard Business School Press, 1997); Joe Badaracco and Allen P. Webb, "Business Ethics: A View from the Trenches," *California Management Review* 37, no. 2 (Winter 1995), pp. 8–28; Patrick E. Murphy, "Corporate Ethics Statements: Current Status and Future Prospects," *Journal of Business Ethics* 14 (1995), pp. 727–40; and Lynn Sharp Paine, "Managing for Organizational Integrity," *Harvard Business Review* 72, no. 2 (March–April 1994), pp. 106–17.

[18]See Mark S. Schwartz, "A Code of Ethics for Corporate Codes of Ethics," *Journal of Business Ethics* 41, nos. 1–2 (November–December 2002), p. 27.

[19]For a study of the status of formal codes of ethics in large corporations, see Emily F. Carasco and Jang B. Singh, "The Content and Focus of the Codes of Ethics of the World's Largest Transnational Corporations," *Business and Society Review* 108, no. 1 (January 2003), pp. 71–94, and Patrick E. Murphy, "Corporate Ethics Statements: Current Status and Future Prospects," *Journal of Business Ethics* 14 (1995), pp. 727–40. For a discussion of the strategic benefits of formal statements of corporate values, see John Humble, David Jackson, and Alan Thomson, "The Strategic Power of Corporate Values," *Long Range Planning* 27, no. 6 (December 1994), pp. 28–42. An excellent discussion of whether one should assume that company codes of ethics are always ethical is presented in Schwartz, "A Code of Ethics for Corporate Codes of Ethics," pp. 27–43.

[20]The Business Roundtable, *Corporate Ethics: A Prime Asset,* February 1988, pp. 4–10.

[21]Robert C. Ford, "Darden Restaurants CEO Joe Lee on the Importance of Core Values: Integrity and Fairness," *Academy of Management Executive* 16, no. 1 (February 2002), pp. 31–36.

[22]For some cautions in implementing ethics compliance, see Robert J. Rafalko, "A Caution about Trends in Ethics Compliance Programs," *Business and Society Review* 108, no. 1 (January 2003), pp. 115–26. A good discussion of the failures of ethics compliance programs can be found in Megan Barry, "Why Ethics and Compliance Programs Can Fail," *Journal of Business Strategy,* 26, no. 6 (November–December 2002), pp. 37–40.

[23]For documentation of cross-country differences in what is considered ethical, see Robert D. Hirsch, Branko Bucar, and Sevgi Oztark, "A Cross-Cultural Comparison of Business Ethics: Cases of Russia, Slovenia, Turkey, and United States," *Cross Cultural Management* 10, no. 1 (2003), pp. 3–28, and P. Maria Joseph Christie, Ik-Whan G. Kwan, Philipp A. Stoeberl, and Raymond Baumhart, "A Cross-Cultural Comparison of Ethical Attitudes of Business Managers: India, Korea, and the United States," *Journal of Business Ethics* 46, no. 3 (September 2003), pp. 263–87.

[24]For a discussion of this dimension of leadership, see Alexander and Wilson, "Leading across Cultures," pp. 287–94.

[25]For an excellent survey of the problems and pitfalls in making the transition to a new strategy and to fundamentally new ways of doing business, see John P. Kotter, "Leading Change: Why Transformation Efforts Fail," *Harvard Business Review* 73, no. 2 (March–April 1995), pp. 59–67. See also Thomas M. Hout and John C. Carter, "Getting It Done: New Roles for Senior Executives," *Harvard Business Review* 73, no. 6 (November–December 1995), pp. 133–45, and Sumantra Ghoshal and Christopher A. Bartlett, "Changing the Role of Top Management: Beyond Structure to Processes," *Harvard Business Review* 73, no. 1 (January–February 1995), pp. 86–96.

[26]Fred Vogelstein, "Winning the Amazon Way," *Fortune,* May 26, 2003, p. 64.

[27]For a more in-depth discussion of the leader's role in creating a results-oriented culture that nurtures success, see Benjamin Schneider, Sarah K. Gunnarson, and Kathryn Niles-Jolly, "Creating the Climate and Culture of Success," *Organizational Dynamics,* Summer 1994, pp. 17–29.

[28]Jeffrey Pfeffer, "Producing Sustainable Competitive Advantage through the Effective Management of People," *Academy of Management Executive* 9, no. 1 (February 1995), pp. 55–69.

[29]James Brian Quinn, *Strategies for Change: Logical Incrementalism* (Homewood, IL: Richard D. Irwin, 1980), pp. 20–22.

[30]Ibid., p. 146.

[31]For a good discussion of the challenges, see Daniel Goleman, "What Makes a Leader," *Harvard Business Review* 76, no. 6 (November–December 1998), pp. 92–102; Ronald A. Heifetz and Donald L. Laurie, "The Work of Leadership," *Harvard Business Review* 75, no. 1 (January–February 1997), pp. 124–34; and Charles M. Farkas and Suzy Wetlaufer, "The Ways Chief Executive Officers Lead," *Harvard Business Review* 74, no. 3 (May–June 1996), pp. 110–22.